*Property of
Charles A. Owen Jr.
Medieval Studies Library*

ALBERT E. HARTUNG
GENERAL EDITOR

A Manual of the Writings in Middle English

1050–1500

ALBERT E. HARTUNG
GENERAL EDITOR

A Manual of the Writings in Middle English

1050–1500

*By Members of the Middle English Division of the
Modern Language Association
of America*

Based upon
A Manual of the Writings in Middle English 1050–1400
by John Edwin Wells, New Haven, 1916
and Supplements 1–9, 1919–1951

THE CONNECTICUT ACADEMY OF ARTS AND SCIENCES, NEW HAVEN, CONNECTICUT
MDCCCCLXXX

Library of Congress Cataloging in Publication Data (Revised)

Main entry under title:

A Manual of the writings in Middle English, 1050–1500.

 Vols. 6– by members of the Middle English Group under its later name: Middle English Division.
 Vols. 1–2: general editor: J. B. Severs; v. 3– : A. E. Hartung.
 "Based upon A manual of the writings in Middle English, 1050–1400, by John Edwin Wells, New Haven, 1916, and supplements 1–9, 1919–1951."
 1. English literature–Middle English (1100–1500)–History and criticism. 2. English literature–Middle English (1100–1500)–Bibliography. I. Wells, John Edwin, 1875–1943. A manual of the writings in Middle English, 1050–1400. II. Severs, Jonathan Burke, ed. III. Hartung, Albert E., 1923– ed. IV. Modern Language Association of America. Middle English Group. V. Modern Language Association of America. Middle English Division.
PR255.M3   016.82′09′001   67–7687
ISBN 0-208-01220-6 (v. 3)

© 1980 by The Connecticut Academy of Arts and Sciences
Published for The Connecticut Academy of Arts and Sciences by Archon Books/The Shoe String Press, Inc., Hamden, Connecticut 06514

Printed in the United States of America

Publication of this book was assisted by a grant from the publications program of the National Endowment for the Humanities, an independent federal agency.

Volume 6

XIV. CAROLS

by

Richard Leighton Greene

XV. BALLADS

by

David C. Fowler

XVI. JOHN LYDGATE

by

Alain Renoir and C. David Benson

EDITORIAL AND ADVISORY COMMITTEE

Larry D. Benson • *E. Talbot Donaldson* • *Albert E. Hartung*
Lillian Herlands Hornstein • *Robert E. Kaske* • *Siegfried Wenzel*
Rossell Hope Robbins, Chairman

PREFACE

A collaborative project of the Middle English Division (formerly Group) of the Modern Language Association of America, this manual of Middle English literature has now reached six volumes with the present publication. The chapters comprising the earlier volumes are, for each volume, as follows: 1–The Romances; 2–The *Pearl* Poet, Wyclyf and His Followers, Translations and Paraphrases of the Bible, Saints' Legends, and Instructions for Religious; 3–Dialogues, Debates, and Catechisms, Thomas Hoccleve, and Malory and Caxton; 4–Middle Scots Writers and the Chaucerian Apocrypha; 5–Dramatic Pieces and Poems Dealing with Contemporary Conditions. The present volume 6 includes chapters XIV (Carols), XV (Ballads), and XVI (John Lydgate). Chapters XIV and XV are intended to be complete for all serious studies up to 1978; chapter XVI to Spring 1977. A full account of the principles followed by the editors of the work will be found in the Preface to volume 1.

The following chapters, as copy for them becomes available, are projected for future volumes: Tales; Chronicles; Homilies; Proverbs, Precepts, and Monitory Pieces; Piers Plowman; Works of Religious Information and Instruction; Science, Information, and Documents; Geography and Travel; Letters; Legal Writings; Rolle and His Followers; Lyrics; Gower; Undistributed Prose (i.e., those prose works suitable for inclusion which are not included in the above categories). It is expected that these chapters, together with a Master Index for all the chapters, will be completed in an additional four volumes for a total of ten. It is thus gratifying to the General Editor that with the publication of the present volume the project is now nearer to its completion than its beginning.

On behalf of the Middle English Division and on his own behalf, the General Editor is deeply grateful to the Connecticut Academy of Arts and Sciences for its undertaking the publication of this *Manual*, as it had undertaken the publication of the original. The scholarly community cannot sufficiently acknowledge its debt to the Academy. The General Editor also wishes to thank the National Endowment for the Humanities for its financial support (now continued over several years) of the indispensable contribution made to the project by his capable editorial assistant, Mrs. Marilyn C. Dunlap. Mrs. Dunlap, whose association with the *Manual* began with its third volume and has continued since then, has been a constant and effective help.

Albert E. Hartung
General Editor

CONTENTS

	Commentary	Bibliography
Preface	7	
XIV. Carols	1743	1940
By Richard Leighton Greene		
XV. Ballads	1753	2019
By David C. Fowler		
XVI. John Lydgate	1809	2071
By Alain Renoir and C. David Benson		
Table of Abbreviations	1923	
Index	2177	

XIV. CAROLS

by

Richard Leighton Greene

The genre which the later Middle Ages designate by the term "carol" is distinguished from other Middle English lyrics by its form, which consists of a burden or chorus sung *at the beginning of the piece* and after each stanza and any desired number of stanzas of uniform verse-structure. It is a song designed for social singing. The stanza is by origin a solo part, but in the polyphonic music which appears with about one quarter of the five-hundred-odd preserved carols, the stanzas as well as the burdens are set for more than one voice. The carol corresponds in its form to the French *chanson à carole*, the German *Reigenlied*, and the Italian *ballata*, all of which take their origin from the songs used in the round dance known in French as the *carole*. This ring-dance (which could at any time be opened into a serpentine chain and closed again) was extremely popular with all classes on the Continent and in England, and, while it ceases to be fashionable soon after 1500, it survives much longer in humbler and countrified places and particularly in Scotland, where it persists into fairly modern times. It is alive today in children's games in France, England, and America, and in South-east Europe it is still danced by adults.

The characteristic burden-and-stanza structure of the carol results from the essential division of the dance into alternate periods of standing still or marking time in place, during which the leader of the *carole* sang the stanzas, and of vigorous motion of the ring of dancers (always to the left, or sunwise, except for the *caroles* of witches, which went widdershins) while the whole company sang the unvarying burden. Sometimes, conversely, the burden seems to have been sung standing and the stanzas during the motion. Often the burden is connected by rime to the last lines of the stanzas. Both burdens and stanzas are found in many different verse-forms, but the most frequent type of burden is a couplet of four-measure lines, and the most frequent stanza-form is that of four four-measure lines rimed *aaab*.

Most of the fourteenth- and fifteenth-century carols are found in manuscripts coming from religious houses, and most are anonymous, though there are 26 by John Audelay, a chaplain in the Augustinian Haughmond Abbey in Shropshire, and more than 100 by James Ryman, a friar of the Franciscan house at Canterbury. One of the finest collections is in the commonplace book of Richard Hill, grocer of London (MS Balliol College Oxford 354), which, though written in the first four decades of the sixteenth century, contains many carols known from their occurrence in other manuscripts to have been current in the fifteenth. Other important anthologies of carols are: MS British Museum Sloane 2593, from the great monastery of Bury St. Edmunds; MS Bodleian Library 29734 (Eng poet e.1), probably from Beverley Minster; MS St. John's College Cambridge 259 (S.54), of undetermined provenance but clearly from East Anglia. Two manuscripts important for the music to which their carols are set are MS Bodleian Library 3340 (Arch Selden B.26) and MS British Museum Egerton 3307, the former probably from Worcester, the latter not yet certainly located but definitely not from St. George's Chapel at Windsor. Between these and other manuscripts there are many correspondences of texts, usually too nearly alike to be regarded as orally transmitted. There was clearly a nation-wide exchange in clerical circles of carol-texts which were usually religious or at least edifying in content and which must be regarded as in an entirely different category from the folk-songs of the completely uneducated.

The principal use of both religious and secular carols appears to have been entertainment at feasts or other gatherings in secular or monastic halls, as is shown both by many references in historical documents and by phrases in the texts themselves (e.g., "Wolcum be ye that arn here / Wolcum alle, and mak good chere," or "Lett no man cum into this hall / . . . But that sum sport he bryng withall"). The annual ceremony of the Boar's Head Carol at the Queen's College, Oxford, is the most authentic modern survival (or revival) of this custom. It is not likely that carols were used in actual services in church (except possibly at certain seasons as substitutes for the *Benedicamus Domino*), and there is no satisfactory evidence for their use in processions in churchyard or church in place of the prescribed Latin texts, though this has been suggested.

Many of the carols embody Latin phrases, usually whole lines, sometimes composed specially for the piece itself so as to make true macaronic verse, sometimes borrowed from liturgical texts, most frequently from the hymns of the Office but also from proses or sequences and from antiphons. This borrowing is another sign of the manuscript carols' having been current in clerical surroundings.

The carols of religious content are thus to be regarded as the products of a widespread process, much used, for example, by the Franciscans in Italy, of composing sacred or moralizing lyrics in the verse-forms and to the tunes of songs already known to the people which churchmen regarded as objectionable or at least frivolous. This process should be carefully distinguished from religious parody, properly defined as actual echoing of the secular model. Both procedures are found in the Scottish *Gude and Godlie Ballatis* of post-Reformation times. The following of the burden-and-stanza form required for the dance of the *carole* gives us the English carol as it gives us similar lyrics in the other vernaculars and, when used for compositions in Latin, a large number of extra-liturgical *cantilenae*, many of them obviously for use in Christmas and other festivities. That this substitution was accepted by at least some of the lay folk is shown by the survival in modern traditional folk-song of a few of the manuscript carols (e.g., [79], [144], [154], [325]).

In their themes and in their phraseology the carols show many likenesses to Middle English lyrics cast in other forms, but the qualities of directness, simplicity, informality, and singability are notable in the whole corpus when it is compared to the rest of Middle English verse. The particular combination of piety and festivity surviving in the modern "Christmas carol" (which is no longer restricted to the burden-and-stanza form) pervades most of the medieval carols, especially those which relate to the principal feasting-time of the year, the Nativity season.

The Middle English carols of the fourteenth and fifteenth centuries may be arranged by subject-matter and summarized as follows. The order in general follows that of Greene E E Carols.

(1) Carols of Advent, [1–3]. [1] and [2] are sacred and based on two of the Advent antiphons; [3] is secular and concerns the fasting in Advent.

(2) Carols of the Nativity, [4–94]. This class of carols is the most numerous of all, and its dominance is reflected in the post-medieval use of "carol" to designate any song specifically for Christmas. Several types may be distinguished within the group: carols which greet the Christmas season personified as a visitor [4–6]; carols which call the roll of the Christmas feast-days

[7, 8]; carols emphasizing the conviviality of Christmas and specifically mentioning a feast [9–10, 12, 14]; the large group in which the religious significance of the Nativity is foremost [11, 13, 15–73, 82–94]; carols which present the visit of the shepherds to the Christ Child [74–81].

(3) Carols of the Saints of the Christmas Season, [95–114]. These pieces are in honor of St. Stephen, whose day is December 26 [95–99]; St. John the Evangelist, December 27 [100–105]; the Holy Innocents, December 28 [106–109]; St. Thomas of Canterbury, December 29 [110–114].

(4) Carols of the New Year, [115–119]. Three of these are wholly festive in spirit; the last strikes a note of misgiving for the future.

(5) Carols of the Epiphany, [120–132]. Most of these record the visit of the Three Kings; three relate to the baptism of Christ on the anniversary of the Epiphany [126, 131, 132].

(6) Carols of the Boar's Head, [133–136]. The famous carol [133] still used at the Queen's College, Oxford, is paralleled by the others, all obviously designed for singing at Christmas feasts.

(7) Carols of Holly and Ivy, [137–141]. The two favorite evergreens used for Christmas decorations are presented in an opposition which relates holly to the male and ivy to the female sex [137, 138], two carols associate ivy with the Virgin [139, 140], and one praises it for its therapeutic and masonry-preserving qualities as well as for its greenness in winter [141].

(8) Carols of Candlemas, [142, 143]. These two carols follow the tradition which makes the Purification rather than the Epiphany the end of the Christmas season, and both contain "farewells."

(9) Lullaby Carols, [144–157, 470]. The theme of the Virgin lulling her child is developed in most of these carols to include dialogue between the two in which Christ's sufferings are foretold.

(10) Carols of the Passion, [158–171]. These include dialogues of Mary and her son [158, 159], *planctus Mariae* [161, 162], and a long monologue by Christ addressed to His mother [167].

(11) Carols of and to the Virgin, [172–231]. Some of the carols in honor of Mary naturally include specific reference to the Nativity and were doubtless much used at Christmas. Several adopt the figure of a rose or a rose-tree for Mary [172–176], and many of them, especially those by James Ryman, include a selection of the "types" of the Virgin found in the Old Testament (e.g., the fleece of Gideon, the rod of Aaron, and the burning bush of Moses).

Several of Ryman's carols use the petition "Sancta Maria, ora pro nobis" as a burden [222–228].

(12) Carols of the Joys of Mary, [232–235]. In all of these the number of the Joys is five; the other numbers found in traditional songs do not appear.

(13) Carols of the Annunciation, [236–259]. Almost all of the carols on this theme are narrative in structure and follow closely the scriptural account of the visit of Gabriel. One is on the particular subject of the Magnificat [259].

(14) Carols of Joseph, [260–262]. The three carols deal with "the trouble of Joseph" and the angel's explanation to him of Mary's being with child; one is a *chanson d'aventure* in which Joseph himself explains the situation.

(15) Carols of the Virgin's Motherhood, [263, 264]. The first of these is a sacred parody of a lament of an abandoned girl, with Mary rejoicing in instead of bewailing her condition; the second is an address of Christ to His mother using the imagery of the Song of Songs.

(16) Carols of Christ's Pleading, [265–270]. Three of these carols are on the theme "I desire not the death of a sinner" [266–268]; two are addresses of Christ to sinful man [269–270].

(17) Carols of Christ, [271–276]. These carols are rather conventional pleas for mercy and salvation.

(18) Carols of the Trinity, [277–307]. Most of this group are by James Ryman and are based on the *Te Deum laudamus*; one is on "the knot of the Trinity" [283].

(19) A Carol on the Well of Mercy, [308]. This carol briefly develops the familiar metaphor for divine forgiveness.

(20) Carols of Purgatory, [309, 310]. The first of these is a prayer for the suffering souls; the second presents a voice that speaks to man about purgatory.

(21) A Litany, [311]. A single stanza found in many manuscripts is made into a carol in one of them by the addition of a burden.

(22) Carols of Saints, [312–319]. The saints other than those whose days fall in the Christmas season who have carols addressed to them are Francis of Assisi [312], Anne [313], George [314], Edmund [315], Catherine [316], Winifred (a long narrative by Audelay) [317], and Nicholas [318, 319].

(23) Carols of the Eucharist, [320–324]. The first three of these carols describe and praise the bread which becomes Christ's body; the other two make symbolic use of the wheat from which the bread is made.

(24) The Corpus Christi Carol, [325]. This impressive carol, often called "mysterious," has challenged many commentators. Its earliest appearance is in Richard Hill's commonplace book (Balliol College Oxford MS 354), in which it has been entered at a time later than that of the material which surrounds it. There are two traditional versions from England and one from Scotland, both recorded in the nineteenth century, and one twentieth-century version from the U. S. A. The early interpretations given to the carol, by Anne G. Gilchrist and Edith C. Batho respectively, see in it a series of allusions to the Grail Legend, the hall standing for the Castle of the Grail, the knight for the wounded keeper of the Grail and so on, or a poem on the Entombment of Christ and the figure of the Wounded Knight. Neither reading has proved entirely satisfactory to readers and admirers of the poem. R. L. Greene, in two articles and in the notes in the second edition of *The Early English Carols*, sees in the burden a clear reference to Anne Boleyn, whose well-known badge was a white falcon, and to her winning away of the "mak" of Queen Catherine of Aragon, who was reputed to weep night and day within sight of the Host when she had been banished. This interpretation has troubled a few commentators, but no systematic refutation has yet been published. (See also p. 1772 below.)

(25) A Carol of a Mass, [326]. This carol, recalling the Last Supper as the prototype of the Mass, presents Christ, the disciples, SS. Thomas, Nicholas(?), John, and George, and the Virgin at a Mass in a chapel.

(26) Carols of Religious Counsel, [327–340]. The subjects of the good advice in this group of didactic carols include the Commandments [327], the Seven Deadly Sins [328], the Seven Works of Mercy [329], the Seven Gifts of the Holy Ghost [330], and the five senses [331]; general pious precepts [332], hope in God [333], swearing by the Mass [334], thankfulness [335], Christ's sacrifice [336–338], the Fall of Man [339], and amending the wrongdoer rather than speaking ill of him [340].

(27) Carols of Moral Counsel, [341–360]. This second group of didactic carols, less religious and more prudential than the preceding, includes pieces against haste [341], against a wicked tongue [342–345], against boasting [346, 347], on cheerful endurance [348], on trusting old servants [349], on keeping one's proper "estate" [350–352], against covetousness [353, 354], on death [355, 356], on doing well [357], against pride [358], on making amends [359], and on events warning of God's wrath [360].

(28) Carols of Repentance, [361–363]. These exhort man to the timely seeking of God's grace and mercy.

(29) Carols of Doomsday, [364–367]. These carols are conventional urgings to think of the Last Judgment.

(30) Carols of Mortality, [368–381]. The most striking of this group are the carols which make use of the phrase "Timor mortis conturbat me" [372–375]. One is a *chanson d'aventure* about a bird which sings that all flesh is grass [381].

(31) Satirical Carols, [382–397]. The carols in which satire is predominant use some of the themes found in other Middle English poetry and in several cases include proverbs or proverbial phrases in their burdens. The subjects include "Service is no heritage" [384], the faithlessness of executors [385], "guile" [386, 387], the banishment of truth [388], the prevalence of various vices [389, 390], the unreliability of friends [391], the wisdom of trying friends before they are needed [392], and the power of money [393–396]. One is unique in satirizing a named person in a particular village, Jon Clerke of Great Torrington, Devon [397].

(32) Carols of Women, [398–407]. These carols include praise of womankind associated with the excellence of the Virgin [398–400], Audelay's commendations of virginity [401, 402], and cynical pieces in the medieval antifeminist tradition [403–407]. The last of these is a puzzle-song or "Christmas game" made into a carol [407].

(33) Carols of Marriage, [408–416]. The carols on wedded life generally take the unfavorable view and present wives as shrews, but Audelay's concern is with unequal marriages which impair the quality of inheritance [416].

(34) Carols of Childhood, [417, 418]. Audelay praises children for their freedom from the vices of adults [417], and a schoolboy complains of the harsh discipline enforced by a hated master [418].

(35) Picaresque Carols, [419–424]. Vagabondage is the theme of three carols [419–421]; in one a braggart with a dagger is worsted by a carter with a whip [422]; one is a warning against a wandering life [423]; and one is on a strutting "gallant" [424].

(36) Convivial Carols, [425–431]. A carol to speed the plow [425], probably made from a song originally in another form, has the tone of some later traditional plowmen's songs and may well have been sung on Plow Monday. A song of the fox raiding the poultry-yard [426] has many modern

analogues in folk-song. The "good gossips" meet at the alehouse [427]; a challenge to singers is issued [428]; the butler is begged for a drink [429]; good ale is called for in a repetitive formula which rejects various viands [430]; and the effects of drunkenness from ale are recounted [431].

(37) A Carol of Hunting, [432]. A gay song of hunting the hart with hound and horn.

(38) Political Carols, [433–443]. A carol, unique of its kind, contrasts a good citizen, presumably of Ashford, Kent, with a traitorous one under the types of rose-briar and periwinkle respectively [433]. The carols on larger public personages and events include one on the execution of Archbishop Scrope for rebellion in 1405 [434], the famous "Agincourt Carol" [435], a celebration of Henry V as the "Rose of Ryse" [436], Audelay's prayer for the opening reign of Henry VI [437], a loyal address to Edward IV [438], "Willikin's Return" on Warwick and Henry VI [439], a long account of the Battle of Towton in 1461 [440], Lancastrian verses on the ship of state [441], a dull ceremonial Garter poem on Henry VII [442], and a plea to Jesus to send peace [443].

(39) A Complaint, [444]. The one carol of this type, formal and subjective in style, laments the separation of the speaker from his sovereign by the contrariness of Fortune.

(40) Amorous Carols, [445–465]. This group, which may be presumed to represent a much larger number of love-carols which have not been preserved, includes the important "Ichot a burde in boure bryht," the only one of the MS Harley 2253 lyrics in full carol form [445], a jolly piece in praise of a servingman as a lover [446], the early *chanson d'aventure* of a forsaken maiden with the burden beginning "Nou sprinkes the spray" [447], and a complaint of the strangeness of a beloved man [448]. Two carols recorded in a student's notebook, the most remarkable of all for realism and sexual frankness, narrate the holiday adventures of a serving-maid and are very similar in style [449, 450]. The latter is especially important as showing the connection of the carole with sexual looseness which is so much lamented by preachers. Three pieces are monologues by betrayed girls, one of whom has lost her virtue to a priest at a "well-waking" [458]. A plain-spoken piece commends another "Sir John" as a lover [459]. A girl's account of Jankyn the holy-water clerk with its refrain of "Kyrieleyson" is a kind of sacrilegious trope of the Mass [460]. Four carols, one of a maid and a miller, one of "puddings," and two

of a friar and a nun, are of undiluted obscenity, the last two irreverent as well [461–464]. In another one, purporting to be an expression of relief at escape from love, the gender of the "I" of the speaker has been debated [465].

(41) Humorous Carols, [466–469]. The first of these is a mock-lament of a forsaken lover: "When I sleep I may not wake" [466]; two are excellent examples of the "lying song" or list of disconnected statements [467, 468], and the last is a macaronic nonsense parody of the Christmas services [469].

(42) Miscellany, [471–475]. Five poems on various subjects are listed here as pieces which should be noticed by any reader with an interest in Middle English carols. They are not included in Greene E E Carols, and the reader can judge for himself whether the editor was unjust to these pieces in leaving them out.

A short song [471] which combines Christmas potation and Christmas piety has been well explicated by M. F. Bukofzer, who is followed by Stevens. Bukofzer has pointed out that if the Latin lines added by a later hand are disregarded a regular carol remains recognizable through the efforts of someone to "improve" it.

"A Song of the Blessed Virgin and Joseph" (Carleton Brown's title) [472] was printed by Brown from MS Advocates 18.7.21, where it has sixteen stanzas and no indicated burden. It appears in the later Selden manuscript with music making the first stanza a burden and turning the four-line stanzas into eight-line stanzas arranged in a narrative order less logical than that of the Advocates version. Stevens points out that the musical form given to it is that of the French *virelai* and adds the important comment: "It is interesting to find the only known English *virelai* with music in the middle of a collection of carols."

In "A Song to the Virgin" on the Annunciation [473], the one trite stanza is of little poetical value, and the burden which reappears as a chorus after the stanza with differing music presents merely the first two phrases of the *Ave Maria*. It is, of course, in excellent company in the Selden manuscript. Robbins prints it in his *Early English Christmas Carols*, marking the chorus "Concluding Burden."

A song in praise of Henry VII, "For Victory in France (1492)" (Robbins' title) [474], a patriotic piece which resembles some carols in its rhetoric, was first presented by E. F. Rimbault without division into stanzas. One is not required to be sure of Rimbault's claim of his having it in a manuscript other than MS Cotton Domitian xviii. When Robbins first published it, he was reluctant to call it a carol, and when he presented it in his *Historical Poems* he attached to his note the sensible comment that the text is "obviously contaminated." A consistent rime-scheme is not maintained, and it is not certain that the first two lines are really a burden. It might be said that it "is trying to be a carol" or that there has been some imperfect transmission from memory.

In Friar John Grimestone's "preaching book," MS Advocates 18.7.21, there is a dialogue of the Virgin and her son [475], with a couplet spoken by Christ and two four-line stanzas spoken by Mary. Though it has been reckoned a carol by Robbins (MLN 53.243), there seems to be no repetition of the opening couplet as a burden.

Various fragments have been collected under item [476] in the Bibliography.

XV. BALLADS

by

David C. Fowler

I should like to acknowledge here the late MacEdward Leach, who was the original editor of this chapter, assigned to it at the time of the *Manual's* inception, but unfortunately unable to complete it before his death in 1967. It is gratifying to me to follow in the footsteps of a teacher, fellow scholar, and friend, who did much to foster in me the love of balladry.

David C. Fowler

The ballad may be defined as a traditional narrative song. Calling it "narrative" distinguishes it from the folk song, which is primarily lyrical; calling it "traditional" distinguishes it from artistic compositions that exist apart from the folk; and finally, calling it a "song" separates it from the folk tale and other traditional narratives that are recited without melodic accompaniment. A definition of the ballad that goes beyond these three primary characteristics inevitably suffers a loss of precision. Even the famous "impersonal style" and "dramatic mode" of balladry are not always present, and the use of a refrain, commonly associated with the ballad, is by no means universal. Considerable variation in these secondary characteristics is a marked feature of the European ballad community.

The English and Scottish popular ballads, which are the subject of this chapter, have in a sense been defined progressively by the collections in which they appear down through the centuries. The first such collection in which ballads are included in significant numbers is the Percy Folio MS (ca. 1650), which contains romances, metrical histories, over one hundred miscellaneous songs, and forty-five ballads. In this fine manuscript of minstrelsy, ballads are not distinguished from other forms; all are mingled here in a single great collection. In the early eighteenth century, songbooks increased in numbers and popularity: some, like Ramsay's *Tea-Table Miscellany* (1723–37) and Thomson's *Orpheus Caledonius* (1733), made money for their publishers; others, like Elizabeth Cochrane's songbook (ca. 1730), were compiled and preserved in unpublished form by individuals or families, in the tradition of the commonplace book. All of these songbooks tended to eliminate romances and histories, but commingled ballads and songs without discrimination. The same mixture is evident in the latter half of the century, both in Bishop Percy's *Reliques of Ancient English Poetry* (1765), and in the important though less influential *Scottish Songs* of David Herd (1769–76). It is not until we encounter the repertoire of that famous ballad informant, Mrs. Brown of Falkland, that we find a collection (manuscripts dated 1783–1800) devoted exclusively to ballads as they are now defined. The manuscripts of Mrs. Brown contain thirty-three ballads in fifty-one versions.

The final, authoritative definition of the ballad canon was provided by Francis J. Child, editor of *The English and Scottish Popular Ballads* 5 vols. (Child; 1882–98). This edition consists of 305 numbered "Child ballads" together with the texts of all known variant versions of each ballad designated by letters of the alphabet. Thus *Thomas Rymer* (Child, no. 37) may be more specifically designated no. 37A, with the "A" in this case referring to a version preserved in one of the manuscripts of Mrs. Brown. This convenient method of reference, used by most modern editors and critics, will be employed in the present chapter in reference to specific ballads. The order of presentation of texts in Child's edition is less than satisfactory, but in general subsequent editors have followed his practice of grouping ballads by type. MacEdward Leach, *The Ballad Book* (Leach BB; 1955), follows Child's order almost exactly, and then adds ballads not known or not included by Child. A. B. Friedman, *The Viking Book of Folk Ballads* (Friedman VBFB; 1956), and James Kinsley, *The Oxford Book of Ballads* (Kinsley OBB; 1969), offer different categories, but in general follow Child's typological organization. As against this modern tendency, the present chapter will treat the ballads in chronological order, according to the date of the earliest known version.

Child did not live to write a critical introduction to *The English and Scottish Popular Ballads*, and this circumstance left the field of interpretation wide open for modern ballad criticism. The full story is told by D. K. Wilgus, *Anglo-American Folksong Scholarship since 1898* (1959), but here it will be possible only to mention a few highlights. The question of ballad origins, concerning which Child had very little to say, absorbed the attention of the "Harvard school" under the ambivalent leadership of G. L. Kittredge. The theory of communal origin, or primitive composition by the singing, dancing throng, was derived from the famous *obiter dictum* of the brothers Grimm "Das Volk dichtet," and held the field in England and America during the first two decades of this century. The most articulate spokesman for this point of view was F. B. Gummere, who elaborated his thesis in several books, notably *The Beginnings of Poetry* (1901). Though Gummere was in some sense a literary critic, his concern with origins led to an anthropological emphasis in ballad study which has survived to the present day. But his communal theory was strongly attacked by Louise Pound in her *Poetic Origins and the Ballad* (1921), and tactfully compromised by G. H. Gerould, *The Ballad of Tradition* (1932). In his book Gerould sought, by invoking the concept of "communal recreation," to establish a consensus of ballad scholarship somewhere between the theories of communal and individual authorship.

While the controversy over origins was running its course, great progress was being made in field collecting of ballads and folk songs. The British musicologist, Cecil Sharp, gathered such songs as he could find from rural English counties at the turn of the century and then, to his amazement, stumbled on a much richer harvest in America. The results of his American field work are set forth in *English Folk-Songs from the Southern Appalachians* 2 vols. (1932), a book which had an important influence in turning the attention of students to the music of the ballad, in contrast to Child, who had focussed on the words. The climax of this emphasis on music, as far as balladry is concerned, is the monumental collection by B. H. Bronson, *The Traditional Tunes of the Child Ballads* (Bronson TTCB; 1959–72), which contains the definitive corpus of known melodies associated with the ballads, arranged and numbered in conformity with Child's edition. Along with this attention to the collection of texts and music from modern tradition, ballad bibliography received increased attention, pioneered by S. B. Hustvedt, *Ballad Criticism in Scandinavia and Great Britain during the Eighteenth Century* (1916), and *Ballad Books and Ballad Men* (1930). To match the work of Child for English and Scottish balladry, American ballad bibliographies were compiled by Tristram P. Coffin, *The British Traditional Ballad in North America* (Coffin BTBNA; 1950, revised 1963), and G. Malcolm Laws, *Native American Balladry* (1950, revised 1964) and *American Balladry from British Broadsides* (1957). British materials since Child are represented in Margaret Dean-Smith, *A Guide to English Folk Song Collections, 1822–1952* (Dean-Smith; 1954), and supplemented or expanded by Claude M. Simpson, *The British Broadside Ballad and Its Music* (Simpson BBBM; 1966).

The maturing of balladry as a field of scholarly study is indicated by the growing interest in the international ballad in the context of the European ballad community. An influential pioneer study was Archer Taylor, *"Edward" and "Sven I Rosengård"* (1931), and an important survey of this entire field was undertaken by William Entwistle, *European Balladry* (1939). Since then considerable progress in methodology has been achieved in successive studies of individual ballads: Paul Christophersen, *The Ballad of Sir Aldingar* (1952), Paul G. Brewster, *The Two Sisters* (1953), H. O. Nygard, *The Ballad of Heer Halewijn* (1958), Eleanor Long, *"The Maid" and "The Hangman"* (1971), and the forthcoming study of *Earl Brand* by W. I. Siegmund. On the other hand, as might be expected, much more attention has been devoted to the English and Scottish ballads and their American descendants. A brief but excellent British study by M. J. C. Hodgart, *The Ballads* (1950), combines an interest in literature, music, and folklore; while an American viewpoint predominates in E. K. Wells, *The Ballad Tree* (1950), a thorough, well-illustrated survey of the ballad tradition. The focus of such studies has tended to be modern, but a few works also pay attention to the medieval origins and development of balladry, especially E. K. Chambers, in his chapter on the ballads in *English Literature at the Close of the Middle Ages* (Chambers OHEL; 1945), and D. C. Fowler, *A Literary History of the Popular Ballad* (1968). A recent work, important both for its analysis of the early development of the broadside ballad and for its treatment of the ballad revival in the eighteenth century, is A. B. Friedman, *The Ballad Revival* (1961).

In English literature anthologies, ballads usually appear with literature of the fifteenth century, and partly for this reason it is deemed appropriate to include them here in the *Manual*. Yet in fact scarcely more than a half dozen of the 305 Child ballads actually survive in a form earlier than the year 1500, and the majority of versions were collected in the nineteenth century. Yet there are advantages to studying the ballads as a literary unit, and some justification for assuming that a certain number, at least, existed in oral tradition for a considerable period before they were written down in the form that survives today. In light of this, one possibility might have been to include in this chapter, in addition to the few that actually appear before 1500, only those ballads that seem from internal evidence to have a medieval origin. But not only would this procedure be highly subjective, it would also effectively destroy the unity of the ballad canon.

We have decided, therefore, on a chronological arrangement of the ballads, modified only to the extent necessary to group them according to the sources in which each ballad first appears. Thus each of the twenty-five numbered items of this chapter will represent a ballad source, and each item will contain a discussion of the ballad or ballads in that source. As we proceed chronologically through this list, the nature of the ballad "source" changes to accommodate historical developments. The first fifteen items stand for single manuscripts which contain usually no more than one or two ballads each. Items [16] to [25] represent various chronological groupings according to the type and date of collection or publication, whether manuscript, broadside, songbook, or anthology. The last item, [25], by far the largest, comprises all Child ballads first collected in the nineteenth century—more than one hundred. Within each item, where necessary, the discussion will be organized so as to give prominence or preferential position in that item to those ballads showing evidence of medieval origin. No doubt disagreements will exist over the question of order or preference, but at least it can be said that no ballad is ignored completely, and all are represented equally in the Bibliography. Moreover—and this is important—the actual nature and chronology of ballad sources is explicitly represented in the twenty-five items. In this way we hope to retain the unity of the ballad canon in the *Manual* without misrepresenting the history of balladry.

While it is possible to define the ballad, as indicated at the beginning of this chapter, in terms of its primary characteristics, there is at the same time an evolution of balladry which our chronological arrangement tends to make evident. In the early, formative period, ballads identified as such by Child tend to resemble one or another of several medieval forms: the carol, lyric, riddle, chanson d'aventure, romance, or metrical tale. It is not until the late sixteenth century that the ballad achieves its own identity, best typified perhaps in *Captain Car* (Child, no. 178). This ambiguity in form of the earliest ballads is well illustrated in various chapters of the *Manual*. Under Romances (vol. 1), for example, are included the *Ballad of Hind Horn*, I [3], and, among seventeen romances from the Percy Folio MS, two which Child defined as ballads: *The Marriage of Sir Gawain*, I [35], and *King Arthur and King Cornwall*, I [37]. Further, among miscellaneous romances and Breton lays in the last three sections of chap. I, some two dozen are cross-referenced to the ballad tradition in the Bibliography. In chap. IV, Translations and Paraphrases of the Bible (vol. 2), *Iacob and Iosep*, IV [3], is described as having the characteristics of ballad poetry, and the *Ballad of Twelfth Day*, IV [43], is cross-referenced to Ballads along with *Judas* (see [1] below), which appears in the same manuscript (Trinity Cambridge 323). Finally in chap. VII, Dialogues, Debates, and Catechisms (vol. 3), we find *Inter Diabolus et Virgo*, VII [17], the earliest known form of Child's *Riddles Wisely Expounded* (Child, no. 1); and several texts having important ballad connections: *De Clerico et Puella* (*pastourelle*), VII [54], related perhaps to *Clerk Saunders* (Child, no. 69); *The Nut-Brown Maid*, VII [61], very influential generally but perhaps especially relevant to the ballad of *Child Waters* (Child, no. 63); *Ballad of a Tyrannical Husband*, VII [64], resembling a motif widespread in folktale and folk song; and *The Fermorar and His Dochter*, VII [66], a felicitous example of the chanson d'aventure, which brings to mind *The Carnal and the Crane* (Child, no. 55), *Robyn and Gandeleyn* (Child, no. 115), and especially *Crow and Pie* (Child, no. 111).

In summary, we may characterize the medieval phase of balladry as an incubation period. The first eight sections below, representing texts probably in existence by 1500, illustrate the variety of medieval forms that led to the making of ballad tradition. [1] below has *Judas* and *Twelfth Day*, paraphrases of the Bible; [2] below has *Inter Diabolus et Virgo*, a dialogue involving a girl and a supernatural (demonic) opponent; [3] below has *Robin Hood and the Monk*, a metrical tale of the greenwood; [4] below includes a carol, *St. Stephen and Herod*, a chanson d'aventure with a greenwood setting, *Robyn and Gandeleyn*, and a riddle song, *I Have a Young Sister*, all three texts found in a single medieval songbook (British Museum Sloane 2593); [5] below has *Robin Hood and the Potter* and *King Edward the Fourth and a Tanner of Tamworth*, both metrical tales, one of Robin Hood and the other a type known as King and Subject, perhaps best exemplified in *John the Reeve* (in the Percy Folio MS); [6] and [7] below are *A Gest of Robin Hode* and *Adam Bell*, metrical romances of the greenwood in early printed form; and finally [8] below is a commonplace book containing the *Corpus Christi Carol*, a text not in Child, but included in modern ballad anthologies. In none of the above is there documentary evidence of the existence of tunes, though it is not unreasonable to assume that there were melodies for [4] and [8]. The task of identifying ballads in the late medieval period is indeed precarious, but it is nevertheless a very important aspect of ballad study, and we must be grateful to Child for reaching back with cool confidence to the cradle, so to speak, and choosing for inclusion in the canon these few important medieval forerunners of the ballad tradition.

Chronological List of Ballad Sources

MS TRINITY COLLEGE CAMBRIDGE 323 (B.14.39) [1]. An early commonplace book, compiled about the middle of the thirteenth century by various hands in Latin, French, and English. Carleton Brown regarded it as the product of a religious house, possibly Dominican (Brown ELxiiiC, p. xx), but David Jeffrey believes it to be of Franciscan provenance (*The Early English Lyric and Franciscan Spirituality*, Lincoln Neb 1975, p. 207). Contents: *De Ordine Creaturarum* (folios 1–19), a Latin treatise by an Irish monk dated 650 AD and traditionally ascribed to Isidore of Seville; a miscellany of lyrics, saints' legends, biblical paraphrases, debates, homilies, and proverbs (folios 19–48, 81–87); a legend of St. Nicholas attributed to Wace (folios 48–56) and stories taken from the gospels (folios 58–72), both in French verse; and various sermons and tracts in Latin and French (folios 72–80). Toward the end (folio 83) is a Latin epitaph in memory of Bishop Robert Grosseteste (died 1253).

It may help in envisioning the variety of English texts in the Trinity MS to note how they have been categorized by modern editors, and where they are distributed in the chapters of this *Manual*. Most of the lyrics appear in Brown ELxiiiC (1932), nos. 14–34, 38 supplemented by H. A. Person, *Cambridge Middle English Lyrics*, Seattle 1953, nos. 19, 24, 27, 28, 54, and find a place in the *Manual* in the chapter on lyrics. The *Life of St. Margaret* (folios 20–24) is an early quatrain version discussed under V [184] in vol. 2. *Wise Admonitions* (folio 26) and the *Proverbs of Alfred* (folios 85–87) belong in the chapter on Proverbs, Precepts, and Monitory Pieces. For the *Trinity Poem on Biblical History* (folios 36–42), see IV [50] in vol. 2. A final category of English text is *The Debate between the Body and the Soul* (folios 29–32), for which see VII [18] in vol. 3.

Some of the English lyrics in the Trinity MS have also been regarded as representative of other literary forms. Four of these lyrics appear in VII [18] as examples of *The Debate between the Body and the Soul*. Thus *Shroud and Grave* (Brown ELxiiiC, no. 20), *Doomsday* (Brown ELxiiiC, no. 28a), *The Latemest*

Day (Brown ELxiiiC, no. 29A), and *Over the Bier of the Worldling* (Brown ELxiiiC, no. 38) find a place, respectively, in subsections (d), (g), (h), and (j) of VII [18]. *The Journey of the Three Kings* (Brown ELxiiiC, no. 26) is in IV [43] (see *Manual*, vol. 2), with the title *Ballad of Twelfth Day*. *Of One That Is So Fair and Bright* (Brown ELxiiiC, no. 17A) appears as a carol in Greene R L, *The Early English Carols*, Oxford 1935 (Greene E E Carols, no. 191Bb) and hence belongs also in the chapter on Carols. Finally, and most important for present purposes, *The Bargain of Judas* (Brown ELxiiiC, no. 25) was considered by Child to be the earliest known example of a ballad, and was included in his *English and Scottish Popular Ballads*, Boston 1882, vol. 1, p. 242, entitled *Judas* (Child, no. 23).

On Maundy Thursday Jesus gives Judas 30 pieces of silver and tells him to go to Jerusalem to buy food. Judas meets his "sister" who rebukes him for following a false prophet. She directs him to "go thou on the rock, high upon the stone," and then persuades him to put his head in her lap and go to sleep. When he awakens the silver has been stolen, and he begins to tear his hair. In this condition he meets the "rich Jew" Pilate, who asks him if he would sell his Lord. Judas replies that he will sell him for nothing but the 30 pieces of silver that he had been entrusted with. When the disciples come to the table, Jesus tells them that he has been sold for their food. Judas asks "Is it I?" and Peter protests that he would fight for the love of the Lord against Pilate and all his knights. Jesus predicts that Peter will forsake him thrice before cockcrow.

Child's classification of *Judas* as a ballad may have been based on the presence of popular elements in the narrative, such as the treacherous sister who seemingly casts a spell over Judas (plausibly identified by Dronke as his mistress), and the extraordinary explanation of the selling of Jesus for 30 pieces of silver. Folklore alone, however, cannot establish the identity of ballads, and Child may have given some weight also to the couplet form of *Judas*, which somewhat resembles that of *St. Stephen and Herod* (Child, no. 22), for which see [4] below. The evidence for regarding *Judas* as a ballad remains weak, but Child's view has been accepted by most modern editors and critics, who regard it as the earliest known example of the popular ballad.

Modern editors misrepresent the form of *Judas* by regularly repeating lines 8, 25, and 30, which in the Trinity MS are marked with a ".ii." in the right-hand margin. Skeat took this (Child, vol. 5, p. 288) to be a device for calling attention to the fact that a triplet was being used in place of the usual couplet, as for example in lines 24–26:

[2]

> In him com ur lord gon as is postles setten at mete.
> wou sitte ye postles ant wi nule ye ete.   .ii.
> ic am iboust and isold to day for oure mete.

Most anthologies repeat the middle line above to form two couplets, but surely Skeat was correct in interpreting the mark as indicating a momentary change in the rime scheme. Skeat's view has been supported recently by Mitsui, who however also believes that the ".ii." is a sign to the singer to repeat the second stave of the ballad tune so as to adapt it to the triplet form.

MS BODLEIAN LIBRARY OXFORD 15444 (RAWLINSON D.328) [2]. A mid-fifteenth-century collection of wisdom literature in Latin and English. The *Distichs of Cato* in Latin (folio 1a) is followed by miscellaneous prose and verse in Latin and English (folio 7a). Lydgate's *Stans Puer ad Mensam* in Latin and English (folio 159a), and Benedict Burgh's version of *Cato Minor* (folio 161a), belong respectively in the chapter on Lydgate, and the chapter on Proverbs, Precepts, and Monitory Pieces.

The ballad in this manuscript is *Inter Diabolus et Virgo* (folio 174b), which Child discovered late and included in his last volume (vol. 5, p. 283) under the title *Riddles Wisely Expounded* (Child, no. 1).

> This dialogue between a devil and a maid takes the form of a contest. The devil promises to teach the girl all the wisdom of this world if she will be his lover. He then proceeds to ask her a series of questions, such as What is higher than the tree? What is deeper than the sea? In conclusion he implies that she must perforce be his lover unless she can answer the questions. The maid answers them all satisfactorily, and thus escapes the devil's clutches. Some of the riddles seem to have sexual overtones, and the outcome thus suggests that the girl's naive, correct answers are also an affirmation of her innocence.

Since this text has been treated under VII [17] (see *Manual*, vol. 3) as an example of riddling dialogue, discussion here is limited to a few supplementary observations on later versions.

Some three dozen versions of *Riddles Wisely Expounded* have been collected in Britain and America under various titles, notably *The Devil's Nine Questions*. Most forms identify the questioner as diabolical, although in a few, notably a seventeenth-century broadside (Child, no. 1A), the devil is demythologized and identified as "a knight of noble worth," who agreeably marries the girl when she has successfully answered his questions. In a version in Motherwell's manuscript (1825), the devil flies away in a blazing flame when the girl names him (Child, no. 1C). The perennial fascination of riddles and no doubt a continuing interest in the devil have combined to keep this medieval ballad alive to this day.

MS CAMBRIDGE UNIVERSITY LIBRARY Ff.5.48 [3]. Aside from two short pieces in Latin—a charm against thieves (folio 10ᵇ) and some prognostications (folio 66ᵇ)—this fifteenth-century manuscript consists entirely of English texts. It is a miscellany containing some religious instruction, prophecy, wisdom, and lyrics, but most of all metrical tales. Elsewhere in this *Manual* the *Southern Passion* (folio 87ᵇ) has been dealt with in IV [58], the *South English Legendary* (folio 79ᵃ) in V [1], the *Northern Passion* (folio 11ᵃ) in V [303] (see vol. 2), and *The Clerk and the Nightingale* (folio 57ᵃ) in VII [48] (see vol. 3). Other works in the manuscript are likewise suited to chapters of the *Manual*. To the chapter on Poems Dealing with Contemporary Conditions (*Manual*, vol. 5, XIII [290]) belongs *Tomas of Ersseldoune* (folio 119ᵃ), related to the ballad *Thomas Rymer* (Child, no. 37) which is discussed below in [24]. To the chapter on Tales belong the following: *A Tale of an Incestuous Daughter* (folio 44ᵃ); *A Tale of King Edward and the Shepherd* (folio 48ᵇ), a humorous narrative type identified as *The King and the Subject*, associated with the ballad of *King Edward the Fourth and a Tanner of Tamworth* (Child, no. 273) which is treated below in [5]; *The Tale of the Basin* (folio 58ᵃ); *The Turnament of Totenham* (folio 62ᵃ); *The Adulterous Falmouth Squire* (folio 67ᵃ); *The Hunting of the Hare* (folio 112ᵇ); *The Feast of Tottenham* (folio 115ᵃ); and *The Lady Who Buried the Host* (folio 116ᵇ). To the chapter on Chronicles belongs *The Short Metrical Chronicle of England* (folio 95ᵃ). To the chapter on Proverbs, Precepts, and Monitory Pieces belongs *The ABC of Aristotle* (folio 8ᵃ). To the chapter on Science, Information, Documents belong *Prognostications (Emb þunre)* (folio 9ᵇ), and *Prognostications (Seasons)* (folio 114ᵃ). To the chapter on Works of Religious Information and Instruction belongs Mirk's *Instructions for Parish Priests* (folio 2ᵃ), with which the manuscript begins. To the chapter on Lyrics belong the following: *Signs of Death* (folio 43ᵇ), *Wounds of Christ* (folio 43ᵇ), *A Lament of the Blessed Virgin* (folio 71ᵃ), *The Lamentation of the Blessed Virgin* (folio 73ᵃ), and *An Orison to the Blessed Virgin* (folio 74ᵇ). Finally, to the chapter on Carols belongs *The Betrayed Maiden's Lament* (folio 114ᵇ).

The ballad in this manuscript is *Robin Hood and the Monk* (folio 128ᵇ), the last item in the collection, following immediately after the text of *Thomas of Erceldoune*.

> On a beautiful May morning in Whitsontide, Robin Hood and Little John, on their way to Nottingham to hear Mass, quarrel over the amount won by John in a shooting contest. The latter angrily returns to Sherwood Forest, while Robin continues on to Nottingham and enters the church. There he is recognized by a great-headed monk whom Robin had once robbed of 100 pounds. The monk rushes out of the service, bars the gates of the city, and alerts the sheriff. The sheriff and his men storm the church with staves, and Robin defends himself nobly, all the time wishing that Little John were at his side. At last his sword breaks in a moment of peril, and he is taken prisoner. Meanwhile Little John and Much make plans to intercept the monk, who is on his way with letters to the king, intending to accuse Robin Hood. The two outlaws kill the monk and his page, and take the letters to the king, telling him that the monk died on the way. The king rewards Much and Little John, and sends them back to the sheriff of Nottingham with a safe-conduct for Robin who is ordered to appear before the king. Little John uses the safe-conduct to trick the sheriff and free his master from prison. Robin and John are reconciled, and celebrate their return to Sherwood Forest by drinking wine and eating pasties of venison. When word of Robin's escape reaches court, the king exclaims, with reluctant admiration, "John has beguiled us all!"

The text is divided into 90 stanzas, which may be thought of as seven-stress, riming couplets, but in the manuscript they are written as quatrains riming xaxa. A gap in the narrative at stanza 30 leaves obscure the method by which Little John and Much learn of Robin's imprisonment. Although this is one of the best of the Robin Hood pieces, no other versions survive in later tradition. Like other tales in this manuscript, it is called a "talking" (stanza 90), and there is little evidence that it ever had a tune (see Bronson TTCB). The best indication that it may nevertheless have been a ballad is the striking lyrical character of the two opening stanzas.

MS BRITISH MUSEUM SLOANE 2593 [4]. A mid-fifteenth-century songbook containing carols, lyrics, and miscellaneous pieces. Of the 74 items in the manuscript, only three are in Latin; all the rest are in English. The nature of this collection can perhaps briefly be indicated in the choices made by modern editors for inclusion in their respective canons. Richard L. Greene chose 57 of these texts for publication in his *Early English Carols* (Greene E E Carols; 1935). Carleton Brown picked twelve for his *Religious Lyrics of the*

Fifteenth Century (Brown RLxvC; 1939), and R. H. Robbins chose ten for his *Secular Lyrics of the Fourteenth and Fifteenth Centuries* (Robbins SL; 1952). A scattering of Sloane texts may be found in most modern anthologies of medieval English lyrics.

Child chose two pieces from the Sloane manuscript for inclusion in the ballad canon: *St. Stephen and Herod* (Child, no. 22) and *Robin and Gandeleyn* (Child, no. 115). He also called attention to "I have a young sister," the riddle song used in the later ballad of *Captain Wedderburn's Courtship* (Child, no. 46), discussed below in [23]. Further evidence that the Sloane manuscript draws on oral tradition may be seen in its preservation of two amorous songs, "I have a new garden," which seems to lie behind *The Twelve Days of Christmas*, and "I have a gentle cock," possibly related to a later ballad, *The Grey Cock* (Child, no. 248), included below in [23].

St. Stephen and Herod (Child, no. 22) is properly characterized by Joseph Ritson in his *Ancient Songs* (Ritson AS; 1790) as *A Carol for St. Stephen's Day*. The medieval church calendar, which memorialized the martyrdom of Stephen (Acts 7:58–60) on December 26, is no doubt responsible for the fact that Stephen is here unbiblically depicted as prophesying the birth of Christ to Herod, for which heresy he is then stoned. The piece is composed in twelve seven-stress couplets.

> St. Stephen, a clerk in King Herod's hall, is bringing the boar's head from the kitchen when he suddenly sees the star of Bethlehem. Casting down the boar's head he renounces his allegiance to Herod and declares that a child has been born in Bethlehem who is above all. "Do you lack meat or drink, gold or fee?" asks Herod. When Stephen reiterates his proclamation, Herod denies it, saying that it is no more true than the likelihood that the capon prepared for his dinner will rise up and crow. Immediately the capon crows "Christus natus est!" whereupon Herod directs his torturers to take Stephen out of the town and stone him to death. That is why his martyrdom is celebrated on the day after Christmas.

Robin and Gandeleyn (Child, no. 115) seems to have nothing to do with Robin Hood, and does not survive in later versions. Unlike the other texts in the Sloane manuscript, it is written continuously, without division into lines or stanzas, but the rime scheme suggests that the form intended is seven-stress couplets. Three of these couplet stanzas, however, have extra riming lines (similar to those of the ballad *Judas* noted above in [1]), and a burden, "Robynn lyth in grene wode bowndyn," occurs at the beginning and again at the end of the text.

I heard a clerk talking of Robin and Gandeleyn. He said that they were hunting in the wood when an arrow came from the west and killed Robin. Looking around, Gandeleyn saw a boy called Wrennok of Donne, who challenged him to an exchange of shots. Wrennok shot first and barely missed. Then Gandeleyn shot back and pierced Wrennok through the heart. "Now shalt thou never boast, Wrennok," said Gandeleyn, "at wine nor at ale, that thou hast slain good Robin, and Gandeleyn his knave."

Although no musical notations are preserved in the Sloane manuscript, there can be little doubt that most if not all of the texts included in it were sung. The matter has been disputed, but it may well be that this collection is representative of the repertoire of popular minstrelsy in the fifteenth century, and is therefore one of the best manuscripts available for study of the emergence of the popular ballad from the folk song tradition.

MS CAMBRIDGE UNIVERSITY LIBRARY Ee.4.35 [5]. Part 2 of this volume, containing a fourteenth-century version of *The Prick of Conscience*, is for all practical purposes a separate manuscript. We are concerned here only with part 1, a manuscript of about 1500, containing miscellaneous tales and lyrics. It opens with two metrical tales, *The Adulterous Falmouth Squire* (folio 1a) and *The Lady Who Buried the Host* (folio 3a), both appearing also in the Cambridge manuscript discussed above under [3]. Then there are two monitory pieces, one on the seven virtues and the seven sins (folio 5b), the other on the ten commandments (folio 6a). These are followed by three more metrical tales: *The Child and His Stepdame* (folio 6b), otherwise known as *The Friar and the Boy*, under which title it appears also in the Percy Folio MS (see [17] below); *Robin Hood and the Potter* (folio 14b); and *The King and the Barker* (folio 19b). After these come two moral pieces: *The Book of Courtesy*, otherwise known as *The Little Children's Little Book* (folio 22b), and eight lines on the *Signs of Death* (folio 24a). Thus once again, as in [3] above, we find ballads preserved in a miscellany devoted largely to metrical narratives.

The first ballad in this manuscript is *Robin Hood and the Potter* (Child, no. 121).

Robin Hood sees a potter passing by who has never paid toll, and declares that he will stop him and require him to pay. Little John offers to wager 40 shillings that Robin will not be able to make him do it. While his men watch, Robin stops the potter and a fight ensues. Seizing a staff from his cart, the potter strikes the buckler out of Robin's hand, and gives him a blow on the neck that knocks him to the ground. Robin agrees that Little John has won his 40 shillings, and promises the potter that he may come and go as he pleases without paying toll. Nevertheless he persuades the potter to exchange clothes with him and remain with his men while Robin takes the pots to Nottingham to sell. In Nottingham Robin sells the pots below cost, to the amusement of the citizenry, until he has only five left. These he sends as a gift to the sheriff's wife, and she invites him to dinner. During the meal with the sheriff and his wife, Robin learns of a shooting contest about to be held, with a prize of 40 shillings going to the winner. In his disguise as the potter, Robin enters the contest and easily wins the prize. When the sheriff compliments him on his skill, the "potter" remarks that he has a bow in his cart given to him by Robin Hood. The sheriff exclaims that he'd give 100 pounds to meet the outlaw, and Robin promises to take him to him. The next day, when they reach the forest, Robin blows his horn and his men appear, to the consternation of the sheriff. Robin remarks that if it weren't for his regard for the sheriff's wife, he would have been much harder on the sheriff. As it is, he takes the sheriff's possessions, and sends him home with a white palfrey as a gift for the wife, who is amused by the whole affair. Meanwhile, back in the forest, Robin gives the potter ten pounds for the pots that he had taken to Nottingham, and tells him he will always be welcome in the greenwood.

This piece is composed in about 80 quatrains (some defective). There is no other known version of it in tradition, but parts were adapted for use in *The Playe of Robyn Hode* (see XII [37] in *Manual*, vol. 5), which was first printed in William Copland's edition of *A Mery Geste of Robyn Hode* (London, n.d.) about the middle of the sixteenth century (Child, no. 121, Appendix). Nevertheless *Robin Hood and the Potter* is important as the earliest representative of a type of ballad in which Robin Hood is bested by numerous assorted butchers, tanners, tinkers, shepherds, and beggars.

Child evidently did not regard *The King and the Barker* (Child, no. 273, Appendix I) as a ballad, yet this metrical tale cannot be genetically distinguished from the Robin Hood pieces thus far considered, and therefore we give it here an equal place in the ballad canon.

Once when the king was hunting deer, he overtook a tanner (or barker) of Dantre, who was riding along with a load of cowhides slung over his horse. Instructing his men to keep their distance, the king decided to have some fun by asking the tanner directions without disclosing his identity as king. The tanner tells the king the way to Drayton Basset, but becomes suspicious when the king invites him to go with him to Lord Basset's for dinner. When he sees the king's men approaching, the tanner fears that the king is a thief and that these are his outlaw companions. Stalling for time, the tanner agrees to accompany them to Drayton Basset. The king continues to be affable, and asks the tanner what tidings he has heard. The latter, not much of a conversationalist, replies only that the price of cowhides has gone up. "What do you know of Lord Basset?" asks the king. "I have nothing to do with him," says the tanner, "because he will never buy from me so much as a piece of leather to patch his shoes with." The king then persuades him to join in the deer hunt, and also to exchange horses with him. The tanner, still suspicious, puts the cowhides on the king's horse and follows the king through the woods. Unaccustomed to carrying a load of hides on his back, the king's horse is frightened and throws the tanner, much to the king's amusement. They exchange horses again, and the king thanks the tanner for his service and promises to be his friend. For his part, the tanner seems impressed by his companion, and offers to buy him a drink if they ever meet in Dantre. As they ride together talking, they meet Lord Basset and his men, who immediately fall to their knees when they see the king. "Alas," thinks the tanner, "this must be the king and I shall be hanged!" When they reach Drayton Hall the tanner takes his leave, and the king gives him 100 shillings to mend his cowhides.

There is some evidence that the text, printed in 57 quatrains, has suffered a dislocation, and that stanzas 30–33 should be moved to a position following stanza 54. The above summary of the narrative takes this into account. *The King and the Barker* is a fine example of late medieval minstrelsy of that type which contributed a great deal to the development of the popular ballad. Later versions of it appear under the title *King Edward the Fourth and A Tanner of Tamworth* (Child, no. 273). The earliest of these appeared in 1596 and is characterized as a history, "verie pleasant and merrie to read" (Child, no. 273, Appendix II). The version which Child regarded as a true ballad is a seventeenth-century broadside, obviously descended from the "Historie," and sung to what is described as "an excellent new tune" (Child, no. 273). An analogue is *King Henry II and the Miller of Mansfield* (Child, no. 273, Appendix III), preserved in the Percy Folio MS. The general type of story represented by *The King and the Barker* is often identified as "the king and the subject". We have already taken note, in [3] above, of *A Tale of King Edward and the Shepherd*, and will encounter another famous example in the Percy Folio MS (discussed in [17] below), *John the Reeve*. See also the discussion in vol. 1 of this *Manual* of *The Taill of Rauf Coilyear*, I [59].

A GEST OF ROBYN HODE (INCUNABULUM) [6]. This metrical tale of Robin Hood appears in printed form near the end of the fifteenth century, possibly from the press of William Caxton himself (Baugh LHE, p. 315). Two early fragments surviving from the presses of Wynkyn de Worde and Richard Pynson (see E. G. Duff, Fifteenth-Century English Books, nos. 361, 362) show that the text was in print by the year 1500. The earliest complete copy, *A Lytell Geste of Robyn Hode*, has the imprint of Wynkyn de Worde but is undated; Pollard and Redgrave believe that it was published before 1519 (STC, no. 13689), but current opinion (Katharine F. Pantzer) dates it more precisely in or around the year 1506. An imperfect copy, with over half of the *Geste* missing, was assigned by David Laing with some hesitation to the press of Chepman and Myllar in Edinburgh. Laing may have been influenced initially by the fact that this text, preserved in the Advocate's

Library in Edinburgh, was bound in a single volume with nine pieces from the press of Chepman and Myllar. Modern opinion assigns this defective edition to Jan van Doesborch (John of Dousborowe), a printer of English books in Antwerp, with the approximate date 1510–15. Other editions followed later in the century by William Copland (1560?) and Edward White (ca. 1590?). Child used as the basis for his text the imperfect copy in the Advocate's Library, perhaps in part because it was thought to be the product of a Scottish press, and in part because linguistically it seemed more archaic than the other texts (Child, vol. 3, p. 40, note[†]). In Child's edition the portions missing from the Edinburgh copy are supplied by recourse to Wynkyn de Worde's complete version in the Cambridge University Library (Catalogue, no. 225).

Robin Hood, the most courteous of outlaws, refuses to eat until he can entertain some strange guest. He sends Little John and two other outlaws to find someone, and they return with a poor knight, Sir Richard at the Lee, who dines with Robin Hood and tells of his misfortune and his debt of 400 pounds, owed to the abbot of Saint Mary's. Robin lends him the money on the security of Our Lady (stanzas 1–81). The poor knight, Sir Richard, finds the abbot at dinner and first pleads for an extension of time, but is cruelly refused. He then pays the debt to the consternation of the abbot and sets out to return to Robin Hood his money (stanzas 82–143). Meanwhile, Little John secretly takes service with the hated sheriff of Nottingham. One day after quarreling with the sheriff's butler, who refuses to serve him any dinner, John makes friends with the cook (after fighting him to a draw), and the two of them join Robin in the greenwood, bringing with them much of the sheriff's silverware and a considerable amount of money. The sheriff, meanwhile, is in the forest hunting, and little John tricks him into an ambush, with the result that he is forced to have dinner and spend the night with Robin Hood and the outlaw gang before being allowed to return to Nottingham (stanzas 144–204). In the greenwood Robin Hood refuses to dine until he has sent Little John and two other outlaws to find some strange guest. They return with a monk of Saint Mary's abbey, who dines with the outlaws and then is forced to surrender his money. Robin sends the monk on his way and says that Our Lady has discharged the knight's debt; when Sir Richard returns to the greenwood and attempts to repay the outlaw, Robin will take nothing (stanzas 205–280). When Robin Hood and his men come to Nottingham to participate in an archery contest, the sheriff tries to capture them but they escape and are given protection by their friend Sir Richard (stanzas 281–316). The frustrated sheriff seeks the help of King Edward and furthermore captures the knight with a view to executing him quickly. But Sir Richard's wife appeals to Robin, who rescues the knight and kills the sheriff (stanzas 317–353). At last the King arrives with the intention of capturing Robin Hood, and, disguised as an abbot, he is stopped by the gang and forced to dine on his own deer before he is recognized by the outlaws, who ask forgiveness. The King grants them a pardon, on condition that Robin Hood and his men will come into the King's service (stanzas 354–417). For sport the King and his men are clothed in Lincoln green and all return happily to Nottingham. Robin Hood is unhappy in the King's household, and after a little more than a year he returns to the greenwood and never again enters the King's service. Eventually he is treacherously slain by the prioress of Kyrkesly (stanzas 418–456).

The text consists of 456 seven-stress couplets (written as quatrains) and is divided into eight sections or "fyttes." Child and others have speculated that the story is an amalgam of various Robin Hood ballads from perhaps as early as 1400. No doubt the reference to "rymes of Robyn Hood" in *Piers Plowman* (B-text, Passus V, line 402) has encouraged such speculations, but there is no real evidence to suggest that ballads as we know them existed at that early date (1377–83), or that the *Gest of Robyn Hode* itself had a long life before finding its way into print. The most that can be said is that it is probably based on traditional materials, some going back to the fourteenth century. The art of the surviving narrative, however, is undoubtedly attributable to its late fifteenth-century minstrel composer.

ADAM BELL, CLIM OF THE CLOUGH, AND WILLIAM OF CLOUDESLY [7]. This metrical tale of the greenwood appeared in a dozen printed editions of the sixteenth and seventeenth centuries, but it has not been easy to determine the date of its first appearance. Child's designation of the two earliest fragments, Child, nos. 116a (John Byddell, London 1536) and 116b (unidentified, supplied by J. Payne Collier), indicates that he regarded the Byddell fragment as the earlier of the two, although in a footnote he quotes Hazlitt's opinion that the type used in the Collier fragment is clearly earlier than Copeland's (Child, no. 116c) and is very likely Wynkyn de Worde's. But Child's hesitation to pronounce on the dates may be explained by the fact that he obtained the text only in a copy made for him by Collier in 1857. The original dropped out of sight, and was not available to Child when he was preparing *Adam Bell* for the final edition of the *English and Scottish Popular Ballads* (1882–98), nor was it recorded in the *Short Title Catalogue* (STC; 1927) of Pollard and Redgrave. Eventually it was acquired by the National Library of Scotland, however, where it now is (L.C. 3117), and was examined by F. S. Ferguson, who identified it in his (unpublished) collation cards as "London, Wynkyn de Worde, 1510?". After a recent examination of the fragment, Katharine F. Pantzer, who is at work on a revision of the *Short Title Catalogue*, reports that a more precise date would be ca. 1505, which is here adopted for the purposes of our ballad chronology. Taken together, the bibliographical evidence suggests that *Adam Bell* was quite popular, and that it appeared in print about the same time as *A Gest of Robyn Hode* [6].

Adam, Clim, and William are outlawed for violating the game laws. They swear to be blood brothers and retire to the forest of Inglewood. Later William goes to Carlisle to visit his family. There he is betrayed by an old woman he had befriended, taken by the sheriff, and condemned to be hanged. Informed of William's plight by the village swineherd, Adam and Clim, pretending to have a message from the king, gain access to the city just in time to kill the sheriff and the justice and rescue William from the major and the guards. All return to the greenwood where they have a happy reunion with William's family. Voluntarily the three outlaws, accompanied by William's eldest son, seek out the king to ask pardon. The king refuses them until the queen, claiming a boon promised before, but not yet specified, asks for and obtains their freedom. There follows a shooting contest at which the three outlaws excell. Finally William suggests that he can prove his supremacy as an archer by shooting an apple from his son's head at six score paces. He is of course successful, whereupon the king makes him a royal bowman and chief rider of the north country, and gives other appropriate rewards to William's wife and brothers-at-arms.

The text has 170 quatrains divided into three fits, and very much resembles in style and spirit *A Gest of Robyn Hode*. Shooting an apple off the boy's head recalls early German and Norse tradition, best known in the legend associated with the name of William Tell. Adam Bell, however, belongs with Robin Hood at the close of the Middle Ages, and is distinguishable in name only from his more famous counterpart in Sherwood forest.

MS BALLIOL COLLEGE OXFORD 354 [8]. Knowledge of the existence of this important manuscript in modern times is first attested by its inclusion in H. O. Coxe's Quarto Catalogue of manuscripts in the Oxford Colleges (1852). According to William Chappel (*Popular Music of the Olden Time*, vol. 1, p. 50) it lay undetected for years behind a bookcase in Balliol College Library. Samples of its contents were printed in *Fraser's Magazine* in 1858 by J. A. Froude, who called for publication of the entire manuscript. A goodly portion of it appeared in *Anglia* in 1903, edited by Flügel, and a full edition of the songs and miscellaneous pieces (but excluding longer works already in print) was published in 1907 by R. Dyboski (EETSES 101).

The manuscript is a commonplace book kept in London by Richard Hill, servant of John Wynger (died 1505), and various efforts have been made to narrow the span of time covered by Hill's entries. The safest conclusion, however, is probably that of Mynors in his *Catalogue of the Manuscripts of Balliol College Oxford* (1963), who places it in the first third of the sixteenth century. The latest dated entry is 1536.

Apart from the songs and carols which are our main interest, the manuscript contains a curious assortment of literary texts. *Godfrydus of Rome*, a minor piece taken from the *Gesta Romanorum*, is followed by *The Boke of Marchalsie*, a treatise on the care of horses. Then come *The Seven Sages of Rome*, some excerpts from Gower's *Confessio Amantis*, *The Frere and the Boy* (already noticed in [5] above and to be found also in the Percy Folio MS described below in [17]), *The Siege of Rouen*, *The Trental of St. Gregory*, and *The Boke of Curtasie*. These items are followed by nearly 100 songs, interspersed with a few unrelated items such as further excerpts from *Confessio Amantis*, a Latin treatise for priests in the confessional, miscellaneous proverbs, a list of mayors and sheriffs for the period 1414–1536, and, at the end, a small collection of humorous and satirical pieces.

We focus now on the songs, which are the reason for our present interest, because they include the *Corpus Christi Carol*. Of the 95 songs I have tabulated, 63 are carols and are included in Greene E E Carols (1935). This leaves 32 that might more appropriately be called lyrics on the basis of Greene's definition of the carol, but they are just as likely as the carols to have been intended for singing. Perhaps ten of the carols could be classed as disputed, in the sense that they also appear in modern editions of early English lyrics. Both carols and lyrics agree in subject matter: they celebrate mutually the major feastdays of the church calendar, and contain similar exhortations relating to such matters as matrimony, riches, and mortality. Some critics have speculated that Hill copied his texts from other collections rather than oral tradition, and there is some evidence that this is so (several items seem to have come from Caxton). But it is well to make note of a remarkable fact: eight of the lyrics and 38 of the carols are unique. Without this manuscript, the canon of Middle English carols and lyrics would have been decidedly the poorer. Of the humorous and satirical pieces occurring near the end of the manuscript, one, *The Jolly Juggler* (folio 251), has been called a ballad, notably by Sidgwick (1906) and Bryant (1913).

Among the unique songs of Richard Hill's book is *Corpus Christi*, which appears on folio 165^b with an Epiphany carol (Greene E E Carols, no. 126). It may well be, as Greene suggests, that these two texts were added as an afterthought, since they are not listed in the table of contents of the manuscript. Mynors agrees with this judgment: "The two poems on clxv^v are late additions, but in Hill's hand" (Balliol Catalogue, p. 353). Thus *Corpus*

Christi probably was copied down some time near 1536. Its actual age, as W. W. Greg remarks (RES 13.88), must be considerably greater than the manuscript; how much older it is impossible to say.

There can be no doubt that *Corpus Christi* is a carol. But when is a carol also a ballad? Child chose *St. Stephen and Herod* from a large number of carols in the Sloane manuscript (see [4] above), perhaps partly because of its use of the ballad stanza, and partly because of its apocryphal materials. The *Corpus Christi Carol* had been published first in 1858 (*Fraser's Magazine* 58.134), but it may never have come to Child's attention. If it had, perhaps he might have included it, based on the precedent of *St. Stephen and Herod*. In any case Bryant in his *History of English Balladry* (1913), p. 132, and Gerould in his influential book *The Ballad of Tradition* (1932), p. 33, seem to have regarded it as a ballad, and it appears in more recent ballad collections such as that of MacEdward Leach, *The Ballad Book* (Leach BB; 1955), p. 692. At the same time, the custodians of Middle English carols and lyrics have by no means relinquished their hold on *Corpus Christi*. Significantly, perhaps, Kinsley does not include it in the new *Oxford Book of Ballads* (Kinsley OBB; 1969), while the Sisams do have it in *The Oxford Book of Medieval English Verse* (1970). Hence its inclusion here in the *Manual* continues the struggle for possession of the *Corpus Christi* text. (See also p. 1748 above.)

> The burden of *Corpus Christi* consists of two lines, the first associated with the lullaby (Lully lulley, etc.), and the second an expression of mourning: the falcon hath borne my mate away (death has taken away my beloved).
> He bore him to an orchard brown, in which there was a hall hung with purple and pall. In that hall was a bed hung with gold so red, and in that bed lies a knight, his wounds bleeding day and night. Beside the bed kneels a maid, and she weeps night and day. Beside the bed stands a stone, "Corpus Christi" written theron.

In 1910 A. C. Gilchrist set forth her theory (anticipated by Dyboski) that the text contains images from the legend of the Holy Grail, an interpretation that has remained popular despite occasional dissent from some more recent critics. On the political level R. L. Greene has identified the falcon of *Corpus Christi*'s refrain with Anne Boleyn, and sees the song as a lament expressive of the exile of Catherine of Aragon (1533), whom he identifies as the weeping maiden (MÆ 29.10; 33.53). My own interpretation (*A Literary History of the Popular Ballad*, p. 58) sees the song primarily as a *pietà* placed in a Nativity frame (the lullaby). Thus the later versions (nineteenth and twentieth centuries), which drift toward a more explicit Nativity setting, are nevertheless faithful to the original conception. The remarkable survival of this song in modern oral tradition is no doubt attributable in part to the stability of Christmas as the occasion for singing it. The early version (Richard Hill's) is in six four-stress couplets, preceded by the burden, which appears separate. Some modern versions, however, incorporate the burden in the stanzas as an interlaced refrain.

MS BODLEIAN LIBRARY OXFORD 12653 (RAWLINSON C.813) [9]. A somewhat neglected manuscript containing pieces adapted from the works of Chaucer and various fifteenth-century poets, as well as a few courtly lyrics of the Tudor period. The manuscript itself is dated 1530–40, and the entire corpus of 51 songs was printed by F. M. Padelford in *Anglia* 31.309 in 1908. Of these only 22 were included in the Brown-Robbins *Index*, but the other 29 were added in the Robbins-Cutler *Supplement* (1965). Several love lyrics show the influence of Chaucer, and one is taken practically verbatim from various passages in *Troilus and Criseyde* (Padelford, no. 30). Others represented in the collection are Stephen Hawes (from the *Pastime of Pleasure*), several poems by Lydgate and by Richard Roos, and anonymous pieces like *The Adulterous Falmouth Squire*, from which is reproduced the lament of a soul in torment (Padelford, no. 6).

From this group of courtly lyrics, satires, and elegies (there is even included a dream-vision), Child chose a single song, *Crow and Pie* (Child, no. 111), as a traditional ballad, perhaps because it seemed the prototype of such later pieces as *The Knight and the Shepherd's Daughter* (Child, no. 110).

> While riding through a forest the young man met a fair maid and spoke to her of love. To all his entreaties she responded with clever denials, and even showed reluctance to accept his offer of a gold ring. Each of her replies concluded with a teasing refrain: "Therefore the crow shall bite you." But at last the young man kissed her, took her about the middle small, and laid her on the green. Afterwards the girl wanted to know if he would marry her. "I will be advised, Gyll," he replied, and then added his own refrain line, "for now the pie hath pecked you." In like manner he refused to pay her anything or even give her his name. What he does offer her finally is the moral of the story: "Maidens, let no man throw you down, or you will regret it, and the pie will peck you." The girl bids him farewell and defies him with a new refrain of her own: "Christ's curse go with you!"

This merry example of the battle of the sexes did not endure in tradition. No other versions are known, and in fact the piece rarely appears in modern ballad anthologies. Two other texts in this manuscript (Padelford, nos. 42 and 43) are composed in a similar spirit, and might well have been included by Child. Nevertheless *Crow and Pie* is perhaps the best example of a type of song that undoubtedly influenced the development of the ballad tradition in the sixteenth and seventeenth centuries.

MS BRITISH MUSEUM COTTON CLEOPATRA C.IV [10]. The date of this manuscript has been disputed and indeed one authority states that "it is not really a single MS, but a made-up collection" (O. Arngart, *Two English Border Ballads*, p. 25). Hence we need not be concerned with its other contents, but only take note of the fact that the leaves containing *The Battle of Otterburn* (Child, no. 161) belong to the first half of the sixteenth century. Another ballad, closely associated with this one, appears in Child's edition with the title *The Hunting of the Cheviot* (Child, no. 162), though it is sometimes called *Chevy Chase* by other editors (see [11] below). Most critics acknowledge a connection between the two ballads, and modern opinion gives priority to *The Battle of Otterburn*. My own view is that *Cheviot* is the earlier of the two in date of composition (Western Folklore 25.165), but in the present chapter priority of position is given to *Otterburn* because its manuscript slightly predates that of the *Cheviot* ballad.

> At Lammastide Douglas and his allies go on a raid deep in Northumberland as far as Newcastle. There they find Percy, and challenge him and his men to come forth from the castle and fight, telling him that they have burnt his domain in Northumberland. Percy tells them that because they have done this, he will fight them until either he or Douglas is killed, and that he will meet them at Otterburn for the battle. Percy orders a cask of wine to be lowered from the walls so that they can all drink to the meeting. To Douglas's surprise, Percy and 9,000 Englishmen appear the next day for battle. Percy's father sends word to Percy that he should wait until he and his men can join them, but Percy, impatient, refuses. They drive off their horses and join battle with the Scots. The battle rages fiercely. Finally, Percy and Douglas meet on the field, and Percy, after a hard fight, succeeds in killing Douglas. The battle continues through the night. All the Scots are killed except eighteen and all the English except 500. Percy is captured by the Scots but is exchanged for Sir Hugh Montgomery who had been taken by the English.

The text consists of 70 seven-stress couplets. A full and stirring account of this battle, which took place in August 1388, can be found in Froissart's *Chronicle*, chaps. 136–43 (translated by Bourchier, London 1523–25). Shorter modern versions of the Otterburn ballad survive in editions by David Herd and Sir Walter Scott, and are printed by Child (vol. 3, p. 299).

See also XIII [67] in *Manual*, vol. 5.

MS BODLEIAN LIBRARY OXFORD 6933 (ASHMOLE 48) [11]. A mid-sixteenth-century minstrel's book apparently compiled by Richard Sheale, whose name occurs with several of the texts including *The Hunting of the Cheviot*, the one ballad chosen by Child from this collection. The argument for regarding the manuscript as a minstrel's book is given elsewhere (D. C. Fowler, *A Literary History of the Popular Ballad*, p. 96). Suffice it to say here that the form of *Cheviot* is much too old to have been composed by a sixteenth-century minstrel. By attaching his name to it, Sheale was perhaps merely claiming this venerable ballad as his professional property, identifying it as a part of his repertoire.

> Percy vowed he would hunt in Cheviot hills despite anything the bold Douglas might do. The drivers and bowmen advanced, and greyhounds darted through the groves. By noon on Monday 100 fat harts lay dead. While Percy is watching the slaughtering of the deer, Douglas arrives with a mighty company, and asks, "Who gave you leave to hunt in this Cheviot Chase?" Percy defies him, and the two heroes, at Douglas's suggestion, prepare to meet in single combat. But Witherington, a squire of Northumberland, speaks for all when he says, "I will never see my captain fight on a field, and stand myself and look on." In the general mêlée that follows, Douglas and Percy meet and exchange blows. Douglas admires Percy's fighting ability and offers him a year's wages if he will yield, but Percy refuses. At that moment an arrow strikes Douglas and he falls dying while urging his men to fight on. Percy takes the dead warrior by the hand and declares that he has never seen a better man in all the north country. Then Percy is slain by Montgomery who in turn is killed by a Northumbrian archer, and the battle continues by the light of the moon. At the end, only 55 Scots and 73 English survive. The widows come weeping in the morning to bury their dead. The kings of England and Scotland are disturbed at the news. This was the hunting of the Cheviot. Old men call it the battle of Otterburn.

The ballad is written in 68 rather irregular riming couplets. Recently D. Hamer has sought to restore the text to a more regularized form (RES 20.1). The connection with *The Battle of Otterburn* has been referred to above under [10]. *Cheviot* has been very popular down through the centuries, and survives in numerous broadside copies. It has earned the praise of Sidney, Jonson, and Addison.

See also XIII [68] in *Manual*, vol. 5.

MS CORPUS CHRISTI COLLEGE OXFORD 255 [12]. The earliest version of *King John and the Bishop* (Child, no. 45) was discovered by Carleton Brown in this manuscript of miscellaneous items from the sixteenth and seventeenth centuries. The contents are various and do not concern us, since they do not constitute a single collection. Our ballad occurs at folio 105 by manuscript numbering, but still bears an earlier pagination 416–17 from the (unknown) collection to which it originally belonged. Expert opinion dates this leaf about 1550–70.

> King John, hearing of the wealth of the Bishop of Canterbury, sends for him with the idea of asking him three impossible questions, and seizing his lands if he cannot answer. The Bishop kneels before the King. The three questions are: What am I worth? How soon may I go around the world? What am I thinking? The Bishop has 40 days to find the answers. He inquires at Oxford and Cambridge but without success, and returns home despondent. A shepherd (his brother-in-law) offers to dress as the Bishop and go before the King in his place, and the Bishop agrees. When the King repeats the three questions, the disguised shepherd answers as follows: What are you worth? 29 pence, one penny less than Jesus; how soon may you go around the earth? follow the sun, and it will take you 24 hours; what are you thinking? you think I am the Bishop of Canterbury—but I am really just a shepherd. Whereupon the King pardons the Bishop and rewards the shepherd with 100 pounds a year.

The text has 166 lines in riming couplets and is not divided into stanzas. There is some evidence of memorial transmission (PMLA 46.1026), but nothing to indicate that a melody was ever attached to this early text (see Bronson TTCB, 1.354).

MS YORK MINSTER LIBRARY [13]. According to James Raine (Surtees Society 85.64) this manuscript, in a hand of the sixteenth century, "was originally No. 25 of a ballad-book in small quarto." Unfortunately the remainder of the collection is apparently lost. But we are fortunate to have here the earliest surviving text of *Sir Andrew Barton* (Child, no. 167), a spirited account of a sea battle between the English and the Scots based on events of the year 1511.

> In response to an appeal from London merchants, King Henry sends Lord Charles Howard to capture Andrew Barton, a Scottish pirate whose robbing of merchant ships in the Channel was making trade with the Continent unprofitable. Howard chooses a good gunner, Peter Simond, and a noble bowman, William Horsley, to head up his crew. While sailing in search of Barton, Howard is fortunate enough to encounter Harry Hunt, a former prisoner of the pirate, who agrees to lead the English to the enemy. The battle is fierce, but it is finally decided by the skill of the English archer, Horsley, who prevents the Scots from releasing the "beams" on their mainmast. Apparently if they could have been dropped, they would have assured victory for the Scottish crew. The archer Horsley, however, shoots down the men who attempt to climb the mast, including finally Barton himself. "Fight, masters," said the wounded pirate, "stick stiffly to Sir Andrew Barton, fight while you hear my whistle blow." When the whistle could no longer

be heard, the English seized the Scottish vessel, and Lord Howard returned to the king with Barton's head. The king thanked and rewarded all the participants, including the Scottish survivors.

The York version is in 81 stanzas, and agrees rather closely with the text in the Percy Folio (82 stanzas). The numerous broadsides of the seventeenth century tend to be slightly abbreviated (Child, no. 167B is 64 stanzas) and considerably inferior. The vivid picture of Sir Andrew telling his gold in the light (Child, no. 167, York version, stanza 38) is blurred or eliminated in subsequent versions (Child, nos. 167A, stanza 36; 167B, stanza 32). This ballad is similar in spirit to *Cheviot*, and shows the same kind of balanced appreciation of heroism on both sides. Its popularity continues to the present day, commonly with the title *Henry Martyn*, which Child classified as a separate but related ballad (Child, no. 250).

MS BRITISH MUSEUM HARLEIAN 367 [14]. A collection of miscellaneous papers, most of which belonged to John Stow (died 1605), some in his own hand. The piece that concerns us in this volume, *Flodden Field* (Child, no. 168 Appendix), is copied in a bold professional hand (certainly not that of Stow, as Fleugel thought, *Anglia* 21.320), apparently the same scribe who made the copy of *Ladye Bessie* on folios 89–100 which Halliwell dates about 1600 (Percy Society, vol. V, pt. 4, p. vi). The battle of Flodden Field took place on 9 September 1513.

After the battle of Flodden, in which the English are victorious and the Scottish King James was slain, the Earl of Surrey sent the good news in a message to King Henry VIII, who was on the Continent at the siege of Tournay, accompanied by certain of his lords, including the Earl of Derby. In his report Surrey said that Derby's men fled the field, and king Henry rebuked Derby for their cowardice. Sir Ralph Egerton and others come to the Earl's defense, explaining that if his men did retreat, it was because Derby was not there to lead them. Discouraged by the news and by the king's hostility, Derby bids emotional farewell to his kinsmen and his lands. Then one of his faithful retainers, Jamie Garsed, is brought in and accused of slaying two of his own comrades and wounding three others. The king sends word that Jamie shall hang, but Derby and his friends intercede on his behalf, giving Jamie the opportunity to explain that his victims had called the Earl of Derby a coward. At this news the king forgives Jamie his trespass. The next day comes a messenger from the queen, reporting that the battle of Flodden was won by the forces of the Earl of Derby, Lancashire, and Cheshire. The king then rewards Derby and his friends, and hands over to Derby the judgment of the offence of the Earl of Surrey in sending him the false report of the battle. "Then is his life saved," said Derby. The king commends him for his patience, and assigns him a position beside the Earl of Shrewsbury at the siege. Within the space of three days, Tournay is captured. God save our noble prince and the Earl of Derby!

The text is in 103 loosely structured stanzas reminiscent of the metrical form of *Chevy Chase*. Child calls it a "poem," but it has features in common with balladry, notably the "farewell" stanzas which are the emotional center of *Flodden Field* and which appear also in *Johnie Armstrong* (Child, no. 169C, stanzas 29–31), *Jock o the Side* (Child, no. 187A, stanzas 20–24), and *Lord Maxwell's Last Goodnight* (Child, no. 195), the latter consisting almost entirely of this formula. Near the beginning of *Flodden Field* the King asks the messenger from Surrey, "Who did fight and who did flee? . . . And who is false and who is true to me?" Later, in almost the same words he addresses the messenger from the queen. This parallelism heightens the contrast between the true and false reports, a device very common in balladry. Other versions of *Flodden Field* (see XIII [220] in *Manual*, vol. 5) appear in MS Harley 293, and the Percy Folio MS (the latter having eighteen additional stanzas of a later date). A short ballad of twelve stanzas (Child, no. 168) is quoted in Thomas Deloney's *Jack of Newbury* (1597).

MS BRITISH MUSEUM COTTON VESPASIAN A.25 [15]. A miscellany of Renaissance carols, "ballets," and songs, some with tunes indicated and at least one with musical notations appended (folio 173). The manuscript was copied in the late sixteenth century, and the songs have been printed (somewhat imperfectly) by Böddeker in JfRESL ns 2(1875).81, 210, 347; 3.92. They are now available in a modern edition by Peter J. Seng, *Tudor Songs and Ballads from MS Cotton Vespasian A-25*, Harvard 1978. There are various prose pieces in Latin and English, along with prophecies, miracles, and sermons. The songs reflect various moods, from religious piety to secular exuberance. One in particular, "a mery Ballet of the Hathorne tre, to be songe after Donkin Dargeson," is signed "G[eorge]. Peele" (transcribed by Böddeker as "G. Poete"), but it is not in the original hand of the manuscript, which is too early to have included anything by Peele.

The last song in the collection is the ballad *Captain Car* (folios 187–88), which is signed at the end, "Finis per me, William Asheton clericum." The leaf containing the conclusion of the ballad (folio 188) is partly torn away, but on the verso are traces of musical notation and a few words, mostly illegible except for "quene Elizabethe." If the music was intended for *Captain*

Car, the surviving fragment of it nevertheless does not seem to match any phrase of the refrain given by Simpson ("Sicke sicke and very sicke;" see Simpson **BBBM**, p. 661). The events related in the ballad took place in November 1571, not long before William Asheton copied the words in the manuscript.

> At Martinmas, when the weather grows cold, Captain Car tells his men that they must take a hold. Crecrynbroghe is suggested, but the captain prefers to go to a castle (Towie) where he knows the laird is away. As the lady and her family are sitting down to supper, Captain Car and his men surround the castle. He offers to sleep with her and promises that she will plow his land. The lady refuses, and from the wall she fires at the captain, missing him but killing three of his men. The castle is then set afire, and the lady pleads with Car to save her eldest son. He agrees to guarantee his safety, but when she lets the child down over the wall in a sheet, Captain Car cuts out his heart and tongue, wraps them in a handkerchief and throws them up to the lady. Before they all die in the flames the lady defies her enemies, including John Hamilton, the servant who defected and apparently started the fire. Meanwhile Lord Hamilton was at Carnall, where he dreamed that his halls were all afire and his lady dead. Arriving home with his men, he finds the dream a reality. He blows a trumpet and summons his relatives from the surrounding countryside. The ballad ends with Lord Hamilton mourning the loss of his lady, and wishing that he could have died in her place.

Thirty quatrains with four-line refrain "Sicke sicke" etc. repeated after each stanza. This is the first ballad in our chronological survey (possibly excepting *Robyn and Gandeleyn* in [4] above) with a refrain, and certainly the first to exhibit most of the features characteristic of later balladry. Its quatrains are much more tightly structured than the loose stanzas of such minstrel pieces as *The Hunting of the Cheviot* (Child, no. 162). Moreover *Captain Car* is remarkable for its persistence in tradition through the nineteenth century. Important versions appear in the Percy Folio MS of 1650, and a Glasgow print of 1755 edited by David Dalrymple, Lord Hailes (entitled *Edom o Gordon*).

RENAISSANCE BALLAD COMPOSERS AND COLLECTORS [16]. At this point in our survey of ballad sources the grouping of the ballads begins to change from those based purely on the survival of manuscripts to groups of ballads of a particular sort which appeared within a certain time span. This will be especially true of broadside ballads to be considered in chronological groups representing the seventeenth and eighteenth centuries. The present set of ballads [16] first appeared in the late sixteenth or early seventeenth century, and have in common the fact that a name is associated with each one, either as composer of the ballad or as in some capacity responsible for its publication. Thus *The Fair Flower of Northumberland* (Child, no. 9) first appeared in Thomas Deloney's *Jack of Newbury* (1597); *The Three Ravens* (Child, no. 26), *The Baffled Knight* (Child, no. 112), and *John Dory* (Child, no. 284) were published in the songbooks of Thomas Ravenscroft (1609–11); *The Famous Flower of Serving Men* (Child, no. 106) and *Robin Hood's Golden Prize* (Child, no. 147) are signed by Lawrence Price; *The True Tale of Robin Hood* (Child, no. 154) by Martin Parker, and a piece which Child entitles *The King of Scots and Andrew Browne* (Child, no. 180 Appendix) is signed by William Elderton and licensed for publication on May 30, 1581. The latter provided the impetus for the ballad of *King James and Brown* (Child, no. 180), preserved in the Percy Folio MS (see below in [17]).

Another change in the treatment of ballad groups is that from this section forward not all ballads will be singled out for discussion, though all of them will be represented in the bibliography. The ones treated or summarized will be those which appear for one reason or another to be in contact with medieval tradition. Identifying medieval features in an oral tradition extending over a period of 600 years is not easy, and the editor does not claim infallibility. By consulting the bibliography, however, it will be possible for the student to identify the group of ballads from which selections are made, and make an independent judgment in the matter.

The one ballad in this section which can claim a connection with medieval tradition is *The Three Ravens* (Child, no. 26). Though it first appears in Ravenscroft's *Melismata* (London 1611), it has been singled out by numerous editors as a sterling example of the medieval ballad, and Bronson has even suggested (Bronson TTCB, 1.308) that it pre-dates the *Corpus Christi Carol* which, as we have seen in [8] above, belongs to the period 1500–36. On the other hand, it is possible that this beautiful song is itself influenced by *Corpus Christi* thus taking the form of a secularized *pietà*.

> Three ravens are sitting on a tree, and one asks where they should take breakfast. Another replies that there is a knight slain in the field, who is so carefully guarded by his hounds and hawks that no fowl dares come nigh him. Then down comes a fallow doe (the sweetheart), great with young. She lifts up his bloody head and kisses his wounds. She gets him upon her back and carries him to the earthen lake (pit or grave). She buried him before the prime, and was dead herself before evensong time. God grant to every gentleman such hawks, such hounds, and such a leman.

The ballad is in ten couplets with triple repetition of the first line and interlaced refrain, a common pattern in folk song, very similar to *When Johnnie Comes Marching Home*. The exceptional quality of the 1611 version of *The Three Ravens* may be the reason that no competing versions have developed in modern times. All we have are analogues like the Scottish *Twa Corbies*, or parodies like the American *Billy Magee Magaw*.

MS BRITISH MUSEUM ADDITIONAL 27879 (PERCY FOLIO) [17]. Since the Percy Folio MS (ca. 1650) is so well known, lists of its contents are easily accessible (see Bibliography), and there is no need to give a detailed description here. Suffice it to say that there are nearly 200 texts in the more than 500 pages of the volume, and these may be roughly classified as follows: seventeen romances, 24 metrical histories, over 100 miscellaneous songs, and 45 Child ballads. Of the ballads Child selected from the manuscript, six exist in versions of an earlier date, and hence have been treated in previous sections of this chapter: Child, nos. 116 in [7], 162 in [11], 45 in [12], 167 in [13], 178 in [15], and 180 in [16]. Of the 39 remaining ballads in the Percy Folio MS, eighteen seem clearly too recent to be classified as medieval: Child, nos. 108, 109, 122, 123, 124, 140, 142, 145, 165, 166, 171, 172, 174, 175, 176, 177, 187, 267. All of these are nevertheless represented in the Bibliography.

We are left with 21 ballads which in some sense can be called medieval, but even here some distinctions are in order. Four of these, though they are important for their medieval background, are in some way deficient: a fragment of *Earl Brand* (Child, no. 7), the earliest known English form of an important international ballad; *Sir Lionel* (Child, no. 18), which Bronson has shown (Bronson TTCB, 1.265) to be related to the romance of *Sir Eglamour of Artois* (see I [79] in *Manual*, vol. 1); *King Estmere* (Child, no. 60), which has important Scandinavian analogues but which survives only in Percy's hand-written copy, almost certainly containing the Bishop's own additions; and *Robin Hood's Death* (Child, no. 120), a fragmentary text which belongs with the earliest of the Robin Hood pieces. Two ballads have a fourteenth-century setting, but appear to be of much later origin: *Hugh Spencer's Feats in France* (Child, no. 158), and *Durham Field* (Child, no. 159; see XIII [55] in *Manual*, vol. 5). Six other ballads seem to have medieval features, but for the most part are composites of various earlier motifs or revivals of older themes: *Young Andrew* (Child, no. 48), a pastiche of traditional motifs; *Glasgerion* (Child, no. 67), a composite based on the assignation theme; *Old Robin of Portingale* (Child, no. 80), a marriage of January and May (as in Chaucer's *Merchant's Tale*) with violent ending; *Little Musgrave and Lady Barnard* (Child, no. 81), a classic and influential representative of the adulterous assignation; *Child Maurice* (Child, no. 83), a highly dramatic ballad with interesting variations on the assignation theme adapted from *Little Musgrave*; and *Will Stewart and John* (Child, no. 107), a finely constructed and nostalgic minstrel narrative of courtship and marriage. All six of these are important ballads for the student of medieval tradition, but they exhibit features which suggest a Renaissance interest in medieval themes and settings rather than a medieval origin.

After all the filtering, there remain nine substantial ballads from the Percy Folio MS that probably have a medieval origin. One is *The Maid and the Palmer* (Child, no. 21), an international ballad which dramatizes Christ's encounter with the woman at the well (John 4:6–26) with apocryphal additions, and which in most European versions identifies the woman as Mary Magdalen.

> While the maid is washing at the well, an old palmer (Jesus) comes and asks her for a drink of water. When she makes excuses the old palmer chides her by saying that if he were her lover she would give him a drink, which prompts her to swear that she has no lover. The palmer replies, "Peace, fair maid, you are foresworn," tells her she has borne nine children, and reveals where they are buried. The maid now realizes that she is speaking to the man that all the world believes upon, and asks for penance. He assigns her seven years a stepping stone, seven more a clapper in a bell, and another seven to lead an ape in hell. "When thou hast thy penance done, then thoust come a mayden home."

This ballad has a stanza form like that of *The Three Ravens* (Child, no. 26), with thrice repeated first line and interlaced refrain. In its reference to murdered children and the mother's penance it also has important connections with *The Cruel Mother* (Child, no. 20). Recently David Buchan has called attention to an important version of *The Maid and the Palmer* preserved in a manuscript of ballads from Glenbuchat parish in Aberdeenshire, and offers a persuasive explanation for the relationship of *The Maid* and *The Cruel Mother*. The latter appears first as a seventeenth-century broadside, treated in [18] below.

Robin Hood and Guy of Gisborne (Child, no. 118) may well be one of the earliest of all the Robin Hood ballads. A fragment of a play with a similar plot was preserved with the Fenn papers and dates from about 1475.

> Robin Hood dreams that two men have beaten and disarmed him. When he awakens he and Little John go in search of the men, and come upon a man dressed in a horsehide. Little John wishes to accost the stranger but Robin berates him, quite unreasonably it seems, and Little John returns to Barnstable. There he gets into a fight with the sheriff and his twenty men. Little John and all of Robin Hood's men are captured. Meanwhile Robin has fought with the stranger, now identified as Guy of Gisborne. He kills Guy, disfigures him and changes clothes with him. Then he blows Guy's horn and so summons the sheriff, who thinks that Guy has killed Robin Hood. Robin releases Little John and together they dispose of the sheriff and his men.

This ballad has the characteristic quatrain of the late medieval metrical tale, and there is no evidence of the existence of a tune. No other versions have survived.

We now come to a group of six ballads in the Percy Folio MS derived from medieval romance: *The Boy and the Mantle* (Child, no. 29), *King Arthur and King Cornwall* (Child, no. 30), and *The Marriage of Sir Gawain* (Child, no. 31), all three from Arthurian tradition; *Sir Aldingar* (Child, no. 59), an international ballad with numerous romance motifs; *Sir Cawline* (Child, no. 61), for which an important Scottish analogue has recently been discovered; and *The Lord of Lorn and the False Steward* (Child, no. 271), based on the romance of *Rosewall and Lillian* (see I [101] in *Manual*, vol. 1).

The Boy and the Mantle (Child, no. 29) has the popular medieval motif of the chastity test in a form resembling that of the French fabliau *Cort Mantel*.

> A boy richly dressed appears at Arthur's court and announces that he has a mantle that will fit only a woman who is true to her husband. Guenivere and all the ladies at court try the magic mantle; it fits none of them but Craddock's wife. Then the boy kills a wild boar and announces that no cuckold can carve it. Craddock alone passes the test. Then the boy shows a horn which will betray any cuckold; again only Craddock can pass the test.

There are numerous European analogues, but no other English version of this piece survives. It has 45 irregular stanzas with an occasional triplet.

King Arthur and King Cornwall (Child, no. 30) and *The Marriage of Sir Gawain* (Child, no. 31) are treated in volume 1 of this *Manual* (see I [35] and [37]) and need not be repeated here. They do not survive in modern versions.

Sir Aldingar (Child, no. 59) has many Scandinavian analogues, the earliest dating from the mid-sixteenth century. Since the story is found in William of Malmesbury's *Gesta Regum Anglorum* (1125), some scholars have believed that the ballad of *Sir Aldingar*, or one very like it, was in existence in the twelfth century, but evidence for this is lacking.

> When queen Elinor spurns the approaches of the false steward, Sir Aldingar, he deceives a poor leper and persuades him to lie in the queen's bed. Then Aldingar goes to the king, telling him that the queen has chosen a new love, and shows him the leper. When the king confronts the queen with this evidence, she realizes that Aldingar is responsible. Lamenting her plight, she describes a dream in which a griffin carried her crown away, and would have taken her to his nest also, had it not been for a little hawk who slew the griffin and rescued her. She then appeals for a knight who will engage in a trial by combat with Aldingar to maintain the justice of her cause. Messengers are sent out, and one of them meets a little child, who promises to help the queen, and repeats her dream almost verbatim. On the day when the queen is to be burned, the child appears and challenges the contemptuous Aldingar to fight. The steward allows the first stroke to the boy, who proceeds to cut off both his legs at the knee. Aldingar calls for a priest, confesses his guilt, and obtains forgiveness from the queen before he dies.

A later form of this ballad survives in Scottish tradition (Child, no. 59B), but the Percy Folio MS version is the one that was influential in shaping the narrative technique of other assignation ballads (especially Child, nos. 81, 80, and 83).

Child speculated in his introduction that *Sir Cawline* (Child, no. 61) might "be formed upon a romance in stanzas" (citing stanzas 8 and 11), and noted the similarity of the first adventure to the romance of *Eger and Grime* (see I [100] in *Manual*, vol. 1). The recent discovery by Marion Stewart of a sixteenth-century Scottish analogue *Sir Colling* sheds much new light on this interesting piece, and suggests that it is in all likelihood of Scottish origin.

> The story consists of three episodes. The first tells of the love sickness of Cawline for the king's daughter. The king, unaware of the cause of the knight's indisposition, sends his daughter to attend him. Cawline tells her that he is ill for love of her. She sends him to fight an "eldrige" king, so that he may prove himself worthy of her. At midnight the eldrige king arrives accompanied by his lady. The two men fight; Cawline cuts off the ring-laden hand of the king, but at the lady's request spares his life. The second episode recounts the coming of a five-headed giant, who demands the princess, unless he can be worsted in battle. Sir Cawline takes him on, using the eldrige sword, and kills him and cuts off his five heads. The king now agrees to the marriage, but that morning as Cawline is walking in the garden, the false steward releases a lion, "Sir Cawline for to teare." Cawline wraps his mantle of green around his arm and thrusts it down the lion's throat to burst its heart. At last the two lovers are married and have fifteen sons.

The Scottish *Sir Colling* clears up a number of uncertainties in the Percy Folio MS version. Indeed the first two stanzas which Child, thinking they belonged to another ballad, printed separately in his introduction (Child, vol. 2, p. 56), are shown by the new version to belong with the text, and constitute an appropriate introduction to it (*Sir Colling*, lines 1–10):

> Jesus Chryst and triniti
> Yat deitt wes on ye ruid,
> to send him grace in all digrie
> yat luiffis ye Scottis bluid:
> Yis be ane knycht corporall,
> hardie vas and guid.
> Sir Coling vas ye knychtis name,
> ane kingis sone vas hie;
> with Edvaird ye bruce he fuir to fecht
> In Irland biyond ye sie.

We see here also the kind of rime scheme that Child suspected: ababcbdefe. Elsewhere the rimes indicate a Scottish original, as when the author rimes *small* and *away* (lines 184, 186). There are of course certain minor differences of detail in the story: The anonymous king of the Folio text is the lord of Argyll in the Scottish version; Sir Cawline hears a bugle blow as the eldrige king approaches, while Sir Colling is instructed to blow his horn to summon him; in the English text the giant has five heads, while the Scottish giant has only three; Cawline's mantle is green, and Colling's is gray. But the Scottish text also provides significant clarifications. At stanzas 12–13 Child thought there had been a loss, yet the correct form of the stanza is clear in *Sir Colling* (lines 52–55):

> Gif yat I be sa sempill ane knycht
> I may not be thy peir,
> sum deidis of armis ʒe wald me wiss
> to be ʒowr bachleir.

We now know that the girl did not abruptly assign him the eldrige hill adventure, but did so on his invitation. Child compares the eldrige knight who haunts the moors to Grendel, and adds "but there is only a hint of that supernatural terror which attends the awful 'march-stepper' in Beowulf."

This is perhaps more appropriately said of *Sir Cawline* (stanza 19) than of *Sir Colling*, where more care is taken to set the stage (lines 80–83):

> At midnyt quan ye mone did ryss
> it schewe him littill lyt;
> he saw betwein him and ye sey
> full fast cumand ane knyt. . . .

Stanza 29 in Child's edition seems to be a snatch of conversation interrupted by the sudden appearance of the giant. Comparison with *Sir Colling* shows this to be not entirely the case (lines 148–51):

> Quhan yai had eittin and drukin veill
> and greit mirth yai had maid,
> four and tventie greit schipis
> vas strukin in ye raid.

It seems the English copyist failed to understand (see stanza 29, lines 3–4) that four and twenty great ships, with their sails struck and at anchor in the road, marked the arrival of the giant.

Besides affording this type of clarification, the Scottish *Sir Colling* has a general literary superiority which has been ably demonstrated by Stewart (*Scottish Studies* 16.23). In the same article she has also emphasized the important fact that the modern Scottish versions of Mrs. Harris and Peter Buchan, which Child relegated to an appendix, are in direct line of descent from *Sir Colling*, and thus testify to the authenticity of Scottish oral tradition. It speaks well for Bronson that he defended the Scottish versions against Child's disparagement (Bronson TTCB, 2.37) before the existence of *Sir Colling* was known. Discoveries of this kind (see also below, *King Orfeo*, in [25]) suggest that greater weight should be given to the role of Scotland in the creation of the ballad form. We have noted already the possibility of a Scottish origin for *Chevy Chase* (above, in [10] and [11]), and the first clear use of a refrain stanza in the Scottish *Captain Car* (above, in [15]). To this question we will return in [24] below, in connection with the ballad of *Thomas Rymer* (Child, no. 37).

The Folio version of *The Lord of Lorne and the False Steward* (Child, no. 271) is the earliest, but a broadside of the same title was registered in 1580, and the romance of *Roswall and Lillian* (see I [101] in *Manual*, vol. 1), on which the ballad seems to be based, was composed in the late fifteenth century.

> The son of the Lord of Lorne, having mastered all the books in Scotland, is sent under the protection of the steward to France to complete his education. The steward changes clothes with him and impersonates him at the court. The boy meanwhile is forced to become a shepherd, using the name Disaware. The steward, working fast, is pledged in marriage to the princess. One day the princess out hunting sees Disaware and after a conversation with him—he does not betray his identity—takes him to court in her service, as chamberlain. When the steward objects, Disaware is made groom. One day the lady overhears a remark that Disaware makes to his horse and asks him to tell his story. He replies that he cannot since he has sworn not to. The princess suggests that he can tell the story to the horse, since he has sworn only not to reveal it to a human being. Disaware agrees, tells the horse the story, the princess overhears, rushes into the castle, and sends a letter posthaste to Disaware's father. When the father arrives, the steward is apprehended and executed and the boy and the princess are married.

A somewhat shorter form of the story appears in broadsides of the later seventeenth century (Child, no. 271B), but the ballad does not survive in modern times.

Child Waters (Child, no. 63) is reminiscent of Chaucer's *Clerk's Tale* of patient Griselda, and is the most thoroughly medieval selection in the entire Percy Folio MS. Though the man's name, Waters, reminds us of Chaucer's Walter, the ballad is a treatment of the subject that has its own integrity. Indeed it might be said in some respects to be more successful in handling its difficult theme than the *Clerk's Tale*, where the Clerk's Envoy, skillful as it is, could be interpreted as a failure of nerve. In some inscrutable fashion the ballad poet has managed to suggest the godlike, otherworldly character of Child Waters, without which his testing of fair Ellen would be intolerable. Hence the ending of the ballad, like the restoration of Job's fortunes in the Bible, comes as a solemn benediction.

> Fair Ellen tells Child Waters that she is carrying his child. In response he offers her land, but she says that she would prefer a kiss, or a twinkling of his eye, to all the lands of Cheshire and Lancashire. Child Waters must go on a journey, and, at her urging, he allows Ellen to run by his side disguised as a footpage. While he rides, she runs barefoot through the broom; and when she inquires why he rides so fast, he simply calls her attention to the water he is about to cross. Ellen manages to get past the water with the help of our Lady, and they come to a castle of red gold, the home, Child Waters tells her, of his paramour. That evening he orders fair Ellen to bring him a woman of the streets to sleep with him, and to carry her to his bed to avoid defiling of her feet. Ellen does all of this without complaint, but asks to sleep at his bed's feet. Early in the morning he instructs her to get up and feed his horse. While in the stable, she is seized with labor pains,

and groans aloud. The mother hears, and tells her son that there is a ghost in the stable, or else a woman in childbirth. Child Waters gets up, puts on his silken clothes, and listens silently at the door of the stable. Then he comforts fair Ellen, promising that the bridal and the churching shall be on one day.

Later Scottish versions of *Child Waters* survive, of which the best are undoubtedly the two obtained from Mrs. Brown of Falkland (see below in [24]), one in 1783 and the other in 1800. In these versions (Child, no. 63Ba, b) the characterization of Child Waters (here called Lord John) is understandably altered in the direction of making him seem more concerned for the welfare of Burd Ellen.

The Percy Folio MS is a miscellany, but more precisely it is a collection of late medieval minstrelsy. The presence of both romances and ballads, sometimes difficult to separate from each other, reminds us that these two genres are ultimately related. For it was the romances that provided the style and narrative technique that governed the evolution of the popular ballad at the end of the Middle Ages.

SEVENTEENTH-CENTURY BROADSIDES [18]. There are 35 ballads in this group, and it is almost certain that none of them could be of medieval origin. On the other hand, many of them do have a medieval setting. This is true for example of one subgroup, the fifteen Robin Hood ballads: Child, nos. 126, 127, 128, 129, 130, 133, 135, 136, 138, 139, 141, 143, 146, 148, 149. One of these, *Robin Hood Newly Revived* (Child, no. 128), is based on the romance of *Gamelyn* (see I [9] in *Manual*, vol. 1), but there is no evidence of any oral tradition behind it.

Another subgroup is made up of ten ballads that lend themselves to a chronological arrangement such as Child has followed in his edition: Child, nos. 156, 160, 169, 170, 191, 209, 285, 286, 287, 292. Taking these in order we observe first that *Queen Eleanor's Confession* (Child, no. 156) is set in the late twelfth century, *The Knight of Liddesdale* (Child, no. 160) was assassinated in 1353, *Johnie Armstrong* (Child, no. 169) was hanged in 1530, *The Death of Queen Jane* (Child, no. 170) occurred in 1537, *Hughie Grame* (Child, no. 191) was probably executed around 1550, and *Geordie* (Child, no. 209), if he is indeed to be identified with George Gordon, fourth earl of Huntly, was arrested in 1554. There is no need to inquire into the other four, since they clearly belong to events of the seventeenth century. The only ballad here that might seem to be medieval is *Queen Eleanor's Confession* (Child, no. 156). If, as has been suggested, George Peele's *Edward I* (1593) is indebted to the ballad, we have evidence of its existence almost a century earlier than the broadside. But the tale of the husband who takes the shrift-father's place and hears his wife's confession was widely available (as in Thomas Twyne's *The Schoolmaster*, London 1576, IV.viii), and there are no verbal echoes of the ballad in the play, such as we find, for example, of *Little Musgrave* in Beaumont and Fletcher, *The Knight of the Burning Pestle* (1611). The existence as early as 1593 of an oral form of *Queen Eleanor's Confession* with the "friar's daughter" stanza preserved only in Kinloch (Child, no. 156E, stanza 16) seems unlikely. In all probability, therefore, the ballad is a seventeenth-century creation, based on the wide-spread fabliau which itself goes back to medieval sources (Child, vol. 3, p. 258).

Ten other ballads of indeterminate date complete our survey of the seventeenth-century broadsides: Child, nos. 2, 10, 20, 73, 74, 105, 110, 243, 272, 276. Most of these were published late in the century, but stanza 5 of *Fair Margaret and Sweet William* (Child, no. 74) is quoted in *The Knight of the Burning Pestle* (1611), and stanza 15 of *The Knight and the Shepherd's Daughter* (Child, no. 110) occurs in Fletcher's *The Pilgrim* (1621). Child inclines also to the belief (vol. 5, p. 100) that the ballad *The Friar in the Well* (Child, no. 276) is referred to in Skelton's *Colin Cloute* (1522), but here again we lack the kind of verbal echo needed for proof. Skelton's reference may simply be to the fabliau that lies behind the ballad. Certainly none of these contain evidence of pre-sixteenth-century origin. As we approach the date of Defoe's *The Apparition of Mrs. Veal* (1706), broadside balladry increasingly reflects a popular interest in the supernatural. Thus we find *The Suffolk Miracle* (Child, no. 272), a version of the Specter Bridegroom tale; *James Harris* (*The Daemon Lover*) (Child, no. 243), concerning a dead lover who returns from the sea; *Fair Margaret and Sweet William* (Child, no. 74), mentioned above, in which the ghost of Margaret haunts William's bride-bed; and *The Elfin Knight* (Child, no. 2), wherein a supernatural suitor and a young maid match wits in setting impossible tasks for each other as prerequisites for marriage. Moreover a revenant ending appears in *The Cruel Mother* (Child, vol. 2, p. 500), and such endings are added to two other ballads of the present group in later versions: *The Twa Sisters* (Child, no. 10N–Q), and *Lord Thomas and Fair Annet* (Child, no. 73E–H). The rather casual treatment of the supernatural in *The Elfin Knight* (Child, no. 2) suggests that it may be the earliest in this group, though it falls far short of the antiquity of *Riddles Wisely Expounded* (Child, no. 1) (see above under [2]). Paradoxically, as we shall see below in [23], the ballad of *Clerk Saunders* (Child, nos. 69, 77), first collected nearly 100 years later than *The Suffolk Miracle* (Child, no. 272), presents a treatment of the revenant theme much more ancient than anything of the sort found in these broadsides.

The rather disappointing results of our survey of seventeenth-century broadsides may perhaps be attributed to the form of their publication. While it is true that ballads of the broadside type appear in the Percy Folio MS, ballads like *Child Waters* apparently did not find a welcome reception in the broadside market. Hence it may be that our grouping of these ballads together leaves the impression that the medieval influence in balladry comes to an end during this period. But the impression is misleading, as we shall see in some of the following sections devoted to ballads first recovered in the eighteenth century.

EIGHTEENTH-CENTURY BROADSIDES [19]. Of the 25 ballads in this section, a dozen can be eliminated immediately from consideration: Child, nos. 104, 173, 179, 184, 192, 199, 227, 237, 283, 288, 289, 295. To these I add, somewhat reluctantly, *Bewick and Graham* (Child, no. 211), which in both style and content echoes an earlier era of balladry, with its structural parallelism and its characterization of the two young men respectively as *clericus* and *miles*. Of the twelve remaining, eight are Robin Hood ballads: Child, nos. 125, 131, 132, 134, 150, 151, 152, 153. The setting in these is medieval, but none of them has any sign of antiquity. *King Henry Fifth's Conquest of France* (Child, no. 164) relates the battle of Agincourt (1415), but is clearly of late composition. *Lady Isabel and the Elf Knight* (Child, no. 4) gains prestige from its association with the European *Heer Halewijn*, but the English versions are poor and late. *Lady Alice* (Child, no. 85) was known to Child only in nineteenth-century versions, but William Shenstone's *Miscellany* (1759–63) has a version which shows that this ballad may originally have been a part of *Clerk Colvill* (Child, no. 42), a ballad included in the *Songs* of David Herd (see [23] below).

The one ballad that offers itself as possibly of medieval origin is *Gude Wallace* (Child, no. 157), treating events of about 1300, and celebrating a hero who earlier appeared in Blind Harry's *Wallace* (ca. 1460). The ballad survives in a chapbook of about 1745, very near the time of the battle of Culloden (1746). This story, depicting heroism against superior numbers, seems based on Blind Harry's *Wallace* (bk. 5, lines 1080–1119) and its promulgation at this time is readily understandable. I conclude that the ballad is not likely to have survived in tradition since the fifteenth century, but rather expresses Scottish national feeling in the eighteenth century.

EIGHTEENTH-CENTURY SONGBOOKS [20]. The five eighteenth-century songbooks represented in this section are Ramsay's *Tea Table Miscellany* (1723–37), Thomson's *Orpheus Calidonius* (1733), Elizabeth Cochrane's songbook (ca. 1730), Johnson's *Scots Musical Museum* (1787–1803), and Ritson's *Scotish Song* (1794). A sixth songbook, encountered too late for systematic inclusion here, should not be overlooked: *A Collection of Diverting Songs, Epigrams, &c.*, n.d., ca. 1738 (C. H. Wilkinson copy, in the Library of Worcester College, Oxford), which has more than two dozen ballad versions unknown to Child along with a rich assortment of over 1300 songs.

Twelve ballads appear for the first time in one or another of the five songbooks represented here: in Ramsay are Child, nos. 84, 181, and 200; in Cochrane are Child, nos. 5, 76, 144, and 293; in Thomson is Child, no. 215; in Johnson are Child, nos. 16, 240, and *Lady Mary Ann*, Robert Burns' version of the traditional ballad *A-Growing* which Child unfortunately omitted from his edition; and in Ritson is Child, no. 196, *The Fire of Frendraught*. No attempt is made here or in the following sections of this chapter to present the full range of ballad manuscripts and their contents. For details the student is advised to consult the dissertation of William Montgomerie in Edinburgh University Library, parts of which have appeared in "A Bibliography of the Scottish Ballad Manuscripts 1730–1825," SSL 4(1966).3, 79, 194; 5.107; 6.91; 7.60, 238.

The twelve songbook ballads include four that are to some degree connected with medieval tradition. *Gil Brenton* (Child, no. 5) is an international ballad especially rich in Scandinavian analogues, and it appears in Britain in three important eighteenth-century collections: Elizabeth Cochrane's songbook (ca. 1730), Herd's *Ancient and Modern Scots Songs* (1769), and Mrs. Brown's manuscripts (1783). The story in the songbook version (Child, no. 5E) is as follows.

Lord Benwall has gone hunting and while walking alone he meets with a young lady whom he detains all night. When they part in the morning he gives her a pair of gloves and a gay gold ring. Lord Benwall next goes wooing and marries the youngest of seven ladies. As they are journeying towards his home, the bride moans, but when questioned she refuses to explain her sadness. Having reached Lord Benwall's home, the bride is seized by labor pains while they are at supper. When questioned this time she confesses to the groom that she is with child. Lord Benwall calls her a common whore, but his mother (apparently) tells him to go cheer up his merry men while she hears a further explanation from the bride regarding her condition. The girl explains that once when she was walking alone a lord met her and detained her all night, after which he gave her a pair of gloves and a gay gold ring. She offers to show these tokens to the mother, who in turn goes and challenges her son to produce the ring she had given him. Lord Benwall confesses that he gave the ring to a lady whom he now wishes, somewhat belatedly, he might have in his bower, whereupon his mother triumphantly announces that he now has in his home that very lady. When the heir is born, Benwall's name is found written on his breastbone. Overjoyed, Lord Benwall orders his lady clothed in silk and his young son fed with milk.

Herd's version of *Gil Brenton* (Child, no. 5G) is defective, but clearly like the songbook version summarized above. Mrs. Brown's text (Child, no. 5A), however, is twice the length of the others, and contains unique features: a chastity test (stanzas 15–26), with the consequent substitution of a maid in the bridal bed reminiscent of Brangwain's role in the romance of Tristan and Iseult; the use of a miraculous talking bed (stanzas 27–32) to reveal the fraudulent substitution of the maid and the pregnancy of the bride; and the bride's account of the seduction (stanzas 41–60) is made to suggest a fairy encounter similar to that related in *Tam Lin* (Child, no. 39).

The fragment of *Sheath and Knife* in Johnson's *Scots Musical Museum* (Child, no. 16C) was the earliest bit of this ballad known to Child, but the recent discovery of a related seventeenth-century text, published by Mrs. H. M. Shire in 1960, points up the antiquity of this ballad, and shows its close connection with *Leesome Brand* (Child, no. 15) and *Gil Brenton* (Child, no. 5). The desperate plight of a girl, accompanied by her lover, giving birth to a child under adverse conditions is common to all three, but the incest theme occurs only in *Sheath and Knife* and in some analogues of *Leesome Brand*. The seventeenth-century Scottish text is found in the commonplace book of Robert Edward, minister of the Murroes, compiled ca. 1635 and preserved for many years in the library of the earls of Dalhousie, Panmure House (since 1957 on indefinite loan to the National Library of Scotland, MS 9450). It is interesting that the Panmure version contains the incest motif as an integral part of the story.

A brother loves his sister, and urges her not to tell his deed. The girl fears that her condition will be discovered when she attends the father's feast in her finest clothes, and she warns that her brother John will burn them both on a hill. To avoid discovery they flee on horseback, but before they have ridden a mile she begins to quake and groan. He asks if there is water in her shoes, or wind in her gloves, or does she think him too simple a knight to ride with her? She evidently dismisses him from her presence, instructing him to bend his bow when he hears her cry, and sound his horn when he sees her lying still. "I would give all my father's land," she says, "for one woman at my command." When the brother returns, he finds the baby born and the girl dead (as in *Leesome Brand*), and so takes his young son to a milk woman. Drawing his sword, he wounds himself sorely and asks his mother to make his bed, mourning the loss of his knife and its sheath: "ther is no cutlar in this land / can mak a kniffe so at my comand." Turning his face to the wall, he gives up the ghost. Brother and sister are buried in Mary's Kirk and Quire, and birk and brier grow out of their graves, a sign that they were lovers.

The stanzas in the Panmure manuscript occasionally shift into four lines (or even six), but the normal form is a two-line stanza with interlaced refrain, as in the opening:

Ther was a sister and a brother
   the sun gois to under the wood
Who most intirelie lovid othir
   god give we had nevir beine sib.

The relationship of *Sheath and Knife*, *Gil Brenton*, and *Leesome Brand* is evidently close, but it is not easy to decide whether the incest theme is original. The symbolic knife, however, unconnected with incest, occurs in the Percy Folio MS abridgment of *The Squire of Low Degree* (see I [104] in *Manual*, vol. 1) simply entitled "The Squire" (PFMS, 3.263). This abridgment, dating from perhaps 1560, has the heroine mourn the apparent loss of her beloved under circumstances that require concealing the loss from her father. When the father asks her why she is sad, she explains that she has lost her knife ("The Squier," lines 123–26):

"My daughter," he sayes, "if itt be but a blade,
I can gett another as good made."
"Father," she sais, "there is never a smith but one
That can smith you such a one."

In any case the discovery of a seventeenth-century version of the ballad in the Panmure manuscript is of the greatest importance, strengthening as it does the possibility of a medieval origin for this group, and providing yet another instance of the importance of early Scottish tradition in the evolution of balladry.

The Lass of Roch Royal (Child, no. 76) is especially well represented in eighteenth-century versions: Elizabeth Cochrane's songbook (Child, no. 76A), a broadside of about 1740 entitled *The Lass of Ocram* in the Roxburghe collection (Child, vol. 3, p. 510), David Herd's manuscripts (Child, no. 76B), and two versions by Mrs. Brown of Falkland (Child, no. 76D, E). Since a synoptic view of these versions is given elsewhere (*Journal of American Folklore* 71.553), our epitome of the narrative is based solely on the broadside, *The Lass of Ocram*, which appears to preserve the archetypal form of the story.

> The Lass of Ocram is sailing all alone in a rich ship when she meets a proud merchant man. She identifies herself to him, saying that she is in search of Lord Gregory. The merchant man apparently recognizes her and directs her to yonder island. She asks at the gate to be let in, but Gregory's mother, speaking as if she were Gregory, demands that she name three tokens which the lovers had exchanged. The lass mentions linen, rings, and her maidenhead, suggesting reproachfully in the process that the value of the various tokens is symbolic of their love relationship: her ring was of the beaten gold, his was of block tin. At the mention of maidenhead, the mother tells her to be gone, "or else in the deep seas / you and your babe shall fall." Whereupon the girl asks who will shoe her bonnie feet, etc., concluding with "Who's to be father of my child / if Lord Gregory is none?" The mother's answer is: let your own family (brother, sister, mother, father) take care of you, and "let God be father of your child, / for Lord Gregory is none." Lord Gregory has apparently been asleep during this conversation, and when he finally awakens he tells his mother of a dream in which he saw the Lass of Ocram floating on the flood. His mother advises him to lie still and rest, for, she says, the maid passed by here not half an hour ago. Lord Gregory then curses his mother for not waking him, and declares his heart will break for the Lass of Ocram.

The history of the transmission of this ballad from the eighteenth century to the present is one of erosion and eventual disintegration, leaving as the emotional center the free-floating "shoe-my-foot" stanzas which have attached themselves to nearly 100 different ballads and songs. But a vertical analysis of the earliest versions shows a familiar narrative: the heroine is banished from kith and kin to sail alone on the sea, and after finally coming to land she is rebuffed (as she thinks) by her true love through the machinations of his malevolent mother and is therefore mercilessly driven, with her young babe in her arms, back once more to her ship to sail the seas in peril of her life. The situation is that of the Accused Queen, renowned heroine of medieval folktale and romance, best known as Constance in Chaucer's *Man of Law's Tale*. Barring the discovery of an earlier Scottish version (the broadside rimes *alone* and *main*), the process whereby our heroine's story was transmitted from the Middle Ages to the eighteenth century must remain a mystery.

The Gypsy Laddie (Child, no. 200) is preserved in two eighteenth-century versions, one in Ramsay's *Tea-Table Miscellany* (Child, no. 200A), and the other a broadside of about the same date (Child, no. 200G).

> The gypsies come to our good lord's gate, and sing so sweetly that the lady comes down to them. When they see her beauty, they cast their glamor over her, and she leaves her comfortable home to go with them. The lady vows that she shall go to bed with Johnny Faa, and her lord shall no more come near her. When the lord comes home and learns of the loss of his lady, he vows to go seek her. The gypsies mourn their fall because of a fair young wanton lady.

This summary follows the highly lyrical version in Ramsay; the broadside has a more detailed story (the lord is "the Earl of Castle"), it specifies that the gypsies were to be hanged, and replaces the spell-casting with a homelier example of gypsy influence (Child, no. 200G, stanza 3):

> They gave to her a nutmeg brown,
> And a race of the best ginger;
> She gave to them a far better thing,
> 'Twas the ring from off her finger.

This comic touch in the broadside, together with the predominantly satirical treatment of gypsies in the seventeenth century (see *Come My Dainty Doxeys* in the Percy Folio, PFMS 3.313), suggested to Judith Knoblock (Western Folklore 19.35) that *The Gypsy Laddie* had its origin in a parody of the romance of *Sir Orfeo* (see I [86] in *Manual*, vol. 1). According to this theory the fairy troop that abducted Heurodis is replaced by a band of gypsies, and the bathos of the implied comparison provides a basis for satire. This is not the kind of thing that endures in tradition, however, and indeed the romantic treatment of gypsy life was perhaps an inevitable development in the eighteenth century. In any case the satire has been entirely eliminated in the lyric version of Ramsay, and leaves only a slight trace in the broadside. If the theory is correct, *The Gypsy Laddie*, though not itself of medieval origin, has close ties with a version of the Orpheus story. And the recent discovery of a sixteenth-century form, *King Orphius* (see below under [25]), together with the existence of a tune, "Lady Cassilles Lilt," as early as 1630 (Bronson TTCB, 3.198), suggests a channel for oral transmission of both narrative and melody, and also reminds us of the importance of Scottish tradition in tracing the genesis and development of particular ballads.

PERCY'S RELIQUES [21]. Considering the importance of Bishop Percy's *Reliques of Ancient English Poetry* (London 1765), it is surprising that, among the large number of selections included, there are only four traditional ballads previously unknown, and one of these, *Young Waters* (Child, no. 94) had actually appeared as a pamphlet in Glasgow in 1755. The other three, *Edward* (Child, no. 13B), *Sir Patrick Spens* (Child, no. 58A), and *The Jew's Daughter* (Child, no. 155B), all came to Percy (along with *Lord Thomas and Fair Annet*, a ballad already discussed in section [18] above) in a single packet from Edinburgh in August 1763, just in time for inclusion in the first edition of the *Reliques*. All three of these new texts have been recognized as outstanding specimens of the ballad, and appear regularly in English literature anthologies. Their literary excellence is undeniable, but it is much more difficult to say whether they are ballads that derive from medieval tradition which simply were not recorded until the time of Percy's *Reliques*. That such a gap between time of origin and transcription can occur is dramatically illustrated, as we have seen, by the recovery in modern times of oral versions of the *Corpus Christi Carol*, where there is a gap of nearly 400 years. But the stability of occasion for singing a carol has been provided by the church calendar, whereas it is not so easy to explain a centuries-long persistence of *Edward*, *Sir Patrick Spens*, and *Sir Hugh, or the Jew's Daughter*. The last named would presumably have existed in some form from the time of the alleged event (1255) and hence have an unrecorded oral history of over 500 years. An analysis of the structure of *Sir Hugh*, and especially its apparent indebtedness to *The Cruel Mother* (see D. C. Fowler, *A Literary History of the Popular Ballad*, p. 258), suggest that it is a ballad of modern date, despite its impressive medieval setting. Even more obvious, I believe, is the case of *Edward* and *Sir Patrick Spens*. *Edward* is simply an example of domestic tragedy with that flair for the dramatic which we have found to be characteristic of the eighteenth century, despite its connections with European analogues. *Sir Patrick Spens* emerges, like *Gude Wallace*, at a time when Scottish national feeling was at its height. While these are the conclusions I have reached, I should add that MacEdward Leach was of the opinion that *Sir Hugh* probably, and *Sir Patrick Spens* possibly were in existence prior to 1500. Whatever the truth of the matter, I certainly agree with Leach that *Sir Patrick*, with its dramatic intensity and felicitous language, is "one of the finest of all ballads."

PERCY PAPERS: MSS IN THE HARVARD LIBRARY [22]. After the publication of the *Reliques of Ancient English Poetry*, Percy received, between 1766 and 1780, copies of ballads from correspondents all over the country. These were never published in Percy's lifetime, but were eventually acquired by the Harvard library and used by Child in the preparation of his edition. The Percy papers are thus a miscellaneous collection, united only by the fact that they came from readers of the *Reliques* who wished to add to the Bishop's accumulation of ballad texts. Among these papers we find the earliest known versions of no less than thirteen ballads: Child, nos. 12, 75, 93, 95, 100, 114, 185, 188, 189, 195, 214, 217, 238. None of this group is of medieval origin. *Lord Randall* (Child, no. 12) and *The Maid Freed from the Gallows* (Child, no. 95) can claim a certain antiquity by virtue of their European analogues, but nothing suggests that either is any earlier than the sixteenth century. *Johnie Cock* (Child, no. 114) is a fine ballad, but the reference to wolves does not necessarily indicate a medieval setting (Child, vol. 3, p. 2), and Johnie's "shoes of the American leather" (Child, no. 114A, stanza 13, line 3) point in the other direction. The only other ballad that might boast an early origin is *Lamkin* (Child, no. 93), but this is one of those domestic tragedies of no particular time or place; it is difficult to believe that *Lamkin* could be earlier than the sixteenth or seventeenth century.

DAVID HERD: MSS BRITISH MUSEUM ADDITIONAL 22311-12 AND PRINTED EDITIONS OF 1769 AND 1776 [23]. One of the most reliable ballad collectors and editors in the eighteenth century was David Herd (1732-1810), who lived in Edinburgh most of his life but was able to gather an impressive variety of ballads and songs from rural Scotland. A selection of these he first published in 1769, and then issued an enlarged edition (two volumes) in 1776. From this vast storehouse Child selected 44 ballads for inclusion in his edition, and of these 27 are the earliest known versions: Child, nos. 11, 14, 38, 39, 42, 43, 46, 50, 51, 62, 64, 66, 68, 69(77), 88, 91, 182,

204, 210, 213, 220, 221, 248, 274, 275, 277, 279. Four of these have at least a modest claim to the attention of the medievalist. *The Wee Wee Man* (Child, no. 38) is related to a poem in eight-line stanzas in a fourteenth-century manuscript (British Museum Cotton Julius A.5, folio 175ª). *Tam Lin* (Child, no. 39) contains a fairy abduction reminiscent of *Sir Orfeo*, though it concentrates on shape shifting and the handling of the supernatural seems in some ways post-medieval. Estimates of the antiquity of *Clerk Colvill* (Child, no. 42) appear to have been affected by its connection with the great Danish ballad *Elveskud*, which spread over Europe in the sixteenth century; but the English version is much later and inferior to its continental analogues, and, as we have seen in section [19] above, the process of disintegration is indicated by the splitting of *Lady Alice* (Child, no. 85) from the main line of descent. *The Grey Cock, or, Saw You My Father* (Child, no. 248) looks to be of modern composition, but it does recall the medieval literary tradition of the dawn-song, or *aube*, as found for example in Chaucer's *Troilus and Criseyde* and *The Reeve's Tale*.

There is, however, one ballad, *Clerk Saunders* (Child, nos. 69 and 77), which justifies all of David Herd's efforts, even if he had discovered nothing else in his entire career. The story of *Clerk Saunders* has a revenant ending which appears separately under the title *Sweet William's Ghost* (Child, no. 77) in Ramsay's *Tea-Table Miscellany* vol. IV (1740), at least two decades before Herd collected his complete version (Herd's MSS, A, I, 177). For this reason Child decided that there were originally two separate ballads, and hence he divided Herd's text into two parts (Child, nos 69A and 77B) even though they are united in the manuscript. The argument for the unity of Herd's *Clerk Saunders* is given elsewhere (D. C. Fowler, *A Literary History of the Popular Ballad*, p. 193), and provides the basis for the following summary.

> Clerk Saunders and May Margret are in love, but she resists his suggestion that they lie together before they are married because she fears they will be discovered by her seven brothers. To enable her to swear her innocence and "save her oath" Saunders suggests that she lift the doorlatch with his sword, so she can say she never let him in; wear a blindfold, so she can say she never saw him; and carry him to her bed, so she can say he never trod her bower floor. Margret agrees, but all their precautions are wasted, for that night the seven brothers burst into the room with their torches burning bright and find the lovers asleep in each other's arms. There is a moment of suspense as six of the brothers, in turn, express their sympathy for the couple and refuse to harm them. But the seventh says, "Altho there wear no a man but me, I bear the brand, I'le gar him die" (Child, no. 69A, stanza 14). He pierces the sleeping Saunders through and through with the cold iron. In the morning Margret looks between her and the wall, "and dull and heavy was his eeen" (Child, no. 69A, stanza 18, line 4). When she sees the blood of Saunders' fair body and

realizes that he is dead, she utters the traditional vow of austerities, climaxed by her resolution to wear "nought but dowy black." Her father offers her consolation, but she refuses to be comforted.

In the evening, when all men have gone to bed, Clerk Saunders comes to Margret's window and asks her to return the faith and troth he has given her. Margret asks first for a kiss, but he warns her that his mouth is cold, and if she did, her days would not be long. Then with a note of urgency he asks again for the return of the troth for, he says, cocks are crowing on merry middle-earth, and the singing of birds foretells the coming of day. Margret delays him with a question: what becomes of women who die in childbirth? When he assures her that "their beds are made in the heavens high," she stretches the troth out the window to him on a wand. Saunders heartily thanks her and departs, after promising to return for her "gin ever the dead come for the quick." Margret follows him back to the grave and asks for room to lie beside him. But Saunders warns her that he sleeps among the worms, with no coverlet but cold meal and a winding sheet.

No single source for this ballad has been found, though elements of it are scattered through European balladry (Child, vol. 2, p. 156). But the text is a remarkable composite of themes and motifs from medieval romance. The temptation of the lovers to anticipate their marriage is reminiscent of an episode in Malory's *Sir Gareth of Orkney*, and the device of "saving" one's oath echoes several situations in the story of Tristan and Iseult, notably the "ordeal by iron" in Béroul. The seven brothers connect with early abduction narratives such as that of *Earl Brand*, and they are much more functional than the brothers who appear briefly in *Fair Margaret and Sweet William* (Child, no. 74A, stanzas 11, 14), a ballad in existence in 1611. Margret's vow of austerities is at least as old as *The Squire of Low Degree* (ca. 1500). But all of these themes and motifs relate to the first part of the ballad. What of the revenant ending? This too, it seems to me, can be traced to medieval romance and didactic literature. Among the treasuries of tradition that present a picture of life after death are *The Trental of Gregory* and collections such as the *Gesta Romanorum*. These in turn had an influence on secular literature like *The Awntyrs of Arthure at the Terne Wathelyne*, in which the ghost of Guenevere's mother appears to Gawain and the queen, delivers certain pronouncements and answers questions. Another metrical piece, *The Child of Bristowe*, has a revenant, the child's father, who demands the return of a troth. Thus all of the features of the revenant ending of *Clerk Saunders* come ultimately from medieval sources: the questioning of the ghost, the troth-return, and even the *memento mori* ending, reminiscent of Guenevere's mother's moral exhortation in *The Awntyrs of Arthure*. With these are blended the folk beliefs regarding the departure of the dead at cock-crow, and the kiss of death. But beyond even these is an impressive organic unity, and a Boethian theme of consolation reminiscent of the Middle English *Pearl*, and Chaucer's *Book of the Duchess*. We are left to wonder how this luminous ballad found its way through the centuries, unrecorded in full until the latter half of the eighteenth century.

MRS. BROWN OF FALKLAND: JAMIESON'S BROWN MANUSCRIPT, 1783 (J–B); WILLIAM TYTLER'S BROWN MANUSCRIPT, 1783 (WT–B); ALEXANDER FRASER TYTLER'S BROWN MANUSCRIPT, 1800 (AFT–B), AND ROBERT JAMIESON'S *POPULAR BALLADS AND SONGS*, 1806 (PBS) [24]. Anna Gordon Brown (1747–1810) was the most important single contributor to Child's canon, providing a total of 33 ballads in 51 versions. Even more impressive is the fact that 23 of these were unknown to the world before they were obtained from Mrs. Brown: Child, nos. 6, 32, 34, 35, 37, 53, 65, 82, 89, 90, 92, 96, 97, 98, 99, 101, 102, 103, 203, 216, 222, 247, 252. The details concerning her ballad manuscripts are provided by W. Montgomerie (SSL 7.60, 238). Suffice it to say here that J–B was compiled in 1783 and later given to Robert Jamieson for use in his *Popular Ballads and Songs*; this first manuscript had twenty ballad texts but no music. WT–B was done later in 1783 at the request of the musicologist William Tytler, this time with music but repeating only fourteen of the original twenty ballads in J–B, and adding one not given before. AFT–B was obtained by Alexander Fraser Tytler from Mrs. Brown in 1800 on behalf of Walter Scott, who was then collecting materials for his *Minstrelsy of the Scottish Border* (1802), and this manuscript has nine ballads, seven of them appearing for the first time in Mrs. Brown's repertoire; there is no music for these, despite the fact that Mrs. Brown's letter of transmittal seems to say that AFT–B had music as well as words. Finally Jamieson obtained six more ballads, four of them previously unknown, directly from Mrs. Brown between 1800 and 1806, when his edition (PBS) was published.

Of the ballads obtained from Mrs. Brown in 1783, there are perhaps three "grotesques" that are related to medieval tradition: *King Henry* (Child, no. 32), an offshoot of *The Marriage of Sir Gawain* (Child, no. 31) in the Percy Folio MS (see [17] above); *Kemp Owyne* (Child, no. 34B), in which the romance hero Owain is made the hero of an unspelling quest; and *Allison Gross* (Child, no. 35), another unspelling wherein the speaker is turned into an "ugly worm" by the witch of the north country, and restored by the queen of the fairies. This group illustrates Mrs. Brown's interest in magic and witchcraft, and one of them, *King Henry*, was printed by Matthew Gregory Lewis in his *Tales of Wonder* (1801). Accordingly it is not unreasonable to assume that these ballads reflect an eighteenth-century Gothic interest, rather than that they represent authentic survival of medieval tradition.

One of Mrs. Brown's early ballads, however, *Young Beichan* (Child, no. 53), is an important example of the persistence of medieval legend. She has left us two versions of this in three copies. What Child designates as no. 53A appears to be a broadside version, resembling a text in the Glenriddell manuscripts (Child, no. 53B), and is preserved in J–B only; the other version, much expanded (from 23 to 36 stanzas), seems to be Mrs. Brown's re-creation, with its text preserved in both J–B and WT–B, the latter with tune included (Bronson TTCB, 1.464 from Ritson's copy). The following summary is based on Mrs. Brown's "broadside" version (Child, no. 53A).

> Young Beichan sails from London and is imprisoned by a Moor, whose daughter frees him on condition he will marry her within seven years. She gives him bread and wine, and he returns to London. After seven long years the girl sails to London and reaches young Beichan's gates just as he is about to marry another. Beichan returns the young bride to her mother and declares he will marry the Moorish lady.

The origin of this story is found in the legendaries of the Middle Ages, in particular the account of the life of St. Thomas à Becket designed to be read each year on his day (7 July). The text is best preserved in the *South English Legendary* (EETS 236.610). For detailed references see V [276] in *Manual*, vol. 2. All this is not to say that Child, no. 53A has a medieval texture like that of *Clerk Saunders* (Child, nos. 69A, 77B); on the other hand, I am inclined to believe, as Bronson seems to indicate (Bronson TTCB, 1.409), that the text of *Young Beichan* which Mrs. Brown provides is the end result of oral transmission from pre-Reformation times and is not a late, Gothic reprise of the old story. Despite the Reformation strictures, ballads and songs generated under the influence of the medieval church calendar (like *Corpus Christi* in [8] above) have tended to persist in tradition for a remarkably long time, thanks to the stability of occasion for singing provided by the temporale and the sanctorale.

For the student of medieval literature, the most crucial case in the repertoire of Mrs. Brown is the ballad of *Thomas Rymer* (Child, no. 37A). It first comes to light in the AFT–B manuscript of 1800 and was used by Scott (with some changes) for the first edition of *Minstrelsy of the Scottish Border*

(1802), and subsequently appears, more faithfully reproduced, in Jamieson's *Popular Ballads and Songs*. Five other versions of this ballad were collected in the early nineteenth century mostly from the border area, three of them in the region of the Eildon Hills, the setting of the story.

> As Thomas lay on Huntlie bank, a beautiful lady came riding by. Thomas thought she was the queen of Heaven, but she assured him that she was only queen of Fairyland. She invited Thomas to go with her and serve her for seven years. He agreed. For 40 days and nights they waded through blood; then they came to a green garden. After forbidding Thomas to eat of the fruit of that country, the queen gave him bread and wine which she had brought, and then showed him the three roads, one leading to heaven, one leading to hell, and one leading to Elfland. Thomas is warned that no matter what they see, he is not to say a word. They departed on the last road and for seven years Thomas was not seen on earth.

This obviously has some connection with the fourteenth-century *Tomas of Ersseldoune* (see XIII [290] in *Manual*, vol. 5), which tells in a prologue how Thomas received the soothsayer's gift, and appends a series of prophecies. Three types of relationships with the ballad may be postulated. First, the ballad may be a part of the resurgence of Scottish culture in the eighteenth century, composed directly from the manuscript. Second, the ballad may be an authentic survival in oral tradition, based ultimately on the medieval narrative in the manner of *Young Beichan* (though without the support of the Sanctorale). Third, as has been proposed recently by Emily B. Lyle, the ballad may have had an independent existence in medieval times, itself reflecting a version prior to and influencing *Tomas of Ersseldoune*.

I must confess a long-standing inclination toward the first hypothesis, with even a hunch that Mrs. Brown herself, who "read everything in the marvelous way," was the author rather than simply the transmitter of her version. The nineteenth-century texts, in this view, would then be local variants stimulated by the impact of *Minstrelsy of the Scottish Border*. On the other hand, recent discoveries and developments in the study of ballads should caution us against too easily assuming an eighteenth-century origin. We have already noted the recently recovered early Scottish versions of *Sir Cawline* and *Sheath and Knife* (in [17] and [20] above), and will encounter below (in [25]) the sixteenth-century version of *King Orphius*, all of which compel respect for a Scottish oral tradition of great antiquity. In the specific case of *Thomas Rymer* Lyle has shown (*Scottish Studies* 13.65) that the configuration of placenames in the border versions are confirmed in medieval documents in a way that makes it difficult (to say the least) to maintain a theory of modern adaptation from Scott's *Minstrelsy*. This being the case, our second hypothesis now seems more plausible, namely that *Tomas of Ersseldoune* was preserved orally (minus the prophecies) in *Thomas Rymer* for over 400 years until finally written down for the first time in 1800. Having abandoned my original theory in the light of new evidence, I may perhaps be forgiven a continuing skepticism regarding the third hypothesis, which envisions a ballad something like the surviving one (in quatrains abcb) circulating in the fourteenth century and influencing the composition of *Tomas of Ersseldoune*. Our chronological survey of the ballads suggests that it is difficult to substantiate the existence of ballads in the form that we now know them before (let us say) the appearance of *Captain Car* in 1571.

BALLADS COLLECTED IN THE NINETEENTH CENTURY [25]. In this final section we include all remaining Child ballads (over 100 of them) plus a number of carols. The only unity here is a negative one: none of these is known to exist in a version earlier than the nineteenth century. Ideally, of course, these ballads should be studied with the same concern for date and source that is required for those in the preceding sections. But the task of tracing texts to their sources for this period is only now getting underway, perhaps best illustrated in the work of Scottish editors (William Montgomerie, David Buchan, Emily Lyle). In any case, with a few important exceptions, these ballads are only remotely connected with medieval tradition. In what follows no attempt is made to speak of them all (though all are listed in the Bibliography), but only to refer to those that are of particular interest to medievalists.

Two ballads, though they are separated in the Child canon, really are attached to other ballads already treated, and need not concern us here: *Leesome Brand* (Child, no. 15) belongs with *Sheath and Knife* (Child, no. 16), discussed in [20] above; and *Henry Martyn* (Child, no. 250) is a late form of *Sir Andrew Barton* (Child, no. 167), discussed in [13] above. Two other ballads should be classified as of possible early date: *Hind Etin* (Child, no. 41) is an international ballad with Danish versions surviving from the sixteenth century; *The Battle of Harlaw* (Child, no. 163), fought on 24 July 1411, is mentioned as a song title in the *Complaynt of Scotland* (1549), with early evidence of a tune (Bronson TTCB, 3.117), and a poem on the subject first printed in

Ramsay's *Ever Green* (1724), vol. 1, p. 78 (reprinted by Foulis in 1748), and a chapbook form of the poem published in Aberdeen 1801 (Bodleian Library, *A Right Merrie Book of Garlands and Songs*, no. 59). Two more ballads could be said to represent modern imitations of medieval style: *Proud Lady Margaret* (Child, no. 47) is a Gothic reconstruction of the *memento mori* theme using the riddle formula; and *The Wife of Usher's Well* (Child, no. 79) is an imaginative re-creation of the revenant experience.

A few important carols, of a type represented by *Corpus Christi* discussed in [8] above, appear to have had a long life in oral tradition before being recovered in the nineteenth and twentieth centuries. In this group are *The Cherry Tree Carol* (Child, no. 54), *The Carnal and the Crane* (Child, no. 55), *Dives and Lazarus* (Child, no. 56), and *The Unquiet Grave* (Child, no. 78). The last-named is not strictly speaking a carol, but perhaps fits best in this category for historical reasons. Outside the Child canon, but worthy of inclusion here, are several religious songs that have been preserved for centuries in oral tradition and appear to be pre-Reformation in origin: *The Bitter Withy*, *The Holy Well*, *Sweet Jesus*, *Gloria Tibi Domine*, and perhaps the *Boar's Head Carol* (Greene E E Carols, no. 132) traditionally associated with Queen's College, Oxford, and *The Bold Fisherman* (for the latter see L. Broadwood, Journ of the Folk-Song Soc 5.132).

The Cherry Tree Carol (Child, no. 54) preserves the miracle of the tree bowing down to permit the Virgin to gather cherries. In the Middle English *Childhood of Jesus* (Arch 74.327) this episode occurs during the flight into Egypt. Mary is weary from travel and Joseph seats her under a palm tree to rest. When she expresses a desire for the fruit of the tree, the Christ child orders the tree to bow down. In the carol, however, this event forms a part of the courtship of Joseph and Mary, that moment when Joseph first learns that she is with child; hence the child, unborn, speaks miraculously from his mother's womb. The scene is thus moved from the desert to an orchard, the tree is a cherry, and Mary's desire for the fruit is not from weariness of travel but the understandable craving of an expectant mother. The new setting ties the carol to the Nativity feast in the church calendar, where it has remained firmly rooted for some five centuries.

The Carnal and the Crane (Child, no. 55) is a mosaic of doctrinal and biblical themes. The central episode is the flight into Egypt, to which apocryphal incidents have been added resembling those in the *Childhood of Jesus*. The miraculous sowing and harvesting of the crop on a single day (stanzas 18–28), reminiscent of the impossible tasks in *The Elfin Knight* (Child, no. 2), is used here to deceive Herod into giving up his pursuit of the holy family. This carol also shows the signs of reshaping that have made it a nativity song (stanza 30), and thus preserved it in a protestant culture where Christmas remained the one enduring occasion when carols are sung in popular religious observances.

Dives and Lazarus (Child, no. 56), a retelling of the parable in Luke 16:19–31, does not have the distinctive apocryphal features that suggest medieval origin, and hence there is some uncertainty about its age. The style suggests that it is a product of oral tradition, but it may be post-Reformation in origin.

In the beautiful lyric, *The Unquiet Grave* (Child, no. 78), a lover sits mourning on his sweetheart's grave for a twelvemonth and a day, after which the sweetheart (in some versions the sexes are reversed) asks who is disturbing her sleep. When the lover asks for a kiss, the dead warns that a kiss would be fatal. In the earliest version a moral conclusion exhorts the lover to make himself content until God calls him away; in others the song ends with a haunting stanza wherein the departed sweetheart promises to return when the autumn leaves turn green and spring up again. This last is a striking variation on the paraphrases of "never" which occur at the end of ballads like *Edward* (Child, no. 13), while at the same time it appears to hold out a promise of reunion of the lovers at the Resurrection. Obviously this is no ordinary carol, but we place it here because its musical settings, which are rich and varied, are carol-like, and because it appears to be descended from a medieval carol which begins "There blows a colde wynd todaye, todaye" (Greene E E Carols, no. 170), as pointed out by Bronson (Bronson TTCB, 2.234).

Of the carols not included in Child, *Gloria Tibi Domine* occurs in a Cornish carol book dated 1767 (MS Harvard College Library 25258.27.5*), which was first printed by Greene in 1940; *Sweet Jesus* appeared as a broadside ca. 1822 and was subsequently reprinted in nineteenth-century collections. Both of these carols survive in medieval manuscripts and were preserved in oral tradition as was *Corpus Christi*. Detailed references are available in R. L. Greene, "The Traditional Survival of Two Medieval Carols" (ELH 7.223).

Gloria Tibi Domine and *Sweet Jesus* are so clearly carols both in form and content that they have not been inserted in the modern ballad canon. The case is quite otherwise with *The Bitter Withy* and *The Holy Well*.

A fragment of *The Bitter Withy* appeared in *Notes and Queries* (18 January 1868), and a full version taken from a letter dated 31 December 1888 was published in *Notes and Queries* (29 July 1905). The earliest versions are about nine stanzas in length.

> On a holy day our Savior asked his mother Mary if he might play at ball. On his way ("it was upling scorn and downling scorn") he met three jolly jerdins, who refused to play ball with him since they were high-born and he was low-born. Our Savior built a bridge of sunbeams and crossed over it, but when the jolly jerdins tried to do the same, they fell and were drowned. Hearing of this, Mary called home her child and gave him three slashes with a handful of withy branches. The child curses the withy, saying that it shall be the first tree that perishes at the heart.

Over a dozen versions have been collected in modern times, and an added popularity has resulted from *Mary Mild*, a version produced by the Kingston Trio ca. 1960 in their album "Last Month of the Year" (Capitol T–1446). It is indeed remarkable to find such a song, with incidents from the apocryphal New Testament, preserved through the centuries and finally caught up in the electronic folk song revival of the mid-twentieth century.

A related song is *The Holy Well*, which appears in broadsides of the late eighteenth and early nineteenth centuries, and subsequently was printed in nineteenth-century carol collections. The earliest is a version of fourteen stanzas, published in William Sandys, *Christmas Carols Ancient and Modern* (London 1833).

> On a holy day Jesus asked his dear mother if he might go out to play. He went to yonder town as far as the holy well, and invited some children to play with him. They refused, considering him too low-born, and Jesus went home weeping to tell his mother of his rebuff. Mary heatedly suggested that he take away those sinful souls, and dip them deep in hell. But Jesus replied that sinful souls needed his help. In the last stanza Gabriel announces that Jesus, although but a maiden's child, is the king of heaven.

It has been suggested by Janet Graves (*Western Folklore* 26.13) that this is a divergent form of *The Bitter Withy*, adapted to suit a protestant viewpoint. Some twenty versions survive, and a composite text was recorded in 1956 for "Great British Ballads not included in the Child Collection" (Riverside Recording Company, RLP 12–629).

There are, in conclusion, two ballads collected in the nineteenth century that have ties with medieval romance. The first is *Hind Horn* (Child, no. 17), found in Motherwell's manuscript (1827) and subsequently in many other versions in Britain and America.

> Horn is in love with the king's daughter Jean, and she with him. When they perforce must part she gives him a magic ring which, by the degree of brightness of its seven diamonds, will reveal the lady's condition. Later when the ring pales, Horn returns home and learns that Jean is about to be married to another. He then trades clothes with a beggar so that he may beg food at the castle gate, and by this ruse communicate with Jean. When she gives him, a supposed beggar, a cup of wine, he drops the ring in the cup. She recognizes it, demands an explanation which he gives, and then immediately renounces her bridegroom and marries Horn.

The earliest medieval form of this story occurs in the Anglo-Norman *Horn et Rimenild* (ca. 1170–80), followed by *King Horn* (ca. 1225) and *Horn Child* (ca. 1320), both of which English texts may have influenced the shaping of the ballad (see I [1–4] in *Manual*, vol. 1). There is no evidence of the early existence of *Hind Horn*, but its existence in the eighteenth century may perhaps be inferred from echoes of it in ballads like *The Kitchie Boy* (Child, no. 252).

A final and most interesting case is *King Orfeo* (Child, no. 19), surviving as a testimonial to the medieval fascination with the classical myth of Orpheus and Eurydice. Until recently it has been generally assumed that the ballad is derived from the Middle English *Sir Orfeo* (see I [86] in *Manual*, vol. 1) which dates from the beginning of the fourteenth century. In view of the recent discovery of a fragmentary Scottish *King Orphius*, however, in a manuscript of the sixteenth century (see M. Stewart, *Scottish Studies* 17.1), this assumption seems untenable. Child gives a single version published in 1880, and since then other Shetland forms of the same song have been recovered in 1947 (*Journ of the Eng Folk-Dance and Song Soc* 5.77) and more recently in a version collected by Collinson (Archive, School of Scottish Studies, rec. No. 1955/145/6), both included in Bronson TTCB, 1.275; 4.455. The text is in couplets, with an obscure interlaced refrain, *Scowan ürla grün / Whar giorten han grün oarlac*, the first half of which Child interprets as Danish *Skoven årle grön* (Early green's the wood).

> A king of the east went hunting, leaving his queen Isabel at home. To her came the fairy king, who pierced her heart with a dart and so cast a spell over her and carried her away. When the king of the east discovered this and tried to follow them, he found a gray stone blocking the door

they had entered (Child, no. 19A, stanza 5). Whereupon he played his pipes, first the joyful music, then the sad music, then the music that would heal a sick heart. As a result of his playing, he was invited inside. There he again played so wonderfully that he was asked to name what he would have for a reward. He asked for his lady Isabel, and the fairy king granted the request. The king of the east took his wife home, where "noo he's king ower a' his ain."

That this is an authentic survival from the Middle Ages can scarcely be doubted, and it demonstrates dramatically the power and persistence of oral tradition. In noting the change of the heroine's name from Eurydice (Middle English Heurodis) to Isabel, we might be tempted to conclude that this is a late influence from balladry, where the name Isabel is legion. But indeed it preserves intact the name of the queen in the medieval Scottish text, where we read of "Orpheus ye king / and Issabell ye worthy quine" (lines 79–80). *King Orfeo* is a very appropriate example, therefore, with which to conclude our chronological survey of the ballad tradition, re-enforcing as it does the statement of Lajos Vargyas in his *Researches into the Medieval History of Folk Ballad* (Budapest 1967, p. 7) that "the ballad is a mediaeval genre."

XVI. JOHN LYDGATE

by

Alain Renoir and C. David Benson

(The works of John Lydgate have attracted an unusually large number of alternate titles. These alternate titles where present have been included in parentheses after the numbered main title in both the commentary and bibliography. All titles, both main and alternate, have been separately indexed. Works, therefore, may be located through any of their titles by consulting the Index.)

John Lydgate (1370?–1449?) was a monk of the Benedictine Abbey of Bury St. Edmund's and is credited with the composition of some 145,000 lines of verse and one major prose work (*The Serpent of Division* [167]). The significance of this figure becomes obvious when one recalls that it exceeds the combined totals of the preserved writings of Chaucer and Shakespeare, but the impressive bulk of his production has not exactly endeared him to the official literary taste of modern times: since the end of the eighteenth century, he has repeatedly attracted the adjectives *prolix* and *voluminous* as well as *dull* and has been reproached with having lived thirty years too long. In contradistinction, his own contemporaries in nearly all walks of life between kings and guildsmen obviously thought enough of him to commission his work, and the next century went on considering him equal to Chaucer. Presumably as a result of this early reputation, his works have been preserved in multitudinous manuscripts and were among the first to be printed and reprinted in England.

Just as Lydgate wrote for several kinds of patrons, so his writings cover nearly the whole range of literary possibilities: from translations to original creations, from religious didacticism to courtly love, from legends of saints to actual history, from monumental epics and romances to brief pieces designed to accompany the various courses at a coronation banquet, from philosophy to satire, from prayers to semi-dramatic pieces, and so on. Regardless of the patron or the genre, his work tends to express the kind of sentiments which we have come to associate with the established powers, and it expresses them often and without reservation: Holy Church is always right, and the Lollards deserve merciless repression; the King is all good, and his opponents would hurt the entire nation; England is perfect, and her enemies are despicable slanderers. Notwithstanding these observations, we must avoid the conclusion that Lydgate automatically praised those whose approval he needed, as the following fact will suggest. When Duke Humphrey of Gloucester–the powerful patron who commissioned his adaptation of Laurence de Premierfait's French version of Boccaccio's *De Casibus* into the English *Fall of Princes* [47]–divorced his wife, Jacqueline of Hainault, Lydgate proved independent enough to express unequivocally his sympathy for the latter in a *Complaint for My Lady of Gloucester and Holland* [69] which was surely not designed to earn him the Duke's approbation.

Lydgate's association with Duke Humphrey naturally brings up a question concerning his relation to early English humanism, since the Duke seems to have taken enough interest in the humanistic enterprise to bring Tito Livio Frulovisi and Antonio Beccaria to England and commission Latin translations of Aristotle's *Politics* and Plato's *Republic*. Although there have been arguments on both sides, the majority verdict seems to be that Lydgate had nothing to do with humanism and remained typical of the Middle Ages to the very end. This view–which, incidentally, is not wholly shared by the present writer–finds corroboration in his innumerable references to Chaucer and his having presented his *Siege of Thebes* [169] as an addition to *The Canterbury Tales*, both of which have warranted his classification as an English Chaucerian. He often refers to Chaucer as his master and usually contrasts the latter's talent to his own ineptitude, a practice which has made it possible for critics to agree on the point of his humility.

As one who adapted into English both French and Latin works, who wrote on subjects that can be traced back to remotest antiquity (i.e., *Troy Book* [189]) through the Middle Ages and classical Rome, who reflects the influence of both Continental and English authors, and whose own influence has been found geographically in both England and Scotland and chronologically far into the Renaissance, Lydgate has attracted the attention of students of literary history and the history of ideas. As one who wrote for different patrons over a long period of time during which the English language was supposedly changing, he has commanded the attention of linguists. As one whose works were copied and recopied in innumerable manuscripts, he has been a veritable gold mine for textual scholars. Until fairly recent times, however, he did not provide a marked stimulus for literary critics, except for those who acted on the understandable urge to demonstrate that works of his that had been previously ascribed to Chaucer were in fact not by Chaucer. Since the Second World War, two indispensable books have been published by literary scholars. One is Walter F. Schirmer's *John Lydgate: Ein Kulturbild aus dem 15. Jahrhundert* (subsequently translated into English by Ann E. Keep as *John Lydgate: A Study in the Culture of the XVth Century*) and the other is Derek Pearsall's *John Lydgate*. Most of the matters mentioned in the following pages or listed in the bibliography are discussed in detail in these books, which are likely to remain central to the study of Lydgate for years to come.

SS. ALBAN AND AMPHIBAL [1]. 638 rime royal stanzas in three books followed by a prayer also in rime royal.

Book 1 opens with an invocation to Clio where Lydgate proclaims his own ineptitude and offers an interpretation of Alban's name. The narrative proper begins with Julius Caesar's conquest of Britain. Later, King Severus of Britain sends 1500 young men, including Amphibal and Alban, to be knighted in Rome by Diocletian. Along with some other Briton youths, Amphibal is converted to Christianity and chooses a life of poverty in hiding. After a futile search for the Christians, Diocletian proceeds to confer knighthood on the faithful Britons in a long and detailed ceremony followed by a tournament during which Alban proves superior to all others and fights in an armor which will someday be used by King Offa, founder of St. Alban's Monastery. The newly knighted Britons return home, except for Alban, who will stay behind and serve Diocletian for seven years. When an usurper assumes the crown of Britain, the Romans take over once again to re-establish order, and Alban soon returns as Steward of Britain. The first book ends with Lydgate's statement that he is translating the story at the Abbot of St. Albans' request.

Book 2 opens with a prologue and an encomium of Alban, who is reunited with Amphibal in Verulamium. At Alban's home, Amphibal explains how the Son of God kept him safe and helped him return to Britain undetected, expatiates on the virgin birth of Jesus, discusses the Annunciation, predicts that Alban will accept Christianity and be released from the sorrows of the world through martyrdom, and urges him to forsake his worthless gods. Alban warns Amphibal that such views are likely to cost him his head and offers to protect him. That night, he dreams of the Crucifixion, Resurrection, and Ascension. Amphibal explains the dream, blames the Jews, tells the story of Adam and Jesus, and concludes with an account of Good Friday and the Harrowing of Hell. Alban accepts Christianity, weeps, kisses the cross, and receives baptism. Amphibal now determines to go, but Alban persuades him to stay another week and give him further instruction in the nature and practices of Christianity. While praying together at night, they are seen by a pagan, with the result that they must appear before a judge, but Alban exchanges garments with Amphibal, sends him on his way, and stays behind. Because of a death decree against those who fail to worship the gods, the pagans invade Alban's house at dawn and find him kneeling before the cross. Alban is now a knight of Christ and keeps clutching the cross despite both physical torture and the judge's attempts to win him back to paganism; when the crowd drags him to a pagan temple, he earns himself a merciless whipping by refusing to light a sacrificial fire, but he continues praying to God until the judge sentences him to six months in prison. In sympathy with the martyr, the elements dry up the earth, but the pagans miss the point of the lesson and attribute their deprivations to some kind of sorcery. The King of Britain, who hesitates to have Alban executed, writes to Diocletian, who answers that all Christians are to be put to death, except Alban, who should be won back to the pagan faith; if Amphibal is found, he should have his bowels pulled out. While some pagans hold Alban responsible for the sterility of the earth, others take the opposite view, and a convocation of wise men exonerates him. Fearing to lose his opportunity for martyrdom, however, Alban launches on a tirade against idolatry, and the pagans decide to take him to Holmhurst and behead him. On their way there, some fall off a narrow bridge and drown in the river; when Alban prays that they may be saved to witness the remainder of his passion, the river dries up, and the dead are brought back to life. His prospective executioner is so impressed that he repents and forsakes the pagan gods in favor of Jesus, thus enraging the pagans, who break all the teeth in his mouth and bones in his body before leaving him helpless on the ground. As the procession resumes, Alban performs another miracle, for which the pagans thank the sun, thus illustrating the blindness of idolatry. His head is eventually cut off, and the beheader's eyes fall to the ground. On the way back from the execution, the judge comes upon the maimed would-be executioner and mockingly tells him to take Alban's head back to the body where it belongs and ask to be healed. When the judge sees his mocking suggestion turn into a reality, he has the man's head cut off, and the crowd begins protesting the cruelty and madness of the action, thus showing that truth will out. That night a light shines from Alban's tomb to illuminate Britain while angels sing his praise. Lydgate asks the martyr's forgiveness for deficiencies in the text he has written and for his help in writing the third book and Amphibal's martyrdom.

Book 3 begins with the pagans' realization that the miracles which are taking place that night are the work of God, and one of them exhorts the others to give up their false gods and search for the man who converted Alban and must have been sent by Jesus himself. Their search for Amphibal takes 1000 of them to Wales, where they find him and receive baptism. Back in Verulamium, the pagans learn of the conversion and go after Amphibal and the new converts, whom they meet at Lichfield. When the converts refuse to abjure Christianity, their pursuers set upon them and slaughter 999 of them, accidentally sparing a cripple who could not get there to be killed; they then proceed to drag badly wounded Amphibal toward Verulamium. On the way, they meet the cripple who escaped the slaughter, and Amphibal makes him whole, thus greatly impressing the pagans but not converting them. Back in Verulamium, the rumor spreads that Amphibal and his 1000 converts have abjured Christianity, but the inhabitants soon learn the truth and begin weeping and cursing Amphibal. We now learn that God spoke to the martyrs, that all 999 souls ascended straight to Heaven, that their mangled corpses were mended, that their blood turned to milk, and that an eagle and a wolf were sent by God to watch over them. The pagans are so impressed that they begin praising the Lord Jesus, but the obdurate judge so effectively argues and threatens that one pagan pulls out Amphibal's bowels and ties them to a stake while the others cast sundry projectiles at the martyr, who continues preaching while being disembowelled. Those whom he converts are put to death, while the others urge Amphibal to accept the pagan gods and he answers that God will have mercy on those who accept baptism. At the height of his martyrdom, he sees Jesus and Alban in Heaven, and two angels appear as a voice informs that he will join his friend and receive his reward among martyrs. While angels take his soul to Heaven, a convert buries his body in a secret place, and the tormentors are suddenly afflicted with paralysis, thus frightening Verulamium into accepting Christianity. The veracity of the original story was declared in Rome. Miraculous cures occurred when King Offa found Alban's remains where they had appeared to him in a vision. Offa had a church built there and went to Rome to obtain many special graces for it. When Germanus and Lupus later came to Britain to put down the Pelagian Heresy, they visited Alban's grave. Offa spared neither gold nor silver to honor St. Alban, who loved both God and his neighbor. The poem ends with a prayer asking St. Alban to pray for practically everybody and everything, and all but three of the stanzas thereof end with the line, "O Prothomartir of Brutis Albion."

This hagiographic poem is based primarily on the *Interpretatio Guilielmi* of an otherwise unknown William and on an anonymous *Tractatus de Nobilitate*, with much of the concluding materials derived from Matthew Paris' *Vita Secondi Offae* and Bede's *Historia*. It has been argued that the fact that Lydgate was commissioned by the Abbot of St. Albans to write *SS. Alban and Amphibal* bears witness to the inroads of early humanism into the cloister. The poem was presumably held in high respect during the sixteenth century, since it was one of the few lives of saints to go to an English press after 1525 and its influence has been traced in both Hawes and Spenser. It seems to parallel Lydgate's own *SS. Edmund and Fremund* [42] and is typical of its author in other ways, such as the general tone, the numerous apologies for poetic ineptitude, the habit of reiterating points which have already been made at length, and the tendency to elaborate upon a text which is supposedly being translated.

BALLADE ON AN ALE SELLER [2]. Eleven rime royal stanzas with slightly varying refrain.

> Recalling how fickle and double-dealing was the person whom he is addressing, the speaker writes to inform her that he will no longer trust her. He reproaches her with putting on wanton looks only to make money and causing her admirers to go into debt for her as soon as they run out of cash. Her enticements bring men into trouble, and the speaker will not compare her to Griselda. With her ale, kissing, and clever behavior, she lures men into spending plenty; but she is deceitful despite her physical endowments and deserves to be treated as she treats others. In contrast, faithful women deserve praise.

This basically antifeminist poem is an early example of its genre and is said to have influenced Dunbar.

BALLADE ON AN ALE SELLER BECOME CONSTANT (also **BALLADE PER ANTIPHRASIM**) [3]. Four eight-line stanzas ababbcbc, with refrain.

The speaker tells the person whom he is addressing that she is as honest and faithful as he is free, but he is tied with a line.

See [2] above for comments.

AMEROUS BALADE (also **A LOVER'S NEW YEAR'S GIFT** and **NEW YEAR'S VALENTINE**) [4]. One five-line stanza and 22 three-line stanzas.

The speaker says that, in keeping with custom, he must remember his lady on this high feast and renew his choice to serve her faithfully forever. The very thought of her cheers him up, and he has asked the moon and the sun to put in a word for him with her, but a cloudy thought assailed his heart and made him despair of her mercy. Hope then cleared the storm even though the peerless lady was far away. He lists beautiful and faithful women whom his lady exceeds in all respects, and he says that he would rather enjoy a single look from her eyes than possession of all the other women. The only thing he can give her is his heart, which he sends her and which will be happy with her. He further asks his little song to go to her and confirm his intentions.

Although authorship has been claimed for Richard Roos, this poem is generally assumed to be Lydgate's and has been considered one of his finest.

AMOR ET PECUNIA (also **AMOR VINCIT OMNIA MENTIRIS QUOD PECUNIA** and **A DEMAWNDE BY LYDGATE**) [5]. Seventeen eight-line stanzas ababbcbc, with slightly varying refrain with exception of stanza 16.

Everyone has his own opinion as to whether love or money is more valuable, but in practice gold always comes first, as books make it clear even when the servants of Cupid disagree. Thinking of Troilus and others or reading Ovid makes it clear that love weighs nothing against a heavy purse. It is customary for human beings to betray each other for gain, and the misadventures of famous lovers of old confirm the fact. Ovid says that gods take pleasure in gifts, and so do princes, so that love may not count on friends in need, and money leads the dance. Fortune is fickle, and prosperity makes for friendship, so that one should test one's friends to see whether they prefer love or money. Some men are so blind that they cannot see the signature on their seals, and promises can be like a tree that blooms in April but bears no fruit in August. We should therefore turn to God, who gives us the kind of perfect love that will not fail a friend in need. There we shall find joy in a love that exceeds everything, and we should think of the heavenly mansion, more beautiful than the greatest cities of old. Whoever says *amor vincit omnia* is wrong about earthly love but right about heavenly love.

This poem has been praised for its sophistication and is said to have been aimed at a humanistic audience.

PRAISE OF ST. ANNE [6]. Two rime royal stanzas.

He who would love the daughter should also love the mother, so that he who worships Our Lady must also worship St. Anne. The following prayer to the latter alone was said by a holy man who saw them both on his deathbed.

Though a separate poem, these stanzas really constitute a prologue to *Prayer to St. Anne* [143].

ASSEMBLY OF GODS (also ACCORD OF REASON AND SENSUALITY IN THE FEAR OF DEATH, and ASSEMBLE DE DYEUS, and INTERPRETACYON OF THE NATURES OF GODDYS AND GODDESSES) [7]. 301 rime royal stanzas.

As Phebus has almost run his course in the Crab, we find the speaker wondering how to bring reason and sensuality into agreement and falling asleep in the process. Morpheus takes him to the Court of Minos, where Pluto is likewise present and where Eolus is brought in by Cerberus to answer the accusations of Diana and Neptune, who want him punished for having destroyed the former's forests and tampered with the workings of the latter's ocean. Minos proposes to hear Eolus' side, but a messenger from Apollo comes in to request suspension of the trial and invite the gods to a banquet. The speaker goes along to the palace of Apollo, where many gods are already assembled. Because Diana refuses to sit until Eolus has been tried, Pluto sums up the complaints against the latter. At Apollo's request, Diana conditionally drops her charges, and Phoebe is appointed arbiter between Neptune and Eolus. Athena then requests that the gods be seated at the banquet in the proper order, and the next nineteen stanzas describe the seating process, beginning with Aurora and ending with Apollo himself. Philosophers and poets wait at the table while Orpheus and Pan provide the music.

When Discord arrives belatedly and is refused a seat, she leaves in anger and meets with Atropos, who takes her part and enters the palace to intimidate the gods with a recital of his achievements as a bringer of death to all but one whom he does not name. The gods vow to use their respective powers to bring death upon the unnamed exception, and Eolus wins Neptune's forgiveness with a promise to use his blasts against the prospective enemy. Pluto now bethinks himself of inquiring about that enemy's name. Upon being told by Atropos that it is Virtue, he declares that he is indeed dealing with his worst enemy and dispatches Cerberus to bring Vice to the rescue. Cerberus soon returns with Vice followed by the seven deadly sins and an immense army of lesser sins and sinners led by Idleness. When Apollo suggests that a formal challenge be issued to Virtue, Vice immediately objects, but Morpheus sneaks out and warns him anyway. With the help of Imagination, Virtue gathers his host and moves toward an unnamed field presumably to do battle. Baptism, who has been sent ahead on a scouting mission, is seen by Original Sin, who runs away in terror while Virtue enters the field on a chariot guided by the four cardinal virtues and followed by six lesser virtues leading a great many additional virtues of all kinds. Virtue turns down offers of help from Nigromancy, Palmistry, and their ilk, so that they join forces with Vice, while Moderate Diet, Love of Learning, and others join forces with Virtue and bring with them an army of founders of churches, lovers of Christ, and all kinds of virtuous people. We now learn that the prospective battlefield is named Microcosm, that five highways lead to it, and that Conscience sits in the middle thereof to judge the outcome of the battle. As the two armies march onto the field, Vice bestows knighthood upon Falsehood, Dissimulation, and twelve others, and Virtue does the same thing with Faith, Hope, and twelve others. The lord of the field is Freewill, who receives envoys from both parties but sides with neither. Vice has Sensuality sow the field with weeds in which the forces of Virtue become entangled, but they rest under the sign of the cross and ward off enemy projectiles with the shield of the Holy Trinity. Because Freewill temporarily takes Vice's side, Virtue is forced off the field, but Baptism, Faith, Hope, and their crew hold their ground until the arrival of Perseverance gives Virtue the will to mount a victorious attack in the name of Jesus. Impressed by Virtue's victory, Freewill asks for advice from Conscience, who refers him to Humility, and he finally reaches Penance after having visited Confession, Contrition, and Satisfaction. From Heaven, Alpha and Omega send two ladies down: the one, named Prescience, drives Vice into hell along with all who still believe in him; the other, named Predestination, gives the palm of victory to Virtue, who falls on his knees along with his entire army to thank God. Some of the vanquished go to Peace and are eventually sent to Baptism and Virtue. Freewill is summoned by Virtue and blames Sensuality for his misbehavior during the battle. He is nevertheless permitted to control Microcosm, but under the supervision of Reason, and Sensuality is restrained and ordered to mend his ways. Because of Nature's protests, however, Virtue grants Sensuality freedom within Microcosm under the supervision of Sadness. Virtue thanks Morpheus and leaves for his castle. Atropos complains that he has been foiled in his rightful attempt to bring Death to Virtue, but Apollo explains that Death holds sway only within the realm of Nature and that Virtue is outside that realm. Recidivation makes an unsuccessful visit to Microcosm, and Reason and Sadness clear the weeds which Sensuality had sown earlier. In a state of dejection, Atropos calls upon Reason to ask the way to the Lord of Light, and he is directed to Virtue's castle, where Righteousness tells him that he is in fact a servant of the Lord, that his name has been changed to Death, and that the false gods whom he previously served are doomed to hell and oblivion. Virtue then sends Priesthood with the Eucharist to the field, which is cleansed so that the Lord may be properly received, and Holy Unction anoints the five highways. As Death begins claiming his due, however, the grass withers and the gates are shut. No sooner have these things taken place than Death vanishes and Virtue is suddenly exalted above the firmament. Morpheus approaches the speaker, who asks him the meaning of what he has seen.

In answer to his request, the speaker is led by Morpheus to a four-walled arbor into which they are admitted by Wit and which turns out to be Dame Doctrine's school. Around Doctrine, sit Holy Text, Gloss, and Moralization, and Scripture is the scribe. On one wall, the speaker sees pictures of Adam, Eve, and other personages from the Old Testament; on the opposite wall, he sees pictures of Peter, Paul, and other personages from the New Testament as well as Church Fathers. Doctrine beckons the speaker and explains the vision. In her explanation, Minos stands for God's judgment of human beings according to their deeds, and the complaint of Diana and Neptune against Eolus illustrates the folly of attempting the impossible. After the Fall, the people of the world slept in pagan law, and the poets invented false gods and fostered various superstitions until Moses received the Tables, thus leading mankind out of the Time of Deviation into the Time of Revocation, which lasted until the Incarnation and ushered in the Time of Reconciliation, all three of which are painted on three other walls. On the fourth wall is painted the Time of Pilgrimage, or Time of Dangerous Passage, which is what the battle between Vice and Virtue was meant to represent, just as the complaint of Atropos was meant to represent the joint constraint of Discord and Death upon friendship. The battle between Vice and Virtue also illustrates the inward struggle which each human being must experience, and Microcosm is the individual. The other allegories are likewise explained, and the poet looks at the images of poets and philosophers on the fourth wall. His contemplation is interrupted by Doctrine, who expatiates upon the pictures of the Times. Just as he asks Doctrine how Reason and Sensuality might be reconciled, the conversation is interrupted by the entrance of Death, of whom he is terrified. Reason and Sensuality follow, and both are of the same mind in making excuses for his cowardice on grounds that Death is indeed to be avoided. Doctrine points out that their agreement has answered the speaker's question, and Death, Reason, and Sensuality vanish. Doctrine interprets the vision, and the speaker now clearly understands that Reason and Sensuality are necessarily reconciled in the presence of Death. Doctrine vanishes, and Morpheus takes the speaker back to his bed before likewise vanishing. The speaker awakens and realizes that his adventure was nothing more than a dream, which he decides to write down. He asks prospective readers to leave the chaff and take only the grain from his vision, and to fight the devil, the flesh, and the world so that virtue may reign in them: then will there be glory in Heaven. He says that we must pray to God and magnify His name, and he asks Jesus to grant eternal bliss to the audience of his book.

This dream vision reflects most of the conventions of its genre as well as reflecting a typical Christian attitude toward the ancient gods. It has been said to show the influence of Peter Comestor and is accepted as a source for Henryson's *Testament of Cresseid* (see X [4] in *Manual*, volume 4); its treatment of the Seven Deadly Sins puts one in mind of Spenser's *Faerie Queene*. Although its concept of the relationship between reason and sensuality is clearly similar to that found in *Reson and Sensuallyte*, [161] below, and the poem was attributed to Lydgate by Wynken de Worde in the fifteenth century as well as by its first modern editor and other scholars, its authorship is extremely uncertain and has been questioned or rejected on both internal and external grounds by some of the most eminent mediaevalists.

LEGEND OF ST. AUSTIN AT COMPTON [8]. 51 eight-line stanzas ababbcbc, including envoy.

As told in the Bible, Abel initiated the custom of paying the tithe, and it was continued by Melchizedek, so that we should also pay it, as did Jacob. Whoever would withold it should recall what happened when St. Austin came from Rome to preach the faith in Kent, where he wrought miracles and brought the people out of darkness by baptizing them when Ethelred was king. In the village of Compton, he was asked by the priest to convince the lord to pay the tithe like everyone else, but the lord refused to be convinced by reason. Austin then went to mass and asked that every person out of grace should leave, whereupon an unprepossessing corpse rose from his grave and walked out of the churchyard in everybody's sight. Upon being questioned, the corpse informed Austin that he had been enduring all kinds of torments for over 150 years because he had been cursed for refusing to pay the tithe when he was alive. Austin found the burial place of the priest who had pronounced the curse, made him arise, and convinced him to forgive the culprit as Jesus would have done. The Lord's mercy can accomplish anything, and Trajan was saved in the same manner by St. Gregory. The priest, given the choice of going with St. Austin or returning to the grave, wisely chose the latter alternative, and the lord repented and agreed to pay the tithe.

AVE JESSE VIRGULA [9]. Nineteen eight-line stanzas ababbcbc, with slightly varying refrain ending with "Ave Jesse Virgula," and with initial letters of first five lines of stanzas 15–17 reading M-A-R-I-A.

Hail blessed lady, mother of Christ! Hail wholesome cypress, lady of virginity, window of Heaven, victorious laurel, fresh rose, green emerald, burning tree, celestial sapphire, patient beryl, Eva turned into Ave, woman clothed in a sun, etc., etc! Above all women you are endowed with the four cardinal virtues, and the letters in your name stand for all kinds of virtues and other good things. Help your servants, and be with us when we shall die.

This is a heavily aureate macaronic poem with strong echoes in the Scottish Chaucerians; its direct influence on Dunbar has been both demonstrated and denied.

AVE REGINA CELORUM [10]. Six eight-line stanzas ababbcbc with Latin refrain.

Hail luminary, excellent virgin, mother of compassion, queen of the skies, etc., etc! Since you have entered England, ask your son to protect us from pestilence. Holy maiden who has fostered Tetragrammaton, fairest of all women, mirror of meekness, pray gentle Jesus that we may go to Heaven.

An aureate macaronic poem which has been argued to reflect contemporary preoccupation with the Black Death and to have influenced Dunbar.

BALLAD BY JOHN LUCAS [11]. Four rime royal stanzas.

Take heed, people of the world, for you will be punished after death for your trespasses against God. Learn to die by repenting and following the lessons of Jesus, who was crucified for our redemption. Heeding his commandments will take us back to paradise, whence our father Adam fell. O Jesus, bring us to that glory.

This poem also occurs as stanzas 5–8 of *Death's Warning* [31], which should be consulted for scholarship and edition.

A BALLADE OF HER THAT HATH ALL VIRTUES [12]. Seven rime royal stanzas including envoy, with slightly varying refrain.

Nature has given you as much beauty, prudence, truth, and a host of other qualities as the most wonderful women of old, so that you have all the virtues except pity, which Danger has withheld from you. Go, little ballade, and recommend me to my lady, but first make sure that Danger and Disdain be not present.

This poem has been said to reflect French and Chaucerian influence and to illustrate Lydgate's ability to produce inconsequential verse on demand. Its authorship has been contested.

BENEDICTUS DEUS IN DONIS SUIS [13]. Nine eight-line stanzas ababbcbc, with slightly varying refrain.

> The gifts of God are manifold, and He should be blessed for all of them. He gave purity to Noah, faith to Abraham, wisdom to Solomon, conquest to Alexander, prophecy to the Sybil, etc., etc. He has also given patience to wives, but not to all of them. In conclusion, let the Lord be blessed for all His gifts, and think of the changes of fortune that befell Job, David, and Nebuchadnezzar.

THE EIGHT VERSES OF ST. BERNARD, VERSION 1 [14]. Nine eight-line stanzas ababbcbc, each with Latin prose introduction.

> Illumine my eyes so that Satan may have no power upon me at the time of death. I commend my spirit into Your hands, Lord; cause me to know my end and the number of my days so that I may rise again when Gabriel blows his horn. You have broken my bonds, and I shall do penance. You are my only refuge, and I cry to You. Make the sign of the cross on my forehead to confound my spiritual enemies, and forget the trespasses of my youth.

Stanza 9 of this adaptation from the Latin is similar to stanza 1 of Lydgate's own *Prayer in Old Age* [156]; it and several other stanzas recur in similar forms in Version 2 [15].

THE EIGHT VERSES OF ST. BERNARD, VERSION 2 [15]. Eleven eight-line stanzas ababbcbc.

> Illumine my eyes so that my enemy may have no power against me at the time of death. Since Your blood bought me, I commend my spirit into Your hands. Cause me to know the end and number of my days. You have broken my bonds, and I shall praise You; do not despise my prayer. There is no flight but into Your grace, and I kneel before You for guidance. I call to You and say You are my hope. Make me a sign to protect me from my enemies, and be my comfort. You are the well of mercy; forget the trespasses of my youth. Have mercy on me, Lord, and remember that Your blood was our redemption. Since I am Your servant, grant that my actions may please You, and have mercy when I die.

This poem was composed for Henry V. Several stanzas are identical to stanzas in Version 1 [14], and stanza 9 is nearly identical.

BEWARE OF DECEITFUL WOMEN (also AGAINST WOMEN and THE BLYNDE MAN ETETH MANY A FLYE) [16]. Six rime royal stanzas with refrain.

Be circumspect, lovers, for Samson and Solomon themselves were deceived, and the blind man eats many a fly. Do not trust women, for they are two-faced and inconstant. Whoever trusts them will lose everything, for all that shines is not gold. The efforts of the whole world could not make women constant, and it is foolish to trust them. By nature, they can deceive, spin, and weep. Even though the earth were parchment, the ocean were ink, and all men were scribes, it would be impossible to record all the treacheries of women. The blind man eats many a fly.

This is a conventional satire against women, and the traditional reference to their natural gifts calls to mind Chaucer's Wife of Bath.

FRAGMENT OF HYMN TO BLESSED VIRGIN [17].

The opening two stanzas are almost completely lost, and the authorship is very much in doubt.

BYCORNE AND CHYCHEVACHE [18]. Nineteen rime royal stanzas with occasional prose commentaries to introduce speakers.

Take heed, wise people, and remember the following story about husbands and wives and two beasts who eat men and women. Bicorne eats patient men, and Chichevache eats patient women. Then Bicorne will speak thus: I am quite fat, but my poor wife Chichevache finds hardly anything to eat, while my diet consists of men who dare not contradict their wives. Then a group of men will speak thus: Take heed, fellows, how Bicorne is preparing to eat all humble men and we shall be devoured because our wives rule us; only he who rules his wife can escape. Then a woman being eaten by Chichevache will speak thus: Take your cue from me, noble wives; avoid humility, or Chichevache will swallow you. Then Chichevache will speak thus: I am terribly hungry and am embarrassed to show my emaciated body, but I can eat only meek women, and I found only one Griselda all these lean years. Then an old man will speak thus: My wife has been eaten by this horrible beast, and I shall never find another one because the others know better than to practice humility, but husbands are bound in a double chain by their wives and Bicorne.

This satire is based on a French text with analogues in other languages. It is explicitly designed to accompany pictorial representations but the theory that it may have been intended for dramatic presentation has been advanced. The poem has been considered typical of Lydgate's satire and suggestive of Chaucer's influence.

A CALENDAR [19]. 52 rime royal stanzas.

The poem begins in January with the speaker asking Jesus to save him from confusion on the Circumcision, and it proceeds from saint's day to saint's day with statements concerning the various saints and members of the heavenly hierarchy whose help is being sought. It ends in December with St. Thomas of Canterbury and St. Silvester. A presumably spurious fifty-third stanza asks again for Jesus' mercy.

This poetic calendar may be suggestive of the feasts observed at Lydgate's own monastery.

VERSES ON CAMBRIDGE [20]. Fourteen rime royal stanzas.

According to both Bede and Alfred the Chronicler, the name Cambridge comes from Canteber, after whom the river Cantabro was named, and the city was founded 4388 years after the world began. Canteber was schooled in Athens, whence he brought Anaximander and Anaxagoras to Cambridge, and thus did the university begin. Cassibelanus added to the university, which attracted a great many scholars, some of whom Julius Caesar took to Rome with him. In all these years, Cambridge has never been blamed for heresy.

THE CHURL AND THE BIRD [21]. 54 rime royal stanzas and one eight-line stanza ababbcbc.

Parables grounded on Scripture are useful, as when the Bible tells how the trees once chose a king among them, and the fables poets make up about beasts and plants can tell the truth under cover. I have therefore decided to tell a story from the French about three proverbs and a bird. A certain churl had a lovely garden with a tree in which a bird used to sing a heavenly melody toward evening and at dawn. He caught the bird and began making a cage for her, but the bird explained that one cannot sing in prison, and she offered to sing for the churl if he would let her go free. She explained that the poor plowman is happier than the rich man who is shackled by his possessions. When she repeated that she simply would not sing in a cage, the churl said that he would have to eat her. She answered that she would make a very small meal and offered to present him with three extremely valuable pieces of wisdom if he let her go. As soon as she was free, she vowed never to get caught again, but kept her bargain by advising the churl that one should never be gullible, never desire the impossible, and never grieve over losses that may not be recovered. Then she told him that he was an ignorant fool to let her go, for she had inside her a precious stone worth the ransom of a king and endowed with all kinds of magical powers, although these things would have been wasted on him, and she added that he would never get it again and that she was wasting her time trying to talk sense into him. The churl wept at his loss, and the bird told him that he had obviously forgotten everything she had taught him, since he had proved gullible enough to believe that a little bird could carry such a precious stone, was grieving over a loss that could not be recovered, and had desired the impossible. She also told him that trying to teach wisdom to an ass would be a waste of time, that like seeks like, that each man sticks to his trade, and that churls cannot tell the difference between one bird and another. The author now asks people to remember that a churlish churl will always meet disaster and that freedom is worth more than all worldly riches. He asks his little book to recommend him to his master.

This morality, which has several analogues in Latin and French, has been said to reflect the influence of Chaucer and the fabliaux. Its popularity with its own time and immediately thereafter may be inferred from the number of manuscripts and early prints.

COMPLAINT FOR LACK OF MERCY [22]. Four eight-line stanzas ababbcbc with slightly varying refrain.

None has greater cause for sorrow than I; salt tears fall from my eyes for lack of mercy. What good do virtue and beauty without mercy? But for hope, I should die for lack of mercy.

This poem has been considered representative of Lydgate's mature style.

COMPLAINT OF THE BLACK KNIGHT (also COMPLAINT OF A LOVER'S LIFE and THE MAYING AND DISPORT OF CHAUCER) [23]. 95 rime royal stanzas and an envoy of two eight-line stanzas ababbcbc.

The poet speaks: in May, when Flora had clad the soil in green, red, and white, and Lucifer had chased away the night to bid lovers awake and enjoy themselves, I woke up with a sigh and went into the forest to hear the birds sing. By a river, I came upon a small park enclosed by a wall, and I went in to listen to the birds, who were singing as if their hearts would burst. The ground cover was lush, and there were several kinds of beautiful trees. In the middle of a patch of soft grass, there was a lovely well with clear water. Unlike the well of Narcissus or Pegasus or Diana, it was so wholesome that it would refresh those in distress. I drank of its water and felt relieved of my sorrow. Proceeding into the park, I found a green arbor in which a pale man in black was lying and groaning as though he were in pain. Wondering what this might be, I hid behind a bush to observe and saw that he was extremely handsome. It seemed fitting to record the words he was speaking, but I need help in this task for I am only a scrivener and have no personal experience of the subject matter. If there be anyone here who has suffered for love, let him listen to this man's account of his mortal woe.

The black knight now speaks: my mournful experience explains only part of my sorrow. I alternate between sweating and shivering as a result of my lady's aloofness, my return for faithful service. Envy and other hostile forces have conspired to slay Truth, and Falsehood has taken over. Cruelty judged Truth in the latter's absence and without due process, and I die for Truth. This must be the result of blind chance, since I have loved a woman and will continue to do so even if I am banished from her and must die. The faithful man always seems to lose out, as illustrated by the misadventures of Palamides, Hercules, Jason, etc., etc. They suffered for Love, who rewards falsehood rather than virtue and suffering. My woeful heart breaks for lack of mercy from her who laughs at my sorrow. I complain to you, God of Love, and charge you with fickleness, for you slay the faithful and let false ones go their way. I must beg mercy from my foe, and I die for Truth. Nature has been good to my lady, but Disdain is her chamberlain,

Despite controls her, and I am being killed with sharp words. Queen of my life, I ask only to die in your service. Either order my death or save me; I ask for mercy but will be content with dying in your service. If you know my truth before I die, I shall gladly submit. I send her my heart and commend myself to her mercy.

The poet resumes speaking: with these words, he sighed as if his heart would break, and I wept at his woe until he got up and went into a lodge nearby. Because night was drawing near, I took my pen and hurriedly began writing down word for word what I had heard. Blame me if anything be wrong with the narrative, since it will be the result of my ineptitude, and I ask forgiveness. As I was writing, I thought that I saw Venus rising in the West, and I prayed to her thus: O Lady Venus, let not this man die; let the streams of your influence help the faithful man who was lying in the arbor as well as all faithful men, and cause his lady to show mercy. When Venus was gone, I went home to bed. Since I cannot keep awake, I say farewell to you, lovers; I pray God to grant each of you to hold his lady in his arms and be avenged upon Jealousy, who has so long waged war against Truth. May it please you, Princess, to keep this little poem in mind and to take your faithful man back into your grace. Go, little book, to the queen of my heart, and rejoice that she will see you while I am left behind in pain.

Although the authorship has been questioned, this poem is generally assumed to be Lydgate's. It has been said to be typical of Lydgate's handling of nature, to reflect the influence of Froissart and Chaucer, and to have influenced Spenser. It has also been considered a companion piece to *A Lover's Lament* [110].

A COMPLEYNT THAT CRIST MAKETH OF HIS PASSIOUN (also CRISTES PASSIOUN) [24]. Fifteen eight-line stanzas ababbcbc, with slightly varying refrain.

To end your exile from paradise, O man, I hang upon the cross: look at My wounds and think of My passion. Remember My bloody face and the scorn I endured, and think of My passion. Think of Calvary, of the false accusations against Me, and of the torments I endured: all was for love of you. Naked on the cross, I fought Satan for your sake. My flesh was torn to pieces for you, and I found no mercy before Pilate or anyone else. Imprint these things on your mind, and remember that blood and water will wash away sin and corruption. The Church began when Longinus's spear went through My heart, and Adam was returned to happiness through My passion. There were palpable tokens, as when bodies rose out of their graves. Call to mind, man, how My mother fainted by the cross. Go, little bill, and hang before the cross, where people who see you will think of Christ's passion.

This poem has been said to reflect Lydgate's fondness for the aureate style.

A COMPLAINT THAT CRIST MAKETH OF HIS PASSIOUN (SCOTTISH VERSION) [25]. See also [24].

Dunbar's authorship has been proposed for this version. (See X [108] in *Manual*, volume 4.)

CONSULO QUISQUIS ERIS (also **CONCORDS OF COMPANY** and **UTTER THY LANGUAGE**) [26]. Fifteen eight-line stanzas ababbcbc, with slightly varying refrain.

> I advise you, whoever you may be, to conform to the customs around you and to suit your language to your audience if you would live in peace. Be foxy with foxes, drunken with the drunk, holy with holy men; price your wares according to the market, and God may protect you as He did Daniel. Talk about philosophy with philosophers and about poetry with poets: suit your language to your audience. But above all, I urge you to love God and avoid sin. Be content with little, as advised by Socrates and Cato, and keep in mind the respective fates of Diogenes and Alexander or of Paul and Caesar and Pompey. I once saw on a wall a picture of a virtuous and beautiful man: let us pray Jesus to awaken such a figure in our conscience, and let us suit our language to His pleasure.

This poem has been said to reflect the influence of the *Disticha Catonis*, the Bestiary, and Chaucer.

CRISTE QUI LUX ES ET DIES [27]. Seven eight-line macaronic stanzas ababbcbc, with pairs of identical Latin statements serving as both captions and eighth lines.

> Christ, Who are our day and light, be our succor; we pray for Your protection in the night, so that our flesh may not bring our spirit to ruin. Let our eyes rest and our spirit stay awake to serve You. Protect us from our foes, be our champion, and govern Your servants, whom You bought with Your blood. Remember us, benign Lord, since You bought us at such cost. Glory be to the Father, the Son, and the Holy Ghost.

This paraphrase of a Latin hymn has been noted for its uncommon use of Latin lines.

THE DAUNCE OF MACHABREE (also **THE DAUNCE OF DEATH**) [28]. 73 eight-line stanzas ababbcbc.

> O reasonable creatures wishing for eternal life, you may find here a doctrine to guide your mortal life and learn from this dance, for Death spares neither the high nor the low. In this mirror, everyone may see that the order in which one dies depends on God's decree.
> Death to the Pope: you who are so high in dignity and rule the Church, you must begin the dance first, as befits your papal rank. The Pope's answer: it behooves me to lead this dance, since I was highest in my see, and I may not flee Death, thus illustrating the worthlessness of temporal honors. Death to the Emperor: you must forsake scepter and sword and join my dance, for all of Adam's children must die. The Emperor's answer: to whom may I appeal? There is no help, and great lords have little advantage once wrapped in a shroud. Death to the

Cardinal: you seem disconcerted and frightened, Sir Cardinal, but you must nevertheless follow the others in this dance. The Cardinal's answer: I dread losing so suddenly my ermine and red hat, and I perceive that all joy ends in sorrow. Death to the Empress, the King, the Patriarch, etc., etc. Finally, Death to the Hermit. The Hermit's answer: solitary life in the desert is no protection against Death, but I welcome that which is sent by God's grace, and I humbly thank my Lord for His gifts.

You who look upon this text, remember always and above all that you will turn into food for worms regardless of your rank. Man's life is but a puff of wind, and you who read this story, keep the content in mind, and it will lead you into spiritual life. Be not afraid to think about this text, for it will not make you die any sooner but will lead you into virtue, and I dare say you will be the better for it.

This translation from a French text belongs to a long tradition of macabre literature, and its influence has been detected in Dunbar and Elizabethan tragedy.

THE DAUNCE OF MACHABREE WITH FIVE-STANZA PROLOGUE [29]. 84 eight-line stanzas ababbcbc, including prologue and envoy.

O people with hearts of stone who think that the world will last forever, take heed and see that Death slays both young and old as well as high and low. Death spares neither popes nor kings nor emperors despite their might. Consider this, wise people, and keep it in mind like the example which I found painted on a wall in Paris and which I am translating from the French. I am making a plain translation so that proud people may see their ugly end as though in a mirror and change their ways. This dance is depicted at the Holy Innocents to show that life is but a pilgrimage. I shall proceed immediately to show the end of our journey. (The remainder follows the pattern of [28] with several additions until the envoy, which is summed up herewith.) My lords and masters, I beg you be kind to my translation and make such corrections as seem necessary. My French is not good enough for a word-for-word translation, and my language is graceless. My name is John Lydgate.

ON DE PROFUNDIS (also PSALM 129) [30]. 21 eight-line stanzas ababbcbc.

While I was wondering in my simple mind what we can do for the souls in purgatory, I was asked to explain why the *De Profundis* is said for Christian souls. I have no eloquence, but I shall try to answer in my inadequate style. Jonas uttered the original lamentation while he was inside the whale, and both Augustine and Jerome agreed in respect to it that certain things can be of help to dead souls. David divides the psalm in eight parts. To understand why it is said especially for dead souls, we must recall how the examples of Jonas, Daniel, Joseph, Jesus, and Judith show that prayers may deliver souls from purgatory, as do other examples. Masses, especially the Requiem, are likewise effective, as are the incantations of priests, alms, and various other things. Let our prayer reach Your ears, O Christ Jesus, so that those in purgatory may be released of their pains. Who, O Lord, could bear the brunt of Your punishment if You treated people as they deserve? Pity and mercy live in Heaven, where they are our advocates and plead in the name of the Passion. My soul abides in Your word, my trust is in Your Passion, and I shall go wherever You assign me my penance. From the gray morning onward, the hope of Israel to endure till night depends on the Resurrection. This is to say that Christ rose from the grave on Easter morning to insure that we may gain eternal life and may claim mercy before justice in His Passion. David records how Mercy, Patience, and Pity plead for us. The Lord has redeemed Israel, paid our ransom with His blood, and will convey our souls to the reign of glory. The Lord brought Israel out of captivity through Cyrus, and Jesus' triumph on the cross delivers souls out of purgatory. This treatise was compiled in my old age at William Curteys' request so that it may hang on a wall in his church.

This poem has been said to throw light on the use of the psalter in the fifteenth century.

DEATH'S WARNING (also **DEATH'S WARNING TO THE WORLD** and for stanzas 5–8 alone **BALLAD BY JOHN LUCAS,** [11] above) [31]. Eight rime royal stanzas.

Since you want my image in your book, remember that I spare neither young nor old, and be ready before I ring my bell. No armor can withstand my spear, nor is there any reprieve for those whom I mark, even though the time of my coming is uncertain. Remember that life goes by very fast. One should pray, for no one knows the hour of my coming and there is no shutting me out; everyone must eventually die because of Adam's sin. (For the remainder, see *Ballad by John Lucas* [11].)

The authorship of this poem has been contested.

THE DEPARTYNG OF THOMAS CHAUCER [32]. Eleven rime royal stanzas.

O Lucina, empress of all waters, watch over the voyage of my master Chaucer; and, Neptune, protect him from wind and waves. God, keep him healthy while he is in France, for the sun of hospitality is now in eclipse: Ceres and Bacchus were ever present when he entertained gentlemen and was loved of rich and poor for his generosity. It is no wonder, my Lord Moeleyns, that you should sigh when your friend is away, but he will soon be back. And you, tender creature, leave off weeping, however hard his absence must be on one so true and kind as you are. You, gentlemen of the neighborhood, may well grieve, for there is no hunting or fun in his absence. Forget him not, and pray St. Julian to come home again and bring joy to the whole shire. As for me, I feel sadder than I can express, and I shall pray God that he may soon return.

This poem has been considered a companion piece to *The Complaint of the Black Knight* [23], and its authorship has been questioned.

DEUS IN NOMINE TUO SALUUM ME FAC (also PSALM 53) [33].
Nine eight-line stanzas ababcbcb, with slightly varying refrain.

> God, make me safe and sound, and rectify whatever is sick in my soul, so that I may improve while I have time before I die. Hear my prayer, as You bought me on the Cross; if I be tempted by the Fiend, let my resting place be in Your right side while I have time. Powerful aliens have sought my soul, but without avail because they do not look at You; may Your Passion be imprinted upon my thought. God has helped me and freed me: whom shall I thank but You? You do not forsake the sinner. Turn evil unto my mortal foes who would cause me to disobey You, and save me from deadly sin. I shall sacrifice unto You and despise worldly wealth; I beseech You of grace. You have delivered me, and I shall try to repay You. Help me, maiden and mother full of grace. Joy to the Father, the Son, and the Holy Ghost, three in one without beginning or end: heal the hurt of my sin.

DIETARY (also A DIETARY AND A DOCTRINE FOR PESTILENCE and MEDICINA STOMACHI) [34]. Eighteen eight-line stanzas ababbcbc. See also [35] below.

> For health of body, keep your head from cold, avoid raw meat, drink good wine, and do not eat too much; aged women, do not drink before sleep. Eat good bread a day-and-a-half old, avoid overwork, and do not sleep at noon. Put sage and rue in your drinks, and avoid excess; bid aged men go to bed early. A replete stomach causes great damage, but a glad heart and a temperate diet are wholesome for everyone. Caraway is a good medicine; overeating and drinking late in the evening cause phlegm, and a moderate diet is the best physician. If leeches fail, try a temperate diet, moderate work, and the avoidance of melancholy; do not believe every tale you hear, and be courteous and prudent. Hate double talk, and suffer no detraction to go on at your table. Dress according to your rank, keep your word, and do not fight with a subject. Light a fire in the morning and at bedtime against the black mist and the air of pestilence; pray in the morning, visit the poor, and practice compassion, and God will be good to you. Do not sleep after meals, stand up for your rights, but swear no false oath. Clear air makes for good digestion, but avoid drinking between meals. Thus the good of soul and body depends on moderation and charity. This recipe is not to be bought from the apothecary but is available to all.

This *Dietary*, which may be found immediately following *A Doctrine for Pestilence*, [36] below, with lines and stanzas numbered accordingly, is presumably based on a twelfth-century Latin text, and its recognized popularity may be inferred from the number of extant manuscripts and prints.

DIETARY IN DISARRANGED ORDER [35].
This poem corresponds to stanzas 2, 1, 8, 9, 3, 6, 5, and 10 of *Dietary* [34];

consult bibliography under both entries and *Dietary: a Doctrine for Pestilence* [36].

DIETARY: A DOCTRINE FOR PESTILENCE (also A DOCTRYNE FOR PESTILENCE) [36]. Three stanzas ababbcbc.

Whoever would avoid sickness and pestilence, let him avoid sadness, drink good wine, walk in clean air, rise early, avoid incontinence, eat no fruit, but eat chicken with sauce, and sleep in the morning as protection against black mists.

This poem may be considered a companion piece to *Dietary* [34], whose bibliography should also be consulted.

BEWARE OF DOUBLENESSE [37]. Thirteen eight-line stanzas ababbcbc, each ending with the word *doublenesse*.

This world is full of change in everything, so that I find security in nothing except women: beware of duplicity. Summer flowers fade with winter showers, so that there can be no trust except in women: beware of duplicity. The moon changes, as does everything except women. Sunshine turns to darkness at night. The tides come and go, and rain follows drought. The wheel of fortune turns continually: who can restrain the wind or hold a snake by the tail? Women know how to row along with duplicity, so that they always reach a haven. Therefore, those who accuse them of duplicity are in collusion. Although clerks accuse them of duplicity, women are merely lucky. Samson found out first-hand that women are faithful, and the stories of Cleopatra and Rosamond will confound those who accuse them of duplicity. O women, though you naturally incline to be pure and faithful, protect yourself with a mighty shield of duplicity.

The authorship of this satire against women has been questioned.

DUODECIM ABUSIONES (also GO FORTH KYNG, ADVICE TO THE SEVERAL ESTATES, and TO THE ESTATES) [38]. Two rime royal stanzas with six-line Latin prologue.

King without wisdom, bishop without doctrine, etc., etc. Go forth, king, and rule through wisdom; bishop, administer doctrine; rich man, give alms; people, obey your king, etc., etc. Poor man, remember that your lot is ordained by God and do your share.

EAGLE AS NEW YEAR GIFT (also BALLADE ON A NEW YEAR'S

GIFT OF AN EAGLE PRESENTED TO KING HENRY VI) [39]. Eleven rime royal stanzas, including envoy, with two different refrains.

> This imperial bird is humbly offered to you on this New Year's Day to add to your glory. This stately bird soars very high; because it has won the crown among birds, it is offered to your glory. This bird, which in heaven is sacred to Jupiter, which brought the olive of peace to Octavian at the Nativity, and which Ezekiel saw in a vision, is offered to your glory. This royal bird with piercing sight is also offered to the queen, for it is the empress of birds, and a great goddess sends it to you, Princess. May this gracious alliance bring peace in England and France. This bird is on the arms of emperors and appeared in Rome in the time of Julius Caesar when Jesus was born; for this reason, this eagle is offered to you, O Princess. This bird has held a parliament with other birds under the presidency of Nature, and they did their best to send you all the good things of life. Most noble Prince, this eagle is presented to you, and it will also bring you, Princess, joy, health, and prosperity.

This occasional poem has been said to reflect the influence of Chaucer and to treat nature in a typically Lydgatian manner.

BANNER OF ST. EDMUND [40]. Ten stanzas in long lines riming ababbcbc, followed by two short Latin prayers in prose.

> Blessed Edmund, king, martyr, and virgin, conquered the serpent's venom. His banner had the figure of Adam to show the sovereignty of reason and a lamb of gold high in a tree to betoken humility and our redemption. The banner's field of gules showed his sufferance while at war with the Danes. This standard was always with him and did miracles. This virtuous banner will protect this land from enemies and shall be borne in war by Henry VI, who will be under Edmund's protection. The other standard had three crowns, which were granted to Edmund for kingship, virginity, and martyrdom. The historical meaning of these three crowns is that Henry is king of France and England and will later receive a heavenly crown. All who say this prayer to St. Edmund will be granted 200 days of pardon: (brief prayer in Latin prose follows).

This short prayer, which reveals Lydgate's taste for allegorical interpretation, serves as the prologue in several manuscripts to the *Life of SS. Edmund and Fremund* (see [42] below). The claim that Edmund's three crowns signify that Henry VI is king of both England and France is reminiscent of Lydgate's many other poems on Henry's dual monarchy (see, for example, [74], [75], [80], and [81] below).

MIRACLES OF ST. EDMUND [41]. An opening stanza in rime royal, followed by 57 stanzas riming ababbcbc.

Sovereign lord, may it please you to take this treatise which, between hope and dread, is presented to you. For Edmund's sake, defend and champion the Church.

I will rehearse a miracle that occurred in London on November 20, 1041, at the bridge over the Thames. A passing ox-cart knocked a small child into the river, but Christ preserved the boy until a boatman rescued him. Meanwhile, the distraught mother, having been told of the accident, asked whose feast it was. Told it was Edmund's, she prayed for her child's safety. When she went to the river she saw her son getting out of a boat and calling for her. She then vowed always to keep the saint's feast. This miracle must be ascribed to God and not to man.

We pray to the saints to work miracles through the Lord. Christ is an example of a martyr's passion. One such is enshrined in Britain: Edmund, who performed many miracles and I will rehearse two late ones. I have little eloquence, but, like the widow in the gospel, I will make this present to the martyr. On April 27, 1444, a two-year-old girl fell into the river near Northgate and was thought drowned. When the body was recovered, a woman held it by the legs and much water ran out from the mouth and nose. Then the child's mother and father and all the others prayed to St. Edmund and promised him devotion. They then bore the child to the saint's shrine, and Jesus, seeing their devotion, revived the child. Do not forget this miracle. Abbot William celebrated it and the child was borne in procession through Bury. All said this prayer: "Gem of martyrs, who died young, remember the town of Bury." In another miracle, a two-year-old child was run over by a cart. The body was brought home and all prayed. The body lay dead for an hour; at noon the people prayed again to the holy martyr, and Christ restored the child to life. The people went to Edmund's shrine in procession to proclaim this further evidence of Edmund's power in heaven. Now let us ask three things from the martyr: to defend his Church, his town, and his country against all enemies.

Once considered a first draft of Lydgate's *Life of SS. Edmund and Fremund* (see [42] below), this work was more probably composed in 1444 as an addition to the miracles related in Book III of the *Life*. The style is less grand than that of *Edmund and Fremund*, and a ballad stanza is used instead of the early poem's rime royal. The focus on miracles involving small children has been compared to Chaucer's *Prioress's Tale*. The poem's realistic detail of everyday life has been noted, along with its description of practices in the monastery at Bury.

LIFE OF SS. EDMUND AND FREMUND [42]. 3,508 long lines in rime royal (for prologue and epilogues found in some manuscripts see [40] above and [78] and [80] below).

Book I. I will tell the life of St. Edmund, martyr, virgin, and king, born in Saxony of royal blood. I depend more on grace than on eloquence. I began this translation when Henry VI visited Bury for the feast of Christmas (1433). Holy Edmund shall protect Henry. Abbot William charged me to translate this noble story from Latin to give to the king, but first I will pray to the holy martyr.

Alkmond was the excellent king of Saxony and his noble wife was Siware. Alkmond, urged by a revelation, went on a pilgrimage to Rome, where he stayed with a holy widow. She saw a light shine in four beams from his breast and prophesied that he would have a son who would illuminate the four parts of the world. After Alkmond returned home, Siware bore Edmund in 841. Offa, king of Estyngland (East Anglia), had no heir. On his way to the Holy Land, he visited his cousin Alkmond. Impressed by the young Edmund, he declared him his heir. On his return, Offa fell mortally ill and ordered his men to bring Edmund home as their king. After a tearful farewell from his parents, Edmund set sail for East Anglia. Upon landing, Edmund prayed and five miraculous wells sprang forth. He built a town near the wells and after a year went to Athelborgh. When Bishop Kunbertus called the lords together, Edmund's right to the kingship was revealed, and soon after he was crowned at Bury in 856. Edmund established good laws and policies (described at length) and was a virtuous king to all the realm. His fame increased and reached even Denmark.

Book II. The king of Denmark, Lothbroc, a pagan, had two sons, Hingwar and Ubba, who were pirates. They boasted of their manhood, but their father replied that Edmund surpassed them. One day Lothbroc's boat was blown to Norfolk. He was treated so courteously by Edmund that he asked to stay. Lothbroc hunted with Bern, the king's huntsman, but the latter, growing envious of the Dane's success, murdered Lothbroc and hid his body in the bushes. When Bern's guilt was discovered, he was condemned to be set adrift in a boat and landed in Denmark where he told Hingwar and Ubba that Edmund had slain their father. The sons went to England with an army and slew every Christian in the North. After several years, Hingwar arrived in East Anglia to attack Edmund. A great battle was fought, which Edmund won, but he later regretted the loss of life and resolved never to shed blood again. Hingwar, with help from Ubba, demanded that Edmund surrender and renounce Christianity. Edmund refused and, offering no defence, was brought before Hingwar like Christ before Pilate. Affirming his faith, Edmund was bound and beaten; then Hingwar tied him to a tree and shot him full of arrows like St. Sebastian. Finally Edmund's head was cut off and hidden by the Danes in a thicket, though miraculously preserved by a wolf. After the Danes left, the Christians searched a long time for the head until Christ permitted it to say, "here, here." The head was then miraculously joined to the body and a sepulchre built for it. The martyrdom occurred in December when Edmund was 30. Glorious martyr, inspire my pen to tell the story of St. Fremund, thy cousin.

Book III. I fear I am presumptuous in writing about saints. Now I think of St. Edmund and his cousin, St. Fremund, who avenged him, but I am too old to write such a high thing. I follow Burchardus, Fremund's secretary, who wrote his life. Fremund was the son of King Offa, who reigned in Mershlond (Mercia) and of Bothild, sister to St. Edmund. A three-day-old child prophesied that Offa would have a son in his old age who would do miracles and be king, martyr, and virgin. He was to be called Fremund. When the boy was born, a rainbow appeared for nine days. When he grew up, Fremund converted the people, including his parents, from idolatry to Christianity. Though he wanted to be a contemplative, Fremund was forced to rule by the people, but after a year he went off to a desert island with two companions. Seven years later, Offa, too old to avenge the murder of Edmund by the Danes, sent for Fremund. Fremund was undecided until an angel told him to return and fight the Danes with God's help. Against Hingwar, Fremund with twenty-four companions and guided by Christ slew forty thousand. Duke Oswy, a traitor and apostate, desired to be king and, finding Fremund kneeling in prayer, cut off his head. But the king's blood burned the murderer fiercely until he called for mercy and was absolved by the head of Fremund. After Fremund's death, his body performed many miracles. Three virgins were cured at Fremund's sepulchre and were then told by an angel to remove Fremund's body. They built a tomb on a plain by a river, but the next morning the body and the tomb were gone. They were distraught until calmed by a revelation. An English pilgrim at Jerusalem was told to return home and recover the body of Fremund on the plain. With the Pope's blessing he did so and took the body to Dunstable. There it performed more miracles. Holy Fremund, protect thy servants and save Henry VI and all this land.

Miracles of St. Edmund: In 1013 the Danes under Sven forced King Ethelred to flee and demanded tribute. The East Anglians refused and prayed to Edmund. The saint appeared to his servant Ayllewyn and ordered him to go to Sven and demand that the Danes release his people from tribute. Sven refused and Edmund appeared before him as a knight and killed him. Other tyrants were punished. Sheriff Leoffstan attempted to try a woman at the saint's tomb. She cried out to Edmund and a fiend possessed Leoffstan and killed him. Five knights who tried to steal a horse from Edmund's court were driven mad until they confessed. A briber falsely kissed Edmund's tomb and his teeth stuck to it until he confessed. Eight thieves were enchanted when they tried to rob the church at night. Osgothus, a Danish lord, scorned Edmund, but he was driven mad one day in Edmund's tomb. King Edward had the monks pray until he was restored to health and then he became devout. Ayllewyn brought Edmund's body to London for three years. The bishop tried to steal the body to prevent its return, but it remained fixed as a mountain. When Ayllewyn came for the body, however, it moved easily and performed wonderful miracles as it passed through each town. Baldewynus, third abbot of Bury, built a new church as a shrine for Edmund and moved him there with great ceremonies in 1095, two hundred and twenty-five years after his passion.

This highly ornate life of Lydgate's own patron saint (and the life of his cousin Fremund) was written, as the poet tells us at the beginning of Book III, in his old age. According to Lydgate himself, Abbot William Curteys commissioned the work as a gift to Henry VI, following the king's stay at Bury St. Edmunds to celebrate the feast of Christmas in 1433. A rich presentation copy of the poem, almost certainly made at Bury, is extant (MS Harley 2278), which contains a miniature of Lydgate offering the poem to Henry VI (the king to whom he addressed so many other pieces). The poem concerns two of Lydgate's most persistent subjects: the church and the throne. St. Edmund was not only a martyr and the patron of the poet's own monastery, he was also an English king. Lydgate therefore takes the opportunity to discuss proper political rule as well as sainthood.

The legend of St. Edmund has its origin in a brief notation in the *Anglo-Saxon Chronicle* for the year 870, which says little more than that King Edmund fought with the Danes and was killed. Nevertheless, veneration of Edmund began almost immediately and a long hagiographical tradition precedes the present work with lives of the saint in Latin, Old English, Anglo-Norman, and Old French. It has been said that until he was replaced by Thomas à Becket, Edmund was the national saint of England. Lydgate's own source for Edmund's life was a Latin prose compendium (MS Bodley 240), which he probably supplemented with oral traditions concerning the saint's miracles. It has been shown that Lydgate handles his sources with independence. This last and most important literary monument to Saint Edmund seems to have had a significant influence on fifteenth-century hagiographers.

A double legend (like Lydgate's later *SS. Alban and Amphibal*, see [1] above), *Edmund and Fremund* is an elaborate poem of high ambition. The poet is often elaborately rhetorical, especially in his prologue and epilogues, and makes many classical and biblical allusions. The legends illustrate the pacifism found in Lydgate's other works, and the poem's relation to secular romance has been noted. The critical assessment of *Edmund and Fremund* as a literary work has been mixed. The poem has been called a failed epic, but the narrative achievement of its first two books has been praised by another critic as revealing Chaucer's influence on the monk at its best. Likewise, although the last book has been dismissed as weak and structurally confused, especially in its list of Edmund's miracles, it has recently been argued that these miracles are chosen to create an artistic balance and that they reveal the poet's conscious literary skill.

EPISTELL TO SIBILLE [43]. Twenty rime royal stanzas, including envoy, with nineteen of them ending with word *besynesse*.

> Keeping busy is the best way to avoid sloth, just as Martha ministered to Jesus, and so did Mary by contemplation. Nobody today could find such two, who avoid idleness and provide example through womanly diligence. Their praise and price go far, for labor is at war with vice. Men should commend diligent women. A husband with such a wife may trust her, for she will help him in all things and be humble. She resembles a merchant ship insofar as she provides for her household and keeps busy with her work. Her candle will never go out at night. [Missing line here in only MS] Her fingers did their work with weaving, she gave to the poor, and she taught virtue to her servants. Her garment was silk and purple in that royal city where her husband renders justice. She made rich cloth of gold and silk and sold it; her own garment was made of strength, cleanness, and honesty, and she will earn Heaven through virtuous diligence. She spoke with wisdom and in low tones; she never ate her bread in idleness, and she was respected by her husband and children, so that she excelled many women of antiquity. Worldly business is but vanity, but a provident woman is worthy of praise. Wives, widows, and maidens, I humbly ask you to remember that idleness is the mother of vices. Go, little epistle, and recommend me to Lady Sibyl; ask her to have pity on my dull style and to avoid idleness.

This poem has been shown to be based on Proverbs 31 and said to reflect the influence of Christine de Pisan.

EVERYTHING DRAWETH TO HIS SEMBLABLE (also **EVERY THING TO HIS SEMBLABLE** and **A NATURAL BALADE BY LYDEGATE**) [44]. 25 eight-line stanzas ababbcbc, each ending with word *semblable*.

Treat each man as he likes it: the knight likes to hear about war and the squire about distress in love, the conqueror about his victories, philosophers about philosophy, versifiers about metrics, the smith about forging, etc., etc. The nightingale likes singing, the wolf likes eating flesh, the scorpion likes to sting, and minerals are likewise attracted to certain things. Each creature draws to its like. Man lived in paradise until he listened to the serpent and departed from God, Whom he resembled and Who had given him heavenly intelligence. Heaven is ordained for contemplative people; the good go up and the cursed go to hell. O God, Who made man in Your own image, give us Heaven. Lift up your eyes, man, toward your Redeemer, Who pleased to make you in His own image.

This poem, which has been called a compendium of medieval occupations, resembles in some respects *Consulo Quisquis Eris* [26].

AN EXORTACION TO PRESTYS (also POEMS ON THE MASS, I) [45]. Seven eight-line stanzas ababbcbc, including envoy.

Holy priests, remember at Mass to receive the Lord with both love and dread. Shrive yourself and beg Jesus' mercy before you receive the sacrament. Be contrite, pray for all, and think of the Lord's five wounds. You must remember His Passion, which He endured for your redemption. Love Him alone, and make your heart His dwelling place. Go, little book that has been composed in humility, and pray holy priests to read this ditty.

This poem has been treated as a companion piece to *Interpretacio Misse* [87] and *On Kissing at Verbum Caro* [103 and 104]; the three have been printed together under the title of *Poems on the Mass*.

FABULA DUORUM MERCATORUM [46]. 130 rime royal stanzas, including envoy.

I have read that there once lived in Egypt, a rich and abundant land by the Red Sea, a merchant both rich and virtuous as well as true to his word. This worthy Egyptian merchant met another from a country called Baldak, and they became such close friends that the fame of their mutual love soon spread far abroad: the light of virtue may not be hidden. Nature links with love similarly virtuous people, and honor is wedded to worthiness. These good merchants held their wares in common and were of such accord that only death could end their love. The merchant of Baldak once went to Egypt on business and was overjoyed to visit with his friend, for separation is painful to those who love each other truly, and the end thereof is as sweet as honey after gall. The Egyptian was delighted to see his friend, and he welcomed him to his home and all his possessions. He dined, wined, and entertained him with hunting in the company of beautiful ladies and maidens; his friend thanked him, and they spent a happy summer together until the visitor fell seriously ill and insisted upon being left alone in his room. His illness was love, and the object thereof was the very woman whom his friend loved above all others. The many doctors who came to his bedside tried in vain every possible cure for every known disease until they concluded that he was suffering of love melancholy, which is brought on by one's love for a woman and causes a frenetic condition for which there is practically no known cure. The Egyptian begged his friend to name the object of his desire and caused all the women of the household to parade through the latter's room until the truth became evident. He generously gave the woman to his friend and arranged a splendid wedding, after which the friend joyfully returned home with the most loving and obedient wife in the world–but it is common knowledge that all wives are meek and patient. The Egyptian was so distressed by his friend's departure that I shall be unable to account for his sorrow and the following doleful matter unless I have the help of Megaera, Tisiphone, and Mirrha, for Fortune played him false, so that he lost his wealth and all his friends. He pitifully recalled the days of his prosperity, but nobody took heed of his plight, and he could only lament the fickleness of his former friends and proclaim the worthlessness of wealth and vanity: the world deludes all of us when we most trust it. I feel my hands quake at the thought of writing down this poor man's woe, but we must learn to endure adversity and to accept Seneca's opinion that no man is virtuous until he has been tested. God was presumably testing the merchant, who praying to Him for comfort thought to seek out his friend in Baldak. There the merchant, too ashamed of his poverty to show himself to his friend, went to sleep in an old temple where, as he slept, a murderer put a corpse. Found out by the crowd, the merchant was blamed for the crime, to which he confessed out of despair, hoping that a sentence of death would release him from his misery. As he was being taken to the place of execution, however, his friend recognized him and took the murder upon himself to secure his release. The latter was about to be executed when the real murderer, after praying for God's mercy, came forward to confess his deed. The two merchants and the murderer were taken to the king, who pardoned all three and marvelled at the power of friendship. It would be hard to find anything like it today in this realm. The merchant of Baldak gave his friend half of his possessions and assured him of his lasting love before the latter returned to Egypt. There is no more to say about their friendship, and I do not wish to be tedious. Have mercy on my unskilled narrative, and may God make all friends as true as these two merchants.

FALL OF PRINCES [47]. Nine books, for a total of 36,365 lines, in rime royal with a few envoys in eight-line stanzas, ababbcbc.

Book I. Prologue: discussion of Laurent and Boccaccio and praise of Chaucer and Gloucester. Stories of Adam and Eve (envoy) and of Nimrod. Against Proud Princes (envoy). Stories of Saturn, Vixoses, Thanaus, Zoroaster, Ninus, Moses, Ogygus, flood in Thessaly, plague in Athens, Isis, Erysichthon, Danaus, and Philomela and Procne (envoy). Stories of Jupiter and Europa and of Cadmus and family (envoy). Stories of Aeetes, Jason, Medea, Pelias, Creusa, Aegeus, Minos, Scylla, Nisus, Minotaur, Pasiphae, Taurus; stories of Theseus: Hippolyte, Ariadne, and Phaedra and Hippolytus; stories of Sisera, Deborah, and Gideon (envoy). Stories of Jabin and of Oedipus, Laius, Jocasta, Tiresias, Eteocles, Polynices, and Creon (envoy). Story of Atreus and Thyestes (envoy). Stories of Theseus: Centaurs, Pirithous, Creon, Ariadne, Phaedra, Hippolytus (envoy). On Unstable Princes, A Mock Defense of Women, On Human Nature (envoy). Stories of Althaea and Meleager and of Hercules: Eurystheus, Iole, his labors, and Deianeira (envoy). Stories of Narcissus and Echo, Byblis, Myrrha, Adonis, Orpheus and Eurydice, and Marpessa (envoy). Story of Priam and of the Troy Book. On the Pride of Wealth and in Praise of Poverty (with mention of Zenocrates, Diogenes, and Alexander [envoy]). Story of Samson and Delilah (envoy). On the Malice of Women (with mention of Hercules, Agamemnon, Samson, Phyllis, Scylla, Semiramis, Esther, Alceste). Stories of Pyrrhus: Polyxena, Andromache, and Hermione, and of Canace and Macareus (envoy).

Book II. Prologue on Fortune and Virtue. Story of Saul: David and Witch of Endor (envoy). On the Virtue of Obedience. Story of Rehoboam (envoy). On Good Government. Stories of Mucius Scaevola, Lucrece, Appius and Virginia (envoy). Stories of Jeroboam and Jadan, Zerah, Adab, Zimri, Ahab and Jezebel, and Athaliah (envoy). Story of Dido (envoy). Mock

Envoy on Widows. Story of Sardanapalus. In Praise of Industry and Invention (with mention of Pythagoras, Tubal, Lucius Tarquin, children of Seth, Enoch, Cam, Catacrismus, Ezra, Abraham, Isis, Phoenicians, Carmentis, Homer, Tully, Callicrates, Mirmecides, Pan, Mercury, Bacchus, Perdix, Euclid, Phoebus, Albumasar, Minerva, Jason, Ceres, Dionysus, Bellona, Etholus, Aristaeus, Piroides, Pallas, and Fido[envoy]). Stories of Amaziah, Jehoash, Uzziah (an exhortation not to offend God). Stories of Hoseah, Sennacherib, and Zedekiah (envoy). Stories of Astyages (nobility comes from grace not blood) and youth of Cyrus (envoy). Stories of Candaules and Gyges, Midas, Belshazzar and Daniel (envoy). Stories of Croesus and of Cyrus (envoy). Stories of Romulus and Remus (against the deifying of men) and of Metius. Against Fraud and Deceit. Story of Hostilius. Envoy on Rome.

Book III. Prologue on the poet's inadequacy with mention of Boccaccio and Fortune. Dispute between Fortune and Poverty. Stories of Hostilius, Ancus Marcius, and Lucinio (envoy). Story of Tarquin and Lucrece (with complaint of Lucrece). Boccaccio on the Lechery of Princes (with mention of David and Bathsheba, Samson and Delilah, Solomon; advice of Scipio and Cato; punishments of Tarquin, Apius Claudius, Shechem, Paris and Helen, the Gibeonites, and Holofernes [envoy]). Stories of Cambyses, Smerdis, Oropastes, Otanes, and Darius. Stories of Coriolanus and Volumnia, Miltiades, and Cynaegeirus (envoy). Story of Xerxes (envoy). Stories of Artabanus and Darius, Phalanthus and the Spartans, and Ceso Quintius and Cloelius Gracchus. Story of Apius and the falseness of judges (envoy). In Praise of the Justice of the Former Age (with mention of Phoroneus, Minos, Mercury, Solon, and Lycurgus). Against Dishonest Officials and Judges in Rome and Italy. Story of Alcibiades (with exclamation of his death and envoy). On the Ambitions of Worldly People. In Praise of Industrious Men. On Poets. Story of Machaeus and Cartalus (envoy). Stories of Himilco and of Hanno (envoy). Against Covetousness (with mention of its punishments and of Pompey, Diogenes, Croesus, Sardanapalus, Sophodius, Cincinnatus, Masinissa, and Xerex. Stories of Evagoras, Theo, Amyntas and Eurydice, Philip of Macedon, Epaminondas, Haman and Mordecai, and Artaxerxes and Cyrus and Darius (envoy).

Book IV. Prologue on Poets and Writing (with mention of Prosper, Seneca, Vegetius, Persius, Vergil, Ovid, Petrarch, Homer, Aesop, Juvenal, and Dante). Story of Marcus Manlius and Description of Roman Triumphs (envoy). Stories of Nectanebes, Pausanias, Heliarchus and Leonides, and Dionysius of Syracuse (envoy). Against Princes Who Consider Themselves Gods. Stories of Polycrates and of Callisthenes and Alexander (envoy). Stories of Alexander of Epirus and of Alexander the Great and Darius (envoy). On the Ruin of War (with mention of Troy, Greece, Persia, Rome, Carthage, and the heirs of Alexander). Story of Eumenes and Antigonus (envoy). Story of Queen Olympias (envoy). Story of Agathocles (envoy). Stories of the murders of Cassander. Stories of Antipater and Thessalonica, Demetrius, Peucestas and Amyntas, Sandrocottus, Seleucus, and Arsinoe and Ceraunus (envoy). Stories of the deaths of Ceraunus, Belgius, and Brennus (envoy). Stories of Pyrrhus of Epirus, Aristotimus, and Arsinoe, wife of Magas, and Demetrius.

Book V. Boccaccio's Disdain of Those Who Delight in Physical Beauty, with story of Spurina (envoy). Stories of Seleucus and Antiochus, Laodameia, Cleomenes, Hiero, Cornelius, Hannibal, Xanthippus, and Marcus Regulus (envoy). Stories of Ptolemy · Philopator, Britomaris, and Viridomarus, Hannibal and Scipio, Syphax (Masinissa, Hasdrubal, and Scipio), Nabis, Wars between Rome and Carthage, Perseus, Destruction of Corinth, Philip Philermene, Democritus, and Antiochus and Atilius (envoy). Stories of Hieronymus of Syracuse, Ingratitude of Rome to Scipio Africanus and Asiaticus, Philopoemen, and Ingratitude to Scipio Nasica (envoy). Story of Hannibal (envoy). Stories of Prusias and Nicomedes, Persa, Azariah, Ammonius, Andriscus, and Alexander Balas (envoy). Stories of Caius and Tiberius Cracchus, Hasdrubal's wife, Jonathan Maccabeus, Demetrius II, Zebina, Bituitus, Cleopatra and Euergetes, and Jugurtha (envoy).

Book VI. Fortune appears to Boccaccio. Fortune tells the stories of Saturnine, Drusus, Scipio, Fanaticus, Athenion, Spartacus, Viriathus, Marius, Mithridates, Orodes, and Pompey. Story of

Gaius Marius and of Sulla, with discussion of Virtue and mention of the three Cleopatras. Story of Mithridates (envoy). Stories of Eucratides, Orodes, Fimbria, Albinus, Adrian, and Sothimus. Description of Thrace and stories of Pompey and his Wars with Caesar (envoy). Stories of Caesar, Pompey, and Juba. Digression on Clothes. Stories of Aristobolus, the last Scipio, Pompey's son Pompey, and the Death of Caesar (envoy). Story of Octavian and the murderers of Caesar. The Career of Cicero (Tully). On Rhetoric and Oratory. Stories of Sextus Pompey and of Anthony and Cleopatra.

Book VII. Stories of those killed by Octavian: Anthony's son Anthony, Caesarius, Julia, Agrippa, Cassius, and Galbus. Story of Herod (envoy). Story of Herod Antipas. Quarrel between Messalina, Caligula, and Tiberius. Story of Nero (envoy). Stories of Eleazar, Galba, Piso, Otho, and Vitellius. On Gluttony. On the Golden Age and against Gluttony (with mention of John the Baptist and Diogenes [envoy]). Story of the Jews, their Unkindness to Jesus, and the Destruction of Jerusalem.

Book VIII. Prologue: Sloth attacks Boccaccio and then Petrarch appears to inspire him; Lydgate also vows to continue. Stories of the Roman Emperors: Domitian, Commodus, Helvius Pertinax, Julian, Severus, Antonius, Macrinus, Antonius Aurelius, Marcus Aurelius, Maximus, Gordian, the two Philips, Decius, Gallus, Volusian, Aemilian, Valerian (rebuke of Valerian), Gallien, Quintilius, Aurelian the Dane, Tacitus, Florianus, Probus, and Clarus and his sons. Story of Queen Zenobia. Stories of Diocletian, Carausius, Maximian, Galerius, Maxentius, Licinius. Constantine and Crispus, Arius, Constans and Constantius, and Vetranio. Story of Constantine the Great. Story of Julian the Apostate (against blasphemy and oaths). Stories of Valens, Theodosius I, Hermanric, Gratian, and Theodosius the Great. Stories of Honorius, Alaric, Radagaisus, Rufinus, Stilicho, Constans and Constantine, Gerontius, Attalus, and Heraclian. On the Ruin and Conduct of Kings. Story of Odoacer. On the Fall of Rome. Stories of Trasilla, Busar, Philete, Marcian, Leo and Zeno, and Symmachus, and Boethius. Story of King Arthur (envoy). Against Those Who Are Unkind to Kindred. Stories of Gelimar, Amarales, Sindbal, and Turisund and Queen Rosamond.

Book IX. Stories of the Emperor Maurice, Muhammad, and Brunhilde (envoy and excuse for her). Stories of Heraclius, his son Constantine, Constantine's son Constantine, Gisulf and Romilda, Justinian Temerarius, and Philippicus. On Covetousness Causing Division in the Church. Stories of Four Lombard Kings: Lupus, Alahis, Aribertus, and Desiderius. Stories of Pope Joan and of Arnulph. Against the Pride of Princes. Stories of Pope John XII, Charles of Lorraine, Kings Salomon and Pietro of Hungary, Diogenes Romanus, Robert of Normandy and Henry I, Josselyn of Rages, and Andronicus I (envoy). Stories of Emperor Isaac, three Sultans, Robert Surrentine, William of Sicily, Robert Guiscard, Tancred, his son William, Guy de Lusignan, John of Brienne, and Henry, son of Frederick II. Commendation of Love between Kindred. Stories of Manfred of Naples, Enzio of Sardinia (a special well and herb in Sardinia), Frederick, son of Alphonse of Castile, Maumetus of Persia and Argones, and Charles of Anjou (envoy). Stories of Ugolino of Pisa, Aiton of Armenia, Pope Boniface VIII, the Order of Templars, Commendation of Three Philosophers for Their Patience (Theodorus, Anaxarchus, and Scaevola). Commendation of Patience. The Story of Philip the Fair and his Sons. Dante appears to Boccaccio and tells him to write the story of Duke Gaultier of Florence. Story of Philipot Cathenoise (envoy). Stories of King Sancho of Majorca, King Louis of Jerusalem and Sicily, and King John of France (envoy). On Fortune. Envoy to Duke Humphrey and Final Envoy. The Translator's Words to His Book.

This massive encyclopedia of the world's rulers and their unfortunate falls, written between about 1431 and 1439, was Lydgate's most popular work and certainly his most influential. Thirty-four manuscripts of the full poem are extant, with an almost equal number of manuscripts of extracts in addition to several early editions. The *Fall of Princes* begins with the story of Adam and Eve and ends with that of the fourteenth-century King John of France; included along the way are accounts of both classical and Biblical figures. As a collection of historical and legendary stories, Lydgate's work is similar to John Gower's *Confessio Amantis* or Chaucer's *Legend of Good Women*; because of its special emphasis on the ruin of great men, its closest English analogue is undoubtedly Chaucer's *Monk's Tale*, though Lydgate appears to take the form a good deal more seriously than Chaucer.

The *Fall of Princes* was begun at the command of Humphrey, Duke of Gloucester, whom some have seen as the first humanistic patron of letters in England and others have judged an inappropriate sponsor for a work that argues that public men should be moderate and without ambition or sin. Lydgate's connection with Gloucester goes back to at least 1422, but the patron's support of the *Fall of Princes*, though enthusiastic at first, seems to have waned over the years.

The ultimate source of Lydgate's poem is Boccaccio's *De casibus virorum illustrium*, a Latin prose work written during 1355–60. A line of famous men and women appear before Boccaccio, sometimes telling their own stories, sometimes listening as he tells about them. The *De casibus* is a skillful and artistic work; it varies its basic structure with disputes and digressions and presents some stories at full length while giving others briefly or in a group. Its view of the great is often severe. Lydgate apparently did not know Boccaccio's work directly and, although he mentions the Italian author frequently, his immediate source is Laurent de Premierfait's *Des cas des nobles hommes et femmes*, a French prose work commissioned by the famous Jean, Duc de Berry, and finished in 1409. Laurent had produced an earlier translation of the *De casibus* that is fairly literal, but this second and more popular version is much expanded and more encyclopedic. Laurent adds so much biographical, historical, and geographical material that the dramatic shape and power of Boccaccio's work is lost.

Just as Laurent had done with Boccaccio, Lydgate often expands his source, especially with information from Ovid and with passages of rhetorical decoration. Sometimes he even omits material: a prominent example is his brief treatment of the Trojan War, which he notes he had already told at length in the *Troy Book* [189]. The most interesting group of original passages in the *Fall of Princes* are the *envoys* that Lydgate appends to many of his stories. He tells us (2.141-61) that his patron Gloucester requested these passages, which would offer a remedy against the blow of fortune just narrated, a remedy especially applicable to kings and princes. Modern criticism does not rate the literary skill of the *Fall of Princes* very high, but some of the *envoys* have been seen as happy exceptions.

Lydgate also differs from his source in the moral stance he adopts. His practice, much more than Laurent's, is to see sin as the direct cause of bad fortune. As a practical and optimistic moralist, Lydgate tends to the belief that man can learn from past examples how to avoid a fall. He is not consistent in this view, however, and in the *Fall of Princes* his presentation of Fortune is confused. At times the goddess is merely fickle, causing ruin and prosperity without reason or justification; at other times, she is a divine agent of retribution, carrying out God's justice on this earth through the punishment of sin. Lydgate is not a deep or original thinker (the political views expressed in the *Fall*, for example, are traditional), and he seems finally to value the number of conventional sentiments he can include over their consistency. More surprising is Lydgate's attempt to imitate the humor of his master Chaucer, whose influence is felt throughout the *Fall of Princes* and whose praises the poet frequently sings. Abandoning the role of serious moralist, Lydgate makes comedy out of Boccaccio's tired, and apparently sincere, denunciations of women.

Perhaps the liveliest critical debate over the *Fall of Princes* concerns the degree to which it contains Renaissance or humanistic elements. Many have seen the poem as a transitional work between the Middle Ages and the Renaissance, and it is often considered more forward-looking than Lydgate's earlier poems. Although this is still the general view, it has come under some attack recently by those who argue that the *Fall* is a retreat, both intellectually and artistically, from Boccaccio. However, the *Fall* has been said to anticipate future attitudes in three main areas: morality, classical antiquity, and literary style. Lydgate's greater stress on divine retribution as the primary cause of ruin, though an extremely materialistic and mechanical view of justice, has been seen as a tentative step toward the new view of human responsibility that underlies Renaissance tragedy. Others have seen a new appreciation of the classical past, of its ideals and heroes, which does not depend on the values of Christian morality or chivalry. Finally, Lydgate's rhetorical efforts have been shown to exert a great influence on the next few generations of English writers. Consolidating and simplifying the achievements of Chaucer, Lydgate in the *Fall of Princes* taught his literary descendents much about the possibilities of English poetry.

The influence of Lydgate's poem on later English writers was enormous. The *Fall of Princes* is a great storehouse of traditional stories and moral lessons. Writers like Peter Idley and John Cavendish used it directly, and its conception of tragedy was important to Renaissance drama, even perhaps to Shakespeare. The *Fall of Princes* was the primary inspiration for the *de casibus* tradition in English literature, and especially for the popular *Mirror for Magistrates*, which deliberately presents itself as a continuation of Lydgate's work. The *Fall of Princes* is a limited success as a literary work, but its importance in the history of English poetry is real.

FALL OF PRINCES, BK 2.4432–38: DECEYT DECEYVYTH [48]. One stanza in rime royal.

Deceit shall itself be deceived. Deceit returns to him who is s deceiver. He who practices fraud is rewarded with fraud.

Apparently the single most popular stanza in the *Fall of Princes*; it achieved an almost proverbial status and almost half of the surviving examples of these commonplace sentiments are scribbled on fly-leaves. In the *Fall* itself the stanza concludes a section of five stanzas entitled "Bochas ageyn doubilnes and fals symulacion," which follows the story of Metius.

FALL OF PRINCES, EXTRACTS COMBINED WITH CHAUCER'S MONK'S TALE [49]. Approximately 1450 lines of extracts from the first three books of the *Fall of Princes* in rime royal and 752 consecutive lines (B 3205–3956) from the *Monk's Tale* in an eight-line ballad stanza, ababbcbc.

This manuscript is clearly an attempt to produce an anthology of tragedies. The extracts from the *Fall* are almost entirely Lydgate's original envoys, which give remedies for individual falls. The selections include most of the envoys from the first three books with an occasional bit of narration and sometimes a moralization translated from Lydgate's source. The single selection from the *Monk's Tale*, which is the second item in the collection, includes almost the whole tale and is thus primarily narration.

FALL OF PRINCES, THE TONGUE [50]. Seven stanzas, first three in rime royal from Lydgate's *Fall of Princes* (I.4621–41), combined with three stanzas in rime royal from Chaucer's *Troilus* (III.302–22) and one anonymous tetrameter stanza which also rimes ababbcc.

> Lydgate: No pestilence is worse than a flattering tongue; woe to a false, slanderous tongue. We should say the best about others and be slow to judge if we have no evidence. Chaucer: O tongue, you have caused sorrow to women unjustly; a braggart about love is always also a liar. Anonymous: Because of Fortune, I am bound in love service.

An example of the popularity of the *Fall*, especially in excerpt, even in unlikely contexts. Here Lydgate's version of Boccaccio's sentiments on the instability of princes is combined with some of Pandarus's advice to Troilus, and all is given an apparently personal application by the anonymous compiler.

THE FIFFTENE TOKYNS AFORN THE DOOM [51]. Eleven eight-line stanzas ababbcbc.

> As St. Jerome knew by inspiration and the Scriptures tell us, there will be fifteen tokens before Judgment Day. On the first day, the sea will rise above the hills, and, on the second, it will fall so low as to be nearly invisible. On the third day, all animals will tremble with fear; on the fourth, the waters will burn; on the fifth, the birds will fly away and refuse to eat; on the sixth, a fiery flood will destroy houses and castles; on the seventh, stones will burst to pieces. The eighth token will be an earthquake. On the ninth day, high mountains will be levelled, and, on the tenth, people will come out of caves and run about mad and speechless. On the eleventh day, as the Scriptures tell us, skeletons will arise and stand on their graves until the setting of the bloody sun; on the twelfth, there will be lightnings and the stars will fall from the sky; on the thirteenth, everything living will die and subsequently rise; on the fourteenth day, both Heaven and earth will be consumed into ashes. On the last and fifteenth day, as St. Jerome says, Heaven and earth will be made new again. May God grant that all human beings may be taught by Christ's Passion before that day and may come to bliss.

This poem has been said to belong to the tradition of the Dance Macabre.

SONG AGAINST FLEMINGS (also A BALLADE IN DESPYTE THE FLEMYNGES) [52]. Five eignt-line stanzas ababbcbc, each ending with word *semblable*.

> Let him who searches for the source of fraudulent falseness go to Flanders and seek out the Black Lion who presumptuously maligned England. Let us remember that the murder of his

father evoked manly compassion in Henry V—but you have caused Flanders to malign England. You swore an oath upon the sacrament and received the absolution at Arras but spoke under a veil of deception instead of bringing about a perfect union between the two realms. What have you done at Calais with all your guns? You are a cowardly cockney who dares not fight but can malign.

This poem has been called a rather moderate attack against Philip of Burgundy.

THE FLOURE OF CURTESY [53]. 38 rime royal stanzas and a four-line abab envoy.

In February, during the night of St. Valentine, when birds choose their mates, I heard a lark bid lovers awake to serve Love forever as Venus and Cupid may order. I got up and went to a grove to watch the birds choose their mates. I was very thirsty, and I sat under a laurel as Aurora began distilling her crystal tears. I saw the birds mating, and I wondered why it was that they were free to follow their natural inclination while man alone was barred from such pleasures by statute of Nature. My woe is like an improperly healed wound, and Fortune has treated me so badly that I am unlikely ever to succeed in love. False suspicion is causing me to die, but I shall continue to serve while dying, and I shall do my humble best to write something in my lady's praise although I cannot rime. I speak out of duty without presumption, and the reader should know that my commendation of her is written under correction.

Just as the sun surpasses the stars, so my lady surpasses other women. She has the richness of the ruby and the sweetness of the rose; she is the mirror both of beauty and of conduct. She is cheerful but lets reason guide her desires; she is so devoid of pride that she herself is a guide to virtue; she is discrete and equally kind to high and low: she is called the Flower of Courtesy. She is wonderfully feminine in every respect: she consoles those in need; she is demure and well spoken; she never lends ear to evil words against either friend or foe; she is steadfast and truthful, and goodness and beauty are knit together in her person. I am too clumsy to do justice to her virtues, and I must accordingly ask to be forgiven for not knowing any muse. All I can say is that Nature would find nothing to improve in her: she is as good as Polyxena, as fair as Helen, as steadfast as Dorigen, etc., etc. She surpasses all others in goodness and beauty, and I am too ignorant to describe her virtues, so that I can only try to make up for my ineptness by humbly writing a little ballade. I fear the meter will be lame, for Chaucer is dead, who was fairest of tongue; we may try to imitate his style, but all in vain. Thus I can only say to her what follows: I choose to love you, as I heard the birds say to each other on St. Valentine's morning; I love you though I find no mercy, and I would die to please you, as I heard the birds; and I shall never repent of my love, and I thought that I heard all the birds sing. Princess of beauty, I present you with this simple ditty and am as faithful as the birds I heard sing.

This poem, whose authorship has been questioned by one scholar, has been said to be a nearly flawless example of Lydgate's craft and to be typical of his attitude toward Chaucer. It contains similarities to the *Parliament of Fowls*, and its influence on Milton has been argued. It is illustrative of Lydgate's fondness for self-deprecation.

FOUR THINGS THAT MAKE A MAN A FOOL: THER BEOTHE FOURE THINGES (also included in SAYINGS OF DAN JOHAN) [54]. One rime royal stanza.

> There are four things that make a man a fool: honor, old age, women, and wine.

This poem, once ascribed to Chaucer, reads like an elaboration on a Latin text on the same subject and has been said to show a possible debt to Gower.

FOUR THINGS THAT MAKE A MAN A FOOL: THER BEON FOURE THINGES (also included in SAYINGS OF DAN JOHAN) [55]. One rime royal stanza.

> There are four things that cause great folly: honor, old age, women, and wine. Learn, therefore, to practice humility.

See [54] for commentary.

FOUR THINGS THAT MAKE A MAN A FOOL: WURSHIP, WOMEN, WINE, UNWELDY AGE (also included in SAYINGS OF DAN JOHAN) [56]. One rime royal stanza.

> Worship, women, wine, and old age cause men to lose their reason, but women are the worst.

This stanza occurs in several poems by Lydgate and others; see [54] for general commentary.

FOUR THINGS THAT MAKE A MAN A FOOL: ON WORLDLY WORSHIP (also included in SAYINGS OF DAN JOHAN) [57]. One rime royal stanza.

> Worldly worship is vainglorious and prejudicial to the soul.

See [54] for commentary.

FOUR THINGS THAT MAKE A MAN A FOOL: BALADE DE

BONE COUNSEYLE (also BALLADE DE BONE CONSEYLL, included in SAYINGS OF DAN JOHAN) [58]. One rime royal stanza.

When suffering adversity, you should thank the Lord and remember Christ and the Cross.

A FREOND AT NEODE [59]. Seventeen eight-line stanzas ababbcbc, each ending with word *nede*.

As I was walking by myself one morning, I heard a lark sing and say that Fortune changes, so that it is well to have a friend at need. One has many friends in prosperity, but the crowds that gather around the tree vanish as soon as the branches are bare. The rich man has many friends, but nobody seeks the poor man's company, and it is rare to have a friend at need. Faithful friends were Orestes and Pylades, Achilles and Patroclus, Protesilaus and Theseus, David and Jonathan, and Amis and Amiloun. Cicero says that a friend at need is a precious treasure. Do not change old friends, and beware of parasites who are like weathercocks. Cicero compares friendship to the sun, and Solomon advises being selective in choosing friends and never letting go of one whose loyalty has been proved. Avoid temporary friends and seek the one who will be with you in need. Jesus, Sirach's son, warns against those who speak fair words but will be no real friends when needed; he says that a friend who does no good is no better than an enemy who does no harm. Solomon says that there are true friends and false friends. Blessed be the man who helps his friend; he is worth more than a precious jewel. O Christ, who suffered the Passion and whose friendship never fails, be our protection and help those who call on you in need.

GAUDE FLORE VIRGINALI [60]. Eight rime royal stanzas, each preceded by a Latin line, the first seven of which begin with the word *gaude*.

May there be joy with the pure virginal flower in heaven where angels live. Spouse of God, glorious lantern who gives the light of peace, help us love your Son. Hail, vessel of virtuous radiance, Jesus'mother praised by the angels. Joy to you, whose requests will always be granted by Jesus. Joy to the merciful mother of sinners through whom the Father will grant forgiveness and heaven. Joy to the blessed virgin mother of Christ who sits beside the Trinity. Joy to the Blessed Virgin, queen of heaven. Chosen spouse of God, show us the way to heaven and keep our souls from the devil.

This poem is adapted from a Latin text; Lydgate's authorship has been questioned and very convincingly rejected on metrical grounds.

GAUDE VIRGO MATER CHRISTI [61]. Seven rime royal stanzas, including envoy, all with a slightly varying refrain and each of the first six preceded by a Latin line beginning with the word *gaude*.

Be glad, mother of Christ, who conceived by hearing when the Holy Ghost entered your breast and Gabriel brought the news; and have mercy on us. Be glad that you bore God in chastity to redeem mankind, and do not disdain to save your servants. Rejoice, mother who endured the Passion and felt the joy of the Resurrection, and have mercy on us. Be glad of the Ascension, and have mercy; be glad that you also ascended to heaven, where angels and saints praise your chastity, and have mercy. Now, most merciful queen, maid, and mother, have mercy. Princess of Mercy, in the name of your five joys take us where you reign with your son.

This poem is an adaptation of the Latin *Gaude Virgo*.

A GENTLEWOMAN'S LAMENT (also A LOVER'S COMPLAINT) [62]. Seven eight-line stanzas ababbcbc.

Alas! how can I endure the womanly sorrow of loving one in whose grace I am unlikely to stand? The distance is too great between his station and my simplicity, but I shall love him even without hope of success. When we were children we gathered flowers together, and love put in my heart a knot of remembrance which can never be unbound, for I shall always be his woman: would God that he knew. He is always present in my sight, for he is my chosen knight even though he does not know it. He stands imprinted forever upon my inward thoughts, and I shall never live in peace without his love. I have been true to him since childhood, and I always think of him whether I wake or sleep.

This poem has been said to reflect both Chaucerian and French influence, and the authorship has been questioned.

LEGEND OF ST. GEORGE [63]. 35 rime royal stanzas.

You who have access to this story may see the martyrdom of St. George, in whose honor the Order of the Garter was founded. The name George stands for both holiness and knighthood, as my author says, as well as for the defeat of the Fiend by Christ's own knight. He was born in Cappadocia and in youth took pleasure in practicing virtue and avoiding vice. In the name of Christ, he later left home to take up arms for the sake of the Church, widows, and virginity. Meanwhile in Libya a great dragon was besieging a city. The king, queen, and council tried to pacify it with a daily offering of two sheep; when this device proved futile, they decided to offer human beings drawn by lot. To the king's and queen's sorrow, the lot eventually fell upon their daughter. Splendidly arrayed, she was sent out to be devoured, but on the way she met a knight sent by the Lord to protect her. It was St. George, Our Lady's own knight, and the princess was afraid that he might be eaten along with her. When he saw her tears, he determined to be her champion and risk his life for her. When he saw the dragon lift his head, he charged and wounded him with his spear. He then told the princess to use her girdle to lead the wounded dragon into the city, where he cut off its head in front of the assembled citizens. He then taught them Christianity, baptized everyone, and told the king to revere the Church, honor the priesthood, keep the poor in mind, and hear Mass daily. At that time, a tyrant named Dacian was intent upon destroying Christianity and slaying the Christians. St. George, dressed like a pauper, called upon him to give up idolatry, with the result that he was arrested and submitted to all kinds of tortures for his faith in Christ. In his prison cell, he was comforted by Christ, who promised him the heavenly laurel of martyrdom. He was then made to drink poison, but his poisoner repented and converted to Christianity. Then St. George was ordered broken on the wheel and boiled in lead, but he survived unharmed. When he was brought to a temple, he defied the Mohammedan gods, who were suddenly turned to ashes by a bolt of fire from heaven, and Dacian's wife was converted to Christianity. In the end, he was beheaded by Dacian's order and died praying for those who would pray to him. A voice from heaven announced that his prayer had been granted, and Dacian was struck dead by lightning.

This poem, presumably based on the *Legenda Aurea*, is believed to have been intended for pictorial display.

LIFE OF ST. GILES [64]. 368 lines in an eight-line ballad stanza, ababbcbc.

May St. Giles, born under Agamemnon's rule, inspire me. I was asked to translate your story from Latin, St. Giles. Your father was Theodorus, your mother Pellagia–both of royal blood. As a child you gave away your coat, then your inheritance. Other miracles followed, but you fled the country to avoid vainglory and did other marvels. You spent three years in the desert where God miraculously fed you through a hind (she was your cook and butler). Fluent, king of Burgundy, lived nearby and one day while hunting, he chased your hind to your feet. The king saw you wounded by an arrow and in recompense he built you a monastery where you kept your wound open in memory of Christ, an example to all and a perfect abbot. King Charles sent for you to pray for his sins; a letter written in gold came from heaven that absolved the king and gave you the power to forgive other repentant sinners. Returning to your monastery, you healed a duke's son and then made a pilgrimage to Rome. The Pope granted you freedom and his protection and gave twelve doors to your monastery which told the lives of the twelve apostles. You foresaw your death and gave up the ghost among your weeping brethren. Prayer: Gracious Giles, save the poor and needy and pray for our sins. Teach us to love the Lord and save us from the world, the flesh, and the devil.
Lenvoye: St. Giles, think of the author and all who trust in your prayer.

A short, quite original life of a saint popular in England. Lydgate claims to be translating from a Latin original, but his immediate source has been identified as an Old French version by the Anglo-Norman Guillaume de Berneville. The author addresses the saint throughout in the second person singular, thus turning the narrative into a kind of prayer. Lydgate tries in this poem to create an intimate, yet elegant and sonorous style. He is clearly charmed by the deer which succors Giles. Perhaps because of his own monkish vocation, Lydgate describes Giles as an ideal abbot and stresses the good a monastery can do for others and the need for it to be free and independent.

GLORIOSA DICTA SUNT DE TE (also **BALADE OF OURE LADYE BY LIDEGATE**) [65]. 29 eight-line stanzas ababbcbc, all ending with word *thee* and all but three with slightly varying refrain.

> On holy hills I saw the foundation of a city above the rainbow. Its name is the dwelling place of deity, and it is written that upon the walls glorious things are sung and said of you, so David sang upon the mountains of Sion. You are the lodestar of all cities; authors used to praise Troy and Rome, but all their boasting must now end, so glorious things are said and sung of you. You are the city chosen by God the Father for the Holy Ghost to descend in your tabernacle, and Anne offered your virginity to God. You are the temple where Christ chose to dwell for reasons which I am too inept to express. There was a city of champions and a refuge of sinners; a tree of life sprang from it, according to Ecclesiastes, and Ezekiel also saw a city within which the Lord and Lords had sovereignty. You were a star passing all other heavenly bodies in your Conception and Assumption. As David had a thousand shields, so you have a thousand virtues, and your chastity was offered to God. You were the most perfect of women; like Judith killing Holofernes, you defeated the fiend and saved mankind. Consolation of sinful men, you have been called temple of Solomon; you are the city seen by St. John and built of precious stones: sapphire for truth, chalcedony against the enemies of right, emerald to comfort blind eyes, etc., etc. Glory of the patriarchs and mirror of chastity for the virgins, blessed lady whom clerks call empress of hell, be our succor when we pass away and cause us to dwell where glorious things are said and sung of you.

This poem combines one of the Psalms with part of Revelation.

APPEAL TO GLOUCESTER (also **LETTER TO GLOUCESTER** and **UPON THE EMPTINESS OF HIS PURSE**) [66]. Eight eight-line stanzas ababbcbc, including envoy, with varying refrain.

> Mighty prince, condescend to look at this little note which I wrote with quaking hand when my purse was sick. Although I asked physicians and apothecaries, there was no adequate remedy to be found in the town of Bury for lack of a ship to bring it to shore. There was no plate or other token from the Tower; it is hard to get honey out of marble, and my purse and I are fallen into indigence, which you could cure with plate or coinage. Gold is the best cordial; *aurum potabile* is good for old age, especially in the form of coinage. Little poem, why are you not ashamed of your impudence? *Nihil habet* makes old men faint and coinage is the best remedy. Explain as an excuse that there is neither cross nor pile in your sanctuary. May God send a better remedy with the sound of coinage.

This poem, which has been said to owe much to Chaucer and Jean de Meun, has been rated one of Lydgate's better short pieces.

EPITAPH ON GLOUCESTER [67]. See *Manual*, volume 5, Poems on Contemporary Conditions, XIII [229], for Rossell Hope Robbins' commentary and bibliography.

MARRIAGE OF GLOUCESTER (also ON GLOUCESTER'S APPROACHING MARRIAGE) [68]. 27 rime royal stanzas and an eight-line envoy ababbcbc.

Through Venus and Cupid hearts have often been joined. Heaven does many things beyond human comprehension, including causing hearts to fall in love within Jupiter's chains. Thus did the knot of alliance first come between countries, for nobody can escape a course set by Heaven, and marriage was established by the Eternal Lord. Books and authentic chronicles tell us how countries have been united by marriage, as in the case of England and France, and I hope that the war between these will be ended by the union of Catherine and Henry V and that Holland may be joined to England. The old hatred between the two will be ended by a new sun brought in by one who is the flower of womanhood: Jacqueline, Duchess of Holland, who is as meek as Esther, as wise as Judith, etc., etc. In addition, she is compassionate, celestial, and feminine. Her colors are black, white, and red in token of truth, purity, and perfect sobriety. Since she comes of the noblest blood, I hope that her visit to this land will result in her marriage to the best knight in war and peace, one who surpasses all and deserves to be registered in the House of Fame and is the equal of the Nine Worthies. He reads with understanding the Scriptures, poetry, and philosophy, and he has Solomon's wisdom, Julius Caesar's prowess, Cicero's eloquence, etc., etc. May God grant that this knight and the lovely duchess be joined so that there may be peace between this land and its mortal foes. Everyone in the land is praying for this union: may God grant the request. May Hymen, Juno, etc., etc., as well as Fortune, help with this matter. Princess of goodness, I humbly pray that you take no heed of my ineptitude and that you have mercy upon my ignorance, since I wrote this poem only to please you.

This poem has been said to contain strong parallels to Lydgate's own *Temple of Glas*, [176] below, and has been praised for the dexterity with which it avoids awkward political issues.

A COMPLAINT FOR MY LADY OF GLOUCESTER AND HOLLAND [69]. Eighteen rime royal stanzas.

A solitary man sat weeping by a river, as did many others in hope that the sun would shine and disperse the clouds of their sorrow and that God would send back home to them the one for whom they were calling. They complained that Fortune did nothing to help them, and thus the women of all degrees cried for the return of the princess who would end their woe: send her home soon to dispel the rage of those who complain for her sake. While they were speaking, there appeared a mermaid looking like a sorceress surrounded by witches, and they strove night and day to turn the prince's heart against right: may vengeance fall upon them! They used false incantations to turn the prince's heart against that fair princess and make him lose his good name. In his dream, the solitary man heard the women of the country pray for the return of the princess: God bring her home to gladden us. He wrote down his dream, and 300,000 people of that region were in agreement with him. Their names will be known as soon as God chases the bawds and other rascals who may not long prevail against truth. Under the color of this dream the solitary man bears witness to the fact that rich and poor pray each day for the return of the princess; she is beloved throughout the land, especially by her godson.

This poem, whose authorship has been seriously questioned, is generally considered illustrative of the indignation caused by Gloucester's desertion of Jacqueline of Hainault.

GOD IS MYN HELPERE [70]. Thirteen eight-line stanzas ababbcbc with slightly varying refrain.

God is my help, and I fear no man despite my impotence. I trust Him for He was my Redeemer. He has helped me in many ways and has never deceived any man who trusted Him with all his heart. I have often been in danger, but God has always helped me. Fortune is fickle, and worldly prosperity may not last, but I fear no man while God is helping me. In gladness or in sorrow, under a bright or a cloudy sky, during summer or other seasons, as long as men live righteously there is no cause for fear when He pleases to help. Who say the best shall never repent, and God will help. Regardless of the circumstances, He will not fail those who call upon Him; there is no cause for fear when God pleases to help.

GUY OF WARWICK [71]. 74 eight-line stanzas ababbcbc.

In 927 King Athelstan was reigning over England while the Danes were persecuting everyone, slaughtering even pregnant women, and wasting the land around Winchester. They showed no pity, and the streams ran red with blood: perhaps it was a punishment for some old sin. This realm was almost brought to destruction, but God is merciful while punishing. God has chastised many a great city: Jerusalem, Paris, Rome, etc., etc. The Danes were now shedding English blood, but God was ready to turn Athelstan's troubles into prosperity: the sun follows the rain. I read in the chronicle that the estates met at Winchester to find the means to set things right, but the Danes demanded that Athelstan send them immediately either tribute or a champion to fight the Danish giant Colebrand. Athelstan and his lords could only weep and pray, for Guy of Warwick had become a pilgrim and Herald of Harderne (the best knight next to Guy himself) had temporarily left the realm in search of Guy's son, who had been abducted by merchants. As Athelstan was weeping and begging God to forgive him his trespasses, he fell asleep, and an angel appeared to tell him to get up with the sun and go to the north gate of the city, where he would find a pilgrim who would do battle for him and triumph through the might of God. It was the just-returned Guy, whom Athelstan not recognizing beseeched in God's name to fight Colebrand. The old pilgrim and the giant met in combat at Hide Meadow on July 12. When Guy's sword broke, Colebrand refused him a new one, but Guy smote off his head with a poleax. The Danes left the land, and the English went to the cathedral, where Guy meekly offered the ax, which is still kept in the vestiary. He then donned once more his pilgrim's garb and revealed his identity to Athelstan under the seal of secrecy before returning to Warwick incognito. There he found his wife feeding the poor, and he took alms from her three days in a row before retiring to a nearby hermitage where he spent two solitary years. Upon learning from God that the time of his death was near, he sent his ring to his wife with the request that he be buried without pomp by the small altar where he lay. She wept, kissed his body, and did as he had requested. She died soon thereafter, having first made the necessary arrangements for their son to succeed to the title and earldom of Warwick. For additional facts, consult Gerard Cornubiensis; if anything be wrong with this text, put the blame for dullness on Lydgate: he never gathered flowers in Tully's garden but prays everyone not to disdain the contents.

This poem, whose immediate source is generally assumed to be Girardus Cornubiensis, has been said to illustrate Lydgate's lowest style.

A DITTY AGAINST HASTE [72]. Twenty eight-line stanzas ababbcbc with refrain in first fifteen stanzas and variations thereof in remainder.

> Haste without discretion is odious, especially when it helps various sins against conscience: he hastens well who knows how to wait. The hasty man must endure all kinds of woes: he hastens well, etc., etc. Rancor follows foolish haste, which causes one to regret one's actions. Solomon speaks of three men who were both hasty and evil: such people always die early. A sudden wind will shake down hasty blossoms, and hasty fruit will putrify. Everything is best taken in due time: think of Asael, Patroclus, Hector, etc., etc. Beware of hasty speech. Haste is good when it hastens toward virtue, and sloth is good when it slows down vengeance. Hastening with love and fear toward Christ is good. A good beginning requires a good conclusion: hasten toward Christ's passion, embrace that banner, and abide thereby.

This poem has been noted for its use of both classical and Biblical references.

HENRY V'S EXPEDITION INTO FRANCE (also THE SIEGE OF HARFLEUR, usually linked with BATTLE OF AGINCOURT and SIEGE OF CALAIS) [73]. 292 tetrameter lines with irregular basic rime pattern abab.

> Our king was in Winchester and said he would go to fight in France. The Duke of Clarence approved, and they went through London, where they were greeted by the mayor and the guilds before going on to Southampton. There our king found 1500 ships awaiting him and executed several traitors before crossing the sea to Normandy. He and Clarence prepared to besiege Harfleur, and he told the French that he would play tennis with balls of stone unless they surrendered their town. They dug mines and countermines, and the English guns shot balls of stone that brought many walls down during this game until the French decided to surrender if the dauphin did not rescue them. When the French surrendered, our king thanked God and said he would now march against Calais.

For commentary and bibliography for the subsequent companion pieces, *The Siege of Calais* and *The Battle of Agincourt*, see XIII [51] and [72], in *Manual*, volume 5. Lydgate's authorship of this poem has been questioned by some and rejected by others; the present writer can find nothing reminiscent of Lydgate in the text.

HENRY VI: HIS CLAIM TO FRANCE (also ENGLISH TITLE TO THE CROWN OF FRANCE and TITLE AND PEDIGREE OF HENRY

VI; followed by ROUNDEL ON THE CORONATION OF HENRY VI [81] in only manuscript) [74]. 329 decasyllabic lines of riming couplets and one triplet.

In order to set troubled hearts at ease and to settle arguments concerning the lineage of England and France, I followed the precept and command of the wise Lord of Warwick, who was then present in Paris. He does not hesitate to show the right of his sovereign, the five-year-old Henry VI. To this end, the Regent of France, My Lord of Bedford, had a search conducted by the best qualified clerk through the chronicle, and I humbly obeyed the command to translate that clerk's French into English. I have followed the original as carefully as possible although I lack the flowers of rhetoric.

Jesus Christ, seeing the trouble between the kings of England and of France and seeing also how the dauphin ordered the iniquitous murder of John of Burgundy and thereby lost his claim to the kingdom—considering these things, God has mercifully provided a rightful heir for the two realms. The pedigree shows beyond doubt that he comes in straight line from the stock of St. Louis, and God has provided this Henry to put an end to all disagreement and be king of England and of France. By the treaty of Troyes, Henry (V) became heir to the crown of France, and his marriage to Katherine in St. John's Church reinforced his claim. No man was better suited than worthy King Henry to bring two realms under one crown. Being descended from royal stock and St. Louis through Henry (V) and Katherine, Henry VI was born to wear the crowns of England and of France. All this is clearly shown in the French pedigree which My Lord of Warwick asked me to translate, and which I began translating on July 20, when Saturn is in the Scorpion. May God grant him a place in heaven.

This poem, which has been considered both worthless and skillful, is believed to have been designed to be posted in churches.

HENRY VI: BALLADE UPON HIS CORONATION [75]. Eighteen eight-line stanzas ababbcbc including envoy.

Most noble of all Christian princes, descended from St. Edward and St. Louis, love and dread God, who gave glory to your ancestors. By divine ordinance the throne of France must be firm in faith, and you must accordingly protect the Church, uphold truth, and be fair and merciful. May God send you the virtues of Solomon, David, Hector, etc., etc. Repress heretics and Lollards like Sigismund; be filled with manhood like your father and with goodness like your blessed mother. I pray to God that you may be like them in your virtuous conduct in England and France. Excellent prince, love God, be liberal, cherish the Church, have mercy on the poor, keep your word, etc. etc., and God will bless your royal state from above.

HENRY VI: SOTELTIES AT THE CORONATION BANQUET [76]. Three eight-line stanza ababbcbc.

Behold St. Edward and St. Louis and the branch of their blessed blood; may God grant that Henry VI be like them. Both Sigismund and Henry V fought miscreants to provide an example for this branch. Blessed Virgin and St. George, may you help this youth reign over England and France.

Each stanza is preceded by the menu for the accompanying course.

HENRY VI: TRIUMPHAL ENTRY INTO LONDON [77]. 77 rime royal stanzas including envoy.

On a Thursday toward the end of windy February, when Phebus was in the Fish, the return of Henry VI, rightfully crowned king of France, caused the weather to be fair in London. No cloud was seen, and the citizens blessed the day. Like Jerusalem after David's victory, they were glad to receive their king. The mayor and notables dressed in scarlet, the guilds and other citizens in white, and even aliens came to meet the king. They lined up in two rows at Blackheath, where the mayor greeted the king in the name of all his loving subjects. I shall describe what took place, but I have no eloquence. At the entrance of the bridge of this noble town there was the likeness of a gigantic champion with his sword drawn against the enemies of the king, and two antelopes stood on either side with the arms of England and of France. In the middle of the bridge there was a tower covered with gold cloth whence the empresses Nature, Grace, and Fortune presented the king with the gifts of science, fairness, prosperity, etc., etc., and seven maidens presented him with the gifts of the Holy Ghost. There were also seven virgins in white who presented the king with the crown of glory, the scepter of pity, etc., etc., and who sang a roundel of welcome for his return from France. At Cornhill there was a tabernacle where Lady Sapience was surrounded by the seven liberal sciences and held a sign advising kings to govern according to her rules. At the Conduit the king was received by the ladies Mercy, Truth, and Clemency, and two judges and eight sergeants stood before him with a sign in praise of equity. There were water fountains where Mercy, Grace, and Pity ministered to the king and where various trees bore all kinds of fruit while two old men named Enoch and Elijah addressed him. Then the king rode toward a green castle upon whose towers was displayed his pedigree and title to the crowns of England and of France. There were two green trees representing St. Edward and St. Louis, as well as a tree of Jesse. At St. Paul's there was a likeness of the Trinity surrounded by angels charged with watching over the king, and the archbishop and other notables of the Church were waiting to meet the king, who was then solemnly escorted to Westminster to receive St. Edward's scepter while a *Te Deum* was sung. The following Saturday the mayor presented the king with £1000 in the name of the officials of London. Be glad, O London, for Rome never received Julius Caesar as London did the king on his return from France. I praise London for seven things: truth, faith, etc., etc., and I hope, O noble mayor, that you will have mercy on this simple product of my ineptitude.

This poem, which has been considered one of the earliest accounts of a pageant, has been said to reflect Chaucerian influence and to have influenced Thomas Middleton's *Triumph of Truth*.

ENVOY TO HENRY VI (at end of LIFE OF SS. EDMUND AND FREMUND [42]) [78]. Five stanzas in rime royal, with the same rime scheme throughout and "correction" the last word of each stanza.

Go, little book, and be fearful in such a high presence. Humbly submit yourself to correction. You have no rhetorical colors save black and white. May God grant you mercy for you lack eloquence.

This brief envoy occurs at the end of nine manuscripts of the *Life of SS. Edmund and Fremund* (see [42] above) and was apparently addressed to Henry VI for whom the double legend was written. It contains many mythological and humanistic allusions and, like other examples of the modesty topic, asserts its rhetorical incompetence in lines of much skill and ingenuity.

A PRAYER FOR HENRY VI, HIS QUEEN AND PEOPLE (also AB INIMICIS) [79]. Twelve rime royal stanzas with slightly varying two-line refrain.

> Blessed Jesus, deliver us from our foes and preserve the king, the queen, the people, and the land. Consider our affliction and shadow us with Your protection; look at us with Your benign face and forgive our sins. Hear our call for help and have mercy on us, Son of God. Do not disdain us, and bring fortune to this realm, O Christ who died on the cross for us. Protect Henry VI, Your own knight born to inherit France, and do not forget his mother, Katherine, or those who work for his inheritance here and in France. Give him grace to be crowned soon here and in France.

This poem has been presented as evidence of Lydgate's ability to handle any kind of material.

A PRAYER TO ST. EDMUND FOR HENRY VI (also PRAYERS TO ST. EDMUND) [80]. Eight stanzas, riming ababbcbc, with repeated rime scheme and refrain.

> O glorious martyr, who suffered horrible death, pray for the inheritor of England and France. Be our shield from foreign enemies. Pray for the Church and all the estates. Help and support priests, women, innocents, and the needy. Pray for craftsmen, laborers, pilgrims, sailors, and peace. Bring about unity, comfort the sick, restore exiles, and deliver prisoners. Increase the prowess of Henry VI and preserve his two kingdoms.

This highly ornamented prayer follows the *Life of SS. Edmund and Fremund* (see [42] above) in several manuscripts, but it is also found alone. Written in Lydgate's best invocatory rhetoric, its stylistic ambition is revealed by the refrain, "Pray for the inheritor of England and France," at the end of each stanza and by the use of a single rime scheme throughout. Like *Edmund and Fremund* itself, the poem combines both patriotic and religious themes and has been compared to *A Prayer for Henry VI, His Queen and People* (see [79] above). The insistence that Henry is king of both England and France is also found in many other poems by Lydgate on the dual monarchy (see, for example, [40], [74], [75], and [81]). The language and style of this poem have been compared to other Lydgate pieces like his less political appeal to St. Edmund (see [147] below) and his prayers to St. Denis and St. Thomas of Canterbury (see [146] and [154] below).

ROUNDEL ON THE CORONATION OF HENRY VI [81]. Ten lines ababababba.

Rejoice, England and France, for God has sent the blood of St. Edward and St. Louis to rule. O heavenly blossom, may God grant that you be like your father.

This poem follows *Henry VI: His Claim to France* [74] in the only known manuscript.

DEFENSE OF HOLY CHURCH [82]. 21 rime royal stanzas.

Laud and honor to you, most worthy prince who has protected the Spouse of Christ who was oppressed in Jerusalem and suffered in Babylon until you had pity upon her woe and delivered her from Nebuchadnezzar so that the Temple may be rebuilt in Jerusalem and protected from those who would threaten the patrimony of Peter. You saw to it that Noah's ship be safe from Scylla and Charybdis, and I now urge God's knight to protect the Ark from the Philistines. Think how Saul was false to David, and be sure to separate the grain from the chaff. Just as David cleared the lame out of Zion, so rid yourself of the lame in faith and let rigor hold the scales. Emulate Saul, Samuel, and Elijah, and remember the fates of Antiochus and Belshazzar.

The authorship of this religious and political poem has been questioned.

DEBATE OF THE HORSE, GOOSE, AND SHEEP [83]. 77 rime royal stanzas and an envoy of fifteen eight-line stanzas ababbaba with varying refrain.

The old custom was to have judges settle disagreements after all concerned had presented their arguments. I recently saw a wall painting in which the lion and the eagle were the judges and the horse, goose, and sheep were arguing which of the three was most useful to man.

The horse spoke first: Is there any other beast as useful in both peace and war as the horse? Remember Alexander's horse, and Hector's, and Perseus', and note that in various languages the word for a knight indicates connection with horses. Without a horse, weapons would be of no avail to princes, and Chaucer told of a horse of brass. Zacharias saw four horses that stood for boldness, soberness, the defense of Holy Church, and the cardinal virtues. Without horses there could be no tournaments or transportation. Horses will carry a poor man's grain as well as wine and other things, and they carry hay and oats to the granary. In August they carry sheaves, as well as water, timber etc., etc. You, prudent judges, decide whether the goose or sheep can compare to the horse. I have told the truth; let the goose speak now.

The words of the goose: I will speak my truth. While you are confined to your pasture, I am at home on land, water, and air, and wild geese foretell storms for the good of men. The grease of ganders is good for medical purposes goose feathers for arrows, goose quills for writing, and goose down for pillows. Goose excrement is good for burns, while horse dung is good only for furnaces; and a dead horse is only a carcass, while a fat goose is served at a king's table. The best English arrows are made with goose, swan, or peacock feathers and have won many a victory for Englishmen, as illustrated by the capture of the French king at Poitiers. The Duke of Clarence got in trouble when he spurned goose feathers. A gander saved Rome; did a horse ever do any such thing? In the book of the Knight of the Swan, royal children born with chains turned into swans when those chains were torn off. Recently a Lombard was turned into a goose for seven years, and his kin now wear a goose on their livery. Weigh these things and see whether a horse can compare to a gander or a goose. In Rome the gander was deified; let us see if the sheep can do better.

The sheep was meek, but he addressed the judges after a Latin exordium: According to St. Augustine, the chaste sheep named Mary brought forth the royal lamb Jesus who endured the Passion for mankind. Did such solemn thing ever happen to a horse or a goose? This lamb was Christ, descended from Abraham and called lamb for his meekness. None contributes to the common good as does the sheep, for the lamb vanquished Satan. The goose may cackle and the horse prance, but neither equals the sheep, for English wool is the best in the world and is used for furs, garments, etc., etc. Mutton is especially wholesome meat and cures all kinds of ills, and the sheep never seeks a quarrel. Therefore, give the prize to the sheep and stop all war.

No, said the horse, the sheep is the cause of war since it was for wool that the Duke of Burgundy attacked Calais and reckless men are attracted to places where there is plenty of wool. You talk peace but cause war; and, without war, there would be no call for great horses. Nor, said the goose, for my feathers nor for the arrows which will protect us from our enemies despite the sheep. Without war, said the horse, we could not protect our right, but this sheep cares only about eating in peace; and there would be no jobs for armorers, and knighthood would no longer flourish. Peace brings wealth, which brings pride, which brings war, which causes people to want peace. Since wealth comes from wool, the sheep is the real cause of war. The horse is fallen in dotage, said the sheep, for it is not the sheep's fault that men shear him of the wool for which they subsequently fight.

When the lion and the eagle saw that the horse, the goose, and the sheep were equally necessary to the common good, they decreed that they should cease arguing and that each should henceforth act as nature intended: the horse by working, the goose by swimming, and the sheep by grazing. Nobody should wrong or oppress others, and comparisons breed hatred, and this fable shows that he who has the greater portion of virtuous gifts should share with others, for no man has all virtues and no man should despise another.

Envoy: Understand the meaning of this fable: no man, however brave, holy, or rich, should ever presume to despise his neighbor. The steed wears trappings of gold while the sheep meekly grazes in the pasture, but wool is used to make rich garments and down to make featherbeds: do not despise your neighbor. Tyrants oppress the poor: do not despise your subjects. After the sun comes rain; poets have implicitly reproved tyrants with fables about horse, sheep, goose, or other beasts: do not despise the poor. In nature the big fish eats the little one, the churl hates the nobleman, and beggars and fools rise to despise their neighbors, but death comes to all creatures to teach the proud not to despise their neighbors. In Alexander's time, a king once gave up his purple to show that poor and rich were all one: princes, do not despise your subjects, for both high and low were made of earth. Both the head and the feet are necessary, and horse, sheep, and goose ought not to quarrel. He does well who refrains from despising his neighbor. Nature has a law for all creatures, and nobody has the right to despise his neighbor.

This poem has been considered especially illustrative of Lydgate's didacticism.

HOW THE PLAGUE WAS SESYD IN ROME [84]. Six rime royal stanzas.

Not even the greatest doctors could make a medicine like the Lord. In King Gilbert's time, when a dreadful pestilence killed more than half the population of Rome and Pavia, a good and an evil angel smote people by the thousand. When a holy man had a revelation and erected an altar to St. Sebastian, the plague ceased. No medicine would do any good, but God ended the pestilence through his martyr.

BALLADE ON THE IMAGE OF OUR LADY (also IMAGE OF OUR LADY) [85]. Five eight-line stanzas ababbcbc.

Behold this glorious image of Our Lady painted like the picture of St. Luke in Rome. Those who worship it at the Assumptions and other feasts will have 500 years of pardons, and those who help this church will have 1500. Ralph Gelebronde bought the pardons in Rome through the labor of Archdeacon John Thornton: may God take them both in His grace.

This poem is believed to have been intended to accompany a picture.

ON THE IMAGE OF PITY (also PITY TO THE WRETCHED SINNER) [86]. Five eight-line stanzas ababbcbc.

O wretched sinner, kneel and behold Christ's mother mourning for her child who suffered for your sins, and pray to the mother and maid. Remember that, but for Adam's fall, she would not have been crowned Queen of Heaven, and run to a priest to confess, and you will be saved. If you should be tempted to sin, think on this sorrowful woman holding her dead son. Learn this lesson and be saved: images showing holy stories were made for that purpose.

This poem is considered to have been intended to be posted with a picture.

INTERPRETACIO MISSE (also INTERPRETACION AND VIRTUES OF THE MASS, POEMS ON THE MASS II, PRAYER AT THE HOLY COMMUNION, PRAYER TO THE HOLY SACRAMENT, and VIRTUES OF THE MASS; contains a third version of ON KISSING AT VERBUM CARO [103–104]) [87]. 83 eight-line stanzas ababbcbc including envoy.

You who would hear Mass, consider first the meaning of the spiritual armor that is the priest's vestment. Know that the Mass is medicine for spiritual ailments, and attend it every morning for protection. Kneel humbly while the priest dons his vestments, make no noise, do not gaze about, and do not leave until the end. Pope Celestine ordered priests to say *Judica me Deus* at Mass. This Psalm laments the Babylonian Captivity, and I shall translate it in my simple manner: Judge me, O Lord, O gracious Jesus, for You are my support; send Your light down to guide me, and I shall enter up to Your altar to be shriven in the name of the Crucifixion. Why are you sad, O my soul, since Christ has bought you with His Passion? Trust in God, Who bled for my sake. First, the priest dons the amice, then the alb, etc., etc., and stands before the altar as Christ's champion, while burning candles signify that Christ is light. He sings the *Kyrie* in Greek and the *Gloria* as a token of unity; he then goes on to the *Orison* and the *Epistle*, which stands for the coming of Christ, and he proceeds to the *Graduale*, the *Alleluia*, etc., etc. until the end of the service. With all your might say a prayer at the elevation of the Sacrament: Hail Holy Jesus, grant me clean shrift before death; let me receive You and grant me repentance before death; let me see and receive You daily, and have mercy on me. If recited with charity, the *Pater Noster* is a most effective prayer since Christ Himself taught it to His disciples, but no prayer will do any good without charity. Beware, you priests, that charity be not absent when you celebrate Mass. The *Pater Noster* includes all perfection. The *Agnus Dei* is said three times. Christ as a lamb was offered on the cross, and this lamb is mentioned in the Song of Songs. This lamb was rubified in blood and rose on Easter to turn into the Lion of Judah. The Nativity brought peace to the world, so that people now kiss the *pax* to signify that peace is the cause of felicity. At the Postcommunion the priest greets the people the way Jesus appeared to His disciples-after the Resurrection and greeted His mother and the other Maries who sought His sepulcher out of love. Let us rise as early as they did and hear Mass. After the priest says *ite missa est*, the people depart as the children of Israel departed through the Red Sea and the prisoners left Babylon to rebuild Jerusalem. As the children of Israel were fed with manna, we should take our spiritual food at daily Mass. Lord, grant that we may hear Mass correctly.

According to St. Bernard, Mass yields great rewards and helps pilgrims; it also helps laborers endure their work and makes merchants lucky and people meek while bringing luck to everyone. Hearing Mass brings assistance from St. Nicholas, St. Julian, St. Christopher, etc., etc. The Mass is our spear and shield. The day a man hears Mass devoutly, his steps are counted by angels and his venial sins forgiven. Hearing Mass helps with travel, and he who dies after hearing Mass receives credit for communion as well. Mass before a meal improves the quality of food just as manna helped the children of Israel. Just as the head is above the other parts of the body, so Jesus Christ has placed the Mass above all other means of help. The Mass helps sailors, poor people, women in labor, and even souls out of purgatory. In view of all these things, let people rise early to go to Mass. Go, little treatise, and pray those who read you to correct your author's well-meaning simplicity where they see need to do so.

This poem, which has been said to illustrate Lydgate's religious conservatism, seems to form a sequence with *An Exortacion to Prestys* [45] and *On Kissing at Verbum Caro* [103–104]; the three have been printed together under the title of *Poems on the Mass*.

ISOPES FABULES (including THE COCK AND THE PRECIOUS STONE, THE WOLF AND THE LAMB, THE FROG AND THE MOUSE, THE HOUND AND THE SHEEP, THE WOLF AND THE

CRANE, THE SUN'S MARRIAGE, and THE HOUND AND THE CHEESE) [88]. 137 rime royal stanzas.

Wisdom is worth more than gold. This is why the Roman poet laureate Aesop composed instructive animal fables which, like oysters, may contain pearls of wisdom, and this is why I am translating them into English, but I was born in Lydgate and never passed the gate of Tully's garden to gather flowers of rhetoric. May the readers forgive my ineptitude and make such corrections as seem needed. Like my author, I begin with a cock.

The cock has a red crest that gives him courage; he keeps time at night, protects his brood, and awakens folks at dawn by praising the Trinity with his crowing, for which he deserves praise. He stands against vice and sings to show us how to praise the Lord. This cock once walked out and found a jacinth stone in a dunghill, but he continued looking for food, thus teaching us to earn our livelihood through honest labor. Idleness breeds robbery and sends people to Tyburn. Lazy people are beasts, for virtue begins with work. The cock spoke thus to the stone: A jeweler who found you would set you in gold; the best Ethiopian jacinths have great virtues, but they are of no use to me, and you belong to jewelers. Wisemen like wisdom, but fools despise it; steel is for the armor and lead for the church roof; the swan likes to swim and I to scratch for grain; people act according to their nature. The moral of this fable is that people should be diligent, take whatever God sees fit for them, and thank the Lord.

There can be no compromise between virtue and vice, and there is a great division between rancor and humble patience. Big pikes eat smaller fishes, and the wolf looks contemptuously upon the lamb, as shown by Aesop. A wolf was drinking at a river upstream from a lamb and accused him of muddying his water. The lamb replied that it could not be so since he was downstream, but the wolf accused him of duplicity and devoured him. The lamb was killed for saying the truth, and yet he gives us cheese, milk, and wool, and a ram bore the Golden Fleece, but the wolf goes free. What does the poor man get when he goes to court? After death, however, the lamb is served at the king's table while the wolf is not even worthy of being fed to dogs, and poor men have their reward in heaven. The moral of Aesop's fable is that the lamb is praised for his meekness, and the wolf is rebuked for his ravenous nastiness.

Whoever tries to deceive another will be repaid accordingly. Some men like truth and others fraudulence, and Aesop tells of a deceitful frog who tricked a mouse who had invited him to dinner at home. The mouse was poor and happy: I am better off than Croesus, I sleep better than Midas, and this place is good enough for me. He invited the frog to spend the night, but the other wanted a drink, so that the two went to the river. There the frog invited the mouse to his home on the other side. Because the mouse could not swim, the frog tied a string to his neck to pull him across, but he really intended to drown him. As they were getting on their way, a kite caught them both by the thread and ate the frog first because he was fat. The thread broke, and the mouse escaped. Ingratitude is the worst of all vices. In this fable the mouse was innocent but the frog was undone through his own attempt to deceive his friend: who uses fraud will be repaid with fraud.

False jurors and false witnesses are monstrous people whose cankered lips hinder rightful causes. Aesop wrote about a big dog who forced an innocent sheep to appear before a judge. He swore that he had lent the sheep a loaf when the latter was hungry but that the sheep had never returned it. The sheep was astounded but humbly denied the charge. When the judge asked for witnesses, the dog produced two whom he called the faithful wolf and the gentle kite, who perjured themselves: may they hang by the neck. The sheep had to sell his fleece to pay, so that he died of cold in winter, and his carcass was eaten by the wolf and kite: poor folks are always devoured by the rich, and those who have no conscience cut large thongs out of others' leather. False witnesses are worse than barbed arrows, for there is no defense against them. They should be gelded to prevent them from multiplying. Holcot says that a perjured person is a traitor to God and that he who swears falsely on the Bible offers himself to the devil. God has forbidden man to bear false witness, and the trespass of perjury is huge. Aesop calls perjurers harpies, and they deserve damnation. The false juror will be damned unless he repents and does penance before death.

Aesop continues, writing of ingratitude, telling how a wolf was unkind to a crane who had done him a good turn. While the animals held a feast, a wolf began choking on a bone and promised the crane a great reward to take it out. When the crane asked for his reward, however, the wolf denied having promised anything and argued that the crane was lucky not to have been eaten while picking the bone. This is the way tyrants act with poor people who work for them. Poor people have no choice but to obey. Fair promises gladden fools, but the rich man has everything and gives nothing away. The moral of this tale is that tyrants know no mercy and it is folly to play with them.

Aesop writes another fable against tyranny. When the sun fell into dotage and yearned after a wife, he called a council of gods, but they decided that earthly creatures could not endure the heat of two suns. Likewise a single tyrant in a shire is enough to set all the country afire, and his heirs are likely to be worse. Merchants fear thieves and one cannot win against many. Aesop's lesson is that one tyrant may go hard on people but two are worse.

Aesop has composed a moral fable about covetise. A dog carrying a cheese in his mouth was going over a bridge and saw his own reflection in the water. Thinking that there was another cheese there, he opened his mouth and lost the one he had. Thus one sees that covetise often fails: one should be content with what little one has.

These tales, which are part of a medieval tradition, have been said to reflect the influence of Marie de France.

A BALLADE OF JACK HARE (also A SATYRICAL BALLAD) [89].
Ten eight-line stanzas ababbcbc with varying refrain, including envoy.

A sluggard knave who can pluck the lining out of a bowl, this boy Maymond, the son of Idleness, is the brother of every vice; he talks and drinks too much, snatches purses, and is the worst there can be. He is a truant who plays dice and spends his winnings on ale. Health to Maymond and his lousy pate: he is unthrifty, unwashed, and unlaced. You are the best of your kind, and you snore like a hog; so health to you who can drink so much ale.

This poem has been said to show the influence of Chaucer and the *Disciplina Clericalis*. The last three stanzas are probably spurious.

JESUS TO BLESSED VIRGIN ROSE OF WOMANHOOD (also THE CHILD JESUS TO MARY THE ROSE) [90]. Three rime royal stanzas with varying refrain.

Because of your meekness, My Father sent His spirit into your breast, Rose of Womanhood, so that I now play with roses before you and rejoice in your presence. Benign mother, Rose of Judah, I rejoice in your presence. Among My wounds there are five roses which conquer the Fiend to save mankind.

LEGEND OF DAN JOOS (also **THE MONK WHO HONORED THE VIRGIN**) [91]. Twenty rime royal stanzas.

O well of sweetness whose Nativity saved mankind from death, give me a drop of thy grace so that my ineptitude may not deface your miracle as I retell it. Vincent tells how a monk once heard a bishop recite five Latin psalms in honor of the flower that gave birth to Jesus. The monk memorized these psalms and recited them daily. One night, when the monk, Dan Joos, was missing at prayer time, his superior went to his cell, where he found him dead with five roses in his mouth, nose, and ears, and the name Maria was written in gold on them. After seven days, three famous bishops saw the miracle and said praise to the heavenly Judge and His mother. Never did I hear of such joy as occurred when they told the story of this holy monk. O fresh lovers who live in duplicity, give up your blind fantasies and write your poems to Maria so that you may earn heaven. She is so perfect that she pities all human beings. Benign lady, reward them as you did Dan Joos.

This poem has been considered one of Lydgate's more pleasant works.

ORISON ON THE FIVE JOYS (also **TO MARY THE STAR OF JACOB** and **AN ORISON TO THE BLESSED VIRGIN OF THE FIVE JOYS**) [92]. Seven rime royal stanzas.

O Star of Jacob, let your stream of grace shine upon me for the joy of the Annunciation. Save me in the name of your joy at the Nativity, and protect me tonight in the name of your joys at the Ascension, the Assumption, and the Resurrection. I shall kneel to you nightly in humility. I stand assured against spiritual enemies while I remember your five joys.

ON THE FIVE JOYS (also **TO MARY QUEEN OF HEAVEN**) [93]. Ten eight-line stanzas ababbcbc and one four-line stanza abba, including envoy; refrain in stanzas 1–7, varying refrain in 8–10, and none in 11.

Queen of Heaven, Empress of Hell, Lady of this World, look down with mercy on your servants who pray to your five joys. Celestial Cypress, Yard of Aaron, Rose of Jericho, Judith the Second, pray for your servants who pray to your five joys. You were shown to St. John in the Apocalypse; green olive, help your servants in the name of your son's Passion and His five wounds. Go, little poem, and pray to this pure Virgin that she may enlighten us who are bound to remember the five joys. Our hope lies in her whose five joys will be our salvation. When tempted, think of Christ's Passion.

THE FIFTEEN JOYS OF OUR LADY (also **FIFTEEN JOYS OF MARY**) [94]. 28 rime royal stanzas.

Blessed Lady, Princess of Mercy who bore Jesus Christ nine months and gave him the milk of your breasts, pray your Son to have mercy upon me so that I may do penance and receive the sacrament before death. Grant that I may kneel fifteen times before your image. O Queen of Heaven and Empress of Hell, you felt joy when Gabriel spoke to you; pray to your Son that I may please Him. For your joy at meeting Elizabeth, be my succor. For your joy at feeling your Son inside your body, be my defense. For your joy when Christ was born, when the shepherds found you, when the Three Kings visited you, when Simeon made his prophecy, when you found your Son in Jerusalem, when the water was turned into wine, when Christ fed 5000 with five loaves, when your Son endured the Passion for us, when He was resurrected, when He ascended, when the Holy Ghost came down from above, and when your Assumption occurred, pray your Son that I may confess and have full remission of my sins before death. Have mercy upon my friends, my kindred, and all those who love you.

THE FIFTEEN JOYS AND SORROWS OF OUR LADY (also THE FIFTEEN JOYS AND SORROWS OF MARY) [95]. 45 rime royal stanzas including envoy.

Between midnight and the gray morning, I opened a book in which I found a meditation with a picture of Mary, and accounts of her fifteen joys and fifteen sorrows were marked off in red and black. I saw someone kneel and recite a *Pater Noster* and ten *Ave*'s at the end of each ballade. The sight did my heart such good that I wrote these ballades as they stand here. Blessed Branch that sprang from Jesse, pray for your servants in the name of the joy which you felt when the angels served you, when Gabriel came to you, when Elizabeth met with you, when your chastity was made clear, when you bore Jesus Christ, when the Three Kings brought you gifts, when you escaped Herod's power, when you found your Son in Jerusalem, when Jesus turned water into wine, when He rose from the dead, when He ascended, when Gabriel brought you a palm from Jesus, when the apostles came to you, and Jesus Christ sent angels to convey you to Heaven.

Just as you have heard the joys, so were the fifteen sorrows following in order thereafter with prayers in between, and I have reproduced them with quaking pen. God grant that I may not displease her. O glorious maid, you endured sorrow when you were forced to marry, when your chastity was questioned, when Simeon said that a sword would pierce your heart, when Christ was left behind in Jerusalem, when Jesus called you a woman, when Jesus was taken by the Jews, when you were not permitted to see your Son, when Jesus bore the cross to Calvary, when you saw Jesus' hands and feet nailed on the Cross, when Jesus spoke to you from the Cross, when Jesus cried out to His Father and gave up the ghost, when you saw Jesus taken down after the Crucifixion, when He was laid in the grave: have mercy on us. These sorrows are set down here, O merciful Queen, so that we may know what Christ suffered for us. Let all those who would serve Mary remember this compilation although it is lame in meter and eloquence. Go, little treatise: accept criticism, and ask the authors thereof to correct you where you have failed.

A SONG OF JUST MESURE (also ALLE THYNGES IN MESURE and ON MODERATION) [96]. Thirteen eight-line stanzas ababbcbc with varying refrain.

Ancient authors write that nothing is praised unless it be done according to the proper measure. Music, carpentry, etc., etc., require measure. When measure is missing, justice turns into madness. A Scottish hare similar to a griffin would be out of proportion. The proverb says that measure is treasure, and this principle applies to rhetoric, poetry, medicine, etc., etc. Lack of measure yields tyranny; the cook seasons by measure, and measure is needed in peace and war. He is blessed who does everything according to measure: you will receive the same measure as you give others.

HYMN TO SS. KATHERINE, MARGARET, AND MAGDALENE (also DE TRIBUS VIRGINIBUS KATARINA MARGARETA ET MAGDALENA) [97]. Four eight-line stanzas ababbcbc.

Katherine and Margaret, make heavenly grace shine upon us; Mary Magdalene, pray Jesus for us. Lord, grant us remission of our sins in the name of these three women, and have mercy on us for the love of them.

THE THREE KINGS OF COLOGNE [98]. Fragment of 123 rime royal stanzas with two lines of first stanza missing.

... They never ceased for either wind or rain, and they went to the highest mountain in the East to seek the star that would announce the birth of Him Who should guide the world. The star appeared brighter than any other; it was like the sun, and in it they saw a child holding a cross. They heard a voice saying that the King of the Jews was born and that they should go and worship Him. Your work, O Lord, is marvelous; You are God and You are born in a stall. Multitudes had come to the city to pay tribute to Caesar, so that Joseph and Mary could find no room except that stall where the King of Glory was born. The shepherds saw and heard the angels sing, so that they came to Bethlehem, and the ox and the ass worshipped Him. In India, clerks informed three kings that the King was born: His star betokens the birth of the Savior. At that time there were three kings–Melchior, Balthasar, and Caspar–who lived in different parts of far-away India, and they came with rich presents for the King: gold and valuables because He was human and incense because He was God. While they travelled, the star guided them and people marvelled at them. They reached Jerusalem separately on the thirteenth day, and the star vanished under a cloud.

Melchior waited on Calvary, and Balthasar went to the village of Galilee, but the star had vanished when the cloud dissipated. King Caspar also arrived, and the three met and saluted each other, for each one understood the others' languages. The star still did not appear, and they wondered where the King of the Jews might be. They said this is the place, this is the King's home; and their presence and their words greatly disturbed Herod, for he knew that the Jews did not like him. When he decided to find a remedy and inquired where Christ should be born, the princes of the law said it would be in Bethlehem. Then he called the three kings and asked them to let him know when and where He would be born so that he might go worship Him, but he really wanted to avenge himself on God: O false Herod, O blind Jews, who will ever forgive you? O cursed king and cursed people! As the three kings left town, the star was shining brighter than the sun. They recognized it, and it took them where Christ was born. As it stood still above the house, the three kings entered and reverently offered Him their treasures, thanking Him because they knew that He was both God and man. I cannot rehearse their joy and the honor they did to the Child and Virgin. They spent the day in prayer and provided food and drink. O blissful Lord, none can resist Your will; You have the power to make a star, but man is simple. O little Child, You can make the stars Your subjects. O mighty Lord, where are the men of Your household, except for Joseph and Your mother: will You be found in Your ox stall? O little house, the King of Glory lies within your walls, and the kings of the Orient kneel before Him. O noble kings, well ought you to be glad; now go to sleep, for you must leave in the morning to spread the word.

Guided by an angel, they escaped Herod and made their way back toward their respective countries. They retell the glorious event as they travel; their fame will last forever throughout India. They reach their homes in two years' time. To worship the King of the Jews, they soon built a chapel on the mountain whence they first saw the star; they promised to visit the moutain once a year, and they chose that place for their sepulture. They visited thirty years in a row, until the Passion, after which St. Thomas came, baptized them, and consecrated the chapel. By the mountain, they built a city, where Prester John still resides and where St. Thomas remains the spiritual guide. Then Thomas made the three kings bishops, caused the Mohammedan temples to be abandoned and priests to be ordained to baptize and preach the Gospel. Where he was martyred, people are now born with dog faces. After his death, the three kings endowed churches, and the people thus taught became firm in the true faith. The three kings go on working from year to year in perfect humility.

They thus remained simple and humble all their lives, and they lived in chastity without wives or children, but they trained spiritual sons, so that they are considered the originators of their nation although they lived in virginity. A year before their deaths, they gathered the lay and religious leaders in St. Thomas' place to select a spiritual governor, whom they named Thomas in honor of the saint and whom they obey as we do the Pope. The noble kings also gave the temporal power to a clerk who had come with Thomas, and they ordered the appointment of someone with power to chastise those who stray from the faith or doubt the doctrine. This temporal lord is called Prester John to emphasize the importance of priesthood: because priests wield God's power but lay rulers are lower in dignity, the governor is called priest rather than king or emperor; and he is called John after the Evangelist, who was the best of his time. Thus the three kings followed Thomas' advice and spent their lives in prayer until a star appeared at the Feast of the Nativity to let them know that the end of their natural days was nearing. They prepared their tombs for the last passage. At the age of 150, King Melchior died at Mass on the eighth day after Christmas, Balthazar died five days later at the Epiphany, and Caspar followed on the day of the funeral service: the three friends are buried side by side on earth and are together in Heaven with the God who reigns in three persons. Their corpses remained in perfect condition until heresy began spreading, at which time their flesh began disintegrating, and the wicked Nestorians took Caspar's remains back to the island of his birth.

St. Elene went to Greece 234 years after the birth of Christ, obtained the two bodies from Prester John and Patriark Thomas, and sent to India to retrieve Caspar's body from the Nestorians, who exchanged it for St. Thomas's corpse, so that the three friends came together again. She placed them in St. Sophia along with the relics of Christ and Mary which she had brought from Jerusalem. She had also visited His birthplace in Bethlehem, where the Jews scorned that house and kept it sealed until her visit. The three kings and the mementos of Christ remained in Constantinople until King Charles of France brought them home with him. After Elene's death, Julian turned against the Church, heresy began spreading, and the Greeks rebelled against Rome, so that Constantine's corpse lay in neglect and the Saracens took over until the Roman Emperor restored the land to the Greeks. It eventually befell that a learned Greek clerk became Bishop of Milan and secured permission to bring the three kings there. In time Milan rebelled against Emperor Frederick, who took the city with the help of the Bishop of Cologne. The three kings were then transferred to Cologne, where the inhabitants received them with joy and solemnity. Their three corpses now lie in one tomb, and they perform daily grace in the name of Him whom they sought in Bethlehem.

The authorship of this poem is considered at best doubtful.

CHARTERS OF THE KINGS OF ENGLAND (also CARTAE VERSIFICATAE) [99]. 98 rime royal stanzas.

Canute's Charter. In the name of the Monarch of Heaven to Whose power all powers must obey, Whose bounties are incomparable, etc., etc., I, King Canute, on the advice of the local spiritual lords, decree that the Monks of St. Benedict shall dwell permanently in Bury, where they shall have full lordship and where no bishop or anyone may interfere with them. This decree is in the name of holy Edmund, martyr and virgin, whom King Edmund worshiped because they bore the same name. I, Canute, am likewise moved by the martyr, and I want his church to prosper through taxes and subsidies from the town. I shall myself give yearly alms to the convent. May anyone who tries changing this status against my intention suffer damnation. Men may see that this charter was confirmed by the lords of the land, as well as by two archbishops, six bishops, etc., etc.

Hardecanute's Charter. In the name of the Holy Trinity, here follows the franchise which King Hardecanute gave to St. Edmund: It is a terrible thing that worldly men concern themselves only with false riches despite the lessons of holy saints. I accordingly believe that we should heed the Gospel and endow the Church faithfully, for kings ought by custom to maintain the Church, for the Lord will reward us as we have deserved. Keeping these things in mind and recalling how my father endowed the church of Bury so that the monks may dwell there permanently, I, Hardecanute, want to insure that neither bishop nor nobleman may ever interfere, and I do so especially for the health of my father's and my mother's souls. May anyone who presumes to break this decree be doomed to hell for eternity. I, Hardecanute, confirm this donation with the sign of the cross; I, Emma, Hardecanute's mother, also confirm it with a cross, and I, Bishop Egelnold, etc., etc. Now everyone who sees this charter will want to abide by it.

Edward's Charter. I, King Edward, make known to all my vassals my will that Canute's charter be respected, that the monastery be the property of the monks, that no bishop have any power over them, that the monks be free to choose their own abbot, and that nobody may hinder their freedom. May anyone who transgresses be accursed. I send my wishes for health and welfare to all my barons, and I forbid that any bishop be so hardy as to injure the church despite the protection which my predecessors and I have provided. Those who read this charter should be careful not to offend St. Edward.

William the Conqueror's Charter. In his charter, this worthy Duke of Normandy and King of England notifies the archbishops, bishops, earls, etc., etc. here assembled of the controversy whereby Bishop Arfast has attempted to trespass against the jurisdiction and royal freedom of St. Edmund. The abbot wisely explained how King Canute had given the monks a perpetual charter, how the first abbots were consecrated, and how they had been granted perpetual independence from bishops by three kings. Then the Archbishop of York, the Earl of Kent, and my brother Odo decreed that the charter should stand, and all the lords present gave assent. I concur and command that Bishop Arfast and his successor should never again transgress: no bishop shall have dominion over the town or the church where St. Edmund lies enshrined. I, William, have ratified this with a cross, and I, Mathilda, have confirmed it, and I, Lanfranc, etc., etc. There were three saints as well as many others among the bishops present.

There is agreement on the probability but not the certainty of the authorship of this poem.

VERSES ON THE KINGS OF ENGLAND, FIRST REDACTION (also THE KINGS OF ENGLAND SITHEN WILLIAM CONQUEROUR) [100]. Fifteen rime royal stanzas.

This mighty William, made King of Brutus' Albion by conquest, put out Harold and took possession. Next came his son, William Rufus, who is buried at Winchester, and then his brother Henry I, who reigned 33 years and upon whose death his cousin Stephen sailed to England to be crowned by the archbishop. Henry II, son of the Empress, was crowned next, followed by Richard I, John, Henry III, Edward I, Edward II, Edward III, Richard II, Henry IV, Henry V, and Henry VI.

MS Harley 2251 (see MS 22, Bibliography) has an additional stanza on Edward IV. This poem is believed to have been written to accompany portraits.

VERSES ON THE KINGS OF ENGLAND, SECOND REDACTION WITH 15 INTRODUCTORY STANZAS (also THE KINGS OF ENGLAND SITHEN WILLIAM CONQUEROUR) [101]. 30 rime royal stanzas.

We are told that 224 kings reigned between the time of Brutus and devout Alfred, who reigned 29 years. Next in order came his son Edward, who repaired churches and was followed by Athelstan, who made great donations to churches, followed by Edmund, Edreed, Edwyne, Edgar, Edward, Egelreed, Edmund, Canute, Harald Harfoot, Hardecanute, St. Edward, Harold. This mighty William . . . .

See [100] for summary of the remainder.

VERSES ON THE KINGS OF ENGLAND, THIRD REDACTION IN COUPLETS (also THE KINGS OF ENGLAND SITHEN WILLIAM CONQUEROUR) [102]. 92 couplets and one eight-line stanza ababbcbc.
See [100] for summary.

ON KISSING AT VERBUM CARO, FIRST VERSION [103]. Four eight-line stanzas ababbcbc.

Devout people who kiss stone, wood, earth, or iron in church, think on the Cross and the Passion for which these things stand, and lift up your heart toward the East when the priest says *verbum caro factum est*.

For remarks, see the second version, [104] below.

ON KISSING AT VERBUM CARO, SECOND VERSION (also A CALL TO DEVOTION) [104]. Four eight-line stanzas ababbcbc.

Roughly the same outline as the first version [103] except that lines 12–16 contain different illustrations.

On Kissing at Verbum Caro seems to form a sequence with *An Exortacion to Prestys* [45] and *Interpretacio Misse* [87], the latter of which contains a third and totally different version thereof. The three poems have been printed together under the title of *Poems on the Mass*.

LAMENTACIOUN OF OUR LADY MARIA (also QUIS DABIT MEO CAPITI FONTEM LACRIMARUM) [105]. Nineteen eight-line stanzas ababbcbc with varying refrain.

Who shall give me a well of bitter tears to show my sorrow at the sight of my Son bleeding on a cross? Who shall give me enough weeping for the blood of my sweet Son on the cross? The Jews have done me wrong in crucifying my sweet Son. Have compassion upon my sighs, O daughters of Jerusalem; and you, ladies and virgins, go see the wounds of your true Spouse and remember His dreadful victory and my sorrow. How should I restrain my weeping? O unkind people, see the Lord of Heaven and Hell crucified. It is no wonder though I swoon; I can hardly stand, for my pains exceed all torments old and new: my dear Son wore a crown of thorns and was crucified for mankind; He was slain for Adam's sin. Because of His love for mankind, He was offered in sacrifice like a lamb. He might be called Eleazar the second, or Hercules, and He conquered death with death. Let every man and woman see His bleeding wounds and trust in His mercy, and I shall kneel before Him and be mediator for all mankind.

This poem was once attributed to Chaucer.

A TRETISE FOR LAVANDRES (stanza 3 often printed separately as ON WINE; also TREATISE FOR LAUNDRESS) [106]. Three rime royal stanzas with two Latin lines forming another stanza before the last.

You who are duly paid to care for my lady's attire, look to it that you wash her clothes clean from stains. Wash wine stains in milk, and oil spots in lye.

The Latin lines are found printed separately as *On Wine*.

LETABUNDUS [107]. 39 eight-line stanzas ababbcbc.

Through lineal descent from the time of Abraham and the patriarchs, *Letabundus* has been the proper hymn to sing at the feast of the Virgin, and the chorus of prophets in Heaven likewise sings it for the empress named Mary to express joy for Him Who was born in Bethlehem and is named Immanuel. These prophets ask you to sing also how Gabriel brought the news that the King of Kings would be born of a maid, as David had prophesied, and the prophets and patriarchs rejoiced. It is your duty to sing *Letabundus*. The Angel of Counsel spoke to Tobit and later came down with the key of David to set His throne in a pure maid, the Star of the Sea. Malachis calls Him the Sun of Righteousness, and Mary shines like a star in virginity and motherhood: O Blessed Queen, let your light shine on us. The shepherds rejoiced at the star that had brought three kings to Bethlehem, and worshipers should sing *Letabundus* to celebrate this feast. The cedar and the hyssop together symbolize the union of the Old and New Testament: Christ came like the green plants in March, and His blood is the red thread that binds these trees in Leviticus. Christ was the word of the Highest, as Isaiah sang in the synagogue and as the Sibyl's verses tell us despite the pride of the Jews: why will you not believe, unhappy people? Prophecy told of the Nativity and was fufilled in Mary. Now, all people present should remember *Letabundus*.

LIFE OF OUR LADY (the MAGNIFICAT also printed separately) [108]. Six books totalling 836 rime royal stanzas and (the *Magnificat* in Bk. 2) ten eight-line stanzas ababbcbc.

Book I. O thoughtful hearts plunged in distress, look at the light of the fair Star of Jacob that surpasses even the Pleiades; and you, Star of all Stars, shed the liquor of your grace into my pen as I begin my praise of you with an account of your birth. Flower of Virtue which saved man from death, this flower, O Nazareth, makes your name more royal than Rome or Troy: therefore, rejoice that the Holy Ghost would rest on this flower, for this is the rose and the lily that God beheld and whose birth the angel announced when he told Joachim and Anne that their virgin daughter would be chosen of God. Nine months later, at the birth of this pure maid, the night of death was dissipated; and as Minerva is both a virgin and the mother of patience, so this Heavenly Queen eventually proved both a mother and a virgin. At the age of three, she was taken to the temple, where she immediately ascended the fifteen steps to the high altar, so that her mother vowed to let her live in the temple to be guided by the Holy Ghost. The maid's thought was wholly on God; her conversation was serious and demure, she spent most of her time in prayer, and an angel would come down to bring her food at noon, so that she gave to the poor the normal food given her. Her face was brighter than the sun, and she surpassed Helen of Troy, Dido, Judith, etc., etc. in both beauty and perfection. As St. Anselm says, she was a daughter of David by descent, as well as God's servant and spouse, and she received seven gifts from the Holy Ghost: fear of the Lord, pity, knowledge, fortitude, prudence, understanding, and wisdom. She was also the throne void of sin, strong in virtue, full of compassion, etc., etc. I find it written that this maid of Nazareth said seven prayers each day, begging the Lord to give her grace to observe the First Commandment, to love her neighbor, to please the Lord, to be humble, that she may see and worship the chosen virgin who will bear the Son, to obey His statutes, and to see that the temple be kept from harm and that His people be virtuous. Thus did this Virgin spend her time until she reached the age of thirteen and was to leave the temple and be married to a bishop's son, but she preferred to keep her vow of virginity. The bishops then decided to find a keeper for Mary, and, when a dove landed on Joseph's yardstick, they knew he should have her, and they blessed him accordingly. She was immediately assigned to him, but he had to be persuaded that it was the will of God, for he was worried by his own advanced age. Five maidens came with her and did chores, but Mary cared for the purple silk, whose color belongs only to a king, for Heaven meant her to be the mother of the King who would spread His banner of purple on Calvary to redeem mankind. Now I leave this blissful virgin in Nazareth, where she leads a life too perfect for description and thus provides an example for all of us. The house where you lived was blessed, as was the table where you ate and those who beheld you there. Who can tell the melody that angels made in your holy place? I am too inept to tell these things, and I stand at your mercy, my Lady for whom I have compiled this first book, beseeching those who read it to forgive my mistakes.

Book II. Whoever is fettered in prison thinks about deliverance, and whoever languishes in exile and knows no means of escaping death thinks of old felicity while waiting for grace. Who could tell of greater joy than the man who was created to dwell in paradise? But he was banished into hell and must abide in prison, for he has so lost his honor, his joy, and his wellbeing that, when Mercy would have granted him a pardon, Justice denied it, and, when Peace would have redeemed him, Truth flatly said he could get no grace. These four were assembled to discuss this matter and argued back and forth until Mercy and Peace brought the problem before the King of Glory and spoke in the heavenly consistory: remember, Lord, that mercy always abides with You, and take into Your grace the woeful caitiff who has so long been away from Your face; give him now remission from thraldom. The Judge gave benign audience but said that Justice and Truth must also be consulted, and Truth spoke openly: if it be true that this sinner has not died for his iniquity, then my sister and I have been deprived of both freedom and jurisdiction unless he be punished; and Peace is doing us wrong in trying to help him against our wish. Then Justice spoke: though he were my brother, he must die unless someone else dies in his place. Mercy, however, argued that the death of a sinner is no pleasing sacrifice to God, so that the death of an innocent must be devised, for rust may not be scoured with rust, and Biblical tradition shows that he who would die for man's ransom must be as pure as a lamb; this request is not against either Justice or Truth, and our Judge may thus satisfy them while helping man. Now the High Judge mercifully inclined to condescend, and He finally said that a pure innocent should meekly die to pay the ransom for man's transgression: My own Son shall be sent down to wrap Himself in the mortal nature of man, and He shall build His palace in a virgin on whose lap the unicorn shall sleep and to whom Gabriel shall now bring the news. Without wasting time, the angel came down to deliver his message, and St. Bernard later composed a poem on the subject, which I am unworthy to repeat. Gabriel told the Virgin that a child should be conceived within her womb by the Holy Ghost and that He should be named Jesus. Thus was pride vanquished by humility. She was the castle whose crystal wall no one might open; she was the gate which Ezekiel saw in his vision; she was the urn in which was kept the manna of our salvation; she was the woman whom St. John saw in Heaven and who represented the first wall of Holy Church. O blind man, why will you not see how Jesus could come through the gate without breaking it and thus be born of a perfect virgin. Just as Pliny speaks of a place where the earth is so virtuous that it will heal any wound, so Mary was chosen of God to bear the fruit of our redemption. Although she remained cold to the flesh, she burnt with love and could thus be both virgin and mother: I hold him mad who would dispute this point, for He who created the world with a word can also create a virgin mother just as He showed the flaming bush to Moses, made Balaam's ass speak, fed a multitude with five loaves, etc., etc. Just as the phoenix can regenerate himself after burning down to ashes, so the Lord took flesh and blood within a virgin to regenerate our sinful kind. If anyone doubts Mary's virginity, I can only ask mercy for his great offence. Mary went out of Nazareth to tell the news to Elizabeth, who was also pregnant and called her blessed among women, and she sang as follows: My soul magnifies the Eternal Lord, my spirit rejoices for He has noticed the humility of His handmaid; He is mighty in His magnificence; His mercy is immense toward those who fear Him; He has humbled tyrants and exalted the humble, etc., etc. After she had completed this song and Elizabeth had given birth to John the Baptist, Mary remained there three months, living in contemplation and burning with the love of God. When Joseph, who had been practicing his carpenter's craft in Capernaum, returned to Nazareth, he was greatly puzzled at finding his wife pregnant, and he spoke thus: What shall I say now that she is with child, God knows, not by me? I shall never accuse her of breaking her vow of chastity, but have mercy, O Lord, and help me reconcile my conviction that she is innocent with the fact that no woman has ever conceived without a man. Joseph then burst out in tears, but the maidens in attendance on Mary consoled him and vouched for her chastity. He would nevertheless have gone away, but an angel of the Lord appeared to him in his sleep and so changed his mind that upon waking up he declared that his night of error had turned into day. In time the bishops heard that Mary was with child, and they summoned Joseph, who assured them that she was still a virgin, but they decided to test them both with the water of jealousy, the drinking of which changes the complexion of the guilty. Since the truth need not pull in its horns but shines like the sun, they were proved innocent; before drinking, Mary prayed to God to let His grace rain down from Heaven and make an open demonstration of her chastity. Thereupon the people began to fear punishment for their previous distrust, and threw themselves on the ground to kiss her feet, but she returned to her chamber to wait her day with the Holy Ghost for her guide. Only with her support shall I be able to go on with this poem, for the rhetoric of Tully and Petrarch is dead, and my master Chaucer is dead, who might have corrected the errors of my inept pen, so that I shall have to proceed without his help. Be you my guide, O chaste tower of the Holy Ghost.

Book III. When all was hushed and all was silence, Your Word, O Lord, suddenly descended upon earth to shed light for our salvation 5199 years after the creation of the world, when Augustus ordered a census for the purpose of taxation, and during the reign of Herod Joseph and Mary went to Bethlehem to pay their taxes. As they were going along, Mary suddenly said that she could see two people on the road and that one was rejoicing while the other was complaining, but Joseph could see no such thing and told her to hold her peace. Then an angel appeared and reproached him with his conduct: the two people whom Mary saw were the Jews bemoaning the coming demise of the Synagogue and the Pagans welcoming the approach of the time of grace. In Bethlehem Joseph and Mary could find no better lodging than a little stall in a stable. No sooner had Mary entered therein than a light far brighter than the sun began shining upon her; and the Son was born there about midnight totally painlessly and without any assistance, for Joseph had gone out to look for midwives. When Joseph and the midwives returned, they found Jesus in the stall with the ox and the ass and Mary praying to Him as both her child and our Savior, and the midwives were afraid of the great light therein. Balaam had prophesied that a star should arise from the line of Jacob, and a star shone above the ox stall at the Nativity. Now Mary humbly asked the midwives in, and they saw the beasts kneeling before the Child and perceived that He was born without offence to virginity and that the milk He was suckling was sent from Heaven. When one of them presumed to touch the Child without the proper devotion, however, her arm immediately died, but she begged for forgiveness and was made whole again. While these things were going on, a star appeared to shepherds in the field, and an angel told them to seek the newborn Savior in Bethlehem. After singing for joy, they did as they were told, and the hymn *Gloria in Excelsis Deo* celebrates the event. It is a wondrous thing that God chose to be born on earth to save what was lost and that a virgin could become a mother. Isaiah had asked the Lord to send down a lamb to save us, and David had also prayed to the Lord, as had Solomon, etc., etc., and Jacob had prophesied that the world should find salvation in One born of Mary, who is like a garnet apple. In Egypt, Joseph had also foreseen the event, for it was known that the Lamb of God should come to slay the lion, and now the prophesies have been fulfilled through the miracle of a virgin mother. At the Nativity, the Temple of Apollo in Rome tumbled down in accordance with a prediction that it would do so when a child would be born of a virgin; and the water of a well was turned into oil and ran into the Tiber as the wise Sibyl had said it would when the Savior would be born. The Senate wanted to proclaim Emperor Octavian a god, but he saw a circle of gold around the sun and therein a virgin holding a child in her arms; when the Sibyl explained the phenomenon, the Emperor worshipped at the altar and declined deification because he understood that there could be only one god. At the same time in Engedi, the vines produced balm instead of wine, and in Egypt the false idols fell to the ground. The Romans had erected a huge brass statue which they called God, but the sculptor told them that it would stand only until a virgin gave birth to a child before Whom Rome would humbly bow, and the Sibyl said that the child's mother would be of the Hebrew race and that He would be both God and man together. Obediah prophesied that One would come to Judea to be the joy and salvation of mankind, and Baruch also prophesied His coming, as did Daniel, etc., etc. We read in Esdras that a woman is superior to wine or a king since the Holy Ghost would fructify a pure virgin for the salvation of mankind. Now He is born, the rightful Heir who will rebuild Jerusalem, which the tyrant Herod falsely rules. O my Lady, how rich God has made you! You alone have what the angels desire, and, as St. Augustine writes, we must ask you, Flower of Virginity, not to spare your milk. How happy you are to have Him touch your breasts with His lips and feel your mouth and eyes with His finger, for here is the remedy for venom brought into the world when the snake made Adam dine on the apple. Your milk is like manna, which is the food of angels, O fair Rose of Jericho who brought into the world Him Who is both God and man. Now, fair Cedar, Cypress of Zion, etc., etc., you are named the Glory of Jerusalem, and are the soil of our salvation. Grant that your servants may sing, pray, and serve you in honor of your Son on the Feast of the Nativity; and, my Lady, think of your men this month of December.

Book IV. Early in January, I began thinking upon the Feast of the Circumcision. Luke tells how the Child wept when He was circumcised seven days after the Nativity, and His mother burst into tears; and Alcuin writes that He was circumcised four times: with the knife of poverty at the Nativity, with an actual knife at the Circumcision, with the knife of adversity while He lived as a man, and finally when He suffered the Passion. Christ still suffers four kinds of circumcision in the world through detraction, through the deeds of men without conscience, through the deeds of heretics who disobey Holy Church, and through the bloody deeds of tyrants who act against the Faith. He also shed His blood five times during His lifetime: upon the Circumcision, when He sweated blood on the hill before the Passion, when He was tied to a pillar by the Jews, when He was nailed on the Cross for our good, and when His heart was pierced by a spear on Calvary. Upon the Circumcision, He was given the name of Jesus, but my wit is too inept to elaborate on the worth of that name, which has been sacred from eternity and which is certain comfort against all diseases. St. Bernard says that this name refreshes the world like the four streams of sapience, righteousness, holiness, and redemption. It is the name specified by prophets and magnified by the apostles, and it enabled the martyrs to endure their passions with firm hearts and to win victory. It is the feast of virginity and the oil of grace which has anointed prophets, priests, kings, and champions, and we must note that Jesus Christ was all four of these. O Jesus, I cry to You for Your daily help: let Your pity have mercy on us. You are both just and merciful, hence Your being called both a lamb and a lion. O Lord of Pity, have mercy on us on the Circumcision, save us from temptation, let Your name be our protection, and save those who have faith and trust in Your name.

Book V. O Lord, let Your light dispel my darkness to speak of Your Epiphany, and let me be touched by the majesty of the star which appeared to three kings at the Nativity as was predicted by Balaam. As a result of his prediction, twelve men watched from a hilltop to see the star that would annouce the birth of Christ. Three kings saw that star and followed it to the place where the King was born. In Jerusalem, their inquiries about the King of the Jews so troubled Herod that he summoned them and falsely said that he would go worship Him if they told him where He could be found. Just as a snake hides under flowers until he is ready to strike with venom, so you, Herod, practiced mortal deceit, but all in vain. Who can tell the joy of these kings when they saw the star shining over the house where the Child was born. They went in and humbly presented their gifts to the Child: gold as the proper tribute to a king, frankincense as the symbol of sacrifices to God, and myrrh as a token of the fact that He would die for mankind. How could anyone endure being proud after considering the meekness of her who was Queen of Heaven and Earth? O pride, root of our distress, take heed how humbly she behaved with three kings kneeling before her. Was there any cloth of gold to be found about her, or a palace, or silk? Note, you women with your pearls, how your queen wore no expensive fur and yet was the fairest to see, and give up your pride. Isolde, Helen, Dido are dead and forgotten, but not so the meekness of her who sat on the ground with her child. That night an angel warned the three kings to beware of Herod, and they returned home safely. The Feast of the Epiphany has especially miraculous powers because it coincides with four events in the life of Christ: the visit of the three kings, the baptism of Jesus by St. John, Jesus' turning the water into wine, and His feeding 5000 people with five loaves. Now Jesus, on this high feast we beseech You to protect us. During our pilgrimage make us strong against our enemies who would take from us through persecution the gold of perfect charity, for the day of truth has turned into night. Christ Jesus Who may amend all that, grant us the gold of faith on this High Feast, as well as the gold of love. And you, Blissful Queen who gave your Son the chaste milk of virginal cleanness, guide us toward the court of Heaven. What a thing it must be to see the Lord lying in a manger, and we feel comfort at the thought of the three kings kneeling before you. Now, in remembrance of that day when you were honored with gold and myrrh and frankincense, be our lodestar to eternal life when we shall leave this life.

Book VI. Glory unto you, O Blissful Queen who was God's chaste tower shut with the key of virginity and who never burned with fleshly heat! Although you were pure, you humbly came in due time to the temple to be purified, but the law applied only to mothers who had conceived through contact with a man, and these were to offer a lamb and a pigeon, or two doves if they were destitute. Despite the special prerogative that nature had given her, the Virgin humbly brought two doves to the temple, where old Simeon joyfully embraced the Child Jesus. The old man had been promised by the Holy Ghost that he should see Christ, and he had come to witness the Presentation. He held Him, prayed to Him, and declared himself ready to die in peace now that he had seen the Savior of Israel and of the world; and Mary and Joseph wondered as he predicted the Passion. Likewise, an old woman named Anna saw the Child Jesus in the temple, and she fell on her knees and openly proclaimed that our salvation was nearing. Now it seems to me proper that on this Feast of the Purification every man should be merry and offer both a turtle dove and a dove: the one stands for chastity and the other for humility, as shown by their actual behavior. This feast is also called Candlemas because the Romans used to take burning tapers to the Temple of Februa every fifth year on February 1 and went on doing so after adopting the Faith, but Pope Sergius had the idea of turning the custom into a means of honoring Our Lady, who is the best mediator between her Son and us. This feast also takes its name from the procession of Anna and Simeon when they met Him with great devotion when He took His flesh and blood from a meek Virgin in order to save us. On this occasion, all Christians must offer a taper uniting faith, work, and good intention, for the taper would be worthless without these three. Christ, let the sun of Your mercy shine upon us for the sake of the Virgin who went to the temple to present You; because of her prayers grant that we may hold our tapers before You when we die. Grant, O Lord, that while we are alive we may keep our tapers burning bright on this day from year to year in honor of the Queen to whom this feast is dedicated. Blessed Queen, protect your servants on the Feast of Candlemas.

This poem, whose popularity is attested by its 47 extant manuscripts and several early prints, has been said to owe much to St. Bernard and St. Bonaventura and to reflect the influence of Chaucer. It has also been evaluated by different critics as a dull piece of work and as a high point in the history of English religious writings, and it contains what is perhaps Lydgate's best known encomium of Chaucer.

LOOK IN THY MEROUR (also LYDGATE'S PROVERBS) [109]. 27 eight-line stanzas ababbcbc with slightly varying refrain, including envoy.

Toward the end of frosty January a thrush flew to the front of my study and spoke to me: Look in your mirror and do not judge others. Even the bright peacock ought to look at his own feet to control his pride; the royal eagle must come down after flying high; the beautiful swan has black feet and beak in token of mourning; the hardy lion must eventually lose his strength. The tiger is swift, the fox preys on chickens, etc., etc.; everyone has something but nobody has everything. Though you have power, obey the Scriptures and do not oppress the poor; a beggar raised to worldly dignity is like an ass raised to royalty. Tyrants are like ferocious beasts, and humble people are like peaceful beasts; some people are friendly and some cantankerous; some are impatient and some patient, etc., etc. Nobody is free of blemish, and opposites do not agree, so that a poor man ought not to be proud. Some men are false and others deceitful, for nature can create both Thersites and Hector, and one man may be just as strong as another is weak, but the rose grows on thorns and there is seldom a clear day without a cloud. Let each one try to avoid pride and cultivate humility in himself. Vicious men find evil in others while they ought to look in their mirror. All men are sinful, so that judges ought to look in their mirror before allowing the sword to punish the culprit. Go little book, and ask your readers to have mercy on John Lydgate and look in their mirror.

This poem has been said to be reminiscent of John Gower and to reflect the influence of the classics, the Bestiary, Isidore of Seville, and Chaucer.

A LOVER'S LAMENT (also MY LADY DERE and THOMAS CHAUCER'S COMPLAINT) [110]. Sixteen eight-line stanzas ababbcbc with slightly varying refrain, including envoy.

Every natural creature is happiest where the source of his pleasure resides, and I live in sorrow except when I see my beloved lady. Elsewhere, I feel like a man thinking of Heaven while in purgatory. The sun and the stars shine beautifully, but I cannot enjoy them except when I am with my beloved lady. Then I feel as though the black clouds can no longer hide the beams of Phebus, and I forget my sorrow. I rejoice like the birds in May or like the beasts playing in the forests and the marshes. When I do not see her, however, my heart is struck by death just as a fish out of water must die: the ruby is best in the gold ring, the daisies grow in the sun, etc., etc., and I am happy when I see my beloved lady. When I part from her, the sky grows dark and I wear black till I see her again: let me see her soon again, Immortal God. Go, little letter, and pray the sovereign of my heart to show enough pity to be my sovereign beloved lady. Take the seventeenth letter of the ABC first and last around E, and you will see my beloved lady.

This poem has been considered a companion piece to *Complaint of the Black Knight* [23] and thought representative of the poetry of Thomas Chaucer's circle.

ADVICE TO LOVERS (also ADVICE TO AN OLD GENTLEMAN WHO WISHED FOR A YOUNG WIFE and PROHEMY OF A MARRIAGE BETWIX AN OLDE MAN AND A YONGE WIFE) [111]. 72 rime royal stanzas and an envoy of two eight-line stanzas ababbcbc.

A secular philosopher had a friend who had reached the age at which the mind grows unclear but who had been encouraged by flatterers to take a wife. When asked for advice, the philosopher answered as follows: My friend, as you are approaching dotage, you want to know whether you ought to marry an attractive young woman, and I urge you to think on Chaucer's story of May and January. Consider that you have only a few years left and are getting progressively feebler. You say that she is demure and loves you and that you cannot help yourself, but I tell you that you can indeed help yourself, and I remind you that many an old rooster sits on a dunghill while a younger one plays with the hens. You say that she will help you look after your property, but I say that you could find a man to do the same thing. Consider that your pitiful physical state is getting worse even though you pretend to feel well. You also argue that, since you practiced wantonness in youth, you need the sanction of marriage in old age, but I say that there are safer ways to holiness. You told me yourself the story of a woman who felt sexual fever nine times each night, so you can assume that a young woman will marry an old man only in hope that he may soon die and leave her free to turn to a young one. Furthermore, the two of you will constantly fight to determine who will be in charge, and I tell you that she will win the contest. Everyone knows the story of the woman who was widowed seven times but mourned only her last husband because she had no prospect of an eighth one: get a wife and you will soon lead the dance of death while a younger man—perhaps a servant whom you hated—will sleep in your nest. With a woman, you are deceived when you begin to trust. One recalls the tale of the old man who wanted to marry a young woman but confessed to her that he had three failings: he grew angry too fast, he grew angry without cause, and he was impotent. She declared that these failings were of no consequence since she had remedies for them, but they were hardly married before she began reproaching her husband with his failure to satisfy her erotic cravings. When he inquired about her remedies, she said that she could get angrier than he could, that she would give him plenty of causes for anger, and that she could use his possessions to procure a substitute for the erotic debt which he was unable to pay her. Thus the old man learned that beautiful apples are often rotten at the core, and I urge you to think about this man and old January. As for your possessions, you can use them for alms as well as leave them to your heir. Only he who cannot keep continent should heed St. Paul's advice that it is better to marry than to burn, but you are too old to need such frailties. Pray God that you may think on this little lesson. Go, little book, and be cautious, since you may displease jolly bodies that bring old men to their undoing; your words are true, and silly dotards should do their best to keep out of the snare.

This antimatrimonial poem, which concludes with the fabliau tale of December and January, explicitly cites Chaucer's *Merchant's Tale* and seems to refer to *The Wife of Bath's Tale* and possibly to other *Canterbury Tales*. Partly because of the lively tone of the speaking voice, the authorship is very much in doubt with scholars. The poem has received very little critical attention and has not been edited since 1840.

LIFE OF ST MARGARET [112]. 77 rime royal stanzas including an eleven-stanza prologue and an envoy of three stanzas with similar rimes and last word.

I intend to compile a life of St. Margaret to honor her, even though I have no rhetoric. We know, however, that a royal ruby may be wrapped in sackcloth, and I shall accordingly disregard my lack of eloquence in order to account for her holiness, chastity, and martyrdom. This daisy despised worldly glory to put all her faith in Christ, and she was named after a precious gem called margarite. Like a pearl, she was white through virginity, and she was small through humility, but she earned the heavenly palm through her triumph. She was a comfort to men because she vanquished the devil and sacrificed her flesh to the Lord Who died upon the cross for our redemption. O gem of gems, shed your aureate liquor upon my quaking pen to guide me as I err, and remember my Lady March, who ordered me to retell your martyrdom and virginity on the basis of French and Latin sources.

Born in Antioch of a father who was a Pagan patriarch, this blessed virgin was entrusted to a nurse who had her baptized very young, thus infuriating her father. By the age of fifteen, when she was a mirror of meekness generally beloved for her inner virtue, she kept her nurse's sheep in the pasture. The Prefect Olibrius happened by and was so taken by her beauty that he wondered who she could be and determined to have her as wife or concubine. When asked about her identity, she demurely answered that her name was Margaret and that she was a Christian intent upon living and dying in the Faith. The judge advised her that one of her nobility and beauty ought not to believe on Him Who died on the Cross, but she answered that He had shed His blood for our redemption, and the judge sent her to prison. Next day he urged her to return to the pagan gods, but she refused and was condemned to hang and be torn apart. While she was being tortured, the spectators begged her to save herself by recanting, but she called the judge an insatiable lion and explained that her soul would remain faithful though her body be rent to pieces, and he ordered her sent back to prison alive. There she prayed the Lord that she might see her enemy, and a fierce dragon named Satan appeared and swallowed her, but she crossed herself and burst out of his middle. He then turned himself into a man but was again defeated and begged for mercy. She then cast him down, put her foot upon his back, and told him to remember how he had been vanquished by the feminine power of a pure virgin. The serpent acknowledged that he had been vanquished by her innocence and lamented having been brought low by a woman rather than a man, especially since her parents had been devout followers of his. When she asked him how he attacked mankind, he answered that he acted strictly through lies and that he felt such envious hatred of virtue that he must continue seeking revenge against Heaven although knowing himself doomed to hell for eternity. After all, he knew that Solomon kept all the fiends inside a bottle until men broke it to look for a treasure and let them out again. The virgin then let the malicious serpent go, and he vanished. The next day she was stripped naked, burnt with brands, and thrown in boiling water, but an earthquake occurred, and 5000 spectators were converted, but the judge nevertheless ordered the virgin beheaded. She requested only enough time to pray, and her prayer was for her tormentors and for such people as would thereafter call to her for help, especially women in childbirth. From the mansion of Heaven a voice announced that God granted her prayer, and she spoke to the executioner: my dear brother, do not hesitate to smite. A holy saint has written about this virgin that she avoided anything evil and should stand as an example to all virgins, for she forsook father, mother, and life for Christ. Lift up your hearts, noble ladies, and pray to St. Margaret whenever you are sick or in trouble. Now, chaste gem, be a shield to your servants.

AGAINST MARRIAGE (also PAIN AND SORROW OF EVIL MARRIAGE and WARNING AGAINST MARRIAGE) [113]. Seventeen rime royal stanzas.

Glory be to God, John, Peter, and Lawrence, who have spared me the mortal pestilence of the yoke of marriage. I once thought of marrying a fair maiden on the advice of married men who obviously wanted another companion in their sorrow, but God saved me through the advice of three angels who rescued me from the perils of hell. John Chrysostom showed me that women were inconstant, and Peter confirmed that they were full of duplicity, unbearably bossy, always complaining, etc, etc., as well as prone to go on pilgrimages to kiss lusty young images rather than relics. In conclusion, there is no worse poison than wedlock. Therefore, young men, withdraw your foot before you fall in the snare.

This poem, whose authorship has been questioned, is based on Latin and French sources and is said to have influenced Dunbar.

MESOUR IS TRESOUR [114]. Nineteen eight-line stanzas ababbcbc.

Men long ago wrote that measure was treasure. Measure is the root of all good policy, and it causes popes and prelates to act properly in all respects. Power and possessions can do no good to emperors, kings, and other lords unless they act according to just measure, as is obvious from the fate of Alexander, who conquered the world but neglected measure. Hannibal and Scipio came to bad ends for lack of measure. Knighthood should support the Church and protect widows, maidens, and the poor, as well as work for the common good and punish those who work against just measure. Honest judges should practice mercy and measure, as well as heed God's truth and remember how Cambises departed from measure by oppressing the poor. Mayors and other officials should be guided by measure, as should merchants, artisans, various tradesmen, laborers, and plowmen. Just as shepherds watch over their flocks, so spiritual shepherds should watch over Christ's fold so that heretics may not quench the Faith and just measure. Isaac and Jacob were shepherds, and those who govern should follow their example to repress wrong, support right, and keep this house safe while allowing themselves to be guided by just measure.

This poem has been said to be intended to accompany a painting; its authorship has been questioned.

MIDSOMER ROSE (also ON THE MUTABILITY OF HUMAN AFFAIRS) [115]. Fifteen eight-line stanzas ababbcbc.

Let no man boast of virtue, wealth, knowledge, or anything worldly, for everything comes from Jesus and changes like a midsummer rose as the Lord pleases. The flower is sweet-smelling, the thorn is sharp, night differs from day, and everything changes like a midsummer rose. The flowers open in April and May, the cuckoo and the nightingale are different, as are the wolf and the lamb accused of muddying the water. All worldly things must change, such as the seasons or day and night. Where is David, where is Solomon, Julius, Tullius, Homer, the Peers of France, and the deeds of chivalry? The martyrs of Thebes are no more, but their martyrdom is remembered better than any midsummer rose. The memory of worthy knights is built upon righteousness, and high nobility is worthless without truth, but these martyrs' bloody torment was no mere summer rose but Jesus Himself, the Rose of Jericho Whose five roses printed a rose in your heart.

This poem is part of the ubi-sunt tradition and has been said to reflect the influence of the Bible, the *Legenda Aurea*, Seneca, Cicero, and others.

AGAINST MILLERS AND BAKERS [116]. Three eight-line stanzas ababbcbc.

Put out his head and arms. False bakers should be sent to the pillory, and a chapel should be built under it.

This poem has been considered typical of Lydgate's satire.

MISERICORDIAS DOMINI IN ETERNUM CANTABO (also PSALM 88) [117]. 24 eight-line stanzas ababbcbc with slightly varying refrain.

All creatures should sing songs in praise of the Lord, and this is why, O Lord, I shall sing Your mercies eternally as long as I live. David sang with his harp and slew Goliath with his meekness, and Jesus slew Satan with the humility of the Crucifixion and sang *Benedictus Dominus Meus*. There are songs of conquest and victory, but I prefer singing Your mercies eternally. Virgil sang of Aeneas, Dares of Hector; others sing of Hannibal, Bellerophon, and so forth, but I eternally sing of His mercies. People sing woeful tragedies and funny comedies, and the Muses sang of Mercury and Philology, while Circe turned men into beasts with song and the Sirens lured them with tunes, but I sing Your mercies. Deborah sang a canticle to the Lord, as did Anna, Moses, the three children in the fire, and Judith when she slew Olofernes, but I sing His mercies. Isaiah sang the *Confiteor* to save the people, and David sang, as did Hezekiah, Habakkuk, etc. Our Mediatrix, Mary, sang the *Magnificat*. Patriarchs, apostles, martyrs, bishops, women, maidens, etc. sing hosanna in Heaven. This is the best song, and I eternally sing Your mercies.

This poem has been noted for its many classical references.

MUMMING AT BISHOPSWOOD [118]. Sixteen rime royal stanzas including envoy.

Mighty Flora, the goddess of fresh flowers, has clothed the soil in lusty green for the delight of the estates assembled here. Spring has sent her own daughter to make vegetation grow and the birds sing now that winter is gone. Spring brings felicity to all the estates of this region: victory to princes and peace to the people. Winter shall pass, and buds of truth and unity shall exile duplicity so that all human beings will act according to their respective callings, and righteousness will repress extortion. These are the tidings of Spring, and Summer will soon follow: let her be welcome. May is here to present your Excellency with an abundance of fresh flowers. This princess has repaired the damage caused by Winter, and Zephyrus has carpeted the hills with red and white, while the nightingale now sings to defy Winter. The Muses sing on Parnassus, and May has come to bring happiness to your Highness.

The innovative form and presentation of this mumming have been the subject of scholarly investigation.

MUMMING AT ELTHAM [119]. Twelve rime royal stanzas including envoy; two different refrains.

Bacchus, Juno, and Ceres send wine, wheat, and oil to your Majesty as tokens of peace and happiness. These gifts stand for peace with your lieges, abundance, and happiness. Isaac gave Jacob his blessing with three gifts, and the Lord will undo the rebels to your cause so that Mars will have to desist and your renown will spread through both your realms. Likewise, Juno sends you knighthood, victory, and honor for your martial deeds against infidels. To you, Princess, they also bring similar tokens as well as gladness of heart. To your Highness, they give this olive, and Juno sends you the love of all people so that luck, health, and grace may be your guides. Take these gifts, excellent Prince, and may you have joy and gladness of heart.

The use of classical materials in this mumming has been considered innovative.

MUMMING AT HERTFORD [120]. 254 lines in riming couplets.

The complaint of the peasants to the king: Most noble Prince, certain peasants have come here to complain about their fierce wives, and we know from the philosophers that life with a wife is the worst of earthly torments. Hobbe the Reeve complains of Beatrice Bittersweet, who drinks and does not cook his dinner. Poor Robin gets hit over the head with a distaff if he utters a word, and Colin gets a similar treatment from Cecily Sourcheer, who gives him the silent treatment and spends his money on drink. These husbandmen could also tell how Mabel scratches with her nails or how Bartholomew the butcher cowers before Pernelle, etc. These holy martyrs request your protection and hope that you will so amend the situation that their wives will henceforth temper their customary rights with mercy. It is no joke to play with wives, except for fools who are willing to die.
The answer of the wives: We six wives are fully agreed to fight for our cause in tournament if words will do no good. We have on our side the worthy Wife of Bath, who can show how wives win Heaven for their husbands by teaching them patience. We mend their clothes and clout their backs. Fie on the cowards! We request confirmation of the old status.

The King's answer to both: This noble prince will not give a quick answer here and now, for he proposes to examine the matter and let reason be his guide. He feels compassion for the poor husbands but must also weigh the custom which women invoke, so that the wives will retain the mastery for a year while he searches for a legal solution. Let men beware, however, before they let themselves be caught in the bond of wedlock, for it is a prison even though the walls may be painted with gold.

This poem has been said to owe much to Chaucer, the Noah tradition, and the French debate.

MUMMING AT LONDON (also DESGUISING OF DAME FORTUNE) [121]. 342 basically octosyllabic lines in riming couplets.

The Coming of Fortune: Behold the lady of mutability named Fortune; according to *The Romance of the Rose*, she dwells on an island where the fair weather is wont to turn suddenly into a storm, and her hall is beautiful on one side and ugly on the other. She is as deceitful as her house is unstable: she exalted Alexander and then cast him down, and she did the same thing to Caesar. The two tuns in her cellar are filled respectively with sweet syrup and with gall. Old stories tell us how changes come about, as in the cases of Gyges and a thousand more. But four ladies are now coming who will overpower her if she dares show her double face in this place.

The Coming of Prudence: Behold the lady whom poets call Prudence and who uses foresight against Fortune. Seneca says that she has three eyes in order to consider past, present, and future. She guides the mirror of providence, and she can free those in the power of Fortune.

The Coming of Righteousness: Behold this lady, Righteousness, who is princess of all the virtues. She puts aside friendship, love, and fear so that her decisions may never be bought. She has no hand to take bribes and no eye to see who is powerful and who is weak. There was once a judge who never pronounced dishonest judgment. Three hundred years after his death, his body had putrified, but his mouth and lips had remained whole, thus illustrating the power of Righteousness over the mutability of Fortune.

The Coming of Fortitude: Take heed of Fortitude, whom philosophers also call Magnificence. She fights against all vices and is afraid of nothing as she undertakes great things for the common good. She armed ancient philosophers, as may be seen in respect to Diogenes, Plato, and Socrates; and she encouraged Scipio, Hector, and the Nine Worthies as well as Henry V. In order to put Fortune under foot, let her be welcome here this Christmas.

The Coming of Temperance: This fourth lady whom you see here is called Temperance, and she keeps vices in check with the help of her cousin Soberness. She keeps us away from pride and gluttony, teaches us to say the best, and keeps us from hasty revenge. Whoever is governed by Prudence, Righteousness, Magnificence (Fortitude), and Temperance may go free from Fortune.

This mumming has been noted for its innovations and its debt to *The Romance of the Rose*.

MUMMING AT WINDSOR [122]. Fourteen rime royal stanzas.

Most noble of all Christian princes, you may be pleased to have men recall before you how France was converted when the Lord cast His eyes down on Clovis and shed His grace upon him through St. Clotilda, whose devotion put an end to Mohammedanism in France and brought in Our Lord Jesus when an angel presented a hermit with a blue shield adorned with three fleurs-de-lis. St. Clotilda always spoke the truth—which is no wonder, since it is the nature of women to do so—and she converted Clovis to the Faith. He put the three fleurs-de-lis on his shield and was baptized by St. Remigius with oil from a golden ampulla which was brought from Heaven by an angel, is still kept at Rheims, and will soon serve to anoint Henry VI. The story of the fleur-de-lis will now be shown in the high presence of your Royal Excellence.

MUMMING FOR THE GOLDSMITHS OF LONDON [123]. Fourteen rime royal stanzas.

The worthy David has come with the twelve tribes to this city to visit the noble mayor and bring him gifts that are both heavenly and moral. From his own city of Jerusalem, he has brought the Ark to insure grace and prosperity. Sing, O Levites, who bear the Ark of the Lord, for it is more effective than the Palladium of Troy, so that it behooves all estates, and especially the ministers of the Church, to emulate David, who humbly danced and sang before it. Rise, O Lord, in Your Ark, to protect the Mayor and citizens of this new Troy. Worthy David brings you, O noble Mayor, the power to govern in wisdom, peace, and righteousness, as a writ within the Ark will show. The High Lord will bless you and insure peace, prosperity, and unity in this city during your time.

MUMMING FOR THE MERCERS OF LONDON [124]. Fifteen rime royal stanzas.

Most mighty Jupiter, whose mansion is above the sunbeams, whence Phebus shines upon the Euphrates toward Jerusalem, came down where Mars built his palace upon the red sand, where Bacchus dwells by the river Tagus, and by the well from which Tully drank—as did Virgil, Ovid, etc.—until he saw a boat with a fisherman who caught no fish and with signs reading *grande travayle* and *nulle avayle*. He went on until he reached the British Sea and found clear weather as he entered Brutus' Albion by the Thames, where he saw a ship with a sign proclaiming that every man must thank God. Near it, there was another boat with a fisherman catching a great load of fish and with signs reading *grande peyne* and *grande gayne*. When Paul's light showed him that he was near London, he landed where certain vessels now lie at anchor. Certain estates wish to visit the Mayor of London and hope that he will receive them.

This mumming offers a particularly dense concentration of classical allusions.

MUMMING FOR QUEEN MARGARET (also PAGEANT VERSES FOR QUEEN MARGARET and QUEEN MARGARET'S ENTRY

INTO LONDON) [125]. Ten eight-line stanzas ababbcbc and thirteen rime royal stanzas.

Most Christian Princess, your city and subjects welcome you, and your people in England and France hope for peace since you are like the dove that brought the branch of peace to Noah on the ark. May Grace be your guide in life, and may Truth, Mercy, Justice, and Peace watch over the two realms, for these four sisters will bring peace. The people ask the Lord for peace. The angels of peace will triumph, and peace will replace war because of the blessed Margaret, so that the wicked angels will no longer cause trouble. In his psalm David has praised grace in life and glory afterwards as well as the wonders of the tabernacle of the Lord. Eat and drink, friends, for there shall be peace. O celestial song, no earthly joy may equal you. Who can praise the palace of God and its eternal glory? But, Princess, God has blessed this pageant and your entry into your city, where you are welcome with greater joy than anyone can say. May we all reach the city of Jerusalem. O Mother of Christ, pray for our queen, so that she may live here a long time and have eternal bliss thereafter. Each man will have to present his account when the Last Trumpet calls, and those who have lived well will be saved.

SAYENGE OF THE NYGHTYNGALE [126]. 54 rime royal stanzas.

One evening in June, after the birds had finished their song, I heard a nightingale sing upon a thorn, and I wondered about the meaning of the melody. I think that she was asking Venus to punish false lovers but to cherish those who languish in true affection, and I suddenly fell asleep. I dreamed that a messenger was sent to me, not by Cupid, but by the Lord. He bid me follow him to understand the meaning of that song, which had nothing to do with the garden of the rose but betokens pure love. See how this little bird sings as though she would dismember herself. She sings not of the flesh but only of the injuries done to the Lord Who died for us on the Cross. Day and night she bids us slay those who do not think with love about the Lord Who opened for us the five wounds that formed a rose upon His death. Who could see this sight without feeling pity? He was the same whom Isaiah saw and Who vanquished Satan. When asked why His garment was red, He answered that it was because He has pressed the wine alone on the Cross, sustained only by His Mother and John, and He did so for the sake of mankind and because of the sins of man. He was beaten and nailed to the tree. Thus the bird said to slay those who are unkind and have forgotten the Passion: against pride, think of My meekness; against lechery, think of My purity, etc., etc. In His generosity, He gave His body to man, His clothing to the Jews, His blessed corpse to His disciples, His Mother to John, and His spirit to His Father. He conquered the deadly sins. It was a thing beyond comparison, for the Son to die to free His servant so that he might inherit Heaven. Let us not forget His kindnesses. His Cross is our best protection against the Fiend; it is the palm of victory, the key of Heaven, etc., etc. Forsake the world, O sinful soul, and make your way to the garden of perfect lovers to gather the flowers of virtue. This world is but an exile, whereas the God of Love dwells in that garden, calling His spouse just as the nightingale calls the human soul with heavenly harmony. He calls it His spouse by affinity of grace and His sister because He was born of the Virgin who bore the fruit that slew Satan.

This poem has fared somewhat better with modern criticism than most of Lydgate's work.

NIGHTINGALE AS SYMBOL OF CHRIST (also THE NIGHTINGALE) [127]. 59 rime royal stanzas including proem.

Go, little poem, and humbly beg the Duchess of Buckingham for a place among her books until she decides to read you to the members of her following who want to hear about the amorous song of the nightingale, and she commands them to listen to the spiritual meaning of the nightingale whose song and death are here set in English. When May banishes the cold of winter, all creatures must sleep at night, but the nightingale alone sings all night. On a night near the end of April, I was lying awake and thinking about this troubled world. Long before daybreak, the nightingale began singing, and I thought that she was calling me by name and asking me to get up. I obeyed and walked until I found her singing on a laurel, and I suddenly understood that she was singing of her coming death. At dawn she seemed to say that she must die in spite of her mirth and song; at prime she said that her life would soon end, at tierce that she had to die, and at sext that death was welcome. She ended her song and died at nones. I found this story in a Latin book, and the nightingale stands for Christ Himself and every Christian soul. Dawn stands for the beginning of the world and the fall of the angels which ought to teach you humility. At this hour of dawn Adam and Eve sinned through envy, and we were all doomed to hell until Christ came down out of pity. Do not forget that death may come suddenly and that God has given you free will to live or die forever, and remember your sins each morning. Christ was betrayed at dawn, the time also called matin, and taken by the Jews: O, sinful man, think of Your Lord who died for you. Prime stands for the time when the world was destroyed by water and God spared only Noah and seven others because of their righteousness, hence the reason for living virtuously. God does not take vengeance quickly, and He rejoices when you turn to virtue, but there is no pardon for him who dies in deadly sin. The seed of Noah forgot the lesson of the flood and turned to vice: think of the sins of your forefathers. God has protected you in youth, and you must now pray and think of the pains that Christ endured to set an example for us. Restrain yourselves, young gallants, and think of what Solomon said about the wantonness of youth. Tierce stands for the third age of the world, when Abraham led a perfect life but many others behaved so abominably that the Trinity destroyed Sodom and Gomorrah, thus providing an example for people in their later years. The Fiend tries to deceive your souls, but you may escape by thinking of Christ and the Jews who mocked Him when He bore the Cross to Calvary for your sake. Be careful, mighty princes, for death will come of a sudden. Death took the Duke of Warwick in the tierce of life, and it will take high and low without warning. The nightingale continued singing from tierce to sext, which stands for the time when Dathan and Abiram were swallowed by the earth. In all ages people like to serve the devil, but you who are in the hour of sext ought to think of Christ and His rewards. He was crucified, and we must be sure never to forget His torments while He remained nailed on the Cross from sext to nones. Adam lived in prosperity until he was banished as well as all his offspring until Christ gave up the ghost unto His Father. Thus has the nigntingale, thus has the Lord dearly bought our souls upon the Cross and thus given us cause to serve Him. After the Lord's ascension, the Holy Ghost sent us His body to be received for our salvation. All those who are fed here at this glorious feast may be glad, and we beseech Him to grant us eternal joy when we shall leave this world.

Recent scholarship rejects Lydgate's authorship of this poem.

NINE PROPERTIES OF WINE [128]. One eight-line stanza ababbcbc.

Wine comforts and does wonderful things for the eyes, heart, stomach, wits, courage, wounds, the palate, and feasts.

FIFTEEN O'S OF CHRIST [129]. 42 eight-line stanzas ababbcbc.

O blessed Lord, You are the chief wealth and comfort of those who love You; let Your grace shine on them. Think on Your mortal grief and Your prayer to Your Father to translate the chalice of the Passion while You were sweating both blood and water. You were brought to judgment by false accusers and condemned to death, and You were scourged and crowned with thorns. O gracious Jesus, imprint on my heart the memory of Your sufferings on the Cross and let me remember how You were crucified between two thieves for our sake. When You were covered with blood from head to foot, You prayed Your Father to forgive those who tortured You. Give me the grace to remember Your Passion. When Your enemies stood around You like tigers, You showed Your love. Defend us from our enemies. When You were hanging on the Cross, forsaken by all except Your mother and John, You told her to behold her son, and she remembered Simeon's prophecy. Grant that we may find support in Your Passion. Gracious Jesus, our comfort, Your friends left You hanging on the Cross alone, except for Your mother and John. To You I say this prayer so that You grant me shrift before I pass hence. You are the well of mercy; set our hearts afire to rid us of carnal lust. Grant us to receive Your body and blood before we go hence. Merciful Jesus, for Your distress on the Cross, forsake us not when we cry to You for help. O Jesus, called Alpha and Omega, remember how You bled to wash our sins with Your precious blood. Our redemption was shown in the blood and water of Your Passion. O truthful Jesus born of a pure virgin and slain in Jerusalem for Your servants, write Your Passion with Your blood in my heart. O mighty Jesus, Lion of Judah, You slew death with death and were made weak only to show Your power. O Jesus, called the Son of Your Father's wisdom, plenteous Grape and Vine, grant that I may be wounded as You were so that the rust of my life may be washed away with tears and I may join the saints in the heavenly mansions.

THE ORDER OF FOOLS (also A TALE OF THRESCORE FOLYS AND THRE) [130]. 22 stanzas ababbcbc.

The Order of Fools was founded by Marcolf under Bacchus and Juno and numbers sixty-three. First among fools is the person who neither loves nor fears God, then the person who pays no attention to the Church, or to the saints, or to the poor, etc., etc. Then comes the steadfast in sin, the backbiter, the deceitful, etc., etc., and finally the sleepy shepherd, the fat prince of lean people, and those who preach abstinence from a full stomach. All these have a pardon from Bishop Nullatensis, but none will thrive.

This poem has been said to belong to the tradition of the *Speculum Stultorum* and to reflect the influence of the Bible, Chaucer, and Isidore of Seville.

BALADE IN COMMENDATION OF OUR LADY (also BALLADE AT THE REVERENCE OF OUR LADY) [131]. Twenty rime royal stanzas.

I could tell a thousand stories to show how Cupid pierces the heart of his servants, but I shall instead speak of one who will not fail. I am unworthy, but she is most merciful, and I shall kneel and praise her. O Star of Stars, have mercy on me for your five joys. Clean Chamber of Chastity, Fructifying Olive, and Redolent Cedar, remember sinners and protect us. Protector of wanderers, O you mirth of the martyrs and ruby rubified in the Passion, etc., etc., you were chosen for Joseph and gave birth miraculously without knowing him.

This very aureate poem, which seems heavily indebted to the *Anticlaudianus*, has been rated among Lydgate's best and said to have influenced Dunbar.

VALENTINE TO OUR LADY (also VALENTINE TO HER I LOVE and VALENTINE TO HER THAT EXCELLETH ALL) [132]. Twenty rime royal stanzas with varying refrain, including envoy.

Every year on Saint Valentine's Day, men search Cupid's calendar to select a beloved, but I love one who excels all others. Some choose for fairness and others for station or wealth, but I love one who excels all others. I chose that flower long ago, and she excels Lucrece, Dido, Rachel, etc., etc. She is Mary, and her humility prompted the Lord to let her bear the fruit that would save us all. She is clothed in the sun in St. John's *Apocalypse*, the virgin in Octavius' vision, and the woman saluted by Gabriel. St. Catherine was good, and so were St. Margaret, St. Mary Magdalene, etc., etc., but I love one best who excels all others, and I shall choose her from year to year on St. Valentine's Day. With humble heart I beseech that Virgin to shed her grace on Henry VI and his mother. May Jesus Christ have mercy on us when we call for help in the name of her who excels all others.

PAGEANT OF KNOWLEDGE (also SEVEN WISE COUNSELS) [133]. 39 stanzas in four groups totaling fourteen eight-line stanzas ababbcbc alternating with three groups totaling 25 rime royal stanzas; stanzas 19-37 with varying refrain.

This world is borne by seven estates, each of which has a specific responsibility: princes must govern, priests must live in perfection, etc., etc. Prudence bids us consider past, present, and future and weigh all matters before acting; justice bids us hold the balance carefully and beware of flatterers; temperance bids us avoid acting in anger; discretion is mother of all virtues; reason is the celestial empress that curbs our sensuality; pleasance and good will beseech us to be of good cheer after satisfying our needs; and courtesy and nurture bid us be content with what we have. Jubal was the father of song and music; Saturn first taught tillage, Mars taught war, Minerva taught eloquence, etc., etc. Of the seven liberal sciences, grammar teaches writing, philosophy teaches the nature of things, etc., etc. Priscian taught grammar, Euclid excelled in geometry, etc., etc. The planet Saturn stirs a man to melancholy, the planet Jupiter stirs him to great deeds, etc., etc. Aries is choleric and governs the head, Taurus governs the throat, etc., etc. How then could a man's life be steadfast? How can a creature made of earth, air, fire, and water have a stable life? Fire turns earth into liquid and liquid into air; air gives man breath for his heart, and water changes from liquid to ice and is affected by the moon. The sanguine man is bold and inclined to love, the phlegmatic is slow, etc., etc. Man endures dryness and heat in summer, strange infirmities in autumn, cold in winter, and lust in the spring. The weather changes with the months, Fortune is transmutable, storms follow the sunshine, and youth changes into old age. Then raise your eyes to Heaven and pray the Lord to grant you grace to repent before death so that you may attain everlasting joy.

This poem has been considered particularly illustrative of the medieval view of the nature of medicine. Consult [134–136] for different version and excerpts copied as individual poems.

PAGEANT OF KNOWLEDGE, STANZAS 23–END, IN DIFFERENT VERSION [134]. Eighteen eight-line stanzas ababbcbc, the first sixteen with varying refrain.

How could a creature made of earth, air, fire, and water have a stable life? He has joints, flesh, and bones of earth, humors of water, air in his arteries, and fire in his heart. He has dryness and moisture in spring, dryness and heat in summer, infirmities in autumn, and cold and humidity in winter. Man has cold and humidity in winter, when the daisy droops. Fire turns earth into water and water into air, and faith, hope, and charity can overcome all despair even though there is no steadfastness in life. Air is good for a man's heart, and water congeals to crystal. The sanguine man is bold, the phlegmatic is slow, etc., etc. The planet Saturn stirs a man's heart to melancholy, the planet Jupiter stirs him to great deeds, etc., etc. The world is uncertain and Fortune transmutable; each season changes, and the winds make man insecure and fearful. Storms follow the sunshine, and nature dies with winter. Consider also the transmutation from youth into old age. Man! raise your eyes to Heaven and pray the Lord to grant you grace to repent before death so that you may attain everlasting joy.

For other version and excerpts copied as individual poems, consult [133], [135], and [136].

PAGEANT OF KNOWLEDGE, STANZA 23 ALONE [135]. One rime royal stanza.

The world so wide, man so insignificant: how can a creature made of earth, air, fire, and water have a stable life?

This stanza also appears in *Debate of the Horse, Goose, and Sheep* [83] and differs somewhat from that in *Pageant of Knowledge* [133]; its authorship is considered very doubtful. See under [133], [134], and [136] for context and additional scholarship.

PAGEANT OF KNOWLEDGE, STANZAS 3-9 [136]. Nine rime royal stanzas.

For summary, see [133]: Prudence bids us ..., and courtesy and nurture bid us be content with what we have.

The order of the stanzas is 5, 4, 3, 6, 7, 8, 9. See *Pageant of Knowledge* [133] for context, and consult [134] and [135] for additional scholarship.

EXPOSITION OF PATER NOSTER [137]. 42 eight-line stanzas ababbcbc.

I stand in trembling reverence, for my wit is feeble and my torch is burnt out, so that I can only count on hope to help me expound the *Pater Noster*. Four things must be remembered in respect to prayer, but I do not mean the four Evangelists, or the four spheres of Ezekiel, or the four winds, or the four cardinal virtues, or the four wheels of Elijah's chariot: I pass all these things to speak of prayer and seven petitions which surpass all prayers, and yet I have no mouth worthy of speaking of the Trinity. The word *Pater* shows God's might and gives us assurance of remedy against worldly distress. In this word stands all our hope to be accepted as His children, and the seven petitions equal the seven gifts of the Holy Ghost. We make bold to ask these things by sanctifying Your name and praying that Your kingdom may come to us in this life and then in Heaven, that Your will be done and that we may remember the Passion, that we may fulfill Your Commandments and receive Your body in the form of bread which was kneaded before Pilate and baked in the Passion. This bread gives us life; it is the bread of angels. O Lord, forgive us our debts and consider our frailty: I am worse than any man, for I am soiled with the Seven Sins but can nevertheless resent a small fault in my neighbor while finding means of ignoring my own horrible trespasses. Who shows no mercy to others shall receive none himself; your prayers are worthless unless you love both friends and enemies. O Lord Jesus, let us not fall into temptation and deliver us from evil during this fearful pilgrimage. The *Pater Noster* is the most powerful of all prayers. I have acted like a gleaner in a field full of texts, but my own soil is dry and dull. Let this be laid on my breast with my Testament when I am dead. Though I was dull in my devotions, I said the seven petitions daily with all my heart. On my knees I pray that my masters who will read this compilation may be merciful enough to correct it when they have time.

PARAPHRASE OF PATER NOSTER [138]. Seven rime royal stanzas with Latin refrain in 1-6.

Our Glorious Father etc., etc.

PELERINAGE DE LA VIE HUMAINE (also PILGRIMAGE OF THE LIFE OF MAN) [139]. 24,832 lines in the printed edition, mostly in short couplets but also including a prologue in long-line couplets, a long prose

section, Chaucer's *ABC*, and the prayer that is separately dealt with as item [147] below.

    Translator's Prologue: Worldly folk should learn that this life is fleeting and only a pilgrimage to Jerusalem or Babylon. Only divine grace can help; learn from this book, which Lord Salisbury commanded me to translate. I began in 1426. Pay attention to the sentence, for I lack eloquence.
    Author's Prologue: In 1330 I had a wonderful dream. I wrote it down, but it was taken from me. Now I shall rewrite it and send it out.
    My dream urged me to go to Jerusalem. I saw many pilgrims dying on the road; many others were helped into the city. After nine months I met a lady, Grace Dieu, who said I could only enter the city by her. She took me into her house founded 1330 years ago. Grace Dieu explained baptism and confirmation and I underwent both. Reason appeared and lectured on the ointments. She spoke with Moses about his horns and staff, discussed marriage, and explained tonsure. Moses appointed his servants and gave Grace Dieu to the pilgrims. Reason preached on the sword and keys also given to all pilgrims. I received sword and keys, and Reason explained them further. Moses dined on bread and wine. Reason made Nature object to the miraculous change of bread and wine in the Eucharist, but Grace Dieu defended the sacrament. Two ladies appeared. The first was Penance with a hammer and broom to destroy sin and sweep it away. The second lady was Charity who explained her activities among men. She then read the testament of Christ. The pilgrims were fed from Moses' table. I went to Grace Dieu for proof of what I'd seen and she taught me about the Eucharist and answered the objections of Aristotle and Nature. I asked Grace Dieu for bread from Moses' table. She advised me on the use of the senses and gave me scrip and staff (the allegorical significance of each is explained at length and Latin poems are inserted). Grace Dieu gave me allegorical pieces of armor (which I disliked and threw off), left, but then returned with David's stones. I got ready for my journey, but Grace Dieu criticized my fleshly weakness and said the soul should rule the body. I set out on my pilgrimage and was stopped by a churl, Rude Entendement, whose objections were answered at length by Reason. Then I met Youth who, at the fork of Labor and Idleness (each of whom describes himself), urged me to take the wrong path. Moral Virtue said I should keep to the right path. I met Mortification of the Body and wept and blamed my flesh. Grace Dieu appeared and explained the weakness of the body using wheel analogies. Youth bore me aloft and threw me down where I met Gluttony, who described herself; Venus joined us and recounted her actions. The two bound and dragged me. I was then attacked by Sloth, who described her office, until I was finally freed by a white dove. I saw Pride, who told me about herself, and then I saw Envy, who also described herself. She and her daughters (Treason and Detraction) attacked me and I was again saved by a white dove. I then met Wrath, who described himself and then attacked me along with Tribulation. Helpless before Tribulation, I prayed to Mary in St. Bernard's words (a long prose insert on the various consolations for an afflicted heart). Tribulation said she had driven many to Mary. I came into a wild wood and saw Avarice, who described herself. She attacked me and I was saved by Youth. I was bidden by a messenger to come to Necromancy, whose actions he described, but I refused. I met Heresy and her father, Satan, who barred my way. I attempted to swim away and in the sea of the world I saw other pilgrims progressing with various degrees of difficulty or success. I escaped Satan by crossing myself and, while swimming, was cast on the wheel of Fortune. Fortune explained herself and then I was thrown from her wheel. In jeopardy I lamented the loss of Grace Dieu, when the dove reappeared with Chaucer's *ABC*. I reached a hill of sand where I debated with Astrology and then Geomancy about their teachings, especially the denial of human free will. I sailed away and on another island met Idolatry. There I was threatened by the one who made the idol and, fleeing, I met Sorcery, whose teachings I denounced. By the sea, I was threatened by Scylla (or Conspiracy) and her hounds. Alone and entranced, I saw a

revolving tower built by Satan, the significance of which was explained by a monstrous Worldly Gladness before she threw me into the sea. Youth abandoned me on my island and I was desolate until Grace Dieu sailed up. After a second baptism, I was able to enter her ship Religion and there I chose the castle of the Cistercian order. The ship set sail and on board I met, and learned about from talking with, Lesson, Hagiography, Obedience, Abstinence, Chastity, Poverty, and Prayer. Prayer offered to show me the way to the city. Obedience said the way to Jerusalem is hard and she bound me for thirty-nine years. One day Envy attacked me in the castle; Ovid pitied me and when the king returned he arrested my enemies. I visited other castles and with Grace Dieu saw religious who had broken their bonds. I met Sterility and Apostasy. Two messengers, Age and Sickness, came to me and warned of Death's approach. Mercy came to help me and explained her function. Prayer and Alms were to prepare my way to Jerusalem, but I could use only the latter. Death arrived and, in fear, I woke up.

The *Pélerinage* is as long as several of Lydgate's other important translations, but is generally regarded as an inferior piece of work. Begun in 1426 at the request of Thomas Montacute, earl of Salisbury and the second husband of Alice Chaucer, the *Pélerinage* is a translation of Guillaume de Deguileville's second, expanded version of the *Pélerinage de la vie humaine*, the first of Deguileville's allegorical trilogy (he also produced the *Pélerinage de l'ame* and the *Pélerinage de Jésus Christ*). The *Pélerinage de la vie humaine* shows the unmistakable influence of the *Roman de la rose*, and, in English literature, it may later have been used by Spenser, Milton, and perhaps even Bunyan.

The sixteenth-century identification of Lydgate as the translator has been questioned by some. Although the English poem is considerably expanded from its source (24,832 lines from 18,123), very little of substance has been added. The poem has an importance in the history of allegory, but it is usually considered unsuccessful as a work of art, despite the praise of some for its dialogue and realism. The allegory is intellectual rather than imaginative, and the literal story is often confusing and rarely of much value in itself.

PRAYER INSERTED IN PELERINAGE DE LA VIE HUMAINE (also **PRAYER TO BLESSED VIRGIN**) [140]. Four stanzas in long lines, each riming ababbcbc.

O blessed maid, be merciful and the refuge of sinners. Queen of heaven, lodestar of the sea, help them to arrive at felicity. O holy star, without mutability, in whom the Son took on humanity, be our refuge in tribulation. Lenvoye: Princess, pray thy Son to have mercy on me since my trust is only in you.

This short prayer, distinct in style from the rest of the *Pèlerinage*, is inserted after the long prose homily on the Virgin from St. Bernard. The poem has been highly praised, especially in comparison with the rest of the *Pèlerinage*, and is somewhat similar to Lydgate's many other prayers to the Virgin: see, for example, *Orison on the Five Joys* [92], *Ave Regina Celorum* [10], *Regina Celi Letare* [162], and *Stella Celi Extirpavit* [173 and 174].

LIFE OF ST. PETRONILLA (also LEGEND OF ST. PETRONILLA) [141]. Twenty eight-line stanzas ababbcbc and one four-line stanza abab, including ballade.

This is to put in remembrance the perfect life of a most gracious virgin named Petronilla, who was Peter's daughter and was humble although she surpassed all other virgins in beauty. She was firm in Christ's law and never complained although she was an invalid. In the Lord's sight, she was one of the five maidens to bear their lights before Jesus. When asked by Titus why he did not cure Petronilla as he did others, Peter made her whole and told her to wait upon them. After she had done so, he ordered her back to bed and her infirmity. On the point of marrying Flaccus, she asked for an escort of women, but she lay in prayer and died a virgin. Afterwards Flaccus ordered both her closest woman friend and her confessor put to death. Petronilla died on the last day of May, which is the time when all birds sing. Like the nightingale, she was ever wakeful in Jesus' service. Virgin of great virtue, you served with humble diligence. Pray Jesus to ease our sickness for your father's sake. Whoever comes before her on a pilgrimage may be certain to have his petition granted.

This poem is presumably based on the *Legenda Aurea* and is thought to have been written for St. Petronilla's hospital in Bury.

PRAISE OF PEACE [142]. 24 eight-line stanzas ababbcbc with varying refrain.

Mercy and Truth met on a mountain while Peace and Justice were walking on the plain, and Charity joined these four sisters. Pity leads to Pax, and *P* stands for prudence, *A* for authority, and *X* for Christ, Who died for our sins so that we may live in peace. There is both inward and outward peace, as well as the contemplative peace of holy living which perfect men lead in solitude and fasting. Peace is daughter of Charity and was most praised by Socrates; she is patient and makes the sword rust. He who wants to live in peace should love Jesus. Gabriel brought the word of peace; when the angels sang, the star guided the shepherds to Bethlehem, where they found the King of Peace and praised God. The seven daughters of the Holy Ghost— Charity, Patience, etc., etc.—all worked for peace, just as Mary did when the King of Peace lay in a manger. At the birth of Jesus the Sibyl had a vision of an empress holding in her arms a child who was the Lord of Peace, and Herod ordered children to be slain. St. John had a vision of a rider with a bloody sword who was the cause of all kinds of proud wars contrary to peace. May God send peace between England and France. Henry V did not hesitate to stand for his rights, and he died as all of us must eventually do. May God grant us His peace, which Christ died to bring us.

PRAYER TO ST. ANNE (also INVOCATION TO ST. ANNE) [143]. Eleven rime royal stanzas.

Prime Mover of Everything, inspire my inept breast so that I may write about St. Anne, for my wit is barren without Your help. Shed Your aureate liquor from above so that I may praise St. Anne. You too, St. Anne, help me with my writing and help us gain salvation, you from whose breast sprang our lodestar. O, blissful Anne who brought forth the ark that bore the holy manna, you who were predestined to bear the Virgin who should neutralize the serpent's venom, have mercy on us so that God may also have pity on us before passing judgment. O blissful sugar cane, help us sing the praise of the Lamb Who killed death and bought us with His blood.

PRAYER TO BLESSED VIRGIN (also ORISON TO THE BLESSED VIRGIN and PRAYER TO MARY IN WHOM IS AFFIAUNCE) [144]. Three eight-line stanzas ababbcbc.

Sweetest balm, pray your Son for me; as Eve brought sorrow to the world, so you brought us joy. My request in your presence is that I may have long life, plenty of wealth, and eternal bliss.

The authorship of this poem has been questioned.

PRAYER TO BRITISH SAINTS, ESPECIALLY ST. URSULA (also ST. URSULA AND THE ELEVEN THOUSAND VIRGINS) [145]. Three eight-line stanzas ababbcbc.

You, British martyrs famous for perfection, and you, eleven thousand virgins whose martyrdom earned you crowns of red roses: may Jesus forgive us our trespasses in your name with the help of Ursula.

PRAYER TO ST. DENIS (also DEVOWTE INVOCACIOUN TO ST. DENIS) [146]. Nine eight-line stanzas ababbcbc with varying refrain.

Blessed Denis, chosen of God and protector of France, remember how Christ grants their requests to those who pray to you, and preserve us from our foes. Give us humility for pride, chastity for lechery, etc., etc.; give us faith, hope, and charity; let us not trust in Fortune, but in the Lord Who died upon a cross. We have full faith in you, St. Denis; be present when death comes, O star of Paris, and pray God to accept our prayer.

This poem was presumably written for Charles VII.

PRAYER TO ST. EDMUND [147]. Ninety-six lines in stanzas riming ababbcbc.

> Glorious Edmund, protect your servants. You chose to die rather than forsake Christ; pray for us. Gracious king, be our means to Jesus who gave mercy to others. As prince of this region, pray for us. Pray to Christ that we may all live in charity and peace: You are our protector and defence. Flower of martyrs, your holy relics are preserved. You are king, martyr, and virgin, symbolized by roses and lilies. You help thy servants, as has been seen. Pray for those who come on pilgrimage, for those who dwell in your town, and for your monks, who call to you each day.

This prayer, in Lydgate's magnificent invocatory style, may have been written on his return from Paris (about 1429) to be sung in the monastery at Bury. The piece is less political than Lydgate's other prayer to St. Edmund, which follows at the end of the martyr's legend (see [80] above); its language has been compared to the *Prayer to St. Denis* (see [146] above).

PRAYER TO GABRIEL [148]. One eight-line stanza ababbcbc.

> Blessed Gabriel, who first told Mary that she should bear a child in virginity, be our help.

The authorship of this poem has been questioned.

PRAYER TO ST. LEONARD [149]. Five eight-line stanzas ababbcbc with varying refrain, and one six-line stanza aabbcc.

> Refuge of disconsolate people, blessed Leonard, remember prisoners, exiled people, the poor, etc., etc., and all those who resort to this place so that they may repent and join you in eternity. Merciful Leonard, show your servants a palpable sign of coming salvation.

PRAYER TO ST. MICHAELL [150]. One eight-line stanza ababbcbc.

> O Michael, be the grace of Jesus Christ, be our shield and protection, and present our prayer to the Lord.

The authorship of this poem has been questioned.

PRAYER TO ST. OSITHA [151]. Three eight-line stanzas ababbcbc with varying refrain.

Hail, holy Sitha, you who served the Lord Jesus and beat your breast with a little stone; you who help the sorrowful, O blessed Sitha, support all those who call to you in need.

This poem has been considered typical of Lydgate's style, and the identity of the saint has been questioned.

PRAYER TO ST. ROBERT OF BURY [152]. Five eight-line stanzas ababbcbc with varying refrain.

O blessed Robert, who was sacrificed by the Jews, pray to Christ for all those who revere your passion. You, who were slain as a child for Christ before you could speak a word, remember Bury, where you have a chapel and a shrine.

PRAYER TO ST. THOMAS [153]. Two eight-line stanzas ababbcbc.

Blessed Thomas, who stood as a pillar of Holy Church, have mercy on us, be our protection, and keep us from sin for Jesus' sake.

The authorship of this poem has been questioned.

PRAYER TO ST. THOMAS OF CANTERBURY [154]. Fifteen eight-line stanzas ababbcbc with varying refrain, including envoy.

Singular shepherd, guardian of Christ's fold, pray for all who call to you in their need. Strong in virtue, you watched over Christ's garden, in whose defense your garment was bloodied, and the water of your well turned once to milk and four times to blood as token of your chastity and martyrdom. No danger deterred you from weeding our wheat fields to save your sheep. Blessed be the kingdom in which you were born and predestined to be martyred, and where you earned the palm despite your foes. Jewel of martyrs, neither Caesar nor Hannibal can compare with you. For your love our Lord from Heaven set alight extinguished tapers. Remember those who come to visit your holy place, pray for the Church, the king, your chaplains, your church, your town, your monastery, the knights, the yeomen, etc., etc., and pray to Jesus to put an end to bloodshed. Go, little tablet, to this martyr to whom I offer your content in hope that those who read it will correct it so that the martyr may help us in our need.

The authorship of this poem has been questioned.

PRAYER TO TEN SAINTS [155]. Twelve eight-line stanzas ababbcbc with two varying refrains in stanzas 1–7 and 8–12.

Blessed St. Denis, whose preaching won France to Christ's faith, pray for your servants and protect those who remember your passion. Glorious George, who slew the dragon, pray for Henry VI and for those who remember your passion. Holy Christopher, who carried Jesus, Bishop Blaise, torn with iron combs, St. Giles, who lived in the wild woods, pray for those who remember you. May all five of you pray for us. O Catherine broken on the wheel, Margaret devoured by a dragon, St. Martha who slew the dragon, Blessed Christina, who endured sword and flames, and Blessed Barbara, whose holiness repels gunshots, have pity on us for your virginity.

PRAYER IN OLD AGE [156]. Four eight-line stanzas ababbcbc.

Forgive, Jesus, the sins of my ignorant youth and the misspent time of my middle years when I did not understand the changes of Fortune. Forsake me not, Lord, in my old age, and grant me a sign in the name of Your Passion.

Opening stanza is the same as that of *The Eight Verses of St. Bernard* (see [14] and [15] above).

PROCESSION OF CORPUS CHRISTI [157]. 28 eight-line stanzas ababbcbc.

To celebrate this high feast which is most heavenly and divine, these mysteries based on Scripture will be declared in your presence. First consider how Christ was crucified for Adam's sin; remember also how Melchizedek offered bread and wine, how Abraham offered bread, and so forth through the apostles. Holy Jerome cleaned the faith from heresy; moral Gregory explained how the bread is flesh taken from a pure virgin, and blessed Augustine explained how we improve in all respects when Christ is eaten. Ambrose has written that the sacrament enables us to triumph over Satan, and holy Thomas Aquinas had a vision of the Host as symbol of the Trinity. Receive these figures with reverence, and may God grant an eternal supply of this celestial manna where the angels sing hosannah.

This poem, in which scholars have seen the influence of the *Legenda Aurea* and the Church Fathers, has been thought to have been connected with some sort of dramatic presentation but to be nonetheless different from the Corpus Christi plays.

PROVERBS (also SEE MYCHE, SAY LYTELL, AND LERNE TO SOFFAR IN TYME) [158]. Five rime royal stanzas.

See much, say little, and learn to suffer in time: keep these things in mind, for the world changes like the moon. Would God that all false tongues were bound until the world be safe from Satan. A little spark often lights a fire that cannot be stopped. Deal not with doubleness; see much, etc., etc.

Lydgate's authorship of this poem is considered extremely doubtful.

PSALM 102 (also BENEDIC ANIMA MEA DOMINO) [159]. 22 eight-line stanzas ababbcbc.

Give praise to the Lord, O my soul, and give thanks to Him Who bought you at such cost with His precious blood upon the Cross and is the most merciful of lords. He is ever steadfast in love and will restore your youth in a mantle of immortality. Lord, grant me mercy before You judge. He protected His beloved Israel from Pharaoh: now grant me Lord to repent before I die. I dare not come before Him when He shall judge, for my salvation depends on His mercy. He has set our sins aside and delayed judgment so that we may come to grace, and He has pity upon His children like a merciful father. He remembers that we are dust, for the spirit of man shall soon pass: Lord, let mercy grant that we may reign in Your glory. Your mercies, Lord, are eternal and will extend to those who keep Your Commandments: grant that I be among the faithful. God has built a mansion in Heaven, and my only safeconduct there is Your mercy. All the angels bless the Lord, and nothing may disobey His word: have mercy upon my sinfulness before I die. Bless the Lord and all His works, O my soul, for life and death depend upon His grace, as will our redemption when You shall judge us.

This poem is based on Psalm 102 (in the Vulgate numbering).

RAMMESHORNE [160]. Seven eight-line stanzas ababbcbc with slightly varying refrain.

Righteousness sits crowned like an empress, and the law has defied bribery and set up Truth as a goddess: everything is going straight as a ram's horn. Princes support what is right, prelates live in holiness, knights endure no falsehood, etc., etc. The rich are so generous that the poor complain for no reason and charity rules everyone. Hypocrisy has become virtuous, so that deceit no longer dares spread its wings, and women have exchanged pride for meekness. Note how virtue is now in charge and heretics have lost their boldness so that everyone is going straight as a ram's horn.

RESON AND SENSUALLYTE [161]. 7042 lines in short rimed couplets.

I present this book, which tells how I was mated by a Queen, to all lovers of chess. Do not judge it harshly, but correct its mistakes. Fortune gives both joy and sorrow. One beautiful spring morning, as I lay in bed, Lady Nature appeared to me (she is described) and urged me to rise and follow the right path to perfection. She said God has given man two virtues: his senses and his reason. The latter should rule because it leads to heaven. Reason and Nature are sisters. Nature left and I went into the lovely fields and wandered from my path. I saw the goddesses Pallas (Minerva), Juno, and Venus, with Mercury (all described in detail). After recounting the Judgment of Paris, Mercury asked me if I thought the Trojan's decision was correct; I said it was. All leave except Venus, who declared she would give me a woman more beautiful than Helen. I told Venus I would follow her, though I also meant to keep Nature's commands. Venus assured me that she and Nature always agree. Venus's two sons are Deduit (Delight) and Cupid. I was told to go to the Garden of Deduit and there find my promised lady. On the way to the garden, I met Diana in an evergreen forest (she is described). Diana rebuked me and urged me to repent. She said Venus now rules everywhere with her lust (it was different in King Arthur's day), even among the gods. She said that my choice of Venus over Juno and Pallas was foolish. She warned me against the dangers of Venus and urged me not to enter the Garden of Deduit, which is full of sorrowful folk and terrible perils that often seem attractive on the surface (these are described at length). She told me of the sorrows that have been suffered in the garden by Narcissus, Pygmalion, Pasiphae, Mirra, Menaphron, Phaedra, Tereus, Silla, Medea, Phyllis, Dido, and Pyramus and Thisbe. Diana described the beauty of her forest of chastity. I refused to stay in the forest, for I had promised to serve Venus. Diana claimed that I was falling into a trap and that I had misinterpreted Nature's commandment. But I was determined to see the Garden of Deduit and so Diana left. I reached the garden, which is described in the *Romance of the Rose*. It was a beautiful place with pictures on the wall. Courtesy welcomed me and said I might go where I liked. Cupid rules there (his crown and clothing are described) and he has three ladies with him and two bows, each with five arrows as described in the *Romance of the Rose*, plus a crowd of followers. I heard wonderful music in the garden and saw the well of Narcissus. All crowded around to watch Deduit play chess with a beautiful maiden. I forgot Juno and Pallas and wanted to stay there. The chess game was drawn and the maid said she would next play with me. The maiden's pawns (all are described in detail) were youth, beauty, simplicity, sweet looks, deportment, foresight, kindness, and nobility; her queen was grace; her knights were shame and timidity; her rooks were welcome and sweet appearance; her bishops were meekness and obedience; her king was constancy in love. My pawns were idleness, sight, sweet thought, delection ... [unfinished].

This love allegory, which was apparently not a commissioned piece, has received as much modern praise and approval as any of Lydgate's works. Although the evidence for authorship is slight, Lydgate's claim, while disputed, is still generally affirmed. The poem is usually dated between about 1406 to 1412, and there is general agreement that it is an early work, written before more ponderous historical works like the *Troy Book* and the *Fall of Princes*.

Lydgate's source is the first 4873 lines of the French *Les Échecs amoureux*; these he turns into slightly more than 3500 couplets. The French poem continues on to finish the game of chess and offers a detailed description of both the laws of love and the traditional remedies against love; it then effectively abandons allegory to consider at great length the different modes and stations of life, concluding with a mass of practical information about everything from when to wean a baby to where to locate a wine cellar. The landscape of the part Lydgate translated is familiar from the *Roman de la rose*, and the French author also draws on Alain de Lille, Ovid, manuals on chess, and general mythographic lore. Lydgate expands his source throughout and, as usual, is always eager to show off his knowledge, especially of classical stories; in particular, he adds much original material to the descriptions of the gods during the Judgment of Paris and to the allegorical explanations of the various chess pieces. Lydgate himself later used some of this mythographic material in the *Troy Book*; other echoes of *Reson and Sensuallyte* have been detected in Dunbar and in the *Floure and the Leafe*.

Reson and Sensuallyte is generally considered one of the most pleasant and readable of Lydgate's works. It has been praised for the vigor and beauty with which it describes the spring landscape and for the psychological accuracy of its portrait of the would-be lover, who wishes to follow the right path of Nature but is nevertheless dazzled by the delights of love. The poem is a happy combination of the courtly and the homiletic: its moral vision is clear and orthodox, yet there is a real appreciation for the physical beauty of nature and the pleasures of love. During the chess game, Lydgate introduces much satire on women, which takes the form of mock praise. Here as elsewhere, the Fairfax MS includes a series of Latin sidenotes, probably not by Lydgate, which explain the true moral lesson.

REGINA CELI LETARE [162]. Five rime royal stanzas, each with an additional line in Latin.

O joyful light descended from David, mother of your Lord, virgin and mother, rejoice. Remember that sin was the reason for your elevation and that your Son died for us. O happy sin! Because of it we rejoice in your honor and the birth of the Creator. Daughter of Pharaoh, pray for us when we must appear for judgment. O Queen of Glory, because of your virginity and motherhood, we all say halleluiah.

RIGHT AS THE CRABBE GOTH FORWARD (also SATYRICAL BALLAD ON THE TIMES) [163]. Seven eight-line stanzas, octosyllabic, ababbcbc, with slightly varying refrain modified in envoy.

This world is full of stability and without any variance, so that everything goes straight as the crab goes forward. Right is so strong that there is no falsehood and Fortune is now stable. Princes uphold right, knighthood protects truth, the law no longer takes bribes, flattery no longer works, each man has what he needs, etc., etc., just as the crab goes forward. Even women have banished newfangledness just as the crab goes forward, but the heavenly sign shows that the crab goes backward.

This translation of a French poem has been said to have influenced Dunbar and to be typical of Lydgate's satire.

RIME WITHOUT ACCORD (also **ON THE INCONSISTENCY OF MEN'S ACTIONS**) [164]. Eleven eight-line stanzas ababbcbc with refrain in 1-10.

Everything draws to its like, except that human beings crave both carnal and spiritual satisfaction, and yet fire and water burning within one person may well rime but do not agree. For a man to serve two lords, for a mighty king to rule a poor country, for a priest to fight in battle, for a doctor to thrive when there is no illness, for a good wife to run around, etc., etc., it may well rime, but it does not agree. Almighty God, deliver us from such inconsistencies and bring us into Your inheritence.

SALUTACIO ANGELICA (also **AVE MARIA**) [165]. Nine eight-line stanzas ababbcbc, 1-8 with lines 6 and 8 in Latin.

Hail, glorious Lady and Queen of Heaven, help us worship. Blessed may he be who called you Mary, and now we call to you, hail Mary. God was made man through a virgin: this was your marriage, and you suckled Jesus. Flower of purity, remember our frailty and comfort us in the name of your Son Who shed His blood in the Passion. Mention us in your prayers so that we may earn the blessed light. Forgive our presumption and be our comfort. Farewell, Lady, pray for us to your sweet Son.

SECREES OF OLD PHILISOFFRES (also **THE GOVERNAUNCE OF KINGS AND PRINCES** and **SECRETA SECRETORUM**) [166]. 390 rime royal stanzas, of which 214-227 have varying refrain.

God Almighty, save our king, confirm him in all virtues, and increase the glory of his realm; may he govern wisely, punish evil, reward virtue, etc., etc. Excellent Prince, forgive my inept style: I am only a humble servant without eloquence, and I write at your command. This book is entitled *Secrees of Old Philisoffres* and was compiled by Aristotle for Alexander. Aristotle was prudent, wise, devoted to his studies, etc., etc. He was endowed with the gift of prophecy, allowed by God to be called an angel, and even granted a glimpse of Heaven. His advice helped Alexander conquer the world, and the two carried on a correspondence. Alexander wrote to describe Persia and its government and to ask advice on how he might conquer it. Aristotle advised forethought, warned against attempting any enterprise unlikely to succeed, advised reliance upon philosophers for the purpose of insuring good government, and promised God's approval of virtuous conduct. Thus did Alexander conquer Persia with Aristotle's advice. Philip of Paris, who was skilled in both languages and rhetoric, did his best to seek out hidden mysteries. I (i.e., Johannes) did everything possible to understand the things that philosophers sought, and I travelled to Arabia to find some of their secrets. There I met a hermit who clearly explained to me the book of Aesculapius, and I returned home, where I gave thanks to God. I (i.e., Lydgate) stopped for a moment to consider what I should do next, and my mind turned to him who had translated the text from Greek and Arabic into Latin, whom my author names Philip and who addressed his preface to Bishop Guido as follows: Under your gracious support, I write with quaking pen for lack of rhetoric; I have no colors to paint your high renown, the virtues of your name, your wide learning, and the qualities which you share with Noah, Abraham, Cicero, etc., etc., as well as your eagerness to avoid vice, your saintly conduct, your dedication to the reformation of the wicked, your study of the seven sciences, and your humility, which are such that to know you is like attending a university. May God multiply your years. I lack words to account for the learning you gathered while drinking from the well of Helicon along with Homer and Virgil, when you proved both a philosopher and a poet. This book, which came to your attention in Antioch, was translated from Arabic into Latin at your bidding; I undertook the task in all humility as your disciple and clerk, and I have done the translation inexpertly and not word for word.

Although Aristotle was too old and weak to do so, Alexander wanted the philosopher to visit him and reveal his secrets concerning astronomy, astrology, magic, alchemy, etc., etc. Aristotle succeeded in pleasing the king while keeping some of his secrets to himself, for certain kinds of knowledge ought not to be available to everyone. One should search in the Scriptures for explanations of natural mysteries, including such stones as will cure illnesses, but I (i.e., Lydgate) lack the knowledge to deal with these matters as Aristotle did when he taught Alexander how to separate the four elements. This kind of undertaking is not for poor people. The first translator of this book was a Spaniard named John, whose father had received it from a hermit who lived in the place built by Aesculapius near the oracle of the sun. I now began translating the letter which Aristotle wrote to Alexander because he was too weak to visit him. He advised the king to practice the imperial virtues, to disregard flatterers, and to listen to truth. As is reported in Greek books, Aristotle had visited the Lord in Heaven and thus learned secrets which he revealed only through symbolism, for the grain is to be found under the chaff. There are various ways of looking upon royal liberality; the Italians, the Indians, and the Persians hold diverse opinions on the subject, and I believe that temperance and discretion are best. One should reward people according to their desert, and Aristotle makes it clear that a king should provide both for himself and for his subjects and ought not to be greedy. A king careful of his reputation must share what Fortune has sent him and must practice liberality in keeping with just measure so that the sun of his virtue may shine. A king must follow reason and show his generosity to both the nobility and his subjects, and Aristotle suggests avoiding both prodigality and avarice. Measure should rule to make sure that people are rewarded according to their desert, for there is a difference between truth and flattery, and flatterers sting worse than briars. He who would build a reputation must weigh the merits of both high and low in order to reward the worthy but not the unwise; he should help those who have fallen into undeserved poverty but not those who have lost their possessions through vainglory, for prodigality is not honorable, and a king must both avoid avarice and know the difference between liberality and prodigality. In respect to the philosopher's stone, Aristotle wrote to Alexander thus: You must separate fire and water from air and purify all three; a resultant citron color will do for gold, and white for silver. Hermogenes taught Philip such secrets as a king should know. A king should avoid excess of both liberality and appetite, and be on guard against avarice. In order to insure a good reputation, he should avoid vice, keep his subjects from fighting among themselves, be merciful and just, and especially eager to chastise heretics and other enemies of Holy Church. He should look proper and dignified. O, noble Prince, consider how great is the virtue of chastity. According to Roman custom, kings are wont to show themselves in full state so that their subjects may both love and fear them. The king's commands must be obeyed and his rights maintained. A king should surround himself with music so commoners may enjoy his presence, and he should keep a splendid court. His grace should be like the rain that comforts both grass and trees, and he should be merciful, true to his promises, and both the university and the clergy to give the example to his people. For the health of his body, the king must have a physician who is a good astronomer, so as to produce correct diagnoses. O Alexander, trust only a physician proved by experience, for such a one will keep a king in health. Natural philosophers are in agreement that man's body is made of four humors and that an excess of any one of these is harmful. Even in the absence of a physician, one should try controlling one's diet, workload, and melancholy, for a moderate diet does for the body what charity does for the soul. Spring is the season when nature comes to life and birds choose their mates; it is the season which lovers praise and the season when we can act like fools or like prudent people. Summer is the hot and dry season of flowers when fruit and grain ripen and young people enjoy various feasts; therefore, Alexander, thank God for whatever He sends you and keep in mind that you will be rewarded according to your work. Autumn is the time when people work hard at mowing and reaping and when the leaves fall; it is a time of sickness and pestilence and resembles old age, so that you should weigh all actions, Alexander. Winter is the season when trees are bare and the nights long, and we may not return to the spring that gave us strength, for we are now decrepit, and death will consume everything.

Youth and lack of eloquence have delayed the work which I (i.e., Burgh, after Lydgate's death) humbly submit to your consideration in hope that you will enlighten the dullness of my pen. When the flower of knighthood refuses to fight, then the dwarf has no choice but to enter the battle. How can I follow the subtle traces of John Lydgate, since I am not acquainted with the nine Muses? I lack the necessary techniques, as well as Cicero's rhetoric or Ptolemy's astronomy, so that I consider both the royal command and the nasty remarks which detractors will make, and I find myself between Scylla and Charybdis but must do this translation as I have been ordered. Death, Alexander, came either naturally through old age or accidentally as a result of fortune. The body may be kept healthy by sleeping much, eating well, etc., etc., as well as by making certain to vomit once a month. Too little eating, too much drinking, bathing in sulphur water, etc., etc., are harmful. Consider, Alexander, that the body has four principal parts. The first is the head, and dim eyes, etc., etc., are signs of disease there, but aloes boiled in wine is a good remedy for ailments of the head; the second is the breast, and a bitter mouth, aching limbs, etc., etc., are signs of disease there, but vomiting or eating spice will help; the third is the belly, and bloating there or redness of the knee indicate a condition which must be treated with purgation, for it may result in a back-ache, poor digestion, etc., etc.; the fourth is the genitals, and lack of appetite or redness of the testicles indicates illness, which must be treated with fennel and various roots before it may engender calculus. I have read somewhere that a mighty king once gathered the best physicians of Greece and India to teach him such medicines as would prevent disease. The former prescribed water in the morning, and the other prescribed milk and fasting, but in my opinion, Alexander, the way to keep healthy includes the proper amount of sleep, raisins and other such things in the morning, and nuts, figs, and rue. Furthermore, certain foods listed here produce good blood, some are good for laborers but not for other people, and the perch is a particularly good fish. Running water is good, but sleepy and bitter water cause diseases; water immediately before or during meals is bad, and one should drink water cold in summer and warm in winter. Hill-grown wine is best, especially for old people; thick red wine is good for the blood, but not if taken to excess. Good wine comes from grapes grown in large fields and is between red and gold in color; it has fourteen properties, including promoting good digestion, producing pure blood, etc., etc., but too much of it brings about contrary effects, just as rhubarb can turn into a deadly poison if one eats too much of it. I marvel at the foolishness of people who neglect the help of good bread, meat, and wine, or who overeat, overwork themselves, or overdrink. Willows and sandalwood ointment are good following the heavy use of wine, but one must not cease drinking all of a sudden. The duty of a king is to protect his subjects' lives and possessions and to rule with righteousness, and the Indians believe that the former is especially important. During council meeting, you will do well to listen to all opinions but keep your own to yourself until the appropriate time and be slow in deliberation and quick in action. I have read the Indian story of a weaver's son who insisted upon studying with wise men and eventually became chief councilor while the king's son would learn nothing except metalwork. The wise men explained that this situation was the result of the constellations and that it showed that kings must respect wisdom regardless of its origin. A great man once wrote to his son that one should always listen to the advice of the wise, reject bad advice, never put his power into one man's hands, and test one's officers by pretending to be in need. Never trust a covetous man or one who can be corrupted, but trust one in whom these fifteen virtues are in evidence: physical fitness, intelligence, love of wise men, etc., etc. In contrast, gluttony is detestable in an officer of state, as is avarice. As old philosophers remind us, man is called the little world, and he is indeed brave as a lion, fearful as a hare, etc., etc., so that he is indeed a little world. In addition, Alexander, be sure that your private secretary will keep your letters confidential and record your thoughts in beautiful language before you reward him. Make sure that you have swift messengers who are the ears, eyes, and tongues of their lord, but avoid indiscreet drunkards and high-ranking officers prone to treason. Consider how much a realm profits from a king who governs honorably for the good of his subjects and protects them according to custom. Appoint good officers, or your subjects will rebel, and be sure to appoint honest judges and establish courts of appeal. In war, do not take part in battles yourself; know the feelings of your soldiers, make encouraging speeches, make camp in the proper places, have plenty of food for the army, etc., etc., poison the enemy's wells, and make use of efficient spies, but keep in mind that it is better to get what you need without war. Philomon was the discoverer of physiognomy. When he was reproached with having analyzed a picture of Hippocrates and found in it lechery and deceit, he answered that he had referred to the natural disposition rather than to the actual deeds, and Hippocrates acknowledged the validity of the verdict, thus showing that kings should learn physiognomy. Avoid colorless men, choose a man who laughs heartily, and flee from deformed men. The best are well-proportioned, have a good voice, soft ears, plenty of hair, etc., etc. There are twelve signs of a good man: sweet looks, full ears, rather large eyes, etc., etc. Note all aspects, and do not judge by one alone.

Go, little book, and apologize for me to the reader. Do not defend me if anyone objects to my ineptitude, but ask him to make such corrections as are needed.

This poem, whose reading is often made somewhat irritating by frequent, inconsistent, and unannounced shifts in point of view as well as by the lack of a clear principle of organization, was completed by Benedict Burgh after Lydgate's death. It is a translation of the *Secreta Secretorum* and has been said to borrow from the Bible.

SERPENT OF DIVISION [167]. Prose with one four-line stanza aabb inserted and an envoy of three eight-line stanzas ababbcbc with refrain.

According to old books, Rome was first governed by kings and then by counselors until the latter changed their title to that of dictator in the time of the triumvirate of Pompey, Crassus, and Julius Caesar. Rome flowered in prosperity while the three worked in unison, but the contagious serpent of division put an end to their worthiness through Caesar's pride and Pompey's envy. The time came when Crassus was sent with legions against the Parthians, and Caesar was sent across the Alps, where he promptly conquered all territories on his path except

Britain, which held out until the defeat of its king. Crassus was so cruel to the Parthians that they eventually killed him. Pompey feared the power which Caesar was acquiring through his conquests, and he seized upon the death of his wife, who was Caesar's daughter, as an excuse for having him recalled to Rome. Thus did the snake of mistrust and envy begin to kindle the fire of envy. When Caesar found reasons for remaining in the field, Pompey succeeded in having him declared a traitor. Unaware of this development, the other decided to return to Rome if he were granted the triumph which his accomplishment deserved, but Pompey made certain to have the request denied, and the denial so irritated Caesar that it became the root of the division between them and the cause of the civil war, as Lucan writes in his book. Also according to Lucan, there were three logical reasons for these events. The first was necessity, since pomp and pride must fall like everything else in this world. The second was consuetude, since Fortune always casts down those whom she has raised on her wheel. The third was willfulness, since the contenders were so blinded by their prosperity that neither would listen to the other. Now Caesar led his army across the Alps back into Italy and stopped at the Rubicon. As he was about to cross that river, the likeness of a sorrowful old woman appeared to him and begged him recall his allegiance to Rome, but she had no sooner vanished than he prayed aloud to Jupiter and proclaimed that he was crossing the river not as an enemy but as the defender of a just cause who would live and die for the good of the city. The Romans were divided between those who favored Pompey and those who favored Caesar, and thus began a division which was never completely healed and which should serve as an example for all nations. Valerius tells of an old philosopher who tried to illustrate the situation by showing that, while a strong man could not pull off the tail of a horse with one pull, a weak man could easily pull it one hair at a time. Soon the city was filled with omens of war: flaming stars were seen, dogs ceased barking, the Sibyl predicted destruction, the priest found discoloration in the entrails of sacrificial victims, etc., etc., so that I may conclude that division separates man from God. Caesar skirted Dyrrachium and went into Thessaly where he defeated Pompey, who fled to Egypt. Caesar followed, defeated King Ptolemy, and installed Cleopatra on the throne. After he had gone on to conquer Africa and received tribute from Spain, he had a dream in which he copulated with his own mother, and the philosophers interpreted it as meaning that he should become emperor of the world. He accordingly returned to Rome, where he was made emperor. Caesar's death was announced by various omens: a tomb was opened in which was found a tablet predicting his murder, his wife had a dream in which the pinnacle of the imperial palace collapsed, etc., etc. The engineer of the murder was Brutus Cassius, who made a pact with others to knife him to death in the senate. My master Chaucer has written of this deed that it shows that one should never trust Fortune. Let everyone consider the dangers of mutability, and let every head of state think of Caesar's fate as an illustration of the contagious perils of division, pride, and envy, for the city of Rome was thus despoiled of both her treasure and her knights. I undertook this translation at the command of my most worshipful sovereign. This little prose work exposes the damage that befell Rome as a result of division and the ambition of Caesar and Pompey. Christ Himself says that no divided country can endure. No one may count on Fortune, but one can avoid dissension by recalling the example of Pompey and Caesar.

This work has been said to have drawn on Chaucer in addition to French and Latin sources, and the handling of Fortune has been considered reminiscent of Boethius.

SERVANT OF CUPYDE FORSAKEN (also **COMPLAYNT LYDE-GATE** and **NEW YEAR GIFT**) [168]. Nine eight-line stanzas ababbcbc in octosyllabic verse with varying refrain, including envoy.

I have served Cupid a long time and have been mercilessly forsaken over and over again because of Danger and Disdain. I found disdain in high estate and debate in lower places. I loved some beautiful women who neglected me, and some wealthy women who passed me by, and service got me only scorn from young and old. The harder I tried, the more I was forsaken. I accordingly direct this complaint to all women.

The authorship of this poem has been questioned.

SIEGE OF THEBES [169]. Prologue and three parts for a total of 4716 decasyllabic couplets.

Prologue. When bright Phebus had passed the Ram in the middle of April, at the time when *The Canterbury Tales* were written by the flower of all British poets and chief register of this pilgrimage, I came to Canterbury to fulfill my vows to the saint after an illness, and I accidentally entered the inn where the Pilgrims were staying. In answer to the Host's command, I said that my name was Lydgate, Monk of Bury, and that I was about fifty years old. He invited me to join the Pilgrims for supper and to return home with them the next day with the understanding that I should also tell a tale, and I agreed to do so, as you will now hear.

Part I. Sirs, I said, my wits are barren, but I shall obey the Host's command and tell a wondrous tale about the siege and destruction of Thebes, which was erected by the warbles of King Amphion's harp, as both my author and Boccaccio have written. Other authors say that Cadmus first built the city but was eventually exiled by Amphion, who was the ancestor of King Layus, who was Jocasta's husband. When Jocasta became pregnant, the oracles predicted that she would bear a son who would grow to kill his father. Layus accordingly told her to have the child killed as soon as he was born, but the two men charged with the deed found him too beautiful to die, so that they pierced his feet and hung him thereby on a tree, where he was found by huntsmen who took him to King Polibon of Arcadia, who named him Oedipus and raised him with the intention of making him his heir. Oedipus grew so unbearably proud and overbearing that someone eventually told him that he was a mere foundling. After obtaining Polibon's confirmation of the fact, he went to the Temple of Apollo, where an unclean spirit inside a gold statue told him to travel to Thebes to find his lineage. On the way he stopped by a castle to take part in a tournament organized by King Layus and accidentally killed the latter. Since nobody knew exactly who had killed the king, Oedipus said nothing and promptly resumed his journey toward Thebes. On the way, he met a monster called the Sphinx, who made it a practice to slay all passers-by who could not solve a riddle which he set them. Contrary to expectation, Oedipus solved the problem and cut off the Sphinx's head. As a result of his deed, he was given a warm welcome in Thebes and soon asked to marry the late king's widow and become king himself, so that he both killed his father and married his mother. God does not suffer blood to touch blood: Herod married his brother's wife and thus caused the death of John the Baptist. We should learn from Oedipus, who was punished although he acted in ignorance. The wedding was unhappy, and none of the Muses was there: they had gone to the wedding of Mercury and Philology, which has been described by Marcianus Capella. The wedding that took place in Thebes eventually brought about the destruction of the city, and the guests included Cerberus, Herebus, Night and her daughters, Dread, Fraud, etc., etc. Oedipus reigned a long time in prosperity and had two sons and two daughters by Jocasta, but Fortune cast him off her wheel when he was at the very top. One night Jocasta noticed the old wounds on his feet, and the terrible truth soon became evident to both of them. Moral Seneca tells in a tragedy how Oedipus lost his mind and tore his eyes out, and how his sons threw his corpse into a pit. Only unnatural blood comes from cursed stock: those who do not honor their parents will find Fortune contrary and end badly. Be warned by the story of Oedipus' sons, and I shall continue the story as soon as we have passed this vale.

Part II. When we had passed Boughton, I went on with my tale and explained how Oedipus' sons began striving for the crown as soon as their father was dead. The Thebans decided that Eteocles should be crowned because he was the elder, but the younger brother, Polynices, refused to abide by this decision, and it was finally decided that each of them would take turn reigning a year at a time. Since Eteocles was to reign first, Polynices rode out of town and travelled until he reached a forest by the sea. After weathering a particularly fierce storm, he crossed the forest and near midnight reached the palace of Adrastus, King of Argos, who had two lovely daughters and no male heir, and who had dreamt that they should marry a wild boar and a fierce lion. Finding everybody asleep in Argos, Polynices tied his horse and went to sleep on a porch. He had hardly gone to sleep when another knight, Tideus, rode in, who had been banished from Calidonia for accidentally shooting his brother, as Statius tells us. Polynices jumped to his feet and began abusing Tideus, who politely answered that he too had been driven by the storm and would like to share the same porch for the rest of the night, but Polynices insisted on fighting. Awakened by the noise of the combat, Adrastus separated them and confiscated their swords before asking who they were; he then arranged a reconciliation, invited them to stay, and had them meet his daughters, with whom they immediately fell in love. The next day, when he noticed that their coats of arms included respectively a boar and a lion, he asked them to marry his daughters with the understanding that each would inherit half his possessions and that he would immediately abdicate the throne in their favor, and so it was done. Upon hearing news of these events, Eteocles called his allies and officers and told them that he would never be at peace until his brother was dead. The good ones among them told him that a king must keep his word. Truth is indeed above everything else, as illustrated in the Bible; truth is the preserver of kingdoms, for God sees all, and note that Thebes was destroyed by Eteocles' duplicity. But at the end of his year's reign, Eteocles listened to the flatterers who advised him to go back on his word and keep the crown. Meanwhile Polynices listened to Adrastus' advice not to go to Thebes himself, and Tideus decided to go there as his messenger. In Thebes, Tideus, finding Eteocles sitting with his lords in the hall, boldly reminded him of the agreement whereby he must now relinquish the throne for a year. Eteocles turned pale and asked why Polynices should want Thebes now that he had everything he needed in Argos. He then declared the agreement void and boasted that his brother would not get even a half-foot of Thebes. Tideus politely but firmly answered that his lack of faith would cause Argos and the rest of Greece to make war on him and that God would punish him; he defied him in the name of Polynices and called on the Theban lords to live up to the agreement. No sooner had he left the hall, than Eteocles sent fifty knights in pursuit to kill him. Tideus, however, took his stand on a hill and killed all his enemies but one, whom he sent back to tell Eteocles what had taken place. Severely wounded and weakened by loss of blood, he nevertheless got on his horse and rode on until he reached King Lycurgus' castle, where he dismounted and lay exhausted in the garden until the king's daughter found him and dressed his wounds. Although invited to stay, he left the next day for Argos, where his wife embraced him. Polynices grieved to see him so wounded, and Adrastus sent for doctors to heal him. Back in Thebes, Eteocles was so furious that he began cursing his dead knights as cowards, but the survivor answered that it was his breaking the agreement that brought about the disaster, and he then killed himself. Sorrow and destruction will fall upon the king and the entire region because truth was not kept, as my tale will show if you care to hear the rest of it.

Part III. Why, cruel Mars, were you so angry with the people of Thebes, whose city was burnt to the ground? Was it because of Original Sin? King Adrastus decided to conquer Thebes and called a meeting of Greek kings and lords who would take part in the campaign. Tideus sent to Chalcedon for warriors, and many knights also came from Thebes because they considered themselves honor-bound to help Polynices. Adrastus housed and fed everyone well: a prince, especially a conqueror, must practice liberality if he wants to secure his people's love, which is worth more than gold. In Thebes, Eteocles assembled his lords and friends, placed soldiers on the walls, bestowed gifts upon the knights, filled the stores, and strengthened the fortifications. Meanwhile, the Greeks decided to seek the advice of a wise bishop named Amphiaraus, but he knew that the campaign would kill most of the Greek kings and that he himself would meet his death if he went along. He accordingly decided to hide and let only his wife know of his hiding place, but she was forced to reveal it. Despite his remonstrations, the Greeks went along with the wishes of the younger men, who wanted immediate war: Youth likes to act on catastrophic impulses. What good would all the wisest men do if nobody listened to them? On the way to Thebes, the Greeks ran out of water while crossing a desert, and Tideus and Capaneus rode out on a scouting mission until they found a garden in which a beautiful young woman named Ipsiphyle was watching over King Lycurgus' infant son. They convinced her to leave the child alone for a few minutes so that she might guide them to a nearby river where the host would quench their thirst. Ipsiphyle explained that she was a king's daughter who had been forced to flee her own country after saving her father's life when the women had decided to kill all the men and take over. Read Boccaccio if you want to know the whole story. While she was talking and showing the river to the Greeks, a snake bit the king's child, and only the intercession of the Greeks saved Ipsiphyle from the wrath of the grieving Lycurgus. It would take a very long time to describe the sorrow and lamentations that took place during the burial. Adrastus reminded Lycurgus that death comes to everyone sooner or later and that only those who show mercy shall receive mercy, but the queen swooned and demanded that either Ipsiphyle or the snake be killed. The Greeks killed the snake and arranged a reconciliation between Lycurgus and Ipsiphyle, but Boccaccio says that she left the country and books tell us that he eventually went to Athens to fight with Palamon against Arcite and eventually came to a bad end for destroying Bacchus' vines. The Greeks now resumed their march and soon reached Thebes and began laying waste the countryside. Eteocles called a meeting to seek advice. When Jocasta reminded him that he was at fault and advised him to keep the agreement, he said that he might let Polynices reign for a year but would keep the sovereignty. Since no Theban would agree to deliver this message to the Greek camp, Jocasta offered to take her daughters along and act as an intermediary between her sons, but Polynices proved as intractable as Eteocles. While she was with the Greeks, they killed a pet tiger escaped from Thebes because they thought it was wild. The Thebans came out to avenge the tiger, and the actual fighting thus began, even though Jocasta convinced Polynices to recall his soldiers temporarily. Jocasta tried to convince Adrastus to make peace, but he would accept only such terms as Tideus would work out, and my author says that the latter would not risk his men's lives by entering Thebes. Before leaving the Greek camp, Jocasta had promised Polynices to make a last attempt at convincing Eteocles to live up to his agreement, but she had no success there either. Next morning the Greeks took to the field, and the earth opened and swallowed Amphiaraus: the devil paid him the wages of idolatry. Because of the death of Amphiaraus, some Greeks began thinking about giving up, but Adrastus summoned a meeting where it was decided that withdrawal would be cowardice and that they should stay there until Thebes had been destroyed. Then they made Terdimus bishop to replace Amphiaraus. Tideus inflicted enormous losses on the Thebans but was himself killed by a crossbow quarrel; even the best knight could not avoid death. Polynices wounded Eteocles to death, but the latter stabbed him in the heart, so that both died. The thunder of the guns was hideous as Thebans and Greeks slaughtered each other at the gates. Of the Greek lords, only Adrastus and Capaneus survived, but the Thebans succeeded in barring the gates. The next day they buried Eteocles, and an old tyrant named Creon was elected king of Thebes. After the news of the slaughter had reached Greece, the Greek widows put on black, and between one and two thousand of them set out barefoot for Thebes to bury their dead. Upon reaching their destination, they swooned at the sight of the corpses which Creon had ordered left unburied to be eaten by the dogs. As my master Chaucer has written, they waited until Theseus came by, and they asked him to redress their grievances. He was moved by their plight and went on to kill Creon and level Thebes to the ground. I shall not describe the details of this action. Adrastus returned to Argos, where he soon died and lies buried. These events took place four hundred years before the foundation of Rome, and the blood of both Greece and Thebes was spilled. Everybody suffers in war, which is something which began in Heaven with the pride of Lucifer. Covetousness and ambition are the roots of all evil, but the venom of war shall be proscribed, and peace and love shall again spread through the world. Let us pray that He Who is both one and two and three and gave His blood for mankind may send us peace here and eternal joy when we die.

This poem, which is presented as an addition to *The Canterbury Tales*, is assumed to be based on a French version of the story of Thebes and to reflect the influence of Boccaccio, Chaucer, Martianus Capella, the Bible, and Seneca. The subject matter belongs to an amply attested medieval tradition, and this particular version has been said to suggest something of Lydgate's possible importance to the history of early Humanism.

SODEIN FAL OF PRINCES (also **FALLS OF SEVEN PRINCES**) [170]. Seven rime royal stanzas.

Behold the great Prince Edward II: he was deposed and murdered in prison. See how Richard was glorious but died in prison. See Charles of France, the Duke of Orleans, Thomas of Gloucester, the Duke of Burgundy, and the Duke of Ireland.

This poem has been considered a tapestry piece, a mumming, and a processional.

STANS PUER AD MENSAM (normal version) [171]. Fourteen rime royal stanzas including envoy.

My dear son standing at table before your lord, learn these rules with all your heart. Keep your hands and feet still. Do not wiggle, lean against the post, pick your nose, or scratch. Walk demurely, avoid dissolute language, pare your nails, wash your hands, be quiet, eat and drink properly without picking your teeth with your knife, avoid ribaldry and offending noises, etc., etc. Children's quarrels are not serious, and a rod will reform their insolence. Who spares the rod sets virtue aside. Go, little poem without eloquence, and pray little children to heed your lessons. If ought be wrong, put the blame on John Lydgate.

This poem is usually considered an adaptation of a Latin original. The number of manuscripts suggests the popularity of the subject matter, presumably with grownups. Consult [172] for expanded version with prologue.

STANS PUER AD MENSAM (expanded version with 6-stanza prologue) [172]. 30 eight-line stanzas ababbcbc, one (15) six-line stanza ababcc, and one (32) four-line stanza abab, including prologue.

> May Jesus Christ, Who died on the Cross, give me grace to teach children to flee from vice. My intent is to teach them courtesy because it will avail both rich and poor. A vicious child never learns anything or thrives at all, and nobody likes him. Therefore, pay attention to my lesson: work while you are young, learn to help yourself, never act against reason, and listen to my teaching.

See the normal version of *Stans Puer ad Mensam* [171] for remainder of summary and for comment.

STELLA CELI EXTIRPAVIT, VERSION 1 [173]. Four eight-line stanzas ababbcbc.

> Heavenly Queen who suckled Jesus, drive away the war of pestilence and restrain the mist of infected air. Protect us in the name of the Passion. Virgin mother, you can save your servants from pestilence just as the sun chases the black mist.

See also Version 2 [174].

STELLA CELI EXTIRPAVIT, VERSION 2 [174]. Four eight-line stanzas ababbcbc with varying refrain.

> O Blessed Queen, look at us and be our shield against pestilence. Adam's sin brought death, but you brought life to mankind. Drive off the air of pestilence, and grant me long life, wealth, and eternal bliss.

See also Version 1 [173].

SUPPLICATIO AMANTIS (also THE COMPLEYNT) [175]. 628 octosyllabic lines in riming couplets.

> Alas, my lady, I can find no remedy for my woe since I went away from you, and I am like a fish out of water whenever I do not see you. I turn pale and remember how I was unable to express my feelings when I took leave of you: in your presence I have a tongue but no words. I always think of you, and you know that my heart is constantly suing for mercy, but you have no

compassion for your servant since you will not bid him serve you. How have I offended you? Queen of my heart, I entreat your womanly mercy to save my life by giving me a task to do for you. You can see my piteous countenance and notice how I shake for sorrow. When I had to leave you, I felt as though a sword of sorrow had gone through my side, and I was angry at the sun because it shone so brightly while I endured suffering. The sun would meet Diana on March 31, but I was sad at leaving my lady. I may well complain of March, that caused my separation from the flower of womanhood. She has wisdom, honesty, etc., etc., and lacks nothing except pity. Alas, Fortune, your wheel and cheer are so constantly changing; I must die unless you turn your wheel so that I may have the lovely daisy named Margaret, the most wonderful of flowers. May God bring me within sight of her, and may Fortune help me. Noble lady, I suffer for you alone and wish to be your man. You are my joy, my sorrow, my mirth, my malady, etc., etc. I burn with fever at the oratory of Venus, and I have been faithful ever since I first looked at your bright eyes. I have therefore written this poem, at which I beseech you to look before you throw it in the fire. If it is fated to be torn to pieces, I pray that it will be with your soft hands; and, if you read it, I shall desire no other reward. I shall remain your man from year to year whether I live or die.

This poem, which is not normally attributed to Lydgate, seems to have been intended as a continuation of *Temple of Glas* [176].

TEMPLE OF GLAS [176]. 1403 lines of which the formal speeches are in rime royal and the narrative is in long-line couplets.

One night in the middle of December, I fell asleep in distress and was carried away to a round, dazzling Temple of Glass. Inside were pictures of famous lovers who had complaints for Venus (Dido, Penelope, Griselda, Paris and Helen, Mars and Venus, Canace, and others are named). There were thousands of other lovers complaining to the goddess of various ills and misfortunes in love. At last I saw a lady who surpassed the rest. In her hand was a bill of complaint: "O Venus, grant me thy grace. I have no liberty to choose freely. I am bound to one I do not love. What I secretly desire I may not possess." Venus answered: "I promise you relief and an end to your sorrow. I will bind the heart of the one you love to you." The lady then prayed in thanks to Venus. Venus gave the lady hawthorn branches to teach her to be unchanging. Next in my dream I saw a crowd offering to the goddess and then a solitary man. He lamented, saying: "Alas, I am ensnared in love for that woman in the temple. I am caught between hope and dread." He then entered an oratory and prayed: "O Cytherea, you alone can help me. Constrain her to love me; for I dread to ask for grace from one so virtuous. I will always be true to her. I ask you to grant me release." Venus answered: "Cupid and I will help you, but be not too hasty. Let Reason govern desire. Thou must kneel and ask thy lady for pity." The knight was afraid, but made his complaint to the lady thus: "Queen and mistress of women, I am your servant. I would rather die than offend you. Let me obtain mercy or die in your service." The lady blushed and in pity said: "I accept you, but we must submit to Venus's will." Then I saw the lovers before the goddess, who united their hearts, saying: "My daughter, accept this man in your mercy. And, my son, be steadfast and courteous to all. Seek virtue and avoid vice. In the end you shall win her. Kiss him, daughter. Your heart shall be locked by my golden key." Then the lady kissed her servant. All in the temple praised Venus and Cupid, and the goddess promised that the love of these two would endure forever. A ballad was then sung before the goddess. With this melody I awoke, sad to lose sight of that beautiful lady. For her I write this treatise and send it to her for correction.

This somewhat puzzling and yet completely conventional courtly love poem has been dated anywhere between 1400 and 1420. Although the *Temple of Glas* has no direct source, its debt to the courtly tradition, especially as embodied in the *Roman de la rose*, and to Chaucer (especially his *House of Fame, Parliament of Foules, Knight's Tale, Squire's Tale, Troilus and Criseyde, Anelida and Arcite, Legend of Good Women*, and *Complaint of Mars*) is immense. The poem's popularity in the fifteenth century is attested to by the large number of prints and surviving manuscripts, and its influence on Spenser and the *Kingis Quair* has been argued.

Three different versions of the poem are found in the manuscripts, whose relationship has been variously defined, with the standard modern text usually accepted as the final version. What some consider the first draft of the poem is quite different from the final one, principally in its presentation of the lady's psychology and in the inclusion of a long complaint by the poet on leaving his mistress, which is usually not considered to be by Lydgate. The occasion of the poem is also in dispute. Some argue that it was written for a marriage, perhaps a Paston marriage because the lady's motto (*De mieulx en mieulx*) is also theirs, but others deny this, arguing that the relationship between the lovers, though never stated directly, must be adulterous. A real story may indeed lie behind the poem, but the narrative is probably too vague to permit any definite identification. Individual theories are thus possible: it has been argued by one scholar that the lovers have engaged in a clandestine marriage, and by another that the author is Richard Roos.

The *Temple of Glas* has been praised for its technical skill, though it often reads like an anthology of traditional speeches and has little narrative development. Abstract and serious, but almost totally lacking real allegory, the poem has little philosophical or psychological complexity. It is generally similar to Lydgate's *Complaint of the Black Knight* [23] and *The Floure of Curtesy* [53].

THE TESTAMENT [177]. 118 eight-line stanzas ababbcbc in five sections, with different varying refrain in each of sections I, III, and V.

Section I. How wholesome is the memory of Jesus! It is a triumphant name with which to vanquish Satan. No song is so sweet as Jesus, Who will pardon all those who are contrite and have done penance, and in Whom stands all our hope. Ignacius' heart was marked with His name in gold letters. Jesus redeemed us on Calvary. No language or word can tell the worth of Jesus. Merciful Jesus, have mercy on all those who bow to You on their knees. The Lord was slain so that the servant may go free: is not man bound to kneel before Him? The name of Jesus appears 660 times in Paul's epistles. No enemy can hurt him who bows to Jesus, whose name will always be my sovereign guide. While He was on the Cross, Jesus granted Paradise to a thief so that no man may ever despair. His name is effective remedy for all kinds of ailments. Patriarchs, prophets, the Apostles, beasts, birds, etc., etc., must humbly bow before Him, and there can be no perfect love unless it be grounded in Him. The name of Jesus means our Savior, our Sampson, and our Orpheus, and its letters stand for jocunditas, eternitas, sanitas, ubertas, and suavitas, or for joy, everlasting sufficiency, salvation, the five wounds, and the sacrament, just as the *J* stands for Jacob and the *C* for Christ. Have mercy on us, Jesus, when we die. In my old age and infirmity, I pray to Jesus with my whole heart so that He may forgive my sins. With Jesus' help, I am intent upon writing my testament before I pass hence, for age calls me to my grave. Mercy, Jesus, in the name of the Passion! I shall now confess the sins of my life.

Section II. The past years of my youth have brought me the calends of death. I was summoned by one of his beadles, feebleness; then came sickness, followed by remembrance and regret. Lying alone, I began to think about the four seasons of the departed year. Spring brings about a rebirth of nature, with honeysuckles and other flowers, sunshine, amorous birds, and dewdrops; it is the time of joy and greenness, and stirs fresh hearts and makes the birds sing. In all these respects, it resembles childhood. It is the moist and hot season when Flora covers mountains and vales with her cheerful wardrobe, and it is a favorite with childhood, which is the time of life when the blood is moist and hot and goes to the head. At this time of life, desire holds the bridle, and it changes just as spring weather suddenly changes from sunshine to rain, and death can also overcome a child. Spring lasts only a short time, and I remember well when I was happy and thoughtless in that season. Before I tell the trespasses of my tender age, Jesus, grant me to die in state of grace, and may Your Passion guide me.

Section III. O Mighty Lord, grant me confession, communion, and repentance before I die. You are merciful though mighty, and I am a sinful wretch. Receive my confession, O Jesus, and bridle my sinfulness under Your discipline. Let Your grace lead me, and do not suffer me to find pleasure in anything but Your name, for there is no lord but Jesus, Who endured the Passion on the Cross for our sake. I am inspired to praise the name of Jesus above everything else. Let me not rest; fill my soul to make it sing for mercy, for my faith and hope call to You, Jesus, and there is no god but You. Let me speak to You, for You are the health of my soul. Show Your face and let the merciful light of Your eyes shine upon Your servant, as You save me in Your mercy. You are my refuge; let me receive the Holy Sacrament, which is the food of my old age. My heart is impure, but You can purify my soul as a carpenter repairs a broken house. I cry that You accept me, Jesus Who died on the Cross. Grant me constant remembrance of Your five wounds and the other tokens of the Passion, and let the name of Jesus enlighten my mind. I humbly end my prayer with the hope that you will grant me confession, communion, and repentance before I die.

Section IV. During the season of my green years, I was silly, willful, unwilling to learn, easily angered, and guided only by passions; I stole apples and other fruits, enjoyed playing practical jokes, did not care for my prayers, and sneered at those who would have taught me better. In fact, I acted like a truant and enjoyed doing so. After I entered into religion, I was taught the Benedictine Rule but took little heed of it and would not mount the nine steps of humility. I was impatient, disobedient, foul-spoken, gluttonous, fond of listening to fables, unattracted by holy histories and contemplation, etc., etc. until I reached the age of fifteen and saw a crucifix with a caption that read thus: behold My meekness, O child, and give up your pride. I shall now write a poem in remembrance.

Section V. Behold, O man! Lift up your eyes and see what pain I endure for your sins. Behold the ropes with which I was bound, behold how I was sold by Judas, behold how I was condemned to death, behold how I was offered like a lamb in sacrifice. See My body beaten and nailed to the Cross, and behold My bleeding wounds. See how My disciples forsook Me and the knights cast dice for My clothes. Behold My love and give Me yours in return; give Me your heart and keep these things engraved in your memory. Remember how I gave proof of My mercy by granting Paradise to a thief, and come home, My brother for whom I offered My blood in sacrifice.

This poem has been said to reflect the influence of the *Legenda Aurea*, Isidore of Seville, and Chaucer and to have influenced Dunbar. Some critics rate it as one of Lydgate's best works.

SONG OF THANKSGIVING (also TE DEUM) [178]. Thirteen eight-line macaronic stanzas ababbcbc with Latin refrain.

We praise You, O God Who sits in splendor among sun and stars. All the angels, the seraphim, etc., etc., sing sanctus and praise You. Heaven and earth proclaim Your majesty and charity, as do the apostles, the martyrs, and the Church. When You had overcome death, Jesus King of Glory, You sat at the right of God, and You will be the judge on the Day of Judgment. Grant us eternal glory, Lord, and let us praise Your name in this world. Have mercy on us, Lord, since our hope is entirely in You, and let us not suffer perdition.

This free translation of the *Te Deum* is said to have influenced other religious poems.

THAT NOW IS HAY THAT SUMTYME WAS GRASSE [179]. Seventeen eight-line stanzas ababbcbc including envoy, of which sixteen have the same refrain.

There is little security in this world except in change, which occurs just as the grass turns to hay. The flowers that adorn the meadow in April will be cut by the scythe in June, the roses of midsummer will soon lose their fragrance, and the nightingale of summer will cease singing in winter. Old age defaces all beauty. Polyxena, who was so fair, is dead, as are Helen, Dido, David, Hector, Arthur, etc., etc. Now it is day, now night; now we are happy in love, now we despair, etc., etc. Let us not belabor the point, since anyone can see that everything changes. Go forth, little poem, and bid people remember that only the celestial City has grass that never turns to hay.

THEY THAT NO WHILE ENDURE, VERSION 1 [180]. Seven eight-line stanzas ababbcbc with varying refrain.

This world is so big that no one can control it, as shown in the lives of Alexander and Croesus. The power of mighty princes does not endure, and the same holds true of those who think the world will last forever, those who are foolhardy, the women who sell their beauty, etc., etc. Pray to God, therefore, and endure through mercy and grace.

This poem should be examined in connection with Version 2 [181].

THEY THAT NO WHILE ENDURE, VERSION 2 [181]. Eight rime royal stanzas with identical refrain.

The bold knight, the amorous squire, the hawk, or the greyhound: not one of these will endure in the natural order of things, and the same holds true of the cutpurse, the liar, the drunkard, etc., etc.

This poem should be examined in connection with Version 1 [180].

THOROUGHFARE OF WOE (also **ON THE WRETCHEDNESS OF WORLDLY AFFAIRS**) [182]. 24 eight-line stanzas ababbcbc with identical refrain.

Lift up your eyes, you who are blinded with worldly vanity, for this world is a thoroughfare of woe. Boethius bids us beware of mutability in a world in which everything is as transitory as a painting on a stage. See how Adam and Eve were cast out of Paradise. Even the wealthiest lords tempt Fortune through greed and must endure change. None was braver than Joshua, fairer than Absalom, etc., etc., but they were only pilgrims passing to and fro. Paris was wrecked by the Armagnacs and Burgundians, and mighty Henry V has died, as did the Duke of Exeter, the earl of Salisbury, etc., etc., for death spares neither emperor nor king. God sends summons to all, and sickness and languor are the beadles. The Lord Himself, Who gave Heaven to His children, received nothing but scorn on earth, for this life always fails, and even triumphant kings are only transitory shadows. Masters who read this ditty, remember that I took the refrain from my master Chaucer, who declared long ago that this world is a thoroughfare of woe.

This poem has been selected both as an example of Lydgate's solid craftsmanship and as an example of his failure to understand Chaucerian humor.

TYED WITH A LINE (also **ON THE INSTABILITY OF HUMAN AFFAIRS**) [183]. Twelve rime royal stanzas, with identical refrain in 1–7 and varying refrain in 9–12.

The more I go, the more I am behind; the longer I serve, the more I am neglected: is this fortune or infortune? Though I go loose, I am tied with a line. The fuller the belly, the greedier in eating; a warlike peace and peace within the war, etc., etc., thus is the world in variance, and no man goes loose but he be tied with a line. Defy Fortune and look at the dance of death. Trust in God, for Christ's Passion will redeem us.

The authorship of some stanzas has been questioned.

TYED WITH A LINE, STANZA 1 ONLY (recorded and printed as separate poem) [184].

See [183] for summary.

The authorship has been questioned. See complete version [183] for additional comment.

TIMOR MORTIS CONTURBAT ME (also WOURLDLY MUTABILITE) [185]. Sixteen eight-line stanzas of octosyllabic verse ababbcbc with Latin refrain.

As I lay on my bed the other night, I began to think about worldly mutability and to realize that the fear of death disturbs me. I considered how Adam was deceived into eating an apple and was then threatened by fear of death. But for his trespass, we would not know the fear of death, but there has been no remedy for this disease from that time to the present through Noah, Abraham, Isaac, etc., etc. St. John writes that he saw a rider on a pale horse and that his name was Death and he had power over everything. Even the Nine Worthies fell under the stroke of death, as did Judith, Dido, Penelope, etc., etc. Neither power nor wealth avails against the fear of death that disturbs me, for winter follows summer and man has no protection against the fear of death. Keep in mind that worldly good will do you no good when death comes and that the only help is the Passion of Christ.

This poem has been assumed to have influenced Dunbar's *Lament for the Makaris*, X [29] in *Manual*, volume 4.

GUARD YOUR TONGUE (also ADVICE TO TITTLE-TATTLERS and THE COCK HATH LOWE SHOONE) [186]. Twenty-two eight-line stanzas ababbcbc with refrain in all stanzas except 17.

The wise man keeps quiet, for it is folly to speak out of turn and the old proverb says that, although we go quietly, the cock has low shoes. Think plenty, but say little and speak advisedly.

At night the cock watches over Dame Pertelote when the fox comes near to discuss peace, for there may be fraud hidden under false peace. Contraries never agree, but the world is turned upside-down: no officer dares misbehave under a prince, and neither do the friars, pardoners, etc., etc. Even bishops pretend to be honest, but keeping quiet is worth a groat. The eagle flies during the day and the goatsucker at night; the eagle flies aloft and the snail crawls on the ground, etc., etc. The rich man always wins, and the poor is found guilty; nobody is so pompous as the newly rich. Nobody is really happy, and no animal lives in peace; those who speak the truth get into trouble. A beggar's appetite is always good, and the dole of poor men is never certain. Bones do not satisfy the appetite of a hungry man. Hear everything, be patient, avoid quarrels, etc., etc. However quietly we go, the cock has low shoes.

This series of proverbs belongs to an otherwise attested genre and has been said to reflect the influence of Chaucer and the *Disticha Catonis*.

WIKKED TONGUE (also **BALLAD OF GOOD COUNSEL** and **A WICKED TUNGE WILLE SEY AMYS**) [187]. Nineteen rime royal stanzas with varying refrain.

No matter how powerful, rich, wise, or prudent you may be, you cannot avoid being judged, and a wicked tongue will say nasty things. If you dress nicely, people will call you vain, and they will call you sluggard if you dress poorly; if you are fair, they will call you amorous, and they will call you vicious if you are ugly; if you have a wife, they will pretend to be sorry for you, and they will call you impotent if you live in chastity, etc., etc. Even if you had the courage of Hector, the eloquence of Tully, etc., etc., or if you were a woman with the virtue of Esther, the patience of Griselda, etc., etc., some wicked tongue will say nasty things. Since nobody can escape the sword of tongues, woe to the tongues that say nasty things. Noble princes, remember that discretion is a virtue most pleasing to Christ, and avoid listening to nasty things.

This poem, which has been considered especially typical of Lydgate's techniques, is believed to be adapted from the Latin and to have influenced Dunbar.

TRETYSE OF CRYSTYS PASSYOUN (also **THE DOLEROUS PYTE OF CRYSTES PASSIOUN**) [188]. Seven eight-line stanzas ababbcbc with varying refrain.

Look on this painting morning and evening. Kneel and consider My bloody wounds, which are a spiritual mirror known as the pity of My Passion. The wounds of My heart will protect you against the devil, and I shall be your trusty champion when you behold this pity. Take heed of My picture, for My blood was shed for the sake of mankind and My death was victory over death. A *Pater Noster*, a *Creed*, and an *Ave* before this pity over thirty days will earn you 26,000 years of pardons.

TROY BOOK (also HYSTORYE, SEGE, AND DESTRUCCYON OF TROYE) [189]. Five books, for a total of 30,117 lines, in rimed couplets.

Prologue. Mars and Othea, help me. I undertake this work for Prince Henry. Writers enable us to know the past. Some authors have lied about Troy, but Dares and Dictys told the truth. I follow Guido delle Colonne.

Book I. King Peleus of Thessaly secretly hates his nephew Jason and urges him to seek the Golden Fleece. Jason with Hercules and others sails for Colchis. They land at Troy, but Laomedon, suspecting their intentions, forces them to leave. The Argonauts are welcomed to Colchis by King Cethes; his daughter Medea falls in love with Jason and, by her magic, helps him to win the Golden Fleece. Jason becomes king of Thessaly and, with the aid of Hercules, assembles a fleet which sails to Troy to revenge Laomedon's insult. The Trojan army is ambushed, the city taken, and Laomedon killed. His daughter, Hesione, is given to Telamon as a concubine.

Book II. Priam rebuilds Troy into a glorious city. Then he seeks his revenge. Antenor is sent to Greece to demand Hesione's return, but he is refused. Paris is then allowed to go to Greece, in accordance with his dream, where he abducts Helen and returns with her to Troy. Menelaus learns of this and, with Agamemnon, assembles an army. Achilles is sent to the oracle at Delphi (digression on the rise of idolatry) where he learns the Greeks will win and where Calchas deserts to the Greek side. The Greeks sail toward Troy and from Tenedos send ambassadors to demand the return of Helen and compensation. The Trojans refuse. While the Greeks send Achilles to Messina for provisions, many allies arrive to aid Troy. Finally the Greeks sail to Troy itself and, after a furious battle, achieve a landing.

Book III. In the first regular battle many are wounded and slain (including Patroclus) in fierce combat. The Trojans are on the point of total victory when Hector recalls them at the request of his cousin Ajax Telamoun. A truce is set during which Cassandra warns the Trojans and Palamedes challenges Agamemnon's leadership. Another fierce battle occurs which the Trojans win. That night the Greek leaders plot to kill Hector. More fighting. The Trojans decide not to kill their prisoner Thoas and a terrible storm damages the Greek tents. In a new battle, Diomedes slays the Centaur and Antenor is captured. The next day the Trojans lose and a truce is set during which Antenor is exchanged for Thoas and Cresseid also goes over to the Greeks. Hector and Achilles meet and agree to a single combat that will decide the war but neither side allows it. Lydgate praises Chaucer. When the fighting resumes, it continues savagely for thirty days with the Greeks getting the worst of it. Another truce is set during which Priam buries six of his natural sons. There is more fighting and another truce. Andromache dreams that Hector will die in battle the next day. Although his wife and others keep him from battle for a time, Hector eventually enters the fighting and, after accomplishing marvels, is slain in a cowardly attack by Achilles. The city and Lydgate lament Hector.

Book IV. The Greeks are confident of victory and Palamedes is elected commander. To avenge Hector, Priam himself leads the Trojans and they put the Greeks to flight. A truce is called and during the celebration of the anniversary of Hector's death, Achilles sees Polyxena at Troy and falls in love. Priam agrees to give his daughter to Achilles if he will make peace between the armies. But the Greeks refuse Achilles' appeals to end the war and he angrily withdraws from the fighting. The war begins again and Deiphobus, Sarpedon, and Palamedes are killed. Agamemnon is re-elected commander. Led by Troilus, the Trojans get the best of the Greeks and a truce is called. Ulysses tries in vain to get Achilles to fight again; the Greeks become discouraged, but Calchas urges them to fight on. Troilus performs marvels and another truce is called. Achilles allows the Myrmidons to fight and they are routed by Troilus. When the fighting resumes after another truce, the Greeks are driven to their tents by Troilus before

Achilles rejoins the fighting and saves the army. Achilles plots and accomplishes the cowardly slaughter of Troilus, whose body he drags around the walls of Troy. Achilles also slays Menon by treachery. Hecuba plans an ambush for Achilles, which Paris carries out. Agamemnon vows to continue the war after Achilles' death and sends for the hero's son Pyrrhus. In a new battle, Paris and Ajax kill one another. Priam refuses to let his men fight until the Amazons, led by Penthesilea, arrive to help Troy for Hector's sake. Penthesilea is successful in a number of single combats, but is finally killed by Pyrrhus. Lydgate scolds Mars. Antenor and Aeneas plot with the Greeks to betray the city and Priam is helpless to stop them: a fraudulent peace is arranged during which Priam is forced to bring the bronze horse into Troy. That night the Greek army, which had pretended to leave, returns and joins with those in the horse to sack Troy. Thousands of Trojans are killed including Priam. Polyxena is cruelly sacrificed at the advice of Calchas, and Hecuba, driven mad, is stoned to death. Lydgate curses the false gods and mourns Troy's fate.

Book V. Discord occurs among the Greeks who are preparing to return home. Ulysses wins a dispute with Ajax Telamon. Ajax is then murdered and Ulysses flees. Aeneas and then Antenor are banished from Troy. A tempest from Minerva brings disaster to the Greek fleet. A false tale about the murder of Palamedes incites Naulus to cause the wreck of 200 Greek ships. Agamemnon returns home and is murdered by his wife. Because of other lies, Diomedes' wife will not let him return immediately. Orestes avenges his father's murder and later marries Hermione, the daughter of Helen and Menelaus. Ulysses has many adventures before returning home. Pyrrhus returns to Thessaly with Andromache, avenges his grandfather, and becomes king. He later ravishes Hermione and is killed by Orestes. Eventually Thessaly is ruled by Hector's son. A strange tale about Menon's queen follows. Ulysses is killed by his unknown son by Circe who was looking for his father. This is all Dares and Dictys say. I hope for peace from Henry V's marriage. Forgive my poor verse. This story shows the vicissitudes of Fortune.

Lenvoy. Henry, best of knights and equal to past heroes, I beg you to accept my poem kindly. I will pray for you. Little book, accept correction humbly.

The most popular of the English poetic versions of the medieval history of Troy, the *Troy Book* was begun in 1412 at the command of Prince Hal, who wished the ancient story to be available in English, and was finally completed in 1420. This enormous work is not without its intellectual, historical, moral, and even literary interest, but, in general, Lydgate's ambition outruns his achievement.

Lydgate's principal source is Guido delle Colonne's *Historia Destructionis Troiae* (1287), a Latin prose translation of Benoît de Sainte-Maure's lavish *Roman de Troie* (ca. 1160); both works claim to tell the full and accurate story of the Trojan War based on the eyewitness diaries of Dares and Dictys. Guido's *Historia* was accepted as genuine history throughout Europe in the late Middle Ages and two other Middle English verse translations of it were made: the *Laud Troy Book* and the alliterative *Destruction of Troy* (see I [74] and [72] in *Manual*, volume 1). Efforts to prove a relationship between these three poems have been unsuccessful.

Lydgate is careful to preserve the historical truth of his source (names, battles, speeches, etc.), but he also supplements Guido from other authorities: Ovid is his favorite and the *Troy Book* also contains material from such diverse writers as Isidore of Seville, John Trevisa, and Christine de Pisan, The influence of Chaucer, whom Lydgate several times praises in the poem, is evident throughout in both added material and the general poetic texture. The *Troy Book* was extremely popular in its day, as its twenty extant manuscripts and two early prints attest; but, though it has been shown to have influenced Marlowe, Thomas Kyd, John Pikeryng, and Shakespeare's *Troilus and Cressida*, Lydgate's poem was overshadowed in the Renaissance by Caxton's *Recuyell of the Histories of Troy* (see IX [21] in *Manual*, volume 3), which presents the same material in a more convenient form.

Even though the subject of the *Troy Book* is today considered to be the stuff of romance or legend, Lydgate presents his work as serious history and takes pains to remain faithful to the factual truth (as he thought) of his source. Little is omitted from Guido and the extensive additions are almost always clearly supplementary. Lydgate's actual knowledge is more limited than his many citations would suggest (much of his Virgilian material, for example, comes from Chaucer), but he is genuinely well-read and adds much classical and other learned material to the *Troy Book*: some have judged his additions an imitation of Chaucer while others see a foretaste of humanistic practice. Lydgate's tendency is to tell all he knows when a name is mentioned and so he turns Guido's version of the Judgment of Paris and his digression on idolatry into small encyclopedias of mythographic lore. On occasion he will add a second version of a story, like that of the sacrifice of Iphigenia at Aulis, to Guido's account. Although some have suggested that Lydgate's attitude toward the classical past is hostile, it has recently been argued that the poet works hard to create a believable picture of the ancient world in the *Troy Book* and that he reveals a genuine, if limited, sense of anachronism, especially in his portrayal of pagan rites.

Unlike the two other Middle English histories of Troy, Lydgate imitates and even extends Guido's practice of moralization and rhetorical elaboration. The poet loves to instruct his readers and, in addition to his more academic digressions, he is always finding moral lessons in the story of Troy. But these lessons are not really as profound or central to the work as some have thought; instead they are decorative, detachable from the narrative, and never the result of allegorization. Lydgate's most frequent message is the value of prudence; he tries to give practical, optimistic advice and echoes little of Guido's pessimism. Occasionally he even has some awkward Chaucerian fun with his source's moralizations, as in his mock defenses of women. The serious lessons Lydgate finds in the story are almost always facile and conventional, however; and, because they are *ad hoc* and proverbial, they are frequently contradictory. Lydgate's presentation of Fortune is particularly confused. He personifies and makes more rhetorically elaborate the vague forces of fate in Guido, but cannot decide if the goddess is a random figure of chance or the agent of divine retribution. A similar contradiction is found in his attitude toward the war itself. He glories in the pageantry and heroism of battle and yet bitterly denounces Mars and the horrors war brings. The peace-loving monk is in conflict with the court poet of Henry V.

Lydgate praises the rhetorical skills of Guido as beyond his own powers, but, in fact, he employs many of the devices of medieval literary theory to amplify and decorate the poem. The *Troy Book* often reads like a rhetorical manual come to life. The narrative is expanded throughout (Lydgate's famous prolixity), and an elaborate prologue plus such things as invocations, astrological references, and classical mythology are added to make the story more elaborate and formal. Lydgate makes no attempt to reorder or seriously reinterpret the story of Troy; he sees himself a craftsman and historian, and not as a creative artist. Without fundamentally changing the factual essence of the story of Troy, the monk finds a series of familiar tropes in the narrative (from the organization of an army for battle to the evils of cupidity or envy) that he automatically turns into conventional rhetorical set-pieces. The *Troy Book* never fully comes alive as a story, but some of Lydgate's additions, especially his laments for the dead and meditations on the vicissitudes of human life, have a real power and dignity.

Although it sometimes appears to be almost on the verge of genuine tragedy, the *Troy Book* finally disappoints. Lydgate seems to understand much of what his master had done in the *Troilus* (he would have made a good teacher of Chaucer), but lacks the ability to equal it in his own work. Lydgate's failure is not from want of trying, however. In the *Troy Book* he aims to play a number of roles: rhetorician, scholar, moralist, and historian. It is usually his fate to exercise one of these offices only at the expense of the others; but occasionally, as in the retelling of Hector's death, he makes all his various roles work together. At such rare moments, Lydgate's ability and ambition are one.

SCOTTISH FRAGMENTS INSERTED IN TROY BOOK [190]. One fragment of 596 lines in riming couplets and another of 3,118 lines also in riming couplets.

The fragments correspond approximately to Lydgate's *Troy Book*, Bk. I, lines 935–1688 (the story of Jason), and Bk. IV, line 5332-Bk. V, line 3340 (from Aeneas' and Antenor's ambassy to Priam to the end of the story proper). The fragments have been attributed to Barbour. Consult *Troy Book*, [189] above, and see Barbour in the chapter on Chronicles.

VENUS MASS (also LOVER'S MASS) [191]. 145 lines in poetry and some prose at the end. The verse is in couplets and in various stanzas, including three stanzas riming aababbab and one riming abbabcbc.

> Introibo: I will go to the altar of the mighty god of Love and make sacrifice. I will always be his man. Confiteor: Although I am young and inexperienced, I would put myself forward as a servant of Love. Misereatur: Folk who repent their time vainly spent in sloth will be accepted into grace by the god of Love by the will of Dame Venus and Bishop Genius. Officium: I honor Cupid that he may be my guide and have pity on my distress. Kyrie: I cry for mercy against danger and disdain. Christe: Hope and dread make me pale. She will not listen to me. Kyrie: I will keep my truth in joy or sorrow and ever serve her. Gloria in excelsis: Worship to the god of Love. May he send his true and stable servants their desires, and after winter storms the joy of spring. Orison: Most mighty lord, you know lovers' hearts. Have mercy on the stable. Epistel in prose: From the poor, probationary lover to the loyal brotherhood and all stable religious: Health and abide in truth perpetually. Pilgrims on a long journey are accustomed to rest and refresh themselves and recall the part they have accomplished and then complete the rest with new vigor. And thus I, as a pilgrim in the service of the god of Love, recall my struggles and see the end of my predecessors in love: Troilus, Penelope, Polyxena, Dido, Tristan and Isolde, and Palamedes. When they were recalled, it seemed I was one of the worst in grace despite my long pilgrimage; but I will persevere until my life's end. I beseech you, my brothers, to remember me in your prayers that I might sometime find mercy.

An incomplete work that follows a long tradition in the Middle Ages of using Church ritual to describe the plight of human lovers. The work is metrically intricate and changes its verse to fit various parts of the Mass. There are verbal parallels to Chaucer and Lydgate, but the authorship of the latter has generally not been accepted.

SONG OF VERTU (also THE TRIUMPH OF VIRTUE) [192]. Thirteen eight-line stanzas ababbcbc with varying refrain in 1–12.

Just as men gather honey from sweetness and make hippocras out of wine and spices, so they may learn virtue from prudent people. Welling springs comfort the sight, wine derives its quality from the vine, and he who seeks virtue will learn virtue, for everything draws to its own nature. Fire burns, but smoke angers many a cook, and men learn wisdom from the wise and slander from backbiters. Mariners set their course by the needle and lodestar: love Holy Church, divide your time between prayer, work, and the reading of old books, work hard, shun the bestial urges of the flesh, and go to confession so that you may dwell above the stars with Him Who bought you on the Cross.

VEXILLA REGIS PRODEUNT [193]. Nine eight-line stanzas ababbcbc, of which 2–8 end with Latin or partly Latin lines.

The royal banners of the King, with the Cross as His standard, march toward battle to slay death. The fruit of a tree caused our loss, but He died upon the Cross to slay death and slew pride with His humility, and Longius pierces His heart with a lance. It was all done according to prophecy, and the Cross is now the fairest tree in Heaven and the best remedy for our own ills. O Christ, You are our protection and are called One, and Two, and Three. Glory be to the Father, the Son, and the Holy Ghost.

WHO SEITH THE BEST SHALL NEVER REPENT (also SAY THE BEST AND NEVER REPENT) [194]. Sixteen eight-line stanzas ababbcbc in octosyllabic lines with varying refrain in all but next-to-last stanza.

I once found a written statement aimed at people who speak ill of others, which said that who says the best shall never repent. It never hurts to say the best, and there is none so virtuous as to be immune to venomous speech. False statements have injured many a creature, for a spoken word cannot be recalled and a backbiter is likely to hurt innocents. Tongues that enjoy saying the worst are most blameworthy, as pointed out by Cato and St. John, and many a lady has suffered through slander. Solomon held false tongues in abhorrence, but good words please God and man. There is nothing worse than making lies appear truer than the truth. Nature asks God for revenge upon false tongues, but who says the best shall never repent.

The authorship of this poem has been questioned, and stanza 15 (20 if introductory ballade, [195] below, is counted) is considered spurious.

BALLADE INTRODUCTORY TO WHO SEITH THE BEST SHALL NEVER REPENT [195]. Five rime royal stanzas with varying refrain.

Who says the best shall never repent, and wise men know that a tongue will break bones though it itself has none. Crooked language robs innocents of their reputation, so that it is better to be fed on raw beef than on slander. Evil speech is the worst of vices, for it can put an end even to old friendship.

See under *Who Seith the Best Shall Never Repent* [194].

WHY ARTOW FROWARD (also IN CRUCE SUM PRO TE, A PRAYER UPON THE CROSS, and UPON THE CROSS) [196]. Five eight-line stanzas ababbcbc with varying refrain, including envoy and concluding prayer.

I was nailed upon the Cross for you; forsake your sins for My sake: why are you so slack since I am so merciful? Look at My wounds, and recall that I had mercy on Peter and Magdalen because of their contrition. Come to school, and learn your lesson from My sacrifice. Lord, grant that Your five wounds may wash away our sins, and have mercy on us in Your mother's name.

EXAMPLES AGAINST WOMEN (also FALL OF PRINCES, EXTRACTS) [197]. Fifteen rime royal stanzas.

Christ gave Adam and Eve control over everything in Paradise except the forbidden fruit, but they were both banished when Eve took the apple from the serpent and gave it to Adam. Solomon was punished when he listened to women, Rachel stole her father's goods and mocked him, Judith killed Holofernes with his own sword, Job's wife let her husband lie in misery on a dunghill, Delilah's perfidy caused Samson to be blinded and enslaved. There is no pestilence so grievous as the perfidy of women, and these old examples should teach men to beware, but there are nevertheless some faithful women.

AGAINST THE HORNS OF WOMEN (also A DYTE OF WOMENHIS HORNYS, BALLAD ON THE FORKED HEAD-DRESSES OF LADIES, and HORNS AWAY) [198]. Nine eight-line stanzas ababbcbc with varying refrain, including envoy.

All beauty comes from God and nature, and artifices are worthless, for beauty will show even though horns were away. Real jewels withstand the test, while counterfeits do not. In his famous book, Alanus represented Nature with only a kerchief upon her head, and the ancient poets depicted Helen, Penelope, Polyxena, and Lucretia without horns. Clerks tell us that horns are for animals, but fierce archwives will not cast theirs away. Noble princesses, take no offense at this inept little ditty and cast your horns away, for humility is greatest of all virtues. Note how Mary wore only a kerchief at Christ's birth although she was the highest of degree. Follow her example, and cast your horns away.

This poem has been considered part of the ship-of-fools tradition. See also XIII [136–138] in *Manual*, volume 5.

THE WORLD IS VANITY (also THE WORLD IS VARIABLE) [199].

Fourteen eight-line stanzas ababbcbc with refrain, including envoy.

As I was walking alone at dawn on a December morning, I began thinking about the fickleness of fortune and concluded that experience shows that the world is variable, as shown by the ancient philosophers and tragic poets. The beggar who rises to power forgets his own kind, but during the golden age everyone acted correctly, and courage at the service of the community was respected by the senators. The owl differs from the eagle, and the lamb from the lion; Delilah deluded Samson, Venus draws Mars away from war, but the tidy shepherd minds his own sheep. Each one should mind his business within the body politic. Those who falsely spend Church property purchase Christ's curse. As Aristotle teaches, uncontrolled talking is a failure. Go, little statement, and show this proverb to every estate, for experience shows that the world is variable.

This poem has been said to be virtually unintelligible.

FRAGMENT IN STYLE OF LYDGATE: THE WORLD IS VANITY [200].

Bibliography

Table of Abbreviations

For abbreviations and shortened forms not appearing in this table consult the list of background books at the beginning of the appropriate chapter of the Bibliography.

AAGRP	Ausgaben und Abhandlungen aus dem Gebiete der romanischen Philologie
AC	Archaeologica Cantiana
Acad	Academy
AEB	Kölbing E, Altenglische Bibliothek, Heilbronn 1883–
AELeg 1875	Horstmann C, Altenglische Legenden, Paderborn 1875
AELeg 1878	Horstmann C, Sammlung altenglischer Legenden, Heilbronn 1878
AELeg 1881	Horstmann C, Altenglische Legenden (Neue Folge), Heilbronn 1881
AESpr	Mätzner E, Altenglische Sprachproben, Berlin 1867–
AF	Anglistische Forschungen
AfDA	Anzeiger für deutsches Alterthum
AHR	American Historical Review
AJ	Ampleforth Journal
AJA	American Journal of Archaeology
AJP	American Journal of Philology
ALb	Allgemeines Literaturblatt
ALg	Archivum linguisticum
Allen WAR	Allen H E, Writings Ascribed to Richard Rolle Hermit of Hampole and Materials for His Biography, MLA Monograph Series 3, N Y 1927
Angl	Anglia, Zeitschrift für englische Philologie

TABLE OF ABBREVIATIONS

AnglA	Anglia Anzeiger
AnglB	Beiblatt zur Anglia
AN&Q	American Notes and Queries
Antiq	Antiquity
APS	Acta philologica scandinavica
AQ	American Quarterly
AR	Antioch Review
Arch	Archiv für das Studium der neueren Sprachen und Literaturen
Archaeol	Archaeologia
Ashton	Ashton J, Romances of Chivalry, London 1890
ASp	American Speech
ASR	American Scandinavian Review
ASt	Aberystwyth Studies
Athen	Athenaeum
BA	Books Abroad
BARB	Bulletin de l'Académie royale de Belgique
Baugh LHE	Baugh A C, The Middle English Period, in A Literary History of England, N Y 1948; 2nd edn 1967
BB	Bulletin of Bibliography
BBA	Bonner Beiträge zur Anglistik
BBCS	Bulletin of the Board of Celtic Studies (Univ of Wales)
BBGRP	Berliner Beiträge zur germanischen und romanischen Philologie
BBSIA	Bulletin bibliographique de la Société internationale arthurienne
Bennett OHEL	Bennett H S, Chaucer and the Fifteenth Century, Oxford 1947
Best BIP	Best R I, Bibliography of Irish Philology, 2 vols, Dublin 1913
BGDSL	Beiträge zur Geschichte der deutschen Sprache und Literatur
BHR	Bibliothèque d'humanisme et renaissance
BIHR	Bulletin of the Institute of Historical Research
Billings	Billings A H, A Guide to the Middle English Metrical Romances, N Y 1901

Blackf	Blackfriars
Bloomfield SDS	Bloomfield M W, The Seven Deadly Sins, Michigan State College of Agriculture and Applied Science Studies in Language and Literature, 1952
BNYPL	Bulletin of the New York Public Library
Böddeker AED	Böddeker K, Altenglische Dichtungen des MS Harl 2253, Berlin 1878
Bossuat MBLF	Bossuat R, Manuel bibliographique de la littérature française du moyen âge, Paris 1951; supplément Paris 1955; deuxième supplément Paris 1961 [the item numbers run consecutively through the supplement]
BPLQ	Boston Public Library Quarterly
BQR	Bodleian Quarterly Record (sometimes Review)
Brandl	Brandl A, Mittelenglische Literatur, in Paul's Grundriss der germanischen Philologie, 1st edn, Strassburg 1893, $2^1.609$ ff, Index $2^2.345$
Brown ELxiiiC	Brown C F, English Lyrics of the 13th Century, Oxford 1932
Brown Reg	Brown C, A Register of Middle English Religious and Didactic Verse, parts 1 and 2, Oxford (for the Bibliographical Society) 1916, 1920
Brown RLxivC	Brown C F, Religious Lyrics of the 14th Century, Oxford 1924
Brown RLxvC	Brown C F, Religious Lyrics of the 15th Century, Oxford 1939
Brown-Robbins	Brown C and R H Robbins, The Index of Middle English Verse, N Y 1943; see also Robbins-Cutler
Bryan-Dempster	Bryan W F and G Dempster, Sources and Analogues of Chaucer's Canterbury Tales, Chicago 1941
BrynMawrMon	Bryn Mawr College Monographs, Bryn Mawr 1905–
BSEP	Bonner Studien zur englischen Philologie
BUSE	Boston University Studies in English
CASP	Cambridge Antiquarian Society Publication
CBEL	Bateson F W, Cambridge Bibliography of English Literature, 5 vols, London and N Y 1941, 1957
CE	College English

CFMA	Les classiques français du moyen âge; collection de textes français et provençaux antérieurs a 1500, Paris 1910–
Chambers	Chambers E K, The Mediaeval Stage, 2 vols, Oxford 1903; rptd from corrected sheets 1925, 1948, 1954
Chambers OHEL	Chambers E K, English Literature at the Close of the Middle Ages, Oxford 1945
CHEL	Ward A W and A R Waller, The Cambridge History of English Literature, vols 1 and 2, Cambridge 1907, 1908
CHR	Catholic Historical Review
ChS	Publications of the Chaucer Society, London 1869–1924
Ch&Sidg	Chambers E K and F Sidgwick, Early English Lyrics, London 1907; numerous reprints
CJ	Classic Journal
CL	Comparative Literature
CMLR	Canadian Modern Language Review
Comper Spir Songs	Comper F M M, Spiritual Songs from English Manuscripts of Fourteenth to Sixteenth Centuries, London and N Y 1936
Conviv	Convivium
Courthope	Courthope W J, History of English Poetry, vol 1, London 1895
CP	Classical Philology
Craig HEL	Craig H, G K Anderson, L I Bredvold, J W Beach, History of English Literature, N Y 1950
Cross Mot Ind	Cross T P, Motif Index of Early Irish Literature, Bloomington Ind 1951
Crotch PEWC	Crotch W J B, The Prologues and Epilogues of William Caxton, EETS 176, London 1928
CUS	Columbia University Studies in English and in Comparative Literature, N Y 1899–
DA, DAI	Dissertation Abstracts, Dissertation Abstracts International

DANHSJ	Derbyshire Archaeological and Natural History Society Journal
de Julleville Hist	de Julleville L Petit, Histoire de la langue et de la littérature française, vols 1 and 2, Paris 1896–99
de Ricci Census	de Ricci S and W J Wilson, Census of Medieval and Renaissance Manuscripts in the United States of America and Canada, vols 1–3, N Y 1935, 1937, 1940
Dickins and Wilson	Dickins B and R M Wilson, Early Middle English Texts, Cambridge 1950
DLz	Deutsche Literaturzeitung
DNB	Stephen L and S Lee, Dictionary of National Biography, N Y and London 1885–1900, and supplements
DomS	Dominican Studies: An Annual Review, Blackfriars Publications, London
DUJ	Durham University Journal
EA	Études anglaises
EBEP	Erlanger Beiträge zur englischen Philologie
EC	Essays in Criticism
EETS	Publications of the Early English Text Society (Original Series), 1864–
EETSES	Publications of the Early English Text Society (Extra Series), 1867–
EG	Études germaniques
EGS	English and Germanic Studies
EHR	English Historical Review
EIE, EIA	English Institute Essays (Annual), N Y 1939–
EJ	English Journal
ELH	Journal of English Literary History
Ellis EEP	Ellis G, Specimens of Early English Poetry, 3 vols, London 1811
Ellis Spec	Ellis G, Specimens of Early English Metrical Romances, 3 vols, London 1805; rvsd Halliwell, 1 vol, Bohn edn 1848 (latter edn referred to, unless otherwise indicated)

Enc Brit	Encyclopaedia Britannica, 11th edn
Engl	English: The Magazine of the English Association
E&S	Essays and Studies by Members of the English Association, Oxford 1910–
E&S Brown	Essays and Studies in Honor of Carleton Brown, N Y 1940
Esdaile ETPR	Esdaile A, A List of English Tales and Prose Romances Printed before 1740, London 1912
EStn	Englische Studien
ESts	English Studies
ETB	Hoops J, Englische Textbibliothek, 21 vols, Heidelberg 1898–1935?
Expl	Explicator
Farrar-Evans	Farrar C P and A P Evans, Bibliography of English Translations from Medieval Sources, N Y 1946
FFC	Folklore Fellows Communications
FFK	Forschungen und Fortschritte: Korrespondenzblatt der deutschen Wissenschaft und Technik
Flügel NL	Flügel E, Neuenglisches Lesebuch, Halle 1895
FQ	French Quarterly
FR	French Review
FS	French Studies
Furnivall EEP	Furnivall F J, Early English Poems and Lives of Saints, Berlin 1862 (Transactions of Philological Society of London 1858)
Gautier Bibl	Gautier L, Bibliographie des chansons de geste, Paris 1897
Gayley	Gayley C M, Plays of Our Forefathers, N Y 1907
GdW	Gesamtkatalog der Wiegendrucke, Leipzig 1925–
Germ	Germania
Gerould S Leg	Gerould G H, Saints' Legends, Boston 1916
GGA	Göttingische gelehrte Anzeiger
GJ	Gutenberg Jahrbuch
GQ	German Quarterly
GR	Germanic Review

Greene E E Carols	Greene R L, The Early English Carols, Oxford 1935; 2nd edn 1977
GRM	Germanisch-Romanische Monatsschrift
Gröber	Gröber G, Grundriss der romanischen Philologie, Strassburg 1888–1902, new issue 1897–1906, 2nd edn 1904– (vol 2^1 1902 referred to, unless otherwise indicated)
Gröber-Hofer	Hofer S, Geschichte der mittelfranzösischen Literatur, 2 vols, 2nd edn, Berlin and Leipzig 1933–37
Hall Selections	Hall J, Selections from Early Middle English 1130–1250, 2 parts, Oxford 1920
Hammond	Hammond E P, Chaucer: A Bibliographical Manual, N Y 1908
Hartshorne AMT	Hartshorne C H, Ancient Metrical Tales, London 1829
Hazlitt Rem	Hazlitt W C, Remains of the Early Popular Poetry of England, 4 vols, London 1864–66
Herbert	Herbert J A, Catalogue of Romances in the Department of MSS of the British Museum, London 1910 (vol 3 of Ward's Catalogue)
Hermes	Hermes
Hibbard Med Rom	Hibbard L, Medieval Romance in England, N Y 1924
HINL	History of Ideas News Letter
Hisp	Hispania
HispR	Hispanic Review
HJ	Hibbert Journal
HLB	Harvard Library Bulletin
HLF	Histoire littéraire de la France, Paris 1733– ; new edn 1865–
HLQ	Huntington Library Quarterly
Holmes CBFL	Cabeen D C, Critical Bibliography of French Literature, vol 1 (the Medieval Period), ed U T Holmes jr, Syracuse N Y 1949
HSCL	Harvard Studies in Comparative Literature

HSNPL	Harvard Studies and Notes in Philology and Literature, Boston 1892–
HudR	Hudson Review
IER	Irish Ecclesiastical Review
IS	Italian Studies
Isis	Isis
Ital	Italica
JAAC	Journal of Aesthetics and Art Criticism
JBL	Journal of Biblical Literature
JCS	Journal of Celtic Studies
JEGGP	Jahresbericht über die Erscheinungen auf dem Gebiete der germanischen Philologie
JEGP	Journal of English and Germanic Philology
JEH	Journal of Ecclesiastical History
JfRESL	Jahrbuch für romanische und englische Sprache und Literatur
JGP	Journal of Germanic Philology
JHI	Journal of the History of Ideas
JPhilol	Journal of Philology
JPhilos	Journal of Philosophy
JRLB	Bulletin of the John Rylands Library, Manchester
Kane	Kane G, Middle English Literature: A Critical Study of the Romances, the Religious Lyrics, Piers Plowman, London 1951
Kennedy BWEL	Kennedy A G, A Bibliography of Writings on the English Language from the Beginning of Printing to the End of 1922, Cambridge Mass and New Haven 1927
Kild Ged	Heuser W, Die Kildare-Gedichte, Bonn 1904 (BBA 14)
Körting	Körting G, Grundriss der Geschichte der englischen Literatur von ihren Anfängen bis zur Gegenwart, 5th edn, Münster 1910
KR	Kenyon Review
Krit Jahresber	Vollmüller K, Kritischer Jahresbericht über die Fortschritte der romanischen Philologie, München

	und Leipzig 1892–1915 (Zweiter Teil, 13 vols in 12)
KSEP	Kieler Studien zur englischen Philologie
Lang	Language
LB	Leuvensche Bijdragen, Periodical for Modern Philology
LC	Library Chronicle
Leeds SE	Leeds Studies in English and Kindred Languages, School of English Literature in the University of Leeds
Legouis	Legouis E, Chaucer, Engl trans by Lailvoix, London 1913
Legouis HEL	Legouis E and L Cazamian, trans H D Irvine and W D MacInnes, A History of English Literature, new edn, N Y 1929
LfGRP	Literaturblatt für germanische und romanische Philologie
Libr	The Library
Litteris	Litteris: An International Critical Review of the Humanities, New Society of Letters
LMS	London Medieval Studies
Loomis ALMA	Loomis R S, Arthurian Literature in the Middle Ages, A Collaborative History, Oxford 1959
LP	Literature and Psychology
LQ	Library Quarterly
Lund SE	Lund Studies in English
LZ	Literarisches Zentralblatt
MÆ	Medium ævum
Manly CT	Manly J M, Canterbury Tales by Geoffrey Chaucer, with an Introduction, Notes, and a Glossary, N Y 1928
Manly Spec	Manly J M, Specimens of the Pre-Shakespearean Drama, vol 1, 2nd edn, Boston 1900
Manly & Rickert	Manly J M and E Rickert, The Text of the Canterbury Tales Studied on the Basis of All Known Manuscripts, 8 vols, Chicago 1940
Manual	A Manual of the Writings in Middle English

	1050–1500, New Haven 1967– (vols 1 and 2, ed J B Severs; vols 3–6, ed A E Hartung)
MBREP	Münchener Beiträge zur romanischen und englischen Philologie
MED	Kurath H and S M Kuhn, Middle English Dictionary, Ann Arbor 1952– (M S Ogden, C E Palmer, and R L McKelvey, Bibliography [of ME texts], 1954, p 15)
MH	Medievalia et humanistica
MHRA	MHRA, Bulletin of the Modern Humanities Research Association
Migne PL	Migne, Patrologiae Latinae cursus completus
Minor Poems	Skeat W W, Chaucer: The Minor Poems, 2nd edn, Oxford 1896
MKAW	Mededeelingen van de Koninklijke akademie van wetenschappen, afdeling letterkunde
ML	Music and Letters
MLF	Modern Language Forum
MLJ	Modern Language Journal
MLN	Modern Language Notes
MLQ (Lon)	Modern Language Quarterly (London)
MLQ (Wash)	Modern Language Quarterly (Seattle, Washington)
MLR	Modern Language Review
Monat	Monatshefte
Moore Meech and Whitehall	Moore S, S B Meech and H Whitehall, Middle English Dialect Characteristics and Dialect Boundaries, University of Michigan Essays and Studies in Language and Literature 13, Ann Arbor 1935
Morley	Morley H, English Writers, vols 3–6, London 1890
Morris Spec	Morris R (ed part 1), R Morris and W W Skeat (ed part 2), Specimens of Early English, part 1, 2nd edn, Oxford 1887; part 2, 4th edn, Oxford 1898
MP	Modern Philology
MS	Mediaeval Studies
MSEP	Marburger Studien zur englischen Philologie, 13 vols, Marburg 1901–11

MUPES	Manchester University Publications, English Series
NA	Neuer Anzeiger
Neophil	Neophilologus, A Modern Language Quarterly
NEQ	New England Quarterly
New CBEL	Watson G, The New Cambridge Bibliography of English Literature, 4 vols, Cambridge 1969–74; Index, compiled J D Pickles, Cambridge 1977
NLB	Newberry Library Bulletin
NM	Neuphilologische Mitteilungen: Bulletin de la Société neophilologique de Helsinki
NMQ	New Mexico Quarterly
NNAC	Norfolk and Norwich Archaeological Society
N&Q	Notes and Queries
NRFH	Nueva revista de filologia hispánica
NS	Die neueren Sprachen, Zeitschrift für den neusprachlichen Unterrecht
O'Dell CLPF	O'Dell S, A Chronological List of Prose Fiction in English Printed in England and Other Countries, Cambridge Mass 1954
OMETexts	Morsbach L and F Holthausen, Old and Middle English Texts, 11 vols, Heidelberg 1901–26
Oxf Ch	Skeat W W, The Works of Geoffrey Chaucer, Oxford 1894–1900 (6 vols; extra 7th vol of Chaucerian Poems)
Palaes	Palaestra, Untersuchungen und Texte
PAPS	Proceedings of the American Philosophical Society
Paris Litt Franç	Paris G P B, La littérature française au moyen âge, 4th edn, Paris 1909
Patterson	Patterson F A, The Middle English Penitential Lyric, N Y 1911
Paul Grundriss	Paul H, Grundriss der germanischen Philologie, 3 vols, 1st edn, Strassburg 1891–1900; 2nd edn 1900–
PBBeitr	Paul H and W Braune, Beiträge zur Geschichte der deutschen Sprache und Literatur, Halle 1874–
PBSA	Papers of the Bibliographical Society of America
PBSUV	Papers of the Bibliographical Society, Univ of Virginia

PFMS	Furnivall F J and J W Hales, The Percy Folio MS, 4 vols, London 1867–69; re-ed I Gollancz, 4 vols, London 1905–10 (the earlier edn is referred to, unless otherwise indicated)
Philo	Philologus
PMLA	Publications of the Modern Language Association of America
PMRS	Progress of Medieval and Renaissance Studies in the United States and Canada
Pollard 15CPV	Pollard A W, Fifteenth Century Prose and Verse, Westminster 1903
PP	Past and Present
PPR	Philosophy and Phenomenological Research
PPS	Publications of the Percy Society
PQ	Philological Quarterly
PR	Partisan Review
PS	Pacific Spectator
PSTS	Publications of the Scottish Text Society, Edinburgh 1884–
PULC	Princeton University Library Chronicle
QF	Quellen und Forschungen zur Sprach- und Culturgeschichte der germanischen Völker
QQ	Queen's Quarterly
RAA	Revue anglo-américaine
RadMon	Radcliffe College Monographs, Boston 1891–
RB	Revue britannique
RC	Revue celtique
RCHL	Revue critique d'histoire et de littérature
REH	The Review of Ecclesiastical History
Rel Ant	Wright T and J O Halliwell, Reliquiae antiquae, 2 vols, London 1845
Ren	Renascence
Renwick-Orton	Renwick W L and H Orton, The Beginnings of English Literature to Skelton 1509, London 1939; rvsd edn 1952
RES	Review of English Studies

RevP	Revue de philologie
RF	Romanische Forschungen
RFE	Revista de filología espanola
RFH	Revista de filología hispánica
RG	Revue germanique
RHL	Revue d'histoire littéraire de la France
Rickert RofFr, RofL	Rickert E, Early English Romances in Verse: Romances of Friendship (vol 1), Romances of Love (vol 2), London 1908
Ringler BEV	Ringler W, A Bibliography and First-Line Index of English Verse Printed through 1500, PBSA 49.153
Ritson AEMR	Ritson J, Ancient English Metrical Romances, 3 vols, London 1802, rvsd E Goldsmid, Edinburgh 1884 (earlier edn referred to, unless otherwise indicated)
Ritson APP	Ritson J, Ancient Popular Poetry, 2nd edn, London 1833
Ritson AS	Ritson J, Ancient Songs from the Time of Henry III, 2 vols, London 1790, new edn 1829; rvsd W C Hazlitt, Ancient Songs and Ballads, 1 vol, London 1877 (last edn referred to, unless otherwise indicated)
RLC	Revue de littérature comparée
RLR	Revue des langues romanes
RN	Renaissance News
Robbins-Cutler	Supplement to Brown-Robbins, Lexington Ky 1965
Robbins-HP	Robbins R H, Historical Poems of the 14th and 15th Centuries, Oxford 1959
Robbins SL	Robbins R H, Secular Lyrics of the 14th and 15th Centuries, 2nd edn, Oxford 1955
Robson	Robson J, Three Early English Metrical Romances, London (Camden Society) 1842
Rolls Series	Rerum Britannicarum medii aevi scriptores, Published by Authority of the Lords Commissioners of Her Majesty's Treasury, under the Direction of the Master of the Rolls, London 1857–91
Rom	Romania

RomP	Romance Philology
RomR	Romanic Review
Root	Root R K, The Poetry of Chaucer, Boston 1906
Rot	Rotulus, A Bulletin for MS Collectors
Roxb Club	Publications of the Roxburghe Club, London 1814–
RSLC	Record Society of Lancashire and Cheshire
RUL	Revue de l'Université laval
SA	The Scottish Antiquary, or Northern Notes and Queries
SAQ	South Atlantic Quarterly
SATF	Publications de la Société des anciens textes français, Paris 1875–
SB	Studies in Bibliography: Papers of the Bibliographical Society of the University of Virginia
SBB	Studies in Bibliography and Booklore
ScanSt	Scandinavian Studies
Schipper	Schipper J, Englische Metrik, 2 vols, Bonn 1881–88
Schofield	Schofield W H, English Literature from the Norman Conquest to Chaucer, N Y 1906
SciS	Science and Society
Scrut	Scrutiny
SE	Studies in English
SEER	Slavonic and East European Review
SEP	Studien zur englischen Philologie
ShJ	Jahrbuch der deutschen Shakespeare-Gesellschaft
SHR	Scottish Historical Review
Skeat Spec	Skeat W W, Specimens of English Literature 1394–1579, 6th edn, Oxford
SL	Studies in Linguistics
SN	Studia neophilologica: A Journal of Germanic and Romanic Philology
SP	Studies in Philology
Spec	Speculum: A Journal of Mediaeval Studies
SR	Sewanee Review
SRL	Saturday Review of Literature
SSL	Studies in Scottish Literature

STC	Pollard A W and G R Redgrave, A Short-Title Catalogue of Books Printed in England, Scotland, and Ireland and of English Books Printed Abroad 1475–1640, London 1926
StVL	Studien zur vergleichenden Literaturgeschichte
Summary Cat	Madan F and H H E Craster, A Summary Catalogue of Western Manuscripts Which Have Not Hitherto Been Catalogued in the Quarto Series, Oxford 1895–1953
SUVSL	Skriften utgivna av Vetenskaps-societeten i Lund
SWR	Southwest Review
Sym	Symposium
Ten Brink	Ten Brink B A K, Early English Literature, English Literature, trans Kennedy et al, vol 1, vol 2 (parts 1–2), London and N Y 1887–92 (referred to as vols 1–3)
Texas SE	Texas Studies in English
Thompson Mot Ind	Thompson S, Motif Index of Folk-Literature, 6 vols, Helsinki 1932–36
Thoms	Thoms W J, A Collection of Early Prose Romances, London 1828; part ed Morley, Carlsbrooke Library, whole rvsd edn, London (Routledge); new edn, Edinburgh 1904
TLCAS	Transactions of Lancashire and Cheshire Antiquarian Society
TLS	[London] Times Literary Supplement
TNTL	Tijdschrift voor nederlandse taal- en letterkunde
TPSL	Transactions of the Philological Society of London
Trad	Traditio, Studies in Ancient and Medieval History, Thought, and Religion
TRSL	Transactions of the Royal Society of Literature
TTL	Tijdschrift voor taal en letteren
Tucker-Benham	Tucker L L and A R Benham, A Bibliography of Fifteenth-Century Literature, Seattle 1928
UKCR	University of Kansas City Review
UQ	Ukrainian Quarterly
Utley CR	Utley F L, The Crooked Rib: An Analytical Index

	to the Argument about Women in English and Scots Literature to the End of the Year 1568, Columbus O 1944
UTM	University of Toronto Monthly
UTQ	University of Toronto Quarterly
VMKVA	Verslagen en mededeelingen der Koninklijke vlaamsche academie
VQR	Virginia Quarterly Review
Ward	Ward H L D, Catalogue of Romances in the Department of MSS of the British Museum, 2 vols, London 1883–93 (see Herbert for vol 3)
Ward Hist	Ward A W, A History of English Dramatic Literature to the Death of Queen Anne, 3 vols, new edn, London 1899
WBEP	Wiener Beiträge zur englischen Philologie
Weber MR	Weber H W, Metrical Romances of the 13th, 14th, and 15th Centuries, 3 vols, Edinburgh 1810
Wehrle	Wehrle W O, The Macaronic Hymn Tradition in Medieval English Literature, Washington 1933
Wells	Wells J E, A Manual of the Writings in Middle English 1050–1400, New Haven 1916 (Supplements 1–9, 1919–51)
Wessex	Wessex
WHR	Western Humanities Review
Wilson EMEL	Wilson R M, Early Middle English Literature, London 1939
WMQ	William and Mary Quarterly
WR	Western Review
Wright AnecLit	Wright T, Anecdota literaria, London 1844
Wright PPS	Wright T, Political Poems and Songs from the Accession of Edward III to That of Richard III, 2 vols, London (Rolls Series) 1859–61
Wright PS	Wright T, Political Songs of England from the Reign of John to That of Edward III, Camden Society, London 1839 (this edn referred to, unless otherwise

	indicated); 4 vols, rvsd, privately printed, Goldsmid, Edinburgh 1884
Wright SLP	Wright T, Specimens of Lyric Poetry Composed in England in the Reign of Edward I, Percy Society, 2 vols, London 1896
Wülcker	Wülcker R P, Geschichte der englischen Literatur, 2 vols, Leipzig 1896
YCGL	Yearbook of Comparative and General Literature
YFS	Yale French Studies, New Haven 1948–
Yksh Wr	Horstmann C, Yorkshire Writers, Library of Early English Writers, 2 vols, London 1895–96
YR	Yale Review
YSCS	Yorkshire Society for Celtic Studies
YSE	Yale Studies in English, N Y 1898–
YWES	Year's Work in English Studies
YWMLS	Year's Work in Modern Language Studies
ZfCP	Zeitschrift für celtische Philologie (Tübingen)
ZfDA	Zeitschrift für deutsches Alterthum und deutsche Litteratur
ZfDP	Zeitschrift für deutsche Philologie
ZfFSL	Zeitschrift für französische Sprache und Literatur
ZfÖG	Zeitschrift für die österreichischen Gymnasien
ZfRP	Zeitschrift für romanische Philologie
ZfVL	Zeitschrift für vergleichende Litteraturgeschichte, Berlin

Other Commonly Used Abbreviations

ae	altenglische	AN	Anglo-Norman	OF	Old French
af	altfranzösische	c	copyright	ON	Old Norse
engl	englische	ca	circa	pt	part
f	für	crit	criticized by	re-ed	re-edited by
me	mittelenglische	f, ff	folio, folios	rptd	reprinted
u	und	ME	Middle English	rvsd	revised
z	zu	n d	no date	unptd	unprinted

XIV. CAROLS

by
Richard Leighton Greene

BACKGROUND BOOKS: The following important, frequently listed entries, here given full statement, are referred to in abbreviated form in the pages that follow. For abbreviations not appearing in this list, consult the general Table of Abbreviations.

Beeching	Beeching H C, A Book of Christmas Verse, 2nd edn, N Y 1926
Davies	Davies R T, Medieval English Lyrics, London 1963
Early Bodleian Music	Stainer Sir J, Early Bodleian Music, London 1901
Flügel Fest R Hildebrand	Flügel E, Englische Weihnachtslieder aus einer Handschrift des Balliol College zu Oxford, Forschungen zur deutschen Philologie, Festgabe für Rudolf Hildebrand, Leipzig 1894
Greene Selection	Greene R L, A Selection of English Carols, Oxford 1962
Luria & Hoffman	Luria M S and R L Hoffman, Middle English Lyrics, N Y 1974
OBC	Dearmer P, R Vaughan Williams and M Shaw, The Oxford Book of Carols, London 1928; music edn, London 1928; rvsd edn, London 1964
Oliver	Oliver R, Poems without Names: The English Lyric, 1200–1500, Berkeley 1970
Reed Christmas Carols	Reed E B, Christmas Carols Printed in the Sixteenth Century, Cambridge Mass 1932
Rickert Anc Eng Chr Carols	Rickert E, Ancient English Christmas Carols, London 1914

Robbins Christmas Carols	Robbins R H, Early English Christmas Carols, N Y 1961
Silverstein	Silverstein T, Medieval English Lyrics, London 1971
Sisam	Sisam C and K, The Oxford Book of Medieval English Verse, Oxford 1970
Stevens Med Carols	Stevens J, Mediaeval Carols, Musica Britannica 4, 2nd edn, London 1958
Stevick	Stevick R D, One Hundred Middle English Lyrics, Indianapolis Ind 1964
Terry Med Carol Book	Terry Sir R R, A Mediaeval Carol Book, London [1931]
Weston	Weston J L, Old English Carols, London 1911
Woolf	Woolf R, The English Religious Lyric in the Middle Ages, Oxford 1968

DESCRIPTIVE LIST OF MSS CONTAINING FIVE OR MORE CAROLS

British Museum, Egerton 3307. Vellum, $11\frac{1}{2} \times 8\frac{3}{4}$ in, 88 folios (mid 15 cent).

This is a very important musical MS, acquired by the British Museum about 1945 from a London bookseller. It was not known to be extant when the first edition of Greene E E Carols was published. It contains portions of the Mass and processional music in polyphony, by anonymous composers and chiefly for Holy Week, a motet in honor of St Dunstan, a Goliardic drinking song found also in *Carmina Burana*, Latin *cantilenae*, and English carols. All the carols are in one of the four hands in which the MS is written.

Carols [22](MS 3), [39], [99](MS), [113], [125], [126], [141], [181], [191](MS 2), [280], [314], [340](MS 4).

There are close correspondences with Bodl 3340 in both music and verbal texts. The history of the MS before its sale to the British Museum is not known, and its place of origin or medieval ownership is uncertain. Bertram Schofield's assignment of it to Windsor (Musical Quart 32.514) cannot stand. R L Greene (Journ of the American Musicological Soc 7.15) has suggested Meaux Abbey, Yorkshire, on the basis of the occurrence of two crosses patonce (the principal charge in the Abbey's arms) and the "words" or mottoes, assumed to be punning, "Mieulx en de cy" and "En de cy mieulx," as well as on the basis of the language of the English carols.

British Museum, Sloane 2593. Paper, $5\frac{7}{8} \times 4\frac{3}{8}$ in, 37 folios (mid 15 cent).

One of the most important carol MSS, defective at the beginning, at least 47 leaves having been lost. It contains English and Latin carols and songs and two English ballads. It has no music. It has many correspondences with other MSS, especially Bodl 29734 and Balliol 354.

Carols [6](MS 2), [7](MS 2), [15], [23], [24], [26](MS 3), [27], [67], [85](MS 3), [86], [111](MS 3), [120](MS 3), [121](MS 2), [122](MS 1), [124](MS 3), [145], [147](MS 2), [150](MS 2), [159](MS 2), [169], [170], [175](MS 3), [180](MS 2), [186](MS 2), [189], [233], [236](MS 4), [238], [244], [315], [318], [319], [320], [323], [332], [339], [342], [344], [358] (MS 2), [359](MS 2), [360], [366], [368], [371], [384], [386], [387], [388], [393], [395], [399] (MS 2), [408], [410], [421], [422], [460], [476]e.

From Bury St Edmunds, probably from the great Benedictine abbey with its fine library.

British Museum, Addit 5665. The "Ritson MS." Paper and vellum, 10 × 7 in, ff 1–149 (late 15 cent).

A musical MS, with settings in two and three parts, of English carols, sacred and secular, and Latin masses and motets. Some of the Latin pieces derive from the Sarum Processional, but the MS as a whole is not made up of processional music. Composers whose names occur are listed by John Stevens as follows: "Richard Smert; John Trouluffe; John Cornish; Henry Petyr, Sir Thomas Packe; Sir William Hawte, *miles*; Edmund Sturges (Turges?); T B (B T?); J Norman; W P; and, by implication, Henry VIII ['Passetyme with good cumpanye', two versions]" (Music and Poetry in the Early Tudor Court, p 338).

Carols [1], [2], [5], [12], [13](MS 2), [30](MS 3), [56–58], [84], [88], [90](MS 1a & b), [94], [97], [101](MS 5a & b), [107–09], [114], [116], [132](MS 2), [134], [187], [261], [277], [308], [309], [333], [340](MS 3), [351], [357], [362](MS 4), [370], [378], [390], [443].

The relatively few correspondences are with several other important carol MSS.

The MS appears to be from Devonshire. Smert was rector of Plymtree near Exeter from 1435 to 1477 (Stevens Med Carols, p 125).

Oxford, Bodleian Library 3340 (Arch Selden B.26), Part I. Parchment, $10\frac{1}{4}$ × $7\frac{1}{8}$ in, 37 folios (mid 15 cent).

Part I, which contains all the carols, is bound with four other unrelated MSS. It also contains English songs and Latin *cantilenae* not in carol form, all with anonymous music in two and three parts. All the carols except [333](MS 1), and the accompanied words of [17](MS 1), [29](MS 1), and [33] are in one hand.

Carols [4], [13](MS 1), [17](MS 1), [28], [29](MS 1), [30](MS 1), [31–33], [68], [72], [115](MS 1), [176], [179], [183], [186](MS 1), [191](MS 1), [236](MS 1), [340](MS 1), [341](MS 1), [362](MS 1), [425], [435](MS 1), [472] (MS 1), [473].

The MS has correspondences chiefly with Trinity Coll Camb 1230, BM Addit 5665, Sloane 2593, Bodl 29734, Balliol 354, and Egerton 3307. It is very probably from Worcester. There is no valid evidence to connect it with Windsor.

Oxford, Bodleian Library 21876 (Douce 302). Parchment, $10\frac{3}{4}$ × $7\frac{7}{8}$ in, ff ii–36 (early 15 cent).

The volume contains the poems of John Audelay, a chaplain at Haughmond Abbey (Augustinian) in Shropshire. There is no music. There are three hands. All the carols are in one hand, with corrections by a second.

Carols [6](MS 1), [95], [100], [106], [110], [115](MS 2), [120](MS 1), [172](MS 1), [177], [232](MS 1), [272], [312], [313], [317], [327–31], [350], [372], [401], [402], [416], [417], [437].

The volume is imperfect at the beginning, and there are gaps after ff 7[b] and 19. An erased note on f 35[a] names as an owner of the book John Barker, a canon of the Augustinian priory of Launde, Leicestershire, to whom it was given by one Wyatt ("Wm Vyott a mynstrall yn Coventre" in another erased note).

The occurrence of five of the carols in other MSS not associated with Audelay casts some doubt on his original authorship in these cases.

Oxford, Bodleian Library 29734 (Eng poet e.1). Paper, $4\frac{3}{8}$ × 6 in (page size), 65 folios (ff 11–62 constitute MS proper; mid 15 cent).

The contents, which include English and Latin poems in other than carol form, are written in two hands. There is music only for the burden of one carol and for one Latin hymn.

Carols [7](MS 1), [20](MS 1), [30](MS 2), [36–38], [40], [41], [42](MS), [43], [78](MS 1), [85](MS 2), [92], [101](MS 1), [102], [112], [124](MS 1), [135], [138], [139], [142], [147](MS 1), [152](MS 1), [153](MS 1), [159](MS 1), [175](MS 1), [180](MS 1), [185], [208], [234](MS 1), [239](MS 1), [240](MS 1), [241](MS 1a & b), [263], [283], [311](MS 1), [335], [337], [340](MS 2), [343], [345], [347], [359](MS 1), [361], [373](MS 1), [385], [389](MS 1), [391], [392](MS 1), [403](MS 1), [405](MS 1), [406](MS 1), [407], [409], [411], [412], [414], [415](MS 1), [419], [427](MS 1), [430](MS 1), [431], [444].

The MS is probably from Beverley Minster in Yorkshire, where there was a strong college of secular canons. It has a great many correspondences, especially with Sloane 2593 and Balliol 354.

Oxford, Balliol College 354. Paper, 11½ × 4½ in, 255 folios (early 16 cent; dated entries range from 1502 to 1536).

The commonplace book of Richard Hill, grocer of London. It contains poems by Lydgate, Gower, and Dunbar, miscellaneous and anonymous pieces in verse and prose, collectanea and family memoranda. It is written for the most part in one hand, probably that of Hill himself.

Carols [10], [19], [20](MS 2), [26](MS 1), [34](MS 2), [44–51], [76], [77], [78](MS 2), [98], [101](MS 2), [103], [111](MS 1), [118], [120](MS 2), [121](MS 1), [127], [132](MS 1), [133] (MS), [137](MS 1), [143], [152](MS 2), [154](MS 2), [155], [160], [164], [165](MS), [167], [172](MS 2), [175](MS 2), [178], [184], [188](MS 1), [232](MS 2), [234](MS 2), [235], [236](MS 2), [239](MS 2), [240](MS 2), [241](MS 2), [242], [243], [273], [324], [325], [334] (MS 1), [348], [349], [353], [354], [358](MS 1), [362](MS 2), [364], [373](MS 2), [375], [376], [377], [389](MS 2), [392](MS 2), [403](MS 2), [405](MS 2), [406](MS 2), [413], [415](MS 2), [418](MS 2), [427](MS 2), [428], [429], [432](MS), [467].

There are many correspondences with other carol MSS, especially Sloane 2593, Bodl 29734, and Trinity Coll Camb 1230. Though written after 1500, this MS preserves largely fifteenth-century or earlier material.

Cambridge, University Library Ee.1.12. Parchment, 7⅞ × 5½ in, 110 folios (late 15 cent).

Three leaves are missing between ff 108, 109.

The volume contains English songs and translations of Latin hymns by Friar James Ryman of the Franciscan house at Canterbury. One of the three hands in the MS may be Ryman's own. His authorship is asserted by the following colophon on f 80[a]:

Explicit liber ympnorum et canticorum quem composuit Frater Iacobus Ryman ordinis Minorum ad laudem omnipotentis dei et sanctissime matris eius marie omniumque sanctorum anno domini millesimo cccc[mo] lxxxxii[o].

Carols [3], [20] (MS 3), probably not by Ryman; carols by Ryman: [52–55], [61–66], [69–71], [73–75], [80] (MS), [81], [83], [87], [91], [128–31], [156], [161], [162], [174], [190], [193–201], [203–07], [209–14], [216–31], [245](MS 1a & b), [246–57], [259], [260], [264], [267–69], [275], [276], [279], [281], [282], [284–90], [292–307], [321], [355], [356], [363].

Cambridge, Gonville and Caius College 383. Paper, 8⅞ × 5⅞ in, 108 folios (mid 15 cent).

The volume is the exercise and commonplace book of Wymundus London, a trilingual student, probably at Oxford. In the miscellaneous material are a number of place names from Oxfordshire. All the carols are in one hand, apparently that of London himself, and are written in odd spaces along with other notes and memoranda.

Carols [111] (MS 2), [188] (MS 2), [423], [449], [450], [452], [453], [466], [476]b.

There are two correspondences with Balliol 354 and one with Sloane 2593.

Cambridge, St John's College 259 (S.54). Paper, 5¾ × 4⅛ in, 14 folios (mid 15 cent).

Defective at the beginning and much worn and torn. The binding is unique among carol MSS, a wallet-like wrapper of vellum designed to make the volume easily portable. There is no reason to associate it with minstrels. It has no music and is written in four different hands. In addition to complete carols and carol-fragments, it contains one Epiphany piece not in carol form.

Carols [82], [89], [124](MS 2), [140], [144](MS 1), [150](MS 1), [151](MS 2), [234](MS 3), [266] (MS 1), [274], [316], [369], [394], [404], [420], [451], [476]c, [476]d, [476]f.

The correspondences with other carol MSS include Sloane 2593, Bodl 29734, and Balliol 354. There is no indication of provenance except the language, which points to East Anglia.

Cambridge, Trinity College 1230 (0.3.58). A vellum roll, 6 ft 8 in × 7 in (mid 15 cent).

A unique specimen of the roll format with a collection of carols, considerably worn and faded. There is music for all the carols. On the dorse of the roll are four masses. All the carols are written in one hand.

Carols [16] (MS 2), [17] (MS 2), [18], [20] (MS 4), [21], [96], [101] (MS 3), [115] (MS 3), [173], [236] (MS 3), [237] (MS 2), [341] (MS 2), [435] (MS 2).

The correspondences with other carol MSS are mostly with Bodl 29734, Bodl 3340, and Balliol 354. There is no satisfactory evidence of the provenance of the roll.

Lord Harlech: on deposit in the Nat Libr Wales, Porkington 10. Parchment and paper, 5½ × 4¼ in, 211 folios (mid 15 cent).

The contents of this miscellany, written in several different hands, include romances, practical treatises, narrative and lyric verse, both secular and religious. The dialect is chiefly West Midland. The volume has been the private property of the family of Ormsby-Gore for more than a century and has apparently been in Wales in earlier times. Porkington was the name once in use for the family estate now known as Brogyntyn.

Carols [122](MS 2), [136], [154](MS 3), [326], [338].

There are correspondences with Sloane 2593, Balliol 354, and Bodl 798.

GENERAL TREATMENTS OF THE CAROL.

Sandys W, Christmas Carols, Ancient and Modern, London 1833; Christmastide, Its History, Festivities, and Carols, London 1852.
Husk W H, Songs of the Nativity, London [1868], sig b₁ʳ.
Padelford F M, Transition English Song Collections, CHEL, 2.422.
Chambers E K and F Sidgwick, Fifteenth-Century Carols by John Audelay, MLR 5.473.
Duncan E, The Story of the Carol, London 1911.
Rickert Anc Eng Chr Carols, p xiii.
Helmore T, Carols, in J Julian, A Dictionary of Hymnology, London 1915, p 205.
Phillips W, Carols: Their Origin, Music, and Connection with Mystery-Plays, London [1921].
Ch&Sidg, London 1926, p 259.
Reed Christmas Carols, p xi.
Wehrle.
Greene E E Carols.
Brown RLxvC, p xix.
Sahlin M, Étude sur la carole médiévale, Upsala 1940.
Chambers OHEL, p 66.
Greene R L, Carol, Collier's Encyclopedia, N Y 1949, 4.541.
Bukofzer M F, Studies in Medieval and Renaissance Music, N Y 1950, p 148.
Miller C K, The Early English Carol, RN 3.61.
Wells E K, The Ballad Tree, N Y 1950, p 195.
Kane, p 165.
Moore A K, The Secular Lyric in Middle English, Lexington Ky 1951.
Stevens J E, Carol, in F Blume, Die Musik in Geschichte und Gegenwart, Kassel and Basel 1952, vol 2, col 856.
Stevens J [E], H J Lincoln and J Marshall, Carol, in E Bloom, Grove's Dictionary of Music and Musicians, 5th edn, London 1954, 2.78.
Dean-Smith M, A Guide to English Folk Song Collections 1822–1952, Liverpool 1954, p 19.
Robbins SL, p xvii.

Harrison F Ll, Music in Medieval Britain, London 1958.
Routley E, The English Carol, London 1958.
Stevens Med Carols, p xiii.
Robbins R H, Middle English Carols as Processional Hymns, SP 56.559.
Stevens J [E], Music and Poetry in the Early Tudor Court, London 1961.
Robbins Christmas Carols.
Greene Selection.
Manning S, Wisdom and Number, Lincoln Neb 1962.
OBC, rvsd edn, p v.
Robbins R H, The Earliest Carols and the Franciscans, MLN 53.239.
Woolf.
Robbins R H, The Burden in Carols, MLN 57.16.
Gray D, Themes and Images in the Medieval English Religious Lyric, London 1972.
Jeffrey D L, The Early English Lyric and Franciscan Spirituality, Lincoln Neb 1975.
Stevens J [E], Early Tudor Songs and Carols, Musica Britannica 36, London 1975.

[1] O OF IESSE THOW HOLY ROTE.

MS. BM Addit 5665, ff 19ᵇ–20ᵃ (late 15 cent; music).
Brown-Robbins, no 2533.
Editions. Fehr B, Arch 106.268.
Greene E E Carols, p 3; 2nd edn, p 1.
Modernization. Stevens Med Carols, p 77 (with music).
Commentary. Greene E E Carols, p 352; 2nd edn, p 342.

[2] O DAUID THOW NOBELL KEY.

MS. BM Addit 5665, ff 20ᵇ–22ᵃ (late 15 cent; music).
Brown-Robbins, no 2409.
Editions. Fehr B, Arch 106.268.
Greene E E Carols, p 3; 2nd edn, p 1.
Modernization. Stevens Med Carols, p 78 (with

music).
Commentary. Greene E E Carols, p 352; 2nd edn, p 342.
Stevens Med Carols, p 121.

[3] WITH PACIENS THOU HAS VS FEDDE (James Ryman?).

MS. Camb Univ Ee.1.12, ff 58ᵇ–59ᵃ (ca 1492).
Brown-Robbins, no 4197.
Editions. Zupitza J, Arch 89.238.
Greene E E Carols, p 4; 2nd edn, p 1.
Little A G, Archaeologia Cantiana 54.2.
Greene Selection, p 53.
Sisam, p 504.
Filmer R M, A Chronicle of Kent 1250–1760, London n d, p 28.
Modernizations. Davies, p 231.
Luria & Hoffman, p 234.
Commentary. Zupitza, Arch 95.274.
Greene E E Carols, p 353 (questions Ryman's authorship); 2nd edn, p 342.
Jacob E F, Chichele and Canterbury, Studies in Medieval History Presented to Frederick Maurice Powicke, ed R W Hunt et al, Oxford 1948, p 396.
Greene Selection, p 186.
Davies, p 354.

[4] GO DAY SYRE CRYSTEMAS OUR KYNG.

MS. Bodl 3340 (Arch Selden B.26), f 8ᵃ (mid 15 cent; music).
Brown-Robbins, no 1004.
Editions. Early Bodleian Music, 2.107 (with music).
Padelford F M, Angl 36.89.
Ch&Sidg, p 233.
Greene E E Carols, p 5; 2nd edn, p 3.
Modernizations. Rickert Anc Eng Chr Carols, p 219.
Terry Med Carol Book, p 39 (with music).
Stevens Med Carols, p 12 (with music).
Robbins Christmas Carols, p 16 (with music).
Stevens J, Tidings True, London [1976], p 22 (with music).
Commentary. Robbins Christmas Carols, p 16.

[5] DIEVS WOUS GARDE BYEWSSER TYDYNGES Y YOW BRYNG.

MS. BM Addit 5665, ff 8ᵇ–9ᵇ (late 15 cent; music by Richard Smert).
Brown-Robbins, no 681.
Editions. Ritson AS 1790, p 128; 1829, 2.17; 1877, p 61.
Stafford Smith J, Musica Antiqua, [London 1812], p 26 (with music; in part).
Sandys W, Christmas Carols, London 1833, p 17.
Wright T, Carols, PPS 4.51.
Sandys W, Christmastide, London 1852, p 224.
Bullen A H, Carols and Poems, London 1885, half-title, verso.
Flügel NL, p 123.
Fehr B, Arch 106.266.
Julian J, A Dictionary of Hymnology, 2nd edn, London 1925, p 209.
Greene E E Carols, p 6; 2nd edn, p 3.
Modernizations. Sylvester J pseud, A Garland of Christmas Carols, Ancient and Modern, London 1861, p 165.
Husk W H, Songs of the Nativity, London 1868, p 127.
Phillips W J, Carols: Their Origin, Music, and Connection with Mystery Plays, London [1921], p 120.
Rickert Anc Eng Chr Carols, p 218.
OBC, p 21; music edn, p 40; rvsd edn, p 41.
Terry Med Carol Book, p 57 (with music).
Beeching, p 157.
Stevens Med Carols, p 67 (with music).
Robbins Christmas Carols, p 9 (with music).
Commentary. Beeching, p 157.
Greene E E Carols, p 353; 2nd edn, p 343.
Stevens Med Carols, p 120 (notes Smert as composer).
Robbins Christmas Carols, p 9.

[6] WOLCUM BE ÞU HEUENE KYNG (John Audelay?).

MSS. 1, Bodl 21876 (Douce 302), ff 28ᵃ–28ᵇ (mid 15 cent); 2, BM Sloane 2593, f 32ᵃ (mid 15 cent).
Brown-Robbins, no 3877.
Editions. Ritson AS 1790, p 81; 1829, 1.140; 1877, p 120 (MS 2).
Sandys W, Christmas Carols, London 1833, p 3 (MS 2); Christmastide, London 1852, p 218 (MS 1).
Wright T, Carols, PPS 4.4 (MS 2); Carols, Publ Warton Club 4.93 (MS 2).
Ch&Sidg, p 232 (MS 2).
Chambers E K and F Sidgwick, MLR 5.483 (MS 1).
Duncan E, The Story of the Carol, London 1911, p 63 (MS 2).
Whiting E K, EETS 184.186 (MS 1).
Greene E E Carols, p 6; 2nd edn, p 3 (MSS 1, 2).

Greene Selection, p 55 (MS 1).
Modernizations. [Vizetelly H], Christmas with the Poets, London 1851, p 7 (MS 2).
Sylvester J pseud, A Garland of Christmas Carols, London 1861, p 79 (MS 2).
Husk W H, Songs of the Nativity, London 1868, p 6 (MS 2).
Bullen A H, Carols and Poems, London 1885, p 2 (MS 2).
Rickert Anc Eng Chr Carols, p 121 (MS 2).
Hutchins C L, Carols Old and Carols New, Boston 1916, p 673 (with supplied music; omits burden; MS 2).
Phillips W J, Carols: Their Origin, Music, and Connection with Mystery Plays, London [1921], p 119 (MS 1).
Beeching, p 3 (MS 2).
OBC, p 213; music edn, p 368; rvsd edn, p 364 (with modern music; MS 2).
Young P M, Carols for the Twelve Days of Christmas, London 1953, p 112 (MS 2).
Routley E, The English Carol, London 1958, p 74 (MS 2).
Commentary. Whiting E K, EETS 184.250.
Greene E E Carols, p 354; 2nd edn, p 344.
Greene Selection, p 187.

[7] ÞE FERSTE DAY OF ȝOL HAN WE IN MYNDE.

MSS. 1, Bodl 29734 (Eng poet e.1), ff 22^a–22^b (mid 15 cent); 2, BM Sloane 2593, ff 33^b–34^a (mid 15 cent).
Brown-Robbins, no 3343.
Editions. Wright T, Carols, PPS 4.17 (MS 2); 23.24 (MS 1); Carols, Publ Warton Club 4.98 (MS 2).
Greene E E Carols, p 7 (MS 1 with collation of MS 2); 2nd edn, p 4.
Greene Selection, p 56 (MS 1).
Modernizations. Husk W H, Songs of the Nativity, London 1868, p 8 (MS 1).
Rickert Anc Eng Chr Carols, p 223 (MS 1).
Adamson M R, A Treasury of ME Verse, London 1930, p 109 (omits burden; MS 1).
Davies, p 167 (MS 1).
Commentary. Greene E E Carols, p 354; 2nd edn, p 344.
Greene Selection, p 187 (MS 1).
Davies, p 338.

[8] NOW YS CUM OWRE SAUEOWRE.

MS. Huntington Libr HM. 147, f 113^a (ca 1500).
Brown-Robbins, no 2334.
Editions. Schulz H C, Huntington Libr Bull 6.166.
Greene E E Carols, p 8; 2nd edn, p 5.
Brown RLxvC, p 122.
Commentary. Greene E E Carols, p 354; 2nd edn, p 344.
Brown RLxvC, p 319.

[9] NOW YS ȝOLE COMYN W^t GENTYLL CHERE.

MS. BM Addit 14997, ff 44^b–45^a (1500).
Brown-Robbins, Robbins-Cutler, no 2343.
Editions. Hammerle K, Arch 166.204.
Greene E E Carols, p 9; 2nd edn, p 5.
Robbins SL, p 3.
Greene Selection, p 57.
Silverstein, p 117.
Sisam, p 513.
Modernizations. Stevick, p 166.
Luria & Hoffman, p 136.
Commentary. Greene E E Carols, p 355; 2nd edn, p 344.
Robbins SL, p 228.
Greene Selection, p 188.

[10] LETT NO MAN CUM INTO THIS HALL.

MS. Balliol 354, f 223^b (early 16 cent).
Brown-Robbins, Robbins-Cutler, no 1866.
Editions. Flügel Fest R Hildebrand, p 69.
Flügel NL, p 123.
Flügel E, Angl 26.241.
Pollard 15CPV, p 86.
Ch&Sidg, p 234.
Frost L, Come Christmas, N Y 1935, p 261.
Dyboski R, EETSES 101.15.
Greene E E Carols, p 9; 2nd edn, p 6.
Robbins SL, p 3.
Greene Selection, p 58.
Kaiser R, Medieval English (3rd edn of Alt- und me Anthologie), Berlin West 1958, p 290.
Sisam, p 527.
Modernizations. Rickert Anc Eng Chr Carols, p 220.
Beeching, p 158.
OBC, p 211; music edn, p 358; rvsd edn, p 359 (with supplied music).
Davies, p 277.
Stevick, p 170.
Oliver, p 110.
Luria & Hoffman, p 133.
Commentary. Ch&Sidg, p 373.
Greene E E Carols, p 355; 2nd edn, p 345.
Schoeck R J, Angl 71.356.
Greene Selection, p 189.

[11] A CHILD IS BOREN AMONGES MAN.

MSS. I, Bodl 1871 (Bodley 26), f 202^b (mid 14 cent); 2, Univ of London 657, p 287 (14 cent; stanza 3).
Brown-Robbins, Robbins-Cutler, no 29.
Editions. Brown RLxivC, p 110 (MS 1).
Greene E E Carols, p 9 (MS 1 with collation of MS 2); 2nd edn, p 6.
Chambers OHEL, p 80 (MS 1).
Obertello A, Liriche religiose Inglesi del secolo quattordicesimo, Milan 1947, p 104 (MS 1 with Italian trans).
Greene Selection, p 59 (MS 1).
Sisam, p 183 (MS 1).
Modernization. Stevick, p 65.
Commentary. Brown RLxivC, p 272.
Greene E E Carols, pp lxxxiii, cxxv, cxli, 355; 2nd edn, pp ciii, cliv, clxviii, 345.
Sahlin M, Étude sur la carole médiévale, Upsala 1940, pp 58, 182.
Chambers OHEL, p 80.
Jeffrey D L, The Early English Lyric and Franciscan Spirituality, Lincoln Neb 1975, p 179.
Greene Selection, p 189.
Manning S, Wisdom and Number, Lincoln Neb 1962, pp 28, 31.

[12] A KYNGES SONE AND AN EMPEROURE.

MS. BM Addit 5665, ff 39^b–40^a (late 15 cent; music).
Brown-Robbins, no 3587 (under "This day ys borne a chylde of grace"); Robbins-Cutler, no 54.5.
Editions. Sandys W, Christmas Carols, London 1833, p 14.
Wright T, Carols, PPS 4.53.
Fehr B, Arch 106.274.
Greene E E Carols, p 10; 2nd edn, p 7.
Modernizations. Rickert Anc Eng Chr Carols, p 217.
Beeching, p 164.
Stevens Med Carols, p 96 (with music).
Robbins Christmas Carols, p 82 (with music).
Oliver, p 32.
Commentary. Greene E E Carols, p 355; 2nd edn, p 346.
Stevens Med Carols, p 122.

[13] NOW WEL MAY WE MERTHIS MAKE.

MSS. 1, Bodl 3340 (Arch Selden B.26), f 10^a (mid 15 cent; music); 2, BM Addit 5665, ff 36^b–37^a (late 15 cent; music); 3, Bridgwater Corp Muniments 123, on back of indenture (late 15 cent).
Brown-Robbins, Robbins-Cutler, no 2377.
Editions. Early Bodleian Music, 2.109 (with music; MS 1).
Fehr B, Arch 106.273 (MS 2).
Padelford F M, Angl 36.91 (MS 1).
Reports of the Historical MSS Commission 3. Appendix, p 316 (MS 3).
Dilks T B, Pilgrims in Old Bridgwater, Bridgwater 1927, p 35 (MS 3).
Greene E E Carols, p 10 (MS 3 with collation of MSS 1 and 2); 2nd edn, p 7.
Greene Selection, p 60 (MS 3).
Modernizations. Terry Med Carol Book, p 2 (with music; MS 1).
Stevens Med Carols, pp 14 (with music; MS 1), 94 (with music; MS 2).
Robbins Christmas Carols, p 20 (with music; MS 2).
Commentary. Wehrle, pp 66, 67.
Greene E E Carols, pp lxxxi, xcviii, 355; 2nd edn, pp cii, cxxii, 346.
Greene Selection, p 190.

[14] THIS HOLY TYME OURE LORD WAS BORNE.

MS. Bodl 15353 (Rawlinson C.506), f 31^b (early 15 cent).
Brown-Robbins, no 3609.
Editions. Macray W D, Catalogi Manuscriptorum Bibliothecae Bodleianae Pt 5 Fasc 2, Oxford 1878, p 266.
Greene E E Carols, p 11; 2nd edn, p 8.
Commentary. Greene E E Carols, p 356; 2nd edn, p 347.

[15] IN þIS TYME A CHYLD WAS BORN.

MS. BM Sloane 2593, ff 27^a–27^b (mid 15 cent).
Brown-Robbins, no 1574.
Editions. Wright T, Carols, Publ Warton Club 4.78; Carols, PPS 4.12.
Greene E E Carols, p 11; 2nd edn, p 8.
Commentary. Greene E E Carols, p 356; 2nd edn, p 347.

[16] A PRYNCYPAL POYNTH OF CHARYTE.

MSS. 1, Corp Christi Camb 233, f 95^b (late 15 cent); 2, Trinity Camb 1230 (0.3.58), no 5 (mid 15 cent; music).
Brown-Robbins, Robbins-Cutler, no 88.

Editions. Fuller Maitland J A and W S Rockstro, English Carols of the 15th Century, London [1891], p 11 (with music; MS 2).
Patterson F A, in B Matthews and A H Thorndike, Shaksperian Studies, N Y 1916, p 444 (MS 1).
Greene E E Carols, p 12 (MS 1 with collation of MS 2); 2nd edn, p 8.
Modernizations. Rickert Anc Eng Chr Carols, p 203 (MS 2).
Terry Med Carol Book, p 48 (with music; MS 2).
Stevens Med Carols, p 4 (with music; MS 2).
Robbins Christmas Carols, p 30 (with music; MS 2).
Stevens J, Tidings True, London [1976], p 8 (with music; MS 2).
Commentary. Robbins Christmas Carols, p 30.

[17] IN BEDLEM THIS BERDE OF LYF.

MSS. 1, Bodl 3340 (Arch Selden B.26), f 27ᵇ (mid 15 cent; music); 2, Trinity Camb 1230 (0.3.58), no 2 (mid 15 cent; music).
Brown-Robbins, no 1473.
Editions. Fuller Maitland J A and W S Rockstro, English Carols of the 15th Century, London [1891], p 5 (with music; MS 2).
Early Bodleian Music, 2.155 (with music; MS 1).
Padelford F M, Angl 36.110 (MSS 1, 2).
Greene E E Carols, p 13 (MS 2 with collation of MS 1), 2nd edn, p 9.
Brown RLxvC, p 111 (MS 2).
Modernizations. Terry Med Carol Book, pp 36 (with music; MS 1), 42 (with music; MS 2).
Stevens Med Carols, pp 2 (with music; MS 2), 27 (with music; MS 1).
Commentary. Greene E E Carols, p 356; 2nd edn, p 347.
Stevens Med Carols, p 119 (corrects Greene on music: two versions essentially the same composition).

[18] THIS BABE TO VS THAT NOW IS BORE.

MS. Trinity Camb 1230 (0.3.58), no 4 (mid 15 cent; music).
Brown-Robbins, no 3574 (with [19] below).
Editions. Dyboski R, EETSES 101.177.
Fuller Maitland J A and W S Rockstro, English Carols of the 15th Cent, London [1891], p 9 (with music).
Greene E E Carols, p 13; 2nd edn, p 9.
Modernizations. Rickert Anc Eng Chr Carols, p 169.
Terry Med Carol Book, p 46 (with music).
Stevens Med Carols, p 4 (with music).
Commentary. Greene E E Carols, p 356; 2nd edn, p 347.

[19] THIS BABE TO VS NOW IS BORN.

MS. Balliol 354, f 227ᵇ (early 16 cent).
Brown-Robbins, no 3574 (with [18] above).
Editions. Flügel Fest R Hildebrand, p 76.
Flügel E, Angl 26.254.
Dyboski R, EETSES 101.30.
Ch&Sidg, p 116.
Greene E E Carols, p 14; 2nd edn, p 10.
Modernizations. Segar M G, A Mediaeval Anthology, London 1915, p 43.
Comper Spir Songs, p 91.
Weston, p 32.
Commentary. Greene E E Carols, p 356; 2nd edn, p 347.

[20] IN BEDLEEM IN THAT FAIR CETE.

MSS. 1, Bodl 29734 (Eng poet e.1), f 35ᵇ (mid 15 cent); 2, Balliol 354, f 222ᵇ (early 16 cent); 3, Camb Univ Ee.1.12, f 1ᵃ (late 15 cent; music); 4, Trinity Camb 1230 (0.3.58), no 6 (mid 15 cent; music); 5, BM Addit 31042, f 94ᵇ (15 cent; fragment).
Brown-Robbins, Robbins-Cutler, no 1471.
Editions. Fuller Maitland J A and W S Rockstro, English Carols of the 15th Cent, London [1891], p 13 (with music; MS 4).
Flügel Fest R Hildebrand, p 67 (MS 2).
Flügel E, Angl 26.239 (MS 2).
Wright T, Carols, PPS 23.52 (MS 1).
Ch&Sidg, p 138 (MS 4).
Dyboski R, EETSES 101.12 (MS 2).
Wehrle, p 72 (MSS 1, 2, 4).
Greene E E Carols, p 14 (MSS 1–4); 2nd edn, pp 10 (MSS 1–4), 11 (MS 5).
Greene Selection, p 61 (MS 2).
Hodder K, Arch 205.378 (MS 5), 380 (facsimile).
Modernizations. Rickert Anc Eng Chr Carols, pp 50 (MS 1), 183 (MS 2).
OBC, p 148 (MS 1); music edn, p 242; rvsd edn, p 252 (MS 1 with editorially supplied music). with editorially supplied music).
Terry Med Carol Book, p 49 (MS 4 with music).
Stevens Med Carols, pp 5 (MS 4 with music), 111 (MS 3 with music; burden only).
Commentary. Ch&Sidg, p 355.
Dyboski, EETSES 101.173.
Wehrle, p 72.
Greene E E Carols, p 357; 2nd edn, p 348.
Stevens Med Carols, p 123.
Greene Selection, p 191.

[21] NOW GOD ALMYTHTY DOUN HATH SENT.

MS. Trinity Camb 1230 (0.3.58), no 8 (mid 15 cent; music).
Brown-Robbins, no 2315.
Editions. Fuller Maitland J A and W S Rockstro, English Carols of the 15th Cent, London [1891], p 17 (with music).
Greene E E Carols, p 16; 2nd edn, p 11.
Modernizations. Rickert Anc Eng Chr Carols, p 204.
Terry Med Carol Book, p 50 (with music).
Stevens Med Carols, p 7 (with music).
Robbins Christmas Carols, p 22 (with music).
Commentary. Greene E E Carols, p 357; 2nd edn, p 348.

[22] AS HOLY KYRKE MAKYS MYND.

MSS. 1, BM Harley 275, ff 146b–147a (late 15 cent); 2, Advocates 19.3.1, ff 59a–59b (late 15 cent); 3, BM Egerton 3307, ff 65b–66a (mid 15 cent); 4, Bodl fragment.
Brown-Robbins, Robbins-Cutler, no 340.
Editions. Turnbull W B D D, The Visions of Tundale, Edinburgh 1843, p 139 (MS 2).
Breul K, Zwei Mittelenglische Christmas Carols, EStn 14.402 (MS 2).
Ch&Sidg, p 134 (MS 2).
Williams J, N&Q 2s 9.439 (MS 1).
Greene E E Carols, p 16 (MSS 1, 2); 2nd edn, pp 12 (MSS 1, 2), 13 (MSS 3, 4).
Brown RLxvC, p 123 (MS 2).
Greene Selection, p 62 (MS 3).
Modernization. Stevens Med Carols, p 52 (MS 3 with music).
Commentary. Breul, EStn 14.405.
Ch&Sidg, p 354.
Wehrle, p 100.
Greene E E Carols, pp lxxii, 357; 2nd edn, pp xciii, 348.
Brown RLxvC, p 319.
Stevens Med Carols, p 120.
Greene R L, Journ of the American Musicological Soc 7.80.
Greene Selection, p 192.

[23] BLYSSID BE þAT MAYDE MARY.

MS. BM Sloane 2593, f 4b (mid 15 cent).
Brown-Robbins, no 527.
Editions. Sandys W, Christmas Carols, London 1833, p 6.
Wright T, Carols, PPS 4.5; Carols, Publ Warton Club 4.9.
Fehr B, Arch 107.48.
Julian J, A Dictionary of Hymnology, London 1925, p 208.
Greene E E Carols, p 18; 2nd edn, p 14.
Modernizations. Rickert Anc Eng Chr Carols, p 45.
Hutchins C L, Carols Old and Carols New, Boston 1916, p 603 (with supplied music, altered).
Beeching, p 22.
Woodward G R, The Cowley Carol Book, Oxford n d (altered).
Commentary. Wehrle, p 70.
Greene E E Carols, p lxxiii; 2nd edn, p xciv.

[24] þE SUNNE OF GRACE HYM SCHYNIT IN.

MS. BM Sloane 2593, f 11b (mid 15 cent).
Brown-Robbins, Robbins-Cutler, no 3472.
Editions. Wright T, Carols, Publ Warton Club 4.34.
Fehr B, Arch 109.51.
Greene E E Carols, p 18; 2nd edn, p 14.
Sisam, p 436.
Modernizations. Rickert Anc Eng Chr Carols, p 209.
Comper Spir Songs, p 73.
Sitwell E, The Atlantic Book of British and American Poetry, Boston 1958, p 11.
Commentary. Greene E E Carols, pp xcvi, 357; 2nd edn, pp cxx, 349.
Manning S, Wisdom and Number, Lincoln Neb 1962, p 23.

[25] ALL THIS WORLDE WAS FUL OF GRACE.

MS. BM Addit 40166(C3), ff 12b–13a (15 cent).
Brown-Robbins, no 226.
Edition. Greene E E Carols, p 19; 2nd edn, p 14.
Commentary. Greene E E Carols, p 358; 2nd edn, p 349.

[26] IN þIS TYME CRYST HAʒT VS SENT.

MSS. 1, Balliol 354, f 220a (early 16 cent); 2, BM Royal 20.A.i, f 120a (early 15 cent); 3, BM Sloane 2593, ff 24a, 24b (mid 15 cent).
Brown-Robbins, no 1575.
Editions. Flügel Fest R Hildebrand, p 61 (MS 1).
Wright T, Carols, PPS 4.11 (MS 3); Carols, Publ Warton Club 4.68 (MS 3).
Flügel E, Angl 26.231 (MS 1).
Dyboski R, EETSES 101.7, 170 (MSS 1, 3).
Frost L, Come Christmas, N Y 1935, p 262 (MS 1).

Greene E E Carols, p 19; 2nd edn, p 15 (MSS 1–3).
Modernizations. Weston, p 18 (MS 1).
Rickert Anc Eng Chr Carols, pp 52, 47 (MSS 1, 3).
Commentary. Greene E E Carols, p 358; 2nd edn, p 350.

[27] þIS TYME IS BORN A CHYLD FUL GOOD.

MS. BM Sloane 2593, f 28^a (mid 15 cent).
Brown-Robbins, no 3643.
Editions. Wright T, Carols, PPS 4.14; Carols, Publ Warton Club 4.80.
Greene E E Carols, p 20; 2nd edn, p 16.
Greene Selection, p 63.
Modernizations. Rickert Anc Eng Chr Carols, p 48.
Beeching, p 19.
Commentary. Greene E E Carols, p 358; 2nd edn, p 350.
Greene Selection, p 192.

[28] EXORTUM EST IN LOUE & LYSSE.

MS. Bodl 3340 (Arch Selden B.26), f 7^a (mid 15 cent; music).
Brown-Robbins, no 753.
Editions. Early Bodleian Music, 2.104 (with music).
Padelford F M, Angl 36.87.
Greene E E Carols, p 21; 2nd edn, p 16.
Copley J, Seven English Songs and Carols of the Fifteenth Century, Leeds School of English Language Texts and Monographs no 6, Leeds 1940, p 16 (with music).
Modernizations. Rickert Anc Eng Chr Carols, p 166.
OBC, p 82; music edn, p 128; rvsd edn, p 135.
Terry Med Carol Book, p 32 (with music).
Stevens Med Carols, p 11 (with music).
Robbins Christmas Carols, p 32 (with music).
Routley E, The English Carol, London 1958, p 34.
Greenberg N, An English Songbook, Garden City N Y 1961, p 68 (with music).
Stevens J, Tidings True, London [1976], p 6 (with music).
Commentary. Wehrle, p 111.
Greene E E Carols, p 358; 2nd edn, p 350.
Robbins Christmas Carols, p 32.

[29] OWT OF ȜOUR SLEPE ARYSE & WAKE.

MSS. 1, Bodl 3340 (Arch Selden B.26), f 14^b (mid 15 cent; music); 2, Camb Univ Ll.1.11, f 32^a (mid 15 cent; music).
Brown-Robbins, Robbins-Cutler, no 2733.
Editions. Early Bodleian Music, 2.122 (MS 1 with music).
Ch&Sidg, p 115 (MS 1).
Padelford F M, Angl 36.96 (MS 1).
Greene E E Carols, p 21; 2nd edn, p 16 (MS 1).
Blume F, Die Musik in Geschichte und Gegenwart, Kessel and Basel 1952, vol 2, cols 857–58 (MS 1; facsimile).
Greene Selection, p 64 (MS 1).
Gray D, Themes and Images in the Medieval English Religious Lyric, London 1972, p 96; A Selection of Religious Lyrics, Oxford 1975, p 7.
Modernizations. Rickert Anc Eng Chr Carols, p 165 (MS 1).
Terry Med Carol Book, p 34 (MS 1 with music).
Stevens Med Carols, pp 18 (MS 1 with music), 114 (MS 2 with music).
Robbins Christmas Carols, p 18 (MS 1 with music).
OBC, p 216; music edn, p 376; rvsd edn, p 369 (MS 1 with supplied music).
Davies, p 195.
Oliver, p 115.
Greene E E Carols, 2nd edn, p 17 (MS 2).
Commentary. Greene E E Carols, p 359; 2nd edn, p 350.
Bukofzer M F, Some Sources of 15 Cent English Music, RN 2.65 (first notice of MS 2).
Stevens Med Carols, p 124.
Greene Selection, p 193.
Manning S, Wisdom and Number, Lincoln Neb 1962, p 143.
Gray D, Themes and Images in the Medieval English Religious Lyric, London 1972, p 96.

[30] A PATRE UNIGENITUS.

MSS. 1, Bodl 3340 (Arch Selden B.26), f 15^a (mid 15 cent; music); 2, Bodl 29734 (Eng poet e.1), ff 32^b–33^a (mid 15 cent); 3, BM Addit 5665, ff 28^b–29^a (late 15 cent; music).
Brown-Robbins, no 18.
Editions. Wright T, Carols, PPS 4.58 (MS 3); 23.48 (MS 2).
Fehr B, Arch 106.270 (MS 3).
Early Bodleian Music, 2.122 (MS 1 with music).
Padelford F M, Angl 36.98 (MSS 1–3).
Greene E E Carols, p 22 (MS 1 with collation of MSS 2 and 3); 2nd edn, p 17.
Greene Selection, p 65 (MS 1).
Modernizations. Rickert Anc Eng Chr Carols, p 53 (MS 2).
Terry Med Carol Book, p 28 (MS 1 with music).

Stevens Med Carols, pp 19 (MS 1 with music), 85 (MS 3 with music).
Routley E, The English Carol, London 1958, p 33 (MS 1).
Robbins Christmas Carols, pp 25 (MS 3 with music), 28 (MS 1 with music).
OBC, p 28 (MS 1); music edn, p 48; rvsd edn, p 46 (MS 1).
Sayre E, A Christmas Book, N Y 1966, p 93 (MS 1).
Commentary. Wehrle, p 124.
Greene E E Carols, pp lxi, lxxiv, 359; 2nd edn, pp lxxxii, xciv, 351.
Greene Selection, p 193.

[31] THIS IS THE SONGE þAT ȝE SHUL HERE.

MS. Bodl 3340 (Arch Selden B.26), f 23ᵇ (mid 15 cent; music).
Brown-Robbins, no 3619.
Editions. Early Bodleian Music, 2.146 (with music).
Padelford F M, Angl 36.108.
Greene E E Carols, p 23; 2nd edn, p 18.
Modernizations. Rickert Anc Eng Chr Carols, p 172.
Terry Med Carol Book, p 4 (with music).
Stevens Med Carols, p 23 (with music).

[32] A SONGE TO SYNG Y HAUE GOD RYȜT.

MS. Bodl 3340 (Arch Selden B.26), f 28ᵃ (mid 15 cent; music).
Brown-Robbins, no 93.
Editions. Early Bodleian Music, 2.157 (with music).
Padelford F M, Angl 36.112.
Greene E E Carols, p 23; 2nd edn, p 18.
Modernizations. Stevens Med Carols, p 28 (with music).
Oliver, p 30.
Robbins Christmas Carols, p 42 (with music).
Commentary. Wehrle, p 68.
Greene E E Carols, p 359; 2nd edn, p 351.
Raw B C, MLR 55.413.

[33] THAT LORD þᵗ LAY IN ASSE STALLE.

MS. Bodl 3340 (Arch Selden B.26), f 28ᵇ (mid 15 cent; music).
Brown-Robbins, no 3283.
Editions. Early Bodleian Music, 2.158 (with music).
Padelford F M, Angl 36.112.
Greene E E Carols, p 23; 2nd edn, p 18.

Brown RLxvC, p 118.
Modernizations. Stevens Med Carols, p 29 (with music).
Robbins Christmas Carols, p 34 (with music).
Commentary. Greene E E Carols, p 359; 2nd edn, p 351.
Brown RLxvC, p 318.

[34] A LITIL CHILDE þER IS I-BORE.

MSS. 1, Bodl 7589 (Ashmole 1393), f 69ᵇ (mid 15 cent); 2, Balliol 354, f 231ᵇ (early 16 cent).
Brown-Robbins, nos 63, 3635; Robbins-Cutler, no 3635.
Editions. Flügel Fest R Hildebrand, p 82 (MS 2).
Early Bodleian Music, 2.65 (MS 1).
Flügel E, Angl 26.268 (MS 2).
Pollard 15CPV, p 95 (MS 2).
Ch&Sidg, p 132 (MS 1).
Dyboski R, EETSES 101.49 (MS 2).
Greene E E Carols, p 24; 2nd edn, p 19 (MSS 1, 2).
Modernizations. Weston, p 91 (MS 2).
Rickert Anc Eng Chr Carols, pp 42, 43 (MSS 1, 2).
Beeching, p 20 (MS 2).
Sayre E, A Christmas Book, N Y 1966, p 45 (MS 1).
Commentary. Ch&Sidg, p 353.
Greene E E Carols, p 359; 2nd edn, p 351.

[35] BE GLAD LORDYNGES BEþE MORE & LESSE.

MSS. 1, Camb Univ Ii.4.11, f 170ᵇ (early 15 cent); 2, BM Harley 5396, f 280ᵇ (mid 15 cent); 3, Public Record Office Chancery Miscellany, bundle 34, file 1, no 12, f 1ᵃ (early 15 cent).
Brown-Robbins, Robbins-Cutler, no 463.
Editions. Rel Ant, 1.203 (MS 1).
Wright T, Carols, PPS 4.33 (MS 2).
Ch&Sidg, p 118.
Greene E E Carols, p 25 (MS 1 with collation of MSS 2 and 3); 2nd edn, p 19.
Modernization. Rickert Anc Eng Chr Carols, p 22 (MS 2).
Commentary. Wehrle, p 71.
Greene E E Carols, p 360; 2nd edn, p 352.

[36] A FERLY THING IT IS TO MENE.

MS. Bodl 29734 (Eng poet e.1), ff 18ᵇ–19ᵇ (mid 15 cent).
Brown-Robbins, no 34.
Editions. Wright T, Carols, PPS 23.15.

Greene E E Carols, p 26; 2nd edn, p 20.
Sisam, p 469.
Commentary. Greene E E Carols, p 360; 2nd edn, p 352.

[37] THIS MAY I PREVE WITHOUȜTEN LETT.

MS. Bodl 29734 (Eng poet e.1), f 19ᵇ (mid 15 cent).
Brown-Robbins, no 3630.
Editions. Wright T, Carols, PPS 23.17.
Greene E E Carols, p 26; 2nd edn, p 21.
Modernizations. Rickert Anc Eng Chr Carols, p 44.
Adamson M R, A Treasury of ME Verse, London 1930, p 105.
Commentary. Wehrle, p 87.
Greene E E Carols, p 360; 2nd edn, p 352.

[38] GODES SONNE FOR þE LOUE OF MANE.

MS. Bodl 29734 (Eng poet e.1), f 21ᵃ (mid 15 cent).
Brown-Robbins, no 997.
Editions. Wright T, Carols, PPS 23.21.
Greene E E Carols, p 27; 2nd edn, p 21.
Modernization. Rickert Anc Eng Chr Carols, p 173.
Commentary. Wehrle, p 71.
Greene E E Carols, p 360; 2nd edn, p 352.

[39] OMNES GENTES PLAUDITE.

MS. BM Egerton 3307, f 51ᵇ (mid 15 cent; music).
Robbins-Cutler, no 2674.5.
Editions. Greene Selection, p 68.
Greene E E Carols, 2nd edn, p 22.
Modernization. Stevens Med Carols, p 36 (with music).
Commentary. Greene Selection, p 195.
Greene E E Carols, 2nd edn, p 352.

[40] A MAN WAS þE FYRST GYLT.

MS. Bodl 29734 (Eng poet e.1), ff 27*ᵇ–28ᵃ (mid 15 cent).
Brown-Robbins, no 76.
Editions. Wright T, Carols, PPS 23.39.
Ch&Sidg, p 117.
Greene E E Carols, p 27; 2nd edn, p 22.
Modernizations. Rickert Anc Eng Chr Carols, p 164.
Sayre E, A Christmas Book, N Y 1966, p 57.
Commentary. Greene E E Carols, p 360; 2nd edn, p 352.

[41] THE FYRST DAY WAN CRIST WAS BORNE.

MS. Bodl 29734 (Eng poet e.1), ff 29ᵃ–29ᵇ (mid 15 cent).
Brown-Robbins, no 3344.
Editions. Wright T, Carols, PPS 23.42.
Ch&Sidg, p 140.
Greene E E Carols, p 28; 2nd edn, p 22.
Modernizations. Rickert Anc Eng Chr Carols, p 180.
Stevick, p 144.
Commentary. Greene E E Carols, p 360; 2nd edn, p 353.
Manning S, Wisdom and Number, Lincoln Neb 1962, p 12.

[42] WELCOME BE THYS BLISSED FEEST.

MS. Bodl 29734 (Eng poet e.1), ff 53ᵃ–53ᵇ (mid 15 cent). PRINT: Huntington Libr, Christmas carolles newely Inprynted (Richard Kele), pp [28, 29] (ca 1550; STC, no 5205).
Brown-Robbins, Robbins-Cutler, no 3876.
Editions. Wright T, Carols, PPS 23.83 (MS).
Reed Christmas Carols, p 46 (facsimile of PRINT).
Greene E E Carols, p 28 (MS with collation of PRINT); 2nd edn, p 23.
Commentary. Reed Christmas Carols, p 81.

[43] GODDYS SONNE IS BORNE.

MS. Bodl 29734 (Eng poet e.1), ff 52ᵇ–53ᵃ (mid 15 cent).
Brown-Robbins, Robbins-Cutler, no 998.
Editions. Wright T, Carols, PPS 23.82.
Ch&Sidg, p 136.
Greene E E Carols, p 29; 2nd edn, p 24.
Modernization. Rickert Anc Eng Chr Carols, p 41.
Davies, p 222.
Commentary. Greene E E Carols, p 361; 2nd edn, p 353.

[44] A VIRGYN PURE.

MS. Balliol 354, f 178ᵃ (early 16 cent).
Brown-Robbins, no 103.
Editions. Flügel Fest R Hildebrand, p 55.
Flügel NL, p 117.
Flügel E, Angl 26.195.
Dyboski R, EETSES 101.3.
Greene E E Carols, p 30; 2nd edn, p 24.
Modernizations. Rickert Anc Eng Chr Carols, p 51.
Weston, p 7.

Commentary. Wehrle, p 93.
Greene E E Carols, p 361; 2nd edn, p 353.

[45] MARY FLOWR OF FLOWERS ALL.

MS. Balliol 354, f 221ª (early 16 cent).
Brown-Robbins, no 2097.
Editions. Flügel Fest R Hildebrand, p 63.
Flügel NL, p 116.
Flügel E, Angl 26.234.
Dyboski R, EETSES 101.8.
Frost L, Come Christmas, N Y 1935, p 266.
Greene E E Carols, p 30; 2nd edn, p 25.
Modernizations. Rickert Anc Eng Chr Carols, p 170.
Weston, p 9.

[46] GLORIOUS GOD HAD GRET PITE.

MS. Balliol 354, f 227ª (early 16 cent).
Brown-Robbins, no 916.
Editions. Flügel Fest R Hildebrand, p 74.
Flügel E, Angl 26.253.
Dyboski R, EETSES 101.29.
Greene E E Carols, p 31; 2nd edn, p 25.
Modernization. Rickert Anc Eng Chr Carols, p 190.
Commentary. Greene E E Carols, p 361; 2nd edn, p 354.

[47] FOR HIS LOVE Þt BOWGHT VS ALL DERE.

MS. Balliol 354, f 229ª (early 16 cent).
Brown-Robbins, no 825.
Editions. Flügel Fest R Hildebrand, p 77.
Flügel E, Angl 26.260.
Dyboski R, EETSES 101.37.
Ch&Sidg, p 139.
Brougham E M, Corn from Olde Fieldes, 2nd edn, London 1918, p 8.
Greene E E Carols, p 32; 2nd edn, p 26.
Modernizations. Rickert Anc Eng Chr Carols, p 188.
Comper Spir Songs, p 96.
Commentary. Greene E E Carols, p 362; 2nd edn, p 354.

[48] THE SON OF THE FADER OF HEVYN BLYS.

MS. Balliol 354, f 221ᵇ (early 16 cent).
Brown-Robbins, no 3473.
Editions. Flügel Fest R Hildebrand, p 64.
Flügel E, Angl 26.235.
Dyboski R, EETSES 101.9.
Greene E E Carols, p 32; 2nd edn, p 26.
Modernization. Rickert Anc Eng Chr Carols, p 185.

Commentary. Greene E E Carols, p 362; 2nd edn, p 354.

[49] IN-TO THIS WORLDE THIS DAY DIDE COM.

MS. Balliol 354, f 229ᵇ (early 16 cent).
Brown-Robbins, no 1601.
Editions. Flügel Fest R Hildebrand, p 78.
Flügel E, Angl 26.260.
Pollard 15CPV, p 92.
Dyboski R, EETSES 101.38.
Greene E E Carols, p 32; 2nd edn, p 26.
Modernizations. Rickert Anc Eng Chr Carols, p 189.
Weston, p 31.

[50] NOW IOY BE TO THE TRYNYTE.

MS. Balliol 354, f 230ᵇ (early 16 cent).
Brown-Robbins, Robbins-Cutler, no 2346.
Editions. Flügel Fest R Hildebrand, p 80.
Flügel E, Angl 26.265.
Dyboski R, EETSES 101.45.
Frost L, Come Christmas, N Y 1935, p 259.
Greene E E Carols, p 33; 2nd edn, p 27.
Greene Selection, p 66.
Modernizations. Rickert Anc Eng Chr Carols, p 243.
Weston, p 39.
Commentary. Greene E E Carols, p 362; 2nd edn, p 354.
Greene Selection, p 194.

[51] CRYST KEPE VS ALL AS HE WELL CAN.

MS. Balliol 354, f 241ᵇ (early 16 cent).
Brown-Robbins, no 608.
Editions. Flügel Fest R Hildebrand, p 82.
Flügel E, Angl 26.271.
Pollard 15CPV, p 96.
Dyboski R, EETSES 101.49.
Greene E E Carols, pp lxviii, 33; 2nd edn, pp lxxxix, 27.
Modernization. Rickert Anc Eng Chr Carols, p 187.
Commentary. Greene E E Carols, p lxvii; 2nd edn, p lxxxviii.

[52] THIS CHIELDE IS WAS AND AY SHALL BE (James Ryman).

MS. Camb Univ Ee.1.12, ff 43ª–43ᵇ (ca 1492).
Brown-Robbins, no 3585.
Editions. Zupitza J, Arch 89.210.
Greene E E Carols, p 34; 2nd edn, p 28.
Commentary. Zupitza, Arch 94.395.

[53] MARY SO MYELDE AND GOOD OF FAME (James Ryman).

MS. Camb Univ Ee.1.12, f 76ª (ca 1492).
Brown-Robbins, no 2122.
Editions. Zupitza J, Arch 89.275.
Greene E E Carols, p 34; 2nd edn, p 28.
Commentary. Zupitza, Arch 96.167.
Greene E E Carols, p 363; 2nd edn, p 355.

[54] NOW FORTO SYNG I HOLDE IT BEST (James Ryman).

MS. Camb Univ Ee.1.12, f 85ᵇ (ca 1492).
Brown-Robbins, no 2310.
Editions. Zupitza J, Arch 89.292.
Greene E E Carols, p 35; 2nd edn, p 28.
Commentary. Zupitza, Arch 96.316.
Greene E E Carols, p 363; 2nd edn, p 355.

[55] THE FADERS SONE OF HEUEN BLYS (James Ryman).

MS. Camb Univ Ee.1.12, f 86ª (ca 1492).
Brown-Robbins, no 3334.
Editions. Zupitza J, Arch 89.293.
Greene E E Carols, p 36; 2nd edn, p 29.
Commentary. Zupitza, Arch 96.317.
Wehrle, p 150.
Greene E E Carols, p 363; 2nd edn, p 355.

[56] TYDYNGS TREW TOLDE THER YS TREWE.

MS. BM Addit 5665, ff 33ᵇ–34ª (late 15 cent; music).
Brown-Robbins, no 3737.
Editions. Fehr B, Arch 106.272.
Greene E E Carols, p 36; 2nd edn, p 29.
Modernizations. Stevens Med Carols, p 91 (with music).
Robbins Christmas Carols, p 39 (with music).
Commentary. Greene E E Carols, p 363; 2nd edn, p 355.

[57] A CHILDE YS BORN OF A MAYDE.

MS. BM Addit 5665, ff 34ᵇ–35ª (late 15 cent; music).
Brown-Robbins, no 31.
Editions. Fehr B, Arch 106.272.
Greene E E Carols, p 37; 2nd edn, p 30.
Modernization. Stevens Med Carols, p 92 (with music).

[58] BI THI BURTHE þᵘ BLESSED LORD.

MS. BM Addit 5665, ff 52ᵇ–53ª (late 15 cent; music by Richard Smert).
Brown-Robbins, no 581.
Editions. Fehr B, Arch 106.278.
Greene E E Carols, p 37; 2nd edn, p 30.
Robbins R H, MLN 57.19.
Modernizations. Rickert Anc Eng Chr Carols, p 181.
Stevens Med Carols, p 109 (with music).
Robbins Christmas Carols, p 36 (with music).
Routley E, The English Carol, London 1958, p 31 (in part; with music).
Commentary. Robbins R H, The Burden in Carols, MLN 57.19.

[59] THAT IX MONEYTHES [W]AS ENCLUS.

MS. Yale Univ, Osborn Collection, Osborn Shelves a.1, p [306] (14 cent).
Not in Brown-Robbins or Robbins-Cutler.
Edition. Greene E E Carols, 2nd edn, p 30.
Commentary. Greene E E Carols, 2nd edn, p 355.

[60] OF MARY A MAYDE WITHOWT LESYNG (James Ryman).

MS. Camb Univ Addit 7350, Box 2, f 1ᵇ (late 15 cent).
Robbins-Cutler, no 2635.5.
Editions. Robbins R H, PMLA 81.309.
Greene E E Carols, 2nd edn, p 31.
Commentary. Robbins R H, PMLA 81.308.
Greene E E Carols, 2nd edn, p 356.

[61] THE FADERS SONNE OF HEUEN BLIS (James Ryman).

MS. Camb Univ Ee.1.12, ff 44ª–44ᵇ (ca 1492).
Brown-Robbins, no 3332.
Editions. Zupitza J, Arch 89.212.
Greene E E Carols, p 38; 2nd edn, p 31.
Commentary. Zupitza, Arch 94.397.
Greene E E Carols, p 363; 2nd edn, p 356.

[62] THE SONNE OF GOD AND KING OF BLIS (James Ryman).

MS. Camb Univ Ee.1.12, ff 45ᵇ–46ª (ca 1492).
Brown-Robbins, no 3467.
Editions. Zupitza J, Arch 89.214.
Greene E E Carols, p 38; 2nd edn, p 32.
Commentary. Zupitza, Arch 94.401.

[63] THE SONE OF GOD SO FULL OF MYGHT (James Ryman).

MS. Camb Univ Ee.1.12, ff 104ᵃ–104ᵇ (ca 1492).
Brown-Robbins, no 3470.
Editions. Zupitza J, Arch 89.324.
Greene E E Carols, p 39; 2nd edn, p 32.
Commentary. Zupitza, Arch 97.141.
Greene E E Carols, p 363; 2nd edn, p 356.

[64] BOTHE YONGE AND OLDE TAKE HEDE OF THIS (James Ryman).

MS. Camb Univ Ee.1.12, ff 24ᵃ–24ᵇ (ca 1492).
Brown-Robbins, no 546.
Editions. Zupitza J, Arch 89.186.
Greene E E Carols, p 40; 2nd edn, p 33.
Modernization. Routley E, The English Carol, London 1958, p 41.
Commentary. Zupitza, Arch 93.390.
Greene E E Carols, pp lxxxvii, 364; 2nd edn, pp cx, 356.
Stevens Med Carols, p 119.

[65] BEHOLDE & SE HOW THAT NATURE (James Ryman).

MS. Camb Univ Ee.1.12, ff 23ᵃ–24ᵃ (ca 1492).
Brown-Robbins, no 488.
Editions. Zupitza J, Arch 89.185.
Greene E E Carols, p 41; 2nd edn, p 34.
Greene Selection, p 67.
Commentary. Zupitza, Arch 93.383.
Greene E E Carols, p 364; 2nd edn, p 356.
Stevens Med Carols, p 119.
Greene Selection, p 194.

[66] THE PROPHESY FULFILLED IS (James Ryman).

MS. Camb Univ Ee.1.12, ff 74ᵇ–75ᵇ (ca 1492).
Brown-Robbins, no 3450.
Editions. Zupitza J, Arch 89.272.
Greene E E Carols, p 41; 2nd edn, p 34.
Commentary. Zupitza, Arch 96.165.
Greene E E Carols, p 364; 2nd edn, p 357.

[67] ADAM OUR FADER WAS IN BLIS.

MS. BM Sloane 2593, ff 4ᵃ–4ᵇ (mid 15 cent).
Brown-Robbins, no 118.
Editions. Wright T, Carols, Publ Warton Club 4.7.
Fehr B, Arch 109.43.

Greene E E Carols, p 42; 2nd edn, p 35.
Modernization. Rickert Anc Eng Chr Carols, p 162.
Commentary. Wehrle, p 69.
Greene E E Carols, p 364; 2nd edn, p 357.

[68] THIS WORLE WONDREþ OF AL THYNGE.

MS. Bodl 3340 (Arch Selden B.26), f 29ᵃ (mid 15 cent; music).
Brown-Robbins, no 3659.
Editions. Early Bodleian Music, 2.160 (with music).
Padelford F M, Angl 36.113.
Greene E E Carols, p 43; 2nd edn, p 36.
Modernization. Stevens Med Carols, p 30 (with music).
Commentary. Greene E E Carols, p 364; 2nd edn, p 357.

[69] THUS IT IS SAIDE IN PROPHECYE (James Ryman).

MS. Camb Univ Ee.1.12, ff 37ᵇ–38ᵇ (ca 1492).
Brown-Robbins, no 3724.
Editions. Zupitza J, Arch 89.203.
Greene E E Carols, p 43; 2nd edn, p 36.
Commentary. Zupitza, Arch 94.200.
Greene E E Carols, p 364; 2nd edn, p 357.

[70] A MEYDEN MYELDE HATH BORNE A CHIELDE (James Ryman).

MS. Camb Univ Ee.1.12, ff 41ᵇ–42ᵃ (ca 1492).
Brown-Robbins, no 67.
Editions. Zupitza J, Arch 89.209.
Greene E E Carols, p 44; 2nd edn, p 37.
Commentary. Zupitza J, Arch 94.391.
Greene E E Carols, p 365; 2nd edn, p 357.

[71] THIS IS THE STONE KUT OF THE HILLE (James Ryman).

MS. Camb Univ Ee.1.12, ff 75ᵇ–76ᵃ (ca 1492).
Brown-Robbins, no 3620.
Editions. Zupitza J, Arch 89.274.
Greene E E Carols, p 45; 2nd edn, p 37.
Commentary. Zupitza, Arch 96.166.
Wehrle, p 151.
Greene E E Carols, p 365; 2nd edn, p 357.

[72] A NYWE WERK IS COME ON HONDE.

MS. Bodl 3340 (Arch Selden B.26), ff 21ᵇ–22ᵃ (mid 15 cent; music).

Brown-Robbins, no 81.
Editions. Early Bodleian Music, 2.140 (with music).
Padelford F M, Angl 36.106.
Greene E E Carols, p 45; 2nd edn, p 38.
Modernizations. Stevens Med Carols, p 22 (with music).
Sayre E, A Christmas Book, N Y 1966, p 103.
Commentary. Greene E E Carols, p 364; 2nd edn, p 358.

[73] OUTE OF YOURE SLEPE ARRYSE AND WAKE (James Ryman).

MS. Camb Univ Ee.1.12, ff 39^a–40^a (ca 1492).
Brown-Robbins, no 2734.
Editions. Zupitza J, Arch 89.206.
Greene E E Carols, p 46; 2nd edn, p 38.
Commentary. Zupitza, Arch 94.203.
Greene E E Carols, p 365; 2nd edn, p 358.

[74] VPON A NYGHT AN AUNGELL BRIGHT (James Ryman).

MS. Camb Univ Ee.1.12, ff 33^a–34^a (ca 1492).
Brown-Robbins, Robbins-Cutler, no 3837.
Editions. Zupitza J, Arch 89.197.
Greene E E Carols, p 47; 2nd edn, p 39.
Commentary. Zupitza, Arch 94.188.
Wehrle, p 153.
Greene E E Carols, pp lxi, 365; 2nd edn, pp lxxxii, 358.
Davies, p 229.

[75] WHENNE CRISTE WAS BORNE AN AUNGELL BRIGHT (James Ryman).

MS. Camb Univ Ee.1.12, ff 34^a–34^b (ca 1492).
Brown-Robbins, no 3930.
Editions. Zupitza J, Arch 89.199.
Greene E E Carols, p 47; 2nd edn, p 39.
Commentary. Zupitza, Arch 94.190.

[76] AS I CAM BY THE WAY.

MS. Balliol 354, f 231^b (early 16 cent).
Brown-Robbins, no 343.
Editions. Flügel Fest R Hildebrand, p 81.
Flügel E, Angl 26.267.
Pollard 15CPV, 94.
Dyboski R, EETSES 101.48.
Greene E E Carols, p 48; 2nd edn, p 40.
Modernization. Rickert Anc Eng Chr Carols, p 102.
Commentary. Greene E E Carols, p 365; 2nd edn, p 358.

[77] THE SHEPARD UPON A HILL HE SATT.

MS. Balliol 354, ff 224^a–224^b (early 16 cent).
Brown-Robbins, Robbins-Cutler, no 3460.
Editions. Flügel Fest R Hildebrand, p 70.
Flügel NL, p 117.
Flügel E, Angl 26.243.
Pollard 15CPV, p 87.
Ch&Sidg, p 127.
Dyboski R, EETSES 101.16.
Cook A S, A Literary ME Reader, Boston 1915, p 468.
Frost L, Come Christmas, N Y 1935, p 270.
Greene E E Carols, p 49; 2nd edn, p 40.
Cecil Lord D, The Oxford Book of Christian Verse, Oxford 1940, p 2.
Kermode F, English Pastoral Poetry, London 1952, p 50.
Greene Selection, p 69.
Sisam, p 529.
Silverstein, p 115.
Gray D, Themes and Images in the Medieval English Religious Lyric, London 1972, p 116; A Selection of Religious Lyrics, Oxford 1975, p 9.
Modernizations. Ancient Carols, The Shakespeare Head Press Booklets, no 1, Stratford-on-Avon 1906, p 5.
Rickert Anc Eng Chr Carols, p 99.
Manning Foster A E, Christmas Carols of England, London 1915, p 67.
Beeching, p 15.
Adamson M R, A Treasury of ME Verse, London 1930, p 143.
Commentary. Greene E E Carols, p 366; 2nd edn, p 358.
Greene Selection, p 196.
Woolf, p 303.

[78] ABOWT THE FYLD THEI PYPED FUL RIGHT.

MSS. 1, Bodl 29734 (Eng poet e.l), f 60^a (mid 15 cent); 2, Balliol 354, f 222^a (early 16 cent); 3, MS formerly owned by Thomas Sharp, destroyed 1879 (16 cent; music).
Brown-Robbins, no 112.
Editions. Sharp T, A Dissertation on the Pageants or Dramatic Mysteries, Coventry 1825, pp 113, 115, 118 (MS 3 with music).
Flügel Fest R Hildebrand, p 66 (MS 2).
Flügel NL, p 117 (MS 2).
Craig H, EETSES 87.31, 32 (MS 3).
Wright T, Carols, PPS 23.95 (MS 1).

Pollard 15CPV, pp 272, 273 (MS 3).
Flügel E, Angl 26.237 (MSS 1, 2).
Ch&Sidg, p 126 (combined text).
Dyboski R, EETSES 101.11 (MS 2 with collation of MS 1).
Brougham E M, Corn from Olde Fieldes, 2nd edn, London 1918, p 6 (stanzas 6 and 7 from MS 1).
Frost L, Come Christmas, N Y 1935, p 269 (MS 2).
Greene E E Carols, p 50 (MSS 1, 3 with collation of MS 2); 2nd edn, p 41.
Greene Selection, p 71 (MS 1).
Kermode F, English Pastoral Poetry, London 1952, p 50.
Silverstein, p 115.
Gray D, A Selection of Religious Lyrics, Oxford 1975, p 8 (MS 1).
Modernizations. Bullen A H, Carols and Poems, London 1886, p 19 (MS 1).
Duncan E, The Story of the Carol, London 1911, p 76 (MS 3 with music).
Rickert Anc Eng Chr Carols, pp 97, 99 (MSS 1, 3).
Segar M G, A Mediaeval Anthology, London 1915, p 101 (MS 2); Some Minor Poems of the Middle Ages, London 1917, p 9 (MS 2).
Phillips W J, Carols: Their Origin, Music, and Connection with Mystery Plays, London [1921], p 105 (MS 3).
OBC, p 208 (MS 2); music edn, p 338; rvsd edn, p 342 (MS 2 with modern music).
Sitwell E, The Atlantic Book of British and American Poetry, Boston 1958, p 12.
Commentary. Munro J, N&Q 11s 1.125.
Ch&Sidg, p 352.
Greene E E Carols, p 366; 2nd edn, p 359.
Greene Selection, p 197.
Carpenter N C, Music in English Mystery Plays, Music in English Renaissance Drama, ed J H Long, Lexington Ky 1968, p 27.
Cutts J C, RN 10.5.
Greene R L, RN 10.42.
Woolf, p 303.

[79] WHEN CRYST WAS BORN OF MARY FRE.

MS. BM Harley 5396, f 273b (mid 15 cent).
Brown-Robbins, Robbing-Cutler, no 3932.
Editions. Sandys W, Christmas Carols, London 1833, p 2.
Wright T, Carols, PPS 4.32.
Ch&Sidg, p 130.
Cook A S, A Literary ME Reader, Boston 1915, p 464.
Greene E E Carols, p 51; 2nd edn, p 42.
Modernizations. Cundall J, A Booke of Christmas Carols, London 1846, unpaged.
[Vizetelly H], Christmas with the Poets, London 1851, p 11.
Husk W H, Songs of the Nativity, London 1868, p 53.
Sylvester J pseud, A Garland of Christmas Carols, Ancient and Modern, London 1861, p 78.
Bramley H R and J Stainer, Christmas Carols New and Old, London [1871], p 42 (with modern music).
Bullen A H, Carols and Poems, London 1885, p 6.
A Garland of Christmas Verse, Hampstead and London [ca 1904], p 4.
Rickert Anc Eng Chr Carols, p 46.
Manning Foster A E, Christmas Carols of England, London 1915, p 8.
Hutchins C L, Carols Old and Carols New, Boston 1916, pp 88 (with supplied music), 493 (with supplied music).
Beeching, p 18 (omits burden).
OBC, p 217; music edn, p 378; rvsd edn, p 372 (with supplied music).
Loomis R S and R Willard, Medieval English Verse and Prose, N Y 1948, p 389.
Traditional version. "Christ is born of maiden fair."
Gillington A E, Old Christmas Carols of the Southern Counties, London 1910, p 15 (with music).
Hutchins, Carols Old and Carols New, p 293 (with music).
Commentary. Greene E E Carols, pp cvii, 367; 2nd edn, pp cxxxii, 360.
Dean-Smith M, A Guide to English Folk Song Collections, Liverpool 1954, pp 35, 58.
Greene Selection, p 22.

[80] NOW IN BETHELEME THAT HOLY PLACE (James Ryman).

MS. Camb Univ Ee.1.12, ff 38b–39a (ca 1492).
PRINT: Huntington Libr, Christmas carolles newly Inprynted (Richard Kele), p [25] (ca 1550; STC, no 5205).
Brown-Robbins, Robbins-Cutler, no 2332.
Editions. [Bliss P], Bibliographical Miscellanies, Oxford 1813, p 56 (PRINT).
Sandys W, Christmas Carols, London 1833, p 20 (PRINT).
Wright T, Carols, PPS 4.58 (PRINT).
Husk W H, Songs of the Nativity, London [1868], p 54 (PRINT).

Zupitza J, Arch 89.204 (MS).
Phillips W J, Carols: Their Origin, Music and Connection with Mystery Plays, London [1921], p 108.
Reed Christmas Carols, p 43 (facsimile of PRINT).
Greene E E Carols, pp 51 (MS), 52 (PRINT); 2nd edn, p 43 (MS, PRINT).
Greene Selection, p 72 (MS).
Modernizations. Bramley H R and J Stainer, Christmas Carols New and Old, London [1871], p 68 (PRINT with modern music).
Bullen A H, Carols and Poems, London 1885, p 10 (PRINT).
Rickert Anc Eng Chr Carols, p 104 (MS).
Beeching, p 18 (PRINT).
Commentary. Zupitza, Arch 94.202.
Greene R L, Review of Reed Christmas Carols, MLN 48.133 (identifies Kele's and Ryman's pieces as same carol).
Greene E E Carols, p cxxvi; 2nd edn, p clv.
Greene Selection, p 198.

[81] TO THE SHEPEHERDES KEPING THEIRE FOLDE (James Ryman).

MS. Camb Univ Ee.1.12, ff 34ª–35ᵇ (ca 1492).
Brown-Robbins, no 3775.
Editions. Zupitza J, Arch 89.200.
Greene E E Carols, p 52; 2nd edn, p 44.
Commentary. Zupitza, Arch 94.193.
Wehrle, p 146.
Greene E E Carols, p 367; 2nd edn, p 361.

[82] X FOR CRYSTES HYM SELFE WAS DYTH.

MS. St John's Camb 259 (S.54), f 1ª (mid 15 cent).
Brown-Robbins, Robbins-Cutler, no 4241.
Editions. James M R and G C Macaulay, MLR 8.69.
Greene R L, BQR 7.40.
Greene E E Carols, p 53; 2nd edn, p 44.
Commentary. Greene E E Carols, p 367; 2nd edn, p 361.
Brown B D, BQR 7.2 (possible source in MS Bodl Don c.13).

[83] MANKYENDE WAS SHENT AND AY FORLORE (James Ryman).

MS. Camb Univ Ee.1.12, ff 40ª–40ᵇ (ca 1492).
Brown-Robbins, no 2087.
Editions. Zupitza J, Arch 89.207.
Greene E E Carols, p 53; 2nd edn, p 44.
Commentary. Zupitza, Arch 94.205.

[84] MAN BE MERY I THE REDE.

MS. BM Addit 5665, ff 11ᵇ–12ª (late 15 cent; music).
Brown-Robbins, no 2044.
Editions. Wright T, Carols, PPS 4.55.
Fehr B, Arch 106.267.
Greene E E Carols, p 54; 2nd edn, p 45.
Modernizations. Ancient Carols, The Shakespeare Head Press Booklets, no 1, 2nd edn, Stratford-on-Avon 1906, p 20.
Rickert Anc Eng Chr Carols, p 209.
Beeching, p 157.
Adamson M R, A Treasury of ME Verse, London 1930, p 142.
Stevens Med Carols, p 69 (with music).
Sayre, p 53.
Commentary. Greene E E Carols, p 367; 2nd edn, p 362.

[85] SALUATOR MUNDI DOMINE.

MSS. 1, Bodl 6777 (Ashmole 189), f 107ª (15 cent); 2, Bodl 29734 (Eng poet e.l), f 20ª (mid 15 cent); 3, BM Sloane 2593, ff 9ᵇ–10ª (mid 15 cent).
Brown-Robbins, Robbins-Cutler, no 3070.
Editions. Fehr B, Arch 109.49 (MS 3).
Wright T, Carols, PPS 23.18 (MS 2); Carols, Publ Warton Club 4.28 (MS 3).
Greene E E Carols, p 54; 2nd edn, p 45 (MSS 1–3).
Brown RLxvC, p 117 (MS 1).
Modernization. Rickert Anc Eng Chr Carols, pp 178, 179 (MSS 1, 3).
Commentary. Wehrle, p 122.
Greene E E Carols, p 368; 2nd edn, p 362.
Brown RLxvC, p 318.
Oliver, p 20.

[86] IHESU AS þᵘ ART OUR SAUYOUR.

MS. BM Sloane 2593, f 5ᵇ (mid 15 cent).
Brown-Robbins, no 1662.
Editions. Wright T, Carols, PPS 4.6; Carols, Publ Warton Club 4.12.
Greene E E Carols, p 55; 2nd edn, p 46.
Modernization. Rickert Anc Eng Chr Carols, p 176.

[87] AUCTOR OF HELTHE CRISTE HAUE IN MYENDE (James Ryman).

MS. Camb Univ Ee.1.12, ff 37ª–37ᵇ (ca 1492).

Brown-Robbins, no 449.
Editions. Zupitza J, Arch 89.203.
Greene E E Carols, p 56; 2nd edn, p 46.
Commentary. Zupitza, Arch 94.199.
Greene E E Carols, p 368; 2nd edn, p 362.

[88] OFF MARY CRIST WAS BORE.

MS. BM Addit 5665, ff 17b–18a (late 15 cent; music).
Brown-Robbins, Robbins-Cutler, no 2636.
Editions. Wright T, Carols, PPS 4.55.
Fehr B, Arch 106.268.
Greene E E Carols, p 56; 2nd edn, p 47.
Modernizations. The Oxford History of Music, 2nd edn, Oxford 1932, 2.340 (with music).
Stevens Med Carols, p 75 (with music).
Commentary. Stevens Med Carols, p 121.

[89] IHESU RESTYD IN A MAY.

MS. St John's Camb 259 (S.54), f 2a (mid 15 cent).
Brown-Robbins, no 1744.
Editions. James M R and G C Macaulay, MLR 8.69.
Greene E E Carols, p 57; 2nd edn, p 47.
Commentary. Greene E E Carols, p 368; 2nd edn, p 363.

[90] IHESU OF A MAYDE þOU WOLDIST BE BORNE.

MS. 1a, BM Addit 5665, ff 43b–44a (late 15 cent; music by Richard Smert); 1b, ibid, ff 29b–30a (music by Richard Smert).
Brown-Robbins, no 1738.
Editions. Wright T, Carols, PPS 4.54 (MS 1a).
Fehr B, Arch 106.271 (MS 1b), 275 (MS 1a).
Greene E E Carols, p 57; 2nd edn, p 47 (MSS 1a, 1b)
Modernizations. Rickert Anc Eng Chr Carols, p 181.
Julian J, A Dictionary of Hymnology, 2nd edn, London 1925, p 209 (omits stanza 1).
Stevens Med Carols, pp 101, 86 (with music).
Stevens J, Tidings True, London [1976], p 19 (with music).
Commentary. Wehrle, p 94.
Greene E E Carols, p 368; 2nd edn, p 363.

[91] THOU ART SOLACE IN ALLE OURE WOO (James Ryman).

MS. Camb Univ Ee.1.12, f 104b (ca 1492).
Brown-Robbins, no 3667.

Editions. Zupitza J, Arch 89.325.
Greene E E Carols, p 58; 2nd edn, p 48.
Commentary. Zupitza, Arch 97.141.

[92] SWET IHESUS IS CUM TO VS.

MS. Bodl 29734 (Eng poet e.1), ff 45b–47b (mid 15 cent).
Brown-Robbins, Robbins-Cutler, no 3235.
Editions. Wright T, Carols, PPS 23.69.
Greene E E Carols, p 58; 2nd edn, p 48.
Greene Selection, p 74.
Davies, p 241.
Commentary. Greene E E Carols, p 369; 2nd edn, p 363.
Greene Selection, p 198.
Davies, p 356.

[93] A MERVELUS þYNG I HAFE MUSYD IN MY MYNDE.

MS. BM Lansdowne 379, f 38a (ca 1500).
Brown-Robbins, no 78.
Editions. Greene E E Carols, p 60; 2nd edn, p 50.
Brown RLxvC, p 109.
Modernization. Rickert Anc Eng Chr Carols, p 159.
Commentary. Wehrle, p 92.
Greene E E Carols, p 369; 2nd edn, p 364.

[94] O BLESSE GOD IN TRINITE.

MS. BM Addit 5665, ff 26b–27a (late 15 cent; music).
Brown-Robbins, no 2388.
Editions. Wright T, Carols, PPS 4.56.
Fehr B, Arch 106.270.
Greene E E Carols, p 62; 2nd edn, p 52.
Miller C K, The Early English Carol, RN 3.62 (in part; with music).
Modernizations. Rickert Anc Eng Chr Carols, p 179.
Stevens Med Carols, p 83 (with music).
Commentary. Stevens Med Carols, p 121.

[95] SAYNT STEUEN þE FIRST MARTERE (John Audelay).

MS. Bodl 21876 (Douce 302), f 28b (early 15 cent).
Brown-Robbins, no 3057.
Editions. Chambers E K and F Sidgwick, MLR 5.483.
Whiting E K, EETS 184.187.
Greene E E Carols, p 62; 2nd edn, p 52.
Commentary. Whiting, EETS 184.250.
Greene E E Carols, p 370; 2nd edn, p 364.

[96] OF THIS MARTIR MAKE WE MENDE.

MS. Trinity Camb 1230 (0.3.58), no 11 (mid 15 cent).
Brown-Robbins, no 2665.
Editions. Fuller Maitland J A and W S Rockstro, English Carols of the Fifteenth Century, London [1891], p. 23 (with music).
Greene E E Carols, p 63; 2nd edn, p 52.
Modernizations. Rickert Anc Eng Chr Carols, p 122.
Terry Med Carol Book, p 54 (with music).
Stevens Med Carols, p 9 (with music).
Commentary. Wehrle, p 104.
Greene E E Carols, p 370; 2nd edn, p 364.

[97] IN THIS VALE OF WRECCHEDNESSE.

MS. BM Addit 5665, ff 22^b–23^a (late 15 cent; music).
Brown-Robbins, no 1578.
Editions. Fehr B, Arch 106.269.
Greene E E Carols, p 63; 2nd edn, p 52.
Modernizations. Rickert Anc Eng Chr Carols, p 122.
Stevens Med Carols, p 80 (with music).
Commentary. Wehrle, p 82.
Greene E E Carols, p 370; 2nd edn, p 365.

[98] WHAN SEYNT STEVYN WAS AT IERUȝALEM.

MS. Balliol 354, f 288^a (early 16 cent).
Brown-Robbins, no 4012.
Editions. Flügel NL, p 113.
Flügel E, Angl 26.256.
Dyboski R, EETSES 101.32.
Greene E E Carols, p 63; 2nd edn, p 53.
Modernization. Rickert Anc Eng Chr Carols, p 124.
Commentary. Wehrle, p 96.
Greene E E Carols, p 370; 2nd edn, p 365.

[99] I SCHAL YOW TELL ÞIS ILK NYGHT.

MS. BM Egerton 3307, f 54^b (mid 15 cent; music).
PRINT: 1a, Huntington Libr, Christmas carolles newely Inprynted (Richard Kele), pp [33–35] (ca 1550; STC, no 5205); 1b, Ibid, p [42].
Robbins-Cutler, nos 1363.5, 2652.5.
Editions. Reed Christmas Carols, pp 51, 60 (facsimile of PRINT 1a, 1b).
Greene E E Carols, p 64 (PRINT); 2nd edn, pp 53 (PRINT), 54 (MS).
Greene Selection, p 78 (MS).
Modernization. Stevens Med Carols, p 39 (with music).
Commentary. Greene E E Carols, p 370 (on PRINT); 2nd edn, p 365.
Greene Selection, p 199.

[100] SYNT ION IS CRISTIS DERLYNG DERE (John Audelay).

MS. Bodl 21876 (Douce 302), f 28^b (early 15 cent).
Brown-Robbins, no 2929.
Editions. Chambers E K and F Sidgwick, MLR 5.484.
Whiting E K, EETS 184.188.
Greene E E Carols, p 65; 2nd edn, p 55.
Commentary. Whiting, EETS 184.250.
Greene E E Carols, p 370; 2nd edn, p 365.

[101] TO THE NOW CRISTIS DERE DERLYNG.

MSS. 1, Bodl 29734 (Eng poet e.1), f 40^a (mid 15 cent); 2, Balliol 354, f 222^a (early 16 cent); 3, Trinity Camb 1230 (0.3.58), no 12 (mid 15 cent; music); 4, BM Harley 4294, f 81^b (early 16 cent); 5a, BM Addit 5665, ff 37^b–38^a (late 15 cent; music); 5b, Ibid, ff 48^b–49^a (music).
Brown-Robbins, Robbins-Cutler, no 3776.
Editions. Fuller Maitland J A and W S Rockstro, English Carols of the 15th Cent, London [1891], p 25 (MS 3 with music).
Wright T, Carols, PPS 23.60 (MS 1).
Fehr B, Arch 106.273 (MS 5a with collation of MS 5b).
Flügel E, Angl 26.237 (MS 2).
Dyboski R, EETSES 101.11, 172 (MSS 2, 5a with collation of MSS 1, 3).
Greene E E Carols, p 66 (MSS 3, 4 with collation of MSS 1, 2, 5a, 5b); 2nd edn, p 55.
Greene Selection, p 79 (MS 1).
Davies, p 157 (MS 3).
Modernizations. Weston, p 42 (MS 2).
Rickert Anc Eng Chr Carols, p 126 (MS 2).
Segar M G, A Mediaeval Anthology, London 1915, p 103 (MS 2).
Terry Med Carol Book, p 55 (MS 3 with music).
Comper Spir Songs, p 235 (MS 2).
Stevens Med Carols, pp 10 (MS 3 with music), 95 (MS 5a with music), 105 (MS 5b with music).
Commentary. Wehrle, p 95.
Greene E E Carols, pp lxii, cv, 370; 2nd edn, pp

lxxxiii, cxxx, 366.
Stevens Med Carols, p 117.
Greene Selection, p 199.

[102] O GLORIUS IOHAN
EVANGELYSTE.

MS. Bodl 29734 (Eng poet e.1), f 39ᵇ (mid 15 cent).
Brown-Robbins, Robbins-Cutler, no 2443.
Editions. Wright T, Carols, PPS 23.59.
Greene E E Carols, p 67; 2nd edn, p 56.
Commentary. Wehrle, p 81.
Greene E E Carols, p 371; 2nd edn, p 366.

[103] THOW DERESTE DISCIPLE OF IHU CRISTE.

MS. Balliol 354, ff 228ᵇ–229ᵃ (early 16 cent).
Brown-Robbins, no 3669.
Editions. Flügel E, Angl 26.258.
Dyboski R, EETSES 101.35.
Greene E E Carols, p 68; 2nd edn, p 57.
Modernizations. Rickert Anc Eng Chr Carols, p 126.
Comper Spir Songs, p 236.
Commentary. Wehrle, p 80.
Greene E E Carols, p 371; 2nd edn, p 366.

[104] O BLESSYD JOHAN THE EUANGELYST.

MSS. No MS extant. PRINT: Huntington Libr, Christmas carolles newely Inprynted (Richard Kele), p [35] (ca 1550; STC, no 5205).
Robbins-Cutler, no 2392.5.
Editions. Reed Christmas Carols, p 53 (facsimile).
Greene E E Carols, p 68; 2nd edn, p 57.

[105] THE NAME OF IOHAN WEL PRAYS I MAY.

MSS. No MS extant. PRINT: Huntington Libr, Christmas carolles newely Inprynted (Richard Kele), p [5] (ca 1550; STC, no 5205).
Robbins-Cutler, no 3438.8.
Editions. Reed Christmas Carols, p 23 (facsimile).
Greene E E Carols, p 69; 2nd edn, p 57.
Commentary. Greene E E Carols, p 371; 2nd edn, p 366.

[106] CRIST CRID IN CRADIL MODER BA BA (John Audelay).

MS. Bodl 21876 (Douce 302), ff 28ᵇ–29ᵃ (early 15 cent).
Brown-Robbins, no 601.
Editions. Chambers E K and F Sidgwick, MLR 5.485.
Whiting E K, EETS 184.189.
Greene E E Carols, p 69; 2nd edn, p 58.
Greene Selection, p 79.
Commentary. Whiting, EETS 184.250.
Greene E E Carols, p 372; 2nd edn, p 367.
Greene Selection, p 200.

[107] DIC ERODES IMPIE.

MS. BM Addit 5665, ff 6ᵇ–7ᵃ (late 15 cent; music).
Brown-Robbins, no 680.
Editions. Fehr B, Arch 106.265.
Greene E E Carols, p 70; 2nd edn, p 58.
Modernization. Stevens Med Carols, p 65 (with music).
Commentary. Wehrle, p 112.
Greene E E Carols, p 372; 2nd edn, p 368.

[108] WHEN GOD WAS BORNE OF MARY FRE.

MS. BM Addit 5665, ff 23ᵇ–24ᵃ (late 15 cent; music).
Brown-Robbins, Robbins-Cutler, no 3950.
Editions. Fehr B, Arch 106.269.
Greene E E Carols, p 70; 2nd edn, p 59.
Modernizations. Rickert Anc Eng Chr Carols, p 128.
Stevens Med Carols, p 81 (with music).
Commentary. Wehrle, p 87.

[109] HERODE þᵗ WAS BOTHE WYLDE & WODE.

MS. BM Addit 5665, ff 24ᵇ–25ᵃ (late 15 cent; music).
Brown-Robbins, Robbins-Cutler, no 1212.
Editions. Sandys W, Christmas Carols, London 1833, p 18.
Fehr B, Arch 106.269.
Greene E E Carols, p 71; 2nd edn, p 59.
Modernizations. Rickert Anc Eng Chr Carols, p 128.
Stevens Med Carols, p 82 (with music).
Commentary. Greene E E Carols, p 373; 2nd edn, p 368.

[110] FOR ON A TEWSDAY THOMAS WAS BORNE.

MS. Bodl 21876 (Douce 302), f 29ᵃ (early 15 cent).
Brown-Robbins, no 838.
Editions. Chambers E K and F Sidgwick, MLR 5.486.

Whiting E K, EETS 184.190.
Greene E E Carols, p 71; 2nd edn, p 60.
Commentary. Whitihg, EETS 184.251.
Greene E E Carols, p 373; 2nd edn, p 368.

[111] LESTENYTȝ LORDYNGIS BOþE GRETE AND SMALE.

MSS. 1, Balliol 354, ff 227ᵇ–228ᵃ (early 16 cent); 2, Caius Camb 383, p 68 (mid 15 cent); 3, BM Sloane 2593, ff 23ᵇ–24ᵃ (mid 15 cent); 4, Public Record Office Chancery Miscellany, bundle 34, file 1, no 12, f 1ᵃ (early 15 cent).
Brown-Robbins, no 1892.
Editions. Wright T, Songs and Carols, London 1836, no 11 (MS 3); Carols, Warton Club 4.66 (MS 3).
Flügel NL, p 113 (MS 1).
Flügel E, Angl 26.255 (MS 1).
Dyboski R, EETSES 101.31, 177 (MS 1 with collation of MS 3).
Greene E E Carols, p 72 (MS 3 with collation of MSS 1, 2, 4); 2nd edn, p 60.
Brunner K, Angl 61.151 (MS 2).
Brown RLxvC, p 189 (MS 2).
Greene Selection, p 82 (MS 3).
Modernizations. Rickert Anc Eng Chr Carols, p 129 (MS 1).
Segar M G, Some Minor Poems of the Middle Ages, London 1917, p 19 (MS 1).
Tydeman W, English Poetry 1400–1580, London 1970, p 51.
Luria & Hoffman, p 152 (MS 2).
Commentary. Wright, Warton Club 4.118.
Wehrle, p 83.
Greene E E Carols, pp lxii, 373; 2nd edn, pp lxxxiii, 369.
Brown RLxvC, p 331.
Greene Selection, p 202.

[112] AS STORYS WRYGHT AND SPECYFY.

MS. Bodl 29734 (Eng poet e.1), ff 35ᵃ–35ᵇ (mid 15 cent).
Brown-Robbins, no 405.
Editions. Wright T, Carols, PPS 23.51.
Greene E E Carols, p 73; 2nd edn, p 61.
Commentary. Greene E E Carols, p 374; 2nd edn, p 370.

[113] AL HOLY CHYRCH WAS BOT A THRALL.

MS. BM Egerton 3307, ff 62ᵇ–63ᵃ (mid 15 cent; music).

Robbins-Cutler, no 187.5.
Editions. Greene R L, Journ of the American Musicological Soc 7.7.
Greene Selection, p 80.
Greene E E Carols, 2nd edn, p 62.
Modernization. Stevens Med Carols, p 48 (with music).
Commentary. Greene Selection, p 200.
Greene E E Carols, 2nd edn, p 370.

[114] OUTE OF THE CHAFFE WAS PURED THIS CORNE.

MS. BM Addit 5665, ff 41ᵇ–42ᵃ (late 15 cent; music).
Brown-Robbins, no 2731.
Editions. Fehr B, Arch 106.275.
Greene E E Carols, p 74; 2nd edn, p 62.
Modernization. Stevens Med Carols, p 98 (with music).
Commentary. Greene E E Carols, p 374; 2nd edn, p 371.

[115] A BABE IS BORN OF HEY NATURE (John Audelay?).

MSS. 1, Bodl 3340 (Arch Selden B.26), ff 15ᵇ–16ᵃ (mid 15 cent; music); 2, Bodl 21876 (Douce 302), f 29ᵃ (early 15 cent); 3, Trinity Camb 1230 (0.3.58), no 10 (mid 15 cent; music).
Brown-Robbins, no 21.
Editions. Fuller Maitland J A and W S Rockstro, English Carols of the 15th Cent, London [1891], p 21 (MS 3 with music).
Early Bodleian Music, 2.125 (MS 1 with music).
Chambers E K and F Sidgwick, MLR 5.487 (MS 2).
Padelford F M, Angl 36.99 (MSS 1, 3).
Whiting E K, EETS 184.191 (MS 2).
Greene E E Carols, p 74 (MS 2 with collation of MSS 1 and 3); 2nd edn, p 62.
Greene Selection, p 83 (MS 2).
Sisam, p 386.
Modernizations. Rickert Anc Eng Chr Carols, p 167 (MS 3).
Hutchins C L, Carols Old and Carols New, Boston 1916, p 560 (MS 3 with music).
Terry Med Carol Book, pp 8 (MS 1 with music), 52 (MS 3 with music).
Comper Spir Songs, p 17 (MS 2).
OBC, p 49 (MS 1); music edn, p 84; rvsd edn, p 78 (MS 1 with music).
Stevens Med Carols, pp 8 (MS 3 with music), 20 (MS 1 with music).
Robbins Christmas Carols, p 78 (MS 2 with music).

Sayre E, A Christmas Book, N Y 1966, p 43 (MS 2).
Commentary. Chambers and Sidgwick, MLR 5.477.
Whiting, EETS 184.251.
Greene E E Carols, p 375; 2nd edn, p 372.
Chambers OHEL, p 103.
Stevens Med Carols, p 118.
Copley J, N&Q 204.387.
Greene Selection, p 204.
Utley F L, Manual, 3.687 (VII[10]).

[116] GABRIELL BRYȜTHER THEN THE SONE.

MS. BM Addit 5665, ff 12ᵇ–13ᵃ (late 15 cent; music).
Brown-Robbins, no 887.
Editions. Fehr B, Arch 106.267.
Greene E E Carols, p 76; 2nd edn, p 63.
Modernizations. Rickert Anc Eng Chr Carols, p 31.
Stevens Med Carols, p 70 (with music).
Commentary. Greene E E Carols, p 375; 2nd edn, p 372.

[117] MAKE WE MERY IN HALL AND BOURE.

MSS. No MS extant. PRINT: Huntington Libr, Christmas carolles newely Inprynted (Richard Kele), p [23] (ca 1550; STC, no 5205).
Robbins-Cutler, no 2039.5.
Editions. [Bliss P,] Bibliographical Miscellanies, Oxford 1813, p 54.
Reed Christmas Carols, p 41 (facsimile).
Greene E E Carols, p 76; 2nd edn, p 64.
Commentary. Greene E E Carols, p 375; 2nd edn, p 372.

[118] LYFT VP YOUR HARTIS & BE GLAD.

MS. Balliol 354, f 223ᵇ (early 16 cent).
Brown-Robbins, no 1873.
Editions. Flügel Fest R Hildebrand, p 69.
Flügel NL, p 123.
Flügel E, Angl 26.242.
Frost L, Come Christmas, N Y 1935, p 261.
Dyboski R, EETSES 101.15.
Greene E E Carols, p 77; 2nd edn, p 64.
Greene Selection, p 84.
Modernizations. Rickert Anc Eng Chr Carols, p 219.
Weston, p 41.
Davies, p 288.
Commentary. Dyboski, EETSES 101.173.
Greene E E Carols, p 375; 2nd edn, p 372.

Greene Selection, p 205.
Davies, p 367.

[119] ANODER YERE HIT MAY BETYDE.

MS. BM Addit 40166 (C3), f 12ᵇ (15 cent).
Brown-Robbins, no 320.
Editions. Greene E E Carols, p 77; 2nd edn, p 64.
Robbins-HP, p 62.
Greene Selection, p 85.
Modernization. Stevick, p 165.
Commentary. Greene E E Carols, p 376; 2nd edn, p 373.
Robbins-HP, p 278.
Greene Selection, p 205.
Oliver, p 34.

[120] ÞER IS A BABE BORN OF A MAY (John Audelay?).

MSS. 1, Bodl 21876 (Douce 302), f 31ᵃ (early 15 cent); 2, Balliol 354, f 221ᵇ (early 16 cent); 3, BM Sloane 2593, ff 27ᵇ–28ᵃ (mid 15 cent).
Brown-Robbins, nos 20, 3526.
Editions. Sandys W, Christmastide, London 1852, p 226 (MS 3).
Wright T, Carols, PPS 4.13 (MS 3); Carols, Warton Club 4.79 (MS 3).
Flügel Fest R Hildebrand, p 65 (MS 2).
Flügel E, Angl 26.239 (MS 2).
Dyboski R, EETSES 101.10, 171 (MSS 2, 3).
Chambers E K and F Sidgwick, MLR 6.70 (MS 1).
Whiting E K, EETS 184.198 (MS 1).
Greene E E Carols, p 77; 2nd edn, p 67 (MSS 1–3).
Kaiser R, Alt- und mittelenglische Anthologie, Berlin 1955, p 42 (MS 1); Medieval English (3rd edn of Anthologie), Berlin West 1958, p 295 (MS 1 in part).
Modernizations. Husk W H, Songs of the Nativity, London 1868, p 52 (MS 3).
Bramley H R and J Stainer, Christmas Carols, New and Old, London 1871, p 104 (MS 3 with modern music).
Weston, p 27 (MS 2).
Rickert Anc Eng Chr Carols, pp 49 (MS 3), 52 (MS 2).
Hutchins C L, Carols Old and Carols New, Boston 1916, p 447 (MS 3 with supplied music; omits burden).
OBC, p 145; music edn, p 236; rvsd edn, p 246 (MS 3 with supplied music).
Frost L, Come Christmas, N Y 1935, p 348 (MS 3).
Young P M, Carols for the Twelve Days of Christmas, London 1953, p 64 (MS 3 with supplied music; altered).

Simon H W, Christmas Songs and Carols, Boston 1955, p 39 (MS 3).
Commentary. Dyboski, EETSES 101.171.
Whiting, EETS 184.252.
Wehrle, p 73.
Greene E E Carols, pp lxxii, 376; 2nd edn, pp xciii, 376.

[121] THER YS A BLOSSUM SPRONG OF A THORN.

MSS. 1, Balliol 354, f 222^b (early 16 cent); 2, BM Sloane 2593, ff 12^a–13^a (mid 15 cent).
Brown-Robbins, nos 2730, 3527.
Editions. Wright T, Carols, Warton Club 4.36 (MS 2).
Flügel Fest R Hildebrand, p 67 (MS 1).
Fehr B, Arch 109.52 (MS 2).
Flügel E, Angl 26.239 (MS 1).
Dyboski R, EETSES 101.12 (MS 1).
Greene E E Carols, p 79; 2nd edn, p 68 (MSS 1, 2).
Brown RLxvC, p 126 (MS 2).
Greene Selection, p 86 (MS 1).
Modernizations. Weston, p 21 (MSS 1, 2).
Rickert Anc Eng Chr Carols, p 117 (MSS 1, 2).
Commentary. Greene E E Carols, pp lxii, xcvii, cxxxiv, 376; 2nd edn, pp lxxxiv, cxxi, clxi, 376.
Brown RLxvC, p 321.
Greene Selection, p 206.

[122] IHESU WAS BORN IN BEDLEM IUDE.

MSS. 1, BM Sloane 2593, ff 14^a–14^b (mid 15 cent); 2, Nat Libr Wales, Porkington 10, ff 198^b–199^b (mid 15 cent).
Brown-Robbins, no 1785.
Editions. Wright T, Carols, Warton Club 4.40 (MS 1).
Fehr B, Arch 109.54 (MS 1).
Greene E E Carols, p 80; 2nd edn, p 69 (MSS 1, 2).
Brown RLxvC, p 124 (MS 2).
Commentary. Greene E E Carols, p 376; 2nd edn, p 377.
Brown RLxvC, p 320.

[123] TRUTH IT IS FUL SEKYRLY.

MS. Canterbury Cathedral, Addit 68, ff 100^a–101^b (late 15 cent).
Robbins-Cutler, no 3810.3.
Editions. Woodruff C E, A XVth Cent Guidebook to the Principal Churches of Rome Compiled c 1470 by William Brewyn, London 1933, p 81.

Greene E E Carols, 2nd edn, p 71.
Commentary. Greene E E Carols, 2nd edn, p 377.

[124] NOW IS þE TWELþE DAY I-COME.

MSS. 1, Bodl 29734 (Eng poet e.1), ff 31^b–32^b (mid 15 cent); 2, St John's Camb 259 (S.54), ff 7^b–9^a (mid 15 cent); 3, BM Sloane 2593, ff 17^a–18^b (mid 15 cent); 4, BM Harley 541, ff 214^a–214^b (15 cent).
Brown-Robbins, nos 2333, 2339.
Editions. Wright T, Carols, PPS 4.23 (MS 4); 23.46 (MS 1); Carols, Warton Club 4.49 (MS 3).
Edmond J P, N&Q 6s 6.506 (text from Lumley's Bibliographical Advertiser, 1841; MS 4).
Sandys W, Christmastide, London 1852, p 220.
Fehr B, Arch 107.55 (MS 4).
James M R and G C Macaulay, MLR 8.77 (MS 2).
Greene E E Carols, p 82 (MSS 2–4 with collation of MS 1); 2nd edn, p 72.
Greene Selection, p 87 (MS 3).
Modernizations. [Vizetelly H], Christmas with the Poets, London 1851, p 8 (MSS 1, 4; combined text).
Sylvester J pseud, A Garland of Christmas Carols, Ancient and Modern, London 1861, p 9 (MSS 1, 4; combined text).
Husk W H, Songs of the Nativity, London 1868, p 79 (MS 4).
Bullen A H, Carols and Poems, London 1885, p 250 (MS 4).
Hutchins C L, Carols Old and Carols New, Boston 1916, p 544 (MS 1 with supplied music, altered).
Rickert Anc Eng Chr Carols, pp 110 (MS 4), 112 (MS 3).
Beeching, p 5 (MS 4).
OBC, p 211; music edn, p 363; rvsd edn, p 362 (MS 4 with supplied music).
Sayre E, A Christmas Book, N Y 1966, p 109 (MS 2).
Commentary. Greene E E Carols, pp cxxxiv, 377; 2nd edn, pp clxi, 378.
Greene Selection, p 207.

[125] HAYL, MOST MYGHTY IN THI WERKYNG.

MS. BM Egerton 3307, f 55^a (mid 15 cent; music).
Robbins-Cutler, no 1070.5.
Editions. Greene Selection, p 90.
Greene E E Carols, 2nd edn, p 76.
Modernization. Stevens Med Carols, p 40 (with music).
Commentary. Greene Selection, p 208.
Greene E E Carols, 2nd edn, p 378.

[126] HYS SIGNE YS A STER BRYTH.

MS. BM Egerton 3307, ff 58ᵇ–59ᵃ (mid 15 cent; music).
Robbins-Cutler, no 1220.5.
Editions. Greene Selection, p 90.
Greene E E Carols, 2nd edn, p 76.
Modernization. Stevens Med Carols, p 43 (with music).
Commentary. Greene Selection, p 208.
Greene E E Carols, 2nd edn, p 378.

[127] OWT OF þE EST A STERRE SHON BRIGHT.

MS. Balliol 354, f 165ᵇ (early 16 cent).
Brown-Robbins, no 2732.
Editions. Flügel NL, p 122.
Flügel E, Angl 26.176.
Dyboski R, EETSES 101.1.
Frost L, Come Christmas, N Y 1935, p 258.
Greene E E Carols, p 86; 2nd edn, p 76.
Modernizations. Rickert Anc Eng Chr Carols, p 116.
Weston, p 19.
Sayre E, A Christmas Book, N Y 1966, p 101.
Commentary. Greene E E Carols, p 377; 2nd edn, p 378.

[128] THRE KINGIS ON THE XIJᵗʰ DAYE (James Ryman).

MS. Camb Univ Ee.1.12, ff 51ᵇ–52ᵇ (ca 1492).
Brown-Robbins, no 3710.
Editions. Zupitza J, Arch 89.224; Alt- und mittelenglisches Uebungsbuch, 8th edn, Vienna and Leipzig 1907, p 191.
Greene E E Carols, p 87; 2nd edn, p 77.
Commentary. Zupitza, Arch 94.419.
Wehrle, p 154.
Greene E E Carols, p 377; 2nd edn, p 379.

[129] ON XIJᵗʰᵉ DAY CAME KINGIS THRE.

MS. Camb Univ Ee.1.12, ff 52ᵇ–53ᵃ (ca 1492).
Brown-Robbins, no 2690.
Editions. Zupitza J, Arch 89.225.
Greene E E Carols, p 88; 2nd edn, p 78.
Commentary. Zupitza, Arch 94.420.

[130] ON XIJᵗʰᵉ DAY THIS STERRE SO CLERE (James Ryman).

MS. Camb Univ Ee.1.12, ff 53ᵃ–54ᵃ (ca 1492).
Brown-Robbins, no 2691.
Editions. Zupitza J, Arch 89.226.
Greene E E Carols, p 88; 2nd edn, p 78.
Commentary. Zupitza, Arch 95.259.
Greene E E Carols, p 377; 2nd edn, p 379.

[131] NOWE THIS TYME REX PACIFICUS (James Ryman).

MS. Camb Univ Ee.1.12, f 58ᵃ (ca 1492).
Brown-Robbins, no 2367.
Editions. Zupitza J, Arch 89.236.
Greene E E Carols, p 90; 2nd edn, p 79.
Commentary. Zupitza, Arch 95.272.
Greene E E Carols, p 377; 2nd edn, p 379.

[132] WHEN IHŪS CRISTE BAPTY3ED WAS.

MSS. 1, Balliol 354, ff 178ᵃ–178ᵇ (early 16 cent); 2, BM Addit 5665, ff 40ᵇ–41ᵃ (late 15 cent; music by John Trouluffe and Richard Smert).
Brown-Robbins, Robbins-Cutler, no 3975.
Editions. Flügel Fest R Hildebrand, p 55 (MS 1).
Fehr B, Arch 106.274 (MS 2).
Flügel E, Angl 26.196 (MS 1).
Dyboski R, EETSES 101.4, 169 (MS 1 with collation of MS 2).
Greene E E Carols, p 90 (MS 2 with collation of MS 1); 2nd edn, p 79.
Modernization. Stevens Med Carols, p 97 (MS 2; with music).
Commentary. Greene E E Carols, p 378; 2nd edn, p 379.

[133] THE BORIS HED IN HONDES I BRYNGE.

MS. Balliol 354, f 228ᵃ (early 16 cent). PRINT: Bodleian Libr, Rawlinson 4to.598(10) (Wynkyn de Worde; 1521).
Brown-Robbins, no 3313.
Editions. Ritson AS 1790, p 125; 1829, 2.16; 1877, p 159. (PRINT).
Ames J, Typographical Antiquities, ed T F Dibdin, London 1810–19, 2.251 (PRINT).
Cundall J, A Booke of Christmas Carols, London 1846, p [9] (PRINT).
Sandys W, Christmastide, London 1852, p 231 (PRINT).
Wright T, Carols, PPS 4.26 (PRINT).
Sylvester J pseud, A Garland of Christmas Carols, Ancient and Modern, London 1861, p 155 (PRINT).
Husk W H, Songs of the Nativity, London 1868, p 119 (PRINT).
Bullen A H, Carols and Poems, London 1885, pp 170, 231 (PRINT).

Flügel E, Angl 12.587 (PRINT); 26.257 (MS).
Flügel Fest R Hildebrand, p 77 (MS).
Flügel NL, p 123 (MS, PRINT).
Furnivall F J, EETS 32.398 (MS).
Pollard 15CPV, p 92 (MS).
Ch&Sidg, p 235 (MS).
Dyboski R, EETSES 101.33 (MS).
Rickert Anc Eng Chr Carols, p 260 (PRINT).
Beeching, p 163 (PRINT).
Greene E E Carols, pp cvi (PRINT), 91 (MS, PRINT); 2nd edn, pp cxxx (PRINT), 80 (MS, PRINT).
Young P M, Carols for the Twelve Days of Christmas, London 1953, p 37 (PRINT).
Robbins SL, p 48 (PRINT).
Greene Selection, p 91 (MS).
Davies, p 278.
Sisam, p 532.
Luria & Hoffman, p 139 (PRINT).
Traditional Versions from Queen's College, Oxford. Greene E E Carols, p 92; 2nd edn, p 80.
OBC, p 24; music edn, p 37; rvsd edn, p 39.
Modernizations. [Vizetelly H], Christmas with the Poets, London 1851, p 20.
Segar M G, Some Minor Poems of the Middle Ages, London 1917, p 14.
Loomis R S and R Willard, Medieval English Verse and Prose, N Y 1948, p 390.
Commentary. Wehrle, p 84.
Greene E E Carols, pp 378, 379; 2nd edn, pp 379, 380.
Robbins SL, p 243.
Routley E, The English Carol, London 1958, p 39.
Greene Selection, p 208.
Oliver, p 19.

[134] THE BORYS HEDE THAT WE BRYNG HERE.

MS. BM Addit 5665, ff 7ᵇ–8ᵃ (late 15 cent; music).
Brown-Robbins, no 3315.
Editions. Stafford Smith J, Musica Antiqua, [London 1812], p 22 (with music).
Ritson AS 1790, p 127; 1829, 2.16; 1877, p 160.
Sandys W, Christmas Carols, London 1833, p 16.
Hampson R T, Medii Aevi Kalendarium, London 1841, 1.95.
Wright T, Carols, PPS 4.50.
Sandys, Christmastide, London 1852, p 223.
Flügel NL, p 124.
Greene E E Carols, p 92; 2nd edn, p 81.
Greene Selection, p 91.
Modernizations. [Vizetelly H], Christmas with the Poets, London 1851, p 17.
Sylvester J pseud, A Garland of Christmas Carols Ancient and Modern, London 1861, p 157.

Husk W H, Songs of the Nativity, London 1868, p 124.
Bullen A H, Carols and Poems, London 1886, p 267.
Rickert Anc Eng Chr Carols, p 258.
Beeching, p 164.
Stevens Med Carols, p 66 (with music).
Robbins Christmas Carols, p 13 (with music).
Commentary. Greene E E Carols, pp 378, 379; 2nd edn, pp 379, 381.
Greene Selection, p 209.

[135] AT THE BEGYNNYNG OF THE METE.

MS. Bodl 29734 (Eng poet e.1), f 29ᵇ (mid 15 cent).
Brown-Robbins, no 436.
Editions. Wright T, Carols, PPS 23.42.
Greene E E Carols, p 92; 2nd edn, p 81.
Robbins SL, p 48.
Modernizations. Husk W H, Songs of the Nativity, London 1868, p 118.
Rickert Anc Eng Chr Carols, p 257.
Luria & Hoffman, p 139.
Commentary. Greene E E Carols, pp 378, 379; 2nd edn, pp 379, 381.
Robbins SL, p 243.

[136] THE BORIS HEDE IN HOND I BRYNG.

MS. Nat Libr Wales, Porkington 10, ff 202ᵃ–202ᵇ (mid 15 cent).
Brown-Robbins, no 3314.
Editions. Sandys W, Christmastide, London 1852, p 230.
Wright T, Carols, PPS 4.3.
Rel Ant, 2.30.
Furnivall F J, EETS 32.397.
Greene E E Carols, p 93; 2nd edn, p 81.
Robbins SL, p 49.
Silverstein, p 145.
Modernizations. [Vizetelly H], Christmas with the Poets, London 1851, p 19.
Sylvester J pseud, A Garland of Christmas Carols Ancient and Modern, London 1861, p 152.
Husk W H, Songs of the Nativity, London 1868, p 116.
Rickert Anc Eng Chr Carols, p 257.
Beeching, p 162.
Luria & Hoffman, p 140.
Commentary. Greene E E Carols, pp 378, 379; 2nd edn, pp 379, 381.
Robbins SL, p 243.

[137] HOLY BERITH BERIS BERIS REDE YNOWGH.

MSS. 1, Balliol 354, ff 251ᵃ–251ᵇ (early 16 cent); 2, BM Harley 5396, f 275ᵇ (mid 15 cent).
Brown-Robbins, no 1226.
Editions. Ritson AS 1790, p 74; 1829, 1.132; 1877, p 114 (MS 2).
Sandys W, Christmas Carols, London 1833, p 1 (MS 2).
Flügel Fest R Hildebrand, p 83 (MS 1).
Arber E, The Dunbar Anthology, London 1901, p 145 (MS 2).
Flügel E, Angl 26.279 (MS 1).
Dyboski R, EETSES 101.116, 189 (MSS 1, 2).
Russell C, N&Q 12s 6.22 (MS 2).
Ch&Sidg, p 239 (MS 1).
Greene E E Carols, p 93; 2nd edn, p 82 (MSS 1, 2).
Greene Selection, p 92 (MSS 1, 2).
Davies, pp 175 (MS 2), 280 (MS 1).
Sisam, p 451 (MS 2).
Modernizations. [Vizetelly H], Christmas with the Poets, London 1851, p 29 (MS 2).
Sylvester J pseud, A Garland of Christmas Carols Ancient and Modern, London 1861, p 144 (MS 2).
Bullen A H, Carols and Poems, London 1886, p 68 (MS 2).
Duncan E, The Story of the Carol, London 1911, p 192 (MS 2).
Rickert Anc Eng Chr Carols, pp 265, 264 (MSS 1, 2).
Beeching, p 161 (MS 2).
Routley E, The English Carol, London 1958, p 72 (MS 1).
Commentary. Flügel Fest R Hildebrand, p 83.
Greene E E Carols, pp xcix, 380; 2nd edn, pp cxxiii, cxxvi, 382.
Utley CR, p 144.
Greene Selection, pp 32, 209.
De la Mare W, Come Hither, new edn, London 1928, p 650.
Moore A K, The Secular Lyric in Middle English, Lexington Ky 1959, p 168.
Davies, p 340.
Utley F L, Manual, 3.725 (VII [51] c).

[138] HER COMMYS HOLLY þAT IS SO GENT.

MS. Bodl 29734 (Eng poet e.1), ff 53ᵇ–54ᵃ (mid 15 cent).
Brown-Robbins, no 1195.
Editions. Wright T, Carols, PPS 23.84.
Ch&Sidg, p 238.
Patterson F A, in B Matthews and A H Thorndike, Shaksperian Studies, N Y 1916, p 444.
Greene E E Carols, p 94; 2nd edn, p 83.
Robbins SL, p 46.
Modernizations. [Vizetelly H], Christmas with the Poets, London 1851, p 30 (incomplete).
Sylvester J pseud, A Garland of Christmas Carols Ancient and Modern, London 1861, p 143.
Husk W H, Songs of the Nativity, London 1868, p 129.
Bullen A H, Carols and Poems, London 1885, p 255.
Rickert Anc Eng Chr Carols, p 262.
Beeching, p 159.
Luria & Hoffman, p 137.
Commentary. Greene E E Carols, pp ciii, 380; 2nd edn, pp cxxvii, 383.
Utley CR, p 142.
Utley F L, Manual, 3.725 (VII [51] b).

[139] þE MOST WORTHYE SHE IS IN TOWNE.

MS. Bodl 29734 (Eng poet e.1), f 54ᵃ (mid 15 cent).
Brown-Robbins, no 3438.
Editions. Wright T, Carols, PPS 23.85.
Ch&Sidg, p 236.
Greene E E Carols, p 95; 2nd edn, p 83.
Robbins SL, p 46.
Greene Selection, p 93.
Sisam, p 480.
Modernizations. Davies, p 228.
[Vizetelly H], Christmas with the Poets, London 1851, p 30.
Husk W H, Songs of the Nativity, London 1868, p 130.
Rickert Anc Eng Chr Carols, p 263.
Beeching, p 160.
Luria & Hoffman, p 137.
Commentary. Ch&Sidg, p 374.
Wehrle, p 97.
Greene E E Carols, pp lxiii, ciii, 380; 2nd edn, pp lxxxiv, cxxvii, 383.
Utley CR, p 250.
Robbins SL, p 242.
Greene Selection, p 210.
Davies, p 353.
Woolf, p 300.
Utley F L, Manual, 3.725 (VII[51]b).

[140] OUER ALL GATIS THAT I HAFF GON.

MS. St John's Camb 259 (S.54), ff 12ᵃ–12ᵇ (mid 15 cent).
Brown-Robbins, no 2735.

Editions. James M R and G C Macaulay, MLR 8.83.
Greene E E Carols, p 95; 2nd edn, p 83.
Commentary. Greene E E Carols, pp ciii, 381; 2nd edn, pp cxxvii, 383.
Utley CR, p 223.
Utley F L, Manual, 3.725 (VII[51]d).

[141] IUY IS BOTH FAIR & GREN.

MS. BM Egerton 3307, ff 59^b–60^a (mid 15 cent; music).
Robbins-Cutler, no 1651.5.
Editions. Greene Selection, p 94.
Greene E E Carols, 2nd edn, p 84.
Modernization. Stevens Med Carols, p 44 (with music).
Commentary. Greene Selection, p 211.
Greene E E Carols, 2nd edn, p 384.

[142] BEHOLD WHAT LYFE THAT WE RYNE INE.

MS. Bodl 29734 (Eng poet e.1), ff 38^a–38^b (mid 15 cent).
Brown-Robbins, no 503.
Editions. Wright T, Carols, PPS 23.56.
Greene E E Carols, p 96; 2nd edn, p 84.
Greene Selection, p 95.
Commentary. Greene E E Carols, p 381; 2nd edn, p 384.
Greene Selection, p 212.

[143] HERE HAUE I DWELLYD WITH MORE AND LASSE.

MS. Balliol 354, f 224^b (early 16 cent).
Brown-Robbins, no 1198.
Editions. Flügel Fest R Hildebrand, p 72.
Flügel NL, p 126.
Flügel E, Angl 26.245.
Pollard 15CPV, p 89.
Dyboski R, EETSES 101.18.
Frost L, Come Christmas, N Y 1935, p 328.
Greene E E Carols, p 96; 2nd edn, p 85.
Greene Selection, p 96.
Sisam, p 531.
Modernizations. Rickert Anc Eng Chr Carols, p 225.
Beeching, p 184.
Loomis R S and R Willard, Medieval English Verse and Prose, N Y 1948, p 391.
Commentary. Greene E E Carols, p 381; 2nd edn, p 384.
Greene Selection, p 212.

[144] A CHYLD YS BORN E-WYS.

MSS. 1, St John's Camb 259 (S.54), ff 6^b–7^a (mid 15 cent); 2, Westminster Abbey 20, f 20^a (15 cent).
Brown-Robbins, no 30.
Editions. Robinson J A and M R James, The MSS of Westminster Abbey, Cambridge 1909, p 76 (MS 2).
James M R and G C Macaulay, MLR 8.76 (MS 1).
Greene E E Carols, p 97 (MS 1 with collation of MS 2); 2nd edn, p 85.
Greene R L, The Traditional Survival of Two Medieval Carols, ELH 7.225 (MS 2).
Greene Selection, p 97 (MS 1).
Traditional Versions. 1, Bodleian Libr, Douce Addit 137, broadside [Birmingham 1822]; rptd R L Greene, ELH 7.228 (version 1 with collation of versions 2, 3); Greene E E Carols, 2nd edn, p 86.
2, A Good Christmas Box Containing a Choice Collection of Christmas Carols, Dudley 1847, p 96.
3, Sidgwick F, Popular Carols, London 1908, p 29.
Commentary. Greene E E Carols, p 381; 2nd edn, p 385.
Greene, ELH 7.223.
Greene Selection, p 213.
Utley F L, Manual, 3.673 (VII[1]b).

[145] I SAW A FAYR MAYDYN SYTTYN & SYNGE.

MS. BM Sloane 2593, f 32^a (mid 15 cent).
Brown-Robbins, no 1351.
Editions. Wright T, Carols, Warton Club 4.94.
Fehr B, Arch 107.49.
Ch&Sidg, p 131.
Greene E E Carols, p 98; 2nd edn, p 87.
Greene Selection, p 98.
Gray D, A Selection of Religious Lyrics, Oxford 1975, p 12.
Modernizations. Rickert Anc Eng Chr Carols, p 66.
Beeching, p 10.
Segar M G, A Mediaeval Anthology, London 1915, p 66.
OBC, p 220; music edn, p 396; rvsd edn, p 386 (with modern music).
Bullett G, The English Galaxy of Shorter Poems, London 1947, p 7.
Davies, p 166.
Sayre E, A Christmas Book, N Y 1966, p 125.
Commentary. Greene E E Carols, p 382; 2nd edn, p 385.

Manning S, Wisdom and Number, Lincoln Neb 1962, p 26.
Utley F L, Manual, 3.675 (VII[1]i).
Greene Selection, p 214.

[146] I SAW A SWETE SEMLY SYGHT.

MS. BM Addit 5666, ff 4ᵇ–5ᵃ (early 15 cent; music).
Brown-Robbins, no 1352.
Editions. Ritson AS 1790, p xxxviii (with music); 1829, l.liv (with music); 1877, p xlvii (with music).
Greene E E Carols, p 98; 2nd edn, p 87.
Modernizations. Duncan E, The Story of Minstrelsy, London 1907, p 87 (with music).
Rickert Anc Eng Chr Carols, p 59.
Duncan E, The Story of the Carol, London 1911, p 56 (with music).
Phillips W J, Carols: Their Origin, Music, and Connection with Mystery Plays, London [1921], p 69.
Bukofzer M F, Journ of the American Musicological Soc 7.74.
Stevens Med Carols, p 1 (with music).
Robbins Christmas Carols, p 70 (with music).
Stevens J, Tidings True, London [1976], p 12 (with music).
Commentary. Greene E E Carols, p 382; 2nd edn, p 385.

[147] AS I ME ROS IN ON MORWENYNG.

MSS. 1, Bodl 29734 (Eng poet e.1), ff 34ᵃ–34ᵇ (mid 15 cent); 2, BM Sloane 2593, ff 16ᵇ–17ᵃ (mid 15 cent).
Brown-Robbins, no 361.
Editions. Wright T, Carols, PPS 23.50 (MS 1); Carols, Publ Warton Club 4.48 (MS 2).
Ch&Sidg, p 141 (composite text).
Greene E E Carols, p 98 (MS 1 with collation of MS 2); 2nd edn, p 88.
Modernizations. Rickert Anc Eng Chr Carols, p 68 (MS 1).
Comper Spir Songs, p 27 (MS 2).
Sitwell E, The Atlantic Book of British and American Poetry, Boston 1958, p 7.
Sayre E, A Christmas Book, N Y 1966, p 123 (MS 1).
Commentary. Greene E E Carols, p 382; 2nd edn, p 386.

[148] THIS ENDURS NYGHT.

MSS. 1, BM Harley 2380, ff 70ᵇ–71ᵃ (15 cent); 2, BM Addit 5465, ff 50ᵇ–53ᵃ (early 16 cent; music).
Brown-Robbins, no 3597.
Editions. Sandys W, Christmas Carols, London 1833, p 11 (MS 2).
Madrigals by English Composers of the 15th Century, Plainsong and Mediaeval Music Society, London 1893, no 5 (MS 2 with music).
Fehr B, Arch 106.60 (MS 2).
Ch&Sidg, p 157 (MS 2).
Greene E E Carols, p 99; 2nd edn, p 88 (MSS 1, 2).
Brown RLxvC, p 4 (MS 1).
Stevens J [E], Music and Poetry in the Early Tudor Court, p 366; Early Tudor Songs and Carols, Musica Britannica 36, London 1975, p 78 (MS 2).
Modernizations. Bullen A H, Carols and Poems, London 1885, p 21 (MS 2).
Rickert Anc Eng Chr Carols, p 62 (MS 2).
Segar M G, A Mediaeval Anthology, London 1915, p 72 (MS 2).
Comper Spir Songs, p 21 (MS 2).
Commentary. Greene E E Carols, p 382; 2nd edn, p 386.
Brown RLxvC, p 293.
Chambers OHEL, p 107.
Utley F L, Manual, 3.677 (VII[1]v).

[149] HOW SULD I NOW þᵘ FAYRE MAY FALL APONE A SLEPE.

MS. Bodl 29003 (Addit A.106), ff 14ᵇ–15ᵃ (late 15 cent).
Brown-Robbins, no 1264.
Editions. Greene E E Carols, p 101; 2nd edn, p 90.
Brown RLxvC, p 3.
Tydeman W, English Poetry 1400–1580, London 1970, p 48.
Silverstein, p 107.
Commentary. Greene E E Carols, p 383; 2nd edn, p 387.
Brown RLxvC, p 293.
Utley F L, Manual, 3.675 (VII[1]h).

[150] THE FADER OF HEUENE HIS OWYN SONE HE SENT.

MSS. 1, St John's Camb 259 (S.54), ff 11ᵃ–11ᵇ (mid 15 cent); 2, BM Sloane 2593, ff 16ᵃ–16ᵇ (mid 15 cent).
Brown-Robbins, no 3329.
Editions. Wright T, Carols, PPS 4.8 (MS 2); Carols, Publ Warton Club 4.46 (MS 2).

James M R and G C Macaulay, MLR 8.83 (MS 1).
Brougham E M, Corn from Olde Fieldes, 2nd edn, London [1918], p 5 (MS 2, in part).
Greene E E Carols, p 102; 2nd edn, p 91 (MSS 1, 2).
Brown RLxvC, p 120 (MS 2).
Thomas R S, The Penguin Book of Religious Verse, Harmondsworth 1963, p 43 (in part).
Modernization. Rickert Anc Eng Chr Carols, p 65 (MS 2).
Commentary. Greene E E Carols, p 383; 2nd edn, p 387.
Manning S, Wisdom and Number, Lincoln Neb 1962, p 26.

[151] ALS I LAY VP-ON A NITH.

MSS. 1, Camb Univ Addit 5943, f 169^a (early 15 cent); 2, St John's Camb 259 (S.54), ff 4^a–4^b (mid 15 cent); 3, BM Harley 2330, f 120^a (15 cent); 4, Advocates 18.7.21, ff 3^b–4^b (1372).
Brown-Robbins, no 352.
Editions. M[ayer] L S, Music Cantelenas Songs Etc, London 1906, sheet i (MS 1).
James M R and G C Macaulay, MLR 8.72 (MS 2).
Sandison H E, BrynMawrMon 12.103 (MS 3).
Brown RLxivC, p 70 (MS 4).
Greene E E Carols, p 103 (MS 4 with collation of MSS 1–3); 2nd edn, p 92.
Obertello A, Liriche religiose Inglesi del secolo quattordicesimo, Milan 1947, p 110 (MS 4 with Italian trans).
Modernizations. Comper Spir Songs, p 50 (MS 4, incomplete and with additions from MS 3).
Stevens Med Carols, p 110 (MS 1 with music).
Robbins Christmas Carols, p 73 (MS 1 with music).
Davies, p 112 (MS 4).
Sayre E, A Christmas Book, N Y 1966, p 131 (MS 4).
Weber S A, Theology and Poetry in the Middle English Lyric, Columbus O 1969, p 61 (MS 4).
Commentary. Greene E E Carols, p 383; 2nd edn, p 387.
Obertello, p 224.
Davies, p 323.
Weber, pp 69, 243 (MS 4).
Jeffrey D L, The Early English Lyric and Franciscan Spirituality, Lincoln Neb 1975, p 241 (MS 4).
Utley F L, Manual, 3.674 (VII[1]d).

[152] THIS LOUELY LADY SAT AND SONG.

MSS. 1, Bodl 29734 (Eng poet e.1), ff 17^b–18^b (mid 15 cent); 2, Balliol 354, ff 226^a–226^b (early 16 cent); 3, BM Royal Appendix 58, ff 52^b–54^b (early 16 cent; music); 4, Advocates 19.3.1, ff 210^b–211^a (late 15 cent).
Brown-Robbins, no 3627.
Editions. Rel Ant, 2.76 (MS 4).
Wright T, Carols, PPS 23.12 (MS 1).
Flügel NL, p 119 (MSS 2, 3).
Flügel E, Angl 12.270 (MS 3); 26.250 (MS 2).
Ch&Sidg, p 121 (MS 1).
Dyboski R, EETSES 101.25, 175, 174 (MSS 2–4 with collation of MS 1).
Julian J, A Dictionary of Hymnology, 2nd edn, London 1925, p 209 (MS 1).
Budd F E, A Book of Lullabies 1300–1900, London 1930, p 34 (MS 1).
Greene E E Carols, p 106; 2nd edn, p 95 (MSS 1–4).
Cecil Lord D, The Oxford Book of Christian Verse, Oxford 1940, p 17 (MS 2; omits burden).
Brandl A and O Zippel, Middle English Literature, 2nd edn, N Y 1949, p 114 (MS 4).
Greene Selection, p 99 (MS 4).
Sisam, p 466 (MS 1).
Modernizations. [Vizetelly H], Christmas with the Poets, London 1851, p 12 (MS 1).
Sylvester J pseud, A Garland of Christmas Carols, Ancient and Modern, London 1861, p 5 (MS 1).
Husk W H, Songs of the Nativity, London 1868, p 13 (MS 1).
Bramley H R and J Stainer, Christmas Carols New and Old, London 1871, p 53 (composite text with modern music).
Bullen A H, Carols and Poems, London 1886, p 15 (MS 1).
Weston, p 14 (MS 2).
Rickert Anc Eng Chr Carols, p 59 (MS 1 with additions from MS 3).
Segar M G, A Mediaeval Anthology, London 1915, p 68 (MS 2).
Hutchins C L, Carols Old and Carols New, Boston 1916, p 342 (MS 4 with supplied music, altered).
Segar M G, Some Minor Poems of the Middle Ages, London 1917, p 44 (MS 2).
Beeching, p 8 (MS 1).
OBC, p 47 (MS 1); music edn, p 76; rvsd edn, p 70 (composite text with music from MS 3).
Terry Med Carol Book, p 60 (MS 3 with music).
Comper Spir Songs, p 58 (MS 2 with one stanza of MS 1).

Commentary. Ch&Sidg, p 351.
Dyboski R, EETSES 101.175 (erroneous reference to BM Addit 31922).
Greene E E Carols, p 384; 2nd edn, p 388.
Greene Selection, p 214.
Manning S, Wisdom and Number, Lincoln Neb 1962, p 49.
Utley F L, Manual, 3.678 (VII[1]w).

[153] THIS ENDRYS NY3T.

MSS. 1, Bodl 29734 (Eng poet e.1), ff 20ª–21ª (mid 15 cent); 2, Camb Univ Addit 5943, f 145ª (early 15 cent); 3, BM Addit 5666, ff 2ᵇ–3ª (early 15 cent; music).
Brown-Robbins, Robbins-Cutler, no 3596.
Editions. Wright T, Carols, PPS 23.19 (MS 1).
Ritson AS 1877, p xlviii (MS 3, in part).
M[ayer] L S, Music Cantelenas Songs Etc, London 1906, sheet x (MS 2).
Ch&Sidg, p 119 (MS 1).
Cook A S, A Literary ME Reader, Boston 1915, p 466 (MS 1).
Greene E E Carols, p 110; 2nd edn, p 98 (MSS 1–3).
Sisam, p 472 (MS 1).
Modernizations. Rickert Anc Eng Chr Carols, p 69 (MS 1).
Hutchins C L, Carols Old and Carols New, Boston 1916, p 527 (MS 1 with supplied music).
Stevens Med Carols, p 110 (MS 3, burden only; with music).
Robbins Christmas Carols, p 72 (MS 3, burden only, with music).
Commentary. Ch&Sidg, p 351.
Greene E E Carols, p 384; 2nd edn, p 389.
Stevens Med Carols, p 123 (corrects Greene on music of MS 3).
Utley F L, Manual, 3.677 (VII[1]u).

[154] A BABE IS BORN OUR BLYSSE TO BRYNGE.

MSS. 1, Bodl 798 (Laud misc 683), f 105ᵇ (15 cent); 2, Balliol 354, f 225ᵇ (early 16 cent); 3, Nat Libr Wales, Porkington 10, ff 201ª–202ᵇ (mid 15 cent).
Brown-Robbins, Robbins-Cutler, no 22.
Editions. Flügel Fest R Hildebrand, p 73 (MS 2).
Flügel E, Angl 26.247 (MS 2).
Pollard 15CPV, p 90 (MS 2).
Dyboski R, EETSES 101.21 (MS 2).
MacCracken H N, MLN 24.225 (MS 1 with collation of MS 2).
Greene E E Carols, p 112 (MS 2 with collation of MSS 1, 3); 2nd edn, p 100.
Brown RLxvC, p 1 (MS 3).
Greene R L, ELH 7.232 (MS 2).
Greene Selection, p 101 (MS 2).
Traditional Versions. 1, Harvard Coll Libr, HCL 25258.27.5*, Carol Book A, p 8 (1767).
2, Harvard Coll Libr, HCL 25258.27.5*, Carol Book B, p 58 (1777).
3, Sandys W, Christmas Carols, Ancient and Modern, London 1833, p 122.
4, Sylvester J pseud, A Garland of Christmas Carols, Ancient and Modern, London 1861, p 41.
Editions of Traditional Versions 1–3. Greene R L, ELH 7.235.
Greene E E Carols, 2nd edn, p 101.
Modernizations. Weston, p 28 (MS 2).
Rickert Anc Eng Chr Carols, p 72 (MS 2).
Segar M G, A Mediaeval Anthology, London 1915, p 76 (composite text; in part).
Comper Spir Songs, p 47 (MS 2).
Davies, p 197 (MS 2).
Commentary. Dyboski R, EETSES 101.173.
Wehrle, p 91.
Greene E E Carols, p 384; 2nd edn, p 389.
Greene R L, ELH 7.223.
Greene Selection, p 215.
Brown RLxvC, p 293.
Utley F L, Manual, 3.673 (VII[1]c).

[155] SO BLESSID A SIGHT IT WAS TO SEE.

MS. Balliol 354, f 226ª (early 16 cent).
Brown-Robbins, Robbins-Cutler, no 3161.
Editions. Flügel NL, p 119.
Flügel E, Angl 26.249.
Dyboski R, EETSES 101.23.
Frost L, Come Christmas, N Y 1935, p 267.
Greene E E Carols, p 113; 2nd edn, p 102.
Modernizations. Rickert Anc Eng Chr Carols, p 74.
Comper Spir Songs, p 42.
Commentary. Greene E E Carols, p 384; 2nd edn, p 390.
Utley F L, Manual, 3.676 (VII[1]q).

[156] THAT MEYDEN MYLDE HERE CHILDE DID KEPE (James Ryman).

MS. Camb Univ Ee.1.12, ff 102ᵇ–103ᵇ (ca 1492).
Brown-Robbins, no 3284.
Editions. Zupitza J, Arch 89.321.
Greene E E Carols, p 114; 2nd edn, p 102.
Sisam, p 507.
Modernization. Stevick, p 155.

Commentary. Zupitza, Arch 97.139.
Greene E E Carols, p 384; 2nd edn, p 390.
Utley F L, Manual, 3.677 (VII[1]s).

[157] LULLAY LULLAY LITEL CHILD.

MSS. 1, BM Harley 7358, f 12[b] (late 14 cent); 2, Advocates 18.7.21, f 6[a] (1372).
Brown-Robbins, Robbins-Cutler, no 2024.
Editions. Heuser W, BBA 14.211 (MS 1).
Brown RLxivC, p 80 (MS 2).
Greene E E Carols, p 115 (MS 2 with collation of MS 1); 2nd edn, p 103.
Cecil Lord D, The Oxford Book of Christian Verse, Oxford 1940, p 17 (MS 2; omits burden).
Obertello A, Liriche religiose Inglesi del secolo quattordicesimo, Milan 1947, p 118 (MS 2 with Italian trans).
Greene Selection, p 103 (MS 2).
Gray D, A Selection of Religious Lyrics, Oxford 1975, p 13 (MS 2).
Modernizations. Comper Spir Songs, p 25 (MS 1 with one stanza from MS 2).
Williams M, Glee-wood, N Y 1949, p 456 (MS 2, in part).
Sayre E, A Christmas Book, N Y 1966, p 59 (MS 2).
Owen L J and N H, Middle English Poetry: Anthology, Indianapolis Ind 1971, p 17 (MS 2).
Luria & Hoffman, p 194 (MS 2).
Commentary. Brown RLxivC, p 264.
Greene E E Carols, pp cxxv, 384; 2nd edn, pp cliv, 390.
Greene Selection, p 216.
Manning S, Wisdom and Number, Lincoln Neb 1962, p 24.
Owen, p 356.

[158] O MY DERE SONNE WHY DOEST THOU SOO (James Ryman).

MS. Camb Univ Ee.1.12, f 69[b] (ca 1492).
Brown-Robbins, no 2530.
Editions. Zupitza J, Arch 89.263.
Greene E E Carols, p 116; 2nd edn, p 104.
Commentary. Zupitza, Arch 95.403.
Woolf, p 252.
Utley F L, Manual, 3.675 (VII[1]l).

[159] MARY MODER CUM & SE.

MSS. 1, Bodl 29734 (Eng poet e.1), ff 27*[a]–27*[b] (mid 15 cent); 2, BM Sloane 2593, ff 23[a]–23[b] (mid 15 cent); 3, Advocates 18.7.21, f 121[a] (1372); 4, BM Addit 31042, f 94[b] (15 cent; fragment). PRINT: 5, Huntington Libr, Christmas carolles newely Inprynted (Richard Kele), pp [31–33] (ca 1550; STC, no 5205).
Brown-Robbins, nos 1219, 2036, 2111.
Editions. [Bliss P], Bibliographical Miscellanies, Oxford 1813, p 49 (PRINT).
Wright T, Carols, PPS 4.10 (MS 2); 23.38 (MS 1); Carols, Publ Warton Club 4.65 (MS 2).
Ch&Sidg, p 146 (MS 1).
Brown RLxivC, p 85 (MS 3).
Reed Christmas Carols, pp 49 (facsimile of PRINT), 82 (MSS 2, 3).
Greene E E Carols, p 117; 2nd edn, pp 105 (MSS 1–3, PRINT), 107 (MS 4).
Cecil Lord D, The Oxford Book of Christian Verse, Oxford 1940, p 41 (MS 1).
Greene Selection, p 104 (MS 1).
Hodder K, Arch 205.378 (MS 4), 380 (facsimile).
Modernizations. Segar M G, A Mediaeval Anthology, London 1915, p 41 (MS 1).
Watts N, Love Songs of Sion, London 1924, p 91 (MS 2; omits burden).
Comper Spir Songs, p 109 (MS 2 with additions from MS 3).
Commentary. Thien H, Über die englischen Marienklagen, Kiel 1906, p 45.
Brown RLxivC, p 266.
Reed Christmas Carols, p 82 (treats [157] as variant).
Greene E E Carols, pp cxxv, cxxxv, 385; 2nd edn, pp cliv, clxii, 391.
Greene Selection, p 217.
Woolf, p 250.
Utley F L, Manual, 3.675 (VII[1]k).

[160] THYS BLESSYD BABE þ[t] THOU HAST BORN.

MS. Balliol 354, f 223[a] (early 16 cent).
Brown-Robbins, no 3575.
Editions. Flügel NL, p 112.
Flügel E, Angl 26.240.
Dyboski R, EETSES 101.13.
Reed Christmas Carols, p 84.
Greene E E Carols, p 119; 2nd edn, p 107.
Modernization. Comper Spir Songs, p 111.
Commentary. Thien H, Über die englischen Marienklagen, Kiel 1906, p 46.
Greene E E Carols, p 385; 2nd edn, p 391.
Woolf, p 252.
Utley F L, Manual, 3.677 (VII[1]t).

[161] WHEN FALS IUDAS HER SON HAD SOLDE (James Ryman).

MS. Camb Univ Ee.1.12, ff 77[a]–77[b] (ca 1492).
Brown-Robbins, no 3944.

Editions. Zupitza J, Arch 89.277.
Greene E E Carols, p 120; 2nd edn, p 107.
Commentary. Zupitza, Arch 96.169.
Greene E E Carols, p 385; 2nd edn, p 391.

[162] IN PROPHESY THUS IT IS SAIDE
(James Ryman).

MS. Camb Univ Ee.1.12, f 78ᵃ (ca 1492).
Brown-Robbins, no 1524.
Editions. Zupitza J, Arch 89.280.
Greene E E Carols, p 120; 2nd edn, p 108.
Commentary. Zupitza, Arch 96.172.
Greene E E Carols, p 386; 2nd edn, p 391.

[163] WITH FAUOURE IN HIR FACE
FERR PASSYNG MY REASON.

MSS. 1, Trinity Camb 1450 (0.9.38), ff 63ᵇ–64ᵃ (late 15 cent); 2, Rylands Libr 18932, ff 120ᵃ–120ᵇ (15 cent).
Brown-Robbins, Robbins-Cutler, no 4189.
Editions. Brydges E, Censura Literaria, London 1805, 10.186 (MS 2).
Furnivall F J, EETS 24.126 (MS 1).
Ch&Sidg, p 144 (MS 1).
Greene E E Carols, p 121 (MS 2 with collation of MS 1); 2nd edn, p 108.
Brown RLxvC, p 17 (MS 2).
Sisam, p 486 (MS 2).
Silverstein, p 102 (MS 2).
Reiss E, The Art of the ME Lyric, Athens Ga 1972, p 144 (MS 2).
Gray D, A Selection of Religious Lyrics, Oxford 1975, p 21 (MS 2).
Modernization. Stevick, p 150 (MS 2).
Commentary. Greene E E Carols, p 386; 2nd edn, p 392.
Brown RLxvC, p 298.
Kane, p 173.
Reiss, edn, p 145.
Woolf, p 265.

[164] BOWGHT & SOLD FULL
TRAYTORSLY.

MS. Balliol 354, f 230ᵃ (early 16 cent).
Brown-Robbins, Robbins-Cutler, no 548.
Editions. Flügel E, Angl 26.263.
Dyboski R, EETSES 101.41.
Greene E E Carols, p 122; 2nd edn, p 109.
Modernizations. Segar M G, A Mediaeval Anthology, London 1915, p 80; Some Minor Poems of the Middle Ages, London 1917, p 48.
Comper Spir Songs, p 102.

Commentary. Greene E E Carols, p 386; 2nd edn, p 392.
Kane, p 172.

[165] WHAN Þᵗ MY SWETE SONE WAS
XXXᵗⁱ WYNTER OLD.

MS. Balliol 354, f 230ᵃ (early 16 cent). PRINT: Huntington Libr, Christmas carolles newely Inprynted (Richard Kele), pp [14–16] (ca 1550; STC, no 5205).
Brown-Robbins, no 4023.
Editions. [Bliss P], Bibliographical Miscellanies, Oxford 1813, p 51 (PRINT).
Flügel E, Angl 26.262 (MS).
Ch&Sidg, p 142 (MS).
Dyboski R, EETSES 101.40 (MS).
Reed Christmas Carols, p 32 (facsimile of PRINT).
Greene E E Carols, p 122 (MS with collation of PRINT); 2nd edn, p 109.
Sisam, p 533 (MS).
Modernizations. Comper Spir Songs, p 100.
Sitwell E, Planet and Glow-worm, London 1944, p 75; The Atlantic Book of British and American Poetry, Boston 1958, p 18.
Commentary. Thien H, Über die englischen Marienklagen, Kiel 1906, p 19.
Ch&Sidg, p 356.
Reed Christmas Carols, p 76.
Greene E E Carols, p 386; 2nd edn, p 392.
Kane, p 172.

[166] AS I WENT THIS ENDERS DAY.

MSS. No MS extant. PRINT: Huntington Libr, Christmas carolles newely Inprynted (Richard Kele), p [17] (ca 1550; STC, no 5205).
Robbins-Cutler, no 377.5.
Editions. Reed Christmas Carols, p 35 (facsimile).
Greene E E Carols, p 123; 2nd edn, p 111.
Commentary. Greene E E Carols, p 386; 2nd edn, p 392.

[167] I WAS BORN IN A STALL.

MS. Balliol 354, f 225ᵃ (early 16 cent).
Brown-Robbins, no 1383.
Editions. Flügel NL, p 121.
Flügel E, Angl 26.246.
Dyboski R, EETSES 101.19.
Greene E E Carols, p 125; 2nd edn, p 111.
Modernizations. Rickert Anc Eng Chr Carols, p 78.
Comper Spir Songs, p 33.
Commentary. Greene E E Carols, p 387; 2nd edn, p 393.

[168] THERE WAS SUIM TEME BYFALLE A CAS.

MS. BM Royal 20.A.i, ff 120ª–120ᵇ (early 15 cent).
Brown-Robbins, no 3550.
Edition. Greene E E Carols, p 126; 2nd edn, p 111.
Commentary. Greene E E Carols, p 387; 2nd edn, p 393.

[169] MAN IF þᵘ HAST SYNNYD OWTH.

MS. BM Sloane 2593, ff 22ª–22ᵇ (mid 15 cent).
Brown-Robbins, Robbins-Cutler, no 2061.
Editions. Wright T, Carols, Publ Warton Club 4.61.
Fehr B, Arch 109.62.
Greene E E Carols, p 126; 2nd edn, p 112.
Commentary. Greene E E Carols, p 388; 2nd edn, p 393.

[170] IHESU OF HIS MODER WAS BORN.

MS. BM Sloane 2593, ff 28ª–28ᵇ (mid 15 cent).
Brown-Robbins, no 1739.
Editions. Wright T, Carols, Publ Warton Club 4.81.
Fehr B, Arch 109.67.
Greene E E Carols, p 127; 2nd edn, p 113.
Modernization. Comper Spir Songs, p 93.

[171] THYS WYNDE BE RESON YS CALLYD TENTACYON.

MS. Bodl 7683 (Ashmole 1379), pp 32–34 (ca 1500).
Brown-Robbins, Robbins-Cutler, no 3525 (indexed by first line of burden).
Editions. Greene E E Carols, p 127; 2nd edn, p 113.
Greene Selection, p 105.
Sisam, p 491.
Modernizations. Stevick, p 42.
Luria & Hoffman, p 150.
Commentary. Greene E E Carols, p 388; 2nd edn, p 393.
Robbins R H, The Burden in Carols, MLN 57.22 (prefers to regard as not a carol).
Greene Selection, p 217.
Bronson B H, The Traditional Tunes of the Child Ballads, Princeton 1962, 2.234.
Woolf, p 198.

[172] þIS FLOUR IS FAIRE & FRESCHE OF HEUE (John Audelay).

MSS. 1, Bodl 21876 (Douce 302), f 31ᵇ (early 15 cent); 2, Balliol 354, f 220ª (early 16 cent).
Brown-Robbins, Robbins-Cutler, no 3603.
Editions. Flügel Fest R Hildebrand, p 60 (MS 2).
Flügel NL, p 115 (MS 2).
Flügel E, Angl 26.230 (MS 2).
Ch&Sidg, p 110 (MS 1).
Dyboski R, EETSES 101.6 (MS 2).
Chambers E K and F Sidgwick, MLR 6.73 (MS 1).
Haberly L, Alia Cantalena de Sancta Maria, Long Crendon Bucks 1926 (MS 1).
Whiting E K, EETS 184.202 (MS 1).
Greene E E Carols, p 129 (MS 1 with collation of MS 2); 2nd edn, p 115.
Sisam, p 388 (MS 1).
Modernizations. Weston, p 23 (MS 2).
Rickert Anc Eng Chr Carols, p 160 (composite text).
Segar M G, A Mediaeval Anthology, London 1915, p 44 (MS 2, in part).
Adamson M R, A Treasury of ME Verse, London 1930, p 167 (MS 2).
Comper Spir Songs, p 28 (MS 1).
Sitwell E, The Atlantic Book of British and American Poetry, Boston 1958, p 8.
Sayre E, A Christmas Book, N Y 1966, p 1 (MS 1).
Commentary. Dyboski, EETSES 101.169.
Greene E E Carols, p 388; 2nd edn, p 394.
Greene Selection, p 217.
Copley J, ESts 39.210.

[173] THER IS NO ROSE OF SWYCH VERTU.

MS. Trinity Camb 1230 (O.3.58), no 13 (mid 15 cent; music).
Brown-Robbins, Robbins-Cutler, no 3536.
Editions. Fuller Maitland English Carols, p 27 (with music).
Ch&Sidg, p 105.
Greene E E Carols, p 130; 2nd edn, p 116.
Greene Selection, p 107.
Manning S, Wisdom and Number, Lincoln Neb 1962, p 155.
Sisam, p 408.
Gray D, Themes and Images in the Medieval English Religious Lyric, London 1972, p 88.
Oliver R, Poems without Names: The English Lyric 1200–1500, Berkeley Calif 1970, p 82.
Modernizations. Rickert Anc Eng Chr Carols, p 8.

Segar M G, A Mediaeval Anthology, London 1915, p 65.
Watts N, Love Songs of Sion, London 1924, p 132 (omits burden).
Terry Med Carol Book, p 56 (with music).
Bullett G, The English Galaxy of Shorter Poems, London 1947, p 5.
Stevens Med Carols, p 10 (with music).
Robbins Christmas Carols, p 66 (with music).
Routley E, The English Carol, London 1958, p 29 (with music).
Stevens J, There Is No Rose of Such Virtue, London 1951; Tidings True, London [1976], p 9 (with music).
Commentary. Ch&Sidg, p 348.
Wehrle, p 67.
Greene E E Carols, pp lxxxii, 389; 2nd edn, pp cii, 395.
Greene Selection, p 218.
Manning, p 155.
Robbins Christmas Carols, p 66.
Routley, p 29.
Woolf, p 288.
Gray, edn, p 88.

[174] TO THIS ROOSE AUNGELL GABRIELL (James Ryman).

MS. Camb Univ Ee.1.12, ff 24ᵇ–25ᵃ (ca 1492).
Brown-Robbins, no 3779.
Editions. Zupitza J, Arch 89.187.
Greene E E Carols, p 131; 2nd edn, p 116.
Commentary. Zupitza, Arch 93.393.
Greene E E Carols, p 389; 2nd edn, p 395.
Woolf, p 288.

[175] LYTH AND LYSTEN BOTH OLD AND ȝONG.

MSS. 1, Bodl 29734 (Eng poet e.1), ff 21ᵃ–21ᵇ (mid 15 cent); 2, Balliol 354, f 220ᵇ (early 16 cent); 3, BM Sloane 2593, ff 6ᵇ–7ᵃ (mid 15 cent).
Brown-Robbins, nos 1893, 1914.
Editions. Wright T, Songs and Carols, London 1836, no 5 (MS 3); Carols, PPS 23.21 (MS 1); Carols, Publ Warton Club 4.16 (MS 3).
Flügel Fest R Hildebrand, p 62 (MS 2).
Flügel NL, p 116 (MS 2).
Flügel E, Angl 26.232 (MS 2).
Pollard 15CPV, p 85 (MS 2).
Stobart J C, The Chaucer Epoch, London [1906], p 16.
Ch&Sidg, p 103 (MS 3).
Dyboski R, EETSES 101.170, 177 (MSS 1–3).

Quiller-Couch A, The Oxford Book of English Verse, Oxford 1925, p 12 (MS 3).
Greene E E Carols, p 131; 2nd edn, p 116 (MSS 1–3).
Cecil Lord D, The Oxford Book of Christian Verse, Oxford 1940, p 30 (MS 3).
Greene Selection, p 108 (MS 1).
Sisam, p 429 (MS 3).
Modernizations. Ancient Carols, The Shakespeare Head Press Booklets No 1, 2nd edn, Stratford-on-Avon 1906, p 10 (MS 3).
Weston, p 25 (MS 2).
Rickert Anc Eng Chr Carols, p 9 (MS 2).
Watts N, Love Songs of Sion, London 1915, p 123 (MS 2).
Beeching, p 25 (MS 3).
Sitwell E, The Atlantic Book of British and American Poetry, Boston 1958, p 6.
Oliver, p 20 (MS 1).
Stevick, p 146 (MS 1).
Commentary. Greene E E Carols, p 389; 2nd edn, p 395.
Spitzer L, Explication de Texte Applied to Three Great ME Poems, ALg 3.137; rptd Essays on English and American Literature, ed A Hatcher, Princeton 1962, p 193.
Greene Selection, p 219.

[176] THIS ROSE IS RAILED ON A RYS.

MS. Bodl 3340 (Arch Selden B.26), f 9ᵇ (mid 15 cent; music).
Brown-Robbins, no 3638.
Editions. Early Bodleian Music, 2.108 (with music).
Padelford F M, Angl 36.90.
Greene E E Carols, p 133; 2nd edn, p 118.
Modernizations. Rickert Anc Eng Chr Carols, p 11.
Terry Med Carol Book, p 10 (with music).
Stevens Med Carols, p 13 (with music).
Robbins Christmas Carols, p 68 (with music).
Stevens J, Tidings True, London [1976], p 10 (with music).
Commentary. Wehrle, p 76.
Greene E E Carols, p 389; 2nd edn, p 395.

[177] BLESSID MOT þᵘ BE þᵘ BERD SO BRYȝT (John Audelay).

MS. Bodl 21876 (Douce 302), f 30ᵃ (early 15 cent).
Brown-Robbins, no 536.
Editions. Chambers E K and F Sidgwick, MLR 6.75.
Whiting E K, EETS 184.205.
Greene E E Carols, p 134; 2nd edn, p 118.

Modernization. Comper Spir Songs, p 5.
Commentary. Whiting, EETS 184.254.
Greene E E Carols, p 389; 2nd edn, p 395.

[178] FAYRE MAYDYN WHO IS THIS BARNE.

MS. Balliol 354, f 177ᵇ (early 16 cent).
Brown-Robbins, no 755.
Editions. Flügel Fest R Hildebrand, p 53.
Flügel NL, p 111.
Flügel E, Angl 26.189.
Pollard 15CPV, p 83.
Dyboski R, EETSES 101.2.
Greene E E Carols, p 134; 2nd edn, p 119.
Modernizations. Comper Spir Songs, p 19.
Watts N, Love Songs of Sion, London 1924, p 39.
Beeching, p 21.
Weston, p 12.
Sayre E, A Christmas Book, N Y 1966, p 148.
Commentary. Wehrle, p 91.
Greene E E Carols, p 389; 2nd edn, p 395.
Utley F L, Manual, 3.675 (VII[1]g), 687 (VII[9]).

[179] WORSHYP BE þE BIRTH OF þE.

MS. Bodl 3340 (Arch Selden B.26), f 14ᵃ (mid 15 cent; music).
Brown-Robbins, no 4229.
Editions. Early Bodleian Music, 2.121 (with music).
Padelford F M, Angl 36.95.
Greene E E Carols, p 134; 2nd edn, p 119.
Modernizations. Terry Med Carol Book, p 26 (with music).
Stevens Med Carols, p 17 (with music).
Commentary. Wehrle, p 103.
Greene E E Carols, p 390; 2nd edn, p 396.

[180] IT WERN FOWRE LETTERYS OF PURPOSY.

MSS. 1, Bodl 29734 (Eng poet e.1), ff 25ᵃ–25ᵇ (mid 15 cent); 2, BM Sloane 2593, f 24ᵇ (mid 15 cent).
Brown-Robbins, Robbins-Cutler, no 1650.
Editions. Wright T, Carols, PPS 23.31 (MS 1); Carols, Publ Warton Club 4.69 (MS 2).
Fehr B, Arch 109.64 (MS 2).
Greene E E Carols, p 135; 2nd edn, p 120 (MSS 1, 2).
Greene Selection, p 109 (MS 1).
Sisam, p 479 (MS 1).
Modernization. Rickert Anc Eng Chr Carols, p 7 (MS 2).
Davies, p 163.

Commentary. Greene E E Carols, p 390; 2nd edn, p 396.
Greene Selection, p 219.
Woolf, p 293.
Borroff M, N&Q 221.294.

[181] HAYLE BE THOU MARY MOST OF HONOWR.

MS. BM Egerton 3307, f 67ᵃ (mid 15 cent; music).
Robbins-Cutler, no 1030.5.
Editions. Greene Selection, p 109.
Greene E E Carols, 2nd edn, p 119.
Modernization. Stevens Med Carols, p 54 (with music).
Commentary. Greene Selection, p 220.
Greene E E Carols, 2nd edn, p 386.

[182] THAT WAS IHU OURE SAUEOUR.

MS. Trinity Camb 652 (R.2.20), f 169ᵇ (late 15 cent).
Brown-Robbins, no 3297.
Editions. Greene E E Carols, p 136; 2nd edn, p 120.
Brown RLxvC, p 110.

[183] LO MOISES BUSH SHYNYNGE VN-BRENT.

MS. Bodl 3340 (Arch Selden B.26), f 24ᵃ (mid 15 cent; music).
Brown-Robbins, no 1931.
Editions. Early Bodleian Music, 2.147 (with music).
Padelford F M, Angl 36.108.
Greene E E Carols, p 136; 2nd edn, p 120.
Modernization. Stevens Med Carols, p 24 (with music).
Commentary. Greene E E Carols, p 391; 2nd edn, p 397.
Woolf, p 285.

[184] VPON A LADY FAYRE & BRIGHT.

MS. Balliol 354, f 177ᵇ (early 16 cent).
Brown-Robbins, no 3835.
Editions. Flügel Fest R Hildebrand, p 54.
Flügel NL, p 126.
Flügel E, Angl 26.190.
Dyboski R, EETSES 101.2.
Greene E E Carols, p 136; 2nd edn, p 121.
Modernization. Adamson M R, A Treasury of ME Verse, London 1930, p 146 (omits burden).
Commentary. Greene E E Carols, p 391; 2nd edn, p 397.

[185] OF ALL þI FRENDES SCHE IS þE
FLOWRE.

MS. Bodl 29734 (Eng poet e.1), ff 33ª–33ᵇ (mid
15 cent).
Brown-Robbins, no 2618.
Editions. Wright T, Carols, PPS 23.49.
Greene E E Carols, p 137; 2nd edn, p 121.
Commentary. Greene E E Carols, p 391; 2nd edn,
p 397.

[186] HOLY MAYDYN BLYSSID þOU BE.

MSS. 1, Bodl 3340 (Arch Selden B.26), f 10ᵇ (mid
15 cent; music); 2, BM Sloane 2593, ff 25ª–25ᵇ
(mid 15 cent).
Brown-Robbins, no 1230.
Editions. Wright T, Carols, Publ Warton Club
4.71 (MS 2).
Fehr B, Arch 109.64 (MS 2).
Early Bodleian Music, 2.110 (MS 1 with music).
Padelford F M, Angl 36.91, 92 (MSS 1, 2).
Greene E E Carols, p 137; 2nd edn, p 122 (MSS
1, 2).
Modernizations. Rickert Anc Eng Chr Carols, p 18
(MS 2).
Terry Med Carol Book, p 24 (MS 1 with music).
Stevens Med Carols, p 14 (MS 1 with music).
Commentary. Greene E E Carols, p 391; 2nd edn,
p 398.
Manning S, Wisdom and Number, Lincoln Neb
1962, p 165.

[187] BENYNG LADY BLESSED MOTE
THOW BE.

MS. BM Addit 5665, ff 4ᵇ–5ª (late 15 cent;
music).
Brown-Robbins, Robbins-Cutler, no 507.
Editions. Stafford Smith J, Musica Antiqua, [London 1812], p 23 (with music; in part).
Fehr B, Arch 106.265.
Padelford F M, Angl 36.92.
Brougham E M, Corn from Olde Fieldes, 2nd edn,
London [1918], p 11 (stanzas in order 2, 3, 1).
Greene E E Carols, p 138; 2nd edn, p 122.
Modernizations. Stevens Med Carols, p 62 (with
music).
Robbins Christmas Carols, p 56 (with music).

[188] ALLE ȜE MOUWEN OF IOYE
SYNGE.

MSS. 1, Balliol 354, f 249ᵇ (early 16 cent); 2,
Caius Camb 383, p 68 (mid 15 cent); 3, BM
Printed Book C.21.c.12, MS entry on C₄ᵛ
(early 16 cent).
Brown-Robbins, Robbins-Cutler, no 236.
Editions. Flügel E, Angl 26.274 (MS 1).
Dyboski R, EETSES 101.49 (MS 1).
Greene E E Carols, p 139 (MSS 1, 2); 2nd edn,
p 123 (MSS 1–3).
Brunner K, Angl 61.150 (MS 2).
Brown RLxvC, p 33 (MS 2).
Commentary. Greene E E Carols, p 391; 2nd edn,
p 398.
Brunner, Kirchenlieder aus dem 15 Jahrhundert,
Angl 61.149.

[189] MARY IS A LADY BRYȜT.

MS. BM Sloane 2593, f 8ᵇ (mid 15 cent).
Brown-Robbins, no 2103.
Editions. Wright T, Carols, Publ Warton Club
4.23.
Fehr B, Arch 109.48.
Ch&Sidg, p 108.
Greene E E Carols, p 139; 2nd edn, p 123.
Modernizations. Rickert Anc Eng Chr Carols, p 16.
Brougham E M, Corn from Olde Fieldes, 2nd
edn, London [1918], p 10.
Commentary. Wehrle, p 77.

[190] BEHOLD AND SEE O LADY FREE
(James Ryman).

MS. Camb Univ Ee.1.12, ff 13ᵇ–14ª (ca 1492).
Brown-Robbins, Robbins-Cutler, no 489.
Editions. Zupitza J, Arch 89.172.
Greene E E Carols, p 140; 2nd edn, p 124.
Commentary. Zupitza, Arch 93.299.
Wehrle, p 156.
Greene E E Carols, p 392; 2nd edn, p 398.

[191] THOW HOLY DOUȜTER OF
SYON.

MSS. 1, Bodl 3340 (Arch Selden B.26), f 25ᵇ (mid
15 cent; music); 2, BM Egerton 3307, f 53ª
(mid 15 cent; music).
Brown-Robbins, Robbins-Cutler, no 3674.
Editions. Early Bodleian Music, 2.151 (MS 1 with
music).
Padelford F M, Angl 36.109 (MS 1).
Greene E E Carols, p 140 (MS 1); 2nd edn, p 124
(MSS 1, 2).
Greene Selection, p 110 (MS 2).
Modernizations. Rickert Anc Eng Chr Carols, p 17
(MS 1).
Stevens Med Carols, p 36 (MS 2 with music).

Commentary. Greene Selection, p 221.
Greene E E Carols, 2nd edn, p 398.

[192] A LADY þAT WAS SO FEYRE
AND BRIʒT.

MS. Bodl 7589 (Ashmole 1393), f 69ᵇ (mid 15 cent).
Brown-Robbins, no 61.
Editions. Early Bodleian Music, 2.65.
Greene E E Carols, p 141; 2nd edn, p 125.
Brown RLxvC, p 34.
Modernization. Rickert Anc Eng Chr Carols, p 5.
Source. Of on þat is so fayr and briʒt (Brown-Robbins, no 2645).
Ch&Sidg, p 345.
Greene E E Carols, p 141; 2nd edn, p 120.
Hunt R W, Mediaeval and Renaissance Stud 5.54.
Quiller-Couch A, The Oxford Book of English Verse, Oxford 1939, p 11 (incomplete).
Sisam, p 13.
Stevick, p 15.
Commentary. Ch&Sidg, p 345.
Patterson, p 179.
Wehrle, pp 30, 101.
Greene E E Carols, pp cxxxiv, 392; 2nd edn, pp clxi, 399.
Manning S, Wisdom and Number, Lincoln Neb 1962, pp 8, 126.
Woolf, p 126.

[193] O CLOSED GATE OF EZECHIEL
(James Ryman).

MS. Camb Univ Ee.1.12, ff 14ᵇ–15ᵃ (ca 1492).
Brown-Robbins, no 2404.
Editions. Zupitza J, Arch 89.173.
Greene E E Carols, p 142; 2nd edn, p 126.
Commentary. Zupitza, Arch 93.307.
Greene E E Carols, p 392; 2nd edn, p 399.
Jeffrey D L, The Early English Lyric and Franciscan Spirituality, Lincoln Neb 1975, p 235.

[194] O CLOSED GATE OF EZECHIELL
(James Ryman).

MS. Camb Univ Ee.1.12, ff 15ᵃ–16ᵃ (ca 1492).
Brown-Robbins, no 2405.
Editions. Zupitza J, Arch 89.174.
Greene E E Carols, p 143; 2nd edn, p 127.
Commentary. Zupitza, Arch 93.313.
Greene E E Carols, p 392; 2nd edn, p 399.

[195] HAILE PERFECT TRONE OF
SALAMON (James Ryman).

MS. Camb Univ Ee.1.12, ff 16ᵃ–17ᵃ (ca 1492).
Brown-Robbins, no 1074.
Editions. Zupitza J, Arch 89.175.
Greene E E Carols, p 143; 2nd edn, p 127.
Commentary. Zupitza, Arch 93.317.

[196] O QUENE OF GRACE AND OF
CONFORTE (James Ryman).

MS. Camb Univ Ee.1.12, f 17ᵃ–17ᵇ (ca 1492).
Brown-Robbins, no 2543.
Editions. Zupitza J, Arch 89.176.
Greene E E Carols, p 144; 2nd edn, p 128.
Commentary. Zupitza, Arch 93.326.
Greene E E Carols, p 392; 2nd edn, p 399.

[197] SITH THY SONNE IS BOTH GOD
AND MAN (James Ryman).

MS. Camb Univ Ee.1.12, ff 17ᵇ–18ᵃ (ca 1492).
Brown-Robbins, no 3152.
Editions. Zupitza J, Arch 89.177.
Greene E E Carols, p 145; 2nd edn, p 129.
Commentary. Zupitza, Arch 93.328.
Greene E E Carols, 2nd edn, p 400.

[198] SITH CRISTE HATH TAKE BOTH
FLESSHE & BLODE (James Ryman).

MS. Camb Univ Ee.1.12, f 18ᵃ–18ᵇ (ca 1492).
Brown-Robbins, no 3123.
Editions. Zupitza J, Arch 89.178.
Greene E E Carols, p 145; 2nd edn, p 129.
Commentary. Zupitza, Arch 93.330.

[199] SITH OF RIGHT THOU MAYST
NOT FORSAKE (James Ryman).

MS. Camb Univ Ee.1.12, ff 18ᵇ–19ᵇ (ca 1492).
Brown-Robbins, no 3136.
Editions. Zupitza J, Arch 89.179.
Greene E E Carols, p 146; 2nd edn, p 129.
Commentary. Zupitza, Arch 93.334.
Greene E E Carols, p 393; 2nd edn, p 400.

[200] O QUENE OF MERCY AND OF
GRACE (James Ryman).

MS. Camb Univ Ee.1.12, ff 19ᵇ–20ᵇ (ca 1492).
Brown-Robbins, no 2544.
Editions. Zupitza J, Arch 89.180.

Greene E E Carols, p 146; 2nd edn, p 130.
Commentary. Zupitza, Arch 93.369.
Greene E E Carols, p 393; 2nd edn, p 400.

[201] O HEUENLY STERRE SO CLERE AND BRIGHT (James Ryman).

MS. Camb Univ Ee.1.12, ff 20b–21a (ca 1492).
Brown-Robbins, no 2460.
Editions. Zupitza J, Arch 89.181.
Greene E E Carols, p 147; 2nd edn, p 131.
Commentary. Zupitza, Arch 93.374.
Greene E E Carols, p 393; 2nd edn, p 400.

[202] ALL HEYLE MARY AND WELL YOU BE.

MS. Glasgow Univ Hunterian 83, f 21a (late 15 cent; music).
Brown-Robbins, Robbins-Cutler, no 182.
Editions. Robbins R H, MLN 58.41.
Greene E E Carols, 2nd edn, p 131.
Modernization. Stevens Med Carols, p 111 (with music).

[203] HAILE FUL OF GRACE CRISTE IS Wt THE (James Ryman).

MS. Camb Univ Ee.1.12, f 21b (ca 1492).
Brown-Robbins, no 1042.
Editions. Zupitza J, Arch 89.182.
Greene E E Carols, p 148; 2nd edn, p 131.
Commentary. Zupitza, Arch 93.378.
Wehrle, p 147.

[204] HAILE SPOWSE OF CRISTE OURE SAVIOURE (James Ryman).

MS. Camb Univ Ee.1.12, ff 22a–22b (ca 1492).
Brown-Robbins, no 1080.
Editions. Zupitza J, Arch 89.183.
Greene E E Carols, p 148; 2nd edn, p 132.
Commentary. Zupitza, Arch 93.379.

[205] AS AARON YERDE WtOUTE MOISTURE (James Ryman).

MS. Camb Univ Ee.1.12, ff 25a–26a (ca 1492).
Brown-Robbins, no 328.
Editions. Zupitza J, Arch 89.188.
Greene E E Carols, p 149; 2nd edn, p 132.
Commentary. Zupitza, Arch 93.395.
Greene E E Carols, p 393; 2nd edn, p 400.

[206] O QUENE OF BLISSE THY SON IHESUS (James Ryman).

MS. Camb Univ Ee.1.12, ff 78a–78b (ca 1492).
Brown-Robbins, Robbins-Cutler, no 2542.
Editions. Zupitza J, Arch 89.280.
Greene E E Carols, p 150; 2nd edn, p 133.
Commentary. Zupitza, Arch 96.173.
Greene E E Carols, p 393; 2nd edn, p 401.
Copley J, ESts 39.210.

[207] O QUENE OF PITEE AND OF GRACE (James Ryman).

MS. Camb Univ Ee.1.12, ff 79a–80a (ca 1492).
Brown-Robbins, no 2545.
Editions. Zupitza J, Arch 89.283.
Greene E E Carols, p 150; 2nd edn, p 133.
Commentary. Zupitza, Arch 96.175.
Greene E E Carols, p 393 (colophon naming Ryman as author of hymns and songs in the MS); 2nd edn, p 401.

[208] O BLYSSEDFULL BERD FULL OF GRACE.

MS. Bodl 29734 (Eng poet e.1), f 25b (mid 15 cent).
Brown-Robbins, no 2400.
Editions. Wright T, Carols, PPS 23.32.
Greene E E Carols, p 151; 2nd edn, p 134.
Modernization. Rickert Anc Eng Chr Carols, p 15.

[209] HAYLE OURE LOD STERRE BOTH BRIGHT & CLERE (James Ryman).

MS. Camb Univ Ee.1.12, ff 77b–78a (ca 1492).
Brown-Robbins, no 1072.
Editions. Zupitza J, Arch 89.278.
Greene E E Carols, p 152; 2nd edn, p 135.
Commentary. Zupitza, Arch 96.170.

[210] O IESSE YERDE FLORIGERAT (James Ryman).

MS. Camb Univ Ee.1.12, ff 87b–88a (ca 1492).
Brown-Robbins, Robbins-Cutler, no 2466.
Editions. Zupitza J, Arch 89.295.
Greene E E Carols, p 152; 2nd edn, p 135.
Commentary. Zupitza, Arch 96.320.

[211] O STRONGE IUDITH SO FULL
OF MYGHT (James Ryman).

MS. Camb Univ Ee.1.12, ff 88ª–88ᵇ (ca 1492).
Brown-Robbins, no 2559.
Editions. Zupitza J, Arch 89.297.
Greene E E Carols, p 153; 2nd edn, p 136.
Commentary. Zupitza, Arch 96.321.
Greene E E Carols, p 394; 2nd edn, p 401.

[212] O FAYRE RACHEL SEMELY IN
SYGHT (James Ryman).

MS. Camb Univ Ee.1.12, ff 88ᵇ–89ᵇ (ca 1492).
Brown-Robbins, no 2426.
Editions. Zupitza J, Arch 89.298.
Greene E E Carols, p 154; 2nd edn, p 136.
Commentary. Zupitza, Arch 96.322.
Greene E E Carols, p 394; 2nd edn, p 401.
Woolf, p 284.

[213] ADAM AND EVE THATTE WERE
VNWYSE (James Ryman).

MS. Camb Univ Ee.1.12, f 89ᵇ (ca 1492).
Brown-Robbins, no 116.
Editions. Zupitza J, Arch 89.299.
Greene E E Carols, p 154; 2nd edn, p 137.
Commentary. Zupitza, Arch 96.323.
Wehrle, p 148.

[214] O PRYNCES OF ETERNALL PEAS
(James Ryman).

MS. Camb Univ Ee.1.12, ff 97ª–97ᵇ (ca 1492).
Brown-Robbins, no 2540.
Editions. Zupitza J, Arch 89.312.
Greene E E Carols, p 155; 2nd edn, p 137.
Commentary. Zupitza, Arch 97.134.

[215] O UERY LYFE OF SWETNES AND
HOPE.

MSS. No MS extant. PRINT: Huntington Libr,
  Christmas carolles newely Inprynted (Richard
  Kele), p [44] (ca 1550; incomplete at end;
  STC, no 5205).
Robbins-Cutler, no 2577.3.
Editions. Reed Christmas Carols, p 62 (facsimile).
Greene E E Carols, p 155; 2nd edn, p 138.
Commentary. Reed Christmas Carols, p 89.
Greene E E Carols, p 394; 2nd edn, p 401.

[216] PERLES PRYNCES OF EUERY
PLACE (James Ryman).

MS. Camb Univ Ee.1.12, ff 9ª–10ª (ca 1492).
Brown-Robbins, no 2745.
Editions. Zupitza J, Arch 89.335.
Greene E E Carols, p 155; 2nd edn, p 138.
Commentary. Zupitza, Arch 97.149.

[217] CHILDRYN OF EVE BOTH
GRETE AND SMALL (James Ryman).

MS. Camb Univ Ee.1.12, ff 96ª–96ᵇ (ca 1492).
Brown-Robbins, no 597.
Editions. Zupitza J, Arch 89.311.
Greene E E Carols, p 156; 2nd edn, p 139.
Commentary. Zupitza, Arch 97.132.
Wehrle, p 152.

[218] O FLOURE OF ALL UIRGINITE
(James Ryman).

MS. Camb Univ Ee.1.12, ff 96ᵇ–97ª (ca 1492).
Brown-Robbins, no 2435.
Editions. Zupitza J, Arch 89.312.
Greene E E Carols, p 157; 2nd edn, p 139.
Commentary. Zupitza, Arch 97.133.

[219] O IESSE YERDE FLORIGERAT
(James Ryman).

MS. Camb Univ Ee.1.12, ff 102ª–102ᵇ (ca 1492).
Brown-Robbins, no 2467.
Editions. Zupitza J, Arch 89.320.
Greene E E Carols, p 157; 2nd edn, p 140.
Commentary. Zupitza, Arch 97.138.
Greene E E Carols, p 395; 2nd edn, p 402.

[220] REGINA CELI LETARE (James
Ryman).

MS. Camb Univ Ee.1.12, ff 101ª–101ᵇ (ca 1492).
Brown-Robbins, no 2801.
Editions. Zupitza J, Arch 89.319.
Greene E E Carols, p 158; 2nd edn, p 140.
Commentary. Zupitza, Arch 97.137.

[221] SITH THOU HAST BORN THE
KYNG OF GRACE (James Ryman).

MS. Camb Univ Ee.1.12, ff 103ᵇ–104ª (ca 1492).
Brown-Robbins, no 3148.
Editions. Zupitza J, Arch 89.323.
Greene E E Carols, p 158; 2nd edn, p 140.
Commentary. Zupitza, Arch 97.140.

[222] O MODER MYLDE MAYDE VNDEFYLDE (James Ryman).

MS. Camb Univ Ee.1.12, f 5ᵃ (ca 1492).
Brown-Robbins, no 2527.
Editions. Zupitza J, Arch 89.327.
Greene E E Carols, p 159; 2nd edn, p 141.
Modernization. Stevick, p 158.
Commentary. Zupitza, Arch 97.143.
Greene E E Carols, p 395; 2nd edn, p 402.

[223] O UIRGYN CHAST BOTH FURST AND LAST (James Ryman).

MS. Camb Univ Ee.1.12, ff 5ᵃ–5ᵇ (ca 1492).
Brown-Robbins, no 2578.
Editions. Zupitza J, Arch 89.328.
Greene E E Carols, p 159; 2nd edn, p 141.
Commentary. Zupitza, Arch 97.144.

[224] O LILLY FLOWRE OF SWETE ODOWRE (James Ryman).

MS. Camb Univ Ee.1.12, f 5ᵇ (ca 1492).
Brown-Robbins, no 2480.
Editions. Zupitza J, Arch 89.328.
Greene E E Carols, p 159; 2nd edn, p 141.
Commentary. Zupitza, Arch 97.144.
Wehrle, p 149.

[225] O SPOWSESSE MOST DERE MOST BRY3T MOST CLERE (James Ryman).

MS. Camb Univ Ee.1.12, ff 5ᵇ–6ᵃ (ca 1492).
Brown-Robbins, no 2554.
Editions. Zupitza J, Arch 89.328.
Greene E E Carols, p 160; 2nd edn, p 142.
Commentary. Zupitza, Arch 97.144.

[226] O TRYCLYN OF THE TRINITE (James Ryman).

MS. Camb Univ Ee.1.12, ff 6ᵃ–6ᵇ (ca 1492).
Brown-Robbins, no 2575.
Editions. Zupitza J, Arch 89.330.
Greene E E Carols, p 160; 2nd edn, p 142.
Commentary. Zupitza, Arch 97.145.
Greene E E Carols, p 395; 2nd edn, p 402.

[227] O SPOWSESS OF CRIST AND PARAMOUR (James Ryman).

MS. Camb Univ Ee.1.12, f 6ᵇ (ca 1492).
Brown-Robbins, no 2555.
Editions. Zupitza J, Arch 89.330.
Greene E E Carols, p 161; 2nd edn, p 142.
Commentary. Zupitza, Arch 97.145.

[228] O MEKE HESTER SO MYLDE OF MYNDE (James Ryman).

MS. Camb Univ Ee.1.12, f 7ᵃ (ca 1492).
Brown-Robbins, no 2508.
Editions. Zupitza J, Arch 89.331.
Greene E E Carols, p 161; 2nd edn, p 143.
Commentary. Zupitza, Arch 97.146.

[229] O BLESSID MAYDE MODER AND WYFFE (James Ryman).

MS. Camb Univ Ee.1.12, ff 7ᵃ–7ᵇ (ca 1492).
Brown-Robbins, no 2396.
Editions. Zupitza J, Arch 89.331.
Greene E E Carols, p 161; 2nd edn, p 143.
Commentary. Zupitza, Arch 97.147.

[230] SITH THOU HAST BORN THE KYNG OF GRACE (James Ryman).

MS. Camb Univ Ee.1.12, ff 7ᵇ–8ᵃ (ca 1492).
Brown-Robbins, no 3149.
Editions. Zupitza J, Arch 89.332.
Greene E E Carols, p 162; 2nd edn, p 143.
Commentary. Zupitza, Arch 97.147.

[231] O SWEETE LADY O UIRGYN PURE (James Ryman).

MS. Camb Univ Ee.1.12, ff 8ᵇ–9ᵃ (ca 1492).
Brown-Robbins, no 2563.
Editions. Zupitza J, Arch 89.334.
Greene E E Carols, p 162; 2nd edn, p 144.
Commentary. Zupitza, Arch 97.149.
Wehrle, p 154.

[232] GAUDE MARIA CRISTIS MODER (John Audelay?).

MSS. 1, Bodl 21876 (Douce 302), ff 31ᵇ, 30ᵃ (early 15 cent); 2, Balliol 354, f 219ᵃ (early 16 cent).
Brown-Robbins, no 895.
Editions. Flügel Fest R Hildebrand, p 56 (MS 2).
Flügel E, Angl 26.226 (MS 2).
Pollard 15CPV, p 84 (MS 2).
Dyboski R, EETSES 101.65 (MS 2).
Chambers E K and F Sidgwick, MLR 6.74 (MS 1).
Whiting E K, EETS 184.203 (MS 1).

Greene E E Carols, p 163 (MS 2 with collation of MS 1); 2nd edn, p 144.
Commentary. Husk W H, Songs of the Nativity, London 1868, p 87.
Whiting, EETS 184.253.
Wehrle, p 79.
Greene E E Carols, p 396; 2nd edn, p 403.
Woolf, p 297.

[233] ÞE FERSTE IOYE AS I ȜU TELLE.

MS. BM Sloane 2593, ff 9a–9b (mid 15 cent).
Brown-Robbins, no 3347.
Editions. Sandys W, Christmas Carols, London 1833, p 58.
Wright T, Carols, Publ Warton Club 4.26.
Fehr B, Arch 109.48.
Duncan E, The Story of the Carol, London 1911, p 166.
Greene E E Carols, p 164; 2nd edn, p 145.
Modernizations. Rickert Anc Eng Chr Carols, p 205.
Phillips W J, Carols: Their Origin, Music, and Connection with Mystery Plays, London [1921], p 91.
Commentary. Greene E E Carols, 2nd edn, p 403.
Wells E K, The Ballad Tree, N Y 1950, p 200.

[234] MARY FOR THE LOUE OF THE.

MSS. 1, Bodl 29734 (Eng poet e.1), f 45a (mid 15 cent); 2, Balliol 354, f 223b (early 16 cent); 3, St John's Camb 259 (S.54), ff 2a–2b (mid 15 cent).
Brown-Robbins, no 2098.
Editions. Wright T, Carols, PPS 23.68 (MS 1).
Flügel E, Angl 26.242 (MS 2).
Dyboski R, EETSES 101.15 (MS 2), 173 (collation of MS 1).
James M R and G C Macaulay, MLR 8.70 (MS 3).
Greene E E Carols, p 164; 2nd edn, p 145 (MSS 1–3).
Greene Selection, p 111 (MS 1).
Modernization. Watts N, Love Songs of Sion, London 1924, p 143 (MS 1; omits burden).
Commentary. Wehrle, p 78.
Greene Selection, p 221.

[235] GAUDE TO WHOM GABRYELL WAS SENT.

MS. Balliol 354, f 228b (early 16 cent).
Brown-Robbins, no 898.
Editions. Flügel E, Angl 26.257.
Dyboski R, EETSES 101.33.

Greene E E Carols, p 166; 2nd edn, p 147.
Modernization. Sayre E, A Christmas Book, N Y 1966, p 17.

[236] AS I LAY VPON A NYȜT.

MSS. 1, Bodl 3340 (Arch Selden B.26), f 13b (mid 15 cent; music); 2, Balliol 354, f 222a (early 16 cent); 3, Trinity Camb 1230 (0.3.58), no 3 (mid 15 cent; music); 4, BM Sloane 2593, f 30b (mid 15 cent).
Brown-Robbins, Robbins-Cutler, no 354.
Editions. Wright T, Carols, Publ Warton Club 4.88 (MS 4).
Fuller Maitland J A and W S Rockstro, English Carols of the 15th Century, London [1891], p 7 (MS 3 with music).
Early Bodleian Music, 2.119 (MS 1 with music).
Fehr B, Arch 109.68 (MS 4).
Flügel E, Angl 26.238 (MS 2).
Ch&Sidg, p 106 (MS 3).
Dyboski R, EETSES 101.12, 172 (MSS 2–4).
Padelford F M, Angl 36.93 (MSS 1–4).
Greene E E Carols, p 166; 2nd edn, p 147 (MSS 1–4).
Brown RLxvC, p 108 (MS 3).
Modernizations. Rickert Anc Eng Chr Carols, p 14 (MS 3).
Watts N, Love Songs of Sion, London 1924, p 122 (MS 3, in part; wrong MS reference).
Terry Med Carol Book, p 44 (MS 3 with music).
Stevens Med Carols, pp 3 (MS 3 with music), 16 (MS 1 with music).
Stevens J, Tidings True, London [1976], p 4 (MS 1 with music).
Commentary. Ch&Sidg, p 349.
Greene E E Carols, p 396; 2nd edn, p 404.

[237] THE HOLY GOST IS TO THE SENT.

MSS. 1, Bodl 3340 (Arch Selden B.26), f 23a (mid 15 cent; music); 2, Trinity Camb 1230 (0.3.58), no 1 (mid 15 cent; music). PRINT: 3, Huntington Libr, Christmas carolles newely Inprynted (Richard Kele), p [43] (ca 1550; STC, no 5205).
Brown-Robbins, Robbins-Cutler, no 3385.
Editions. Fuller Maitland J A and W S Rockstro, English Carols of the 15th Cent, London [1891], p 3 (MS 2 with music).
Early Bodleian Music, 2.144 (MS 1 with music).
Padelford F M, Angl 36.107 (MS 1).
Reed Christmas Carols, p 61 (facsimile of PRINT 3).
Greene E E Carols, p 168 (MS 1 with collation of MS 2 and PRINT 3); 2nd edn, p 148.

Brown RLxvC, p 110 (MS 1).
Greene Selection, p 112 (MS 1).
Modernizations. Rickert Anc Eng Chr Carols, p 12 (MS 1).
Terry Med Carol Book, pp 22 (MS 1 with music), 40 (MS 2 with music).
Stevens Med Carols, p 2 (MS 1 with music).
Robbins Christmas Carols, p 60 (MS 2 with music).
Commentary. Reed Christmas Carols, p 88.
Greene E E Carols, p 396; 2nd edn, p 404.
Stevens Med Carols, p 117.
Greene Selection, p 222.
Robbins Christmas Carols, p 60.

[238] NOWEL EL BOþE ELD & ȝYNG.

MS. BM Sloane 2593, ff 28b–29a (mid 15 cent).
Brown-Robbins, Robbins-Cutler, no 2384.
Editions. Wright T, Carols, PPS 4.15; Carols, Publ Warton Club 4.83.
Greene E E Carols, p 169; 2nd edn, p 149.
Modernizations. Rickert Anc Eng Chr Carols, p 28.
Sayre E, A Christmas Book, N Y 1966, p 15.
Commentary. Greene E E Carols, p 397; 2nd edn, p 404.

[239] GABRIELL THAT ANGELL BRYȝT.

MSS. 1, Bodl 29734 (Eng poet e.1), f 26a (mid 15 cent); 2, Balliol 354, f 221b (early 16 cent).
Brown-Robbins, Robbins-Cutler, no 890.
Editions. Wright T, Carols, PPS 23.33 (MS 1).
Flügel Fest R Hildebrand, p 65 (MS 2).
Flügel E, Angl 26.236 (MS 2).
Dyboski R, EETSES 101.10 (MS 2), 171 (collation of MS 1).
Greene E E Carols, p 169; 2nd edn, p 150 (MSS 1, 2).
Modernizations. Weston, p 8.
Rickert Anc Eng Chr Carols, p 29.
Segar M G, A Mediaeval Anthology, London 1915, p 85.

[240] GABRYELL OF HYȝE DEGREE.

MSS. 1, Bodl 29734 (Eng poet e.1), ff 27a–27b (mid 15 cent); 2, Balliol 354, f 219b (early 16 cent); 3, Glasgow Hunterian 83, f iiib (late 15 cent; music).
Brown-Robbins, no 889.
Editions. Wright T, Carols, PPS 23.36 (MS 1).
Flügel Fest R Hildebrand, p 58 (MS 2).
Flügel E, Angl 26.229 (MS 2).
Dyboski R, EETSES 101.5 (MS 2), 169 (collation of MS 1).
Frost L, Come Christmas, N Y 1935, p 264 (MS 2).
Greene E E Carols, p 170 (MSS 1, 2); 2nd edn, pp 150 (MSS 1, 2), 151 (MS 3).
Robbins R H, MLN 58.40 (MS 3).
Modernizations. Weston, p 5 (MS 2).
Rickert Anc Eng Chr Carols, p 30 (MS 2).
Stevens Med Carols, p 111 (MS 3 with music).
Robbins Christmas Carols, p 64 (MS 3 with music).
Greenberg N, An English Songbook, Garden City N Y 1961, p 66 (MS 3 with music).
Stevens J, Tidings True, London [1976], p 6 (MS 3 with music).
Commentary. Greene E E Carols, p 397; 2nd edn, p 405.
Stevens Med Carols, p 123.
Robbins Christmas Carols, p 64.

[241] TYDYNGES TREW þER BE CUM NEW.

MSS. 1a, Bodl 29734 (Eng poet e.1), f 41a (mid 15 cent); 1b, ibid, f 51b (music); 2, Balliol 354, f 229b (early 16 cent); 3, Yale Univ Libr 365 (formerly Brome), f 79b (late 15 cent).
Brown-Robbins, Robbins-Cutler, no 3736.
Editions. Wright T, Carols, PPS 23.62 (MSS 1a, 1b with music), 79.
Toulmin Smith L, A Common-place Book of the 15th Cent, [London] 1886, p 122 (MS 3).
Flügel Fest R Hildebrand, p 78 (MS 2).
Early Bodleian Music, 2.183 (MS 1b with music).
Flügel E, Angl 26.261 (MS 2).
Pollard 15CPV, p 93 (MS 2).
Dyboski R, EETSES 101.39 (MS 2), 177 (collation of MSS 1b, 3).
Greene E E Carols, p 171 (MS 1b with collation of MSS 1a, 2, 3); 2nd edn, p 152.
Greene Selection, p 113 (MS 1b).
Modernizations. Chappell W, Old English Popular Music, London 1893, p 30.
Weston, p 1 (MS 2).
Rickert Anc Eng Chr Carols, p 35 (MS 2).
Phillips W J, Carols: Their Origin, Music, and Connection with Mystery Plays, London [1921], pp 29 (MS 1a), 103 (MS 1b with music).
Watts N, Love Songs of Sion, London 1924, p 145 (MS 1a; omits burden).
Beeching, p 24 (MS 1a).
OBC, p 42 (MS 2); music edn, p 76 (MS 2, with misleading note); rvsd edn, p 70.
Terry Med Carol Book, p 30 (MS 1a with music).
Stevens Med Carols, p 110 (MS 1a with music).

Robbins Christmas Carols, p 62 (MS 1b with music).
Stevens J, Tidings True, London [1976], p 3 (MS 1b with music).
Commentary. Greene E E Carols, p 397; 2nd edn, p 405.
Stevens Med Carols, p 123.
Robbins Christmas Carols, p 62.
Greene Selection, p 222.

[242] FROM HEVYN WAS SENT AN ANGELL OF LIGHT.

MS. Balliol 354, f 219^b (early 16 cent).
Brown-Robbins, Robbins-Cutler, no 878.
Editions. Flügel Fest R Hildebrand, p 57.
Flügel NL, p 114.
Flügel E, Angl 26.228.
Dyboski R, EETSES 101.4.
Frost L, Come Christmas, N Y 1935, p 263.
Greene E E Carols, p 172; 2nd edn, p 153.
Modernizations. Rickert Anc Eng Chr Carols, p 32.
Weston, p 3.
Segar M G, A Mediaeval Anthology, London 1915, p 83; Some Minor Poems of the Middle Ages, London 1917, p 11.
Commentary. Wehrle, p 74.
Greene E E Carols, p 397; 2nd edn, p 405.

[243] I SHALL YOU TELL A GRET MERVAYLL.

MS. Balliol 354, f 230^b (early 16 cent).
Brown-Robbins, no 1363.
Editions. Flügel Fest R Hildebrand, p 79.
Flügel E, Angl 26.264.
Dyboski R, EETSES 101.44.
Greene E E Carols, p 173; 2nd edn, p 153.
Modernization. Rickert Anc Eng Chr Carols, p 34.
Commentary. Greene E E Carols, p 397; 2nd edn, p 405.

[244] MARY MODER MEKE & MYLDE.

MS. BM Sloane 2593, f 10^a (mid 15 cent).
Brown-Robbins, no 2113.
Editions. Sandys W, Christmas Carols, London 1833, p 7.
Wright T, Carols, PPS 4.7; Carols, Publ Warton Club 4.29.
Greene E E Carols, p 174; 2nd edn, p 154.
Greene Selection, p 114.
Modernization. Rickert Anc Eng Chr Carols, p 13.
Commentary. Wehrle, p 76.
Greene E E Carols, 2nd edn, p 405.
Greene Selection, p 222.

[245] THE AUNGELL SEYDE OF HIGH DEGREE (James Ryman).

MS. 1a, Camb Univ Ee.1.12, ff 11^a–11^b (ca 1492); 1b, ibid, ff 81^b–82^a.
Brown-Robbins, no 3304.
Editions. Zupitza J, Arch 89.167, 286 (MSS 1a, 1b).
Greene E E Carols, p 174 (MS 1a with collation of MS 1b); 2nd edn, p 154.
Commentary. Zupitza, Arch 93.281; 96.311.
Greene E E Carols, 2nd edn, p 406.

[246] THE AUNGELL SEIDE OF HIGH DEGREE (James Ryman).

MS. Camb Univ Ee.1.12, ff 11^b–12^b (ca 1492).
Brown-Robbins, no 3303.
Editions. Zupitza J, Arch 89.169.
Greene E E Carols, p 175; 2nd edn, p 155.
Commentary. Zupitza, Arch 93.294.

[247] HAYLE FULL OF GRACE CRISTE IS W^t THE (James Ryman).

MS. Camb Univ Ee.1.12, ff 12^b–13^b (ca 1492).
Brown-Robins, no 1043.
Editions. Zupitza J, Arch 89.170.
Greene E E Carols, p 176; 2nd edn, p 155.
Commentary. Zupitza, Arch 93.297.
Wehrle, p 147.

[248] AS LONGE BEFORE PROPHESY SEYDE (James Ryman).

MS. Camb Univ Ee.1.12, ff 40^b–41^b (ca 1492).
Brown-Robbins, no 398.
Editions. Zupitza J, Arch 89.208.
Greene E E Carols, p 177; 2nd edn, p 156.
Commentary. Zupitza, Arch 94.389.

[249] THE HIGH FADER OF BLISSE ABOVE (James Ryman).

MS. Camb Univ Ee.1.12, ff 67^b–68^a (ca 1492).
Brown-Robbins, no 3378.
Editions. Zupitza J, Arch 89.258.
Greene E E Carols, p 177; 2nd edn, p 157.
Commentary. Zupitza, Arch 95.396.
Greene E E Carols, p 398; 2nd edn, p 406.

[250] THAT ARCHAUNGELL SHYNYNG FULL BRIGHT (James Ryman).

MS. Camb Univ Ee.1.12, ff 68^a–68^b (ca 1492).
Brown-Robbins, no 3267.
Editions. Zupitza J, Arch 89.260.

Greene E E Carols, p 178; 2nd edn, p 157.
Commentary. Zupitza, Arch 95.398.
Greene E E Carols, p 398; 2nd edn, p 406.

[251] THUS TO HER SEIDE AN
AUNGELL THOO (James Ryman).

MS. Camb Univ Ee.1.12, f 77ᵃ (ca 1492).
Brown-Robbins, no 3726.
Editions. Zupitza J, Arch 89.277.
Greene E E Carols, p 179; 2nd edn, p 158.
Commentary. Zupitza, Arch 96.169.
Greene E E Carols, p 398; 2nd edn, p 406.

[252] AN ANGELLE THAT WAS FAYRE
AND BRYGHT (James Ryman).

MS. Camb Univ Ee.1.12, ff 82ᵃ–83ᵃ (ca 1492).
Brown-Robbins, no 283.
Editions. Zupitza J, Arch 89.288.
Greene E E Carols, p 179; 2nd edn, p 158.
Commentary. Zupitza, Arch 96.311.

[253] AN ANGELLE BRIGHT (James
Ryman).

MS. Camb Univ Ee.1.12, ff 83ᵃ–84ᵃ (ca 1492).
Brown-Robbins, no 278.
Editions. Zupitza J, Arch 89.289.
Greene E E Carols, p 180; 2nd edn, p 159.
Commentary. Zupitza, Arch 96.313.

[254] O MAN OF MOLDE (James
Ryman).

MS. Camb Univ Ee.1.12, ff 84ᵃ–85ᵃ (ca 1492).
Brown-Robbins, no 2501.
Editions. Zupitza J, Arch 89.291.
Greene E E Carols, p 181; 2nd edn, p 160.
Commentary. Zupitza, Arch 96.314.

[255] AN ANGELLE CAME VNTO
THATTE MAYDE (James Ryman).

MS. Camb Univ Ee.1.12, ff 85ᵃ–85ᵇ (ca 1492).
Brown-Robbins, no 279.
Editions. Zupitza J, Arch 89.292.
Greene E E Carols, p 181; 2nd edn, p 160.
Commentary. Zupitza, Arch 96.316.

[256] AN ANGELLE SEIDE TO THATTE
MEYDE SO FRE (James Ryman).

MS. Camb Univ Ee.1.12, ff 87ᵃ–87ᵇ (ca 1492).
Brown-Robbins, no 282.
Editions. Zupitza J, Arch 89.294.

Greene E E Carols, p 182; 2nd edn, p 160.
Commentary. Zupitza, Arch 96.319.
Greene E E Carols, p 399; 2nd edn, p 407.

[257] AN ANGELLE CAME WITH FULLE
GRETE LIGHT (James Ryman).

MS. Camb Univ Ee.1.12, f 10ᵃ (ca 1492).
Brown-Robbins, no 280.
Editions. Zupitza J, Arch 89.336.
Greene E E Carols, p 182; 2nd edn, p 161.
Commentary. Zupitza, Arch 97.151.
Greene E E Carols, p 399; 2nd edn, p 407.

[258] LORDES & LADYES ALL
BYDENE.

MSS. No MS extant. PRINT: Huntington Libr,
  Christmas carolles newely Inprynted (Richard
  Kele), p [26] (ca 1550; STC, no 5205).
Robbins-Cutler, no 1984.5.
Editions. [Bliss P,] Bibliographical Miscellanies,
  Oxford 1813, p 57.
Sandys W, Christmas Carols Ancient and Modern,
  London 1833, p 21.
Reed Christmas Carols, p 44 (facsimile).
Greene E E Carols, p 183; 2nd edn, p 161.
Commentary. Greene E E Carols, p 399; 2nd edn,
  p 407.

[259] THUS SEIDE MARY OF GRETE
HONOURE (James Ryman).

MS. Camb Univ Ee.1.12, ff 26ᵃ–27ᵃ (ca 1492).
Brown-Robbins, no 3725.
Editions. Zupitza J, Arch 89.189.
Greene E E Carols, p 183; 2nd edn, p 162.
Commentary. Zupitza, Arch 94.161.
Greene E E Carols, p 399; 2nd edn, p 407.

[260] IOSEPHE WOLDE HAUE FLED FRO
THAT MAYDE (James Ryman).

MS. Camb Univ Ee.1.12, ff 68ᵇ–69ᵃ (ca 1492).
Brown-Robbins, no 1802.
Editions. Zupitza J, Arch 89.260.
Greene E E Carols, p 184; 2nd edn, p 162.
Commentary. Zupitza, Arch 95.399.
Greene E E Carols, p 399; 2nd edn, p 407.

[261] I IOSEP WONDER HOW THIS MAY
BE.

MS. BM Addit 5665, ff 10ᵃ–11ᵃ (late 15 cent;
  music).
Brown-Robbins, Robbins-Cutler, no 1322.

Editions. Stafford Smith J, Musica Antiqua, London 1812, p 24 (with music).
Sandys W, Christmas Carols, Ancient and Modern, London 1833, p 13.
Wright T, Carols, PPS 4.52.
Fehr B, Arch 106.266.
Julian J, A Dictionary of Hymnology, 2nd edn, London 1925, p 209 (omits burden).
Greene E E Carols, p 185; 2nd edn, p 163.
Greene Selection, p 115.
Modernizations. Rickert Anc Eng Chr Carols, p 24.
Stevens Med Carols, p 68 (with music).
Sayre E, A Christmas Book, N Y 1966, p 23.
Stevens J, Tidings True, London [1976], p 16 (with music).
Commentary. Greene E E Carols, p 399; 2nd edn, p 407.
Greene Selection, p 222.

[262] CONCEYUED MAN HOW MAY THAT BE BY REASON BROGHT ABOWTE.

MS. BM Addit 20059, ff 6ᵇ–7ᵇ (late 15 cent). Transcript by Joseph Hunter in BM Addit 24542, f 178ᵇ (19 cent).
Brown-Robbins, Robbins-Cutler, no 651.
Editions. Greene E E Carols, p 185 (from Hunter's transcript); 2nd edn, p 164 (from original MS).
Brown RLxvC, p 184.
Commentary. Greene E E Carols, p 399; 2nd edn, p 407.
Brown RLxvC, p 330 (on identification of original MS by B N H Geary).

[263] VNDER A TRE.

MS. Bodl 29734 (Eng poet e.1), ff 47ᵇ–48ᵃ (mid 15 cent).
Brown-Robbins, no 3822.
Editions. Wright T, Carols, PPS 23.73.
Greene E E Carols, p 186; 2nd edn, p 164.
Greene Selection, p 116.
Modernizations. Rickert Anc Eng Chr Carols, p 20.
Davies, p 236.
Silverstein, p 114.
Commentary. Greene E E Carols, p 400; 2nd edn, p 408.
Greene Selection, p 223.
Davies, p 355.

[264] COME MY DERE SPOWSE AND LADY FREE (James Ryman).

MS. Camb Univ Ee.1.12, ff 22ᵇ–23ᵃ (ca 1492).

Brown-Robbins, no 641.
Editions. Zupitza J, Arch 89.184.
Greene E E Carols, p 187; 2nd edn, p 165.
Commentary. Zupitza, Arch 93.380.
Greene E E Carols, p 400; 2nd edn, p 408.
Woolf, p 299.

[265] THE KINGES BANER ON FELDE IS PLAYD.

MSS. No MS extant. PRINT: Huntington Libr, Christmas carolles newely Inprynted (Richard Kele), p [2] (ca 1550; STC, no 5205).
Brown-Robbins, Robbins-Cutler, no 3404; Robbins-Cutler, no 1119.
Editions. [Bliss P], Bibliographical Miscellanies, Oxford 1813, p 48.
Dyce A, The Poetical Works of John Skelton, London 1843 (and later printings), 1.144.
Reed Christmas Carols, p 20 (facsimile).
Greene E E Carols, p 189; 2nd edn, p 167.
Henderson P, The Complete Poems of John Skelton Laureate, 3rd edn, London 1959, p 16.
Commentary. Reed Christmas Carols, p 71.
Greene E E Carols, p 401; 2nd edn, p 409.

[266] FADYR I AM þIN OWYN CHYLDE.

MSS. 1, St John's Camb 259 (S.54), f 9ᵃ (mid 15 cent); 2, BM Addit 15233, f (3)hᵃ (mid 16 cent; burden and 23 6-line stanzas); 3, BM Addit 29372(7), f 8ᵇ (1616; music by Thomas Morley; 2 stanzas); 4, Folger Shakespeare Libr, Losely 58 (1589–92; 23 6-line stanzas).
Brown-Robbins, Robbins-Cutler, no 782.
Editions. Halliwell [-Phillipps] J O, The Moral Play of Wit and Science, Shakespeare Soc Publ no 37, London 1848, p 68 (MS 2).
James M R and G C Macaulay, MLR 8.79 (MS 1).
Greene E E Carols, p 190; 2nd edn, p 168 (MS 1).
Greene Selection, p 118 (MS 1).
Modernization. Comper Spir Songs, p 177.
Commentary. Greene E E Carols, p 401; 2nd edn, p 409.
Greene Selection, p 223 (MS 1).

[267] HAUE MYENDE FOR THE HOW I WAS BORNE (James Ryman).

MS. Camb Univ Ee.1.12, f 47ᵃ (ca 1492).
Brown-Robbins, no 1124.
Editions. Zupitza J, Arch 89.217.
Greene E E Carols, p 191; 2nd edn, p 168.
Commentary. Zupitza, Arch 94.406.
Greene E E Carols, p 401; 2nd edn, p 410.

[268] YF THOW THY LYFE IN SYNNE HAUE LEDDE (James Ryman).

MS. Camb Univ Ee.1.12, f 47ᵇ (ca 1492).
Brown-Robbins, no 1434.
Editions. Zupitza J, Arch 89.217.
Greene E E Carols, p 191; 2nd edn, p 168.
Commentary. Zupitza, Arch 94.407.
Greene E E Carols, p 401; 2nd edn, p 410.

[269] HAUE MYENDE HOWE I MANKYENDE HAUE TAKE (James Ryman).

MS. Camb Univ Ee.1.12, ff 47ᵇ–48ᵇ (2 additional stanzas at f 3ᵃ; ca 1492).
Brown-Robbins, no 1125.
Editions. Zupitza J, Arch 89.218, 337.
Greene E E Carols, p 192; 2nd edn, p 169.
Silverstein, p 117.
Modernizations. Comper Spir Songs, p 148.
Stevick, p 159.
Commentary. Zupitza, Arch 94.407.
Greene E E Carols, p 401; 2nd edn, p 410.

[270] MANKEND I CALE.

MS. BM Royal 17.B.xliii, ff 184ᵃ–184ᵇ (late 15 cent).
Brown-Robbins, Robbins-Cutler, no 2086.
Editions. Greene E E Carols, p 192; 2nd edn, p 170.
Greene Selection, p 118.
Modernizations. Davies, p 256.
Silverstein, p 117.
Commentary. Greene E E Carols, p 402; 2nd edn, p 410.
Greene Selection, p 224.
Silverstein, p 119 (rejects iconoclastic meaning stated by Greene).
Davies, p 359.

[271] ÞU SIKEST SORE.

MS. Advocates 18.7.21, f 124ᵇ (1372).
Brown-Robbins, Robbins-Cutler, no 3691.
Editions. Brown RLxivC, p 87.
Greene E E Carols, p 193; 2nd edn, p 170.
Sisam, p 198.
Davies, p 111.
Silverstein, p 62.
Modernizations. Comper Spir Songs, p 81.
Williams M, Glee-wood, N Y 1949, p 454.
Commentary. Brown RLxivC, p 267.
Greene E E Carols, p 402; 2nd edn, p 412.
Kane, p 136.

[272] FOR LOUE IS LOUE & EUER SCHAL BE (John Audelay).

MS. Bodl 21876 (Douce 302), f 30ᵇ (early 15 cent).
Brown-Robbins, no 831.
Editions. Chambers E K and F Sidgwick, MLR 6.79.
Whiting E K, EETS 184.210.
Greene E E Carols, p 193; 2nd edn, p 170.
Sisam, p 390.
Modernization. Comper Spir Songs, p 77.
Commentary. Whiting, EETS 184.xviii.
Greene E E Carols, p 402; 2nd edn, p 412.

[273] O WORTHY LORD & MOST OF MYGHT.

MS. Balliol 354, f 223ᵃ (early 16 cent).
Brown-Robbins, no 2586.
Editions. Flügel Fest R Hildebrand, p 68.
Flügel E, Angl 26.241.
Dyboski R, EETSES 101.14.
Greene E E Carols, p 194; 2nd edn, p 171.
Modernization. Rickert Anc Eng Chr Carols, p 184.
Commentary. Dyboski, EETSES 101.173.
Wehrle, p 102.

[274] GOD þᵗ ALL THIS WORD HAS WRO3TH.

MS. St John's Camb 259 (S.54), f 10ᵃ (mid 15 cent).
Brown-Robbins, no 972.
Editions. James M R and G C Macaulay, MLR 8.81.
Greene E E Carols, p 194; 2nd edn, p 171.

[275] O SWEETE IHESU SO MEKE AND MYLDE (James Ryman).

MS. Camb Univ Ee.1.12, f 8ᵇ (ca 1492).
Brown-Robbins, no 2561.
Editions. Zupitza J, Arch 89.333.
Greene E E Carols, p 195; 2nd edn, p 172.
Commentary. Zupitza, Arch 97.148.
Wehrle, p 155.

[276] O KING OF GRACE AND INDULGENCE (James Ryman).

MS. Camb Univ Ee.1.12, ff 46ᵇ–47ᵃ (ca 1492).
Brown-Robbins, Robbins-Cutler, no 2476.
Editions. Zupitza J, Arch 89.216.
Greene E E Carols, p 195; 2nd edn, p 172.
Commentary. Zupitza, Arch 94.404.

Greene E E Carols, p 403; 2nd edn, p 412.

[277] GLORIUS GOD IN TRINITE.

MS. BM Addit 5665, ff 32ᵇ–33ᵃ (late 15 cent).
Brown-Robbins, Robbins-Cutler, no 918.
Editions. Fehr B, Arch 106.272.
Patterson, p 71.
Greene E E Carols, p 196; 2nd edn, p 172.
Modernizations. Rickert Anc Eng Chr Carols, p 183.
Stevens Med Carols, p 90 (with music).
Commentary. Patterson, p 170.
Greene E E Carols, p 403; 2nd edn, p 412.

[278] MOOST SOUERAYN LORDE CHRYSTE [JESU].

MSS. No MS extant. PRINT: Huntington Libr, Christmas carolles newely Inprynted (Richard Kele), p [47] (ca 1550; STC, no 5205).
Robbins-Cutler, no 2217.5.
Editions. Reed Christmas Carols, p 65 (facsimile).
Greene E E Carols, p 196; 2nd edn, p 173.
Commentary. Greene E E Carols, p 403; 2nd edn, p 413.

[279] O ORIENT LIGHT SHYNYNG MOOST BRYGHT (James Ryman).

MS. Camb Univ Ee.1.12, ff 36ᵃ–37ᵃ (ca 1492).
Brown-Robbins, no 2534.
Editions. Zupitza J, Arch 89.202.
Greene E E Carols, p 196; 2nd edn, p 173.
Commentary. Zupitza, Arch 94.196.
Greene E E Carols, p 403; 2nd edn, p 413.

[280] FADER & SON AND HOLY GOST.

MS. BM Egerton 3307, f 55ᵃ (mid 15 cent; music).
Robbins-Cutler, no 772.5.
Editions. Greene Selection, p 120.
Greene E E Carols, 2nd edn, p 174.
Modernization. Stevens Med Carols, p 40 (with music).
Commentary. Greene Selection, p 225.
Greene E E Carols, 2nd edn, p 413.

[281] I LOUE A LOUER THAT LOUETH ME WELL (James Ryman).

MS. Camb Univ Ee.1.12, f 42ᵇ (ca 1492).
Brown-Robbins, no 1328.
Editions. Zupitza J, Arch 89.210.
Greene E E Carols, p 197; 2nd edn, p 174.
Modernization. Comper Spir Songs, p 99.

Commentary. Zupitza, Arch 94.392.
Greene E E Carols, p 403; 2nd edn, p 413.

[282] ADAM AND EVE DID GEVE CONCENT (James Ryman).

MS. Camb Univ Ee.1.12, ff 43ᵇ–44ᵃ (ca 1492).
Brown-Robbins, no 115.
Editions. Zupitza J, Arch 89.211.
Greene E E Carols, p 198; 2nd edn, p 174.
Commentary. Zupitza, Arch 94.396.
Greene E E Carols, p 403; 2nd edn, p 413.

[283] AN AUNGELL FRO HEVYN GAN LYTH.

MS. Bodl 29734 (Eng poet e.1), f 31ᵃ (mid 15 cent).
Brown-Robbins, no 281.
Editions. Wright T, Carols, PPS 23.45.
Breul K, EStn 14.404.
Greene E E Carols, p 198; 2nd edn, p 175.
Commentary. Greene E E Carols, p 403; 2nd edn,

[284] O LORDE BY WHOME AL THING IS WROUGHT (James Ryman).

MS. Camb Univ Ee.1.12, ff 44ᵇ–45ᵃ (ca 1492).
Brown-Robbins, no 2485.
Editions. Zupitza J, Arch 89.213.
Greene E E Carols, p 199; 2nd edn, p 175.
Commentary. Zupitza, Arch 94.399.

[285] O FADER Wᵗ OUTE BEGYNNYNG (James Ryman).

MS. Camb Univ Ee.1.12, ff 50ᵃ–50ᵇ (ca 1492).
Brown-Robbins, no 2432.
Editions. Zupitza J, Arch 89.222.
Greene E E Carols, p 199; 2nd edn, p 176.
Greene Selection, p 120.
Modernization. Comper Spir Songs, p 178.
Commentary. Zupitza, Arch 94.415.
Greene E E Carols, p 404; 2nd edn, p 414.
Greene Selection, p 226.

[286] THY CREATURES TERRESTRIALL (James Ryman).

MS. Camb Univ Ee.1.12, ff 59ᵃ–59ᵇ (ca 1492).
Brown-Robbins, no 3728.
Editions. Zupitza J, Arch 89.240.
Greene E E Carols, p 200; 2nd edn, p 176.
Commentary. Zupitza, Arch 95.276.
Wehrle, p 157.

Greene E E Carols, p 404; 2nd edn, p 414.

[287] O GOD & MAN SEMPITERNALL (James Ryman).

MS. Camb Univ Ee.1.12, ff 59^b–60^a (ca 1492).
Brown-Robbins, no 2448.
Editions. Zupitza J, Arch 89.241.
Greene E E Carols, p 200; 2nd edn, p 177.
Commentary. Zupitza, Arch 95.277.
Greene E E Carols, p 404; 2nd edn, p 414.

[288] O FADER OF HIGH MAIESTE (James Ryman).

MS. Camb Univ Ee.1.12, f 60^b (ca 1492).
Brown-Robbins, no 2431.
Editions. Zupitza J, Arch 89.243.
Greene E E Carols, p 201; 2nd edn, p 177.
Commentary. Zupitza, Arch 95.280.
Greene E E Carols, p 404; 2nd edn, p 414.

[289] FADER AND SONNE & HOLI GOOST (James Ryman).

MS. Camb Univ Ee.1.12, ff 60^b–61^a (ca 1492).
Brown-Robbins, no 781.
Editions. Zupitza J, Arch 89.244.
Greene E E Carols, p 202; 2nd edn, p 178.
Commentary. Zupitza, Arch 95.281.

[290] THE HIGH FADER OF BLISSE ABOUE (James Ryman).

MS. Camb Univ Ee.1.12, f 61^a (ca 1492).
Brown-Robbins, no 3379.
Editions. Zupitza J, Arch 89.245.
Greene E E Carols, p 202; 2nd edn, p 178.
Commentary. Zupitza, Arch 95.282.
Greene E E Carols, p 404; 2nd edn, p 414.

[291] THE FATHER OF HEUYN FROM ABOUE (James Ryman).

MS. Camb Univ Addit 7350, Box 2, f 1^a (late 15 cent).
Robbins-Cutler, no 3328.5.
Editions. Robbins R H, PMLA 81.309.
Greene E E Carols, 2nd edn, p 179.
Commentary. Robbins, PMLA 81.308.
Greene E E Carols, 2nd edn, p 415.

[292] OF A MAYDE CRISTE DID NOT FORSAKE (James Ryman).

MS. Camb Univ Ee.1.12, ff 61^a–61^b (ca 1492).
Brown-Robbins, no 2603.
Editions. Zupitza J, Arch 89.246.
Greene E E Carols, p 203; 2nd edn, p 179.
Commentary. Zupitza, Arch 95.284.

[293] O FADER OF ETERNALL BLYS (James Ryman).

MS. Camb Univ Ee.1.12, f 90^a (ca 1492).
Brown-Robbins, no 2429.
Editions. Zupitza J, Arch 89.299.
Greene E E Carols, p 203; 2nd edn, p 180.
Commentary. Zupitza, Arch 96.324.
Wehrle, p 156.

[294] O ENDLES GOD OF MAGESTE (James Ryman).

MS. Camb Univ Ee.1.12, ff 90^a–90^b (ca 1492).
Brown-Robbins, no 2419.
Editions. Zupitza J, Arch 89.300.
Greene E E Carols, p 204; 2nd edn, p 180.
Commentary. Zupitza, Arch 96.324.

[295] FADERE OF BLISSE OMNIPOTENT (James Ryman).

MS. Camb Univ Ee.1.12, ff 90^b–91^a (ca 1492).
Brown-Robbins, no 785.
Editions. Zupitza J, Arch 89.301.
Greene E E Carols, p 204; 2nd edn, p 181.
Commentary. Zupitza, Arch 96.325.
Greene E E Carols, p 405; 2nd edn, p 415.

[296] O ENDLES GOD OF MAIESTE (James Ryman).

MS. Camb Univ Ee.1.12, ff 91^a–91^b (ca 1492).
Brown-Robbins, no 2417.
Editions. Zupitza J, Arch 89.301.
Greene E E Carols, p 205; 2nd edn, p 181.
Commentary. Zupitza, Arch 96.325.

[297] THE SONNE OF GOD THATTE ALL HATH WROUGHT (James Ryman).

MS. Camb Univ Ee.1.12, f 91^b (ca 1492).
Brown-Robbins, no 3471.
Editions. Zupitza J, Arch 89.302.
Greene E E Carols, p 205; 2nd edn, p 181.
Commentary. Zupitza, Arch 96.326.
Greene E E Carols, p 405; 2nd edn, p 415.
Woolf, p 306.

[298] O ENDLES GOD OF MAIESTE
(James Ryman).

MS. Camb Univ Ee.1.12, ff 92ª–92ᵇ (ca 1492).
Brown-Robbins, no 2418.
Editions. Zupitza J, Arch 89.303.
Greene E E Carols, p 205; 2nd edn, p 182.
Commentary. Zupitza, Arch 96.326.
Greene E E Carols, p 405; 2nd edn, p 415.

[299] O SWETE IHESU WE KNOWLEGE
THIS (James Ryman).

MS. Camb Univ Ee.1.12, ff 92ᵇ–93ª (ca 1492).
Brown-Robbins, no 2562.
Editions. Zupitza J, Arch 89.304.
Greene E E Carols, p 206; 2nd edn, p 182.
Commentary. Zupitza, Arch 96.327.
Wehrle, p 162.
Greene E E Carols, p 405; 2nd edn, p 415.
Woolf, p 306.

[300] O FADER OF HIGH MAIESTE
(James Ryman).

MS. Camb Univ Ee.1.12, f 93ª (ca 1492).
Brown-Robbins, no 2430.
Editions. Zupitza J, Arch 89.305.
Greene E E Carols, p 207; 2nd edn, p 183.
Commentary. Zupitza, Arch 96.328.

[301] THE SONNE OF GOD OURE
LORDE IHESUS (James Ryman).

MS. Camb Univ Ee.1.12, f 93ª–93ᵇ (ca 1492).
Brown-Robbins, no 3469.
Editions. Zupitza J, Arch 89.306.
Greene E E Carols, p 207; 2nd edn, p 183.
Commentary. Zupitza, Arch 96.329.

[302] THE FADERS SONNE OF HEUEN
BLIS (James Ryman).

MS. Camb Univ Ee.1.12, f 93ᵇ (ca 1492).
Brown-Robbins, no 3333.
Editions. Zupitza J, Arch 89.306.
Greene E E Carols, p 207; 2nd edn, p 184.
Commentary. Zupitza, Arch 96.329.
Woolf, p 306.

[303] THE SONNE OF GOD HATH
TAKE NATURE (James Ryman).

MS. Camb Univ Ee.1.12, ff 94ª–94ᵇ (ca 1492).
Brown-Robbins, no 3468.

Editions. Zupitza J, Arch 89.307.
Greene E E Carols, p 208; 2nd edn, p 184.
Commentary. Zupitza, Arch 97.129.
Greene E E Carols, p 405; 2nd edn, p 416.
Woolf, p 306.

[304] TO CRIST IHESU THATTE
LORDE AND KYNG (James Ryman).

MS. Camb Univ Ee.1.12, ff 93ᵇ–94ª (ca 1492).
Brown-Robbins, no 3751.
Editions. Zupitza J, Arch 89.307.
Greene E E Carols, p 208; 2nd edn, p 184.
Commentary. Zupitza, Arch 96.330.
Greene E E Carols, p 405; 2nd edn, p 416.

[305] ETERNALL GOD FADER OF
LIGHT (James Ryman).

MS. Camb Univ Ee.1.12, ff 94ᵇ–95ª (ca 1492).
Brown-Robbins, no 731.
Editions. Zupitza J, Arch 89.308.
Greene E E Carols, p 209; 2nd edn, p 185.
Commentary. Zupitza, Arch 97.130.
Greene E E Carols, p 406; 2nd edn, p 416.
Woolf, p 306.

[306] O ENDLES GOD BOTHE IIJ AND
ONE (James Ryman).

MS. Camb Univ Ee.1.12, f 95ᵇ (ca 1492).
Brown-Robbins, no 2416.
Editions. Zupitza J, Arch 89.310.
Greene E E Carols, p 210; 2nd edn, p 185.
Commentary. Zupitza, Arch 97.131.
Greene E E Carols, p 406; 2nd edn, p 416.

[307] O HIGHE FADER OF HEUEN
BLYS (James Ryman).

MS. Camb Univ Ee.1.12, f 8ª (ca 1492).
Brown-Robbins, no 2462.
Editions. Zupitza J, Arch 89.333.
Greene E E Carols, p 210; 2nd edn, p 186.
Commentary. Zupitza, Arch 97.148.

[308] I HAUE Y-SO3TE IN MANY A
SYDE.

MS. BM 5665, ff 46ᵇ–47ª (late 15 cent; music).
Brown-Robbins, no 1315.
Editions. Flügel NL, p 113.
Greene E E Carols, p 210; 2nd edn, p 186.
Modernization. Stevens Med Carols, p 104 (with music).

Commentary. Greene E E Carols, p 406; 2nd edn, p 416.

[309] O GOD WE PRAY TO THE IN SPECYALL.

MS. BM Addit 5665, ff 51ᵇ–52ᵃ (late 15 cent; music).
Brown-Robbins, no 2453.
Editions. Fehr B, Arch 106.278.
Greene E E Carols, p 211; 2nd edn, p 186.
Modernization. Stevens Med Carols, p 108 (with music).
Commentary. Greene E E Carols, p 406; 2nd edn, p 416.

[310] WHY SITTIST þOU SO SYNGYNG þENKYST þOU NOTHYNG.

MS. Rylands Libr Lat 395 (formerly 18932), f 119ᵇ (15 cent).
Brown-Robbins, Robbins-Cutler, no 4163.
Editions. Brydges E, Censura Literaria, London 1805, 8.401.
Greene E E Carols, p 211; 2nd edn, p 187.
Brown RLxvC, p 254.
Commentary. Greene E E Carols, p 406; 2nd edn, p 416.
Brown RLxvC, p 342.

[311] IHESUS FOR THI HOLY NAME.

MS. Bodl 29734 (Eng poet e.1), ff 49ᵃ–50ᵃ (mid 15 cent).
Brown-Robbins, no 1704.
For 11 other MSS containing the first stanza, the prayer by the Holy Name, see Brown-Robbins, no 1703.
Editions. Wright T, Carols, PPS 23.76.
Patterson, p 68.
Greene E E Carols, p 212 (with collation of 9 other MSS); 2nd edn, p 187 (with collation of 10 other MSS).
Commentary. Patterson, p 169.
Greene E E Carols, p 407; 2nd edn, pp xxvii, 417.
Manning S, Wisdom and Number, Lincoln Neb 1962, p 64.
Gray D, N&Q 212.131.
Hirsh J C, N&Q 215.44.

[312] A HOLE CONFESSOURE þᵘ WERE HONE (John Audelay).

MS. Bodl 21876 (Douce 302), f 32ᵃ (early 15 cent).
Brown-Robbins, no 44.
Editions. Chambers E K and F Sidgwick, MLR 6.81.
Whiting E K, EETS 184.212.
Greene E E Carols, p 213; 2nd edn, p 188.
Greene Selection, p 122.
Commentary. Whiting, EETS 184.255.
Greene E E Carols, pp cxxvii, 407; 2nd edn, pp clvi, 417.
Greene Selection, p 226.

[313] SWETE SAYNT ANNE WE þE BESECHE (John Audelay).

MS. Bodl 21876 (Douce 302), f 31ᵃ (early 15 cent).
Brown-Robbins, no 3244.
Editions. Chambers E K and F Sidgwick, MLR 6.71.
Whiting E K, EETS 184.200.
Greene E E Carols, p 214; 2nd edn, p 189.
Commentary. Whiting, EETS 184.253.
Greene E E Carols, pp cxxxviii, 407; 2nd edn, pp clxv, 418.
Woolf, p 297.

[314] WORSCHIP OF VERTU YS þE MEDE.

MS. BM Egerton 3307, f 63ᵇ (mid 15 cent; music).
Robbins-Cutler, no 4229.5.
Editions. Schofield B, Musical Quart 32.513.
Copley J, N&Q 203.239.
Greene Selection, p 124.
Greene E E Carols, 2nd edn, p 190.
Modernizations. Stevens Med Carols, p 49 (with music).
Davies, p 185.
Commentary. Greene Selection, p 227.
Greene E E Carols, 2nd edn, p 418.

[315] A NEWE SONG I WIL BEGYNNE.

MS. BM Sloane 2593, ff 25ᵇ–26ᵃ (mid 15 cent).
Brown-Robbins, no 80.
Editions. The Suffolk Garland, Ipswich 1818, pp 349, 351.
Ritson AS 1790, p 84; 1829, 1.143; 1877, p 123.
Wright T, Songs and Carols, London 1836, no 13; Carols, Publ Warton Club 4.73.
Greene E E Carols, p 215; 2nd edn, p 190.
Greene Selection, p 124.
Modernization. Duncan E, The Story of the Carol, London 1911, p 66.
Commentary. Greene E E Carols, p 408; 2nd edn, p 419.

Greene Selection, p 228.

[316] LYSTYN LORDYNGYS QWATTE I XALL SAY.

MS. St John's Camb 259 (S.54), ff 3ᵃ–3ᵇ (mid 15 cent).
Brown-Robbins, no 1900.
Editions. James M R and G C Macaulay, MLR 8.71.
Greene E E Carols, p 215; 2nd edn, p 191.
Commentary. Greene E E Carols, p 408; 2nd edn, p 420.

[317] ALS þᵘ WERE MARTER & MAYD CLENE (John Audelay).

MS. Bodl 21876 (Douce 302), ff 26ᵃ–26ᵇ (early 15 cent).
Brown-Robbins, no 413.
Editions. Whiting E K, EETS 184.171.
Greene E E Carols, p 216; 2nd edn, p 191.
Commentary. Gerould S Leg, p 256.
Whiting, EETS 184.247.
Greene E E Carols, p 408; 2nd edn, p 420.

[318] SEYNT NICHOLAS WAS OF GRET POSTE.

MS. BM Sloane 2593, f 2ᵇ (mid 15 cent).
Brown-Robbins, no 3034.
Editions. Wright T, Songs and Carols, London 1836, no 2; Carols, Publ Warton Club 4.4.
Greene E E Carols, p 218; 2nd edn, p 193.
Commentary. Wright, Carols, Publ Warton Club 4.105
Greene E E Carols, p 409; 2nd edn, p 421.

[319] IN PATRAS þER BORN HE WAS.

MS. BM Sloane 2593, f 34ᵃ (mid 15 cent).
Brown-Robbins, no 1522.
Editions. Wright T, Songs and Carols, London 1856, no 19; Carols, Publ Warton Club 4.99.
Greene E E Carols, p 218; 2nd edn, p 193.
Greene Selection, p 125.
Commentary. Greene E E Carols, p 410; 2nd edn, p 421.
Greene Selection, p 229.

[320] IT IS BRED FRO HEUENE CAM.

MS. BM Sloane 2593, ff 21ᵇ–22ᵃ (mid 15 cent).
Brown-Robbins, no 1627.
Editions. Wright T, Carols, Publ Warton Club 4.60.

Fehr B, Arch 109.62.
Greene E E Carols, p 219; 2nd edn, p 193.
Brown RLxvC, p 180.
Modernization. Comper Spir Songs, p 245.
Commentary. Greene E E Carols, p 410; 2nd edn, p 422.

[321] THIS BREDE GEVETH ETERNALL LYFE (James Ryman).

MS. Camb Univ Ee.1.12, ff 49ᵇ–50ᵃ (ca 1492).
Brown-Robbins, Robbins-Cutler, no 3583.
Editions. Zupitza J, Arch 89.221.
Greene E E Carols, p 219; 2nd edn, p 194.
Greene Selection, p 126.
Modernization. Comper Spir Songs, p 247.
Commentary. Zupitza, Arch 94.413.
Greene E E Carols, p 410; 2nd edn, p 422.
Robbins R H, MP 36.344.
Greene Selection, p 230.
Manning S, Wisdom and Number, Lincoln Neb 1962, p 140.
Jeffrey D L, The Early English Lyric and Franciscan Spirituality, Lincoln Neb 1975, p 237.

[322] MAN þᵗ IN ERTH ABYDYS HERE.

MS. Balliol 354, f 223ᵃ (early 16 cent).
Brown-Robbins, Robbins-Cutler, no 2076.
Editions. Dyboski R, EETSES 101.14.
Greene E E Carols, p 220; 2nd edn, p 194.
Modernizations. Segar M G, A Mediaeval Anthology, London 1915, p 40 (in part).
Comper Spir Songs, p 241.
Watts N, Love Songs of Sion, London 1924, p 21 (in part).
Commentary. Greene E E Carols, p 410; 2nd edn, p 422.

[323] QWETE IS BOTHE SEMELY AND SOTE.

MS. BM Sloane 2593, f 13ᵇ (mid 15 cent).
Brown-Robbins, Robbins-Cutler, no 3920.
Editions. Wright T, Carols, Publ Warton Club 4.38.
Fehr B, Arch 109.53.
Greene E E Carols, p 220; 2nd edn, p 195.
Modernization. Comper Spir Songs, p 249.
Commentary. Greene E E Carols, p 411; 2nd edn, p 422.

[324] ON CRISTIS DAY I VNDERSTOND.

MS. Balliol 354, f 228ᵇ (early 16 cent).

Brown-Robbins, no 2681.
Editions. Flügel NL, p 112.
Flügel E, Angl 26.258.
Dyboski R, EETSES 101.34.
Greene E E Carols, p 221; 2nd edn, p 195.
Greene Selection, p 127.
Modernizations. Rickert Anc Eng Chr Carols, p 186.
Comper Spir Songs, p 95.
Commentary. Greene E E Carols, p 411; 2nd edn, p 423.
Greene Selection, p 230.
Manning S, Wisdom and Number, Lincoln Neb 1962, pp 112, 175.

[325] HE BARE HYM VP HE BARE HYM DOWN.

MS. Balliol 354, f 165ᵇ (early 16 cent).
Brown-Robbins, no 1132.
Editions. Flügel NL, p 142.
Flügel E, Angl 26.175.
Ch&Sidg, p 148.
Dyboski R, EETSES 101.103.
Gilchrist A G, Journ of the Folk-Song Soc 4.53.
CHEL, 2.433.
Segar M G, A Mediaeval Anthology, London 1915, p 35.
Cook A S, A Literary ME Reader, Boston 1915, p 440.
OBC, music edn, p 127; rvsd edn, p 134.
Greene E E Carols, p 221; 2nd edn, p 195.
Greg W W, RES 13.8.
Quiller-Couch A, The Oxford Book of English Verse, Oxford 1939, p 36.
Williams M, Glee-wood, London 1940, p 459.
Cecil Lord D, The Oxford Book of Christian Verse, Oxford 1940, p 43.
Chambers OHEL, p 111.
Leach M, The Ballad Book, N Y 1953, p 692.
Speirs J, Medieval English Poetry: The Non-Chaucerian Tradition, London 1957, p 76.
Mason H A, Humanism and Poetry in the Early Tudor Period, London 1959, p 146.
Greene Selection, p 128.
Davies, p 272.
Stevick, p 171.
Sisam, p 524.
Fowler D C, A Literary History of the Popular Ballad, Durham N C 1968, p 58.
Tydeman W, English Poetry 1400–1580, London 1970. p 53.
Oliver, p 108.
Grigson G, The Faber Book of Popular Verse, London 1971, p 308.
Owen L J and N H, Middle English Poetry: An Anthology, Indianapolis Ind 1971, p 16.

Gray D, Themes and Images in the Medieval English Religious Lyric, London 1972, p 104.
Luria & Hoffman, p 221.
French Translation. Dubois M–M, La Littérature anglaise du Moyen Âge, Paris 1962, p 132.
Traditional Versions. 1, "Over yonder's a park."
ETK, N&Q 3s 2.103.
Rickert Anc Eng Chr Carols, p 194.
Journ of the Folk-Song Soc 4.53.
OBC, p 222; music edn, p 402; rvsd edn, p 392 (with music by Martin Shaw).
Greene E E Carols, p 222; 2nd edn, p 196.
Greene Selection, p 128.

2, "Down in yon forest."
Vaughan Williams R, Eight Traditional Carols, London 1919, p 14 (with music); Journ of the Folk-Song Soc 4.63 (with music).
OBC, p 81; music edn, p 126; rvsd edn, p 134. (with music).
Greene E E Carols, p 222; 2nd edn, p 196.
Nettel R, Sing a Song of England, London 1954, p 65 (inaccurate).
Greene Selection, p 129.

3, "The heron flew east, the heron flew west."
Hogg J, The Mountain Bard, Edinburgh 1807, p 13.
Batho E C, E&S 9.93; The Ettrick Shepherd, Cambridge 1927, p 30.
Greene E E Carols, p 222; 2nd edn, p 126.
Mason H A, Humanism and Poetry in the Early Tudor Period, London 1959, p 147.
Greene Selection, p 130.

4, "Down in yon forest be a hall."
G[ilchrist] A G, Journ of the English Folk Dance and Song Soc 4.122 (with music).
Greene E E Carols, 2nd edn, p 197.
Brice D, The Folk-Carol of England, London 1967, p 72 (with music).
Modernizations. Rickert Anc Eng Chr Carols, p 193.
Segar M G, A Mediaeval Anthology, London 1915, p 35.
Comper Spir Songs, p 106.
Loomis R S and R Willard, Medieval English Verse and Prose, N Y 1948, p 392.
Commentary. Sidgwick F, N&Q 10s 4.181.
Ch&Sidg, p 357.
Gilchrist A G, F Sidgwick, R Vaughan Williams, J A Fuller Maitland, and G R S Mead, Journ of the Folk-Song Soc 4.52.
Batho E C, The Life of Christ in the Ballads, E&S 9.93.
Gerould G H, The Ballad of Tradition, Oxford 1932, pp 33, 124.

Le May Sister M de L, The Allegory of the Christ-Knight in English Literature, Washington 1932, p 65.
Greene E E Carols, pp xciv, 411; 2nd edn, pp lxx, lxxi, 423.
Chambers OHEL, p 112.
Kane, p 174.
Berry F, A Medieval Poem and Its Secularized Derivative, Essays in Criticism, 5.299; Poets' Grammar, London 1958, chap 2, pt 3, appendix 1.
Nettel R, Sing a Song of England, London 1954, p 64.
Speirs J, Medieval English Poetry: The Non-Chaucerian Tradition, London 1957, p 76.
Routley E, The English Carol, London 1958, p 61.
Bronson B H, The Traditional Tunes of the Child Ballads, Princeton 1959, 1.308.
Mason H A, Humanism and Poetry in the Early Tudor Period, London 1959, p 147.
Greene R L, The Meaning of the Corpus Christi Carol, MÆ 29.10.
TLS, 20 Jan 1961, p 47.
Greene Selection, p 230.
Greene R L, The Burden and the Scottish Variant of the Corpus Christi Carol, MÆ 33.53.
Manning S, Wisdom and Number, Lincoln Neb 1962, pp 115, 135.
Davies, p 363.
Brice D, The Folk-Carol of England, London 1967, p 70.
Fowler D C, A Literary History of the Popular Ballad, Durham N C 1968, p 63.
Oliver, p 108.
Owen L J and N H, Middle English Poetry: An Anthology, Indianapolis Ind 1971, p 355.
Gray D, Themes and Images in the Medieval English Religious Lyric, London 1972, p 164.
Stevens J, Medieval Romance, London 1973, p 113.
Jeffrey D L, The Early English Lyric and Franciscan Spirituality, Lincoln Neb 1975, p 252.

[326] AND BY A CHAPELL AS Y CAME.

MS. Nat Libr Wales, Porkington 10, ff 198ª–198ᵇ (mid 15 cent).
Brown-Robbins, no 298.
Editions. Sandison H E, BrynMawrMon 12.102.
Greene E E Carols, p 223; 2nd edn, p 197.
Brown RLxvC, p 183.
Chambers OHEL, p 111.
Greene Selection, p 130.
Sisam, p 423.
Modernizations. Comper Spir Songs, p 250.

Oliver, p 119.
Tydeman W, English Poetry 1400–1580, London 1970, p 52.
Grigson G, The Faber Book of Popular Verse, London 1971, p 313.
Luria & Hoffman, p 220.
Commentary. Greene E E Carols, pp xcv, 412; 2nd edn, p 428.
Robbins R H, The Burden in Carols, MLN 57.20 (suggests reading line 1 as line 4).
Chambers OHEL, p 111.
Greene Selection, p 231.
Gray D, N&Q 208.431; Themes and Images in the Medieval English Religious Lyric, London p 164.

[327] AND LOUE þI GOD OUER AL þYNG (John Audelay).

MS. Bodl 21876 (Douce 302), f 27ᵇ (early 15 cent).
Brown-Robbins, no 304.
Editions. Chambers E K and F Sidgwick, MLR 5.479.
Whiting E K, EETS 184.181.
Greene E E Carols, p 223; 2nd edn, p 197.
Commentary. Whiting, EETS 184.249.
Greene E E Carols, p 413; 2nd edn, p 428.

[328] FORE-SAKE þI PRIDE & þYN ENUY (John Audelay).

MS. Bodl 21876 (Douce 302), ff 27ᵇ–28ª (early 15 cent).
Brown-Robbins, no 858.
Editions. Chambers E K and F Sidgwick, MLR 5.480.
Whiting E K, EETS 184.182.
Greene E E Carols, p 223; 2nd edn, p 198.
Commentary. Greene E E Carols, p 413; 2nd edn, p 429.

[329] FEDE þE HUNGERE þE þIRSTE ȜIF DRENKE (John Audelay).

MS. Bodl 21876 (Douce 302), f 28ª (early 15 cent).
Brown-Robbins, no 792.
Editions. Chambers E K and F Sidgwick, MLR 5.480.
Whiting E K, EETS 184.183.
Greene E E Carols, p 224; 2nd edn, p 198.
Commentary. Whiting, EETS 184.249.
Greene E E Carols, p 413; 2nd edn, p 429.

[330] MYND RESUN VERTU & GRACE
(John Audelay).

MS. Bodl 21876 (Douce 302), f 28ᵃ (early 15 cent).
Brown-Robbins, no 2173.
Editions. Chambers E K and F Sidgwick, MLR 5.482.
Whiting E K, EETS 184.185.
Greene E E Carols, p 224; 2nd edn, p 198.
Commentary. Whiting, EETS 184.249.
Greene E E Carols, p 414; 2nd edn, p 429.

[331] þE FURST Hᵗ IS þI HERYNG
(John Audelay).

MS. Bodl 21876 (Douce 302), f 28ᵃ (early 15 cent).
Brown-Robbins, no 3346.
Editions. Chambers E K and F Sidgwick, MLR 5.481.
Whiting E K, EETS 184.184.
Greene E E Carols, p 225; 2nd edn, p 199.
Commentary. Whiting, EETS 184.249.
Greene E E Carols, p 414; 2nd edn, p 429.

[332] EUERY DAY þᵘ MYȝT LERE.

MS. BM Sloane 2593, f 4ᵇ (mid 15 cent).
Brown-Robbins, no 739.
Editions. Wright T, Carols, Publ Warton Club 4.10.
Fehr B, Arch 109.44.
Ch&Sidg, p 180.
Greene E E Carols, p 225; 2nd edn, p 199.
Modernization. Davies, p 156.
Commentary. Greene E E Carols, p 414; 2nd edn, p 430.
Wenzel S, NM 77.85.

[333] WHEN LORDECHYPPE YS LOSTE & LUSTI LEKYNG WITH ALL.

MS. BM Addit 5665, ff 30ᵇ–31ᵃ (late 15 cent; music).
Brown-Robbins, no 3988.
Editions. Fehr B, Arch 106.271.
Greene E E Carols, p 226; 2nd edn, p 200.
Modernization. Stevens Med Carols, p 87 (with music).
Commentary. Greene E E Carols, p 414; 2nd edn, p 430.

[334] THE MASSE IS OF SO HIGH DIGNYTEE.

MSS. 1, Balliol 354, ff 230ᵃ–230ᵇ (early 16 cent);
2, Trinity Camb 1450 (0.9.38), f 69ᵇ (late 15 cent).
Brown-Robbins, no 3424.
Editions. Flügel E, Angl 26.263 (MS 1).
Dyboski R, EETSES 101.42 (MS 1).
Greene E E Carols, p 226 (MS 2 with collation of MS 1); 2nd edn, p 201.
Modernization. Comper Spir Songs, p 243 (MS 1).

[335] MAN AND WOMAN IN EVERY PLACE.

MS. Bodl 29734 (Eng poet e.1), f 27ᵇ (mid 15 cent).
Brown-Robbins, no 2041.
Editions. Wright T, Carols, PPS 23.37.
Greene E E Carols, p 227; 2nd edn, p 202.

[336] CRYSTE MADE MANE YN þIS MANER OF WYSE.

MS. Bodl 6777 (Ashmole 189), ff 104ᵃ–104ᵇ (15 cent).
Brown-Robbins, no 610.
Editions. Greene E E Carols, p 228; 2nd edn, p 202.
Brown RLxvC, p 162.
Commentary. Greene E E Carols, p 415; 2nd edn, p 431.
Kane, p 132.

[337] WHAN NO THYNG WAS BUT GOD ALONE.

MS. Bodl 29734 (Eng poet e.1), ff 24ᵇ–25ᵃ (mid 15 cent).
Brown-Robbins, Robbins-Cutler, no 4000.
Editions. Wright T, Carols, PPS 23.30.
Greene E E Carols, p 229; 2nd edn, p 203.
Sisam, p 478.
Commentary. Greene E E Carols, p 415; 2nd edn, p 432.
Brown RLxvC, p 331.

[338] WHANE NOþING WHAS BUT GOD ALONE.

MS. Nat Libr Wales, Porkington 10, ff 200ᵃ–200ᵇ (mid 15 cent).
Brown-Robbins, no 4001.
Editions. Greene E E Carols, p 229; 2nd edn, p 204.
Brown RLxvC, p 187.
Commentary. Greene E E Carols, p 415; 2nd edn, p 432.
Brown RLxvC, p 331.

[339] IN þE VALE OF ABRAHAM.

MS. BM Sloane 2593, ff 2ª–2ᵇ (mid 15 cent).
Brown-Robbins, no 1568.
Editions. Wright T, Songs and Carols, London. 1836, no 1; Carols, Publ Warton Club 4.2.
Greene E E Carols, p 230; 2nd edn, p 204.
Sisam, p 426.
Modernization. Stevick, p 100.
Commentary. Wright, Carols, Warton Club 4.103.
Greene E E Carols, pp cxliv, 416; 2nd edn, pp clxxi, 432.

[340] HOLY WRIT SEY3T WHECH NO THYNG YS SOTHER.

MSS. 1, Bodl 3340 (Arch Selden B.26), f 5ª (mid 15 cent; music); 2, Bodl 29734 (Eng poet e.1), ff 24ª–24ᵇ (mid 15 cent); 3, BM Addit 5665, ff 31ᵇ–32ª (late 15 cent; music); 4, BM Egerton 3307, f 66ᵇ (mid 15 cent; music).
Brown-Robbins, no 1234.
Editions. Wright T, Carols, PPS 23.29 (MS 2).
Early Bodleian Music, 2.87 (MS 1 with music).
Fehr B, Arch 106.271 (MS 3).
Padelford F M, Angl 36.86 (MS 1).
Greene E E Carols, p 230 (MS 1 with collation of MSS 2, 3); 2nd edn, p 205 (MSS 1 and 4, with collation of MSS 2,3).
Brown RLxvC, p 278 (MS 2).
Greene Selection, p 131 (MS 4).
Sisam, p 416 (MS 4).
Modernizations. Adamson M R, A Treasury of ME Verse, London 1930, p 141 (MS 2; omits burden).
Stevens Med Carols, pp 53 (MS 4 with music), 88 (MS 3 with music).
Commentary. Greene E E Carols, pp cix, 416; 2nd edn, pp cxxxiv, 433.
Stevens Med Carols, p 117.
Greene Selection, p 232.

[341] ABYDE I HOPE IT BE THE BESTE.

MSS. 1, Bodl 3340 (Arch Selden B.26), f 29ᵇ (mid 15 cent; music); 2, Trinity Camb 1230 (0.3.58), no 9 (mid 15 cent; music).
Brown-Robbins, no 111.
Editions. Fuller Maitland J A and W S Rockstro, English Carols of the 15th Cent, London [1891], p 19 (MS 2 with music).
Early Bodleian Music, 2.161 (MS 1 with music).
Ch&Sidg, p 189 (MS 1).
Padelford F M, Angl 26.114 (MS 1).
Greene E E Carols, p 231 (MS 1 with collation of MS 2); 2nd edn, p 206.
Modernization. Stevens Med Carols, pp 8 (MS 2 with music), 31 (MS 1 with music).
Commentary. Ch&Sidg, p 364.
Greene E E Carols, p 416; 2nd edn, p 433.
Stevens Med Carols, p 117 (corrects Greene on division of burden and stanza).

[342] þI TUNGE IS MAD OF FLEYCH & BLOD.

MS. BM Sloane 2593, f 7ª (mid 15 cent).
Brown-Robbins, no 3733.
Editions. Rel Ant, 2.165.
Wright T, Carols, Publ Warton Club 4.18.
Greene E E Carols, p 232; 2nd edn, p 206.
Commentary. Greene E E Carols, p 417; 2nd edn, p 433.

[343] ITTES KNOWYN IN EUERY SCHYRE.

MS. Bodl 29734 (Eng poet e.1), ff 28ᵇ–29ª (mid 15 cent).
Brown-Robbins, no 1633.
Editions. Wright T, Carols, PPS 23.41.
Masters J E, Rymes of the Minstrels, Shaftesbury 1927, p 12.
Greene E E Carols, p 232; 2nd edn, p 207.
Commentary. Greene E E Carols, p 417; 2nd edn, p 433.

[344] þER IS NON GRES þᵗ GROWIT IN GROUND.

MS. BM Sloane 2593, ff 30ª–30ᵇ (mid 15 cent).
Brown-Robbins, Robbins-Cutler, no 3537.
Editions. Rel Ant, 2.167.
Wright T, Carols, Publ Warton Club 4.87.
Ch&Sidg, p 191.
Greene E E Carols, p 233; 2nd edn, p 207.
Greene Selection, p 132.
Sisam, p 444.
Commentary. Ch&Sidg, p 364.
Greene E E Carols, p 417; 2nd edn, p 434.
Greene Selection, p 233.

[345] WITH PETY MOVYD I AM CONSTREYNYD.

MS. Bodl 29734 (Eng poet e.1), ff 50ᵇ–51ª (mid 15 cent; music, burden only).
Brown-Robbins, Robbins-Cutler, no 4198 (erroneous duplicate entry, Brown-Robbins, no 2612, corrected by Robbins-Cutler, no 2612).

Editions. Wright T, Carols, PPS 23.78.
Greene E E Carols, p 233; 2nd edn, p 207.
Modernizations. Stevens Med Carols, p 111 (burden only, with music).
Stevick, p 148.
Commentary. Greene E E Carols, p 417; 2nd edn, p 434.

[346] ... SIT AMONGES THE KNYGHTES ALL.

MS. BM Harley 4294, f 81[b] (late 15 cent).
Brown-Robbins, no *50; Robbins-Cutler, no *3119.5.
Editions. Rel Ant, 1.252.
Greene E E Carols, p 234; 2nd edn, p 208.
Commentary. Greene E E Carols, p 418; 2nd edn, p 434.

[347] BLOWYNG WAS MAD FOR GRET GAME.

MS. Bodl 29734 (Eng poet e.1), f 22[a] (mid 15 cent).
Brown-Robbins, Robbins-Cutler, no 543.
Editions. Wright T, Carols, PPS 23.23.
Ch&Sidg, p 192.
Masters J E, Rymes of the Minstrels, Shaftesbury 1927, p 8.
Greene E E Carols, p 234; 2nd edn, p 208.
Sisam, p 474.
Commentary. Ch&Sidg, p 365.
Greene E E Carols, p 418; 2nd edn, p 434.

[348] BE MERY & SUFFER AS I THE VISE.

MS. Balliol 354, f 231[a] (early 16 cent).
Brown-Robbins, no 470.
Editions. Flügel NL, p 141.
Flügel E, Angl 26.265.
Dyboski R, EETSES 101.46.
Greene E E Carols, p 235; 2nd edn, p 209.
Greene Selection, p 133.
Modernization. Segar M G, A Mediaeval Anthology, London 1915, p 111.
Commentary. Greene E E Carols, p 418; 2nd edn, p 435.
Greene Selection, p 233.

[349] AN OLD SAID SAWE: ON-KNOWEN ON-KYSTE.

MS. Balliol 354, f 231[a] (early 16 cent).
Brown-Robbins, no 294.

Editions. Flügel E, Angl 26.266.
Dyboski R, EETSES 101.47.
Greene E E Carols, p 235; 2nd edn, p 209.
Modernization. Segar M G, A Mediaeval Anthology, London 1915, p 112 (in part).
Commentary. Greene E E Carols, pp cxliv, 418; 2nd edn, pp clxx, 435.

[350] IN WAT ORDER OR WHAT DEGRE (John Audelay).

MS. Bodl 21876 (Douce 302), f 29[b] (early 15 cent).
Brown-Robbins, no 1588.
Editions. Chambers E K and F Sidgwick, MLR 6.68.
Whiting E K, EETS 184.195.
Greene E E Carols, p 235; 2nd edn, p 209.
Kaiser R, Alt- und mittelenglische Anthologie, Berlin 1955, p 442; Medieval English (3rd edn of Anthologie), Berlin West 1958, p 295.
Davies, p 171.
Commentary. Greene E E Carols, p 419; 2nd edn, p 435.

[351] THE HYERE MEN CLYMMETH THE SORERE YS THE FALL.

MS. BM Addit 5665, ff 14[b]-15[a] (late 15 cent; music).
Brown-Robbins, Robbins-Cutler, no 3382.
Editions. Fehr B, Arch 106.267.
Greene E E Carols, p 236; 2nd edn, p 210.
Modernization. Stevens Med Carols, p 72 (with music).
Commentary. Greene E E Carols, p 419; 2nd edn, p 436.

[352] IF Y HALDE THE LOWE ASYSE.

MS. Camb Univ Addit 5943, f 145[b] (early 15 cent).
Brown-Robbins, no 1415.
Editions. M[ayer] L S, Music Cantelenas Songs Etc, London 1906, sheet b.
Greene E E Carols, p 237; 2nd edn, p 210.
Brown RLxvC, p 285.
Greene Selection, p 134.
Sisam, p 374.
Commentary. Greene E E Carols, p 420; 2nd edn, p 436.
Brown RLxvC, p 350.
Greene Selection, p 234.

[353] I WAS Wᵗ POPE & CARDYNALL.

MS. Balliol 354, f 226ᵇ (early 16 cent).
Brown-Robbins, no 1386.
Editions. Flügel NL, p 141.
Flügel E, Angl 26.252.
Dyboski R, EETSES 101.26.
Greene E E Carols, p 237; 2nd edn, p 211.
Commentary. Greene E E Carols, pp cxlv, 420; 2nd edn, pp clxxi, 437.

[354] YF GOD SEND þE PLENTUOWSLY RICHES.

MS. Balliol 354, f 178ᵃ (early 16 cent).
Brown-Robbins, no 1412.
Editions. Flügel E, Angl 26.195.
Dyboski R, EETSES 101.3.
Greene E E Carols, p 237; 2nd edn, p 211.
Commentary. Greene E E Carols, p 420; 2nd edn, p 437.

[355] O MAN WHICHE ART THE ERTHE TAKE FROO (James Ryman).

MS. Camb Univ Ee.1.12, ff 48ᵇ–49ᵃ (ca 1492).
Brown-Robbins, no 2506.
Editions. Zupitza J, Arch 89.219.
Greene E E Carols, p 238; 2nd edn, p 211.
Commentary. Zupitza, Arch 94.410.
Greene E E Carols, p 420; 2nd edn, p 437.

[356] I HAD RICHESSE I HAD MY HELTH (James Ryman).

MS. Camb Univ Ee.1.12, ff 49ᵃ–49ᵇ (ca 1492).
Brown-Robbins, no 1298.
Editions. Zupitza J, Arch 89.220.
Greene E E Carols, p 238; 2nd edn, p 212.
Modernization. Stevick, p 153.
Commentary. Zupitza, Arch 94.412.
Greene E E Carols, p 420; 2nd edn, p 437.

[357] NOW TO DO WELL HOW SHALT þᵘ DO.

MS. BM Addit 5665, ff 35ᵇ–36ᵃ (late 15 cent; music).
Brown-Robbins, no 2370.
Editions. Fehr B, Arch 106.272.
Greene E E Carols, p 239; 2nd edn, p 212.
Modernization. Stevens Med Carols, p 93 (with music).
Commentary. Greene E E Carols, p 420; 2nd edn, p 437.

[358] PRYDE IS OUT & PRIDE IS INE.

MSS. 1, Balliol 354, f 249ᵇ (early 16 cent); 2, BM Sloane 2593, f 9ᵃ (mid 15 cent).
Brown-Robbins, no 2771.
Editions. Rel Ant, 2.166 (MS 2).
Wright T, Carols, Publ Warton Club 4.24 (MS 2).
Flügel E, Angl 26.274 (MS 1).
Dyboski R, EETSES 101.50 (MS 1).
Ch&Sidg, p 183 (MS 2).
Greene E E Carols, p 239 (MS 2 with collation of MS 1); 2nd edn, p 212.
Commentary. Greene E E Carols, pp cxliv, 421; 2nd edn, pp clxxi, 438.

[359] þOW þᵘ BE KYNG OF TOUR & TOWN.

MSS. 1, Bodl 29734 (Eng poet e.1), ff 30ᵇ–31ᵃ (mid 15 cent); 2, BM Sloane 2593, f 6ᵃ (mid 15 cent).
Brown-Robbins, no 3707.
Editions. Wright T, Carols, PPS 23.44 (MS 1); Carols, Publ Warton Club 4.15 (MS 2).
Fehr B, Arch 109.45 (MS 2).
Ch&Sidg, p 186 (MS 2).
Greene E E Carols, p 240 (MS 2 with collation of MS 1); 2nd edn, p 213.
Commentary. Greene E E Carols, p 421; 2nd edn, p 438.

[360] THYNK MAN QWEROF þᵘ ART WROUT.

MS. BM Sloane 2593, ff 26ᵃ–26ᵇ (mid 15 cent).
Brown-Robbins, no 3566.
Editions. Wright T, Carols, Publ Warton Club 4.73.
Greene E E Carols, p 241; 2nd edn, p 213.
Greene Selection, p 135.
Commentary. Wright, Warton Club 4.118.
Greene E E Carols, p 421; 2nd edn, p 438.
Greene Selection, p 234.
Whitfield D W, N&Q 223.203.

[361] GAME AND ERNEST EUER AMONG.

MS. Bodl 29734 (Eng poet e.1), ff 28ᵃ–28ᵇ (mid 15 cent).
Brown-Robbins, no 893.
Editions. Wright T, Carols, PPS 23.40.
Greene E E Carols, p 241; 2nd edn, p 214.
Modernization. Adamson M R, A Treasury of ME Verse, London 1930, p 151.

Commentary. Wehrle, p 94.
Greene E E Carols, p 422; 2nd edn, p 439.

[362] MAN HAUE IN MYNDE HOW HERE BYFORE.

MSS. 1, Bodl 3340 (Arch Selden B.26), f 7ᵇ (mid 15 cent; music); 2, Balliol 354, f 220ᵇ (early 16 cent); 3, Lincoln Coll Oxf Lat 89, f 27ᵇ (mid 15 cent); 4, BM Addit 5665, ff 42ᵇ–43ᵃ (late 15 cent; music).
Brown-Robbins, no 2053.
Editions. Early Bodleian Music, 2.106 (MS 1 with music).
Fehr B, Arch 106.275 (MS 4).
Flügel E, Angl 26.233 (MS 2).
Dyboski R, EETSES 101.8, 171 (MSS 2, 4).
Padelford F M, Angl 36.87 (MSS 1, 2, 4).
Greene E E Carols, p 242 (MSS 2, 4 with collation of MS 1); 2nd edn, p 214 (MSS 2–4 with collation of MS 1).
Modernizations. Terry Med Carol Book, p 38 (MS 1 with music).
Stevens Med Carols, pp 12 (MS 1 with music), 100 (MS 4 with music).
Commentary. Greene E E Carols, p 422 (MSS 1, 2, 4); 2nd edn, p 439.

[363] THAT HOLY CLERKE SEINT AUGUSTYNE (James Ryman).

MS. Camb Univ Ee.1.12, ff 46ᵃ–46ᵇ (ca 1492).
Brown-Robbins, no 3272.
Editions. Zupitza J, Arch 89.215.
Greene E E Carols, p 243; 2nd edn, p 215.
Commentary. Zupitza, Arch 94.402.
Greene E E Carols, p 422; 2nd edn, p 439.

[364] ATT DOMYS DAY WHEN WE SHALL RYSE.

MS. Balliol 354, f 221ᵃ (early 16 cent).
Brown-Robbins, no 425.
Editions. Flügel E, Angl 26.234.
Dyboski R, EETSES 101.9.
Greene E E Carols, p 243; 2nd edn, p 216.
Commentary. Greene E E Carols, p 422; 2nd edn, p 439.

[365] A DOUMS DAY WE SCHULL Y-SEE.

MS. Bridgwater Corporation Muniments 123, on strip with indenture (late 15 cent).
Brown-Robbins, no 17.

Editions. Reports of the Historical MSS Commission 3.316 (Appendix).
Greene E E Carols, p 244; 2nd edn, p 216.

[366] ȜYNG MEN þᵗ BERN HEM SO GAY.

MS. BM Sloane 2593, f 8ᵃ (mid 15 cent).
Brown-Robbins, no 4281.
Editions. Wright T, Carols, Publ Warton Club 4.21.
Fehr B, Arch 109.47.
Greene E E Carols, p 244; 2nd edn, p 217.
Commentary. Greene E E Carols, p 422; 2nd edn, p 440.
Wenzel S, NM 77.85.

[367] THIS VOYCE BOTH SHARP & ALSO [SHYLL].

MSS. No MS extant. PRINT: Huntington Libr, Christmas carolles newely Inprynted (Richard Kele), pp [48], [45], [46] (ca 1550; STC, no 5205).
Robbins-Cutler, no 3645.8.
Editions. Reed Christmas Carols, pp 63 (facsimile), 66.
Greene E E Carols, p 245; 2nd edn, p 217.
Commentary. Greene R L, MLN 48.133.
Greene E E Carols, p 423; 2nd edn, p 440.

[368] þIS WORD LORDINNGGIS I VNDERSTONDE.

MS. BM Sloane 2593, ff 3ᵃ–3ᵇ (mid 15 cent).
Brown-Robbins, no 3658.
Editions. Wright T, Carols, Publ Warton Club 4.5.
Ch&Sidg, p 181.
Fehr B, Arch 109.42.
Greene E E Carols, p 245; 2nd edn, p 217.
Commentary. Ch&Sidg, p 362.
Greene E E Carols, p 423; 2nd edn, p 440.

[369] þIS WORLD IS FALCE I DARE WYLL SAY.

MS. St John's Camb 259 (S.54), ff 10ᵇ–11ᵃ (mid 15 cent).
Brown-Robbins, no 3654.
Editions. James M R and G C Macaulay, MLR 8.82.
Greene E E Carols, p 246; 2nd edn, p 218.
Greene Selection, p 136.
Commentary. Greene E E Carols, p 423; 2nd edn, p 440.

Greene Selection, p 236.
Woolf, p 343.

[370] THIS WORLDE YS BUT A VANITE.

MS. BM Addit 5665, ff 49b–50a (late 15 cent; music).
Brown-Robbins, no 3652.
Editions. Fehr B, Arch 106.277.
Greene E E Carols, p 246; 2nd edn, p 219.
Modernization. Stevens Med Carols, p 106 (with music).
Commentary. Greene E E Carols, p 423; 2nd edn, p 441.

[371] I AM A CHYLD & BORN FUL BARE.

MS. BM Sloane 2593, ff 7b–8a (mid 15 cent).
Brown-Robbins, no 1268.
Editions. Wright T, Carols, Publ Warton Club 4.20.
Fehr B, Arch 109.46.
Ch&Sidg, p 184.
Greene E E Carols, p 247; 2nd edn, p 219.
Commentary. Greene E E Carols, p 424; 2nd edn, p 441.
Woolf, p 333.

[372] DRED OF DEþ SOROW OF SYN (John Audelay).

MS. Bodl 21876 (Douce 302), ff 30b, 32a (early 15 cent).
Brown-Robbins, Robbins-Cutler, no 693.
Editions. Chambers E K and F Sidgwick, MLR 6.80.
Whiting E K, EETS 184.211.
Greene E E Carols, p 247; 2nd edn, p 219.
Sisam, p 391.
Silverstein, p 105.
Modernizations. Comper Spir Songs, p 230.
Davies, p 170.
Commentary. Whiting, EETS 184.255.
Greene E E Carols, p 424; 2nd edn, p 442.
Davies, p 339.
Woolf, p 335.

[373] AS I WENT IN A MERY MORNYNG.

MSS. 1, Bodl 29734 (Eng poet e.1), ff 38b–39a (mid 15 cent); 2, Balliol 354, f 176b (early 16 cent). PRINT: 3, Huntington Libr, Christmas carolles newely Inprynted (Richard Kele), p [41] (ca 1550; STC, no 5205).
Brown-Robbins, Robbins-Cutler, no 375.
Editions. Wright T, Carols, PPS 23.57 (MS 1).
Flügel E, Angl 26.191, 192 (MSS 1, 2).
Ch&Sidg, p 150 (MS 2).
Dyboski R, EETSES 101.3 (MS 2), 169 (collation of MS 1).
Patterson, p 102 (MS 1).
Reed Christmas Carols, p 59 (facsimile; PRINT 3).
Greene E E Carols, p 248 (MS 1 with collation of MS 2 and PRINT 3); 2nd edn, p 220.
Greene Selection, p 137 (MS 1).
Sisam, p 525 (MS 2).
Wilhelm J J, Medieval Song, N Y 1971, p 363 (MS 1).
Modernizations. Segar M G, A Mediaeval Anthology, London 1915, p 100 (MS 2); Some Minor Poems of the Middle Ages, London 1917, p 41 (MS 2).
Stevick, p 135 (MS 1).
Commentary. Ch&Sidg, p 357.
Brabant F G, Oxfordshire, London 1919, p 257.
Reed Christmas Carols, p 86.
Greene E E Carols, p 424; 2nd edn, p 442.
Greene Selection, p 236.
Woolf, p 333.
Gray D, N&Q 205.303.

[374] AS I WENT ME FORE TO SOLASE.

MS. Bodl 29734 (Eng poet e.1), ff 48a–49a (mid 15 cent).
Brown-Robbins, Robbins-Cutler, no 376.
Editions. Wright T, Carols, PPS 23.74.
Flügel E, Angl 26.193.
Patterson, p 100.
Greene E E Carols, p 249; 2nd edn, p 220.
Modernization. Stevick, p 137.
Commentary. Patterson, p 181.
Greene E E Carols, pp 424, 425; 2nd edn, p 443.

[375] ILLA IUVENTUS THAT IS SO NYSE.

MS. Balliol 354, f 229a (early 16 cent).
Brown-Robbins, no 1444.
Editions. Flügel E, Angl 26.259.
Dyboski R, EETSES 101.36.
Ch&Sidg, p 149.
Patterson, p 103.

Greene E E Carols, p 249; 2nd edn, p 221.
Modernization. Davies, p 279.
Commentary. Patterson, p 182.
Wehrle, p 89.
Greene E E Carols, pp lxi, 424, 425; 2nd edn, pp lxxxii, 443.

[376] O MARCYFULL GOD MAKER OF ALL MANKYND.

MS. Balliol 354, f 210^a (early 16 cent).
Brown-Robbins, Robbins-Cutler, no 2511.
Editions. Flügel E, Angl 26.223.
Dyboski R, EETSES 101.92.
Greene E E Carols, p 250; 2nd edn, p 221.
Silverstein p 122.
Commentary. Greene E E Carols, pp lxxxiii, 425; 2nd edn, pp ciii, 444.
Robbins SL, p 268 (interprets as epitaph).

[377] IN XX^{ti} YERE OF AGE REMEMBRE WE EUERYCHON.

MS. Balliol 354, f 210^a (early 16 cent).
Brown-Robbins, Robbins-Cutler, no 1587.
Editions. Flügel E, Angl 26.224.
Dyboski R, EETSES 101.93.
Greene E E Carols, p 250; 2nd edn, p 222.
Commentary. Greene E E Carols, p 425; 2nd edn, p 444.

[378] WHILE Y WAS ȝONGE & HADDE CORAGE.

MS. BM Addit 5665, ff 45^b–46^a (late 15 cent; music).
Brown-Robbins, Robbins-Cutler, no 4077.
Editions. Fehr B, Arch 106.276.
Patterson, p 100.
Greene E E Carols, p 251; 2nd edn, p 222.
Modernization. Stevens Med Carols, p 103 (with music).
Commentary. Patterson, p 180.
Wehrle, p 86.
Greene E E Carols, p 426; 2nd edn, p 444.

[379] DETHE BEGAN BY CAUSE OF SYN.

MSS. No MS extant. PRINT: Huntington Libr, Christmas carolles newely Inprynted (Richard Kele), pp [7]-[10] (ca 1550; STC, no 5205).
Robbins-Cutler, no 672.4.
Editions. Reed Christmas Carols, p 25 facs.
Greene E E Carols, p 251; 2nd edn, p 222.

[380] HOW SCHOWLD I BOT I THOGHT ON MYN ENDYNG DAY.

MS. Trinity Camb 899 (R.14.26), f 21^a (early 15 cent).
Brown-Robbins, no 1263.
Edition. Greene E E Carols, p 252; 2nd edn, p 223.

[381] AS I ME RODE IN A MEY MORNYNG.

MS. Advocates 19.3.1, ff 95^b–96^a (late 15 cent).
Brown-Robbins, no 358.
Edition. Greene E E Carols, p 253; 2nd edn, p 224.
Commentary. Greene E E Carols, p 426; 2nd edn, p 444.

[382] YOUGTH LUSTE RECHES OR MANHOD.

MS. Trinity Camb 1157 (0.2.53), ff 57^a–58^a (late 15 cent).
Brown-Robbins, no 4285.
Edition. Greene E E Carols, p 253; 2nd edn, p 224.

[383] THEN ALL YOUR DOYNGS SCHOLD HERE IN EARTHE.

MS. Trinity Camb 1359 (0.7.31), ff 202^b–203^a; ff 203^b–204^a (second copy incomplete; ca 1500).
Brown-Robbins, no 3515.
Edition. Greene E E Carols, p 254 (with collation of second copy); 2nd edn, p 225.

[384] IF þOU SERUE A LORDE OF PRYS.

MS. BM Sloane 2593, ff 8^a–8^b (mid 15 cent).
Brown-Robbins, no 1433.
Editions. Wright T, Carols, Publ Warton Club 4.22.
Fehr B, Arch 109.47.
Ch&Sidg, p 185.
Greene E E Carols, p 255; 2nd edn, p 226.
Greene Selection, p 138.
Sisam, p 431.
Modernization. Davies, p 154.
Commentary. N&Q 1s 8.586.
Ch&Sidg, p 363.
Greene E E Carols, pp cxlv, 427; 2nd edn, pp clxxi, 445.
Greene Selection, p 238.

[385] MAN BE WAR þE WAY YS SLEDER.

MS. Bodl 29734 (Eng poet e.1), f 13ª (mid 15 cent).
Brown-Robbins, no 2050.
Editions. Wright T, Carols, PPS 23.4.
Greene E E Carols, p 255; 2nd edn, p 226.
Commentary. Wright, PPS 23.99.
Greene E E Carols, pp cix, 427; 2nd edn, pp cxxxiv, 445.

[386] GYLE & GOLD TOGEDERE ARN MET.

MS. BM Sloane 2593, ff 5ᵇ–6ª (mid 15 cent).
Brown-Robbins, no 1020.
Editions. Wright T, Carols, Publ Warton Club 4.13.
Fehr B, Arch 107.49.
Greene E E Carols, p 256; 2nd edn, p 227.
Commentary. Greene E E Carols, p 427; 2nd edn, p 445.

[387] SEMENAUNT IS A WONDER þING.

MS. BM Sloane 2593, ff 29ᵇ–30ª (mid 15 cent).
Brown-Robbins, no 3085.
Editions. Rel Ant, 2.166.
Wright T, Carols, Publ Warton Club 4.86.
Ch&Sidg, p 190.
Greene E E Carols, p 256; 2nd edn, p 227.

[388] A MAN þᵗ XULD OF TREWþE TELLE.

MS. BM Sloane 2593, ff 7ª–7ᵇ (mid 15 cent).
Brown-Robbins, Robbins-Cutler, no 72.
Editions. Rel Ant, 2.165.
Wright T, Carols, Publ Warton Club 4.19.
Ch&Sidg, p 187.
Greene E E Carols, p 257; 2nd edn, p 227.
Robbins-HP, p 146.
Greene Selection, p 139.
Sisam, p 430.
Modernizations. Adamson M R, A Treasury of ME Verse, London 1930, p 133 (omits burden).
Stevick, p 106.
Commentary. Robbins-HP, p 329.

[389] VYCYCE BE WYLD AND VERTUES LAME.

MSS. 1, Bodl 29734 (Eng poet e.1), ff 60ᵇ–61ª (mid 15 cent); 2, Balliol 354, f 227ª (early 16 cent).
Brown-Robbins, no 3852.
Editions. Wright T, Carols, PPS 23.96 (MS 1).
Flügel E, Angl 26.252 (MS 2).
Dyboski R, EETSES 101.27 (MS 2), 176 (collation of MS 1).
Greene E E Carols, p 257 (MS 1 with collation of MS 2); 2nd edition, p 228.
Modernization. Adamson M R, A Treasury of ME Verse, London 1930, p 163 (MS 2).
Commentary. Greene E E Carols, p 428; 2nd edn, p 446.

[390] GOD SENDE VS PESE & VNITE.

MS. BM Addit 5665, ff 50ᵇ–51ª (late 15 cent; music).
Brown-Robbins, Robbins-Cutler, no 962.
Editions. Fehr B, Arch 106.277.
Greene E E Carols, p 258; 2nd edn, p 228.
Modernization. Stevens Med Carols, p 107 (with music).
Commentary. Greene E E Carols, p 428; 2nd edn, p 446.
Stevens Med Carols, p 122.

[391] EUERY MANE IN HYS DEGRE.

MS. Bodl 29734 (Eng poet e.1), ff 16ᵇ–17ᵇ (mid 15 cent).
Brown-Robbins, no 743.
Editions. Wright T, Carols, PPS 23.10.
Greene E E Carols, p 258; 2nd edn, p 229.

[392] VNDER A FOREST þᵗ WAS SO LONG.

MSS. 1, Bodl 29734 (Eng poet e.1), ff 23ᵇ–24ª (mid 15 cent); 2, Balliol 354, ff 231ª–231ᵇ (early 16 cent).
Brown-Robbins, no 3820.
Editions. Wright T, Carols, PPS 23.28 (MS 1).
Flügel E, Angl 26.267 (MS 2).
Ch&Sidg, p 193 (MS 1).
Dyboski R, EETSES 101.47 (MS 2), 178 (collation of MS 1).
Greene E E Carols, p 259 (MS 1 with collation of MS 2); 2nd edn, p 229.
Greene Selection, p 140 (MS 1).
Sisam, p 534 (MS 2).
Commentary. Greene E E Carols, p 428; 2nd edn, p 447.
Greene Selection, p 238.

[393] QUAN I HAUE IN MYN PURS INOW.

MS. BM Sloane 2593, f 6ᵃ (mid 15 cent).
Brown-Robbins, Robbins-Cutler, no 3959.
Editions. Wright T, Songs and Carols, London 1836, no 4; Carols, Publ Warton Club 4.14.
Greene E E Carols, p 260; 2nd edn, p 230.
Greene Selection, p 141.
Sisam, p 428.
Modernization. Stevick, p 105.
Commentary. Greene E E Carols, pp cxliv, 428; 2nd edn, pp clxx, 447.
Greene Selection, p 238.
Mustanoja J F, The Suggestive Use of Christian Names in Middle English Poetry, Medieval Literature and Folklore Studies: Essays in Honor of Francis Lee Utley, New Brunswick N J 1970, p 60.

[394] IN EUERY PLAS QWERE þAT I WENDE.

MS. St John's Camb 259 (S.54), f 3ᵇ (mid 15 cent).
Brown-Robbins, Robbins-Cutler, no 1484.
Editions. James M R and G C Macaulay, MLR 8.72.
Greene E E Carols, p 260; 2nd edn, p 230.
Commentary. Greene E E Carols, pp cxliv, 429; 2nd edn, pp clxx, 448.

[395] PENY IS AN HARDY KNYGHT.

MS. BM Sloane 2593, f 26ᵇ (mid 15 cent).
Brown-Robbins, Robbins-Cutler, no 2747.
Editions. Wright T, Songs and Carols, London 1836, no 4; Carols, Publ Warton Club 4.75; The Latin Poems Commonly Attributed to Walter Mapes, Camden Soc 17, London 1841, p 361.
Ritson AS 1790, p 76; 1829, 1.134; 1877, p 16.
Hazlitt Rem, 4.359.
Arber E, The Dunbar Anthology, London 1901, p 79.
Greene E E Carols, p 261; 2nd edn, p 231.
Robbins SL, p 50.
Kaiser R, Alt- und mittelenglische Anthologie, Berlin 1955, p 317; Medieval English (3rd edn of Anthologie), Berlin West 1958, p 550.
Sisam, p 441.
Modernization. Luria & Hoffman, p 114.
Commentary. Greene E E Carols, p 429; 2nd edn, p 448.

Robbins SL, p 244.

[396] ABOUE ALL TH[I]NG THOW ARTE A KYNG.

MS. BM Royal 17.B.xlvii, ff 160ᵇ–162ᵃ (late 15 cent).
Brown-Robbins, no 113.
Editions. Halliwell-[Phillipps] J O, Nugae Poeticae, London 1844, p 46.
FitzGibbon H M, Early English and Scottish Poetry, London 1888, p 233 (in part).
Greene E E Carols, p 261; 2nd edn, p 231.
Robbins-HP, p 134.
Modernization. Luria & Hoffman, p 116.
Commentary. Greene E E Carols, p 429; 2nd edn, p 449.
Robbins-HP, p 322.

[397] ION CLERKE OF TORYTON I DAR AVOW.

MS. Stanbrook Abbey 3, f iiiᵃ (late 15 cent).
Robbins-Cutler, no 1793.6.
Editions. Ker N R, MÆ 34.231.
Greene E E Carols, 2nd edn, p 232.
Commentary. Greene E E Carols, 2nd edn, p 449.

[398] SCHE SAW þEIS WOMEN ALL BEDENE.

MS. St John's Camb 259 (S.54), f 7ᵃ–7ᵇ (mid 15 cent).
Brown-Robbins, Robbins-Cutler, no 3098.
Editions. James M R and G C Macaulay, MLR 8.76.
Greene E E Carols, p 263; 2nd edn, p 233.
Commentary. Greene E E Carols, p 429; 2nd edn, p 449.
Utley CR, p 230.

[399] WYMMEN BEþ BOþE GOUD AND SCHENE.

MSS. 1, BM Harley 7358, f 8ᵃ (late 14 cent); 2, BM Sloane 2593, f 5ᵃ (mid 15 cent).
Brown-Robbins, Robbins-Cutler, no 4219.
Editions. Wright T, Carols, Publ Warton Club 4.106, 11 (MSS 1, 2); Songs and Carols, London 1836, no 3 (MS 2).
PFMS, 3.545 (MS 2).
Ch&Sidg, p 198 (MS 1).
Greene E E Carols, p 263 (MS 1 with collation of MS 2); 2nd edn, p 233.

Greene Selection, p 142 (MS 1).
Modernization. Segar M G, A Mediaeval Anthology, London 1915, p 108.
Commentary. Greene E E Carols, p 430; 2nd edn, p 450.
Utley CR, p 310.
Greene Selection, p 239.

[400] TO ONPREYSE WEMEN YT WERE A SHAME.

MS. BM Harley 4294, f 81[a] (early 16 cent).
Brown-Robbins, Robbins-Cutler, no 3782.
Editions. Rel Ant, 1.275.
Ch&Sidg, p 197.
Greene E E Carols, p 264; 2nd edn, p 234.
Robbins SL, p 31.
Kaiser R, Alt- und mittelenglische Anthologie, Berlin 1955, p 297; Medieval English (3rd edn of Anthologie), Berlin West 1958, p 470.
Sisam, p 521.
Modernizations. Adamson M R, A Treasury of ME Verse, London 1930, p 118.
Grigson G, The Faber Book of Popular Verse, London 1971, p 207.
Davies, p 283.
Luria & Hoffman, p 39.
Commentary. Greene E E Carols, p 430; 2nd edn, p 450.
Utley CR, p 271.
Robbins SL, p 237.

[401] BLESSID MOT BE OURE HEUENE QUEN (John Audelay).

MS. Bodl 21876 (Douce 302), f 30[a] (early 15 cent).
Brown-Robbins, Robbins-Cutler, no 535.
Editions. Chambers E K and F Sidgwick, MLR 6.76.
Whiting E K, EETS 184.206.
Greene E E Carols, p 264; 2nd edn, p 234.
Commentary. Greene E E Carols, p 430; 2nd edn, p 450.
Utley CR, p 115.

[402] IN WORD IN DED IN WIL IN þOȝT (John Audelay).

MS. Bodl 21876 (Douce 302), ff 30[a]–30[b] (early 15 cent).
Brown-Robbins, Robbins-Cutler, no 1595.
Editions. Chambers E K and F Sidgwick, MLR 6.77.
Whiting E K, EETS 184.207.

Greene E E Carols, p 265; 2nd edn, p 235.
Commentary. Whiting, EETS 184.254.
Greene E E Carols, p 430; 2nd edn, p 451.
Utley CR, p 168.

[403] IN EUERY PLACE YE MAY WELL SEE.

MSS. 1, Bodl 29734 (Eng poet e.1), ff 55[b]–56[a] (mid 15 cent); 2, Balliol 354, f 250[a] (early 16 cent).
Brown-Robbins, Robbins-Cutler, no 1485.
Editions. Wright T, Carols, PPS 23.88 (MS 1).
Flügel E, Angl 26.275 (MS 2).
Dyboski R, EETSES 101.112 (MS 2), 188 (collation of MS 1).
Masters J E, Rymes of the Minstrels, Shaftesbury 1927, p 28 (MS 1).
Greene E E Carols, p 265 (MS 2 with collation of MS 1); 2nd edn, p 235.
Robbins SL, p 35 (MS 2).
Kaiser R, Alt- und mittelenglische Anthologie, Berlin 1955, p 311 (MS 1); Medieval English (3rd edn of Anthologie), Berlin West 1958, p 478 (MS 1).
Greene Selection, p 143 (MS 2).
Davies, p 221 (MS 2, in part).
Modernization. Luria & Hoffman, p 63.
Commentary. Wehrle, p 98.
Greene E E Carols, p 431; 2nd edn, p 451.
Utley CR, p 165.
Robbins SL, p 238.
Greene Selection, p 240.
Davies, p 352.

[404] STEL IS GUD I SEY NO ODYR.

MS. St John's Camb 259 (S.54), f 9[b] (mid 15 cent).
Brown-Robbins, Robbins-Cutler, no 3214.
Editions. James M R and G C Macaulay, MLR 8.80.
Greene E E Carols, p 266; 2nd edn, p 236.
Commentary. Greene E E Carols, p 431; 2nd edn, p 452.
Utley CR, p 238.

[405] SUM BE MERY AND SUM BE SADE.

MSS. 1, Bodl 29734 (Eng poet e.1), ff 56[b]–57[a] (mid 15 cent); 2, Balliol 354, ff 250[a]–250[b] (early 16 cent); 3, Lambeth 306, ff 135[a]–135[b] (late 15 cent).
Brown-Robbins, Robbins-Cutler, no 3171.

Editions. Rel Ant, 1.248 (MS 3).
Wright T, Carols, PPS 36.89, 103 (MSS 1, 3).
Flügel E, Angl 26.276 (MS 2).
Furnivall F J, EETS 12.23 (MS 3).
Ch&Sidg, p 214 (composite text).
Dyboski R, EETSES 101.113, 188, 189 (MSS 2, 3; collation of MS 1).
Masters J E, Rymes of the Minstrels, Shaftesbury 1927, p 30 (MS 1).
Greene E E Carols, p 267 (MS 2 with collation of MSS 1, 3); 2nd edn, p 236.
Modernizations. Roberts D K, Straw in the Hair, London 1953, p 151.
Luria & Hoffman, p 72 (MS 2).
Commentary. Ch&Sidg, p 368.
Greene E E Carols, p 431; 2nd edn, p 452.
Utley CR, p 234.

[406] WHEN NETTULS IN WYNTER BRYNG FORTH ROSYS RED.

MSS. 1, Bodl 29734 (Eng poet e.1), ff 43^b–45^a (mid 15 cent); 2, Balliol 354, f 250^b (early 16 cent); 3, in BM printed book 1.B.55242, Bartholomaeus Anglicus, De Proprietatibus Rerum, flyleaves (early 16 cent).
Brown-Robbins, Robbins-Cutler, no 3999.
Editions. Wright T, Carols, PPS 23.66 (MS 1).
Flügel E, Angl 26.277 (MS 2).
Dyboski R, EETSES 101.114 (MS 2), 189 (collation of MS 1).
Garrett R M, Angl 32.358 (MS 3).
Masters J E, Rymes of the Minstrels, Shaftesbury 1927, p 18 (MS 1).
Greene E E Carols, p 269 (MS 1 with collation of MSS 2, 3); 2nd edn, p 238.
Utley F L, PMLA 60.346 (MS 3).
Kaiser R, Alt- und mittelenglische Anthologie, Berlin 1955, p 312 (MS 1, in part).
Robbins SL, p 103 (MS 1; omits burden).
Tydeman W, English Poetry 1400–1580, London 1970, p 58 (MS 1).
Silverstein, p 151 (MS 1).
Modernizations. FitzGibbon H M, Early English and Scottish Poetry, London 1888, p 200 (MS 1).
Wells C, A Nonsense Anthology, N Y 1903, p 186 (MS 3).
Roberts D K, Straw in the Hair, London 1953, p 149 (MS 3).
Davies, p 223 (MS 2).
Luria & Hoffman, p 65 (MS 2).
Commentary. Greene E E Carols, p 432; 2nd edn, p 453.
Robbins SL, p 264.

Utley CR, p 295.
Utley F L, PMLA 60.346 (close comparison of versions and argument for priority of MS 3).
Davies, p 352.

[407] THER WER iij WYLLY; 3 WYLY THER WER.

MS. Bodl 29734 (Eng poet e.1), f 13^a (mid 15 cent).
Brown-Robbins, Robbins-Cutler, no 3552.
Editions. Wright T, Carols, PPS 23.4.
Masters J E, Rymes of the Minstrels, Shaftesbury 1927, p 20.
CHEL, 2.437.
Silverstein, p 153.
Greene E E Carols, 2nd edn, p 239.
Sisam, p 466
Commentary. Toulmin Smith L, A Common-place Book of the Fifteenth Century, London 1886, p 12.
Greene E E Carols, 2nd edn, p 454.

[408] LOKE ER þIN HERTE BE SET.

MS. BM Sloane 2593, f 9^b (mid 15 cent).
Brown-Robbins, Robbins-Cutler, no 1938.
Editions. Wright T, Carols, Publ Warton Club 4.27.
Fehr B, Arch 109.49.
Greene E E Carols, p 270; 2nd edn, p 239.
Robbins SL, p 37.
Silverstein, p 130.
Modernization. Luria & Hoffman, p 66.
Commentary. Wright, Carols, Warton Club 4.107.
Greene E E Carols, p 432; 2nd edn, p 456.
Utley CR, p 179.
Robbins SL, p 239.

[409] ȜYNG MEN I RED THAT YE BEWAR.

MS. Bodl 29734 (Eng poet e.1), ff 29^b–30^a (mid 15 cent).
Brown-Robbins, Robbins-Cutler, no 4278.
Editions. Wright T, Carols, PPS 23.43.
Ch&Sidg, p 209.
Masters J E, Rymes of the Minstrels, Shaftesbury 1927, p 23.
Greene E E Carols, p 271; 2nd edn, p 240.
Commentary. Greene E E Carols, p 433; 2nd edn, p 456.
Utley CR, p 317.
Moore A K, The Secular Lyric in ME, Lexington Ky 1951, p 176.

[410] YING MEN I WARNE YOU EUERICHONE.

MS. BM Sloane 2593, ff 24^b–25^a (mid 15 cent).
Brown-Robbins, Robbins-Cutler, no 4279.
Editions. Wright T, Songs and Carols, London 1836, no 12; Carols, Publ Warton Club 4.70.
Ch&Sidg, p 207.
Greene E E Carols, p 271; 2nd edn, p 240.
Robbins SL, p 38.
Kaiser R, Alt- und mittelenglische Anthologie, Berlin 1955, p 309; Medieval English (3rd edn of Anthologie), Berlin West 1958, p 475.
Sisam, p 440.
Oliver, p 78.
Tydeman W, English Poetry 1400–1580, London 1970, p 57.
Greene Selection, p 144.
Modernizations. Luria & Hoffman, p 67.
Stevick, p 104.
Commentary. Greene E E Carols, p 433; 2nd edn, p 457.
Utley CR, p 317.
Robbins SL, p 240.
Moore A K, The Secular Lyric in Middle English, Lexington Ky 1951, p 177.
Greene Selection, p 241.
Oliver, p 51.

[411] ALL THAT I MAY SWINK OR SWETE.

MS. Bodl 29734 (Eng poet e.1), ff 23^a–23^b (mid 15 cent).
Brown-Robbins, Robbins-Cutler, no 210.
Editions. Wright T, Carols, PPS 23.26.
Ch&Sidg, p 208.
Masters J E, Rymes of the Minstrels, Shaftesbury 1927, p 9.
Greene E E Carols, p 272; 2nd edn, p 240.
Sisam, p 475.
Modernizations. FitzGibbon H M, Early English and Scottish Poetry, London 1888, p 239.
Williams C, The New Book of English Verse, Oxford 1938, p 63.
Auden W H, The Oxford Book of Light Verse, Oxford 1938, p 63.
Stevick, p 139.
Luria & Hoffman, p 68.
Commentary. Ch&Sidg, p 367.
Greene E E Carols, pp cviii, 433; 2nd edn, pp cxxxiii, 457.
Utley F L, How Judicare Came in the Creed, MS 8.304.
Utley CR, p 106.

Moore A K, The Secular Lyric in Middle English, Lexington Ky 1951, p 177.

[412] DAYLY IN ENGLOND MERUELS BE FOWND.

MS Bodl 29734 (Eng poet e.1), ff 42^b–43^b (mid 15 cent).
Brown-Robbins, Robbins-Cutler, no 667.
Editions. Wright T, Carols, PPS 23.64.
Masters J E, Rymes of the Minstrels, Shaftesbury 1927, p 14.
Greene E E Carols, p 272; 2nd edn, p 241.
Commentary. Wright, PPS 23.102.
Greene E E Carols, p 433; 2nd edn, p 457.
Utley CR, p 121.
Moore A K, The Secular Lyric in ME, Lexington Ky 1951, p 176.

[413] A LYTYLL TALE I WILL YOU TELL.

MS. Balliol 354, f 249^a (early 16 cent).
Brown-Robbins, no 65.
Editions. Flügel E, Angl 26.271.
Dyboski R, EETSES 101.110.
Greene E E Carols, p 273; 2nd edn, p 242.
Commentary. Utley CR, p 100.

[414] THYS INDRYS DAY BEFEL A STRYFE.

MS. Bodl 29734 (Eng poet e.1), f 34^b (mid 15 cent).
Brown-Robbins, Robbins-Cutler, no 3593.
Editions. Wright T, Carols, PPS 23.51.
Masters J E, Rymes of the Minstrels, Shaftesbury 1927, p 27.
Greene E E Carols, p 274; 2nd edn, p 243.
Sisam, p 481.
Commentary. Greene E E Carols, p 434; 2nd edn, p 458.
Utley CR, p 263.

[415] MANY A MAN BLAMYS HIS WYFFE PERDE.

MSS. 1, Bodl 29734 (Eng poet e.1), ff 54^b–55^a (mid 15 cent); 2, Balliol 354, f 241^a (early 16 cent).
Brown-Robbins, Robbins-Cutler, no 2090.
Editions. Wright T, Carols, PPS 23.86 (MS 1).
Flügel E, Angl 26.269 (MS 2).
Dyboski R, EETSES 101.109 (MS 2).
Masters J E, Rymes of the Minstrels, Shaftesbury

1927, p 24 (MS 1).
Greene E E Carols, p 275 (MS 2 with collation of MS 1); 2nd edn, p 243.
Commentary. Greene E E Carols, p 434; 2nd edn, p 458.
Utley CR, p 187.

[416] HIT IS FUL HEUE CHASTITE
(John Audelay).

MS. Bodl 21876 (Douce 302), f 30^b (early 15 cent).
Brown-Robbins, Robbins-Cutler, no 1630.
Editions. Chambers E K and F Sidgwick, MLR 6.78.
Whiting E K, EETS 184.208.
Greene E E Carols, p 276; 2nd edn, p 244.
Commentary. Whiting, EETS 184.254.
Greene E E Carols, p 434; 2nd edn, p 459.
Utley CR, p 169.

[417] FORE PRIDE IN HERTE HE HATIS ALLE ONE.

MS. Bodl 21876 (Douce 302), ff 29^b, 31^a (early 15 cent).
Brown-Robbins, no 840.
Editions. Chambers E K and F Sidgwick, MLR 6.69.
Whiting E K, EETS 184.197.
Greene E E Carols, p 277; 2nd edn, p 245.
Commentary. Haberly L, TLS Jan 12 1928, p 28.
Whiting, EETS 184.xviii.
Greene E E Carols, p 435; 2nd edn, p 459.

[418] I WOLD FAYN BE A CLARKE.

MSS. 1, Bodl 1491 (Laud misc 601), f 115^b (late 15 cent; fragment); 2, Balliol 354, f 252^a (early 16 cent).
Brown-Robbins, no 1399.
Editions. Flügel E, Angl 26.283 (MS 2).
Furnivall F J, EETS 32.403 (MS 2).
White B, EETS 187.xii (MS 2).
Bennett H S, England from Chaucer to Caxton, London 1928, p 45 (MS 2).
Greene E E Carols, p 277 (MS 2); 2nd edn, pp 245 (MS 2), 246 (MS 1).
Kaiser R, Medieval English (3rd edn of R Kaiser, Alt- und me Anthologie), Berlin West 1958, p 559 (MS 2, omits burden).
Greene Selection, p 145 (MS 2).
Davies, p 289 (MS 2).
Sisam, p 544 (MS 2).

Commentary. Greene E E Carols, p 435; 2nd edn, p 459.
Greene Selection, p 241.

[419] IN ALL THIS WARLD [N]IS A MERYAR LIFE.

MS. Bodl 29734 (Eng poet e.1), f 23^b (mid 15 cent).
Brown-Robbins, Robbins-Cutler, no 1468.
Editions. Wright T, Carols, PPS 23.27.
Ch&Sidg, p 210.
Masters J E, Rymes of the Minstrels, Shaftesbury 1927, p 7.
Bennett H S, England from Chaucer to Caxton, London 1928, p 31.
Greene E E Carols, p 278; 2nd edn, p 246.
Robbins SL, p 6.
Sisam, p 477.
Modernizations. Stevick, p 141.
Luria & Hoffman, p 81.
Commentary. Greene E E Carols, p 435; 2nd edn, p 461.
Utley CR, p 163.
Robbins SL, p 230.

[420] QWYLL MEN HAUE HER BORNYS FULL.

MS. St John's Camb 259 (S.54), f 9^b (mid 15 cent).
Brown-Robbins, no 4078.
Editions. James M R and G C Macaulay, MLR 8.80.
Greene E E Carols, p 278; 2nd edn, p 246.
Commentary. Greene E E Carols, p 435; 2nd edn, p 461.

[421] WE BERN ABOWTYN NON CATTES SKYNNYS.

MS. BM Sloane 2593, ff 26^b–27^a (mid 15 cent).
Brown-Robbins, no 3864.
Editions. Wright T, Songs and Carols, London 1836, no 16; Carols, Publ Warton Club 4.76.
Greene E E Carols, p 279; 2nd edn, p 246.
Robbins SL, p 6.
Tydeman W, English Poetry 1400–1580, London 1970, p 64.
Modernizations. Oliver, p 106.
Luria & Hoffman, p 81.
Commentary. Greene E E Carols, p 436; 2nd edn, p 461.
Robbins SL, p 229.

[422] LESTENIT LORDYNGES I YOU BESEKE.

MS. BM Sloane 2593, ff 29ᵃ–29ᵇ (mid 15 cent).
Brown-Robbins, no 1896.
Editions. Wright T, Songs and Carols, London 1836, no 17; Carols, Publ Warton Club 4.84.
Fairholt F W, Satirical Songs and Poems on Costume, PPS 27.50.
Ch&Sidg, p 243.
Greene E E Carols, p 279; 2nd edn, p 247.
Sisam, p 442.
Commentary. Greene E E Carols, p 436; 2nd edn, p 462.

[423] WAN IC WENTE BYYONDE THE SEE.

MS. Caius Camb 383, p 41 (mid 15 cent).
Brown-Robbins, Robbins-Cutler, no 3971.
Editions. Greene E E Carols, p 280; 2nd edn, p 247.
Greene Selection, p 146.
Commentary. Robbins-HP, p 323.
Greene Selection, p 242.
Greene E E Carols, 2nd edn, p 462.

[424] GALAWNT PRIDE THY FATHER YS DEDE.

MS. Bodl Rawl poet 34, f 4ᵇ (late 15 cent).
Brown-Robbins, no 892.
Editions. Furnivall F J, Acad 50.146.
Robbins-HP, p 138.
Greene E E Carols, 2nd edn, p 248.
Commentary. Greene E E Carols, 2nd edn, p 463.

[425] I BLESSYD BE CRISTES SONDE.

MS. Bodl 3340 (Arch Selden B.26), f 19ᵃ (mid 15 cent; music).
Robbins-Cutler, no 1405.5.
Editions. Early Bodleian Music 2.132 (with music).
Padelford F M, Angl 36.104.
Ch&Sidg, p 241.
Chambers OHEL, p 95.
Robbins-HP, p 97.
Greene Selection, p 147.
Sisam, p 382.
Greene E E Carols, 2nd edn, p 248.
Modernization. Stevens Med Carols, p 112 (with music).
Commentary. Bukofzer M F, Journ of the American Musicological Soc 7.64.
Stevens Med Carols, p 124.

Greene Selection, p 243.
Greene E E Carols, 2nd edn, p 464.

[426] IT FELL AGEYNS THE NEXT NYGHT.

MS. BM Royal 19.B.iv, f 97ᵇ (late 15 cent).
Brown-Robbins, no 1622.
Editions. Bowers R H, JEGP 51.393.
Robbins SL, p 43.
Perkins G, Journ of American Folklore 74.235.
Sisam, p 511.
Greene E E Carols, 2nd edn, p 249.
Modernization. Luria & Hoffman, p 125.
Commentary. Robbins R H, MLN 57.22.
Perkins, Journ of American Folklore 74.235; 77.263 (long and important study, listing many modern analogues).
Greene E E Carols, 2nd edn, p 466.

[427] I SHALL YOU TELL A FULL GOOD SPORT.

MSS. 1, Bodl 29734 (Eng poet e.1), ff 57ᵇ–59ᵇ (mid 15 cent); 2, Balliol 354, ff 206ᵇ–207ᵇ (early 16 cent); 3, BM Cotton Titus A.xxvi, ff 161ᵃ–162ᵃ (15 cent); 4, BM Cotton Vitel D.xii, f 43ᵇ (15 cent).
Brown-Robbins, nos 1362, *32; Robbins-Cutler, no 2358.5.
Editions. Ritson AS 1790, p 77; 1829, 1.136; 1877, p 117 (MS 3).
Wright T, Carols, PPS 23.91, 104 (MSS 1, 3).
Flügel NL, p 149 (MS 2).
Flügel E, Angl 26.208 (MS 2), 213 (MS 1 in part).
Dyboski R, EETSES 101.106, 187 (MSS 2, 3 with collation of MS 1).
Cook A S, A Literary ME Reader, Boston 1915, p 372 (MS 2).
Masters J E, The Gossips, Shaftesbury 1926 (MS 1).
Bennett H S, England from Chaucer to Caxton, London 1928, p 134 (MS 1, in part).
Robbins R H, Brit Mus Quart 27.12 (MS 4).
Greene E E Carols, p 280 (MSS 2, 3 with collation of MS 1); 2nd edn, pp 249 (MSS 1, 3), 253 (MS 4).
Coulton G G, Life in the Middle Ages, Cambridge 1954, 3.141 (MS 1).
Kaiser R, Medieval English (3rd edn of R Kaiser, Alt- und me Anthologie), Berlin West 1958, p 479 (MS 1, in part).
Greene Selection, p 148 (MS 2).
Pollet M, John Skelton, Paris 1962, p 251 (MS 1).
Sisam, p 437 (MS 2).

Modernization. Arber E, The Dunbar Anthology, London 1901, p 108 (MS 1).
Commentary. Robbins, Brit Mus Quart 27.12.
Greene E E Carols, p 436; 2nd edn, p 466.
Utley CR, p 152.
Edwards H L R, Skelton: The Life and Times of a Tudor Poet, London 1949, p 117.
Greene Selection, p 246.
Pollet, John Skelton, pp 131, 251.

[428] IS þER ANY GOOD MAN HERE.

MS. Balliol 354, f 251ᵇ (early 16 cent).
Brown-Robbins, no 1609.
Editions. Flügel E, Angl 26.280.
Dyboski R, EETSES 101.117.
Greene E E Carols, p 284; 2nd edn, p 253.
Robbins SL, p 1.
Sisam, p 540.
Modernizations. Stevick, p 167.
Luria & Hoffman, p 141.
Commentary. Greene E E Carols, p 437; 2nd edn p 468.
Robbins SL, p 227.

[429] JENTILL BUTLER BELL AMY.

MS. Balliol 354, ff 251ᵇ–252ᵃ (early 16 cent).
Brown-Robbins, no 903.
Editions. Flügel E, Angl 26.282.
Dyboski R, EETSES 101.118.
Ch&Sidg, p 227.
Greene E E Carols, p 285; 2nd edn, p 254.
Robbins SL, p 10.
Mason H A, Humanism and Poetry in the Early Tudor Period, London 1959, p 151.
Greene Selection, p 153.
Sisam, p 542.
Silverstein, p 147.
Modernizations. Davies, p 276.
Luria & Hoffman, p 144.
Commentary. Ch&Sidg, p 371.
Greene E E Carols, p 437; 2nd edn, p 468.
Robbins SL, p 232.
Greene Selection, p 247.

[430] BRING US IN NO BROWNE BRED FOR THAT IS MADE OF BRANE.

MSS. 1, Bodl 29734 (Eng poet e.1), ff 41ᵇ–42ᵃ (mid 15 cent); 2, BM Harley 541, f 214ᵇ (15 cent).
Brown-Robbins, no 549.
Editions. Ritson AS 1790, p xxiv; 1829, l.xlix (MS 2).
Wright T, Carols, PPS 23.63, 102 (MSS 1, 2).
Chappell W, Popular Music of the Olden Time, London [1853], 1.43 (MS 1).
Furnivall F J, EETS 32.363 (MS 1).
Sandys W, Festive Songs, PPS 23.16 (MS 1).
Chener P, N&Q 2s 10.471 (MS 2).
Gutch E, Notes on the Months, London 1866, p 418 (MS 1).
Hackwood F W, Inns, Ales, and Drinking Customs of Old England, N Y n d, p 328 (MS 1).
Wright T, Gentleman's Magazine ns 17.597 (MS 1).
Early Bodleian Music, 2.184 (MS 1).
Ch&Sidg, p 222 (MS 1).
Masters J E, Rymes of the Minstrels, Shaftesbury 1927, p 21 (MS 1).
Greene E E Carols, p 285; 2nd edn, p 254 (MSS 1, 2).
Robbins SL, p 9 (MS 1).
Kaiser R, Alt- und mittelenglische Anthologie, Berlin 1955, p 311 (MS 1); Medieval English (3rd edn of Anthologie), Berlin West 1958, p 478 (MS 1).
Greene Selection, p 154 (MS 1).
Sisam, p 482 (MS 1).
Silverstein, p 146 (MS 1).
Modernizations. [Vizetelly H], Christmas with the Poets, London 1851, p 24 (MS 1).
Bullen A H, Carols and Poems, London 1885, p 187 (MS 1).
Rickert Anc Eng Chr Carols, p 245 (MS 1).
Bullett G, The English Galaxy of Shorter Poems, London 1947 (in part).
Davies, p 217 (MS 1).
Stevick, p 142 (MS 1).
Oliver, p 104 (MS 1).
Luria & Hoffman, p 143 (MS 1).
Commentary. Ch&Sidg, p 370.
Greene E E Carols, pp xcv, 437 (corrects often-repeated statement that this carol has music); 2nd edn, pp cxx, 468.
Moore A K, The Secular Lyric in Middle English, Lexington Ky 1951, p 171.
Robbins SL, p 232.
Greene Selection, p 247.
Oliver, p 104.

[431] ALE MAK MANY A MANE TO STYK AT A BRERE.

MS. Bodl 29734 (Eng poet e.1), ff 52ᵃ–52ᵇ (mid 15 cent).
Brown-Robbins, no 163.
Editions. Wright T, Carols, PPS 23.81.
Sandys W, Festive Songs, PPS 23.17.

Ch & Sidg, p 224.
Masters J E, Rymes of the Minstrels, Shaftesbury 1927, p 22.
Greene E E Carols, p 287; 2nd edn, p 255.
Roberts D K, Straw in the Hair, London 1953, p 470.
Greene Selection, p 155.
Sisam, p 483.
Modernization. [Vizetelly H], Christmas with the Poets, London 1851, p 26 (incomplete).
Commentary. Greene E E Carols, p 438; 2nd edn, p 470.
Moore A K, The Secular Lyric in Middle English, Lexington Ky 1951, p 171.
Utley CR, p 165.
Speirs J, Medieval English Poetry: The Non-Chaucerian Tradition, London 1957, p 88.
Greene Selection, p 248.
Hackwood F W, Inns, Ales, and Drinking Customs of Old England, N Y n d, p 327.

[432] AT A PLACE WHERE HE ME SETT.

MS. Balliol 354, f 177^b (early 16 cent). PRINT: Bodleian Libr, Rawlinson 4to.598 (10) (Wynkyn de Worde; 1521).
Brown-Robbins, no 418.
Editions. Haslewood J, The Book containing the Treatises of Hawking, Hunting ... printed at Westminster by Wynkyne de Worde ..., London [1811], p 58 (PRINT).
Flügel NL, p 151 (PRINT).
Flügel E, Angl 12.587 (PRINT); 26.194 (MS, PRINT).
Ch & Sidg, p 245 (PRINT).
Dyboski R, EETSES 101.103 (MS), 186 (PRINT).
Padelford F M, Early Sixteenth Century Lyrics, Boston 1907, pp 75 (MS), 138 (PRINT).
Greene E E Carols, pp 287 (MS), 288 (PRINT); 2nd edn, p 256 (MS, PRINT).
Sisam, p 526 (MS).
Commentary. Greene E E Carols, p 438; 2nd edn, p 471.

[433] DET PERUYNKKLE HED YKOWMBYRGHT OWRE TOWN.

MS. County Archives Office, Maidstone, Kent, K.A.O.U 182 Z1, verso (late 15 cent).
Not in Brown-Robbins or Robbins-Cutler.
Edition. Greene E E Carols, 2nd edn, p 257.
Commentary. Greene E E Carols, 2nd edn, p 471.

[434] THE BYSSHOPE SCROPE THAT WAS SO WYSE.

MS. Trinity Camb 652 (R.4.20), f 171^a (late 15 cent).
Brown-Robbins, no 3308.
Editions. James M R, The Western MSS in the Libr of Trinity Coll Cambridge, Cambridge 1901, 2.148 (in part).
Furnivall F J, EETS 24.128.
Greene E E Carols, p 288; 2nd edn, p 257.
Robbins-HP, p 91.
Modernization. Brougham E M, Corn from Olde Fieldes, 2nd edn, London [1918], p 163.
Commentary. Greene E E Carols, p 438; 2nd edn, p 474.
Robbins-HP, p 294.

[435] OWRE KYNGE WENT FORTH TO NORMANDY.

MSS. 1, Bodl 3340 (Arch Selden B.26), ff 17^b–18^a (mid 15 cent; music); 2, Trinity Camb 1230 (0.3.58), no 7 (mid 15 cent; music).
Brown-Robbins, Robbins-Cutler, no 2716.
Editions. Percy T, Reliques of Ancient English Poetry, London 1765, 2.24 (MS 1; music at end of vol).
Rimbault E F, The Ancient Vocal Music of England, London [1847], no 19 (MS 1).
Stafford Smith J, A Collection of English Songs, London [1774], p 7 (MS 1; incomplete).
Burney C, A General History of Music, London 1776–89, 2.383 (MS 1).
Fuller Maitland J A and W S Rockstro, English Carols of the Fifteenth Century, London [1891], p 15 (MS 2 with music).
Early Bodleian Music, 2.128 (MS 1 with music).
Padelford F M, Angl 36.101 (MSS 1, 2).
Hecht H and L Schücking, Die englische Literatur, Potsdam 1927, facing p 144 (MS 1 facsimile).
Wooldridge H E, The Oxford History of Music, 2nd edn, London 1932, 2.7 (MS 1 in part, with music).
Greene E E Carols, p 289 (MS 1 with collation of MS 2); 2nd edn, p 257.
Robbins-HP, p 91 (MS 1).
Greenberg N, An English Songbook, Garden City N Y 1961, p 62 (MS 1), facing p 61 (facsimile).
Greene Selection, p 156 (MS 1).
Davies, p 168 (MS 1).
Sisam, p 381 (MS 1).
Modernizations. Duncan E, The Story of Minstrelsy, London 1907, p 93 (MS 2 with music).

Stevens Med Carols, p 6 (MS 2 with music).
Routley E, The English Carol, London 1958, p 37 (MS 1).
Stevick, p 94 (MS 1).
Stevens J, Tidings True, London [1976], p 27 (MS 2 with music).
Commentary. Padelford F M, Angl 36.84.
Greene E E Carols, pp civ, 439; 2nd edn, pp cxxix, 474.
Moore A K, The Secular Lyric in ME, Lexington Ky 1951, p 160.
Robbins-HP, p 296.
Greene Selection, p 250.
Routley, English Carol, p 37.

[436] THE ROSE IT ES THE FAIREST FLOUR.

MS. BM Addit 31042, f 110^b (mid 15 cent).
Brown-Robbins, Robbins-Cutler, no 3457.
Editions. Furnivall F J, N&Q 5s 12.124.
Greene E E Carols, p 290; 2nd edn, p 258.
Robbins-HP, p 92.
Greene Selection, p 157.
Modernization. Rickert Anc Eng Chr Carols, p 142.
Commentary. Greene E E Carols, p 439; 2nd edn, p 475.
Robbins-HP, p 297.
Greene Selection, p 251.

[437] FORE HE IS FUL ȜONG TENDER OF AGE (John Audelay).

MS. Bodl 21876 (Douce 302), ff 29^a–29^b (mid 15 cent).
Brown-Robbins, no 822.
Editions. Halliwell[-Phillipps] J O, PPS 14.viii.
Chambers E K and F Sidgwick, MLR 5.488.
Whiting E K, EETS 184.193.
Greene E E Carols, p 290; 2nd edn, p 258.
Robbins-HP, p 108.
Commentary. Whiting, EETS 184.251.
Greene E E Carols, p 440; 2nd edn, p 475.
Robbins-HP, p 305.

[438] SITHE GOD HATHE CHOSE ÞE TO BE HIS KNYȜT.

MS. Lambeth 306, f 136^a (late 15 cent).
Brown-Robbins, no 3127.
Editions. Halliwell[-Phillipps] J O, Archaeol 29.130.
Furnivall F J, EETS 15.4.

Parry E, Royal Visits and Progresses to Wales, Chester 1850, p 265.
Greene E E Carols, p 291; 2nd edn, p 259.
Robbins-HP, p 221.
Commentary. Gairdner J, Three Fifteenth-Century Chronicles, Camden Soc ns 28, London 1880, p 85.
Greene E E Carols, p 440; 2nd edn, p 476.
Robbins-HP, p 381.

[439] TYLL HOME SULL WYLEKYN THIS JOLY GENTYL SCHEPE.

MS. BM Addit 19046, f 74^a (late 15 cent).
Brown-Robbins, Robbins-Cutler, no 3742.
Editions. Greene E E Carols, p 292; 2nd edn, p 260.
Robbins-HP, p 198.
Commentary. Greene E E Carols, p 441; 2nd edn, p 477.
Brotanek R, Mittelenglische Dichtungen aus der Handschrift 432 des Trinity College in Dublin, Halle/Saale 1940, p 141.
Chambers OHEL, p 89.
Robbins-HP, p 361.

[440] I WARNE YOU EUERYCHONE FOR YE SHULD VNDERSTONDE.

MS. Trinity Dublin 432 (D.4.18), ff 70^b–73^a (late 15 cent).
Brown-Robbins, Robbins-Cutler, no 1380.
Editions. Madden F, Archaeol 29.343.
Parry E, Royal Visits and Progresses to Wales, Chester 1850, p 266.
Greene E E Carols, p 292; 2nd edn, p 260.
Thornley I, England under the Yorkists, London 1921, p 15 (in part).
Brotanek R, Mittelenglische Dichtungen aus der Handschrift 432 des Trinity College in Dublin, Halle/Saale 1940, p 138.
Robbins-HP, p 215.
Commentary. Madden, Archaeol 29.343.
Greene E E Carols, p 441; 2nd edn, p 477.
Brotanek, Me Dichtungen, p 141.
Robbins-HP, p 374.

[441] OUR SHYP IS LAUNCHED FROM THE GROUNDE.

MS. Trinity Coll Dublin 516 (E.5.10), ff 30^a–31^a (mid 15 cent).
Brown-Robbins, Robbins-Cutler, no 2727.
Editions. Madden F, Archaeol 29.326.
Robbins-HP, p 191.

Greene E E Carols, 2nd edn, p 262.
Commentary. Robbins-HP, p 356.
Greene E E Carols, 2nd edn, p 478.

[442] O MOOST NOBLE KING, THY FAME DOTH SPRING AND SPREDE.

MS. BM Cotton Julius B.xii, f 50^b (1488). PRINT: The Institution, Laws & Ceremonies of the Most Noble Order of the Garter (Elias Ashmole), London 1672, pp 594–595 (from MS penes Arth Com Anglesey, f 169).
Brown-Robbins, no 2526 (entry erroneous; corrected by Robbins-Cutler, no 2526).
Editions. The Poetical Works of John Skelton, ed after A Dyce, Boston 1856, 2.345 (often reprinted; PRINT).
Greene E E Carols, 2nd edn, p 264 (MS).
Commentary. Greene E E Carols, 2nd edn, p 480.

[443] JHESU FOR THY WONDES FYFF.

MS. BM Addit 5665, ff 44^b–45^a (late 15 cent; music).
Brown-Robbins, Robbins-Cutler, no 1710.
Editions. Fehr B, Arch 106.276.
Greene E E Carols, p 296; 2nd edn, p 266.
Robbins-HP, p 242.
Modernization. Stevens Med Carols, p 102 (with music).
Commentary. Greene E E Carols, p 443; 2nd edn, p 481.
Robbins-HP, p 390.
Stevens Med Carols, p 122.

[444] WHYLOME I PRESENT WAS WITH MY SOFFREYNE.

MS. Bodl 29734 (Eng poet e.1), ff 14^a–15^b (mid 15 cent).
Brown-Robbins, no 4075.
Editions. Wright T, Carols, PPS 23.5.
Greene E E Carols, p 298; 2nd edn, p 267.
Commentary. Greene E E Carols, pp cix, 444; 2nd edn, cxxxiv, 483.

[445] ICHOT A BURDE IN BOURE BRYHT.

MS. BM Harley 2253, ff 72^b–73^a (early 14 cent).
Brown-Robbins, no 1395.
Editions. Ritson AS 1790, p 26; 1829, 1.58; 1877, p 50.

Wright T, Specimens of Lyric Poetry, PPS 4.51.
Böddeker AED, p 168.
Wülcker R P, Altenglisches Lesebuch, Halle 1874, 1.108.
Cook A S, A Literary ME Reader, Boston 1915, p 412.
Kluge F, Mittelenglishes Lesebuch, 2nd edn Halle 1912, p 82.
Brandl A and O Zippel, ME Sprach- und Literaturproben, Berlin 1917; 2nd edn, Middle English Literature, N Y 1949, p 127.
Brown ELxiiiC, p 148.
Greene E E Carols, p 299; 2nd edn, p 268.
Quiller-Couch A, The Oxford Book of English Verse, Oxford 1939, p 5.
Brook G L, The Harley Lyrics, Manchester 1948, p 48.
Mossé F, A Handbook of ME, trans J A Walker, Baltimore 1952, p 208.
Kaiser R, Alt- und Mittelenglische Anthologie, Berlin 1955, p 294; Medieval English (3rd edn of Anthologie), Berlin West 1958, p 467.
Sitwell E, The Atlantic Book of British and American Poetry, Boston 1958, p 22 (in part).
Stemmler T, Die Englischen Liebesgedichte des MS Harley 2253, Bonn 1962, p 22.
Greene Selection, p 158.
Davies, p 88 (in part).
Sisam, p 122.
Silverstein, p 88.
Modernizations. Segar M G, Some Minor Poems of the Middle Ages, London 1917, p 30.
Stevick, p 43.
Luria & Hoffman, p 31.
Commentary. Bödekker AED, p 167.
Heider O, Untersuchungen zur mittelenglischen erotischen Lyrik (1250–1300), Halle 1905, p 35.
Ch&Sidg, p 277.
Greene E E Carols, pp cxxxix, 445; 2nd edn, pp clxvi, 483.
Robbins R H, SP 56.577.
Dickins and Wilson, p 228.
Brown ELxiiiC, p 230.
Wilson EMEL, p 261.
Brook, Harley Lyrics, pp 6, 12, 16, 82.
Moore A K, The Secular Lyric in ME, Lexington Ky 1951, p 65.
Spitzer L, Explication de Texte Applied to Three Great ME Poems, ALg 3.2; rptd Essays on English and American Literature, ed A Hatcher, Princeton 1962, p 193.
Stemmler, Die Englischen Liebesgedichte, p 168.
Greene Selection, p 252.
Davies, p 317.

[446] OFF SERUYNG MEN I WYLL BEGYNE.

MS. BM Sloane 1584, f 45^b (15 cent).
Brown-Robbins, no 2654.
Editions. Ritson AS 1790, p 92; 1829, 2.8; 1877, p 154.
Fairholt F W, PPS 27.58.
Furnivall F J, Captain Cox, His Ballads and Books, London 1871, pp xiii, cxxix.
Greene E E Carols, p 303; 2nd edn, p 272.
Robbins SL, p 32.
Stemmler T, Medieval English Love-Lyrics, Tübingen 1970, p 111.
Modernization. Luria & Hoffman, p 55.
Commentary. Greene E E Carols, p 446; 2nd edn, p 486.

[447] ALS I ME ROD THIS ENDRE DAI.

MS. Lincoln's Inn, Hale 135, f 135^b (early 14 cent).
Brown-Robbins, no 360.
Editions. Woodbine G E, MLR 4.236.
Skeat W W, MLR 5.105.
Sandison H E, BrynMawrMon 12.47.
Sisam K, Fourteenth Century Verse and Prose, Oxford 1921, p 163.
Brown ELxiiiC, p 119.
Greene E E Carols, p 305; 2nd edn, p 274.
Kermode F, English Pastoral Poetry, London 1955, p 45.
Kaiser R, Alt- und mittelenglische Anthologie, Berlin 1955, p 291; Medieval English (3rd edn of Anthologie), Berlin West 1958, p 463.
Greene Selection, p 161.
Sisam, p 98.
Stemmler T, Medieval English Love-Lyrics, Tübingen 1970, p 10.
Reiss E, The Art of the ME Lyric, Athens Ga 1972, p 44.
Modernizations. Adamson M R, A Treasury of ME Verse, London 1930, p 19.
Davies, p 77.
Stone B, Medieval English Verse, Baltimore 1964, p 100.
Stevick, p 36.
Luria & Hoffman, p 16.
Commentary. Skeat, MLR 5.104.
Sandison, BrynMawrMon 12.47.
Brown ELxiiiC, p 214.
Greene E E Carols, p 447; 2nd edn, p 487.
Robbins R H, SP 577.
Wilson EMEL, p 263.

Onions C T, MÆ 17.32.
Chambers OHEL, p 77.
Moore A K, The Secular Lyric in ME, Lexington Ky 1951, p 58.
Kermode, Eng Pastoral Poetry, p 239.
Sitwell E, The Atlantic Book of British and American Poetry, Boston 1958, p 24.
Greene Selection, p 254.
Reiss, edn, p 45.
Utley F L, Manual, 3.726 (VII[52]).

[448] THE MAN THAT I LOUED ALTHERBEST.

MS. Camb Univ 5943, f 178^b (early 15 cent).
Brown-Robbins, Robbins-Cutler, no 3418.
Editions. M[ayer] L S, Music Cantelenas Songs Etc, London 1906, sheet k.
Greene E E Carols, p 306; 2nd edn, p 275.
Robbins SL, p 16.
Kaiser R, Alt- und mittelenglische Anthologie, Berlin 1955, p 297; Medieval English (3rd edn of Anthologie), Berlin West 1958, p 470.
Sisam, p 375.
Stemmler T, Medieval English Love-Lyrics, Tübingen 1970, p 69.
Modernization. Luria & Hoffman, p 53.
Commentary. Greene E E Carols, p 447; 2nd edn, p 488.
Robbins SL, p 234.

[449] ALL THIS DAY IC HAN SOUGHT.

MS. Caius Camb 383, p 41 (mid 15 cent).
Brown-Robbins, Robbins-Cutler, no 225.
Editions. Greene E E Carols, p 306; 2nd edn, p 275.
Robbins SL, p 24.
Greene Selection, p 162.
Sisam, p 452.
Stemmler T, Medieval English Love-Lyrics, Tübingen 1970, p 83.
Modernization. Luria & Hoffman, p 86.
Commentary. Greene E E Carols, pp xcv, 447; 2nd edn, p 488.
Robbins SL, p 236.
Greene Selection, p 255.

[450] LADD Y THE DAUNCE A MYSSOMUR DAY.

MS. Caius Camb 383, p 41 (mid 15 cent).
Brown-Robbins, no 1849.
Editions. Greene E E Carols, p 307; 2nd edn, p 276.

Robbins SL, p 22.
Kaiser R, Alt- und mittelenglische Anthologie, Berlin 1955, p 310; Medieval English (3rd edn of Anthologie), Berlin West 1958, p 476.
Greene Selection, p 164.
Davies, p 204.
Stemmler T, Medieval English Love-Lyrics, Tübingen 1970, p 81.
Silverstein, p 134.
Modernizations. Stevick, p 125.
Luria & Hoffman, p 85.
Commentary. Greene E E Carols, pp xcv, 447; 2nd edn, p 489.
Robbins SL, p 236.
Moore A K, The Secular Lyric in ME, Lexington Ky 1951, p 180.
Greene Selection, p 256.
Davies, p 347.

[451] þIS ENDY DAY I METE A CLERKE.

MS. St John's Camb 259 (S.54), ff 2ᵇ–3ᵃ (mid 15 cent).
Brown-Robbins, no 3594.
Editions. James M R and G C Macaulay, MLR 8.71.
Greene E E Carols, p 308; 2nd edn, p 277.
Robbins SL, p 18.
Stemmler T, Medieval English Love-Lyrics, Tübingen 1970, p 87.
Modernization. Luria & Hoffman, p 82.
Commentary. Greene E E Carols, p 448; 2nd edn, p 490.
Robbins SL, p 234.

[452] Y LOUEDE A CHILD OF THIS CUNTRE.

MS. Caius Camb 383, p 210 (mid 15 cent).
Brown-Robbins, no 1330.
Editions. Greene E E Carols, p 308; 2nd edn, p 277.
Robbins SL, p 17.
Greene Selection, p 166.
Sisam, p 456.
Tydeman W, English Poetry 1400–1580, London 1970, p 60.
Stemmler T, Medieval English Love-Lyrics, Tübingen 1970, p 86.
Modernization. Luria & Hoffman, p 54.
Commentary. Greene E E Carols, p 448; 2nd edn, p 491.
Robbins SL, p 234.
Greene Selection, p 258.

[453] MYN OWNE DERE LADI FAIR AND FRE.

MS. Caius Camb 383, p 210 (mid 15 cent; music).
Brown-Robbins, no 2185.
Editions. Greene E E Carols, p 300; 2nd edn, p 269.
Robbins SL, p 13.
Stemmler T, Medieval English Love-Lyrics, Tübingen 1970, p 85.
Modernizations. Stevens Med Carols, p 111 (burden only; with music).
Luria & Hoffman, p 38.
Commentary. Robbins SL, p 233.
Stevens Med Carols, p 123.

[454] I SAW NEUER JOY LYK TO THAT SIGHT.

MS. Lincoln Coll Oxf Lat 100, f 2ᵇ (mid 15 cent).
Brown-Robbins, no 2232 (indexed by first line of burden).
Editions. Robbins SL, p 145.
Stemmler T, Medieval English Love-Lyrics, Tübingen 1970, p 72.
Greene E E Carols, 2nd edn, p 269.
Commentary. Greene E E Carols, 2nd edn, p 484.

[455] SOME TYME Y LOUED AS YE MAY SEE.

MS. Camb Univ Ff.1.6, ff 136ᵇ–137ᵃ (late 15 cent).
Brown-Robbins, no 3179.
Editions. Ritson AŞ 1829, 1.129.
Rel Ant, 1.24.
Arber E, The Dunbar Anthology, London 1901, p 118.
Greene E E Carols, p 301; 2nd edn, p 269.
Commentary. Robbins R H, The Findern Anthology, PMLA 69.610 (detailed and important).

[456] ALAS GOOD MAN MOST YOW BE KYST.

MS. Canterbury Cathedral, Christ Church Letters, vol 2, no 173 (ca 1500).
Brown-Robbins, no 150.
Editions. Reports of the Historical MSS Commission, 5, Appendix p 458 (in part).
Ebworth J W, Bagford Ballads, London 1878, 1.519.
Greene E E Carols, p 301; 2nd edn, p 270.
Robbins SL, p 28.

Sisam, p 521.
Stemmler T, Medieval English Love-Lyrics, Tübingen 1970, p 107.
Modernization. Luria & Hoffman, p 78.
Commentary. Greene E E Carols, p 445; 2nd edn, p 485.
Utley F L, Manual, 3.728 (VII [55]).

[457] THAT HART MY HART HATH IN SUCHE GRACE.

MS. Canterbury Cathedral, Christ Church Letters, vol 2, no 174 (ca 1500).
Brown-Robbins, Robbins-Cutler, no 3271.
Editions. Reports of the Historical MSS Commission, 5, Appendix p 458.
Greene E E Carols, p 302; 2nd edn, p 271.
Commentary. Greene E E Carols, p 446; 2nd edn, p 485.

[458] THE LAST TYME I THE WEL WOKE.

MS. Camb Univ Ff.5.48, f 114[b] (late 15 cent).
Brown-Robbins, Robbins-Cutler, no 3409.
Editions. Rel Ant, 1.1.
Brand T, Popular Antiquities, London 1849, 2.379.
Hazlitt W C, Faiths and Folklore, London 1905, 2.617.
Greene E E Carols, p 309; 2nd edn, p 278.
Robbins SL, p 19.
Stemmler T, Medieval English Love-Lyrics, Tübingen 1970, p 70.
Modernizations. Luria & Hoffman, p 82.
Grigson G, The Faber Book of Popular Verse, London 1971, p 142.
Commentary. Greene E E Carols, p 448; 2nd edn, p 491.
Robbins SL, p 235.
Moore A K, The Secular Lyric in ME, Lexington Ky 1951, p 179.

[459] O LORDE SO SWETT SER IOHN DOTHE KYS.

MS. Huntington Libr EL.1160, f 11[b] (ca 1500).
Brown-Robbins, no 2494.
Editions. Robbins SL, p 20.
Stemmler T, Medieval English Love-Lyrics, Tübingen 1970, p 105.
Silverstein, p 133.
Greene E E Carols, 2nd edn, p 278.
Modernization. Luria & Hoffman, p 83.

Commentary. Robbins SL, p 235.
Greene E E Carols, 2nd edn, p 492.

[460] AS I WENT ON YOLE DAY IN OURE PROSESSION.

MS. BM Sloane 2593, ff 34[a]–34[b] (early 15 cent).
Brown-Robbins, Robbins-Cutler, no 377.
Editions. Wright T, Songs and Carols, London 1836, no 20; Carols, Publ Warton Club 4.100.
Ch&Sidg, p 220.
Greene E E Carols, p 309; 2nd edn, p 278.
Robbins SL, p 21.
Kaiser R, Alt- und mittelenglische Anthologie, Berlin 1955, p 312; Medieval English (3rd edn of Anthologie), Berlin West 1958, p 477.
Greene Selection, p 166.
Sisam, p 445.
Stemmler T, Medieval English Love-Lyrics, Tübingen 1970, p 89.
Tydeman W, English Poetry 1400–1580, London 1970, p 59.
Silverstein, p 129.
Modernizations. Auden W H, The Oxford Book of Light Verse, Oxford 1938, p 53.
Speirs J, Medieval English Poetry: The Non-Chaucerian Tradition, London 1957, p 82.
Davies, p 162.
Oliver, p 122.
Grigson G, The Faber Book of Popular Verse, London 1971, p 141.
Luria & Hoffman, p 84.
Owen L J and N H, Middle English Poetry: An Anthology, Indianapolis Ind 1971, p 14.
Commentary. Ch&Sidg, p 370.
Greene E E Carols, pp lxiii, 449; 2nd edn, pp lxxxiv, 492.
Sahlin M, Étude sur la carole médiévale, Upsala 1940, pp 57, 84, 121.
Robbins SL, p 235.
Greene Selection, p 259.
Davies, p 336.
Owen, ME Poetry, p 349.

[461] IT WAS A MAYDE OF BRENTEN ARS.

MSS. No MS extant. PRINT: Huntington Libr, Christmas carolles newely Inprynted (Richard Kele), p [18] (ca 1550; STC, no 5205).
Robbins-Cutler, no 1641.5.
Editions. Reed Christmas Carols, p 36 (facsimile).
Greene E E Carols, p 311; 2nd edn, p 280.

Grigson G, The Faber Book of Popular Verse, London 1971, p 106.
Commentary. Greene E E Carols, p 450; 2nd edn, p 496.

[462] I PRAY YOW, MAYDENS EUERYCHONE.

MS. Camb Univ Addit 7350, Box 2, f 2ª (late 15 cent).
Robbins-Cutler, no 1344.5.
Editions. Robbins R H, PMLA 81.310.
Greene E E Carols, 2nd edn, p 280.
Commentary. Robbins, PMLA 81.309.
Greene E E Carols, 2nd edn, p 496.

[463] THE NUNNE WALKED ON HER PRAYER.

MSS. No MS extant. PRINT: Huntington Libr, Christmas carolles newely Inprynted (Richard Kele), p [19] (ca 1550; STC, no 5205).
Robbins-Cutler, no 3443.5 (erroneous).
Editions. Reed Christmas Carols, p 37 (facsimile).
Greene E E Carols, p 311; 2nd edn, p 281.
Robbins R H, PMLA 81.308.
Grigson G, The Faber Book of Popular Verse, London 1971, p 106.
Commentary. Greene E E Carols, p 450; 2nd edn, p 496.

[464] THER WAS A FRIER OF ORDER GRAY.

MS. Camb Univ Addit 7350, Box 2, f 2ª (late 15 cent).
Robbins-Cutler, no 3443.5.
Editions. Robbins R H, PMLA 81.309.
Greene E E Carols, 2nd edn, p 281.
Commentary. Robbins, PMLA 81.308.
Greene E E Carols, 2nd edn, p 497.

[465] SOMTYME Y LOUID SO DO Y YUT.

MS. Camb Univ Ff.1.6, f 139ᵇ (late 15 cent).
Brown-Robbins, Robbins-Cutler, no 3180.
Editions. Ritson AS 1790, p 72; 1829, 1.129; 1877, p 111.
Rel Ant, 1.202.
Greene E E Carols, p 316; 2nd edn, p 288.
Sisam, p 489.
Modernization. Adamson M R, A Treasury of ME Verse, London 1930, p 149.

Commentary. Greene E E Carols, p 452; 2nd edn, p 502.
Utley CR, p 236.
Robbins SL, p 277.
Moore A K, The Secular Lyric in ME, Lexington Ky 1951, p 178.
Robbins R H, The Findern Anthology, PMLA 69.610.

[466] I AM SORY FOR HER SAKE.

MS. Caius Camb 383, p 68 (mid 15 cent).
Brown-Robbins, Robbins-Cutler, no 1280.
Editions. Greene E E Carols, p 317; 2nd edn, p 288.
Robbins SL, p 34.
Greene Selection, p 167.
Sisam, p 454.
Stemmler T, Medieval English Love-Lyrics, Tübingen 1970, p 84.
Modernizations. Stevick, p 128.
Oliver, p 112.
Luria & Hoffman, p 40.
Commentary. Greene E E Carols, p 452; 2nd edn, p 503.
Utley CR, p 146.
Robbins SL, p 238.
Greene Selection, p 260.

[467] I SAWE A DOGE SETHYNG SOWSE.

MS. Balliol 354, f 241ᵇ (early 16 cent).
Brown-Robbins, Robbins-Cutler, no 1350.
Editions. Flügel E, Angl 26.270.
Dyboski R, EETSES 101.110.
Greene E E Carols, p 317; 2nd edn, p 289.
Modernization. Grigson G, The Faber Book of Popular Verse, London 1971, p 87.
Commentary. Greene E E Carols, p 453; 2nd edn, p 504.

[468] MY LADY WENT TO CAUNTERBURY.

MSS. No MS extant. PRINT: Huntington Libr, Christmas carolles newely Inprynted (Richard Kele), p [20] (ca 1550; STC, no 5205).
Robbins-Cutler, no 2250.8.
Editions. [Bliss P,] Bibliographical Miscellanies, Oxford 1813, p 53.
Husk W H, Songs of the Nativity, London 1868, p 134.
Ch&Sidg, p 254.
Reed Christmas Carols, p 38 (facsimile).

Greene E E Carols, p 318; 2nd edn, p 290.
Auden W H, The Oxford Book of Light Verse, Oxford 1938, p 87.
Roberts D K, Straw in the Hair, London 1953, p 155.
Greene Selection, p 168.
Modernization. Rickert Anc Eng Chr Carols, p 143.
Commentary. Reed Christmas Carols, p 78.
Greene E E Carols, p 453; 2nd edn, p 504.
Greene Selection, p 202.

[469] IPSE MOCAT ME.

MSS. No MS extant. PRINT: Huntington Libr, Christmas carolles newely Inprynted (Richard Kele), p [22] (ca 1550; STC, no 5205).
Robbins-Cutler, no 1605.5
Editions. Reed Christmas Carols, p 40 (facsimile).
Greene E E Carols, p 319; 2nd edn, p 291.
Commentary. Reed Christmas Carols, p 79.
Greene E E Carols, p 454; 2nd edn, p 506.

[470] YE BEN MY FATHER BY CREATION.

MS. Stanbrook Abbey 3, f 241[b].
Robbins-Cutler, no 4242.5.
Editions. Ker N R, MÆ 34.233.
Greene E E Carols, 2nd edn, p 87.
Commentary. Greene E E Carols, 2nd edn, p 385.

[471] FETYS BEL CHERE.

MS. Bodl 3340 (Arch Selden B.26), f 24[a] (mid 15 cent; music).
Brown-Robbins, Robbins-Cutler, no 795.
Editions. Early Bodleian Music, 2.150 (with music).
Padelford F M, Angl 36.109.
Modernizations. Stevens Med Carols, p 113 (with music).
Luria & Hoffman, p 133.
Commentary. Stevens Med Carols, p 124.
Bukofzer M F, Journ of the American Musicological Soc 7.64.

[472] HERE LOKYNG WAS SO LOUELY.

MSS. 1, Bodl 3340, f 18[a] (mid 15 cent; music); 2, Advocates 18.7.21, f 5[b] (late 14 cent).
Brown-Robbins, Robbins-Cutler, no 353 (indexed by first line of burden of MS 1).
Editions. Early Bodleian Music, 2.132 (MS 1 with music).

Padelford F M, Angl 36.102 (MS 1).
Copley J, Seven English Songs and Carols of the Fifteenth Century, Leeds School of English Language Texts and Monographs No 6, p 14 (MS 1 with music).
Brown RLxivC, p 78 (MS 2).
Modernization. Stevens Med Carols, p 112 (MS 1 with music).
Commentary. Stevens Med Carols, p 123 (MS 1).
Brown RLxivC, p 264 (MS 2).

[473] HAYL BLESSID FLOUR OF VIRGINITE.

MS. Bodl 3340, f 26[a] (mid 15 cent; music).
Brown-Robbins, Robbins-Cutler, no 1036.
Editions. Early Bodleian Music, 2.152 (with music).
Padelford F M, Angl 36.110.
Modernizations. Stevens Med Carols, p 25 (with music).
Robbins Christmas Carols, p 49 (with music).
Commentary. Stevens Med Carols, p 118.

[474] AND SAVE THYS FLOWRE WYCHE YS OWRE KYNG.

MS. BM Cotton Domit xviii, f 248[b] (1492).
Robbins-Cutler, no 306.8.
Editions. Rimbault E F, A Little Book of Songs and Ballads, London 1851, p 33.
Flügel NL, p 160.
Robbins R H, NM 55.293.
Robbins-HP, p 96.
Commentary. Robbins, NM 55.289.
Robbins-HP, p 300.

[475] ALLAS WO SAL MYN HERTE SLAKEN.

MS. Advocates 18.7.21, f 121[b] (late 14 cent).
Brown-Robbins, no 162.
Edition. Robbins R H, MLN 53.244.
Commentary. Robbins, MLN 53.243.

[476] FRAGMENTS OF TEXTS PROBABLY IN CAROL FORM.

a. "... cristus...."
MS. Bodl 2265, 12 strips removed from binding (15 cent; music).
Not in Brown-Robbins or Robbins-Cutler.
Edition. Greene E E Carols, 2nd edn, p 295.

b. "Mari milde haþ boren a chylde."

MS. Caius Camb 383, p 210 (mid 15 cent).
Brown-Robbins, no 2109.
Edition. Greene E E Carols, p 320; 2nd edn, p 292.

c. "The borys hed haue we in broght."
MS. St John's Camb 259 (S.54), f 1ª (mid 15 cent).
Brown-Robbins, no *56; Robbins-Cutler, no *3312.
Editions. James M R and G C Macaulay, MLR 8.68.
Greene E E Carols, p 321; 2nd edn, p 293.
Greene Selection, p 209.
Commentary. James and Macaulay, MLR 8.86.

d. "... ye xall ete."
MS. St John's Camb 259 (S.54), ff 13ᵇ–14ª (mid 15 cent).
Brown-Robbins, no *77; Robbins-Cutler, no *4256.3.
Editions. James M R and G C Macaulay, MLR 8.85.
Greene E E Carols, p 321; 2nd edn, p 293.

e. "þᵘ wost wol lytyl ho is thi foo."
MS. BM Sloane 2593, f 2ª (mid 15 cent).
Brown-Robbins, no *67; Robbins-Cutler, no 3700.5.
Editions. Wright T, Carols, Publ Warton Club 4.1.
Fehr B, Arch 109.41.
Greene E E Carols, p 322; 2nd edn, p 293.

f. "In evyn yer sitte a lady...."
MS. St John's Camb 259 (S.54), f 13ª (mid 15 cent).
Brown-Robbins, Robbins-Cutler, no 1492.
Editions. James M R and G C Macaulay, MLR 8.85.
Greene E E Carols, p 322; 2nd edn, p 294.
Commentary. Utley CR, p 166.

g. "Wymmen ben fayre for t...."
MS. Camb Univ Addit 5943, last flyleaf, recto (early 15 cent).
Brown-Robbins, Robbins-Cutler, no 4218.
Edition. Greene E E Carols, p 322; 2nd edn, p 294.
Commentary. Utley CR, p 310.

h. "This ender day wen me was wo."
MS. BM Addit 5666, f 3ᵇ (early 15 cent; music).
Brown-Robbins, no 3595.
Editions. Ritson AS 1877, p xlvi (with music).
Duncan E, The Story of Minstrelsy, London 1907, p 86 (with music).
Wilson R M, The Lost Literature of Medieval England, London 1952, p 180.
Greene E E Carols, p 323; 2nd edn, p 294.
Modernization. Stevens Med Carols, p 110 (with music).

i. "Of Mary de...."
MS. Camb Univ Addit 2764(1).C, recto (15 cent; music).
Robbins-Cutler, no *2636.5.
Edition. Greene E E Carols, 2nd edn, p 294.

XV. BALLADS

by
David C. Fowler

BACKGROUND BOOKS: The following important, frequently listed entires, here given full statement, are referred to in abbreviated form in the pages that follow. For abbreviations not appearing in this list, consult the general Table of Abbreviations.

Bronson TTCB	Bronson B H, The Traditional Tunes of the Child Ballads, 4 vols, Princeton N J 1959–72.
Child	Child F J, ed, The English and Scottish Popular Ballads, 5 vols, Boston and N Y 1882–98; rptd N Y 1956, 1962, 1965.
Coffin BTBNA	Coffin T P, The British Traditional Ballad in North America, Phila 1950; rvsd 1963.
Dean-Smith	Dean-Smith M, A Guide to English Folk Song Collections 1822–1952, Liverpool 1954.
Friedman VBFB	Friedman A B, The Viking Book of Folk Ballads, N Y 1956.
Kinsley OBB	Kinsley J, The Oxford Book of Ballads, Oxford 1969.
Leach BB	Leach MacE, The Ballad Book, N Y 1955.
Sargent and Kittredge	Sargent H C and G L Kittredge, English and Scottish Popular Ballads, Boston 1904.
Simpson BBBM	Simpson C M, The British Broadside Ballad and Its Music, New Brunswick N J 1966.

The following general sections (BIBLIOGRAPHIES, SURVEYS AND HISTORIES OF BALLAD RESEARCH, GUIDES TO BALLAD VARIANTS, EDITIONS, and STUDIES) have been prepared with the special help of William I. Siegmund.

BIBLIOGRAPHIES.

Stevenson T G, The Bibliography of James Maidment, Edinburgh 1883.
Child, Bibliography, 5.503; Sources of the Texts of the English and Scottish Ballads, 5.397.
Cameron J, A Bibliography of Peter Buchan's Publications, Edinburgh 1901.
Fairley J A, Bibliography: Peter Buchan, Aberdeen 1914.
Volkskundliche Bibliographie 1917–37/38, Berlin 1919–57 (continued by the Internationale volkskundliche Bibliographie).
MLA International Bibliography of Books and Articles on the Modern Languages and Literatures 1921– , N Y 1921– (published as a suppl to PMLA. The title varies: MLA American Bibliography, 1921–55; Annual Bibliography, 1956–62; MLA International Bibliography, 1963–).
Pound L, Oral Literature, in The Cambridge History of American Literature, Cambridge and N Y 1921, 4.502, 799.
Mattfield J, The Folk Music of the Western Hemisphere: A List of References in the N Y Public Libr, N Y 1925.
Holmes T J and G W Thayer, English Ballads and Songs in the John G White Collection of Folklore and Orientalia of the Cleveland Public Libr and in the Libr of Western Reserve Univ, Cleveland 1931.
Fox-Strangways A H and M Karpeles, Cecil Sharp's Publications, in their Cecil Sharp, London 1933; 2nd edn N Y 1955, p 221.
Henry M E, A Bibliography for the Study of American Folksongs, London 1937.
Boggs R S, Folklore Bibliography for 1937–63, Southern Folklore Quart 2(1938)–28(1964) (annual; continued by M E Simmons' Folklore Bibliography).
Check List of the Writings of Phillips Barry, in The New Green Mountain Songster, ed H H Flanders et al, New Haven Conn 1939; rptd Hatboro Pa 1966, p 273.
Day C L and E B Murrie, English Song Books 1651–1702, London 1940.
Lomax A and S R Cowell, American Folk Song and Folk Lore: A Regional Bibliography, N Y 1942.
Internationale volkskundliche Bibliographie/International Folklore Bibliography/Bibliographie internationale des arts et traditions populaires 1939/41– , Bonn 1949.
Bonser W, A Bibliography of Folklore as Contained in the First Eighty Years of the Publications of the Folklore Society, Folklore Soc Publ no 121, London 1951.
Haywood C, A Bibliography of North American Folklore and Folksong, 2 vols, N Y 1951; 2nd edn N Y 1961.
Dean-Smith.
Montgomerie W, Bibliography of the Scottish Ballad Manuscripts 1730–1825, diss Edinburgh 1954.
Annual Folklore Bibliography for 1954–62, Journ American Folklore 68(1955)–76(1963) (the annual bibliographies for 1963 and 1964 were published in Abstracts of Folklore Stud).
Lawless R M, Folksingers and Folksongs in America: A Handbook of Biography, Bibliography, and Discography, N Y 1960; new rvsd edn N Y 1965.
Abstracts of Folklore Stud 1(1962)– .
Brednich R W, Verzeichnis der Schriften Erich Seemanns, Jahrbuch für Volksliedforschung 9(1964).171.
Richmond W E, Annual Bibliography [of Folklore] 1963–64, in Abstracts of Folklore Stud 3(1964)–4(1965).
Simmons M E, Folklore Bibliography for 1964–72, Southern Folklore Quart 29(1965)–37 (1973) (annual; preceded by R S Boggs' Folklore Bibliography).
Gillis F and A P Merriam, Ethnomusicology and Folk Music: An International Bibliography of Dissertations and Theses, Middletown Conn 1966.
Montgomerie W, A Bibliography of the Scottish Ballad Manuscripts 1730–1825; pt 1: Scottish Ballad MSS and the Libraries Where They are Deposited, SSL 4.3; pt 2: Elizabeth Cochrane Her Songbook, SSL 4.79; pt 3: David Herd's MS, SSL 4.194; pt 4: The Mansfield MS, SSL 5.107; pt 5: The Glenriddell Ballad MS [and An Old Lady's Complete Set of Ballads], SSL 6.91; pts 6–7: Mrs Brown's MSS, SSL 7.60, 238.
Vetterl K, A Select Bibliography of European Folk Music, Prague 1966.
Andraschke P, Verzeichnis der Schriften John Meiers, Jahrbuch für Volksliedforschung 14 (1969).124.
Annual Biblio of Scottish Literature 1970, The Bibliotheck suppl no 1– .
Jahresbibliographie der Volksballadenforschung 1(1968)– , compiled by Z Kumer, R W Brednich and O Sirovátka, Ljubljana 1970–.
Chapple J A V, Miscellanies, Anthologies and

Collections of Poetry, in New CBEL, vol 2, col 327 (a thorough chronological list for the years 1660–1800 followed by a select list for the 19th cent).

Rogers P, Thomas Percy, in New CBEL, vol 2, col 242.

Bronson TTCB, 4.517.

Randolph V, Ozark Folklore: A Bibliography, Indiana Univ Publ, Folklore Institute Monograph Series, Bloomington 1972, vol 24 (a model biblio of the folklore of a region; very well annotated; songs and ballads, p 1).

Simmons M E, Folklore Biblio for 1973, Indiana Univ Publ, Folklore Institute Monograph Series, Bloomington 1975, vol 28.

Vaughan Williams Memorial Libr Catalogue of the Eng Folk Dance and Song Soc: Acquisitions to the Libr of Books, Pamphlets, Periodicals, Sheet Music and MSS from Its Inception to 1971, London 1973.

Davies R T, Ballads, in New CBEL, vol 1, col 711.

SURVEYS AND HISTORIES OF BALLAD RESEARCH.

Wilgus D K, Anglo-American Folksong Scholarship since 1898, New Brunswick N J 1959.

Lundell J A, Skandinavische Volkspoesie, in Paul Grundriss, 2nd edn, 2.1135.

Meier J, Deutsche und niederländische Volkspoesie, in Paul Grundriss, 2nd edn, 2.1176.

Hustvedt S B, Ballad Criticism in Scandinavia and Great Britain during the 18th Cent, Scandinavian Monographs 11, N Y 1916; Ballad Books and Ballad Men: Raids and Rescues in Britain, America and the Scandinavian North since 1800, Cambridge Mass 1930; rptd N Y 1970 (Appendix A: The Grundtvig-Child Correspondence; Appendix B: The Grundtvig-Child Index of English and Scottish Ballads).

Dal E, Nordisk folkeviseforskning siden 1800, Universitets Jubilæets Danske Samfund [publ no] 376, Copenhagen 1956 (a fairly detailed English summary of this comprehensive survey of Scandinavian ballad research from 1800 until roughly the middle of this century begins on p 410).

Friedman A B, The Ballad Revival: Studies in the Influence of Popular on Sophisticated Poetry, Chicago 1961.

Hildeman K-I, Modern Scandinavian Ballad Research, in J C H R Steenstrup, The Medieval Popular Ballad, Seattle 1968, p xi.

GUIDES TO BALLAD VARIANTS.

Shearin H G and J H Combs, A Syllabus of Kentucky Folk-Songs, Transylvania Univ Stud in Eng, Lexington 1911, vol 2.

Pound L, Folk-Song of Nebraska and the Central West: A Syllabus, Nebraska Acad of Sciences Publ, Lincoln 1915, vol 9, no 3.

Davis A K Jr, Folk Songs of Virginia: A Descriptive Index and Classification of Material Collected under the Auspices of the Virginia Folklore Soc, Durham N C 1949.

Coffin BTBNA.

White E A, An Index of English Songs Contributed to the Journ of the Folk Song Soc 1899–1931 and Its Continuation The Journ of the Eng Folk Dance and Song Soc to 1950, ed M Dean-Smith, London 1951.

Dean-Smith.

Wilgus D K, A Syllabus of Kentucky Folksongs, Kentucky Folklore Record 1(1955).31.

Laws G M, American Balladry from British Broadsides: A Guide for Students and Collectors of Traditional Song, Publ of the American Folklore Soc Bibliographical and Special Series, Phila 1957, vol 8.

Simpson BBBM.

Lewis M E B, A Bibliography of Ballads from Selected Collections of Scottish Ballads and Songs, diss Univ of Pa 1969; DA 29.3545A.

Rosenberg B A, The Folksongs of Virginia: A Checklist of the WPA Holdings of Alderman Libr Univ of Virginia, Charlottesville 1969.

EDITIONS.

Percy T, Reliques of Ancient English Poetry, 3 vols, London 1765; 2nd edn 1767; 3rd edn 1775; 4th edn 1794 (there were many edns of the work during the 19th cent; standard edn is by H B Wheatley, 3 vols, London 1876–77; rptd N Y 1966).

Ritson J, A Select Collection of English Songs, 3 vols, London 1783.

Ritson AS.

Ritson J, Scotish Song, 2 vols, London 1794; rvsd edn Glasgow 1869; Robin Hood, 2 vols, London 1795.

Scott W, Minstrelsy of the Scottish Border, 3 vols; vols 1–2, Kelso 1802; vol 3, Edinburgh 1803; 2nd edn Edinburgh 1803 (given its appeal and Scott's renown, the work was published approximately a dozen times before his death in 1832 and roughly once a decade after that for the rest of the 19th cent; standard edn is by T F Henderson, 4 vols, London and N Y 1902; reissued 1932).

Jamieson R, Popular Ballads and Songs from Tradition, Manuscripts and Scarce Editions with Translations of Similar Pieces from the Danish Language and a Few Originals by the Editor, 2 vols, Edinburgh 1806.

Finlay J, Scottish Historical and Romantic Ballads, 2 vols, Edinburgh 1808.

Gilchrist J, A Collection of Ancient and Modern Scottish Ballads, 2 vols, Edinburgh 1815.

Campbell A, Albyn's Anthology, 2 vols, Edinburgh 1816–18; rptd Norwood Pa 1970.

Buchan P, Gleanings of Scotch, English and Irish Scarce Old Ballads, Peterhead 1825; republished with the title Gleanings of Scarce Old Ballads, Aberdeen 1891; Aberdeen edn rptd Norwood Pa 1970.

Kinloch G R, Ancient Scottish Ballads, London 1827.

Motherwell W, Minstrelsy: Ancient and Modern, Glasgow 1827.

Lyle T, Ancient Ballads and Songs, London 1827; rptd Norwood Pa 1970.

Buchan P, Ancient Ballads and Songs of the North of Scotland, 2 vols, Edinburgh 1828; republished Edinburgh 1875; 1875 edn rptd Norwood Pa 1970.

Dauney W, Ancient Scotish Melodies, Edinburgh 1838.

Chappell W, A Collection of National Airs, 2 vols, London 1838–40.

Chambers R, Twelve Romantic Scottish Ballads, Edinburgh 1844.

Dixon J H, Scottish Traditional Versions of Ancient Ballads, London 1845; Ancient Poems, Ballads, and Songs of the Peasantry of England, PPS 42, London 1846; rvsd edn by R Bell, London 1857.

Rimbault E F, Musical Illustrations of Bishop Percy's Reliques of Ancient English Poetry, London 1850; rptd Norwood Pa 1970.

Chappell W, Popular Music of the Olden Time, 17 pts, London 1855–59; 2 vols, London 1859; rptd with an introd by F W Sternfeld, N Y 1965.

Bell R, Early Ballads Illustrative of History, Traditions and Customs, London 1856; Ancient Poems, Ballads and Songs of the Peasantry of England, London 1857 (a rvsd edn of Dixon, Ancient Poems, Ballads and Songs of the Peasantry, PPS 42).

Child F J, English and Scottish Ballads, 8 vols, Boston 1857–58; London 1861.

Aytoun W E, The Ballads of Scotland, 2 vols, Edinburgh and London 1858.

PFMS.

Bruce J C and J Stokoe, Northumbrian Minstrelsy: A Collection of the Ballads, Melodies and Small-Pipe Tunes of Northumbria, Newcastle-upon-Tyne 1882; rptd with a foreword by A L Lloyd, Hatboro Pa 1965.

Child.

Sumner H, The Besom-Maker and Other Country Folk Songs, London 1888.

Baring-Gould S and H F Sheppard, Songs and Ballads of the West, 4 pts, London 1889–92; 2nd edn London 1891–95.

Stokoe J and S Reay, Songs and Ballads of Northern England, Newcastle-on-Tyne and London ca 1890.

Kidson F, Traditional Tunes: A Collection of Ballad Airs Chiefly Obtained in Yorkshire and the South of Scotland, Oxford 1891; rptd Wakefield 1970.

Lang A, Border Ballads, London 1895.

Hecht H, Songs from David Herd's Manuscripts, Edinburgh 1904.

Sargent and Kittredge.

Campbell O and C J Sharp, English Folk Songs from the Southern Appalachians, N Y 1917.

Pound L, American Ballads and Songs, N Y 1922; rptd with a foreword by K S Goldstein, N Y 1972.

Cox J H, The Ballads and Songs of West Virginia, diss Harvard 1923.

Williams A, Folk Songs of the Upper Thames, London 1923; rptd Detroit 1968.

Gray R P, Songs and Ballads of the Maine Lumber-Jacks, Cambridge Mass 1924.

Cox J H, Folk-Songs of the South, Cambridge Mass 1925; rptd Hatboro Pa 1963 and N Y 1967.

Greig G, Last Leaves of Traditional Ballads and Ballad Airs Collected in Aberdeenshire, ed A Keith, Aberdeen 1925.

Eckstorm F H and M W Smyth, Minstrelsy of Maine: Folk-Songs and Ballads of the Woods and the Coast, Boston 1927.

Hudson A P, Specimens of Mississippi Folklore, Ann Arbor Mich 1928.

Mackenzie W R, Ballads and Sea Songs from Nova Scotia, Cambridge Mass 1928; rptd with a foreword by G M Laws Jr, Hatboro Pa 1963.

Barry P, F Eckstorm and M W Smyth, British Ballads from Maine, New Haven 1929.

Davis A K Jr, Traditional Ballads of Virginia,

Cambridge Mass 1929; rptd Charlottesville Va 1969.

Henry M E, Ballads and Songs of the Southern Highlands, Journ American Folklore 42 (1929). 254.

Ord J, The Bothy Songs and Ballads of Aberdeen, Banff and Moray, Angus and the Mearns, Paisley 1930; rptd Norwood Pa 1971.

Smith R, South Carolina Ballads, Cambridge Mass 1928.

Flanders H H and G Brown, Vermont Folk-Songs and Ballads, Brattleboro Vt 1931; 2nd edn 1932; rptd Hatboro Pa 1968.

Creighton H, Songs and Ballads from Nova Scotia, Toronto 1932; rptd with a bibliographical and autobiographical postscript, N Y 1966.

Major M, British Ballads in Texas, in Tone the Bell Easy, ed J F Dobie, Publ of the Texas Folklore Soc 10.131.

Sharp C J and M Karpeles, English Folk Songs from the Southern Appalachians, 2 vols, London 1932.

Greenleaf E B and G Y Mansfield, Ballads and Sea Songs of Newfoundland, Cambridge Mass 1933; rptd Hatboro Pa 1968.

Henry M E, Songs Sung in the Southern Appalachians, London 1933.

Karpeles M, Folk Songs from Newfoundland, Oxford 1934; rptd Hamden Conn 1970.

Greene E E Carols.

Hudson A P, G Herzog and H Halpert, Folk Tunes from Mississippi, N Y 1937.

Scarborough D, A Song Catcher in Southern Mountains: American Folk Songs of British Ancestry, N Y 1937; rptd N Y 1966.

Henry M E, Folk-Songs from the Southern Highlands, N Y 1938.

Eddy M O, Ballads and Songs from Ohio, N Y 1939.

Flanders H H et al, The New Green Mountain Songster: Traditional Folk Songs of Vermont, New Haven Conn 1939; rptd with an introd by T P Coffin, Hatboro Pa 1966.

Gardener E E and G J Chickering, Ballads and Songs of Southern Michigan, Ann Arbor Mich 1939; rptd with a foreword by A B Friedman, Hatboro Pa 1967.

Belden H M, Ballads and Songs Collected by the Missouri Folk-Lore Soc, Univ of Missouri Stud 15(1940), no 1; rptd Columbia Mo 1955.

Thompson H W, Body, Boots and Britches, Phila 1940; rptd Detroit 1968.

Brewster P G, More Indiana Ballads and Songs, Southern Folklore Quart 5(1941).169.

Randolph V, British Ballads and Songs, Ozark Folksongs, vol 1, Columbia Mo 1946.

Arnold B, Folksongs of Alabama, Birmingham Ala 1950.

Owens W A, Texas Folk Songs, Publ of the Texas Folklore Soc 23, Austin and Dallas 1950.

Beattie W, Border Ballads, Harmondsworth 1952.

Belden H M and A P Hudson, Folk Ballads from North Carolina, in The Frank C Brown Collection of North Carolina Folklore, vol 2, Durham N C 1952.

Flanders H H and M Olney, Ballads Migrant in New England, N Y 1953.

Leach BB.

Schinhan J P, The Music of the Ballads, in The Frank C Brown Collection of North Carolina Folklore, vol 4, Durham N C 1957.

Reeves J, The Idiom of the People: English Traditional Verse ... from the MSS of C J Sharp, London 1958; rptd N Y 1965.

Bronson TTCB.

Davis A K Jr, More Traditional Ballads of Virginia, Chapel Hill N C 1960.

Reeves J, The Everlasting Circle: English Traditional Verse ... from the MSS of S Baring-Gould, H E D Hammond and G B Gardiner, London 1960.

Flanders H H, Ancient Ballads Traditionally Sung in New England, 4 vols, Phila 1960-65 (critical analyses by T P Coffin; music annotations by B Nettl).

Cox J H, Traditional Ballads Mainly from West Virginia, ed H Halpert and G Herzog, American Folk-Song Publ no 3, mimeo; rptd along with the companion edn of folk songs as Traditional Ballads and Folk-Songs Mainly from West Virginia, ed G W Boswell, Publ of the American Folklore Soc Bibliographic and Special Series, vol 15, Phila 1964.

Moore E P and C O, Ballads and Folk Songs of the Southwest, Norman Okla 1964.

Fowke E, Traditional Singers and Songs from Ontario, Hatboro Pa 1965 (musical transcriptions by P Seeger).

Henderson F and F Collinson, New Child Ballad Variants from Oral Tradition, Scottish Stud 9(1965).1.

Hodgart M J C, The Faber Book of Ballads, London 1965.

Peacock K, Songs of the Newfoundland Outports, 1 vol in 3, National Museum of Canada Bull no 197 = Anthropological Series no 65, Ottawa 1965.

Leach MacE, Folk Ballads and Songs of the Lower Labrador Coast, National Museum of Canada Bull no 201 = Anthropological Series no 68,

Ottawa 1965.
Purslow F, Marrow Bones: English Folk Songs from the Hammond and Gardiner MSS, London 1965.
Duncan J B, Folk Songs of Aberdeenshire, ed P N Shuldham-Shaw, London 1967.
Kinsley OBB.
Riddle A, A Singer and Her Songs: Almeda Riddle's Book of Ballads, ed R D Abrahams and G Foss, Baton Rouge La 1970.
Buchan D D, A Scottish Ballad Book, London 1973.
Stewart M and H M Shire, King Orphius, Sir Colling, The Brother's Lament, and Litel Musgray: Poems from Scottish MSS of circa 1586 and circa 1630, Cambridge 1973.
Grigson G, The Penguin Book of Ballads, Harmondsworth 1975 (with introd).
Holloway J and J Black, Later English Broadside Ballads, Lincoln Neb 1975.
Lyle E B, Andrew Crawfurd's Collection of Ballads and Songs, vol 1, Edinburgh 1975; PSTS 4s 9.
Dobson R B and J Taylor, Rymes of Robin Hood: An Introd to the English Outlaw, London 1976.

STUDIES.

Pegge Mr, Observations on Dr Percy's Account of Minstrels among the Saxons, Archaeol 2.100.
Chambers R, The Romantic Scottish Ballads: Their Epoch and Authorship, Edinburgh 1820s, 1859, 1869.
Ritson J, Letters from Joseph Ritson to ... G Paton, ed J Maidment, Edinburgh 1829.
Fiedler E, Geschichte der volkstümlichen schottischen Liederdichtung, 2 vols in 1, Zerbst 1846.
Smith A, Scottish Ballads, Edinburgh 1857.
Wolf F J, Über die Frage in welchen Kreisen sind die jetzt sogenannten Volksballaden entstanden, Leipzig 1857.
Clyne N, The Romantic Scottish Ballads and the Lady Wardlaw Heresy, Aberdeen 1859.
Murray J C, The Ballads and Songs of Scotland in View of their Influence on the Character of the People, London 1874.
Napier J, Old Ballad Folklore, Folklore Record 2.92.
Bennett W C, Contributions to a Ballad History of England and the States Sprung from Her, London 1879.
Child F J, Invitation to Unite in an Effort to Collect Popular Ballads from Oral Tradition, Cambridge Mass 1881.
Meyer R M, Über den Refrain, Zeitschrift für vergleichende Litteraturgeschichte 1.34.

Child F J, Letters to C K Sharpe, ed A Allerdyce, 2 vols, London 1888.
Blackie J S, Scottish Song: Its Wealth, Wisdom, and Social Significance, Edinburgh 1889.
Tappert W, Wandernde Melodien: Eine musikalische Studie, 2nd rvsd and enlarged edn, Berlin 1889.
Hahner L, Kulturhistorisches im engl Volkslied, I: Naturgefühl, Mann und Frau, Eltern und Kinder, Essen und Trinken in den Robin-Hood Balladen, diss Freiburg 1892.
Hales J, Folia Litteraria: Essays and Notes on English Literature, N Y 1893.
Odell G C D, Simile and Metaphor in the English and Scottish Ballads, diss Columbia Univ 1893.
Williams A M, Studies in Folk-Song and Popular Poetry, Boston 1894.
Baring-Gould S, An Historical Sketch of English National Song, London [1895 or later]; rptd London 1962.
Geddie J, The Balladists, Edinburgh 1896.
Gummere F B, The Ballad and Communal Poetry, HSNPL 5.41; rptd in The Critics and the Ballad, ed MacE Leach and T P Coffin, Carbondale Ill 1961, p 20.
Boynton J H, Studies in the English Ballad Refrain with a Collection of Ballad and Early Song Refrains, diss Harvard 1897.
Henderson T F, Scottish Vernacular Literature: A Succinct History, Edinburgh 1898; 2nd rvsd edn, London 1900; 3rd rvsd edn, Edinburgh 1910, p 335.
Flügel E, Zur Chronologie der engl Balladen, Angl 21.312.
Görbing F, Die Elfen in den engl- und schottischen Balladen, diss Halle 1899; Beispiele von realiserten Mythen in den engl und schottischen Balladen, Angl 23.1.
Fehr B, Die formelhaften Elemente in den alten engl Balladen, 1. Teil: Wortformeln, diss Basle 1900.
Bowen E, The Old English Ballad, SR 9.286.
Gummere F B, The Beginnings of Poetry,. N Y 1901; rptd 1965.
Thuren H, Dans og kvaddigtning paa Færøerne, Copenhagen 1901.
Fairley J A, Peter Buchan: Printer and Ballad Collector, Peterhead 1903.
Gummere F B, Primitive Poetry and the Ballad, MP 1.193, 217, 373.
Jaehde W, Religion, Schicksalsglaube, Vorahnungen, Träume, Geister und Rätsel in den engl-schottischen Volksballaden, diss Halle 1905.
Böckel O, Psychologie der Volksdichtung, Leipzig

1906; 2nd edn 1913.
Elliot W F, The Trustworthiness of Border Ballads, Edinburgh 1910.
Hart W M, Professor Child and the Ballad, PMLA 21.755; rptd in Child, 5.[570].
Hillmann W, England und Schottland in den engl-schottischen Volksballaden, diss Halle 1906.
Ibsen H, The Saga and the Ballad, Contemporary Rev 90.318.
Meier J, Kunstlieder im Volksmunde: Materialien und Untersuchungen, Halle 1906.
Schütte P, Die Liebe in den engl und schottischen Volksballaden, diss Halle 1906.
Belden H M, Archaisms in Ballads, MLN 22.263.
Gummere F B, The Popular Ballad, London and Cambridge Mass 1907; rptd N Y 1959; Ballad Origins, The Nation 85.184.
Hart W M, Ballad and Epic, HSNPL 11; rptd N Y 1967.
Rüdiger G, Zauber und Aberglaube in den engl-schottischen Volksballaden, diss Halle 1907.
Clawson W, The Robin Hood Ballads, diss Harvard 1907; Ballad and Epic, Journ American Folklore 21.349.
Baldow G, Ehe und Familie in den engl-schottischen Volksballaden, diss Halle 1908.
Gaussen A C C, Percy: Prelate and Poet, London 1908.
Gummere F B, Ballads, in CHEL 2.449, 553.
Kreusch F, Verstellung, Heuchelei, Hinterlist und Verrat in den engl-schottischen Volksballaden, diss Halle 1908.
Shuldham-Shaw P N and E B Lyle, edd, Folk-Song in the North East: J B Duncan's Lecture 1908, Scottish Stud 18.1.
Thuren H, Folkesangen paa Færφerne, Folklore Fellows Publ Northern Series 2, Copenhagen 1908.
Züge K, Das Verkleidungsmotiv in den engl-schottischen Volksballaden, diss Halle 1908.
Greig G, Folk-Song of the North-East, 2 vols, Peterhead 1909–14; rptd in 1 vol with a foreword by K S Goldstein and A Argo, Hatboro Pa 1963 (articles contributed to the Buchan Observer from Dec 1907 to June 1911 printed in book form).
Ker W P, On the History of the Ballads 1100–1500, Proc of the British Acad 4.179; rptd separately Folcroft Pa 1970.
Liestøl K, Samanhengen millom dei engelske og dei norderlendske folkevisorne, Syn og Segn 13.106; rptd in his Saga og folkeminne, Oslo 1941, p 156.
Mackenzie W R, Ballad-Singing in Nova Scotia, Journ American Folklore 22.327.
Olrik A, Epische Gesetze der Volksdichtung, Zeitschrift für deutsches Altertum 51.1; trans into English, Epic Laws of Folk Narrative, in The Study of Folklore, ed A Dundes, Englewood Cliffs N J 1965, p 129.
Bryant F E, Chapters toward a History of Early English Popular Balladry, diss Harvard 1910.
Elliot W F, Further Essays on Border Ballads, Edinburgh 1910.
Lang A, Sir Walter Scott and the Border Minstrelsy, London 1910.
Wagner A, Die sittlich-religiöse Lebensanschauung des engl und schottischen Volkes nach den Volksballaden, diss Halle 1910.
Jackson G P, From Young Lessing to Percy's Reliques, diss Univ of Chicago 1911.
Leskien A, Zur Wanderung von Volksliedern, Berichte über die Verhandlungen der Königliche Sächsische Gesellschaft der Wissenschaften zu Leipzig, philologisch-historische Klasse 63.177.
Shearin H G, British Ballads in the Cumberland Mountains, SR 19.313.
Belden H M, The Relation of Balladry to Folklore, Journ American Folklore 24.1; Balladry in America, Journ American Folklore 25.1.
Delattre F, English Fairy Poetry from the Origins to the 17th Cent, London and Paris 1912.
Dixon W M, English Epic and Heroic Poetry, London 1912.
Henderson T F, The Ballad in Literature, Cambridge and N Y 1912.
Miller F, The Glenriddell Ballad Manuscript, Arch 128.79.
Bryant F E, A History of English Balladry and Other Studies, Boston 1913 and 1919; rptd Folcroft Pa 1970; rptd with new introd by R Thomson with the title A History of English Balladry through the Reign of Elizabeth, Norwood Pa 1973.
Moore J R, Omission of the Central Action in English Ballads, MP 11.391.
Pound L, The Southwestern Cowboy Songs and the English and Scottish Ballads, MP 11.195.
Barry P, The Transmission of Folk-Song, Journ American Folklore 27.67.
Beatty A, Ballad, Tale and Tradition: A Study in Popular Literary Origins, PMLA 29.473.
Ehrke K, Das Geistermotiv in den schottisch-englischen Volksballaden: Ein Beitrag zur Geschichte der Volksdichtung, diss Marburg 1914.
Sidgwick F, The Ballad, London 1914.
Kidson F and M Neal, English Folksong and

Dance, Cambridge 1915.
Lomax J A, Some Types of American Folk-Song, Journ American Folklore 28.1.
Newbolt H, British Ballads, English Rev 21.452.
Walker W, Peter Buchan and Other Papers on Scottish and English Ballads and Songs, Aberdeen 1915; rptd Norwood Pa 1973.
Firth C, Ballads and Broadsides, in Shakespeare's England, ed S Lee, 2 vols, Oxford 1916–17, 2.511; rptd in his Essays Historical and Literary, ed G Davis, Oxford 1938, p 1.
Moore J R, The Influence of Transmission on the English Ballads, MLR 11.385.
Riemann H, Folkloristische Tonalitätstudien, I: Pentatonik und tetrachordale Melodik im schottischen, irischen, walisischen, skandinavischen, und spanischen Volksliede und im gregorianischen Gesange, Abhandlungen der Kgl Sächsisches Forschungsinstitute zu Leipzig, Forschungsinstitut für Musikwissenschaft heft 1, Leipzig 1916.
Lowie R H, Oral Tradition and History, Journ American Folklore 30.161.
Meier J, Volksliedstudien, Strassburg 1917.
Pound L, The Beginnings of Poetry, PMLA 32.201.
Eicker H, Studien zur engl-schottischen Volksballade historischen Charakters, diss Halle 1918/1924.
McGill J, Old Ballad Burthens, Musical Quart 4.293.
Pound L, The Ballad and the Dance, PMLA 34.360; King Cnut's Song and Ballad Origins, MLN 34.162; The English Ballads and the Church, PMLA 35.161; The Uniformity of the Ballad Style, MLN 35.217; Poetic Origins and the Ballad, N Y 1921.
Mackenzie W R, The Quest of the Ballad, Princeton 1919; rptd N Y 1966, 1969.
Liebermann F, Zu Liedrefrain und Tanz im engl Mittelalter, Arch 140.261.
McKnight G H, Ballad and Dance, MLN 35.464; rptd in The Critics and the Ballad, ed MacE Leach and T P Coffin, Carbondale Ill 1961, p 30.
Mertens K, Die Entwicklung der engl und schottischen Volksballaden in Verhältnis zu den dänischen Folkeviser, diss Halle 1920/1925.
Parsons E C, The Study of Variants, Journ American Folklore 33.87.
Schwebsch E, Schottische Volkslyrik in James Johnson's The Scot's Musical Museum, Palaes 95.
Joy F L, Magic in the English and Scottish Popular Ballads, South Atlantic Quart 20.222.
Leach H G, Angevin Britain and Scandinavia, HSCL 6.
Olrik A, Nogle grundsætninger for sagnforskning, ed H Ellekilde, Danmarks folkeminder no 23, Copenhagen 1921.
Rankin J W, Rhythm and Rime before the Norman Conquest, PMLA 36.401.
Wimberly L C, Minstrelsy, Music and Dance in the English and Scottish Popular Ballads, Univ of Nebraska Stud in Lang, Lit and Criticism no 4.
Stewart G R Jr, Modern Metrical Technique as Illustrated by Ballad Meter 1700–1920, diss Columbia Univ 1922.
Gerould G H, The Making of Ballads, MP 21.15.
Mackensen L, Der singende Knochen, FFC 49.
Smith W, Elements of Comedy in the English and Scottish Ballads, in Vassar Mediaeval Stud, ed C F Fiske, New Haven Conn 1923, p 83.
Watt L MacL, The Scottish Ballads and Ballad Writing, Paisley 1923.
Beckwith M, The English Ballad in Jamaica: A Note upon the Origin of the Ballad Form, PMLA 39.455.
Hewlett M H, Ballad Origins, in his Last Essays, N Y 1924, p 69.
Peinecke A, Hornstoff und Hornballade: Ein Beitrag zur Geschichte der Volksdichtung, diss Marburg 1924.
Pound L, The Term Communal, PMLA 39.440.
Combs J H, Folk-Songs du Midi des États-Unis, Paris 1925.
Ker W P, Collected Essays, ed by C Whibley, 2 vols, London 1925.
Scarborough D, On the Trail of Negro Folk-Songs, Cambridge Mass 1925; rptd with a foreword by R Abrahams, Hatboro Pa 1963.
Stewart G R Jr, The Meter of the Popular Ballad, PMLA 40.933.
Eicker H, Die historische Volksballade der Engländer und Schotten, Neue anglistische Arbeiten 7, Leipzig 1926.
Keith A, Scottish Ballads: Their Evidence of Authorship and Origin, E&S 1s 12.243; rptd in The Critics and the Ballad, ed MacE Leach and T P Coffin, Carbondale Ill 1961, p 39.
Graves R, The English Ballad: A Short Critical Survey, London 1927; rptd Folcroft Pa 1970.
Haworth P, English Hymns and Ballads and Other Studies in Popular Literature, Oxford 1927; rptd Folcroft Pa 1969.
Ruhrmann F G, Studien zur Geschichte und Charakteristik des Refrains in der engl Literatur, AF 64.

Taylor A, Precursors of the Finnish Method of Folklore Study, MP 25.481.
Wimberly L C, Death and Burial Lore in the English and Scottish Popular Ballads, Univ of Nebraska Stud in Lang, Lit, and Criticism no 8; Folklore in the English and Scottish Ballads, Chicago 1928; rptd N Y 1959, 1965.
Wright R L, Hawkers and Walkers in Early America, Phila 1927.
DeVries J, Die Märchen von klugen Rätsellösern, FFC 73.
Powell L F, Percy's Reliques, Libr 4s 9.113.
Davis A K Jr, Some Problems of Ballad Publication, Musical Quart 14.283; On the Collecting and Editing of Ballads, American Speech 5.452.
Fischer G, Das Tragische als ästhetischer Wert in den engl-schottischen Volksballaden, diss Marburg 1929.
Holz F, Die Mädchenräuberballade: Eine kritische Betrachtung von 120 Fassungen aus deutsch- und fremdläandischen Sprachgebieten als Beitrag zur vergleichenden Literaturgeschichte, diss Heidelberg 1929.
Pound L, A Recent Theory of Ballad Making, PMLA 44.622.
Randolph V, The Ozark Play Party, Journ American Folklore 42.201.
Schwietering J, Das Volkslied als Gemeinschaftslied, Euphorion 30.236.
Steinberg H, Studien zur engl-schottische Border-Ballade, diss Marburg 1929.
Child F J, Letters on Scottish Ballads from F J Child to W[illiam] W[alker], Aberdeen 1930; rptd Norwood Pa 1970.
Kahlert A C D, Metaphor und Symbol in der engl-schottischen Volksballaden, diss Marburg 1930.
Krappe A H, The Science of Folklore, N Y 1930; rptd 1964, p 173.
Kühnemund M, Ausdruck der Intensität durch Quantität in den engl-schottischen Volksballade, diss Marburg 1930.
Mark J, Recollections of Folk-Musicians, Musical Quart 16.170.
Seeman E, Variantenbildung im Vortrag desselben Sängers, Jahrbuch f Volksliedforschung 2.74.
Harris C A, The Element of Repetition in Nature and the Arts, Musical Quart 17.302.
Martin B, Allan Ramsay: A Study of his Life and Works, Cambridge Mass 1931.
Randolph V, The Ozarks: An American Survival of Primitive Society, N Y 1931; Ozark Mountain Folk, N Y 1932.

Gerould G H, The Ballad of Tradition, Oxford 1932; rptd N Y 1957.
Humbert G, Literarische Einflüsse in schottischen Volksballaden, Studien zur engl Philologie heft 74, Halle 1932.
Megas G A, Die Ballade von der Losgekauften, Jahrbuch f Volksliedforschung 3.54.
Pound L, On the Dating of the English and Scottish Ballads, PMLA 47.10.
Watkin-Jones A, Bishop Percy and the Scottish Ballads, E&S 18.110.
Willinsky M, Bischof Percys Bearbeitung der Volksballaden und Kunstgedicht seines Folio-Manuskriptes, Beiträge zur engl Philologie heft 22, Leipzig 1932.
Wilson W E, The Making of the Minstrelsy, Cornhill Magazine ns 73.266 (an edn of J E Shortreed, Conversations with my Father on the Subject of his Tours with Sir Walter Scott in Liddesdale).
Borregaard M C, The Epithet in English and Scottish, Spanish and Danish Popular Ballads, The Hague 1933; rptd Norwood Pa 1973.
Fox-Strangways A H and M Karpeles, Cecil Sharp, London 1933; 2nd edn N Y 1955.
Gainer P W, The Refrain in the English and Scottish Popular Ballads, diss St Louis Univ 1933.
Schmidt W, Die Entwicklung der engl-schottischen Volksballaden, Angl 57.1, 113.
Schröder E, Das Tanzlied von Kölbigk, Nachrichten von der Gesellschaft der Wissenschaften zu Göttingen, Philologisch-historische Klasse 1933, p 355.
Barbeau M, How Folk-Songs Travelled, Music and Letters 15.306.
Dennis L, Percy's Essay on the Ancient Metrical Romances, PMLA 49.81.
Herzog G, Speech Melody and Primitive Music, Musical Quart 20.452.
Hudson A P, Folksongs of the Whites, in Culture in the South, ed W T Couch, Chapel Hill N C 1934.
Hyder C, Swinburne and the Popular Ballad, PMLA 49.295.
Marwell H, Thomas Percy: Studien zur Entstehungsgeschichte seiner Werke, diss Göttingen 1934.
Walker A J, Popular Songs and Broadside Ballads in the English Drama 1559–1642, diss Harvard Univ 1934.
Whiting B J, Proverbial Material in the Popular Ballad, Journ American Folklore 47.22.
Chickering G J, The Origin of a Ballad, MLN 50.465.

Hustvedt S B, Grundtvig's Index B of English and Scottish Ballads, PMLA 50.595; A Melodic Index of Child's Ballad Tunes, Publ of UCLA in Langs and Lits 1.51.
Panke F, Die schottischen Liebesballaden: Ein Beitrag zur Entstehung von Variantenbildungen, Neue deutsche Forschungen 53, Berlin 1935.
Williams I A, English Folksong and Dance, London 1935.
Ammermann E, Die schottische Zauberballade, diss Marburg 1936.
Hendren J W, A Study of Ballad Rhythm, Princeton Stud in Eng 14.
Jordans H, The Old French Chansons d'histoire as a Possible Origin of the Eng Popular Ballad, RLC 16.367.
Ogburn V H, New Light on the Life and Works of Bishop Thomas Percy, diss Stanford Univ 1937; Thomas Percy's Unfinished Collection: Ancient Eng and Scottish Poems, ELH 3.183.
Bennett H S, The Author and his Public in the 14th and 15th Centuries, E&S 1s 23.7.
Botkin B A, ed, The American Play-Party Song, Univ Stud of the Univ of Nebraska, Lincoln Neb 1937; rptd N Y 1963, vol 38, nos 1–4.
Bronson B H, Ritson's Bibliographia Scotia, PMLA 52.122; Joseph Ritson: Scholar at Arms, 2 vols, Berkeley 1938.
Taylor G A, Ballads, Dalhousie Rev 17.339.
Dobie M R, The Development of Scott's Minstrelsy, Trans of the Edinburgh Biblio Soc 2.65.
Reichenbach H, The Tonality of Eng and Gaelic Folksong, ML 19.268.
Spivacke H, The Archive of American Folk-Song in the Libr of Congress, Southern Folklore Quart 2.31.
Schmidt W, Die Überlistungsszene in der Volksballade vom Mädchenmörder, GRM 27.383.
Entwistle W J, Ballads and Tunes Which Travel, Folklore 50.333; European Balladry, Oxford 1939; corrected re-issue 1951; Notation for Ballad Melodies, PMLA 55.61.
Buchanan A, A Neutral Mode in Anglo-American Folk Music, Southern Folklore Quart 4.77.
Hagedorn M, Das Percy-Folio MS: Die Stellung der Volksballaden des Percy-Folio MSS in der Engl-schottischen Volksballaden-Tradition, Studien zur Volksliedforschung: Beihefte zum Jahrbuch Volksliedforschung heft 3, Berlin 1940.
Taylor A, The Themes Common to Eng and German Balladry, MLQ 1.23.
Bate W J, Percy's Use of his Folio-MS, JEGP 43.337.
Bayard S P, Ballad Tunes and the Hustvedt Indexing Method, Journ American Folklore 55.248.
Dennis L, Thomas Percy: Antiquarian vs Man of Taste, PMLA 57.140.
Gordon P, The Music of the Ballads, Southern Folklore Quart 6.143.
Martin B, The Folk Ballad, Dalhousie Rev 22.455.
Poladian S, The Problems of Melodic Variation in Folk Song, Journ American Folklore 55.204.
Pound L, Literary Anthologies and the Ballad, Southern Folklore Quart 6.127.
Percy Bishop T, The Percy Letters, ed D N Smith and C Brooks, 6 vols, Baton Rouge La 1944–61.
Bronson B H, The Interdependence of Ballad Tunes and Texts, California Folklore Quart 3.185; rptd in his Ballad as Song, Berkeley and Los Angeles 1969, p 37; also rptd in The Critics and the Ballad, ed MacE Leach and T P Coffin, Carbondale Ill 1961, p 77.
Bronson, Mrs Brown and the Ballad, California Folklore Quart 4.129; rptd in his Ballad as Song, p 64.
Chambers OHEL, vol 2, pt 2; rptd with corrections Oxford 1947, pp 122, 223.
Bronson, Folksong and the Modes, Musical Quart 32.37; rptd in his Ballad as Song, p 79.
Hudson A P, Byron and the Ballad, SP 42.594.
Mackenzie E K A, Percy and Ballad Correctness, RES 1s 21.
Keel F, The Folk Song Society 1898–1948, Journ of Eng Folk Dance and Song Soc 5.111.
Liestøl K, Scottish and Norwegian Ballads, Studia Norvegica no 1, Oslo 1946.
Millar B P, British Balladry in the 18th Cent, diss Harvard 1946.
Richmond W E, Ballad Place Names, Journ American Folklore 59.263.
Farmer H G, A History of Music in Scotland, London 1947.
Lomax J A, Adventures of a Ballad Hunter, N Y 1947.
Richmond W E, Place Names in the Eng and Scottish Popular Ballads and their American Variants, diss Ohio State Univ 1947.
Richmond W K, Poetry of the People, London 1947.
Toschi P, Fenomenologia del Canto popolare, Rome 1947.
Howes F, Man, Mind and Music, London 1948; rptd Freeport N Y 1970.
Baldi S, Studî sulla poesia popolare d'Inghilterra e di Scozia, Rome 1949.
Bronson B H, Mechanical Help in the Study of

Folk Song, Journ American Folklore 62.81.

Dean-Smith M, The Preservation of Eng Folk-Song and Popular Music, Journ of Eng Folk Dance and Song Soc 6.29; The Preservation of Eng Folk Song in the Journ of the Folk Song Soc, Journ of Eng Folk Dance and Song Soc 6.69.

Entwistle W J, New Light on the Epic-Ballad Problem, Journ American Folklore 62.375.

Meier J, Volksliedwanderung u Volksliedforschung, Archiv f Literatur u Volksdichtung 1.177.

Seeger C, Professionalism and Amateurism in the Study of Folk Music, Journ American Folklore 62.107; rptd in The Critics and the Ballad, ed MacE Leach and T P Coffin, Carbondale Ill 1961, p 151.

Seeman E, Wolfdietrichepos u Volksballade: Ein Beitrag zur Geschichte der mittelalterlichen Balladendichtung (1. Folge), Archiv f Literatur u Volksdichtung 1.119.

Bronson B H, Some Observations about Melodic Variation in British-American Folk Tunes, Journ American Musicological Soc 3.120; Melodic Stability in Oral Transmission, Journ of International Folk Music Council 3.50.

Hodgart M J C, The Ballads, London 1950; 2nd edn 1962.

Hudson A P, La Poesia folklorica, Folklore Americas 10, nos 1, 2.

Millar B P, 18th Cent Views of the Ballad, Western Folklore 9.124.

Wells E K, The Ballad Tree: A Study of British and American Ballads... together with 60 Traditional Ballads and their Tunes, N Y 1950.

Baine R M, Percy's Own Copies of the Reliques, HLB 5.

Bayard S P, Principal Versions of an International Folk Tune, Journ of International Folk Music Council 3.44.

Halpert H, Vitality of Tradition and Local Songs, Journ of International Folk Music Council 3.35.

Karpeles M, Some Reflections on Authenticity in Folk Music, Journ of International Folk Music Council 3.10.

Karpeles M and A Baké, Manual for Folk Music Collectors, London 1951.

Morokoff G E, Whole-Tale Parallels of the Child Ballads as Cited or Given by Child or in FFC 74, Journ American Folklore 64.203.

Poladian S, Melodic Contour in Traditional Music, Journ of International Folk Music Council 3.30.

Randolph V and R A Musick, Folksong Hunters in Missouri, Midwest Folklore 1.23.

Richmond W E, Some Effects of Scribal and Typographical Error on Oral Tradition, Southern Folklore Quart 15.159; rptd in The Critics and the Ballad, ed MacE Leach and T P Coffin, Carbondale Ill 1961, p 225.

Roberts W E, Comic Elements in the Eng Traditional Ballad, Journ of International Folk Music Council 3.76.

Saygun A A, Authenticity in Folk Music, Journ of International Folk Music Council 3.7.

Simeone W E, The May Games and the Robin Hood Legend, Journ American Folklore 64.265.

Boswell G W, Reciprocal Influences of Text and Tune in the Southern Traditional Ballad, diss George Peabody Coll for Teachers 1951; The Epic of Folksong: A Radio Program, Tennessee Folklore Soc Bull 18.74.

Beck H P, Down East Ballads and Songs, diss Univ of Pa 1952.

Blaich H-W, Bell Robertson's Volksballaden: Studien zur Familien- u Landschaftstradition des schottischen Nordostens, diss Bonn 1952.

Friedman A B, A Selective Hist of the Ballad Revival, diss Harvard 1952.

Krohmann H, Die dänischen u engl-schottischen Liebesballaden, diss Bonn 1952.

Lowe B, Robin Hood in the Light of History, Journ of Eng Folk Dance and Song Soc 7.228.

Parker H, Affiliations of British and West Scandinavian Ballads: A Preliminary Stud, diss Univ of Calif at Berkeley 1952.

Richmond W E, A Note in the Case against Peter Buchan, Folklore 63.124.

Scheithauer L J, Rhythmus u Volkslied: Ein Beitrag zum methodischen Problem der Rhythmusanalyse, diss Leipzig 1952.

Simeone W E, Still More about Robin Hood, Journ American Folklore 65.418; The Historic Robin Hood, Journ American Folklore 66.303.

Bronson B H, On the Union of Words and Music in the Child Ballads, Western Folklore 11.233; rptd in his Ballad as Song, Berkeley and Los Angeles 1969, p 112; Good and Bad in British-American Folk Song, Journ of International Folk Music Council 5.64.

Bayard S P, American Folksongs and their Music, Southern Folklore Quart 17.122.

Miles J, The Language of the Ballads, RomP 7.1.

Pound L, American Folksong: Origins, Texts and Modes of Diffusion, Southern Folklore Quart 17.114.

Reppert J D, F J Child and the Ballad, diss Harvard 1953.

Stewart J K, The Ballad in Relation to 18th Cent Critical Theory 1700–65, diss Princeton 1953.

Taylor A, Trends in the Study of Folksong 1937–50, Southern Folklore Quart 17.97.

Nettl B, Stylistic Change in Folk Music, Southern Folklore Quart 17.216; La Musica folklorica, Folklore Americas 14, no 2.

Abrahamsen S, The English-Scottish and the Scandinavian Ballads, Edda 54.123.

Bronson, Habits of the Ballad as Song, in Five Gayley Lectures 1947–54, Univ of Calif Publ Eng Stud, Berkeley 1954, 10.21; rptd in his Ballad as Song, Berkeley and Los Angeles 1969, p 92.

Bronson, The Morphology of the Ballad Tunes: Variation, Selection and Continuity, Journ American Folklore 67.1; rptd in his Ballad as Song, p 144.

Friedman A B, The First Draft of Percy's Reliques, PMLA 69.1233; Percy's Folio MS Revalued, JEGP 53.524.

Greenway J, The Flight of the Grey Goose: Literary Symbolism in the Ballad, Southern Folklore Quart 18.165.

Hendren J W, The Scholar and the Ballad Singer, Southern Folklore Quart 18.139; rptd in The Critics and the Ballad, ed MacE Leach and T P Coffin, Carbondale Ill 1961, p 3.

Hodgart M J C, Medieval Lyrics and the Ballads, in The Age of Chaucer, ed B Ford, A Guide to Eng Lit, Harmondsworth 1954, 1.159.

Unwin R, The Rural Muse: Stud in the Peasant Poetry of England, London 1954.

White A, Children in the Ballads, Southern Folklore Quart 18.205.

Amann W F, Folksong Definitions: A Critical Analysis, Midwest Folklore 5.101.

Ames R A, The Story of American Folk Song, N Y 1955; reissued 1960.

Bayard S P, Decline and Revival of Anglo-American Folk Music, Midwest Folklore 5.69; published in rvsd form in Folklore in Action, ed H P Beck, Phila 1962, p 21.

Hinton S, The Singer of Folk Songs and his Conscience, Western Folklore 14.170.

Mendoza V T, The Frontiers between Popular and Folk, Journ of International Folk Music Council 7.24.

Ritchie J, Singing Family of the Cumberlands, N Y 1955.

Shelton A J Jr, Social Criticism in Eng and Scottish Folk Ballads, diss St Louis Univ 1955.

Wilgus D K, Ballad Classification, Midwest Folklore 5.95.

Chambers G B, Folksong—Plainsong: A Study in Origins and Musical Relationships, London 1956; N Y 1957.

Folk Music Collected in the British Isles: Some English MS and Recorded Collections Accessible to the Public, Journ of Eng Folk Dance and Song Soc 8.160.

Greenway J, Aunt Molly Jackson and Robin Hood: A Study in Folk Re-creation, Journ American Folklore 69.23.

Karpeles M, Cecil Sharp: Collector of Eng Folk Music, in Studia memoriae Belae Bartok sacra, Budapest 1956, p 445.

Lomax A, Folk Song Style: Notes on a Systematic Approach to the Study of Folk Song, Journ of International Folk Music Council 8.48.

Mackenzie M L H, The Scottish Ballad in the 18th Cent: A Bibliographical Stud, diss Univ of Toronto 1956.

Montgomerie W, Sir Walter Scott as Ballad Editor, RES ns 7.158; Sketch for a Hist of the Scottish Ballad, Journ of Eng Folk Dance and Song Soc 8.40.

Reppert J D, William MacMath and F J Child, PMLA 71.510.

Sellers W E, The Folklore of Kinship in the British Traditional Ballads, diss Boston Univ 1956; Kinship in the British Ballads: The Historical Evidence, Southern Folklore Quart 20.199; Kindred and Clan in the Scottish Border Ballads, Boston Univ Stud in Eng 3.1.

Taylor A, Una comparación tentative de temas de baladas Inglesas y Espanolas, Folklore Americano 4, no 4, p 5.

Wells E K, Some Currents of British Folk Song in America 1916–58, Journ of Eng Folk Dance and Song Soc 8.129.

Bayard S P, A Miscellany of Tune Notes, in Stud in Folklore in Honor of... Stith Thompson, ed W E Richmond, Indiana Univ Publ Folklore Series no 9, Bloomington 1957, p 151.

Bronson B H, About the Commonest British Ballads, Journ of International Folk Music Council 9.22; rptd in his Ballad as Song, Berkeley and Los Angeles 1969, p 162; The Riverside Recordings of the Child Ballads: A Review Article, Western Folklore 16.189.

Dober V, The Marital Status of Child Ballad Heroines, Southern Folklore Quart 21.93.

Freeman L C, The Changing Function of a Folksong, Journ American Folklore 70.215.

Gower H, Traditional Scottish Ballads in the United States, diss Vanderbilt Univ 1957.

Hyman S E, The Child Ballad in America: Some Aesthetic Criteria, Journ American Folklore 70.235.

Kinne F, A Comparative Study of British Traditional Ballads and American Indigenous Ballads, diss Johann Wolfgang Goethe Univ 1957.

Leach MacE, Folksong and Ballad–A New Emphasis, Journ American Folklore 70.205.

McNeil N L, The British Ballad West of the Appalachian Mountains, diss Univ of Texas 1957.

Speirs J, Medieval English Poetry: The Non-Chaucerian Tradition, London 1957.

Stewart J K, The Ballad and the Genres in the 18th Cent, ELH 24.120.

Simeone W E, Robin Hood Ballads in North America, Western Folklore 7.197; The Mythical Robin Hood, Western Folklore 17.21; Robin Hood and Some Other Outlaws, Journ American Folklore 71.27.

Taylor A, Some Recent Stud in Folksongs, Midwest Folklore 7.229.

Bronson B H, The Music of the Ballads, VQR 34.474.

Elliot K, Scottish Song 1500–1700, Proc of Royal Musical Assoc 84.1.

Karpeles M, ed, The Collecting of Folk Music and Other Ethno-musicological Material: A Manual for Field Workers, London 1958.

Matthäi S, Rittertum u Adel in den engl und schottischen Folksballaden, diss Frei Univ Berlin 1958.

Montgomerie W, William Motherwell and Robert A Smith, RES ns 9.152 (Smith was one of Motherwell's informants).

Moore A, The Literary Status of the Eng Popular Ballad, CL 10.1; rptd in Middle Eng Survey, ed E Vasta, Notre Dame 1965, p 309.

Sanders J B, The Ballads as a Source of Nursery Rhymes, Midwest Folklore 8.189.

Bascom W R, The Main Problems of Stability and Change in Tradition, Journ of International Folk Music Council 11.7.

Bronson, Toward the Comparative Analysis of British-American Folk-Tunes, Journ American Folklore 72.165; rptd in his Ballad as Song, Berkeley and Los Angeles 1969, p 172.

Cazden N, Regional and Occupational Orientations of American Traditional Song, Journ American Folklore 72.310.

Coffin T P, The Folk Ballad and the Literary Ballad: An Essay in Classification, Midwest Folklore 9.5; rptd in Folklore in Action, ed H P Beck, Phila 1962, p 58.

Lomax A, Folk-Song Style, American Anthropologist 61.927.

Rennick R, The Disguised Lover Theme and the Ballad, Southern Folklore Quart 23.215.

Sebeok T, Approaches to the Analysis of Folksong Texts, Ural-Altaische Jahrbücher 31.392.

Bouillon E, Zum Verhältnis von Text u Melodie in den engl-schottischen Volksballaden, diss Bonn 1960.

Creighton H, Songs from Nova Scotia, Journ of International Folk Music Council 12.84.

Friedman A B, Addison's Ballad Papers and the Reaction to Metaphysical Wit, CL 12.1.

Greenway J, Folk Songs as Socio-Historical Documents, Western Folklore 19.1.

Hand W D and G O Arlt, edd, Humaniora: Essays in Literature, Folklore [and] Bibliography Honoring Archer Taylor, Locust Valley N Y 1960.

Horn D, Tune Detecting in 19th Cent Hymnals, Tennessee Folklore Soc Bull 26.99.

Lord A B, The Singer of Tales, HSCL 24; rptd N Y 1965.

Miller E J W, The Rag-Bag World of Balladry, Southern Folklore Quart 24.217.

Nettl B, An Introd to Folk Music in the United States, Wayne State Univ Stud 7; rvsd edn Detroit 1962.

Nygard H O, Ballads and the Middle Ages, Tennessee Stud in Lit 5.85.

Reeves J, Cecil Sharp and Eng Traditional Verse, Journ of Eng Folk Dance and Song Soc 9.55.

Salmen W, Der Fahrende Musiker im europäischen Mittelalter, Die Musik im alten u neuen Europa 4, Kassel 1960.

Winkelman D M, Musicological Techniques of Ballad Analysis, Midwest Folklore 10.197.

Armour E, The Melodic and Rhythmic Characteristics of the Music of the Traditional Ballad Variants Found in the Southern Appalachians, diss NYU 1961; DA 22.4368.

Barry P, The Part of the Folksinger in the Making of Folk Balladry, in The Critics and the Ballad, ed MacE Leach and T P Coffin, Carbondale Ill 1961, p 59.

Bayard S P, Prolegomena to a Study of the Principal Melodic Families of British-American Folk Song, Journ American Folklore 63.1; rptd in The Critics and the Ballad, ed MacE Leach and T P Coffin, Carbondale Ill 1961, p 103.

Brewster P G and G Tarsouli, Handjeris and Lioyenneti and Child 76 and 110: A Stud in Similarities, FFC 183.

Browne E W, Variant Forms of Eng and Scottish Popular Ballads in America, diss USC 1961; DA 21.3768.

Friedman A B, The Ballad Revival: Stud in the Influence of Popular on Sophisticated Poetry, Chicago 1961; The Formulaic Improvisation Theory of Ballad Tradition: A Counterstatement, Journ American Folklore 74.113.

Jones J H, Commonplace and Memorization in

the Oral Tradition of the English and Scottish Popular Ballads, Journ American Folklore 74.97 (compare A B Friedman's appended counter-statement).

Keen M H, The Outlaws of Medieval Legend, London 1961.

Leach MacE, The Singer or the Song, in Singers and Storytellers, ed M C Boatright, M Hudson and A Maxwell, Dallas 1961, Publ Texas Folklore Soc 30.30; Problems of Collecting Oral Literature, PMLA 77.335.

Leach MacE and T P Coffin, edd, The Critics and the Ballad, Carbondale Ill 1961; rptd 1973.

Nygard H O, The Critic and the Ballad, in Stud in Honor of John C Hodges and Alwin Thaler, ed R B Davis, Knoxville 1961, Tennessee Stud in Lit special no, p 11.

Richmond W E, Romantic Nationalism and Ballad Scholarship: A Lesson for Today from Norway's Past, Southern Folklore Quart 25.91.

Speirs J, The Scottish Ballads, Scrut 4.35; rptd in The Critics and the Ballad, ed MacE Leach and T P Coffin, Carbondale Ill 1961, p 236.

Taylor A, The Buried Lover Escapes, in Stud in Medieval Lit in Honor of Albert C Baugh, ed MacE Leach, Phila 1961, p 209.

Utley F L, Folk Literature: An Operational Definition, Journ American Folklore 74.193; rptd in The Study of Folklore, ed A Dundes, Englewood Cliffs N J 1965, p 7.

Beck H P, ed, Folklore in Action: Essays for Discussion in Honor of MacE Leach, American Folklore Soc Bibliographical and Special Series 14, Phila 1962.

Bowra C M, Primitive Song, London and Cleveland 1962; rptd N Y 1963.

Bush D, Eng Lit in the Earlier 17th Cent, Oxford Hist of Eng Lit vol 5, 2nd edn Oxford 1962 (popular literature, pp 39, 478).

Ehrenpreis A H, Swinburne's [Unpublished] Edition of Popular Ballads, PMLA 77.559.

Lomax A, Song Structure and Social Structure, Ethnology 1.425.

Sachs C, The Wellsprings of Music, ed J Kunst, The Hague 1962; rptd N Y 1965.

Siuts H, Volksballaden–Volkserzählungen: Motiv- u Typen-register, Fabula 5.72.

Smith J O, The Fifth Act and the Chorus in the Eng and Scottish Ballads, Dalhousie Rev 42.329.

Sydow A, Das Lied: Ursprung, Wesen u Wandel, Göttingen 1962.

Abrahams R D, Folklore in Culture: Notes toward an Analytic Method, Univ Texas Stud in Lang and Lit 5.98.

Bauman R, The Dowie Dens o'Yarrow, Scottish Stud 7.115.

Ben-Amos D, The Situation Structure of the Non-Humorous English Ballad, Midwest Folklore 13.163.

Buermann T B, A History of the North Carolina Folklore Soc, North Carolina Folklore 11, no 2, p 1.

Clarke K W and M Clarke, Introducing Folklore, N Y 1963.

Crawford T, Scottish Popular Ballads and Lyrics of the 18th and Early 19th Centuries: Some Preliminary Conclusions, SSL 1.49.

Elder M, Ballad Country: The Scottish Border, Edinburgh 1963.

Fowke E, British Ballads in Ontario, Midwest Folklore 13.133.

Greig G, Folk-Song in Buchan, Trans of Buchan Field Club 9(1906–07).2; rptd in his Folk-Song in Buchan and Folk-Song of the North-East, Hatboro Pa 1963.

James T G, The Eng and Scottish Popular Ballads of Francis J Child, Journ American Folklore 46.51; rptd in condensed form in The Critics and the Ballad, ed MacE Leach and T P Coffin, Carbondale Ill 1961, p 12.

McMillan D J, Five Traditional Medieval Historical Ballads and the Nature of Oral Transmission, diss Univ of Maryland 1963; DA 24.4138 (based on Child, nos 159, 161–63, and 168); Folk Projection and Historic Truth, AN&Q 2.149 (based on Child, nos 159, 161–63, and 168).

Montgomerie W, William MacMath and the Scott Ballad MSS, SSL 1.93.

Röhrich L, Die Volksballade von Herrn Peters Seefahrt u die Menschenopfer-Sagen, in Märchen, Mythos, Dichtung: Festschrift ... Friedrich von der Leyen, ed H Kuhn and K Schier, Munich 1963, p 177 (Child, nos 24 and 57; DgF, no 376; Continental analogues).

Sackett S J, Metaphor in Folksong, Folklore and Folk Music Archivist 6, no 3, p 6; Simile in Folksong, Midwest Folklore 13.5.

Bailey F, The Historical Ballad: Its Tradition in Britain and America, diss Univ of Tenn 1964; DA 25.395.

Brednich R W, Die Legende vom Elternmörder in Volkserzählung u Volksballade, Jahrbuch f Volksliedforschung 9.116.

Bronson B H, Folk-Song in the United States 1910–1960, Jahrbuch f Volksliedforschung 9.1 (1964; = Festschrift zum 75, Geburtstag von Erich Seemann); rptd in his Ballad as Song, Berkeley and Los Angeles 1969, p 243.

Coffin T P, Folksong and Folksong Scholarship, I: On a Peak in Massachusetts: The Literary and Aesthetic Approach, in A Good Tale and a

Bonny Tune, ed M C Boatright, W M Hudson and A Maxwell, Publ Texas Folklore Soc 32.201, 265.

Flanders H H, Ancient Themes and Characteristics Found in Certain New England Folk Songs, Journ American Folklore 77.32.

Foss G, Folksong and Folksong Scholarship, V: The Transcription and Analysis of Folk Music, in A Good Tale and a Bonny Tune, ed M C Boatright, W M Hudson, and A Maxwell, Publ Texas Folklore Soc 32.237, 268.

Goldstein K S, A Guide for Field Workers in Folklore, Memoirs of American Folklore Soc 52, Hatboro Pa 1964.

Gower H, The Scottish Palimpsest in Traditional Ballads Collected in America, in Reality and Myth: Essays in American Lit in Memory of R C Beatty, ed W E Walker and R L Welker, Nashville 1964, p 117.

Greenway J, Folksong and Folksong Scholarship, II: Folksong as an Anthropological Province: The Anthropological Approach, in A Good Tale and a Bonny Tune, ed M C Boatright, W M Hudson and A Maxwell, Publ Texas Folklore Soc 32.209, 266.

Henderson H, Scots Folk-song Today, Folklore 75.48.

Ives E D, Larry Gorman: The Man Who Made the Songs, Bloomington Ind 1964.

Mackenzie M L H, The Great Ballad Collectors: Percy, Herd and Ritson, SSL 2.213.

McMillan D J, A Survey of Theories Concerning the Oral Transmission of the Traditional Ballad, Southern Folklore Quart 28.299.

Parades A, Some Aspects of Folk Poetry, Texas Stud in Lit and Lang 6.213.

Richmond W E, Folksong and Folksong Scholarship, III: The Comparative Approach: Its Aims, Techniques and Limitations, in A Good Tale and a Bonny Tune, ed M C Boatright, W M Hudson and A Maxwell, Publ Texas Folklore Soc 32.217, 266.

Rutherford F, The Collection and Publishing of Northumbrian Folksong, Archaeologia Aeliana 42.261.

Sternfeld F W, Music and Ballads, Shakespeare Survey 17.214.

Taylor A, The Parallels between Ballads and Tales, Jahrbuch f Volksliedforschung 9.104.

Thomas F, A Study of Narrative Technique and Figurative Language in the Ballads, diss Univ of Wisconsin 1964; DA 25.2502.

Thomas J, Ballad Makin' in the Mountains of Kentucky, N Y 1964.

Toelken J B, Some Poetic Functions of Folklore in the Eng and Scottish Traditional Ballads, diss Univ of Oregon 1964.

Wilgus D K, Folksong and Folksong Scholarship IV: The Rationalistic Approach, in A Good Tale and a Bonny Tune, ed M C Boatright, W M Hudson and A Maxwell, Publ Texas Folklore Soc 32.227, 268.

Bascom W R, Four Functions of Folklore, Journ American Folklore 67.333; rptd in The Study of Folklore, ed A Dundes, Englewood Cliffs N J 1965, p 279.

Bødker L, International Dictionary of Regional European Ethnology and Folklore vol 2: Folk Literature (Germanic), Copenhagen 1965.

Brunvand J H, Folk Song Stud in Idaho, Western Folklore 24.231.

Coffin T P, Remarks Preliminary to a Study of Ballad Meter and Ballad Singing, Journ American Folklore 78.149.

Ford I W, Traditional Music of America, Hatboro Pa 1965.

Fowler D C, Toward a Literary Hist of the Popular Ballad, N Y Folklore Quart 21.123.

Kennedy P H, Present Status of Ballad Collecting and Geographical Ballad Distributions in North Carolina, in Folklore Stud in Honor of A P Hudson, North Carolina Folklore, Chapel Hill 1965, vol 13, nos 1–2, p 66.

Muir W, Living with Ballads, N Y 1965.

Nettl B, Folk and Traditional Music of the Western Continents, Englewood Cliffs N J 1965; 2nd edn 1973.

Petzoldt L, Volksballade, Sage u Exempel: Zur Stoff- u Überlieferungsgeschichte der Volkserzählung vom Beleidigten Totenschädel, Jahrbuch f Volksliedforschung 12.103.

Pratt S R S, The Eng Folk Dance and Song Soc, Journ of Folklore Institute 2.294.

Sinclair J M, When Is a Poem Like a Sunset? Rev of Eng Lit 6.76.

Stekert E J, Two Voices of Tradition: The Influence of Personality and Collecting Environment upon the Songs of Two Traditional Folksingers, diss Univ of Pa 1965; DA 26.7251.

Abrahams R D, Patterns of Structure and Role Relationships in the Child Ballad in the U S, Journ American Folklore 79.448.

Browne R B, D M Winkelman and A Hayman, edd, New Voices in American Stud, Lafayette Ind 1966.

Collinson F, The Traditional and National Music of Scotland, London and Nashville Tenn 1966.

Danckert W, Das Volkslied im Abendland, Bern 1966.

Mackenzie M L H, Ballad Collectors in the 18th Cent, Humanities Assoc Bull 18[1](1966).33.

Steckmesser K L, Robin Hood and the American

Outlaw: A Note on Hist and Folklore, Journ American Folklore 79.348.

Suppan W, Volkslied: Seine Sammlung u Erforschung, Stuttgart 1966.

Taylor A, The English Riddle Ballads, in Stud in Lang and Lit in Honour of Margaret Schlauch, ed M Brahmer, S Helsztýnski and J Krzýzanowski, Warsaw 1966, p 445.

Tyeryar G L, Supernatural Agents in Child's Eng and Scot Popular Ballads, diss Univ of Wisconsin 1966.

Winkelman D M, Some Rhythmic Aspects of the Child Ballad, in New Voices in American Studies, ed R B Browne et al, Lafayette Ind 1966, p 151; Poetic/Rhythmic Stress in the Child Ballads, Keystone Folklore Quart 12.103.

Bailey F, The Dramatic Tendency and Historicity in the Ballads, Southern Folklore Quart 31.310; The Historical Ballad: A Problem of Definition, Southern Folklore Quart 32.260.

Boswell G W, Reciprocal Controls Exerted by Ballad Texts and Tunes, Journ American Folklore 80.169; Stanza Form and Music Imposed Scansion in Southern Ballads, Southern Folklore Quart 31.320.

Combs J H, Folk-Songs of the Southern United States, ed D K Wilgus, Publ American Folklore Soc Bibliographical and Special Series 19, Austin Texas 1967.

Djoudjeff S, Esquisse d'une métode musicologique pour l'étude des vers populaires, in To Honor Roman Jakobson, Janua linguarum series maior 31, The Hague 1967, vol 1, p 523.

Foss G, A Methodology for the Description and Classification of Anglo-American Traditional Tunes, Journ of Folklore Institute 4.102.

Karpeles M, Cecil Sharp, London 1967.

Lomax A, The Good and the Beautiful in Folksong, Journ American Folklore 80.212.

Nygard H O, Popular Ballad and Medieval Romance, in Folklore International: Essays in Traditional Lit, Belief and Custom in Honor of Wayland Debs Hand, ed D K Wilgus, Hatboro Pa 1967, p 161.

Pinon R, Philologie et folklore musical: Les chants de[s] pâtres avant leur émergence folklorique, Jahrbuch f Volksliedforschung 12.141.

Sirovátka O, Stoff u Gattung–Volksballade u Volkserzählung, Fabula 9.162.

Toelken J B, An Oral Canon for the Child Ballads: Construction and Application, Journ of Folklore Institute 4.75.

Vargyas L, Researches into the Mediaeval Hist of Folk Ballad, trans A H Whitney, Budapest 1967.

Wolf J Q, Folksingers and the Re-creation of Folksong, Western Folklore 26.101.

Abrahams R D and G Foss, Anglo-American Folksong Style, Englewood Cliffs N J 1968.

Bausinger H, Formen der Volkspoesie, Grundlagen der Germanistik 6, Berlin 1968.

Bronson B H, Cecil Sharp and Folksong: A Review Article, Western Folklore 27.200; rptd in his Ballad as Song, Berkeley and Los Angeles 1969, p 162.

Brunvand J H, The Study of American Folklore: An Introd, N Y 1968, pp 149, 252 (ballads).

Caldwell H B, The Child Tragic Ballad: A Comparison with Medieval Literary Tragedy–Boccaccio, Chaucer, Lydgate, diss Vanderbilt Univ 1968; DA 29.865A.

Dorson R M, The British Folklorists: A History, Chicago 1968.

Dronke P, The Medieval Lyric, London 1968.

Fowler D C, A Literary History of the Popular Ballad, Durham N C 1968.

Leach MacE and H Glassie, A Guide for Collectors of Oral Traditions and Folk Cultural Material in Pennsylvania, Harrisburg 1968.

List G, Toward the Indexing of Ballad Texts, Journ American Folklore 81.44.

Lomax A, ed, Folk Song Style and Culture: A Staff Report on Cantometrics, Washington 1968.

Lord T T, English Ballad Collecting and Editing from 1898 to World War II, diss Univ of Pa 1968; DA 30.1141A.

Pop M, Der formelhafte Charakter der Volksdichtung, Deutsches Jahrbuch f Volkskunde 14.1.

Rogers E R, The Open Code of Ballads, diss Univ of Colorado 1968; DA 29.3585A.

Steenstrup J C H R, The Medieval Popular Ballad, trans E G Cox, Univ of Wash Publ Eng 3, Boston 1914; rptd with new foreword by D C Fowler and a biblio essay by K-I Hildeman, Seattle 1968.

Stekert E J, Tylor's Theory of Survivals and National Romanticism: Their Influence on Early American Folksong Collectors, Southern Folklore Quart 32.209.

Tallmadge, The Scotch-Irish and British Traditional Ballad in America, N Y Folklore Quart 24.261.

Taylor A, Lists and Classifications of Folksongs, Jahrbuch f Volksliedforschung 13.1.

Boswell G W, Text-Occasioned Ornamentation in Folksinging, Southern Folklore Quart 33.333.

Bronson B H, The Ballad as Song, Berkeley and Los Angeles 1969; Fractures in Tradition among the Child Ballads, in his Ballad as Song, p 257;

Of Ballads, Songs and Snatches, in his Ballad as Song, p 282.
Clissold I et al, Alfred Williams and the Folk Songs of the Upper Thames: A Symposium, Folk Music Journ 1.293.
Howes F, Folk Music in Britain and Beyond, London 1969.
Pinon R, Philologie et folklore musical: Les instruments de musique des pâtres au moyen age et à la renaissance, Jahrbuch f Volksliedforschung 14.85.
Shire H M, Song, Dance and Poetry of the Court of Scotland under King James VI, Cambridge 1969.
Wiora W, Zur Fundierung allgemeiner Thesen über des Volkslied durch historische Untersuchungen, Jahrbuch f Volksliedforschung 14.1.
Abrahams R D, Creativity, Individuality and the Traditional Singer, Stud in the Literary Imagination 3[1](Apr 1970).5.
Burns T, A Model for Textual Variation in Folksong, Folklore Forum 3[2](1970).49.
Caldwell H B, The Multiple Effects of the Tragic Event in the Child Ballad, N Y Folklore Quart 26.14.
Danckert W, Das europäische Volkslied, 2nd rvsd and enlarged edn, Bonn 1970.
Gower H and J Porter, Jeannie Robertson: The Child Ballads, Scottish Stud 14.275; Jeannie Robertson: The Other Ballads, Scottish Stud 16.139.
Richmond W E, The Development of the Popular Ballad: A New Theory, Genre 3(1970).198.
Johnson E, Sir Walter Scott: The Great Unknown, 2 vols, N Y 1970.
Munro L, Lizzie Higgins and the Oral Transmission of Ten Child Ballads, Scottish Stud 14.155.
Sirovátka O, Die zwischenstaatlichen Beziehungen in der Volksdichtung u die Kontaktzonen, Ethnologica Slavica 1 (1970 for 1969).157.
Syndergaard L E, English-Scottish and Danish Popular Ballads: A Comparative Study, diss Univ of Wisconsin 1970; DA 31.5377A.
Wilgus D K, A Type-Index of Anglo-American Traditional Narrative Songs, Journ of Folklore Institute 7.161.
Zug C G, Sir Walter Scott and the Ballad Forgery, SSL 8.52.
Boswell G W, A Note-Commentary on J Barre Toelken's An Oral Canon for the Child Ballads, Journ of Folklore Institute 8.57.
Buchan D D, Nicol, Scott and the Ballad Collectors, Ariel: A Rev of International Eng Lit, 2[3](July 1971).88; The Ballad and the Folk, London 1972.
Charlton L E, The Balladry of Northumbria, Eng Dance and Song 33.112.
Ives E D, Lawrence Doyle: The Farmer-Poet of Prince Edward Island, A Stud in Local Songmaking, Univ of Maine Stud 92.
Krohn K, Folklore Methodology, trans R L Welsch, American Folklore Soc Publ Bibliographical and Special Series 21, Austin Texas 1971.
Rossel S, Den litterære vise i folketraditionen, Danmarks folkeminder 81, Copenhagen 1971.
Wood H H, Scott and Jamieson: The Relationship between Two Ballad-Collectors, SSL 9.71.
Caldwell H B, Ballad Tragedy and the Moral Matrix: Observations on Tragic Causation, N Y Folklore Quart 28.209.
Henderson H, Jeannie Robertson as Storyteller, Tocher 6.169.
Johnson D, Music and Society in Lowland Scotland in the 18th Cent, London 1972.
Laws G M Jr, The British Literary Ballad: A Study in Poetic Imitation, Carbondale Ill 1972.
Lyle E B, The Matching of Andrew Blakie's Ballad Tunes with their Texts, Scottish Stud 16.175.
Metzner E E, Zur frühesten Geschichte der europäischen Balladendichtung: Der Tanz in Kölbigk, Frankfurter Beiträge zur Germanistik 14.
Richmond W E, Narrative Folk Poetry, in Folklore and Folklife: An Introd, ed R M Dorson, Chicago 1972, p 85.
Shield H, The Dead Lover's Return in Modern English Ballad Tradition, Jahrbuch f Volksliedforschung 17.98; Old British Ballads in Ireland, Folk Life 10(1972).68.
Thigpen K A Jr, An Index to the Known Oral Sources of the Child Collection, Folklore Forum 5.55.
Turner J W, A Morphology of the True Love Ballad, Journ American Folklore 85.21.
Vartin S, Thomas Percy's Reliques: Its Structure and Organization, diss NYU 1972; DA 33.734A.
Fraser R D, Verbal Parallelism in the Ballad and the Medieval Lyric, diss Univ of Oregon 1973; DA 33.6869A.
Grobman N R, 18th-Cent Scottish Philosophers on Oral Tradition, Journ of Folklore Institute 10.187.
Holbek B, The Ballad and the Folk, Arv [= Journ of Scandinavian Folklore] 29–30(1973–74).5.
Hostettler A, Symbolic Tokens in a Ballad of the Returned Lover, Western Folklore 32.33.
Johnson H S, The Hist of Anglo-Irish Ballad

Traditions, diss Univ of Pa 1973; DA 34.14083A.
McLaren C A and M A Stephen, Reports and Surveys of Archives in Northern Scotland, Northern Scotland 1²(1973).223.
Nicolaisen W F H, Place-Names in Traditional Ballads, Folklore 84.299.
Reed J, The Border Ballads, London 1973.
Thigpen K A Jr, A Reconsideration of the Commonplace Phrase and Commonplace Theme in the Child Ballads, Southern Folklore Quart 37.385.
Anders W, Balladensänger u mündliche Komposition: Untersuchungen zur engl Traditionsballade, Bochumer Arbeiten zur Sprach- u Literaturwissenschaft 8, Munich 1974.
Brednich R W, L Röhrich and W Suppan, edd, Handbuch des Volksliedes, 2 vols, Motive: Freiburger folkloristische Forschungen 1, Munich 1974.
McCullough L, An Historical Sketch of Traditional Irish Music in the United States, Folklore Forum 7.177.
Nicolaisen W F H, Place-Names in Traditional Ballads, Literary Onomastics Stud 1.84.
Reppert J D, F J Child and the Ballad, in The Learned and the Lewed, ed L D Benson, Harvard Stud Eng 5.197.
Thomson R S, The Development of the Broadside Ballad Trade and its Influence upon the Transmission of English Folksongs, diss Cambridge Univ 1974.
Bratton J S, The Victorian Popular Ballad, London 1975.
Brander N, Scottish and Border Battles and Ballads, London 1975.
Bronson B H, Traditional Ballads Musically Considered, Critical Inquiry 2(1975).29.
Elbourne R, The Study of Change in Traditional Music, Folklore 86.181.
Grobman N R, David Hume and the Earliest Scientific Method for Collecting Balladry, Western Folklore 34.16.
Harry K W, The Sources and Treatment of Traditional Ballad Texts in Sir Walter Scott's Minstrelsy of the Scottish Border and Robert Jamieson's Popular Ballads and Songs, diss Aberdeen 1975.

Noto V S, Scottish Ballad and Scottish Folk, Archivio Storico Lombardo 7(1975).59.
Rogers E, Clothing as a Multifarious Ballad Symbol, Western Folklore 34.261.
Short D D, Some Scottish Variants of a Burnsville Folk Song Fragment, North Carolina Folklore Journ 23.16.
Wehse R, Broadside Ballad and Folksong: Oral Tradition vs Literary Tradition, Folklore Forum 8.2.
Gardner-Medwin A, Miss Reburn's Ballads: A 19th-Cent Repertoire from Ireland, in Ballad Studies, ed E B Lyle, Cambridge 1976, p 9.
Gower H, The Scottish Element in Traditional Ballads Collected in America, in Ballad Studies, ed E B Lyle, Cambridge 1976, p 117.
Munro A, Abbotsford Collection of Border Ballads: Sophia Scott's Manuscript Book with Airs, Scottish Stud 20.91.
Lyle E B, Child's Scottish Harvest, HLB 25.125.
Hilton R H, Peasants, Knights and Heretics, Cambridge 1976 (chaps 10–14 on Robin Hood).
Lyle E B, Ballad Studies, Cambridge 1976.
Bronson B H, The Singing Tradition of Child's Popular Ballads, Princeton 1976 (abridgement of Bronson TTCB).
Dronke P, Learned Lyric and the Popular Ballad in the Early Middle Ages, Studi Medievali (Roma) 17(1976).1.
Bekker-Nielsen H, Oral Tradition—Literary Tradition: A Symposium, Odense Univ 1977.
Coffin T P, The British Traditional Ballad in North America, rvsd edn (PAFS 2), Univ of Texas 1977.
Kupke L, Erscheinungsformen und Funktionen des Achtergewichts in der engl-schottischen Volksballade, Frankfurt 1977.
Roth K, Ehebruchschwänke in Liedform: Eine Untersuchung zur deutsch- und englischsprachigen Schwankballade, Munich 1977.
Conroy P, Ballads and Ballad Research: Selected Papers of the International Conference on Nordic and Anglo-American Ballad Research, Univ of Washington (Seattle), May 2–6 1977, Seattle 1978.
Holzapfel O, The European Medieval Ballad: A Symposium, Odense Univ 1978.

Chronological List of Ballad Sources

[1] MS TRINITY COLLEGE CAMBRIDGE 323 (B.14.39)(1225–75).

MS. Skeat W W, The Proverbs of Alfred, TPSL 1895–98, p 399.
James M R, Catalogue of MSS in Trinity Coll Camb, 1.438.
Greg W W, Facsimiles of Twelve Early English Manuscripts in the Library of Trinity College Cambridge, Oxford 1913, no V (Judas, f 34ª).
Brown ELxiiiC, p xx.
Jeffrey D, The Early English Lyric and Franciscan Spirituality, Lincoln Neb 1975, p 206.
MS Contents. De Ordine Creaturarum, f 1, see Migne PL, 83.913.
Lyrics, f 19 etc, see Brown ELxiiiC, nos 14–34, 38; H A Person, Cambridge Middle English Lyrics, Seattle 1953, nos 19, 24, 27, 28, 54.
Life of St Margaret, f 20, see Manual, vol 2, V [184](c).
Wise Admonitions, f 26, see K Brunner, EStn 70.225.
Debate between the Body and the Soul, ff 27ª, 29ᵇ, 43ª, 43ᵇ, 84ª, see Manual, vol 3, VII [18] (d), (f), (g), (h), (j).
Trinity Poem on Biblical History, f 36, see Manual, vol 2, IV [50].
Proverbs of Alfred, f 85, see O Arngart, The Proverbs of Alfred, Lund 1955, pp 30, 70.
On the Epiphany (Twelfth Day), f 35, see Manual, vol 2, IV [43].
Carol (Of One That Is So Fair and Bright), f 24, see Greene E E Carols, no 191Bb.

    Judas (Child, no 23).
Editions. Rel Ant, 1.144.
AESpr, 1.114.
Child, 1.243; 5.288.
Sargent and Kittredge, p 41.
Cook A S, A Literary Middle English Reader, Boston 1915, p 470.
Sisam K, Fourteenth Century Verse and Prose, Oxford 1921, p 168.
Brown ELxiiiC, p 38.
Niles J J, Carol Study Book, N Y 1948, p 5.
Mossé F, Handbook of Middle English, Baltimore 1952, p 205.
Leach BB, p 108.
Friedman VBFB, p 56.
Davies R T, Medieval English Lyrics, London 1963, p 75.
Sisam C and K Sisam, Oxford Book of Medieval English Verse (no 30), Oxford 1970, p 54.
Sources and Literary Relations. Child, 1.242.
Bryant F E, History of English Balladry, Boston 1913 and 1919, p 55; rptd Folcroft Pa 1970; rptd with introd by R Thomson, Norwood Pa 1973.
Baum P F, The English Ballad of Judas Iscariot, PMLA 31.181, 481.
Pound L, Poetic Origins and the Ballad, N Y 1921, pp 164, 179.
Chambers OHEL, p 151.
Buchheit G, Judas Iskarioth: Legende, Geschichte, Deutung, Gütersloh 1954.
Mackey J R, Medieval Metrical Saints' Lives and the Origin of the Ballad, diss Univ of Pa 1968; DA 29.2162A.
Dronke P, The Medieval Lyric, London 1968, p 67.
Mitsui T, Notes on the Stanzaic Division and the Metre of Judas, Studies in English Literature (ELS Japan) 44.209.
Crowther J D W, The Bargain of Judas, ELN 13. 245.
Schueler D G, The Middle English Judas: An Interpretation, PMLA 91.840.
Bibliography. Brown-Robbins, Robbins-Cutler, no 1649.

[2] MS BODLEIAN LIBRARY OXFORD 15444 (RAWLINSON D.328) (shortly after 1444–45).

MS. Catalogus Codicum MS Bibl Bodl, pt V, fasc iii, Oxford 1878, col 165.
MS Contents. Stans Puer ad Mensam, see Brown-Robbins, Robbins-Cutler, no 2233.
Burgh's version of Cato Minor, see Brown-Robbins, Robbins-Cutler, no 3955.

    Riddles Wisely Expounded (Child, no 1).
Editions. Furnivall F J, Three ME Poems, EStn 23.444.
Child, 5.283.
Sargent and Kittredge, p 1.
Leach BB, p 47.
Sources and Analogues. Child, 1.1, 484; 2.495; 3.496; 4.439; 5.205, 284.
Wimberly L C, Folklore in the English and Scottish Ballads, Chicago 1928, p 301; rptd N Y 1959 and 1965.
Barry P, Bull of the Folk-Song Soc of the North-East 10.9; 12.9.

Taylor A, English Riddles from Oral Tradition, Berkeley 1951.
Thompson S, The Types of the Folktale, FFC 184, Helsinki 1961, no 1093.
Leach MacE, Folk Ballads and Songs of the Lower Labrador Coast, Ottawa 1965, p 27.
Toelken J B, Riddles Wisely Expounded, Western Folklore 25.1.
Bibliography. Brown-Robbins, Robbins-Cutler, no 4169.
Dean-Smith, p 84 (Lay the Bent to the Bonny Broom).
Coffin BTBNA (1963), p 22.
Bronson TTCB, 1.3; 4.439.
Simpson BBBM, p 431.
Utley F L, Manual, 3.845 (VII [17]).

[3] MS CAMBRIDGE UNIVERSITY LIBRARY Ff.5.48 (2nd half 15 cent).

MS. Downing J Y, A Critical Edition of Cambridge University MS Ff.5.48, diss Univ of Wash 1969.
Hardwick C and H R Luard, Catalogue of MSS in the Library of Cambridge Univ, 2.505.
Foster F, The Northern Passion, London 1913, EETS 145, p 14.
Zettl E, An Anonymous Short English Metrical Chronicle, London 1935, EETS 196, p xiii.
MS Contents. Lyrics, f 43[b] etc, see Brown-Robbins, Robbins-Cutler, nos 4035, 4185, 1899, 2619, 2119.
Carol (The Betrayed Maiden's Lament), f 114[b], see Greene E E Carols, no 456.

Robin Hood and the Monk (Child, no 119).
Editions. Jamieson R, Popular Ballads and Songs, 2 vols, Edinburgh 1806, 2.54.
Hartshorne C H, Ancient Metrical Tales, London 1829, p 179.
Ritson J, Robin Hood, 2 vols, London 1832, 2.221.
Gutch J M, A Lytyll Geste of Robin Hode, 2 vols, London 1847, 2.7.
Child, 3.97.
Gummere F B, Old English Ballads, Boston 1894, p 77.
Sargent and Kittredge, p 282.
Cook A S, A Literary Middle English Reader, Boston 1915, p 158 (abridged).
Leach BB, p 340.
Friedman VBFB, p 327.
Kinsley OBB, p 405.
Dobson R B and J Taylor, Rymes of Robin Hood: An Introd to the English Outlaw, London 1976, p 113 (Child, no 119).

Sources and Analogues. Child, 3.94.
Chambers OHEL, p 132.
Keen M, Outlaws of Medieval Legend, Toronto 1961, p 121.
Bessinger J B Jr, Robin Hood: Folklore and Historiography 1377–1500, Tenn Stud in Lit 11.61.
Dobson R B and J Taylor, The Medieval Origins of the Robin Hood Legend: A Reassessment, Northern History 7.1.
Bibliography. Brown-Robbins, Robbins-Cutler, no 1534.
Gable J H, Bibliography of Robin Hood, Lincoln 1939, no 774.
Bronson TTCB, 3.17.

[4] MS BRITISH MUSEUM SLOANE 2593 (1450).

MS. Wright T, Songs and Carols, London 1856.
Fehr B, Die Lieder der MS Sloane 2593, Arch 109.33.
Greene E E Carols, p 330.
Fowler D C, A Literary History of the Popular Ballad, Durham N C 1968, p 33.
MS Contents. Carols, f 1[a] etc, see Greene E E Carols, nos 7B, 8B, 16, 24, 25, 27A, 28, 68, 86A, 87, 114A, 122B, 123B, 124A, 125A, 143, 145B, 148A, 157C, 168, 169, 175C, 180B, 185A, 188, 231, 234C, 236, 242, 312, 315, 316, 317, 320, 329, 336, 339, 341, 355A, 356A, 357, 363, 365, 368, 381, 383, 384, 385, 390, 392, 395B, 403, 405, 416, 417, 457, App v.
Lyrics, see Brown RLxvC, nos 18, 72, 78, 79, 81, 83, 84, 87, 88, 90, 114, 123; Robbins SL, nos 4, 5, 7, 21, 27, 41, 43, 45, 46, 57.

St Stephen and Herod (Child, no 22).
Robin and Gandeleyn (Child, no 115).
The Riddle Song (Child, no 46 App; see also Captain Wedderburn's Courtship under [23] below).
Editions. Ritson AS, pp 49, 83 (Child, nos 115, 22).
Sandys W, Christmas Carols, London 1833, no 4 (Child, no 22).
Wright T, Songs and Carols, London 1856, nos 29, 35, 44 (Child, nos 46 App, 115, 22; all except Child, no 22 previously published in T Wright, Songs and Carols, London 1836).
Gutch J M, A Lytyll Geste of Robin Hode, 2 vols, London 1847, 2.36 (Child, no 115).
Sylvester J, Garland of Christmas Carols, London 1861, p 2 (Child, no 22).
Bullen A H, Carols and Poems, London 1866, p 33 (Child, no 22).

Husk W H, Songs of the Nativity, London 1868, p 40 (Child, no 22).
Wülcker R P, Altenglische Lesebuch, 2 vols, Halle 1874–80, 2.122 (Child, no 46 App).
Child, 1.241, 415; 3.13 (nos 22, 46 App, 115).
Gummere F B, Old English Ballads, Boston 1894, p 295 (Child, no 22).
Sargent and Kittredge, pp 40, 83, 244 (Child, nos 22, 46 App, 115).
Rickert E, Ancient English Christmas Carols, London 1910, p 123 (Child, no 22).
Manly J M, English Prose and Poetry, Boston 1907, p 84 (Child, no 22).
Williams C, New Book of English Verse, N Y 1936, p 67 (Child, no 46 App).
Oxford Book of Christian Verse, Oxford 1940, p 42 (Child, no 22).
Auden W H and N H Pearson, Poets of the English Language, N Y 1950, 1.27 (Child, no 46 App).
Oxford Dictionary of Nursery Rhymes, Oxford 1951, p 386 (Child, no 46 App).
Robbins SL, no 45 (Child, no 46 App).
Leach BB, pp 107, 158, 332 (Child, nos 22, 46 App, 115).
Davies R T, Medieval English Lyrics, London 1963, p 164 (Child, no 46 App).
Kinsley OBB, pp 3, 374 (Child, nos 22, 115).
Sisam C and K Sisam, Oxford Book of Medieval Verse, Oxford 1970, pp 56, 435, 437 (Child, nos 22, 46 App, 115).
Dobson R B and J Taylor, Rymes of Robin Hood: An Introd to the English Outlaw, London 1976, p 255 (Child, no 115).
Sources and Analogues. Child, 1.233, 414; 3.12.
Batho E C, The Life of Christ in the Ballads, E&S 9.70.
Toelken J B, Riddles Wisely Expounded, Western Folklore 25.1.
Strömböck D, St Stephen in the Ballads, Arv: Journ of Scandinavian Folklore 24.133.
Bibliography. Brown-Robbins, Robbins-Cutler, nos 1302, 1303, 1317, 3058.
Dean-Smith, pp 100 (Riddle Song); 21 and n 39 (I have a new garden).
Coffin BTBNA (1963), pp 45, 53, (Child, nos 22, 46).
Bronson TTCB, 1.297, 376; 4.462.

[5] MS CAMBRIDGE UNIVERSITY LIBRARY Ee.4.35 (1500).

MS. Hardwick C and H R Luard, Catalogue of MSS in the Library of Cambridge Univ, 2.167.
MS Contents. Monitory pieces, f 5^b etc, see Brown-Robbins, Robbins-Cutler, nos 469, 3685, 1920, 4035.
Metrical tales, f 1^a etc, see Brown-Robbins, Robbins-Cutler, nos 2052, 622, 977.
Robin Hood and the Potter (Child, no 121).
The King and the Barker (Child, no 273 App I).
Editions. Ritson J, Pieces of Ancient Popular Poetry, London 1791, p 57 (Child, no 273 App I); Robin Hood, 2 vols, London 1795, 1.82 (Child, no 121).
Gutch J M, A Lytyll Geste of Robin Hode, 2 vols, London 1847, 2.23 (Child, no 121).
Hazlitt Rem, 1.4 (Child, no 273 App I).
Child, 3.109 (no 121); 5.78 (no 273 App I).
Sargent and Kittredge, p 289 (Child, no 121).
Leach BB, p 352 (Child, no 121).
Dobson R B and J Taylor, Rymes of Robin Hood: An Introd to the English Outlaw, London 1976, p 123 (Child, no 121).
Sources and Analogues. Child, 3.108; 4.497; 5.67, 303.
Keen M, Outlaws of Medieval Legend, Toronto 1961, p 116.
Bessinger J B Jr, Robin Hood: Folklore and Historiography 1377–1500, Tenn Stud in Lit 11.61.
Fowke E, The King and the Tinker, Journ American Folklore 79.469.
Fowler D C, A Literary History of the Popular Ballad, Durham N C 1968, p 83.
Dobson R B and J Taylor, The Medieval Origins of the Robin Hood Legend: A Reassessment, Northern History 7.1.
Walsh E, The King in Disguise, Folklore 86(1975).3.
Utley F L and B Ward, Manual, 5.1384, 1623 (XII [37]).
Bibliography. Brown-Robbins, Robbins-Cutler, nos 1533, 4168.
Gable J H, Bibliography of Robin Hood, Lincoln 1939, no 782.
Dean-Smith, p 82.
Bronson TTCB, 4.92.

[6] A GEST OF ROBYN HODE (INCUNABULUM) (1500).

PRINTS. STC, nos 13687–92.
Duff E G, 15th Century English Books, Oxford 1917, nos 361, 362.
Early English Printed Books in the University Library Cambridge (1475–1640), 4 vols, Cam-

bridge 1900–07, 1.50 (no 225, Wynkyn de Worde).
A Short-Title Catalogue of Foreign Books Printed up to 1600 . . . Now in the Nat Libr Scotland and the Libr of the Faculty of Advocates, Edinburgh 1970, p 179 (J van Doesborch).
Proctor R G C, Jan van Doesborgh Printer at Antwerp An Essay in Bibliography (Bibl Soc Illust Monograph, no 2), London 1894.
Isaac F, English and Scottish Printing Types 1501–35, 1508–41, Oxford 1930, Figures 92, 93.
Editions and Facsimiles. Ritson J, Robin Hood, London 1795, 1.2.
Laing D, The Knightly Tale of Golagros and Gawane and Other Ancient Poems Printed by W Chepman and A Myllar in the Year MDVIII, Edinburgh 1827 (only 76 copies survived a fire in the bookbinder's).
Gutch J M, A Lytyll Geste of Robin Hode, 2 vols, London 1847, 1.145.
Morley H, Shorter English Poems, London 1876, p 82.
Child, 3.56 (no 117).
Gummere F B, Old English Ballads, Boston 1894, p 1.
Flügel NL, p 171.
Pollard 15CPV, p 35.
Sargent and Kittredge, p 256.
Tudor Facsimile Texts, 1914.
Stevenson G, PSTS 65.267.
Beattie W, The Chepman and Myllar Prints (Edinburgh Bibl Soc), Edinburgh 1950, pp xv, 197.
Kinsley OBB, p 420.
Dobson R B and J Taylor, Rymes of Robin Hood: An Introd to the English Outlaw, London 1976, p 71.
Sources and Literary Relations. Child, 3.39, 519; 4.496; 5.240, 297.
Chambers OHEL, p 134.
Parsons L, The Meaning of Robin Hood, Hibbert Journ 55.268.
Keen M, Outlaws of Medieval Legend, Toronto 1961, p 100.
Bessinger J B Jr, Robin Hood: Folklore and Historiography 1377–1500, Tenn Stud in Lit 11.61.
Fowler D C, A Literary History of the Popular Ballad, Durham N C 1968, p 72.
Parker D, Popular Protest in A Gest of Robyn Hode, MLQ 32.3.
Dobson R B and J Taylor, The Medieval Origins of the Robin Hood Legend: A Reassessment, Northern History 7.1.
Bessinger, The Gest of Robin Hood Revisited in

The Learned and the Lewed: Studies in Chaucer and Medieval Literature, ed L D Benson, Cambridge Mass 1974, p 355; Harvard Stud in Eng 5.355.
Bibliography. Brown-Robbins, Robbins-Cutler, no 1915.
Gable J H, Bibliograph of Robin Hood, Lincoln 1939, no 528.
Bronson TTCB, 3.13.

[7] ADAM BELL, CLIM OF THE CLOUGH, AND WILLIAM OF CLOUDESLY (ca 1505).

PRINTS. STC, nos 1806–1813; revised STC, no 1805.7.
Isaac F, English and Scottish Printing Types 1501–35, Oxford 1930, Figure 3 (a page from STC, no 5199, with an early form of w^2 in Wynkyn de Worde which also occurs in revised STC, no 1805.7).
Editions. Percy T, Reliques of Ancient English Poetry, London 1765, 1.129.
Ritson J, Pieces of Ancient Popular Poetry, London 1791, p 5.
Hazlitt Rem, 2.138.
Child, 3.22 (no 116).
Sargent and Kittredge, p 246.
Kinsley OBB, p 380.
Dobson R B and J Taylor, Rymes of Robin Hood: An Introd to the English Outlaw, London 1976, p 255.
Literary Relations. Child, 3.14, 518; 4.496; 5.297.
Keen M, The Outlaws of Medieval Legend, Toronto 1961, p 124.
Bibliography. Bronson TTCB, 3.12.
New CBEL 1.1080.

[8] MS BALLIOL COLLEGE OXFORD 354 (1500–36).

MS. Coxe H O, Catalogus Codicum, Oxon 1852, 1.110 (rptd 1972).
Chappell W, Popular Music of the Olden Time, 2 vols, London 1855–57, 1.50.
Froude J A, The Commonplace Book of Richard Hill, Fraser's Magazine 58(1858).127.
Flügel, Angl 26.94.
Dyboski, edn, EETSES 101.
Bryant F E, History of English Balladry, Boston 1913, p 132.
Hills W P, N&Q 177.452 (Richard Hill).
Mynors R A B, Catalogue of the Manuscripts of Balliol College Oxford, Oxford 1963, p 352.
MS Contents. Godfrydus of Rome, f iii, see S J H

Herrtage, ed, Gesta Romanorum, EETSES 33.180.
The Boke of Marchalsie, f vii, see Brown-Robbins, Robbins-Cutler, no 3318.
The Seven Sages of Rome, f xviii, see K Brunner, ed, EETS 191; Brown-Robbins, Robbins-Cutler, no 3187.
Gower, Confessio Amantis (excerpts), f lv, see Works, ed G C Macaulay, Oxford 1901; Brown-Robbins, Robbins-Cutler, no 2662.
The Frere and the Boy, f xcviii, see Brown-Robbins, Robbins-Cutler, no 977.
Miscellaneous pieces, f c, see Brown-Robbins, Robbins-Cutler, nos 4148, 3307.
The Siege of Rouen, f cxxviii, see H Huscher, ed, Kölner Anglistische Arbeiten, Leipzig 1927; Brown-Robbins, Robbins-Cutler, no 979.
The Trental of St Gregory, f cxxxix, see Horstmann, ed, EETS 98.260; Brown-Robbins, no 1653.
The Boke of Curtasie, f cxli, see Dyboski, ed, Bausteine: Zeitschrift für neu-englische Wortforschung, Berlin 1905/6, p 329; Brown-Robbins, Robbins-Cutler, no 1920.
Miscellaneous songs and carols, f cxliv etc, see Brown-Robbins, Robbins-Cutler, nos 2385, 2410, 374, 506, 1055, 1032, 2060, 4246, 2413, 1454, 350, 1891, 2233, 324, 3074, 4181, 4137, 1919, 1132, 2732, 2784, 2678, 755, 3835, 375, 1412, 103, 3975, 1259, 1488, 769, 1941, 346, 704, 1163, 914, 2511, 1587, 1286, 1817, 3087, 3969, 895, 878, 889, 3603, 1575, 1914, 2053, 2097, 425, 3473, 890, 20, 3776, 112, 354, 1471, 3527, 3575, 2586, 2076, 1873, 2098, 3460, 1383, 22, 3161, 3627, 1386, 3852, 916, 3574, 1892, 4012, 898, 2681, 3669, 1444, 825, 1601, 3736, 4023, 548, 3424, 1363, 2346, 470, 294, 3820, 343, 3635, 608, 236, 2771.

Corpus Christi Carol (Greene E E Carols, no 126).
Editions. N&Q 3s 2(1862).103 (Staffordshire version).
Flügel NL, p 142.
Flügel E, Angl 26.175.
Sidgwick F, N&Q 10s 4(1905).181.
Dyboski R, Songs Carols and Other Miscellaneous Poems, EETSES 101, London 1907, p 103.
Manly J M, English Poetry 1170–1892, Boston 1907, p 65.
Rickert E, Ancient English Xmas Carols, London 1910, p 193.
Vaughan Williams R, Journ of the Folk-Song Soc 4(1910).63 (Derbyshire version).
Ch&Sidg, p 148.

Cook A S, A Literary ME Reader, Boston 1915, p 440.
Segar M, Medieval Anthology, London 1915, p 35.
Hogg J, The Mountain Bard (Edinburgh 1807), note to Sir David Graeme; rptd in E C Batho, The Ettrick Shepherd, Cambridge 1927, p 31 (Scottish analogue).
Niles J J, Ten Christmas Carols, N Y 1935, p 2.
Greene E E Carols, p 221.
Williams C, New Book of English Verse, N Y 1936, p 112.
Wells E K, Journ of the Eng Folk-Dance and Song Soc 4(1942).122 (North Carolina version).
Leach BB, p 692.
Greene R L, A Selection of English Carols, Oxford 1962, p 128.
Davies R T, Medieval English Lyrics, London 1963, p 272.
Stevick R, One Hundred Middle English Lyrics, N Y 1964, p 171.
Haskell A S, A Middle English Anthology, N Y 1969, p 344.
Sisam C and K Sisam, Oxford Book of Medieval English Verse (no 30), Oxford 1970, p 542.
Tydeman W, English Poetry 1400–1580, London 1970, p 53.
Literary Criticism. Gilchrist A C, Journ of the Folk-Song Soc 4(1910).53.
Bryant F E, A History of English Balladry, Boston 1919, p 134.
Batho E C, The Life of Christ in the Ballads, E&S 9.93.
Gerould G H, The Ballad of Tradition, Oxford 1932; rptd N Y 1957, pp 33, 124n.
Greg W W, RES 13.88.
Greene R L, The Traditional Survival of Two Medieval Carols, ELH 7.223.
Chambers OHEL, p 111.
Kane G, Middle English Literature, London 1951, p 174.
Speirs J, Medieval English Poetry, London 1957, p 76.
Mason H A, Humanism and Poetry in the Early Tudor Period, London 1959, p 146.
Greene R L, The Meaning of the Corpus Christi Carol, MÆ 29.10.
Manning S, Wisdom and Number, Lincoln 1962, p 115.
Greene R L, The Burden and the Scottish Variant of the Corpus Christi Carol, MÆ 33.53.
Fowler D C, A Literary History of the Popular Ballad, Durham N C 1968, p 58.
Oliver R, Poems without Names; The English Lyric 1200–1500, Berkeley 1970, p 108.

Owen L J and N H, Middle English Poetry: An Anthology, N Y 1971, p 354.
Gray D, Themes and Images in the Medieval English Religious Lyric, London 1972, p 164.
Bibliography. Brown-Robbins, Robbins-Cutler, no 1132.
Dean-Smith, p 64 (Down in Yon Forest).

[9] MS BODLEIAN LIBRARY OXFORD 12653 (RAWLINSON C.813) (1530–40).

MS. Catalogus Codicum MS Bibl Bodl, pt V, fasc ii, Oxford 1878, col 415.
Padelford, edn, Angl 31.309; 35.178.
Bolle W, Zur Lyric der Rawlinson-HS. C.813, Angl 34.273.
Power K H J, A Critical Edition of the English Lyrics in Rawlinson MS C.813 in the Bodleian Libr, D Phil thesis, Univ of Western Australia (in progress).
Hawes S, Pastime of Pleasure, ed W E Mead, EETS 173.xxxviii nl.
Robbins SL, nos 129, 130, 200, 204, 207.
Robbins-HP, no 74.
Stevens J, Music and Poetry in the Early Tudor Court, London 1961, pp 365 (no F28), 424 (no H108).
Seaton E, Sir Richard Roos c 1410–1482 Lancastrian Poet, London 1961, passim (attributes Padelford, nos 23, 24, 26, 27, 32, to Roos through the discovery of anagrams).
MS Contents. Miscellaneous lyrics, Brown-Robbins, nos 1768, 172, 430, 2228, 2532, 2822, 2496, 368, 3804, 4210, 1180, 1329, 2529, 649, 2421, 2498, 729, 767, 2547, 366, 4190, 2821; Robbins-Cutler, nos 2757.3, 340.5, 1349.5, 2271.6, 2261.8, 2827.5, 159.8, 79.5, 2532.5, 2482.5, 3962.5, 2552.5, 3098.3, 1450.5, 1841.5, 1926.5, 2409.5, 1017.5, 2560.5, 3713.5, 2245.1, 642.5. 4020.3, 1328.7, 3785.5, 3228.5, 3917.8, 2500.5, 2439.5.

Crow and Pie (Child, no 111).
Editions. Halliwell J O, Nugae Poeticae, London 1844, p 42.
Child, 2.478.
Sargent and Kittredge, p 238.
Padelford F M, The Songs in MS Rawlinson C.813, Angl 31.374 (no 40); rptd Univ of Wash 1909; Angl 35.178.
Literary Relations. Child, 2.478.
Bryant F E, A History of English Balladry, Boston 1919, p 128.
Fowler D C, A Literary History of the Popular Ballad, Durham N C 1968, p 29.

Bibliography. Robbins-Cutler, no 3713.5.

[10] MS BRITISH MUSEUM COTTON CLEOPATRA C.IV (1st half 16 cent).

MS. Catalogue of MSS in the Cottonian Library, London 1802, p 580, item 12.
Arngart O, Two English Border Ballads, Acta Universitatis Lundensis sectio 1, no 18, Lund 1973, p 25.

The Battle of Otterburn (Child, no 161).
Editions. Percy T, Reliques of Ancient English Poetry, 3rd edn London 1775, 1.21.
Ritson J, The Northumberland Garland: or Newcastle Nightingale, Newcastle 1793, p 3; rptd Northern Garlands, 1810.
Ritson AS, 2nd edn London 1829, 1.94.
Child, 3.295.
Gummere F J, Old English Ballads, Boston 1894, p 94.
Flügel NL, p 192.
Arber E, The Dunbar Anthology 1401–1508, London 1901, p 50.
Sargent and Kittredge, p 387.
Sidgwick F, Popular Ballads of the Olden Time, 4 vols, London 1903–12, 3.18.
Witham R A, English and Scottish Popular Ballads, N Y 1909, p 60.
Leach BB, p 436.
Robbins-HP, p 64.
Kinsley OBB, p 491.
Literary Relations. White R, History of the Battle of Otterburn, London 1857.
Child, 3.289, 520; 4.499; 5.243, 297.
Lang A, Sir Walter Scott and the Border Minstrelsy, London 1910, p 53.
Bryant F E, A History of English Balladry, Boston 1919, p 147.
Arngart O, The Battle of Otterburn and the Hunting of the Cheviot, SN 47.7.
Bland D S, Macbeth and the Battle of Otterburn, N&Q 194.335; The evolution of Chevy Chase and The Battle of Otterburn, N&Q 196.160.
Clark J W, Popular Ballads: The Heroic and Tragic Voice of the Common Man, Minnesota Rev 6(1966).219.
Fowler D C, The Hunting of the Cheviot and The Battle of Otterburn, Western Folklore 25.165.
McMillan D J, Some Popular Views of Four Medieval Ballads, Southern Folklore Quart 30.179.
Tranter N, It fell about the Lammastide, Scots Magazine ns 93(1970).540.
Arngart, Two Eng Border Ballads.

Bibliography. Brown-Robbins, Robbins-Cutler, no 1620.
Bronson TTCB, 3.109.
Dean-Smith, p 51.
New CBEL, 1.711.
Robbins R H, Manual, 5.1662.

[11] MS BODLEIAN LIBRARY OXFORD 6933 (ASHMOLE 48) (1560).

MS. Black W H, Catalogue of Ashmole MSS, Oxford 1845, col 83.
Wright, edn.
Rollins H E, MLN 34.340.
Fowler D C, A Literary History of the Popular Ballad, Durham N C 1968, p 96.
Arngart O, Two English Border Ballads, Acta Universitatis Lundensis sectio 1, no 18, Lund 1973, p 50.

The Hunting of the Cheviot (Child, no 162).

Editions. Hearne T, Guilielmi Neubrigensis Historia, Oxford 1719, 1.82.
Percy T, Reliques of Ancient English Poetry, 1st edn London 1765, 1.4.
Annual Register 8(1766).261.
Ritson AS, 1.105.
Wright T, Songs and Ballads, London 1860, p 24.
Allingham W, The Ballad Book, London 1879, p 48.
Skeat Spec, p 67.
Child, 3.307.
Gummere F B, Old English Ballads, Boston 1894, p 325.
Flügel NL, p 198.
Arber E, The Dunbar Anthology 1401–1508, London 1901, p 63.
Sargent and Kittredge, p 393.
Sidgwick F, Popular Ballads of the Olden Time, 4 vols, London 1903–12, 3.3.
Bronson W C, English Poems, 4 vols, Chicago 1907–10, 1.216.
Witham R A, English and Scottish Popular Ballads, N Y 1909, p 66.
Leach BB, p 447.
Friedman VBFB, p 277.
Kinsley OBB, p 496.
Literary Relations. Child, 3.303; 4.502; 5.244, 297.
Nessler K, Geschichte der Ballade Chevy Chase, Berlin 1911.
Bryant F E, A History of English Balladry, Boston 1919, p 147.
Sauer O, Die Quellen der Chevy Chaseballade, Halle 1913.

McCutcheon R P, Two 18th-century Emendations to Chevy Chase, MLN 37.436.
Bland D S, The evolution of Chevy Chase and The Battle of Otterburn, N&Q 196.160.
Clark J W, Popular Ballads: The Heroic and Tragic Voice of the Common Man, Minnesota Rev 6(1966).219.
Fowler D C, The Hunting of the Cheviot and The Battle of Otterburn, Western Folklore 25.165.
McMillan D J, Some Popular Views of Four Medieval Ballads, Southern Folklore Quart 30.179.
Truman W C, Shakespeare's Henry IV Part I and the Ballad Chevy Chase, N&Q 211.131.
Hamer D, Towards Restoring The Hunting of the Cheviot, RES 20.1.
Tranter N, It fell about the Lammastide, Scots Magazine ns 93(1970).540.
Steven W M, Richard Sheale and the Ballad of Chevy Chase, AN&Q 9.115.
Thomson R S, The Transmission of Chevy-Chase, Southern Folklore Quart 39.63.
Arngart O, The Battle of Otterburn and the Hunting of the Cheviot, SN 47.7.
Bibliography. Robbins-Cutler, nos 3445.5 and 960.1.
Bronson TTCB, 3.113.
Dean-Smith, p 57.
Coffin BTBNA (1963), p 110.
New CBEL, 1.711.
Simpson BBBM, p 96.
Robbins R H, Manual, 5.1663(XIII [78]).

[12] MS CORPUS CHRISTI COLLEGE OXFORD 255 (1550–70).

MS. Coxe H O, Catalogus Codicum, Oxon 1852, 2.105.
Cornelius, edn, PMLA 46.1025.

King John and the Bishop (Child, no 45).

Edition. Cornelius R D, A New Text of an Old Ballad, PMLA 46.1026.
Literary Relations. Child, 1.403, 508; 2.506; 4.459; 5.216, 291.
Röhrich L, ed, Erzählungen des späten Mittelalters und ihr Weiterleben in Literatur und Volksdichtung bis zur Gegenwart, 2 vols, Bern 1962–67, 1.146, 281 (analogues).
Bibliography. Brown-Robbins, Robbins-Cutler, no 1346.
Bronson TTCB, 1.354; 4.461.
Coffin BTBNA (1963), p 52.
Simpson BBBM, p 172.

[13] MS YORK MINSTER LIBRARY (16 cent).

MS. Publications of the Surtees Soc, 85.64 n 1.

Sir Andrew Barton (Child, no 167).
Editions. Publications of the Surtees Soc, 85.64.
Child, 4.503.
Literary Relations. Child, 3.334; 4.393, 502; 5.245, 302.
Bryant F E, A History of English Balladry, Boston 1919, p 195.
Fowler D C, A Literary History of the Popular Ballad, Durham N C 1968, p 115.
Bibliography. Brown-Robbins, Robbins-Cutler, no 1621.
Bronson TTCB, 3.133; 4.24, 509 (= Henry Martyn).
Coffin BTBNA, p 112.

[14] MS BRITISH MUSEUM HARLEIAN 367.

MS. Catalogue of the Harleian Manuscripts, 1.212.

Flodden Field (Child, no 168 App).
Editions. Webber H, An Edition of Flodden Field, Edinburgh and London 1808.
Evans R H, Old Ballads, London 1810, 3.58.
Child, 3.355.
Literary Relations. Child, 3.351; 4.507; 5.298.
Robbins R H, Manual, 5.1492 (XIII [220]).
Oates J C T, The Trewe Encounter: A Pamphlet of Flodden Field, Trans Cambridge Bibl Soc 1.126.
Bibliography. Robbins-Cutler, no 1011.5.
Robbins, Manual, 5.1698.

[15] MS BRITISH MUSEUM COTTON VESPASIAN A.25 (16 cent).

MS. Catalogue of MSS in the Cottonian Library, London 1802, p 438, item 67, f 187.
Böddeker, edn, JfRESL ns 2(1875).81, 210, 347; 3.92.
Seng, edn.
Bryant F E, A History of English Balladry, Boston 1919, p 193.
MS Contents. Rule of St Benedict in English verse, f 66, see Brown-Robbins, no 218.
Richard de Caistre's hymn, f 171, see Brown-Robbins, Robbins-Cutler, no 1727.
The Dance of Death, f 172, see Brown-Robbins, Robbins-Cutler, no 2590.

For miscellaneous songs, carols, etc see the following:
Ritson AS, p 146.
Evans R H, Old Ballads, London 1810, 1.342.
Dyce A, The Works of George Peele, London 1829, 2.256.
Rel Ant, 1.238, 239, 324; 2.31, 111.
Wright T, Specimens of Old Christmas Carols, PPS 4(1841).34.
Bullen A H, The Works of George Peele, London 1888, 2.370.
Greene E E Carols, pp 60, 317, 325.
Simpson BBBM, pp 157, 165.

Captain Car (Child, no 178).
Editions. Ritson AS, p 137.
Böddeker R, JfRESL ns 3.126.
Furnivall F J, Trans of the New Shakspere Soc, 1880–86, Appendix p 52†.
Child, 3.430.
Sargent and Kittredge, p 434.
Leach BB, p 488.
Seng P J, Tudor Songs and Ballads from MS Cotton Vespasian A-25, Harvard 1978, p 128.
Literary Relations. Child, 3.423, 520; 4.513; 5.247, 299.
Bryant, p 194.
Simpson W D, The Earldom of Mar, Aberdeen 1949, p 145.
Bibliography. Bronson TTCB, 3.156.
Coffin BTBNA, p 116.
Simpson BBBM, p 660.

[16] RENAISSANCE BALLAD COMPOSERS AND COLLECTORS (16–17 cent).

Note: This grouping includes the following titles:
The Fair Flower of Northumberland (Child, no 9; Thomas Deloney; STC, no 6559).
The Three Ravens (Child, no 16; Thomas Ravenscroft; STC, no 20758).
The Famous Flower of Serving Men (Child, no 106; Lawrence Price).
The Baffled Knight (Child, no 112; Thomas Ravenscroft; STC, no 20757).
Robin Hood's Golden Prize (Child, no 147; Lawrence Price).
True Tale of Robin Hood (Child, no 154; Martin Parker; STC, no 19275).
King James and Brown (Child, no 180; William Elderton).
John Dory (Child, no 284; Thomas Raven-

scroft; STC, no 20757).
Editions. Child, 1.113 (no 9), 254 (no 26); 2.430 (no 106), 483 (no 112); 3.209 (no 147), 227 (no 154), 443 (no 180); 5.132 (no 284).
Sargent and Kittredge, pp 16 (Child, no 9), 45 (Child, no 26), 221 (Child, no 106), 239 (Child, no 112), 347 (Child, no 147), 362 (Child, no 154), 441 (Child, no 180), 609 (Child, no 284).
Mann F O, ed, The Works of Thomas Deloney, Oxford 1912, p 33.
Leach BB, pp 71 (Child, no 9), 111 (Child, no 26), 320 (Child, no 112), 420 (Child, no 147).
Friedman VBFB, pp 23 (Child, no 26), 155 (Child, no 112).
Kinsley OBB, pp 272 (Child, no 9), 245 (Child, no 26).
Dobson R B and J Taylor, Rymes of Robin Hood, An Introd to the English Outlaw, London 1976, p 187 (Child, no 154).
Literary Relations. Child, 1.111, 493; 2.498; 3.499; 5.207 (no 9); 1.253; 4.454; 5.212 (no 26); 2.428; 3.518; 4.492 (no 106); 2.479; 3.518; 4.495; 5.239, 296 (no 112); 3.208, 519 (no 147); 3.227 (no 154); 3.442 (no 180); 5.131 (no 284).
Bryant J E, A History of English Balladry, Boston 1919, p 197 (Child, no 26).
Rollins H E, SP 17.199 (William Elderton).
Neumann F W, Die schottische Volksballade von den Drei Raben in Russland, Neuphilologische Monatsschrift 8.120 (Child, no 26).
Schmidt W, Die Volksballade von den Drei Raben, Neuphilologische Monatsschrift 8.81 (Child, no 26).
Hamer D, The Twa Corbies, RES ns 23.355 (Child, no 26).
Locke L G, The Three Ravens, Explicator 4(1946), item 54 (Child, no 26).
Montgomerie W, The Twa Corbies, RES ns 6.227 (Child, no 26).
Chatman V V, The Three Ravens Explicated, Midwest Folklore 13.177 (Child, no 26).
Wiatt W H, The Twa Corbies Again, Keystone Folklore Quart 10.116 (Child, no 26).
Bibliography. Bronson TTCB, 1.138 (Child, no 9), 308; 4.459 (Child, no 26); 2.530; 4.483 (Child, no 106); 2.547 (Child, no 112); 3.68 (Child, no 147); 4.303 (Child, no 284).
Dean Smith, pp 65 (Child, no 9), 111 (Child, no 26), 53 (Blow away the morning dew, Child, no 112).
Coffin BTBNA, pp 46 (Child, no 26), 98 (Child, no 106), 99 (Child, no 112), 116 (Child, no 180).
Simpson BBBM, pp 27 (Child, no 112), 493 (Child, no 180), 398 (Child, no 284).

[17] MS BRITISH MUSEUM ADDITIONAL 27879 (PERCY FOLIO) (1650).

MS. PFMS.
Millican C B, The Original of the Ballad Kinge Arthurs Death in the Percy Folio MS, PMLA 46.1020.
Willinsky M, Bischof Percy's Bearbeitung der Volksballaden und Kunstgedichte seines Folio-Manuskriptes, Beiträge zur englischen Philologie 22, Leipzig 1932; rptd N Y etc 1967.
Hagedorn M, Das Percy Folio-Manuskript, Berlin 1940.
Bate W J, Percy's Use of His Folio Manuscript, JEGP 43.337.
Friedman A B, Percy's Folio Manuscript Revalued, JEGP 53.524; The Ballad Revival, Chicago 1961, p 29.
Fowler D C, A Literary History of the Popular Ballad, Durham N C 1968, p 132.
Wardroper J, Love and Drollery, London 1969 (includes songs from the Percy MS).
Wilson R H, Malory and the Ballad King Arthur's Death, Medievalia et Humanistica 6(1975). 139.
Schwegler R A, Sources of the Ballads in Bishop Percy's Folio Manuscript, diss Chicago 1977.

Earl Brand (Child, no 7).
Editions. PFMS, 1.133.
Child, 1.103.
Sargent and Kittredge, p 13.
Literary Relations. Child, 1.88, 489; 2.498; 3.497; 4.443; 5.207, 285.
Boeckh L, Zur Entwicklung der Earl Brand-Ballade, diss Marburg 1922.
Powers D C, The American Variants of Earl Brand, Western Folklore 17.77.
Siegmund W I, A Comparative Study of Earl Brand (Child, no 7) and Its Danish and Icelandic Analogues, 2 vols, diss Ohio State Univ 1973; DAI 34.2489A.
Bibliography. Bronson TTCB 1.106; 4.443.
Dean-Smith, p 64.
Coffin BTBNA, p 29.

Sir Lionel (Child, no 18).
Editions. PFMS, 1.75.
Child, 1.210.
Sargent and Kittredge, p 34.
Leach BB, p 101.
Literary Relations. Child, 1.208; 2.500; 4.451.
Hornstein L H, Manual, 1.124 (I [79]).
Bibliography. Bronson TTCB, 1.265; 4.455.

Dean-Smith, p 105.
Coffin BTBNA, p 42.

The Maid and the Palmer (Child, no 21).
Editions. PFMS, 4.96.
Child, 1.232.
Sargent and Kittredge, p 40.
Leach BB, p 106.
Literary Relations. Child, 1.228; 2.501; 3.502; 4.451; 5.212, 288.
Buchan D D, The Maid, the Palmer, and the Cruel Mother, Malahat Rev 3(1967).98.
Harris J, Maiden in the Mor Lay and the Medieval Magdalene Tradition, Journ of Medieval and Renaissance Stud 1.59.
Bibliography. Bronson TTCB, 4.457.

The Boy and the Mantle (Child, no 29).
Editions. PFMS, 2.304.
Child, 1.271.
Sargent and Kittredge, p 47.
Leach BB, p 114.
Kinsley OBB, p 31.
Literary Relations. Child, 1.257, 507; 2.502; 3.503; 4.454; 5.212, 289.
Bibliography. Coffin BTBNA, p 49.

King Arthur and King Cornwall (Child, no 30).
Editions. PFMS, 1.61.
Child, 1.283.
Sargent and Kittredge, p 50.
Literary Relations. Child, 1.274, 507; 2.502; 3.503; 5.289.
Walpole R N, The Pèlerinage de Charlemagne: Poem, Legend and Problem, RomP 8.173 (see especially p 184f).
Davis J W, Le Pelerinage de Charlemagne and King Arthur and King Cornwall: A Study in the Evolution of a Tale, diss Indiana Univ 1974; DAI 35.397A.
Newstead H, Manual, 1.67 (I [35]).
Bibliography. Newstead, Manual, 1.247.

The Marriage of Sir Gawain (Child, no 31).
Editions. PFMS, 1.105.
Child, 1.293.
Sargent and Kittredge, p 55.
Leach BB, p 119.
Literary Relations. Child, 1.288, 507; 2.502; 4.454; 5.213, 289.
Newstead H, Manual, 1.66 (I [37]).
Bibliography. Bronson TTCB, 1.317.
Coffin BTBNA, p 49.
Newstead, Manual, 1.247.

Young Andrew (Child, no 48).
Editions. PFMS, 2.328.
Child, 1.432.
Sargent and Kittredge, p 88.
Literary Relations. Child, 1.432.

Sir Aldingar (Child, no 59).
Editions. PFMS, 1.166.
Child, 2.44.
Sargent and Kittredge, p 106.
Leach BB, p 185.
Kinsley OBB, p 23.
Literary Relations. Child, 2.33, 510; 3.508; 4.463; 5.292.
Christophersen P, The Ballad of Sir Aldingar, Oxford 1952.
Taylor D S, The Lineage and Birth of Sir Aldingar, Journ of American Folklore 65.139.
Entwistle W J, Sir Aldingar and the Date of English Ballads, Saga Book of the Viking Soc for Northern Research 13.97.

King Estmere (Child, no 60).
Editions. Child, 2.51.
Sargent and Kittredge, p 111.
Kinsley OBB, p 127.
Literary Relations. Child, 2.49, 510; 3.508; 4.463.

Sir Cawline (Child, no 61).
Editions. PFMS, 3.3.
Child, 2.58.
Sargent and Kittredge, p 115.
Literary Relations. Child, 2.56, 511; 3.508; 4.463.
Stewart M, A Recently-Discovered Manuscript: ane taill of Sir Colling ye knyt, Scottish Stud 16.23.
Hornstein L H, Manual, 1.151 (I [100]).
Stewart M and H M Shire, The Ninth of May, 4(1973).11.
Bibliography. Bronson TTCB, 2.37.

Child Waters (Child, no 63).
Editions. PFMS, 2.269.
Child, 2.85.
Sargent and Kittredge, p 122.
Leach BB, p 201.
Friedman VBFB, p 123.
Kinsley OBB, p 149.
Literary Relations. Child, 2.83, 511; 3.508; 4.463; 5.220.
Bibliography. Bronson TTCB, 2.44.
Coffin BTBNA, p 64.

Glasgerion (Child, no 67).
Editions. PFMS, 1.248.
Child, 2.138.
Sargent and Kittredge, p 136.
Leach BB, p 223.

Friedman VBFB, p 72.
Kinsley OBB, p 123.
Literary Relations. Child, 2.136, 511; 3.509; 4.468; 5.293.
Bibliography. Bronson TTCB, 2.59.
Coffin BTBNA, p 65.

Old Robin of Portingale (Child, no 80).
Editions. PFMS, 1.235.
Child, 2.240.
Sargent and Kittredge, p 170.
Literary Relations. Child, 2.240, 513; 3.514; 4.476; 5.225, 295.

Little Musgrave and Lady Barnard (Child, no 81).
Editions. PFMS, 1.119.
Child, 2.245.
Sargent and Kittredge, p 174.
Literary Relations. Child, 2.242, 513; 4.476; 5.225.
Campbell M, A Study of 25 Versions of Little Musgrave and Lady Barnard in Ballad Collections of North America, Tennessee Folklore Soc Bull 21.14.
Stewart M and H M Shire, The Ninth of May 4(1973).24.
Bibliography. Bronson TTCB, 2.267; 4.474.
Coffin BTBNA, p 79.

Child Maurice (Child, no 83).
Editions. PFMS, 2.502.
Child, 2.264.
Sargent and Kittredge, p 176.
Leach BB, p 274.
Literary Relations. Child, 2.263; 3.514; 4.478.
Bibliography. Bronson TTCB, 2.316; 4.476.
Coffin BTBNA, p 81.

Will Stewart and John (Child, no 107).
Editions. PFMS, 3.216.
Child, 2.433.
Sargent and Kittredge, p 223.
Literary Relations. Child, 2.432; 5.237.

Christopher White (Child, no 108).
Editions. PFMS, 3.494.
Child, 2.439.
Sargent and Kittredge, p 228.
Literary Relations. Child, 2.439.

Tom Potts (Child, no 109).
Editions. PFMS, 3.135.
Child, 2.442.
Sargent and Kittredge, p 229.
Literary Relations. Child, 2.441; 3.518.

Robin Hood and Guy of Gisborne (Child, no 118).
Editions. Percy T, Reliques of Ancient English Poetry, 3 vols, London 1765, 1.74; 4th edn 1794, 1.81.
Ritson J, Robin Hood, London 1795, 1.114.
PFMS, 2.227.
Child, 3.91.
Sargent and Kittredge, p 279.
Leach BB, p 334.
Dobson R B and J Taylor: Rymes of Robin Hood: An Introd to the English Outlaw, London 1976, p 140.
Literary Relations. Child, 3.89.
Bibliography. Bronson TTCB, 3.16.
Coffin BTBNA, p 101.

Robin Hood's Death (Child, no 120).
Editions. PFMS, 1.53.
Child, 3.104.
Sargent and Kittredge, p 286.
Leach BB, p 349.
Dobson and Taylor, p 133.
Literary Relations. Child, 3.102; 5.240, 297.
Bibliography. Bronson TTCB, 3.18.
Coffin BTBNA, p 102.

Robin Hood and the Butcher (Child, no 122).
Editions. PFMS, 1.19.
Child, 3.116.
Sargent and Kittredge, p 294.
Dobson and Taylor, p 150.
Literary Relations. Child, 3.115.

Robin Hood and the Curtal Friar (Child, no 123).
Editions. PFMS, 1.26.
Child, 3.123.
Sargent and Kittredge, p 297.
Dobson and Taylor, p 158.
Literary Relations. Child, 3.120; 5.297.
Bibliography. Bronson TTCB, 3.21.

The Jolly Pinder of Wakefield (Child, no 124).
Editions. PFMS, 1.32.
Child, 3.131.
Sargent and Kittredge, p 301.
Dobson and Taylor, p 146.
Literary Relations. Child, 3.129.
Bibliography. Bronson TTCB, 3.24.

Robin Hood Rescuing Three Squires (Child, no 140).
Editions. PFMS, 1.13.
Child, 3.179.
Sargent and Kittredge, p 332.
Friedman VBFB, p 342.

Literary Relations. Child, 3.177.
Bibliography. Bronson TTCB, 3.53; 4.493.
Coffin BTBNA, p 106.

Little John a Begging (Child, no 142).
Editions. PFMS, 1.47.
Child, 3.188.
Sargent and Kittredge, p 336.
Literary Relations. Child, 3.188.
Bibliography. Bronson TTCB, 3.60.

Robin Hood and Queen Katherine (Child, no 145).
Editions. PFMS, 1.37.
Child, 3.198.
Sargent and Kittredge, p 341.
Literary Relations. Child, 3.196.
Bibliography. Bronson TTCB, 3.65.

Hugh Spencer's Feats in France (Child, no 158).
Editions. PFMS, 2.290.
Child, 3.276.
Sargent and Kittredge, p 378.
Literary Relations. Child, 3.275; 4.499; 5.243.

Durham Field (Child, no 159).
Editions. PFMS, 2.190.
Child, 3.284.
Sargent and Kittredge, p 382.
Literary Relations. Child, 3.282; 5.297.
McMillan D J, Some Popular Views of Four Medieval Ballads, Southern Folklore Quart 30.179.
Robbins R H, Manual, 5.1416.
Bibliography. Robbins, Manual, 5.1661.

Sir John Butler (Child, no 165).
Editions. PFMS, 3.205.
Child, 3.329.
Sargent and Kittredge, p 403.
Literary Relations. Child, 3.327.

The Rose of England (Child, no·166).
Editions. PFMS, 3.187.
Child, 3.332.
Sargent and Kittredge, p 405.
Literary Relations. Child, 3.331.
Bibliography. Coffin BTBNA, p 111.
Robbins R H, Manual, 5.1697.

Thomas Cromwell (Child, no 171).
Editions. PFMS, 1.129.
Child, 3.377.
Sargent and Kittredge, p 419.
Literary Relations. Child, 3.377.

Musselburgh Field (Child, no 172).
Editions. PFMS, 1.123.

Child, 3.378.
Sargent and Kittredge, p 420.
Literary Relations. Child, 3.378; 4.507.
Friedman A B, A New Version of Musselburgh Field, Journ of American Folklore 66.74.
Bibliography. Coffin BTBNA, p 114.

Earl Bothwell (Child, no 174).
Editions. PFMS, 2.260.
Child, 3.400.
Sargent and Kittredge, p 423.
Literary Relations. Child, 3.399; 5.247.

The Rising in the North (Child, no 175).
Editions. PFMS, 2.210.
Child, 3.404.
Sargent and Kittredge, p 424.
Leach BB, p 484.
Literary Relations. Child, 3.401.

Northumberland Betrayed by Douglas (Child, no 176).
Editions. PFMS, 2.217.
Child, 3.411.
Sargent and Kittredge, p 426.
Kinsley OBB, p 526.
Literary Relations. Child, 3.408; 5.299.
Bibliography. Coffin BTBNA, p 115.

The Earl of Westmoreland (Child, no 177).
Editions. PFMS, 1.292.
Child, 3.419.
Sargent and Kittredge, p 430.
Literary Relations. Child, 3.416; 5.299.
Dickson A, The Earl of Westmoreland and Bueve de Hantone, PMLA 43.570.

Jock o the Side (Child, no 187).
Editions. PFMS, 2.203.
Child, 3.477.
Sargent and Kittredge, p 456.
Literary Relations. Child, 3.475.
Robson M, Notes on the Historical Background and Sources of Jock o' the Side, Trans of the Hawick Archaeolog Soc 1971, p 11.
Bibliography. Bronson TTCB, 3.171.
Dean-Smith, p 80.
Coffin BTBNA, p 117.

The Heir of Linne (Child, no 267).
Editions. PFMS, 1.174.
Child, 5.14.
Sargent and Kittredge, p 576.
Literary Relations. Child, 5.11.
Stewart M and H M Shire, The Ninth of May 4(1973).28.
Bibliography. Bronson TTCB, 4.75.
Coffin BTBNA, p 141.

The Lord of Lorn and the False Steward (Child, no 271).
Editions. PFMS, 1.180.
Child, 5.48.
Sargent and Kittredge, p 586.
Literary Relations. Child, 5.42, 280.
Hornstein L H, Manual, 1.152 (I [101]).
Stewart M and H M Shire, The Ninth of May 4(1973).28.
Bibliography. Bronson TTCB, 4.83.

[18] SEVENTEENTH-CENTURY BROADSIDES.

The Elfin Knight (Child, no 2).
Editions. Child, 1.15.
Sargent and Kittredge, p 3.
Leach BB, p 51.
Friedman VBFB, p 7.
Literary Relations. Child, 1.6, 484; 2.495; 3.496; 4.439; 5.205, 284.
Taylor A, The English Riddle Ballads, Stud in Lang and Lit in honour of M Schlauch, Warsaw 1966, p 445.
Toelken J B, Riddles Wisely Expounded, Western Folklore 25.1.
Lindfars B, A Fraudulent Elfin Knight from West Virginia, Western Folklore 27.107.
Bibliography. Bronson TTCB, 1.9; 4.439.
Dean-Smith, p 65.
Coffin BTBNA, p 23.

The Twa Sisters (Child, no 10).
Editions. Child, 1.126.
Sargent and Kittredge, p 18.
Literary Relations. Child, 1.118, 493; 2,498; 3.499; 4.447; 5.208, 286.
Liestøl K, De tvo systar, Maal og Minné 1.37 (with Scandinavian analogue).
Taylor A, The English Scottish and American Versions of the Twa Sisters, Journ American Folklore 42.238.
Parker H, The two sisters–going which way? Journ American Folklore 64.347.
Brewster P G, The Two Sisters, Helsinki 1953 (FFC 147).
Roth K, Die Ballade von den Zwei Schwestern, Jahrbuch f Volksliedforschung 13.71 (East European variants of the Continental analogue).
Bibliography. Bronson TTCB, 1.10, 4.444.
Dean-Smith, p 113.
Coffin BTBNA, p 32.

The Cruel Mother (Child, no 20).
Editions. Child, 2.500.
Sargent and Kittredge, p 37.
Literary Relations. Child, 1.218, 504; 2.500; 3.502; 4.451; 5.211, 287.
Myer M G, Murder with a Penknife–A Children's Song, N&Q ns 13.103.
Buchan D D, The Maid, the Palmer and the Cruel Mother, Malahat Rev 3.98.
Harris J, Maiden in the Mor Lay and the Medieval Magdalene Tradition, Journ of Medieval and Renaissance Stud 1.59.
Bibliography. Bronson TTCB, 1.276; 4.456.
Dean-Smith, p 61.
Coffin BTBNA, p 44.

Lord Thomas and Fair Annet (Child, no 73).
Editions. Child, 2.187.
Sargent and Kittredge, p 153.
Leach BB, p 182.
Literary Relations. Child, 2.179, 512; 3.509; 4.469; 5.223, 293.
Miller E D, Nonsense and New Sense in Lord Thomas, Southern Folklore Quart 1.25.
Beard A, Lord Thomas in America, Southern Folklore Quart 19.257.
Harris R, Lord Thomas and Fair Ellinor; a preliminary study of the ballad, Midwest Folklore 5.79.
Bibliography. Bronson TTCB, 2.88; 4.468.
Dean-Smith, p 85.
Coffin BTBNA, p 68.

Fair Margaret and Sweet William (Child, no 74).
Editions. Child, 2.200.
Sargent and Kittredge, p 157.
Kinsley OBB, p 231.
Literary Relations. Child, 2.199; 5.224, 293.
Bibliography. Bronson TTCB, 2.155; 4.470.
Dean-Smith, p 65.
Coffin BTBNA, p 70.
Simpson BBBM, p 785.

The Bailiff's Daughter of Islington (Child, no 105).
Editions. Child, 2.427.
Sargent and Kittredge, p 220.
Leach BB, p 313.
Friedman VBFB, p 140.
Kinsley OBB, p 342.
Literary Relations. Child, 2.426; 3.518; 5.237.
Gainer P W, The Bailiff's Daughter of Islington, West Virginia Univ Philological Papers 15.70.
Bibliography. Bronson TTCB, 2.515; 4.482.
Dean-Smith, p 51.
Coffin BTBNA, p 97.

Simpson BBBM, p 29.

The Knight and the Shepherd's Daughter (Child, no 110).
Editions. Child, 2.459.
Sargent and Kittredge, p 235.
Literary Relations. Child, 2.457; 4.492; 5.237.
Bibliography. Bronson TTCB, 2.535; 4.486.
Dean-Smith, p 83.
Coffin BTBNA, p 99.
Simpson BBBM, p 658.

Robin Hood and the Tanner (Child, no 126).
Editions. Child, 3.137.
Sargent and Kittredge, p 305.
Leach BB, p 372.
Literary Relations. Child, 3.137.
Bibliography. Bronson TTCB, 3.28; 4.490.
Dean-Smith, p 101.
Coffin BTBNA, p 103.

Robin Hood and the Tinker (Child, no 127).
Editions. Child, 3.141.
Sargent and Kittredge, p 307.
Leach BB, p 376.
Literary Relations. Child, 3.140.
Bibliography. Bronson TTCB, 3.32.

Robin Hood Newly Revived (Child, no 128).
Editions. Child, 3.145.
Sargent and Kittredge, p 309.
Leach BB, p 381.
Literary Relations. Child, 3.144.
Dunn C W, Manual, 1.31 (I [9]).
Bibliography. Bronson TTCB, 3.33.

Robin Hood and the Prince of Aragon (Child, no 129).
Editions. Child, 3.147.
Sargent and Kittredge, p 311.
Literary Relations. Child, 3.147.
Bibliography. Bronson TTCB, 3.34.
Coffin BTBNA, p 103.

Robin Hood and the Scotchman (Child, no 130).
Editions. Child, 3.151.
Sargent and Kittredge, p 314.
Literary Relations. Child, 3.150.
Bibliography. Bronson TTCB, 3.37.

Robin Hood and the Beggar, I (Child, no 133).
Editions. Child, 3.156.
Sargent and Kittredge, p 318.
Leach BB, p 385.

Literary Relations. Child, 3.155.
Bibliography. Bronson TTCB, 3.47.
Coffin BTBNA, p 104.

Robin Hood and the Shepherd (Child, no 135).
Editions. Child, 3.165.
Sargent and Kittredge, p 324.
Literary Relations. Child, 3.165.
Bibliography. Bronson TTCB, 3.49.
Coffin BTBNA, p 105.

Robin Hood's Delight (Child, no 136).
Editions. Child, 3.168.
Sargent and Kittredge, p 325.
Literary Relations. Child, 3.168.
Bibliography. Bronson TTCB, 3.50.

Robin Hood and Allen a Dale (Child, no 138).
Editions. Child, 3.173.
Sargent and Kittredge, p 329.
Leach BB, p 399.
Dobson R B and J Taylor, Rymes of Robin Hood: An Introd to the English Outlaw, London 1976, p 172.
Literary Relations. Child, 3.172.
Bibliography. Bronson TTCB, 3.51.
Coffin BTBNA, p 105.

Robin Hood's Progress to Nottingham (Child, no 139).
Editions. Child, 3.176.
Sargent and Kittredge, p 330.
Leach BB, p 400.
Literary Relations. Child, 3.175.
Bibliography. Bronson TTCB, 3.52.
Coffin BTBNA, p 105.

Robin Hood Rescuing Will Stutly (Child, no 141).
Editions. Child, 3.185.
Sargent and Kittredge, p 334.
Leach BB, p 402.
Literary Relations. Child, 3.185; 4.497.
Bibliography. Bronson TTCB, 3.58.
Coffin BTBNA, p 106.

Robin Hood and the Bishop (Child, no 143).
Editions. Child, 3.191.
Sargent and Kittredge, p 338.
Leach BB, p 409.
Literary Relations. Child, 3.191.
Bibliography. Bronson TTCB, 3.61.
Coffin BTBNA, p 107.

Robin Hood's Chase (Child, no 146).
Editions. Child, 3.206.

Sargent and Kittredge, p 346.
Leach BB, p 206.
Literary Relations. Child, 3.205.
Bibliography. Bronson TTCB, 3.67.

    The Noble Fisherman, or, Robin Hood's Preferment (Child, no 148).
Editions. Child, 3.211.
Sargent and Kittredge, p 349.
Dobson and Taylor, p 179.
Literary Relations. Child, 3.211.
Bibliography. Bronson TTCB, 3.69.

    Robin Hood's Birth, Breeding, Valor, and Marriage (Child, no 149).
Editions. Child, 3.215.
Sargent and Kittredge, p 350.
Literary Relations. Child, 3.214.
Bibliography. Coffin BTBNA, p 107.

    Queen Eleanor's Confession (Child, no 156).
Editions. Child, 3.258.
Sargent and Kittredge, p 372.
Leach BB, p 431.
Literary Relations. Child, 3.257; 4.498; 5.241, 297.
Nørgaard H, Peele's Edward I and Two Queen Elinor Ballads, ESts 45(Suppl).165.
Bibliography. Bronson TTCB, 3.105.
Coffin BTBNA, p 109.

    The Knight of Liddesdale (Child, no 160).
Editions. Hume of Godcroft, History of the Houses of Douglas and Angus, p 77.
Child, 3.288.
Sargent and Kittredge, p 386.
Literary Relations. Child, 3.288.

    Johnie Armstrong (Child, no 169).
Editions. Child, 3.367.
Sargent and Kittredge, p 413.
Leach BB, p 476.
Friedman VBFB, p 240.
Literary Relations. Child, 3.362, 520; 4.507; 5.298.
Armstrong W A, The Armstrong Borderland, Galashiels 1960.
Bibliography. Bronson TTCB, 3.140.
Coffin BTBNA, p 113.
Simpson BBBM, p 401.

    The Death of Queen Jane (Child, no 170).
Editions. Child, 3.373.
Sargent and Kittredge, p 418.
Friedman VBFB, p 285.
Literary Relations. Child, 3.372; 5.245, 298.
Bibliography. Bronson TTCB, 3.144.
Dean-Smith, p 63.
Coffin BTBNA, p 113.

    Hughie Grame (Child, no 191).
Editions. Child, 4.10.
Sargent and Kittredge, p 470.
Literary Relations. Child, 4.8, 518; 5.300.
Bibliography. Bronson TTCB, 3.179.
Dean-Smith, p 74.

    Geordie (Child, no 209).
Editions. Child, 4.127.
Sargent and Kittredge, p 496.
Leach BB, p 555.
Literary Relations. Child, 4.123.
Bibliography. Bronson TTCB, 3.268; 4.498.
Dean-Smith, p 68.
Coffin BTBNA, p 124.

    James Harris (The Daemon Lover) (Child, no 243).
Editions. Child, 4.362.
A Collection of Diverting Songs, Epigrams, &c, n d, ca 1738, p 466 (The Distressed Ship Carpenter, song no MCLVII; C H Wilkinson copy, Worcester Coll Libr, Oxford).
Sargent and Kittredge, p 543.
Leach BB, p 599.
Literary Relations. Child, 4.360, 524.
Burrison J, James Harris in Britain since Child, Journ of American Folklore 80.271.
Lyle E B, The Visions in St. Patricks Purgatory, Thomas of Erceldoune, Thomas the Rhymer, and the Daemon Lover, NM 72.716.
Medwin A G, The Ancestry of the House Carpenter: A Study of the Family History of the American Forms of Child 243, Journ of American Folklore 84.414.
Bibliography. Bronson TTCB, 3.429; 4.508.
Dean-Smith, p 80.

    The Suffolk Miracle (Child, no 272).
Editions. Child, 5.66.
Sargent and Kittredge, p 593.
Leach BB, p 646.
Literary Relations. Child, 5.58, 303.
Delarue P, Le Conte Populaire francais Catalogue, Paris 1957, 1.384.
Mitsakis K, Greek Sources of an English Ballad: The Return of the Dead Brother and The Suffolk Miracle, Comparative Literature Stud (Univ of Maryland) 3.47.
Bibliography. Bronson TTCB, 4.84.
Coffin BTBNA, p 142.

    The Friar in the Well (Child, no 276).
Editions. Child, 5.101.
Sargent and Kittredge, p 601.
Literary Relations. Child, 5.100.
Bibliography. Bronson TTCB, 4.140.

Simpson BBBM, p 240.

The George Aloe and the Sweepstake (Child, no 285).
Editions. Child, 5.134.
Sargent and Kittredge, p 610.
Leach BB, p 665.
Literary Relations. Child, 5.133.
Bibliography. Bronson TTCB, 4.306, 511.
Coffin BTBNA, p 152.

The Sweet Trinity (The Golden Vanity) (Child, no 286).
Editions. Child, 5.136.
Sargent and Kittredge, p 611.
Leach BB, p 667.
Literary Relations. Child, 5.135, 305.
Bibliography. Bronson TTCB, 4.312, 511.
Dean-Smith, p 69.
Coffin BTBNA, p 153.

Captain Ward and the Rainbow (Child, no 287).
Editions. Child, 5.144.
Sargent and Kittredge, p 613.
Leach BB, p 670.
Literary Relations. Child, 5.143, 305.
Thomson R S, The Development of the Broadside Ballad Trade and Its Influence upon the Transmission of English Folksongs, diss Cambridge Univ 1974, p 219.
Bibliography. Bronson TTCB, 4.363.
Coffin BTBNA, p 155.

The West-Country Damosel's Complaint (Child, no 292).
Editions. Child, 5.158.
Sargent and Kittredge, p 617.
Literary Relations. Child, 5.157.
Bibliography. Bronson TTCB, 4.389.

[19] EIGHTEENTH-CENTURY BROADSIDES.

Lady Isabel and the Elf-Knight (Child, no 4).
Editions. Child, 1.59.
Sargent and Kittredge, p 5.
Leach BB, p 54.
Friedman VBFB, p 11.
Literary Relations. Child, 1.22, 485; 2.496; 3.496; 4.440; 5.206, 285.
Kemppinen I, The Ballad of Lady Isabel and the False Knight, Helsinki 1954.
Nygard H O, Narrative Change in the European Tradition of the Lady Isabel and the Elf Knight Ballad, Journ American Folklore 65.1; Ballad Source Study: Child Ballad no 4 as Exemplar, Journ American Folklore 68.141; rptd in The Critics and the Ballad, edd MacE Leach and T P Coffin, Carbondale I11 1961, p 189; The Ballad of Heer Halewijn, Helsinki and Knoxville 1958 (FFC 169).
Lloyd A L, How Outlandish is The Outlandish Knight? Tradition 1.36.
Buchan D D, Lady Isabel and the Whipping Boy, Southern Folklore Quart 34.62.
Long E R, Thematic Classification and Lady Isabel, Journ American Folklore 85.32.
Bibliography. Bronson TTCB, 1.39; 4.442.
Dean-Smith, p 97 (The Outlandish Knight).
Coffin BTBNA, p 25.

Lady Alice (Child, no 85).
Editions. Child, 2.279.
Sargent and Kittredge, p 181.
Literary Relations. Child, 2.279; 3.514; 5.225.
Bayard S P, The Johnny Collins Version of Lady Alice, Journ American Folklore 58.73.
Parker H, The Clerk Colvill Mermaid, Journ American Folklore 60.265.
Shenstone's Miscellany 1759–1763, ed I A Gordon, Oxford 1952, p 18.
Bibliography. Bronson TTCB, 2.392.
Dean-Smith, p 58 (Clerk Colvill).
Coffin BTBNA, p 86.

Prince Heathen (Child, no 104).
Editions. Child, 2.424.
Sargent and Kittredge, p 219.
Literary Relations. Child, 2.424; 5.296.

Robin Hood and Little John (Child, no 125).
Editions. Child, 3.134.
Sargent and Kittredge, p 302.
Leach BB, p 367.
Dobson R B and J Taylor, Rymes of Robin Hood: An Introd to the English Outlaw, London 1976, p 165.
Literary Relations. Child, 3.133; 5.297.
Kirkland E C, The Effect of Oral Tradition on Robin Hood and Little John, Southern Folklore Quart 4.15.
Bibliography. Bronson TTCB, 3.26; 4.489.
Dean-Smith, p 101.
Coffin BTBNA, p 102.

Robin Hood and the Ranger (Child, no 131).
Editions. Child, 3.152.
Sargent and Kittredge, p 315.
Literary Relations. Child, 3.152.
Bibliography. Bronson TTCB, 3.38; 4.491.

The Bold Pedlar and Robin Hood (Child, no 132).
Editions. Child, 3.154.
Sargent and Kittredge, p 316.
Leach BB, p 383.
Literary Relations. Child, 3.154; 5.240.
Bibliography. Bronson TTCB, 3.40; 4.491.
Dean-Smith, p 101 (Robin Hood and the Bold Pedlar).
Coffin BTBNA, p 104.

Robin Hood and the Beggar, II (Child, no 134).
Editions. Child, 3.159.
Sargent and Kittredge, p 320.
Leach BB, p 388.
Literary Relations. Child, 3.158.
Bibliography. Bronson TTCB, 3.48.

Robin Hood and Maid Marion (Child, no 150).
Editions. Child, 3.218.
Sargent and Kittredge, p 354.
Leach BB, p 423.
Dobson and Taylor, p 176.
Literary Relations. Child, 3.218, 519.
Bibliography. Bronson TTCB, 3.70.

The King's Disguise, and Friendship with Robin Hood (Child, no 151).
Editions. Child, 3.220.
Sargent and Kittredge, p 356.
Literary Relations. Child, 3.220.

Robin Hood and the Golden Arrow (Child, no 152).
Editions. Child, 3.223.
Sargent and Kittredge, p 358.
Literary Relations. Child, 3.223; 5.241.

Robin Hood and the Valiant Knight (Child, no 153).
Editions. Child, 3.225.
Sargent and Kittredge, p 360.
Dobson and Taylor, p 183.
Literary Relations. Child, 3.225.
Bibliography. Bronson TTCB, 3.71.

Gude Wallace (Child, no 157).
Editions. Child, 3.266.
Sargent and Kittredge, p 375.
Leach BB, p 433.
Literary Relations. Child, 3.265; 5.242.
Bibliography. Bronson TTCB, 3.107.
Coffin BTBNA, p 110.

King Henry Fifth's Conquest of France (Child, no 164).

Editions. Child, 3.323.
Sargent and Kittredge, p 402.
Leach BB, p 464.
Literary Relations. Child, 3.320; 5.245.
Bibliography. Bronson TTCB, 3.127.
Coffin BTBNA, p 111.

Mary Hamilton (Child, no 173).
Editions. Child, 3.384.
Sargent and Kittredge, p 421.
Leach BB, p 482.
Friedman VBFB, p 184.
Literary Relations. Child, 3.379; 4.507; 5.246, 298.
Tolman A H, Mary Hamilton: The Group Authorship of Ballads, PMLA 42.422.
Coffin T P, Mary Hamilton and the Anglo-American Ballad as an Art Form, Journ American Folklore 70.208; rptd in British Traditional Ballad in North America, rvsd edn 1963, p 164; rptd The Critics and the Ballad, edd MacE Leach and T P Coffin, 1961, p 245.
Taplin G B, Andrew Lang as a Student of the Traditional Narrative Ballad, Tulane Stud Eng 14.57.
Drake C C, Mary Hamilton in Tradition, Southern Folklore Quart 33.39.
Tranter N, Who Was the Fourth Mary? Scots Magazine ns 95.520.
Long E R, Ballad Singers, Ballad Makers, and Ballad Etiology, Western Folklore 32.225.
Bibliography. Bronson TTCB, 3.150; 4.494.
Coffin BTBNA, p 114.

Rookhope Ryde (Child, no 179).
Editions. Child, 3.439.
Sargent and Kittredge, p 439.
Literary Relations. Child, 3.439.

The Lads of Wamphray (Child, no 184).
Editions. Child, 3.459.
Sargent and Kittredge, p 448.
Leach BB, p 495.
Literary Relations. Child, 3.458, 520.

The Lochmaben Harper (Child, no 192).
Editions. Child, 4.17.
Sargent and Kittredge, p 472.
Literary Relations. Child, 4.16; 5.300.

The Bonnie House o Airlie (Child, no 199).
Editions. Child, 4.56.
Sargent and Kittredge, p 482.
Leach BB, p 537.
Literary Relations. Child, 4.54; 5.252.
Bibliography. Bronson TTCB, 3.191.
Coffin BTBNA, p 118.

Bewick and Graham (Child, no 211).
Editions. Child, 4.146.
Sargent and Kittredge, p 499.
Leach BB, p 561.
Literary Relations. Child, 4.144, 522.
Bibliography. Bronson TTCB, 3.292.

Bonny Lizie Baillie (Child, no 227).
Editions. Child, 4.267.
Sargent and Kittredge, p 524.
Leach BB, p 585.
Literary Relations. Child, 4.266; 5.265.
Bibliography. Bronson TTCB, 3.369.

The Duke of Gordon's Daughter (Child, no 237).
Editions. Child, 4.333.
Sargent and Kittredge, p 536.
Literary Relations. Child, 4.332; 5.273.
Bibliography. Bronson TTCB, 3.407; 4.506.

The Crafty Farmer (Child, no 283).
Editions. Child, 5.129.
Sargent and Kittredge, p 608.
Leach BB, p 662.
Literary Relations. Child, 5.128.
Bibliography. Bronson TTCB, 4.282, 511.
Coffin BTBNA, p 151.

The Young Earl of Essex's Victory over the Emperor of Germany (Child, no 288).
Editions. Child, 5.146.
Sargent and Kittredge, p 614.
Literary Relations. Child, 5.145.
Bibliography. Bronson TTCB, 4.369.

The Mermaid (Child, no 289).
Editions. Child, 5.149.
Sargent and Kittredge, p 615.
Leach BB, p 673.
Literary Relations. Child, 5.148.
Bibliography. Bronson TTCB, 4.370, 512.
Dean-Smith, p 88.
Coffin BTBNA, p 157.

The Brown Girl (Child, no 295).
Editions. Child, 5.167.
Sargent and Kittredge, p 621.
Literary Relations. Child, 5.166.
Bibliography. Bronson TTCB, 4.402, 512.
Dean-Smith, p 56.
Coffin BTBNA, p 159.

[20] EIGHTEENTH-CENTURY SONGBOOKS.

Elizabeth Cochrane's Songbook (Harvard MS Eng 512) (ca 1730).

Ramsay A, Tea-Table Miscellany, 4 vols, Edinburgh 1723–37.
Thomson W, Orpheus Caledonius, 2 vols, 2nd edn London 1733.
Johnson J, Scots Musical Museum, 6 vols, Edinburgh 1787–1803.
Ritson J, Scotish Song, 2 vols, London 1794.
A Collection of Diverting Songs, Epigrams, &c. n d, ca 1738, C H Wilkinson copy, Worcester College, Oxford.
MS. Montgomerie W, Elizabeth Cochrane Her Songbook, SSL 4(1966).79.

Gil Brenton (Child, no 5; Cochrane).
Edition. Child, 1.76.
Literary Relations. Child, 1.62, 489; 2.498; 3.497; 4.442; 5.207, 285.
Bibliography. Bronson TTCB, 1.101.

Sheath and Knife (Child, no 16; Johnson).
Editions. Child, 1.186.
Shire H M, Poems from Panmure House, The Ninth of May 1(1960). 13 (17-cent text discussed in Introduction p 6).
Literary Relations. Child, 1.185; 2.499; 3.500; 4.450; 5.210.
Bibliography. Bronson TTCB, 1.253.

The Lass of Roch Royal (Child, no 76; Cochrane).
Editions. Child, 2.215.
Sargent and Kittredge, p 161.
Leach BB, p 253.
Literary Relations. Child, 2.213; 3.510; 4.471; 5.225, 294.
Fowler D C, An Accused Queen in The Lass of Roch Royal, Journ of American Folklore 71.553.
Bibliography. Bronson TTCB, 2.218; 4.472.
Coffin BTBNA, p 73.

Bonny Barbara Allan (Child, no 84; Ramsay).
Editions. Child, 2.276.
Sargent and Kittredge, p 180.
Leach BB, p 277.
Kinsley OBB, p 353.
Literary Relations. Child, 2.276; 3.514.
Flanagan J T, An Early American Printing of Barbara Allen, N Y Folklore Quart 20.47.
Cray E, Barbara Allan: Cheap Print and Reprint, in W D Hand festschrift, ed D K Wilgus, Hatboro Pa 1967, p 41.
Kolinski M, Barbara Allan: Tonal Versus Melodic Structure, Ethnomusicology 12.208; 13.1.
Hendren J W, Bonnie Barbara Allen, in Folk Travelers: Ballads, Tales, and Talk, ed M C

Boatwright, W M Hudson and A Maxwell, Publ of the Texas Folklore Soc 25.47.
Millican C B, Barbara Allen, Journ American Folklore 42.303.
Bibliography. Bronson TTCB, 2.321; 4.476.
Dean-Smith, p 51.
Coffin BTBNA, p 82.

Robin Hood and the Bishop of Hereford (Child, no 144; Cochrane).
Editions. Child, 3.195.
Leach BB, p 411.
Literary Relations. Child, 3.193.
Bibliography. Bronson TTCB, 3.62.
Dean-Smith, p 101.

The Bonny Earl of Murray (Child, no 181; Ramsay).
Editions. Child, 3.448.
Sargent and Kittredge, p 443.
Leach BB, p 492.
Kinsley OBB, p 594.
Literary Relations. Child, 3.447; 4.515.
Ives E D, The Bonny Earl of Murray: The Ballad as History, Midwest Folklore 9.133.
Tranter N, The Bonnie Earl o' Moray, Scots Magazine ns 92.11.
Bibliography. Bronson TTCB, 3.159; 4.494.
Coffin BTBNA, p 116.

The Fire of Frendraught (Child, no 196; Ritson).
Editions. Ritson J, Scotish Song, London 1794, 2.35.
Child, 4.47.
Literary Relations. Child, 4.39, 521; 5.251, 301.
Muir W, Living with Ballads, London and N Y 1965, chap 5.
Bibliography. Bronson TTCB, 3.188.

The Gypsy Laddie (Child, no 200; Ramsay).
Editions. Child, 4.65.
Sargent and Kittredge, p 483.
Leach BB, p 539.
Literary Relations. Child, 4.61, 522; 5.252, 301.
Dauney W, Ancient Scottish Melodies, Edinburgh 1838, no 30 Lady Cassilles Lilt, p 228 (Skene MS Nat Libr Scot Advocates 5.2.15, ca 1630).
Rountree T J, Ethnological Implications in the Gypsy Laddie, Tenn Folklore Soc Bull 24 (1958).128.
Knoblock J A, The Gypsy Laddie: An Unrecognized Child of Medieval Romance, Western Folklore 19.35.
Henderson H, How a Bothy Song Came into Being, Scottish Stud 5.212.

Glassie H H, The Gypsy Laddie: Two New Texts With Tunes, Tenn Folklore Soc Bull 30(1964).1.
Portelli A, The Gypsy Laddie, Studi Inglesi (Rome) 2(1975).111.
Bibliography. Bronson TTCB, 3.198; 4.494.
Coffin BTBNA, p 119.

Rare Willie Drowned in Yarrow (Child, no 215; Thomson).
Editions. Child, 4.179.
Sargent and Kittredge, p 506.
Literary Relations. Child, 4.178; 5.256.
Belden H M, Boccaccio, Hans Sachs, and the Bramble Briar, PMLA 33.327.
Bibliography. Bronson TTCB, 3.328.
Coffin BTBNA, p 130.

The Rantin Laddie (Child, no 240; Johnson).
Editions. Child, 4.351.
Sargent and Kittredge, p 541.
Leach BB, p 597.
Literary Relations. Child, 4.351; 5.274.
Bibliography. Bronson TTCB, 3.423; 4.508.
Coffin BTBNA, p 136.

John of Hazelgreen (Child, no 293; Cochrane).
Editions. Child, 5.160.
Leach BB, p 674.
Friedman VBFB, p 143.
Literary Relations. Child, 5.159.
Zug C G III, Scott's Jock of Hazeldean: The Recreation of a Traditional Ballad, Journ of American Folklore 86.152; John of Hazelgreen and His American Progeny, Southern Folklore Quart 39.83.
Bibliography. Bronson TTCB, 4.390.
Coffin BTBNA, p 158.

A-Growing (Johnson, Lady Mary Ann).
Editions. Johnson J, Scots Musical Museum, vol 4(1792), no 377 (Lady Mary Ann by Robert Burns).
Aberdeen Univ Libr MS 2181, 1.25 (MS of Rev Robert Scott, Glenbuchat Parish; ballads collected prior to 1818; Craigston's Growing printed in PQ 52.102).
Songs from David Herd's Manuscript, ed H Hecht, Edinburgh 1904, p 145.
C K Sharpe copy in Broughton House (see ed D Buchan, Scottish Ballad Book, London 1973, p 223).
Maidment J A, A North Country Garland, Edinburgh 1824, p 21 (Young Laird of Craigston).
Literary Relations. Spaulding J, Memorialls of the

trubles in Scotland and in England 1624–1645, Aberdeen 1850.
Lewis M E B, The Progress of Lady Mary Ann, PQ 52.97.
Bibliography. See M E B Lewis above, to which add the following: Disley H, London n d, Harvard collection, vol 14, p 42 (broadside).
Such. British Museum, 1871, also in Harvard collection, vol 11, p 63; rptd Journ of the Folk-Song Soc 2(1906).275 (broadside).
Wehman H J, N Y ca 1880, no 756 (broadside).
Baring-Gould S, British Museum L R 271 c 2, vol 6, p 33; rptd in J Reeves, The Everlasting Circle, N Y 1960 (broadside).
The Works of Robert Burns, ed by the Ettrick Shepherd and William Motherwell, 5 vols, n d, 3(= 1835).41 (My Bonnie Laddie's Lang o' Growing; 7 stanzas "preserved in the west of Scotland").
The Trees Are Growing Tall, Journ of the Eng Folk-Dance and Song Soc 8(1956).20 (Irish version).
MacColl E, in Sing Out! vol 13, no 2(1963), p 35.
Buchan D, ed, A Scottish Ballad Book, London 1973, no 40 (The Young Laird of Craigston).

[21] **PERCY'S RELIQUES** (1765).

Edward (Child, no 13).
Editions. Child, 1.169.
Sargent and Kittredge, p 25.
Leach BB, p 86.
Friedman VBFB, p 156.
Kinsley OBB, p 239.
Literary Relations. Child, 1.167, 501; 2.499; 3.499; 5.209, 287.
Schmidt E, Edward, in F R Heinzel festschrift, Weimar 1898, p 29.
Taylor A, The Texts of Edward in Percy's Reliques and Motherwell's Minstrelsy, MLN 45.225; Edward and Sven i Rosengård: A Study in the Dissemination of a Ballad, Chicago 1931.
Schmidt W, Die Entwicklungsgeschichte der Edward-Ballade, Angl 57.277; Der Anlass zum Streit in der Edward-Ballade, Angl 61.222.
Bronson B H, Edward, Edward: A Scottish Ballad, Southern Folklore Quart 4.1, 159; rptd Ballad as Song, Berkeley and Los Angeles 1969, p 1.
Staedler E, Die schottische Edwardballade, Dichtung und Volkstum [= Euphorion] 42.109.
Coffin T P, The Murder Motive in Edward, Western Folklore 8.314.
Blum M M, Edward and the Folk Tradition, Southern Folklore Quart 21.131.
Taylor A, Svend i Rosengård og Edward, Danske Studier 53.105.
Helgason J, The Ballad of Edward in Icelandic Tradition, Saga och Sed (1960), p 21.
Schmidt-Hidding W, Edward, Edward in der Balladenwelt, Theador Spira festschrift, Heidelberg 1961, p 100.
Wilgus D K, The Oldest (?) Text of Edward, Western Folklore 25.77.
Twitchell J, The Incest Theme and the Authenticity of the Percy Version of Edward, Western Folklore 34.32.
Porter J, Jeannie Robertson's My Son David: A Conceptual Performance Model, Journ American Folklore 89.7.
Bibliography. Bronson TTCB, 1.237; 4.451.
Coffin BTBNA, p 39.

Sir Patrick Spens (Child, no 58).
Editions. Child, 2.20.
Sargent and Kittredge, p 103.
Leach BB, p 179.
Friedman VBFB, p 298.
Kinsley OBB, p 311.
Literary Relations. Child, 2.17, 510; 5.220.
Tranter N, No, Sir Patrick! Scots Magazine ns 90.420.
Matchett W H, The Integrity of Sir Patrick Spens, MP 68.25.
Albright R L N, The Fate of Sir Patrick Spens: The Ballad as a Strategy for Living, Keystone Folklore Quart 17.19.
McNeil N L, Origins of Sir Patrick Spens, in Hunters and Healers: Folklore Types and Topics, ed W M Hudson, Publ Texas Folklore Soc 35.65.
Bibliography. Bronson TTCB, 2.29; 4.468.
Coffin BTBNA, p 62.

Young Waters (Child, no 94).
Editions. Child, 2.343.
Sargent and Kittredge, p 200.
Kinsley OBB, p 321.
Literary Relations. Child, 2.342; 3.516.
Bibliography. Bronson TTCB, 2.446.

Sir Hugh, or, The Jew's Daughter (Child, no 155).
Editions. Child, 3.244.
Sargent and Kittredge, p 370.
Literary Relations. Child, 3.233, 519; 4.497; 5.241, 297.
Hart W M, English Popular Ballads, N Y 1916, p 30.
Rinker B F, The Ballad of the Jew's Daughter, Journ American Folklore 39.212.
Woodall J R, Sir Hugh, a Study in Balladry,

Southern Folklore Quart 19.77.
Hippensteel F, Sir Hugh: The Hoosier Contribution to the Ballad, Indiana Folklore 2.75.
Edmundson L J, Theme and Countertheme: The Function of Child Ballad 155, Sir Hugh or The Jew's Daughter in James Joyce's Ulysses, DAI 36.2216A.
Burton T G, Sir Hugh in Sullivan County, Tennessee Folklore Soc Bull 31.42.
Stamper F C and W H Jansen, Water Birch: An American Variant of Sir Hugh of Lincoln, Journ American Folklore 71.16.
Langmuir G I, The Knight's Tale of Young Hugh of Lincoln, Spec 47.459.
Bibliography. Bronson TTCB, 3.72.
Dean-Smith, p 85.
Coffin BTBNA, p 107.

[22] PERCY PAPERS: MSS IN THE HARVARD LIBRARY (1766-80).

Lord Randal (Child, no 12).
Edition. Child, 1.501.
Literary Relations. Child, 1.151, 498; 2.498; 3.499; 4.499; 5.208, 286.
Shearin H G, Lord Randall in America, MLR 14.211.
Whiting B, The Ballad of Lord Randal, Journ of American Folklore 39.81.
Taylor A, A Contamination in Lord Randal, MP 29.105.
Beck T T, A Variant of Lord Randal, N&Q 209.34; Lord Randal in Louisiana, McNeese Rev 15.18.
Flatto E, Lord Randal, Southern Folklore Quart 34.331.
Kash G S, The Poisoning in Lord Randal, Tennessee Folklore Soc Bull 36.6.
Bibliography. Bronson TTCB, 1.191; 4.451.
Dean-Smith, p 85.
Coffin BTBNA, p 36.

Lord Lovel (Child, no 75).
Editions. Child, 2.207.
Sargent and Kittredge, p 159.
Leach BB, p 250.
Literary Relations. Child, 2.204, 512; 3.510; 4.471; 5.225, 294.
Bibliography. Bronson TTCB, 2.189; 4.471.
Dean-Smith, p 85.
Coffin BTBNA, p 72.

Lamkin (Child, no 93).
Editions. Child, 2.333.
Sargent and Kittredge, p 199.
Literary Relations. Child, 2.320, 513; 3.515; 4.480;
5.229, 295.
The Letters of Sir Walter Scott 1787-1807, ed H J C Grierson (1932), p 4.
Gilchrist A C, Lambkin, Journ of the Eng Folk-Dance and Song Soc 1(1932).1; rptd The Critics and the Ballad, edd MacE Leach and T P Coffin, Carbondale Ill 1961, p 204.
Niles J D, Lamkin: The Motivation of Horror, Journ of American Folklore 90.49.
Bibliography. Bronson TTCB, 2.428; 4.479.
Dean-Smith, p 83.
Coffin BTBNA, p 89.

The Maid Freed from the Gallows (Child, no 95).
Editions. Child, 2.350.
Sargent and Kittredge, p 200.
Leach BB, p 296.
Friedman VBFB, p 132.
Literary Relations. Child, 2.346, 514; 3.516; 4.481; 5.231, 296.
Pohl E, Die Deutsche Volksballade von der Losgekauften, Helsinki 1934 (Folklore Fellows Communications, no 105).
Urcia I, The Gallows and the Golden Ball: An Analysis of The Maid Freed From the Gallows, Journ of American Folklore 79.463.
Coffin T P, The Golden Ball and the Hangman's Tree, W D Hand festschrift, Hatboro Pa 1967, p 23.
Long E R, Child 95 The Maid Freed from the Gallows: A Geographical-Historical Study, diss UCLA 1968; DA 29(1968-69).2620A.
Long E, The Maid and The Hangman: Myth and Tradition in a Popular Ballad, Berkeley Calif 1971.
Bibliography. Bronson TTCB, 2.448; 4.80.
Dean-Smith, p 86.
Coffin BTBNA, p 91.

Willie o Winsbury (Child, no 100).
Editions. Child, 2.401.
Sargent and Kittredge, p 211.
Literary Relations. Child, 2.398, 514; 3.517; 4.491; 5.296.
Bibliography. Bronson TTCB, 2.495; 4.481.
Dean-Smith, p 117.
Coffin BTBNA, p 96.

Johnie Cock (Child, no 114).
Editions. Child, 3.3.
Sargent and Kittredge, p 241.
Leach BB, p 325.
Friedman VBFB, p 234.
Literary Relations. Child, 3.1; 4.495.
Becker H, Die Ballade von Johnie Cock, in Max

Deutschbein festschrift, Leipzig 1936, p 191.
Hopkins R H, A Note on Johnie Cock, N&Q 204.24.
Bibliography. Bronson TTCB, 3.3.
Coffin BTBNA, p 100.

    Dick o the Cow (Child, no 185).
Editions. Child, 3.464.
Sargent and Kittredge, p 449.
Leach BB, p 498.
Kinsley OBB, p 538.
Literary Relations. Child, 3.461.
Bibliography. Bronson TTCB, 3.165.
Coffin BTBNA, p 117.

    Archie o Cawfield (Child, no 188).
Editions. Child, 3.487.
Sargent and Kittredge, p 461.
Leach BB, p 509.
Literary Relations. Child, 3.484; 4.516.
Bibliography. Bronson TTCB, 3.175.
Coffin BTBNA, p 117.

    Hobie Noble (Child, no 189).
Editions. Child, 4.2.
Sargent and Kittredge, p 465.
Literary Relations. Child, 4.1.

    Lord Maxwell's Last Goodnight (Child, no 195).
Editions. Child, 4.36.
Sargent and Kittredge, p 476.
Leach BB, p 533.
Literary Relations. Child, 4.34; 5.251.
Bibliography. Bronson TTCB, 3.186.

    The Braes o Yarrow (Child, no 214).
Editions. Child, 4.164.
Sargent and Kittredge, p 504.
Friedman VBFB, p 99.
Literary Relations. Child, 4.160, 522; 5.255.
Belden H M, Boccaccio, Hans Sachs, and the Bramble Briar, PMLA 33.327.
Coffin T P, The Braes of Yarrow Tradition in America, Journ of American Folklore 63.328.
Bibliography. Bronson TTCB, 3.314; 4.498.
Dean-Smith, p 64 (The Dowie Dens of Yarrow).
Coffin BTBNA, p 127.

    The Broom of Cowdenknows (Child, no 217).
Editions. Child, 4.193.
Sargent and Kittredge, p 510.
Literary Relations. Child, 4.191, 523; 5.257.
Bibliography. Bronson TTCB, 3.338; 4.500.
Coffin BTBNA, p 131.

    Glenlogie, or, Jean o Bethelnie (Child, no 238).

Edition. Child, 4.343.
Literary Relations. Child, 4.338; 5.273, 302.
Bibliography. Bronson TTCB, 3.414; 4.507.

[23] DAVID HERD: MSS BRITISH MUSEUM ADDITIONAL 22311-12 AND PRINTED EDITIONS OF 1769 AND 1776.

    The Cruel Brother (Child, no 11).
Edition. Child, 1.148.
Literary Relations. Child, 1.141, 496; 2.498; 3.499; 4.449; 5.208, 286.
Bibliography. Bronson TTCB, 1.185; 4.447.
Dean-Smith, p 61.
Coffin BTBNA, p 36.

    Babylon, or, The Bonnie Banks o Fordie (Child, no 14).
Edition. Child, 1.174.
Literary Relations. Child, 1.170, 501; 2.499; 3.499; 4.450; 5.209, 287.
Bibliography. Bronson TTCB, 1.248; 4.453.
Coffin BTBNA, p 40.

    The Wee Wee Man (Child, no 38).
Editions. Child, 1.330.
Sargent and Kittredge, p 66.
Leach BB, p 135.
Kinsley OBB, p 11.
Literary Relations. Child, 1.329.
Lyle E B, The Wee Wee Man and Als y Yod on ay Mounday, Scottish Literary News 3(1973).21.
Bibliography. Bronson TTCB, 1.326.
Coffin BTBNA, p 50.

    Tam Lin (Child, no 39).
Edition. Child, 1.345.
Literary Relations. Child, 1.335, 507; 2.505; 3.504; 4.455; 5.215, 290.
Lyle E B, The Ballad Tam Lin and the Traditional Tales of Recovery from the Fairy Troop, SSL 6.175; The Opening of Tam Lin, Journ of American Folklore 83.33; The Teind to Hell in Tam Lin, Folklore 81.177; The Burns Text of Tam Lin, Scottish Stud 15.33.
Haden W D, The Scottish Tam Lin, Tenn Folklore Soc Bull 38.42.
Niles J D, Tam Lin: Form and Meaning in a Traditional Ballad, MLQ 38.336.
Bibliography. Bronson TTCB, 1.327; 4.459.
Dean-Smith, p 55 (Brian O'Lynn).
Coffin BTBNA, p 50.

    Clerk Colvill (Child, no 42).
Editions. Child, 1.388.
Sargent and Kittredge, p 75.
Leach BB, p 149.

Friedman VBFB, p 30.
Kinsley OBB, p 85.
Literary Relations. Child, 1.371; 2.506; 3.506; 4.459; 5.215, 290.
Forslin A, Balladen om riddar Olof och älvorna: En traditions-undersökning, Arv [Journ of Scandinavian Folklore] 18–19.1; also publ as Meddelanden fran Svenskt Visarkiv no 19, Stockholm 1964.
Parker H, The Clark Colvill Mermaid, Journ of American Folklore 60.265.
Bibliography. Bronson TTCB, 1.334.
Dean-Smith, p 58.
Coffin BTBNA, p 51.

The Broomfield Hill (Child, no 43).
Editions. Child, 1.394.
Sargent and Kittredge, p 77.
Literary Relations. Child, 1.390, 508; 2.506; 3.506; 4.459; 5.290.
Harvey R, Moriz von Craûn and the Chivalric World, Oxford 1961.
Bibliography. Bronson TTCB, 1.336; 4.460.
Dean-Smith, p 56.
Coffin BTBNA, p 51.

Captain Wedderburn's Courtship (Child, no 46).
Editions. Child, 1.419.
Sargent and Kittredge, p 83.
Leach BB, p 158.
Literary Relations. Child, 1.414; 2.507; 3.507; 4.459; 5.216, 291.
Taylor A, The English Riddle Ballads, Margaret Schlauch festschrift, Warsaw 1966, p 445.
Toelken J B, Riddles Wisely Expounded, Western Folklore 30.1.
Bibliography. Bronson TTCB, 1.362; 4.462.
Coffin BTBNA, p 53.

The Bonny Hind (Child, no 50).
Editions. Child, 1.446.
Sargent and Kittredge, p 92.
Friedman VBFB, p 172.
Kinsley OBB, p 201.
Literary Relations. Child, 1.444; 5.218.

Lizie Wan (Child, no 51).
Editions. Child, 1.448.
Sargent and Kittredge, p 93.
Friedman VBFB, p 159.
Leach BB, p 167.
Literary Relations. Child, 1.447.
Bibliography. Bronson TTCB, 1.403.
Coffin BTBNA, p 57.

Fair Annie (Child, no 62).
Editions. Child, 2.74.
Sargent and Kittredge, p 118.
Literary Relations. Child, 2.63, 511; 4.463; 5.220.
Bibliography. Bronson TTCB, 2.40.
Coffin BTBNA, p 63.

Fair Janet (Child, no 64).
Editions. Child, 2.106.
Literary Relations. Child, 2.100; 3.508; 4.464; 5.222, 292.
Tuschke L, Fair Janet und Kong Valdemar og hans Søster, ein Beitrag zur Frage der Beziehungen zwischen englischen-schottischen und skandinavischen Volksballaden (Studien zur Volksliedforsch 2), Berlin 1940.
Meier J, Die Ballade vom Grausamen Bruder, Jahrbuch f Volksliedforschung 8.1.
Bibliography. Bronson TTCB, 2.47.

Lord Ingram and Chiel Wyet (Child, no 66).
Editions. Child, 2.131.
Literary Relations. Child, 2.126, 511; 3.508; 5.223, 292.
Bibliography. Bronson TTCB, 2.58.
Coffin BTBNA, p 65.

Young Hunting (Child, no 68).
Editions. Child, 2.144.
Sargent and Kittredge, p 139.
Leach BB, p 230.
Kinsley OBB, p 87.
Literary Relations. Child, 2.142, 512; 3.509; 4.468; 5.223.
Bibliography. Bronson TTCB, 2.60.
Coffin BTBNA, p 66.

Clerk Saunders (Child, no 69).
Editions. Child, 2.158.
Sargent and Kittredge, p 143.
Leach BB, p 234.
Friedman VBFB, p 94.
Kinsley OBB, p 76.
Literary Relations. Child, 2.156, 512; 3.509; 4.468; 5.223, 293.
Fowler D C, A Literary History of the Popular Ballad, Durham N C 1968, p 193.
Rodgers E, The Moral Standing of the Unkept Unkempt, Southern Folklore Quart 36.144.
Bibliography. Bronson TTCB, 2.83.

Sweet William's Ghost (Child, no 77).
Editions. Child, 2.230.
Sargent and Kittredge, p 166.
Literary Relations. Child, 2.226, 512; 4.474; 5.225, 294.
Shields H, The Dead Lover's Return in Modern English Ballad Tradition, Jahrbuch für Volksliedforschung 17(1972).98.

Bibliography. Bronson TTCB, 2.229; 4.473.
Coffin BTBNA, p 75.

  Young Johnstone (Child, no 88).
Editions. Child, 2.289.
Sargent and Kittredge, p 186.
Leach BB, p 283.
Literary Relations. Child, 2.288.
Bibliography. Bronson TTCB, 2.411; 4.477.
Coffin BTBNA, p 88.

  Fair Mary of Wallington (Child, no 91).
Editions. Child, 2.312.
Literary Relations. Child, 2.309, 513; 3.515; 4.479; 5.227.
Parker H, The Scobs Was in Her Mouth, Journ of American Folklore 71.532.
Bibliography. Bronson TTCB, 2.417.

  The Laird o Logie (Child, no 182).
Editions. Child, 3.453.
Sargent and Kittredge, p 446.
Literary Relations. Child, 3.449, 520; 4.515; 5.299.
Lyle E B, An Eighteenth Century Record of The Laird o Logie, Scottish Stud 17.162.
Bibliography. Bronson TTCB 3.162.

  Jamie Douglas (Child, no 204).
Edition. Child, 4.103.
Literary Relations. Child, 4.90.
Bibliography. Bronson TTCB, 3.290.
Coffin BTBNA, p 123.

  Bonnie James Campbell (Child, no 210).
Editions. Child, 4.143.
Sargent and Kittredge, p 497.
Leach BB, p 560.
Literary Relations. Child, 4.142.
Bibliography. Bronson TTCB, 3.290.
Coffin BTBNA, p 126.

  Sir James the Rose (Child, no 213).
Editions. Child, 4.159.
Sargent and Kittredge, p 503.
Literary Relations. Child, 4.155.
Bibliography. Bronson TTCB, 3.300; 4.498.
Coffin BTBNA, p 126.

  The Bonny Lass of Anglesey (Child, no 220).
Editions. Child, 4.215.
Sargent and Kittredge, p 513.
Literary Relations. Child, 4.214.

  Katharine Jaffray (Child, no 221).
Editions. Child, 4.219.
Sargent and Kittredge, p 514.
Leach BB, p 578.
Literary Relations. Child, 4.216, 523; 5.260.

Bibliography. Bronson TTCB, 3.352.
Coffin BTBNA, p 132.

  The Grey Cock, or, Saw You My Father? (Child, no 248).
Editions. Child, 4.390.
Sargent and Kittredge, p 551.
Leach BB, p 612.
Literary Relations. Child, 4.389; 5.302.
Baskerville C R, English Songs of the Night Visit, PMLA 36.565.
Friedman A B, The Grey Cock–A Drollery Version, Journ of American Folklore 67.285.
Schelp H, Die Tradition der Alba und die Morgenszene in Chaucers Troilus and Criseyde, GRM 15(1965).251.
Hatto A T, ed, Eos. An Enquiry into the Theme of Lovers' Meetings and Partings at Dawn in Poetry, La Haye 1965.
Shields H, Une alba dans la poésie populaire anglaise? RLR, bk 2 (1971), p 461 (Actes du VIème Congrès International de Langue et Littérature d'oc et d'études Franco-Provencales, Montpellier Sept 1970); Grey Cock: Dawn Song or Revenant Ballad? Ballad Stud (1976), p 67.
Sisam C and K Sisam, Oxford Book of Medieval English Verse (no 30), Oxford 1970, p 433.
Bibliography. Bronson TTCB, 4.15.
Dean-Smith, p 71.
Coffin BTBNA, p 139.

  Our Goodman (Child, no 274).
Editions. Child, 5.91.
Sargent and Kittredge, p 597.
Leach BB, p 654.
Friedman VBFB, p 445.
Literary Relations. Child, 5.88, 281, 303.
Bibliography. Bronson TTCB, 4.95.
Dean-Smith, p 70.
Coffin BTBNA, p 143.

  Get Up and Bar the Door (Child, no 275).
Editions. Child, 5.98.
Sargent and Kittredge, p 600.
Literary Relations. Child, 5.96, 281, 304.
Bibliography. Bronson TTCB, 4.130, 509.
Coffin BTBNA, p 145.

  The Wife Wrapt in Wether's Skin (Child, no 277).
Edition. Child, 5.104.
Literary Relations. Child, 5.104, 304.
Gelber M, The Wife Wrapt in Wether's Skin or Old Dandoo, Western Folklore 22.273.
Brunvand J H, Child 277: Ballad and Tale, Western Folklore 23.117.

Bibliography. Bronson TTCB, 4.143, 509.
Coffin BTBNA, p 146.

 The Jolly Beggar (Child, no 279).
Edition. Child, 5.111.
Literary Relations. Child, 5.109.
Bibliography. Bronson TTCB, 4.213.
Coffin BTBNA, p 150.

[24] MRS BROWN OF FALKLAND: JAMIESON'S BROWN MANUSCRIPT, 1783 (J-B), WILLIAM TYTLER'S BROWN MANUSCRIPT, 1783 (WT-B), ALEXANDER FRASER TYTLER'S BROWN MANUSCRIPT, 1800 (AFT-B), AND ROBERT JAMIESON'S *POPULAR BALLADS AND SONGS,* 1806 (PBS).

MSS. Montgomerie W, Mrs Brown's Manuscripts, SSL 7(1969–70).60, 238.

 Willie's Lady (Child, no 6).
Editions. Child, 1.86.
Sargent and Kittredge, p 9.
Leach BB, p 64.
Friedman VBFB, p 18.
Literary Relations. Child, 1.81; 2.498; 3.497; 5.207, 285.
Bibliography. Bronson TTCB, 1.104.
Coffin BTBNA, p 28.

 King Henry (Child, no 32).
Editions. Child, 1.298.
Sargent and Kittredge, p 58.
Kinsley OBB, p 64.
Literary Relations. Child, 1.297; 2.502; 4.454; 5.289.
Bibliography. Bronson TTCB, 1.319.

 Kemp Owyne (Child, no 34).
Editions. Child, 1.309.
Sargent and Kittredge, p 60.
Literary Relations. Child, 1.306; 2.502; 3.504; 4.454; 5.213, 290.
Bibliography. Bronson TTCB, 1.322.

 Allison Gross (Child, no 35).
Editions. Child, 1.314.
Sargent and Kittredge, p 62.
Leach BB, p 128.
Kinsley OBB, p 54.
Literary Relations. Child, 1.313; 3.504; 5.214.

 Thomas Rymer (Child, no 37).
Editions. Child, 1.323.
Sargent and Kittredge, p 64.
Leach BB, p 131.
Friedman VBFB, p 39.
Literary Relations. Child, 1.317; 2.505; 3.504; 4.454; 5.290.

Murray J A H, ed, Thomas of Erceldoune, London 1875 (EETS 61).
Brandl A, ed, Thomas of Erceldoune, Berlin 1880.
Burnham J, A Study of Thomas of Erceldoune, PMLA 23.375.
Saalbach A, Entstehungsgeschichte der schottischen Volksballade Thomas Rymer, Halle 1913.
Flasdieck H M, Tom der Reimer: von keltischen Feen und politischen propheten, Breslau 1934.
Schmidt W, Die Volksballaden von Tom dem Reimer, Angl 61.193.
Nixon I, Thomas of Erceldoune, diss Edinburgh Univ 1947.
Albrecht W P, The Loathly Lady in Thomas of Erceldoune, Albuquerque N M 1954 (Univ of N M Publs in Lang and Lit, no 11).
Miller H C, A Study of Thomas of Erceldoune, diss Lehigh Univ 1965; DA 26.7299.
Nelson C E, The Origin and Tradition of the Ballad of Thomas Rymer: A Survey, in New Voices in American Stud, Lafayette Ind 1966 (Purdue Univ Stud), p 138.
Lyle E B, Thomas of Erceldoune: The Prophet and the Prophesied, Folklore 79.111; A Reconsideration of the Place Names in Thomas the Rymer, Scottish Stud 13.65; A Comment on the Rhyme Scheme of Two Stanzas of Thomas of Erceldoune, N&Q 214.48; The Relationship between Thomas the Rymer and Thomas of Erceldoune, Leeds Stud in English 4(1970).23; The Turk and Gawain as a Source of Thomas of Erceldoune, Forum Mod Lang Stud 6(1970).98.
Briggs K M, The Fairies and the Realms of the Dead, Folklore 81.81.
Lyle, The Celtic Affinities of the Gift in Thomas of Erceldoune, Eng Lang Notes 8.161; The Visions in St Patrick's Purgatory, Thomas of Erceldoune, Thomas the Rymer, and The Daemon Lover, NM 72.716.
Scott H and T Scott, True Thomas the Rhymer and Other Tales, Oxford 1971.
Goedhals J B, The Romances and Prophecies of Thomas of Erceldoune, UNISA (Univ of South Africa) Eng Stud 10.1.
Lyle, Sir Landevale and the Fairy-Mistress Theme in Thomas of Erceldoune, MÆ 42.244.
Alfred W, A Deliberate Analogue of Fitt I of Thomas of Erceldoune, in The Learned and the Lewed: Studies in Chaucer and Medieval Literature, ed L D Benson, Cambridge Mass 1974, p 385.
Robbins R H, Manual, 5.1526 (XIII [290]).

Bibliography. Bronson TTCB, 1.324.
Coffin BTBNA, p 49.

Young Beichan (Child, no 53).
Editions. Child, 1.463.
Sargent and Kittredge, p 95.
Literary Relations. Child, 1.454; 2.508; 3.507; 4.460; 5.218, 291.
Thiemke H, Die ME Thomas Beket-Legende des Gloucester-legendars, Berlin 1919 (Palaes 131).
Brown P A, The Development of the Legend of Thomas Becket, Phila 1930.
Bibliography. Bronson TTCB, 1.409; 4.465.
Dean-Smith, p 85 (Lord Bateman).
Coffin BTBNA, p 58.

Lady Maisry (Child, no 65).
Editions. Child, 2.114.
Sargent and Kittredge, p 128.
Leach BB, p 208.
Kinsley OBB, p 295.
Literary Relations. Child, 2.112; 3.508; 4.466; 5.222, 292.
Bibliography. Bronson TTCB, 2.50.
Dean-Smith, p 83.
Coffin BTBNA, p 64.

The Bonny Birdy (Child, no 82).
Editions. Child, 2.260.
Sargent and Kittredge, p 174.
Literary Relations. Child, 2.260.

Fause Foodrage (Child, no 89).
Editions. Child, 2.298.
Sargent and Kittredge, p 188.
Literary Relations. Child, 2.296, 513; 3.515; 4.479.
Bibliography. Bronson TTCB, 2.414.

Jellon Grame (Child, no 90).
Editions. Child, 2.303.
Sargent and Kittredge, p 191.
Kinsley OBB, p 164.
Literary Relations. Child, 2.302, 513; 3.515; 4.479; 5.226, 295.
Bibliography. Bronson TTCB, 2.416.
Coffin BTBNA, p 89.

Bonny Bee Hom (Child, no 92).
Editions. Child, 2.318.
Sargent and Kittredge, p 195.
Leach BB, p 287.
Literary Relations. Child, 2.317; 5.229.
Bibliography. Bronson TTCB, 2.418.
Coffin BTBNA, p 89.

The Gay Goshawk (Child, no 96).
Editions. Child, 2.357.
Sargent and Kittredge, p 202.
Leach BB, p 300.

Kinsley OBB, p 222.
Literary Relations. Child, 2.355; 3.517; 4.482; 5.234, 296.
Bibliography. Bronson TTCB, 2.476.
Dean-Smith, p 81 (The Jolly Gay Goshawk).
Coffin BTBNA, p 94.

Brown Robin (Child, no 97).
Editions. Child, 2.368.
Sargent and Kittredge, p 205.
Literary Relations. Child, 2.368.
Bibliography. Bronson TTCB, 2.479.

Brown Adam (Child, no 98).
Editions. Child, 2.374.
Sargent and Kittredge, p 207.
Literary Relations. Child, 2.373.
Bibliography. Bronson TTCB, 2.482.

Johnie Scot (Child, no 99).
Editions. Child, 2.379.
Sargent and Kittredge, p 208.
Leach BB, p 303.
Literary Relations. Child, 2.377; 4.486; 5.234.
Jones J H, Commonplace and Memorization in the Oral Tradition of the English and Scottish Popular Ballads, Journ of American Folklore 74.97, 113.
Thigpen K A Jr, A Reconsideration of the Commonplace Phrase and Commonplace Theme in the Child Ballads, Southern Folklore Quart 37.385.
Bibliography. Bronson TTCB, 2.484.
Coffin BTBNA, p 95.

Willie o Douglas Dale (Child, no 101).
Editions. Child, 2.407.
Sargent and Kittredge, p 211.
Leach BB, p 310.
Literary Relations. Child, 2.406; 3.517; 5.235.
Bibliography. Bronson TTCB, 2.507.
Coffin BTBNA, p 96.

Willie and Earl Richard's Daughter (Child, no 102).
Editions. Child, 2.412.
Sargent and Kittredge, p 213.
Dobson R B and J Taylor, Rymes of Robin Hood: An Intro to the English Outlaw, London 1976, p 195.
Literary Relations. Child, 2.412; 3.518.
Bibliography. Bronson TTCB, 2.509; 4.482.
Coffin BTBNA, p 97.

Rose the Red and White Lily (Child, no 103).
Editions. Child, 2.417.
Sargent and Kittredge, p 216.

Literary Relations. Child, 2.415.
Bibliography. Bronson TTCB, 2.511.

The Baron of Brackley (Child, no 203).
Edition. Child, 4.86.
Literary Relations. Child, 4.79, 522; 5.253.
Bibliography. Bronson TTCB, 3.255; 4.495.

The Mother's Malison, or, Clyde's Water (Child, no 216).
Editions. Child, 4.188.
Sargent and Kittredge, p 509.
Literary Relations. Child, 4.185; 5.256, 301.
Bibliography. Bronson TTCB, 3.332; 4.499.

Bonny Baby Livingston (Child, no 222).
Editions. Child, 4.233.
Sargent and Kittredge, p 517.
Leach BB, p 579.
Literary Relations. Child, 4.231, 523; 5.261.
Bibliography. Bronson TTCB, 3.359; 4.502.

Lady Elspat (Child, no 247).
Editions. Child, 4.387.
Sargent and Kittredge, p 550.
Literary Relations. Child, 4.387.
Bibliography. Bronson TTCB, 4.13.

The Kitchie-Boy (Child, no 252).
Edition. Child, 4.405.
Literary Relations. Child, 4.400; 5.277.
Nelles W R, The Ballad of Hind Horn, Journ of American Folklore 22.42.
Bibliography. Bronson TTCB, 4.58.
Coffin BTBNA, p 141.

[25] BALLADS COLLECTED IN THE NINETEENTH CENTURY.

The Fause Knight upon the Road (Child, no 3).
Editions. Child, 1.21.
Sargent and Kittredge, p 4.
Graves R, The English Ballad, London 1927, p 43; English and Scottish Ballads, London 1957, p 1.
Literary Relations. Child, 1.20, 485; 2.496; 3.496; 4.440.
Gerould G H, An Irish Version of the False Knight Upon the Road, MLN 53.596.
List G, An Ideal Marriage of Ballad Text and Tune, Midwest Folklore 7.95.
Bibliography. Bronson TTCB, 1.34; 4.442.
Coffin BTBNA, p 24.

Erlinton (Child, no 8).
Editions. Child, 1.107.
Sargent and Kittredge, p 14.

Literary Relations. Child, 1.106; 3.498; 4.445.
Bibliography. Coffin BTBNA, p 30.

Leesome Brand (Child, no 15).
Editions. Child, 1.182.
Sargent and Kittredge, p 27.
Leach BB, p 91.
Literary Relations. Child, 1.177, 501; 2.499; 3.500; 4.450; 5.209, 287.
Shire H M, Poems from Panmure House, The Ninth of May 1(1960).13 (17 cent text, discussed in Introd, p 6).

Hind Horn (Child, no 17).
Editions. Child, 1.201.
Sargent and Kittredge, p 31.
Leach BB, p 97.
Friedman VBFB, p 112.
Literary Relations. Child, 1.187, 502; 2.499; 3.501; 4.450; 5.210, 287.
Kealy J K, The Americanization of Horn, Southern Folklore Quart 37.4; The Horn Hero in Romance and Ballad Tradition, diss Stanford Univ 1971; DA 32.6932A.
Nelles W R, The Ballad of Hind Horn, Journ of American Folklore 22.42.
McLaughlin J, The Return Song in Medieval Romance and Ballad: King Horn and King Orfeo, Journ of American Folklore 88.304.
Bibliography. Bronson TTCB, 1.254; 4.454.
Coffin BTBNA, p 41.

King Orfeo (Child, no 19).
Editions. Child, 1.217.
Sargent and Kittredge, p 37.
Shuldham-Shaw P N, The Ballad King Orfeo, Scottish Stud 20.124.
Literary Relations. Child, 1.215; 2.500; 3.502; 4.451; 5.211.
Friedman J B, Orpheus in the Middle Ages, Cambridge Mass 1970.
Stewart M, King Orphius, Scottish Stud 17.1; The Ninth of May 4(1973).7 (16 cent text; discussed, p 18).
McLaughlin, Return Song, Journ of American Folklore 88.304.
Bibliography. Bronson TTCB, 1.274; 4.455.
Coffin BTBNA, p 44.

Bonnie Annie (Child, no 24).
Editions. Child, 1.245.
Sargent and Kittredge, p 42.
Literary Relations. Child, 1.244; 4.452.
Bibliography. Bronson TTCB, 1.298.
Coffin BTBNA, p 46.

Willie's Lyke-Wake (Child, no 25).

Editions. Child, 1.250.
Sargent and Kittredge, p 44.
Leach BB, p 110.
Literary Relations. Child, 1.247, 506; 2.502; 3.503; 4.453; 5.212, 289.
Bibliography. Bronson TTCB, 1.305.
Coffin BTBNA, p 46.

The Whummil Bore (Child, no 27).
Editions. Child, 1.255.
Sargent and Kittredge, p 46.
Literary Relations. Child, 1.255; 5.212.
Davis A K Jr and P C Worthington, A New Traditional Ballad from Virginia: The Whummil Bore, Southern Folklore Quart 21.187.
Bibliography. Bronson TTCB, 1.316.
Coffin BTBNA, p 48.

Burd Ellen and Young Tamlane (Child, no 28).
Editions. Child, 1.256.
Sargent and Kittredge, p 46.
Literary Relations. Child, 1.256, 507; 3.503.

Kempy Kay (Child, no 33).
Edition. Child, 1.301.
Literary Relations. Child, 1.300; 5.213, 289.
Bibliography. Bronson TTCB, 1.321.

The Laily Worm and the Machrel of the Sea (Child, no 36).
Editions. Child, 1.316.
Sargent and Kittredge, p 62.
Literary Relations. Child, 1.315; 5.214, 290.
Bibliography. Coffin BTBNA, p 49.

The Queen of Elfan's Nourice (Child, no 40).
Editions. Child, 1.359.
Sargent and Kittredge, p 69.
Literary Relations. Child, 1.358; 2.505; 3.505; 4.459; 5.215, 290.
Bibliography. Bronson TTCB, 1.332.
Coffin BTBNA, p 51.

Hind Etin (Child, no 41).
Editions. Child, 1.367.
Sargent and Kittredge, p 70.
Leach BB, p 142.
Literary Relations. Child, 1.360, 508; 2.506; 3.506; 4.459; 5.215.
Bibliography. Bronson TTCB, 1.333.

The Twa Magicians (Child, no 44).
Editions. Child, 1.402.
Sargent and Kittredge, p 77.
Kinsley OBB, p 51.
Literary Relations. Child, 1.399; 2.506; 3.506; 4.459; 5.216, 290.

Bibliography. Bronson TTCB, 1.348.
Coffin BTBNA, p 52.

Proud Lady Margaret (Child, no 47).
Editions. Child, 1.426.
Sargent and Kittredge, p 86.
Leach BB, p 162.
Literary Relations. Child, 1.425; 4.460; 5.291.
Bibliography. Bronson TTCB, 1.382.
Coffin BTBNA, p 55.

The Twa Brothers (Child, no 49).
Editions. Child, 1.438.
Sargent and Kittredge, p 91.
Leach BB, p 165.
Friedman VBFB, p 169.
Kinsley OBB, p 234.
Literary Relations. Child, 1.435; 2.507; 3.507; 4.460; 5.217, 291.
Bibliography. Bronson TTCB, 1.384; 4.462.
Coffin BTBNA, p 55.

The King's Dochter Lady Jean (Child, no 52).
Editions. Child, 1.450.
Sargent and Kittredge, p 94.
Literary Relations. Child, 1.450.
Bibliography. Bronson TTCB, 1.407; 4.464.

The Cherry Tree Carol (Child, no 54).
Editions. Child, 2.2.
Sargent and Kittredge, p 98.
Leach BB, p 175.
Friedman VBFB, p 59.
Kinsley OBB, p 1.
Graves R, The English Ballad, London 1927, p 74; English and Scottish Ballads, London 1957, p 25.
Literary Relations. Child, 2.1, 509; 5.220.
Cutting E E, The Cherry Tree Carol, N Y Folklore Quart 1(1945).48.
Bibliography. Bronson TTCB, 2.3; 4.467.
Dean-Smith, p 57.
Coffin BTBNA, p 60.

The Carnal and the Crane (Child, no 55).
Editions. Child, 2.8.
Sargent and Kittredge, p 100.
Literary Relations. Child, 2.7, 509; 3.507; 4.462; 5.220.
Bibliography. Bronson TTCB, 2.15.
Dean-Smith, p 56.

Dives and Lazarus (Child, no 56).
Editions. Child, 2.11.
Sargent and Kittredge, p 101.
Leach BB, p 177.
Literary Relations. Child, 2.10, 510; 3.507; 4.462;

5.220, 292.
Bibliography. Bronson TTCB, 2.17; 4.468.
Dean-Smith, p 63.
Coffin BTBNA, p 61.

Brown Robyn's Confession (Child, no 57).
Editions. Child, 2.16.
Sargent and Kittredge, p 102.
Literary Relations. Child, 2.13, 510; 3.508; 4.462; 5.220, 292.
Bibliography. Bronson TTCB, 2.24.

Willie and Lady Maisry (Child, no 70).
Editions. Child, 2.167.
Sargent and Kittredge, p 146.
Literary Relations. Child, 2.167.
Bibliography. Bronson TTCB, 2.85.

The Bent Sae Brown (Child, no 71).
Editions. Child, 2.171.
Sargent and Kittredge, p 148.
Literary Relations. Child, 2.170; 3.509; 4.469; 5.223.
Bibliography. Bronson TTCB, 2.86.

The Clerk's Twa Sons o Owsenford (Child, no 72).
Editions. Child, 2.175.
Sargent and Kittredge, p 150.
Leach BB, p 237.
Literary Relations. Child, 2.173, 512; 3.509; 4.469; 5.293.
Bibliography. Bronson TTCB, 2.87.

The Unquiet Grave (Child, no 78).
Editions. Child, 2.236.
Sargent and Kittredge, p 167.
Leach BB, p 262.
Friedman VBFB, p 32.
Kinsley OBB, p 96.
Graves R, The English Ballad, London 1927, p 96; English and Scottish Ballads, London 1957, p 47.
Literary Relations. Child, 2.234, 512; 3.512; 4.474; 5.225, 294.
Harvey R, The Unquiet Grave, Journ of the Eng Folk-Dance and Song Soc 4(1941).49.
Davis A K Jr, The Unquiet Grave: A New-Old Ballad from Virginia, in English Stud in Honor of James S Wilson, Univ of Virginia Stud 4.99.
Griffith G, The Unquiet Grave, Southern Folklore Quart 31.314.
Bickford S S, A Twelve-Month and a Day: A Note on Child no 78, Calcutta Rev ns 2.193.
Bibliography. Bronson TTCB, 2.234; 4.473.
Dean-Smith, p 113.
Coffin BTBNA, p 77.

The Wife of Usher's Well (Child, no 79).
Editions. Child, 2.238.
Sargent and Kittredge, p 168.
Leach BB, p 263.
Kinsley OBB, p 94.
Graves R, The English Ballad, London 1927, p 52; English and Scottish Ballads, London 1957, p 58.
Literary Relations. Child, 2.238; 3.513; 5.294.
Puhvel M, The Revenants in The Wife of Usher's Well: A Reconsideration, Folklore 86.175.
Bibliography. Bronson TTCB, 2.246; 4.474.
Coffin BTBNA, p 77.

Young Benjie (Child, no 86).
Editions. Child, 2.282.
Sargent and Kittredge, p 183.
Leach BB, p 281.
Literary Relations. Child, 2.281; 4.478.
Bibliography. Bronson TTCB, 2.408.
Coffin BTBNA, p 88.

Prince Robert (Child, no 87).
Editions. Child, 2.284.
Sargent and Kittredge, p 183.
Kinsley OBB, p 203.
Literary Relations. Child, 2.284; 5.295.
Munnelly T, Lord O'Bore and Mary Flynn, Irish Folk Music Stud 1(1972-3).28.
Bibliography. Bronson TTCB, 2.410.
Coffin BTBNA, p 88.

The Great Silkie of Sule Skerry (Child, no 113).
Editions. Child, 2.494.
Sargent and Kittredge, p 240.
Leach BB, p 321.
Friedman VBFB, p 27.
Kinsley OBB, p 91.
Literary Relations. Child, 2.494; 3.518; 4.495.
Bruford A, The Grey Selkie, Scottish Stud 18.63.
Bibliography. Bronson TTCB, 2.564.

Robin Hood and the Pedlars (Child, no 137).
Editions. Child, 3.171.
Sargent and Kittredge, p 327.
Literary Relations. Child, 3.170.

The Battle of Harlaw (Child, no 163).
Editions. Child, 3.318.
Sargent and Kittredge, p 401.
Literary Relations. Child, 3.316; 5.245.
Mackay W, The Battle of Harlaw: Its True Place in History, Trans of the Gaelic Soc of Inverness 30(1919-22).267.
McMillan D J, Some Popular Views of Four

Medieval Ballads, Southern Folklore Quart 30.179.
Buchan D, History and Harlaw, Journ of the Folklore Institute (Ind Univ) 5.58.
Robbins R H, Manual, 5.1425 (XIII[70]).
Bibliography. Bronson TTCB, 3.117; 4.494.

    Willie Macintosh (Child, no 183).
Editions. Child, 3.457.
Sargent and Kittredge, p 446.
Friedman VBFB, p 266.
Literary Relations. Child, 3.465; 4.516.
Bibliography. Bronson TTCB, 3.164.
Coffin BTBNA, p 117.

    Kinmont Willie (Child, no 186).
Editions. Child, 3.472.
Sargent and Kittredge, p 453.
Leach BB, p 505.
Kinsley OBB, p 559.
Literary Relations. Child, 3.469; 4.516.
Elliott W F, The Trustworthiness of the Border Ballads, Edinburgh and London 1906.
Lang A, Sir Walter Scott and the Border Minstrelsy, London 1910.
Brown J W, Kinmont Willie in Ballad and History, Carlisle 1922.
Fraser G M, The Steel Bonnets: The Story of the Anglo-Scottish Border Reivers, London 1971, p 329.
Rice H A L, Kinmont Willie, Scotland's Magazine, March 1974, p 35.
Bibliography. Bronson TTCB, 3.168.

    Jamie Telfer of the Fair Dodhead (Child, no 190).
Editions. Child, 4.6.
Sargent and Kittredge, p 467.
Kinsley OBB, p 549.
Literary Relations. Child, 4.4, 518; 5.249, 300.

    The Death of Parcy Reed (Child, no 193).
Editions. Child, 4.25.
Sargent and Kittredge, p 473.
Leach BB, p 522.
Literary Relations. Child, 4.24, 520.
Bibliography. Bronson TTCB, 3.184.
Dean-Smith, p 62.

    The Laird of Wariston (Child, no 194).
Editions. Child, 4.31.
Sargent and Kittredge, p 474.
Leach BB, p 529.
Literary Relations. Child, 4.28.

    James Grant (Child, no 197).
Editions. Child, 4.50.
Sargent and Kittredge, p 481.

Literary Relations. Child, 4.49; 5.251.

    Bonny John Seton (Child, no 198).
Editions. Child, 4.52.
Sargent and Kittredge, p 481.
Leach BB, p 535.
Literary Relations. Child, 4.51; 5.251.

    Bessy Bell and Mary Gray (Child, no 201).
Editions. Child, 4.76.
Sargent and Kittredge, p 485.
Friedman VBFB, p 302.
Kinsley OBB, p 617.
Literary Relations. Child, 4.75, 522; 5.253.
Bibliography. Bronson TTCB, 3.251.
Coffin BTBNA, p 123.

    The Battle of Philiphaugh (Child, no 202).
Editions. Child, 4.78.
Sargent and Kittredge, p 486.
Literary Relations. Child, 4.77.
Bibliography. Bronson TTCB, 3.254.

    Loudon Hill, or, Drumclog (Child, no 205).
Editions. Child, 4.107.
Sargent and Kittredge, p 491.
Literary Relations. Child, 4.105.

    Bothwell Bridge (Child, no 206).
Editions. Child, 4.109.
Sargent and Kittredge, p 492.
Leach BB, p 551.
Literary Relations. Child, 4.108.
Bibliography. Bronson TTCB, 3.262.

    Lord Delamere (Child, no 207).
Editions. Child, 4.112.
Sargent and Kittredge, p 493.
Literary Relations. Child, 4.110.

    Lord Derwentwater (Child, no 208).
Editions. Child, 4.117.
Sargent and Kittredge, p 494.
Leach BB, p 553.
Literary Relations. Child, 4.115, 522; 5.254.
Bibliography. Bronson TTCB, 3.264.
Dean-Smith, p 85.
Coffin BTBNA, p 124.

    The Duke of Athole's Nurse (Child, no 212).
Editions. Child, 4.151.
Sargent and Kittredge, p 502.
Leach BB, p 566.
Kinsley OBB, p 344.
Literary Relations. Child, 4.150.
Bibliography. Bronson TTCB, 3.295.

    The False Lover Won Back (Child, no 218).

Editions. Child, 4.210.
Sargent and Kittredge, p 511.
Leach BB, p 575.
Literary Relations. Child, 4.209.
Bibliography. Bronson TTCB, 3.345.
Coffin BTBNA, p 132.

The Gardener (Child, no 219).
Editions. Child, 4.212.
Sargent and Kittredge, p 513.
Leach BB, p 577.
Literary Relations. Child, 4.212; 5.258.
Bibliography. Bronson TTCB, 3.348; 4.501.
Dean-Smith, p 103 (The Seeds of Love).
Coffin BTBNA, p 132.

Eppie Morrie (Child, no 223).
Editions. Child, 4.239.
Sargent and Kittredge, p 519.
Literary Relations. Child, 4.239; 5.262.
Bibliography. Bronson TTCB, 3.361.

The Lady of Arngosk (Child, no 224).
Editions. Child, 4.243.
Sargent and Kittredge, p 520.
Literary Relations. Child, 4.241.

Rob Roy (Child, no 225).
Editions. Child, 4.245.
Sargent and Kittredge, p 521.
Leach BB, p 583.
Literary Relations. Child, 4.243, 523; 5.262.
Bibliography. Bronson TTCB, 3.363.
Coffin BTBNA, p 133.

Lizie Lindsay (Child, no 226).
Editions. Child, 4.256.
Sargent and Kittredge, p 522.
Literary Relations. Child, 4.255, 524; 5.264.
Bibliography. Bronson TTCB, 3.365; 4.502.
Coffin BTBNA, p 133.

Glasgow Peggie (Child, no 228).
Editions. Child, 4.271.
Sargent and Kittredge, p 526.
Leach BB, p 588.
Literary Relations. Child, 4.270; 5.266.
Bibliography. Bronson TTCB, 3.370; 4.502.

Earl Crawford (Child, no 229).
Editions. Child, 4.277.
Sargent and Kittredge, p 527.
Leach BB, p 589.
Literary Relations. Child, 4.276; 5.301.
Bibliography. Bronson TTCB, 3.376.

The Slaughter of the Laird of Mellerstain (Child, no 230).
Editions. Child, 4.281.

Sargent and Kittredge, p 528.
Literary Relations. Child, 4.281.

The Earl of Errol (Child, no 231).
Editions. Child, 4.283.
Sargent and Kittredge, p 529.
Literary Relations. Child, 4.282; 5.267.
Bibliography. Bronson TTCB, 3.378.

Richie Story (Child, no 232).
Editions. Child, 4.293.
Sargent and Kittredge, p 530.
Leach BB, p 592.
Literary Relations. Child, 4.291; 5.270.
Bibliography. Bronson TTCB, 3.380.
Coffin BTBNA, p 134.

Andrew Lammie (Child, no 233).
Editions. Child, 4.302.
Sargent and Kittredge, p 532.
Literary Relations. Child, 4.300.
Bibliography. Bronson TTCB, 3.385; 4.503.
Coffin BTBNA, p 135.

Charlie MacPherson (Child, no 234).
Editions. Child, 4.309.
Sargent and Kittredge, p 533.
Literary Relations. Child, 4.308; 5.301.

The Earl of Aboyne (Child, no 235).
Editions. Child, 4.312.
Sargent and Kittredge, p 534.
Leach BB, p 593.
Literary Relations. Child, 4.311; 5.270, 301.
Bibliography. Bronson TTCB, 3.391.

The Laird o Drum (Child, no 236).
Editions. Child, 4.323.
Sargent and Kittredge, p 535.
Literary Relations. Child, 4.322; 5.272.
Bibliography. Bronson TTCB, 3.395; 4.506.
Coffin BTBNA, p 135.

Lord Saltoun and Auchanachie (Child, no 239).
Editions. Child, 4.347.
Sargent and Kittredge, p 539.
Leach BB, p 595.
Literary Relations. Child, 4.347; 5.273.
Bibliography. Bronson TTCB, 3.422.
Coffin BTBNA, p 136.

The Baron o Leys (Child, no 241).
Edition. Child, 4.355.
Literary Relations. Child, 4.355; 5.275.
Bibliography. Bronson TTCB, 3.427.

The Coble o Cargill (Child, no 242).
Editions. Child, 4.359.
Sargent and Kittredge, p 542.

Literary Relations. Child, 4.358.

James Hatley (Child, no 244).
Editions. Child, 4.371.
Sargent and Kittredge, p 546.
Leach BB, p 606.
Literary Relations. Child, 4.370.

Young Allan (Child, no 245).
Editions. Child, 4.377.
Sargent and Kittredge, p 547.
Leach BB, p 608.
Literary Relations. Child, 4.375; 5.275.
Bibliography. Bronson TTCB, 4.3.

Redesdale and Wise William (Child, no 246).
Editions. Child, 4.383.
Sargent and Kittredge, p 549.
Literary Relations. Child, 4.383; 5.276.
Bibliography. Bronson TTCB, 4.11.

Auld Matrons (Child, no 249).
Editions. Child, 4.391.
Sargent and Kittredge, p 552.
Literary Relations. Child, 4.391.

Henry Martyn (Child, no 250).
Editions. Child, 4.393.
Sargent and Kittredge, p 553.
Leach BB, p 615.
Friedman VBFB, p 358.
Literary Relations. Child, 4.393; 5.302.
Bibliography. Bronson TTCB, 4.24, 509.
Dean-Smith, p 72.
Coffin BTBNA, p 140.

Lang Johnny More (Child, no 251).
Editions. Child, 4.397.
Sargent and Kittredge, p 554.
Literary Relations. Child, 4.396, 524.
Bibliography. Bronson TTCB, 4.47.

Thomas o Yonderdale (Child, no 253).
Editions. Child, 4.409.
Sargent and Kittredge, p 559.
Literary Relations. Child, 4.409.
Bibliography. Bronson TTCB, 4.60.

Lord William, or, Lord Lundy (Child, no 254).
Editions. Child, 4.411.
Sargent and Kittredge, p 560.
Leach BB, p 621.
Literary Relations. Child, 4.411.
Bibliography. Bronson TTCB, 4.62.

Willie's Fatal Visit (Child, no 255).
Editions. Child, 4.415.
Sargent and Kittredge, p 561.

Leach BB, p 623.
Literary Relations. Child, 4.415.
Bibliography. Bronson TTCB, 4.64.

Alison and Willie (Child, no 256).
Editions. Child, 4.416.
Sargent and Kittredge, p 562.
Leach BB, p 625.
Literary Relations. Child, 4.416.
Bibliography. Bronson TTCB, 4.66.

Burd Isabel and Earl Patrick (Child, no 257).
Editions. Child, 4.418.
Sargent and Kittredge, p 563.
Leach BB, p 626.
Literary Relations. Child, 4.417; 5.278.
Bibliography. Bronson TTCB, 4.67.

Broughty Wa's (Child, no 258).
Editions. Child, 4.424.
Sargent and Kittredge, p 565.
Literary Relations. Child, 4.423.
Bibliography. Bronson TTCB, 4.68.

Lord Thomas Stuart (Child, no 259).
Editions. Child, 4.425.
Sargent and Kittredge, p 565.
Leach BB, p 629.
Literary Relations. Child, 4.425; 5.279.

Lord Thomas and Lady Margaret (Child, no 260).
Editions. Child, 4.427.
Sargent and Kittredge, p 566.
Leach BB, p 631.
Literary Relations. Child, 4.426.
Bibliography. Bronson TTCB, 4.70.

Lady Isabel (Child, no 261).
Editions. Child, 4.430.
Sargent and Kittredge, p 567.
Leach BB, p 633.
Literary Relations. Child, 4.429.

Lord Livingston (Child, no 262).
Editions. Child, 4.432.
Sargent and Kittredge, p 569.
Literary Relations. Child, 4.431.

The New-Slain Knight (Child, no 263).
Editions. Child, 4.434.
Sargent and Kittredge, p 571.
Literary Relations. Child, 4.434; 5.279.

The White Fisher (Child, no 264).
Editions. Child, 4.436.
Sargent and Kittredge, p 571.
Literary Relations. Child, 4.435.
Bibliography. Bronson TTCB, 4.71.

The Knight's Ghost (Child, no 265).
Editions. Child, 4.437.
Sargent and Kittredge, p 573.
Literary Relations. Child, 4.437.
Bibliography. Bronson TTCB, 4.72.

John Thomson and the Turk (Child, no 266).
Editions. Child, 5.9.
Sargent and Kittredge, p 574.
Literary Relations. Child, 5.1, 279.
Bibliography. Bronson TTCB, 4.74.
Coffin BTBNA, p 141.

The Twa Knights (Child, no 268).
Editions. Child, 5.25.
Sargent and Kittredge, p 580.
Literary Relations. Child, 5.21.
Rountree J T, Old Lady Grant, another Child ballad no 268? Journ of American Folklore 83.458.
Bibliography. Coffin BTBNA, p 142.

Lady Diamond (Child, no 269).
Editions. Child, 5.35.
Sargent and Kittredge, p 583.
Leach BB, p 635.
Literary Relations. Child, 5.29, 303.
Bibliography. Bronson TTCB, 4.79.

The Earl of Mar's Daughter (Child, no 270).
Editions. Child, 5.40.
Sargent and Kittredge, p 584.
Leach BB, p 641.
Literary Relations. Child, 5.38.
Bibliography. Bronson TTCB, 4.82.

The Farmer's Curst Wife (Child, no 278).
Editions. Child, 5.108.
Sargent and Kittredge, p 605.
Leach BB, p 661.
Friedman VBFB, p 452.
Literary Relations. Child, 5.107, 305.
Bibliography. Bronson TTCB, 4.174, 510.
Dean-Smith, p 66.
Coffin BTBNA, p 148.

The Beggar-Laddie (Child, no 280).
Editions. Child, 5.116.
Sargent and Kittredge, p 606.
Literary Relations. Child, 5.116, 305.
Bibliography. Bronson TTCB, 4.250.

The Keach i the Creel (Child, no 281).
Edition. Child, 5.122.
Literary Relations. Child, 5.121.
Bibliography. Bronson TTCB, 4.257, 511.
Dean-Smith, p 82.

Coffin BTBNA, p 151.

Jock the Leg and the Merry Merchant (Child, no 282).
Editions. Child, 5.126.
Sargent and Kittredge, p 607.
Literary Relations. Child, 5.126.
Bibliography. Bronson TTCB, 4.278.

The Wylie Wife of the Hie Town Hie (Child, no 290).
Edition. Child, 5.153.
Literary Relations. Child, 5.153.
Bibliography. Bronson TTCB, 4.388.

Child Owlet (Child, no 291).
Editions. Child, 5.157.
Sargent and Kittredge, p 617.
Literary Relations. Child, 5.156, 305.

Dugall Quin (Child, no 294).
Editions. Child, 5.165, 305.
Sargent and Kittredge, p 620.
Literary Relations. Child, 5.165, 305.

Walter Lesly (Child, no 296).
Editions. Child, 5.168.
Sargent and Kittredge, p 623.
Literary Relations. Child, 5.168.

Earl Rothes (Child, no 297).
Editions. Child, 5.170.
Sargent and Kittredge, p 624.
Leach BB, p 682.
Literary Relations. Child, 5.170.

Young Peggy (Child, no 298).
Editions. Child, 5.171.
Sargent and Kittredge, p 624.
Leach BB, p 683.
Literary Relations. Child, 5.171.
Bibliography. Bronson TTCB, 4.423.

Trooper and Maid (Child, no 299).
Editions. Child, 5.172.
Leach BB, p 684.
Literary Relations. Child, 5.172, 306.
Bibliography. Bronson TTCB, 4.424.
Coffin BTBNA, p 161.

Blancheflour and Jellyflorice (Child, no 300).
Editions. Child, 5.175.
Sargent and Kittredge, p 625.
Literary Relations. Child, 5.175.

The Queen of Scotland (Child, no 301).
Editions. Child, 5.176.
Sargent and Kittredge, p 626.
Literary Relations. Child, 5.176.

Fraser S, The Queen of Scotland, Folklore 73.41.

Young Bearwell (Child, no 302).
Editions. Child, 5.178.
Sargent and Kittredge, p 627.
Literary Relations. Child, 5.178.

The Holy Nunnery (Child, no 303).
Editions. Child, 5.180.
Sargent and Kittredge, p 628.
Leach BB, p 686.
Literary Relations. Child, 5.179.

Young Ronald (Child, no 304).
Editions. Child, 5.182.
Sargent and Kittredge, p 629.
Literary Relations. Child, 5.181.

The Outlaw Murray (Child, no 305).
Editions. Child, 5.191.
Sargent and Kittredge, p 632.
Kinsley OBB, p 363.
Literary Relations. Child, 5.185, 307.

Popular Carols

Broadwood L, The Bold Fisherman, Journ of the Folk-Song Soc 5.132.
Greene R L, The Traditional Survival of Two Medieval Carols, ELH 7.223 (Gloria Tibi Domine and Sweet Jesus).
Friedman A B, A Carol in Tradition, in Chaucer and Middle English Studies in Honour of Rossell Hope Robbins, ed B Rowland, London 1974, p 298.

The Bitter Withy.
Editions. C F S, N&Q 4s 1(Jan 18 1868).53 (fragment).
Sidgwick F, N&Q 10s 4(July 29 1905).84.
Williams R V, Journ of the Folk-Song Soc 8(1906).205.
Gerould G H, The Ballad of the Bitter Withy, PMLA 23.145.
Sidgwick F, Popular Carols, London 1908.
Leather E M, Journ of the Folk-Song Soc 14(1910).31.
Notes and Queries of Evesham 1(1911).215.
Sharp C J, English Folk Carols, London 1911.
Leather E M, Folklore of Herefordshire, London 1912, p 181.
Journ of the Folk-Song Soc 18(1914).2.
Sharp C J, Journ of the Folk-Song Soc 31(1927).31.
Niles J J, The Anglo-American Carol Study Book, N Y 1948, p 32.
Literary Relations. Gerould, PMLA 23.141.
Barry P, The Bridge of Sunbeams, Journ of American Folklore 27.77.
Batho E C, The Life of Christ in the Ballads, E&S 9(1923).70.
Titland W J, The Bitter Withy and Its Relationship to the Holy Well, Journ of American Folklore 80.49.

The Holy Well.
Editions. Sandys W, Christmas Carols Ancient and Modern, London 1833.
Howitt W, The Rural Life of England, London 1840, p 468.
Hotten J C (pseud J Sylvester), A Garland of Christmas Carols, London 1861, p 32.
Rimbault E F, A Collection of Old Christmas Carols, London n d (= 1863).
Husk W, Songs of the Nativity, London 1868, p 91.
Bramley H R and J Stainer, Christmas Carols New and Old, London n d (= 1871 and 1878), p 136.
A Garland of Christmas Carols, Newcastle-upon-Tyne: R Robertson, 1880.
Burne C S, Shropshire Folk-Lore, London 1883–86, p 567.
Sidgwick F, Popular Carols, London n d.
Dunstan R, A Second Book of Carols, London n d (= 1909), p 67.
Journ of the Folk-Song Soc 4(1910).26.
The Oxford Book of Ballads, ed Quiller-Couch, Oxford 1910, p 458.
Sharp C J, English Folk Carols, London 1911, p 59.
Shaw M and P Dearmer, edd, The English Carol Book, London and Oxford 1913, p 32.
Journ of the Folk-Song Soc 5(1914).1.
Leather E M and V Williams, Twelve Traditional Christmas Carols, London 1920.
Dearmer P, V Williams, and M Shaw, edd, The Oxford Book of Carols, London 1928, no 56.
Literary Relations. Graves J M, The Holy Well: A Medieval Religious Ballad, Western Folklore 26(1967).13.
Titland W J, The Bitter Withy and Its Relationship to the Holy Well, Journ of American Folklore 80.49.

XVI. JOHN LYDGATE

by

Alain Renoir and C. David Benson

BACKGROUND BOOKS: The following important, frequently listed entries, here given full statement, are referred to in abbreviated form in the pages that follow. For abbreviations not appearing in this list, consult the general Table of Abbreviations.

Duschl	Duschl J, Das Sprichwort bei Lydgate, Weiden 1912
Gattinger	Gattinger E, Die Lyrik Lydgates, WBEP 4
Halliwell PPS 2	Halliwell J O, A Selection from the Minor Poems of Dan John Lydgate, in Early English Poetry, Ballads, and Popular Literature of the Middle Ages, PPS 2, London 1840
MacCracken EETSES 107	MacCracken H N, The Minor Poems of John Lydgate, Pt 1, EETSES 107, London 1911
MacCracken EETS 192	MacCracken H N, The Minor Poems of John Lydgate, Pt 2, EETS 192, London 1934
MacCracken TPSL	MacCracken H N, The Lydgate Canon, TPSL 1907–10
PearsallLydgate	Pearsall D, John Lydgate, Charlottesville 1970 (crit D Fox, N&Q ns 18(216).308; J Mitchell, JEGP 70.528; R Pryor, MÆ 40.206; D Brewer, New Statesman 79.587; D Mehl, Angl 90.383; R M Wilson, MLR 67.164; P J Frankis, RES ns 23.472; M C Seymour, NM 73.729; R J Simon, EA 26.352; A S G Edwards, ESts 54.504)

Reger	Reger H, Die epische Cäsur in der Chaucerschule, Bayreuth 1910
RenoirLydgate	Renoir A, The Poetry of John Lydgate, Cambridge Mass and London 1967 (crit TLS 8 June 1967, p 510; W F Schirmer, Angl 85.460; J Milosh, Cithara 7.77; J A W Bennett, SN 40.242; J Mitchell, JEGP 67.144; S Manning, ELN 5.210; D S Brewer, Spec 44.317; S Deligiorgis, CL 21.273; P J Frankis, RES ns 20.79; J Norton-Smith, MÆ 38.88; F L Utley, Renaissance Quart 22.47; J Norton-Smith, ESts 52.361)
Rossi	Rossi S, Poesia cavalleresca e poesia religiosa inglese nel Quattrocento, Milano 1960
SchirmerLydgate	Schirmer W F, John Lydgate: Ein Kulturbild aus dem 15 Jahrhundert, Tübingen 1952 (crit M A Manzalaoui, MÆ 24.29; H Lüdeke, ESts 36.116)
trans Keep	Schirmer W F, John Lydgate: a Study in the Culture of the XVth Century, trans A E Keep, Berkeley and Los Angeles 1961 (crit TLS 29 Dec 1961, p 930; J Speirs, New Statesman 63.90; H S Bennett, MLR 57.407; R H Robbins, Angl 80.454; A Renoir, JEGP 63.767; L E Nathan, MP 61.312; J Norton-Smith, MÆ 33.80; S Deligiorgis, CL 21.273)
Seaton	Seaton E, Sir Richard Roos, London 1961

GENERAL TREATMENTS.

Language. Schick J, Lydgate's Temple of Glas, EETSES 60.63 (vocabulary less indigenous, more modern than Chaucer's).

Skeat W W, Principles of English Etymology, 2s, Oxford 1891.

Dibelius W, John Capgrave und die engl Schriftsprache, Angl 23.153, 323.

Hingst R, Die Sprache John Lydgates aus seinen Reimen, Greiswald 1908.

Reismüller G, Romanische Lehnwörter bei Lydgate, MBREP 58 (lists ca 850 Lat and Fr words first used by L, 150 first used by Chaucer and then by L; discusses influence of sources and contemporaries on L's vocabulary).

Babcock C W, A Study of the Meterical Use of the Inflectional e in ME, PMLA 29.59 (treatment of final e similar to Chaucer's).

Hüttmann E, Das Partizipium Präsentis bei Lydgate im Vergleich mit Chaucers Gebrauch, Kiel 1914.

Royster J F, The Do Auxiliary 1400 to 1450, MP 12.449 (Do Auxiliary appears in 45 of 68 poems printed by MacCracken in EETSES 107; numerous Do Auxiliaries in L's poetry, none in his prose).

Juhl H, Der syntaktische Gebrauch des Infinitives bei John Lydgate, Kiel 1921 (a 4-page summary of a dissertation).

Tillman N P, Lydgate's Rhymes as Evidence of His Pronunciation, Univ Wisconsin Summaries of Doctoral Dissertations 6(1942).293.

Pearsall D, The English Chaucerians, in Chaucer and Chaucerians, ed D S Brewer, Univ Alabama 1966, p 206 (L's language imitates Chaucer's); PearsallLydgate, pp 50, 58.

Versification. Puttenham G, The Art of English Poesie, London 1588, bk 2, chap 3 (L's awkward caesura).

Schipper, 1.492.

Schick, EETSES 60.1iv (classifies L's meters into 3 types).

Courthope, 1.321 (emphasis on metrical incompetence).

Pollard 15CPV, p xi (weakening of final e partly responsible for L's failure in following Chaucer's meters).

MacCracken TPSL, appendix 2.iii (L's rimes); rptd EETSES 107.vi.

Reger, passim (counts certain, probable, and doubtful epic caesurae in L's poetry; computes percentage of those that are certain; finds that percentage increases chronologically).

Saintsbury G, Historical Manual of English Prosody, London 1910, pp 52, 287 (on Lydgatian line); A History of English Prosody, London 1923, 1.218; 2.275; 3.389, 543 (emphasis on L's metrical deficiencies).

Berdan J M, The Influence of Medieval Latin Rhetorics on the English Writers of the Early Renaissance, RomR 7.288.

Hammond E P, English Verse between Chaucer and Surrey, Durham 1927, p 76; Hammond, p 498 (definition of Lydgatian line).

Spindler R, Engl Metrik, Munich 1927, p 60.

Young G, An English Prosody on Inductive Lines, Cambridge 1928, p 38 (effect of shortening pentameter line on L's meters).

Pyle F, The Pedigree of Lydgate's Heroic Line, Hermathena 50.26 (characteristics of Lydgatian line exist as early as Poema Morale; L's use of that line).

Lewis C S, The 15-Cent Heroic Line, E&S 24.28 (a general theory of 15-cent metrics).

Southworth J G, Verses of Cadence, Oxford 1954, p 78 (L's prosody rhythmic and not metrical but less flexible than Chaucer's).

Manzalaoui M A, Lydgate and English Prosody, Cairo Stud in English, ed M Wahba, Cairo 1960, p 87 (harmonizes theories of Schick and Lewis and claims L's rhythm is relaxed).

Pearsall, English Chaucerians, p 204; PearsallLydgate, p 60 (L's versification an imitation of Chaucer's).

Fox D, Chaucer's Influence on 15-Cent Poetry, in Companion to Chaucer Stud, ed B Rowland, Toronto N Y and London 1968, p 389.

Mitchell J, Thomas Hoccleve, Urbana Chicago and London 1968, p 100 (brief summary of views of L's meter).

Eliason N E, Chaucer's 15-Cent Successors, Medieval and Renaissance Stud 5.112 (L's versification an attempt and failure to imitate Chaucer's).

Hascall D L, The Prosody of John Lydgate, Language and Style 3.122 (applies modified Halle-Keyser theory to L).

Robinson I, Chaucer's Prosody, Cambridge 1971, pp 67 (surveys views of L's metrical incompetence), 199 (claims L's basic meter is balanced pentameter).

Authorship. Bale J, Catalogus, 1557, p 586 (erratic list of L's works); Index Britanniae Scriptorum, ed R L Poole and M Bateson from MS notebook, Oxford 1902, p 228.

Stowe J, list appended to Siege of Thebes in Speght's Chaucer, 1598 (usually cited from MSS, more reliable than Bale).

Pits J, Relationum Historicarum de Rebus Anglicis, Paris 1619, 1.632 (list based on Bale).

Tanner T, Bibliotheca Britannico-Hibernica, ed D Wilkins, 1748, p 489.

Ritson J, Bibliographia Poetica, London 1802, p 66 (attributes 251 titles to L).

Schick, EETSES 60.cxlii (L's principal works).

MacCracken TPSL, appendix 2.iii (establishes canon and discusses earlier lists); rptd with minor corrections EETSES 107.v (crit E P Hammond, AnglB 24.140).

Brusendorff A, The Chaucer Tradition, London 1925, p 466 (prints and discusses John Shirley's list).

SchirmerLydgate, p 228; trans Keep, p 264 (L's works classified according to genre).

Seaton, p 110 (argues that Shirley was wrong in his attribution of courtly poems to L; many should be assigned to Richard Roos).

Sources and Literary Relations. Flügel E, Kleinere Mitteilungen aus Handschriften, Angl 14.463 (prints and discusses ME texts that show L's influence).

Gattinger, passim.
Förster M, Über Benedict Burghs Leben und Werke, Arch 101.29 (influence of L on later Chaucerians).
MacCracken H N, Lydgatiana, Arch 126.365; 127.322; 129.50; 130.286; 131.40 (prints and discusses ME poems that show L's influence).
Spurgeon C, Chaucer devant la critique en Angleterre et en France, Paris 1911, p 7 (lists and location of Chaucer allusions in L's works); Five Hundred Years of Chaucer Criticism and Allusion, ChS 2s 48.14 (prints L's allusions to Chaucer).
Duschl, passim (number, source, and classification of proverbs in L).
Brusendorff, Chaucer Tradition, passim (relationship to Chaucer).
Hammond, English Verse, p 77.
Schirmer W F, Dichter und Publikum zu Ende des 15 Jahrhunderts in England, Zeitschrift f Ästhetik u allgemeine Kuntwissenschaft 28.209 (L's general stylistic relationship to Chaucer).
Glunz H H, Die Literarästhetik des europäischen Mittelalters, Bochum-Lagendreer 1937 (notes Italian influence on L).
Bennett OHEL, p 111.
Moore A K, The Secular Love Lyric in ME, Lexington 1951, p 106 (L's testimonies regarding Chaucer's production are worthless).
Enkvist N E, The Seasons of the Year, Societas Scientiarum Fennica Commentationes Humanarum Litterarum 22.4, Helsingfors 1957, p 118 (L's work a catalogue of topics and commonplaces that occur in descriptions of the seasons).
Wickham G, Early English Stages 1300 to 1660, London and N Y 1959, 1.207 (discusses elements from which L made his mummings), 180 (argues for great influence of L's theatrical pieces on secular drama through the Renaissance).
Ferguson A B, The Indian Summer of English Chivalry, Durham 1960, p 210 (notes influence on Hawes and discusses L as a transitional figure).
Seaton, p 521 (discusses influence of L on Roos and their rivalry).
Pearsall, English Chaucerians, p 204 (discusses L's imitations of Chaucer); Gower and Lydgate, London 1969, p 23 (discusses how L differs from Gower and Chaucer); PearsallLydgate, pp 32 (influence on L of library at Bury and of monastic learning), 49, 63 (notes influence of Chaucer on L).
Gluck F, The Minor Poems of Stephen Hawes, DA 27.3426A (mentions influence of L in notes).

RenoirLydgate, pp 28, 55 (believes it is a mistake to judge L by Chaucer), 137 (discusses influence of aureate style in Renaissance).
Fox, Chaucer's Influence, p 392 (notes L's general debt to Chaucer).
Eliason, Medieval and Renaissance Stud 5.103 (notes understanding of Chaucer's art by L and other 15-cent writers and their attempt to imitate it).
Mitchell, Thomas Hoccleve, p 34 (L's religious poetry characterized and compared with Hoccleve's).
Blake N F, The 15th Cent Reconsidered, NM 71.146 (only passing mention of L but contains literary and linguistic survey of the period).
Kean P M, Chaucer and the Making of English Poetry, London and Boston 1972, 2.211 and passim (comparisons of Chaucer and Lydgate).
Hertzig M J, The Early Recension and Continuity of Certain ME Texts in the 16th Cent, DAI 34.1913A (L a continual force throughout the 16th cent).
Walsh E, John Lydgate and the Proverbial Tiger, The Learned and the Lewed, ed L Benson, Harvard Eng Stud 5, Cambridge Mass 1974, p 291 (L is responsible for the view in Eng literature of the tiger as a fierce beast).
Miskimin A S, The Renaissance Chaucer, New Haven and London 1975, pp 121, 134 (L's use of modesty topos compared with Chaucer's), 234, 239, 244 (notes that L's works were included among Chauceriana).

Other Scholarly Problems: Biography. Bokenham O, Legend of St Elizabeth, ca 1443–47, ed C Horstmann, Osbern Bokenham's Legenden, Heilbronn 1883, p 265 (speaks of L as still alive).
Zupitza J, Zur Biographie Lydgates, Angl 3.532 (prints royal grant of annual pension to L in 1446).
Morley, 6.101.
Schick, EETSES 60.1xxxv (L's life and chronology of his writings).
Brandl, 2.686.
Fiedler G, Zum Leben Lydgates, Angl 15.391 (extracts from documents concerning L's stay at Hatfield).
Ten Brink, 2¹.220; 2².7.
Steele R, Lydgate and Burgh's Secrees of Old Philisoffres, EETSES 66.xvi (prints documents concerning L's life).
DNB, 12.306.
MacCracken H N, The Death of Lydgate, The Nation (N Y) 94.209 (argues evidence of Metham's *Amoryus and Cleopes* fixes L's death between Easter and 1 Sept 1449).

Kingsford C L, English Historical Literature in the 15th Cent, Oxford 1913, p 4 (L's patrons).
Craig H, The Works of John Metham, EETS 132.xii (argues evidence of Metham's *Amoryus and Cleopes* fixes L's death before Henry VII reached age 27).
Gerould S Leg, p 256.
Schleich G, Die me Umdichtung von Boccaccios *De claris mulieribus*, Palaes 144.105 (improbability of L's Italian journey).
Hammond, English Verse, p 77.
Utley CR, p 14 and no 201 (L must have written for mixed audience; importance of Ragman Roll as key to L's attitude toward women).
Schirmer W F, Geschichte der engl Literatur, Halle 1937, pp 166, 178; SchirmerLydgate, p 1; trans Keep, p 3 (L's life and cultural background).
Knowles D, The Religious Orders in England, Cambridge 1955, 2.273 (discusses L as a royal poet outside the cloister).
Emden A B, A Biographical Register of the Univ of Oxford to A D 1500, Oxford 1958, 2.1185 (life).
Dédéyan C, Dante en Angleterre, Les Lettres Romanes 13.179, 183 (general treatment of L's life and knowledge).
Norton-Smith J, John Lydgate Poems, Oxford 1966, p xiii (brief biography and chronology).
Mathew G, The Court of Richard II, N Y 1968, p 58 (L a court poet more than a monk).
PearsallLydgate, pp 4, 22, 160, 223, 293, passim.
Scattergood V J, Politics and Poetry in the 15th Cent, London 1971, p 16.
Other Scholarly Problems. [anonymous] Brydle Paths: Clapgate and Lydgate, N&Q 182.358 (term Lydgate Lane used to designate bridle paths near Birmingham today).
Tillyard E M W, The English Renaissance: Fact or Fiction?, London 1952, pp 67, 74, 93 (L transition figure between Middle Ages and Renaissance).
Cary G, The Medieval Alexander, ed D J A Ross, Cambridge 1956, pp 255, 277, 319 (notes different views of Alexander in L's works).
Renoir A, A Note on Saintsbury's Criticism of Lydgate, NM 58.69 (claims it doubtful Saintsbury had read L carefully); John Lydgate Poet of the Transition, English Miscellany 11.9 (L a representative transitional figure between Middle Ages and Renaissance in attitudes toward antiquity, rulers, and nationalism); Attitudes toward Women in Lydgate's Poetry, ESts 42.1 (summary of previous criticism on this topic); RenoirLydgate, pp 10 (claims L knew he was dull), 50 (L as a transitional figure), 61 (L's attitude toward classical antiquity), 79 (L's attitude toward women).
Conley J, Four Studies in Aureate Terms, DA 17.353 (L coined the term aureate); Aureate a Stylistic Term, N&Q ns 13(211).369 (a rare word in 15th and 16th cents except in L).
Wickham, Early English Stages, 1.191 (defines the new form of L's mummings and disguisings), 398 (claims Harley portrait is probably a good likeness of L).
Seaton, p 159 (discusses L's method of including ladies' names in his poems).
Norton-Smith, John Lydgate Poems, p 192 (has note on L's aureate diction).
Pearsall, English Chaucerians, p 215 (discusses L's techniques of amplifications); Pearsall-Lydgate, pp 23 (L's relations to Bury St Edmunds), 73 (L's association with Shirley), 110 (L sees world operating by contraries), 167 (discusses L's relations with the Warwick family).
Robbins R H, A Middle English Prayer to St Mary Magdalen, Traditio 24.458 (verse prayers to saints not common in ME, but L wrote 3).
Mitchell, Thomas Hoccleve, p 50 (L's attitude toward women is ambiguous but primarily amused).
Edwards A S G, Lydgate's Attitudes to Women, ESts 51.436.
Williamson M, Antony and Cleopatra in the Late Middle Ages and Early Renaissance, Michigan Academician 5.147 (discusses L's double presentation of Cleopatra).
Crosby D L, The Presenter in Elizabethan Drama, DAI 33.2887A (L's mummings discussed).
Pearsall D and E Salter, Landscapes and Seasons of the Medieval World, Toronto 1973, p 193 (brief description of nature miniatures in 3 MSS).
Literary Criticism. Sherry R, A Treatise of Schemes and Tropes, London 1550, f Aii[b] (Chaucer, Gower, L are examples of best style).
Peacham H, The Compleat Gentleman 1625, pr STC, no 19502, p 95 (reproaches L with lack of imagination).
Cooper E, The Muses' Library, 1737 (perhaps first frankly adverse criticism of L for purely literary reasons).
Ritson J, Bibliographia Poetica, London 1802, p 87 (insists on L's worthlessness).
Brydges S E, Restituta, London 1816, pp 29, 199 (prints Renaissance opinions of L).
Campbell T, Specimens of the British Poets, London 1919, 1.89.
Warton T, History of English Poetry, ed W C Hazlitt, London 1871, 3.53 (surveys L's con-

tribution).
Schick, EETSES 60.cxlii (precise reference to early evaluations of L).
Lounsbury T, Studies in Chaucer, N Y 1892, 1.438, 500; 2.25; 3.304 (considers L beneath contempt).
Jusserand J J, Literary History of the English People, N Y and London 1895, p 498.
Ker W P, John Gower Poet, Quarterly Rev 197.437; rptd as Gower, W P Ker Essays on Medieval Literatures, p 101 (Dunbar's testimony regarding L's reputation).
Moorman F W, The Interpretation of Nature in English Poetry, QF 95.125 (argues L not so dull as usually assumed).
Vickers K H, Humphrey Duke of Gloucester, London 1907, p 390 (dismisses L's production as worthless for either history or literature).
Licklider A H, Chapters on the Metric of the Chaucerian Tradition, Baltimore 1910, p 3 (surveys L criticism to 1907).
CHEL, 2.197 (insists on L's deficiencies).
Reufs F, Das Naturgefühl bei Lydgate, Arch 122.269 (argues L's original perception of nature ruined by monastic interpretation).
Kingsford, English Hist Lit in the 15th Cent, p 229 (sees no historical significance in most of L's poems).
Cohen H L, The Ballade, N Y 1915, p 222 (evaluation of L's ballades and ballade-like sections of longer works).
Saintsbury G, A History of English Criticism, Edinburgh and London 1925, pp 30, 62, 254 (lists opinions of L).
Aurner N S, Caxton Mirrour of 15-Cent Letters, London and Boston 1926, p 225 (prints Caxton's commendation of L in epilogue of Bk 2 of IX [21]).
Hammond, English Verse, p 97 (L's reputation).
Schirmer W F, Dichter und Publikum zu Ende der 15 Jahrhunderts in England, Zeitschrift f Ästhetik u algemeine Kunstwissinschaft 28.209 (L's style in the light of his age and influence of Chaucer); Das Ende des Mittelalters in England, Kleine Schriften, Tübingen 1950, p 25 (discusses aspects of L's style and subject matter that made him typical of his age); Schirmer-Lydgate, p 223; trans Keep, p 255 (L's reputation).
Bennett H S, The Author and His Public in the 14th and 15th Cent, E&S 23.7 (L exemplifies worst results of patronage system); Bennett OHEL, p 30; English Books and Readers 1475–1557, London 1952, p 4 (gives illustrations of L's popularity during period studied).

Lewis C S, The Allegory of Love, Oxford 1936, p 76 (argues L better poet than usually assumed).
Sampson G, The Concise Cambridge History of Eng Literature, Cambridge and N Y 1941, p 84.
Moore, Secular Love Lyric in ME, p 106 (suggests L marks low point of Eng poetic tradition).
Renoir A, The Binding Knot Three Uses of One Image in Lydgate's Poetry, Neophil 41.202; RenoirLydgate, p 1 (survey of opinions about L).
Murphy J J, A 15-Cent Treatise on Prose Style, Newberry Libr Bull 6.205 (this work anticipates L's style).
Rossi, pp 35 (L as translator), 59 (L's use of rhetoric), 92 (general assessment).
Norton-Smith, John Lydgate Poems, p ix (general assessment of work and style).
Pearsall, English Chaucerians, p 203 (discussion of L's importance); PearsallLydgate, pp 1 (discusses L's reputation), 67 (L as a 15-cent poet), 99 (L's amplifications in personal description), 103 (brief assessment of the shorter love poems).
Marotta J G, John Lydgate and the Tradition of Medieval Rhetoric, DAI 33.729A (L on the art of poetry).
Hayes J J, The Court Lyric in the Age of Chaucer, DAI 34.4205A.
Stouck M, Studies in English Verse Hagiography 1300–1500, DAI 36.1538A (has a section on L's hagiographic poetry).
General References. Smith C G, The Transition Period, N Y 1900, p 7.
Wylie J H, The Reign of Henry V, Cambridge 1914 (numerous references to L for historical evidence).
Mullet C F, John Lydgate: a Mirror of Medieval Medicine, Bull of the History of Medicine 22.403 (L's preoccupation with pestilence and views on medicine typical of his time: knowledge is to be sought as means of exalting God–not as end in itself).
Schirmer W F, Geschichte der engl u amerikanischen Literatur, Tübingen 1954, p 166.
Schlauch M, English Medieval Literature and Its Social Foundation, Warszawa 1956, p 290 (brief discussion of L's career).
Weiss R, Humanism in England during the 15th Cent, 2nd edn, Oxford 1957 (background of L's world).
Zesmer D, Guide to English Literature from Beowulf through Chaucer and Medieval Drama, N Y 1961, p 260.
Baugh LHE, p 295.

Pearsall D, Gower and Lydgate, London 1969, p 23 (brief description of various poems).
Gray D, Later Poetry The Courtly Tradition, in The Middle Ages, ed W F Bolton, London 1970, p 322.
Tydeman W, English Poetry 1400–1580, London 1970, p 161.
Bibliography. Ames J, Typographical Antiquities, London 1749 (bibliography of early prints).
Blades W, The Life and Typography of William Caxton, London 1861, 1.73 (lists L's works printed by Caxton).
Collier J P, A Bibliographical and Critical Account of the Rare Books of the English Language, N Y 1866, 1.123 (gives account of L in W Bullein's Dialogue 1573).
Hazlitt W C, Handbook of the Popular Poetical and Dramatic Literature of Great Britain, London 1867, p 357.
Aurner, Caxton Mirrour, pp 41, 170 (lists L's works printed by Caxton before 1480).
Hammond, English Verse, p 98.
Tucker-Benham, p 228.
Bennett, English Books, p 4 (occasional bibliographical details).
Norton-Smith, John Lydgate Poems, p xvi.
Matthews W, Old and ME Literature, N Y 1968, p 70 (brief).
Fox D, Chaucer's Influence on 15-Cent Poetry, in Companion to Chaucer Stud, ed B Rowland, Toronto N Y and London 1968, p 400.
PearsallLydgate, p 301.
Edwards A S G, A Lydgate Bibliography 1928–68, BB 27.95.
New CBEL, 1.639.

[1] SS ALBAN AND AMPHIBAL.

MSS. 1, Trinity Oxf 38, ff 1^a–66^b (1450–1500); 2, Lansdowne 699, ff 96^a–176^b (1450–1500); 3, Inner Temple 511, pt 11, ff 1^a–66^b (15 cent); 4, Lincoln Cath 129, ff 1^a–67^b (1450–1500; begins imperfectly); 5, Huntington Libr HM 140 (formerly Phillipps 8299), ff 1^a–67^b (1450–80). PRINT: 6, John Herford, St Albans 1534 (rptd C Horstmann, Festschrift zu dem 50 jährigen Jubiläum der Königlichen Realschule zu Berlin, 1882).
MS of Extract. MS Fitzwilliam Museum 40–1950, f 135^a (1450–1500; 5 stanzas of concluding prayer to St Alban).
Brown-Robbins, Robbins-Cutler, no 3748.
Royal Commission on Historical MSS, 11th Report, London 1888, 7.231 (on MS 3).
Manly & Rickert, 1.433, 638, 641 (describes MS 5 and lists owners).
Bennett H S, English Books and Readers 1475–1557, Cambridge 1952, p 72 (PRINT 6 one of very few saints' lives printed after 1525).
van der Westhuizen, edn, p 3 (discusses all MSS and PRINT 6).
Edition. van der Westhuizen J E, The Life of Saint Alban and Saint Amphibal, Leiden 1974 (crit J Norton-Smith, MÆ 44.325; A Renoir, Spec 52.397; A S G Edwards, ESts 57.369); p 47 (abstract).
Language. Dibelius W, John Capgrave und die engl Schriftsprache, Angl 23.153, 323.
Hingst R, Die Sprache John Lydgates aus seinen Reimen, Greiswald 1908.
Hüttmann E, Das Partizipium Präsentis bei Lydgate im Vergleich mit Chaucer's Gebrauch, Kiel 1914.
Versification. Reger, pp 49, 78 (finds 13.64 percent lines have epic caesurae).
Date. Warton T, History of English Poetry, ed W C Hazlitt, London 1871, 3.66 (dates poem 1439).
Schick J, Lydgate's Temple of Glas, EETSES 60.cvii.
Gerould S Leg, p 263.
van der Westhuizen, edn, p 22.
Authorship. MacCracken TPSL, appendix 2.xxii; rptd EETSES 107.xxv.
van der Westhuizen, edn, p 22.
Sources and Literary Relations. Warton, 3.66 (argues influence of elegiac poem by Robert of Dunstable).
Duschl, p 9 (sources and classifications of proverbs).
MacCracken H N, Lydgatiana, Arch 129.50 (prints [98] below and argues organization based on [1] and [42]).
Spurgeon C, Five Hundred Years of Chaucer Criticism and Allusion, ChS 2s 48.44.
Patch H R, The Goddess Fortuna in Mediaeval Literature, Cambridge Mass 1927, pp 43, 100, 109 (discusses treatment of Fortune in L's poem and other texts).
SchirmerLydgate, p 144; trans Keep, p 166 (poem is parallel to [42] below; shows relations to Tractatus de nobilitate vita et martyrio Albani et Amphibali).
van der Westhuizen, edn, p 26 (general tradition and specific sources; relationship to Interpretatio Guilielmi and Tractatus de Nobilitate).
Miskimin A S, The Renaissance Chaucer, New Haven and London 1975, p 285 (influence on Hawes and Spenser).
Renoir A, Crist Ihesu's Beasts of Battle A Note

on Oral-Formulaic Theme Survival, Neophil 60.455 (changes in a formula from Old English to L).
Other Scholarly Problems. Schirmer W F, Der engl Frühhumanismus, Leipzig 1931, p 84; rvsd edn, Tübingen 1963, p 75 (commissioning of L to write [1] suggests inroad of humanism into cloister).
van der Westhuizen, edn, p 60 (notes L's chronological error concerning Pelagian heresy and the attempt to correct it in PRINT 6).
Literary Criticism. PearsallLydgate, p 283.
van der Westhuizen, edn, p 64.
General References. SchirmerLydgate, p 144; trans Keep, p 166 (briefly discusses all aspects of the poem).
Rossi, p 209.
Bibliography. Gerould S Leg, p 270.
van der Westhuizen, edn, p 316.

[2] BALLADE ON AN ALE SELLER.

MS. Bodl 11914 (Rawl C.48), ff 131^b–133^a (15 cent; slightly imperfect).
Brown-Robbins, Robbins-Cutler, no 2809.
Edition. MacCracken EETS 192.429.
Abstract. Utley CR, no 249.
Authorship. MacCracken EETSES 107.xi.
SchirmerLydgate, p 229; trans Keep, p 266.
Sources and Literary Relations. Nichols P H, William Dunbar as a Scottish Lydgatian, PMLA 46.214 ([2] and [3] are earliest examples of their genre in English and influenced Dunbar).
General References. SchirmerLydgate, p 82; trans Keep, p 97.
Renoir A, Attitudes to Women in Lydgate's Poetry, ESts 42.9 (antifeminist).

[3] BALLADE ON AN ALE SELLER BECOME CONSTANT (also BALLADE PER ANTIPHRASIM).

MS. Bodl 11914 (Rawl C.48), f 133^{a-b} (15 cent; slightly imperfect).
Brown-Robbins, Robbins-Cutler, no 3823.
Edition. MacCracken EETS 192.432.
Abstract. Utley CR, no 334 (also traces term Antiphrasim to Shirley).
Authorship. MacCracken TPSL, appendix 2.x; rptd EETSES 107.xii.
SchirmerLydgate, p 229; trans Keep, p 266.
Literary Relations. Nichols P H, William Dunbar as a Scottish Lydgatian, PMLA 46.214 ([3] and [2] are earliest examples of their genre in English and influenced Dunbar).

Literary Criticism. Moore A K, The Secular Lyric in ME, Lexington 1951, p 139.
General References. SchirmerLydgate, p 82; trans Keep, p 97.
PearsallLydgate, p 216.

[4] AMEROUS BALADE (also A LOVER'S NEW YEAR'S GIFT and NEW YEAR'S VALENTINE).

MS. BM Addit 16165, ff 253^b–254^b (1425–75).
Brown-Robbins, no 1496.
Hammond E P, The Departing of Chaucer, MP 1.331; Omissions from the Editions of Chaucer, MLN 19.37.
Editions. Hammond E P, Lydgate's New Year's Valentine, Angl 32.194 (introd argues departure from usual Lydgatian conventions).
MacCracken EETS 192.424.
Versification. Raymond J C, Lydgate's Verse and the Nature of English Prosody, DAI 34.5925A.
Date. Seaton, p 157 (1430–39).
Authorship. MacCracken TPSL, appendix 2.xix; rptd EETSES 107.xxii.
SchirmerLydgate, p 229; trans Keep, p 265.
Seaton, p 157 (argues for Richard Roos).
Sources and Literary Relations. Stillwell G, Chaucer's Eagles and Their Choice on February 14, JEGP 53.546 (unlike Chaucer's Parliament, [4] bears witness to tradition of humility in courtly lovers).
Other Scholarly Problems: Biography. Hammond, Angl 32.194 (argues contents of MS suggest that L may have been Complete Letter Writer for unknown lady).
Seaton, p 157 (argues that poem contains name cryptograms).
Literary Criticism. Lewis C S, The Allegory of Love, Oxford 1936, p 243 (poem shows L at his best).
Seaton, p 157 (brief).
General Reference. SchirmerLydgate, p 30; trans Keep, p 35.

[5] AMOR ET PECUNIA (also AMOR VINCIT OMNIA MENTIRIS QUOD PECUNIA and A DEMAWNDE BY LYDGATE).

MSS. 1, Bodl 693 (Ashmole 59), ff 41^a–43^a (Shirley MS); 2, Harley 2251, ff 46^b–48^b (1464–83); 3, BM Addit 29729, ff 124^b–126^a (John Stowe; 1558).
Brown-Robbins, Robbins-Cutler, no 698.
Hammond E P, Two British Museum MSS, Angl 28.1 (detailed study of MS 2).
Manly & Rickert, 1.241 (description of MS 2).

Edition. MacCracken EETS 192.744 (MS 2; collations from MSS 2, 3).
Abstract. Utley CR, no 57.
Authorship. MacCracken TPSL, appendix 2.ix; rptd EETSES 107.xi.
SchirmerLydgate, p 234; trans Keep, p 272.
Literary Criticism. PearsallLydgate, p 207 (relatively sophisticated in allusions and variation).
General Reference. SchirmerLydgate, p 177; trans Keep, p 203 (argues poem aimed at humanistically cultivated public).

[6] PRAISE OF ST ANNE.

MSS. 1, Trinity Camb 601, f 169[b] (1461–83); 2, Harley 2251, f 76[b] (1464–83).
Brown-Robbins, no 1152.
Hammond E P, Two British Museum MSS, Angl 28.1 (detailed study of MS 2).
Manly & Rickert, 1.241 (description of MS 2).
Bennett OHEL, p 116 (L's poem one of several works suggestive of John Shirley's purpose in compiling MSS).
Edition. MacCracken EETSES 107.130 (MS 2; collations from MS 1).
Authorship. MacCracken TPSL, appendix 2.xxii; rptd EETSES 107.xxv.
SchirmerLydgate, pp 232, 239; trans Keep, pp 271, 280.
General References. SchirmerLydgate, p 166; trans Keep, p 190 (notes that poem is really prologue to [143] below).
Woolf R, The English Religious Lyric in the Middle Ages, Oxford 1968, p 295 (L fuses different traditions).

[7] ASSEMBLY OF GODS (also ACCORD OF REASON AND SENSUALITY IN THE FEAR OF DEATH, and ASSEMBLE DE DYEUS, and INTERPRETACYON OF THE NATURES OF GODDYS AND GODDESSES).

MSS. 1, Trinity Camb 599, ff 68[a]–98[a] (1475–1525); 2, Royal 18.D.ii, ff 167[a]–181[a] (1498–1525; copy of PRINT 3). PRINTS: 3, de Worde, 1498 (Canterbury Tales; STC, no 17005); 4, de Worde, post 1499 (STC, no 17006; facsimile rptd Jenkinson, Cambridge 1906); 5, de Worde, ca 1500 (STC, no 17007); 6, Pynson, ca 1505 (STC, no 17007.5); 7, Redman, 1540; 8, Redman, 1540; 9, Redman, n d.
Brown-Robbins, Robbins-Cutler, no 4005.
Hoops J, 15-Cent Facsimiles, EStn 39.111.
Duff E G, 15-Cent English Books, Oxford 1917, entries 253–55 (description of PRINTS 6, 7, 8, 9).
Simpson P, Proof-reading in the 16th, 17th, and 18th Cents, London 1935, p 59 (printer's marks show MS 1 to have been used by de Worde).
Schulz H C, MS Printer's Copy for a Lost Early English Book, Libr 4s 22.138 (PRINT 3 illustrates small number of extant printer's copies).
Ringler BEV, p 153.
Stevenson A, Tudor Roses from John Tate, SB 20.15 (discusses PRINT 3, whose paper was made by Tate).
Fletcher B Y, The Textual Tradition of The Assembly of Gods, PBSA 71.191 (discusses the relations of MSS and PRINTS).
Edition. Triggs O L, The Assembly of Gods, Chicago 1895, and EETSES 69 (MS 1; introd on MSS, authorship, date, versification, language and literary relations).
Language. Dibelius W, John Capgrave und die engl Schriftsprache, Angl 23.153, 323.
Hingst R, Die Sprache John Lydgates aus seinen Reimen, Greiswald 1908, p 66.
Versification. Licklider A H, Chapters on the Metric of the Chaucerian Tradition, Baltimore 1910, pp 38, 201 (discusses L's use of divided stress and arsis-thesis variations).
Reger, pp 66, 78 (13.15 percent lines have certain epic caesurae).
Saintsbury G, A History of English Prosody, London 1923, 1.228 (ascribes metrical deficiencies to L's ineptitude rather than to scribal errors).
Date. Schick J, Lydgate's Temple of Glas, EETSES 60.cxii (ca 1403).
Bühler C F, The Assembly of Gods and Christine de Pisan, ELN 4.251 (notes different suggested dates).
Authorship. Stowe's list in Speght's Chaucer, 1598.
Schick, EETSES 60.cix (questions L's authorship).
Rudolph A, Lydgate und die Assembly of Gods, Berlin 1909 (rejects L's authorship).
Kern J H, Iets over London Likkepeny, Neophil 3.287 (argues that L was probably dead before composition of poem and rimes are un-Lydgatian).
Hammond, p 407 (questions validity of ascription to L by de Worde and Stowe).
Lewis C S, The Allegory of Love, Oxford 1936, p 260 (rejects L's authorship on basis of meter).
Bonner F W, The Genesis of the Chaucer Apocrypha, SP 48.461 (on former ascription to Chaucer).
SchirmerLydgate, p 237; trans Keep, p 277 (rejects L's authorship on internal grounds).

Bühler, ELN 4.251 (rejects L with no new proof).
Sources and Literary Relations. Keiller M M, The Influence of Piers Plowman on the Macro Play of Mankind, PMLA 26.339 (influence of [7] on Macro Play not so real as that of Piers).
Lowes J L, Spenser and the Mirour de l'Omme, PMLA 29.488 (compares animal symbols for 7 deadly sins in [7] and Faerie Queene).
Smart W K, Some English and Latin Sources and Parallels for the Morality of Wisdom, Chicago 1912, p 42 (concept of reason and sensuality similar to that in St Augustine and [161] below).
Cook J D, Euhemerism: a Mediaeval Interpretation of Classical Paganism, Spec 2.396 (euhemerism in [7] reflects influence of Peter Comestor).
Patch H R, The Goddess Fortuna in Mediaeval Literature, Cambridge Mass 1927, pp 43, 65, 75, 157 (discusses treatment of Fortuna in L's poem and other texts).
Stearns M, A Note on Henryson and Lydgate, MLN 60.101 (Assembly is important source for Henryson's Testament of Cresseid).
Bühler, ELN 4.251 (borrows from Epitre d'Othea but unclear whether French original or ME trans by Scrope).
Other Scholarly Problems. Bennett OHEL, pp 119, 214 ([7] typical of 15-cent interest in pious tales).
Chew S C, The Pilgrimmage of Life, New Haven and London 1962, pp 246, 382n (conception of the fates).
Literary Criticism. Knowlton E C, Nature in ME, JEGP 20.186 (finds typically Lydgatian handling of nature in [7]).
Gradon P, Form and Style in Early English Literature, London 1971, pp 62, 370 (allegory is thin and pictorial).

[8] LEGEND OF ST AUSTIN AT COMPTON.

MSS. 1, Camb Univ Hh.4.12, ff 35^a–40^a (1475–1500); 2, Harley 2255, ff 24^a–32^b (1448?–49?); 3, Harley 4826, ff 46^a–50^b (15 cent); 4, Lansdowne 699, ff 35^a–41^b (1450–1500); 5, Lincoln Cath 129, ff 75^a–76^a (15 cent; lines 1–128 lacking); 6, Leyden Univ Vossius 9, ff 8^b–17^a (15 cent).
Brown-Robbins, Robbins-Cutler, no 1875.
Utley CR, no 199 (suggests MS 2 compiled ca 1448–49).
van Dorsten J A, The Leyden Lydgate MS, Scriptorium 14.315 (MS 6).
Editions. Halliwell PPS 2.135 (MS 2).
MacCracken EETSES 107.193 (MS 2; collations from all other MSS).
Textual Emendations. Gattinger, p 84.
Language. Hingst R, Die Sprache John Lydgates aus seinen Reimen, Greiswald 1908, p 15.
Versification. Reger, pp 41, 77 (finds certain epic caesurae in 11 percent lines).
Authorship. MacCracken TPSL, appendix 2.xxii; rptd EETSES 107.xxv.
SchirmerLydgate, p 230; trans Keep, p 268.
Sources and Literary Relations. SchirmerLydgate, p 139; trans Keep, p 160 (source is Chronicle of Johannes Bromtonus, now in Bollandists' Acta Sanctorum 6.396).
Literary Criticism. Gattinger, pp 33, 72, 84 (discusses style).
Gerould S Leg, p 264.
General References. SchirmerLydgate, pp 65, 139, 148; trans Keep, pp 75, 160, 170.
PearsallLydgate, p 279.

[9] AVE JESSE VIRGULA.

MSS. 1, Trinity Camb 601, ff 163^a–165^a and again ff 234^a–236^b (1461–83); 2, Harley 2251, ff 30^b–32^b (1464–83); 3, Harley 2255, ff 140^a–141^b (stanzas 1–7 lacking; 1448?–49?).
Brown-Robbins, no 1037.
Hammond E P, Two British Museum MSS, Angl 28.1 (detailed study of MS 2).
Manly & Rickert, 1.241 (description of MS 2).
Utley CR, no 194 (suggests MS 3 compiled ca 1448–49).
Edition. MacCracken EETSES 107.299 (MSS 2, 3; collations from MS 1).
Authorship. MacCracken TPSL, appendix 2.ix; rptd EETSES 107.xii.
SchirmerLydgate, p 233; trans Keep, p 271.
Sources and Literary Relations. MacCracken H N, Lydgatiana, Arch 131.40 (prints Acrostic on Maria which imitates L's poem).
SchirmerLydgate, p 242; trans Keep, p 285.
Nichols P H, William Dunbar as a Scottish Lydgatian, PMLA 46.214 (demonstrates direct influence of poem on Dunbar's New Stanzas); Lydgate's Influence on the Aureate Terms of the Scottish Chaucerians, PMLA 47.516.
Jack R D S, Dunbar and Lydgate, SSL 8.219 (denies influence on Dunbar claimed by Nichols above).
Other Scholarly Problems. Woolf R, The English Religious Lyric in the Middle Ages, Oxford 1968, p 283 (unusual reference to foreign

iconographic forms).
Literary Criticism. SchirmerLydgate, p 171; trans Keep, p 195 (calls poem arsenal of aureate style).

[10] AVE REGINA CELORUM.

MSS. 1, Trinity Camb 601, f 162^{a-b} and again f 233^{a-b} (1461–83); 2, Harley 2251, ff 34^a–35^b (1464–83).
Brown-Robbins, no 1056.
Hammond E P, Two British Museum MSS, Angl 28.1 (detailed study of MS 2).
Manly & Rickert, 1.241 (description of MS 2).
Edition. MacCracken EETSES 107.291 (MS 1; collations from MS 2).
Authorship. MacCracken TPSL, appendix 2.x; rptd EETSES 107.xii.
SchirmerLydgate, p 233; trans Keep, p 271.
Sources and Literary Relations. SchirmerLydgate, p 242; trans Keep, p 285 (mentions poems in imitation of this poem).
Jack R D S, Dunbar and Lydgate, SSL 8.220 (influenced Dunbar's ANE BALLAT OF OUR LADY, X[103]).
Other Scholarly Problems. Wehrle W O, The Macaronic Hymn Tradition in Medieval English Literature, Washington 1933, p 136 (poem reflects influence of Black Death).
Mullet C F, John Lydgate: a Mirror of Medieval Medicine, Bull of the History of Medicine 22.403 (poem representative of contemporary preoccupation with pestilence).
Literary Criticism. SchirmerLydgate, p 168; trans Keep, p 192 (style less Latinate than [165] below).
PearsallLydgate, p 272 (L's high style).

[11] BALLAD BY JOHN LUCAS.

MSS. 1, Bodl 21896 (Douce 322), f 20^a (15 cent); 2, Harley 1706, ff 19^b–20^a (15 cent); 3, Camb Univ Ff.5.45, ff 13^b–14^a (1400–25).
Brown-Robbins, Robbins-Cutler, no 2585.
Edition and Scholarship. See [31] below.

[12] A BALLADE OF HER THAT HATH ALL VIRTUES.

MSS. 1, Trinity Camb 600, pp 34–35 (1450–75); 2, BM Addit 29729, f 157^{a-b} (John Stowe, 1558).
Brown-Robbins, Robbins-Cutler, no 869.
Hammond E P, Lydgate's Mumming at Hertford, Angl 22.364 (describes MS 1).

Brusendorff A, The Chaucer Tradition, London 1925, pp 208, 466, and passim (discusses Shirley's marginalia in MS 1).
Editions. MacCracken EETS 192.379 (MS 1; collations from MS 2).
Robbins SL, p 129 (MS 1).
Stevick R D, One Hundred ME Lyrics, Indianapolis and N Y 1964, p 116 (MS 1; normalized with glosses at foot of page).
Date. Seaton, p 156 (1430–39).
Authorship. MacCracken TPSL, appendix 2.x; rptd EETSES 107.xii.
SchirmerLydgate, p 229; trans Keep, p 265.
Seaton, p 156 (argues for Richard Roos).
Sources and Literary Relations. SchirmerLydgate, p 30; trans Keep, p 35 (argues influence of French and Chaucer's Anelida).
Other Scholarly Problems. Seaton, p 156 (argues that poem contains name cryptograms).
Literary Criticism. Moore A K, The Secular Love Lyric in ME, Lexington 1951, p 138 (argues poem illustrative of L's gift for twaddle).

[13] BENEDICTUS DEUS IN DONIS SUIS.

MSS. 1, Bodl 798 (Laud Misc 683), ff 31^b–33^a (15 cent); 2, Harley 2255, ff 142^a–143^a (1448?–49?).
Brown-Robbins, no 943.
Utley CR, no 194 (suggests MS 2 compiled ca 1448–49).
Edition. MacCracken EETSES 107.7 (MS 1; collations from MS 2).
Authorship. MacCracken TPSL, appendix 2.x; rptd EETSES 107.xii.
SchirmerLydgate, p 234; trans Keep, p 273.
Other Scholarly Problems. Wylie J H, The Reign of Henry the Fifth, Cambridge 1914–29, 2.397 (reference to horned Moses throws light on Duke of Berry's tomb).
General Reference. SchirmerLydgate, p 178; trans Keep, p 204.

[14] THE EIGHT VERSES OF ST BERNARD, VERSION 1.

MS. Bodl 798 (Laud Misc 683), ff 27^a–29^a (15 cent).
Brown-Robbins, no 2553.
Edition. MacCracken EETSES 107.206.
Authorship. MacCracken TPSL, appendix 2.xxii; rptd EETSES 107.xxv.
SchirmerLydgate, p 232; trans Keep, p 270.
Other Scholarly Problems. SchirmerLydgate, p 163;

trans Keep, p 187 (stanza 9 is octosyllabic version of [156] below).

[15] THE EIGHT VERSES OF ST BERNARD, VERSION 2.

MSS. 1, Camb Univ Kk.1.3 pt 12, f 18[b] (15 cent; lines 1–50 only); 2, BM Addit 29729, ff 126[b]–127[b] (John Stowe; 1558).
Brown-Robbins, no 2553.
Edition. MacCracken EETSES 107.209 (MS 2; collations from MS 1).
Authorship. MacCracken TPSL, appendix 2.xxii; rptd EETSES 107.xxv.
SchirmerLydgate, p 232; trans Keep, p 270.
Other Scholarly Problems. SchirmerLydgate, p 163; trans Keep, p 187 (written for Henry V; stanza 9 is octosyllabic version of [156] below).

[16] BEWARE OF DECEITFUL WOMEN (also AGAINST WOMEN and THE BLYNDE MAN ETETH MANY A FLYE).

MSS. 1, Trinity Camb 599, f 207[a-b] (1450–1500); 2, Trinity Camb 1450, f 28[a-b] (1425–75); 3, Harley 2251, f 154[b] (1464–83); 4, Rome Eng Coll 1306 (also numbered 127 and A.347), f 75[b] (1436–56). PRINT: 5, Stowe, Chaucer 1561 (STC, no 5075; rptd R Anderson, A Complete Edition of the Poets of Great Britain, London 1795, 1.586; rptd A Chalmers, The Works of the English Poets, London 1810, 1.564).
Brown-Robbins, Robbins-Cutler, no 1944.
Hammond E P, Two British Museum MSS, Angl 28.1 (detailed study of MS 3).
Manly & Rickert, 1.241 (description of MS 3).
Klinefelter R A, A Newly Discovered 15-Cent English MS, MLQ (Wash) 14.3 (contents of MS 4).
Robbins R H, A ME Diatribe against Philip of Burgundy, Neophil 39.131 (description and contents of MS 4).
Rigg A G, Some Notes on Trinity Coll Camb MS O.9.38, N&Q ns 13(211).324; A Glastonbury Miscellany of the 15th Cent, Oxford 1968, p 59 (MS 2).
Editions. Oxf Ch, 7.295 (MS 1; collations from MSS 2, 3, and PRINT 5).
Hammond E P, English Verse between Chaucer and Surrey, Durham 1927, p 413.
Robbins SL, pp 224, 290 (MS 1).
Davies R T, Medieval Eng Lyrics, London 1962, pp 238 (all MSS except MS 4; slightly normalized with glosses at foot of page), 356 (briefly discusses conventions and lists poem as anonymous).
Textual Matters. Robbins SL, p 290 (notes rearrangement of stanzas and 7th added in MS 2).
Rigg, N&Q ns 13(211).328; Glastonbury Miscellany, p 60.
Language. Dibelius W, John Capgrave und die engl Schriftsprache, Angl 23.153, 323.
Hingst R, Die Sprache John Lydgates aus seinen Reimen, Greiswald 1908, p 20.
Versification. Reger, pp 62, 77 (no certain epic caesurae in poem).
Rigg, N&Q ns 13(211).329 (altered rime scheme in different MSS).
Authorship. Skeat W W, The Chaucer Canon, Oxford 1900, p 124 (argues probable authorship of L on basis of Tyrwhitt).
Hammond, p 412 (finds no sign of L's authorship).
MacCracken EETSES 107.xlix (rejects L's authorship on basis of internal evidence and lack of early authority).
Utley CR, no 166 (questions MacCracken's rejection of poem from L canon).
Rigg, N&Q ns 13(211).237; Glastonbury Miscellany, p 60 (argues for L's authorship by claiming allusion to Earl of Suffolk's attacks on L's anti-feminism).
Other Scholarly Problems. Vickers K H, Humphrey Duke of Gloucester, London 1907, p 335 (argues poem probably intended as hint to Humphrey of Gloucester).
Duschl, pp 9, 20 (classifies proverbs).
Literary Criticism. Reufs F, Das Naturgefühl bei Lydgate, Arch 122.269.
Bibliography. Rigg, Glastonbury Miscellany, p 59.

[17] FRAGMENT OF HYMN TO BLESSED VIRGIN.

MS. St John's Oxf 56, ff 84[b]–85[b] (late 15 cent).
Brown-Robbins, no *34; Robbins-Cutler, no *1037.5.
Authorship. MacCracken TPSL, appendix 2.xxvii; rptd EETSES 107.xxx.
Brown-Robbins, no *34 (questions L's authorship).
SchirmerLydgate, p 233; trans Keep, p 271.
General References. SchirmerLydgate, p 168; trans Keep, p 192.

[18] BYCORNE AND CHYCHEVACHE.

MSS. 1, Trinity Camb 599, ff 157[b]–159[a] (1450–75); 2, Trinity Camb 600, pp 10–15 (1450–75); 3, Harley 2251, ff 244[b]–246[b]? (1464–83);

4, BM Addit 29729 (John Stowe, 1558; recorded in Brown-Robbins, not in EETSES 107).
Brown-Robbins, Robbins-Cutler, no 2541.
Hammond E P, Lydgate's Mumming at Hertford, Angl 22.364 (partial contents and description of MS 2); Two British Museum MSS, Angl 28.1 (detailed study of MS 3).
Brusendorff A, The Chaucer Tradition, London 1925, pp 208, 466, and passim (discusses Shirley's marginalia in MS 2).
Manly & Rickert, 1.241, 532 (description of MSS 1, 3).
Editions. Dodsley R, Old Plays, London 1827, 12.297 (MS 3).
Halliwell PPS 2.129 (MS 3); rptd A Montaiglon, Recueil de poèsies françoises des XVe et XVIe siècles, Paris 1855–78, 11.277, with French trans 2.191; rptd H Morley, Shorter English Poems, London 1876, p 54; rptd W A Neilson and K G T Webster, The Chief British Poets of the 14th and 15th Cents, Boston 1916, p 220.
Hammond E P, English Verse between Chaucer and Surrey, Durham 1927, p 115 (MS 1).
MacCracken EETS 192.433 (MS 2; collations from MSS 1, 3).
Abstract. Utley CR, no 227.
Language. Hingst R, Die Sprache John Lydgates aus seinen Reimen, Greiswald 1908, p 15.
Menner R J, Bycorne-Bygorne Husband of Chichevache, MLN 44.455 (Bycorne-Bygorne comes from Latin biscornis: fantastic animal).
Date. Utley CR, no 227 (ca 1420–35).
Authorship. MacCracken TPSL, appendix 2.x; rptd EETSES 107.xiii.
SchirmerLydgate, p 229; trans Keep, p 266.
Sources and Literary Relations. Jubinal A, Mystères inédits du quinzième siècle, Paris 1837, 1.248, 389 (discusses Chychevache in relation to St Genevieve's meakness; prints French analogue).
Montaiglon, Recueil, 11.284 (prints French poem probably similar to L's original).
Gattinger, pp 8, 55, 62, 73, 84 (poem is typical of L's satire; based on a Dit de la Chincheface, ed A Jubinal, Mystères, 1.390; reflects influence of Chaucer).
Bolte J, Bigorne und Chichevache, Arch 106.1 (traces use of Bycorne and Chychevache as grotesque elements in English, French, German and Italian texts); Noch einmal Bigorne und Chichevache, Arch 114.80 (prints and discusses French analogue).
MacCracken H N, Lydgatiana, Arch 126.365 (prints Life of Holy Job and discusses its technical relationship to [18] and other tapestry poems of L).
Other Scholarly Problems. Gerould J H, Legends of St Wulfhad and St Ruffin at Stone Priory, PMLA 32.323 (argues L's poem intended for mural rather than tapestry presentation).
Hammond E P, Lydgate and the Duchess of Gloucester, Angl 27.381 (poem illustrative of L's relation to patronage system).
SchirmerLydgate, p 83; trans Keep, p 98 (poem is a mumming).
Wickham G, Early English Stages 1300 to 1660, London 1959, pp 191, 205 (defines the new form of L's mummings and disguisings).
PearsallLydgate, p 180 (not mumming as claimed by Schirmer above but suggests words on a painted cloth).
Edwards A S G, Lydgate's Attitudes to Women, ESts 51.436 (brief).
General References. Schirmer W F, Das Ende des Mittelalters in England, in Kleine Schriften, Tübingen 1950, p 25; SchirmerLydgate, pp 83, 90, 110; trans Keep, pp 98, 106, 128.
Rossi, p 139.
PearsallLydgate, p 179.
Rogers K M, The Troublesome Helpmate, Seattle and London 1966, p 85.

[19] A CALENDAR.

MSS. 1, Bodl 11755 (Rawl B.408), ff 7ª–12ª (1425–75); 2, Bodl 21803 (Douce 229), ff 1ª–7ª (15 cent); 3, Bodl 21896 (Douce 322), ff 2ª–7ª (15cent); 4, St John's Oxf b.2.24 (formerly Arch A.50; late 15 cent?; MS inserted between Court of Sapience and Pilgrimage of the Soul in vol of Caxton prints; first 2 stanzas lacking); 5, Harley 1706, ff 3ª–8ᵇ (15 cent); 6, Harley 4011, ff 130ª–143ª (1450–1500; lines 1–59 lacking); 7, Lambeth 878, pp 159–183 (15 cent); 8, Longleat 30, ff 1ª–12ᵇ? (15 cent); 9, Huntington Libr HM 142 (formerly Bement), ff 1ª–6ᵇ (1467). PRINT: 10, Matyns of Our Lady, de Worde, 1513 (STC, no 15914).
Brown-Robbins, Robbins-Cutler, no 1721.
Schulz H C, ME Texts from the Bement MS, HLQ 3.443 (notes variants in Calendar and argues MS 9 is twin of MS 8).
Editions. Horstmann C, Nachtrage zu den Legenden, Arch 80.114 (composite text from MSS 1, 3, 6).
Clark A, The English Register of Godstow Nunnery, EETS 129.13 (MS 1).
MacCracken EETSES 107.363 (MS 1; collations from MSS 2, 3, 5, 6, 7).
Selection. Maskell W, Monumenta Ritualia

Ecclesiae Anglicanae, Oxford 1882, 3.224 (January and December).
Language. Dibelius W, John Capgrave u die engl Schriftsprache, Angl 23.153, 323.
Hingst R, Die Sprache John Lydgates aus seinen Reimen, Greiswald 1908.
Authorship. MacCracken TPSL, appendix 2.xvi; rptd EETSES 107.xix.
SchirmerLydgate, p 231; trans Keep, p 269.
Other Scholarly Problems. Duschl, pp 30, 92 (classifies proverbs).
Literary Criticism. Gerould S Leg, p 266.
General Reference. SchirmerLydgate, pp 120, 151; trans Keep, pp 139, 174 (composed for L's own cloister, hence indicative of which feasts were observed there).

[20] VERSES ON CAMBRIDGE.

MSS. 1, Camb Univ Mm.1.35, pp 249–250 (early 18th cent); 2, Harley 367, f 88[a] (1600–25).
Brown-Robbins, no 582.
Editions. Retrospective Rev 2s 1.498 (MS 1).
MacCracken EETS 192.652 (MS 1; collations from MS 2).
Versification. Reger, pp 63, 77 (7.14 percent lines have certain epic caesurae).
Authorship. MacCracken TPSL, appendix 2.xi; rptd EETSES 107.xiii.
SchirmerLydgate, p 231; trans Keep, p 269.
General Reference. SchirmerLydgate, p 207; trans Keep, p 237.

[21] THE CHURL AND THE BIRD.

MSS. 1, Balliol 354, ff 106[a]–112[a] (1518–36; probably a transcript of PRINT 17); 2, Christ Church Oxf 152, ff 277[a]–284[b] (1460–1500; lines 274–341 lacking); 3, Camb Univ Hh.4.12, ff 74[b]–81[a] (1475–1500); 4, Camb Univ Kk.1.6, ff 208[b]–214[b] (15 cent; ends imperfectly); 5, Trinity Camb 599, ff 9[a]–12[a] (1475–1525); 6, Cotton Calig A.ii, ff 17[a]–20[a] (1400–50); 7, Harley 116, ff 146[b]–152[a] (1475–1500); 8, Harley 2407, ff 76[a]–89[b] (no date in Harleian cat; 66 stanzas); 9, Lansdowne 699, ff 28[a]–34[b] (1450–1500); 10, BM Addit 39547, ff 89[a]?–109[a]? (transcript of MS 6 by Bishop Percy); 11, Lincoln Cath 129, ff 68[a]–75[a]? (15 cent; MacCracken EETS 192.468 records text as written on ff cij–cvij; opening page almost entirely torn); 12, Deene Park (formerly Cardigan; formerly Brudenell), ff 304[a]–308[a] (1425–75; lines 1–366 only; Lovell, edn, suggests now in Univ of Texas); 13, Longleat 258, ff 137[a]–147[a] (1460–70); 14, Leyden Univ Vossius 9, ff 42[a]–49[a] (15 cent); 15, Boston Public Libr 92 (formerly Gurney), ff 187[a]–189[b] (16 cent; stanzas 1–16 lacking); 16, Huntington Libr HM.144 (formerly Huth), ff 135[a]–140[a] (1480–1500).
PRINTS: 17, Caxton, 1477–78 (STC, no 17008; rptd Cambridge facsimile 1906); 18, Caxton, ca 1492 (STC, no 17009; rptd Sykes, Roxb Club 1818, p xvi); 19, Pynson, ca 1493 (STC, no 17010); 20, de Worde, ca 1500 (STC, no 17011); 21, Mychel, 1540; 22, Copland, 1550; 23, Ashmole, Theatrum Chemicem Britannicum, 1652, pp 213–26.
Brown-Robbins, Robbins-Cutler, no 2784.
Lewis J, The Life of Mayster Wyllyam Caxton, London 1737.
Dibdin T F, Typographical Antiquities, London 1810–12, 1.307; 2.325 (PRINTS 17, 18, 20).
Lowndes W T, Bibliographer's Manual, ed H G Bohn, London 1864, 3.1418.
Blades W, The Biography and Typography of William Caxton, N Y 1882, p 209 (PRINTS 17, 18).
Robinson F N, On Two MSS of Lydgate's Guy of Warwick, HSNPL 5.177 (describes MS 14).
Hoops J, 15-Cent Facsimiles, EStn 36.111 (Cambridge facsimiles).
Duff E G, 15-Cent Eng Books, Oxford 1917, entries 256–59 (PRINTS 17, 18, 19, 20).
Plomer H R, Wynkyn de Worde and His Contemporaries, London 1925, p 117 (suggests 1493 as date for PRINT 19).
Hammond, edn, p 103 (MS 13).
Bühler C F, Three Notes on Caxton, Libr 4s 17.155 (argues possibility of lost printing; crit E F Bosanquet, Libr 4s 17.362); Two Caxton Editions of The Churl and the Bird, Libr 4s 21.279 (argues copy of Caxton in Pierpont Morgan Libr is 1st print, and copy in Cambridge Univ Libr is 2nd print).
Manly & Rickert, 1.71, 85, 232 (describes MSS 2, 5, 12).
Bennett H S, English Books and Readers 1475–1557, Cambridge 1952, p 184 (notes that Pynson and de Worde printed the poem because of its popularity).
Ringler BEV, p 153.
van Dorsten J A, The Leyden Lydgate MS, Scriptorium 14.315 (MS 14).
Editions. Halliwell PPS 2.179 (MS 7).
Tyroller F, Die Fabeln von dem Mann u dem Vogel in ihrer Verbreitung in der Weltliteratur, Litterarhistorische Forschungen 51.176 (Halliwell's text with emendations; introd traces

development of fable and gives sources of L's poem; analogues are printed after L's text).

Hammond E P, English Verse between Chaucer and Surrey, Durham 1927, p 104 (MS 13 with stanzas 49–50 from MS 11).

MacCracken EETS 192.468 (MS 9; collations from MSS 1, 3, 4, 5, 6, 7, 11, 14 and PRINTS 17, 18, 19, 20, 21, 23; prints on p 485 eight spurious stanzas from Ashmole's Theatrum Chem); rptd W A Neilson and K G T Webster, The Chief British Poets of the 14th and 15th Cents, Boston 1916, p 208.

Lovell R E, John Lydgate's Siege of Thebes and Churl and Bird Edited from the Cardigan-Brudenell MS, DAI 30.2974A (MS 12).

Selections. Bowers R H, Lydgate's The Churl and the Bird MS Harley 2407 and Elias Ashmole, MLN 49.90 (prints from MS 8 eight stanzas found only in that MS and compares them to Ashmole's print).

Bühler C, A Note on Stanza 24 of Lydgate's The Churl and the Bird, JEGP 40.562 (textual variants to EETS text).

Versification. Schick J, Lydgate's Temple of Glas, EETSES 60.lv.

Reger, pp 41, 78 (11.16 percent lines have certain epic caesurae).

Pyle F, The Pedigree of Lydgate's Heroic Line, Hermathena 50.26 (shows that characteristics of L's line go back as far as Poema Morale; discusses L's use of it).

Date. Schick, EETSES 60.cxii (ca 1398).

Authorship. Dibdin, Typ Ant, 1.308.

MacCracken TPSL, appendix 2.xi; rptd EETSES 107.xiii.

SchirmerLydgate, p 229; trans Keep, p 265.

Sources and Literary Relations. Dibdin, Typ Ant, 1.307; 2.325 (believes poem based on Disciplina clericalis).

Blades W, The Life and Typography of William Caxton, London 1861–63, 2.60 (L's poem tells same story as Laborer and Nightingale in Gesta Romanorum, chap 169).

Sauerstein P E, Über Lydgates Aesopübersetzung, Halle 1885, p 6 (relationship to Fables, Disciplina clericalis, and Gesta romanorum).

Gattinger, pp 13, 38, 50, 64, 72, 84 (notes influence of French fabliaux, Bible, Disciplina clericalis, and Chaucer).

Schleich G, Über der Quelle von Lydgates Gedicht The Chorle and the Bird, Arch 99.425 (relationship to Disciplina clericalis, Li lais de l'oiselet, Du vilein et de l'oiselet, Legenda aurea, Gesta romanorum, Barlaam and Josaphat).

Duschl, pp 14, 25, 48, 55, 86, 88 (traces one proverb to Guido delle Colonna and classifies others).

Spurgeon C, Five Hundred Years of Chaucer Criticism and Allusion, ChS 2s 48.15.

Patch H R, The Goddess Fortuna in Mediaeval Literature, Cambridge Mass 1927, pp 64, 159 (discusses concept of fall off Fortune's wheel in L's poem and other texts).

SchirmerLydgate, p 32; trans Keep, p 37 (compares tone to that of similar story in Disciplina clericalis).

Bolton W F, Traditio 14.359n (notes other appearances of apologue of the fowler), 366n (an example of didactic value of literary stories).

Other Scholarly Problems. Brusendorff A, The Chaucer Tradition, London 1925, p 29 (believes that the Master mentioned in the envoy is not necessarily Chaucer).

Bennett OHEL, p 141 (poem is illustrative of L's didactic purpose).

General Reference. RenoirLydgate, p 44 (very medieval poem).

[22] COMPLAINT FOR LACK OF MERCY.

MS. Camb Univ Ff.1.6, ff 152ᵃ–153ᵃ (15 cent).
Brown-Robbins, no 1017.
Edition. MacCracken EETS 192.381.
Authorship. MacCracken EETSES 107.xiii.
SchirmerLydgate, p 229; trans Keep, p 265.
General Reference. SchirmerLydgate, p 30; trans Keep, p 35 (characteristic of L's mature style).

[23] COMPLAINT OF THE BLACK KNIGHT (also COMPLAINT OF A LOVER'S LIFE and THE MAYING AND DISPORT OF CHAUCER).

MSS. 1, Bodl 1782 (Digby 181), ff 31ᵃ–39ᵃ; 2, Bodl 2078 (Bodley 638), ff 1ᵃ–4ᵃ (begins at line 468; 15 cent?); 3, Bodl 3354 (Arch Selden B.24), ff 120ᵇ–129ᵇ (ca 1486); 4, Bodl 3896 (Fairfax 16), ff 20ᵇ–30ᵃ (1400–50); 5, Bodl 10173 (Tanner 346), ff 48ᵇ–59ᵃ (1400–20); 6, Pepys 2006, pp 1–17 (1425–75); 7, BM Addit 16165, ff 190ᵇ–200ᵇ (Shirley MS; 1425–75); 8, Asloan, ff 243ᵃ–246ᵇ, 293ᵃ–300ᵇ (transcript of PRINT 11); 9, Univ Edinb, Laing 450 (not listed in C R Borland, Descriptive Catalogue of the Western Mediaeval MSS in Edinburgh Univ Libr); 10, Nat Libr Scot 1.1.6 (Bannatyne), pp 618–621 (1568; a 21-rime-royal-stanza Scottish version with all courtly material excerpted). PRINTS: 11, Chepman and Myllar, Golagros and Gawane, 1508 (rptd G Stevenson, Pieces from the Malecullick and the Gray MSS together with the Chepman and Myllar Prints, PSTS 65.178; rptd D Laing, Edinburgh 1927; rptd Edinburgh Biblio Soc, The Chepman and Myllar Prints, Edinburgh 1950, p 109; STC, no 5099); 12, de Worde, n d (rptd Roxb Club 1818); 13, Thynne, Chaucer, 1532, ff 308a–312a (rptd A Chalmers, The Works of the English Poets, London 1810, 1.338; STC, no 5068); 14, Stowe, Chaucer, 1561 (STC, no 5075; the 21-stanza Socttish version); 15, Speght, Chaucer, 1602, ff 256b–261a.

Brown-Robbins, Robbins-Cutler, no 1507.

Dibdin T F, Typographical Antiquities, London 1912, 2.372 (discusses PRINT 12).

Hammond E P, The Departing of Chaucer, MP 1.331 (discusses MS 7); Omissions from the Editions of Chaucer, MLN 19.35 (describes MS 7).

Manly & Rickert, 1.406 (description of MS 6).

Editions. Urry J, Chaucer 1721, and subsequent edns of Chaucer to 1878.

Murdoch J B, The Bannatyne MS, Hunterian Club 6.817 (the 21-stanza Scottish version).

Oxf Ch, 7.245 (PRINT 13; collations from MSS 1, 2, 3, 4, 5).

Krausser E, Lydgate's Complaint of the Black Knight, Halle 1896 (all MSS except MS 8; introd discusses MSS, language, meter, authorship, date, and influence of Chaucer); rptd Angl 19.211; crit M Kaluza, Lydgate's Complaint of the Black Knight, LfGRP 20.373.

Craigie W A, The Asloan MS, PSTS ns 16.247.

Ritchie W T, The Bannatyne MS, PSTS ns 26.82 (the 21-stanza Scottish version).

MacCracken EETS 192.383 (MS 4; collations for MSS 1, 2, 3, 5, 6, 7 and PRINTS 11, 13).

Norton-Smith J, John Lydgate Poems, Oxford 1966, pp 47 (MS 4; collations from MSS 3, 5, 7), 160 (discusses MSS relations and textual problems; brief commentary, notes and glossary).

Selection. Tydeman W, Eng Poetry 1400–1580, London 1970, p 25 (lines 1–84 from Norton-Smith edn, with notes).

Modernization. Clarke C C, The Riches of Chaucer, London 1835, p 235.

Language. Skeat B M, The Lamentatyon of Mary Magdaleyne, Cambridge 1897, p 9 (notes Chaucerian vocabulary).

Dibelius W, John Capgrave u die engl Schriftsprache, Angl 23.153, 323.

Hingst R, Die Sprache John Lydgates aus seinen Reimen, Greiswald 1908.

Babcock C F, A Study of the Meterial Use of the Inflectional e in ME with Particular Reference to Chaucer and Lydgate, PMLA 29.59 (L's language bridges gap between Middle Ages and Renaissance).

Versification. Bowen E W, Confusion between q̄ and ō in Chaucer's Rimes (L's use of also: to and also: therto rimes).

Schick J, Lydgate's Temple of Glas, EETSES 60.1v.

Skeat, Lamentatyon, p 23 (relationship between versification of Black K and that of Lamentatyon).

Smith C G, The Transition Period, N Y 1900, p 12 (Chaucerian aspect of L's versification).

Licklider A H, Chapters on the Metric of the Chaucerian Tradition, Baltimore 1910, pp 46, 57, 200 (discusses L's use of resolved stress and arsis-thesis variation).

Reger, pp 54, 77 (finds certain epic caesurae in 2.9 percent of lines).

Hammond E P, The Nine-Syllabled Pentameter Line in Some Post-Chaucerian MSS, MP 23.129 (prints all acephalous and broken-back lines in MS 4 text of [23] and explains them as overzealous attempt to imitate Chaucer's variations on the ten-syllable line).

Pyle F, The Pedigree of Lydgate's Heroic Line, Hermathena 50.26 (shows that characteristics of L's line go back at least to Poema Morale and discusses L's use of that line).

Date. Schick, EETSES 60.cxii (ca 1400–02).

Seaton, p 212 (1433–38).

Norton-Smith, edn p 161 (1398–1412; before change in L after 1412).

Authorship. Schick, EETSES 60.cxxvii.

Oxf Ch, 7.xliii (ascribes [23] to L on basis of internal evidence and Shirley's ascription in MS 7).

Skeat W W, The Chaucer Canon, Oxford 1900, p 102.

MacCracken TPSL, appendix 2.xi; rptd EETSES 107.xiv.

Hammond, p 413.

Kern J H, Iets over London Likkepeny, Neophil 3.287 (believes L's authorship of [23] not beyond question).

Brusendorff A, The Chaucer Tradition, London 1925, p 45 (ascribes [23] to L mostly on basis of Tyrwhitt).

Utley CR, no 345 (discusses earlier arguments for L's authorship and mentions the Scottish abridged version).

SchirmerLydgate, p 229; trans Keep, p 265.

Seaton, p 212 (argues for Richard Roos).

Sources and Literary Relations. Sandras E G, Études sur Chaucer, Paris 1859, p 80 (notes close resemblance between [23] and Froissart's Dit

du bleu chevalier).
Ten Brink B A K, Chaucer Studien, Münster 1870, p 170 (relation of [23] to Froissart's Dit du bleu chevalier, printed p 206; relationship to Chaucer in use of term Complaint).
Skeat W W, Lydgate's Testimony to The Romaunt of the Rose, Athen 1896, p 747 ([23]'s debt to Chaucer's Romaunt frag A); The Chaucer Canon, Oxford 1900, p 72 (notes borrowing of one passage from Chaucer's Romaunt of the Rose frag A, shows possible influence of other passages).
Lange J H, Lydgate u Fragment B des Romaunt of the Rose, EStn 29.397 (argues relationship of [23] and [176] to Romaunt of the Rose frag B much closer than usually assumed).
Spurgeon C, Five Hundred Years of Chaucer Criticism and Allusion, ChS 2s 48.15.
Hibbard L A, Chaucer's Shapen was My Sherte, PQ 1.222 (like Chaucer in Knight's Tale, Troilus, and Legend of Hypermnestra, L uses shirt image to express foreordained death).
Schirmer W F, The Importance of the 15th Cent for the Study of the Eng Renaissance, Eng Stud Today, Oxford 1951, p 164 (on resemblance of [23] to Book of the Duchess); SchirmerLydgate, p 28; trans Keep, p 34 (relationship to Romance of the Rose and to Chaucerian and French traditions in general).
Seaton, p 216.
Norton-Smith, edn, p 161 (discussion and notes).
RenoirLydgate, p 46.
PearsallLydgate, p 84.
Miskimin A S, The Renaissance Chaucer, New Haven and London 1975, p 298 (influenced Spenser's Daphnaida).
Other Scholarly Problems. Bennett OHEL, p 116 ([23] suggestive of Shirley's purpose in compiling MSS).
Bonner F W, The Genesis of the Chaucer Apocrypha, SP 48.461 (former ascription of [23] to Chaucer notably responsible for later erroneous impressions of Chaucer).
Seaton, p 212 (argues poem contains name cryptograms; knight is Edmund Beaufort).
RenoirLydgate, p 84 (attitude toward women).
Pearsall D and E Salter, Landscapes and Seasons of the Medieval World, Toronto 1973, p 193 (garden landscape is traditional and no longer realistic).
Literary Criticism. Godwin W, Life of Chaucer, London 1803, 2.277 (argues [23] first-rate poem, a little weakened by effeminacy).
Moorman F W, The Interpretation of Nature in Eng Poetry, QF 95.127 ([23] reveals fine perception of colors and appreciation of natural scenery).
CBEL, 2.204.
Reufs F, Das Naturgefühl bei Lydgate, Arch 122.269 (concludes that monastic view of nature ruins L's originality).
Knowlton E C, Nature in ME, JEGP 20.186 ([23] typical of L's handling of nature).
Lewis C S, The Allegory of Love, Oxford 1936, p 239 (finds occasional good conceit in [23] and notes that handling of love is more modern than in Machaut or Chaucer).
Norton-Smith, edn, p 161 (brief).
RenoirLydgate, p 24 (brief; L's skill at setting physical background).
Pearsall D, Gower and Lydgate, London 1969, p 81 (analyzes opening nature description); PearsallLydgate, p 84.
Marotta J G, John Lydgate and the Tradition of Medieval Rhetoric, DAI 33.729A.
General Reference. Pearsall D, The English Chaucerians, in Chaucer and Chaucerians, ed D S Brewer, Univ Alabama 1966, p 209.
Bibliography. Hammond E P, Omissions from the Edns of Chaucer, MLN 19.35.
SchirmerLydgate, p 226; trans Keep, p 261.

[24] A COMPLEYNT THAT CRIST MAKETH OF HIS PASSIOUN (also CRISTES PASSIOUN).

MSS. 1, Bodl 798 (Laud Misc 683), ff 12a–14b (15 cent); 2, Camb Univ Kk.1.6, ff 194a–196a (15 cent); 3, Trinity Camb 601, ff 189b–193b (1461–83; 20 stanzas); 4, Harley 372, ff 54a–55a (1440–60); 5, Harley 7333, f 147a–b (1425–75); 6, BM Addit 31042, ff 94a–b, 96a (1425–75).
Brown-Robbins, no 2081.
Stern K, The London Thornton Miscellany A New Description of BM Addit MS 31042, Scriptorium 30.26, 33 (MS 6).
Edition. MacCracken EETSES 107.216 (MS 1; collations from all MSS).
Selection. Kild Ged, p 210 (stanzas 1–2 only, from MS 6).
Authorship. MacCracken TPSL, appendix 2.xii; rptd EETSES 107.xiv.
SchirmerLydgate, p 232; trans Keep, p 270.
Literary Criticism. SchirmerLydgate, p 162; trans Keep, p 185 (aureate style).
Woolf R, The Eng Religious Lyric in the Middle Ages, Oxford 1968, p 208.
General Reference. PearsallLydgate, p 182 (to be hung on scroll by crucifix).

[25] A COMPLEYNT THAT CRIST MAKETH OF HIS PASSIOUN (SCOTTISH VERSION).

MS. Pepys 1576, f 170ᵇ (15 cent).
Brown-Robbins, Robbins-Cutler, no 2497.
Edition. James M R, Catalogue of Manuscripts, 3.16.
Authorship. Nichols P H, William Dunbar as a Scottish Lydgatian, PMLA 46.220 (introd proposes Dunbar's authorship).

[26] CONSULO QUISQUE ERIS (also CONCORDS OF COMPANY and UTTER THY LANGUAGE).

MSS. 1, Bodl 3356 (Arch Selden B.10), ff 205ᵃ–end (ca 1470–80); 2, Bodl 6943 (Ashmole 59), ff 29ᵇ–31ᵇ (1447–56); 3, Camb Univ Hh.4.12, ff 82ᵃ–83ᵇ (15 cent); 4, Jesus Camb 56, ff 22ᵇ–25ᵃ (15 cent); 5, Trinity Camb 601, ff 296ᵇ–298ᵃ (1461–83); 6, Harley 2251, ff 11ᵇ–13ᵃ (1464–83); 7, Harley 2255, ff 1ᵃ–3ᵃ (1448?–49?); 8, BM Addit 34360, ff 70ᵇ–72ᵇ (1461–83).
Brown-Robbins, no 1294.
Hammond E P, Two British Museum MSS, Angl 28.1 (detailed study of MSS 6, 8).
Manly & Rickert, 1.241 (description of MS 6).
Utley CR, no 194 (suggests MS 7 compiled ca 1448–49).
Editions. Halliwell PPS 2.173 (MS 7).
Furnivall F J, Political, Religious, and Love Poems, EETS 15.46 (prints MSS 3 and 7 on opposite pages).
MacCracken EETS 192.750 (MS 7; collations from all other MSS).
Language. Hingst R, Die Sprache John Lydgates aus seinen Reimen, Greiswald 1908, p 17.
Versification. Reger, pp 41, 78 (finds 21.67 percent lines have certain epic caesurae).
Authorship. Hammond, p 461 (ascribes poem to L on basis of Shirley's ascription in MS 2).
MacCracken TPSL, appendix 2.xii; rptd EETSES 107.xiv.
Bonner F W, The Genesis of the Chaucer Apocrypha, SP 48.461 (notes that poem was once attributed to Chaucer).
SchirmerLydgate, p 233; trans Keep, p 272.
Sources and Literary Relations. Gattinger, pp 16, 49, 69, 72, 84 (notes classical references and influence of Disticha Catonis, Bestiary material, and Chaucer).
Duschl, p 51.
General References. SchirmerLydgate, p 174; trans Keep, p 199.
PearsallLydgate, p 209.

[27] CRISTE QUI LUX ES ET DIES.

MSS. 1, Trinity Camb 600, pp 195–197 (1450–75); 2, Harley 2251, ff 235ᵇ–236ᵃ (1464–83).
Brown-Robbins, no 614.
Hammond E P, Lydgate's Mumming at Hertford, Angl 22.364 (describes MS 1); Two British Museum MSS, Angl 28.1 (detailed study of MS 2).
Brusendorff A, The Chaucer Tradition, London 1925, pp 208, 466, and passim (discusses Shirley's marginalia in MS 1).
Manly & Rickert, 1.241 (description of MS 2).
Edition. MacCracken EETSES 107.235 (MS 1; collations from MS 2).
Authorship. MacCracken TPSL, appendix 2.xii; rptd EETSES 107.xiv.
SchirmerLydgate, p 232; trans Keep, p 270.
Sources and Literary Relations. SchirmerLydgate, p 162; trans Keep, p 186 (paraphrase of an ancient Latin hymn).
Literary Criticism. Wehrle W O, The Macaronic Hymn Tradition in Medieval Eng Literature, Washington 1933, p 138 (notes uncommon handling of Latin lines at beginning and end of stanzas).
General Reference. PearsallLydgate, p 260.

[28] THE DAUNCE OF MACHABREE (also THE DAUNCE OF DEATH).

MSS. 1, Bodl 2527 (Bodley 686), ff 208ᵇ–216ᵃ (1430–40); 2, Corp Christi Oxf 237, ff 146ᵃ–157ᵃ? (other foliation 142ᵃ–153ᵃ; 15 cent); 3, Cotton Vesp A.xxv, ff 172ᵃ–178ᵇ? (other foliation 181ᵃ–187ᵇ; 1475–1500; only 49 stanzas); 4, Lansdowne 699, ff 41ᵇ–66ᵇ (1450–1500; reproduced MLA Collection of Photographic Facsimiles 48); 5, Lincoln Cath 129, ff 79ᵇ–end (15 cent); 6, Leyden Univ Vossius 9, ff 29ᵇ–42ᵃ (15 cent; lacks prologue and envoy); 7, Harvard Univ *27282.67.10 (formerly Ashburnham 131), f 44ᵃ (1475–1500; stanza 22 alone inserted in text of Troy Book).
Brown-Robbins, Robbins-Cutler, no 2590 (Robbins-Cutler suggests this version and not [29] below printed by Tottel in 1554 and rptd by Dugdale).
Robinson F N, On Two MSS of Lydgate's Guy of Warwick, HSNPL 5.177 (describes MS 6).
Manly & Rickert, 1.64 (description of MS 1).

van Dorsten J A, The Leyden Lydgate MS, Scriptorium 14.315 (MS 6; also relationship of MS 6 to MSS 4 and 5).
Editions. Böddeker K, Engl Lieder u Balladen aus dem 16 Jahrhundert, JfRESL 15.115 (MS 3; prints 2 stanzas from French version on p 113; includes bibliographical introd).
Warren F and B White, The Dance of Death, EETS 181 (MS 4; collations from all MSS except MS 7; prints French version on p 79; appendices on mural paintings, the word macabre, later analogues, and printed versions); crit H M Léon, N&Q 160.342, 411, 449.
The Dance of Poulys Otherweyes Called Makabre, MLA Collection of Photographic Facsimiles 46.
Selections. Förster M, crit of EETS edn of Lydgate's Fall of Princes, AnglB 36.36 (MS 4).
Bergen H, Lydgate's Troy Book, EETSES 126.45 (prints stanza 22 of Dance found on f 44ª of MS 7).
Modernization and Abstract. Seelman W, Die Totentänze der Mittelalters, Leipzig 1891, p 55 (abstract).
Language. Hammond E P, Lydgate's Prologue to the Story of Thebes, Angl 36.360 (points out borrowings from the French for sake of rime).
Versification. Reger, pp 69, 77 (finds 4.46 percent lines have certain epic caesurae).
Hammond, Angl 36.360.
Pyle F, The Pedigree of Lydgate's Heroic Line, Hermathena 50.26 (shows that characteristics of L's line go back at least to Poema Morale; L's use of that line).
Date. Schick J, Lydgate's Temple of Glas, EETSES 60.cxii (ca 1425).
SchirmerLydgate, p 110; trans Keep, p 128 (1426–30).
Authorship. MacCracken TPSL, appendix 2.xii; rptd EETSES 107.xiv.
SchirmerLydgate, p 230; trans Keep, p 268.
Sources and Literary Relations. Douce F, The Dance of Death, London 1833, pp 29, 52, 72 (argues concept of Machabree the Doctoure not original with L; comparison with other texts).
Langlois E H, Essai historique philosophique et pittoresque sur les dances des morts, Rouen 1852, 1.92, 115, 129 (relationship of L's poem to French).
Humphreys H N, Hans Holbein's Dance of Death, London 1886, p 18 (organization of L's text similar to that of text by Guy Marchand in 1485).
Warton T, History of English Poetry, ed W C Hazlitt, London 1871, 3.55 (erratic history of Dance of Death).
Morley, 6.108 (relationship of L's poem to Walter Map).
Seelmann, Die Totentänze, p 22 (argues L's poem based on 14-cent French text rather than on Dance at the Innocents graveyard).
Flügel E, Liedersammlungen des XVI Jahrhunderts, besonders aus der Zeit Heinrichs VIII: Erth upon Erth, Angl 26.216 (mention of relationship of [28] to Erth upon Erth).
Künstle K, Die Legenden der drei Lebenden u der drei Toten u der Totentanz, Freiburg 1908 (argues L's poem belongs to earlier tradition than lost text in the Innocents graveyard).
Hammond E P, Dance Macabre, MLN 24.63 (term macabre possibly from Laurentius Machabre); Latin Texts of the Dance of Death, MP 8.399 (discusses references to L's poem in MS Balliol Coll Oxf 354 Vado mori); A MS Perhaps Lost, MLN 32.187 (Danse Macabré in Lille Libr Incunabula Dii is closest text to L's poem).
MacCracken H N, Lydgatiana, Arch 126.365 (points out technical relationship between Life of Holy Job and L's so-called tapestry poems).
Duschl, p 9 (sources and classification of proverbs).
Hammond E P, Eng Verse between Chaucer and Surrey, Durham 1927, p 192 (gives history of topics and prints Vado mori).
Patch H R, The Goddess Fortuna in Mediaeval Literature, Cambridge Mass 1927, pp 118, 163 (discusses references to centrifugal force of Fortune's wheel in L's poem and Chaucer).
Léon H M, Macabré, N&Q 161.33 (relationship of concept of macabré to Arabic cemeteries and legend of Adam and Eve).
Nichols P H, William Dunbar as a Scottish Lydgatian, PMLA 46.214 (influence of L's poem on Dunbar's Lament for the Makaris).
Kurtz L P, The Dance of Death and the Macabre Spirit in European Literature, N Y 1934, pp 139, 301 (traces Dance of Death material from antiquity to modern times).
Farnham W, The Mediaeval Heritage of Elizabethan Tragedy, Berkeley 1936, p 183 (L's poem and The Pride of Life).
Williams E C, The Dance of Death in Painting and Sculpture in the Middle Ages, Journ of the British Archaeological Assoc 3s 1.229 (discusses examples of the Dance of Death in England and in other countries).
Stegemeier H, The Dance of Death in Folksong, Chicago 1939 (first 6 lines of L's 8-line stanzas

follow pattern of Dança general).
Charney E F, La Dance Macabré, Manchester 1945, p 2 (meaning of term Macabré and relationship of L's poem to text mentioned in Journal d'un bourgeois de Paris).
Bowers R H, Iconography in Lydgate's Dance of Death, Southern Folklore Quart 12.111 (argues L's poem belongs to mediaeval tradition that ended with 18–cent graveyard poetry).
Eisler R, Danse Macabre, Trad 6.187 (L's Machabree the Doctoure derived from title of leading members in Ashkenazi Jewish burial fraternities).
Clark J M, The Dance of Death in the Middle Ages and the Renaissance, Glascow 1950, p 11 (argues L's poem follows lost mural at Innocents graveyard with addition of female characters).
SchirmerLydgate, pp 108, 111; trans Keep, pp 126, 129 (relation to legend of 3 dead and 3 living).
Cawley A C, ed, Everyman, Manchester 1961, p 31n (relates bailiff in Dance to Death's speech in Everyman).
Anderson M D, Drama and Imagery in Eng Mediaeval Churches, Cambridge 1963, p 76 (discusses relationship of L's Dance of Death to other ME versions especially the painting in the choir of Hexham).
Kolve V A, Everyman and the Parable of the Talents, Medieval Eng Drama, edd J Taylor and A H Nelson, Chicago and London 1972, p 317n (denies bailiff is source for Everyman as claimed by Cawley above).
Tristram P, Figures of Life and Death in Medieval Eng Literature, N Y 1976 (compares poem with Holbein woodcuts).
Other Scholarly Problems. Collier J P, The History of Eng Dramatic Poetry, London 1879, 1.29 (notes mention of at least one contemporary in poem).
Dufour V, La Dance des Morts, Paris 1891, p 4 (title Dance in L's poem means procession).
Smith C G, The Transition Period, N Y 1900, p 15 (L's poem suggests crisis in allegorical mood at end of Middle Ages).
Benham W and C Welch, Mediaeval London, London 1901, p 59 (mostly on St Paul's Cathedral); Old St Paul's Cathedral, London 1902, p 10 (describes building on whose walls L's poem was painted).
Wylie J H, The Reign of Henry 5th, Cambridge 1914–29, 1.51 (mostly on St Paul's Cathedral).
Gerould J H, Legends of St Wulfhad and St Ruffin at Stone Priory, PMLA 32.323 (discusses mural display and objects to label of tapestry poem).
Chew S C, The Pilgrimmage of Life, New Haven and London 1962, p 227 (L adds real person).
Literary Criticism. Gray T, Some Remarks on the Poems of John Lydgate, The Works of Thomas Gray, ed E Gosse, Edinburgh 1902, 1.387.
Reufs F, Das Naturgefühl bei Lydgate, Arch 122.269 (monasticism ruins L's originality).
Rossi, p 134.
PearsallLydgate, p 177.
General References. Warton T, History of Eng Poetry, ed W C Hazlitt, London 1871, 3.55.
Wimsatt J I, Allegory and Mirror, N Y 1970, p 168.
Bibliography. Langlois, Essai historique.
Massmann H F, Literatur der Todtentänze, Serapeum 1.241; 2.161, 209, 225; 3.328 (descriptive biblio regarding continental and Eng Dance of Death up to 1842).
SchirmerLydgate, p 228; trans Keep, p 263.

[29] THE DAUNCE OF MACHABREE WITH FIVE-STANZA PROLOGUE.

MSS. 1, Bodl 1504 (Laud Misc 735), ff 52^b–62^a (15 cent); 2, Bodl 3441 (Arch Selden Supra 53), ff 148^a–158^a (15 cent); 3, Bodl 27627 (Bodley 221), ff 53^b–62^b (15 cent); 4, Trinity Camb 601, ff 278^b–284^a (1461–83); 5, Harley 116, ff 129^a–140^b (15 cent); 6, Coventry Corp Record Office, ff 70^a–74^b (1425–75); 7, Huntington Libr EL 26.A.13 (formerly Ellesmere), ff 6^a–17^b (15 cent); 8, Rome Eng Coll 1306 (also numbered 127 and A.347), ff 111^a–121^a (1436–56; omits stanzas 7 and 52). PRINTS: 9, Fakes, Horae Beate Marie Virginis (ca 1521; 20 stanzas only; STC, no 15932); 10, Tottel, Fall of Princes (1554; rptd W Dugdale, History of St Paul's Cathedral, 1658; rptd W Dugdale, Monasticon Anglicanum, London 1673, 3.367; rptd F Douce?, The Dance of Death Painted by H Holbein and Engraved by H Hollar, London 1790; rptd A Montaiglon, The Celebrated Hans Holbein's Alphabet of Death, Paris 1856, selected stanzas from L's poem along with Holbein's woodcuts).
Brown-Robbins, Robbins-Cutler, no 2591.
Klinefelter R A, A Newly Discovered 15-Cent Eng MS, MLQ (Wash) 14.3 (description and contents of MS 8).
Robbins R H, A ME Diatribe against Philip of Burgundy, Neophil 39.131 (description and contents of MS 8).
Doyle A I and G B Pace, A New Chaucer MS, PMLA 83.22 (MS 6).
Editions. Bergen H, Lydgate's Fall of Princes, EETSES 123.1025 (PRINT 10; collations from MS 5 and MS of [29] without prologue, MS 4 in [28] above); crit M Förster, AnglB 36.33

(prints section of [29] in MS 4 in [28] above).
Hammond E P, Eng Verse between Chaucer and Surrey, Durham 1927, p 131 (MS 2; introd traces history of topic and prints Vado mori).
Warren F and B White, The Dance of Death, EETS 181 (MS 7; collations from PRINT 10 and all MSS except MS 8; prints French version on p 79; appendices on mural paintings, the word macabre, later analogues, and printed versions).
Selection. Tydeman W, Eng Poetry 1400–1580, London 1970, p 33 (lines 169–264 from Hammond edn, with notes; spelling modernized).
Scholarship: see under [28] above.

[30] ON DE PROFUNDIS (also PSALM 129).

MSS. 1, Bodl 798 (Laud Misc 683), ff 8a–11b (15 cent; stanzas 20–21 from MS 3); 2, Jesus Camb 56, ff 58a–60b (15 cent); 3, Harley 2255, ff 40a–43b (1448?–49?).
Brown-Robbins, Robbins-Cutler, no 1130.
Utley CR, no 194 (suggests MS 3 compiled ca 1448–49).
Edition. MacCracken EETSES 107.77 (MS 1; collations from all MSS).
Authorship. MacCracken TPSL, appendix 2.xii; rptd EETSES 107.xiv.
SchirmerLydgate, p 232; trans Keep, p 269.
Other Scholarly Problems. Moore S, Patrons of Letters in Norfolk and Suffolk ca 1450, PMLA 27.188 (argues patronage of de la Pole and William Curteys).
Wylie J H, The Reign of Henry 5th, Cambridge 1914–29, 1.379 (argues poem throws light on use of psalter).
SchirmerLydgate, p 155; trans Keep, p 179 (poem commissioned by William Curteys).
Deanesly M, The Lollard Bible and Other Medieval Biblical Versions, Cambridge 1920, pp 320, 336 (believes L not aware of rule against use of unlicensed Biblical translations, and notes Henry 5th used L's Psalms in private prayers).
General References. Gattinger, p 31.
Vickers K H, Humphrey of Gloucester, London 1907, p 343.
PearsallLydgate, p 259.

[31] DEATH'S WARNING (also DEATH'S WARNING TO THE WORLD and for stanzas 5–8 alone BALLAD BY JOHN LUCAS, [11] above).

MSS. 1, Bodl 21896 (Douce 322), ff 19b–20a (15 cent); 2, Camb Univ Ff.5.45, f 13a–b (1400–25); 3, Harley 1706, ff 19b–20a (15 cent).
Brown-Robbins, Robbins-Cutler, no 3143.
Edition. MacCracken EETS 192.655 (MS 1; collations from other MSS).
Authorship. MacCracken TPSL, appendix 2.xii; rptd EETSES 107.xiv.
Wager W J, Two Poems from the Booke of John Lucas, PQ 15.377 (definitely not by L; suggests Lucas).
SchirmerLydgate, p233; trans Keep, p 272 (acknowledges possibility of Lucas' authorship).
Sources and Literary Relations. MacCracken H N, Additional Light on the Temple of Glas, PMLA 23.128 (identifies stanzas in MSS 1 and 3 as excerpts from [47] below).
Wager, PQ 15.383 (claims not from [47]).
Edwards A S G, Selections from Lydgate's Fall of Princes, A Checklist, Libr 5s 26 (identifies lines from [47], 1.764–70, 806–12, 918–31, 960–66).
General References. SchirmerLydgate, p 173; trans Keep, p 198.
Woolf R, The Eng Religious Lyric in the Middle Ages, Oxford 1968, p 338.

[32] THE DEPARTYNG OF THOMAS CHAUCER.

MS. BM Addit 16165, ff 248a–249b (1425–75).
Brown-Robbins, Robbins-Cutler, no 2571.
Hammond E P, Omissions from the Edns of Chaucer, MLN 19.35 (describes MS).
Editions. Furnivall F J, N&Q 1.381; Thynnes Animadversions, ChS 2s 13.appendix 4.
Hammond E P, The Departing of Chaucer, MP 1.333 (introd describes MS); rptd M B Ruud, Thomas Chaucer, Minneapolis 1926, p 118.
MacCracken EETS 192.657.
Norton-Smith J, John Lydgate Poems, Oxford 1966, pp 2, 119 (with brief commentary, notes, and glossary).
Date. Norton-Smith, edn, p 119 (4 June 1414; lists other theories).
Authorship. MacCracken TPSL, appendix 2.xii; rptd EETSES 107.xv.
SchirmerLydgate, p 231; trans Keep, p 268.
Versification. MacCracken H N, Additional Light on the Temple of Glas, PMLA 23.128 (L's choice of rime royal suggests his hovering between two meters).
Sources and Literary Relations. MacCracken, PMLA 23.128 (points out similarities between L's poem and Verses by a Lady in Paston Letters).
Norton-Smith, edn, p 119 (this genre not much known in Middle Ages).
Other Scholarly Problems. Kittredge G L, The Nation (N Y) 2.309 (L's poem no proof against filiation

of Thomas by Geoffrey Chaucer).
Furnivall F J, Acad (London) 2.597 (L's poem proof against filiation of Thomas by Geoffrey Chaucer).
Ruud, Thomas Chaucer, p 86 (L's poem no proof against filiation of Thomas by Geoffrey Chaucer).
Bennett OHEL, p 116 (L's poem suggestive of Shirley's purpose in compiling MSS).
SchirmerLydgate, p 51; trans Keep, p 59 (L's poem does not prove L's personal acquaintance with Chaucer but suggests his relation to Chaucer's family).
Stevens J, Music & Poetry in the Early Tudor Court, London 1961, p 161 (corrects MacCracken's gloss and suggests name Alice is concealed).
General Reference. PearsallLydgate, p 162.

[33] DEUS IN NOMINE TUO SALUUM ME FAC (also PSALM 53).

MSS. 1, Bodl 6943 (Ashmole 59), ff 69b–70a, 134b (1447–56); 2, Cotton Calig A.ii, ff 64b–65a (1400–50); 3, Harley 116, f 127a (15 cent); 4, Harley 2255, ff 146b–148a (1448?–49?).
Brown-Robbins, no 951.
Utley CR, no 194 (suggests MS 4 compiled ca 1448–49).
Editions. MacCracken EETSES 107.10 (MS 2; collations from all MSS), 13 (prints stanzas 8–10 of other rendition of same psalm attributed to Lydgate on f 148a of MS 2).
Patterson, p 72 (MS 2).
Authorship. MacCracken TPSL, appendix 2.xiii; rptd EETSES 107.xv.
SchirmerLydgate, p 232; trans Keep, p 269.
Sources and Literary Relations. SchirmerLydgate, p 155; trans Keep, p 179 (early counterpart of [30] above; paraphrase of Psalm 53).
Other Scholarly Problems. Deanesly M, The Lollard Bible and Other Medieval Biblical Versions, Cambridge 1920, pp 320, 336 (believes L probably unaware of rule against unlicensed use of Biblical translations, and notes Henry 5th used L's Psalms in private prayers).
General References. Gattinger, 4.31.
Vickers K H, Humphrey of Gloucester, London 1907, p 343.

[34] DIETARY (also A DIETARY AND A DOCTRINE FOR PESTILENCE and MEDICINA STOMACHI).

MSS. 1, Bodl 798 (Laud Misc 683), ff 60a–62a?

(15 cent); 2, Bodl 1885 (Bodley 48), f 332b (late 15-cent hand in early 15-cent MS); 3, Bodl 2527 (Bodley 686), ff 187b–188b (1430–40); 4, Bodl 3510 (e Mus 52), f 80b (1500–25); 5, Bodl 6922 (Ashmole 61), ff 107a–108a (14 cent; not in Brown Reg entry); 6, Bodl 11914 (Rawl C.48), ff 129a–130a? (15 cent); 7, Bodl 11951 (Rawl C.86), f 61a (1475–1500; 10 stanzas only); 8, Bodl 14529 (Rawl poet F.35), ff 17b–18b (1475–1500; 10 stanzas only); 9, Bodl 29179 (Add B.60), ff 122b–125b? (1475–1500; written as prose); 10, Bodl 30437 (Bodley 912), f 15b (15-cent hand in 14-cent MS); 11, Bodl Lat th.d.15, f 132a; 12, Univ Coll Oxf 60, pp 278–280 (15 cent); 13, Jesus Camb 56, ff 44b–46a (15 cent); 14, St John's Camb 191, ff 167b–168a? (1475–1500; 10 stanzas only); 15, Trinity Camb 263, ff 112b–113b (1425–75); 16, Trinity Camb 1117, f 132a–b (15 cent); 17, Fitzwilliam Mus 261, ff 30a–32b (1480–1520); 18, Arundel 168, f 14b (15 cent); 19, Cotton Calig A.ii, ff 15b–17a? (1400–50); 20, Cotton Titus D.xx, ff 93a–94a (begins at line 35; poem not listed in Cottonian cat); 21, Egerton 1995, ff 77b–78b? (15 cent); 22, Harley 541, ff 207a–b, 209b–212a? (16 cent; leaf misplaced); 23, Harley 941, ff 24a–25b? (15 cent); 24, Harley 2251, ff 4b–5b (1464–83); 25, Harley 2252, ff 1b–2a? (16 cent); 26, Harley 4011, f 143a (1450–1500; lines 1–58; ends imperfectly); 27, Harley 5401, f 103a (15–16 cent; lines 1–61); 28, Lansdowne 699, ff 85b–88b (1450–1500; 18 stanzas); 29, Royal 17.B.xlvii, ff 2a–3b? (1425–85; 11 stanzas); 30, Stowe 982, ff 11a–12b (1475–1500); 31, Sloane 775, ff 54a–56b? (15 cent); 32, Sloane 989, ff 134a–136b (1450–1500); 33, Sloane 3534, ff 1a–? (15 cent); 34, BM Addit 10099, ff 211b–? (15 cent; 13 stanzas disarranged); 35, BM Addit 11307, ff 124a–126a (10 stanzas), 126a–end? (13 stanzas; 15 cent); 36, BM Addit 31042, f 97a–b (15 cent by Robert Thornton; lines 1–17 lacking); 37, BM Addit 34360, ff 63a–64b? (1461–83); 38, Nat Libr Scot 1.1.6 (Advocates), ff 73a–74a (1568; Bannatyne MS); 39, Edinburgh Univ 205 (also Laing 149 and Makculloch MS), f 190a–b (MS proper 1477; Dietary insertion 1490–1510); 40, Hunterian Mus 259 (also U.4.17), pp 50–52? (or ff 25b–26b; 1475–1500; 9 stanzas); 41, Lambeth 444, ff 177b–180a (15 cent); 42, Nottingham Univ MeLMl (formerly Mellish), endleaves (15 cent); 43, Soc of Antiquaries 101, ff 43a–44a (15 cent); 44, Wellcome Hist Med Libr 406 (formerly Loscombe, formerly Ashburnham 122), ff 39b–40b 1400–1425); 45, Wellcome Hist Med Libr 411, ff 2b–

3ᵇ (1475–1500); 46, Trinity Dublin 516, ff 27ᵇ–28ᵇ (1450–1500); 47, Trinity Dublin 537 (to stanza 16, variant), f 73ᵃ⁻ᵇ (15 cent); 48, formerly Clumber (sold by Sotheby's, 1937, lot 1129), ff 83ᵇ–?; 49, formerly Schwerdt (Sotheby Sale, 12 March 1942; present location unknown); 50, Leyden Univ Vossius 9, ff 98ᵇ–100ᵇ (15 cent); 51, Lille Univ Libr 204 (1180), ff 1ᵃ–2ᵇ; 52, Rome Eng Coll 1306 (also numbered 127 and A.347), ff 87ᵇ–88ᵇ (1436–56; lines 1–24 and 33–96 lacking); 53, Nat Libr of Medicine 4, ff 64ᵃ–67ᵇ (1400–25; 10 stanzas); 54, Huntington Libr HM.183 (formerly Hawkins), Art 4 (15 cent). PRINTS: 55, Caxton, The Governayle of Helthe, 1489 (STC, no 12138; see MS Egerton 1995; rptd W Blades, last four unnumbered pages of facsimile of Governayle, London 1858); 56, Pynson, The Kalender of Shepherdes, 1506 (rptd H O Sommer, London 1892, 3.118); 57, de Worde, ca 1510 (STC, no 12139).

Brown-Robbins, Robbins-Cutler, no 824.

Blades W, The Biography and Typography of William Caxton, N Y 1882, p 340 (describes PRINT 55).

Robinson F N, On Two MSS of Lydgate's Guy of Warwick, HSNPL 5.177 (describes MS 50).

Hammond E P, Two British Museum MSS, Angl 28.1 (detailed study of MSS 24, 37).

Stevenson, edn, p xiv (MS 39).

Bühler C F, A Note on Lydgate's Verses on the Kings of England, RES 9.47 (lists variations from Halliwell PPS 2 in MS 46).

Mayer C F, A Medieval English Leechbook and Its 14-Cent Poem on Bloodletting, Bull of the History of Medicine 7.381 (describes MS 53).

Manly & Rickert, 1.64, 241 (description of MSS 3, 24).

Klinefelter R A, A Newly Discovered 15-Cent Eng MS, MLQ (Wash) 14.3 (description and contents of MS 52).

Robbins R H, A ME Diatribe against Philip of Burgundy, Neophil 39.131 (description and contents of MS 52).

Ringler BEV, p 153.

van Dorsten J A, The Leyden Lydgate MS, Scriptorium 14.315 (MS 49).

Gray D, A Copy of Lydgate's Dietary at Lille, N&Q ns 15(213). 245 (MS 51).

Davis N, Chaucer's Gentilesse A Forgotten MS with Some Proverbs, RES ns 20.43 (MS 42).

Stern J, The London Thornton Miscellany A New Description of BM Addit MS 31042, Scriptorium 30.26, 201, 216 (MS 36).

Editions. Blades W, The Governayle of Helthe, London 1858, last 4 unnumbered pages of appendix An Annotated Reprint of the Foregoing Tract (PRINT 55; collations from MSS 24, 28, 32; prints stanzas 5–12 in Introd, pp 13–16, from MS 32).

Brydges S E, Censura Literaria, London 1805–09, 7.345 (MS 24; collations from MS 54).

Halliwell PPS 2.66 (MS 24); rptd W A Neilson and K G T Webster, The Chief British Poets of the 14th and 15th Centuries, Boston 1916, p 221.

Murdoch J B, Bannatyne Manuscript, Hunterian Club, Glasgow 1896, 2.196 (MS 40).

Förster M, Kleinere me Texte, Angl 42.182 (MS 33; collations from MSS 7, 8, 14, 18, 24, 32, 39, 40, 41; see MSS of [35] below and Sommer's edn of Pynson's Kalender of Shepherdes; commentary notes that stanzas 13, 19, 21 correspond to stanzas 183–85 of [166] below).

Stevenson G, Pieces from the Makculloch and the Gray MSS, PSTS 65, Edinburgh and London 1918, p 30 (MS 39).

Ritchie W T, The Bannatyne Manuscript, PSTS ns 22.178 (MS 38; incomplete text).

Bühler C, Lydgate's Rules of Health in MS Lansdowne 699, MÆ 3.53 (MS 28; collations from MSS 1, 6, 34, PRINT 56 and Sommer's edn of it, and W Blades' print of Caxton's Governayle of Helthe).

MacCracken EETS 192.703 (MS 28; collations from MSS 12, 50).

Robbins SL, pp 73 (MS 7), 251 (notes poem's enormous popularity).

Selections. Skeat W W, The Bruce, EETSES 21.537 (MS 14; stanzas 4, 13–21 of MacCracken's numbering); The Bruce, PSTS 32.215 (MS 14; stanzas 4, 13–21 of MacCracken's numbering).

Ward T H, The English Poet, London and N Y 1895, 1.121.

Kaiser R, Medieval English, 3rd edn, Berlin 1958, p 507 (stanzas 1–3; MS 33).

Modernization. Heseltine G C, The Kalendar and Compost of Shepherds, London 1931.

Textual Matters. Gattinger, p 83.

Bühler C F, A Note on Lydgate's Verses on the Kings of England, RES 9.47.

Versification. Reger, pp 41, 78 (finds 17.72 percent lines have certain epic caesurae).

Authorship. Blades W, The Biography and Typography of William Caxton, N Y 1882, p 340 (suggests L's authorship on basis of MS Harley 116).

MacCracken TPSL, appendix 2.xiii; rptd EETSES 107.xv.

Bühler, MÆ 3.52 (ascribes poem to L on basis of rime and meter).

Schirmer Lydgate, p 230; trans Keep, p 267.

Sources and Literary Relations. Förster, Angl 42.176 (original is 12-cent Latin Flos medicinæ).
Other Scholarly Problems. Gattinger, p 19 (notes insertion of moral doctrine).
Bennett OHEL, pp 121, 158 (L's poem most popular of 15-cent works dealing with bodily health).
Mullet C F, John Lydgate: a Mirror of Medieval Medicine, Bull of the History of Medicine 22.403 (L's principal argument is against overeating).
General References. SchirmerLydgate, pp 93, 95; trans Keep, pp 109, 111.
PearsallLydgate, p 219.

[35] DIETARY IN DISARRANGED ORDER (stanzas 2, 1, 8, 9, 3, 6, 5, 10).

MSS. 1, Harley 116, ff 166a–167a ? (15 cent); 2, Lambeth 853, pp 182–185 (1425–50).
Brown-Robbins, Robbins-Cutler, no 1418.
Editions. Furnivall F J, The Babees Book, EETS 32.54 (MS 2; prints Latin dietary on opposite pages).
Stevenson G, Pieces from the Makculloch and the Gray MSS, PSTS 65, Edinburgh and London 1918, p 296 (MS 2).
Literary Relations. Brown-Robbins, no 3087 (notes incorporation of and relation to proverbs in -ly).
Scholarship. See under [34] above.

[36] DIETARY: A DOCTRINE FOR PESTILENCE (also A DOCTRYNE FOR PESTILENCE).

MSS. 1, Bodl 798 (Laud Misc 683), f 62a (15 cent; only MS in which Dietary precedes Doctryne instead of following it); 2, Bodl 11914 (Rawl C.48), f 128b (15 cent); 3, Jesus Camb 56, f 44a (15 cent; 1 extra stanza); 4, Lansdowne 699, f 85b (1450–1500; 8 extra stanzas); 5, BM Addit 10099, f 211a (15 cent); 6, Trinity Dublin 537, f 73a–b (15 cent); 7, Leyden Univ Vossius 9, f 98b (15 cent; 8 extra stanzas); 8, Huntington Libr HM.183 (formerly Hawkins), Art 4 (15 cent); 9, Nat Libr of Medicine 4, ff 66b–67a (1400–25). PRINTS: 10, Caxton, The Governayle of Helthe, 1475–1500 (rptd W Blades, 4 unnumbered pages from end of facsimile of Governayle, London 1858); 11, Pynson, The Kalendar of Shepherdes, 1506 (rptd S E Brydges, Censura Literaria, London 1805–09, 7.345; rptd H O Sommer, The Kalendar of Shepherdes, London 1892, 3.118).
Brown-Robbins, Robbins-Cutler, no 4112.
Mayer C F, A Medieval Eng Leechbook and Its 14-Cent Poem on Bloodletting, Bull of the History of Medicine 7.381 (describes MS 9).
van Dorsten J A, The Leyden Lydgate MS, Scriptorium 14.315 (MS 7).
Editions. Brydges S E, Censura Literaria, London 1805–09, 7.345 (MS 8; see above under PRINT 11).
Blades W, The Governayle of Helthe, London 1858, p 12? (MS 4; see above under PRINT 10).
Cohen H L, The Ballade, N Y 1915, p 263 (MS 4; commentary argues Doctryne must have been originally conceived as ballade).
Bühler C F, Lydgate's Rules of Health in MS Lansdowne 699, MÆ 3.52 (MS 4; collations from MSS 1, 2, 5, PRINT 11 and Sommer's reprint, and Blades' reprint of PRINT 10).
MacCracken EETS 192.702 (MS 4).
Modernization. Heseltine G C, The Kalendar and Compost of Shepherds, London 1931, p 116.
Authorship. MacCracken TPSL, appendix 2.xiii; rptd EETSES 107.xv.
Bühler, MÆ 3.52 (ascribes poem to L on basis of rime and meter).
SchirmerLydgate, p 230; trans Keep, p 267.
Other Scholarly Problems. Mullet C F, John Lydgate: a Mirror of Medieval Medicine, Bull of the History of Medicine 22.403 (L's principal argument is against overeating).
General References. SchirmerLydgate, pp 93, 95; trans Keep, pp 109, 111.
PearsallLydgate, p 219.

[37] BEWARE OF DOUBLENESSE.

MSS. 1, Bodl 3896 (Fairfax 16), f 199a–b (1400–50; error in MS pagination); 2, Bodl 6919 (Ashmole 39), end cover (1450–1500; envoy only); 3, Bodl 6943 (Ashmole 59), ff 47b–48b (1447–56; 11 stanzas); 4, Harley 7578, ff 17b–18b (1425–75); 5, BM Addit 16165, ff 252a–253b (1425–75); 6, Naples Nat Libr XIII.B.29, p 146 (1457; envoy only). PRINT: 7, Stowe, Chaucer, 1561 (STC, no 5075; rptd R Anderson, The Complete Edn of the Poets of Great Britain, London 1795, 1.580; rptd A Chalmers, The Works of the Eng Poets, London 1810, 1.557).
Brown-Robbins, Robbins-Cutler, nos 2602 (Envoy only), 3656.
Koch J, Die neapolitanische Handschrift von Chaucer's Clerk's Tale, Beitrage zur neuren Philologie, 1902, p 257.
Hammond E P, The Departing of Chaucer, MP 1.331 (describes MS 5); Ashmole 59 and Other Shirley MSS, Angl 30.320 (describes MS 2 and compares it to other Shirley MSS); Omissions

from the Edns of Chaucer, MLN 19.35 (describes MS 5).
Manly & Rickert, 1.376 (description of MS 6).
Editions. (See edns of Chaucer: Urry, Bell, Anderson, revised Bell).
Oxf Ch, 7.291 (MS 1; collations from PRINT 7).
MacCracken EETS 192.438 (MS 1; collations from MSS 3, 4, 5).
Davies R T, Medieval Eng Lyrics, London 1962, pp 189 (MSS 1, 4, 5; slightly normalized with glosses at foot of page), 343 (briefly discusses poem; notes).
Tydeman W, Eng Poetry 1400–1580, London 1970, p 30 (from MacCracken edn; notes).
Selections. Black W H, Catalogue of Ashmole MSS, Oxford 1845, p 61 (MS 2; envoy only).
Vallese T, La novelle del chierico de Oxford, Naples 1939, p 77 (envoy only).
Lauritis J A, R A Klinefelter and V F Gallagher, A Critical Edn of John Lydgate's Life of Our Lady, Duquesne Stud Philological Series 2, Pittsburgh 1961, p 40 (envoy only from MS 2).
Modernization. Clarke C C, The Riches of Chaucer, London 1835, 2.307.
Abstracts. Utley CR, nos 230 (envoy), 307 (poem).
Language. Hingst R, Die Sprache John Lydgates aus seinen Reimen, Greiswald 1908, p 47.
Authorship. Tyrwhitt T, Account of the Works of Chaucer, Edinburgh 1775 (rejects Chaucer's authorship and accepts L's on basis of Shirley's ascription in MS 3).
Skeat W W, The Chaucer Canon, Oxford 1900, p 119 (accepts L's authorship on basis of MS 1 and Shirley's MSS 3 and 5).
MacCracken TPSL, appendix 2.xiii; rptd EETSES 107.xv.
Hammond, p 421 (accepts L's authorship on basis of MS 3).
SchirmerLydgate, p 229; trans Keep, p 266.
Seaton, p 228 (claims Richard Roos).
Sources and Literary Relations. Patch H R, The Goddess Fortuna in Mediaeval Literature, Cambridge Mass 1927, pp 157, 169 (discusses treatment of Fortune's wheel in L's poem and other texts).
Other Scholarly Problems. Bonner F W, The Genesis of the Chaucer Apocrypha, SP 48.461.
Renoir A, Attitudes to Women in Lydgate's Poetry, ESts 42.9 (antifeminist).
Seaton, p 228 (argues poem contains name anagrams).
Literary Criticism. Reufs F, Das Naturgefühl bei Lydgate, Arch 122.269 (argues monasticism ruins L's originality).
General References. SchirmerLydgate, p 82; trans Keep, p 97.
RenoirLydgate, p 81.
PearsallLydgate, p 216.

[38] DUODECIM ABUSIONES (also GO FORTH KYNG, ADVICE TO THE SEVERAL ESTATES, and TO THE ESTATES).

MSS. No MS extant. PRINTS: 1, de Worde, The Temple of Glas, ca 1498 (STC, no 17032a; rptd E G Duff, 15-Cent Eng Books, Oxford 1917, p 76); 2, de Worde, ca 1500 (STC, no 17033; rptd T F Dibdin, Typographical Antiquities, London 1912, 2.303; Duff, 15-Cent Eng Books, p 77); 3, Thynne, Chaucer, 1532; 4, Stowe, Chaucer, 1561.
Brown-Robbins, Robbins-Cutler, no 920.
Editions. Anderson R, The Works of the British Poets, London 1795, 1.579.
Schick J, Lydgate's Temple of Glas, EETSES 60.68 (PRINT 1).
Oxf Ch, 1.40 (PRINT 4); 7.408 (PRINT 3).
MacCracken EETS 192.707 (PRINT 1).
Robbins-HP, p 232 (PRINT 1).
Modernization. Clarke C C, The Riches of Chaucer, London 1835, 2.305.
Versification. Reger, pp 62, 78 (finds 21.42 percent lines have certain epic caesurae).
Authorship. MacCracken TPSL, appendix 2.xiii; rptd EETSES 107.xvi.
SchirmerLydgate, p 230; trans Keep, p 267.
Sources and Literary Relations. SchirmerLydgate, p 94; trans Keep, p 111 (L's poem is adaptation and illustration of proverb in Latin).
Robbins-HP, p 324 (discusses the tradition).
Other Scholarly Problems. Bonner F W, The Genesis of the Chaucer Apocrypha, SP 48.461.
Literary Criticism. Reufs F, Das Naturgefühl bei Lydgate, Arch 122.269 (argues monasticism ruins L's originality).
General Reference. PearsallLydgate, p 220.
Bibliography. Ringler BEV, p 163.
Robbins-HP, p 387.

[39] EAGLE AS NEW YEAR GIFT (also BALLADE ON A NEW YEAR'S GIFT OF AN EAGLE PRESENTED TO KING HENRY VI).

MSS. 1, Trinity Camb 600, pp 149–152 (1450–75); 2, Harley 2251, ff 249^b–250^b (1464–83); 3, BM Addit 29729, ff 145^b–146^b (John Stowe; 1558).
Brown-Robbins, Robbins-Cutler, no 3604.

Hammond E P, Lydgate's Mumming at Hertford, Angl 22.364 (describes MS 1); Two British Museum MSS, Angl 28.1 (detailed study of MS 2).
Brusendorff A, The Chaucer Tradition, London 1925, pp 208, 466, and passim (discusses Shirley's marginalia in MS 1).
Editions. Halliwell PPS 2.113 (MS 2).
MacCracken, EETS 192.649 (MS 1; collations from all MSS).
Robbins SL, p 88 (MS 1).
Versification. Reger, pp 42, 77 (finds 6.49 percent lines have certain epic caesurae).
Authorship. MacCracken TPSL, appendix 2.xix; rptd EETSES 107.xxii.
SchirmerLydgate, p 230; trans Keep, p 267.
Sources and Literary Relations. Gattinger, pp 20, 68, 72 (occasional poem influenced by Chaucer).
Literary Criticism. Knowlton E C, Nature in ME, JEGP 20.186 (discusses typically Lydgatian handling of nature in the poem).
SchirmerLydgate, p 114; trans Keep, p 133 (argues stately tone of poem looks back to time of Henry 5).
General Reference. Robbins SL, p 258 (occasion for poem).

[40] BANNER OF ST EDMUND.

MSS. 1, Bodl 6930 (Ashmole 46), ff 85^b–87^a? (15 cent); 2, Bodl 10174 (Tanner 347), ff 86^b–88^b? (15 cent); 3, Corp Christi Oxf 61, ff 64^b–65^b? (15 cent); 4, Camb Univ Ee.2.15, ff 88^b–90^a? (Brown-Robbins has f 104^b; 1470–1500); 5, Harley 372, ff 43^b–45^a? (1433–71); 6, Harley 2278, ff 2^a–4^a? (time of Henry 6?).
Brown-Robbins, no 530.
Editions. AELeg 1881, p 376 (MS 6; collations from MS 1).
Hervey F, Corolla Sancti Edmundi, London 1907, p 409 (MS 6).
Scholarship. See under [42] below.

[41] MIRACLES OF ST EDMUND.

MSS. 1, Bodl 798 (Laud Misc 683), f 24^{a-b} (15 cent); 2, Bodl 6930 (Ashmole 46), ff 87^a–97^a? (15 cent); 3, Bodl 10174 (Tanner 347), ff 88^b–end? (15 cent).
Brown-Robbins, no 1843.
Edition. AELeg 1881, p 440 (MS 2).
Date. Schick J, Lydgate's Temple of Glas, EETSES 60.cxii (1444).
Gerould S Leg, p 264 (1444; last of L's saints' legends that can be dated).
SchirmerLydgate, p 143; trans Keep, p 165 (probably 1444).
Authorship. MacCracken TPSL, appendix 2.xviii; rptd EETSES 107.xxi.
SchirmerLydgate, p 231; trans Keep, p 268.
Sources and Literary Relations. SchirmerLydgate, p 143; trans Keep, p 165 (L's poem reminiscent of Chaucer's Prioress' Tale).
Literary Criticism. Gerould S Leg, p 264 (composed as appendix to St Edmund's life and equally dull).

[42] LIFE OF SS EDMUND AND FREMUND.

MSS. 1, Bodl 6930 (Ashmole 46), ff 1^a–84^b? (15 cent); 2, Bodl 10174 (Tanner 347), ff 1^a–86^b? (15 cent; stanzas 1–190); 3, Bodl 11568 (Rawl B.216), ff 162^b–end (15 cent; stanzas 1–190); 4, Corp Christi Oxf 61, ff 1^a–63^b? (15 cent); 5, Camb Univ Ee.2.15, ff 48^a–105^b (1470–1500; lines 1–119 lacking); 6, Harley 247, ff 45^a–48^a? (16 cent; an extract by John Stowe); 7, Harley 372, ff 1^a–42^b? (1440–60); 8, Harley 2278, ff 6^a–end (time of Henry 6?); 9, Harley 4826, ff 4^a–45^a? (15 cent); 10, Harley 7333, ff 136^a–147^a? (1425–75); 11, Chetham Libr 6709, ff 199^a–282^b, Art 6 (1490); 12, Exeter Misc Rolls 59 (1450–1500; fragment containing 1.1032–2.14 used as cover for other MS); 13, Yates Thompson 47 (formerly Mostyn Hall 84), pp 1–end (15 cent).
Brown-Robbins, Robbins-Cutler, no 3440.
Warton T, History of Eng Poetry, ed W C Hazlitt, London 1871, 3.56 (describes MS 8).
Royal Commission on Historical MSS, 4th Report, London 1873, 4.350 (MS 13, then in Mostyn Hall).
Manly & Rickert, 1.82 and 126 (description of MSS 5, 11).
Rickert M, Painting in Britain The Middle Ages, London 1954, p 198 (describes miniatures in MS 8).
Edwards A S G and J I Miller, Stow and Lydgate's St Edmund, N&Q ns 20(218).367 (Stow annotated MS 13).
Editions. AELeg 1881, p 378 (MS 8).
Hervey F, Corolla Sancti Edmundi, London 1907, p 412 (MS 8).
Clarke D E M, A New Lydgate MS, MLR 24.324 (describes and prints MS 12, fragment of 1.1032–2.14).
Selection. Benham W, Old St Paul's Cathedral,

London 1902, p 62 (6 stanzas, lines 3.1331–72 in AELeg).
Textual Matters. Hammond E P, On the Text of Chaucer's Parlement of Foules, Decenial Publications of the Univ of Chicago 1s 7.3 (notes textual changes for sake of meter by scribe of MS 1).
Abstract. Loomis G, The Growth of the St Edmund Legend, HSNPL 14.83.
Language. Schick J, Lydgate's Temple of Glas, EETSES 60.1xix.
Skeat B M, The Lamentatyon of Mary Magdaleyne, Cambridge 1897, p 27 (argues final es usually sounded, final e occasionally sounded, final ed seldom sounded).
Dibelius W, John Capgrave u die engl Schriftsprache, Angl 23.153, 323.
Hingst R, Die Sprache John Lydgates aus seinen Reimen, Greiswald 1908.
Babcock C F, A Study of the Metrical Use of the Inflectional e in ME with Particular Reference to Chaucer and Lydgate, PMLA 29.59 (L's language bridges gap between Middle Ages and Modern Period).
Versification. Schick, EETSES 60.1v.
Reger, pp 46, 78 (finds 16.13 percent lines have certain epic caesurae).
Pyle F, The Pedigree of Lydgate's Heroic Line, Hermathena 50.26 (shows that characteristics of L's line go back to Poema Morale; discusses L's use of that line).
Southworth J G, The Prosody of Chaucer and His Followers, Oxford 1962, p 76 (L's verse is rhythmic not metrical).
Date. Schick, EETSES 60.cxii (1433).
Gerould S Leg, p 262 (begun 1433).
Authorship. MacCracken TPSL, appendix 2.xxii; rptd EETSES 107.xxv.
SchirmerLydgate, p 231; trans Keep, p 268.
Sources and Literary Relations. Butler A, The Lives of the Fathers, Martyrs, and Other Principal Saints, London 1833, 11.416 (gist of legend with references to L's poem and others).
Duschl, p 9 (sources and classification of proverbs).
MacCracken H N, Lydgatiana, Arch 129.50 (organization of [98] below based on [42] and L's legend of St Alban, [1] above).
McKeehan I P, Some Relationships between the Legends of British Saints and Mediaeval Romance, Univ of Chicago Abstracts of Theses, Humanistic Series 2.383 (argues L's poem is last in series of St Edmund lives showing influence of secular heroic romances); St Edmund of East Anglia: the Development of a Romantic Legend, Univ of Colorado Stud 15.13 (L's poem somewhat similar to Denis Pyramus' Vie Seint Edmund le Rey in respect to romantic characteristics).
Loomis, HSNPL 14.83 (L follows composite source; material for early life of Edmund probably taken from Geoffrey of Wells).
SchirmerLydgate, p 141; trans Keep, p 162 (principal sources of L's poem are Latin lives of Edmund and Fremund, printed C Horstmann, Nova Legenda Angliae, Oxford 1891, 2.575, 689).
Wolpers T, Die engl Heiligenlegende des Mittelalters, Tübingen 1964, p 316 (discusses L's sources and his departures from them).
PearsallLydgate, p 280 (influence).
Miller J I, Literature to History Exploring a Medieval Saint's Legend and Its Context, Literature and History, ed I E Cadenhead, Univ of Tulsa Monograph Series no 9, Tulsa 1970, p 59 (independence in use of Latin prose source); Lydgate the Hagiographer as Literary Artist, The Learned and the Lewed, ed L Benson, Harvard Eng Stud 5, Cambridge Mass 1974, p 280.
Edwards and Miller, N&Q ns 20(218).365.
Other Scholarly Problems. Wylie J H, The Reign of Henry 5th, Cambridge 1914–29, 1.476 (L's poem suggests paraphernalia in royal bedrooms).
Moore S, Patrons of Letters in Norfolk and Suffolk ca 1450, PMLA 27.188 (argues poem is proof of patronage of de la Pole and William Curteys).
Literary Criticism. CBEL, 2.203.
Reufs F, Das Naturgefühl bei Lydgate, Arch 122.269 (monasticism ruins L's originality).
Gerould S Leg, p 262.
Wolpers, Heiligenlegende, p 316 (discusses L's splendid style and interest in spiritual rather than narrative possibilities of the story).
PearsallLydgate, p 281.
Miller, Lydgate the Hagiographer, p 279 (poem has carefully balanced literary form).
Bibliography. Lowndes W T, Bibliographer's Manual, ed H Bohn, London 1864, 3.1419.

[43] EPISTELL TO SIBILLE.

MS. Bodl 6943 (Ashmole 59), ff 59^b–62^a (1447–56).
Brown-Robbins, Robbins-Cutler, no 3321.
Hammond E P, Ashmole 59 and Other Shirley MSS, Angl 30.320 (describes MS).
Edition. MacCracken EETSES 107.14.
Abstract. Utley CR, no 283.

Date. PearsallLydgate, p 169 (1422–33).
Authorship. MacCracken TPSL, appendix 2.xvii; rptd EETSES 107.xx.
SchirmerLydgate, p 234; trans Keep, p 273.
Sources and Literary Relations. Utley CR, no 283 (notes use of Proverbs 31.10–31 and similarities with Christine de Pisan's Livre du Duc des Vrais Amans).
SchirmerLydgate, p 178; trans Keep, p 204 (L's poem is a moral-didactic adaptation of Proverbs 31.10–31).
General References. Edwards A S G, Lydgate's Attitudes to Women, ESts 51.437.
PearsallLydgate, p 82 (brief account of L's patron Sibille Boys), p 169 (poem is a skillful amplification of Proverbs 31.10–31).

[44] EVERYTHING DRAWETH TO HIS SEMBLABLE (also EVERYTHING TO HIS SEMBLABLE and A NATURAL BALADE BY LYDEGATE).

MSS. 1, Bodl 6943 (Ashmole 59), ff 18a–21a (1447–56); 2, Harley 2251, ff 19b–23a (1464–83; lacks stanza 23).
Brown-Robbins, Robbins-Cutler, no 3800.
Hammond E P, Two British Museum MSS, Angl 28.1 (detailed study of MS 2); Ashmole 59 and Other Shirley MSS, Angl 30.320 (description of MS 1).
Manly & Rickert, 1.241 (description of MS 2).
Edition. MacCracken EETS 192.801 (MS 1; collations from MS 2).
Authorship. MacCracken TPSL, appendix 2.xxiv; rptd EETSES 107.xxvii.
SchirmerLydgate, p 233; trans Keep, p 272.
General References. SchirmerLydgate, p 174; trans Keep, p 199 (L's poem is a little compendium of mediaeval occupations and cultural history).
PearsallLydgate, p 214.

[45] AN EXORTACION TO PRESTYS (also POEMS ON THE MASS, I).

MSS. 1, Balliol 354, ff 154a–155a (1518–38; text follows upon [87] below without break); 2, Caius Camb 174, pp 453–454 (1475–1500); text follows upon [87] below without break); 3, Trinity Camb 601, f 205a–b (1461–83; with Envoy from MS 2).
Brown-Robbins, Robbins-Cutler, no 4249.
Edition. MacCracken EETSES 107.84 (MS 3; collations from MSS 1, 2).
Modernization. Watts N, Love Songs of Sion, N Y Cincinnati and Chicago 1924, p 10 (based on MS 3).

Authorship. MacCracken EETSES 107.xx (entered with [87]).
SchirmerLydgate, p 231; trans Keep, p 269 (entered with [87]).
General Reference. SchirmerLydgate, p 152; trans Keep, p 175.

[46] FABULA DUORUM MERCATORUM.

MSS. 1, Bodl 14526 (Rawl Poet F.32), ff 38a–53b (1450–1500; ends imperfectly); 2, Camb Univ Hh.4.12, ff 58a–74a (1475–1500); 3, Harley 2251, ff 55a–70a (1464–83); 4, Harley 2255, ff 72a–88a (1448?–49?); 5, Lansdowne 699, ff 3a–18a (1450–1500); 6, BM Addit 34360, ff 4a–18b (1461–83); 7, Leyden Univ Vossius 9, ff 49a–65a (15 cent).
Brown-Robbins, Robbins-Cutler, no 1481.
Robinson F N, On Two MSS of Lydgate's Guy of Warwick, HSNPL 5.177 (describes MS 7).
Hammond E P, Two British Museum MSS, Angl 28.1 (detailed study of MSS 3, 6).
Utley CR, no 194 (suggests MS 4 compiled ca 1448–49).
van Dorsten J A, The Leyden Lydgate MS, Scriptorium 14.315 (MS 7).
Editions. Zupitza J and G Schleich, QF 83 (from all MSS except 2, 7; commentary discusses influence of Chaucer on L).
MacCracken EETS 192.486 (MS 4; collations from all MSS except MS 2).
Language. Dibelius W, John Capgrave u die engl Schriftsprache, Angl 23.153, 323.
Hingst R, Die Sprache John Lydgates aus seinen Reimen, Greiswald 1908.
Hüttmann E, Das Partizipium Präsentis bei Lydgate im Vergleich mit Chaucers gebrauch, Kiel 1914.
Versification. Schick J, Lydgate's Temple of Glas, EETSES 60.1vi.
Reger, pp 61, 78 (finds 11.76 percent lines have certain epic caesurae).
Authorship. MacCracken TPSL, appendix 2.xiii; rptd EETSES 107.xvi.
SchirmerLydgate, p 231; trans Keep, p 268.
Seaton, p 273 (argues for Richard Roos).
Sources and Literary Relations. Herrtage S J H, The Early Eng Versions of the Gesta Romanorum, EETSES 33.xxi (notes influence of Gesta Romanorum on L's poem).
Duschl, p 9 (sources and classification of proverbs).
Lowes J L, Heroes Again, MLN 31.185 (argues that account of merchant's sickness draws more on contemporary lore than upon Chaucer's

Knight's Tale).
Jenkins C, Some Aspects of Medieval Latin Literature, in The Legacy of the Middle Ages, ed C G Crump and E F Jacob, Oxford 1926, p 159 (notes influence of Gesta Romanorum on L's poem).
Hammond E P, Boethius: Chaucer: Walton: Lydgate, MLN 41.534 (argues Boethian influence in contrast to [47] below).
Patch H R, The Goddess Fortuna in Mediaeval Literature, Cambridge Mass 1927, pp 81, 85, 94, 120 (points out similarities in treatment of Fortune in this and other works).
SchirmerLydgate, p 208; trans Keep, p 238 (relation to Petrus Alphonsus' Disciplina clericalis and others).
Seaton, p 274 (argues for Lilium Medicinae and Mandeville).

Other Scholarly Problem. Seaton, p 273 (argues poem contains name anagrams).

Literary Criticism. Reufs F, Das Naturgefühl bei Lydgate, Arch 122.269 (monasticism ruins L's originality).
SchirmerLydgate, p 207; trans Keep, p 237 (discusses L's use of dialogue and soliloquy).
PearsallLydgate, p 202 (L at the height of his powers).

[47] FALL OF PRINCES.

MSS. 1, Bodl 2440 (Bodley 263), ff 1^a–end (1450–1500); 2, Bodl 3681 (e Mus 1), ff 1^a–144^b (1469–1500; very imperfect); 3, Bodl 4130 (Hatton 2), ff 4^a–end (1469–1500); 4, Bodl 12299 (Rawl C.448), ff 1^a–end (1460–70); 5, Corp Christi Oxf 242, ff 13^a–end (1460–70; lacks 1 leaf at beginning, ends imperfectly); 6, Harley 1245, ff 1^a–182^c (1460–70); 7, Harley 1766, ff 5^a–265^b (1450–60?; Harleian Catalogue, p 209, calls it most remarkable); 8, Harley 3486, ff 2^a–177^d (1469–1500; ends with 9.3098); 9, Harley 4197, ff 1^a–163^d (1469–1500; few lines lacking at end); 10, Harley 4203, ff 1^a–181^d (1469–1500); 11, Royal 18.B.xxxi, ff 1^a–216^a (1460–70); 12, Royal 18.D.iv, ff 2^a–168^a (1425–75; incomplete); 13, Royal 18.D.v, ff 1^a–207^b (1450–75); 14, Sloane 4031, ff 4^a–190^b (1469–1500; omits the 2 envoys to Gloucester and other short passages); 15, BM Addit 21410, ff 1^a–168^a (1469–1500; begins with 1.2017); 16, BM Addit 39659 (formerly Curzon), ff 1^a–185^b (ca 1460–70; several omissions and transpositions); 17, Hunterian 1.50, ff 1^a–211^a (1450–75; lacks 1 leaf at beginning); 18, Lambeth 256, ff 1^a–180^b (ca 1460–70; lacks opening leaf, and leaves 3, 4, 6 of section xxii); 19, Rylands Libr, English 2 (formerly Osterley Park), ff 1^a–184^a (1425–75; omits envoys to Gloucester); 20, Belvoir Castle, ff 1^a–end (15 cent); 21, Longleat 254, large paper folio, ff 1^a–185^b (ca 1460–70); 22, formerly Lyell (Quaritch Sale Cat 699, 1952, Item 28); 23, formerly Wollaton Hall (Quaritch Sale Cat 1931, Item 100; Cat 775, Item 5), ff 1^a–223^b (1450–75); 24, Chicago Univ 565 (formerly Phillipps 4255), ff 2^a–278^b (ca 1475–85; bks 1–3, lacks first 65 lines and others; ends imperfectly); 25, Huntington HM.268 (formerly Ecton Hall), ff 1^a–158^b (1460–70; very imperfect: perhaps 114 leaves lost, remainder bound in improper order); 26, Illinois Univ 84, ff 1–386 (1425–75; very imperfect); 27, Morgan Libr 124 (formerly Lee), ff 1^a–185^b (1450–75?); 28, Newberry Libr 33.3 (formerly Silver 4), ff 1^a–201^b (1440–80); 29, Princeton Univ Deposit (formerly Garrett 139; formerly Phillipps 8117), ff 1^a–210^a (1450–75; numerous omissions); 30, John Gribble (Phila) (formerly Phillipps 8118), ff 1^a–206 (1469–1500; omits the 2 envoys to Gloucester); 31, Houghton 9 (Queenstown, Maryland) (formerly Mostyn Hall 272; formerly Rosenbach 477), ff 1^a–255^b (1450–75; lacks stanzas 1–20 of prologue and other passages; ends with 9.2657); 32, Plimpton 225, ff 1^a–54^b (1450–75; begins with 1.5678; ends with 9.1512; lacks other passages); 33, formerly Rosenbach 475 (formerly Harmsworth; formerly Leighton), ff 1^a–?; 34, Rosenbach Foundation 439/16 (formerly Phillips 4254), ff 1^a–212^d (1450–75; ends with 9.2657; omits passages). PRINTS: 35, Pynson, 1494 (STC, no 3175); 36, Pynson, 1527; 37, Tottel, 1554; 38, Wayland, 1554?.

MSS of Extracts. 39, Bodl 1782 (Digby 181), ff 52^a–53^a (15 cent); 40, Bodl 3556 (Arch Selden B.10), ff 200^a–205^a (copied from PRINT 68?); 41, Bodl 6943 (Ashmole 59), ff 13^a–17^b, 28^b–29^b, 59^a–^{b}, 183^a–^{b} (1447–56); 42, Balliol 329, ff 127^a–171^a (15 cent; wrongfully listed in Robbins-Cutler as complete MS no 32; see Edwards, Libr 5s 26.341); 43, Camb Univ Ff.1.6, ff 150^a–151^a (15 cent); 44, Pepys 2011, ff 77^a–78^a (1450?–1500?); 45, St John's Camb 223, ff 94^a–99^b (1475–1525; Brown-Robbins lists as 233); 46, Trinity Camb 599, ff 2^a–3^a (1475–1525; see also ff 170^b–202^a for selections incorporated in Chaucer's Monk's Tale); 47, Trinity Camb 600, pp 368–370 (1450–75); 48, Fitzwilliam McLean 182, ff 11^a–^{b}, 49^b–52^b (15 cent); 49, Arundel 26, f 32^a (16 cent; Robbins-Cutler, no 1637.8, not identified as from Fall); 50, Harley 172, ff 1*a–*b, 2a–3a (15 cent); 51, Harley 367, ff 83b–86a (transcript by Stowe; copied from MS 41 according to Edwards, N&Q ns 16(214). 170); 52, Harley 2202, ff 71a–72b (15 cent; a fragment of two leaves arranged in reverse order; also listed in Brown-Robbins, Robbins-Cutler as nos 2696, 3538.5); 53, Harley 2251, ff 81a–145b (1464–83); 54, Harley 2255, ff 94b–96b (1448?–49?); 55, Harley 4011, ff 1b–2b (1450–1500; envoy to Gloucester); 56, Lansdowne 699, ff 51a–66b, 91b–95b (1450–1500); 57, Sloane 2452 (a fragment of 8 leaves; Edwards, Manuscripta 16.37 argues that this fragment is from MS 25); 58, BM Addit 29729, ff 169b–170b (John Stowe, 1558); 59, Advocates 1.1.6, f 75b (1568; Bannatyne MS; not listed in Robbins-Cutler, but see Edwards, Libr 5s 26.341); 60, Leyden Univ Vossius 9, ff 64b–80a, 104a–106b (15 cent); 61, Lismore, Gaelic xxxvii, p 184 (assigned no 4014.9 by R H Robbins, A New Lydgate Fragment, ELN 5.244 n3); 62, McGill Univ 143 (4 folios only); 63, Phila Free Public Libr Lewis 314 (1 leaf only; Edwards, Manuscripta 15.29, argues that this leaf is from MS 32); 64, Morgan Libr 4, ff 74b–75b (mid–15 cent; see C F Bühler, A New Lydgate-Chaucer Manuscript, MLN 52.1); 65, John E du Pont (Newton Square, Penn) (10 leaves; Sothby's Sale Cat, 11 July 1966, lot 255); 66, formerly Phillips 23554 (1 leaf; Magg's Sale Cat 849, Item 30 A); 67, Tregaskis Sale Cat 1919 (1 leaf of Bk 3, end chap 5 and beg chap 6). PRINT: 68, de Worde, The Proverbes of Lydgate, 1519.

Brown-Robbins, Robbins-Cutler, no 1168; also nos 1637.8, 2696, 3538.5.

MS Scholarship Concerning Both Complete MSS and Extracts. Dibdin T F, Ames' Typographical Antiquities, London 1812, 2.404 (discusses PRINTS 35, 36).

Royal Commission on Historical MSS, 1st Report, London 1870, 1.11 (MS 20); 3rd Report, London 1872, 3.188 (MS in Marquis of Bath libr); 4th Report, London 1873, 4.362 (MS 31, then in Mostyn Hall); 8th Report, London 1878, 1.100. 629; 3.106 (MSS in libraries of Earl of Jersey, Ewelme Almshouse, and Earl of Ashburnham).

Hortis A, Studj sulle opere latine del Boccaccio, Trieste 1879, p 938 (believes MS 7 to be presentation copy to Gloucester).

Robinson F N, On Two MSS of Lydgate's Guy of Warwick, HSNPL 5.177 (describes MS 60).

Scott M A, Elizabethan Translations from the Italian: the Titles of Such Works Now First Collected and Arranged with Annotations, PMLA 11.377 (describes PRINT 36).

Hammond E P, Lydgate's Mumming at Hertford, Angl 22.364 (describes MS 47); Two British Museum MSS, Angl 28.1 (detailed study of MS 53; MS relation of [183] below and [47]); Ashmole 59 and Other Shirley MSS, Angl 30.320 (describes MS 41); The Texts of Lydgate's Danse Macabre, MLN 36.250 (MS 60); The Nine-Syllabled Pentameter Line in Some Post-Chaucerian MSS, MP 23.129 (excerpts of [47] in MS 53 and perhaps in other MSS are in same hand as some MSS of Chaucer's Canterbury Tales).

Werner F, Ein Sammelkapitel aus Lydgates Fall of Princes, München 1914, p 11.

Brusendorff A, The Chaucer Tradition, London 1925, pp 208, 466, and passim (discusses Shirley's marginalia in MS 47).

Plomer R H, Wynkyn de Worde and His Contemporaries, London 1925, p 116 (describes PRINT 35).

Bergen, edn, vol 4, EETSES 124.3 (describes 30 complete MSS and gives biblio of MS scholarship).

Jackson W A, Wayland's Edn of the Mirror for Magistrates, Libr 4s 13.156 (argues PRINT 38 probably precedes PRINT 37).

Tyson M, Hand-List of the Collection of English MSS in the John Rylands Libr, JRLB 13.152 (describes MS 19).

Campbell L B, The Suppressed Edn of A Mirror for Magistrates, Huntington Libr Bull 6.1 (argues PRINT 36 must be dated after 4 June 1555).

Pyle F, A Mirror for Magistrates, TLS Dec 1935, p 904 (argues PRINT 38 must have been out before PRINT 37).

Hearsey M, The Complaint of Henry Duke of Buckingham, New Haven 1936, p 8 (notes that some prints of [47] end with title page of Mirror for Magistrates).

Bühler C F, A New Lydgate-Chaucer Manuscript, MLN 52.1 (describes MS 64).

Manly & Rickert, 1.241, 532, 623 (description of MSS 42, 46, 53, with identification of owners).

Utley CR, no 185 (marginalia in MS 53).

van Dorsten J A, The Leyden Lydgate MS, Scriptorium 14.315 (MS 60).

Notes and News, JRLB 43.273 (briefly describes MS 19 and miniatures).

Friedman J B, Orpheus in the Middle Ages, Cambridge Mass 1970, p 170 (reproduces 2 miniatures from MS 7).

Edwards A S G, Lydgate's Fall of Princes Unrecorded Readings, N&Q ns 16(214).170 (discusses relationship of MS 44 to MS 64, MS 56 to MS 60, and MS 41 to MS 51); A Missing Leaf from the Plimpton Fall of Princes, Manuscripta 15.29 (MSS 33, 63); Selections from Lydgate's Fall of Princes A Checklist, Libr 5s 26.337 (corrects descriptions of all MSS of selections); The Huntington Fall of Princes and Sloane 2452, Manuscripta 16.37 (discusses MS 57 and its relationship to MS 25); The McGill Fragment of Lydgate's Fall of Princes, Scriptorium 28.75 (discusses MS 62 and its relationship to MS 7).

Edition. Bergen H, Lydgate's Fall of Princes, 4 vols, EETSES 121–24, London 1918–19; also Carnegie Foundation, Washington 1923–27 (MS 1; collations from PRINTS 35–38, and all complete MSS then known except MS 33; substantial sections of texts and Boccaccio and Laurent de Premierfait; crit TLS Sept 25 1924, p 590; E P Hammond, AnglB 36.15; M Förster, AnglB 36.33; A Brandl, Arch 149.111).

Extracts. (See also under THE TONGUE [50], EXAMPLES AGAINST WOMEN [197], and PRAISE OF GLOUCESTER).

a. Episode of Alcibiades.
Norton-Smith J, John Lydgate Poems, Oxford 1966, pp 11 (bk 3.3655–82; MS 1; collations from MSS 2, 3, 4), 127 (brief commentary, notes, and glossary).

b. Episode of Canace and Macareus.
Campbell T, Specimens of the British Poets, London 1819, 2.60.
Gilfillan G, Specimens with Memoirs of the Lessknown British Poets, Edinburgh 1860, 1.46.
Hammond E P, Eng Verse between Chaucer and Surrey, Durham 1927, p 166 (MS 13).

c. Episode of Constantine.
Edwards A S G, Lydgate's Fall of Princes Unrecorded Readings, N&Q ns 16(214).170 (1 stanza on Constantine from MS 56; bk 2.4481–87 from MS 40).

d. Episodes of Dido and of Sardanapalus.
Halliwell PPS 2.69, 84 (MS 53).

e. Episode of King Arthur.
Perzl W, Die Arthur-legende in Lydgate's Fall of Princes, München 1911 (MS 7; collations from MSS 1, 3, 4, 6, 8–13, 15, 53).

f. Episodes of Rome, Julius Caesar, Octavian, Cicero, Boethius.
Hammond, Eng Verse, pp 172, 178 (MS 12).

g. Against Proud Men.
Fitzgibbon H M, Early Eng and Scottish Poetry, London ca 1888, p 77 (lines 1.331–37; modernized).

h. Allusions to Chaucer.
Spurgeon C, Five Hundred Years of Chaucer Criticism and Allusion, ChS 2s 48.37 (MS 7).

i. Account of the Golden Age.
Ward T H, The Eng Poets, London 1895, 1.122.

j. Praise of and Thanks to Gloucester.
Turner S, The History of England during the Middle Ages, London 1823, 3.155 (MS 12).
Furnivall F J, Early Eng Meals and Manners, EETS 32.1xxxv (rptd 1897, 1904; MS 12).
Hammond, Eng Verse, p 174 (MS 12).
Sisam C and K, The Oxford Book of Medieval Verse, Oxford 1970, p 399 (bk 9.3387–442; MS 7; modern spelling and glosses at foot of page).

k. Prologues and Envoys.
Hammond, p 58 (general prologue; PRINT 37); Poet and Patron in the Fall of Princes, Angl 38.129, 133 (prologue to bk 3, from MS 13; envoy to bk 3, chap 18, from MS 1); Eng Verse, pp 157, 186 (general prologue and epilogue, from MS 12).

l. Ballade on Women's Chastity (bk 4.2374–87 and bk 3.1373–421; only in MS 46).
John Stowe, Chaucer 1561, and later Chaucer prints.
Chalmers A, The Works of the Eng Poets, London 1810, 1.565.

m. 2 Stanzas on Women: 1.6630–43, a modified version.
Rel Ant, 2.28.
D'Evelyn C, Peter Idley's Instructions to His Son, Boston London and Oxford 1935, p 137 (from MS Camb Univ Ee.4.37 (E)).

n. Various Stanzas on Women.
Edwards A S G, John Lydgate Medieval Antifeminism and Harley 2251, Annuale Mediaevale 13.32 (42 stanzas, all from bk 1 except 1 from bk 3; MS 53).

o. General.
Bowers R H, The ME Oon Sleth the Deer Wyth an Hookid Arwe, Southern Folklore Quart 15.249 (prints Brown-Robbins, no 2696, from MS 52).
Kaiser R, Medieval Eng, 3rd edn, Berlin 1958, p 501 (bk 1.92–98, 6511–66; bk 4.1–14, 50–56; bk 6.1289–1309, 2822–910; bk 8.190–203;

bk 9.3303–16, 3394–442; MS 1).
Abstracts. Morley, 6.110.
Utley CR, nos 41ª (2 stanzas on women), 142 (Ballade on Women's Chastity), 185 (Boccaccio on Women, published separately, bk 1.6511–734; in MS 53), 220 (episode of Dido).
Textual Matters. Utley CR, no 41ª (discusses changes in passage incorporated in Peter Idley's Instructions to His Son).
van Dorsten, Scriptorium 14.318 (describes hiatus and addition to MS 60).
Edwards, N&Q ns 16(214).170 (interesting variants from MSS 40, 44, 54); Scriptorium 28.75 (MS 7 supports unusual readings in MS 61 and both may represent an early version of [47]).
Language. Hall F, On Eng Adjectives in –able, London 1877, pp 103, 105, 106, and passim.
Schick J, Lydgate's Temple of Glas, EETSES 60.lxv, and passim.
Skeat W W, Principles of Eng Etymology, Oxford 1891, p 153 (on L's introd of French words into Eng).
Dibelius W, John Capgrave u die engl Schriftsprache, Angl 23.153, 323.
Hingst R, Die Sprache John Lydgates aus seinen Reimen, Greiswald 1908, p 60.
Hammond E P, Lydgate's Prologue to the Story of Thebes, Angl 36.360 (notes direct transfer of French words from Laurent de Premierfait into [47]).
Nichols P H, William Dunbar as a Scottish Lydgatian, PMLA 46.214 (adds 66 words to Reismüller's list of L's appropriations of Chaucer's French and Latin borrowings).
Whitehall H, The Background of the Word Bask, PQ 14.229.
Miles J, Eras in Eng Poetry, PMLA 70.853 (proportion of adjective-noun-verb in ten lines is 6–16–9—computed along with [176] below).
Versification. Guest E, History of Eng Rhythms, rvsd W W Skeat, London 1882, p 209 (argues rhythmical regularity of certain lines).
Schick, EETSES 60.lv, and passim.
Reger, pp 69, 77 (finds 10.64 percent lines have certain epic caesurae).
Werner, Ein Sammelkapitel, p 71.
Hammond, MP 23.129 (broken-back lines in prologue are less numerous than acephalous lines).
Spindler R, Engl Metrik, München 1927, p 137.
Young G, An Eng Prosody on Inductive Lines, Cambridge 1928, p 1926 (illustrates lack of regular incidence of stress in L).
Pyle, The Pedigree of Lydgate's Heroic Line, Hermathena 50.26 (shows that characteristics of L's line go back as far as Poema Morale).
Date. Schick, EETSES 60.cxii (ca 1430–38).
Schirmer W F, Lydgate's Fall of Princes, Angl 69.301 (1438–39).
Authorship. MacCracken TPSL, appendix 2.xiv; rptd EETSES 107.xvi.
SchirmerLydgate, p 231; trans Keep, p 268.
Authorship of Ballade on Women's Chastity (extract l above). Skeat W W, The Chaucer Canon, Oxford 1900, p 120 (rejects L's authorship on linguistic grounds).
MacCracken EETSES 107.xvi (rejects Skeat's argument and accepts L's authorship).
Sources and Literary Relations: Especially Boccaccio and Chaucer. Ten Brink B, Chaucer, Münster 1870, p 152 (finds L's list of Chaucer's works unreliable).
Warton T, History of Eng Poetry, ed W C Hazlitt, London 1871, 3.68 (relation to Boccaccio and other sources).
Hortis, Studj, pp 419, 428, 442, 627, 640, and passim (relation to Boccaccio).
Koeppel E, Laurent de Premierfait u John Lydgates Bearbeitungen von Boccaccios De casibus virorum illustrium, München 1885 (relation to Boccaccio; influence of Chaucer and Gower); Chauceriana, Angl 13.184 (references in [47] help determine Chaucer's use of Dante).
Cloetta W, Beiträge zur Literaturgeschichte des Mittelalters u der Renaissance, Halle 1890, 1.43, 146 (discusses references to Chaucer and relationship to Myrrour for Magistrates).
Morley, 6.110 (discusses references to Chaucer).
Lounsbury T, Studies in Chaucer, N Y 1892, 1.358, 419; 2.159, 190, 243; 3.394, 408 (relationship to Chaucer canon; argues reference to Chaucer's trans of Dante is to House of Fame).
Ten Brink, 3.227 (relationship of L's text to that of Laurent de Premierfait).
Gattinger, pp 42, 72 (discusses influence of Isidore of Seville, Chaucer, Petrus Comestor, and Vergil).
Hammond, p 58 (discusses list of Chaucer's works in [47]); Chaucer and Lydgate Notes, MLN 27.91 (argues that Prudent Carnotence of [47] is John of Salisbury and that a passage in the poem may help explain expression 'shippes hoppesteres' in Chaucer's Knight's Tale).
Perzl W, Die Arthur-Legende in Lydgate's Fall of Princes, München 1911 (shows that L knew both Laurent de Premierfait's text and Boccaccio's De casibus; argues L's use of Geoffrey of Monmouth and others).
Spurgeon C, Chaucer devant la critique en Angleterre et en France, Paris 1911, p 9 (counts

more allusions to Chaucer in [47] than in any other work of L); Five Hundred Years of Chaucer Criticism and Allusion, ChS 2s 48.36 (prints allusions to Chaucer).

Legouis, p 26.

Werner F, Ein Sammelkapitel aus Lydgates Fall of Princes, München 1914, passim (argues L used Laurent de Premierfait's version of 1409).

Langhans V, Chaucer's Anelide and Arcite, Angl 44.226 (mentions L's list of Chaucer's works and suggests L's thorough acquaintance with Chaucer).

Förster M, Boccaccio's De casibus virorum illustrium in engl Bearbeitung, DLz 45.1943 (relationship, including tone, between versions of Boccaccio, Laurent de Premierfait, and L).

Brusendorff, Chaucer Tradition, passim (enumerates allusions to and mentions of Chaucer; discusses relationship to Romance of the Rose and other sources).

Patch H R, The Goddess Fortuna in Mediaeval Literature, Cambridge Mass 1927, pp 46, 71, 111, and passim (juxtapositions of treatment of Fortune by L and Boccaccio).

Brie F, Mittelalter u Antike bei Lydgate, EStn 64.261 (discusses relationship to Boccaccio and classical antiquity; argues importance of L to early Eng humanism).

Naunin T, Der Einfluss der mittelalterliche Rhetorik auf Chaucers Dichtung, Bonn 1929, p 55 (argues [47] reflects dependence upon Chaucer and weakening of mediaeval rhetoric).

Farnham W, The Mediaeval Heritage of Elizabethan Tragedy, Berkeley 1936, pp 86, 129 (relationship to Boccaccio).

Raith J, Boccaccio in der engl Literatur von Chaucer bis Painters Palace of Pleasure, Leipzig 1936, p 71 (discusses L's relationship to Boccaccio and contributions to Matter of Antiquity).

Sarton G, Introd to the History of Science, Baltimore 1947, 3.1046 and passim (account of Boccaccio's De Casibus and its translations to [47]).

Coghill N, The Poet Chaucer, London 1949, p 84 (illustrates Chaucer's influence).

Schirmer, Das Ende des Mittelalters in England, Kleine Schriften, Tübingen 1950, p 25 and passim (draws line of influence from Chaucer to L and from L to Mirror for Magistrates); Lydgates Fall of Princes, Angl 69.301 (discusses various sources); SchirmerLydgate, p 179; trans Keep, p 206.

Bonner F W, The Genesis of the Chaucer Apocrypha, SP 48.461 (argues list of Chaucer's works in bk 1 proved source of much Chaucer apocrypha).

Moore K, The Secular Love Lyric in ME, Lexington 1951, p 106 (argues references to Chaucerian poems in bk 1 probably represent L's acceptance of Chaucer's own statement rather than actual acquaintance with the poems themselves).

Wright H G, Boccaccio in England from Chaucer to Tennyson, London 1957, pp 5 (brief on sources), 21 (later influence).

Rossi, p 149 (relation to Boccaccio, Dante, Petrarch, and Gower).

Norton-Smith J, John Lydgate Poems, Oxford 1966, p 127 (discusses originality of passage on Alcibiades and relation to [189] below).

Gathercole P M, Lydgate's Fall of Princes and the French Version of Boccaccio's De Casibus, Miscellanea di studi e richerche sul Quattrocento francese, ed F Simone, Torino 1967, p 165; Laurent de Premierfait's Des cas des nobles hommes et femmes, Univ of North Carolina Stud in the Romance Lang and Lit no 74, Chapel Hill 1968, 1.33 (what L did with his immediate source).

Caldwell H B, The Child Tragic Ballad A Comparison with Medieval Literary Tragedy– Boccaccio Chaucer Lydgate, DA 29.865A.

McCray C L, Chaucer and Lydgate and the Uses of History, DA 29.4461A.

Williamson M, Antony and Cleopatra in the Late Middle Ages and Early Renaissance, Michigan Academician 5.145 (how L departs from Chaucer and Boccaccio).

PearsallLydgate, pp 230 (brief summary of sources), 250 (later influence).

Sources and Literary Relations: General. Brydges S E, The British Bibliographer, London 1810, 1.297 (notes L's influence on Sackville).

Guest, Hist Eng Rhythms, p 524 (L's poem throws light on authorship of Prick of Conscience).

Koeppel E, Lydgate's Story of Thebes, München 1884, pp 9, 14, 19 (uses [47] to date [169] below; notes reference to Statius).

Constans L, Le Roman de Thèbes, Paris 1890, 2.clxiii (notes similarities between Oedipus legend in [47] and [169] below).

Scott M A, Elizabethan Translations from the Italian: the Titles of Such Works Now First Collected and Arranged with Annotations, PMLA 11.377 (uses PRINT 36 along with other works to support argument that Italian influence came in after Dante and Petrarch).

Hammond, Angl 28.1 (discusses relationship of [47] and [183] below); Boethius: Chaucer: Walton: Lydgate, MLN 41.534 (though [46] above shows Boethian influence, omissions in [47] suggest L's lack of enthusiasm for Boethius); Lydgate and Coluccio Saluti, MP 25.49 (supplements Bergen's edn in regard to bk 2, lines 974–1,337, and gives parallel passage in Coluccio's Epistolario).

MacCracken H N, Additional Light on the Temple of Glas, PMLA 23.128 (notes passages from [47] in John Lucas' Death's Warning).

Duschl, p 9 and passim (studies sources and gives classification of proverbs).

Montgomery M, Lydgate's Fall of Princes and Hamlet, TLS Oct 1924, p 651 (argues Gonzago story in Hamlet possibly from [47]).

Patch, Fortuna, pp 53, 82, and passim (notes similarities in treatment of Fortune in L's text and others).

D'Evelyn, Peter Idley, p 49 (shows influence of L on Idley, who borrows 46 stanzas from [47]).

Farnham, Mediaeval Heritage, pp 171, 252, 277, 343, and passim (relationship to Boccaccio, Romance of the Rose, Mirror for Magistrates, and Elizabethan Drama).

Hearsey M, The Complaint of Henry Duke of Buckingham, New Haven 1936, p 108 (points out similarities in wording between [47] and Sackville's contribution to Mirror for Magistrates).

Rathborne I E, The Meaning of Spenser's Fairyland, CUS 131.4, 27, 92, 183 (discusses influence of Mirabilia urbis Romae on crystal palace where Arthur is stellified and which is important analogue to Spenser's Panthea).

Campbell L B, The Mirror for Magistrates, Cambridge 1938, p 5 (discusses relationship between [47] and Mirror for Magistrates).

Bühler C F, Lydgate's Horse, Sheep, and Goose and Huntington MS HM 144, MLN 55.563 (points out stanzas which occur in other poems of L, in Court of Sapience, and in Ashby's Active Policy of a Prince).

Utley CR, nos 41a (relation to Peter Idley), 110 (notes that attack on men's lack of faith in 'I think their men are verry fals and vane' belongs to tradition that goes back to L and Boccaccio), 236 (believes anonymous trans of Boccaccio's De claris mulieribus, ed G Schleich, Palaes 144, imitation of [47]), 242 (suggests relationship between A Satire against Wicked Jezebel and [47]), 292 (discusses relationship of The Scholehouse and [47]).

Tillyard E M W, Shakespeare's History Plays, London 1948, pp 72, 129, and passim (finds L nearer to Renaissance spirit than Chaucer; argues influence of [47] on Shakespeare's history plays, especially Richard II); The Eng Renaissance: Fact or Fiction? London 1952, pp 74, 93 (compares Renaissance spirit in [47] to Boccaccio and Mirror for Magistrates); The Eng Epic and Its Background, Oxford 1954 (compares poem to Boccaccio and Mirror for Magistrates to suggest appropriateness of [47] to L's time).

Chapman R, The Wheel of Fortune in Shakespeare's Historical Plays, RES ns 1.1 (compares concept of kings as sport of Fortune in [47] and in Shakespeare's historical plays).

Purdy R R, The Friendship Motif in ME Literature, Vanderbilt Stud in the Humanities 1.113 (argues story of Atreus and Thyestes is representative of mediaeval attitude toward friendship and deceit which may be traced to Plato).

Schirmer, The Importance of the 15th Cent for the Study of the Eng Renaissance, Eng Stud Today, Oxford 1951, p 104 (discusses relationship to Mirror for Magistrates and Shakespeare).

Swallow A, John Skelton: the Structure of His Poems, PQ 32.29 (argues Skelton's elegy On the Death of a Noble Prince is on theme of [47]).

Rossi S, George Cavendish e il tema della Fortuna, Eng Miscellany 9.51 ([47] was a mine of information for later writers and establishes the image of Fortune).

Dédéyan C, Dante en Angleterre, Les Lettres Romanes 13.179 (cites ref to Dante).

Cutts J P, Lear's Learned Theban, Shakespeare Quart 14.477 (cites L's description of Oedipus but does not argue it is a direct influence on Lear).

Renoir A, John Lydgate Poet of the Transition, Eng Miscellany 11.18 (notes L changes source from blame to praise of English); Renoir-Lydgate, p 20 (discusses Canace's sorrow in [47] and in Gower and Ovid).

Scattergood V J, Politics and Poetry in the 15th Cent, London 1971, p 43 (L changes his sources in portrait of King John).

Edwards A S G, Selections from Lydgate's Fall of Princes A Checklist, Libr 5s 26.337 (discusses enormous popularity of selections from [47]); Some Borrowings by Cavendish from Lydgate's Fall of Princes, N&Q ns 18(216).207; Slyppur Is to Grype Ouer Whom Is No Holde, NM 74.126 (minor instance of later reworking of [47]); Douglas's Palice of Honour and Lydgate's Fall of Princes, N&Q ns 21(219).83.

Schibanoff S, Avarice and Cerberus in Coluccio Salutati's De Laboribus Herculis and Lydgate's Fall of Princes, MP 71.390.

Other Scholarly Problems: Humphrey of Gloucester. Hammond E P, Lydgate and the Duchess of

Gloucester, Angl 27.381 (discusses bk 3.18–24 in relation to Gloucester's marriage and desertion of Jacqueline of Hainault).

Vickers K H, Humphrey Duke of Gloucester, London 1907, p 300 (points out that [47] bears witness to Gloucester's violent end).

Wylie J H, The Reign of Henry 5th, Cambridge 1914–29, 1.192 and passim, 283 ([47 bears witness to Gloucester's and Henry's devotion to Church and dislike of Lollardry).

Schirmer, Der engl Frühhumanismus, Leipzig 1931, p 51; rvsd edn Tübingen 1963, p 43 (argues [47] paints conflicting portrait of Gloucester as early humanist patron).

Weiss R, Humanism in England during the 15th Cent, Oxford 1941, pp 22, 64, 117 (argues [47] is evidence of Gloucester's humanism).

Robbins R H, An Epitaph for Duke Humphrey, NM 56.241 (points out that, unlike Epitaph printed in article, passages on Gloucester in [47] are typical of L's attitude toward him).

RenoirLydgate, p 71 (L's praise of Gloucester).

PearsallLydgate, p 223 (Gloucester not a real humanist and did not continue support for [47]).

Other Scholarly Problems: General. Gattinger, pp 19, 42, and passim (discusses L's use of history for didactic abstractions).

Kleineke W, Engl Fürstenspiegel vom Policraticus Johanns von Salisbury bis zum Basilikon Doron König Jakobs I, SEP 40.13 (discusses significance of moralizing envoys).

Sarton G, Introd to the History of Science, Baltimore 1947, 3.47 and passim (L's view of science typical of his time).

Schirmer, Ende des Mittelalters, p 33 ([47] bears witness to humanistic interest of the times); Importance of 15th Cent, p 104 (discusses importance of Fortune; argues L represents transition between Middle Ages and Renaissance).

Wilson R M, The Lost Literature of Medieval England, London 1952, pp 161, 167 (notes mention of [47] in will of Roger Deury of Hawstead, print in Bury Wills and Inventories, Camden Soc 1850, and its probable presence in inventory of the goods of Exeter as Bocas in Sermone Anglico).

Cary G, The Medieval Alexander, Cambridge 1956, pp 115, 255, 277 (poem presents a very hostile conception of Alexander).

Enkvist N E, The Seasons of the Year, Societas Scientiarum Fennica Commentationes Humanarum Litterarum 22.4, Helsingfors 1957, p 122 (L expands on seasonal description from source with cliches).

Renoir, Attitudes toward Women in Lydgate's Poetry, ESts 42.11 (argues for L's serious conception of women); RenoirLydgate, pp 64 (brief mention of L's method of trans), 69 (L's attitude toward classical antiquity), 88 (L's attitude toward women), 100 (nationalism in [47]), 105 (advice for rulers).

Chew S C, The Pilgrimmage of Life, New Haven and London 1962, p 46 (notes new conception of Fortune in [47]).

Norton-Smith, John Lydgate Poems, p 127 (discusses L's attitude toward Fortune and paganism).

Margeson J M R, The Origins of Eng Tragedy, Oxford 1967, p 71 (brief on L's conception of Fortune).

Scattergood, Politics and Poetry, pp 269, 272, 290 (L's political ideas).

Schibanoff, Memory and Later ME Literature, DAI 32.5201A (L recommends prudence and sees value in pagan past).

Kean P M, Chaucer and the Making of Eng Poetry, London and Boston 1972, 2.213 (L placed value on classical past).

Edwards A S G, John Lydgate Medieval Antifeminism and Harley 2251, Annuale Mediaevale 13.32 (L's antifeminist statements gathered from throughout the poem and annotators disagree with these views).

Kurose T, Rekishi-shugi to Rekishi-kankaku-Lydgate Fall of Princes no Baai, Eigo Seinen 118.522 (historical sense in [47]).

Doob P B R, Nebuchadnezzar's Children, New Haven and London 1974, p 106 (discusses L's depiction of Herod's sinful madness).

Kurose, Notes on John Lydgate's Character Drawings of the Goddess Fortune in the Fall of Princes, Stud in Eng Literature 1975 (Eng Number), p 79.

Literary Criticism. Schick, EETS 60.cxi (argues degeneration of style in [47]).

Lounsbury T, Studies in Chaucer, N Y 1892, passim.

Gattinger, p 78 (discusses style).

Jusserand J J, Histoire litteraire du peuple anglais, Paris 1896, 1.518 (insists on L's dullness).

Gray T, Some Remarks on the Poems of John Lydgate, The Works of Thomas Gray, ed E Gosse, London 1902, 1.387 (defends L's poetry on basis of [47]).

Courthope, 1.323; 2.111 (believes that only contemporary demand for historical works can account for popularity of such dull poem as [47]).

Furnivall F J, The Pilgrimmage of the Life of Man,

London 1905, p xiv (uses evidence of [47] to argue L not so incompetent as usually supposed). CHEL, 2.202.
Reufs F, Das Naturgefühl bei Lydgate, Arch 122.269 (concludes that monasticism ruins L's originality).
Cazamian L, The Development of Eng Humor, N Y 1930, 1.142 (finds [47] too wordy and generally devoid of humor).
Farnham, Mediaeval Heritage, pp 161, 279, and passim (discusses L's view of tragedy as retribution for sin).
Bennett H S, The Author and His Public in the 14th and 15th Cents, E&S 23.7 (points to [47] as example of deplorable fecundity encouraged by patronage system); Bennett OHEL, pp 111, 140, 145 (points to [47] as example of L's voluminousness and didactic purpose); Six Medieval Men and Women, Cambridge 1955, pp 19, 24, and passim (argues L uses medical, nautical, and financial metaphors to gratify Gloucester's taste and the result is verbiage).
Brusendorff, Chaucer Tradition, p 462 (prints a few lines from the Ballade on Women's Chastity in bk 4, and then discusses them as especially characteristic of L).
Schirmer, Engl Frühhumanismus, p 53; rvsd edn, p 47; Lydgates Fall of Princes, Angl 69.301; SchirmerLydgate, trans Keep, passim.
Wright H G, Boccaccio in England from Chaucer to Tennyson, London 1957, p 5 (discusses themes, attitudes, and style).
Rossi, p 142.
Pearsall D, Gower and Lydgate, London 1969, p 26 and passim; PearsallLydgate, p 223.
Edwards, Selections, Libr 5s 26.337 (most popular passages were the envoys added by L)
McCay C T, Narrative Technique in John Lydgate's Fall of Princes, DAI 33.1691A (claims L a good poet).
Marotta J G, John Lydgate and the Tradition of Medieval Rhetoric, DAI 33.729A.
General References. Schirmer, Angl 69.301 (discusses all significant aspects of [47]);ced SchirmerLydgate, trans Keep, passim (discusses all aspects of [47]).
Pearsall, The English Chaucerians, Chaucer and Chaucerians, ed D S Brewer, Univ Alabama 1966, p 218.
Bibliography. Utley CR, no 350 (brief biblio of extracts from bks 1 and 2).
SchirmerLydgate, p 226; trans Keep, p 261.
Ringler BEV, p 153.
Edwards, A Lydgate Biblio 1928–68, BB 27.98.

[48] FALL OF PRINCES, BK 2.4432–38: DECEYT DECEYVYTH.

MSS. 1, Bodl 3896 (Fairfax 16), f 195ª (1440–50); 2, Bodl 4119 (Hatton 73), f 122ᵇ (1425–75); 3, Bodl 21619 (Douce 45), f 116ª (15 cent); 4, Trinity Camb 600, p 368 (1450–75; a Shirley MS); 5, Harley 7578, f 20ª (1425–75); 6, Sloane 1825, f 90ᵇ and again f 91ª (1500?–50?); 7, Nat Libr Scot 1.1.6 (Advocates), f 74ᵇ (1568; Bannatyne MS); 8, Advocates 19.3.1, f 61ᵇ (15 cent); 9, Lambeth, Book of Howth, f 20ª (16 cent); 10, Nottingham Univ Libr MS MeLMI (formerly Mellish), f 2ᵇ (15 cent); 11, Porkington 10, f 198ª (1453–1500); 12, Morgan Libr 775, f 320ª (ca 1486); 13, Bodl Auct 7.Q.21, end papers.
Brown-Robbins, Robbins-Cutler, no 674.
Hammond E P, Lydgate's Mumming at Hertford, Angl 22.364 (describes MS 4).
Brusendorff A, The Chaucer Tradition, London 1925, pp 208, 466, and passim (discusses Shirley's marginalia in MS 4).
Kurvinen A, MS Porkington 10, NM 54.33 (MS 11).
Davis N, Chaucer's Gentilesse A Forgotten Manuscript with Some Proverbs, RES ns 20.43 (MS 10; does not note this poem).
Edwards A S G, Selections from Lydgate's Fall of Princes A Checklist, Libr 5s 26.338.
Editions. Halliwell PPS 2.271 (MS 6).
Brewer J S and W Bullen, Calendar of the Carew MSS, London 1871, 5.24 (MS 9).
Murdoch J B, The Bannatyne MS, Hunterian Club 32.202 (MS 7).
Ritchie W T, The Bannatyne MSS, PSTS ns 22.184 (MS 7).
Seymour St J D, Anglo Irish Literature 1200–1582, Cambridge 1929, p 99 (MS 9).
Kurvinen, NM 54.62 (MS 11).
Robbins SL, pp 100, 262 (MS 2).
Scholarship. See above under [47].

[49] FALL OF PRINCES, EXTRACTS COMBINED WITH CHAUCER'S MONK'S TALE.

MS. Trinity Camb 599, ff 171ª–202ª (extracts from bks 1, 2, 3 with extract from Chaucer's Monk's Tale incorporated; 1475–1525).
Brown-Robbins, Robbins-Cutler, no 3983.
Edwards A S G, Selections from Lydgate's Fall of Princes A Checklist, Libr 5s 26.341.
Scholarship. See above under [47].

[50] FALL OF PRINCES, THE TONGUE.

MS. Camb Univ Ff.1.6, f 150^{a-b} (3 stanzas, Bk 1.4621–41, incorporated with 3 stanzas from Chaucer's Troilus, Bk 3.302–22, and 1 anonymous stanza; 15 cent).
Brown-Robbins, Robbins-Cutler, no 3535.
Edition. Furnivall F J, Odd Texts of Chaucer's Minor Poems, ChS 1s nos 23 and 60, see appendix p xi.

[51] THE FIFFTENE TOKYNS AFORN THE DOOM.

MS. Harley 2255, ff 117^a–118^b (1448?–49?).
Brown-Robbins, no 408.
Utley CR, no 194 (suggests MS compiled ca 1448–49).
Editions. Wright T, Chester Plays, Shakespeare Soc 1847 2.222.
MacCracken EETSES 107.117.
Versification. Reger, pp 68, 77 (finds 3.4 percent lines have certain epic caesurae).
Authorship. Koeppel E, AnglA 24.55.
MacCracken TPSL, appendix 2.xiv; rptd EETSES 107.xvii.
SchirmerLydgate, p 231; trans Keep, p 269.
Sources and Literary Relations. Heist W W, The Fifteen Signs before Doomsday, East Lansing 1952, pp 169, 198 (traces sources and development of the legend and its relation to [28]; argues L's text closely follows Voragine).
SchirmerLydgate, p 155; trans Keep, p 178 (L follows traditional theme of Quindecim signa judicii).
Other Scholarly Problems. Wilson R M, The Lost Literature of Medieval England, London 1952, p 165 (Titchfield 15-cent catalogue mentions unidentified De die iudicii in anglicis).

[52] SONG AGAINST FLEMINGS (also A BALLADE IN DESPYTE THE FLEMYNGES).

MS. Lambeth 84, f 201^b (15 cent).
Brown-Robbins, Robbins-Cutler, no 2657.
Editions. Brie F W D, The Brut, EETS 136.600.
MacCracken EETS 192.600 (Brie).
Authorship. MacCracken H N, A New Poem by Lydgate, Angl 33.283 (argues L's authorship from internal evidence); EETSES 107.xvii.
SchirmerLydgate, p 230; trans Keep, p 267.
Other Scholarly Problem. Robbins-HP, p 289 (note on historical situation).

General Reference. SchirmerLydgate, p 200; trans Keep, p 230.

[53] THE FLOURE OF CURTESY.

MS. No MS extant. PRINT: Thynne, Chaucer, 1532, ff 283^b–285^a.
Brown-Robbins, no 1487.
Editions. Chalmers A, Eng Poets, London 1810, 1.515.
Oxf Ch, 7.266.
MacCracken EETS 192.410.
Selection. Cohen H L, The Ballade, N Y 1915, p 253 (prints ballade and envoy).
Language. Hingst R, Die Sprache John Lydgates aus seinen Reimen, Greiswald 1908, pp 21, 32, 37, 51.
Babcock C F, A Study of the Metrical Use of the Inflectional e in ME with Particular Reference to Chaucer and Lydgate, PMLA 29.59 (argues L's language bridges gap between Middle Ages and modern period).
Versification. Schick J, Lydgate's Temple of Glas, EETSES 60.1v.
Reger, pp 62, 77 (finds 2.22 percent lines have certain epic caesurae).
Pyle F, The Pedigree of Lydgate's Heroic Line, Hermathena 50.26 (shows that characteristics of L's line go back at least to Poema morale; discusses L's use of that line).
Date. Schick, EETSES 60.c, cxii (1400–03).
SchirmerLydgate, p 26; trans Keep, p 31 (ca 1400–02).
Seaton, p 154 (1430–39).
Authorship. Skeat W W, Chaucer Canon, Oxford 1900, p 102 (attributes poem to L on basis of Stowe's list).
MacCracken TPSL, appendix 2.xiv; rptd EETSES 107.xvii.
Hammond, p 424 (assigns poem to L on basis of early commentators and printers).
SchirmerLydgate, p 229; trans Keep, p 265.
Seaton, p 154 (argues for Richard Roos).
PearsallLydgate, p 97 (assigns to L on basis of internal evidence).
Sources and Literary Relations. Schick, EETSES 60.cxxviii (notes similarities with Chaucer's Parliament of Fowles and [176] below).
Duschl, pp 9, 16 (traces only proverb in poem to Ecclesiastes).
Spurgeon C, Five Hundred Years of Chaucer Criticism and Allusion, ChS 2s 48.15 (prints allusions to Chaucer).
Patch H R, The Goddess Fortuna in Mediaeval

Literature, Cambridge Mass 1927, p 96 (discusses Fortune's nastiness to lovers in [53] and other texts).
Lewis C S, The Allegory of Love, Oxford 1936, p 243 (notes Milton's borrowing from [53]).
SchirmerLydgate, p 29; trans Keep, p 34 (notes poem is in tradition of Romance of the Rose).
Stillwell G, Chaucer's Eagles and Their Choice on February 14, JEGP 53.546 (argues poem reflects L's misunderstanding of Chaucer's humor in Parliament of Fowls).
Other Scholarly Problems. Bonner F W, The Genesis of the Chaucer Apocrypha, SP 48.461 (notes that poem was once ascribed to Chaucer and considers it representative of L's attitude toward Chaucer).
Literary Criticism. Reufs F, Das Naturgefühl bei Lydgate, Arch 122.269 (monasticism ruins L's originality).
Lewis, Allegory, p 240 (argues nature in [53] is mere setting without any significacio).
RenoirLydgate, p 23 (brief examination of L's craft).
PearsallLydgate, p 97 (briefly examines near-flawless craft).
Marotta J G, John Lydgate and the Tradition of Medieval Rhetoric, DAI 33.729A.
General References. Courthope, 1.322.
Pearsall D, The English Chaucerians, in Chaucer and Chaucerians, ed D S Brewer, Univ Alabama 1966, p 210.

[54] FOUR THINGS THAT MAKE A MAN A FOOL: THER BEOTHE FOURE THINGES (also included in SAYINGS OF DAN JOHAN).

MSS. 1, Trinity Camb 600, p 8 (1450–75); 2, BM Addit 29729, f 132ª (John Stowe, 1558). PRINT: 3, Stowe, Chaucer, 1561, f 332ª (rptd A Chalmers, Eng Poets, London 1810, 1.551; rptd Oxf Ch, 7.297).
Brown-Robbins, Robbins-Cutler, no 3523.
Hammond E P, Lydgate's Mumming at Hertford, Angl 22.364 (describes MS 1).
Brusendorff A, The Chaucer Tradition, London 1925, pp 208, 466, and passim (discusses Shirley's marginalia in MS 1).
Edition. MacCracken EETS 192.708 (MS 1).
Versification. Reger, pp 62, 77 (finds 4.76 percent lines have certain epic caesurae).
Authorship. Skeat W W, The Chaucer Canon, Oxford 1900, p 117 (argues L's authorship on basis of Stowe and internal evidence).
Hammond, p 454 (accepts L's authorship in agreement with Tyrwhitt in his account of Chaucer's works).
Utley CR, no 387.
SchirmerLydgate, p 230; trans Keep, p 267.
Sources and Literary Relations. Brown-Robbins, no 3521 (notes text founded on Latin lines in MSS Bodl 3896 and Harley 7578).
Utley CR, no 387 (points out L may have known similar material in Gower's Confessio amantis; gives biblio of related material).
SchirmerLydgate, p 95; trans Keep, p 111 (notes that text is elaboration of Honor, etas, femina, vinum).
Other Scholarly Problem. Bonner F W, The Genesis of the Chaucer Apocrypha, SP 48.461 (notes that poem was once ascribed to Chaucer).
Literary Criticism. Reufs F, Das Naturgefühl bei Lydgate, Arch 122.269.
General Reference. PearsallLydgate, p 220 (reflects medieval desire to classify and teach by enumeration).

[55] FOUR THINGS THAT MAKE A MAN A FOOL; THER BEON FOURE THINGES (also included in SAYINGS OF DAN JOHAN).

MSS. 1, Camb Univ Gg.4.27, f 35ª (16 cent); 2, Trinity Camb 600, p 9 (1450–75); 3, BM Addit 29729, f 132ª (John Stowe, 1558). PRINT: 4, Stowe, Chaucer, 1561, f 332ᵇ (rptd A Chalmers, Eng Poets, London 1810, 1.552; rptd Oxf Ch, 7.297).
Brown-Robbins, Robbins-Cutler, no 3521.
Hammond E P, Lydgate's Mumming at Hertford, Angl 22.364 (describes MS 2).
Brusendorff A, The Chaucer Tradition, London 1925, pp 208, 466, and passim (discusses Shirley's marginalia in MS 2).
Edition. MacCracken EETS 192.708 (MS 2).
Versification. See [54] above.
Authorship. See [54].
Sources and Literary Relations. See [54].
Other Scholarly Problem. See [54].
Literary Criticism. See [54].

[56] FOUR THINGS THAT MAKE A MAN A FOOL: WURSHIP, WOMEN, WINE, UNWELDY AGE (also included in SAYINGS OF DAN JOHAN).

MSS. 1, Bodl 3896 (Fairfax 16), f 195ª (1400–50); 2, Bodl 6943 (Ashmole 59), f 72ª (1447–56); 3, Trinity Camb 599, f 205ᵇ (1475–1525; Robbins-Cutler, no 4230, notes this same as

stanza 2 of Robbins-Cutler, no 2524); 4, Harley 116, f 125ᵃ (1475–1500); 5, Harley 2251, f 150ᵇ (1464–83); 6, Harley 7578, f 20ᵃ (1425–75); 7, Advocates 19.3.1, f 175ᵃ (15 cent); 8, Copenhagen Royal Libr Thott 110, 4°, f 164ᵃ; 9, Rome Eng Coll 1306 (also numbered 127 and A.347), f 75ᵃ (1436–1456); 10, Morgan Libr 775, f 320ᵃ (ca 1486).
Brown-Robbins, Robbins-Cutler, no 4230.
Hammond E P, Two British Museum MSS, Angl 28.1 (detailed study of MS 5); Ashmole 59 and Other Shirley MSS, Angl 30.320 (discusses MS 2).
Manly & Rickert, 1.241 (description of MS 5).
Klinefelter R A, A Newly Discovered 15-Cent Eng MS, MLQ (Washington) 14.3 (gives contents of MS 9).
Robbins R H, A ME Diatribe against Philip of Burgundy, Neophil 39.131 (description and contents of MS 9).
Editions. Förster M, Kleine Mitteilungen zur me Lehrdichtung, Arch 104.301 (MS 4, incorrectly cited as Harley 4733).
Brusendorff A, The Chaucer Tradition, London 1925, p 465 (MS 5).
Skeat W W, The Chaucer Canon, Oxford 1900, p 124 (MS 3).
MacCracken EETS 192.709 (MS 1; collations from MSS 2, 5).
Bühler C, The Dicts and Sayings of Philosophers, EETSES 211.368 (MS 10).
Abstract. Utley CR, no 387.
Authorship. MacCracken TPSL, appendix 2.xv; rptd EETSES 107.xvii.
Utley CR, no 387.
SchirmerLydgate, p 230; trans Keep, p 267.
Sources and Literary Relations. Bühler C F, Lydgate's Horse Sheep and Goose and Huntington MS HM 144, MLN 55.563 (notes presence of this stanza in other poems of L, in Court of Sapience, and in Ashby's Active Policy of a Prince).
Utley CR, no 387 (notes that L may have known similar material in Gower's Confessio amantis; gives biblio of related material).
SchirmerLydgate, p 95; trans Keep, p 111 (notes that poem is elaboration of Honor, etas, femina, vinum).

[57] FOUR THINGS THAT MAKE A MAN A FOOL: ON WORLDLY WORSHIP (also included in SAYINGS OF DAN JOHAN).

MSS. 1, Harley 2251, f 42ᵃ (1464–83); 2, BM Addit 34360, f 77ᵃ (1461–83).

Brown-Robbins, no 4228.
Hammond E P, Two British Museum MSS, Angl 28.1 (detailed study of MSS).
Edition. MacCracken EETS 192.709 (MS 2).
Authorship. SchirmerLydgate, p 230; trans Keep, p 267 (included under Four Things?).
General Reference. SchirmerLydgate, p 95; trans Keep, p 111 (included under Four Things?).

[58] FOUR THINGS THAT MAKE A MAN A FOOL: BALADE DE BONE COUNSEYLE (also BALLADE DE BONE CONSEYLL, included in SAYINGS OF DAN JOHAN).

MSS. 1, Trinity Camb 600, p 48 (1450–75); 2, BM Addit 29729, f 132ᵇ (John Stowe, 1558).
PRINT: 3, Stowe, Chaucer, 1561 (probably from MS 1; rptd A Chalmers, Eng Poets, London 1810, 1.552; rptd Oxf Ch, 7.297).
Brown-Robbins, Robbins-Cutler, no 1419.
Hammond E P, Lydgate's Mumming at Hertford, Angl 22.364 (describes MS 1).
Brusendorff A, The Chaucer Tradition, London 1925, pp 208, 466, and passim (discusses Shirley's marginalia in MS 1).
Edition. MacCracken EETS 192.710 (MS 1).
Language. Hingst R, Die Sprache John Lydgates aus seinen Reimen, Greiswald 1908, p 49.
Versification. Reger, pp 62, 77 (finds 4.76 percent lines have certain epic caesurae).
Authorship. Skeat W W, The Chaucer Canon, Oxford 1900, p 117 (argues L's authorship on basis of Stowe and internal evidence).
MacCracken TPSL, appendix 2.xv; rptd EETSES 107.xvii.
Hammond, p 427.
Literary Criticism. Reufs F, Das Naturgefühl bei Lydgate, Arch 122.269.

[59] A FREOND AT NEODE.

MS. Bodl 6943 (Ashmole 59), ff 34ᵇ–37ᵃ (1447–56; variant of lines 1–12 by Shirley on f 34ᵇ, continuous poem begins on f 35ᵃ).
Brown-Robbins, Robbins-Cutler, no 1842.
Hammond E P, Ashmole 59 and Other Shirley MSS, Angl 30.320.
Edition. MacCracken EETS 192.755 (ff 35ᵃ–37ᵇ; collations from Shirley's text on f 34ᵇ).
Textual Matters. Brusendorff A, The Chaucer Tradition, London 1925, p 232.
Authorship. MacCracken TPSL, appendix 2.xv; rptd EETSES 107.xvii.
SchirmerLydgate, p 230; trans Keep, p 272.

Sources and Literary Relations. Sandison H E, Chanson d'Aventure in ME, Bryn Mawr 1913, p 143.
SchirmerLydgate, p 176; trans Keep, p 201 (notes mixture of Classical and Biblical materials).
General References. PearsallLydgate, p 208.

[60] GAUDE FLORE VIRGINALI.

MS. Harley 372, f 55^{a-b} (15 cent).
Brown-Robbins, no 1804.
Editions. Hammerle K, Die me Hymnodie, Angl 55.429 (introd p 428 notes original is Latin text, print C Horstmann, Yorkshire Writers, 1.408).
Brown RLxvC, p 63.
Authorship. MacCracken EETSES 107.xlv (omitted from canon on grounds of rime and meter).
Brown-Robbins, no 1804 and p 764 (question authorship).

[61] GAUDE VIRGO MATER CHRISTI.

MSS. 1, Trinity Camb 600, pp 53–55 (1450–75); 2, Trinity Camb 601, f 173^{a-b} (1461–83); 3, Harley 2251, ff 234^b–235^b (1464–83).
Brown-Robbins, no 464.
Hammond E P, Lydgate's Mumming at Hertford, Angl 22.364 (describes MS 1); Two British Museum MSS, Angl 28.1 (detailed study of MS 3).
Brusendorff A, The Chaucer Tradition, London 1925, pp 208, 466, and passim (discusses Shirley's marginalia in MS 1).
Manly & Rickert, 1.241 (description of MS 3).
Edition. MacCracken EETSES 107.288 (MS 1; collations from MS 3).
Authorship. MacCracken TPSL, appendix 2.xv; rptd EETSES 107.xvii.
SchirmerLydgate, p 232; trans Keep, p 271.
Other Scholarly Problem. Brusendorff, p 461 (heading of poem in MS 1 suggests Shirley's personal acquaintance with L).
General References. SchirmerLydgate, p 167; trans Keep, p 192.
PearsallLydgate, p 274.

[62] A GENTLEWOMAN'S LAMENT (also A LOVER'S COMPLAINT).

MSS. 1, Trinity Camb 600, pp 152–154 (1450–75); 2, Harley 2251, ff 250^b, 251^b (1464–83); 3, BM Addit 29729, ff 160^a–161^a (John Stowe, 1558).

Brown-Robbins, no 154.
Hammond E P, Lydgate's Mumming at Hertford, Angl 22.364 (describes MS 1); Two British Museum MSS, Angl 28.1 (detailed study of MS 2).
Brusendorff A, The Chaucer Tradition, London 1925, pp 208, 466, and passim (discusses Shirley's marginalia in MS 2).
Editions. Halliwell PPS 2.220 (MS 2).
MacCracken EETS 192.418 (MS 1; collations from MSS 2, 3).
Textual Matters. Gattinger, p 84 (suggests textual emendations).
Versification. Gattinger, p 77.
Authorship. Koeppel E, Laurents de Premierfait und John Lydgates Bearbeitungen von Boccaccios De casibus virorum illustrium, Munich 1885, p 76 (rejects L's authorship).
MacCracken TPSL, appendix 2.xv; rptd EETSES 107.xvii.
SchirmerLydgate, p 229; trans Keep, p 265.
Seaton, p 368 (argues for Richard Roos).
Sources and Literary Relations. SchirmerLydgate, p 29; trans Keep, p 35 (notes Chaucerian and French influence).
Other Scholarly Problems. Renoir A, Attitudes to Women in Lydgate's Poetry, ESts 42.11.
Seaton, p 368 (argues poem contains name anagrams).
Literary Criticism. Renoir A, The Binding Knot Three Uses of One Image in Lydgate's Poetry, Neophil 41.202 (shows poignant use of binding knot image).
Norton-Smith J, Lydgate's Metaphors, ESts 42.90 (answer to Renoir above; knot image changes within the poem).
PearsallLydgate, p 103 (shows complexity of knot image).

[63] LEGEND OF ST GEORGE.

MSS. 1, Bodl 2527 (Bodley 686), ff 200^a–204^b (1430–40); 2, Trinity Camb 600, pp 74–81 (1450–75); 3, Trinity Camb 601, ff 314^a–317^b (1461–83); 4, Chetham Libr 6709, ff 193^a–198^b Art 5 (1480–85).
Brown-Robbins, Robbins-Cutler, no 2592.
Hammond E P, Lydgate's Mumming at Hertford, Angl 22.364 (describes MS 2).
Brusendorff A, The Chaucer Tradition, London 1925, pp 208, 466, and passim (discusses Shirley's marginalia in MS 2).
Manly & Rickert, 1.64, 82 (description of MSS 1, 4).
Editions. Hammond E P, Two Tapestry Poems by Lydgate: the Life of St George and the

Falls of Seven Princes, EStn 43.13 (MS 1).
MacCracken EETSES 107.145 (MS 2; collations from MSS 1, 3).
Date. Gerould S Leg, p 260 (after 1426).
Hammond, EStn 43.11 (1426 or later).
Authorship. MacCracken TPSL, appendix 2.xxiii; rptd EETSES 107.xxvi.
SchirmerLydgate, p 230; trans Keep, p 268.
Sources and Literary Relations. MacCracken H N, Lydgatiana, Arch 126.365 (technical relationship between Life of Holy Job, [63], and other tapestry poems by L).
SchirmerLydgate, pp 110, 135, 148; trans Keep, pp 128, 157, 170 (notes that poem is based on material from Legenda aurea).
Wolpers T, Die engl Heiligenlegende des Mittelalters, Tübingen 1964, p 315 (compares language and style with [112] below).
PearsallLydgate, p 275 (compares with S Eng Legendary).
Other Scholarly Problems. Wylie J H, The Reign of Henry 5th, Cambridge 1914–29, 2.117 (notes that the poem throws light on contemporary methods of hanging men).
Gerould J H, Legends of St Wulfhad and St Ruffin at Stone Priory, PMLA 32.323 (argues mural display).
SchirmerLydgate, p 136; trans Keep, p 157 (believes poem designed to go along with pictures).
PearsallLydgate, p 181 (believes verses were read out when murals presented to a guild).

[64] LIFE OF ST GILES.

MSS. 1, Bodl 798 (Laud Misc 683), ff 33b–44b (15 cent); 2, Harley 2255, ff 95b–103a (1448?–49?); 3, Lansdowne 699, f 2a (1450?–1500; only last 6 stanzas); 4, Leyden Univ Vossius 9, ff 1a–6b (lacks stanza 22; 15 cent).
Brown-Robbins, no 2606.
Robinson F N, On Two MSS of Lydgate's Guy of Warwick, HSNPL 5.177 (describes MS 4).
Utley CR, no 194 (suggests MS 2 compiled 1448–49).
van Dorsten J A, The Leyden Lydgate MS, Scriptorium 14.315, 320 (describes MS 4 and suggests relationship to MS 2).
Editions. AELeg 1881, p 371 (MS 2).
MacCracken EETSES 107.161 (MS 1; collations from MSS 2, 4).
Language. Dibelius W, John Capgrave u die engl Schriftsprache, Angl 23.153, 323.
Hingst R, Die Sprache John Lydgates aus seinen Reimen, Greiswald 1908.
Babcock C F, A Study of the Metrical Use of the Inflectional e in ME with Particular Reference to Chaucer and Lydgate, PMLA 29.59 (L's language bridges gap between Middle Ages and modern period).
Versification. Reger, pp 46, 77 (finds 10.32 percent lines have certain epic caesurae).
Authorship. MacCracken TPSL, appendix 2.xxiii; rptd EETSES 107.xxvi.
SchirmerLydgate, p 230; trans Keep, p 268.
Sources and Literary Relations. SchirmerLydgate, pp 137, 148; trans Keep, pp 159, 170 (argues poem based on lost Latin text but L had Guillaume de Berneville's text at his disposal).
Other Scholarly Problem. Wylie J H, The Reign of Henry 5th, Cambridge 1914–29, 2.411 (notes that poem throws light on contemporary use of hunting dogs).
Literary Criticism. Reufs F, Das Naturgefühl bei Lydgate, Arch 122.269 (believes monasticism ruins L's originality).
Gerould S Leg, p 264.
General References. SchirmerLydgate, p 164; trans Keep, p 188 (discusses prayer to St Gyle, stanzas 42–46).
PearsallLydgate, p 279 (notes originality in the narrative).

[65] GLORIOSA DICTA SUNT DE TE (also BALADE OF OURE LADYE BY LIDEGATE).

MSS. 1, Trinity Camb 600, pp 1–4 (1450–75); 2, Harley 2251, ff 239a–242b (1464–83); 3, Harley 2255, ff 135a–139b (1448?–49?); 4, BM Addit 29729, ff 146b–149b (John Stowe, 1558); 5, BM Addit 34360, ff 55b–57b (1461–83; 2 versions).
Brown-Robbins, no 2688.
Hammond E P, Lydgate's Mumming at Hertford, Angl 22.364 (describes MS 1); Two British Museum MSS, Angl 28.1 (detailed study of MSS 2, 5).
Brusendorff A, The Chaucer Tradition, London 1925, pp 208, 466, and passim (discusses Shirley's marginalia in MS 1).
Manly & Rickert, 1.241 (description of MS 2).
Utley CR, no 194 (suggests MS 3 compiled 1448–49).
Edition. MacCracken EETSES 107.315 (MS 1; collations from all MSS, including first text only from MS 5).
Authorship. MacCracken TPSL, appendix 2.xv; rptd EETSES 107.xviii.
SchirmerLydgate, p 233; trans Keep, p 271.
Sources and Literary Relations. SchirmerLydgate, p 170; trans Keep, p 195 (notes that poem is

stretching of Psalm 88 (89) [actually 86 (87)] for the Bishop of Exeter).

PearsallLydgate, p 275 (notes that poem combines Psalm 87 and Revelation 21:19).

Other Scholarly Problem. Deanesly M, The Lollard Bible and Other Biblical Versions, Cambridge 1920, pp 320, 336 (believes L unaware of rule against unlicensed use of Biblical translations, and notes Henry 5 used L's Psalms in private prayers).

General References. Gattinger, p 31.

Vickers K H, Humphrey of Gloucester, London 1907, p 343.

[66] APPEAL TO GLOUCESTER (also LETTER TO GLOUCESTER and UPON THE EMPTINESS OF HIS PURSE).

MSS. 1, Pepys 2011, ff 78^a–79^b (1450?–1500?); 2, Harley 2251, ff 6^a–7^a (1464–83); 3, Harley 2255, ff 45^b–47^a (1448?–49?); 4, Lansdowne 699, ff 90^a–91^a (1450?–1500); 5, BM Addit 34360, ff 64^b–65^b (1461–83); 6, Leyden Univ Vossius 9, ff 102^b–104^a (15 cent); 7, Morgan Libr 4, ff 75^b–77^a (1425–75).

Brown-Robbins, Robbins-Cutler, no 2825.

Robinson F N, On Two MSS of Lydgate's Guy of Warwick, HSNPL 5.177 (describes MS 6).

Hammond E P, Two British Museum MSS, Angl 28.1 (detailed study of MSS 2, 5).

Bühler, edn, MLN 52.1 (describes MS 7 and traces genealogy).

Utley CR, no 194 (suggests MS 3 compiled 1448–49).

van Dorsten J A, The Leyden Lydgate MS, Scriptorium 14.315 (MS 6).

Editions. [Nicolas H,] A Chronicle of London, London 1827, p 268 (MS 3).

Halliwell PPS 2.49.

Hammond E P, Poet and Patron in the Fall of Princes, Angl 38.125 (MS 3); Eng Verse from Chaucer to Surrey, Durham 1927, p 149 (MS 3).

MacCracken EETS 192.665 (MS 3; collations from all MSS except MS 7).

Bühler C F, A New Lydgate-Chaucer MS, MLN 52.2 (MS 7).

Norton-Smith J, John Lydgate Poems, Oxford 1966, pp 1, 114 (brief commentary, notes and glossary).

Textual Matters. Gattinger, p 83 (suggests textual emendations).

Versification. Reger, pp 41, 78 (finds 15.62 percent lines have certain epic caesurae).

Authorship. MacCracken TPSL, appendix 2.xvii; rptd EETSES 107.xx.

SchirmerLydgate, p 231; trans Keep, p 269.

van Dorsten, Scriptorium 14.319 (L's name with poem in MS 6).

Sources and Literary Relations. Gattinger, pp 20, 64 (discusses poem as occasional piece reflecting influence of Chaucer and Jean de Meung).

Bühler, edn, MLN 52.1 (notes use of terms also found in [166] below and Rules of Health).

Moore A K, The Secular Lyric in ME, Lexington 1951, pp 135, 212 (argues poem prompted by Chaucer's Complaint to His Purse).

Norton-Smith, edn, p 116 (notes purse had been personified before in ME but L's treatment original).

Other Scholarly Problems. Gattinger, p 20 (notes poem throws light on relationship between L and Gloucester).

Vickers K H, Humphrey Duke of Gloucester, London 1907, p 392 (argues poet attempts to make Gloucester look like Italian humanist).

Hammond, edn, Eng Verse, p 149 (discusses poem's occasion).

Wylie J H, The Reign of Henry 5th, Cambridge 1914–29, 2.4 (notes poem bears witness to custom of painting sails of ships).

Bennett H S, The Author and His Public in the 14th and 15th Cents, E&S 23.7 (considers poem representative of poet-patron relationship).

Norton-Smith, edn, p 114 (reviews textual evidence for relationship between L and Gloucester).

Literary Criticism. SchirmerLydgate, p 188; trans Keep, p 215 (notes saucy humor of envoy).

Gray D, Later Poetry The Courtly Tradition, in The Middle Ages, ed W F Bolton, London 1970, p 324 (argues poem an example of L's poetic virtues).

PearsallLydgate, p 228 (finds poem a minor masterpiece).

[67] EPITAPH ON GLOUCESTER.

MSS. 1, Harley 2251, ff 7^a–8^b (1464–83); 2, BM Addit 34360, ff 65^b–68^a (1461–83).

Brown-Robbins, Robbins-Cutler, no 3206.

Hammond E P, Two British Museum MSS, Angl 28.1 (detailed study of MSS).

Editions. Robbins R H, An Epitaph for Duke Humphrey, NM 56.243 (MS 1); Robbins-HP, pp 180, 346 (MS 1).

Versification. Pyle F, The Pedigree of Lydgate's Heroic Line, Hermathena 50.26 (traces L's line as far back as Poema morale; studies conditions under which it appears).

Authorship. Schick J, Lydgate's Temple of Glas,

EETSES 60.xcvi (questions L's authorship on basis of internal evidence).
Steele R, A Stow MS of Lydgate, Acad 45.395 (argues L's authorship on basis of MS 2).
MacCracken EETSES 107.xl (argues poem in manner of L rather than by L).
SchirmerLydgate, pp 235, 238; trans Keep, pp 275, 279 (poem in manner of L but not by him).
Robbins, NM 56.241 (argues against L's authorship); Robbins-HP, p 346; Manual, 5.1495.
Other Scholarly Problem. Robbins-HP, pp xxxix (refrain suggests poem written on scroll to hang near tomb at burial), 347 (notes suspected murder of Gloucester and prints account in Hall's chronicle).
Literary Criticism. Vickers K H, Humphrey Duke of Gloucester, London 1907, p 390 (cites poem as example of worthless doggerel).
General References. Gattinger, p 21.
Schirmer W F, Der engl Frühhumanismus, Leipzig 1931, p 53; rvsd edn Tübingen 1963, p 4.
Bibliography. Robbins R H, Manual, 5.1699 (XIII [229]).

[68] MARRIAGE OF GLOUCESTER (also ON GLOUCESTER'S APPROACHING MARRIAGE).

MSS. 1, Trinity Camb 600, pp 158–164 (1450–75); 2, Harley 2251, ff 253ᵇ–256ᵇ? (Harleian catalogue gives 279ᵇ–282ᵇ; 1464–83); 3, BM Addit 29729, ff 157ᵇ–160ᵃ (John Stowe, 1558).
Brown-Robbins, Robbins-Cutler, no 3718.
Hammond E P, Lydgate's Mumming at Hertford, Angl 22.364 (describes MS 1); Two British Museum MSS, Angl 28.1 (detailed study of MS 2).
Brusendorff A, The Chaucer Tradition, London 1925, pp 208, 466, and passim (discusses Shirley's marginalia in MS 1).
Editions. Hammond E P, Lydgate and the Duchess of Gloucester, Angl 27.387 (MS 1; text is preceded by historical introd and followed by [69] below); Eng Verse between Chaucer and Surrey, Durham 1927, p 142 (MS 1; text preceded by historical introd).
MacCracken EETS 192.601 (MS 1; collations from other MSS).
Textual Matters. Holthausen F, Zu me Dichtungen, Angl 44.78 (suggests textual emendations).
Versification. Reger, pp 44, 77 (finds 4.57 percent lines have epic caesurae).
Authorship. MacCracken TPSL, appendix 2.xv; rptd EETSES 107.xviii.
SchirmerLydgate, p 229; trans Keep, p 266.

Sources and Literary Relations. MacCracken H N, Additional Light on the Temple of Glas, PMLA 23.128 (finds strong parallels between this poem and [176] below).
Patch H R, The Goddess Fortuna in Mediaeval Literature, Cambridge Mass 1927, p 29 (lists texts that differentiate between Fortune and Fate).
Literary Criticism. Vickers K H, Humphrey Duke of Gloucester, London 1907, p 390.
SchirmerLydgate, p 97; trans Keep, p 114 (a brilliant solution of a difficult task).
PearsallLydgate, p 165 (good of its kind but retreats into abstraction).
Scattergood V J, Politics and Poetry in the 15th Cent, London 1971, p 145 (dexterously avoids controversies over the marriage).
General Reference. Schirmer W F, Der engl Frühhumanismus, Leipzig 1931, p 53; rvsd edn Tübingen 1963, p 46.
Bibliography. Hammond, edn, Eng Verse, p 145 (gives biblio of historical and related material).

[69] A COMPLAINT FOR MY LADY OF GLOUCESTER AND HOLLAND.

MSS. 1, Bodl 6943 (Ashmole 59), ff 57ᵃ–58ᵇ (1447–56; lines 1–110 only); 2, Trinity Camb 600, pp 363–367 (1456?).
Brown-Robbins, no 92.
Hammond E P, Lydgate's Mumming at Hertford, Angl 22.364 (describes MS 2); Ashmole 59 and Other Shirley MSS, Angl 30.320.
Brusendorff A, The Chaucer Tradition, London 1925, p 209 (discusses chronological allusions and MS 1 and other Shirley MSS).
Editions. Hammond E P, Lydgate and the Duchess of Gloucester, Angl 27.393 (MS 2; preceded by historical introd and [68] above).
MacCracken EETS 192.608 (MS 2; collations from MS 1).
Authorship. MacCracken TPSL, appendix 2.xi; rptd EETSES 107.xiii.
SchirmerLydgate, p 229; trans Keep, p 266.
PearsallLydgate, p 166 (unlikely it is by L as it attacks Gloucester).
Scattergood V J, Politics and Poetry in the 15th Cent, London 1971, p 147 (probably not by L).
Other Scholarly Problem. Vickers K H, Humphrey Duke of Gloucester, London 1907, p 205 (considers poem typical of general indignation at Gloucester's desertion of Jacqueline of Hainault).
General References. Schirmer W F, Der engl Frühhumanismus, Leipzig 1931, p 53; rvsd edn

Tübingen 1963, p 46; SchirmerLydgate, p 97; trans Keep, p 115.
PearsallLydgate, p 166.
Scattergood, p 147 (very circumspect poem).

[70] GOD IS MYN HELPERE.

MS. Harley 2255, ff 148ª–150ª (1448?–49?).
Brown-Robbins, no 953.
Utley CR, no 194 (suggests MS compiled 1448–49).
Edition. MacCracken EETSES 107.27.
Authorship. MacCracken TPSL, appendix 2.xv; rptd EETSES 107.xviii.
SchirmerLydgate, p 234; trans Keep, p 273.
Sources and Literary Relations. Duschl, p 29 (merely classifies one proverb).
Patch H R, The Goddess Fortuna in Mediaeval Literature, Cambridge Mass 1927, p 47 (L's concept of Fortune's hair goes back to Boethius).
General Reference. SchirmerLydgate, pp 19n, 178; trans Keep, pp 22n, 204 (notes theme of mutability of earthly things).

[71] GUY OF WARWICK.

MSS. 1, Bodl 798 (Laud Misc 683), ff 65ª–78ª (15 cent); 2, Trinity Camb 601, ff 305ª–314ª (1461–83); 3, Harley 7333, ff 33ª–35ᵇ (15 cent); 4, Lansdowne 699, ff 18ᵇ–27ᵇ (1450?–1500); 5, Peterborough Public Libr, ff 54ª–63ᵇ; 6, Leyden Univ Vossius 9, ff 17ª–29ᵇ (15 cent); 7, Harvard Coll Eng 530, ff 4ᵇ–12ᵇ (1425–75).
Brown-Robbins, Robbins-Cutler, no 875.
Robinson, edn, HSNPL 5.177 (detailed study of MSS 6, 7).
van Dorsten J A, The Leyden Lydgate MS, Scriptorium 14.315, 320 (describes MS 6 and relationship of [71] in it and in MS 1).
Editions. Zupitza J, Zur Literaturgeschichte des Guy von Warwick, Sitzungsberichte der kaiserlichen Akademie der Wissenschaften (Wien) 74.649 (MS 1; crit Kölbing, Germ 21.354).
Robinson F N, On Two MSS of Lydgate's Guy of Warwick, HSNPL 5.197 (MS 7).
MacCracken EETS 192.516 (MS 1; collations from all MSS).
Selections. PFMS 2.520 (MS 3; end of poem only).
Zupitza J, Alt u me Übungsbuch, Wien 1882, p 103 (MS 1; collations from MSS 2, 4; see also later printings and American adaptation by G E MacLean).
Language. Dibelius W, John Capgrave u die engl Schriftsprache, Angl 23.153, 323.
Hingst R, Die Sprache John Lydgates aus seinen Reimen, Greiswald 1908.
Versification. Schipper, 1.494 and passim.
Pyle F, The Pedigree of Lydgate's Heroic Line, Hermathena 50.26 (studies conditions under which L's line occurs in [71]).
Date. Zupitza, edn, p 623 (suggests 1420).
Schick J, Lydgate's Temple of Glas, EETSES 60.cxii (1423?).
Courthope, 1.323 (before 1423).
SchirmerLydgate, p 78; trans Keep, p 92 (between 1423 and 1426).
Authorship. MacCracken TPSL, appendix 2.xv; rptd EETSES 107.xviii.
SchirmerLydgate, p 231; trans Keep, p 268.
Sources and Literary Relations. Zupitza, edn, p 623 (gives source as Girardus Cornubiensis and prints selections from other versions).
Billings, p 32 (traces development of legend since 10th cent).
Duschl, pp 9, 73 (classifies proverbs).
Schleich G, Lydgates Quelle zu seinem Guy of Warwick, Arch 146.49 (prints the Historia Guidonis de Warwyke of Girardus Cornubiensis and accepts it as L's source).
SchirmerLydgate, p 79; trans Keep, p 94 (accepts Chronicle of Girardus Cornubiensis as L's original).
Klausner D N, Didacticism and Drama in Guy of Warwick, MH ns 6.103 (discusses legend in other ME and AN versions).
Other Scholarly Problems. Ker W P, Medieval Eng Literature, N Y and London 1945, p 98 (notes moral and religious strain of poem).
PearsallLydgate, p 167 (Warwick family as L's patron).
Literary Criticism. Reufs F, Das Naturgefühl bei Lydgate, Arch 122.269 (concludes that monasticism ruins L's originality).
SchirmerLydgate, p 79; trans Keep, p 93 (considers poem standard example of L's lowest style).
PearsallLydgate, p 167 (brief).
General References. SchirmerLydgate, pp 116, 226; trans Keep, pp 135, 260.
Klausner, MH ns 6.103 (L sees himself as a hagiographer rather than a romance storyteller).
Mehl D, The ME Romances of the 13th and 14th Cents, London 1967, p 222.

[72] A DITTY AGAINST HASTE.

MSS. 1, Bodl 11951 (Rawl C.86), ff 84ª–87ᵇ (1475?–1500?); 2, Camb Univ Kk.1.6, ff 205ᵇ–208ᵇ (15 cent); 3, Harley 78, ff 77ᵇ–79ª (1460–

70; 14 stanzas only); 4, Harley 2251, ff 26ᵇ–28ᵃ (1464–83).
Brown-Robbins, no 186.
Hammond E P, Two British Museum MSS, Angl 28.1 (detailed study of MS 4).
Manly & Rickert, 1.241 (description of MS 4).
Edition. MacCracken EETS 192.759 (MS 2; collations from all other MSS).
Authorship. MacCracken TPSL, appendix 2.xv; rptd EETSES 107.xviii.
SchirmerLydgate, p 233; trans Keep, p 272.
Sources and Literary Relations. SchirmerLydgate, p 174; trans Keep, p 200 (notes use of both classical antiquity and of Christ).
General Reference. PearsallLydgate, p 208 (L practicing an effect).

[73] HENRY V'S EXPEDITION INTO FRANCE (also THE SIEGE OF HARFLEUR).

MSS. 1, Bodl 11951 (Rawl 86), ff 178ᵃ–186ᵃ (69 stanzas; 1480–1500); 2, Cotton Vitell D.xii, II, f 214 (parts only; 1475–1500); 3, Harley 565, ff 102ᵃ–114ᵃ (1440–50); 4, Rome Eng Coll 1306 (also numbered A.347 and 127), ff 67ᵃ–74ᵃ (1456–1500). PRINT: 5, John Skot, Batayll of Egyngscourte, 1530? (STC, no 198; rptd E Arber, An Eng Garner, London 1896, 8.13; rptd Pollard 15CPV, p 2).
Brown-Robbins, Robbins-Cutler, no 969.
Klinefelter R A, The Siege of Calais: a New Text, PMLA 66.888 (brief description of MS 4); A Newly Discovered 15-Cent Eng MS, MLQ (Washington) 14.3 (lists contents of MS 4).
Robbins R H, A ME Diatribe against Philip of Burgundy, Neophil 39.131 (gives description and contents of MS 4).
Editions. Hearne T, Helmham's Vita Henrici V, Oxford 1727, p 357 (MS 2; rptd H Nicolas, History of the Battle of Agincourt, London 1832, p 301; rptd R H Evans, Old Ballads Historical and Narrative, London 1810, 2.334).
[Nicolas H,] A Chronicle of London, London 1827, p 216 (MS 3).
Authorship. MacCracken EETSES 107.xlvi (rejects L's authorship).
Kingsford C L, Eng Historical Literature in the 15th Cent, London 1913, pp 232, 238 (rejects L's authorship).
Brown-Robbins, no 969 (lists poem as perhaps by L).
SchirmerLydgate, pp 235, 238; trans Keep, pp 275, 279 (rejects L's authorship on stylistic grounds).

Literary Relations. Robbins R H, Manual, 5.1415 (XIII [51]), 1426 (XIII [72]).
Other Scholarly Problems. Vickers K H, Humphrey Duke of Gloucester, London 1907, p 32 (cites poem as historical evidence for Henry's actions).
Kingsford C L, The First Eng Life of King Henry 5th, Oxford 1911, p xliii (notes that poem is evidence for story of tennis balls sent Henry by the French).
Wylie J H, The Reign of Henry 5th, Cambridge 1914–29, 2.38 and passim.
General Reference. SchirmerLydgate, pp 55, 93; trans Keep, pp 62, 109.

[74] HENRY VI: HIS CLAIM TO FRANCE (also ENGLISH TITLE TO THE CROWN OF FRANCE and TITLE AND PEDIGREE OF HENRY VI) followed by ROUNDEL ON THE CORONATION OF HENRY VI [81] in only MS.

MS. Harley 7333, ff 31ᵃ–32ᵇ (15 cent).
Brown-Robbins, Robbins-Cutler, no 3808.
Editions. Wright PPS, 2.131.
MacCracken EETS 192.613.
Versification. Reger, pp 56, 77 (finds certain epic caesurae in 3.82 percent lines).
Pyle F, The Pedigree of Lydgate's Heroic Line, Hermathena 50.26 (shows that characteristics of L's line go back as far as Poema morale).
Date. Parr J, Astronomical Dating for Some of Lydgate's Poems, PMLA 67.251 (suggests 28 July 1426).
SchirmerLydgate, p 101; trans Keep, p 118 (argues for 28 July 1427).
Authorship. MacCracken TPSL, appendix 2.xx; rptd EETSES 107.xxiii.
SchirmerLydgate, p 229; trans Keep, p 266.
Sources and Literary Relations. Floran M, Document relatif à l'entrée du roi d'Angleterre Henry VI à Paris en 1431, Revue des Études Historiques 75.411 (prints French description of Henry 6's entrance).
MacCracken H N, Lydgatiana, Arch 126.365 (points out technical similarities between Life of Holy Job and [74] and other so-called tapestry poems of L; prints Life of Holy Job).
Rowe B J H, King Henry VI's Claim to France in Picture and Poem, Libr ns 13.77 (argues L's poem trans of French original; prints side-by-side excerpts from L's and French texts).
SchirmerLydgate, p 101; trans Keep, p 118 (considers poem trans of Laurence Calot's text of 1427; discusses Calot's work and background

of document).
Robbins-HP, p 248 (notes some lines duplicated in [100] below).
Other Scholarly Problems. Rowe, Libr ns 13.77 (believes poem designed to be posted in churches).
McKenna J W, Henry VI of England and the Dual Monarchy Aspects of Royal Political Propaganda 1422–32, Journ of the Warburg and Courtauld Institutes 28.153 (L a propagandist for domestic audience).
Scattergood V J, Politics and Poetry in the 15th Cent, London 1971, p 71 (discusses poem as a skillful and insistent political work).
Literary Criticism. Kingsford C L, Eng History in Contemporary Poetry, London 1913, 2.19 (considers poem typical of L's worthless official verse but important for historical reasons).
General References. SchirmerLydgate, pp 78n, 79, 91, 110, 112, 123; trans Keep, pp 92n, 93, 107, 128, 131, 142.
PearsallLydgate, p 166 (argues poem not well done).

[75] HENRY VI: BALLADE UPON HIS CORONATION.

MSS. 1, Bodl 6943 (Ashmole 59), ff 54^a–56^b (1447–56); 2, Trinity Camb 600, pp 154–158 (1450–75); 3, Harley 2251, ff 251^b–253^b (1464–83; omits envoy); 4, BM Addit 29729, ff 84^a–86^a (John Stowe, 1558).
Brown-Robbins, no 2211.
Hammond E P, Lydgate's Mumming at Hertford, Angl 22.364 (describes MS 2); Two British Museum MSS, Angl 28.1 (detailed study of MS 3).
Brusendorff A, The Chaucer Tradition, London 1925, pp 208, 466, and passim (discusses Shirley's marginalia in MS 2).
Edition. Wright PPS, 2.141 (MS 3).
MacCracken EETS 192.624 (MS 2; collations from all other MSS).
Versification. Reger, pp 56, 77 (finds certain epic caesurae in 6.94 percent lines).
Authorship. MacCracken TPSL, appendix 2.x; rptd EETSES 107.xii.
SchirmerLydgate, p 230; trans Keep, p 266.
Other Scholarly Problems. Kleineke W, Engl Fürstenspiegel vom Policraticus Johanns von Salisbury bis zum Basilicon Doron König Jacobs I, SEP 40.136 (points out catalogue of princely virtues in poem).
McKenna J W, Henry VI of England and the Dual Monarchy Aspects of Royal Political Propaganda 1422–32, Journ of the Warburg and Courtauld Institutes 28.155 (combines Arthurian and dual monarchy themes).
Scattergood V J, Politics and Poetry in the 15th Cent, London 1971, pp 72, 148 (dual monarchy used).
General References. SchirmerLydgate, pp 112, 114, 120; trans Keep, pp 131, 132, 139.
PearsallLydgate, p 170.

[76] HENRY VI: SOTELTIES AT THE CORONATION BANQUET.

MSS. 1, St John's Oxf 57 (3 stanzas, not paginated; 15 cent); 2, Cotton Julius B.i, ff 79^a–80^a (no date in Cottonian cat); 3, Lansdowne 285, ff 5^b–7^b (1450–75); 4, Egerton 1995, f 177^a (15 cent); 5, London Guildhall 3313, ff 129^b–130^b (1500–25; listed in Brown-Robbins as no 3133); 6, Morgan Libr M 775, f 15^a (ca 1486). PRINT: 7, Fabyan, New Chronicles, London 1516 (STC, no 10659; altered version; rptd G Ellis, Specimens of the Early Eng Poets, London 1811, pp 600–01).
Brown-Robbins, Robbins-Cutler, no 1929.
Editions. [Nicolas H,] A Chronicle of London, London 1827, p 168 (MS 2).
Hammond E P, Two Tapestry Poems by Lydgate: the Life of St George and the Falls of Seven Princes, EStn 43.23 (MS 1; only poem for the 3rd course).
Gairdner J, The Historical Collections of a Citizen of London, Camden Soc 2s 17(1876).169 (MS 4).
Arthur H, On a MS Collection of Ordinances of Chivalry of the 15th Cent Belonging to Lord Hastings, Archaeol 2s 7.57 (MS 6).
MacCracken EETS 192.623 (MS 2; collations from MS 3).
Thomas A H and I D Thornley, The Great Chronicle, London 1938, p 152 (MS 5).
Harvey J, Gothic England, London 1947, p 179.
Robbins SL, pp 98, 261 (MS 5; brief note).
Authorship. MacCracken TPSL, appendix 2.xxv; rptd EETSES 107.xxviii.
SchirmerLydgate, p 230; trans Keep, p 266.
McKenna J W, Henry VI of England and the Dual Monarchy Aspects of Royal Political Propaganda 1422–32, Journ of the Warburg and Courtauld Institutes 28.157.
Other Scholarly Problems. SchirmerLydgate, p 113; trans Keep, p 132 (draws attention to pageant features).
Wickham G, Early Eng Stages 1300 to 1660, London and N Y 1959, 1.211 (describes a

subtilty).
McKenna, Journ of Warburg Courtauld Inst 28.157 (notes political theme, especially dual monarchy).
General References. PearsallLydgate, p 169.
Scattergood V J, Politics and Poetry in the 15th Cent, London 1971, p 74.

[77] HENRY VI: TRIUMPHAL ENTRY INTO LONDON.

MSS. 1, Cotton Cleop C.iv, ff 38ª–48ª (1425–75); 2, Cotton Julius B.ii, ff 89ª–101ª (15 cent); 3, Harley 565, ff 114ᵇ–124ª (1440–50); 4, London Guildhall 3313, ff 132ᵇ–142ª (1500–25; listed in Brown-Robbins as no 3133); 5, Longleat, at end of MS (stanzas 1–23 only); 6, Rome Eng Coll 1306 (also numbered 127 and A.347), ff 67ª–74ª (1436–1456; roundel varies from usual text). PRINT: 7, Pynson, 1516 (rptd R Fabyan, The New Chronicles of England and France, ed H Ellis, London 1811; roundel only).
Brown-Robbins, Robbins-Cutler, no 3799 (notes presence of prose paraphrases in MSS Cotton Vitel A.xvi, College of Arms Arundel 19, and Egerton 1995).
Klinefelter R A, The Siege of Calais: a New Text, PMLA 67.888 (discusses briefly MS 6); A Newly Discovered 15th-Cent Eng MS, MLQ (Wash) 14.3 (description and contents of MS 6).
Robbins R H, A ME Diatribe against Philip of Burgundy, Neophil 39.131 (description and contents of MS 6).
Editions. [Nicolas H,] A Chronicle of London, London 1827, p 235 (MS 2, 3).
Halliwell PPS 2.2 (MS 1).
Kingsford C L, Chronicles of London, Oxford 1905, p 97 (MS 2).
MacCracken EETS 192.630 (MS 2; collations from MSS 1, 3).
Thomas A H and I D Thornley, The Great Chronicle, London 1938, p 156 (MS 4).
Selections. Schleich G, Ein me Rondel, Arch 96.193 (MS 1; with editor's textual restorations; prints only roundel and suggests it must be the one mentioned in Gregory's Collections of a London Citizen as sung for Henry VI by Londoners); rptd H Cohen, Lyric Forms from France, N Y 1922, p 69.
[Thompson R,] Chronicle of London Bridge, London 1927, p 239 (prints lines 1–224, MS 3).
Fabyan R, The New Chronicle of England and France, ed H Ellis (PRINT 7), p 603 (prints roundel).
MacCracken H N, King Henry's Triumphal Entry into London Lydgate's Poem and Carpenter's Letter, Arch 126.75 (roundel only).
Modernization. Malcolm J P, Londinium Redivivum, London 1803, 2.397 (prints modernization of lines 27–224 in EETS 192 text).
Textual Matter. Gattinger, 4.83.
Language. Hingst R, Die Sprache John Lydgates aus seinen Reimen, Greiswald 1908, p 13.
Versification. Reger, pp 39, 78 (finds certain epic caesurae in 13.24 percent lines).
Date. Ward A W, A History of Eng Dramatic Literature, London 1875, 1.80 (believes poem among earliest descriptions of pageants).
Schick J, Lydgate's Temple of Glas, EETSES 60.cxii (1432).
Authorship. MacCracken TPSL, appendix 2.xvii; rptd EETSES 107.xvi.
SchirmerLydgate, pp 120, 230; trans Keep, pp 139, 267 (suggests possibility of Lydgate's authorship of material accompanying poem, printed in Kingsford's Chronicle of London, pp xxv, 301).
Sources and Literary Relations. Herbert W, The History of the Twelve Great Livery Companies of London, London 1837, 1.92, 200 (compares L's relation with other accounts; suggests it as source of Thomas Middleton's Triumph of Truth).
Delpit J, Collection générale des documents français qui se trouvent en Angleterre, Paris 1847, 1.clx (suggests John Carpenter's account, printed on pp 245–48, as source of L's poem).
Gattinger, pp 20, 72 (prints Fabyan's text and suggests Chaucer's influence on L's style).
Lange J H, Zu Fragment B des ME Rosenromans, EStn 31.159 (notes influence of Romance of the Rose).
MacCracken, Arch 126.75 (shows that Carpenter's letter is L's source, and gives biblio of related material).
Kingsford, Eng Historical Literature in the 15th Cent, Oxford 1913, pp 77, 92, and passim (discusses relationship of L's text to Great Chronicle and accepts Carpenter's narrative printed in Liber Albus, Rolls Series 2.457, as L's source).
Withington R, Eng Pageantry, Cambridge 1918–20, 2.33 (minimizes influence of Middleton's Triumph of Truth).
Wickham G, Early Eng Stages 1300 to 1660, London and N Y 1959, 1.83 (claims L anticipates Jonson).
Other Scholarly Problems. Nichols J G, London Pageants, London 1831, p 18 (notes on Fabyan's account and L's poem).

Davidson C, Studies in the Eng Mystery Plays, Yale 1892, p 87 (believes poem illustrates community of custom and literary standards among Eng and French nobility).
Kingsford, Eng Hist Lit, pp 77, 84, 87, 92, 105 (discusses historical value of Chronicle of London where L's poem appears in two texts).
Withington, Eng Pageantry, 1.141 (carefully describes circumstance of poem and argues for its historical importance).
SchirmerLydgate, pp 90n, 118, 122; trans Keep, pp 106n, 137, 141 (gives thorough account of pageant; suggests that use of Seven Liberal Arts looks toward Renaissance).
Wickham, Early Eng Stages, 1.72 (first use of historical person to point a moral), 90 (use of three wells), 91 (use of orchard), 105 (color symbolism).
Scattergood V J, Politics and Poetry in the 15th Cent, London 1971, p 81 (dual monarchy mentioned).
Literary Criticism. Knowlton E C, Nature in ME, JEGP 20.186 (finds handling of nature typically Lydgatian).
Wickham, Early Eng Stages, 1.75 (shows how this work anticipates later theater).
PearsallLydgate, p 170 (poem is a souvenir program; links L with Shakespeare).
Jack R D S, Dunbar and Lydgate, SSL 8.218 (compares poem unfavorably with Dunbar's To Aberdeen).

[78] ENVOY TO HENRY VI (at end of LIFE OF SS EDMUND AND FREMUND [42]).

MSS. 1, Bodl 6943 (Ashmole 59), f 23[b] (1447–56); 2, Bodl 10174 (Tanner 347), f 86[a] (15 cent); 3, Corp Christi Oxf 61, f 65[b] (15 cent); 4, Camb Univ Ee.2.15, f 88[a] (1470–1500); 5, Harley 367, f 86[b] (1600–25; transcript by Stowe); 6, Harley 372, f 43[a] (1440–60), 7, Harley 2278, f 118[b] (time of Henry 6?); 8, Harley 4826, f 45[b] (15 cent); 9, Yates Thompson (formerly Mostyn Hall), p 213 (15 cent).
Brown-Robbins, no 928.
Edition. AELeg 1881, p 440 (MS 7).

[79] A PRAYER FOR HENRY VI, HIS QUEEN AND PEOPLE (also AB INIMICIS).

MSS. 1, Bodl 3896 (Fairfax 16), ff 199*[b]–200[b] (1400–50); 2, Trinity Camb 601, ff 245[a–b] (only 1 stanza of envoy; dedication altered to Edward 4), 318[b]–319[a] (1461–83); 3, Harley 2251, ff 10[b]–11[a] (only 1 stanza of envoy; dedication altered to Edward 4; 1464–83); 4, Harley 7578, f 19[a–b] (1425–75); 5, BM Addit 34360, ff 69[a]–70[b] (only 1 stanza of envoy; dedication altered to Edward 4; 1461–83); 6, BM Addit 5467 (refrain only, quoted by John Shirley in his text of Governance of Princes; 1450–75); 7, Huntington Libr EL 26.A.13 (formerly Ellesmere), flyleaf (15 cent).
Brown-Robbins, Robbins-Cutler, no 2218.
Hammond E P, Two British Museum MSS, Angl 28.1 (detailed study of MSS 3, 5).
Manly & Rickert, 1.241 (describes MS 3).
Editions. Wülker R P, Altenglisches Lesebuch, Halle 1874–79, 2.8 (MS 4).
Rel Ant, 1.227 (MS 4).
Mahir O, Einige religiöse Gedichte John Lydgates, München 1910, p 44 (MS 1).
MacCracken EETSES 107.212 (MS 1; collations from all other MSS).
Robbins-HP, pp 235, 389 (MS 1; collations from MS 3).
Versification. Reger, pp 68, 77 (finds certain epic caesurae in 5.36 percent lines).
Pyle F, The Pedigree of Lydgate's Heroic Line, Hermathena 50.26 (studies conditions under which various aspects of the line appear).
Date. Robbins-HP, p 389 (before Nov 1429).
Authorship. John Shirley attributes poem to L in MS BM Addit 5467 of Governance of Princes.
MacCracken TPSL, appendix 2.xxi; rptd EETSES 107.xxiii.
SchirmerLydgate, p 230; trans Keep, p 267.
Sources and Literary Relations. SchirmerLydgate, pp 112, 115 and passim; trans Keep, pp 131, 133 and passim (considers source Pontificat of Egbert, Bishop of York, print Surtees Soc 27.26).
Robbins-HP, p 389 (considers the poem a paraphrase of Litany for consecration of a church, refers to Surtees Soc 27.33).
General References. PearsallLydgate, p 170 (poem proves L's ability to handle any kind of material).
Scattergood V J, Politics and Poetry in the 15th Cent, London 1971, p 149.
Bibliography. Robbins-HP, p 389.

[80] A PRAYER TO ST EDMUND FOR HENRY VI (also PRAYERS TO ST EDMUND).

MSS. 1, Bodl 6930 (Ashmole 46), f 84[b] (15 cent);

2, Bodl 6943 (Ashmole 59), f 22ᵇ (1447–56); 3, Bodl 10174 (Tanner 347), f 84ᵃ (15 cent); 4, Corp Christi Oxf 61, f 63ᵇ (15 cent); 5, Camb Univ Ee.2.15, f 103ᵃ (1470–1500); 6, Harley 367, f 86ᵃ (1600–25; transcript by Stowe); 7, Harley 372, f 42ᵇ (1440–60); 8, Harley 2278, f 117ᵃ (time of Henry 6?); 9, Harley 4826, f 45ᵃ (15 cent); 10, Chetham Libr 6709, ff 282ᵇ–284ᵃ (1480–85; 9 stanzas); 11, Yates Thompson (formerly Mostyn Hall 84), p 209 (15 cent).

Brown-Robbins, Robbins-Cutler, no 2445.

Hammond E P, Ashmole 59 and Other Shirley MSS, Angl 30.320 (describes MSS).

Edition. AELeg 1881, p 438 (MS 8; collations from MS 1).

Sources and Literary Relations. The Suffolk Garland, Ipswich 1818, p 351 (notes ceremonies at Bury on feast of St Edmund and prints another prayer to him).

[81] ROUNDEL ON THE CORONATION OF HENRY VI (follows [74] above in only MS).

MS. Harley 7333, f 32ᵇ (15 cent).

Brown-Robbins, no 2804.

Editions. Ritson AS 1829, 1.128.

Wright PPS, 2.140.

Guest E, History of Eng Rhythms, rvsd W W Skeat, London 1882, p 646.

MacCracken EETS 192.622.

Authorship. MacCracken TPSL, appendix 2.xxii; rptd EETSES 107.xv.

Brown-Robbins, no 2804 (does not assign poem to L).

SchirmerLydgate, p 230; trans Keep, p 266.

Sources and Literary Relations. Guest, edn, p 646 (shows L's debt to OF models).

Other Scholarly Problems. SchirmerLydgate, p 112; trans Keep, p 131 (gives background and account of poem).

McKenna J W, Henry VI of England and the Dual Monarchy Aspects of Royal Political Propaganda 1422–32, Journ of the Warburg and Courtauld Institutes 28.154 (theme of dual monarchy used).

General References. PearsallLydgate, p 169.

Scattergood V J, Politics and Poetry in the 15th Cent, London 1971, p 72.

[82] DEFENSE OF HOLY CHURCH.

MSS. 1, Harley 1245, ff 182ᵇ–183ᵃ (15 cent); 2, Sloane 1212, f 3ᵃ⁻ᵇ (stanzas 1–8; 15 cent).

Brown-Robbins, no 2219.

MacCracken H N, Additional Light on the Temple of Glas, PMLA 23.128 (partial description of MS 2).

Norton-Smith, edn, p 143 (MS 2).

Editions. MacCracken EETSES 107.30 (MS 1; collations from MS 2).

Norton-Smith J, John Lydgate Poems, Oxford 1966, pp 30 (MSS 1, 2; with glossary); 150 (commentary and notes; argues that poem is complete; discusses Latinate syntax and metrical control; notes curious combination of Church symbols, history of Israel, allusions to contemporary events).

Date. SchirmerLydgate, p 116; trans Keep, p 134 (1431).

Norton-Smith, edn, p 150 (suggests 1413–14).

Authorship. MacCracken TPSL, appendix 2.xii; rptd EETSES 107.xv.

Wylie J H, The Reign of Henry 5th, Cambridge 1914–29, 1.280 (inclines to attribute poem to Hoccleve despite MacCracken; believes prince addressed to be Henry 5).

SchirmerLydgate, p 233; trans Keep, p 271.

Sources and Literary Relations. SchirmerLydgate, pp 116, 120; trans Keep, pp 134, 139 (notes that poem is both political and religious and draws on Bible).

General Reference. Scattergood V J, Politics and Poetry in the 15th Cent, London 1971, p 261 (says poem is anti-Lollard).

[83] DEBATE OF THE HORSE, GOOSE, AND SHEEP.

MSS. 1, Bodl 1475 (Laud Misc 598), ff 46ᵃ–49ᵃ (15 cent); 2, Bodl 6935 (Ashmole 50), ff 1ᵃ–9ᵃ (16 cent?); 3, Bodl 6953 (Ashmole 754), ff 112ᵃ–124ᵃ (15 cent); 4, Bodl 11914 (Rawl C.48), ff 117ᵃ–128ᵃ (15 cent); 5, Bodl 11951 (Rawl C.86), ff 91ᵃ–99ᵃ (1475–1500?); 6, Camb Univ Hh.4.12, ff 46ᵃ–57ᵇ (1475–1500?); 7, Harley 2251, ff 277ᵃ–287ᵃ (other numbering has 306ᵃ–316ᵃ; 1464–83); 8, Lansdowne 699, ff 67ᵃ–78ᵇ (1475–1500?); 9, BM Addit 34360, ff 27ᵃ–34ᵃ (1461–83); 10, Lambeth 306, ff 142ᵃ–145ᵃ (1460?–1525?); 11, Leyden Univ Vossius 9, ff 80ᵇ–92ᵇ (15 cent); 12, Huntington Libr HM.144 (formerly Huth), ff 140ᵇ–144ᵃ (lacks stanzas 1–42; 1480–1500). PRINTS: 13, Caxton, 1478? (STC, no 17018; lines 1–462); 14, Caxton, n d; 15, de Worde, 1499 (STC, no 17020; rptd Roxb Club, 1822; facsimile Cambridge England, 1906); 16, de Worde, n d; 17, de Worde, n d; 18, follower

of Caxton, 1484.
Brown-Robbins, Robbins-Cutler, no 658.
Lewis J, The Life of Mayster Wyllyam Caxton, London 1737, p 104.
Dibdin T F, Typographical Antiquities, London 1810, 1.307; 2.308, 398 (discusses PRINTS 13–17).
Blades W, The Life and Typography of William Caxton, London 1861–63, 2.56, 58 (compares Caxton's printings); see 2nd edn, The Biography and Typography of William Caxton, N Y 1882, p 205.
Lowndes W T, Bibliographer's Manual, ed H G Bohn, London 1864, 3.1418 (series of biblio notes).
Robinson F N, On Two MSS of Lydgate's Guy of Warwick, HSNPL 5.177 (describes MS 11).
Degenhart, edn, MBREP 19.1 (discusses and attempts to date several MSS).
Hammond E P, Two British Museum MSS, Angl 28.1 (detailed study of MSS 7, 9).
Hoops J, 15–Cent Facsimiles, EStn 39.111 (discusses early prints through Cambridge facsimiles).
Duff E G, 15–Cent Eng Books, Oxford 1917, nos 261–65 (describes PRINTS 13–18).
Bühler C F, Lydgate's Horse Sheep and Goose and Huntington MS HM 144, MLN 55.563 (shows that MS 12 was copied from PRINT 13).
Manly & Rickert, 1.241 (describes MS 7).
Bennett H S, Eng Books and Readers 1475–1557, Cambridge England 1952, p 218 (notes that PRINT 15 followed Caxton without noticing a missing leaf).
Ringler BEV, p 153.
van Dorsten J A, The Leyden Lydgate MS, Scriptorium 14.315 (MS 11).
Editions. Degenhart M, Lydgate's Horse Goose and Sheep, MBREP 19.48 (MS 7; collations from MSS 1, 2, 5, 6, 8, 10, 11).
Furnivall F J, Political Religious and Love Poems, EETS 15(1903).15 (MS 8; collations from MS 7 and Roxb Club print of PRINT 15).
MacCracken EETS 192.539 (MS 8; collations from all MSS except MS 12).
Selections. Halliwell PPS 2.117 (MS 7; prints moral only).
Furnivall, edn, EETS 15.15 (MS 10; stanzas 46–77 only).
Bühler, MLN 55.566 (MS 12; 8 stanzas).
Abstract. Auerner N S, Caxton Mirrour of 15–Cent Letters, London and Boston 1926, p 171.
Textual Matters. Gattinger, p 84 (suggests emendations).
Language. Degenhart, edn, MBREP 19.42.
Hingst R, Die Sprache John Lydgates aus seinen Reimen, Greiswald 1908.
Babcock C F, A Study of the Metrical Use of the Inflectional e in ME with Particular Reference to Chaucer and Lydgate, PMLA 29.59 (L's language bridges gap between Middle Ages and modern period).
Hüttmann E, Das Partizipium Präsentis bei Lydgate im Vergleich mit Chaucers Gebrauch, Kiel 1914.
Versification. Degenhart, edn, MBREP 19.32.
Reger, pp 37, 78 (finds certain epic caesurae in 16.84 percent lines).
Date. Schick J, Lydgate's Temple of Glas, EETSES 60.cxii (1398?).
SchirmerLydgate, p 200; trans Keep, p 230 (1437–40).
Degenhart, edn, MBREP 19.29 (1436–40).
Furnivall, edn, EETS 15.35 (after 1421).
PearsallLydgate, p 200 (soon after 1436).
Authorship. Dibdin, Typ Ant, 1.308.
Degenhart, edn, MBREP 19.28.
MacCracken TPSL, appendix 2.xvi; rptd EETSES 107.xviii.
SchirmerLydgate, p 229; trans Keep, p 265.
Sources and Literary Relations. Degenhart, edn, MBREP 19.19 (believes principal sources to be De Membris et ventre and the Gesta Romanorum).
MacCracken H N, A New Poem by Lydgate, Angl 33.283 (shows that sentiments in lines 409–20 are exactly those of [52] above).
Duschl, p 9 (sources and classification of proverbs).
Spurgeon C, Five Hundred Years of Chaucer Criticism and Allusion, ChS 2s 48.34 (prints allusion).
Bühler, MLN 55.563 (points out stanzas that occur in other poems of L, in Court of Sapience, and in Ashby's Active Policy of a Prince).
SchirmerLydgate, p 200; trans Keep, p 230 (shows similarities to [52] above and to Libel of English Policy).
Lampe D E, ME Debate Poems A Genre Study, DAI 30.3910A.
PearsallLydgate, p 202 (author of Libel of English Policy had read this poem).
Other Scholarly Problems. Wylie J H, The Reign of Henry 5th, Cambridge England 1914–29, 2.152 (finds in poem evidence of physical appearance of arrows).
Bennett H S, Chaucer and the 15th Cent, Oxford 1948, p 141 (mentions poem as illustrative of L's didactic purpose).

RenoirLydgate, p 102 (poem reveals a new spirit of nationalism).
PearsallLydgate, p 202 (disagrees with Renoir above that poem has new spirit of nationalism).
Scattergood V J, Politics and Poetry in the 15th Cent, London 1971, p 43 (poem reveals national pride).
Literary Criticism. Gattinger, pp 15, 73 (discusses style).
Reufs F, Das Naturgefühl bei Lydgate, Arch 122.269 (believes monasticism ruins L's originality).
Knowlton E C, Nature in ME, JEGP 20.186 (finds poem typical of L's handling of nature).
PearsallLydgate, p 200 (poem is a successful use of low style but contains much miscellaneous erudition).
Lampe D, Lydgate's Laughter Horse Goose Sheep as Social Satire, Annuale Mediaevale 15.150.
Bibliography. SchirmerLydgate, p 227; trans Keep, p 261.

[84] HOW THE PLAGUE WAS SESYD IN ROME.

MS. BM Addit 29729, ff 4^b–5^a (John Stowe, 1558).
Brown-Robbins, no 3168.
Edition. MacCracken EETSES 107.159.
Authorship. MacCracken TPSL, appendix 2.xvi; rptd EETSES 107.xviii.
Brown-Robbins, no 3168 (perhaps by L).
SchirmerLydgate, p 230; trans Keep, p 268.
Sources and Literary Relations. SchirmerLydgate, pp 137, 148, 154, 167; trans Keep, pp 158, 170, 177, 191 (shows source to be appendix to Legend of St Sebastian in Legenda Aurea).
Other Scholarly Problem. Mullet C F, John Lydgate: a Mirror of Medieval Medicine, Bull of the History of Medicine 22.403 (quotes from L's poem to illustrate contemporary preoccupation with pestilence).

[85] BALLADE ON THE IMAGE OF OUR LADY (also IMAGE OF OUR LADY).

MS. BM Addit 29729, ff 9^b–10^a (John Stowe, 1558).
Brown-Robbins, no 490.
Edition. MacCracken EETSES 107.290.
Authorship. MacCracken TPSL, appendix 2.xvi; rptd EETSES 107.xix.
SchirmerLydgate, p 232; trans Keep, p 271.

Other Scholarly Problems. SchirmerLydgate, pp 110n, 167; trans Keep, pp 128n, 191 (like [84] above, this is a commissioned poem on an image in a Roman church).
Robbins R H, An Epitaph for Duke Humphrey, NM 56.242 (argues poem designed to be posted).
PearsallLydgate, pp 181, 274 (argues this is one of L's picture poems, made to accompany a copy of a painting in the church of St Maria del Populo in Rome).

[86] ON THE IMAGE OF PITY (also PITY TO THE WRETCHED SINNER).

MSS. 1, Bodl 6943 (Ashmole 59), ff 68^b–69^a (4 stanzas; 1447–56); 2, BM Addit 29729, ff 129^b–130^a (John Stowe, 1558).
Brown-Robbins, no 2588.
Edition. MacCracken EETSES 107.297 (MS 2; collations from MS 1).
Authorship. MacCracken TPSL, appendix 2.xxi; rptd EETSES 107.xxiv.
SchirmerLydgate, p 233; trans Keep, p 272.
Other Scholarly Problems. Robbins R H, An Epitaph for Duke Humphrey, NM 56.242 (believes poem intended to be posted).
PearsallLydgate, pp 182, 274 (argues this is one of L's picture poems to be posted by and to explain an image).
General Reference. SchirmerLydgate, p 173; trans Keep, p 198 (notes this is one of several poems by L on human inadequacy and transitoriness).

[87] INTERPRETACIO MISSE (also INTERPRETACION AND VIRTUES OF THE MASS, POEMS ON THE MASS II, PRAYER AT THE HOLY COMMUNION, PRAYER TO THE HOLY SACRAMENT, and VIRTUES OF THE MASS; contains a third version of ON KISSING AT VERBUM CARO [103–104]).

MSS. 1, Bodl 798 (Laud Misc 683), ff 30^b–31^a ? (lines 321–60 only; 15 cent); 2, Bodl 4119 (Hatton 73), ff 1^a–7^a (lines 1–376; 1425–75); 3, Balliol 354, ff 148^a–155^a (1518–36); 4, St John's Oxf 56, ff 74^b–84^b (1475?–1500); 5, Caius Camb 174, pp 451–455 (lines 593–664; 1475?–1500); 6, Trinity Camb 601, ff 205^b–214^a (1461–83); 7, Arundel 396, ff 121^a–end (1425–50); 8, Harley 2251, ff 179^a–188^a (1464–83); 9, BM Addit 31042, ff 103^a–110^a (lacks lines 1–57; 1425?–1475?; in hand of Robert Thornton); 10, Lambeth 344, ff 1^a–8^a (lacks

stanzas 1–23; 15 cent). PRINT: 11, De Worde, 1500? (rptd H Huth, Fugitive Poetical Tracts, 1s, 1875).
Brown-Robbins, Robbins-Cutler, no 4246.
Hammond E P, Two British Museum MSS, Angl 28.1 (detailed study of MS 8).
Manly & Rickert, 1.241 (describes MS 8).
Stern K, The London Thornton Miscellany A New Description of BM Addit MS 31042, Scriptorium 30.26 (MS 9).
Edition. MacCracken EETSES 107.87 (MS 6; collations from PRINT 11 and all MSS except MS 7).
Modernization and Abstract. Watts N, Love Songs of Sion, N Y Chicago Cincinnati 1924, p 12 (lines 537–67, 584–92, 649–56; MS 6).
Authorship. Huth, Fugitive Tracts, p xi.
MacCracken TPSL, appendix 2.xviii; rptd EETSES 107.xx.
SchirmerLydgate, p 231; trans Keep, p 269.
Sources and Literary Relations. Hammond, Two Chaucer Cruces, MLN 22.51 (believes L's poem shows that oath of Chaucer's Prioress is by St Eloi).
Brown-Robbins, no 4246 (suggests relationship with [103–104] below).
SchirmerLydgate, p 152; trans Keep, p 175 (points out that poem forms part of same unit with [45] above and [103–104] below).
Other Scholarly Problems. Moore S, Patrons of Letters in Norfolk and Suffolk c 1450, PMLA 27.188 (gives proofs of patronage of de la Poles and William Curteys).
Wylie J H, The Reign of Henry 5th, Cambridge England 1914–29, 1.288 and passim; 2.137 and passim (believes poem reflects Eng religious conservatism and throws light on use of armor and nature of pax medals).
SchirmerLydgate, pp 53, 152, 204; trans Keep, pp 61, 175, 234 (poem written for Thomas Chaucer's daughter Alice de la Pole).
General Reference. PearsallLydgate, p 258 (poem employs joinery-work for this distinguished commission).

[88] ISOPES FABULES (including THE COCK AND THE PRECIOUS STONE, THE WOLF AND THE LAMB, THE FROG AND THE MOUSE, THE HOUND AND THE SHEEP, THE WOLF AND THE CRANE, THE SUN'S MARRIAGE, and THE HOUND AND THE CHEESE).

MSS. 1, Bodl 6943 (Ashmole 59), ff 24^b–25^a (4 stanzas of Hound and Cheese; 1447–56); 2, Trinity Camb 599, ff 12^a–16^a (6 fables only), 235^a–237^a (1475?–1525?); 3, Harley 2251, ff 262^a–265^a, 269^a–270^b (Brown-Robbins gives f 257^a and Sauerstein's edn has f 283^a; 1464–83).
Brown-Robbins, Robbins-Cutler, no 4178.
Hammond E P, Two British Museum MSS, Angl 28.1 (detailed study of MS 3).
Manly & Rickert, 1.241 (describes MS 3).
Editions. Sauerstein P, Lydgates Æsopübersetzung, Angl 9.1 (MS 3; crit J Zupitza, Arch 85.1).
Zupitza J, Zu Lydgates Isopus, Arch 85.6 (prologue, first 3 fables, and stanzas 1–4 of 4th fable from MS 2; fable 7 from MS 1).
MacCracken EETS 192.566 (959 lines of composite text from MSS 2, 3; collations from MS 1).
Language. Dibelius W, John Capgrave u die engl Schriftsprache, Angl 23.153, 323.
Hingst R, Die Sprache John Lydgates aus seinen Reimen, Greiswald 1908.
Hüttmann E, Das Partizipium Präsentis bei Lydgate im Vergleich mit Chaucers Gebrauch, Kiel 1914.
Royster J F, The Do Auxiliary 1400 to 1450, MP 12.449 (20 instances in Isopes).
Versification. Schick J, Lydgate's Temple of Glas, EETSES 60.lv.
Reger, pp 57, 78 (finds certain epic caesurae in 13 percent lines).
Date. Schick, EETSES 60.cxii (1397?).
Authorship. MacCracken TPSL, appendix 2.xvi; rptd EETSES 107.xix.
SchirmerLydgate, p 229; trans Keep, p 265.
Sources and Literary Relations. Sauerstein P E, Über Lydgates Æsopübersetzung, Halle 1885 (traces genealogy of fables with emphasis on L's debt to Marie de France).
Duschl, p 9 and passim (sources and classification of proverbs).
SchirmerLydgate, pp 5n, 19, 26, 32; trans Keep, pp 8n, 22, 31, 37 (shows that this early work of L is part of a favorite mediaeval tradition).
PearsallLydgate, pp 192 (discusses fable tradition and moral significance of such poetry for Middle Ages), 194 (compares L's fables unfavorably with those of Chaucer and Henryson).
Other Scholarly Problems. Smart W K, Some Eng and Latin Sources and Parallels for the Morality of Wisdom, Chicago 1912, p 62 (poem reflects contemporary corruption in courts of law).
Bennett H S, Chaucer and the 15th Cent, Oxford 1948, pp 122, 141 (argues fables typical of 15 cent and illustrative of L's didactic purpose).
RenoirLydgate, p 61 (L confuses Aesop with his translator).
Literary Criticism. Reufs F, Das Naturgefühl bei

Lydgate, Arch 122.269 (argues monasticism ruins L's originality).
PearsallLydgate, p 194 (straightforward and didactic platitudes).

[89] A BALLADE OF JACK HARE (also A SATYRICAL BALLAD).

MSS. 1, Bodl 798 (Laud Misc 683), ff 54ᵇ–56ᵃ (15 cent); 2, Harley 2251, f 14ᵃ⁻ᵇ (1464–83); 3, Lansdowne 699, ff 88ᵇ–89ᵃ (1475?–1500); 4, Leyden Univ Vossius 9, ff 101ᵇ–102ᵇ (3 additional stanzas; 15 cent).
Brown-Robbins, Robbins-Cutler, no 36.
Robinson F N, On Two MSS of Lydgate's Guy of Warwick, HSNPL 5.177 (describes MS 4).
Hammond E P, Two British Museum MSS, Angl 28.1 (detailed study of MS 2).
van Dorsten J A, The Leyden Lydgate MS, Scriptorium 14.315 (MS 4).
Editions. Halliwell PPS 2.52 (MS 3).
Rel Ant 1.13 (MS 2).
MacCracken EETS 192.445 (MS 1; collations from all MSS; includes 3 probably spurious stanzas in envoy).
Norton-Smith J, John Lydgate Poems, Oxford 1966, pp 12, 130 (MS 1; collations from all other MSS; brief commentary, notes, and glossary).
Sisam C and K, The Oxford Book of Medieval Verse, Oxford 1970, p 397 (MS 1; modern spelling and glosses at the foot of page).
Textual Matters. Gattinger, p 82 and passim (suggests textual emendations).
Language. Dibelius W, John Capgrave u die engl Schriftsprache, Angl 23.153, 323 (notes gessedresse rime).
Versification. Reger, pp 41, 77 (finds certain epic caesurae in 5 percent lines).
Authorship. MacCracken TPSL, appendix 2.xvi; rptd EETSES 107.xix.
SchirmerLydgate, p 229; trans Keep, p 266.
Sources and Literary Relations. Gattinger, pp 12, 54, 62 (finds poem typical of L's satire; believes that it is adaptation of 13-cent De Maimond Mal Esquier, ed Barbazan Méon, 2.166, but ultimate source is Petrus Alfonsi, Disciplina Clericalis; poem shows influence of Chaucer).
Nichols P H, William Dunbar as a Scottish Lydgatian, PMLA 46.214 (shows L's influence on Dunbar).
SchirmerLydgate, p 81; trans Keep, p 96 (argues influence of Disciplina Clericalis and AN poem).
Norton-Smith, edn, p 130 (traces tradition and claims L owes little to it; argues poetic texture from Cook's Tale).
General Reference. PearsallLydgate, p 218 (good low satire).

[90] JESUS TO BLESSED VIRGIN ROSE OF WOMANHOOD (also THE CHILD JESUS TO MARY THE ROSE).

MS. Harley 2251, f 78ᵃ (1464–83).
Brown-Robbins, no 2238.
Hammond E P, Two British Museum MSS, Angl 28.1 (detailed study of MS).
Manly & Rickert, 1.241 (describes MS).
Edition. MacCracken EETSES 107.235.
Authorship. MacCracken TPSL, appendix 2.xi; rptd EETSES 107.xiii.
Brown-Robbins, no 2238 (gives no author).
SchirmerLydgate, p 232; trans Keep, p 271.
Sources and Literary Relations. SchirmerLydgate, pp 163, 167; trans Keep, pp 186, 191 (gives account of poem and notes similarities of tradition with Magnificat in [108] below).

[91] LEGEND OF DAN JOOS (also THE MONK WHO HONORED THE VIRGIN).

MSS. 1, Trinity Camb 601, ff 165ᵇ–167ᵃ, 236ᵃ–237ᵇ (1461–83); 2, Harley 2251, ff 70ᵇ–72ᵃ (1464–83; omits lines 92–119).
Brown-Robbins, Robbins-Cutler, no 2579.
Hammond E P, Two British Museum MSS, Angl 28.1 (detailed study of MS 2).
Manly & Rickert, 1.241 (describes MS 2).
Editions. Halliwell PPS 2.62 (MS 2).
Horstmann C, Originals and Analogues, ChS 3.286 (MS 2).
MacCracken EETSES 107.311 (MS 1, ff 165ᵇ–167ᵃ; collations from MS 2); rptd W A Neilson and K G T Webster, The Chief British Poets of the 14th and 15th Cents, Boston 1916, p 227.
Boyd B, The ME Miracles of the Virgin, San Marino 1964, pp 56 (MS 1; collations from MS 2; glosses at foot of page), 123 (identifies source and discusses literary relations).
Textual Matters. Gattinger, p 82 (suggests textual emendations).
Language. Hall F, On Eng Adjectives in –able, London 1877, p 102 (shows that L used deprived in the sense of to take away).
Versification. Reger, pp 41, 78 (finds certain epic caesurae in 30.35 percent lines).
Authorship. MacCracken TPSL, appendix 2.xvii; rptd EETSES 107.xix.
SchirmerLydgate, p 230; trans Keep, p 268.
Sources and Literary Relations. Gattinger, pp 33, 39,

72 and passim (gives account of poem and discusses its relationship to Vincent of Beauvais' Speculum historiale).
Boyd B, ME Miracles of the Virgin Independent Tales in Verse, DA 16.334; The Literary Background of Lydgate's The Legend of Dan Joos, MLN 72.81.
General References. SchirmerLydgate, pp 140, 148; trans Keep, pp 161, 170 (believes poem one of L's most pleasant legends because of quasi-hymnical quality).
PearsallLydgate, p 280 (profusion of ornament in the poem).
Bibliography. Boyd, edn, p 122.

[92] ORISON ON THE FIVE JOYS (also TO MARY THE STAR OF JACOB and AN ORISON TO THE BLESSED VIRGIN OF THE FIVE JOYS).

MSS. 1, Bodl 798 (Laud Misc 683), ff 29^b–30^b (15 cent); 2, Sidney Sussex Camb 37, ff 145^b–147^a (1440–50); 3, Trinity Camb 601, ff 173^b–174^b (1461–83); 4, Harley 372, f 70^{a-b} (1440–60).
Brown-Robbins, no 2556.
Edition. MacCracken EETSES 107.282 (MS 1; collations from all MSS).
Authorship. MacCracken TPSL, appendix 2.xxv; rptd EETSES 107.xxviii.
SchirmerLydgate, p 233; trans Keep, p 271.
Sources and Literary Relations. SchirmerLydgate, pp 163n, 168; trans Keep, pp 186n, 193 (poem belongs to Gaudia-tradition).

[93] ON THE FIVE JOYS (also TO MARY QUEEN OF HEAVEN).

MSS. 1, Bodl 798 (Laud Misc 683), ff 17^a–18^b (15 cent); 2, Bodl 4119 (Hatton 73), ff 1^a–2^b (Brown-Robbins records f 119^b; 1425–75); 3, Bodl 9936 (Tanner 110), ff 240^a (lines 1–54), 244^{a-b}; 4, Bodl 11914 (Rawl C.48), ff 80^a–81^a (15 cent); 5, Camb Univ Kk.1.6, ff 199^a–200^b (listed as Kk.7.6 in EETSES 107; 15 cent); 6, Jesus Camb 56, ff 71^b–72^b (15 cent); 7, Trinity Camb 601, ff 167^b–168^b (1461–83); 8, Harley 2255, ff 111^b–113^a (1448?–49?); 9, Lambeth 344, ff 11^a–12^a (15 cent).
Brown-Robbins, Robbins-Cutler, no 2791.
Edition. MacCracken EETSES 107.284 (MS 3, ff 244^{a-b}; collations from MS 3, f 240^a, and all other MSS).
Authorship. MacCracken TPSL, appendix 2.xxi; rptd EETSES 107.xxiv.

SchirmerLydgate, p 233; trans Keep, p 271.
Sources and Literary Relations. SchirmerLydgate, p 170; trans Keep, p 195 (considers it artistically significant poem in Gaudia-tradition).
Dwyer R A, Asenath of Egypt in ME, MÆ 39.118 (argues L's information about Asenath is from Vincent of Beauvais' Speculum historiale).
Other Scholarly Problems. Mullet C F, John Lydgate: a Mirror of Medieval Medicine, Bull of the History of Medicine 22.403 (considers poem representative of contemporary preoccupation with pestilence).
General References. Gattinger, p 31.
Woolf R, The Eng Religious Lyric in the Middle Ages, Oxford 1968, pp 280, 289 (notes tradition of concluding envoy and use of rose image).
PearsallLydgate, p 272 (aureate poem).

[94] THE FIFTEEN JOYS OF OUR LADY (also FIFTEEN JOYS OF MARY).

MSS. 1, Trinity Camb 601, ff 170^a–172^b (1461–83); 2, Cotton Titus A.xxvi, ff 157^b–160^a (15 cent); 3, Phillipps 8820, art 4 (15 cent).
Brown-Robbins, no 533.
Edition. MacCracken EETSES 107.260 (MS 2; collations from MS 1).
Authorship. MacCracken TPSL, appendix 2.xiv; rptd EETSES 107.xvii.
SchirmerLydgate, p 233; trans Keep, p 271.
Sources and Literary Relations. Woolf R, The Eng Religious Lyric in the Middle Ages, Oxford 1968, p 298 (the poem may be a trans of a lost French work, as it claims).
General References. SchirmerLydgate, pp 80, 170; trans Keep, pp 94, 194 (suggests poem is in baroque style and Gaudia-tradition).
PearsallLydgate, pp 71, 168.

[95] THE FIFTEEN JOYS AND SORROWS OF OUR LADY (also THE FIFTEEN JOYS AND SORROWS OF MARY).

MSS. 1, Bodl 2527 (Bodley 686), ff 204^a–208^b (1430–40); 2, Jesus Camb 56, ff 53^a–56^a (15 cent); 3, Trinity Camb 601, ff 157^a–161^b, 232^a–238^a (1461–83); 4, Fitzwilliam McLean 182, f 49^a (fragment used as envoy to Lydgate-Burgh Secrees of Old Philisoffres; 15 cent); 5, Cotton App.xxvii, f 1^a (stanzas 8–23; 16 cent); 6, Harley 2255, ff 88^a–93^a (1448?–49?).
Brown-Robbins, Robbins-Cutler, no 447.
Manly & Rickert, 1.64 (describes MS 1).
Edition. MacCracken EETSES 107.268 (MS 6;

collations from MSS 1-3).
Authorship. MacCracken TPSL, appendix 2.xiv; rptd EETSES 107.xvi.
SchirmerLydgate, p 233; trans Keep, p 271.
Literary Criticism. SchirmerLydgate, p 169; trans Keep, p 194 (notes sparing use of aureate style).
Woolf R, The Eng Religious Lyric in the Middle Ages, Oxford 1968, pp 269, 298 (discusses poem's relationship to the tradition of the 15 joys and its formal, elegant style).
General References. Gattinger, p 31.
PearsallLydgate, pp 183, 274 (notes connection with a picture).

[96] A SONG OF JUST MESURE (also ALLE THYNGES IN MESURE and ON MODERATION).

MSS. 1, Harley 2251, ff 27^b–29^b (10 stanzas; 1464-83); 2, BM Addit 29729, ff 123^a–124^a (13 stanzas; John Stowe, 1558).
Brown-Robbins, Robbins-Cutler, no 584.
Hammond E P, Two British Museum MSS, Angl 28.1 (detailed study of MS 1).
Manly & Rickert, 1.241 (describes MS 1).
Editions. Halliwell PPS 2.80 (MS 1).
MacCracken EETS 192.772 (both MSS).
Textual Matters. Gattinger, p 83 (suggests textual emendations).
Versification. Reger, pp 41, 78 (finds certain epic caesurae in 11.25 percent lines).
Pyle F, The Pedigree of Lydgate's Heroic Line, Hermathena 50.26 (notes extra syllables at caesura of line 13).
Authorship. MacCracken TPSL, appendix 2.xviii; rptd EETSES 107.xxi.
SchirmerLydgate, p 234; trans Keep, p 272.
Other Scholarly Problems. Duschl, p 20 (classifies proverbs).
Literary Criticism. Gattinger, pp 19, 72 (discusses style and notes use of music of the spheres).
General References. SchirmerLydgate, p 177; trans Keep, p 203.
PearsallLydgate, pp 204, 211 (notes other ME poems on the same theme).

[97] HYMN TO SS KATHERINE, MARGARET, AND MAGDALENE (also DE TRIBUS VIRGINIBUS KATARINA MARGARETA ET MAGDALENA).

MSS. 1, Jesus Camb 56, f 76^a (15 cent); 2, Harley 2255, f 115^a (1448?-49?).
Brown-Robbins, no 1814.
Edition. MacCracken EETSES 107.134 (MS 2; collations from MS 1).
Authorship. MacCracken TPSL, appendix 2.xxiii; rptd EETSES 107.xxvi.
Brown-Robbins, no 1814, (does not name L as author).
SchirmerLydgate, p 232; trans Keep, p 270.
General Reference. SchirmerLydgate, p 164; trans Keep, p 188.

[98] THE THREE KINGS OF COLOGNE.

MS. BM Addit 31042, ff 110^a–119^b (lacks about 100 lines at beginning; 1425?-1475?).
Brown-Robbins, no *31; Robbins-Cutler, no *854.3.
Edition. MacCracken H N, Lydgatiana: The Three Kings of Cologne, Arch 129.51 (dates poem immediately after 1433).
Authorship. MacCracken, Arch 129.50 (organization based on [1] and [42] below).
Brown-Robbins, no *31 (questions authorship).
SchirmerLydgate, pp 236, 239; trans Keep, pp 275, 280 (rejects L's authorship).

[99] CHARTERS OF THE KINGS OF ENGLAND (also CARTAE VERSIFICATAE).

MS. BM Addit 14848, ff 243^a–254^a (ca 1440?).
Brown-Robbins, no 1513.
Edition. Arnold T, Memorials of St Edmund's Abbey, Rolls Series 1896, 3.215.
Versification. Reger, pp 55, 78 (finds certain epic caesurae in 15.45 percent lines).
Authorship. MacCracken TPSL, appendix 2.xi; rptd EETSES 107.xiii.
Brown-Robbins, no 1513 (suggests only probability of L's authorship).
SchirmerLydgate, p 231; trans Keep, p 268.
Other Scholarly Problem. SchirmerLydgate, p 206; trans Keep, p 236 (believes poem probably written at command of William Curteys).
General Reference. PearsallLydgate, pp 25, 219 (suggests the range poetry could have in this period).

[100] VERSES ON THE KINGS OF ENGLAND, FIRST REDACTION (also THE KINGS OF ENGLAND SITHEN WILLIAM CONQUEROUR).

MSS. 1, Bodl 1797 (Digby 196), ff 65^a–66^b (10 stanzas inserted in Latin prose Chronica angliae; 15 cent); 2, Bodl 1885 (Bodley 48), f 45^{a-b} (late 15-cent hand in early 15-cent MS); 3, Bodl 2527 (Bodley 686), ff 184^b–186^a (1430-40); 4,

Bodl 3896 (Fairfax 16), ff 330ᵇ–336ᵇ? (1400–50); 5, Bodl 6943 (Ashmole 59), ff 75ᵃ–77ᵃ (1447–56); 6, Bodl 10210 (Tanner 383), ff 51ᵃ–55ᵃ (a 17-cent transcription of PRINT 41); 7, Bodl 11914 (Rawl C.48), ff 78ᵇ–80ᵃ (15 cent); 8, Bodl 11951 (Rawl C.86), ff 187ᵃ–end (16 cent); 9, Bodl 12172 (Rawl C.316, ff 121ᵃ–122ᵇ? (15 cent); 10, Bodl 22005 (Douce g2), a roll (15 cent); 11, Bodl 29284, a roll (1425–75); 12, Bodl 30437 (Bodl 912), f 23ᵃ⁻ᵇ (later hand in 14-cent MS); 13, Bodl Firth d.14, ff 96ᵃ–99 (from a 1483 print); 14, Lincoln Coll Oxford; 15, Camb Univ Addit 6686 (formerly Ashburnham 140), pp 272–273 (15 cent); 16, Caius Camb 249, ff 127ᵃ–134ᵇ? (1464); 17, Jesus Camb 56, ff 46ᵃ–47ᵇ (15 cent); 18, Trinity Camb 601, ff 242ᵃ⁻ᵇ, 319ᵃ–320ᵇ (1461–83); 19, Cotton Galba E.viii, f 2ᵃ⁻ᵇ (15 cent); 20, Cotton Titus D.xx, ff 94ᵃ–95ᵃ (Cottonian catalogue gives beginning f as 91ᵃ; 1462–1500?); 21, Egerton 1995, ff 110ᵃ–113ᵃ (15 cent); 22, Harley 2251, ff 2ᵃ⁻ᵇ (1464–83); 23, Harley 2261, ff 446ᵇ–? (not listed in Harleian catalogue); 24, Harley 7333, ff 149ᵃ–? (15 cent); 25, Lansdowne 210, ff 27ᵃ–42ᵇ (interspersed throughout a prose chronicle; time of Queen Mary); 26, Lansdowne 699, ff 79ᵃ–81ᵃ (1450–1500); 27, Lansdowne 762, ff 10ᵃ–11ᵇ? (to Henry 7; 1500–40); 28, Royal 18.D.ii, ff 181ᵃ–184ᵃ (bulk of MS 1455–1462?; L's poem probably added 1516?–1523?; additional stanza to Henry 8); 29, Stowe 69, f 196 (1425–75; to Richard 2; imperfect); 30, BM Addit 31042, ff 96ᵃ–97ᵃ? (15 cent; to Edward 1); 31, BM Addit 34360, ff 60ᵇ–63ᵃ (1461–83; in 8-line stanzas; to Edward 4); 32, Coll of Arms Arundel 58, ff 335ᵃ–341ᵇ (15 cent); 33, Hertford County Record Office 15857A (a roll with no ff; 15 cent); 34, Ipswich Great Doomsday, ff 237ᵇ–239ᵇ (1520); 35, Lambeth 306, ff 17ᵇ–18ᵇ; 36, Nottingham Univ Me LM1 (formerly Mellish), endleaves (15 cent); 37, Trinity Dublin 516, ff 28ᵇ–30ᵃ (1461); 38, Leyden Univ Vossius 9, ff 92ᵇ–94ᵇ (15 cent); 39, Bühler 17 (formerly Lyell, Quaritch Sale Cat 699, no 52), 2nd flyleaf. PRINTS: 40, Pynson, ca 1518 (Bodl Wood 536); 41, De Worde, 1530; 42, Bodl Ashmole 456 (Printed Book).

Brown-Robbins, Robbins-Cutler, no 3632.

Robinson F N, On Two MSS of Lydgate's Guy of Warwick, HSNPL 5.177 (describes MS 38).

Hammond E P, Two British Museum MSS, Angl 28.1 (detailed study of MSS 22, 31).

Bühler C F, A Note on Lydgate's Verses on the Kings of England, RES 9.47 (dates MS 5 as 1461 and lists variations in MS 37).

Manly & Rickert, 1.64, 207 (describes MSS 3, 24).

van Dorsten J A, The Leyden Lydgate MS, Scriptorium 14.315 (MS 38).

Stern K, The London Thornton Miscellany A New Description of BM Addit MS 31042, Scriptorium 30.26, 201, 216 (MS 30).

Editions. Hearne T, Robert of Gloucester, Oxford 1724, 2.585 (MS 8); rptd London 1810.

Gairdner J, Historical Collection of a Citizen of London, Camden Soc ns 17.49 (MS 21); Three 15-Cent Chronicles, Camden Soc ns 28.28 (MS 35; corrupt text printed as prose in MS and edn).

Robbins-HP, pp 3, 248 (MS 7).

Selection. Furnivall F J, Political Religious and Love Poems, EETS 15(1903).42 (2 opening lines from MS 26).

Versification. Reger, pp 39, 78 (finds certain epic caesurae in 12.38 percent lines).

Date. Bühler, RES 9.47 (dates poem not later than 1442).

SchirmerLydgate, p 206; trans Keep, p 236 (accepts 1442).

Authorship. MacCracken TPSL, appendix 2.xvi; rptd EETSES 107.xix.

SchirmerLydgate, p 231; trans Keep, p 268.

Sources and Literary Relations. MacCracken H N, Lydgatiana: The Life of Holy Job, Arch 126.365 (discusses technical relationship between Life of Holy Job and [100–102] and other tapestry poems of L).

Zettle E, An Anonymous Short Eng Metrical Chronicle, EETS 196.cxxxiv (believes L's riming poem based on Short Chronicle rather than on First Redaction, as Brown-Robbins, no 3431).

Robbins-HP, p 248 (last 2 stanzas duplicate lines in [74] above).

Other Scholarly Problems. SchirmerLydgate, pp 110, 206; trans Keep, pp 128, 236 (believes poem written to accompany portraits; accurate recording of historical events).

Robbins R H, An Epitaph for Duke Humphrey, NM 56.242 (believes poem made to be posted).

McKenna J W, Henry 6 of England and the Dual Monarchy Aspects of Royal Political Propaganda 1422–32, Journ of the Warburg and Courtauld Institutes 28.154 (poem contains dual monarchy theme).

Bibliography. Lowndes W T, Bibliographer's Manual, ed H G Bohn, London 1864, 3.1419.

Robbins-HP, p 248.

[101] VERSES ON THE KINGS OF
ENGLAND, SECOND REDACTION
WITH 15 INTRODUCTORY STANZAS
(also THE KINGS OF ENGLAND
SITHEN WILLIAM CONQUEROUR).

MSS. 1, Harley 372, ff 51ª–53ᵇ (Alfred to Henry 6; 1440–60); 2, Peterborough Publ Libr, ff 49ª–52ᵇ.
Brown-Robbins, Robbins-Cutler, no 882.
Edition. MacCracken EETS 192.710 (MS 1; last 15 stanzas collated with MS 26 from [100] above).
General Reference. Gattinger, p 22.
For scholarship concerning all three redactions of VERSES ON THE KINGS OF ENGLAND, see under FIRST REDACTION, [100] above.

[102] VERSES ON THE KINGS OF
ENGLAND, THIRD REDACTION IN
COUPLETS (also THE KINGS OF
ENGLAND SITHEN WILLIAM
CONQUEROUR).

MS. Bodl 29284 (Addit E.7), a roll.
Brown-Robbins, Robbins-Cutler, no 3431.
Edition. MacCracken EETS 192.717.
Sources and Literary Relations. Zettle E, An Anonymous Short Metrical Chronicle, EETS 196.cxxxiv (believes L's poem based on Short Chronicle).
Brown-Robbins, no 3431 (believes [102] based on [100] above).
For scholarship concerning all three redactions of VERSES ON THE KINGS OF ENGLAND, see under FIRST REDACTION, [100] above.

[103] ON KISSING AT VERBUM CARO,
FIRST VERSION.

MSS. 1, Balliol 354, f 155ª (1518–36); 2, Caius Camb 174, p 455 (1450–1500); 3, Trinity Camb 601, f 215ᵇ (1461–83); for other MSS see under [104] below.
Brown-Robbins, no 2413.
Edition. MacCracken EETSES 107.116–7 (MS 3; collations from the other 2 MSS and from MSS 1, 2, 3, 5, 6 in [104] below).
For scholarship, see under [104] below.

[104] ON KISSING AT VERBUM CARO,
SECOND VERSION (also A CALL TO
DEVOTION).

MSS. 1, Bodl 798 (Laud Misc 683), ff 87ᵇ–88ª (15 cent); 2, Bodl 6943 (Ashmole 59), ff 56ᵇ–57ª (1447–56); 3, Jesus Camb 56, ff 72ᵇ–73ª (15 cent); 4, Trinity Camb 600, p 362 (1456?); 5, Harley 2251, f 9ª (1460–70); 6, Harley 2255, ff 113ᵇ–114ª (1448?–49?); 7, BM Addit 34360, f 68ª (3 stanzas; 1461–83); for other MSS see under [103] and [87] above.
Brown-Robbins, no 4245.
Hammond E P, Lydgate's Mumming at Hertford, Angl 22.364 (describes MS 4); Two British Museum MSS, Angl 28.1 (detailed study of MS 7).
Brusendorff A, The Chaucer Tradition, London 1925, pp 208, 466 and passim (discusses Shirley's marginalia in MS 4).
Edition. Halliwell PPS 2.60 (MS 8 of [87] above).
Versification. Reger, pp 41, 78 (finds certain epic caesurae in 15.62 percent lines).
General Reference. Gattinger, p 31.
For other works of scholarship, see under INTERPRETACIO MISSE, [87] above.

[105] LAMENTACIOUN OF OUR LADY
MARIA (also QUIS DABIT MEO
CAPITI FONTEM LACRIMARUM).

MSS. 1, Bodl 798 (Laud Misc 683), ff 78ª–81ᵇ (15 cent); 2, St John's Oxf 56, ff 73ᵇ–76ª (1475–1500); 3, Jesus Camb 56, ff 19ᵇ–22ᵇ (15 cent); 4, Harley 2251, ff 42ᵇ–46ª (1464–83); 5, Harley 2255, ff 66ᵇ–69ᵇ (1448?–49?); 6, Clopton Chantry, Long Melford (stanzas 8, 4, 14, 17–19 carved on cornice).
Brown-Robbins, no 4099.
Hammond E P, Two British Museum MSS, Angl 28.1 (detailed study of MS 4).
Manly & Rickert, 1.241 (description of MS 4).
Trapp J B, Verses by Lydgate at Long Melford, RES ns 6.1 (notes utter dilapidation of text).
Edition. MacCracken EETSES 107.324 (MS 1; collations from all MSS except MS 6).
Authorship. MacCracken TPSL, appendix 2.xxi; rptd EETSES 107.xxiv.
SchirmerLydgate, p 232; trans Keep, p 270.
Sources and Literary Relations. Bonner F W, The Genesis of the Chaucer Apocrypha, SP 48.461 (listed among works once ascribed to Chaucer and responsible for wrong impression of him).
General Reference. SchirmerLydgate, p 162; trans Keep, p 186 (poem is only example of Planctus-genre in L).

[106] A TRETISE FOR LAVANDRES (stanza 3 often printed separately as ON WINE; also TREATISE FOR LAUNDRESS).

MSS. 1, Camb Univ Ff.1.6, f 141[a] (ca 1500; Brown-Robbins records f 164[a]); 2, Harley 762, f 24[a] (stanza 3; no date in Harleian catalogue); 3, Harley 2251, f 76[b] (stanza 3; 1464–83); 4, Harley 3528, f 38[b] (lines 1–2 of stanza 3; no date in Harleian catalogue); 5, Lansdowne 762, f 24 (stanza 3; 1500–40); 6, BM Addit 34360, f 77[b] (stanza 3; 1461–83). Brown-Robbins, no 4254; Brown-Robbins, Robbins-Cutler, no 2668.
Steele R, A Stowe MS of Lydgate, Acad (London) 45.395 (discusses partial list of contents of MS 6).
Hammond E P, Two British Museum MSS, Angl 28.1 (detailed study of MSS 3, 6).
Manly & Rickert, 1.241 (describes MS 3).
Editions. Rel Ant, 1.26 (MS 1).
MacCracken EETS 192.723 (MS 1; collations from MSS 3, 6).
Selections. Steele, Acad 45.395 (prints stanza 3 as On Wine; MS 6).
Bühler C, crit MacCracken edn, RES 12.237 (prints stanza 3; MS 2).
Versification. Reger, pp 68, 77 (finds no certain epic caesura).
Authorship. MacCracken TPSL, appendix 2.xvii; rptd EETSES 107.xix.
SchirmerLydgate, p 230; trans Keep, p 267.
Other Scholarly Problem. SchirmerLydgate, pp 94, 179; trans Keep, pp 110, 205 (considers poem an original piece written for Sibille Boys).

[107] LETABUNDUS.

MSS. 1, Jesus Camb 56, ff 60[b]–66[a] (15 cent); 2, Trinity Camb 601, ff 197[b]–201[a] (1461–83); 3, Harley 2255, ff 120[a]–126[a] (1448?–49?).
Brown-Robbins, no 1019.
Edition. MacCracken EETSES 107.49 (MS 3; collations from other MSS).
Authorship. MacCracken TPSL, appendix 2.xvii; rptd EETSES 107.xx.
SchirmerLydgate, pp 232, 239; trans Keep, pp 270, 281.
Sources and Literary Relations. SchirmerLydgate, p 157; trans Keep, p 180 (poem is adaptation of Bernard of Clairvaux's hymn in H A Daniel, Thesaurus Hymnologicus, 2.61).
PearsallLydgate, p 263 (claims poem is based on a sequence, not a hymn).

Literary Criticism. PearsallLydgate, p 263 (asserts poem is not a trans but an extended rhapsody).

[108] LIFE OF OUR LADY (the MAGNIFICAT also printed separately).

MSS. 1, Bodl 2253 (Bodley 75), ff 1[a]–83[b] (1475–1500; lacks prologue, stanza 1, and several lines); 2, Bodl 2376 (Bodley 596), ff 86[a]–174[b] (15 cent; several omissions); 3, Bodl 4119 (Hatton 73), ff 10[a]–118[b] (1425–75); 4, Bodl 6919 (Ashmole 39), ff 1[a]–109[a] (1450–1500; omissions, transpositions); 5, Bodl 6943 (Ashmole 59), ff 135[a]–182[a] (1447–56; begins and ends imperfectly, omissions, transpositions); 6, Bodl 14634 (Rawl poet F.140), ff 1[a]–109[a] (15 cent; several omissions); 7, Bodl 27643 (Bodley 120), ff 1[a]–94[a] (1450–1500; several omissions, poem ends imperfectly); 8, Corp Christi Oxf 237, ff 158[a]–240[a] (15 cent; omissions, transpositions); 9, St John's Oxf 56, ff 1[a]–74[b] (1450–1500; 2 pages mutilated, omissions, transpositions); 10, Camb Univ Kk.1.3.x, ff 2[a]–94[a] (1420–50; damaged MS, many omissions, transpositions); 11, Camb Univ Mm. 6.5, ff 1[a]–141[a] (1420–50); 12, Camb Univ Addit 3303 (7), ff 1[a]–4[b] (15 cent; 3 passages from Bk 3); 13, Caius Camb 230, ff 54[a]–55[b] (15 cent; Magnificat only; also numbered pp 113–116); 14, Trinity Camb 601, ff 85[a]–156[b] (1461–83); 1 line missing, a few transpositions); 15, Trinity Camb 602, ff 1[a]–109[b] (1421?–50; 1 omission, 1 transposition); 16, Arundel 168, ff 66[a]–85[a] (15 cent; omissions and imperfect–begins with line 1.414 and ends with 3.1208); 17, Cotton App viii, ff 2[a]–108[a] (15 cent; obscurities, omissions); 18, Harley 629, ff 2[a]–97[a] (a few omissions); 19, Harley 1304, ff 1[a]–99[a] (15 cent); 20, Harley 2382, ff 1[a]–74[b] (1470–1500; begins with line 1.427, several omissions, transpositions); 21, Sloane 297, f 88 (fragment from chap 58, 1 leaf from MS 20); 22, Harley 3862, ff 1[a]–end (1450–1500; many transpositions); 23, Harley 3952, ff 1[a]–105[a] (lacks small portion of text at end, several omissions, transpositions); 24, Harley 4011, ff 23[a]–119[b] (1450–1500); 25, Harley 4260, ff 2[a]–108[a] (15 cent; ends imperfectly, a few omissions, transpositions); 26, Harley 5272, ff 1[a]–98[b] (15 cent; begins on line 1.419; several omissions, transpositions); 27, Sloane 1785, ff 14[a]–29[b] (15 cent; begins on line 1.434 and ends on 1.795, very defective); 28, BM Addit 19252, ff 4[a]–end (1520–50; begins on 1.113 and ends imperfectly); 29, BM Addit 19452, ff 2[a]–89[b] (1520–50; begins on 1.31 and ends on 6.277, omissions, transpositions); 30, BM Addit 29729, ff 122ª–123ª (John Stowe, 1558; Magnificat only); 31, Nat Libr Scot 1.1.6 (Advocates), ff 25ᵇ–26ᵇ (1568; Magnificat only, 3 lines missing); 32, Advocates 19.3.1, ff 176ª–210ª (15 cent; bks 4–6, omissions, transpositions); 33, Chetham Libr 6709, ff 6ª–156ª (1490, probably copied from PRINT 48; a few omissions, transpositions); 34, Durham Univ Cosin V.ii.16, 5ª–90ᵇ (1425–50; omits bk 3.1426 and bk 5.532, 2 stanzas inverted, Calendar follows f 90ᵇ); 35, Hunterian 232, ff 1ª–104ᵇ (15 cent; ends imperfectly with line 6.308); 36, Lambeth 344, ff 13ª–99ᵇ (15 cent; omissions, transpositions); 37, Soc of Antiquaries 134, ff 1ª–30ª (15 cent; begins on line 2.222; 3 omissions, 1 transposition); 38, Longleat 15, ff 2ª–104ᵇ (15 cent; ends on line 6.128, omissions, transpositions); 39, formerly Harmsworth (formerly Mostyn Hall 85), ff 2ª–end (15 cent; sold 1920 to Quaritch; Sotheby Sale, 16 Oct 1945, lot 2019; begins with line 118 of chap 3); 40, Trinity Coll Dublin 423, f 122ᵇ (1475–1525; fragment of 3.1–7); 41, Rome Eng Coll 1306 (also numbered 127 and A.347), ff 2ª–66ᵇ (1436–56; imperfect beginning with line 2.365, lines 2.925–1074 omitted); 42, Chicago Univ 566 (formerly Cockerell), ff 2ª–end (15 cent; begins on line 1.173, several omissions); 43, Huntington Libr HM.115 (formerly Hoe), ff 1ª–112ª (1420–50 with 19-cent section; 2 omissions, 2 transpositions); 44, Huntington Libr HM.144 (formerly Huth 7), ff 11ª–20ª (1480–1500; 2.1–504; in Brown Reg dated 1460–70 and begins on p 113ᵈ); 45, Univ of Illinois (formerly Mostyn Hall 257), ff 1–85 (15 cent; begins with line 118 of chap 3); 46, Univ of Missouri Libr, f 178 (15 cent; fragment contains 5.344–64, 372–92); 47, Yale Univ 281, ff 1ª–114ᵇ (15 cent). PRINTS: 48, The Lyf of Our Lady, Caxton, 1484 (STC, no 17023); 49, Caxton, 1484 (4 leaves; frag of PRINT 48 with variations); 50, Redman, 1531 (STC, no 17025; identical copy of PRINT 48).

Brown-Robbins, Robbins-Cutler, no 2574.

Dibdin T F, Typographical Antiquities, London 1810, 1.366 and passim (describes PRINT 48 and omissions therein); Bibliotheca Spenceriana, 4.334 (describes PRINT 48).

Blades W, The Life and Typography of William Caxton, London 1861–63, 2.171 (dates PRINT 48 1484; see 2nd edn, p 298).

Lowndes W T, Bibliographer's Manual, ed H G Bohn, London 1864, 3.1418.

Duff E G, 15-Cent Eng Books, Oxford 1917, nos 266, 266ª (describes PRINTS 48, 49).

Bühler C F, Three Notes on Caxton, Libr 4s 17.155 (dates Caxton's first print 1481–82; suggests possibility of lost print; crit E F Bosanquet, Libr 4s 17.362); Two Caxton Problems, Libr 4s 20.266 (argues possibility of lost Caxton print).

Manly & Rickert, 1.82, 245 (describes MSS 20, 33).

Bennett OHEL, p 165 (discusses contents of MS 32).

Klinefelter R A, Lydgate's Life of Our Lady and the Chetham MS 6709, PBSA 46.396 (argues MS 33 copied from PRINT 48); The Siege of Calais: a New Text, PMLA 67.888 (brief discussion of MS 41); A Newly Discovered 15-Cent Eng MS, MLQ (Wash) 14.3 (describes MS 41).

Robbins R H, A ME Diatribe against Philip of Burgundy, Neophil 39.131 (discusses MS 41).

Ringler BEV, p 153.

Lauritis-Klinefelter-Gallagher, edn, pp 11, 21 (describes 42 MSS, their relationships, and PRINTS).

Robbins, ELN 5.245 (MS 40).

Jones H G, ELN 7.93 (MS 46).

Edwards A S G and A W Jenkins, Lydgate's Life of Our Lady An Unedited MS of Pt of Bk 3, ELN 9.1 (MS 12; argues it is from same MS as MS 46).

Edition. Lauritis J A, R A Klinefelter and V F Gallagher, A Critical Edition of John Lydgate's Life of Our Lady, Duquesne Stud Philological Series 2, Pittsburgh 1961 (MS 34; collations from MS 7; with textual variants at foot of page, general notes, and glossary; crit W F Schirmer, Angl 79.88; W F Bolton, JEGP 61.165; J Richardson, Spec 37.454; N Davis, RES ns 14.182).

Selections. Turnbull W B D D, The Visions of Tundale, Edinburgh 1843, p 84 (bks 4–6; MS 32).

Tame C E, Early Eng Religious Literature, London 1872, vol 2 (64 unnumbered pages, ends with line 2.1095; from unidentified MS in British Museum).

Dibdin T F, Bibliotheca Spenceriana, London 1851, 4.334 (Comendacion of Chaucer, chap 34; PRINT 48).

Murdoch J B, Bannatyne MS, Hunterian Club, Glasgow 1896, 2.64 (Magnificat; MS 31).

Spurgeon C, Five Hundred Years of Chaucer Criticism and Allusion, ChS 2s 48.19 (Commendacion of Chaucer; MS 18).

Ritchie W T, The Bannatyne MS, PSTS ns 22.60

(Magnificat; MS 31).
Klinefelter R A, Lydgate's Life of Our Lady A Critical Edn of Bks 1 and 2, DA 11.345.
Lauritis J A, Lydgate's Life of Our Lady A Critical Edn of Bks 5 and 6, DA 19.1758.
Norton-Smith J, John Lydgate Poems, Oxford 1966, pp 35 (bk 2.519–903; MS 34); 154 (brief commentary, notes, and glossary).
Robbins R H, A New Lydgate Fragment, ELN 5.246 (bk 3.1–7; MS 40).
Jones H G, An Unedited MS of John Lydgate's Life of Our Lady Bk 5 Vv 344–364 and 372–392, ELN 7.95 (MS 46).
Tydeman W, Eng Poetry 1400–1580, London 1970, pp 28, 164 (bk 1.1–56; from Lauritis-Klinefelter-Gallagher edn; with notes).
Modernization and Abstract. Auerner N S, Caxton Mirrour of 15-Cent Letters, London and Boston 1926, p 172 (brief summary of poem).
Versification. Schick J, Lydgate's Temple of Glas, EETSES 60.1v.
Lauritis-Klinefelter-Gallagher, edn, p 183.
Lauritis, Second Thoughts on Style in Lydgate's Life of Our Lady, in Essays and Stud in Language and Literature, ed H Petit, Duquesne Stud Philological Series 5, Pittsburgh 1964, p 19.
Date. Schick, EETSES 60.cxii (1409?–11?).
Gerould S Leg, pp 259, 290 (accepts 1409–10, argues this poem is only one of L's saints' legends that can be dated before 1426).
Klinefelter, DA 11.345 (argues for 1421–22).
SchirmerLydgate, p 35; trans Keep, p 40 (accepts 1409–11).
Norton-Smith, Poems, p 154 (poem is impossible to date).
Parr J, The Astronomical Date of Lydgate's Life of Our Lady, PQ 50.120 (1415–16).
Authorship. Blades, Life and Typography, 2.171 (accepts L's authorship and points out additions by Caxton; see also 2nd edn, p 298).
MacCracken TPSL, appendix 2.xvii; rptd EETSES 107.xx.
SchirmerLydgate, p 230; trans Keep, p 268.
Sources and Literary Relations. Spurgeon, ChS 2s 48.19.
SchirmerLydgate, p 131; trans Keep, p 152 (suggests thematic relationship to St Bernard and St Bonaventura).
Bonner F W, The Genesis of the Chaucer Apocrypha, SP 48.461 (encomium of Chaucer is representative of L's attitude toward Chaucer).
Lauritis-Klinefelter-Gallagher, edn, p 57 (extensive treatment with extracts from sources).
Norton-Smith, Poems, p 155 (suggests influence of Chaucer).

Other Scholarly Problems. Fiedler G, Zum Leben Lydgates, Angl 15.391 (presents plan for edn of poem).
Brusendorff A, The Chaucer Tradition, London 1925, p 29 (believes references to Chaucer serve only to establish L's personal eminence).
Norton-Smith, Poems, p 154 (doubts Henry 5's patronage).
Literary Criticism. Warton T, History of Eng Poetry, ed W C Hazlitt, London 1871, 3.58 (finds poem tedious despite occasionally harmonious lines).
CHEL, 2.203.
Gerould S Leg, pp 259, 290.
Auerner, Caxton, p 172.
SchirmerLydgate, pp 34, 129, 148 and passim; trans Keep, pp 40, 150, 171 and passim (considers poem an epic with the inclusion of prayers, hymns, etc.; notes that last bk is more concerned with Christ than with Mary).
Rossi, pp 71, 169, 176.
Lauritis-Klinefelter-Gallagher, edn, p 208 (analyses L's syntax, reviews critical opinions of poetic quality, and suggests good passages).
Lauritis, Second Thoughts on Style, p 12.
Norton-Smith, Poems, p 155 (argues that poem is organized around the Christmas Cycle).
Pearsall D, Gower and Lydgate, London 1969 (long discussion; claims poem is one of the high points in Eng religious writing).
General References. Pearsall, The English Chaucerians, in Chaucer and Chaucerians, ed D S Brewer, Univ Alabama 1966, p 218.
RenoirLydgate, p 19 (notes touching scene of Mary and Child).

[109] LOOK IN THY MEROUR (also LYDGATE'S PROVERBS).

MSS. 1, Bodl 3356 (Arch Selden B.10), ff 206[b]–209[b] (27 stanzas; lacks stanzas 1–2; ca 1470–80); 2, Bodl 11951 (Rawl C.86), ff 81[b]–83[b] (20 stanzas; 1480–1500); 3, Jesus Camb 56, ff 29[a]–33[a] (15 cent); 4, Trinity Camb 601, ff 293[a]–296[a] (1461–83); 5, Harley 2255, ff 7[b]–11[b] (1448?–49?); 6, Huntington Libr HM 140 (formerly Phillips 8299; 1450–80). PRINT: 7, De Worde, in Lydgate's Proverbs.
Brown-Robbins, Robbins-Cutler, no 3798.
Collier J P, A Bibliographical and Critical Account of the Rare Books in the Eng Language, N Y 1866, 2.289 (discusses PRINT).
Editions. Halliwell PPS 2.156 (MS 5).
MacCracken EETS 192.765 (MS 5; collations from all MSS and PRINT).
Modernization and Abstract. Collier, Bibliographical

Account, 2.289 (gives gist of poem).
Textual Matters. Gattinger, p 84 (suggests emendations).
Versification. Reger, pp 41, 78 (finds 35.19 percent lines have certain epic caesurae).
Authorship. MacCracken TPSL, appendix 2.xviii; rptd EETSES 107.xx.
SchirmerLydgate, p 233; trans Keep, p 272.
Sources and Literary Relations. Gattinger, pp 17, 49, 50, 65, 72 (notes classical references, influence of Bestiary material, Isidore of Seville, and Chaucer).
Duschl, pp 26, 49 (traces proverb to Virgil and Ecclesiastes; notes similarities with Gower).
SchirmerLydgate, p 176; trans Keep, p 201 (notes greater use of Bestiary than of classical material).
Literary Criticism. Gattinger, p 72 (discusses style).
General Reference. PearsallLydgate, p 214.

[110] A LOVER'S LAMENT (also MY LADY DERE and THOMAS CHAUCER'S COMPLAINT).

MSS. 1, Bodl 6943 (Ashmole 59), ff 45ᵇ–47ᵇ (1447–56); 2, Harley 367, f 87ᵃ⁻ᵇ (in hand of John Stowe; 1600–25); 3, BM Addit 16165, ff 249ᵇ–251ᵇ (16 stanzas; 1425–75).
Brown-Robbins, Robbins-Cutler, no 746.
Editions. Furnivall F J, N&Q 4s 9.382 (MS 3); Thynne's Animadversions, ChS 2s 13.122 (MS 1).
MacCracken EETS 192.420 (MS 3; collations from all MSS).
Date. Seaton, p 220 (1433–38).
Authorship. MacCracken TPSL, appendix 2.xxii; rptd EETSES 107.xxii.
SchirmerLydgate, p 229; trans Keep, p 265.
Seaton, p 220 (argues for Richard Roos).
Sources and Literary Relations. Seaton, p 220 (argues poem is a companion piece to [23] above).
Other Scholarly Problems. SchirmerLydgate, p 54; trans Keep, p 61 (poem representative of poetry in Thomas Chaucer's circle).
Seaton, p 220 (argues poem contains name anagrams).
General Reference. PearsallLydgate, p 162.

[111] ADVICE TO LOVERS (also ADVICE TO AN OLD GENTLEMAN WHO WISHED FOR A YOUNG WIFE and PROHEMY OF A MARRIAGE BETWIX AN OLDE MAN AND A YONGE WIFE).

MS. Harley 372, ff 45ᵃ–51ᵃ (1440–60).
Brown-Robbins, Robbins-Cutler, no 86.

Edition. Halliwell PPS 2.27.
Authorship. Lange J H, Zur Verfasser Schaft des Advice, EStn 30.346 (ascribes to L).
MacCracken EETSES 107.xlviii (suggests may be by Hoccleve).
Brown-Robbins, no 86 (suggests perhaps not by L).
SchirmerLydgate, pp 82n, 235, 237; trans Keep, pp 96n, 275, 278 (believes poem by imitator of L).
Sources and Literary Relations. Utley CR, no 9 (notes reworkings of Chaucer and resemblances to other ME and 16-cent poems).
General Reference. Rogers K M, The Troublesome Helpmate, Seattle and London, p 86.

[112] LIFE OF ST MARGARET.

MSS. 1, Bodl 2527 (Bodley 686), ff 193ᵇ–200ᵇ (1430–40); 2, Camb Univ L1.5.18, ff 29ᵇ–41ᵇ (15 cent); 3, Trinity Camb 600, pp 178–195 (1456?); 4, Harley 367, ff 80ᵃ–83ᵇ (in hand of John Stowe; 1600–25); 5, BM Addit 29729, ff 170ᵇ–177ᵇ (John Stowe, 1558); 6, Chetham Libr 6709, art 4, ff 180ᵃ–189ᵇ (1490); 7, Durham Univ Cosin V.ii.14, ff 97ᵇ–106ᵇ (15 cent); 8, Devonshire, ff 275ᵃ–282ᵃ (1450–60).
Brown-Robbins, Robbins-Cutler, no 439.
Hammond E P, Lydgate's Mumming at Hertford, Angl 22.364 (describes MS 3); The Lost Quires of a Shirley Codex, MLN 36.184 (discusses MS 3); The Nine-Syllabled Pentameter Line in Some Post Chaucerian MSS, MP 23.129 (notes similarities between Chaucer's 2nd Nun's Tale in Corpus Christi MS and L's poem in MS 3).
Brusendorff A, The Chaucer Tradition, London 1925, pp 208, 466 and passim (discusses MS 3).
Manly & Rickert, 1.64, 82, 117 (describes MSS 1, 6, 8).
Editions. AELeg 1881, p 446 (MS 7).
MacCracken EETSES 107.173 (MS 7; collations from MSS 1, 2, 4).
Selections. Cohen L C, The Ballade, N Y 1915, p 255.
Language. Dibelius W, John Capgrave u die engl Schriftsprache, Angl 23.153, 323.
Hingst R, Die Sprache John Lydgates aus seinen Reimen, Greiswald 1908.
Babcock C F, A Study of the Metrical Uses of the Inflectional e in ME with Particular Reference to Chaucer and Lydgate, PMLA 29.59 (argues L's language bridges gap between Middle Ages and modern period).
Mendenhall J C, Aureate Terms, Lancaster Pa 1919, p 66 (suggests patron's influence on diction).

Versification. Reger, pp 46, 77 (finds certain epic caesurae in 7.59 percent lines).

Wolpers T, Die engl Heiligenlegende des Mittelalters, Tübingen 1964, p 313 (discusses L's use of strophes).

Date. Schick J, Lydgate's Temple of Glas, EETSES 60.cxii (1430).

Gerould S Leg, p 261 (1429–30).

SchirmerLydgate, p 133; trans Keep, p 154 (1415–26).

Authorship. MacCracken TPSL, appendix 2.xxiii; rptd EETSES 107.xxvi.

SchirmerLydgate, p 230; trans Keep, p 268.

Sources and Literary Relations. SchirmerLydgate, p 133; trans Keep, p 154 (points out L's debt to French source and Legenda aurea).

Wolpers, Heiligenlegende, p 309 (notes L's departure from sources and from other versions of the legend).

Other Scholarly Problems. Wylie J H, The Reign of Henry 5th, Cambridge 1914–29, 1.526 (refers to poem to illuminate life of Anne, daughter of Earl of Stafford and future wife of king).

Bennett OHEL, p 141 (considers poem representative of contemporary taste for saints' lives).

Literary Criticism. CBEL, 2.203 (argues this is best of L's saints' lives).

Reufs F, Das Naturgefühl bei Lydgate, Arch 122.269 (argues monasticism ruins L's originality).

Gerould S Leg, p 261 (discusses style).

SchirmerLydgate, pp 133, 136, 148; trans Keep, pp 155, 157, 171 (notes grotesque element in dragon episode).

Wolpers, Heiligenlegende, p 309 (discusses L's high, liturgical style).

PearsallLydgate, p 278 (notes poem is elaborate but without life or drama; compares it with a popular version of the legend).

[113] AGAINST MARRIAGE (also PAIN AND SORROW OF EVIL MARRIAGE and WARNING AGAINST MARRIAGE).

MSS. 1, Bodl 1782 (Digby 181), ff 7ª–8ᵇ (16 stanzas beginning at stanza 2; 15 cent); 2, Camb Univ Ff.1.6, ff 155ª–156ª (9 stanzas only, ca 1500); 3, Harley 2251, f 155ª⁻ᵇ (1464–83); 4, Rome Eng Coll 1306 (also numbered 1127 and A.347), ff 80ᵇ–82ª (1436–56). PRINT: 5, de Worde, 1509 (STC, no 19119; with additional introductory stanza: Take hede and lerne, thou lytel chylde, and se, from MS Camb Univ Dd.4.54, f 229ᵇ; see Brown-Robbins, no 3250; rptd J P Collier, Old Ballads, PPS 1, appendix p 17; rptd W C Hazlitt, Remains of the Early Popular Poetry of England, London 1864–66, 4.73).

Brown-Robbins, Robbins-Cutler, no 919.

Hammond E P, Two British Museum MSS, Angl 28.1 (detailed study of MS 3).

Klinefelter R A, The Siege of Calais: a New Text, PMLA 67.888 (brief discussion of MS 4); A Newly Discovered 15-Cent Eng MS, MLQ (Wash) 14.3 (describes MS 4).

Robbins R H, A ME Diatribe against Philip of Burgundy, Neophil 39.131 (describes MS 4).

Editions. Wright T, Latin Poems of Walter Mapes, London 1841, p 295 (MS 1; also prints Latin and French sources, pp 77 and 292).

MacCracken EETS 192.456 (composite text from PRINT 5 and all MSS except MS 4).

Modernization and Abstract. Utley CR, no 75 (gives abstract).

Language. Hall F, On Eng Adjectives in -able, London 1877, p 71.

Authorship. Plomer H R, Robert Copeland, Trans of the Biblio Soc 3.211 (suggests possibility of Copeland's authorship).

MacCracken EETSES 107.xxiii.

Wright L B, Middle Class Culture in Elizabethan England, Chapel Hill 1935, p 471 (attributes poem to Copeland).

Brown-Robbins, no 919 (does not mention L's authorship).

SchirmerLydgate, p 229; trans Keep, p 266.

Sources and Literary Relations. Wright, edn, pp 77, 292 (prints De conjuge non ducenda and French source of L).

Wright, Middle Class Culture, p 471 (believes poem typical of popular controversy over women).

Utley CR, no 75 (believes ultimate source to be De conjuge non ducenda).

SchirmerLydgate, p 82; trans Keep, p 97 (believes ultimate source to be De conjuge non ducenda).

Jack R D S, Dunbar and Lydgate, SSL 8.220 (argues poem influenced Dunbar's Tua Mariit Wemen).

Other Scholarly Problems. Renoir A, Attitudes to Women in Lydgate's Poetry, ESts 42.10 (poem is an example of L in antifeminist mood); RenoirLydgate, p 80.

Literary Criticism. SchirmerLydgate, p 82; trans Keep, p 97.

Bibliography. Dibdin T F, Typographical Antiquities, London 1812, 2.387 (discusses PRINT 5).

Utley CR, no 75 (gives bibliography of related works).

[114] MESOUR IS TRESOUR.

MS. Harley 2255, ff 143b–146b (1448?–49?).
Brown-Robbins, no 2152.
Editions. Halliwell PPS 2.208.
MacCracken EETS 192.776.
Language. Hingst R, Die Sprache John Lydgates aus seinen Reimen, Greiswald 1908, p 16.
Versification. Reger, pp 42, 78 (finds certain epic caesurae in 18.42 percent lines).
Authorship. Koeppel E, Laurents de Premierfait und John Lydgates Bearbeitungen von Boccaccios De casibus virorum illustrium, Munich 1885 (rejects L's authorship).
MacCracken TPSL, appendix 2.xviii; rptd EETSES 107.xxi.
SchirmerLydgate, p 234; trans Keep, p 272.
Gattinger, pp 19, 39 (notes learned references and Biblical influence).
Other Scholarly Problems. Duschl, p 20 (classifies proverb).
PearsallLydgate, p 181 (argues poem intended to be read along with a painting).
Literary Criticism. Gattinger, p 39 (discusses style).
General Reference. SchirmerLydgate, p 177; trans Keep, p 203.

[115] MIDSOMER ROSE (also ON THE MUTABILITY OF HUMAN AFFAIRS).

MSS. 1, Bodl 6943 (Ashmole 59), ff 31b–33b (14 stanzas; 1447–56); 2, Camb Univ Hh.4.12, ff 86a–87b (1450–1500); 3, Jesus Camb 56, ff 25a–27b (15 cent); 4, Trinity Camb 601, ff 300a–301b (1461–83); 5, Harley 2251, ff 15a–16b (1464–83); 6, Harley 2255, ff 3b–5b (1448?–49?); 7, Royal 18.A.xiii, f 114a (lines 1–4; 1400–50); 8, Huntington Libr HM.140 (formerly Phillipps 8299), ff 86b–88a (1450–80).
Brown-Robbins, Robbins-Cutler, no 1865.
Hammond E P, Two British Museum MSS, Angl 28.1 (detailed study of MS 5).
Manly & Rickert, 1.243, 433 (describes MSS 5, 8).
Editions. Gray T, Some Remarks on the Poems of Lydgate, The Works of Thomas Gray, ed T J Mathias, London 1814, 2.76 (no title, no mention of MS).
Halliwell PPS 2.22 (MS 3).
MacCracken EETS 192.780 (MS 6; collations from all MSS except MS 7).
Davies R T, Medieval Eng Lyrics, London 1962, pp 191 (MSS 6, 8; slightly normalized with glosses at foot of page), 344 (brief comments on poem; notes discussing the literary tradition).
Norton-Smith J, John Lydgate Poems, Oxford 1966, pp 20, 136 (all MSS except 7; brief commentary, notes, and glossary).
Sisam C and K, The Oxford Book of Medieval Verse, Oxford 1970, p 393 (MS 6).
Textual Matters. Gattinger, p 82 (suggests textual emendations).
Norton-Smith, edn, p 137 (insists there are 2 versions of the poem in the MSS; no MS has absolute claim to textual authority).
Versification. Reger, pp 41, 78 (finds certain epic caesurae in 15.28 percent lines).
Authorship. MacCracken TPSL, appendix 2.xxii; rptd EETSES 107.xxii.
SchirmerLydgate, p 234; trans Keep, p 272.
Sources and Literary Relations. Gattinger, pp 18, 38, 48, 66, 71 (notes influence of Bible, Legenda aurea, Seneca probably through Alanus de Insulis, Cicero probably through Isidore of Seville, and Chaucer).
Duschl, pp 23, 76 (traces proverb to Laurent de Premierfait).
Tupper F, Ubi Sunt—a Belated Postscript, MLN 28.197 (shows that poem belongs to ubi-sunt tradition that goes from earliest times to present in multiple cultures).
Other Scholarly Problems. Koeppel, E, Lydgates Vowes of Pecok, Arch 108.29 (expression vowis of pecok is conventional knightly oath in L's time and bears witness to L's knowledge of French literature).
Seaton, p 522 (argues poem is an attack on Richard Roos).
Literary Criticism. Gattinger, p 72 (studies style).
Moorman F W, The Interpretation of Nature in Eng Poetry, QF 95.127 (notes L's ability to contrast summer and winter time).
SchirmerLydgate, pp 176, 178; trans Keep, pp 202, 204 (considers poem a close-knit piece in ubi-sunt tradition).
Norton-Smith, edn, p 137 (most ambitious of L's poems in this genre).
PearsallLydgate, p 212 (one of L's best poems).
Kean P M, Chaucer and the Making of Eng Poetry, London and Boston 1972, 2.199 (assured handling of an image in the poem).
Gradon P, Form and Style in Early Eng Literature, London 1971, p 191 (complex metaphysical allusion in the poem).

[116] AGAINST MILLERS AND BAKERS.

MS. Harley 2255, f 157a (1448?–49?).
Brown-Robbins, no 2786.
Editions. [Nicolas H,] A Chronicle of London, London 1827, p 273.

Halliwell PPS 2.207.
Furnivall F J, Political Religious and Love Poems, EETS 15.56.
MacCracken EETS 192.448.
Language. Hingst R, Die Sprache John Lydgates aus seinen Reimen, Greiswald 1908, p 15.
Versification. Reger, pp 42, 77 (finds certain epic caesurae in 8.33 percent lines).
Authorship. MacCracken TPSL, appendix 2.xviii; rptd EETSES 107.xxi.
SchirmerLydgate, p 229; trans Keep, p 266.
Sources and Literary Relations. Gattinger, pp 12, 59 (argues poem typical of L's satire, suggestive of Chaucer's exactitude in Reeve's Tale, and reminiscent of Dit des boulangers, ed A Jubinal, Jongleurs et trouvères, p 138).
Other Scholarly Problems. Wylie J H, The Reign of Henry 5th, Cambridge 1914–29, 2.460 (believes poem bears witness to bakers' custom of using light weights).
SchirmerLydgate, p 81; trans Keep, p 96 (suggests influence of actual experience).

[117] MISERICORDIAS DOMINI IN ETERNUM CANTABO (also PSALM 88).

MSS. 1, Jesus Camb 56, ff 41ª–44ª (15 cent); 2, Trinity Camb 601, ff 193ᵇ–196ª (1461–83); 3, Harley 2255, ff 17ª–21ª (1448?–49?).
Brown-Robbins, no 178.
Edition. MacCracken EETSES 107.71 (MS 3; collations from the other MSS).
Language. Mendenhall J C, Aureate Terms, Lancaster Pa 1919, p 67 (notes heavily aureate diction).
Authorship. MacCracken TPSL, appendix 2.xviii; rptd EETSES 107.xvi.
SchirmerLydgate, p 231; trans Keep, p 269.
Sources and Literary Relations. SchirmerLydgate, pp 20, 155; trans Keep, pp 23, 178 (notes that poem is based on Psalm 89 (88) and uses classical material).
Other Scholarly Problems. Deanesly M, The Lollard Bible and Other Medieval Biblical Versions, Cambridge 1920, pp 320, 336 (believes L probably unaware of rule against unlicensed use of Biblical trans, and notes Henry 5 used L's Psalms for private prayers).
General References. Gattinger, p 31.
Vickers K H, Humphrey of Gloucester, London 1907, p 343.
PearsallLydgate, pp 260, 275.

[118] MUMMING AT BISHOPSWOOD.

MS. Bodl 6943 (Ashmole 59), ff 62ᵇ–64ª (1447–56).

Brown-Robbins, no 2170.
Editions. Stow J, A Survay of London, London 1603, p 99 (prints first 2 stanzas).
[Nicolas H,] A Chronicle of London, London 1827, p 257.
MacCracken EETS 192.668.
Norton-Smith J, John Lydgate Poems, Oxford 1966, pp 7 (from the MS), 122 (brief commentary, notes, and glossary).
Wickham G, Eng Moral Interludes, London 1976, p 210.
Authorship. MacCracken TPSL, appendix 2.xviii; rptd EETSES 107.xxi.
SchirmerLydgate, p 230; trans Keep, p 267.
Sources and Literary Relations. Brotanek R, Die engl Maskenspiele, WBEP 15.9 (traces development of Eng masque with much attention to L).
Norton-Smith, edn, p 123 (compares poem to [76] above).
Other Scholarly Problems. SchirmerLydgate, p 87; trans Keep, p 102 (discusses physical setting and union of pantomime and school drama).
Wickham, Early Eng Stages 1300 to 1660, London and N Y 1959, 1.191, 199 (defines the new form of L's mummings and disguisings).
Norton-Smith, edn, p 123 (attempts to deduce the form of presentation).
Literary Criticism. Withington R, Eng Pageantry, Cambridge Mass 1918, 1.106.
Norton-Smith, edn, p 123 (poem attempts to interweave presentation with representation).
General References. PearsallLydgate, p 186 (disagrees with SchirmerLydgate on setting).
Wickham, The Medieval Theatre, London 1974, p 164; edn, p 197.

[119] MUMMING AT ELTHAM.

MSS. 1, Trinity Camb 600, pp 37–40 (1456?); 2, BM Addit 29729, ff 135ᵇ–136ᵇ (John Stowe, 1558).
Brown-Robbins, Robbins-Cutler, no 458.
Hammond E P, Lydgate's Mumming at Hertford, Angl 22.364 (describes MS 1).
Brusendorff A, The Chaucer Tradition, London 1925, pp 208, 466, and passim (discusses Shirley's marginalia in MS 1).
Editions. Brotanek R, Die engl Makenspiele, WBEP 15.306 (MS 1).
MacCracken EETS 192.672 (MS 1; collations from MS 2).
Modernization and Abstract. Reyher P, Les Masques anglais, Paris 1909, p 109 (abstract).
Versification. Reger, pp 36, 77 (finds certain epic caesurae in 7.14 percent lines).
Authorship. MacCracken TPSL, appendix 2.xviii;

rptd EETSES 107.xxi.
SchirmerLydgate, p 230; trans Keep, p 267.
Sources and Literary Relations. Brotanek, edn, p 9 (traces development of Eng masque with much attention to L; discusses use of classical material).
Withington R, Eng Pageantry, Cambridge Mass 1918, 1.107 (points out that L uses classical material in the pageant a century before anyone else).
Other Scholarly Problems. Chambers, 1.396 (believes poem to have been read aloud in the hall).
Reyher, Masques, p 109 (emphasizes mediaeval attitude toward Pagan and Christian deities).
SchirmerLydgate, pp 85, 90; trans Keep, pp 101, 106 (believes poem meant to be recited).
Wickham G, Early Eng Stages 1300 to 1660, London and N Y 1959, 1.191, 199 (defines the new form of L's mummings and disguisings).
Nelson C W, The Insubstantial Pageant A Brief Examination of the Court Masque in England with Particular Attention to Four Examples of Its Development, DAI 32.2650A (has a chapter on this poem).
General References. PearsallLydgate, p 184 (poem is extremely formal).
Wickham, Eng Moral Interludes, London 1976, p 197.

[120] MUMMING AT HERTFORD.

MSS. 1, Trinity Camb 600, pp 40–48 (1456?); 2, BM Addit 29729, ff 136b–140a (John Stowe, 1558).
Brown-Robbins, Robbins-Cutler, no 2213.
Hammond, edn, Angl 22.364 (describes MS 1).
Brusendorff A, The Chaucer Tradition, London 1925, pp 208, 466, and passim (discusses Shirley's marginalia in MS 1).
Editions. Hammond E P, Lydgate's Mumming at Hertford, Angl 22.367 (MS 1).
Neilson W A and K G T Webster, The Chief British Poets of the 14 and 15 Cents, Boston 1916, p 223.
MacCracken EETS 192.675 (MS 1; collations from MS 2).
Wickham G, Eng Moral Interludes, London 1976, p 204.
Modernizations and Abstracts. Reyher P, Les Masques anglais, Paris 1909, p 113 (abstract).
Utley CR, no 190 (abstract).
Textual Matters. Holthausen F, Zu me Dichtungen, Angl 44.78 (proposes textual emendations in relation to Hammond's edn).
Language. Hingst R, Die Sprache John Lydgates aus seinen Reimen, Greiswald 1908.

Versification. Reger, pp 45, 78 (finds certain epic caesurae in 11.42 percent lines).
Pyle F, The Pedigree of Lydgate's Heroic Line, Hermathena 50.26 (studies conditions under which various aspects of this line appear).
Date. Hammond, edn, Angl 22.364 (believes date almost impossible to ascertain).
Brotanek R, Die engl Maskenspiele, WBEP 15.306 (after 1431, since poem mentions siege of Louvier in 1431).
Chambers, 1.398 (after 1431).
Utley CR, no 190 (discusses various attempts at dating).
SchirmerLydgate, p 89; trans Keep, p 105 (1430).
Renoir A, On the Date of John Lydgate's Mumming at Hertford, Archiv 198.32 (1430–31 or just before for the mumming; 1430–31 or later for the prose introd).
Green R F, Three 15-Century Notes, ELN 14.14 (1426–27).
Authorship. MacCracken TPSL, appendix 2.xviii; rptd EETSES 107.xxi.
SchirmerLydgate, p 230; trans Keep, p 267.
Sources and Literary Relations. Brotanek, Maskenspiele, pp 9, 13 (traces development of Eng masque with much attention to L; notes influence of Chaucer's Wife of Bath on poem).
Reyher, Masques, p 113 (argues that poem owes much to Chaucer's Canterbury Tales and looks forward to Gammer Gurton's Needle).
Spurgeon C, Five Hundred Years of Chaucer Criticism and Allusion, ChS 2s 48.35 (prints reference to Wife of Bath).
Robinson F N, Chaucer, Boston 1933, p 804 (suggests debt of L to Chaucer and Walter Map).
SchirmerLydgate, p 89 and passim; trans Keep, p 105 and passim (believes poem owes much to French debate, theme is similar to [18] above, and women are reminiscent of Wife of Bath).
Wickham, Early Eng Stages 1300 to 1660, London and N Y 1959, 1.221 (the kind of speeches in poem still found in Tudor masques).
PearsallLydgate, p 187 (notes debt to Chaucer and to the world of the popular lyric or of the Noah-play).
Norton-Smith J, Geoffrey Chaucer, London and Boston 1974, pp 108, 170n (notes imitation of Chaucer and resemblance to an earlier work of Deschamps).
Other Scholarly Problems. Withington R, Eng Pageantry, Cambridge Mass 1918, 1.111 (argues poem testifies to early use of debate in masque).
Renoir, The Binding Knot Three Uses of One Image in Lydgate's Poetry, Neophil 41.203 (comic use of the image); Attitudes to Women

in Lydgate's Poetry, ESts 42.11 (antifeminist).
Wickham, Early Eng Stages, 1.191, 204 (defines new form of L's mummings and disguisings).
Edwards A S G, Lydgate's Attitudes to Women, ESts 51.436 (expresses secular view of women).
Literary Criticism. Reufs F, Das Naturgefühl bei Lydgate, Arch 122.269 (concludes that monasticism ruins L's originality).
Withington R, Eng Pageantry, Cambridge Mass 1918, 1.106.
PearsallLydgate, p 187 (finds poem very successful).
General References. Chambers, 1.397.
Rogers K M, The Troublesome Helpmate, Seattle and London 1966, p 85.
Wickham, The Medieval Theatre, London 1974, p 163; edn, p 204.

[121] MUMMING AT LONDON (also DESGUISING OF DAME FORTUNE).

MSS. 1, Trinity Camb 600, pp 55–65 (1456?); 2, BM Addit 29729, ff 140a–144a (John Stowe, 1558).
Brown-Robbins, no 1928.
Hammond E P, Lydgate's Mumming at Hertford, Angl 22.364 (describes MS 1).
Brusendorff A, The Chaucer Tradition, London 1925, pp 208, 466 and passim (discusses Shirley's marginalia in MS 1).
Editions. Brotanek R, Die engl Maskenspiele, WBEP 15.309 (MS 1).
MacCracken EETS 192.682 (MS 1; collations from MS 2).
Modernization and Abstract. Reyher P, Les Masques anglais, Paris 1909, p 110 (abstract).
Date. SchirmerLydgate, p 89; trans Keep, p 104 (1427?).
Authorship. MacCracken TPSL, appendix 2.xix; rptd EETSES 107.xxi.
SchirmerLydgate, p 230; trans Keep, p 267.
Seaton, p 194 (argues for Richard Roos).
Sources and Literary Relations. Brotanek, edn, pp 9, 11 (traces development of Eng masque with much attention to L's mummings; notes use of mediaeval allegory).
Reyher, Masques, p 110 (notes use of Romance of the Rose).
Brusendorff, Chaucer Tradition, p 389 (demonstrates influence of Romance of the Rose).
Patch H R, The Goddess Fortuna in Mediaeval Literature, Cambridge Mass 1927, p 128 (notes L's debt to Romance of the Rose and ultimately to Alanus de Insulis).
SchirmerLydgate, p 89; trans Keep, p 104 (believes poem reminiscent of [161] below).
Seaton, pp 195, 198 (argues for parallels with The Isle of Ladies).
Other Scholarly Problems. Withington R, Eng Pageantry, Cambridge England 1918, 1.107 (believes use of abstraction probably L's innovation).
Wickham G, Early Eng Stages 1300 to 1660, London and N Y 1959, 1.191, 204, 216 (defines the new form of L's mummings and disguisings and notes possible scenic devices).
Seaton, p 195 (argues poem contains name anagrams).
Greaves M, The Blazon of Honour, N Y 1964, p 19 (defines conception of magnanimity in the poem).
RenoirLydgate, p 72 (argues for pro-classical attitude in the poem).
Literary Criticism. Withington, Eng Pageants, 1.106.
Seaton, p 195 (general assessment and discusses political situation).
General References. Chambers, 1.397.
PearsallLydgate, p 186 (typical of L to turn entertainment to moral purposes).

[122] MUMMING AT WINDSOR.

MSS. 1, Trinity Camb 600, pp 71–74 (1456?); 2, BM Addit 29729, ff 144a–145b (John Stowe, 1558).
Brown-Robbins, no 2212.
Hammond E P, Lydgate's Mumming at Hertford, Angl 22.364 (describes MS 1).
Brusendorff A, The Chaucer Tradition, London 1925, pp 208, 466 and passim (discusses Shirley's marginalia in MS 1).
Editions. Brotanek R, Die engl Maskenspiele, WBEP 15.317 (MS 1).
MacCracken EETS 192.691 (MS 1; collations from MS 2).
Versification. Reger, pp 36, 77 (finds certain epic caesurae in 4 percent lines).
Date. Gerould S Leg, p 299 (Christmas 1429).
SchirmerLydgate, p 90; trans Keep, p 106 (1424–30).
Authorship. MacCracken TPSL, appendix 2.xix; rptd EETSES 107.xxi.
SchirmerLydgate, p 230; trans Keep, p 267.
Sources and Literary Relations. Brotanek, edn, p 9 and passim (traces development of Eng masque with much attention to L; discusses use of St Clothilda legend).
SchirmerLydgate, pp 90, 117, 221; trans Keep,

pp 106, 136, 253 (shows similarities to [119] above).
Other Scholarly Problems. Chambers, 1.397 (believes Mumming to have been recited by a presenter).
Wickham G, Early Eng Stages 1300 to 1660, London and N Y 1959, 1.191, 205, 216 (defines the new form of L's mummings and disguisings and notes scenic devices).
Literary Criticism. Gerould S Leg, p 262.
Withington R, Eng Pageantry, Cambridge Mass 1918, 1.106.
Moore A K, The Secular Love Lyric in ME, Lexington 1951, p 146 (considers opening laureate drivel typical of period).
General Reference. PearsallLydgate, p 185 (notes moment of levity).

[123] MUMMING FOR THE GOLDSMITHS OF LONDON.

MSS. 1, Trinity Camb 600, pp 175–178 (1456?); 2, BM Addit 29729, ff 134ª–135ᵇ (John Stowe, 1558).
Brown-Robbins, no 3301.
Hammond E P, Lydgate's Mumming at Hertford, Angl 22.364 (describes MS 1).
Brusendorff A, The Chaucer Tradition, London 1925, pp 208, 466 and passim (discusses Shirley's marginalia in MS 1).
Editions. Brotanek R, Die engl Maskenspiele, WBEP 15.323 (MS 1).
MacCracken EETS 192.698 (MS 1; collations from MS 2).
Versification. Reger, pp 36, 78 (finds epic caesurae in 13.26 percent lines).
Authorship. MacCracken TPSL, appendix 2.xix; rptd EETSES 107.xxii.
Bennett OHEL, p 118 (ascribes poem to L on basis of rubric by John Shirley).
SchirmerLydgate, p 230; trans Keep, p 267.
Sources and Literary Relations. Kings 2, chap 6.1–15.
Brotanek, edn, p 9 and passim (traces development of Eng masque with much attention to L).
Other Scholarly Problems. Chambers, 1.396 (believes Mumming to have been read aloud in the hall).
Bennett OHEL, p 118 (discusses didactic purpose).
Wickham G, Early Eng Stages 1300 to 1660, London and N Y 1959, 1.191, 200 (defines the new form of L's mummings and disguisings).
Literary Criticism. Withington R, Eng Pageantry, Cambridge Mass 1918, 1.106.
General References. SchirmerLydgate, p 92; trans Keep, p 108.
PearsallLydgate, pp 73, 185.

Wickham, The Medieval Theatre, London 1974, p 163.

[124] MUMMING FOR THE MERCERS OF LONDON.

MSS. 1, Trinity Camb 600, pp 171–175 (1456?); 2, BM Addit 29729, ff 132ᵇ–134ª (John Stowe, 1558).
Brown-Robbins, no 2210.
Hammond E P, Lydgate's Mumming at Hertford, Angl 22.364 (describes MS 1).
Brusendorff A, The Chaucer Tradition, London 1925, p 466 (discusses Shirley's marginalia in MS 1).
Editions. Brotanek R, Die engl Maskenspiele, WBEP 15.320 (MS 1).
MacCracken EETS 192.695 (MS 1; collations from MS 2).
Versification. Reger, pp 36, 77 (finds certain epic caesurae in 5.17 percent lines).
Date. SchirmerLydgate, p 91; trans Keep, p 107 (probably 1429).
Authorship. MacCracken TPSL, appendix 2.xix; rptd EETSES 107.xxi.
SchirmerLydgate, p 230; trans Keep, p 267.
Sources and Literary Relations. Brotanek, edn, p 9 and passim (traces development of Eng masque with much attention to L; notes early-Renaissance use of classical mythology).
SchirmerLydgate, p 91; trans Keep, p 107 (notes use of mythology).
Other Scholarly Problems. Chambers, 1.396 (believes Mumming to have been read aloud in the hall).
Wickham G, Early Eng Stages 1300 to 1660, London and N Y 1959, 1.191, 200, 216, 232 (defines the new form of L's mummings and disguisings and discusses the use of scenic devices).
Literary Criticism. Withington R, Eng Pageantry, Cambridge Mass 1918, 1.106.
General Reference. PearsallLydgate, pp 73, 184.

[125] MUMMING FOR QUEEN MARGARET (also PAGEANT VERSES FOR QUEEN MARGARET and QUEEN MARGARET'S ENTRY INTO LONDON).

MSS. 1, Harley 542, ff 101ª–102ᵇ (lines 1–39, 155–70; a Stowe MS, ca 1600); 2, Harley 3869, ff 2ª–4ᵇ (15 cent).
Brown-Robbins, Robbins-Cutler, no 2200.
[Thompson R,] Chronicles of London Bridge, London 1827, p 276 (discusses MS 1).
Brown, edn, MLR 7.225, 231 (discusses MS 2).

Withington, edn, MP 13.53 (shows MS 1 not derived from MS 2).
Editions. Brown C, Lydgate's Verses on Queen Margaret's Entry into London, MLR 7.226 (MS 2).
Withington R, Queen Margaret's Entry into London 1445, MP 13.55 (MS 1).
Textual Matters. Brown, edn, MLR 7.231 (considers text incomplete on basis of William Gregory's Chronicle, ed J Gairdner, Historical Collection of a Citizen of London, Camden Soc 1876, p 186).
Versification. Pyle F, The Pedigree of Lydgate's Heroic Line, Hermathena 50.26 (studies conditions under which line appears).
Date. Schick J, Lydgate's Temple of Glas, EETSES 60.cxii (1445?).
Withington, edn, MP 13.53 (dates poem 28 May 1445 on basis of Stowe's marginalia).
Authorship. Stowe J, Annals of England, London 1615, p 385 (mentions verses by L on Queen Margaret's entry).
Taylor A, The Glory of Regality, London 1820, p 268 (accepts Stowe's testimony).
Hone W, Ancient Mysteries Described, London 1823, p 235.
[Thompson,] Chronicles, p 276 (accepts Stowe's testimony).
Kingsford C L, Chronicles of London, Oxford 1905, p 301.
Brown, edn, MLR 7.225 (assigns poem to L on basis of style).
SchirmerLydgate, p 230; trans Keep, p 267.
Sources and Literary Relations. Brotanek R, Die engl Maskenspiele, WBEP 15.9 and passim (traces development of Eng masque with much attention to L).
PearsallLydgate, p 293 (compares poem with [77] above but finds it less mythological and more religious).
Other Scholarly Problems. Taylor, Regality, p 268 (describes Margaret's entry).
Hone, Mysteries, p 235 (gives account of pageant).
Davidson C, Studies in the Eng Mystery Plays, Yale 1892, p 87 (argues poem illustrates community of custom and literary standards among Eng and French nobility).
Brie F W D, The Brut, EETS 136.489, 510 (describes pageant).
Withington, Eng Pageantry, Cambridge Mass 1918, 1.148 (gives account of pageant).
Literary Criticism. [Thompson,] Chronicles, p 276 and passim.
General Reference. SchirmerLydgate, p 210; trans Keep, p 242.

[126] SAYENGE OF THE NYGHTYNGALE.

MSS. 1, Trinity Camb 600, pp 337–348 (1456?); 2, Harley 2251, ff 229a–234a (1464–81); 3, BM Addit 29729, ff 161a–166b (John Stowe, 1558).
Brown-Robbins, Robbins-Cutler, no 1498.
Hammond E P, Lydgate's Mumming at Hertford, Angl 22.364 (describes MS 1); Two British Museum MSS, Angl 28.1 (detailed study of MS 2).
Brusendorff A, The Chaucer Tradition, London 1925, pp 208, 466 and passim (discusses Shirley's marginalia in MS 1 and relationship of all MSS).
Glauning, edn, EETSES 80.xi (description and genealogy of MSS).
Manly & Rickert, 1.241 (describes MS 2).
Editions. Glauning O, Lydgate's Minor Poems, EETSES 80.16 (MS 2).
MacCracken EETSES 107.221 (MS 1; collations from all other MSS).
Language. Glauning, edn, EETSES 80.xxvi.
Hingst R, Die Sprache John Lydgates aus seinen Reimen, Greiswald 1908.
Royster J F, The Do Auxiliary 1400 to 1450, MP 12.449.
Versification. Glauning, edn, EETSES 80.xx.
Licklider A H, Chapters on the Metrics of the Chaucerian Tradition, Baltimore 1910, pp 42, 62, 104 (discusses devices of resolved stress and arsis-thesis variation).
Reger, pp 39, 77 (finds certain epic caesurae in 5.8 percent lines).
Saintsbury G, A History of Eng Prosody, London 1923, 1.229 (discusses lack of metrical correctness in L).
Date. Glauning, edn, EETSES 80.xxxvi (1446).
Authorship. Glauning, edn, EETSES 80.xxxvi.
MacCracken TPSL, appendix 2.xix; rptd EETSES 107.xxii.
SchirmerLydgate, p 232; trans Keep, p 270.
Seaton, p 388 (argues poem by Richard Roos with end by L).
Sources and Literary Relations. Blades W, The Biography and Typography of William Caxton, 2nd edn, N Y 1882, p 354 (believes L's poem paraphrase of work later printed by Caxton ca 1491).
Glauning, edn, EETSES 80.xxxviii (prints Latin poem).
SchirmerLydgate, p 157; trans Keep, p 180 (shows source to be poem by John Peckham).
PearsallLydgate, p 266 (denies L knew Peckham's poem well; notes influence of Chaucer).
Other Scholarly Problem. Seaton, p 389 (argues poem

contains name anagrams).
Literary Criticism. Reufs F, Das Naturgefühl bei Lydgate, Arch 122.269 (argues monasticism ruins L's originality).
Seaton, p 389 (general assessment; argues 2 parts are totally different in style).
Woolf R, The Eng Religious Lyric in the Middle Ages, Oxford 1968, p 232 (finds poem quite moving).
PearsallLydgate, p 266 (motley in construction, but poem is effective and full of life and color).
Bibliography. SchirmerLydgate, pp 227, 240; trans Keep, pp 261, 281.

[127] NIGHTINGALE AS SYMBOL OF CHRIST (also THE NIGHTINGALE).

MSS. 1, Bodl Lat misc C.66 (formerly Capesthorne), ff 107[b]–? (lacks lines 1–22, other parts illegible; 1500–35); 2, Corp Christi Oxf 203, pp 1–21 (1450–1500); 3, Cotton Calig A.ii, ff 59[a]–64[a] (1400–50; with stanzas 1, 2 from MS 2).
Brown-Robbins, Robbins-Cutler, no 931.
Glauning, edn, EETSES 80.xi (description and genealogy of MSS).
Edition. Glauning O, Lydgate's Minor Poems, EETSES 80.2 (composite text from MSS 2, 3).
Language. Glauning, edn, EETSES 80.xxvi.
Hingst R, Die Sprache John Lydgates aus seinen Reimen, Greiswald 1908.
Versification. Glauning, edn, EETSES 80.xx.
Reger, pp 39, 77 (finds certain epic caesurae in 8.96 percent lines).
Saintsbury G, A History of Eng Prosody, London 1923, 1.229 (discusses lack of metrical correctness in L).
Date. Glauning, edn, EETSES 80.xxxviii (believes poem impossible to date).
Authorship. Glauning, edn, EETSES 80.xxxiv.
SchirmerLydgate, p 236; trans Keep, p 275 (rejects L's authorship).
Sources and Literary Relations. Glauning, edn, EETSES 80.xxxviii (prints Latin poem).
Literary Criticism. Reufs F, Das Naturgefühl bei Lydgate, Arch 122.269 (argues monasticism ruins L's originality).
Woolf R, The Eng Religious Lyric in the Middle Ages, Oxford 1968, p 232 (poem is didactic; notes effective use of bird's cry).
General Reference. SchirmerLydgate, p 157; trans Keep, p 180.
Bibliography. SchirmerLydgate, pp 227, 240; trans Keep, pp 261, 281.

[128] NINE PROPERTIES OF WINE.

MSS. 1, Harley 2252, f 2[a] (16 cent?); 2, BM Addit 10106, f 79[a] (15 cent); 3, BM Addit 29729, f 16[a] (John Stowe, 1558).
Brown-Robbins, Robbins-Cutler, no 4175.
Editions. Rel Ant, 1.325 (MS 2).
Steele R, Secrees of Old Philisoffres, EETSES 66.xxx (MS 3).
MacCracken EETS 192.724 (MS 3; collations from MS 1).
Versification. Reger, pp 68, 78 (finds certain epic caesurae in 28.5 percent lines).
Authorship. MacCracken TPSL, appendix 2.xx; rptd EETSES 107.xxii.
Brown-Robbins, no 4175 (does not attribute poem to L).
SchirmerLydgate, p 230; trans Keep, p 267.
Sources and Literary Relations. Robbins-Cutler, no 4175 (notes that line 2 is the same as line 1969 in [166] below).
General References. SchirmerLydgate, p 95; trans Keep, p 111.
PearsallLydgate, p 220 (finds poem an example of mediaeval concern to classify information by number).

[129] FIFTEEN O'S OF CHRIST.

MSS. 1, Bodl 798 (Laud Misc 683), ff 1[a]–8[a] (15 cent); 2, Bodl 11914 (Rawl C.48), ff 111[b]–116[a] (15 cent); 3, Jesus Camb 56, ff 65[b]–70[b] (15 cent); 4, Harley 2255, ff 104[a]–110[b] (1448?–49?); 5, BM Addit 29729, ff 11[a]–16[a], 287[a–b] (John Stowe, 1558).
Brown-Robbins, no 2394.
MacCracken EETSES 107.xvii (notes Scotch version in MS Arundel 285, a different ME version in MS Bodl 14526, and a prose adaptation in MS Harley 172).
Edition. MacCracken EETSES 107.238 (MS 1; collations from all other MSS).
Authorship. MacCracken TPSL, appendix 2.xiv; rptd EETSES 107.xvii.
SchirmerLydgate, p 232; trans Keep, p 270.
Sources and Literary Relations. SchirmerLydgate, pp 162, 165; trans Keep, pp 185, 189 (notes similarities of tone with [147] below and [47] above).

[130] THE ORDER OF FOOLS (also A TALE OF THRESCORE FOLYS AND THRE).

MSS. 1, Bodl 798 (Laud Misc 683), ff 56[a]–60[a] (15 cent); 2, Bodl 2078 (Bodley 638), f 219[a]

(stanzas 1–6; 15 cent?); 3, Bodl 2291 (Bodley 648), ff 19a–21a (1465?); 4, Cotton Nero A.vi, ff 194b–195b (24 stanzas; 1460–70?); 5, Harley 374, item 17 (15 cent; stanzas 6, 10, 12–14; perhaps copied by Stowe; listed as Harley 364 by Robbins-Cutler, no 3444); 6, Harley 2251, ff 274a–276b (24 stanzas; 1464–83); 7, BM Addit 34360, ff 24a–26b (1461–83).
Brown-Robbins, Robbins-Cutler, no 3444.
Hammond E P, Two British Museum MSS, Angl 28.1 (detailed study of MSS 6, 7).
Bowers R H, Lydgate's The Order of Fools in Harley MS 374, MLN 67.534 (MS 5; suggests may have been copied by Stowe).
Editions. Halliwell PPS 2.164 (MS 6).
Furnivall F J, Queene Elizabethes Achademy, EETSES 8.79 (MS 4).
MacCracken EETS 192.449 (MS 1; collations from all MSS except MS 3).
Textual Matters. Gattinger, p 84 (suggests textual emendations).
Bowers, MLN 67.536 (MS 5).
Versification. Reger, pp 41, 78 (finds certain epic caesurae in 19.27 percent lines).
Authorship. MacCracken TPSL, appendix 2.xx; rptd EETSES 107.xxii.
SchirmerLydgate, p 229; trans Keep, p 266.
Sources and Literary Relations. Gattinger, pp 38, 42, 57, 69, 73 and passim (discusses influence of Bible, Isidore of Seville, Chaucer, and especially Les Trente-sis mestre folies, ed A Jubinal, Nouveau recueil de contes dit et fabliaux, Paris 1829–42, vol 2).
Rey A, Skelton's Satirical Poems, Bern 1899, p 21 (argues poem in tradition of Speculum stultorum, and notes borrowings from classical mythology).
Lange J H, Lydgate und Fragment B des Romaunt of the Rose, EStn 29.397 (notes influence of Romance of Rose).
SchirmerLydgate, pp 80, 173; trans Keep, pp 95, 198 (notes debt to Les Trente-sis mestres folies).
Bowers, MLN 67.534 (notes other ME works of this sort).
Other Scholarly Problem. Duschl, pp 27, 86, 88, 97 (classifies proverbs).
Literary Criticism. Gattinger, p 73.

[131] BALADE IN COMMENDATION OF OUR LADY (also BALLADE AT THE REVERENCE OF OUR LADY).

MSS. 1, Bodl 6943 (Ashmole 59), ff 39b–41a (lacks stanzas 10–18; 1447–56); 2, Sloane 1212, ff 101a–102a (1431–50). PRINTS: 3, Thynne, Chaucer, 1532 (rptd W W Skeat, Oxf Ch, 7.275); 4, Stowe, Chaucer, 1561 (19 stanzas; rptd A Chalmers, Eng Poets, London 1810, 1.546).
Brown-Robbins, Robbins-Cutler, no 99.
MacCracken H N, Additional Light on the Temple of Glas, PMLA 23.128 (partial description of MS 2).
Norton-Smith, edn, p 143 (MS 2).
Editions. Anderson R, The Works of the British Poets, London 1795, 1.575.
MacCracken EETSES 107.254 (MS 2; collations from MS 1, PRINT 3).
Schirmer W F, Der Stil in Lydgates religiöser Dichtung, Kleine Schriften, Tübingen 1950, p 50 (MS 1; German trans on p 54).
Norton-Smith J, John Lydgate Poems, Oxford 1966, pp 25 (MS 2; corrected with MS 1), 143 (brief commentary, notes, and glossary).
Selection. Kaiser R, Medieval Eng, 3rd edn, Berlin 1958, p 506 (lines 57–84; MS 2).
Textual Matters. Norton-Smith, edn, p 143 (notes MSS 1, 2 represent wholly different versions of poem, suggests MS 1 may be an early draft).
Language. Skeat B M, The Lamentatyon of Mary Magdaleyne, Cambridge 1897, p 27 (argues that final e was commonly sounded).
Dibelius W, John Capgrave und die engl Schriftsprache, Angl 23.153, 323.
Versification. Reger, pp 62, 78 (finds certain epic caesurae in 12.14 percent lines).
Authorship. Skeat W W, A Ballade of Our Lady by Lydgate, Acad (London) 40.286 (assigns poem to L on basis of MS 1).
MacCracken TPSL, appendix 2.x; rptd EETSES 107.xii.
SchirmerLydgate, p 233; trans Keep, p 271.
Sources and Literary Relations. Skeat, Acad 40.286 (notes influence of Chaucer).
MacCracken H N, Lydgatiana, Arch 131.40 (prints a Lenvoy to Mary, a Regina celi letare, a Five Joys of the Virgin, and a Maria Virgo assumpta est which imitate [131]).
Nichols P H, William Dunbar as a Scottish Lydgatian, PMLA 46.214 (notes influence of [131] on Dunbar's Ane Ballat of Our Lady); Lydgate's Influence on the Aureate Terms of the Scottish Chaucerians, PMLA 47.516.
Wolpers T, Geschichte der engl Marienlyrik im Mittelalter, Angl 69.3 (discusses influence of Latin hymns on L).
Bonner F W, The Genesis of the Chaucer Apocrypha, SP 48.461.
Hyde I, Lydgate's Halff Chongyd Latyne An

Illustration, MLN 70.252 (many phrases from Anticlaudianus of Alanus de Insulis).

Norton-Smith, edn, p 143 (argues for influence of Chaucer's Troilus but not his ABC; notes influence of Anticlaudianus and church material).

PearsallLydgate, p 270 (briefly notes how traditional the phrases and images are).

Pearsall D and E Salter, Landscapes and Seasons of the Medieval World, Toronto 1973, p 114 (briefly notes the influence of 12-cent Latin verse).

Literary Criticism. Reufs F, Das Naturgefühl bei Lydgate, Arch 122.269 (concludes that monasticism ruins L's originality).

Nichols, PMLA 47.516 (discusses artificiality and extravagance in L's diction).

Schirmer, edn, p 40 (discusses aspects of sentence construction which result in aureate style); SchirmerLydgate, pp 64, 130, 171; trans Keep, pp 74, 152, 195 (finds poem typical of aureate style).

Norton-Smith, edn, p 143 (a fine aureate poem).

PearsallLydgate, p 268 (representative of L's poetic tendencies and one of his best).

Gradon P, Form and Style in Early Eng Literature, London 1971, p 353 (discusses as an aureate poem).

[132] VALENTINE TO OUR LADY (also VALENTINE TO HER I LOVE and VALENTINE TO HER THAT EXCELLETH ALL).

MSS. 1, Bodl 6943 (Ashmole 59), ff 52a–54a (1447–56); 2, Bodl 14530 (Rawl poet F.36), f 1a–b (1450–1500); 3, Trinity Camb 600, pp 145–149 (1456?; with 5 stanzas from MS 2); 4, Harley 2251, ff 242b–244b (1464–83); 5, BM Addit 29729, ff 155a–157b (John Stowe, 1558).

Brown-Robbins, Robbins-Cutler, no 3065.

Hammond E P, Lydgate's Mumming at Hertford, Angl 22.364 (describes MS 3); Two British Museum MSS, Angl 28.1 (detailed study of MS 4).

Brusendorff A, The Chaucer Tradition, London 1925, pp 208, 466 and passim (discusses Shirley's marginalia in MS 3).

Manly & Rickert, 1.241 (describes MS 4).

Editions. Mahir O, Einige religiöse Gedichte John Lydgates, München 1910, p 39 (MS 2).

MacCracken EETSES 107.304 (MS 3; collations from all MSS).

Language. Hingst R, Die Sprache John Lydgates aus seinen Reimen, Greiswald 1908, pp 18, 22, 28, 31, 33, 35 and passim.

Authorship. MacCracken TPSL, appendix 2.xxvii; rptd EETSES 107.xxx.

SchirmerLydgate, p 231; trans Keep, p 269.

Sources and Literary Relations. MacCracken H N, Lydgatiana, Arch 131.40 (prints a Lenvoy to Mary, a Five Joys of the Virgin, and a Maria Virgo assumpta est which imitate [132]).

Stillwell G, Chaucer's Eagles and Their Choice on February 14, JEGP 53.546 (unlike Chaucer's Parlement, [132] bears witness to tradition of humility in courtly lover).

General References. SchirmerLydgate, p 78; trans Keep, p 92.

Woolf R, The Eng Religious Lyric in the Middle Ages, Oxford 1968, p 277 (notes use of Biblical and classical comparisons to the Virgin).

PearsallLydgate, p 164.

[133] PAGEANT OF KNOWLEDGE (also SEVEN WISE COUNSELS).

MSS. 1, Trinity Camb 601, ff 287a–289b (1461–83). PRINT: 2, Mars and Venus, Notary ca 1500 (STC, no 5089; stanzas 8–36 only).

Brown-Robbins, Robbins-Cutler, no 3651.

Edition. MacCracken EETS 192.724.

Versification. Reger, pp 42, 78 (finds certain epic caesurae in 24.17 percent lines).

Authorship. MacCracken TPSL, appendix 2.xx; rptd EETSES 107.xxiii.

Brown-Robbins, no 3651 (does not attribute poem to L).

SchirmerLydgate, p 230; trans Keep, p 267.

Sources and Literary Relations. SchirmerLydgate, p 88; trans Keep, p 104 (notes poem based on Ausonius' Septem sapientium Sententiae).

Bühler C F, Lydgate's Horse Sheep and Goose and Huntington MS HM 114, MLN 55.563 (notes certain stanzas also occur in other works of L, in Court of Sapience, and in Ashby's Active Policy of a Prince).

Other Scholarly Problems. Mullet C F, John Lydgate: a Mirror of Medieval Medicine, Bull of the Hist of Medicine 22.403 (believes poem reflects typical mediaeval view of hist and nature of medicine and contemporary fear of pestilence).

PearsallLydgate, p 183 (briefly discusses [133] as a tableau-presentation).

For other Scholarship, see under [134–136] below.

[134] PAGEANT OF KNOWLEDGE, STANZAS 23–END, IN DIFFERENT VERSION.

MSS. 1, Bodl 11951 (Rawl C.86), ff 77a–79b (16

cent); 2, Camb Univ Hh.4.12, ff 88a–89a (1490–1510); 3, Jesus Camb 56, ff 33a–36a (15 cent); 4, Harley 2251, ff 23b–26a, and again stanzas 11–13, ff 79b–80a (1464–83); 5, Harley 2255, ff 14a–17a (1448?–49?).
Brown-Robbins, no 3503.
Hammond E P, Two British Museum MSS, Angl 28.1 (detailed study of MS 4).
Manly & Rickert, 1.241 (describes MS 4).
Editions. Halliwell PPS 2.193 (MS 5).
MacCracken EETS 192.734 (MS 5).
Sources and Literary Relations. Gattinger, pp 17, 39, 41, 66 (notes influence of Isidore of Seville, Vincent of Beauvais, and Chaucer).
Other Scholarly Problem. PearsallLydgate, p 183 (notes that this version, unlike [133] above, is didactic and not meant for performance).
For other scholarship, see under [133, 135–136].

[135] PAGEANT OF KNOWLEDGE, STANZA 23 ALONE.

MSS. 1, Bodl 3896 (Fairfax 16), f 195a (1400–50); 2, Harley 7333, f 148a (15 cent); 3, Harley 7578, f 20a (1425–75); 4, BM Addit 16165, f 244a (1425–75); 5, BM Addit 34360, f 22a (1461–83); 6, Huntington Libr HM.144 (formerly Huth 7), f 144a (1480–1500); 7, Huntington Libr EL 26.A.13, f ii (15 cent).
Brown-Robbins, Robbins-Cutler, no 3504.
Hanmond E P, Two British Museum MSS, Angl 28.1 (detailed study of MS 5).
Bühler, edn, MLN 55.563 (discusses MS 6).
Editions. Rel Ant, 1.234 (MS 2).
Furnivall F J, Chaucer and Lydgate Fragments, N&Q 5s 9.343 (MS 6).
Flügel E, Kleinere Mitteilungen aus Handschriften, Angl 14.31 (MS 2).
South H P, The Question of Halsam, PMLA 50.362 (MS 1).
Brown RLxvC, p 262 (MS 1).
Bühler C F, Lydgate's Horse Sheep and Goose, MLN 55.567 (MS 6).
Authorship. South, edn, PMLA 50.362 (rejects L's authorship and attributes poem to Halsam).
Bühler, edn, MLN 55.567 (rejects evidence for Halsam's authorship).
Brown-Robbins, no 3504 (does not attribute poem to L).
For other scholarship, see under [133–134, 136].

[136] PAGEANT OF KNOWLEDGE, STANZAS 3–9.

MSS. 1, Bodl 6943 (Ashmole 59), ff 70b–71b (1447–56); 2, Camb Univ Ff.1.6, f 151a (ca 1500); 3, Arundel 168, ff 14a–15a (15 cent); 4, Harley 116, f 124a–b (1475–1500); 5, Harley 2251, ff 168a–169a? (1464–83); 6, Ipswich County Hall Deposit Hillwood (formerly Brome), f 80b (1450–1500); 7, Wellcome Hist Med Libr 673, f 7b (3 stanzas; 1450–1500); 8, Rome Eng Coll 1306 (also numbered 127 and A.347), ff 74b–75a (1436–1456).
Brown-Robbins, Robbins-Cutler, no 576.
Hammond E P, Two British Museum MSS, Angl 28.1 (detailed description of MS 5).
Manly & Rickert, 1.241 (describes MS 5).
Klinefelter R A, The Siege of Calais: a New Text, PMLA 67.888 (discusses MS 8); A Newly Discovered 15-Cent Eng MS, MLQ (Wash) 14.3 (discusses MS 8).
Kane, edn, p 50 (MS 7).
Robbins R H, A ME Diatribe against Philip of Burgundy, Neophil 39.131 (describes MS 8).
Editions. Smith L T, A Common-place Book, London 1886, p 19 (MS 6).
Förster M, Kleine Mitteilungen zur me Lehrdichtung, Arch 104.299 (MS 1).
Kane G, The ME Verse in MS Wellcome 1493, London Mediaeval Stud 2, pt 1.60–61, p 54 (MS 7).
For other scholarship, see under [133–135] above.

[137] EXPOSITION OF PATER NOSTER.

MSS. 1, Bodl 798 (Laud Misc 683), ff 81a–87a (15 cent); 2, Jesus Camb 56, ff 47b–53a (15 cent); 3, Harley 2255, ff 32b–39b (stanzas 3 and 4 come after stanza 11; 1448?–49?).
Brown-Robbins, no 448.
Editions. Mahir O, Einige religiöse Gedichte John Lydgates, München 1910, p 1 (MS 2).
MacCracken EETSES 107.60 (MS 1; collations from all other MSS).
Date. SchirmerLydgate, p 154; trans Keep, p 177 (believes date possibly as late as 1445).
Authorship. MacCracken TPSL, appendix 2.xx; rptd EETSES 107.xxiii.
SchirmerLydgate, p 231; trans Keep, p 269.
Sources and Literary Relations. Duschl, p 53 (traces stanza 31 to Gospels).
Patch H R, The Goddess Fortuna in Mediaeval Literature, Cambridge Mass 1927, p 105 (lists texts showing Fortune as stormy queen).
Other Scholarly Problem. Duschl, p 97 (classifies proverb).
General References. Gattinger, p 31.
Wylie J H, The Reign of Henry 5th, Cambridge

1914–29, 2.460.
PearsallLydgate, p 257 (considers poem a tour de force).

[138] PARAPHRASE OF PATER NOSTER.

MSS. 1, Trinity Camb 601, f 274ª⁻ᵇ (1461–83); 2, Longleat 30, f 24ª (15 cent); 3, Huntington Libr HM.142 (formerly Bement), ff 20ᵇ–21ª (1467).
Brown-Robbins, Robbins-Cutler, no 2711.
Editions. Mahir O, Einige religiöse Gedichte John Lydgates, München 1910, p 16 (MS 1).
MacCracken EETSES 107.18 (MS 1).
Versification. SchirmerLydgate, p 154; trans Keep, p 177 (notes that verse form of this poem is not common with L).
Authorship. MacCracken TPSL, appendix 2.xx; rptd EETSES 107.xxiii.
SchirmerLydgate, p 231; trans Keep, p 269.

[139] PELERINAGE DE LA VIE HUMAINE (also PILGRIMAGE OF THE LIFE OF MAN).

MSS. 1, Cotton Tib A.vii, ff 39ª–106ᵇ (lines 18,313–23,676 only; 15 cent); 2, Cotton Vitell C.xiii, ff 2ª–311ᵇ (does not include Chaucer's ABC hymn but leaves space for it; lacking about 2,200 lines; Furnivall, EETSES 92.lxvii has f 39ª ff; 15 cent); 3, Stowe 952, ff 1ª–379ᵇ (Chaucer's hymn to BV included on f 299ª; ff 1–304 are in 1450–1500 hand, remainder is 1600?); 4, Worcester Cath C.i.8, fragment (Ker Pastedowns, no 1894). PRINT: 5, Caxton 1483 (STC, no 17025).
Brown-Robbins, Robbins-Cutler, no 4265.
8th Report of the Royal Commission on Historical MSS, London 1878, 3.30 (notes MS listed among possessions of Earl of Ashburnham).
Furnivall F J, The Pilgrimage of the Life of Man, EETSES 77.v; 92.lxvii (believes MS 3 to be MS mentioned by Speght in his 1598 Chaucer and describes MSS).
Hammond E P, The Lost Quires of a Shirley Codex, MLN 36.184 (discusses possibility of [139] having been recorded in MS Trinity Camb 600).
Editions. Furnivall F J, Pilgrimage of the Life of Man, Roxb Club 1905 (all MSS); Pilgrimage of the Life of Man, EETSES 77 and 83 (all MSS; prayer to BV in MS 3 printed in EETSES 83.454); reference to Chaucer rptd C Spurgeon, Five Hundred Years of Chaucer Criticism and Allusion, ChS 2s 48.34.
Language. Schick J, Lydgate's Temple of Glas, EETSES 60.lv.
Locock C B, The Pilgrimage of the Life of Man, EETSES 92.xli.
Hingst R, Die Sprache John Lydgates aus seinen Reimen, Greiswald 1908.
Babcock C F, A Study of the Metrical Use of the Inflectional e in ME with Particular Reference to Chaucer and Lydgate, PMLA 29.59 (argues L's language bridges gap between Middle Ages and modern period).
Royster J F, The Do Auxiliary 1400 to 1450, MP 12.449 (counts 20 instances in lines 1–4000).
Mendenhall J C, Aureate Terms, Lancaster Pa 1919, pp 47, 60 (discusses use of aureate terms).
Versification. Schick, EETSES 60.lv.
Locock, EETSES 92.xxxi.
Licklider A H, Chapters on the Metrics of the Chaucerian Tradition, Baltimore 1910, pp 45, 74, 102 (discusses use of resolved stress).
Saintsbury G, A History of Eng Prosody, London 1923, 1.229 (believes L more competent with octosyllabic than other meters).
Pyle F, The Pedigree of Lydgate's Heroic Line, Hermathena 50.26 (notes occasional pause after front syllable).
Date. Schick, EETSES 60.cxii (1426–30?).
SchirmerLydgate, p 103; trans Keep, p 121 (1428).
Authorship. Blades W, The Life and Typography of William Caxton, London 1801–03, 2.131 (attributes poem to L and suggests his possible authorship of Pilgrimage of the Soul).
MacCracken H N, Hoccleve and the Poems from Deguileville, The Nation 85.280 (discusses authorship of poems inserted in [139] and Pilgrimage of the Soul); MacCracken TPSL, appendix 2.xx; rptd EETSES 107.xxiii.
Deanesly M, The Lollard Bible and Other Medieval Versions, Cambridge 1920, p 153 (believes L translated Deguileville's Pèlerinage de la vie humaine but not the Pèlerinage Jhesucrist).
Brusendorff A, The Chaucer Tradition, London 1925, pp 239, 283, 468 (assigns poem to L on both internal and external evidence).
SchirmerLydgate, p 230; trans Keep, p 268.
PearsallLydgate, pp 79, 173 (suggests may have been sub-contracted out by L).
Walls K, Did Lydgate Translate the Pèlerinage de la Vie Humaine? N&Q ns 24(222).103 (argues that the attribution is simply an error by Stowe).
Sources and Literary Relations. Warton T, History of Eng Poetry, ed W C Hazlitt, London 1871, 3.67

(discusses relationship to Deguileville).
Blades, Caxton, p 262 (discusses relationship to Deguileville).
Langue J H, Zu Fragment B des ME Rosenromans, EStn 31.159 (notes influence of Romance of Rose).
Locock, EETSES 92.ix, liii (discusses relationship to Romance of Rose and to Bunyan's Pilgrim's Progress).
Wharey J B, A Study of the Sources of Bunyan's Allegories, Baltimore 1904, p 13 and passim (argues L's poem is based on recension 2 of Deguileville's text and is a source of Bunyan's Pilgrim's Progress).
Spurgeon C, Chaucer devant la critique en Angleterre et en France, Paris 1911, p 10 (notes insertion of Chaucer's ABC in L's poem); Five Hundred Years of Chaucer Criticism and Allusion, ChS 2s 48.34 (notes and prints allusions to Chaucer).
Duschl, p 9 and passim (gives sources and classification of proverbs).
MacCracken, Lydgatiana, Arch 131.40 and passim (prints 2 ABCs to Virgin which reflect influence of both Chaucer and [139]).
Knowlton E C, Nature in ME, JEGP 20.186 (argues that L's treatment of nature in [139] had little influence on later Eng literature).
Patch H R, The Goddess Fortuna in Mediaeval Literature, Cambridge Mass 1927, pp 42, 52, 149 (discusses treatment of Fortune in [139] and other texts).
Sarton G, Introd to the History of Science, Baltimore 1947, 3.533 (lists sources and trans of Deguileville's Pèlerinage).
SchirmerLydgate, pp 102, 148; trans Keep, pp 123, 171 (discusses relationship to Deguileville and Romance of the Rose; notes L's additions).
Tillyard E M W, The Eng Epic and Its Background, Oxford 1954, pp 172 and passim, 283, 293 (argues influence on Spenser, Milton, and Bunyan).
Rossi, p 35.
Beck R, A Precedent for Donne's Imagery in Good Friday 1613 Riding Westward, RES ns 19.166 (does not claim as actual source, only as precedent).
Blythe J H, Images of Wrath Lydgate and Langland, DAI 32.908A.
Other Scholarly Problems. Wylie J H, The Reign of Henry 5th, Cambridge 1914–29, 1.239; 2.137 (believes poem throws light on Life of Thomas Walden and some historical events).
Bennett OHEL, pp 111, 119, 140 (believes poem representative of L's voluminousness and didactic purpose, and typical of his time's interest in pious literature).
Tillyard, The Eng Renaissance: Fact or Fiction, London 1952, p 90 (argues that L's poem is essentially mediaeval but handled in a somewhat Renaissance spirit); Eng Epic, p 172 and passim (believes poem both mediaeval and Renaissance).
Wilson R M, The Lost Literature of Medieval England, London 1952, p 165 (notes that [139] was only Eng book at Ewelme Almshouse in 1466–67).
Rickert M, Painting in Britain The Middle Ages, London 1954, p 199 (discusses miniature in MS Harley 4826, f 1, of L presenting the poem).
PearsallLydgate, p 190n (records suggestion that window in Allexton church, Leics, may incorporate a motif from [139]).
Literary Criticism. CHEL, 2.200.
Reufs F, Das Naturgefühl bei Lydgate, Arch 122.269 (concludes that monasticism ruins L's originality).
Lewis C S, The Allegory of Love, Oxford 1936, pp 234, 264 and passim (believes [139] a heavy poem unpleasant to read and far from Renaissance poetry).
Bennett H S, The Author and His Public in the 14th and 15th Cents, E&S 23.7 (considers [139] example of L's lamentable fecundity).
SchirmerLydgate, p 170; trans Keep, p 194 (believes prayer inserted in [139] typical of invocation style).
Rossi, pp 35, 131.
PearsallLydgate, p 172 (argues poem is a failure because it does not embody spiritual concepts in meaningful literary form).
Brief Reference. Schlauch M, Eng Medieval Literature and Its Social Foundations, Warszawa 1956, p 291.
Bibliography. Locock, EETSES 92.lxiii (discusses MSS and edns of Deguileville's Pèlerinage).
Duff E G, 15-Cent Eng Books, Oxford 1917, no 267 (describes PRINT 5).

[140] PRAYER INSERTED IN PELERINAGE DE LA VIE HUMAINE (also PRAYER TO BLESSED VIRGIN).

MS. Stowe 952, f 299ᵃ (1450–1500).
Brown-Robbins, Robbins-Cutler, no 2395.
For edn and scholarship, see under [139] above.

[141] LIFE OF ST PETRONILLA (also LEGEND OF ST PETRONILLA).

MSS. No MS extant. PRINT: Pynson, ca 1495

(STC, no 19812; rptd H Huth, Fugitive Poetical Tracts, 1s, 1875, no p numbers; rptd MacCracken EETSES 107.154).
Brown-Robbins, Robbins-Cutler, no 3446.
Edition. MacCracken EETSES 107.154.
Authorship. MacCracken, TPSL, appendix 2.xxiii; rptd EETSES 107.xxvi.
Gerould S Leg, p 266 (questions L's authorship).
SchirmerLydgate, p 230; trans Keep, p 268.
Sources and Literary Relations. Huth, Fugitive Tracts, p ix (compares poem with material in Legenda aurea).
SchirmerLydgate, pp 136 and passim, 148; trans Keep, pp 157 and passim, 170 (shows source to be Legenda aurea).
Other Scholarly Problem. Mullet C F, John Lydgate: a Mirror of Medieval Medicine, Bull of the Hist of Medicine 22.403 (considers [141] representative of contemporary preoccupation with pestilence).
General Reference. PearsallLydgate, p 277 (assumes poem was written for the lepers' hospital of St Petronilla at Bury; very simple style).
Bibliography. Dibdin T F, Typographical Antiquities, London 1812, 2.538 (discusses PRINT).
Ringler BEV, p 153.

[142] PRAISE OF PEACE.

MSS. 1, Jesus Camb 56, ff 37^b–41^a (15 cent); 2, Trinity Camb 601, ff 290^a–293^a (1461–83); 3, Harley 2255, ff 21^a–24^b (1 leaf has been skipped in numbering so that f 24 is really f 25; 1448?–49?).
Brown-Robbins, no 2156.
Editions. Wright PPS, 2.209 (MS 3).
MacCracken EETS 192.785 (MS 3; collations from MS 1).
Date. Wright PPS, 2.209 (1443).
SchirmerLydgate, p 75; trans Keep, p 88 (1422).
Scattergood V J, Politics and Poetry in the 15th Cent, London 1971, p 102 (after death of Henry 5 and perhaps much later).
Versification. Reger, pp 56, 78 (finds certain epic caesurae in 17.7 percent lines).
Authorship. MacCracken TPSL, appendix 2.xx; rptd EETSES 107.xxiii.
SchirmerLydgate, p 229; trans Keep, p 266.
Other Scholarly Problems. Koeppel E, Lydgates Vowes of Pecok, Arch 108.29 (notes that expression Vowis of Pecok refers to traditional knightly oath in 14th and 15th cent).
SchirmerLydgate, p 75; trans Keep, p 88 (discusses political background).
General References. PearsallLydgate, p 163 (continues peace themes of [169] and [189] below).
Scattergood, Politics and Poetry, p 102 (considers poem elaborate and learned).

[143] PRAYER TO ST ANNE (also INVOCATION TO ST ANNE).

MSS. 1, Bodl 6943 (Ashmole 59), ff 44^b–45^b (1447–56); 2, BM Addit 16165, f 247^{a-b} (1425–75).
Brown-Robbins, no 3671.
Hammond E P, The Departing of Chaucer, MP 1.331 (describes MS 2); Omissions from the Edns of Chaucer, MLN 19.35 (describes MS 2).
Edition. MacCracken EETSES 107.130 (MS 2; collations from MS 1).
Language. Mendenhall J C, Aureate Terms, Lancaster Pa 1919, p 67 (notes aureate diction).
Authorship. MacCracken TPSL, appendix 2.xxii; rptd EETSES 107.xxv.
SchirmerLydgate, p 232; trans Keep, p 271.
Other Scholarly Problem. SchirmerLydgate, p 166; trans Keep, p 190 (notes that poem was composed at request of Countess of Stafford).
Literary Criticism. Woolf R, The Eng Religious Lyric in the Middle Ages, Oxford 1968, p 295 (shows that the Invocation is a skillful blending of different traditions).

[144] PRAYER TO BLESSED VIRGIN (also ORISON TO THE BLESSED VIRGIN and PRAYER TO MARY IN WHOM IS AFFIAUNCE).

MS. Bodl 11914 (Rawl C.48), f 134^a (15 cent).
Brown-Robbins, no 2565.
Edition. MacCracken EETSES 107.296.
Authorship. MacCracken TPSL, appendix 2.xxi; rptd EETSES 107.xxiv.
Brown-Robbins, no 2565 (does not attribute poem to L).
SchirmerLydgate, p 233; trans Keep, p 271.
Other Scholarly Problems. SchirmerLydgate, p 155; trans Keep, p 178 (believes composition prompted by outbreak of plague).
Literary Criticism. SchirmerLydgate, p 169; trans Keep, p 193 (discusses literary style).

[145] PRAYER TO BRITISH SAINTS, ESPECIALLY ST URSULA (also ST URSULA AND THE ELEVEN THOUSAND VIRGINS).

MSS. 1, Jesus Camb 56, f 76^{a-b} (15 cent); 2, Sidney Sussex Camb 37, f 144^a (other num-

bering, f 7ª; 1440–50); 3, Trinity Camb 601, f 169ª⁻ᵇ (1461–83); 4, Harley 2255, f 116ª (1448?–49?).
Brown-Robbins, no 4243.
Editions. Halliwell PPS 2.178 (MS 4).
MacCracken EETSES 107.144 (MS 4; collations from all MSS).
Versification. Reger, pp 41, 78 (finds certain epic caesurae in 20.83 percent lines).
Date. SchirmerLydgate, p 164; trans Keep, p 188 (believes St Ursula an early poem).
Authorship. MacCracken TPSL, appendix 2.xxiv; rptd EETSES 107.xxvii.
SchirmerLydgate, p 232; trans Keep, p 270.
Sources and Literary Relations. Gattinger, pp 31 and passim, 39 (notes influence of Legenda aurea).

[146] PRAYER TO ST DENIS (also DEVOWTE INVOCACIOUN TO ST DENIS).

MS. Bodl 6943 (Ashmole 59), ff 65ª–66ª (1447–56).
Brown-Robbins, no 2566.
Edition. MacCracken EETSES 107.127.
Language. Mendenhall J C, Aureate Terms, Lancaster Pa 1919, p 67 (notes aureate diction).
Date. SchirmerLydgate, p 165; trans Keep, p 189 (1426).
Authorship. MacCracken TPSL, appendix 2.xxii; rptd EETSES 107.xxv.
SchirmerLydgate, p 232; trans Keep, p 271.
Sources and Literary Relations. Patch H R, The Goddess Fortuna in Mediaeval Literature, Cambridge Mass 1927, p 60 (lists other texts representing Fortune as queen with attendants).
Other Scholarly Problems. Wylie J H, The Reign of Henry 5th, Cambridge 1914–29, 2.433 (offers poem as evidence of common knowledge of St Denis' relation to France).
SchirmerLydgate, pp 108, 165; trans Keep, pp 126, 189 (notes that poem was written for Charles 7).
Literary Criticism. SchirmerLydgate, p 165; trans Keep, p 189 (suggests that L's consummate craftsmanship goes back to Parisian period).

[147] PRAYER TO ST EDMUND.

MSS. 1, Bodl 798 (Laud Misc 683), ff 19ª–21ª (15 cent); 2, Camb Univ Kk.1.6, ff 202ª–203ᵇ (15 cent); 3, Harley 2255, ff 152ª–153ª (lacks stanzas 1–3; 1448?–49?).
Brown-Robbins, no 915.
Edition. MacCracken EETSES 107.124 (MS 1; collations from all MSS).
Date. SchirmerLydgate, p 165; trans Keep, p 189 (believes [147] perhaps composed on return from Paris).
Authorship. MacCracken TPSL, appendix 2.xxiii; rptd EETSES 107.xxv.
SchirmerLydgate, p 232; trans Keep, p 271.
Literary Criticism. SchirmerLydgate, p 164 and passim; trans Keep, p 188 and passim (notes majestic style).

[148] PRAYER TO GABRIEL.

MS. Bodl 798 (Laud Misc 683), f 24ª (15 cent).
Brown-Robbins, no 531.
Edition. MacCracken EETSES 107.133.
Authorship. MacCracken TPSL, appendix 2.xxiii; rptd EETSES 107.xxvi.
Brown-Robbins, no 531 (questions authorship).
SchirmerLydgate, p 232; trans Keep, p 270.
General Reference. SchirmerLydgate, p 164; trans Keep, p 188.

[149] PRAYER TO ST LEONARD.

MSS. 1, Bodl 798 (Laud Misc 683), ff 21ª–22ª (15 cent); 2, Jesus Camb 56, ff 75ᵇ–76ᵇ (15 cent); 3, Sidney Sussex Camb 37, f 142ᵇ (other numbering has f 6ª; 1440–50); 4, Harley 2255, f 114ª⁻ᵇ (1448?–49?); 5, Longleat 256, art 17? (15 cent).
Brown-Robbins, no 2812.
Editions. Halliwell PPS 2.205 (MS 4).
MacCracken EETSES 107.135 (MS 1; collations from all MSS except MS 5).
Versification. Reger, pp 42, 78 (finds certain epic caesurae in 21.74 percent lines).
Date. SchirmerLydgate, p 164; trans Keep, p 188 (1422).
Authorship. MacCracken TPSL, appendix 2.xxiii; rptd EETSES 107.xxvi.
SchirmerLydgate, p 232; trans Keep, p 270.
Sources and Literary Relations. SchirmerLydgate, p 164; trans Keep, p 188 (notes style is reminiscent of that of later [155]).
General References. Gattinger, p 31 and passim. PearsallLydgate, p 265.

[150] PRAYER TO ST MICHAELL.

MS. Bodl 798 (Laud Misc 683), f 24ª (15 cent).
Brown-Robbins, no 2513.
Edition. MacCracken EETSES 107.133.
Authorship. MacCracken TPSL, appendix 2.xxiii; rptd EETSES 107.xxvi.

Brown-Robbins, no 2513 (questions authorship).
SchirmerLydgate, p 232; trans Keep, p 270.
General Reference. SchirmerLydgate, p 164; trans Keep, p 188.

[151] PRAYER TO ST OSITHA.

MSS. 1, Jesus Camb 56? (recorded in Brown-Robbins, no 1050, but not in Jesus Camb catalogue; 15 cent); 2, Sidney Sussex Camb 37, f 145a (other numbering has f 5a; 1440–50); 3, Harley 2255, f 116b (1448?–49?).
Brown-Robbins, no 1050.
Edition. MacCracken EETSES 107.137 (MS 3; collations from MS 2).
Authorship. MacCracken TPSL, appendix 2.xxiii; rptd EETSES 107.xxvi.
Brown-Robbins, no 1050 (questions authorship).
SchirmerLydgate, p 232; trans Keep, p 271.
Sources and Literary Relations. SchirmerLydgate, p 164 and passim; trans Keep, p 188 and passim (notes same refrain as in [147] and [154]).
Other Scholarly Problem. PearsallLydgate, p 265 (raises question of whether poem is to St Ositha or St Sitha of Lucca).
Literary Criticism. SchirmerLydgate, p 164 and passim; trans Keep, p 188 and passim (considers poem standard example of L's litany style).

[152] PRAYER TO ST ROBERT OF BURY.

MS. Bodl 798 (Laud Misc 683), ff 22b–23b (15 cent).
Brown-Robbins, no 2399.
Edition. MacCracken EETSES 107.138.
Authorship. MacCracken TPSL, appendix 2.xiv; rptd EETSES 107.xxvii.
SchirmerLydgate, p 232; trans Keep, p 270.
General References. SchirmerLydgate, p 163; trans Keep, p 187.
PearsallLydgate, p 265.

[153] PRAYER TO ST THOMAS.

MS. Bodl 798 (Laud Misc 683), f 23b (15 cent).
Brown-Robbins, no 538.
Edition. MacCracken EETSES 107.139.
Authorship. MacCracken TPSL, appendix 2.xiv; rptd EETSES 107.xxvii.
Brown-Robbins, no 538 (questions authorship).
SchirmerLydgate, p 232; trans Keep, p 270.
General Reference. SchirmerLydgate, p 164; trans Keep, p 188.

[154] PRAYER TO ST THOMAS OF CANTERBURY.

MSS. 1, Bodl 9936 (Tanner 110), ff 242a–243b (lacks lines 1–24), 245a–b (lines 1–80); 2, Wolfenbüttel, Herzoglichen Bibliothek 2819, ff 149b–150b (15 cent).
Brown-Robbins, Robbins-Cutler, no 3115.
Edition. MacCracken EETSES 107.140 (MS 1).
Authorship. MacCracken TPSL, appendix 2.xiv; rptd EETSES 107.xxvii.
Brown-Robbins, no 3115 (questions authorship).
SchirmerLydgate, p 232; trans Keep, p 270.
Sources and Literary Relations. MacCracken EETSES 107.xxvii (notes use of material in other poems of L).
SchirmerLydgate, pp 164, 166; trans Keep, pp 188, 190 (notes use of litany refrain from [147] and [151] above).
Other Scholarly Problems. Wylie J H, The Reign of Henry 5th, Cambridge 1914–29, 1.460 (mentions poem as throwing light on classification of men-at-arms).
PearsallLydgate, p 264 (assumes poem was to be hung before the saint's shrine).
General Reference. PearsallLydgate, p 265 (poem demonstrates L's techniques of amplification through allusion).

[155] PRAYER TO TEN SAINTS.

MSS. 1, Bodl 798 (Laud Misc 683), ff 24a–27b (15 cent); 2, Jesus Camb 56, ff 73b–75a (15 cent); 3, Sidney Sussex Camb 37, ff 139a–142a? (other numbering has ff 7–10; 1440–50); 4, Harley 2255, ff 70a–72b (1448?–49?).
Brown-Robbins, no 529.
Edition. MacCracken EETSES 107.120 (MS 1; collations from all other MSS).
Date. SchirmerLydgate, p 108; trans Keep, p 126 (believes poem composed during Parisian period).
Authorship. MacCracken TPSL, appendix 2.xxvi; rptd EETSES 107.xxix.
SchirmerLydgate, p 232; trans Keep, p 270.
Sources and Literary Relations. Patch H R, The Goddess Fortuna in Mediaeval Literature, Cambridge Mass 1927, p 175 (lists other texts that emphasize importance of Fortune's wheel).
Literary Criticism. SchirmerLydgate, p 163 and passim; trans Keep, p 187 and passim (argues heroic element differentiates poem from other litany poetry).

[156] PRAYER IN OLD AGE.

MSS. 1, Bodl 4119 (Hatton 73), f 116^{a–b} (1425–75); 2, Lambeth 344, f 10^{a–b} (15 cent).
Brown-Robbins, no 222.
Edition. MacCracken EETSES 107.20 (MS 1; collations from MS 2).
Authorship. MacCracken TPSL, appendix 2.xxi; rptd EETSES 107.xxiv.
SchirmerLydgate, p 232; trans Keep, p 270.
Sources and Literary Relations. Brown-Robbins, no 222 (notes that first stanza is also last stanza of [14–15] above).
SchirmerLydgate, p 163; trans Keep, p 187 (notes that stanza 1 is decasyllabic version of last stanza of [14–15] above and compares the two poems).
General Reference. PearsallLydgate, p 255 (poem is an exemplary prayer, not a real one).

[157] PROCESSION OF CORPUS CHRISTI.

MSS. 1, Trinity Camb 600, pp 348–356 (1456?); 2, Harley 2251, ff 224^b–227^b (1464–83); 3, BM Addit 29729, ff 166^a–168^a (John Stowe, 1558).
Brown-Robbins, no 3606.
Hammond E P, Lydgate's Mumming at Hertford, Angl 22.364 (describes MS 1); Two British Museum MSS, Angl 28.1 (detailed study of MS 2).
Brusendorff A, The Chaucer Tradition, London 1925, pp 208, 466 and passim (discusses Shirley's marginalia in MS 1).
Manly & Rickert, 1.241 (describes MS 2).
Editions. Halliwell PPS 2.95 (MS 2).
MacCracken EETSES 107.35 (MS 1; collations from all MSS).
Textual Matters. Gattinger, p 83 (suggests textual emendations).
Versification. Reger, pp 41, 77 (finds certain epic caesurae in 10.31 percent lines).
Authorship. MacCracken TPSL, appendix 2.xxi; rptd EETSES 107.xxiv.
SchirmerLydgate, p 231; trans Keep, p 269.
Sources and Literary Relations. Gattinger, pp 32, 39, 49 (discusses influence of Legenda aurea and Church Fathers).
Nelson A H, The Medieval Eng Stage, Chicago and London 1974, p 4 (unlike any other surviving Corpus Christi play).
Other Scholarly Problems. Chambers, 2.161 (believes that poem suggests possibility of early dramatic performance and may reflect mediaeval misconceptions about classical stage).
Wylie J H, The Reign of Henry 5th, Cambridge 1914–29, 1.298 (notes representation of Gregory the Great as one of the Four Doctors).
Gerould S Leg, pp 265, 266 (believes poem intended to usher in some dramatic spectacle).
SchirmerLydgate, p 152; trans Keep, p 175 (discusses probable physical set-up of procession).
Literary Criticism. Collier J P, The History of Eng Dramatic Poetry, London 1879, 1.21; 2.69 (denies dramatic shape of poem).
Gattinger, p 72 (discusses style).
General References. PearsallLydgate, p 188 (notes use of Biblical figures).
Nelson, Medieval Eng Stage, p 173.

[158] PROVERBS (also SEE MYCHE, SAY LYTELL AND LERNE TO SOFFAR IN TYME).

MSS. 1, Corp Christi Oxf 203, pp 23–24 (3 stanzas; 1450–1500); 2, Royal 2.D.xxxvii, f 153^a (5 stanzas; 15 cent); 3, BM Addit 29729, f 130^{a–b} (John Stowe, 1558); 4, Advocates 19.3.1, f 61^b (1 stanza; 15 cent); 5, Victoria and Albert Mus Dyce 34 (Dyce's transcript of de Worde print).
Brown-Robbins, Robbins-Cutler, no 3083.
Editions. MacCracken EETS 192.800 (MS 3; collations from MSS 1, 2).
Brown RLxvC, p 279 (MS 2).
Authorship. MacCracken TPSL, appendix 2.xxiv (attributes poem to L on basis of Stowe's list and of style, although MS 1 entitles it Proverbium R Stokys); rptd EETSES 107.xxvii.
Brown-Robbins, no 3083 (mentions possible authorship of both L and Stokys).
Brown C, See Myche Say Lytell and Lerne to Suffer in Tyme, MLN 54.131 (by Stokys, not L).
SchirmerLydgate, p 233; trans Keep, p 272.
PearsallLydgate, p 210 (rejects L's authorship).
Sources and Literary Relations. Rigg A G, A Glastonbury Miscellany of the 15th Cent, Oxford 1968, p 56 (notes other similar ME poems).
General References. SchirmerLydgate, p 174; trans Keep, p 199.
PearsallLydgate, p 210.
Bibliography. Lowndes W T, Bibliographer's Manual, ed H G Bohn, London 1864, 3.1419.

[159] PSALM 102 (also BENEDIC ANIMA MEA DOMINO).

MSS. 1, Trinity Camb 600, pp 19–25, 165–170 (1456?); 2, Harley 2251, ff 236a–238b (1464–83); 3, BM Addit 34360, ff 53b–55a (1461–83).
Brown-Robbins, no 2572.
Hammond E P, Lydgate's Mumming at Hertford, Angl 22.364 (describes MS 1); Two British Museum MSS, Angl 28.1 (detailed study of MSS 2, 3).
Brusendorff A, The Chaucer Tradition, London 1925, pp 208, 466 and passim (discusses Shirley's marginalia in MS 1).
Manly & Rickert, 1.241 (describes MS 2).
Editions. Mahir O, Einige religiöse Gedichte John Lydgates, München 1910, 1.20 (MS 3).
MacCracken EETSES 107.1 (MS 1; collations from all MSS).
Authorship. MacCracken TPSL, appendix 2.x; rptd EETSES 107.xii.
SchirmerLydgate, p 231; trans Keep, p 269.
Other Scholarly Problems. Deanesly M, The Lollard Bible and Other Medieval Biblical Versions, Cambridge 1920, pp 320, 336 (believes that L was not aware of rule against unlicensed use of Biblical translations, and notes that Henry 5 used L's Psalms in his private prayers).
Literary Criticism. SchirmerLydgate, p 115; trans Keep, p 134 (notes use of rhetorical ornamentation).
General References. Gattinger, p 31.
Vickers K H, Humphrey of Gloucester, London 1907, p 343.
PearsallLydgate, p 259.

[160] RAMMESHORNE.

MSS. 1, Bodl 2527 (Bodley 686), ff 190b–191b (1430–40); 2, Bodl 6922* (Ashmole 61), ff 5b–6b (14 cent); 3, Pepys 2553, p 187 (1560–85; Rigg, p 57, claims this MS is a mistaken entry in Brown Reg); 4, Trinity Camb 1450, f 27a–b (1425–75); 5, Harley 172, ff 71b–72b (15 cent); 6, Harley 2251, f 20a (last 3 stanzas; 1464–83); 7, Harley 4011, f 1a (incomplete; 1450–1500); 8, Lansdowne 409, f 265b (8 stanzas; 15 cent); 9, BM Addit 12195, f 121b (stanza 6 only; time of Edward 4?); 10, BM Addit 29729, f 10a–b (John Stowe, 1558); 11, Nat Libr Scot 1.1.6 (Advocates), ff 79b–80a (6 stanzas; 1568); 12, Huntington Libr EL 26.A.13 (formerly Ellesmere), f 18a–b (15 cent).
Brown-Robbins, Robbins-Cutler, no 199.
Hammond E P, Two British Museum MSS, Angl 28.1 (detailed study of MS 6).
Manly & Rickert, 1.64, 241 (describes MSS 1, 6).
Rigg A G, A Glastonbury Miscellany of the 15th Cent, Oxford 1968, p 57 (lists all MSS and discusses their relationships).
Hargreaves H, Lydgate's A Ram's Horn, Chaucer Rev 10.255 (argues MS 2 is not Scottish).
Editions. [Lord Hailes,] Ancient Scottish Poems, 1770, p 207 (MS 11).
Sibbald J, Chronicle of Scottish Poetry, Edinburgh and London 1803, 3.221 (MS 11).
Halliwell PPS 2.171 (MS 5).
Murdoch J B, The Bannatyne MS, Hunterian Club 32.219 (MS 11).
Ritchie W T, The Bannatyne MS, PSTS ns 22.201 (MS 11).
MacCracken EETS 192.461 (MS 12; collations from all MSS except MSS 2, 3).
Modernization. Fitzgibbon H M, Early Eng and Scottish Poetry, London ca 1888, p 78 (lines 1–32, 41–56).
Versification. Reger, pp 41, 77 (finds certain epic caesurae in 3.57 percent lines).
Young G, An Eng Prosody on Inductive Lines, Cambridge 1928, p 142 (discusses use of cinquepace and 4-stress lines).
Rigg, Glastonbury Misc, p 60.
Authorship. MacCracken EETSES 107.xxv.
SchirmerLydgate, p 229; trans Keep, p 266.
Rigg, Glastonbury Misc, p 58.
Sources and Literary Relations. Rigg, Glastonbury Misc, p 58 (notes French origins of this kind of satire and other ME examples).
Hargreaves, Chaucer Rev 10.256 (prints variants in MSS 2, 9 showing later adaptation by others for a popular audience).
General References. Gattinger, p 10.
SchirmerLydgate, p 80; trans Keep, p 95.
PearsallLydgate, p 216.
Scattergood V J, Politics and Poetry in the 15th Cent, London 1971, p 304.

[161] RESON AND SENSUALLYTE.

MSS. 1, Bodl 3896 (Fairfax 16), ff 202a–300a (1400–50); 2, BM Addit 29729, ff 184a–286b (John Stowe, 1558).
Brown-Robbins, Robbins-Cutler, no 3746.
Edition. Sieper E, Reson and Sensuallyte, EETSES 84, 89, 92 (MS 1).
Language. Schick J, Lydgate's Temple of Glas, EETSES 60.1v.
Hingst R, Die Sprache John Lydgates aus seinen Reimen, Greiswald 1908.
Courmont A, Studies in Lydgate's Syntax in the

Temple of Glas, Paris 1912, p 16 and passim (argues syntax already affected by transition that led from ME to Modern Eng).
Babcock C F, A Study of the Metrical Use of the Inflectional e in ME with Particular Reference to Chaucer and Lydgate, PMLA 29.59 (argues L's language bridges gap between Middle Ages and modern period).
Royster J F, The Do Auxiliary 1400 to 1450, MP 12.449 (counts 30 instances of do auxiliary in lines 1–4,100).
Onion C T, No Fage, TLS Feb 11 1926, p 99 (discusses expressions no fage and without fage).
Versification. Schick, EETSES 60.1v.
Licklider A H, Chapters on the Metric of the Chaucerian Tradition, Baltimore 1910, p 200 (discusses arsis-thesis variations).
SchirmerLydgate, p 61; trans Keep, p 71.
Date. Schick, EETSES 60.cxii (1406–08?).
SchirmerLydgate, p 33; trans Keep, p 39 (1408).
Seaton, p 261 (1438–50).
PearsallLydgate, p 120 (just before [189]).
Authorship. MacCracken TPSL, appendix 2.xxi; rptd EETSES 107.xxiv.
Brusendorff A, The Chaucer Tradition, London 1925, pp 185, 388 (rejects L's authorship).
SchirmerLydgate, p 229; trans Keep, p 265.
Seaton, p 261 (argues for Richard Roos).
Sources and Literary Relations. Schick, EETSES 60.cxvii (notes influence of Romance of the Rose and Alanus ab Insulis De Planctu naturae); Kleine Lydgate Studien: Reason and Sensuality, AnglB 8.134 (discusses relationship to immediate source: Les Échecs amoureux).
Sieper E, Les Échecs amoureux, Litterarhistorische Forschungen 9.213 and passim (discusses sources of French poem, L's use of his original, and influence of the Romance of the Rose).
Lange J H, Zu Fragment B des ME Rosenromans, EStn 31.159 (discusses influence of the Romance of the Rose).
Duschl, p 9 and passim (gives sources and classification of proverbs).
Smart W K, Some Eng and Latin Sources and Parallels for the Morality of Wisdom, Chicago 1912, p 41 (believes that concept of reason and sensuality comes from St Augustine).
Mackenzie W R, A Source for Medwall's Nature, PMLA 22.189 (argues [161] important source of Medwall's Nature).
Knowlton E C, Nature in ME, JEGP 20.186 (discusses relationship of [161] to Alanus de Insulis and to later Eng literature).
Patch H R, The Goddess Fortuna in Mediaeval Literature, Cambridge Mass 1927, p 82 (traces Fortune's game of shuttlecock to Romance of the Rose, Machaut, and other sources).
SchirmerLydgate, p 43; trans Keep, p 50 (notes L's use of mythology).
Seaton, pp 256, 268 (discusses poem's relationship to and use of Échecs amoureux and Romance of the Rose).
Pearsall D A, ed, The Floure and the Leafe, London and Edinburgh 1962, p 42 (notes parallels in theme and imagery).
Jack R D S, Dunbar and Lydgate, SSL 8.216, 222 (discusses influence on Dunbar, especially on his Golden Targe).
Means M, The Consolatio Genre in Medieval Eng Literature, Univ of Florida Humanities Monograph no 36, p 95 (briefly relates poem to Roman de la Rose and Langland).
Other Scholarly Problems. Knowlton, JEGP 20.186 (believes that lesson in poem accounts for its success with its own age).
Patch, Fortuna, p 32 (argues handling of Fortune typical of L).
Bennett OHEL, pp 120, 141 (believes poem suggestive of importance of courtly poetry in 15 cent and typical of L's didactic purpose).
SchirmerLydgate, pp 33 and passim, 43; trans Keep, pp 39 and passim, 50 (notes that poem is both moral allegory and poem of courtly love).
Seaton, pp 260 (poet not author of sidenotes in MS 1), 261, 383 (argues that poem contains name anagrams).
Literary Criticism. CHEL, 2.202.
Reufs F, Das Naturgefühl bei Lydgate, Arch 122.269 and passim (believes monasticism ruins L's originality).
Cazamian L, The Development of Eng Humor, N Y 1930, 1.143 (discusses elements of spontaneous fancy in poem).
Lewis C S, The Allegory of Love, Oxford 1936, pp 264, 271 and passim (considers poem one of the most beautiful and important pieces between Chaucer and Spenser).
Bennett OHEL, p 148 (considers poem one of L's more readable works).
Rossi, p 133.
PearsallLydgate, p 115 (discusses all aspects of the poem).
Means, Consolatio Genre, p 91.
General References. SchirmerLydgate, pp 66, 89; trans Keep, pp 76, 105.
Pearsall D, The Eng Chaucerians, in Chaucer

and Chaucerians, ed D S Brewer, Univ Alabama 1966, p 211.
Norton-Smith J, Geoffrey Chaucer, London and Boston 1974, p 57.

[162] REGINA CELI LETARE.

MSS. 1, Trinity Camb 601, ff 162b–163a, 233b–234a (1461–83); 2, Harley 2251, ff 35b–36a (1464–83).
Brown-Robbins, no 2570.
Hammond E P, Two British Museum MSS, Angl 28.1 (detailed study of MS 2).
Manly & Rickert, 1.241 (describes MS 2).
Edition. MacCracken EETSES 107.293 (MS 1, ff 162b–163a; collations from MS 2).
Authorship. MacCracken TPSL, appendix 2.xxi; rptd EETSES 107.xxiv.
SchirmerLydgate, p 233; trans Keep, p 271.
Sources and Literary Relations. MacCracken H N, Lydgatiana, Arch 131.40 (discusses and prints a Regina celi letare in imitation of [162]).
SchirmerLydgate, p 168; trans Keep, p 192 (discusses relationship to Latin Easter hymn).
PearsallLydgate, p 273 (briefly notes the poem's freedom and skill and compares it with other ME versions).
Literary Criticism. Wehrle W O, The Macaronic Hymn Tradition in Medieval Eng Literature, Washington 1933, p 132 and passim (notes conscious use of Latin words as cauda).
Bibliography. SchirmerLydgate, p 242; trans Keep, p 285 (notes edns of related works).

[163] RIGHT AS THE CRABBE GOTH FORWARD (also SATYRICAL BALLAD ON THE TIMES).

MSS. 1, Bodl 2527 (Bodley 686), f 189a–b (1430–40); 2, Trinity Camb 600, pp 50–52 (preceded by OF text, pp 49–50; 1430–40); 3, Harley 2251, f 39a–b (1464–83); 4, Harley 4011, f 1a (lines 30–40; 1450–1500); 5. BM Addit 29729, ff 154a–155a (John Stowe, 1558); 6, Huntington EL 26.A.13 (formerly Ellesmere), f 19a–b (15 cent).
Brown-Robbins, Robbins-Cutler, no 3655.
Hammond E P, Lydgate's Mumming at Hertford, Angl 22.265 (describes MS 2); Two British Museum MSS, Angl 28.1 (detailed study of MS 3).
Brusendorff A, The Chaucer Tradition, London 1925, pp 208, 466 and passim (discusses Shirley's marginalia in MS 2).
Manly & Rickert, 1.241 (describes MS 3).

Editions. Halliwell PPS 2.58 (MS 3).
MacCracken EETS 192.465 (MS 2; collations from all MSS; prints OF original on p 464).
Textual Matters. Gattinger, p 83 (suggests textual emendations).
Authorship. MacCracken TPSL, appendix 2.xxv; rptd EETSES 107.xxviii.
SchirmerLydgate, p 229; trans Keep, p 266.
Sources and Literary Relations. Nichols P H, William Dunbar as a Scottish Lydgatian, PMLA 46.214 (argues influence of poem on Dunbar).
Moore A K, The Secular Love Lyric in ME, Lexington 1951, p 119 (argues handling of OF original illustrates L's reluctance to follow fixed form).
Other Scholarly Problem. Duschl, p 53 (classifies proverb).
Literary Criticism. Gattinger, p 10 (considers poem typical of L's satire).
General References. SchirmerLydgate, p 80; trans Keep, p 95.
PearsallLydgate, p 216.
Scattergood V J, Politics and Poetry in the 15th Cent, London 1971, p 303 (notes L liked this kind of poem but he has to explain the joke).

[164] RIME WITHOUT ACCORD (also ON THE INCONSISTENCY OF MEN'S ACTIONS).

MSS. 1, Pepys 2553, p 171 (8 stanzas; 1560–85); 2, Harley 2251, ff 26a–27a (1464–83); 3, Nat Libr Scot 1.1.6 (Advocates), f 79a–b (stanzas 1–5, 8 in disarranged order, and 2 more stanzas; 1568). PRINT: 4, Chepman and Myllar, 1508 (STC, no 11984; 8 stanzas; rptd J Pinkerton, Ancient Scottish Poems, London 1786; rptd G Stevenson, Pieces from the Makculloch and Gray MSS Together with the Chepman and Myllar Prints, PSTS 65.111).
Brown-Robbins, Robbins-Cutler, no 223.
Hammond E P, Two British Museum MSS, Angl 28.1 (detailed description of MS 2).
Manly & Rickert, 1.241 (describes MS 2).
Editions. Halliwell PPS 2.55 (MS 2).
Murdoch J B, The Bannatyne MS, Hunterian Club 32.217 (MS 3).
Craigie W A, The Maitland Folio, PSTS ns 7.195 (MS 1).
Ritchie W T, The Bannatyne MS, PSTS ns 22.199 (MS 3).
MacCracken EETS 192.792 (MS 2).
Textual Matters. Gattinger, p 83 (suggests textual emendations).
Language. Dibelius W, John Capgrave u die engl

Schriftsprache, Angl 23.153, 323.
Versification. Reger, pp 41, 78 (finds certain epic caesurae in 15.9 percent lines).
Authorship. MacCracken TPSL, appendix 2.xxii; rptd EETSES 107.xxiv.
SchirmerLydgate, p 233; trans Keep, p 272.
Sources and Literary Relations. Duschl, pp 47, 52 (classifies proverbs and notes influence of Gospels and Book of Kings).
Other Scholarly Problem. Gattinger, p 15 (notes use of proverbial utterances).
Literary Criticism. PearsallLydgate, p 214 (L seems unaware of the irony within the poem's paradoxes).
General Reference. SchirmerLydgate, p 173; trans Keep, p 198.

[165] SALUTACIO ANGELICA (also AVE MARIA).

MSS. 1, Trinity Camb 601, ff 274ª–275ª (1461–83); 2, Longleat 30, ff 25ª–? (15 cent); 3, Huntington Libr HM.142 (formerly Bement), ff 21ª–22ᵇ (1467).
Brown-Robbins, Robbins-Cutler, no 1045.
Edition. MacCracken EETSES 107.280 (MS 1).
Versification. PearsallLydgate, p 62 (appears to be free 4-stress 8-line stanza in imitation of accentual Latin).
Authorship. MacCracken TPSL, appendix 2.ix; rptd EETSES 107.xii.
SchirmerLydgate, p 232; trans Keep, p 271.
Other Scholarly Problem. Wehrle W O, The Macaronic Hymn Tradition in Medieval Eng Literature, Washington 1933, p 139 (believes poem suggests notion of immaculate conception already common in L's time).
Literary Criticism. SchirmerLydgate, p 167; trans Keep, p 192 (notes Latinate style and elements of Gaudia-tradition).
PearsallLydgate, p 274 (notes post-verbal sophistication of verse).

[166] SECREES OF OLD PHILISOFFRES (also THE GOVERNAUNCE OF KINGS AND PRINCES and SECRETA SECRETORUM).

MSS. 1, Bodl 505 (Laud Misc 673), ff 1ª–73ᵇ (15 cent); 2, Bodl 1479 (Laud Misc 416), ff 255ª–287ᵇ (1459); 3, Bodl 6930 (Ashmole 46), ff 97ª–160ᵇ (15 cent); 4, Balliol 329, ff 80ª–126ᵇ (15 cent); 5, Caius Camb 336, ff 104ª–124ª (fragment containing stanzas 328–31, 353–90, 170–91, 193–94, 195–213, 234–37, 228–33, 238–71, 273–89, 64, 43, 65, 68; 15 cent); 6, Trinity Camb 599, ff 49ª–59ᵇ (stanzas 186–212 only; 1475?–1525?); 7, Trinity Camb 1212, ff 1ª–44ᵇ (lacks stanzas 1–30, ends imperfectly; 15 cent); 8, Fitzwilliam McClean 182, ff 12ª–49ª (lacks lines 1–64; 15 cent); 9, Fitzwilliam McClean 183, ff 1ª–47ᵇ (also numbered 1ª–23ª; lacks lines 1–82 and leaves in middle and at end; 15 cent); 10, Arundel 59, ff 90ª–130ᵇ (also recorded as ff 1ª–130ᵇ; ends at stanza 352; 1450–1500); 11, Harley 2251, ff 188ᵇ–224ᵃ (ends at stanza 352; 1464–83); 12 Harley 4826, ff 52ª–81ª (15 cent); 13, Lansdowne 285, ff 152ª–196ᵇ (1450–75); 14, Sloane 2027, ff 53ª–92ᵇ (1430–40); 15, Sloane 2464, ff 1ª–65ᵇ (1444?–75); 16, BM Addit 14408, ff 1ª–48ᵇ (lacks lines 1–3; 1473); 17, BM Addit 34360, ff 78ª–116ª (1461–83); 18, BM Addit 39922, f 16ª (lines 1268–1309 only; 15 cent); 19, Morgan Libr 775, ff 139ª–195ª (imperfect; ca 1486); 20, Phila Free Libr Lewis 304 (1 single leaf beginning at line 1476). PRINT: 21, Pynson 1511 (STC, nos 12140, 17017; with significant textual variations; rptd DeW T Starnes, The Gouernaunce of Kynges and Prynces, Gainesville 1957); 22, Pynson 1527.
Brown-Robbins, Robbins-Cutler, no 935 (Robbins-Cutler notes MSS of other prose versions).
Steele R, A Stowe MS of Lydgate, Acad (London) 45.395 (discusses MS 17 and compares to other MSS); edn, EETSES 66.xiii (discusses several MSS); An Unknown Lydgate Edn, TLS Feb 16 1922, p 109 (discusses PRINT 21).
Prosiegel T, Die Handschriften zu Lydgates Book of the Governaunce of Kynges and Prynces, München 1903 (discusses MSS 1–3, 10–17, a Douce fragment?, and PRINT 21; crit O Glöde, LfGRP 30.103).
Förster M, Zu Lydgates Secreta Secretorum, Arch 115.169 (notes reclassification of MSS Ashburnham 132 and 134 as MSS Fitzwilliam McClean 180 and 181, i.e., 182 and 183).
Hammond E P, Two British Museum MSS, Angl 28.1 (detailed study of MSS 11, 17); Ashmole 59 and Other Shirley MSS, Angl 30.320 (discusses MS 10 and compares to MS 11); The Nine-Syllabled Pentameter Line in Some Post-Chaucerian MSS, MP 23.129 (believes one MS of [166] possibly transcribed by scribe of excerpts of Fall of Princes, part of one Canterbury Tales MS, and part of another).
Singer D W, Catalogue of Latin and Vernacular Alchemical MSS, Brussels 1928, 1.31 (lists 11 MSS and PRINT 21, and prints opening and

closing lines of various sections).
Manly & Rickert, 1.241, 623 (describes MSS 4, 11 and identifies owners of MS 11).
Starnes, Gouernaunce, p xi (discusses PRINT 21, including woodcuts).
Edition. Steele R, Lydgate and Burgh's Secrees of Old Philisoffres, EETSES 66 (MS 15).
Selection. Kaiser R, Medieval Eng, 3rd edn, Berlin 1958, p 508 (lines 1296–1302, 1366–79, 1394–1400, 1443–9, 1485–91; MS 15).
Textual Matters. Prosiegel, Handschriften (collates the MSS discussed in the study).
Steele, An Unknown Lydgate Edn, TLS March 2 1922, p 141 (notes omissions and misplaced passages in PRINT 21).
Starnes, Gouernaunce, p xiii (notes variants in PRINT 21).
Language. Schick J, Lydgate's Temple of Glas, EETSES 60.lv.
Dibelius W, John Capgrave u die engl Schriftsprache, Angl 23.153, 323.
Hingst R, Die Sprache John Lydgates aus seinen Reimen, Greiswald 1908.
Babcock C F, A Study of the Metrical Use of the Inflectional e in ME with Particular Reference to Chaucer and Lydgate, PMLA 29.59 (argues L's language bridges gap between Middle Ages and modern period).
Royster J F, The Do Auxiliary 1400 to 1450, MP 12.449 (finds 17 instances of do auxiliary in lines 1–1491).
Versification. Schick, EETSES 60.lv.
Steel, edn, EETSES 60.xix.
Reger, pp 64, 78 (finds certain epic caesurae in 14.69 percent lines).
Saintsbury G, A History of Eng Prosody, London 1923, 1.229 (discusses briefly metrical schemes).
Pyle F, The Pedigree of Lydgate's Heroic Line, Hermathena 50.26 (shows that characteristics of line go back at least to Poema Morale; discusses L's use of the line).
Date. Schick, EETSES 60.cxii (1446?).
PearsallLydgate, p 296 (L's last poem).
Authorship. Blades W, The Life and Typography of William Caxton, London 1861–63, 2.54 (attributes 1st half of poem to L on basis of MS 11).
Förster, Ueber Benedict Burghs Leben und Werken, Arch 101.29 (accepts L's authorship of stanzas 1–145, but questions Burgh's authorship of the remainder).
MacCracken TPSL, appendix 2.xxiv (attributes 1st part of poem to L); rptd EETSES 107.xxvii.
Bühler C, Lydgate's Rules of Health in MS Lansdowne 699, MÆ 3.51 (argues that rime

and meter show [166] and [34] to be by one author).
SchirmerLydgate, p 230; trans Keep, p 267.
Starnes, Gouernaunce, p v.
Sources and Literary Relations. Steele, edn, EETSES 66.vii (discusses relation of [166] to original Secreta Secretorum and related texts).
Duschl, p 9 and passim (gives sources and classification of proverbs; notes material from Ecclesiastes).
Förster, Kleinere ME Texte: John Lydgates Gesundheitregeln, Angl 42.145 and passim (notes that [166] borrows several stanzas from [34]).
Patch H R, The Goddess Fortuna in Mediaeval Literature, Cambridge Mass 1927, p 51 (lists other texts that show Fortune under everchanging aspect).
Mullet C F, John Lydgate: a Mirror of Medieval Medicine, Bull of the Hist of Medicine 22.403 (discusses Syriac and later sources).
SchirmerLydgate, pp 96, 216 and passim; trans Keep, pp 112, 248 and passim (gives account of poem and lists related texts, including Secreta Secretorum).
Starnes, Gouernaunce, pp ix, xv.
Manzalaoui M A, The Secreta Secretorum The Mediaeval European Version of Kitāb Sirr-ul-Asrār, Bull of the Faculty of Arts Alexandria Univ 15.96 (relates [166] to the tradition).
PearsallLydgate, p 296 (brief discussion of the tradition).
Other Scholarly Problems. Moore S, The Death of Lydgate, The Nation (N Y) 94.260 (believes testimony of [166] invalidates date of L's death as suggested by Metham's Amoryus and Cleopes, and suggests time between Michaelmas 1449 and Sept 1450).
Wylie J H, The Reign of Henry 5th, Cambridge 1914–29, 1.326 and passim; 2.137 and passim (believes poem throws light on falconry equipment and treatment of lepers).
Kleineke W, Engl Fürstenspiegel vom Policraticus Johanns von Salisbury bis zum Basilikon Doron König Jakobs I, SEP 40.106 (discusses poem's place in literature of regiment of princes, and mentions Scottish version).
Mullet, Bull Hist Med 22.406 (believes poem reflects burden of pestilence).
SchirmerLydgate, p 216 and passim; trans Keep, p 248 and passim.
Scattergood V J, Politics and Poetry in the 15th Cent, London 1971, p 279 (discussion of advice to Henry 6 in [166]).
Uhlig C, Hofkritik im England des Mittelalters u

der Renaissance, Berlin and N Y 1973, p 75 (advice still relevant in L's time).
Literary Criticism. Reufs F, Das Naturgefühl bei Lydgate, Arch 122.269 (concludes that monasticism ruins L's originality).
Knowlton E C, Nature in ME, JEGP 20.186 (finds handling of nature typical of L).
Manzalaoui, Bull Faculty Arts Alexandria Univ 15.96 (description of seasons one of L's finest passages).
PearsallLydgate, p 296 (as worthless as anything of L's).
General References. Talbot C H, Medicine in Medieval England, London 1967, p 189.
PearsallLydgate, pp 101, 146.
Bibliography. Starnes, Gouernaunce, p xix.

[167] SERPENT OF DIVISION.

MSS. 1, Pepys 2006, pp 191–209 (1425–75); 2, Fitzwilliam McClean 182 (formerly Ashburnham App.134), f 9^b (4 stanzas; 15 cent); 3, BM Addit 38179 (formerly Ashburnham), ff 51^b–60^b (18-cent transcript by Ainsworth); 4, Calthorpe Yelverton 35, ff 146^b–156^b (1460?; Robbins-Cutler says to delete, but used in MacCracken edn); 5, Harvard Univ Eng 530, ff 49^a–57^a (1425–59; Robbins-Cutler says to delete, but used in MacCracken edn). PRINT: 6, Treverys Fragment, 1520? (rptd J Haslewood, Brydges' Censura Literaria, London 1809, 9.369); 7, Rogers O, 1559 (from Treverys); 8, Allde E, 1590 (from Rogers' text?, probable basis of Ainsworth's copy).
Brown-Robbins, Robbins-Cutler, no 3625.
Commission on Historical MSS, 2nd Report, London 1871, 2.42 (mentions one MS).
MacCracken, edn, p 45 (brief account of MSS and PRINTS).
Ringler W, Lydgate's Serpent of Division 1559, Edited by John Stowe, Stud in Bibl 14.201 (discusses PRINT 7; argues it is based on PRINT 6 but not on other MSS as claimed by MacCracken; all changes are printer's errors; claims PRINT 8 not from PRINT 7 but from PRINT 6).
Edition. MacCracken H N, The Serpent of Division, London Oxford and New Haven 1911 (composite text from MSS 2, 4; collations from other MSS and PRINT 6; crit J W H Atkins, MLR 7.253).
Selection. Cohen H L, The Ballade, N Y 1915, p 256 (from MacCracken edn).
Modernization and Abstract. SchirmerLydgate, p 71; trans Keep, p 84 (abstract).
Language. Royster J F, The Do Auxiliary 1400 to 1450, MP 12.449 (considers [167] only well-authenticated work of L where do auxiliary is not used).
Date. Smith T L, Gorboduc, Heilbronn 1883, p xxi (argues for 1400 on basis of MSS).
Schick J, Lydgate's Temple of Glas, EETSES 60.cxii (1400?).
MacCracken, edn, p 4 (1422); Lydgate's Serpent of Division, MLR 8.103 (insists on 1422 in answer to crit by Atkins, MLR 7.253).
Hammond E P, Eng Verse between Chaucer and Surrey, Durham 1927, p 177 (questions 1422).
SchirmerLydgate, p 69; trans Keep, p 82 (questions 1422).
Scattergood V J, Politics and Poetry in the 15th Cent, London 1971, p 138 (Dec 1422).
Authorship. Smith, Gorboduc, p xx (assigns [167] to L on basis of MS 4).
MacCracken TPSL, appendix 2.xxiv; rptd EETSES 107.xxvii.
SchirmerLydgate, p 231; trans Keep, p 269.
Sources and Literary Relations. MacCracken, edn, p 8 and passim (discusses OF and Latin sources).
Spurgeon C, Five Hundred Years of Chaucer Criticism and Allusion, ChS 2s 48.14 (prints allusion to Chaucer).
Brusendorff A, The Chaucer Tradition, London 1925, p 388 (discusses L's use of Chaucer in [167]; believes L quoted from memory).
Patch H R, The Goddess Fortuna in Mediaeval Literature, Cambridge Mass 1927, pp 70, 71, 108, 127 (lists similar views of Fortune's wheel from Boethius on and works in which proud men are cast down).
Orwen W R, Spenser and the Serpent of Division, SP 38.198 (compares theme of Spenser's Ruines of Time to [167]).
SchirmerLydgate, pp 70, 191; trans Keep, pp 83, 219 (believes principal sources to be an OF reworking of Lucan's Pharsalia and a few chaps of Vincent of Beauvais' Speculum Historiale).
Other Scholarly Problems. Brie F, Mittelalter u Antike bei Lydgate, EStn 64.261 (shows mixture of mediaevalism and early humanism in [167] and discusses relation of L to early Eng humanism).
Scattergood, Politics and Poetry, p 138 (discusses L's political ideas, especially how men create civil discord).
Literary Criticism. Smith C G, The Transition Period, N Y 1900, p 324 (believes [167] early good omen for Eng prose).
SchirmerLydgate, p 72; trans Keep, p 85 (defends formlessness of work).

Schlauch M, Stylistic Attributes of John Lydgate's Prose, in To Honor Roman Jakobson, The Hague 1967, 3.1757 (discusses specific usages in L's trans and larger questions of style).
General References. SchirmerLydgate, pp 27 and passim, 79; trans Keep, pp 32, 82 and passim, 93.
Bibliography. Lowndes W T, Bibliographer's Manual, ed H G Bohn, London 1864, 3.1419.

[168] SERVANT OF CUPYDE FORSAKEN (also COMPLAYNT LYDEGATE and NEW YEAR GIFT).

MS. BM Addit 16165, ff 255ª–256ª (1425–75).
Brown-Robbins, Robbins-Cutler, no 886.
Edition. MacCracken EETS 192.427.
Abstract. Utley CR, no 72.
Authorship. MacCracken TPSL, appendix 2.xxv (on basis of Shirley's marginal note in MS); rptd EETSES 107.xxviii.
SchirmerLydgate, p 229; trans Keep, p 265.
Seaton, p 410 (argues for Richard Roos).
Literary Criticism. SchirmerLydgate, pp 30, 221; trans Keep, pp 35, 253 (notes satirical tone of complaint).
General Reference. PearsallLydgate, p 103.

[169] SIEGE OF THEBES.

MSS. (All MSS are more or less imperfect except MSS 1, 10, 14.) 1, Bodl 1124 (Laud Misc 557), ff 1ª–68? (15 cent); 2, Bodl 1479 (Laud Misc 416), ff 227ª–254ª (ca 1459); 3, Bodl 1831 (Digby 230), ff 1ª–27ᵇ (begins imperfectly; 1425?–75?); 4, Bodl 2559 (Bodley 776), ff 1ª–73ᵇ (lacks lines 1–8 of Prologue; 15 cent); 5, Bodl 11914 (Rawl C.48), ff 5ª–78ᵇ (15 cent); 6, Christchurch Oxf 152, ff 291ª–350ª (1460–1500); 7, St John's Oxf 256 (described but given no number by G Bone, H C Schulz and P Simpson, below; neither mentioned nor used by Erdmann and Ekwall in EETSES edn; MS 28 in Robbins-Cutler); 8, Camb Univ Add 2707, f 1 (lines 14–16, 18–21, 54–58, 92–98, 134–40; 15 cent); 9, Camb Univ Add 3137, ff 14ª–end (many leaves lost; 1450?–1500); 10, Camb Univ Add 6864 (formerly Gurney 150; formerly Macro 102), ff 1ª–75ᵇ (15 cent); 11, Pepys 2011, ff 1ª–76ᵇ (1450?–1500?); 12, Trinity Camb 652, ff 89ª–169ᵇ (15 cent); 13, Trinity Camb 1283, ff 191ª–211ᵇ (1450?–1500?); 14, Arundel 119, ff 1ª–79ª (1425?–30?); 15, Cotton App XXVII, ff 3ª–51ᵇ (lines 1–3408; 16 cent); 16, Egerton 2864 (formerly Ingilby; formerly Campton Hall), ff 292ᵇ–341ª (1460?–80?); 17, Royal 18.D.ii, ff 147ᵇ–162ª (1460?); 18, BM Addit 5140, ff 358ª–423ᵇ (lines 1–4503; 1470?–1500?); 19, BM Addit 18632, ff 6ª–33ᵇ (1440?); 20, BM Addit 27929, ff 17ª–84ª (1558); 21, Durham Univ Cosin V.ii.14, item 1 (15 cent); 22, Coventry Corp Record Office, ff 137ª–167ᵇ (1425–75; Robbins-Cutler gives beginning f as 98ª); 23, Lambeth 742, ff 1ª–68ᵇ (1425–75); 24, Deene Park (formerly Cardigan; formerly Brudenell), ff 246ª–304ª (1425–75; Lovell, edn, suggests MS is now in Univ of Texas Libr); 25, Longleat 257, ff 1ª–48ᵇ (lacks f 28; 1450?–70?); 26, formerly Campbell (Robinson Sale Cat 74, 1944, no 268); 27, formerly Mostyn Hall 258, ff 1ª–end (sold to Abbot's, London); 28, Old Buckenham Hall, ff 6ª–end; 29, Boston Public Libr 94, ff 1ª–74ᵇ (1420–40); 30, Morgan Libr 4, ff 1ª–74ª (1425–75). PRINT: 31, de Worde, ca 1492 (STC, no 17031); 32, Stowe, Chaucer 1561 (rptd A Chalmers, Eng Poets, London 1810, 1.570).
Brown-Robbins, Robbins-Cutler, no 3928.
Royal Commission on Historical MSS, Report 3, London 1872, 3.188 (notes MS in Marquis of Bath libr); Report 4, London 1873, 4.361 (notes MS in Mostyn Hall); Report 12, London 1891, 9.164 (notes MS in libr of J H Guerney).
Wright W A, Generydes, EETS 55.v (discusses inclusion of [189], [169], and Generydes in MS 13).
Kölbing E, MS 25 der Bibliothek des Marquis of Bath, EStn 10.203 (describes MS 25 and prints opening and concluding lines of [169]).
Duff E G, 15-Cent Eng Books, Oxford 1917, no 268 (describes PRINT 31).
Bone G, Extant MSS Printed by W de Worde with Notes on the Owner Roger Thorney, Libr 4s 12.284 (describes MS 7 and compares text to PRINT 31; gives facsimile of lines 3187–3214).
Erdmann and Ekwall, edn, EETSES 125.36 (describes 21 MSS and the PRINTS; establishes genealogies).
Simpson P, Proof-reading in the 16th 17th and 18th Cents, London 1935, pp 57 and passim, 93 (demonstrates MS 7 used for editio princeps).
Bühler C F, A New Lydgate-Chaucer MS, MLN 52.1 (lists and discusses contents of MS 30).
Manly & Rickert, 1.29, 71, 85, 143, 339, 644 (describes MSS 6, 16, 18, 24, 25).
Schulz H C, MSS Printer's Copy for a Lost Early Eng Book, Libr 4s 22.138 (discusses imperfect copy of PRINT 31).
Ringler BEV, p 153.
Pearsall D, Notes on the MS of Generydes, Libr

5s 16.205 (MS 13).
Doyle A I and G B Pace, A New Chaucer MS, PMLA 83.22 (MS 22).
Edwards A S G, Lydgate's Siege of Thebes A New Fragment, NM 71.133 (MS 8).
Dunn C W and E T Byrnes, ME Literature, N Y 1973, p 27 (describes MS 17, especially miniature of pilgrims on f 148ª).
Editions. [169] is found in older edns of Chaucer down to Urry and Chalmer's Poets.
Erdmann A and E Ekwall, Lydgate's Siege of Thebes, EETSES 108, 125 (MS 14; notes assembled by Ekwall).
Lovell R E, John Lydgate's Siege of Thebes and Churl and Bird Edited from the Cardigan-Brudenell MS, DAI 30.297A (MS 24).
Selections. Skeat Spec, p 28 (MS 14; collations from MSS 12, 13).
Wülker R P, Ae Lesebuch, Halle 1879, 2.105 (PRINT 32).
Manly J M, Eng Poetry, Boston and N Y 1907, p 49.
Hammond E P, Lydgate's Prologue to the Story of Thebes, Angl 36.360, 363 (MS 14).
Spurgeon C, Five Hundred Years of Chaucer Criticism and Allusion, ChS 2s 48.26 (MS 14).
Richmond V B, Laments for the Dead in Medieval Narrative, Duquesne Stud Philological Series 8, Pittsburgh 1966, p 157 (lines 3229–59; from Erdmann edn).
Edwards A S G, Lydgate's Siege of Thebes A New Fragment, NM 71.135 (lines 14–16, 18–21, 54–58, 92–98, 134–40; MS 8).
Dunn C W and E T Byrnes, ME Literature, N Y 1973, p 511 (lines 66–193; from Erdmann edn; with glosses at the side).
Modernizations and Abstracts. Darton F J H, The Story of the Canterbury Pilgrims, N Y 1914, p 240 (much abridged prose version).
Morley, 6.115 (clear summary).
Erdmann and Ekwall, edn, EETSES 125.3 (detailed outline).
SchirmerLydgate, p 55; trans Keep, p 62 (brief outline).
PearsallLydgate, p 151 (brief outline).
Language. Schick J, Lydgate's Temple of Glas, EETSES 60.lv and passim.
Skeat B M, The Lamentatyon of Mary Magdaleyne, Cambridge 1897, p 9 (notes that use of rayle in reference to blood is typical of L).
Dibelius W, John Capgrave u die engl Schriftsprache, Angl 23.153, 323.
Hingst R, Die Sprache John Lydgates aus seinen Reimen, Greiswald 1908.
Onions C T, Sir Gawain and the Green Knight,
TLS Aug 16 1923, p 545 (shows expression no tage, line 2051, means certainly and survives as verb in some dialects).
Erdmann and Ekwall, edn, EETSES 125.22.
Marcus H, Orientalisches Wortgut im Engl, Arch 191.161 (damask is only oriental term in [169]).
Versification. Schipper, 1.492 (discusses L's use of heroic verse).
Schick, EETSES 60.lv and passim.
Reger, pp 53, 77 (finds certain epic caesurae in 2.5 percent lines).
Saintsbury G, Historical Manual of Eng Prosody, London 1910, p 52 (discusses Lydgatian line); A History of Eng Prosody, London 1923, 1.226 (discusses discordant elements in L's versification).
Spindler R, Engl Metrik, München 1927, p 60 (believes L freer than Chaucer with metrical thesis).
Young G, An Eng Prosody on Inductive Lines, Cambridge 1928, p 127 (argues L astray in regard to regular incidence of stress).
Erdmann and Ekwall, edn, EETSES 125.32.
Pyle F, The Pedigree of Lydgate's Heroic Line, Hermathena 50.26 (shows L's line to go back at least to Poema morale, and discusses use of line).
Date. Schick, EETSES 60.cxii (1420?–22?).
Wülker, Lesebuch, 2.105 (1430).
Atkins J W H, rev of edn of [167], MLR 7.253 (insists [169] necessarily completed before 1425).
Erdmann and Ekwall, edn. EETSES 125.8 (1420–22).
Parr J, Astronomical Dating for Some of Lydgate's Poems, PMLA 67.251 (argues poem probably written in 1421).
SchirmerLydgate, p 55; trans Keep, p 62 (1420–22).
Authorship. MacCracken TPSL, appendix 2.xxv; rptd EETSES 107.xxviii.
Bonner F W, The Genesis of the Chaucer Apocrypha, SP 48.461 (notes [169] was once ascribed to Chaucer).
SchirmerLydgate, p 229; trans Keep, p 266.
Sources and Literary Relations. Furnivall F J, Temporary Preface, ChS 2s 3.31 (discusses palace of [169] in relation to Chaucer's Manciple's Tale).
Warton T, History of Eng Poetry, ed W C Hazlitt, London 1871, 3.74 and passim (discusses relationship to Boccaccio and Marcianus de Capella).
Constans L, La Légende d'Oedipe, Paris 1881, p 366, (traces development of Theban legend from remotest antiquity); Le Roman de Thèbes,

Paris 1890, 2.clx (suggests that source of [169] is early prose redaction of Roman de Thèbes on basis of character names).

Koeppel E, Lydgate's Story of Thebes, München 1884 (demonstrates [169] based on prose redaction of Roman de Thèbes); Laurents de Premierfait u John Lydgates Bearbeitungen von Boccaccios De casibus virorum illustrium, München 1885.

Ten Brink, 2^1.225 (discusses relation to Boccaccio's Genealogica Deorum and General Prologue of Chaucer's Canterbury Tales).

Hammond, p 317 (argues [169] reflects L's misreading of Canterbury Tales); Lydgate's Prologue to the Story of Thebes, Angl 36.360 (discusses relation to General Prologue of Canterbury Tales).

Duschl, p 9 and passim (gives sources and classification of proverbs).

Brie F, Zwei ME Prosaromane: The Sege of Thebes u The Sege of Troy, Arch 130.40 (discusses relationship between [169], prose reworking, pseudo Orosius, OF prose Thèbes, and Chaucer; prints prose reworking).

Spurgeon, ChS 2s 48.26.

Patch H R, The Goddess Fortuna in Mediaeval Literature, Cambridge Mass 1927, pp 48 and passim, 156, 163 (lists works with similar treatments of Fortune, including Chaucer's Troilus).

Erdmann and Ekwall, edn, EETSES 125.6, 10 (discusses relationship to Roman de Thèbes, Hystoire de Thèbes, Roman de Edipus, Chaucer, Boccaccio, Martianus de Capella, Bible, and Seneca).

Lewis C S, The Allegory of Love, Oxford 1936, p 162 and passim (discusses relationship to General Prologue of Canterbury Tales).

Long R A, John Heywood Chaucer and Lydgate, MLN 64.55 (notes that as in Heywood's Mery Play Betwene the Pardoner and the Frere, L's Pardoner tells tale to irritate Friar instead of Summoner as in Chaucer).

SchirmerLydgate, p 31; trans Keep, p 36.

Renoir A, Chaucerian Character Names in Lydgate's Siege of Thebes, MLN 71.249 (L uses Chaucerian forms or ones closer to Roman de Edipus than to Ystoire de Thèbes); The Immediate Source of Lydgate's Siege of Thebes, SN 33.86 (argues L's source is a complete text of the Roman de Edipus); The Poetry of John Lydgate, Cambridge Mass 1967, pp 113 (discusses the poem as a continuation of Chaucer's C T), 117 and notes (discusses L's changes from his French source).

Rossi, p 122 (discusses relations to Chaucer's Knight's Tale and the Roman de Thèbes).

Blake N F, Caxton and Chaucer, Leeds SE ns 1.32 (Caxton's praise of Chaucer has echoes of L's praise in [169]).

Cutts J P, Lear's Learned Theban, Shakespeare Quart 14.477 (cites L's description of Oedipus to argue reference in Lear is to him, but does not claim L as a direct source).

PearsallLydgate, pp 2, 55, 59, 64 (notes poem's influence and discusses relationship to Chaucer), 153 (notes use of Boccaccio; disagrees with Renoir's account above of L's improvements to the French source), 154 (compares [169] with [189]).

Schlauch M, Polynices and Gunnlaug Serpent-Tongue A Parallel, Essays and Stud 1972 in Honour of Beatrice White, Eng Assoc, London 1972, p 15.

Other Scholarly Problems. Joly A, Benoît de Sainte-More et le Roman de Troie, Paris 1871, 2.493 (argues great popularity of subject matter).

Moore S, Patrons of Letters in Norfolk and Suffolk c 1450, PMLA 27.188 (argues patronage of de la Pole and William Curteys).

Brusendorff A, The Chaucer Tradition, London 1925, p 29 (believes compliments to Chaucer mere formalities).

Brie, Mittelalter u Antike bei Lydgate, EStn 64.261 (argues mixture and split between humanism and mediaevalism, and shows importance of L to early humanism).

Frampton M G, The Date of the Wakefield Master, PMLA 50.631 (argues Tydeus' dress suggests that gypoun was not armorial garment).

Bennett H S, The Author and His Public in the 14th and 15th Cents, E&S 23.7 (copy in Anne Paston's possession suggests 15-cent demand for historical material).

Schirmer W F, Das Ende des Mittelalters in England, Kleine Schriften, Tübingen 1950, p 30 (argues presence of [169] in Paston libr suggests that middle class was new public of 15 cent); SchirmerLydgate, pp 111, 204; trans Keep, pp 129, 234 (discusses circumstances of composition).

Parr, The Horoscope of Edippus in Lydgate's Siege of Thebes, Essays in Honor of Walter Clyde Curry, Vanderbilt Stud in the Humanities 2.117 (argues horoscope of Oedipus not really professional).

Wilson R M, The Lost Literature of Mediaeval England, London 1952, p 153 (believes [169] to be work mentioned in will of John Baret of Bury).

Ayers R W, Medieval History Moral Purpose and

the Structure of Lydgate's Siege of Thebes, PMLA 73.468 (poem reflects the English political situation).
Renoir, John Lydgate Poet of the Transition, Eng Miscellany 11.15 ([169] shows respect and admiration for pagans and their gods); Renoir-Lydgate, pp 104, 126 (didactic and political lessons in [169]), 121 (attitude to classical antiquity), 134 (nationalism).
Richmond, Laments for Dead, Duquesne Stud Philological Series 8, Pittsburgh 1966, p 76 (use of laments; brief).
Scattergood V J, Politics and Poetry in the 15th Cent, London 1971, pp 100, 288 (discusses advice for rulers in [169], especially views on peace and war).
Literary Criticism. Warton T, Observations on the Faerie Queene of Spenser, London 1784, p 229 (considers marriage of Oedipus worthy of Chaucer).
Courthope, 1.325 (argues [169] illustrates L's poetic deficiencies).
Jusserand J J, Histoire litteraire du peuple anglais, Paris 1896, 1.517 (insists on mediaeval presentation of classical material).
Collins J C, Ephemera Critica, Westminster 1901, p 199 (defends L's handling of prologue).
CHEL, 1.229.
Reufs F, Das Naturgefühl bei Lydgate, Arch 122.269 (believes monasticism ruins L's originality).
Ayers, PMLA 73.463.
Rossi, p 112.
RenoirLydgate, p 110 (discusses poem and its achievement at length).
PearsallLydgate, p 151.
Marotta J G, John Lydgate and the Tradition of Medieval Rhetoric, DAI 33.729A.
Miskimin A S, The Renaissance Chaucer, New Haven and London 1975, pp 122, 234 (discusses use of modesty topos and compares with Chaucer).
General References. Pearsall, The English Chaucerians, in Chaucer and Chauceriens, ed D S Brewer, Univ Alabama 1966, p 218; Pearsall-Lydgate, pp 22, 62.
Robbins R H, The Eng Fabliau before and after Chaucer, Moderna Språk 64.232.
Bibliography. SchirmerLydgate, p 227; trans Keep, p 262.
Edwards, A Lydgate Biblio 1928–68, BB 27.98.

[170] SODEIN FAL OF PRINCES (also FALLS OF SEVEN PRINCES).

MSS. 1, Trinity Camb 600, ff 359^a–361^a (1456?); 2, Harley 2251, f 228^{a-b} (1464–84); 3, BM Addit 29729, ff 169^b–170^a (Stowe MS, 1558).
Brown-Robbins, Robbins-Cutler, no 500.
Hammond E P, Lydgate's Mumming at Hertford, Angl 22.364 (describes MS 1); Two British Museum MSS, Angl 28.1 (detailed study of MS 2).
Brusendorff A, Chaucer Tradition, London 1925, pp 208, 466 and passim (discusses Shirley's marginalia in MS 1).
Editions. Hammond E P, Two Tapestry Poems by Lydgate: the Life of St George and the Falls of Seven Princes, EStn 43.10 (MS 1).
MacCracken EETS 192.660 (MS 1; collations from other MSS).
Robbins-HP, pp 174, 342 (MS 1; collations from other MSS).
Authorship. MacCracken TPSL, appendix 2.xiv; rptd EETSES 107.xvi.
SchirmerLydgate, p 231; trans Keep, p 268.
Other Scholarly Problems. Gerould J H, Legends of St Wulfhad and St Ruffin at Stone Priory, PMLA 32.323 (discusses mural display).
Robbins-HP, p 342 (identifies poem as a mumming).
PearsallLydgate, p 180 (not a mumming as Robbins-HP says but more like a processional).
General References. SchirmerLydgate, p 197; trans Keep, p 226.
PearsallLydgate, p 251.

[171] STANS PUER AD MENSAM (normal version).

MSS. 1, Bodl 798 (Laud Misc 683), ff 62^b–65^a (15 cent); 2, Bodl 1885, ff 331^a–332^b (1450–1500 but rest of MS earlier); 3, Bodl 2527 (Bodl 686), ff 186^a–187^b (1430–40); 4, Bodl 6943 (Ashmole 59), ff 98^a–99^b (1447–56); 5, Bodl 11914 (Rawl C.48), ff 130^a–132^a (15 cent); 6, Bodl 11951 (Rawl C.86), ff 86^b–88^a (1475?–1500); 7, Bodl 14526 (Rawl poet F.32), ff 30^a–31^a (1450–1500); 8, Bodl 15444 (Rawl D.328), ff 159^a–167^a (15 cent); 9, Bodl Deposit Astor A.2, ff 192^a–193^b (1450–1500); 10, Balliol 354, ff 158^b–159^b (1518–36; from PRINT 25); 11, Camb Univ Ff.4.9, ff 86^a–87^b (15 cent); 12, Camb Univ Hh.4.12, ff 31^b–33^b (1450–1500); 13, Jesus Camb 56, ff 77^a–78^b (15 cent); 14, Pembroke Camb 120, a flyleaf (lines 1–18; 15 cent); 15, Cotton Calig A.ii, ff 14^a–20^b? (other numbering 12^a–13^b; 1400–1450); 16, Harley 2251, f 148^{a-b} (1464–83); 17, Harley 4011, f 1^{a-b} (lines 1–53; 1450–1500); 18, Lansdowne 699, ff 83^b–85^a (1450–1500); 19, Royal 5.A.v, f 134^a (4 lines; 16-cent hand in

15-cent MS); 20, Stowe 982, ff 10ᵃ–11ᵃ (stanza 1 in prose; 1475–1500); 21, BM Addit 5467, ff 67ᵃ–68ᵇ (1450–75); 22, Lambeth 853, pp 150–155 (1430?); 23, Leyden Univ Vossius 9, ff 96ᵇ–98ᵇ (15 cent); 24, Nat Libr of Medicine 4, ff 65ᵃ–66ᵇ (1400–1450). PRINTS: 25, Caxton ca 1477 (STC, no 17030; rptd T F Dibdin, Typographical Antiquities, London 1810–12, 2.222); 26, de Worde 1518.

Brown-Robbins, Robbins-Cutler, no 2233.

Lewis J, The Life of Mayster Wyllyam Caxton, London 1737, p 104.

Dibdin T F, Typographical Antiquities, London 1810–12, 1.306; 2.290 (discusses PRINTS 25, 26).

Blades W, The Biography and Typography of William Caxton, N Y 1882, p 199 (discusses PRINT 25).

Robinson F N, On Two MSS of Lydgate's Guy of Warwick, HSNPL 5.178 (describes MS 23).

Hammond E P, Two British Museum MSS, Angl 28.1 (detailed study of MS 16).

Duff E G, 15-Cent Eng Books, Oxford 1917, no 269 (describes PRINT 25).

Aurner N S, Caxton Mirrour of 15-Cent Letters, London and Boston 1926, p 93 (dates PRINT 25 before 1479).

Mayer C F, A Medieval Eng Leechbook and Its 14-Cent Poem on Bloodletting, Bull of the Hist of Medicine 7.381 (describes MS 24).

Manly & Rickert, 1.64, 241 (describes MSS 3, 16).

Ringler BEV, p 153.

van Dorsten J A, The Leyden Lydgate MS, Scriptorium 14.315 (MS 23).

Bühler C, The 15-Cent Book, Phila 1960, p 133 (describes PRINT 25 and its relationship to MSS 5, 10).

Davis N, crit of Robbins-Cutler, RES ns 18.445 (MS 9).

Editions. Rel Ant, 1.156 (MS 13).

Hazlitt Rem, 3.24 (MS 13; collations from MSS 17, 18, 21).

Furnivall F J, The Babees Book, EETS 32(1867), vol 1, p 26 (prints both MSS 16 and 22 with collations from MS 13); rptd EETS 32(1904). 275.

MacCracken EETS 192.739 (MS 1; collations from all MSS and PRINTS except MSS 8, 11, 14, 19).

Selection. Cook A S, A Literary ME Reader, Boston 1915, p 377 (lines 15–42, 57–70; MS 16; collations from MS 22).

Modernizations. Rickert E, The Babee's Book, N Y 1908; rptd 1928, p 26.

Coulton G G, Social Life in Britain, Cambridge 1918, p 90 (from Rickert).

Wells H W, The Boy at the Table, SR 48.217.

Language. Mendenhall J C, Aureate Terms, Lancaster Pa 1919, p 63.

Versification. Reger, pp 68, 77 (finds certain epic caesurae in 9.1 percent lines).

Authorship. Robinson, HSNPL 5.178 (assigns poem to L on basis of MS 23).

MacCracken TPSL, appendix 2.xxv; rptd EETSES 107.xxviii (attributes poem to L on basis of final line).

Brentano M T, Relationship of the Latin Facetus Literature to the Medieval Eng Courtesy Poems, Lawrence Ka 1935, p 49 (rejects L's authorship).

SchirmerLydgate, p 230; trans Keep, p 267.

van Dorsten, Scriptorium 14.319 (L's name appears in connection with [171] in MS 22).

Sources and Literary Relations. Dibdin, Typ Ant, 2.303 (argues L's original is Carmen juvenile de moribus puerorum of Sulpitius).

Blades, The Life and Typography of William Caxton, London 1861–63, 2.51 (argues immediate source is Carmen juvenile de moribus puerorum); Biography and Typography of Caxton, p 199 (considers Carmen juvenile de moribus puerorum L's original).

Furnivall, edn, EETS 32, vol 2, p 32 (prints Latin Stans puer as probable source of L's poem).

Burhenne F, Das ME Gedicht Stans puer ad mensam u sein Verhältnis zu ähnlichen Erzeugnissen des 15 Jhrh, Hersfeld 1889 (compares poem to Latin and OF texts with notes on language).

Hauffen A, Caspar Scheidt: Studien zur Geschichte der grobianischen Litteratur in Deutschland, QF 66.14 (discusses French, Eng, and Latin works on same topic).

Duschl, pp 9, 21 (traces only proverb to inscription at Delphi).

Aurner, Caxton Mirrour, pp 82, 93 (argues [171] based on Carmen juvenile de moribus puerorum and influenced Boke of Curtesye).

Brentano, Relationship, p 46 (argues Carmen juvenile not source of [171]).

Brown-Robbins, no 2233 (notes other ME version).

SchirmerLydgate, p 94; trans Keep, p 110 (suggests poem perhaps based on OF poem, itself based on Latin poem).

Other Scholarly Problem. SchirmerLydgate, p 93; trans Keep, p 109 (points out great popularity of the genre in L's time).

General References. Rossi, p 171.

PearsallLydgate, p 219.

[172] STANS PUER AD MENSAM (expanded version with 6-stanza prologue).

MS. Bodl 6922* (Ashmole 61), ff 17b–18b (1500?).
Brown-Robbins, no 1694.
Edition. Furnivall F J, Queen Elizabethes Achademy, EETSES 8.56.
For scholarship, see under normal version, [171] above.

[173] STELLA CELI EXTIRPAVIT, VERSION 1.

MSS. 1, Jesus Camb 56, f 73a–b (15 cent); 2, Trinity Camb 601, ff 168b–169a (1461–83); 3, Harley 2251, ff 9b–10a (1464–83); 4, Harley 2255, f 103a–b (1448?–49?); 5, BM Addit 34360, f 68b (also recorded as ff 132b–133a; 1461–83); 6, Chetham Libr 6709, ff 284b–285b (7 stanzas; 1480–85).
Brown-Robbins, Robbins-Cutler, no 3673.
Hammond E P, Two British Museum MSS, Angl 28.1 (detailed study of MSS 3, 5).
Manly & Rickert, 1.241 (describes MS 3).
Editions. MacCracken EETSES 107.294 (MS 4; collations from all MSS except MS 6).
Brown RLxvC, p 208 (MS 6).
Authorship. MacCracken TPSL, appendix 2.xxv; rptd EETSES 107.xxviii.
SchirmerLydgate, p 231; trans Keep, p 269.
Other Scholarly Problems. Mullet C F, John Lydgate: a Mirror of Medieval Medicine, Bull of the Hist of Medicine 22.403 (considers poem typical of the contemporary preoccupation with pestilence).
SchirmerLydgate, pp 154, 169n; trans Keep, pp 178, 193n (believes poem perhaps prompted by outbreak of plague).
Woolf R, The Eng Religious Lyric in the Middle Ages, Oxford 1968, p 282 (says cult of Virgin as protection against plague was rare in England).
General References. Gattinger, p 31.
Woolf, Eng Religious Lyric, p 282 (notes elegant conceit).

[174] STELLA CELI EXTIRPAVIT, VERSION 2.

MS. Bodl 11914 (Rawl C.48), ff 133b–134a (15 cent).
Brown-Robbins, no 2398.
Hammond E P, Two British Museum MSS, Angl 28.1.
Edition. MacCracken EETSES 107.295.

Other Scholarly Problems. See under [173] above.

[175] SUPPLICATIO AMANTIS (also THE COMPLEYNT).

MSS. 1, Camb Univ Gg.4.27, Ia, ff 509b–516b (Schick gives ff 476b–482b; 1420–30; lines 1–254, 331–562); 2, Sloane 1212, f 4a–b (lines 439–505 only; 15 cent); 3, BM Addit 16165, ff 231a–241b (Shirley MS, 1450?; lacks lines 157–76).
Brown-Robbins, Robbins-Cutler, no 147.
Edition. Schick J, Lydgate's Temple of Glas, EETSES 60.59 (composite text from MSS 1, 3).
Date. Schick, edn, EETSES 60.clvii (1420–30).
Authorship. Schick, edn, EETSES 60.clvii (rejects L's authorship).

[176] TEMPLE OF GLAS.

MSS. 1, Bodl 2078 (Bodley 638), ff 16b–38a (1470?–80); 2, Bodl 3896 (Fairfax 16), ff 63a–82b (1440–50, dated 1450 on f 1a in Stowe's hand); 3, Bodl 10173 (Tanner 346), ff 76a–97a (1400–20); 4, Camb Univ Gg.4.27, Ia, ff 491a–516b (1420–30); 5, Pepys 2006, pp 17–52 (1470–1500); 6, Sloane 1212, ff 1a (lines 736–54), 2a (lines 98–162) (15 cent); 7, BM Addit 16165, ff 206b–241b (Shirley MS, 1450?); 8, BM Addit 38179, ff 2a–19b (18 cent; Ainsworth's transcript from MS 5); 9, Longleat 258, ff 1a–32a (1460?–70). PRINTS: 10, Caxton ca 1478 (STC, no 17032; rptd Jenkinson, Cambridge 1905); 11, de Worde ca 1498 (STC, no 17032a); 12, de Worde ca 1500 (STC, no 17033); 13, Pynson ca 1505 (STC, no 12954); 14, Berthelet n d (STC, no 12955); 15, Berthelet ca 1530 (Selden D.45; STC, no 17034).
Brown-Robbins, Robbins-Cutler, no 851.
Lewis J, The Life of Mayster Wyllyam Caxton, London 1737.
Dibdin T F, Typographical Antiquities, London 1810, 1.307; 2.303 (discusses earlier scholarship and PRINTS 10–12).
Watt R, Bibliotheca Britannica, London 1824, 1.207c and 475e (mentions PRINTS 10–12).
Blades W, The Life and Typography of William Caxton, London 1861–63, 2.59 (notes rarity of poem in collections of L's poems); The Biography and Typography of William Caxton, N Y 1882, p 208 (describes PRINT 10).
Furnivall F J, Odd Texts of Chaucer's Minor Poems, London 1868–80, p 251 (prints table

of contents from last leaf of MS 9); Trial-Forewards, London 1871, p 34 (argues MS 1 copied from MS 2; MS 3 probably copied from MS 2).
Gairdner J, ed, The Paston Letters, London 1875, 3.37 (letter 690 mentions now lost MS).
Thynne F, Animadversions 1598, ed F J Furnival, London 1876, p 30 (mentions confusion of titles Temple of Glas and Chaucer's Dream in MS 9).
Schick, edn, EETSES 60.xvii (describes MSS and PRINTS and gives genealogy).
Hammond E P, The Departing of Chaucer, MP 1.33 (discusses MS 7); Omissions from the Edns of Chaucer, MLN 19.35 (describes MS 7 and Shirley as editor of Chaucer and L).
Hoops J, no title, EStn 36.265 (compares typography in PRINT 10 and Chaucer's Anelida).
MacCracken H N, Additional Light on the Temple of Glas, PMLA 23.128 (partial description of MS 6).
Duff E G, 15-Cent Eng Books, Oxford 1917, nos 270–72, p 76 (describes PRINTS 10–12).
Manly & Rickert, 1.170, 406 (describes MSS 4, 5).
Ringler BEV, p 153.
Norton-Smith J, Lydgate's Changes in the Temple of Glas, MÆ 27.166 (discusses MS relations); edn, p 176.
Seaton, p 376 (discusses MS relations).
Editions. Schick J, Lydgate's Temple of Glas, EETSES 60 (MS 3; collations from all MSS except 6, 8 and from PRINTS 10–13).
Norton-Smith J, John Lydgate Poems, Oxford 1966, pp 67 (MS 3), 176 (brief commentary, notes, and glossary; some variants in notes).
Selections. Fehr B, Weitere Beiträge zur engl Lyrik des 15 u 16 Jahrhundert, Arch 107.48 (prints on p 50 two very altered fragments of lover's complaint to Venus in [176] without identifying them; see MacCracken, PMLA 23.128 for identification; from MS 6).
Bruner K and R Hittmair, ME Lesebuch, Heidelberg 1929, p 76 (from Schick).
Neilson W A and K G T Webster, Chief British Poets of the 14 and 15 Cents, Boston 1916, p 213 (from Schick).
Abstracts. Warton T, Hist of Eng Poetry, ed W C Hazlitt, London 1871, 3.61.
Schick, Prolegomena zu Lydgate's Temple of Glas, Berlin 1889.
Courthope, 1.356.
Aurner N S, Caxton Mirrour of 15-Cent Letters, London and Boston 1926, p 170.
PearsallLydgate, p 104.

Textual Matters. Schick, edn, EETSES 60.xlix.
Norton-Smith, MÆ 27.166 (argues that 3 drafts of [176] can be seen in the MSS); edn, p 176.
Seaton, p 375 (argues for 3 versions of poem; different from Norton-Smith's interpretation above).
Language. Schick, edn, EETSES 60.lxii.
Dibelius W, John Capgrave u die engl Schriftsprache, Angl 23.153, 323.
Hingst R, Die Sprache John Lydgates aus seinen Reimen, Greiswald 1908, passim.
Courmont A, Studies on Lydgate's Syntax in the Temple of Glas, Paris 1912 (argues L's syntax already affected by transition that led from ME to Modern Eng).
Babcock C F, A Study of the Metrical Use of the Inflectional e in ME with Particular Reference to Chaucer and Lydgate, PMLA 29.59 (argues L's language bridges gap between Middle Ages and modern period).
Hüttmann E, Das Partizipium Präsentis bei Lydgate im Vergleich mit Chaucers Gebrauch, Kiel 1914, passim.
Royster J F, The Do Auxiliary 1400 to 1450, MP 12.449 (finds 21 instances in poem); A Note on Lydgate's Use of the Do Auxiliary, SP 13.69 (notes L's use of do auxiliary in rimes).
Hittmair R, Das Zeitwort Do in Chaucers Prosa, WBEP 51.95 (studies L's use of do in various positions).
Miles J, Eras in Eng Poetry, PMLA 70.853 (shows proportion of adjectives-nouns-verbs to be 6–16–9 in 10 lines, computed with [47]).
Versification. Schick, edn, EETSES 60.lv.
Licklider A H, Chapters on the Metrics of the Chaucerian Tradition, Baltimore 1910, pp 45, 49, 200 (considers especially resolved stress and arsis-thesis variation).
Reger, pp 59, 77 (finds certain epic caesurae in 6.6 percent lines).
Saintsbury G, Historical Manual of Eng Prosody, London 1910, p 52 (discusses Lydgatian line); A History of Eng Prosody, London 1923, 1.227 (discusses shapelessness of L's verses).
Pyle F, The Pedigree of Lydgate's Heroic Line, Hermathena 50.26 (shows that characteristics of L's line go back at least to Poema Morale; discusses L's line).
Date. Schick, Prolegomena (1400–02); edn, EETSES 60.cxii (1403?).
MacCracken, PMLA 23.128 (believes poem composed in 1420 for marriage of William Paston to Agnes Berry).
Parr J, Astronomical Dating for Some of Lydgate's Poems, PMLA 67.251 (shows L's own astro-

nomical dating to be careless).
Bennett OHEL, p 120 (1410).
SchirmerLydgate, p 32; trans Keep, p 37 (1400–03; perhaps 1402).
Seaton, p 375 (1438–50).
Authorship. Dibdin, Typ Ant, 1.307; 2.303 (ascribes poem to L on basis of Hawes' Pastime of Pleasure).
Collier J P, A Bibliographical and Critical Account of the Rare Books in the Eng Language, N Y 1866, 2.126 (ascribes poem to L on basis of Hawes' Pastime and refutes John Bale's ascription to Hawes).
Schick, Prolegomena (ascribes poem to L on basis of MSS 2, 7); edn, EETSES 60.lxxv (discusses early attributions to Hawes and attributes poem to L on the basis of the MSS and internal evidence).
MacCracken TPSL, appendix 2.xxvi; rptd EETSES 107.xxix.
SchirmerLydgate, p 229; trans Keep, p 265.
Seaton, p 375 (argues that poem is by Richard Roos).
Sources and Literary Relations (to Chaucer). Warton, History, 3.63 (discusses relationship to House of Fame).
Courthope, 1.328 (believes poem illustrates L's inability to follow Chaucer).
Smith C G, The Transition Period, N Y 1900, p 9 (discusses influence of Romance of the Rose).
Lange J H, Lydgate u Fragment B des Romaunt of the Rose, EStn 29.397 (poem much closer to Frag B than usually assumed).
Spurgeon C, Five Hundred Years of Chaucer Criticism and Allusion, ChS 2s 48.17.
Jack A A, A Commentary on the Poetry of Chaucer and Spenser, Glasgow 1920, p 108 (poem suggests L knew source of Chaucer's Squire's Tale).
Brusendorff A, The Chaucer Tradition, London 1925, p 387 (notes relation to Romance of Rose).
Lewis C S, The Allegory of Love, Oxford 1938, p 239.
SchirmerLydgate, p 33; trans Keep, p 38 (notes relation to House of Fame).
Norton-Smith, edn, p 177 and notes (discusses reworking of material from many works of Chaucer).
PearsallLydgate, pp 106, 111 (discusses L's reworkings of hints from Chaucer).
Sources and Literary Relations (general). Browning E B, The Book of the Poets, in Essays on the Greek Christian Poets and the Eng Poets, N Y 1877, 2.26 (finds poem precursor of Faerie Queene).
Gattinger, pp 35, 48 (notes influence of Virgil and compares with [177] below).
Skeat B M, The Lamentatyon of Mary Magdaleyne, Cambridge 1897, p 23 (shows versification of poem influenced Lamentation of Mary Magdaleyne).
MacCracken, PMLA 23.128 (notes parallels with [68] above).
Duschl, p 9 and passim (gives sources and classification of proverbs).
Patch H R, The Goddess Fortuna in Mediaeval Literature, Cambridge Mass 1927, pp 56, 78 155 (lists similar descriptions of Fortune in earlier texts).
Rathborne I E, The Meaning of Spenser's Fairyland, CUS 131.42, 48 (believes poem makes it clear that Spenser's Panthea is temple of Venus).
Lewis, Allegory, pp 239, 242 (notes influence of Machaut and compares to Chretien de Troyes).
Seaton, p 382 (notes relationship to Kingis Quair and Court of Love).
von Hendy A, The Free Thrall A Study of the Kingis Quair, SSL 2.144 (notes imitations of [176]).
PearsallLydgate, pp 18, 110 (notes use of poem by poets and lovers in the 15th cent).
Norton-Smith, ed, The Kingis Quair, Oxford 1971, p xii (shows the Kingis Quair strongly influenced by [176]).
Other Scholarly Problems. Moore S, Patrons of Letters in Norfolk and Suffolk c 1450, PMLA 27.188 (gives proofs of patronge of de la Pole and William Curteys).
Wylie J H, The Reign of Henry 5, Cambridge 1914–29, 1.189, 239; 2.137, 266 (shows poem throws light on Henry 5, Humphrey of Gloucester, and Thomas Walden).
Brie F, Mittelalter u Antike bei Lydgate, EStn 64.261 (notes mixture of humanism and mediaevalism and suggests importance of L to early humanism).
Bennett J W, Spenser's Muse, JEGP 31.200 (argues poem is temple of Venus rather than of Fame).
Bennett OHEL, p 120 (argues poem shows importance of courtly love in 15 cent).
Schirmer W F, Das Ende des Mittelalters in England, Kleine Schriften, Tübingen 1950, p 30 (discusses implication of presence of poem in Paston library); SchirmerLydgate, p 32; trans Keep, p 37 (discusses background of poem).
Renoir A, The Binding Knot Three Uses of One

Image in Lydgate's Poetry, Neophil 41.203 (purely technical use of image); Attitudes to Women in Lydgate's Poetry, ESts 42.12 (serious attitude); RenoirLydgate, p 93 (discusses attitude to women in [176]).
Norton-Smith, Lydgate's Metaphors, ESts 42.91 (reply to Renoir above); edn, p 177 (notes L's skillful handling of traditional allegory and adultery theme).
Seaton, p 378 (poem contains name anagrams).
Kelly H A, Love and Marriage in the Age of Chaucer, Ithaca and London 1975, p 291 (poem describes clandestine marriage):
Literary Criticism. Courthope, 1.328, 332 and passim.
Reufs F, Das Naturgefühl bei Lydgate, Arch 122.269 (argues monasticism ruins L's originality).
Knowlton E C, Nature in ME, JEGP 20.186 (finds in poem typically Lydgatian handling of nature).
Cazamian L, The Development of Eng Humor, N Y 1930, 1.143 (discusses spontaneous fancy).
Norton-Smith, MÆ 27.166 (notes intelligent changes in the poem from the conventions and improvement in the different versions); edn, p 176.
Rossi, p 125.
Seaton, p 376.
Schreiber E G, The Figure of Venus in Late ME Poetry, DAI 31.767A.
PearsallLydgate, p 104 (full discussion of poem, including revisions).
Marotta J G, John Lydgate and the Tradition of Medieval Rhetoric, DAI 33.729A.
General References. SchirmerLydgate, pp 31, 32, 111; trans Keep, pp 36, 37, 129.
Pearsall D, The Eng Chaucerians, in Chaucer and Chaucerians, ed D S Brewer, Univ Alabama 1966, p 210; PearsallLydgate, pp 39, 68, 97.
Bibliography. Lowndes W T, Bibliographer's Manual, ed H G Bohn, London 1864, 3.1419.
Schick, Prolegomena; edn, EETSES 60.cxlii (lists previous scholarship).
SchirmerLydgate, p 226; trans Keep, p 260.

[177] THE TESTAMENT.

MSS. 1, Bodl 798 (Laud Misc 683), ff 88^a–108^a (15 cent); 2, Bodl 11951 (Rawl C.86), ff 62^b–66^b (pt 5 only; 1475–1500); 3, Jesus Camb 56, ff 1^a–19^b (15 cent); 4, Trinity Camb 599, ff 162^a–172^a (pts 2, 3, 4; 1475–1525); 5, Arundel 285, ff 170^b–174^b (pt 5 only; 1500–1525); 6, Harley 218, ff 52^b–72^a (15 cent); 7, Harley 2251, ff 41^a–42^a (pt 5 only; 1464–1483); 8, Harley 2255, ff 47^a–65^b (1448?–49?); 9, Harley 2382, ff 87^b–96^b, 108^{a-b}, 128^b–129^b (1470–1500); 10, Royal 18.D.ii, ff 1^a–5^a (lacks pt 1; 1460?); 11, BM Addit 29729, ff 179^b–183^a (pt 1 only; John Stowe, 1558); 12, BM Addit 34193, ff 223^a–235^a (stanzas 1–44; Brown-Robbins gives f 223^b; 15 cent); 13, Victoria and Albert Mus Dyce 33 (transcript of PRINT); 14, Leyden Univ Vossius 9, ff 117^a–135^b (separately bound in last pt of book; 15 cent); 15, Huntington HM.140 (formerly Phillipps 8299), ff 90^a–91^b (stanzas 1–14; 1450–80); 16, Clopton Chantry, Long Melford (stanzas 29, 30, 27, 56–59, 68, 70, 74–79, 110, 114–16, 118 carved on scroll on chantry cornice). PRINT: 17, Pynson, 1515?
Brown-Robbins, Robbins-Cutler, no 2464.
Dibdin T F, Typographical Antiquities, London 1812, 2.545 (discusses PRINT).
Collier J P, A Bibliographical and Critical Account of the Rare Books in the Eng Language, N Y 1866, 2.289 (discusses PRINT).
Conder, edn, p 49 (discusses state of carved text and prints it).
Robinson F N, On Two MSS of Lydgate's Guy of Warwick, HSNPL 5.177 (describes MS 14).
Hammond E P, Two British Museum MSS, Angl 28.1 (detailed study of MS 7).
Manly & Rickert, 1.241, 245, 433 (describes MSS 7, 9, 15).
van Dorsten J A, The Leyden Lydgate MS, Scriptorium 14.315 (MS 14).
Editions. Halliwell PPS 2.232 (MS 8).
Conder E L, Church of the Holy Trinity, London 1887, p 49 (MS 16).
MacCracken EETSES 107.329 (MS 6; collations from PRINT and all MSS except 16).
Beutner H, Lydgate's Testament, München 1914 (from 12 MSS to be identified in unlocated separate vol with introd and notes).
Trapp J B, Verses by Lydgate at Long Melford, RES ns 6.1 (MS 16).
Selection. Rickert E, Chaucer's World, N Y 1948, p 98 (from EETSES 107).
Modernizations and Abstracts. Collier, Bibliographical Account, 2.287 (abstract).
Fitzgibbon H M, Early Eng and Scottish Poetry, London ca 1888, p 72 (lines 614–55, 890–97; modernized).
Watts N, Love Songs of Sion, N Y Cincinnati and Chicago 1924, p 33 (modernization of lines 89–96, 137–44, 193–208, 447–54, 479–86, 535–42, 551–58, 567–74).
SchirmerLydgate, p 158; trans Keep, p 182

(thorough summary).
Textual Matters. Gattinger, p 84.
Language. Hingst R, Die Sprache John Lydgates aus seinen Reimen, Greiswald 1908, p 15.
Babcock C F, A Study of the Metrical Use of the Inflectional e in ME with Particular Reference to Chaucer and Lydgate, PMLA 29.59 (argues L's language bridges gap between Middle Ages and modern period).
Versification. Reger, pp 42, 78 (finds certain epic caesurae in 21.63 percent lines).
Pyle F, The Pedigree of Lydgate's Heroic Line, Hermathena 50.26 (discusses L's use of line and shows that its characteristics go back at least to Poema Morale).
Date. Schick J, Lydgate's Temple of Glas, EETSES 60.1xxxv (1445?).
Authorship. MacCracken TPSL, appendix 2.xxvi; rptd EETSES 107.xxix.
SchirmerLydgate, p 232; trans Keep, p 270.
Sources and Literary Relations. Gattinger, pp 31, 35, 39, 41, 65, 70, 72 and passim, 84 (compares poem to [176] above; discusses influence of Legenda Aurea, Isidore of Seville, and Chaucer).
Skeat B M, The Lamentatyon of Mary Magdaleyne, Cambridge 1897, p 25 and passim (notes influence of poem on anonymous lamentation).
Moorman F W, The Interpretation of Nature in Eng Poetry, QF 95.125 (argues description of Spring shows differences between L and Chaucer).
MacCracken H N, Lydgatiana 5: 14 Short Religious Poems, Arch 131.40 (prints Prayer to Christ's Name in imitation of L).
Nichols P H, William Dunbar as a Scottish Lydgatian, PMLA 46.214 (shows poem to be direct source of opening quatrains in Dunbar's Lament for the Makaris).
SchirmerLydgate, p 240; trans Keep, p 282 (names analogous pieces).
Kolve V A, Everyman and the Parable of the Talents, in Medieval Eng Drama, edd J Taylor and A H Nelson, Chicago and London 1972, p 318 (compares L's use of talent proverb with use in Everyman without claiming [177] as a source).
Other Scholarly Problems. Abbey C J, Religious Thoughts in Old Eng Verse, London 1892, pp 88, 90 (finds poem typical of penitential spirit in 15 cent).
Duschl, p 73 (discusses only proverb).
Bennett OHEL, p 138 (mentions poem as only evidence of L's early life).

Woolf R, The Eng Religious Lyric in the Middle Ages, Oxford 1968, p 207 (notes visualization of objects of devotion in the poem).
Mitchell J, Thomas Hoccleve, Urbana Chicago and London 1968, p 8 (claims [177] should not be taken as personal autobiography).
Scattergood V J, Politics and Poetry in the 15th Cent, London 1971, p 234 (contains examples of laxity in monasteries).
Literary Criticism. Gattinger, pp 31, 72 (notes lack of unity and discusses style).
Knowlton E C, Nature in ME, JEGP 20.186 (finds in poem typically Lydgatian handling of nature).
Bennett OHEL, p 141 (finds poem one of L's best works).
RenoirLydgate, p 17 (notes L's craft in expressing suffering).
PearsallLydgate, p 294.
General Reference. SchirmerLydgate, pp 6, 10; trans Keep, pp 9, 14.
Bibliography. Lowndes W T, Bibliographer's Manual, ed H G Bohn, London 1864, 3.1418.

[178] SONG OF THANKSGIVING (also TE DEUM).

MS. Harley 2255, ff 43^b–45^a (1448?–49?).
Brown-Robbins, no 3261.
Edition. MacCracken EETSES 107.21.
Language. Mendenhall J C, Aureate Terms, Lancaster Pa 1919, p 67 (notes heavily aureate diction).
Authorship. MacCracken TPSL, appendix 2.xxvi; rptd EETSES 107.xxix.
SchirmerLydgate, p 232; trans Keep, p 270.
Sources and Literary Relations. MacCracken H N, Lydgatiana 5: 14 Short Religious Poems, Arch 131.40 (prints a Salve Regina and a Prayer to Mary and the Saints in imitation of [178]).
Wehrle W O, The Macaronic Hymn Tradition in Medieval Eng Literature, Washington 1933, pp 133, 134 (shows poem to be free trans of Te Deum Laudamus with Latin lines kept for functional reasons).
SchirmerLydgate, p 156; trans Keep, p 179 (finds poem fairly independent from Latin original).
Other Scholarly Problem. Berdan J M, The Influence of Medieval Latin Rhetorics on the Eng Writers of the Early Renaissance, RomR 7.288 (argues L's poem shows importance of Latin in England).
Literary Criticism. PearsallLydgate, p 262 (a bad example of L's aureate ambitiousness).

[179] THAT NOW IS HAY THAT SUMTYME WAS GRASSE.

MSS. 1, Bodl 1191 (Rawl C.86), ff 141ª–142ª (ends imperfectly; 1475–1500); 2, BM Addit 29729, ff 127ᵇ–129ᵇ (John Stowe, 1558).
Brown-Robbins, no 3531.
Manly & Rickert, 1.472 (describes MS 2).
Edition. MacCracken EETS 192.809 (MS 2; collations from other MS).
Date. SchirmerLydgate, p 175n; trans Keep, p 200n (possibly 1424).
Authorship. MacCracken TPSL, appendix 2.xxvi; rptd EETSES 107.xxix.
SchirmerLydgate, p 233; trans Keep, p 272.
Sources and Literary Relations. SchirmerLydgate, p 175; trans Keep, p 200 (notes influence of Psalm 90 and compares to Villon's Snows of Yesteryear).
Conley J, The Reference to Judas Maccabeus in Everyman, N&Q ns 14(212).50 (nine worthies linked with ubi sunt found in Everyman and this poem).
Other Scholarly Problem. SchirmerLydgate, p 85; trans Keep, p 102 (poem possibly written for Queen Catherine).
General Reference. PearsallLydgate, pp 75, 164, 211.

[180] THEY THAT NO WHILE ENDURE, VERSION 1.

MS. Harley 2255, ff 118ᵇ–119ᵇ (1448?–49?).
Brown-Robbins, no 3647.
Edition. MacCracken EETS 192.818.
Authorship. MacCracken TPSL, appendix 2.xxvi; rptd EETSES 107.xxix.
Brown-Robbins, no 3647 (questions L's authorship).
SchirmerLydgate, p 233; trans Keep, p 272.
PearsallLydgate, p 212.
Sources and Literary Relations. One stanza is identical with another in [130] above.
SchirmerLydgate, p 173; trans Keep, p 198 (finds theme similar to some refrains in [47] above).
Literary Criticism. PearsallLydgate, p 212 (the 2 versions reveal the obviousness of L's craft).

[181] THEY THAT NO WHILE ENDURE, VERSION 2.

MSS. 1, Trinity Camb 599, f 209ª (1475–1525); 2, BM Addit 36983, ff 262ª–263ª (1425–50).
Brown-Robbins, no 55.

Edition. MacCracken EETS 192.820 (MS 2; collations from MS 1).
Scholarship. See under [180] above.

[182] THOROUGHFARE OF WOE (also ON THE WRETCHEDNESS OF WORLDLY AFFAIRS).

MSS. 1, Trinity Camb 600, pp 25–32 (1456?); 2, Harley 2251, ff 246ᵇ–249ᵇ (1464–83); 3, BM Addit 29729, ff 151ᵇ–154ª (MacCracken gives 152ᵇ–154ª in edn; Stowe MS, 1558).
Brown-Robbins, no 1872.
Hammond E P, Lydgate's Mumming at Hertford, Angl 22.364 (describes MS 1); Two British Museum MSS, Angl 28.1 (detailed study of MS 2).
Brusendorff A, The Chaucer Tradition, London 1925, pp 208, 466 and passim (discusses Shirley's marginalia in MS 1).
Manly & Rickert, 1.241 (describes MS 2).
Editions. Halliwell PPS 2.122 (MS 2).
MacCracken EETS 192.822 (MS 2; collations from MS 3).
Textual Matters. Gattinger, p 72 ff (suggests emendations).
Language. Hall F, On Eng Adjectives in -able, London 1877, p 193 (argues poem testifies to use of remuable as neuter of removeable).
Brusendorff, Chaucer Tradition, p 257 (shows expression first stock to mean first generation of mankind).
Versification. Reger, pp 41, 78 (finds certain epic caesurae in 12.5 percent lines).
Date. SchirmerLydgate, p 176; trans Keep, p 202 (believes poem written in 1430's).
Authorship. MacCracken TPSL, appendix 2.xxvi; rptd EETSES 107.xxix.
SchirmerLydgate, p 234; trans Keep, p 272.
Sources and Literary Relations. Gattinger, pp 18, 36, 49, 60, 68 (notes influence of Bible and Chaucer and argues reference to Boethius no proof of L's acquaintance with Consolation of Philosophy).
Spurgeon C, Five Hundred Years of Chaucer Criticism and Allusion, ChS 2s 48.36 (prints allusion).
Bonner F W, The Genesis of the Chaucer Apocrypha, SP 48.461 (considers poem representative of L's attitude toward Chaucer).
SchirmerLydgate, pp 176, 200n; trans Keep, pp 202, 230n (notes borrowing from Chaucer's Knight's Tale).
Stillwell G, Chaucer's Eagles and Their Choices

on February 14, JEGP 53.546 (argues poem reflects L's misunderstanding of humor in Parliament of Fowls).
Other Scholarly Problems. Duschl, p 83 (classifies proverb).
Mullet C F, John Lydgate: a Mirror of Medieval Medicine, Bull of the Hist of Medicine 22.403 (considers poem typical of contemporary preoccupation with death).
SchirmerLydgate, p 176; trans Keep, p 202 (believes poem looks forward to [47]).
PearsallLydgate, p 212 (notes that L carries examples of fallen heroes down to his own time).
Literary Criticism. PearsallLydgate, p 211 (shows that poem is solid, sober, and elaborate).

[183] TYED WITH A LINE (also ON THE INSTABILITY OF HUMAN AFFAIRS).

MSS. 1, Harley 2251, ff 37^b–39^b (1464–83); 2, BM Addit 29729, ff 131^b–132^a (3 stanzas; Stowe MS, 1558).
Brown-Robbins, Robbins-Cutler, no 3436.
Hammond E P, Two British Museum MSS, Angl 28.1 (detailed study of MS 1).
Manly & Rickert, 1.241 (describes MS 1).
Edwards, edn, ESts 51.527 (MS 2).
Editions. Halliwell PPS 2.74 (MS 1).
MacCracken EETS 192.832 (MS 1).
Edwards A S G, Lydgate's Tyed with a Line and the Question of Halsam, ESts 51.528 (MS 2).
Textual Matters. Robbins-Cutler, no 3436 (notes burden occurs in [4] above).
Edwards, edn, ESts 51.528 (notes stanzas 2 and 3 in MS 2 differ from MacCracken, edn).
Versification. Reger, pp 41, 78 (finds certain epic caesurae in 15.47 percent lines).
Authorship. Hammond, Angl 28.1 (believes opening stanza not by L).
MacCracken TPSL, appendix 2.xxvii; rptd EETSES 107.xxx.
South H P, The Question of Halsam, PMLA 50.362 (argues opening stanza by Halsam).
SchirmerLydgate, p 233; trans Keep, p 272.
Edwards, edn, ESts 51.527 (argues opening stanza by Halsam but stanzas 2, 3 of MS 2 are by L).
Sources and Literary Relations. Gattinger, pp 14, 69 (notes influence of Chaucer).
Other Scholarly Problems. Gattinger, p 14 (notes proverbial utterances).
Duschl, pp 70, 73 (classifies proverb).
SchirmerLydgate, pp 173, 176; trans Keep, pp 198, 202 (points out gnomic utterances of sort common with L).

[184] TYED WITH A LINE, STANZA 1 ONLY (recorded and printed as separate poem).

MSS. 1, Bodl 3896 (Fairfax 16), f 195^a (1425–75); 2, Camb Univ Ff.1.6, f 151^a (ca 1500); 3, Harley 7333, f 148^a (15 cent); 4, Harley 7578, f 20^a (1425–75); 5, BM Addit 5465, f 2^b (1400–50); 6, BM Addit 16165, f 244^a (1425–75); 7, Huntington Libr HM.144 (formerly Huth 7), f 144^a (1480–1500).
Brown-Robbins, Robbins-Cutler, no 3437.
Stevens, edn, p 351 (MS 5).
Editions. Rel Ant, 1.234 (MS 3).
Furnivall F J, Chaucer and Lydgate Fragments, N&Q 5s 9.343 (MS 7).
Flügel E, Kleinere Mitteilungen aus Handschriften, Angl 14.463 (MS 3).
Fehr B, Die Lieder des Fairfax MS, Arch 106.52 (MS 5).
South H P, The Question of Halsam, PMLA 50.362 (MS 1).
Stevens J, Music and Poetry in the Early Tudor Court, London 1961, p 352 (MS 5; with brief notes and glosses at foot of page).
Scholarship. See under [183] above.

[185] TIMOR MORTIS CONTURBAT ME (also WOURLDLY MUTABILITE).

MS. Harley 2255, ff 128^b–131^a (1448?–49?).
Brown-Robbins, no 3160.
Editions. Patterson F A, ME Penitential Lyric, N Y 1911, p 104.
Gollancz I, Parlement of the Three Ages, London 1915, appendix xi.
MacCracken EETS 192.828.
Selections. Koeppel E, AfDA 24.55.
Kölbing E, Parlement of the Three Ages, EStn 25.287 (prints stanzas 7, 8, 10, 11 in crit of Gollancz 1897 edn of Parlement without [185]).
Modernization and Abstract. SchirmerLydgate, p 108; trans Keep, p 126 (abstract).
Authorship. MacCracken TPSL, appendix 2.xxvi; rptd EETSES 107.xxx.
SchirmerLydgate, p 234; trans Keep, p 273.
Sources and Literary Relations. Nichols P H, William Dunbar as a Scottish Lydgatian, PMLA 46.214 (demonstrates influence of poem on Dunbar's Lament for the Makaris).
SchirmerLydgate, p 178; trans Keep, p 203 (puts poem in same category with [115] above and Dunbar's Lament for the Makaris).
PearsallLydgate, pp 205, 211 (notes that the form

of the poem is very common at the time).
Other Scholarly Problem. Mullet C F, John Lydgate: a Mirror of Medieval Medicine, Bull of the Hist of Medicine 22.403 (mentions poem as typical of contemporary preoccupation with death).

[186] GUARD YOUR TONGUE (also ADVICE TO TITTLE-TATTLERS and THE COCK HATH LOWE SHOONE).

MS. Harley 2255, ff 131^b–135^a (1448?–49?).
Brown-Robbins, Robbins-Cutler, no 3173.
Editions. Halliwell PPS 2.150.
Wright PPS, 2.215.
MacCracken EETS 192.813.
Versification. Reger, pp 41, 78 (finds certain epic caesurae in 16.67 percent lines).
Authorship. MacCracken TPSL, appendix 2.xxvi; rptd EETSES 107.xxix.
SchirmerLydgate, p 233; trans Keep, p 272.
Sources and Literary Relations. Gattinger, pp 15, 49, 67, 71 and passim (notes proverbial aspect of theme and influence of Disticha Catonis and Chaucer).
MacCracken H N, Lydgatiana 2: Two Chaucerian Ballades, Arch 127.322 (prints 2 anonymous ballads illustrative of lesson in [186]).
Spurgeon C, Five Hundred Years of Chaucer Criticism and Allusion, ChS 2s 48.46 (prints allusion to Chaucer).
Rigg A G, A Glastonbury Miscellany of the 15th Cent, Oxford 1968, p 56 (notes other similar ME poems).
Other Scholarly Problem. Duschl, pp 27, 30, 87 (classifies proverbs).
Literary Criticism. Gattinger, p 71 and passim (discusses style).
General References. SchirmerLydgate, p 174; trans Keep, p 199.
PearsallLydgate, p 211 (argues that the poem's cryptic catalogue is worthy of study).

[187] WIKKED TONGUE (also BALLAD OF GOOD COUNSEL and A WICKED TUNGE WILLE SEY AMYS).

MSS. 1, Bodl 2527 (Bodley 686), ff 191^b–193^a (1430–40); 2, Camb Univ Ff.1.6, ff 125^a–128^a (Brown-Robbins gives f 147^a; 15 cent); 3, Trinity Camb 600, pp 15–20 (1456?); 4, Harley 2251, ff 151^a–152^b (1464–83); 5, BM Addit 29729, ff 149^b–151^b (John Stowe MS, 1558); 6, Lambeth 344, f 10^b? (15 cent); 7, Rome Eng Coll 1306 (also numbered 127 and A.347), ff 76^a–78^a (1436–56); 8, Huntington Libr EL 26.A.13 (formerly Ellesmere), ff 20^a–22^a (15 cent). PRINT: 9, Thynne, Chaucer 1532.
Brown-Robbins, Robbins-Cutler, no 653.
Hammond E P, Lydgate's Mumming at Hertford, Angl 22.364 (describes MS 3); Two British Museum MSS, Angl 28.1 (detailed study of MS 4).
Sieper E, Reson and Sensuallyte, EETSES 84.xiii (describes MS 5).
Brusendorff A, The Chaucer Tradition, London 1925, pp 208, 466 and passim (discusses Shirley's marginalia in MS 3).
Manly & Rickert, 1.64, 241 (describes MSS 1, 4).
Klinefelter R A, A Newly Discovered 15-Cent Eng MS, MLQ (Wash) 14.3 (gives description and contents of MS 7).
Robbins R H, A ME Diatribe against Philip of Burgundy, Neophil 39.131 (gives description and contents of MS 7).
Editions. Chalmers A, The Works of the Eng Poets, London 1810, 1.555.
Oxf Ch, 7.285 (PRINT 9; collations from MSS 2, 4).
MacCracken EETS 192.839 (MS 8; collations from PRINT and all MSS except MS 7).
Versification. Reger, pp 62, 77 (finds certain epic caesurae in 5.26 percent lines).
Authorship. Sieper, EETSES 84.xvii (mentions Stowe's statement in MS 5 that poem is trans from Latin by L).
Hammond, p 462 (accepts L's authorship on basis of Stowe and Tyrwhit).
MacCracken TPSL, appendix 2.xxvii; rptd EETSES 107.xxxi.
Bonner F W, The Genesis of the Chaucer Apocrypha, SP 48.461 (notes that poem was once ascribed to Chaucer).
SchirmerLydgate, p 233; trans Keep, p 272.
Seaton, p 338 (argues for Richard Roos).
Sources and Literary Relations. Sieper, EETSES 84.xvii (notes Stowe's assertion that work was trans from Latin).
Nichols P H, William Dunbar as a Scottish Lydgatian, PMLA 46.214 (believes poem direct source of Dunbar's catalogue poems).
Jack R D S, Dunbar and Lydgate, SSL 8.222 (argues that the poem influenced Dunbar's Of Deming and How Sall I Governe Me).
Other Scholarly Problems. Duschl, p 89 (discusses proverb).
Seaton, p 368 (argues poem contains name

anagrams).
Literary Criticism. Reufs F, Das Naturgefühl bei Lydgate, Arch 122.269 (believes monasticism ruins L's originality).
General References. SchirmerLydgate, p 175; trans Keep, p 201.
PearsallLydgate, p 210 (an epitome of L's techniques).

[188] TRETYSE OF CRYSTYS PASSYOUN (also THE DOLEROUS PYTE OF CRYSTES PASSIOUN).

MS. Bodl 798 (Laud Misc 673), ff 15^b–17^a (15 cent).
Brown-Robbins, no 702.
Edition. MacCracken EETSES 107.250.
Date. SchirmerLydgate, p 161; trans Keep, p 185 (believes poem possibly earliest of L's religious lyrics).
Authorship. MacCracken TPSL, appendix 2.xxi; rptd EETSES 107.xxiv.
SchirmerLydgate, p 232; trans Keep, p 270.
Sources and Literary Relations. Leach E, Lydgate's The Dolerous Pyte of Crystes Passioun and Herbert's The Sacrifice, N&Q ns 7(205).421 (notes similarities but does not claim L's poem is Herbert's source).
Woolf R, The Eng Religious Lyric in the Middle Ages, Oxford 1968, p 199 (demonstrates how cleverly L used the traditional image of the grapes and the winepress of the Passion).
Other Scholarly Problem. Woolf, p 199 (discusses how poem was intended to be used).
Literary Criticism. Woolf, p 201 (demonstrates L's skill).
General Reference. PearsallLydgate, p 181.

[189] TROY BOOK (also HYSTORYE, SEGE, AND DESTRUCCYON OF TROYE).

MSS. 1, Bodl 1831 (Digby 230), ff 28^a–194^d (1450–1500); 2, Bodl 1833 (Digby 232), ff 1^a–157^c (lines 1–27,498; 1420–50); 3, Bodl 12297 (Rawl C.446), ff 1^a–174^b (lines 1–28,870; 1420–50); 4, Bodl 13679 (Rawlinson D.913), ff 3, 2 (1.460–537, 623–701; 15 cent); 5, Bodl 14638 (Rawl poet F.144), ff 1^a–404^b (incomplete; 1475–1525); 6, Bodl 14714 (Rawl poet F.223), ff i–xi (also numbered 3–12; fragment to bk 1, line 459); 7, Bodl 21722 (Douce 148), ff 1^a–289^b, 301^a–306^a (includes sections of Scottish Troy Fragment in Brown-Robbins, no *8; 1475–1525); 8, Exeter Oxf 129, ff 1^a–139^a (27,000 lines; 1450–1500); 9, St Johns Oxf 6, ff 1^a–134^b (29,800 lines; 1450–75); 10, Camb Univ Kk.5.30, ff 19^a–304^b (lines 1689–5337; includes 2 Scottish Troy Fragments in Brown-Robbins, no *8; mostly 16 cent); 11, Trinity Camb 1283, ff 38^a–190^b (29,300 lines; 1425–75); 12, Arundel 99, ff 1^a–159^d (29,221 lines; 1425–75); 13, Cotton August A.iv, ff 1^a–155^a (30,111 lines; 1420–50); 14, Royal 18.D.ii, ff 6^a–146^a (28,500 lines; 1450–75); 15, Royal 18.D.vi, ff 4^a–139^b (28,000 lines; 1475–1500); 16, Bristol City Ref Libr, ff 1^a–120^b (24,954 lines; 1425–50); 17, Gloucester Cath 5, ff 1^a–373^b (26,426 lines; 1425–75 with incorrect pagination of 17 cent); 18, Inner Temple 524 (part of prologue on flyleaf; 15 cent); 19, Rylands Libr Eng 1 (formerly Osterley Park), ff 2^a–172^b (1450–75); 20, formerly Phillipps 3113, ff 1^a–392^b (28,090 lines; 1475–1525); 21, formerly Temple, Newton Park, Bristol (Sotheby Sale, 16 June 1941, lot 153); 22, Harvard Coll Eng 752 (formerly Ashburnham 131), ff 1^a–365^b (28,000 lines; 1475–1500); 23, Morgan Libr M876 (formerly Helmingham Hall), ff 1^a–102^b (23,868 lines; 1425–50). PRINTS: 24, Pynson 1513; 25, Marshe 1555.
Brown-Robbins, Robbins-Cutler, no 2516.
Dibdin T F, Typographical Antiquities, London 1812, 2.447 (discusses PRINT 24).
Pantan G A and D Donaldson, The Gest Hystoriale of the Destruction of Troy, EETS 39.x (discusses MS 10).
The Royal Commission on Historical MSS, Report no 1, London 1874, 1.60 (notes MS of poem in Helmingham Hall); Report no 8, London 1878, 3.106 (lists MS of poem among Earl of Ashburnham's possessions); Report no 12, London 1891, 9.399 (notes MS of poem in Gloucester Cathedral Libr).
Wright W A, Generides, EETS 55.v (MS 11).
Mathews N, Early Printed Books and MSS in the City Reference Libr Bristol, Bristol 1899, p 68 (describes MS 16).
Bergen H, Description and Genealogy of the MSS and Prints of Lydgate's Troy Book, Bungay 1906; rptd EETSES 126.1.
Spurgeon C, Five Hundred Years of Chaucer Criticism and Allusion, ChS 2s 48.23 (discusses marginalia in MS 15).
Maxwell W G C, An Inventory of the Contents of Markeaton Hall, DANHSJ 51.117 (traces history of MS 19).
Manly & Rickert, 1.461, 614 (describes MS 5 and identifies the William Carraunt whose arms are on flyleaf of MS 19).

Tillyard E M W, Five Poems, London 1948, p 106 (discusses illust in MS 15).

Notes and News, JRLB 43.273 (MS 19).

van Buuren-Veenenbos C C, John Asloan an Edinburgh Scribe, ESts 47.365 (MS 7).

Pearsall D, Notes on the MS of Generydes, Libr 5s 16.205 (MS 11).

Edition. Bergen H, Lydgate's Troy Book, EETSES 97, 103, 106, 126 (MS 13; collations from PRINTS 24, 25 and all MSS except MSS 4, 5, 18, 21).

Selections. Neilson W A and K G T Webster, Chief British Poets of the 14 and 15 Cent, Boston 1916, p 216 (reprints New Troy from Bergen edn).

Norton-Smith J, John Lydgate Poems, Oxford 1966, pp 14 (bk 2.479–710; MS 13; collations from MS 2), 132 (brief commentary, notes, and glossary).

Richmond V B, Laments for the Dead in Medieval Narrative, Duquesne Stud Philological Series 8, Pittsburgh 1966, p 152 (bk 3.3823–69; from Bergen edn).

Modernizations and Abstracts. Heywood T?, The Life and Death of Hector, print Purfoot 1614 (selections may be found in: E Brydges, Censura Literaria, London 1808, 7.121; H Bergen, Description and Genealogy, p xliv; rptd EETSES 126.68. Heywood's authorship is strongly questioned by: C A Rouse, Thomas Heywood and The Life and Death of Hector, PMLA 43.779; A M Clark, Thomas Heywood Playwright and Miscellanist, Oxford 1931, p 340; D Bush, Wm Painter and Thomas Heywood, MLN 54.279).

Warton T, History of Eng Poetry, ed W Hazlitt, London 1871, 3.82 (abstract).

Fitzgibbon H M, Early Eng and Scottish Poetry, London ca 1888, pp 75, 76 (2.447–60, 1.3093–106; modernized).

Kiser J E, John Lydgate's Troy Book A Prose Trans, DAI 33.4349A (incomplete).

Textual Matters. Prothero G W, A Memoir of Henry Bradshaw, London 1888, p 134.

Language. Hall F, On Eng Adjectives in –able, London 1877 (argues that adj Flaskisable means Fickle from OF Flechir); Flaskisable, Nation (N Y) 63.455 (same argument).

Skeat W W, Flaskisable, N&Q 7s 12.146; rptd W W Skeat, A Student's Pastime, Oxford 1896, p 303 (traces Flaskisable to OF Flechir).

Swith S, n t, N&Q 7s 12.215 (believes term Flaskisable comes from Flasque in heraldry).

Skeat B M, The Lamentatyon of Mary Magdaleyne, Cambridge 1897, pp 9, 11 (argues expression Rayle used in respect to blood is typical of L; notes Chaucer's influence on L's vocabulary and L's influence on later Eng).

Hingst R, Die Sprache John Lydgates aus seinen Reimen, Greiswald 1908.

Babcock C F, A Study of the Metrical Use of the Inflectional e in ME with Particular Reference to Chaucer and Lydgate, PMLA 29.59 (believes L's language bridges gap between Middle Ages and modern period).

Hüttmann E, Das Partizipium Präsentis bei Lydgate im Vergleich mit Chaucers Gebrauch, Kiel 1914.

Royster J F, The Do Auxiliary 1400 to 1450, MP 12.449 (finds 13 instances in Troy Book, lines 1–4000).

Whitehall H, The Background of the Word Bask, PQ 14.229 (argues that L uses Bask in sense of To Bathe or To be Suffused in Liquid).

Utley C R, no 151 (believes expression Cast up the bridel, bk 2, line 520, is popular tag).

Manzalaoui M A, Derring-do, N&Q ns 9(107).369 (notes different uses of the expression in [189]).

Versification. Schick J, Lydgate's Temple of Glas, EETSES 60.lv and passim.

Reger, pp 30, 77 (finds certain epic caesurae in 2.23 percent lines).

Bergen, edn, EETSES 97.xi.

Spindler R, Eng Metrik, München 1927, p 60 (finds L freer than Chaucer with metrical thesis).

Pyle F, The Pedigree of Lydgate's Heroic Line, Hermathena 50.26 (shows characteristics of L's line go back at least to Poema Morale, and discusses uses of the line).

Date. Lydgate in line 124 of poem states that he began work in 1412.

Skeat W W, The Date of Lydgate's Siege of Troy, Acad (London) 41.445 (believes poem finished late in 1420).

Bergen, edn, EETSES 97.ix (1412–20).

Parr J, Astronomical Dating for Some of Lydgate's Poems, PMLA 67.251 (questions Skeat's dating).

Authorship. Koeppel E, Laurents de Premierfait und John Lydgates Bearbeitungen von Boccaccios De Casibus virorum illustrium, München 1885, p 76 (questions L's authorship).

MacCracken TPSL, appendix 2.xxvii; rptd EETSES 107.xxx.

Schirmer Lydgate, p 229; trans Keep, p 266.

Sources and Literary Relations (principally to Chaucer). Ward Hist, 1.433.

Lounsbury T, Studies in Chaucer, N Y 1892, 1.109.

Spurgeon, Chaucer Devant la Critique en Angleterre et en France, Paris 1911, p 8 (believes poem throws light on Chaucer's attitude toward younger poets); Five Hundred Years, ChS 2s 48.23 (prints allusions).

Brown C, Lydgate and the Legend of Good Women, EStn 47.59 (argues influence of Legend A Text on [189]).

Rollins H E, The Troilus-Cressida Story from Chaucer to Shakespeare, PMLA 32.383 (believes L adds nothing to Chaucer).

Mendenhall J C, Aureate Terms, Lancaster Pa 1919, p 47 (argues reference in tragedy of Cressida suggests dependence on Chaucer).

Brusendorff A, The Chaucer Tradition, London 1925, pp 30, 160, 326 (believes evidence of poem shows that L never knew Chaucer in person).

SchirmerLydgate, p 37; trans Keep, p 43.

PearsallLydgate, p 55.

Benson C D, Chaucer's Influence on the Prose Sege of Troy, N&Q ns 18(216).127 (this prose redaction of [189] also has material from Chaucer); The Ancient World in John Lydgate's Troy Book, American Benedictine Rev 24.299 (L's sense of history in [189] from Chaucer).

Literary Relations (to Shakespeare). Steevens G, The Plays of William Shakespeare, London 1793, 11.211 (discusses relationship of poem to Guido delle Colonne's Historia and Shakespeare's Troilus).

Douce F, Illustrations of Shakespeare and of Ancient Manners, London 1807, 2.53 (minimizes influence of [189] on Shakespeare's Troilus); rptd 1839.

Blades W, The Life and Typography of William Caxton, London 1861–63, 2.15 (believes [189] not so important source of Shakespeare's Troilus as Caxton's Recueil des Histoires de Troye); The Biography and Typography of William Caxton, N Y 1882, p 172 (minimizes importance of [189] for study of Shakespeare).

Greif W, Die Mittelalterlichen Bearbeitungen der Trojanersage, Marburg 1886, p 68 (believes [189] among sources of Shakespeare's Troilus).

Rollins, PMLA 32.383.

Tillyard E M W, Shakespeare's Problem Plays, London 1950, p 34 and passim (argues influence of [189] on Shakespeare's Troilus).

Presson R K, Shakespeare's Troilus and Cressida and the Legends of Troy, Madison 1953, p 145 (notes possible parallels between [189] and Shakespeare's Troilus).

Kimbrough R, Shakespeare's Troilus and Cressida and Its Setting, Cambridge Mass 1964, passim (occasionally notes use of [189]).

Bullough G, Narrative and Dramatic Sources of Shakespeare, London and N Y 1966, 6.92, 157 (discusses [189] as possible source for Shakespeare's Troilus and prints selections).

Sources and Literary Relations (general). Steevens, Plays of Shakespeare, 11.211 (discusses relationship of [189] to Guido delle Colonne's Historia destructionis Trojae from which it is translated).

Dunger H, Die Sage vom trojanischen Kriege in den Bearbeitungen des Mittelalters und ihren antiken Quellen, Leipzig 1869, p 80 (outlines course of Troy story from Dares and Dictys to Shakespeare but does not mention Shakespeare's debt to L).

Joly A, Benoît de Sainte-More et le Roman de Troie, Paris 1871, 1.494; 2.895 (believes L used Roman de Troie to complement Guido's Historia).

Warton, History, 3.80 (discusses sources with emphasis on Guido's Historia).

Pantan and Donaldson, EETS 39.xlix (argues L's debt to Gest Hystoriale).

Koerting G, Boccaccios Leben u Werke, Leipzig 1880, p 592 (mentions relationship of Troy Book to Filostrato).

Ward, 1.76.

Morley, 6.118 (gives account of Troy story from Dares to L).

Zupitza J, Über die ME Bearbeitung von Boccaccios De claris mulieribus, Festschrift zur Begrüssung des fünften allgemeinen deutschen Neophilologentages, Berlin 1892, p 120 (uses [189] to establish date of De Claris mulieribus).

Scott M A, Elizabethan Trans from the Italian: Trans of Poetry Plays and Metrical Romances, PMLA 11.377 (uses [189] to demonstrate that Italian influence came only after Dante and Petrarch).

Kempe D, A ME Tale of Troy, EStn 29.1 (examines relationship between [189] and Laud Troy Book and discusses Guido and Benoît).

Wülfing J E, Das Laud-Troybook, EStn 29.374 (compares illustrations of contemporary life in both works).

Albert F, Über Thomas Heywoods The Life and Death of Hector, MBREP 42.6 and passim (pp 1–35 printed separately under same title, Kirchhain 1908; studies in detail relationship between the 2 texts; crit A M Clarke, TLS Oct 1924, p 612).

Duschl, p 9 and passim (gives source and classification of proverbs).

Rollins, PMLA 32.383.

Cook J D, Euhemerism: a Medieval Interpretation of Classical Paganism, Spec 2.396 (discusses influence of Peter Comestor and Isidore of Seville).

Patch H R, The Goddess Fortuna in Mediaeval Literature, Cambridge Mass 1927, pp 32, 60, 97, 153, 155 (believes handling of Fortune shows influence of Boccaccio and perhaps of Claudian, Honorius of Autun, and others).

Bush D, Chaucer's Corinne, Spec 4.106 (notes reference to Ovid in bk 4, line 3030).

Erdmann A and E Ekwall, Lydgate's Siege of Thebes, EETSES 125.6 (discusses relationship of [189] to Guido's Historia).

Bergen, edn, EETSES 126.95 (prints relevant sections of Guido's Historia).

Koch H, Zu Lydgate, Troy Book, 1, 491: the fyry cat, Arch 171.207 (traces expression Fyry cat to Aeneid 8.193–267).

Atwood E B, Some Minor Sources of Lydgate's Troy Book, SP 35.25 (minimizes importance of OF sources and argues most important secondary sources are Ovid, Chaucer, and Isidore of Seville).

Day M, Milton and Lydgate, RES 23.144 (believes [189] possible source of several passages in Il Pensoroso and Comus).

Highet G, The Classical Tradition, N Y and London 1949, p 701n (sketches transmission of euhemerism through Isidore of Seville to Guido and Lydgate).

Marquardt W T, A Source for the Passage on the Origin of Chess in Lydgate's Troy Book, MLN 64.87 (shows source to be Jacobus de Cessolis' De Ludo scaccorum).

Combellack R B, The Composite Catalogue of the Sege of Troye, Spec 26.624 (argues L's catalogue of ships is source of counterpart in Sege of Troye).

SchirmerLydgate, p 37; trans Keep, p 42 (lists sources).

Enkvist N E, The Seasons of the Year, Societas Scientiarum Fennica Commentationes Humanarum Litterarum 22.4, Helsingfors 1957, p 123 (L greatly expands his sources).

Wilson E C, ed, The Lamentation of Troy for the Death of Hector, Institute of Elizabethan Stud Publ no 3, Chicago 1959, p xiii (L is probably inspiration and main source for the Lamentation).

Seaton E, Marlowe's Light Reading, in Elizabethan and Jacobean Stud Presented to Frank Percy Wilson, London 1959, p 28 ([189] is Marlowe's chief source for the non-classical story of Troy).

Rossi, p 99.

Blake N F, Caxton and Chaucer, Leeds SE ns 1.26 (Caxton's praise of Chaucer echoes [189]).

Lauritis J A, Second Thoughts on Style in Lydgate's Life of Our Lady, in Essays and Stud in Lang and Lit, ed H Petit, Pittsburgh 1964, p 13 (argues L knew Homer).

Daniel B L, A Note on Lydgate's Corious Flour of Rethorik, Emporia State Research Stud 14(issue 1).29 (L respects his source's truth but has trouble imitating its style).

Richmond V B, Laments for the Dead in Medieval Narrative, Duquesne Stud Philological Series 8, Pittsburgh 1966, p 63 (laments for dead in [189] compared with the Laud Troy Book).

RenoirLydgate, pp 138, 141 (compares [189] with a 17-cent modernization, The Life and Death of Hector).

Dwyer R A, Some Readers of John Trevisa, N&Q ns 14(212).291 (argues L uses Polychronicon for the labors of Hercules).

Cairncross A S, Thomas Kyd and the Myrmidons, Arlington Quart 1.40 (Kyd follows the medieval version of the death of Achilles, probably from L).

PearsallLydgate, pp 15, 122, 154.

Merritt K M, The Source of John Pikeryng's Horestes, RES ns 23.255 (source is [189] and not Caxton).

Benson, Prudence Othea and Lydgate's Death of Hector, Lydgate Newsletter 1.2; rptd American Benedictine Rev 26.115 (use of Christine de Pisan).

Wilson R H, Manual, 3.777.

Norton-Smith, Geoffrey Chaucer, London and Boston 1974, pp 168, 185 (discusses sources for L's description of theater at Troy).

Meek M E, trans, Guido delle Colonne, Historia Destructionis Troiae, Bloomington and London 1974, pp xi (L's sources), 268 and passim (notes compare [189] and Guido's Historia).

Sundwall M, The Destruction of Troy Chaucer's Troilus and Criseyde and Lydgate's Troy Book, RES ns 26.313 ([189] may have influenced the Destruction).

Other Scholarly Problems. Sommer H O, The Recuyell of the Hystoryes of Troye, London 1894, 1.xl (argues [189] most mediaeval of Troy stories and also best).

Courthope, 1.322, 331 (notes [189] is typical of L's habit of self-criticism).

Chambers, 2.208 n2 (suggests [189] typical of mediaeval misconceptions about classical stage).

Hammond E P, Lydgate and the Duchess of Gloucester, Angl 27.381 (considers [189] illustrative of L's relation to patronage system).

Legouis E, Geoffrey Chaucer, London 1913, p 26 (believes poem throws light on Chaucer the man).
Wylie J H, The Reign of Henry 5, Cambridge 1914–29, 1.277n; 2.1n; 3.426 (offers [189] as evidence for events in lives of Henry 5, Oldcastle, and others).
Tatlock J S P, The Siege of Troy in Elizabethan Literature, PMLA 30.673 (notes popularity of [189] in Shakespeare's time).
Curry W C, The ME Ideal of Personal Beauty as Found in the Metrical Romances Chronicles and Legends of the 13, 14, and 15 Cent, Baltimore 1916, p 10.
Brie F, Mittelalter u Antike bei Lydgate, EStn 64.261 (notes mixture of mediaevalism and humanism in [189] and importance of L to Eng humanism).
Rathborne I F, The Meaning of Spenser's Fairyland, CUS 131.197 (finds in poem ideas common with Renaissance poets).
Tillyard, The Eng Renaissance; Fact or Fiction, London 1952, pp 32, 53 (argues attitude toward women is Renaissance but poem itself is mediaeval); The Eng Epic and Its Background, Oxford 1954, p 202 (considers poem very mediaeval).
Bonner F W, The Genesis of the Chaucer Apocrypha, SP 48.461 (mentions poem as representative of L's attitude toward Chaucer).
Wickham G, Early Eng Stages 1300 to 1660, London and N Y 1959, 1.192, 321 (argues L's description of theater in Troy is actually his own mummings), 302 (discusses definitions of comedy and tragedy in [189]).
Renoir A, John Lydgate Poet of the Transition, Eng Miscellany 11.14 (L is suspicious of antiquity in [189]); Attitudes to Women in Lydgate's Poetry, ESts 42.9; RenoirLydgate, pp 62, 66 (attitude toward classical antiquity), 82, 86 (attitude toward women), 96, 100 (notes nationalism and pro-Trojan bias).
Greaves M, The Blazon of Honour, N Y 1964, p 35 (Hector demonstrates the contemporary idea of chivalry).
Sacharoff M, The Traditions of the Troy-Story Heroes and the Problem of Satire in Troilus and Cressida, Shakespeare Stud 6.125 (heroes in [189] are presented in a favorable light).
Studer J, History as Moral Instruction John Lydgate's Record of Troie Toun, Emporia State Research Stud 19(issue 1).8 (use of Fortune in [189]).
PearsallLydgate, pp 129 and passim (discusses L's use of topics for amplification), 134 (discusses the passages about women), 136 (discusses L's descriptions of times and seasons), 138 (political advice in [189] is conventional).
Strohm P, Storie Spelle Geste Romaunce Tragedie Generic Distinctions in the ME Troy Narratives, Spec 46.351 (L regards [189] as authentic history).
Scattergood V J, Politics and Poetry in the 15th Cent, London 1971, pp 44 (notes pro-Trojan bias in [189]), 287 ([189] a mirror for princes).
Bornstein D, Chivalric Idealism in Lydgate's Troy Book, Lydgate Newsletter 1.8 (L values the idealism of chivalry but not its militarism).
Pearsall D and E Salter, Landscapes and Seasons of the Medieval World, Toronto 1973, p 193 (landscape detail taken from painting).
Benson, The Ancient World in John Lydgate's Troy Book, American Benedictine Rev 24.299 (L attempts in [189] to present an accurate picture of the ancient world).
Literary Criticism. Ten Brink 1893, 2(pt 1).224 (discusses graphic descriptions and expression of psychological conditions).
Sommer, Recuyell, 1.xl (considers [189] best of all mediaeval Troy stories).
Jusserand J J, Histoire Litteraire du Peuple Anglais, Paris 1896, 1.518 (insists on lifelessness of poem).
Brandes G, William Shakespeare, London 1898, 2.192 (notes L's ability to handle satire).
Wagner C H A, The Seege of Troy, N Y 1899, p xxv (believes poem the most poetic of all Troy legends in Eng).
CHEL, 2.201.
Reufs F, Das Naturgefühl bei Lydgate, Arch 122.269 (concludes monasticism ruins L's originality).
Knowlton E C, Nature in ME, JEGP 20.186 (believes treatment of nature in poem is typical of L).
Bennett H S, The Author and His Public in the 14 and 15 Cents, E&S 23.7 (points to [189] as example of L's lamentable fecundity); Bennett OHEL, pp 111, 139, 141 (regrets volume of poem).
Hinton N D, A Study of the Medieval Poems Relating the Destruction of Troy, DA 17.2010 (has a chapter on [189]).
Rossi, p 99.
Pearsall D, Gower and Lydgate, London 1969, p 26 and passim (discusses the rhetoric); PearsallLydgate, pp 125 (long discussion mainly on L's techniques of amplification), 41, 98, 99, 101, 181.
Benson, The Medieval Eng Hist of Troy, DAI

31.6539A (has a chapter on [189]).
General References. SchirmerLydgate, p 36 and passim; trans Keep, p 42 and passim.
Pearsall D, The Eng Chaucerians, in Chaucer and Chaucerians, ed D S Brewer, Univ Alabama 1966, p 212.
Bibliography. Lowndes W T, Bibliographer's Manual, ed H G Bohn, London 1864, 3.1419.
SchirmerLydgate, p 227; trans Keep, p 261.
Edwards A S G, A Lydgate Biblio 1928–68, BB 27.98.

[190] SCOTTISH FRAGMENTS INSERTED IN TROY BOOK.

MS of Fragment A. 1, Camb Univ Kk.5.30, ff 11a–19a (596 lines corresponding to Troy Book 1.876; mostly 16 cent); Pt 2, ff 28a–71a (extracts copied in 1612).
MSS of Fragment B. 2, Bodl 21722, ff 290a–300b (lines 1–918), 307a–336b (lines 1181–1562 continuing to line 3118) (1475–1525); 3, Camb Univ Kk.5.30, ff 304b–308a (mostly 16 cent; lines 1–1562). See under [189] for all 3 MSS.
Brown-Robbins, no *8; Robbins-Cutler, no *298.5.
Editions. Horstmann C, Barbours des schottischen Nationaldichters Legendensammlung, Heilbronn 1881, frag A on p 218; frag B on p 229 (both texts).
Scholarship. See under [189] above.

[191] VENUS MASS (also LOVER'S MASS).

MS. Bodl 3896 (Fairfax 16), ff 314a–316b (1425–75).
Brown-Robbins, Robbins-Cutler, no 4186.
Editions. Simmons T F, The Lay Folks Mass Book, EETS 71.390.
Hammond E P, The Lover's Mass, JEGP 7.96; Eng Verse between Chaucer and Surrey, London 1927, p 210.
Belles Lettres Series 18, Boston.
Authorship. Warton T, History of Eng Poetry, ed W Hazlitt, London 1871, 3.60.
Brandl, 2.692 (doubts L's authorship).
Hammond, JEGP 7.95 (attributes poem to L on basis of similarities between prose conclusion and prologue of [47] bk 3; considers verse Lydgatian).

[192] SONG OF VERTU (also THE TRIUMPH OF VIRTUE).

MSS. 1, Bodl 6943 (Ashmole 59), f 184a–b (lacks stanzas 1–5; 1447–56); 2, Bodl 11951 (Rawl C.86), ff 79b–81a (1475–1500); 3, Camb Univ Kk.1.6, ff 203b–205b (15 cent); 4, Jesus Camb 56, ff 36a–37b (15 cent); 5, Trinity Camb 601, ff 298a–299b (1461–83); 6, Harley 2251, ff 151a–152b (Brown-Robbins begins at f 146a; 3 extra stanzas between 3 and 5; 1464–83); 7, Harley 2255, ff 12a–14a (1448?–49?); 8, Huntington Libr HM.140 (formerly Phillipps 8299), ff 88b–90a (1450–80).
Brown-Robbins, Robbins-Cutler, no 401.
Hammond E P, Two British Museum MSS, Angl 28.1 (detailed study of MS 6).
Manly & Rickert, 1.241, 433 (describes MSS 6, 8).
Editions. Halliwell PPS 2.216 (MS 7).
MacCracken EETS 192.835 (MS 7; collations from all MSS).
Language. Skeat B M, The Lamentatyon of Mary Magdaleyne, Cambridge 1897, p 9 (believes use of word Rayle with blood is typical of L).
Versification. Reger, pp 42, 78 (finds certain epic caesurae in 14.42 percent lines).
Authorship. MacCracken TPSL, appendix 2.xxvii; rptd EETSES 107.xxx.
SchirmerLydgate, p 233; trans Keep, p 272.
Sources and Literary Relations. Gattinger, p 38 (notes Biblical influence).
Other Scholarly Problem. Duschl, pp 47, 88 (classifies proverbs).
Literary Criticism. Gattinger, p 16 (notes use of nature images to illustrate didactic theme).
General References. SchirmerLydgate, p 174; trans Keep, p 199.
PearsallLydgate, p 214.

[193] VEXILLA REGIS PRODEUNT.

MS. Cambridge Univ Kk.1.6, ff 198a–199a (15 cent).
Brown-Robbins, no 2833.
Edition. MacCracken EETSES 107.25.
Authorship. MacCracken TPSL, appendix 2.xxvii; rptd EETSES 107.xxx.
SchirmerLydgate, p 232; trans Keep, p 270.
Sources and Literary Relations. Wehrle W O, The Macaronic Hymn Tradition in Medieval Eng Literature, Washington 1933, p 140 (argues poem based on version of Vexilla regis prodeunt older than that in Roman breviary).
SchirmerLydgate, p 156; trans Keep, p 180 (also argues for antiquity of version of Latin hymn used by L [NB: Latin poem printed in present form by G M Dreres, Ein Jahrtausend lateinischer Hymnendictung, Leipzig 1909, 1.38]).
Other Scholarly Problem. Wylie J H, The Reign of

Henry 5, Cambridge 1914–29, 2.137n (believes poem throws light on care of armor).
Literary Criticism. PearsallLydgate, p 260 (discusses L as a translator and compares his version of the hymn with another ME version).

[194] WHO SEITH THE BEST SHALL NEVER REPENT (also SAY THE BEST AND NEVER REPENT).

MS. Bodl 1475 (Laud Misc 598), f 49^{a-b} (15 cent; introd ballade, [195], on f 49^a).
Brown-Robbins, Robbins-Cutler, no 4042.
Edition. MacCracken EETS 192.796.
Authorship. MacCracken TPSL, appendix 2.xxiv; rptd EETSES 107.xxvii.
Brown-Robbins, no 4042 (lists poem as attributed to L).
SchirmerLydgate, p 233; trans Keep, p 272.
PearsallLydgate, p 210 (probably not by L).
General References. SchirmerLydgate, pp 174, 178n; trans Keep, pp 199, 204n.
PearsallLydgate, p 210.

[195] BALLADE INTRODUCTORY TO WHO SEITH THE BEST SHALL NEVER REPENT.

MS. Bodl 1475 (Laud Misc 598), f 49^a (15 cent).
Brown-Robbins, no 4097; Robbins-Cutler, no 102.5.
Edition. MacCracken EETS 192.795.
Scholarship. See under [194] above.

[196] WHY ARTOW FROWARD (also IN CRUCE SUM PRO TE, A PRAYER UPON THE CROSS, and UPON THE CROSS).

MSS. 1, Bodl 798 (Laud Misc 683), ff 14^b–15^b (15 cent); 2, Bodl 1475 (Laud Misc 598), f 60^{a-b} (Brown-Robbins has f 50^a; 15 cent); 3, Bodl 4119 (Hatton 73), f 4^a (stanza 5 only; 1425–75); 4, Bodl 14526 (Rawl poet F.32), f 31^b (1450–1500); 5, St John's Oxf 56, f 84^a (a torn fragment in very poor shape; 1475–1500); 6, Camb Univ Hh.4.12, f 85^a (1475–1500); 7, Camb Univ Kk.1.6, ff 196^b–197^a (15 cent); 8, Jesus Camb 56, f 71^{a-b} (Brown-Robbins has f 70^b; 15 cent); 9, Cotton Calig A.ii, f 134^b (1400–50); 10, Harley 2255, f 111^{a-b} (1448?–49?); 11, Harley 5396, f 294^a (1450–1500); 12, BM Addit 5465, f 67^b (1400–50); 13, BM Addit 29729, f 131^{a-b} (4 stanzas; Stowe, 1558); 14, Huntington Libr HM.140 (formerly Phillipps 8299), ff 83^b–84^a (6 stanzas; 1450–80).

Brown-Robbins, Robbins-Cutler, no 3845.
Manly & Rickert, 1.433 (discusses MS 14).
Stevens, edn, p 351 (dates MS 12 at ca 1500).
Editions. Furnivall F J, Political and Religious Poems, EETS 15.141 (MS 6).
Fehr B, Die Lieder des Fairfax MS, Arch 106.63 (MS 12).
MacCracken, EETSES 107.252 (MS 1; collations from all MSS except 3, 11, 12).
Greene E E Carols, p 187 (MS 12).
Stevens J, Music and Poetry in the Early Tudor Court, London 1961, p 371 (MS 12; with brief notes and glosses at foot of page; includes burden not by L).
Modernization. Watts N, Love Songs of Sion, N Y Cincinnati and Chicago 1924, p 63 (modernization of lines 1–16, 25–32).
Authorship. MacCracken TPSL, appendix 2.xxvii; rptd EETSES 107.xxx.
SchirmerLydgate, p 232; trans Keep, p 270.
General References. SchirmerLydgate, p 161; trans Keep, p 185 (considers poem exceptionally good).
PearsallLydgate, p 265.

[197] EXAMPLES AGAINST WOMEN (also FALL OF PRINCES, EXTRACTS).

MS. Bodl 1782 (Digby 181), ff 8^b–10^a (15 cent).
Brown-Robbins, Robbins-Cutler, no 3744.
Edwards A S G, Selections from Lydgate's Fall of Princes A Checklist, Libr 5s 26.341 (lists extracts).
Edition. MacCracken EETS 192.442.
Abstract. Utley CR, no 317.
Authorship. MacCracken EETSES 107.xvi.
SchirmerLydgate, p 229; trans Keep, p 266.
Sources and Literary Relations. Utley CR, no 317 (gives equivalent stanzas in [47]).
SchirmerLydgate, p 82; trans Keep, p 97 (mentions relation to [47]).
Other Scholarly Problem. Renoir A, Attitudes to Women in Lydgate's Poetry, ESts 42.8 (antifeminist).
General References. Rogers K M, The Troublesome Helpmate, Seattle and London 1966, p 71 (sentiments are only a literary exercise).
PearsallLydgate, p 217.

[198] AGAINST THE HORNS OF WOMEN (also A DYTE OF WOMENHIS HORNYS, BALLAD ON THE FORKED HEADDRESSES OF LADIES, and HORNS AWAY).

MSS. 1, Bodl 798 (Laud Misc 683), ff 53^a–54^b

(9 stanzas; 15 cent); 2, Bodl 6943 (Ashmole 59), ff 33ᵇ–34ᵇ (7 stanzas; 1547–56); 3, Bodl 11951 (Rawl C.86), ff 88ᵇ–89ᵇ (8 stanzas; 1480–1500); 4, Camb Univ Hh.4.12, ff 84ª–85ª (9 stanzas; 1490–1510); 5, Jesus Camb 56, ff 27ᵇ–29ª (no envoy; 15 cent); 6, Trinity Camb 599, ff 206ª–207ª (Brown-Robbins has 206ᵇ; 1500–25); 7, Harley 2251, f 13ᵇ (stanzas 1–4; 1464–83); 8, Harley 2255, ff 6ª–7ª (9 stanzas; 1448?–49?); 9, BM Addit 34360, f 73ª (stanzas 1–4; 1461–83); 10, Leyden Univ Vossius 9, f 102ᵇ (15 cent; listed by Robbins-Cutler but not by van Dorsten).
Brown-Robbins, Robbins-Cutler, no 2625.
Hammond E P, Two British Museum MSS, Angl 28.1 (detailed study of MSS 7, 9).
Utley CR, no 232 (questions earlier assumption that poem was also in MS 10).
van Dorsten J A, The Leyden Lydgate MS, Scriptorium 14.314 (does not list [198] in MS 10).
Editions. [Nicolas H,] A Chronicle of London, London 1827, p 270 (MS 8).
Halliwell PPS 2.46 (from MS 1); rptd F W Fairholt, PPS 27.52.
Rel Ant, 1.79 (MS 1).
Furnivall F J, Political Religious and Love Poems, EETS 15.45; rvsd edn 15.73 (MS 4); rptd W A Neilson and K G T Webster, Chief British Poets of the 14 and 15 Cent, Boston 1916, p 222.
Hammond E P, Eng Verse between Chaucer and Surrey, Durham 1927, p 112 (MS 8).
MacCracken EETS 192.662 (MS 1; collations from all MSS).
Selection. Douce F, Illustrations of Shakespeare and of Ancient Manners, London 1807 and 1839, 1.201 (prints lines 33–48 from MS 8, along with early illust).
Abstracts. Fairholt F W, Costume in England, London 1846, p 187 (gives gist of poem).
Utley CR, no 232 (gives summary of poem).
Textual Matters. Gattinger, p 83.
Versification. Reger, pp 41, 77 (finds certain epic caesurae in 11.11 percent lines).
Date. Utley CR, no 232 (1390–1449).
Authorship. MacCracken TPSL, appendix 2.xvi; rptd EETSES 107.xviii.
SchirmerLydgate, p 229; trans Keep, p 266.
Seaton, p 188 (argues author is Richard Roos).
Sources and Literary Relations. Gattinger, pp 4, 8, 48, 58, 66, 72 (discusses influence of Alanus de Insulis, the Dit des Cornetes, ed A Jubinal,

Jongleurs et Trouvères, p 87; Jean de Meung; Chaucer).
Schirmer W F, Das Ende des Mittelalters in England, Kleine Schriften, Tübingen 1950, p 25 and passim (discusses relationship to ship-of-fools literature).
SchirmerLydgate, pp 82, 84; trans Keep, pp 97, 99 (discusses influence of Alanus de Insulis).
Scattergood V J, Politics and Poetry in the 15th Cent, London 1971, p 341 (notes L's use of learned references in the poem).
Robbins R H, Manual, 5.1460 (XIII [136–138]).
Other Scholarly Problems. Duschl, p 88 (classifies proverb).
Seaton, p 188 (argues poem contains name anagrams).
Literary Criticism. Gattinger, p 83 (discusses style).
Knowlton E C, Nature in ME, JEGP 20.186 (finds poem typical of L's manner).
SchirmerLydgate, p 82; trans Keep, p 97 (discusses tone of poem).
Seaton, p 188.
PearsallLydgate, p 217 (notes L's seriousness though the topic lends itself to light satire).

[199] THE WORLD IS VANITY (also THE WORLD IS VARIABLE).

MS. Harley 2255, ff 126ᵇ–128ª (1448?–49?).
Brown-Robbins, no 3797.
Edition. MacCracken EETS 192.844.
Authorship. MacCracken TPSL, appendix 2.xxvii; rptd EETSES 107.xxxi.
SchirmerLydgate, p 233; trans Keep, p 272.
Sources and Literary Relations. SchirmerLydgate, p 175; trans Keep, p 201 (mentions relation to [47]).
Other Scholarly Problem. Mullet C F, John Lydgate: a Mirror of Medieval Medicine, Bull of the Hist of Medicine 22.403 (mentions poem as representative of contemporary preoccupation with death).
General Reference. PearsallLydgate, p 214 (poem is virtually unintelligible).

[200] FRAGMENT IN STYLE OF LYDGATE: THE WORLD IS VANITY.

MS. Caius Camb 804, fragment (a slip of vellum; 15 cent).
Brown-Robbins, no *25; Robbins-Cutler, no *3844.8.

INDEX

A bold-face number indicates the main reference in the Commentary; a number preceded by B indicates the reference in the Bibliography. Titles are indexed under the first word following an article. Indexed are all literary works and their authors, names of early printers, and main subdivisions. No attempt has been made to index the names of characters and places in the literary works nor the names of scholars.

AB Inimicis, see *Prayer for Henry VI, His Queen and People, A*
Abbreviations, Tables of, 1923, 1939, 1940, 2019, 2071
ABC (Chaucer), 1886
ABC of Aristotle, 1762
Aboue All Th[i]ng Thow Arte a Kyng, **1749,** B2003
Abowt the Fyld Thei Pyped Ful Right, **1745,** B1956
Abyde I Hope It Be the Beste, **1748,** B1996
Accord of Reason and Sensuality in the Fear of Death, see *Assembly of Gods*
Adam and Eve Did Geve Concent (James Ryman), **1747,** B1988
Adam and Eve Thatte Were Vnwyse (James Ryman), **1746,** B1980
Adam Bell, Clim of the Clough, and William of Cloudesly, 1758, **1769,** B2040
Adam Our Fader Was in Blis, **1745,** B1955
Adulterous Falmouth Squire (tale), 1762, 1765, 1773
Advent, Carols of, **1745,** B1944
Advice to an Old Gentleman Who Wished for a Young Wife, see *Advice to Lovers*
Advice to Lovers, **1873,** B2131
Advice to the Several Estates, see *Duodecim Abusiones*
Advice to Tittle-Tattlers, see *Guard Your Tongue*
Against Marriage, **1875,** B2132
Against Millers and Bakers, **1876,** B2133
Against Proud Men (Fall of Princes, Extracts), B2101
Against the Horns of Women, **1919,** B2174
Against Women, see *Beware of Deceitful Women*
Agincourt, Battle of, 1790
Agincourt Carol, see *Owre Kynge Went Forth to Normandy*
A-Growing (Johnson, "Lady Mary Ann"), **1791,** B2055
Al Holy Chyrch Was Bot a Thrall, **1746,** B1962
Alain de Lille, 1895
Alas, Good Man, Most Yow Be Kyst, **1750,** B2014
Alcibiades, Episode of (Fall of Princes, Extracts), B2101
Ale Mak Many a Mane to Styk at a Brere, **1749,** B2009
Ale Seller, see *Ballade on an Ale Seller*
Ale Seller Become Constant, see *Ballade on an Ale Seller Become Constant*

Alison and Willie, B2068
All Heyle Mary and Well You Be, **1746,** B1979
All That I May Swink or Swete, **1749,** B2006
All This Day Ic Han Sought, **1750,** B2013
All This Worlde Was Ful of Grace, **1745,** B1949
Allas Wo Sal Myn Herte Slaken, **1751,** B2017
Alle Thynges in Mesure, see *A Song of Just Mesure*
Alle ȝe Mouwen of Ioye Synge, **1746,** B1977
Allison Gross, **1800,** B2061
Allusions to Chaucer (Fall of Princes, Extracts), B2101
Als I Lay up-on a Nith, **1746,** B1970
Als I Me Rode This Endre Dai, **1750,** B2013
Als þu Were Marter & Mayd Clene (John Audelay), **1747,** B1992
Amerous Balade, **1814,** B2078
Amor et Pecunia, 1814, B2078
Amor Vincit Omnia Mentiris Quod Pecunia, see *Amor et Pecunia*
Amorous Carols, **1750,** B2012
An Old Said Sawe: On-Knowen On-Kyste, **1748,** B1997
Ancient and Modern Scots Songs (David Herd), 1791
And by a Chapell As Y Came, **1748,** B1994
And Loue þi God Ouer Al þyng (John Audelay), **1748,** B1994
And Save Thys Flowre Wyche Ys Owre Kyng, **1751,** B2017
Andrew Lammie, B2067
Anelida and Arcite (Chaucer), 1907
Angelle Bright (James Ryman), *An,* **1747,** B1985
Angelle Came Vnto Thatte Mayde (James Ryman), *An,* **1747,** B1985
Angelle Seide to Thatte Meyde So Fre (James Ryman), *An,* **1747,** B1985
Angelle That Was Fayre and Bryght (James Ryman), *An,* **1747,** B1985
Anglo-Saxon Chronicle, 1832
Annunciation, Carols of the, **1747,** B1982
Anoder Yere Hit May Betyde, **1746,** B1963
Anticlaudianus, 1883
Apparition of Mrs. Veal (Defoe), 1789
Appeal to Gloucester, **1847,** B2112
Archie o Cawfield, B2058
As Aaron Yerde wtoute Moisture (James Ryman), **1746,** B1979

2177

2178 INDEX

As Holy Kyrke Makys Mynd, **1745**, B1949
As I Cam by þ Way, **1745**, B1956
As I Lay Vpon a Nyȝt, **1747**, B1982
As I Me Rode in a Mey Mornyng, **1749**, B2001
As I Me Ros in On Morwenyng, **1746**, B1969
As I Went in a Mery Mornyng, **1749**, B2000
As I Went Me Fore to Solase, **1749**, B2000
As I Went on Yole Day in Oure Prosession, **1750**, B2015
As I Went This Enders Day, **1746**, B1973
As Longe before Prophesy Seyde (James Ryman), **1747**, B1984
As Storys Wryght and Specyfy, **1746**, B1962
Asheton, William, 1778, 1779
Assemble de Dyeus, see *Assembly of Gods*
Assembly of Gods, **1815**, B2079
At a Place Where He Me Sett, **1750**, B2010
At the Begynnyng of the Mete, **1746**, B1966
Att Domys Day When We Shall Ryse, **1749**, B1999
Aungell fro Hevyn Gen Lyth, An, **1747**, B1988
Aungell Seide of High Degree (James Ryman), **1747**, B1984
Aungell Seyde of High Degree (James Ryman), **1747**, B1984
Auctor of Helthe Criste Haue in Myende (James Ryman), **1745**, B1958
Audelay, John, 1744, 1747, 1749, 1750, 1942
Auld Matrons, B2068
Ave Jesse Virgula, **1817**, B2080
Ave Maria, see *Salutacio Angelica*
Ave Regina Celorum, **1818**, 1888, B2081
Awntyrs of Arthure at the Terne Wathelvne, 1799

Babe Is Born of Hey Nature, A (John Audelay?), **1746**, B1962
Babe Is Born Our Blysse to Brynge, A, **1746**, B1971
Babylon, or, *The Bonnie Banks o Fordie*, B2058
Baffled Knight, **1780**, B2044
Bailiff's Daughter of Islington, B2049
Balade in Commendation of Our Lady, **1882**, B2140
Balade of Oure Ladye by Lidegate, see *Gloriosa Dicta Sunt de Te*
Ballad by John Lucas, **1818**, 1826, B2081; see also *Death's Warning*
Ballad of a Tyrannical Husband, 1758
Ballad of Good Counsel, see *Wikked Tongue*
Ballad of Twelfth Day, see *Twelfth Day*
Ballad on the Forked Headdresses of Ladies, see *Against the Horns of Women*
Ballade at the Reverence of Our Lady, see *Ballade in Commendation of Our Lady*
Ballade de Bone Conseyll, see *Four Things That Make a Man a Fool: Balade de Bone Counseyle*
Ballade in Despyte the Flemynges, see *Song against Flemings*
Ballade Introductory to Who Seith the Best Shall Never Repent, **1918**, B2174
Ballade of Her That Hath All Virtues, A, **1818**, B2081
Ballade of Jack Hare, A, **1859**, B2123
Ballade on a New Year's Gift of an Eagle Presented to King Henry VI, see *Eagle as New Year Gift*
Ballade on an Ale Seller, **1813**, B2078

Ballade on an Ale Seller Become Constant, **1813**, B2078
Ballade on the Image of Our Lady, **1856**, B2121
Ballade on Women's Chastity (Fall of Princes, Extracts), B2101
Ballade per Antiphrasim, see *Ballade on an Ale Seller Become Constant*
Ballads, **1753**, B2019; Chronological List of Balled Sources, **1758**, B2037; see also Background Books, B2019; Bibliographies, B2020; Surveys and Histories of Ballad Research, B2021; Guides to Ballad Variants, B2021; Editions, B2021; Studies, B2024; Popular Carols, B2070
Ballads Collected in the Nineteenth Century, **1803**, B2063
Banner of St. Edmund, **1829**, B2096
Barbour, John, 1917
Bargain of Judas, see *Judas*
Barker, John, 1942
Baron o Leys, B2067
Baron of Brackley, B2063
Battle of Agincourt, 1790
Battle of Agincourt, 1850
Battle of Culloden, 1791
Battle of Harlaw, **1803**, B2065
Battle of Otterburn, **1774**, 1775, B2042
Battle of Philiphaugh, B2066
Battle of Towton, 1750
Be Glad Lordynges Beþe More & Lesse, **1745**, B1951
Be Mery & Suffer As I The Vise, **1748**, B1997
Beaumont and Fletcher, 1789
Beccaria, Antonio, 1810
Bede, 1813; *Historia*, 1813
Beggar-Laddie, B2069
Behold and See O Lady Free (James Ryman), **1746**, B1977
Behold What Lyfe That We Ryne Ine, **1746**, B1968
Behold & Se How That Nature (James Ryman), **1745**, B1955
Benedic Anima Mea Domino, see *Psalm 102* (Lydgate)
Benedicamus Domino, 1744
Benedictus Deus in Donis Suis, **1819**, B2081
Benoît de Sainte-Maure, 1914
Bent Sae Brown, B2065
Benyng Lady Blessed Mote Thow Be, **1746**, B1977
Beowulf, 1785
Bessy Bell and Mary Gray, B2066
Bestiary, 1824, 1872
Betrayed Maiden's Lament (carol), 1763
Beware of Deceitful Women, **1820**, B2082
Beware of Doublenesse, **1828**, B2094
Bewick and Graham, **1790**, B2054
Bi Thi Burthe þᵘ Blessed Lord, **1745**, B1954
Bible, 1876, 1882, 1899, 1904
Bibliography, 1921
Billy Magee Magaw, 1781
Bitter Withy (carol), 1804, **1806**, B2070
Blancheflour and Jellyflorice, B2069
Blessed Virgin, see *Fragment of Hymn to the Blessed Virgin*
Blessid Mot Be Oure Heuene Quene (John Audelay), **1749**, B2004

Blessid Mot þᵘ Be þᵘ Berd So Bryʒt (John Audelay), **1746,** B1975
Blind Harry, 1791
Blowyng Was Mad for Gret Game, **1748,** B1997
Blynde Man Eteth Many a Flye, see *Beware of Deceitful Women*
Blyssid Be þat Mayde Mary, **1745,** B1949
Boar's Head, Carols of the, 1744, **1746,** B1965
Boar's Head Carol, 1744, 1804
Boccaccio, 1810, 1838, 1839, 1841, 1904; *De casibus virorum,* 1810, 1838
Boethius, 1900
Boethius, Episode of (Fall of Princes, Extracts), B2101
Boke of Marchalsie, 1771
Bold Fisherman (carol), 1804
Bold Pedlar and Robin Hood, B2053
Boleyn, Anne, 1748, 1772
Bonnie Annie, B2063
Bonnie Banks o Fordie, see *Babylon*
Bonnie House o Airlie, B2053
Bonnie James Campbell, B2060
Bonny Baby Livingston, B2063
Bonny Barbara Allan, B2054
Bonny Bee Hom, B2062
Bonny Birdy, B2062
Bonny Earl of Murray, B2055
Bonny Hind, B2059
Bonny John Seton, B2066
Bonny Lass of Anglesey, B2060
Bonny Lizie Baillie, B2054
Book of Courtesy (Boke of Curtasie), 1765
Book of the Duchess (Chaucer), 1800
Boris Hed in Hondes I Brynge, **1746,** B1965
Boris Hede in Hond I Bryng, **1746,** B1966
"Borys hed haue we in brought" (carol fragment), B2018
Borys Hede That We Bryng Here, **1746,** B1966
Bothe Yonge and Olde Take Hede of This (James Ryman), **1745,** B1955
Bothwell Bridge, B2066
Bowght & Sold Full Traytorsly, **1746,** B1973
Boy and the Mantle, **1783,** B2046
Braes o Yarrow, B2058
Bring Us in No Browne Bred for That Is Made of Brane, **1749,** B2009
Broom of Cowdenknows, B2058
Broomfield Hill, B2059
Broughty Wa's, B2068
Brown Adam, B2062
Brown, Anna Gordon, see Mrs. Brown of Falkland
Brown Girl, B2054
Brown, Mrs. of Falkland, see under Mrs. Brown
Brown Robbin, B2062
Brown Robyn's Confession, B2065
Bunyan, John, 1887
Burd Ellen and Young Tamlane, B2064
Burd Isabel and Earl Patrick, B2068
Burgh, Benedict, 1761, 1898, 1899; *Cato Minor,* 1761
Burns, Robert, 1791
Bycorne and Chychevache, **1820,** B2082
Bydell, John, 1769

Bysshope Scrope That Was So Wyse, **1750,** B2010

Calendar, A, **1821,** B2083
Call to Devotion, A, see *On Kissing at Verbum Caro (Second Version)*
Cambridge, see *Verses on Cambridge'*
Canace and Macareus, Episode of (Fall of Princes, Extracts), B2101
Canterbury Tales (Chaucer), 1810, 1873, 1901, 1904
Candlemas, Carols of, **1746,** B1968
Capella, Martianus, 1904
Captain Car, 1757, **1778,** 1786, 1803, B2044
Captain Ward and the Rainbow, B2052
Captain Wedderburn's Courtship, 1764, B2059
Carmina Burana, 1941
Carnal and the Crane, 1758, **1804,** B2064
Carol for St. Stephen's Day, A, see *St. Stephen and Herod*
Carols, **1743,** B1940; of Advent, **1745,** B1944; of the Nativity, **1745,** B1945; of the Saints of the Christmas Season, **1746,** B1959; of the New Year, **1746,** B1962; of the Epiphany, **1746,** B1963; of the Boar's Head, **1746,** B1965; of Holly and Ivy, **1746,** B1967; of Candlemas, **1746,** B1968; Lullaby, **1746,** B1968; and 2017; of the Passion, **1746,** B1972; of and to the Virgin, **1746,** B1974; of the Joys of Mary, **1747,** B1981; of the Annunciation, **1747,** B1982; of Joseph, **1747,** B1985; of the Virgin's Motherhood, **1747,** B1986; of Christ's Pleading, **1747,** B1986; of Christ, **1747,** B1987; of the Trinity, **1747,** B1988; on the Well of Mercy, **1747,** B1990; of Purgatory, **1747,** B1991; Litany, **1747,** B1991; of Saints, **1747,** B1991; of the Eucharist, **1747,** B1992; Corpus Christi, **1748,** B1993; of a Mass, **1748,** B1994; of Religious Counsel, **1748,** B1994; of Moral Counsel, **1748,** B1996; of Repentance, **1749,** B1998; of Doomsday, **1749,** B1999; of Mortality, **1749,** B1999; Satirical, **1749,** B2001; of Women, **1749,** B2003; of Marriage, **1749,** B2005; of Childhood, **1749,** B2007; Picaresque, **1749,** B2007; Convivial, **1749,** B2008; of Hunting, **1750,** B2010; Political, **1750,** B2010; Complaint, **1750,** B2012; Amorous, **1750,** B2012; Humorous, **1751,** B2016; Miscellaneous, **1751,** B2017; Fragments, **1752,** B2017; see also Background Books, B1940; Descriptive List of MSS Containing Five or More Carols, B1941; General Treatments of the Carol, B1944
Cartae Versificatae, see *Charters of the Kings of England*
Catherine of Aragon, 1748, 1772
Cato Minor (Benedict Burgh), 1761
Cavendish, John, 1840
Caxton, William, 1767, 1771, 1915
Charles VII, 1890
Charlie MacPherson, B2067
Charters of the Kings of England (also *Cartae Versificatae*), **1863,** B2125
Chaucer, Alice, 1887
Chaucer, Geoffrey, 1773, 1782, 1787, 1794, 1798, 1800, 1810, 1811, 1819, 1820, 1823, 1824, 1826,

1829, 1830, 1833, 1838, 1839, 1840, 1841, 1842, 1843, 1845, 1847, 1852, 1859, 1866, 1871, 1872, 1873, 1878, 1882, 1883, 1886, 1900, 1904, 1907, 1909, 1910, 1912, 1915, 1916, 1917; *ABC*, 1886; *Anelida and Arcite;* 1907; *Book of the Duchess*, 1800; *Canterbury Tales*, 1810; 1873, 1901, 1904; *Clerk's Tale*, 1787; *Complaint of Mars*, 1907; *House of Fame*, 1907; *Knight's Tale*, 1907; *Legend of Good Women*, 1838, 1907; *Man of Law's Tale*, 1795; *Merchant's Tale*, 1782, 1783; *Monk's Tale*, 1838, 1840; *Prioress's Tale*, 1830; *Reeve's Tale*, 1798; *Squire's Tale*, 1907; *Troilus and Criseyde*, 1773, 1798, 1841, 1907, 1916; *Wife of Bath's Tale*, 1820, 1873
Chaucer, Allusions to (Fall of Princes, Extracts), B2101
Chepman and Myllar, 1767, 1768
Cherry Tree Carol, **1804,** B2064
Chevy Chase, see *Hunting of the Cheviot*
Child and His Stepdame (tale), see *Friar and the Boy*
Child Is Boren amonges Man, A, **1745,** B1947
Child Jesus to Mary the Rose, see *Jesus to Blessed Virgin Rose of Womanhood*
Child Maurice, **1782,** B2047
Child of Bristowe, 1799
Child Owlet, B2069
Child Waters, 1758, 1787, 1790, B2046
Childe Ys Born of a Mayde, A, **1745,** B1954
Childhood, Carols of, **1749,** B2007
Childhood of Jesus, 1804, 1805
Childryn of Eve Both Grete and Small (Jame Ryman), **1746,** B1980
Christ, Carols of, **1747,** B1987
Christine de Pisan, 1833, 1915
Christmas Season, Carols of the Saints of the, see *Saints of the Christmas Season*
Christopher White, B2047
Christ's Pleading, Carols of, **1747,** B1986
Chronicle (Froissart), 1774
Chronological List of Ballad Sources, **1758,** B2037
Churl and the Bird, **1821,** B2084
Chyld Ys Born E-wys, A, **1746,** B1968
Cicero, 1876
Cicero, Episode of (Fall of Princes, Extracts), B2101
Clerk and the Nightingale, 1762
Clerk Colvill, 1790, **1798,** B2058
Clerk Saunders, 1758, 1790, **1798,** 1801, B2059
Clerke, Jon (of Great Torrington, Devon), 1749
Clerk's Tale, 1787
Clerk's Twa Sons o Owsenford, B2065
Clyde's Water, see *Mother's Malison*
Coble o Cargill, B2067
Cochrane, Elizabeth, see *Elizabeth Cochrane's Songbook*
Cock and the Precious Stone, see *Isopes Fabules*
Cock Hath Lowe Shoone, see *Guard Your Tongue*
Colin Cloute (Skelton), 1789
Collection of Diverting Songs, Epigrams, etc., 1791
Come My Dainty Doxeys, 1795
Come My Dere Spowse and Lady Free (James Ryman), **1747,** B1986
Comestor, Peter, 1817

Complaint, A (carol), **1750,** B2012
Complaint for Lack of Mercy, **1822,** B2085
Complaint for My Lady of Gloucester and Holland, A, 1810, **1848,** B2113
Complaint of a Lover's Life, see *Complaint of the Black Knight*
Complaint of Mars (Chaucer), 1907
Complaint of the Black Knight, **1822,** 1826, 1872, 1907, B2085
Complaynt Lydegate, see *Servant of Cupyde Forsaken*
Complaynt of Scotland, 1803
Compleynt, see *Supplicatio Amantis*
Compleynt That Crist Maketh of His Passioun, A, **1823,** B2087
Compleynt That Crist Maketh of His Passioun (Scottish Version), A, **1823,** B2088
Conceyued Man How May That Be by Reason Broght Abowte, **1747,** B1986
Concords of Company, see *Consulo Quisque Eris*
Confessio Amantis (Gower), 1771, 1838
Constantine, Episode of (Fall of Princes, Extracts), B2101
Consulo Quisque Eris, **1824,** 1834, B2088
Convivial Carols, **1749,** B2008
Copland, William, 1766, 1768, 1769
Cornish, John, 1942
Corpus Christi Carol, **1748,** 1758, **1771,** 1780, 1796, 1801, 1804, 1805, B1993 and 2041
Corpus Christi plays, 1892
Cort Mantel, 1783
Crafty Farmer, B2054
Crist Crid in Cradil Moder Ba Ba (John Audelay), **1746,** B1961
Criste Qui Lux Es Et Dies, **1824,** B2088
Cristes Passioun, see *Compleynt That Crist Maketh of His Passioun*
"... Cristus ..." (carol fragment), B2017
Crow and Pie, 1758, **1773,** B2042
Cruel Brother, B2058
Cruel Mother, 1782, **1789,** 1796, B2049
Cryst Kepe Vs All as He Well Can, **1745,** B1953
Cryste Made Mane Yn þis Maner of Wyse, **1748,** B1995
Culloden, Battle of, 1791
Curteys, Abbot William, 1832

Daemon Lover, see *James Harris*
Dan Joos, see *Legend of Dan Joos*
Dares, 1914
Daunce of Death, see *Daunce of Machabree*
Daunce of Machabree, **1824,** B2088
Daunce of Machabree with Five-Stanza Prologue, **1825,** B2090
David Herd: MSS British Museum Additional 22311–12 and Printed Editions of 1769 and 1776, **1797,** B2058
Dayly in Englond Meruels Be Fownd, 1749, B2006
De casibus virorum (Boccaccio), 1810, 1838
De Clerico et Puella, 1758
De ordine creaturarum (Isidore of Seville), 1759
de Guileville, see *Guillaume de Guileville*
De Profundis, see *On De Profundis*

De Tribus Virginibus Katarina, Margareta et Magdalena, see *Hymn to SS. Katherine, Margaret, and Magdalene*
Death of Parcy Reed, B2066
Death of Queen Jane, **1788,** B2051
Death's Warning, 1818, **1826,** B2091
Death's Warning to the World, see *Death's Warning*
Debate between the Body and the Soul, 1759
Debate of the Horse, Goose, and Sheep, **1854,** 1884, B2119
Deceyt Deceyvyth, see *Fall of Princes Bk 2.4432–38: Deceyt Deceyvyth*
Defense of Holy Church, **1854,** B2119
Defoe, Daniel, 1789
Deloney, Thomas, 1778, 1780
Demawnde by Lydgate, A, see *Amor et Pecunia*
Departyng of Thomas Chaucer, **1826,** B2091
Des cas des nobles hommes et femmes (Laurent de Premierfait), 1838
Descriptive List of MSS Containing Five or More Carols, B1941
Desguising of Dame Fortune, see *Mumming at London*
Destruccyon of Troye, see *Troy Book*
Destruction of Troy, 1914
Det Peruynkkle Hed Ykowmbyrght Owre Town, **1750,** B2010
Dethe Began By Cause of Syn, **1749,** B2001
Deus in Nomine Tuo Saluum Me Fac, **1827,** B2092
Devil's Nine Questions, 1761
Devowte Invocacioun to St. Denis, see *Prayer to St. Denis*
Dic Erodes Impie, **1746,** B1961
Dick o the Cow, B2058
Dictys, 1914
Dido, Episode of (Fall of Princes, Extracts), B2101
Dietary, **1827,** 1828, B2092
Dietary: A Doctrine for Pestilence, 1827, **1828,** B2094
Dietary and a Doctrine for Pestilence, A, see *Dietary*
Dietary in Disarranged Order, **1827,** B2094
Dievs Wous Garde Byewsser Tydynges Y Yow Bryng, **1745,** B1945
Disciplina Clericalis, 1859
Disticha Catonis, 1824, 1912
Distichs of Cato, 1761
Ditty against Haste, A, **1850,** B2114
Dives and Lazarus, 1804, **1805,** B2064
Doctryne for Pestilence, A, see *Dietary: A Doctrine for Pestilence*
Dolerous Pyte of Crystes Passioun, see *Tretyse of Crystys Passioun*
Doomsday, 1759
Doomsday, Carols of, **1749,** B1999
Doublenesse, see *Beware of Doublenesse*
Doums Day We Schull Y-see, A, **1749,** B1999
"Down in Yon Forest," see *He Bare Hym Vp He Bare Hym Down*
"Down in yon forest be a hall," see *He Bare Hym Vp He Bare Hym Down*
Dred of Deþ Sorow of Syn (John Audelay), **1749,** B2000
Drumclog, see *Loudon Hill*
Duc de Berry, see Jean, Duc de Berry
Dugall Quin, B2069

Duke Humphrey, see Gloucester
Duke of Athole's Nurse, B2066
Duke of Gordon's Daughter, B2054
Dunbar, William, 1813, 1818, 1823, 1825, 1875, 1895, 1896, 1909, 1911, 1912, 1943; *Lament of the Makaris,* 1911
Duodecim Abusiones, **1828,** B2095
Durham Field, **1781,** B2048
Dyte of Womenhis Hornys, A, see *Against Horns of Women*

Eagle as New Year Gift, **1828,** B2095
Earl Bothwell, B2048
Earl Brand, 1756, **1781,** 1799, B2045
Earl Crawford, B2067
Earl of Aboyne, B2067
Earl of Errol, B2067
Earl of Mar's Daughter, B2069
Earl of Westmoreland, B2048
Earl Rothes, B2069
Edmund (King and Saint), 1832; see also St. Edmund
Edom o Gordon, 1779
Edward, **1796,** 1805, B2056
Edward I (George Peele), 1789
Edward IV, 1750, 1864, 1865
Edward, Robert, 1792
Eger and Grime, 1784
Eight Verses of St. Bernard, Version 1, **1819,** 1892; B2081
Eight Verses of St. Bernard, Version 2, **1819,** 1892; B2082
Eighteenth-century Broadsides, **1790,** B2052
Eighteenth-century Songbooks, **1791,** B2054
Elderton, William, 1780
Elfin Knight, **1789,** 1805, B2049
Elizabeth Cochrane's songbook, 1753, 1791, 1794
Elveskud, 1798
English and Scottish Popular Ballads (Child), 1754
English Title to the Crown of France, see *Henry VI: His Claim to France*
Entombment of Christ, 1748
Envoy to Henry VI, **1852,** B2118
Epiphany, Carols of the, **1746,** B1963
Epistell to Sibille, **1833,** B2097
Epitaph on Gloucester, **1847,** B2112
Eppie Morrie, B2067
Erlington, B2063
Estates, Advice to, see *Duodecim Abusiones*
Eternall God Fader of Light (James Ryman), **1747,** B1990
Eucharist, Carols of the, **1747,** B1992
Euery Day þᵘ Myȝt Lere, **1748,** B1995
Euery Mane in Hys Degre, **1749,** B2002
Everything Draweth to His Semblable, **1833,** B2098
Everything to His Semblable, see *Everything Draweth to His Semblable*
Examples against Women, **1919,** B2174
Exortacion to Prestys, An, **1834,** 1857, 1866, B2098
Exortum Est in Loue & Lysse, **1745,** B1950
Exposition of Pater Noster, **1885,** B2142
Extracts from *Fall of Princes,* B2101

2182 INDEX

Fader and Son and Holy Gost, **1747**, B1988
Fader and Sonne & Holi Goost (James Ryman), **1747**, B1989
Fader of Heuene His Owyn Sone He Sent, **1746**, B1969
Fadere of Blisse Omnipotent (James Ryman), **1747**, B1989
Faders Sone of Heuen Blys (James Ryman), **1745**, B1954
Faders Sonne of Heuen Blis (James Ryman), **1745**, B1954
Faders Sonne of Heuen Blis (James Ryman), **1747**, B1990
Fadyr I Am þin Owyn Chylde, **1747**, B1986
Faerie Queene (Spenser), 1817
Fair Annie, B2059
Fair Flower of Northumberland, **1780**, B2044
Fair Janet, B2059
Fair Margaret and Sweet William, **1789**, 1799, B2049
Fair Mary of Wallington, B2060
Fall of Princes, 1810, **1835**, 1894, B2099
Fall of Princes, Bk 2.4432–38: Deceyt Deceyvyth, **1840**, B2106
Fall of Princes, Extracts: Episodes of: *Alcibiades*, B2101; *Canace and Macareus*, B2101; *Constantine*, B2101; *Dido*, B2101; *Sardanapalus*, B2101; *King Arthur*, B2101; *Rome, Julius Caesar, Octavian, Cicero, Boethius*, B2101; *Against Proud Men*, B2101; *Allusions to Chaucer*, B2101; *Account of the Golden Age*, B2101; *Praise of and Thanks to Gloucester*, B2101; Prologues and Envoys, B2101; *Ballade on Women's Chastity*, B2101; 2 Stanzas on Women, B2101; Various Stanzas on Women, B2101; General, B2101; and see also *Examples against Women*
Fall of Princes, Extracts Combined with Chaucer's Monk's Tale, **1840**, B2106
Fall of Princes, The Tongue, **1841**, B2107
Falls of Seven Princes, see *Sodein Fal of Princes*
False Lover Won Back, B2066
Famous Flower of Serving Men, **1780**, B2044
Farmer's Curst Wife, B2069
Father of Heuyn from Aboue (James Ryman), **1747**, B1989
Fause Foodrage, B2062
Fause Knight upon the Road, B2063
Fayre Maydyn Who Is This Barne, **1746**, B1976
Feast of Tottenham (tale), 1762
Fede þe Hungere þe þirste ȝif Drenke (John Audelay), **1748**, B1994
Ferly Thing It Is to Mene, A, **1745**, B1951
Fermorar and His Dochter, 1758
Ferste Ioye as I ȝᵘ Telle, **1747**, B1982
Fetys Bel Chere, **1751**, B2017
Fifftene Tokyns Aforn the Doom, **1841**, B2107
Fifteen Joys and Sorrows of Mary, see *Fifteen Joys and Sorrows of Our Lady*
Fifteen Joys and Sorrows of Our Lady, **1861**, B2124
Fifteen Joys of Mary, see *Fifteen Joys of Our Lady*
Fifteen Joys of Our Lady, **1860**, B2124
Fifteen O's of Christ, **1882**, B2139

Fire of Frendraught, **1791**, B2055
Flemings, see *Song against Flemings*
Fletcher, 1789
Flodden Field, **1777**, B2044
Floure and the Leaf, 1895
Floure of Curtesy, **1842**, 1907, B2107
For His Love þᵗ Bowght Vs All Dere, **1745**, B1953
For Loue Is Loue & Euer Schal Be (John Audelay), **1747**, B1987
For on a Tewsday Thomas Was Borne, **1746**, B1961
"For Victory in France," see *And Save Thys Flowre Wyche Ys Owre Kyng*
Fore He Is Ful ȝong Tender of Age (John Audelay), **1750**, B2011
Fore Pride in Herte He Hatis Alle One, **1749**, B2007
Fore-sake þi Pride & þyn Enuy (John Audelay), **1748**, B1994
Four Things That Make a Man a Fool: Balade De Bone Counseyle, **1843**, B2109
Four Things That Make a Man a Fool: On Worldly Worship, **1843**, B2109
Four Things That Make a Man a Fool: Ther Beon Foure Thinges, **1843**, B2108
Four Things That Make a Man a Fool: Ther Beothe Foure Thinges, **1843**, B2108
Four Things That Make a Man a Fool: Wurship, Women, Wine, Unweldy Age, **1843**, B2108
Fragment in Style of Lydgate: The World Is Vanity, **1920**, B2175
Fragment of Hymn to Blessed Virgin, **1820**, B2082
Fragments of Carols, **1752**, B2017; "... cristus ...," B2017; "Mari milde hath boren a chylde," B2017; "The borys hed haue we in broght," B2018; "... ye xall ete," B2018; "Thu wost wol lytyl ho is thi foo," B2018; "In evyn yer sitte a lady ...," B2018; "Wymmen ben fayre for t ...," B2018; "This ender day wen me was wo," B2018; "Of Mary de ...," B2018
Fragments of texts probably in Carol form, see Fragments of Carols
Freond at Neode, A, **1844**, B2109
Friar and the Boy (also *Frere and the Boy*), 1765, 1771
Friar in the Well, **1789**, B2051
Friendship with Robin Hood, and *King's Disguise*, B2053
Frog and the Mouse, see *Isopes Fabules*
Froissart, 1823
Froissart's *Chronicle*, 1774
From Hevyn Was Sent an Angell of Light, **1747**, B1984
Furst Hᵗ Is þi Heryng (John Audelay), **1748**, B1995
Fyrst Day Wan Crist Was Borne, **1745**, B1952

Gabriel, see *Prayer to Gabriel*
Gabriell Bryȝther Then the Sone, **1746**, B1963
Gabriell That Angell Bryȝt, **1747**, B1983
Gabryell of Hyȝe Degree, **1747**, B1983
Galawnt Pride Thy Father Ys Dede, **1749**, B2008
Game and Ernest Euer Among, **1749**, B1998
Gamelyn (romance), 1788

Gardener, B2067
Gaude Flore Virginali, **1844**, B2110
Gaude Maria Cristis Moder (John Audelay?), **1747**, B1981
Gaude to Whom Gabryell Was Sent, **1747**, B1982
Gaude Virgo (Latin), 1845
Gaude Virgo Mater Christi, **1844**, B2110
Gay Goshawk, B2062
General Extracts *(Fall of Princes, Extracts)*, B2101
Gentlewoman's Lament, A, **1845**, B2110
Geordie, **1788**, B2051
George Aloe and the Sweepstake, B2052
Gest of Robyn Hode (Incunabulum), A, 1758, **1767**, 1769, 1770, B2039
Gesta Regum Anglorum, 1784
Gesta Romanorum, 1771, 1799
Get Up and Bar the Door, B2060
Gil Brenton, **1791**, B2054
Girardus Cornubiensis, 1850
Glasgerion, **1782**, B2046
Glasgow Peggie, B2067
Glenlogie, or, *Jean o Bethelnie*, B2058
Gloria Tibi Domine (carol), 1804, 1805, 1806
Gloriosa Dicta Sunt de Te, **1847**, B2111
Glorious God Had Gret Pite, **1745**, B1953
Glorius God in Trinite, **1747**, B1988
Gloucester, Duke Humphrey of, 1810, 1838, 1839, 1847, 1848, 1849; see also *Appeal to Gloucester, A Complaint for My Lady of Gloucester and Holland, Epitaph on Gloucester, Marriage of Gloucester*, and *Praise of Gloucester* (prologue to Bk. 1 off *Fall of Princes*)
Gloucester, Praise of and Thanks to (Fall of Princes, Extracts), B2101
Gloucester's Approaching Marriage, On, see *Marriage of Gloucester*
Go Day Syre Crystemas Our King, **1745**, B1945
Go Forth Kyng, see *Duodecim Abusiones*
God Is Myn Helpere, **1849**, B2114
God Sende Vs Pese & Vnite, **1749**, B2002
God þt All This Word Has Wroȝth, **1747**, B1987
Goddys Sonne Is Borne, **1745**, B1952
Godes Sonne for þe Loue of Mane, **1745**, B1952
Godfrydus of Rome, 1771
Golden Age, Account of the (Fall of Princes, Extracts), B2101
Golden Vanity, see *Sweet Trinity*
Gordon, George (4th earl of Huntly), 1788
Governaunce of Kings and Princes, see *Secrees of Old Philisoffres*
Gower, John, 1771, 1838, 1843, 1872, 1943; *Confessio Amantis*, 1838
Grail Legend, 1748
Great Silkie of Sule Skerry, B2065
Grey Cock, or, *Saw You My Father?*, 1764, **1798**, B2060
Grimestone, Friar John, 1752
Grosseteste, Bishop Robert, 1759
Guard Your Tongue, **1911**, B2167
Gude and Godlie Ballatis, 1745
Gude Wallace, **1790**, 1796, B2053
Guido delle Colonne, 1914, 1915, 1916

Guillaume de Berneville, 1846
Guillaume de Guileville, 1887
Guy of Warwick, **1849**, B2114
Gyle & Gold Togedere Arn Met, **1749**, B2002
Gypsy Laddie, **1795**, B2055

Haile Ful of Grace Criste Is wt The (James Ryman), **1746**, B1979
Haile Perfect Trone of Salamon (James Ryman), **1746**, B1978
Haile Spowse of Criste Oure Savioure (James Ryman), **1746**, B1979
Haste, see *Ditty against Haste, A*
Haue Myende for The How I Was Borne (James Ryman), **1747**, B1986
Haue Myende Howe I Mankyende Haue Take (James Ryman), **1747**, B1987
Hawes, Stephen, 1773, 1813
Hawte, Sir William, 1942
Hayl Blessid Flour of Virginite, **1751**, B2017
Hayl, Most Myghty in Thi Werkyng, **1746**, B1964
Hayle Be Thou Mary Most of Honowr, **1746**, B1976
Hayle Full of Grace Criste Is wt The (James Ryman), **1747**, B1984
Hayle Oure Lod Sterre Both Bright & Clere (James Ryman), **1746**, B1979
He Bare Hym Vp He Bare Hym Down, **1748**, B1993
Heer Halewijn, 1790
Heir of Linne, B2048
Henry V, 1750, 1819, 1850, 1916
Henry V's Expedition into France, **1850**, B2115
Henry VI, 1750, 1829, 1832, 1850, 1851, 1852, 1853
Henry VI: Ballade upon His Coronation, **1851**, B2116
Henry VI: His Claim to France, **1850**, 1854, B2115
Henry VI: Sotelties at the Coronation Banquet, **1851**, B2116
Henry VI: Triumphal Entry into London, **1852**, B2117
Henry VII, 1750, 1751
Henry VIII, 1942
Henry Martyn, 1777, 1803, B2068; see also *Sir Andrew Barton*
Henryson, Robert, 1817; *Testament of Cresseid*, 1817
Her Commys Holly þat Is So Gent, **1746**, B1967
Herd, David, 1754, 1790, 1791, 1792, 1794, 1797, 1798
Here Haue I Dwellyd with More and Lasse, **1746**, B1968
Here Lokyng Was So Louely, **1751**, B2017
Herode þt Was Bothe Wylde & Wode, **1746**, B1961
"Heron flew east, the heron flew west," see *He Bare Hym Vp He Bare Hym Down*
High Fader of Blisse Aboue (James Ryman), **1747**, B1989
High Fader of Blisse Above (James Ryman), **1747**, B1984
Hill, Richard, 1770, 1771, 1744, 1748; 1943; *Commonplace Book*, 1748, 1843
Hind Etin, **1803**, B2064
Hind Horn, 1757, **1807**, B2063
Historia (Bede), 1813
Historia destructionis Troiae (Guido delle Colonne),

1914
Hit Is Ful Heue Chastite (John Audelay), **1749**, B2007
Hobie Noble, B2058
Hole Confessoure þ*u* Were Hone (John Audelay), A, **1747**, B1919
Holly and Ivy, Carols of, **1746**, B1967
Holy Berith Beris Beris Rede Ynowgh, **1746**, B1967
Holy Church, see Defense of Holy Church
Holy Gost Is to The Sent, **1747**, B1982
Holy Innocents, 1746
Holy Maydyn Blyssid þou Be, **1746**, B1977
Holy Nunnery, B2070
Holy Well (carol), 1804, **1806**, B2070
Holy Writ Sey3t Whech No Thyng Ys Sother, **1748**, B1996
Horn Child, 1807
Horn et Rimenild, 1807
Horns Away, see Against the Horns of Women
Horse, Goose, and Sheep, see Debate of the Horse, Goose and Sheep
Hound and the Cheese, see Isopes Fabules
Hound and the Sheep, see Isopes Fabules
House of Fame (Chaucer), 1907
How Schowld I bot I Thogth on Myn Endying Day, **1749**, B2001
How Suld I Now þ*u* Fayre May Fall apone a Slepe, **1746**, B1969
How the Plague Was Sesyd in Rome, **1856**, B2121
Hugh Spencer's Feats in France, **1781**, B2048
Hughie Grame, **1788**, B2051
Humorous Carols, **1751**, B2016
Humphrey of Gloucester, Duke, see Gloucester
Hunting, A Carol of, **1750**, B2010
Hunting of the Cheviot, 1774, **1775**, 1778, 1779, 1786, B2043
Hunting of the Hare (tale), 1762
Hyere Men Clymmeth the Sorere Ys the Fall, **1748**, B1997
Hymn to SS. Katherine, Margaret, and Magdalene, **1862**, B2125
Hys Signe Ys a Ster Bryth, **1746**, 1771, B1965
Hystorye, Sege, and Destruccyon of Troye, see Troy Book

I Am a Chyld & Born Ful Bare, **1749**, B2000
I Am Sory for Her Sake, **1751**, B2016
I Blessyd Be Cristes Sonde, **1749**, B2008
I Had Richesse I Had My Helth (James Ryman), **1748**, B1998
I Haue Y-so3te in Many a Syde, **1747**, B1990
"I have a gentle cock" (song), 1764; see also Grey Cock
"I have a new garden" (song), 1764
"I have a young sister" (song), 1758, 1764; see also Riddle Song and Captain Wedderburn's Courtship
I Iosep Wonder How This May Be, **1747**, B1985
I Loue a Louer That Loueth Me Well (James Ryman), **1747**, B1988
I Louede a Child of This Cuntre, see under Y
I Pray Yow, Maydens Euerychone, **1750**, B2016
I Saw a Fayr Maydyn Syttyn & Synge, **1746**, B1968
I Saw a Swete Semly Syght, **1746**, B1969
I Saw Neuer Joy Lyk to That Sight, **1750**, B2014
I Sawe a Doge Sethyng Sowse, **1751**, B2016
I Schal Yow Tell þis Ilk Nyght, **1746**, B1960
I Shall You Tell a Full Good Sport, **1749**, B2008
I Shall You Tell a Gret Mervayll, **1747**, B1984
I Warne You Euerychone for Ye Shuld Vnderstonde, **1750**, B2011
I Was Born in a Stall, **1746**, B1973
I Was w*t* Pope & Cardynall, **1748**, B1998
I Wold Fayn Be a Clarke, **1749**, B2007
Iacob and Iosep, 1758
Ichot a Burde in Boure Bryht, **1750**, B2012
Idley, Peter, 1840
If God Send þe Plentuowsly Riches, see under Yf
If þou Serue a Lorde of Prys, **1749**, B2001
If Thow Thy Lyfe in Synne Haue Ledde, see under Yf
If Y Halde the Lowe Asyse, **1748**, B1997
Ihesu as þ*u* Art Our Sauyour, **1745**, B1958
Ihesu of a Mayde þou Woldist Be Borne, **1745**, B1959
Ihesu of His Moder Was Born, **1746**, B1974
Ihesu Restyd in a May, **1745**, B1959
Ihesu Was Born in Bedlem Iude, **1746**, B1964
Ihesus for Thi Holy Name, **1747**, B1991
Illa Iuventus That Is So Nyse, **1749**, B2000
Image of Our Lady, see Ballade on the Image of Our Lady
Image of Pity, see On the Image of Pity
In All This Warld [N]IS a Meryar Life, **1749**, B2007
In Bedleem in That Fair Cete, **1745**, B1948
In Bedlem This Berde of Lyf, **1745**, B1948
In Cruce Sum Pro Te, see Why Artow Froward
In Euery Place Ye May Well See, **1749**, B2004
In Euery Plas Qwere þat I Wende, **1749**, B2003
"In evyn yer sitte a lady ..." (carol fragment), B2018
In Patras þer Born He Was, **1747**, B1992
In Prophesy Thus It is Saide (James Ryman), **1746**, B1973
In þe Vale of Abraham, **1748**, B1996
In þis Tyme a Chyld Was Born, **1745**, B1947
In þis Tyme Cryst Ha3t Vs Sent, **1745**, B1949
In This Vale of Wrecchednesse, **1746**, B1960
In Wat Order or What Degre (John Audelay), **1748**, B1997
In Word in Ded in Wil in þo3t (John Audelay), **1749**, B2004
In xx*ti* Yere of Age Remembre We Euerychon, **1749**, B2001
Incestuous Daughter, A Tale of, 1762
Inconsistency of Men's Actions, see Rime without Accord
Instability of Human Affairs, see Tyed with a Line
Instructions for Parish Priests (Mirk), 1762
Inter Diabolus et Virgo, 1758, 1761; see also Riddles Wisely Expounded
Interpretacio Misse, 1834, **1856**, 1866, B2121
Interpretacion and Virtues of the Mass, see Interpretacio Misse
Interpretacyon of the Natures of Goddys and Goddesses, see Assembly of Gods

INDEX

Interpretatio Guilielmi (William), 1813
In-to This Worlde This Day Dide Com, **1745**, B1953
Invocation to St. Anne, see *Prayer to St. Anne*
Ion Clerke of Toryton I Dar Avow, **1749**, B2003
Iosephe Wolde Haue Fled fro That Mayde (James Ryman), **1747**, B1985
Ipse Mocat Me, **1751**, B2017
Is þer Any Good Man Here, **1749**, B2009
Isidore of Seville, 1759, 1872, 1882, 1909, 1915
Isopes Fabules, **1857**, B2122
It Fell ageyns the Next Nyght, **1749**, B2008
It is Bred Fro Heuene Cam, **1747**, B1992
It Was a Mayde of Brenten Ars, **1750**, B2015
It Wern Fowre Letterys of Purposy, **1746**, B1976
Ittes Knowyn in Euery Schyre, **1748**, B1996
Iuy Is Both Fair & Gren, **1746**, B1968

Jack Hare, see *Ballade of Jack Hare*
Jack of Newbury (Thomas Deloney), 1778, 1780
Jacqueline of Hainault, 1810, 1849
James Grant, B2066
James Harris (The Daemon Lover), **1789**, B2051
James Hatley, B2068
Jamie Douglas, B2060
Jamie Telfer of the Fair Dodhead, B2066
Jan van Doesborch, 1768
Jean de Meun, 1847
Jean, Duc de Berry, 1838
Jean o Bethelnie, see *Glenlogie*
Jellon Grame, B2062
Jentill Butler Bell Amy, **1749**, B2009
Jesus to Blessed Virgin, **1859**, B2123
Jew's Daughter, see *Sir Hugh*
Jhesu for Thy Wondes Fyff, **1750**, B2012
Jock o the Side, 1778, B2048
Jock the Leg and the Merry Merchant, B2069
John Dory, **1780**, B2044
John of Dousborowe, see Jan van Doesborch
John of Hazelgreen, B2055
John the Reeve, 1758, 1767
John Thomson and the Turk, B2069
Johnie Armstrong, 1778, **1788**, B2051
Johnie Cock, **1797**, B2057
Johnie Scot, B2062
Jolly Beggar, B2061
Jolly Juggler, 1771
Jolly Pinder of Wakefield, B2047
Joseph, Carols of, **1747**, B1985
Journey of the Three Kings, see *Twelfth Day*
Joys, see *Orison on the Five Joys; On the Five Joys, Fifteen Joys of Our Lady, Fifteen Joys and Sorrows of Our Lady*
Joys of Mary, Carols of the, **1747**, B1981
Judas, 1758, **1760**, 1764, B2037
Judgment of Paris, 1895, 1915
Julius Caesar, Episode of (Fall of Princes, Extracts), B2101
Just Mesure, see *Song of Just Mesure, A*

Katharine Jaffray, B2060
Keach i the Creel, B2069
Kemp Owyne, **1800**, B2061

Kempy Kay, B2064
King and the Barker, 1765, **1766**, B2039; see also *King Edward the Fourth and a Tanner of Tamworth*
King and the Subject (story type), 1762, 1767
King Arthur, Episode of (Fall of Princes, Extracts), B2101
King Arthur and King Cornwall, 1757, **1783**, B2046
King Canute's Charter, 1864
King Edward and the Shepherd, A Tale of, 1762, 1767
King Edward the Fourth and a Tanner of Tamworth, 1758, 1762, 1767
King Edward's Charter, 1864
King Estmere, **1781**, B2046
King Hardecanute's Charter, 1864
King Henry, **1800**, 1801, B2061
King Henry II and the Miller of Mansfield, 1767
King Henry Fifth's Conquest of France, **1790**, B2053
King Horn, 1807
King James and Brown, **1780**, B2044
King John and the Bishop, **1775**, B2043
King of Scots and Andrew Browne, 1780; see also *King James and Brown*
King Orfeo, 1786, **1807**, B2063
King Orphius (Scottish fragment), 1796, 1802, 1807
Kinges Baner on Felde Is Playd, **1747**, B1986
Kinges Sone and an Emperoure, A, see under *Kynges*
Kingis Quair, 1907
King's Disguise, and, Friendship with Robin Hood, B2053
King's Dochter Lady Jean, B2064
Kings of Cologne, see *Three Kings of Cologne*
Kings of England, see *Charters of the Kings of England* and *Verses on the Kings of England*
Kings of England Sithen William Conqueror, see *Verses on the Kings of England* (1st, 2nd, and 3rd Redactions)
Kinmont Willie, B2066
Kissing at Verbum Caro, see *On Kissing at Verbum Caro*
Kitchie-Boy, 1807, B2063
Knight and the Shepherd's Daughter, 1773, **1789**, B2050
Knight of Liddesdale, **1788**, B2051
Knight of the Burning Pestle, 1789
Knight's Ghost, B2069
Knight's Tale (Chaucer), 1907
Kyd, Thomas, 1915
Kynges Sone and an Emperoure, A, **1745**, B1947

Ladd Y the Daune a Myssomur Day, **1750**, B2013
Lads of Wamphray, B2053
Lady Alice, **1790**, 1798, B2052
"Lady Cassilles Lilt" (song), 1796
Lady Diamond, B2069
Lady Elspat, B2063
Lady Isabel, B2068
Lady Isabel and the Elf-Knight, **1790**, B2052
Lady Maisry, B2062
Lady Mary Ann (Robert Burns), see *A-Growing*
Lady of Arngosk, B2067
Lady þat Was So Feyre and Briȝt, A, **1746**, B1978
Lady Who Buried the Host (tale), 1762, 1765

Ladye Bessie, 1777
Laily Worm and the Machrel of the Sea, B2064
Laird o Drum, B2067
Laird o Logie, B2060
Laird of Wariston, B2066
Lament of the Blessed Virgin (lyric), *A*, 1762
Lament of the Makaris (Dunbar), 1911
Lamentacioun of Mary Magdalene, see *Lamentacioun of Our Lady Maria*
Lamentacioun of Our Lady Maria, **1866**, B2127
Lamentation of the Blessed Virgin (lyric), 1762
Lamkin, **1797**, B2057
Lang Johnny More, B2068
Lass of Ocram, see *Lass of Roch Royal*
Lass of Roch Royal, **1794**, B2054
Last Tyme I The Wel Woke, **1750**, B2015
Latemest Day, 1759
Laud Troy Book, 1914
Laurence (Laurent) de Premierfait, 1810, 1838, 1839
Lavandres, see *Tretise for Lavandres, A*
Leesome Brand, 1792, 1793, **1803**, B2063
Legend of Dan Joos, **1860**, B2123
Legend of Good Women (Chaucer), 1838, 1907
Legend of St. Austin at Compton, **1817**, B2080
Legend of St. George, **1845**, B2110
Legend of St. Petronilla, see *Life of St. Petronilla*
Legenda Aurea, 1846, 1876, 1888, 1892, 1909
Les Échecs amoureux, 1894
Lestenit Lordynges I You Beseke, **1749**, B2008
Lestenytʒ Lordyngis Boþe Grete and Smale, **1746**, B1962
Letabundus, **1866**, B2128
Lett No Man Cum into This Hall, **1745**, B1946
Letter to Gloucester, see *Appeal to Gloucester*
Life of Our Lady, **1867**, B2128
Life of SS. Edmund and Fremund, 1813, 1829, **1830**, 1853, B2096
Life of St. Giles, **1846**, B2111
Life of St. Margaret, 1759
Life of St. Margaret, **1874**, B2131
Life of St. Petronilla, **1888**, B2144
Litany, A (carol), **1747**, B1991
Litil Childe þer Is I-bore, A, **1745**, B1951
Little Children's Little Book, see *Book of Courtesy*
Little John a Begging, B2048
Little Musgrave and Lady Barnard, **1782**, 1789, B2047
Lizie Lindsay, B2067
Lizie Wan, B2059
Lo Moises Bush Shynynge Vn-brent, **1746**, B1976
Lochmaben Harper, B2053
Loke Er þin Herte Be Set, **1749**, B2005
London, Wymundus, 1943
Look in Thy Merour, **1872**, B2130
Lord Delamere, B2067
Lord Derwentwater, B2066
Lord Ingram and Chiel Wyet, B2059
Lord Livingston, B2068
Lord Lovel, B2057
Lord Lundy, see *Lord William*
Lord Maxwell's Last Goodnight, 1778, B2058

Lord of Lorne and the False Steward, **1783**, 1786, B2049
Lord Randal, **1797**, B2057
Lord Saltoun and Auchanachie, B2067
Lord Thomas and Fair Annet, **1789**, 1796, B2049
Lord Thomas and Lady Margaret, B2068
Lord Thomas Stuart, B2068
Lord William, or, *Lord Lundy*, B2068
Lordes and Ladyes All Bydene, **1747**, B1985
Loudon Hill, or, *Drumclog*, B2066
Lovers, see *Advice to Lovers* and *A Lover's Lament*
Lover's Complaint, A, see *A Gentlewoman's Lament*
Lover's Lament, A, 1823, **1872**, B2131
Lover's Mass, see *Venus Mass*
Lover's New Year's Gift, A, see *Amerous Ballade*
Lullaby Carols, **1746**, B1968 and 2017
Lullay Lullay Litel Child, **1746**, B1972
Lydgate, John, 1761, 1773, **1809**, 1943, B2071; see also Background Books, B2071; General Treatments, B2072
Lydgate's Proverbs, see *Look in Thy Merour*
Lyft Vp Your Hartis & Be Glad, **1746**, B1963
Lystyn Lordyngys Qwatte I Xall Say, **1747**, B1992
Lytell Geste of Robyn Hode, A, 1767
Lyth and Lysten Both Old and ʒong, **1746**, B1975
Lytyll Tale I Will You Tell, A, **1749**, B2006

Magnificat, 1747
Magnificat, see *Life of Our Lady*
Maid and the Palmer, **1782**, B2046
Maid Freed from the Gallows, **1797**, B2057
Make We Mery in Hall and Boure, **1746**, B1963
Malory, Sir Thomas, 1799
Man and Woman in Every Place, **1748**, B1995
Man Be Mery I The Rede, **1745**, B1958
Man Be War þe Way Ys Sleder, **1749**, B2002
Man Haue in Mynde How Here Byfore, **1749**, B1999
Man If þᵘ Hast Synnyd Owth, **1746**, B1974
Man of Law's Tale (Chaucer), 1795
Man That I Loued Altherbest, **1750**, B2013
Man þᵗ in Erth Abydys Here, **1747**, B1992
Man þᵗ Xuld of Trewpe Telle, A, **1749**, B2002
Man Was þe Fyrst Gylt, A, **1745**, B1952
Mankend I Cale, **1747**, B1987
Mankyende Was Shent and Ay Forlore (James Ryman), **1745**, B1958
Many a Man Blamys His Wyffe Perde, **1749**, B2006
"Mari milde haþ boren a chylde" (carol fragment), B2017
Marie de France, 1859
Marlowe, 1915
Marriage, see *Against Marriage*
Marriage, Carols of, 1749, B2005
Marriage of Gloucester, **1848**, B2113
Marriage of Sir Gawain, 1757, **1783**, 1800, B2046
Mary Flowr of Flowers All, **1745**, B1953
Mary for the Loue of The, **1747**, B1982
Mary Hamilton, B2053
Mary Is a Lady Bryʒt, **1746**, B1977
Mary Magdalen, 1782
Mary Mild, 1806

Mary Moder Cum & Se, **1746,** B1972
Mary Moder Meke & Mylde, **1747,** B1984
Mary So Myelde and Good of Fame (James Ryman), **1745,** B1954
Mass, A Carol of a, **1748,** B1994
Masse Is of So High Dignytee, **1748,** B1995
Maying and Disport of Chaucer, see *Complaint of the Black Knight*
Medicina Stomachi, see *Dietary*
Melismata (Thomas Ravenscroft), 1780
Merchant's Tale (Chaucer), 1782, 1873
Mermaid, B2054
Mervelus þyng I Hafe Musyd in My Mynde, A, **1745,** B1959
Mery Geste of Robyn Hode (William Copland), *A,* 1766
Mesour Is Tresour, **1875,** B2133
Meyden Myelde Hath Borne a Chielde, A, (James Ryman), **1745,** B1955
Middleton, Thomas, 1852; *Triumph of Truth,* 1852
Midsomer Rose, **1875,** B2133
Millers and Bakers, see *Against Millers and Bakers*
Milton, John, 1842, 1887
Minstrelsy of the Scottish Border (ScoH), 1800, 1801, 1802, 1803
Miracles of St. Edmund, **1829,** B2096
Mirror for Magistrates, 1840
Miscellaneous Carols, **1751,** B2017
Miscellany (William Shenstone), 1790
Misericordias Domini in Eternum Cantabo, **1876,** B2134
Monk Who Honoured the Virgin, see *Legend of Dan Joos*
Monk's Tale (Chaucer), 1838, 1840
Montacute, Thomas (Earl of Salisbury), 1887
Moost Souerayn Lorde Chryste [Jesu], **1747,** B1988
Moral Counsel, Carols of, **1748,** B1996
Mortality, Carols of, **1749,** B2001
Most Worthye She Is in Towne, **1746,** B1967
Mother's Malison, or, *Clyde's Water,* B2063
Mrs. Brown of Falkland, 1754, 1788, 1791, 1792, 1794, 1800, 1801, 1802
Mrs. Brown of Falkland: Jamieson's Brown Manuscript (1783); William Tytler's Brown Manuscript (1783); Alexander Fraser Tytler's Brown Manuscript (1800); Robert Jamieson's *Popular Ballads and Songs* (1806), **1800,** B2061
MS Balliol College Oxford 354, **1770,** B2040
MS Bodleian Library Oxford 6933 (Ashmole 48), **1775,** B2043
MS Bodleian Library Oxford 12653 (Rawlinson C.813), **1773,** B2042
MS Bodleian Library Oxford 15444 (Rawlinson D.328), **1761,** B2037
MS British Museum Additional 27879 (Percy Folio), **1781,** B2045; see also under Percy Folio MS
MS British Museum Cotton Cleopatra C.IV, **1774,** B2042
MS British Museum Cotton Vespasian A.25, **1778,** B2044
MS British Museum Harleian 367, **1777,** B2044

MS British Museum Sloane 2593, **1763,** B2038
MS Cambridge University Library Ee.4.35, **1765,** B2039
MS Cambridge University Library Ff.5.48, **1762,** B2038
MS Corpus Christie College Oxford 255, **1775,** B2043
MS Trinity College Cambridge 323 (B.14.39), **1758,** B2037
MS York Minster Library, **1776,** B2044
Mumming at Bishopswood, **1876,** B2134
Mumming at Eltham, **1877,** B2134
Mumming at Hertford, **1877,** B2135
Mumming at London, **1878,** B2136
Mumming at Windsor, **1878,** B2136
Mumming for Queen Margaret, **1879,** B2137
Mumming for the Goldsmiths of London, **1879,** B2137
Mumming for the Mercers of London, **1879,** B2137
Musselburgh Field, B2048
My Lady Dere, see *Lover's Lament, A*
My Lady Went to Caunterbury, **1751,** B2016
Myn Owne Dere Ladi Fair and Fre, **1750,** B2014
Mynd Resun Vertu & Grace (John Audelay), **1748,** B1995

Name of Iohan Wel Prays I May, **1746,** B1961
Nativity, Carols of the, **1745,** B1945
Natural Balade by Lydegate, A, see *Everything Draweth to His Semblable*
New Year, Carols of the, **1746,** B1962
New Year Gift, see *Servant of Cupyde Forsaken*
New Year Valentine, see *Amerous Ballade*
New-Slain Knight, B2068
Newe Song I Wil Begynne, A, **1747,** B1991
Nightingale, see *Nightingale as Symbol of Christ* and *Sayenge of the Nyghtyngale*
Nightingale as Symbol of Christ, **1881,** B2139
Nine Properties of Wine, **1881,** B2139
Noah tradition, 1878
Noble Fisherman, or, *Robin Hood's Preferment,* B2051
Norman, J, 1942
Northern Passion, 1762
Northumberland Betrayed by Douglas, B2048
"Nou sprinkes the sprai," see *Als I Me Rod This Endre Dai*
Now Forto Syng I Holde It Best (James Ryman), **1745,** B1954
Now God Almythty doun Hath Sent, **1745,** B1949
Now in Betheleme That Holy Place (James Ryman), **1745,** B1957
Now Ioy Be to the Trynyte, **1745,** B1953
Now Is þe Twelþe Day I-come, **1746,** B1964
Now Ys Cum Owre Saueowre, **1745,** B1946
Now Ys ȝole Comyn w^t Gentyll Chere, **1745,** B1946
Now to Do Well How Shalt þ^u Do, **1748,** B1998
Now Wel May We Merthis Make, **1745,** B1947
Nowe This Tyme Rex Pacificus (James Ryman), **1746,** B1965
Nowel el Boþe Eld & ȝyng, **1747,** B1983
Nunne Walked on Her Prayer, **1750,** B2016
Nut-Brown Maid, 1758
Nywe Werk Is Come on Honde, A, **1745,** B1955

O Blesse God in Trinite, **1745**, B1959
O Blessid Mayde Moder and Wyffe (James Ryman), **1746**, B1981
O Blessyd Johan the Euangelyst, **1746**, B1961
O Blyssedfull Berd Full of Grace, **1746**, B1979
O Closed Gate of Ezechiel (James Ryman), **1746**, B1978
O Closed Gate of Ezechiell (James Ryman), **1746**, B1978
O Dauid Thow Nobell Key, **1745**, B1944
O Endles God Bothe II J and One (James Ryman), **1747**, B1990
O Endles God of Mageste (James Ryman), **1747**, B1989
O Endles God of Maieste (James Ryman), **1747**, B1989
O Endles God of Maieste (James Ryman), **1747**, B1990
O Fader of Eternall Blys (James Ryman), **1747**, B1989
O Fader of High Maieste (James Ryman), **1747**, B1989
O Fader of High Maieste (James Ryman), **1747**, B1990
O Fader w^{t}oute Begynnyng (James Ryman), **1747**, B1988
O Fayre Rachel Semely in Syght (James Ryman), **1746**, B1980
O Floure of All Uirginite (James Ryman), **1746**, B1980
O Glorius Iohan Evangelyste, **1746**, B1961
O God & Man Sempiternall (James Ryman), **1747**, B1989
O God We Pray to The in Specyall, **1747**, B1991
O Heuenly Sterre So Clere and Bright (James Ryman), **1746**, B1979
O Highe Fader of Heuen Blys (James Ryman), **1747**, B1990
O Iesse Yerde Florigerat (James Ryman), **1746**, B1979
O Iesse Yerde Florigerat (James Ryman), **1746**, B1980
O King of Grace and Indulgence (James Ryman), **1747**, B1987
O Lilly Flowre of Swete Odowre (James Ryman), **1746**, B1981
O Lorde by Whome Al Thing Is Wrought (James Ryman), **1747**, B1988
O Lorde So Swett Ser Iohn Dothe Kys, **1750**, B2015
O Man of Molde (James Ryman), **1747**, B1985
O Man Whiche Art the Erthe Take Froo (James Ryman), **1748**, B1998
O Marcyfull God Maker of All Mankynd, **1749**, B2001
O Meke Hester So Mylde of Mynde (James Ryman), **1746**, B1981
O Moder Mylde Mayde Vndefylde (James Ryman), **1746**, B1981
O Moost Noble King, Thy Fame Doth Spring and Sprede, **1750**, B2012
O My Dere Sonne Why Doest Thou Soo (James Ryman), **1746**, B1972

O of Iesse Thow Holy Rote, **1745**, B1944
O Orient Light Shynyng Moost Bryght (James Ryman), **1747**, B1988
O Prynces of Eternall Peas (James Ryman), **1746**, B1980
O Quene of Blisse Thy Son Ihesus (James Ryman), **1746**, B1979
O Quene of Grace and of Conforte (James Ryman), **1746**, B1978
O Quene of Mercy and of Grace (James Ryman), **1746**, B1978
O Quene of Pitee and of Grace (James Ryman), **1746**, B1979
O Spowsess of Crist and Paramour (James Ryman), **1746**, B1981
O Spowsesse Most Dere Most Bryʒt Most Clere (James Ryman), **1746**, B1981
O Stronge Iudith So Full of Myght (James Ryman), **1746**, B1980
O Sweete Ihesu So Meke and Mylde (James Ryman), **1747**, B1987
O Sweete Lady O Uirgyn Pure (James Ryman), **1746**, B1981
O Swete Ihesu We Knowlege This (James Ryman), **1747**, B1990
O Tryclyn of the Trinite (James Ryman), **1746**, B1981
O Uery Lyfe of Swetnes and Hope, **1746**, B1980
O Uirgyn Chast Both Furst and Last (James Ryman), **1746**, B1981
O Worthy Lord & Most of Myght, **1747**, B1987
Octavian, Episode of (Fall of Princes, Extracts), B2101
Of a Mayde Criste Did Not Forsake (James Ryman), **1747**, B1989
Of All þi Frendes Sche Is þe Flowre, **1746**, B1977
Of Mary a Mayde withowt Lesyng (James Ryman), **1745**, B1945
"Of Mary de . . ." (carol fragment), B2018
Of One That Is So Fair and Bright, 1760
Of This Martir Make We Mende, **1746**, B1960
Off Mary Crist Was Bore, **1745**, B1959
Off Seruyng Men I Wyll Begyne, **1750**, B2013
Old Robin of Portingale, **1782**, B2047
Omnes Centes Plaudite, **1745**, B1952
On Cristis Day I Vnderstond, **1747**, B1992
On De Profundis, **1825**, B2091
On Gloucester's Approaching Marriage, see *Marriage of Gloucester*
On Kissing at Verbum Caro, First Version, 1834, 1857, **1865**, B2127
On Kissing at Verbum Caro, Second Version, 1834, 1857, **1866**, B2127
On Moderation, see *Song of Just Mesure*
On the Five Joys, **1860**, B2124
On the Image of Pity, **1856**, B2121
On the Inconsistency of Men's Actions, see *Rime without Accord*
On the Instability of Human Affairs, see *Tyed with a Line*
On the Mutability of Human Affairs, see *Midsomer Rose*
On the Wretchedness of Worldly Affairs, see *Thorough-*

fare of Woe
On Wine, see *Treatise for Lavandres, A*
On xij^{the} Day Came Kingis Thre, **1746,** B1965
On xij^{the} Day This Sterre So Clere (James Ryman), **1746,** B1965
Order of Fools, **1882,** B2139
Orison on the Five Joys, **1860,** 1888, B2124
Orison to the Blessed Virgin, see *Prayer to Blessed Virgin* (Brown-Robbins, no 2565)
Orison to the Blessed Virgin (lyric), *An,* 1763
Orison to the Blessed Virgin of the Five Joys, An, see *Orison on the Five Joys*
Orpheus and Eurydice story, 1795, 1807
Orpheus Caledonius (Thomson), 1753, 1791
O's of Christ, see *Fifteen O's of Christ*
Ouer All Gatis That I Haff Gon, **1746,** B1967
Our Goodman, B2060
Our Lady, see *Balade in Commendation of Our Lady, Valentine to Our Lady,* and *Ballade on the Image of Our Lady*
Our Shyp Is Launched from the Grounde, **1750,** B2011
Oute of the Chaffe Was Pured This Corne, **1746,** B1962
Oute of Youre Slepe Arryse and Wake (James Ryman), **1745,** B1956
Outlaw Murray, B2070
Over the Bier of the Worldling, 1760
"Over yonder's a park," see *He Bare Hym Vp He Bare Hym Down* Ovid, 1838, 1895, 1915
Owre Kynge Went Forth to Normandy, **1750,** B2010
Owt of þe Est a Sterre Shon Bright, **1746,** B1965
Owt of ȝour Slepe Aryse & Wake, **1745,** B1950

Packe, Sir Thomas, 1942
Pageant of Knowledge, **1883,** B2141
Pageant of Knowledge, Stanza 23 Alone, **1884,** B2142
Pageant of Knowledge, Stanzas 3–9, **1885,** B2142
Pageant of Knowledge, Stanzas 23–End in Different Version, **1884,** B2141
Pageant Verses for Queen Margaret, see *Mumming for Queen Margaret*
Pain and Sorrow of Evil Marriage, see *Against Marriage*
Paraphrase of Pater Noster, **1885,** B2143
Paris Matthew, 1813; *Vita Secondi Offae,* 1813
Parker, Martin, 1780
Parliament of Fowls, 1842
Passion, Carols of the, **1746,** B1972
Pastime of Pleasure, 1773
Pater Noster, see *Exposition of Pater Noster* and *Paraphrase of Pater Noster*
Patre Unigenitus, A, **1745,** B1950
Pearl, 1800
Peele, George, 1778, 1789
Pélerinage de Jésus Christ (Guillaume de Guileville), 1887
Pélerinage de la vie humaine (Guillaume de Guileville), 1887
Pélerinage de la Vie Humaine (Lydgate), **1885,** B2143
Pélerinage de l'ame (Guillaume de Guileville), 1887
Peny Is an Hardy Knyght, **1749,** B2003
Percy, Bishop, 1797
Percy Folio MS (MS British Museum Additional 27879), 1753, 1757, 1765, 1767, 1771, 1777, 1780, **1781,** 1790, 1793, 1795, 1800, B2045
Percy Papers: MSS in the Harvard Library, **1797,** B2057
Percy's *Reliques,* 1754, **1796,** 1797, B2056
Perles Prynces of Euery Place (James Ryman), **1746,** B1980
Petyr, Henry, 1942
Philip of Burgundy, 1842
Picaresque Carols, **1749,** B2007
Piers Plowman, 1768
Pikeryng, John, 1915
Pilgrim (Fletcher), 1789
Pilgrimage of the Life of Man, see *Pelerinage de la Vie Humaine* (Lydgate)
Pity to the Wretched Sinner, see *On the Image of Pity*
Playe of Robyn Hode, 1766
Poems on the Mass, 1857, 1866, and see *On Kissing at Verbum Caro*
Poems on the Mass I, see *Exortacion to Prestys*
Poems on the Mass II, see *Interpretacio Misse*
Political Carols, **1750,** B2010
Politics (Aristotle), 1810
Popular Carols, B2070
Praise of Gloucester, see *Fall of Princes* (poem is prologue to Bk. I)
Praise of Peace, **1888,** B2145
Praise of St. Anne, **1815,** B2079
Prayer at the Holy Communion, see *Interpretacio Misse*
Prayer for Henry VI, His Queen and People, A, **1853,** B2118
Prayer in Old Age, 1819, **1892,** B2148
Prayer Inserted in Pelerinage de la Vie Humaine, **1887,** B2144
Prayer to Blessed Virgin (Brown-Robbins, no 2565), **1889,** B2145
Prayer to Blessed Virgin (Brown-Robbins, no 2395), see *Prayer Inserted in Pelerinage de la Vie Humaine*
Prayer to British Saints, **1889,** B2145
Prayer to Gabriel, **1890,** B2146
Prayer to Mary in Whom Is Affiaunce, see *Prayer to Blessed Virgin* (Brown-Robbins, no 2565)
Prayer to St. Anne, 1815, **1889,** B2145
Prayer to St. Denis, 1854, **1889,** 1890, B2146
Prayer to St. Edmund, 1854, 1886, **1890,** B2146
Prayer to St. Edmund for Henry VI, A, **1853,** 1890, B2118
Prayer to St. Leonard, **1890,** B2146
Prayer to St. Michaell, **1890,** B2146
Prayer to St. Ositha, **1891,** B2147
Prayer to St. Robert of Bury, **1891,** B2147
Prayer to St. Thomas, **1891,** B2147
Prayer to St. Thomas of Canterbury, 1854, **1891,** B2147
Prayer to Ten Saints, **1892,** B2147
Prayer to the Holy Sacrament, see *Interpretacio Misse*
Prayer upon the Cross, A, see *Why Artow Froward*
Prayers to St. Edmund, see *Prayer to St. Edmund for Henry VI*
Price, Lawrence, 1780
Prick of Conscience, 1765
Prince Hal, 1914

2190   INDEX

Prince Heathen, B2052
Prince Robert, B2065
Prioress's Tale (Chaucer), 1830
Procession of Corpus Christi, **1892**, B2148
Prognostications (Emb punre), 1762
Prognostications (Seasons), 1762
Prohemy of a Marriage betwix an Olde Man and a Yonge Wife, see Advice to Lovers
Prologues and Envoys (Fall of Princes, Extracts), B2101
Prophesy Fulfilled Is (James Ryman), **1745**, B1955
Proud Lady Margaret, **1804**, B2064
Proverbs (Book of) 31, 1833
Proverbs (Lydgate?), **1892**, B2148
Proverbs of Alfred, 1759
Pryde Is Out & Pride Is Ine, **1748**, B1998
Pryncypal Poynth of Charyte, A, **1745**, B1947
Psalm 53 (Lydgate), see Deus in Nomine Tuo Saluum Me Fac
Psalm 88 (Lydgate), see Misericordias Domini in Eternum Cantabo
Psalm 102 (Lydgate), **1893**, B2149
Psalm 129 (Lydgate), see On De Profundis
Psalms (Book of), 1847
Purgatory, Carols of, **1747**, B1991
Pynson, Richard, 1767
Pyty to the Wretched Synner, see On the Image of Pity

Quan I Haue in Myn Purs Inow, **1749**, B2003
Queen Eleanor's Confession, **1788**, B2051
Queen Margaret's Entry into London, see Mumming for Queen Margaret
Queen of Elfan's Nourice, B2064
Queen of Scotland, B2069
Quis Dabit Meo Capitis Fontem Lacrimarum, see Lamentacioun of Our Lady Maria
Qwete Is Bothe Semely and Sote, **1747**, B1992
Qwyll Men Haue Her Bornys Full, **1749**, B2007

Rammeshorne, **1893**, B2149
Rantin Laddie, B2055
Rare Willie Drowned in Yarrow, B2055
Ravenscroft, Thomas, 1780
Recuyell of the Histories of Troy (Caxton), 1915
Redesdale and Wise William, B2068
Reeve's Tale (Chaucer), 1798
Regina Celi Letare (James Ryman), **1746**, B1980
Regina Celi Letare (Lydgate), 1888, **1895**, B2151
Reigenlied, 1743
Religious Counsel, Carols of, **1748**, B1994
Reliques of Ancient English Poetry (Percy), see Percy's Reliques
Renaissance Ballad Composers and Collectors, **1779**, B2044
Repentance, Carols of, **1749**, B1998
Republic (Plato), 1810
Reson and Sensuallyte, 1817, **1893**, B2149
Revelation (Book of), 1847
Richie Story, B2067
Riddle Song, **1764**, B2038; see also "I have a young sister"
Riddles Wisely Expounded, 1758, **1761**, 1790, B2037

Right as the Crabbe Goth Forward, **1895**, B2151
Rime without Accord, **1896**, B2151
Rising in the North, B2048
Rob Roy, B2067
Robin and Gandeleyn, 1758, **1764**, 1779, B2038
Robin Hood and Allen a Dale, B2050
Robin Hood and Guy of Gisborne, **1782**, B2047
Robin Hood and Little John, B2052
Robin Hood and Maid Marion, B2053
Robin Hood and Queen Katherine, B2048
Robin Hood and the Beggar I, B2050
Robin Hood and the Beggar II, B2053
Robin Hood and the Bishop, B2050
Robin Hood and the Bishop of Hereford, B2055
Robin Hood and the Butcher, B2047
Robin Hood and the Curtal Friar, B2047
Robin Hood and the Golden Arrow, B2053
Robin Hood and the Monk, 1758, **1763**, B2038
Robin Hood and the Pedlars, B2065
Robin Hood and the Potter, 1758, **1765**, B2039
Robin Hood and the Prince of Aragon, B2050
Robin Hood and the Ranger, B2052
Robin Hood and the Scotchman, B2050
Robin Hood and the Shepherd, B2050
Robin Hood and the Tanner, B2050
Robin Hood and the Tinker, B2050
Robin Hood and the Valiant Knight, B2053
Robin Hood ballads, 1788, 1790
Robin Hood Newley Revived, **1788**, B2050
Robin Hood Rescuing Three Squires, B2047
Robin Hood Rescuing Will Stutly, B2050
Robin Hood's Birth, Breeding, Valor, and Marriage, B2051
Robin Hood's Chase, B2050
Robin Hood's Death, **1781**, B2047
Robin Hood's Delight, B2050
Robin Hood's Golden Prize, **1780**, B2044
Robin Hood's Preferment, see Noble Fisherman
Robin Hood's Progress to Nottingham, B2050
Robyn and Gandeleyn, see Robin and Gandeleyn
Roman de la rose, 1887, 1895, 1907
Roman de Troie (Benoît de Sainte-Maure), 1914
Romance of the Rose, 1878
Rome, Episode of (Fall of Princes, Extracts), B2101
Rookhope Ryde, B2053
Roos, Richard, 1773, 1814, 1907
Rose It Es the Fairest Flour, **1750**, B2011
Rose of England, B2048
"Rose of Ryse," see Rose It Es the Fairest Flour
Rose the Red and White Lily, B2062
Rosewall and Lillian, 1783, 1787
Roundel on the Coronation of Henry VI, 1851, **1854**, B2119
Ryman, Friar James, 1744, 1746, 1747, 1943

SS. Alban and Amphibal, **1811**, 1833, B2077
St. Anne, 1889; Carol of (Audelay), **1747**, B1991; see also Praise of St. Anne and Prayer to St. Anne
St. Austin, see Legend of St. Austin at Campton
St. Bernard, 1871, 1888; see also Eight Verses of St. Bernard
St. Bonaventura, 1871

St. Catherine, Carol of, **1747,** B1992
St. Denis, see *Prayer to St. Denis*
St. Dunstan, 1941
St. Edmund, 1829, 1832, 1864, 1890; Carol of, **1747,** B1991; see also *Banner of St. Edmund, Miracle of St. Edmund, Life of SS. Edmund and Fremund, Prayer to St. Edmund,* and *Prayer to St. Edmund for Henry VI*
St. Francis of Assisi, Carol of, **1747,** B1991
St. Fremund, 1830; see also *Life of SS. Edmund and Fremund*
St. George, 1748; Carol of, **1747,** B1991; see also *Legend of St. George*
St. Giles (St. Gyles), 1846; see also *Life of St. Giles*
St. John, 1748
St. John the Evangelist, 1746
St. Katherine, 1862; see also *Hymn to SS. Katherine, Margaret and Magdalene*
St. Leonard, see *Prayer to St. Leonard*
St. Magdalene, 1862; see also *Hymn to SS. Katherine, Margaret and Magdalene*
St. Margaret, 1862, 1876; see also *Hymn to SS. Katherine, Margaret and Magdalene* and *Life of St. Margaret*
St. Michaell, see *Prayer to St. Michaell*
St. Nicholas, 1748, 1759; Carols of, **1747,** B1992
St. Ositha, see *Prayer to St. Ositha*
St. Petronilla 1888; see also *Life of St. Petronilla*
St. Robert of Bury, see *Prayer to St. Robert of Bury*
St. Stephen, 1746
St. Stephen and Herod, 1758, 1760, **1764,** 1772, B2038
St. Thomas, 1748; see also *Prayer to St. Thomas* and *Prayer to St. Thomas of Canterbury*
St. Thomas à Becket, 1801, 1832
St. Thomas of Canterbury, 1746
St. Ursula and the Eleven Thousand Virgins, see *Prayer to British Saints, Especially St. Ursula*
St. Winifred, Carol of, **1747,** B1992
Saints, Carols of, **1747,** B1991; and see under individual saints
Saints of the Christmas Season, Carols of the, **1746,** B1959; and see under individual saints
Saluator Mundi Domine, **1745,** B1958
Salutacio Angelica, **1896,** B2152
Sardanapalus, Episode of (Fall of Princes, Extracts), B2101
Sarum Processional, 1942
Satirical Carols, **1749,** B2001
Satyrical Ballad, A, see *Ballade of Jack Hare*
Satyrical Ballad on the Times, see *Right as the Crabbe Goth Forward*
Saw You My Father?, see *Grey Cock*
Say the Best and Never Repent, see *Who Seith the Best Shall Never Repent*
Sayenge of the Nyghtyngale, **1880,** B2138
Sayings of Dan Johan, see also *Four Things That Make a Man a Fool* (5 entries)
Saynt Steuen þe First Martere (John Audelay), **1746,** B1959
Sche Saw þeis Women All Bedene, **1749,** B2003
Schoolmaster (Thomas Twyne), 1789

Scotish Song (Ritson), 1791
Scots Musical Museum (Johnson), 1791, 1792
Scott, Walter, 1800, 1801, 1803
Scottish Fragments Inserted in Troy Book, **1917,** B2173
Scottish Songs (David Herd), 1754
Scrope, Archbishop, 1750
Secrees of Old Philisoffres, **1896,** B2152
Secreta secretorum, 1899; and see *Secrees of Old Philisoffres*
See Myche, Say Lytell, and Lerne to Soffar in Tyme, see *Proverbs* (Lydgate)
Sege of Troy, see *Troy Book*
Semenaunt Is a Wonder þing, **1749,** B2002
Seneca, 1876, 1904
Serpent of Division, 1809, **1899,** B2154
Servant of Cupyde Forsaken, **1900,** B2155
Seven Sages of Rome, 1771
Seven Wise Counsels, see *Pageant of Knowledge*
Seventeenth-century Broadsides, **1788,** B2049
Seynt Nicholas Was of Gret Poste, **1747,** B1992
Shakespeare, William, 1809, 1840, 1915, 1916; *Troilus and Cressida,* 1915, 1916
Sheale, Richard, 1775
Sheath and Knife, **1792,** 1802, 1803, B2054
Shenstone, William, 1790
Shepard upon a Hill He Satt, **1745,** B1956
Short Metrical Chronicle of England, 1762
Shroud and Grave, 1759
Siege of Calais, 1850
Siege of Harfleur, see *Henry V's Expedition into France*
Siege of Rouen, 1771
Siege of Thebes, 1810, **1901,** B2155
Signs of Death (lyric), 1762, 1765
Sir Aldingar, 1756, **1783,** B2046
Sir Andrew Barton, **1776,** 1803, B2044; see also *Henry Martyn*
Sir Cawline, **1783,** 1802, B2046
Sir Colling (Scottish), 1784, 1785, 1786
Sir Eglamour of Artois, 1781
Sir Gareth of Orkney (Malory), 1799
Sir Hugh, or, *The Jew's Daughter,* **1796,** B2056
Sir James the Rose, B2060
Sir John Butler, B2048
Sir Lionel, **1781,** B2045
Sir Orfeo, 1795, 1798, 1807
Sir Patrick Spens, **1796,** B2056
... Sit Amonges the Knyghtes All, **1748,** B1997
Sith Criste Hath Take Both Flesshe & Blode (James Ryman), **1746,** B1978
Sith of Right Thou Mayst Not Forsake (James Ryman), **1746,** B1978
Sith Thou Hast Born the Kyng of Grace (James Ryman), **1746,** B1980
Sith Thou Hast Born the Kyng of Grace (James Ryman), **1746,** B1981
Sith Thy Sonne Is Both God and Man (James Ryman), **1746,** B1978
Sithe God Hathe Chose þe to Be His Knyʒt, **1750,** B2011
Skelton, 1789
Slaughter of the Laird of Mellerstain, B2067
Smert, Richard, 1942

So Blessid a Sight It Was to See, **1746,** B1971
Sodein Fal of Princes, **1904,** B2158
Some Tyme Y Loued as Ye May See, **1750,** B2014
Somtyme Y Louid So Do Y Yut, **1750,** B2016
Son of the Fader of Hevyn Blys, **1745,** B1953
Sone of God So Full of Myght (James Ryman), **1745,** B1955
Song against Flemings, **1841,** B2107
Song of Just Mesure, A, **1861,** B2125
Song of Songs, 1747
Song of Thanksgiving, **1909,** B2164
"Song of the Blessed Virgin and Joseph," see *Here Lokyng Was So Louely*
Song of Vertu, **1917,** B2173
"Song to the Virgin," see *Hayl Blessid Flour of Virginite*
Songe to Syng Y Haue God Ryʒt, A, **1745,** B1951
Songs (David Herd), 1790
Sonne of God and King of Blis (James Ryman), **1745,** B1954
Sonne of God Hath Take Nature (James Ryman), **1747,** B1990
Sonne of God Oure Lorde Ihesus (James Ryman), **1747,** B1990
Sonne of God Thatte All Hath Wrought (James Ryman), **1747,** B1989
South English Legendary, 1762, 1801
Southern Passion, 1762
Speculum Stultorum, 1882
Spenser, Edmund, 1813, 1817, 1823, 1887, 1907; *Faerie Queene*, 1817
Squire of Low Degree, 1793, 1799
Squire's Tale (Chaucer), 1907
Stans Puer ad Mensam (expanded version with 6-stanza prologue), **1905,** B2160
Stans Puer ad Mensam (normal version), 1761, **1904,** B2158
Stel Is Gud I Sey No Odyr, **1749,** B2004
Stella Celi Extirpavit, Version 1, 1888, **1905,** B2160
Stella Celi Extirpavit, Version 2, 1888, **1905,** B2160
Stow, John, 1777
Sturges (Turges?), Edmund, 1942
Suffolk Miracle, **1789,** B2051
Sum Be Mery and Sum Be Sade, **1749,** B2004
Sunne of Grace Hym Schynit In, **1745,** B1949
Sun's Marriage, see *Isopes Fabules*
Supplicatio Amantis, **1905,** B2160
Sweet Jesus (carol), see *Swet Ihesus Is Cum to Vs*
Sweet Trinity (The Golden Vanity), B2052
Sweet William's Ghost, **1798,** B2059
Swet Ihesus Is Cum to Vs, **1745,** 1804, 1805, 1806, B1959
Swete Saynt Anne We þe Besecha (John Audelay), see St. Anne, Carol of
Synt Ion Is Cristis Derlyng Dere (John Audelay), **1746,** B1960

Taill of Rauf Coilyear, 1767
Tale of the Basin, 1762
Tale of Threscore Folys and Thre, A, see *Order of Fools*
Tam Lin, 1792, **1798,** B2058

Te Deum, see *Song of Thanksgiving*
Te Deum laudamus, 1747
Tea-Table Miscellany (Ramsay), 1753, 1791, 1795, 1798
Tell, William, 1770
Temple of Glas, 1848, **1906,** B2160
Testament, **1907,** B2163
Testament of Cresseid (Henryson), 1817
Thanksgiving, see *Song of Thanksgiving*
That Archaungell Shynyng Full Bright (James Ryman), **1747,** B1984
That Hart My Hart Hath in Suche Grace, **1750,** B2015
That Holy Clerke Seint Augustyne (James Ryman), **1749,** B1999
That ix Moneythes [W]as Enclus, **1745,** B1954
That Lord þt Lay in Asse Stalle, **1745,** B1951
That Meyden Mylde Here Childe Did Kepe (James Ryman), **1746,** B1971
That Now Is Hay That Sumtyme Was Grasse, **1909,** B2165
That Was Ihū Oure Saueour, **1746,** B1976
þe Ferste Day of ʒol Han We in Mynde, **1745,** B1946
Then All Your Doyngs Schold Here in Earthe, **1749,** B2001
Ther Blows a Cold Wynd Todaye Today, see *Thys Wynde Be Reson Ys Callyd Tentacyon*
þer Is a Babe Born of a May (John Audelay?), **1746,** B1963
Ther Is a Blossum Sprong of a Thorn, **1746,** B1964
Ther Is No Rose of Swych Vertu, **1746,** B1974
þer Is Non Gres þt Growit in Ground, **1748,** B1996
Ther Was a Frier of Order Gray, **1750,** B2016
Ther Wer iij Wylly; 3 Wyly Ther Wer, **1749,** B2005
There Was Suim Teme Byfalle a Cas, **1746,** B1974
They That No While Endure, Version 1, **1909,** B2165
They That No While Endure, Version 2, **1910,** B2165
þi Tunge Is Mad of Fleych & Blod, **1748,** B1996
This Babe to Vs Nou Is Born, **1745,** B1948
This Babe to Vs That Now Is Bore, **1745,** B1948
This Brede Geveth Eternall Lyfe (James Ryman), **1747,** B1992
This Chielde Is Was and Ay Shall Be (James Ryman), **1745,** B1953
"This ender day wen me was wo" (carol fragment), B2018
This Endrys Nyʒt, **1746,** B1971
This Endurs Nyght, **1746,** B1969
þis Endy Day I Mete a Clerke, **1750,** B2014
þhis Flour Is Faire & Fresche of Heue (John Audelay), **1746,** B1974
This Holy Tyme Oure Lord Was Borne, **1745,** B1947
This Is the Songe þat ʒe Shul Here, **1745,** B1951
This Is the Stone Kut of the Hille (James Ryman), **1745,** B1955
This Louely Lady Sat and Song, **1746,** B1970
This May I Preve withouʒten Lett, **1745,** B1952
This Rose Is Railed on a Rys, **1746,** B1975
þis Tyme Is Born a Chyld Ful Good, **1745,** B1950
This Voyce Both Sharp & Also [Shyll], **1749,** B1999
þis Word Lordinngges I Vnderstonde, **1749,** B1999
þis World Is Falce I Dare Wyll Say, **1749,** B1999

This Worlde Ys But a Vanite, **1749**, B2000
This Worle Wondreþ of Al Thynge, **1745**, B1955
Thomas à Becket, see St. Thomas à Becket
Thomas Chaucer's Complaint, see *Lover's Lament, A*
Thomas Cromwell, B2048
Thomas o Yonderdale, B2068
Thomas Rymer, 1754, 1762, 1786, **1801**, B2061
Thoroughfare of Woe, **1910**, B2165
Thou Art Solace in Alle Oure Woo (James Ryman), **1745**, B1959
Thow Dereste Disciple of Ihū Criste, **1746**, B1961
Thow Holy Douʒter of Syon, **1746**, B1977
þow þᵘ Be Kyng of Tour & Town, **1748**, B1998
Thre Kingis on the xijᵗʰ Daye (James Ryman), **1746**, B1965
Three Kings of Cologne, **1862**, B2125
Three Ravens, **1780**, 1782, B2044
þu Sikest Sore, **1747**, B1987
"*þᵘ wost wol lytyl ho is thi foo*" (carol fragment), B2018
Thus It Is Saide in Prophecye (James Ryman), **1745**, B1955
Thus Seide Mary of Grete Honoure (James Ryman), **1747**, B1985
Thus to Her Seidean Aungell Thoo (James Ryman), **1747**, B1985
Thy Creatures Terrestriall (James Ryman), **1747**, B1988
Thynk Man Qwerof þᵘ Art Wrout, **1748**, B1998
Thys Blessyd Babe þᵗ Thou Hast Born, **1746**, B1972
Thys Indrys Day Befel a Stryfe, **1749**, B2006
Thys Wynde be Reson Ys Callyd Tentacyon, **1746**, B1974
Timor Mortis Conturbat Me, **1911**, B2166
Title and Pedigree of Henry VI, see *Henry VI, His Claim to France*
Tito Livio Frulovisi, 1810
To Crist Ihesu Thatte Lorde and Kyng (James Ryman), **1747**, B1990
To Mary Queen of Heaven, see *On the Five Joys*
To Mary the Star of Jacob, see *Orison on the Five Joys*
To Onpreyse Wemen Yt Were a Shame, **1749**, B2004
To the Estates, see *Duodecim Abusiones*
To the Now Cristis Dere Derlyng, **1746**, B1960
To the Shepeherdes Keping Theire Folde (James Ryman), **1745**, B1958
To This Roose Aungell Gabriell (James Ryman), **1746**, B1975
Tom Potts, B2047
Tomas of Ersseldoune (or *Thomas of Erceldoune*), 1762, 1763, 1802, 1803
Tongue, see *Guard Your Tongue, Wikked Tongue, and Fall of Princes, The Tongue*
Tractatus de Nobilitate (anonymous), 1813
Treatise for Laundress, see *Tretise for Lavandres, A*
Trental of St. Gregory, 1771, 1799
Tretise for Lavandres, A, **1866**, B2128
Tretyse of Crystys Passyoun, **1912**, B2168
Trevisa, John, 1915
Trinity, Carols of the, **1747**, B1988
Trinity Poem on Biblical History, 1759
Tristan and Iseult, 1792, 1799

Triumph of Truth (Thomas Middleton), 1852
Triumph of Virtue, see *Song of Vertu*
Troilus and Cressida (Shakespeare), 1915, 1916
Troilus and Criseyde (Chaucer), 1773, 1798, 1841, 1907, 1916
Trooper and Maid, B2069
Trouluffe, John, 1942
Troy Book, 1810, 1838, 1894, 1895, **1913**, 1917, B2168
True Tale of Robin Hood, **1780**, B2044
Truth It Is Ful Sekyrly, **1746**, B1964
Turnament of Totenham (tale), 1762
Twa Brothers, B2064
Twa Corbies, 1781
Twa Knights, B2069
Twa Magicians, B2064
Twa Sisters, 1756, **1789**, B2049
Twelfth Day, 1758, 1760, B2037
Twelve Days of Christmas, 1764
Twyne, Thomas, 1789
Tydynges Trew þer Be Cum New, **1747**, B1983
Tydyngs Trew Tolde Ther Ys Trewe, **1745**, B1954
Tyed with a Line, **1910**, B2166
Tyed with a Line, Stanza 1 only (recorded and printed as separate poem), **1911**, B2166
Tyll Home Sull Wylekyn This Joly Gentyl Schepe, **1750**, B2011

Vnder a Forest þᵗ Was So Long, **1749**, B2002
Vnder a Tre, **1747**, B1986
Unquiet Grave, 1804, **1805**, B2065
Vpon a Lady Fayre & Bright, **1746**, B1976
Vpon a Nyght an Aungell Bright (James Ryman), **1745**, B1956
Upon the Cross, see *Why Artow Froward*
Upon the Emptiness of His Purse, see *Appeal to Gloucester*
Utter Thy Language, see *Consulo Quisque Eris*

Valentine to Her I Love, see *Valentine to Our Lady*
Valentine to Her That Excelleth All, see *Valentine to Our Lady*
Valentine to Our Lady, **1883**, B2141
Venus Mass, **1917**, B2173
Verses on Cambridge, **1821**, B2084
Verses on the Kings of England, First Redaction, **1864**, B2125
Verses on the Kings of England, Second Redaction with 15 Introductory Stanzas, **1865**, B2127
Verses on the Kings of England, Third Redaction in Couplets, **1865**, B2127
Vertu, see *Song of Vertu*
Vexilla Regis Prodeunt, **1918**, B2173
Virgin, Carols of and to the, **1746**, B1974
Virgin's Motherhood, Carols of the, **1747**, B1986
Virgyn Pure, A, **1745**, B1952
Virtues of the Mass, see *Interpretacio Misse*
Vita Secondi Offae (Matthew Paris), 1813
Vycyce Be Wyld and Vertues Lame, **1749**, B2002

Wace, 1759
Wallace (Blind Harry), 1791

Walter Lesly, B2069
Wan lc Wente Byyonde the See, **1749**, B2008
Warning against Marriage, see *Against Marriage*
Warwick, 1750
We Bern abowtyn Non Cattes Skynnys, **1749**, B2007
Wee Wee Man, **1798**, B2058
Welcome Be Thys Blissed Feest, **1745**, B1952
Well of Mercy, A Carol on the, **1747**, B1990
West-Country Damosel's Complaint, B2052
Whan No Thyng Was but God Alone, **1748**, B1995
Whan Seynt Stevyn Was at Ieruȝalem, **1746**, B1960
Whan þt My Swete Sone Was xxxti Wynter Old, **1746**, B1973
Whane Noþing Whas but God Alone, **1748**, B1995
When Cryst Was Born of Mary Fre, **1745**, B1957
When Fals Iudas Her Son Had Solde (James Ryman), **1746**, B1972
When God Was Borne of Mary Fre, **1746**, B1961
"When I sleep I may not wake," see *I Am Sory for Her Sake*
When Ihūs Criste Baptyzed Was, **1746**, B1965
When Johnnie Comes Marching Home, 1781
When Lordechyppe Ys Loste & Lusti Lekyng with All, **1748**, B1995
When Nettuls in Wynter Bryng Forth Rosys Red, **1749**, B2005
Whenne Criste was Borne an Aungell Bright (James Ryman), **1745**, B1956
While Y Was ȝonge & Hadde Corage, **1749**, B2001
White, Edward, 1768
White Fisher, B2068
Who Seith the Best Shall Never Repent, **1918**, B2174
Whummil Bore, B2064
Why Artow Froward, **1919**, B2174
Why Sittist þou So Syngyng þenkyst þou Nothyng, **1747**, B1991
Whylome I Present Was with My Soffreyne, **1750**, B2012
Wicked Tunge Wille Sey Amys, A, see *Wikked Tongue*
Wife of Bath's Tale (Chaucer), 1820, 1873
Wikked Tongue, **1912**, B2167
Wife of Usher's Well, **1804**, B2065
Wife Wrapt in Wether's Skin, B2060
Will Stewart and John, **1782**, B2047
William of Malmesbury, 1783, 1784
William the Conqueror's Charter, 1864
Willie and Earl Richard's Daughter, B2062
Willie and Lady Maisry, B2065
Willie Macintosh, B2066
Willie o Douglas Dale, B2062
Willie o Winsbury, B2057
Willie's Fatal Visit, B2068
Willie's Lady, B2061
Willie's Lyke-Wake, B2063
"Willikin's Return," see *Tyll Home Sull Wylekyn This Joly Gentyl Schepe*
Wise Admonitions, 1759
With Fauoure in Hir Face Ferr Passyng My Reason, **1746**, B1973

With Paciens Thou Has Vs Fedde (James Ryman?), **1745**, B1945
With Pety Movyd I Am Constreynyd, **1748**, B1996
Wolcum Be þu Heuene Kyng (John Audelay?), **1745**, B1945
Wolf and the Crane, see *Isopes Fabules*
Wolf and the Lamb, see *Isopes Fabules*
Women, see *Against the Horns of Women, Beware of Deceitful Women, Examples against Women;* also see *2 Stanzas on Women* and *Various Stanzas on Women* in *Fall of Princes, Extracts;* also see Women, Carols of, below
Women, Carols of, **1749**, B2003
Women, 2 Stanzas an (Fall of Princes, Extracts), B2101
Women, Various Stanzas on (Fall of Princes, Extracts), B2101
World Is Vanity, **1920**, B2175; see also *Fragment in Style of Lydgate: The World Is Vanity*, **1920**, B2175
World Is Variable, see *World Is Vanity*
Worschip of Vertu Ys þe Mede, **1747**, B1991
Worshyp Be þe Birth of þe, **1746**, B1976
Wounded Knight, 1748
Wounds of Christ (lyric), 1762
Wourldly Mutabilite, see *Timor Mortis Conturbat Me*
Wretchedness of Worldly Affairs, see *Thoroughfare of Woe*
Wyatt, William, 1942
Wylie Wife of the Hie Town Hie, B2069
"Wymmen ben fayre for t . . . ," (carol fragment), B2018
Wymmen Beþ Boþe Goud and Schene, **1749**, B2003
Wynkyn de Worde, 1767, 1768, 1769, 1817

X for Crystes Hym Selfe Was Dyth, **1745**, B1958

Y Louede a Child of This Cuntre, **1750**, B2014
Ye Ben My Father by Creation, **1746**, B2017
". . . ye xall ete" (carol fragment), B2018
Yf God Send þe Plentuowsly Riches, **1748**, B1998
Yf Thow Thy Lyfe in Synne Haue Ledde (James Ryman), **1747**, B1987
Yougth Luste Reches or Manhod, **1749**, B2001
Young Allan, B2068
Young Andrew, **1782**, B2046
Young Bearwell, B2070
Young Beichan, **1801**, B2062
Young Benjie, B2065
Young Earl of Essex's Victory over the Emperor of Germany, B2054
Young Hunting, B2059
Young Johnstone, B2060
Young Peggy, B2069
Young Ronald, B2070
Young Waters, **1796**, B2056
Ying Men I Warne You Euerichone, **1749**, B2006
Ȝyng Men I Red That Ye Bewar, **1749**, B2005
Ȝyng Men þt Bern Hem So Gay, **1749**, B1999